Review Form & Free Prize Draw – Paper P7 Advanced Audit and Assurance (International) (6/07)

All original review forms from the entire BPP range, completed with genuine comments, will be entered into one of two draws on 31 January 2008 and 31 July 2008. The names on the first four forms picked out on each occasion will be sent a cheque for £50.

Name: _____   Address: _____

_____

_____

How have you used this Text?
(Tick one box only)

☐ Home study (book only)

☐ On a course: college _____

☐ With 'correspondence' package

☐ Other _____

Why did you decide to purchase this Text? *(Tick one box only)*

☐ Have used BPP Texts in the past

☐ Recommendation by friend/colleague

☐ Recommendation by a lecturer at college

☐ Saw advertising

☐ Saw information on BPP website

☐ Other _____

During the past six months do you recall seeing/receiving any of the following?
(Tick as many boxes as are relevant)

☐ Our advertisement in *ACCA student accountant*

☐ Our advertisement in *Pass*

☐ Our advertisement in *PQ*

☐ Our brochure with a letter through the post

☐ Our website www.bpp.com

Which (if any) aspects of our advertising do you find useful?
(Tick as many boxes as are relevant)

☐ Prices and publication dates of new editions

☐ Information on Text content

☐ Facility to order books off-the-page

☐ None of the above

Which BPP products have you used?

Text	☑	Success CD	☐	Learn Online	☐
Kit	☐	i-Learn	☐	Home Study Package	☐
Passcard	☐	i-Pass	☐	Home Study PLUS	☐

Your ratings, comments and suggestions would be appreciated on the following areas.

	Very useful	Useful	Not useful
Introductory section (Key study steps, personal study)	☐	☐	☐
Chapter introductions	☐	☐	☐
Key terms	☐	☐	☐
Quality of explanations	☐	☐	☐
Case studies and other examples	☐	☐	☐
Exam focus points	☐	☐	☐
Questions and answers in each chapter	☐	☐	☐
Fast forwards and chapter roundups	☐	☐	☐
Quick quizzes	☐	☐	☐
Question Bank	☐	☐	☐
Answer Bank	☐	☐	☐
Index	☐	☐	☐

Overall opinion of this Study Text	Excellent ☐	Good ☐	Adequate ☐	Poor ☐

Do you intend to continue using BPP products?   Yes ☐   No ☐

On the reverse of this page are noted particular areas of the text about which we would welcome your feedback. The BPP author of this edition can be e-mailed at: jaitindergill@bpp.com

Please return this form to: Nick Weller, ACCA Publishing Manager, BPP Learning Media Ltd, FREEPOST, London, W12 8BR

Review Form & Free Prize Draw (continued)

Please note any further comments and suggestions/errors below

Free Prize Draw Rules

1   Closing date for 31 January 2008 draw is 31 December 2007. Closing date for 31 July 2008 draw is 30 June 2008.

2   Restricted to entries with UK and Eire addresses only. BPP employees, their families and business associates are excluded.

3   No purchase necessary. Entry forms are available upon request from BPP Learning Media Ltd. No more than one entry per title, per person. Draw restricted to persons aged 16 and over.

4   Winners will be notified by post and receive their cheques not later than 6 weeks after the relevant draw date.

5   The decision of the promoter in all matters is final and binding. No correspondence will be entered into.

Preface to the First Edition

The aim of this book is to document the history of the Science Fiction film and to serve as a critical guide to the glorious (and many not so glorious) films that it includes. What distinguishes this volume from others is its scope, which is truly encyclopedic, and its structure. The heart of the book is some 1,450 entries, arranged chronologically and alphabetically within each year, which are devoted to individual films. These entries range from a hundred words to a thousand in a direct reflection of the film's interest and/or historical importance in the development of the Science Fiction film. As far as possible, each entry comprises fully researched credits (director, producer, studio, writer, cinematographer, special effects' men and a minimum of six leading players), a brief synopsis of the plot and informed critical comment on the film. Where relevant, cross-reference is made to other movies. Thus it is possible to follow the careers of important stars, directors and producers and key themes of the genre through the book. In addition to the entries, the encyclopedia also contains numerous appendices, including a Critics' Top Ten,

a ranking of Science Fiction films by their rental earnings and a list of Oscars won by Science Fiction films. Taken together, the appendices represent the most comprehensive statistical overview of the genre ever published.

In the course of preparing this volume, I have relied heavily on Walt Lee's invaluable work, *A Reference Guide to Fantastic Films*, a monument to the surrealist approach to scholarship if ever there was one, Bill Warren's *Keep Watching the Skies!* and Jean-Pierre Bouyxou's less well known *La Science Fiction au Cinéma*. I have also made use of the reviews in *Variety* and the *Motion Picture Herald* and, for more recent films, *The Monthly Film Bulletin*. With these to lean on I have sought to construct what, I hope, is the most comprehensive guide in book form to the Science Fiction cinema so far ever produced.

May the Force be with you.

Phil Hardy
London 1984

Preface to the Second Edition

At the end of the Notes on the Entries in the first edition of this book I asked readers for suggestions and corrections. Happily, the most repeated suggestion was that a new edition was required immediately. Well, six years later, here it is: a completely revised and updated edition.

I also asked readers to send in corrections and these came flooding in. So, thank you to Bill Warren of Los Angeles; J.R. Surrey of Bridport, Dorset; Tim Rogerson of Upminster, Surrey; Joseph G. D'Elia of Irvington, New Jersey; Jim Bechtel of Omaha, Nevada; and Dennis Howells of Ilkeston, Derby.

Particular thanks are due to Kim Newman, who wrote all the entries on the new films included in this book from 1985 onwards. Of course, the responsibility for these remains mine, but the credit is wholly his.

Lastly, many people have asked which contributors were responsible for which entries. While it is impossible to be

precise in a short note (particularly at this late date), the following is an indication of the areas in which the various contributors worked. I was responsible for the bulk of the entries, with the proviso that Denis Gifford wrote many of those on silent films, Anthony Masters many of those on fifties' films, Paul Taylor many of those on seventies' and early eighties' films, and Paul Willemen wrote the bulk of the entries on foreign films (i.e. works made outside the Hollywood/London axis). That said, I remain ultimately responsible for the contents of the book.

I hope that this new edition finds as receptive an audience as the original volume.

Keep Watching the Skies!

Phil Hardy
London 1991

Preface to the Third Edition

Once again I have the pleasure of penning a preface to another edition of *Science Fiction*. This, the first paperback edition, adds some 100 films from the period 1991-94, a new Rental Champs list, a number of corrections to existing entries and even acknowledges the completion of the Channel tunnel between the UK and France. That said this is not an 'all singing and dancing' new edition of *Science Fiction*. Rather it is the previous edition made much better.

In the course of putting together this fourth revision of a book originally published in 1984 (and conceived a couple of years before that), it has become clear that the strains of updating and revising without deforming the structure of the book have finally become too much. It might seem that for a book arranged chronologically one could simply bolt on new years and new entries, as indeed we have done so far. But we have reached the point where the past needs re-excavating too. For just as history is usually written by the victors, so different presents create different pasts. Accordingly this will be the last edition of *Science Fiction* in this form. With this in mind I have also left the introduction unchanged. My comments on the nineties appear in the brief introduction to that decade.

The construction of reference books is a rather more complex issue than one might imagine. There was a time when they were dusty tomes like *The Dictionary of National Biography* which, it seemed, merely attempted to remind us of the known facts in a given arena – in that case the leading players of the stirring stories that was British history – and put those lives into some sort of context. But even the *DNB* had a hidden perspective, a set of assumptions that were not made explicit. It is only after careful examination that the bias behind those assumptions becomes apparent. In the case of *DNB*, history was seen as the story of Englishmen (rarely English women) and usually Englishmen of a certain class. In the recently-begun series of volumes of 'missing names' to the *DNB* that agenda has been highlighted and corrected.

When *Science Fiction* first appeared, it was rather like those volumes of 'missing names'. In place of the verities of mad scientists and robots operating on an Anglo-Hollywood English language axis it pushed to the fore curiosities and foreign language films with their own uses of Science Fiction. It also examined the staples of the genre film with new eyes. It did this not to belittle the films of James Whale or Jack Arnold (or of earlier guides like Walt Lee's wide-ranging three volume *Reference Guide to Fantastic Films*) but to place them in a wider context.

It was this impetus that gave *Science Fiction* its moment and its importance. It enlarged the canon of Science Fiction films and provided a rough guide to that newly extended world, and still managed to be a friendly companion to an evening's television and video watching. *Science Fiction* has been criticized (and *Horror* has been criticized in spades) for searching for meaning and offering interpretations rather than mere plot synopses. This has been a central element of the impetus behind the Encyclopedias. I make no apology for this stance. Future editions will continue in this vein. This impetus is what distinguishes the Aurum and Overlook Encyclopedias from other accounts of the genres.

However, the critical perspective that fuelled the first editions of the Encyclopedias is over. Quite simply, the world of Science Fiction is very different now. For example, like the Horror genre, Science Fiction has benefited from the democracy that cheap but effective special effects have brought. This means that the quality of the special effects is no guide to the quality – whatever the budget – of a film. For Science Fiction this is particularly important. It means, for example, that the aesthetic of Hollywood professionalism should perhaps be questioned more rigorously. Or to put it another way, maybe Ed Wood was righter than we ever thought? (Myself I doubt it, but. . .)

In the intervening years other changes have taken place. In part thanks to the early editions of *Science Fiction* and the growing number of well-researched fanzines and specialist magazines that have sprung up in the last decade or so, and in part thanks to the discovery by video distributors and dealers of the value of niche markets, that impetus has been satisfied. Broadly speaking we know what's out there. It used to be an adage among film curators that there were no lost films, only films that hadn't been found. In Science Fiction (and Horror) that finding has been going on apace. As a result more of the past is available now than ever before, certainly in America.

The present is also changing. The arrival of the CD-ROM and full motion video images on the PC has brought forth interactive movies like Hyperbole Studio's *Quantum Gate* (1994) and *The Vortex* (1995), which consists of three CD-ROMs, to interact with. These are minor outings, but future ones may not be. We need to think about them.

Future editions – *and there will be future editions* – will follow the same format but each entry will be considered again, particularly where new information and the recent release of an obscurity has refreshed tired memories. Similarly the appendices, critics' Top Tens and so forth will be done anew. In short, *Science Fiction* (and its companions in the series) will be rethought.

To do this I would appreciate as much help as possible. Accordingly I ask readers of *Science Fiction* (and *Horror* and *The Western*) to send me, via the publishers, suggestions for new entries (from any year) and comments and corrections on existing ones. If you are among those who have already done so, please send them again if you bear to do so as some of the corrections have gone astray – I blame HAL.

Beam me up, Scotty.

Phil Hardy
Crouch End
London 1995

The Science Fiction Film in Perspective

The Realm of Science Fiction

What immediately strikes one after the briefest of surveys of the impossible genre that is Science Fiction cinema is that virtually all the films that comprise it in some way or another call into question the world we live in and accept as absolute. The ideas that run through the films are often fanciful, but at bottom they represent, in however distorted a fashion, attempts to think in a genuinely speculative way about the futures that await us. The 'what if?'s of Science Fiction cinema are generally less corrosive and radical than those of the printed page, but simply because they are constructed in images (rather than mere words) which spring to life in the hands of an imaginative director, their effects are much more immediate and resonant. Such images – Frankenstein's monster watching a little girl pick flowers in a studio set, the cities of the future in **Metropolis** (1926) and **Things to Come** (1936), the virtually non-stop destruction that comprises the text of **Chikyu Boeigun** (1957), the perverse mythology of **Flash Gordon** (1936), the antiseptic beauty of **2001 – A Space Odyssey** (1968) and the squalor of the spaceways in **Der Grosse Verhau** (1970), to name but a few – however crudely conceived, in their visual orchestration force us to stretch our imagination and see the world afresh. It is this impulse, most often raised in a questioning, pessimistic context that runs through the most adventurous Science Fiction films.

If the Science Fiction impulse seems clear enough, as a film genre Science Fiction is, paradoxically, one of the most difficult to define, let alone describe usefully. The name suggests a relationship with the literary genre and the direct association of 'science' and 'fiction' promises an easy definition. Though this might be true in a general sense, it is unhelpful when attempting to discuss specifics. The relationship between the literary genre (and, one might add, a genre in which definitional questions have been well to the fore) and the Science Fiction film has been, at best, uneasy. Not only have relatively few films been made from Science Fiction novels but, until quite recently, Science Fiction writers and critics have shown a marked hostility to the Science Fiction film. **The Thing** (1951), to take just one classic example, was reviled by the (then) Science Fiction establishment for transforming the interesting source story of a shape-changing alien into a mere monster-on-the-loose film.

A comparison between the Science Fiction film and, say, the western or the musical helps demonstrate how elusive a genre Science Fiction is. The western can be broadly described in terms of its content: the American West between the Civil War and World War I provides the setting for most westerns, the others, by and large, are the exceptions that prove the rule. The musical, on the other hand, is best described in terms of form: musicals are those films which feature extensive sequences of singing and dancing. In contrast to these tightly defined genres, Science Fiction is a far looser accumulation of elements. There is no fixed locale for a Science Fiction film, it can be set in the vastness of space (**Dark Star**, 1974) or inside the human body itself (**Fantastic Voyage**, 1966); it can be set in the far future (**In the Year 2889**, 1966), the near future (**Space Men**, 1960), the present (**Close Encounters of the Third Kind**, 1977) or even the past (**Atlantis, the Lost Continent**, 1960). The 'science' in Science Fiction need not be 'good' science, nor even an imaginative extrapolation of the scientific truths of the day. The rocket that propels the explorers to the moon in **Things to Come** (1936) is impossible – the passengers would not be able to withstand the gravitational forces needed to break clear of the Earth using the rocket-gun suggested. Similarly, the giant, radiation-induced, insect monsters of so many fifties films are impossible. As several biologists have pointed out, the ants of **Them!** (1954), the locusts of **The Beginning of the End** (1957) and other similar creatures, far from being able to menace mankind as they do, would simply keel over if they were the size the film-makers made them; their oxygen systems could not be 'geared up' to their new size. In matters of form too, no simple description of the genre is possible. Science Fiction has its clichéd shots (the slow passage of an angular spaceship across the screen in post **2001 – A Space Odyssey** (1968) films, for example) and its formulae (the classic triangle of a scientist in danger rescued by his plucky daughter, who often doubles as a reporter, with the assistance of a hard-headed hero) and at times in the genre's history stereotyped plots can be identified, but the accumulation of such motifs and conventions is not enough to describe the Science Fiction film genre.

A survey of the history of the Science Fiction film presents an immediate problem of definition. Apart from a hard core of films – **Metropolis** (1926), **Le Voyage dans la Lune** (1902), **2001 – A Space Odyssey** (1968), **Star Wars** (1977), **Forbidden Planet** (1956) and **Solaris** (1971), to pick a few obvious examples – the films discussed by critics of the genre vary wildly from history to history. Alternatively, the problem is avoided by discussing not merely Science Fiction but Science Fiction, horror and fantasy films together, as though it were impossible to differentiate between them. Such a strategy makes sense in part because the different genres are clearly related but it doesn't help any attempt to isolate the all-important Science Fiction elements. From this perspective it is interesting to note those films that are ommitted from the histories; for the most part, these include the Frankenstein films, the gadget-ridden serials of the thirties, the James Bond films and all the similar sixties movies, many of the monster films of the fifties and most comedies with Science Fiction elements. All these films are clearly Science Fiction in some

Right: Space travel as seen through the eyes of Irving Pichel, Destination Moon *(1950).*

Clockwise from top left: *The Classics of the Genre:* Metropolis *(1926),* Le Voyage dans la Lune *(1902),* Solaris *(1971),* Star Wars *(1977) and* 2001 – A Space Odyssey *(1968).*

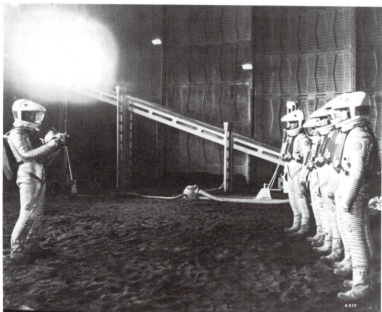

way, yet most histories either gloss over them, as they do most Science Fiction films made outside the Hollywood – London axis, or disregard them completely. The reasons for this are twofold: serials like **The Mysterious Dr Satan** (1940), comedies like **It Happens Every Spring** (1949), not to mention **Abbott and Costello Meet Frankenstein** (1948), and the films detailing the adventures of James Bond and his followers, are clearly marginal compared to **Metropolis** and **Planet of the Apes** (1968). Moreover, on the whole, they are far less respectable than the films the various historians of Science Fiction are trying to elevate as being worth attention. It is undoubtedly true that, until the recent renaissance of the genre in the wake of **Star Wars**, with few exceptions, the genre's films have been made and exhibited within Poverty Row and, as such, have not been deemed worthy of detailed critical attention.

Perhaps the most revealing omissions from most of the histories are the Frankenstein films, which have been regularly claimed, with some justification, by the historians of horror. In production terms James Whale's **Frankenstein** (1931) and Terence Fisher's radical re-interpretation of the legend, **The Curse of Frankenstein** (1957), were part of a cycle of horror films. Bela Lugosi, the star of *Dracula* (1930), which launched the horror boom of the thirties, was originally slated to star in **Frankenstein,** and Hammer, the studio that produced **The Curse of Frankenstein**, quickly followed it with *Dracula* (1957), with Christopher Lee (the creature of the earlier film) in the title role. In both cases, the studios saw the Frankenstein and Dracula films as complementary but the films have far more in common. The Universal cycle, which also included films devoted to the exploits of the Mummy and Lon Chaney's Werewolf, were stylistically uniform. All were clearly influenced equally by German expressionism, and gothic in their lighting effects. Because the Frankenstein films have been so influential in the evolution of the horror film, they will also be covered in the forthcoming horror volume. If, however, the Frankenstein and Dracula films inhabited the same nightmare world, the terrors unleashed in them were significantly different. The terrors of *Dracula* stem from an organized *set of beliefs* (specifically that a person can forswear God and so become a member of the undead), those of **Frankenstein** from an *organized body of knowledge* (specifically of biology, anatomy and so forth). Dracula has no soul (and hence no reflection); Frankenstein is a man of science. Dracula's natural habitat is the crypt and the coffin, Frankenstein's the laboratory. Behind Dracula lie the complex beliefs of Catholicism, behind Frankenstein scientific endeavours to conquer the material world. It is this significant difference that makes one Science Fiction and the other horror.

Our immediate concern here is how the Frankenstein films pinpoint an area of concern that Science Fiction has in common with horror, and how close to our fears of the effects of science and technology are those of the powers of the occult and religion. Indeed, it has been argued that the Science Fiction film is simply a modernization of the horror film. Movies like *The Exorcist* (1973) and *Rosemary's Baby* (1968) demonstrate that the horror film has not been totally supplanted by Science Fiction, but such a view contains an important element of truth. Certainly many of the aliens and robots who populate the Science Fiction film are characterized as latterday vampires and zombies. But more significant than such a specific attempt to bind the two genres together is the more obvious general point that they have in common. Both detail a world in which fear and terror are central. As the two genres developed, the different inflections of that fear and terror became more pointed. In the late fifties, horror supplanted Science Fiction, following the sale of **Frankenstein** (1931) to American TV and Hammer's successful revival of Frankenstein (which it treated in a more gothic manner than had Universal in the thirties) and Dracula. Hammer's commitment to horror is particularly significant as it was the

studio that had led the mini-boom of British Science Fiction with **The Quatermass Xperiment** (1955) a few years before. In America, there was a similar transition in the career of Roger Corman, one of the most important independent director/producers of Science Fiction in the fifties. From **The Day the World Ended** (1956) on, he produced a series of major Science Fiction films before turning decisively to horror with a series of Edgar Allan Poe derived films in the sixties. The contrasting Science Fiction and horror films of Corman and Hammer studios are enlightening. The Science Fiction films, especially Corman's apocalyptic movies, dealt with threats to the survival of mankind; the horror films, though they dwelt equally on the disruption of the natural order and the coming of chaos, were set in isolated communities in which individuals, rather than society itself, were threatened.

The first Science Fiction films, the short trick films of Georges Méliès, Louis Lumière, Stuart Blackton, Ferdinand Zecca and Segundo de Chomon, were all essentially comic in tone. They viewed the new technological world of the 20th century with humour, repeatedly making the simple point that the new-fangled inventions of the century (like the folk remedies of the past) went wrong, to comic effect, as often as they performed correctly. But as the films grew in length and their makers had more time to dwell on the implications of the inventions and emergent technologies that comprised their subject matter, the wonderful innocence of a film like Méliès' **Le Voyage dans la Lune** (1902) swiftly gave way to more sombre thoughts. In common with the popular literature of the period, war and destruction became the major themes of the emerging genre. As early as 1909 and **The Airship Destroyer** – which was inspired by H.G. Wells' novel of a year earlier, *War in the Air*, and promoted as showing 'what might happen in the near future when aeroplanes have been perfected to the point of being practicable engines of war' – film-makers turned their attention to the less beneficial aspects of modern science. This strand of film-making, which intensified in the years immediately preceding World War I, can be traced directly to the present day in **War Games** (1983), by way of the unlikely melodrama **Q Planes** (1937), numerous films of the fifties in which the atomic bomb lurked menacingly behind virtually every image, and **Dr Strangelove, Or How I Learned to Stop Worrying and Love the Bomb** (1964), to name but a few. A similar, though less potent tradition (because the catastrophe imagined was not of man's making) was inaugurated by **The Comet** (1910) which imagined life as we know it to be the result of Earth's collision with a comet or wandering planet. Films of this nature include **Himmelskibet** (1917), **Verdens Undergang** (1916), **When Worlds Collide** (1951) and **Meteor** (1979).

In a different manner, films such as **Alraune** (1918), **Homunculus** (1916) and **Der Golem** (1920) mixed magic and science to produce dark melodramas in which man's meddling with nature was depicted with fearsome effect. As one would expect, these films – like those devoted to Frankenstein, who was first brought to the screen in 1910 – shared many characteristics of the contemporary horror films like *Das Kabinett des Dr Caligari* (1919) and *Nosferatu* (1922). In early Science Fiction literature from H.G. Wells to the pulp magazines that were the forcing ground of Science Fiction, fantasy and science were blended together; *Weird Tales*, one of the first major Science Fiction magazines, cultivated this ambiguity of genre by its very name in the hopes of greater sales.

Against this backdrop, the problem of describing the realm of Science Fiction becomes much simpler. We are not looking for a pure genre, one that can be distinguished from the thriller or horror in some absolute way, but for those films with significant Science Fiction elements. Only in this way can a useful, informative tradition of Science Fiction film-making be created. Science Fiction cannot really be said to exist as a genre until the fifties. Before then, it makes better sense to talk of films with Science Fiction elements. It is for this reason, to establish a Science Fiction tradition, that in the following pages space has been found for the historical curiosities, many of which sadly have been lost, of the early years of the cinema, the Frankenstein films and the gadget-ridden serials and films of the thirties, forties and beyond.

The serials of the thirties and the forties, with their melodramatic adventure plots about megalomaniac villains seeking world domination through the use of the invention of an eccentric and misunderstood scientist and their charmingly naïve special effects, though rarely highlighting the terrors of living in a technological world that man can no longer satisfactorily control, nevertheless remain subdued reflections of the central situation that Science Fiction addresses. The 'what if?' extrapolations of such films may be minor compared to those of Wells' **Things to Come** (1936) and the science closer to pseudo-science but, in their deployment of Science Fiction elements, they are important examples of the parameters of the contemporary would-be Science Fiction genre. Furthermore, they represent a key influence on the Science Fiction films of the present, even from an eighties' viewpoint. When the nuclear holocaust seems a daily possibility, genetic engineering and spare-part surgery are a reality, industrial robots are an everyday sight and domestic robots are promised in a few years, the computer revolution seems about to produce the first intelligent machines and the American government talks of developing **Star Wars**-type weapons' systems, serialdom's cyclotrodes, dynamic vibrators, radio-atomic power transmitters and the like seem as naïve as the predictions of H.G. Wells were wrong-headed. But then, in the phrase employed by Republic to promote **The Crimson Ghost** (1940), the serials were 'ripped from the headlines of the day'. The Science Fiction film, though it deals (mainly) with the future is made in the present, is, in the words of Vivian Sobchack, 'embedded in its [and our] technological, political, social and linguistic present'. Accordingly, though it takes for its subject matter the future, parallel universes and the like, in short that which is literally impossible as things stand in the present, of all the film genres Science Fiction is the most revealing of the times that produced it. Its predictions are regularly overtaken by events but the importance of the predictions is not their correctness but the extrapolative process that produced them.

If only because, since the days of the silent cinema, Hollywood has been the major producer of Science Fiction films, American concerns and aesthetics have been dominant in the genre. This, added to the enormous research problems posed by the Italian and Mexican popular cinemas, say, and the cultural bafflement raised by Science Fiction films in which corpulent masked wrestlers are commonplace and mythological figures regularly fight off aliens, helps to explain why histories of the Science Fiction cinema have been written from a Hollywood perspective. In the entries that follow, we have attempted, successfully I hope, to redress the balance and at least begin to uncover the very distinctive concerns of other countries' contributions to the genre.

The various monster movies (Kaiju Eiga) that form the basis of the Japanese tradition of Science Fiction film-making provide the classic example of just how different Science Fiction can be outside Hollywood. As in so many American films of the fifties and beyond, the trauma of the atomic bomb is palpably present in every image but the questions raised by the bomb and militarism are significantly different in Japan. In the first generation of films, such as **Gojira** (1954) and **Chikyu Boeigun** (1957) – in which aliens from the planet Mysteroid are seeking Earthwomen to mate with because, as a result of a prolonged nuclear war, some 90 per cent of their progeny have to be destroyed at birth – the monsters are, like the Japanese, victims of nuclear aggression. Thus they vent their anger through the repeated destruction of Tokyo – which bizarrely stands in for America – while at the same time showing their cultural identification with the Japanese by

treating the populace with care and concern. The next wave of movies, which includes such films as **Mosura** (1961), sees the monsters – the metaphor for nuclear power – that do battle over the rooftops of Tokyo divided into two camps, good and bad. Thus the nuclear-spawned monsters become the defenders of Japan. The next stage in the genre's development is for the monsters, for example Ghidorah, to become the defenders of the world when space monsters attack Japan/the world. Significantly this shift in the monsters' function paralled the growing pressures (both internal and external) on Japan to re-arm. This in turn was followed by a series of films, beginning with **Gamera Tai Shinkai Kaiju Jigura** (1971), which took the ideologically safer topic of pollution for their subject, the ecological disturbance being created either by industrial waste, as in **Gojira Tai Hedora** (1971), or by aliens, as in **Gojira Tai Gaigan** (1972). The thematic complexity of these films, often hidden by the cultural conditions of their production – many are children's films and all are constructed with a theatricality that is alien to Western audiences – result in Japanese Science Fiction, which is still developing, being one of the most engrossing manifestations of the genre.

The cyclical nature of Japanese Science Fiction, itself an indication of the sheer numbers of films being produced, can also be seen in the Latin cinema. In Italy, as one would expect from the home of international co-productions, the cycles are less evident. As well as relocating vampires and the traditional heroes of the Italian cinema like Maciste (for example, **Maciste e la Regina di Samar**, 1965), in the world of Science Fiction, the Italian cinema, as ever, has been quick to adapt American and other influences. Thus in the sixties, as well as the numerous James Bond lookalikes (including one starring Sean Connery's younger brother, Neil, as James Bond's younger brother – **OK Connery**, 1967), Italy also produced fifties type American space adventures such as **I Criminali della Galassia** (1965) in which the angular histrionics of their American models were transformed into far more seductive and visually exciting forms. If the Science Fiction films of Italy were less pure than those of other Latin countries, because, in the main, they were aimed at the international, rather than the domestic, market those of Spain and, in particular, Mexico, are so introverted as to be unpalatable outside their countries of origin. The numerous Mexican films starring the likes of Santo and the Blue Demon are constructed around such simple pleasures (of narrative, excitement and so forth) and have at their centre such grotesque heroes that Batman and Superman seem rounded, complex characters by comparison. The one strand in Latin Science Fiction that has made its mark in the international film market is a gruesome mix of horror and Science Fiction elements, centred on sadistic surgical and sexual motifs. This sub-genre can be traced back to Jesús Franco's influential **Gritos en la Noche** (1962) and beyond and has in recent years been a strong influence on exploitation films.

The Science Fiction films of Eastern Europe pose a similar problem, but of a political rather than a cultural nature. Though, compared to American films of the fifties, they are surprisingly free of simple propaganda, the political context in which they are produced is an ever-present force. Moreover, like Science Fiction literature, Science Fiction films were generally held in higher regard than in either Britain or America long before **Star Wars** (1977) changed the position of Science Fiction in Hollywood. In part, but only in part, this is because Science Fiction films in Eastern Europe fulfil many of the functions of films of social comment or historical movies in the West. In societies where interrogations of the present and pre-revolutionary past are frowned upon, Science Fiction has become a means of social criticism. The classic example of this is the Polish film **Wojna Świ010atów – Nastepne Stulecie** (1981) which was clearly a response to Russian intervention in Poland. Similarly, **Solaris** (1971), which has generally been seen in the West as a metaphysical film, has been reviewed in the Soviet Union as a political work of art. If, as in the West,

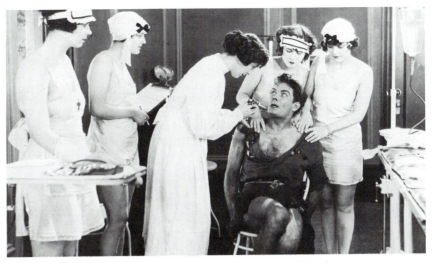

there is a questioning of present trends, albeit more hidden, in the Science Fiction of Eastern Europe, even more marked in the films is their general air of optimism and occasional lyricism, epitomized in the marvellous **Planeta Burg** (1962), sadly best known in the West in the various bastardized versions produced by Roger Corman (**Voyage to a Prehistoric Planet** and **Voyage to the Prehistoric Planet of Women**, both 1966). Certainly the cinema of Eastern Europe is startling in terms of variety and originality.

The Fifties

In his history of Science Fiction literature, *Billion Year Spree,* to best suggest the woeful lack of imagination behind much of the pulpwriting of the twenties, Brian Aldiss offers a description of a characteristic story of the period.

A typical story might relate how a scientist experimenting in his private laboratory found a new way to break up atoms so as to release their explosive powers; in so doing, he sets up a self-perpetuating vortex of energy which kills either the scientist or his assistant, or else threatens the career of his beautiful daughter, before it rolls out of the window and creates great havoc against which the local fire brigade is powerless. The vortex grows bigger and more erratic all the while. Soon it is destroying New York (or Berlin or London or Moscow) and causing great panic. Tens of thousands of lunatics roam the open countryside, destroying everything in their path. The CID (or the militia or the Grenadier Guards or the Red Army) is helpless.

Fortunately, the scientist's favourite assistant, or the reporter on the local newspaper, or the boy friend of the beautiful daughter, has a great idea, which is immediately taken up by the President (or the Chancellor or the King or Stalin). Huge tractors with gigantic electromagnets are built in every country, and these move in on the vortex, which is now very large indeed, having just consumed San Francisco Bridge (or Krupp's works or Buckingham Palace or the Kremlin). Either everything goes well, with the hero and the beautiful daughter riding on the footplate of one of the giant machines as the vortex is repulsed into space – or else things go wrong at the last minute, until a volcanic eruption of unprecedented violence takes place, and shoots the vortex into space.

The hero and the beautiful daughter get engaged (or receive medals or bury daddy or are purged) by the light of a beautiful new moon.

Aldiss' concoction is doubly interesting for the historian of the Science Fiction film, for it is as accurate an account of the world of the serials of the thirties and forties (and with revision would do as a description of the structure of many films of the fifties) as it is of the stories of the twenties. The scripts of those films are certainly as tawdry as the stories Aldiss is parodying, but the films have the saving grace that they are constructed in images rather than Gernsbackian prose. More important here than how good or bad the films were is their uniformity. This highlights one of the most significant preconditions for the existence of a genre: that numerous films of a similar nature should be made. This is precisely what happened in the isolated backwaters of Poverty Row in Hollywood in the thirties and forties where serials and B features were churned out by the likes of Republic and Columbia. The seemingly cast-iron formulae that ruled their construction, whether they were westerns, thrillers or Science Fiction films – or combinations of all three as in the bizarre **Phantom Empire** (1935) in which a singing cowboy takes on crooks and robots in the underground continent of Murania – admitted for the deployment of Science Fiction elements only in the most restricted fashion.

Monsters of the Fifties:
top: The Beginning of
the End *(1957),*
bottom left: Rodan
(1956) and bottom
right: The Thing
(1951).

Following the demise of the serial – undeniably the major source of Science Fiction film-making in the forties – these restrictions were lifted and the various elements coalesced to create the Science Fiction film as a genre in its own right for the first time in its history. In the post-Hiroshima world Science Fiction made emotional sense. The fears that Science Fiction had treated in the past were all too real and the genre flourished as a means of simultaneously highlighting and banishing those fears as film after film depicted the awful consequences of the misapplications of technology and man's ability, after much destruction, to regain control of his destiny. Just how shocking was the realization that we were living in the first atomic age and had the power to destroy mankind (or by extension that there were others in the universe who might care to unleash their 'atomic weapons' on us) can be seen by contrasting the films of the fifties with the earlier future-war films. Prior to World Wars I and II future-war films briefly flourished but once the wars they predicted came about the films ceased to be made. The end of World War II, on the other hand, fuelled Science Fiction film-making in the fifties. Where before imagination had been dulled by the horrifying realities of war, the far more terrifying end to World War II traumatized the imaginations of Science Fiction film-makers.

Equally important to the new found social and emotional relevance of the Science Fiction film was the restructuring of Hollywood that occurred after the war. By the fifties the absolute power of the studios was broken. Before then, the studio contract had dominated all aspects of film-making; after the war as agents, stars, distributors, exhibitors, producers and directors began setting up their own projects, independent productions became more and more common. In this new atmosphere independents like George Pal, producer of the landmark film **Destination Moon** (1950), found it marginally easier to raise finance for their projects. And once teenagers were identified as the major cinema-going audience – as their parents stayed at home in front of their television sets in ever greater numbers – Hollywood became more committed to the once disreputable Science Fiction genre. Accordingly, as the decade passed, more and more films were aimed at this specific market; there were even stories constructed with a specific youth angle in films like **Teenage Monster** (1957), **The Blob, The Space Children** (both 1958) and **Teenagers from Outer Space** (1959). By the mid-fifties, the distribution and exhibition patterns of Science Fiction films, with the exception of the big-budget extravaganzas of the period – **War of the Worlds** (1953), **1984** (1956) – were targeted almost exclusively at the youth audience. By all accounts more Science Fiction films were played in drive-in cinemas (the growth of which in the fifties coincided directly with the Science Fiction boom) than were films of any other genre. This renaissance of Science Fiction resulted in a contraction in the market for westerns simply because the western was far less adaptable to both the new youth audience and the feelings of the period. The career of Roger Corman again provides the classic example of this change. He began his career in 1955 making westerns, traditionally the one area in Hollywood where there was space for independent productions, but after four films switched to Science Fiction before once more decisively switching genres in the early sixties.

Thus, in the fifties, the emotional and social climate in which Science Fiction films could thrive, the restructuring of Hollywood which gave independent producers increased possibilities and a sufficiently large audience combined to make the production of Science Fiction films by independents (and a few major studios) economically viable. From this confluence of factors Science Fiction emerged as a genre in its own right. Hence Susan Sontag, like Brian Aldiss before her, could begin her seminal essay on the Science Fiction film, *The Imagination of Disaster*, by cataloguing and describing 'the typical Science Fiction film' of the period.

In the entries on the individual films and the decade introduction to the fifties, the films are described in detail and various strands and themes are picked out. Here I want to address perhaps the most obvious fact about the films, why so many of them were bad. In the wake of the contemporary vogue for camp, films like **Robot Monster** (1953) and **Plan 9 from Outer Space** (1956), to name but two, have acquired a cult status for their very badness. What lies at the heart of this celebration, which occurred at precisely the time Hollywood was demonstrating with films like **Star Wars** (1977) just how good its special effects were, is a peculiar justification of the professional nature of Hollywood film-making. While it is true there is nothing as funny as an inept special effect – of which there were many in the fifties as director/producers like Bert I. Gordon, Larry Buchanan and Edward D. Wood turned their attention to Science Fiction – those films, and numerous 'better-made' ones are far more revealing of the problems that Science Fiction films faced (and posed) than their cult celebration suggests. Lurking behind every frame of fifties Science Fiction (especially the Japanese films, for obvious reasons) is the fear of a nuclear Armageddon. So much so that by the end of the decade monsters of all shapes and sizes were introduced with nothing but a muttered comment about radiation as the justification for their appearance. And yet, understandably and with few notable exceptions, the films are unable to come to terms with the fears they deal in. If Hiroshima unleashed the possibility of man's annihilation at the hands of his own technology and if that technology held the promise of reducing him to the status of a robot, life in the fifties was unthinkable without the support of that same technology. Thus it is rare in fifties films for scientists or science itself to be held responsible for the monsters they created. In **Them!** (1954), for example, the central situation results from an experiment that simply went terribly wrong. Similarly, the military, the very people who dropped the bomb on Hiroshima, were generally given the role of riding 7th-Cavalry style to the rescue (**Them!** again). Moreover, one of the chief pleasures of the films of the period are the scenes of wholesale destruction they offer.

Faced with the conflicting demands of needing to alarm and reassure their audiences simultaneously, it is hardly surprising that few directors and writers were able to produce aesthetically harmonious works and that so much Science Fiction of the fifties should reflect in a confused way the ambivalent, complex feelings of the period. But, if there is much confusion at the heart of films like **This Island Earth** (1955), especially when compared to the clarity of a Japanese film like **Chikyu Boeigun** (1957), that confusion is richly textured. Certainly, compared to **War of the Worlds** (1953), which retreated to a religious position and suggested that the Martian invasion was to teach man a lesson, films like **This Island Earth**, for all the blandness of their characterization and dialogue, have a power and resonance that remains to this day. **This Island Earth** is in no way a bad film in the manner of so many Science Fiction films of the fifties, but even run-of-the-mill offerings have occasional moments of surrealism that result from the contradictory impulses that set them in motion and, as such, are far more revealing and touching than many of the more respectable films of the decade. The films may represent inadequate responses to the fears they so capably played upon in the name of entertainment, but simply by being made in such numbers they underscored the depth of those fears. All Science Fiction, almost by definition, addresses these fears in some way; what the films of the fifties demonstrate is just how potent the films could be.

Recent Years and the Future

By the mid-eighties it was clear that the Science Fiction film stood at a crossroads. Most of the films that poured forth in increasing numbers from Hollywood had an escapism about them that sat oddly with the tenor of the times that produced them. Ironically, the name of one of the most successful escapist Science Fiction films of the period, **Star Wars**, was taken by the American government, despite the objections of its creator, to help popularize the nuclear weapons system it planned to establish in outer space.

On the one hand, such films were clearly constrained by the need to be profitable, requiring a vast audience to pay for their huge budgets and overwhelming special effects. On the other hand, it was as though three decades of living with fears of imminent devastation had so numbed our imaginations that the reassurance of escapism was demanded by the film-going public. This was all the more understandable in the light of the fact that, after all, the bomb hadn't been dropped (again), space had been understood and mastered, if not exactly conquered, and, as the computer revolution has demonstrated so explicitly, the new technology was far more user-friendly than it was ever expected to be. The resulting placidity was reflected in the extravagant 'space operas' that followed in the wake of *Star Wars* and the (often would-be) aching optimism of the sons of **Close Encounters of the Third Kind** (both 1977).

However, as the eighties proceeded, several significant changes took place. The reception of the telefilm *The Day After* (1983), with its surprisingly matter-of-fact depiction of the immediate effects of a nuclear war, and the sombre **Testament** (1983) and **When the Wind Blows** (1986) demonstrated that Science Fiction films need not be just spectacular. And even when they were, as in the ongoing series of sequels to the decade's big budget success, some reflected the social issues of the day, albeit for the most part in simple-minded fashion. Thus **Star Trek IV: The Voyage Home** (1986) had a fashionable ecological gloss, and **Superman IV: The Quest for Peace** (1987) reflected the fast-developing mood of *glasnost*. More important was **E.T.** (1982), which introduced a new theme – the family in peril – and saw the genre turning away from outer space in response to a broad social concern that was also reflected in other films of the period. Even an action-packed movie like **Back to the Future** (1985) and its even faster-paced sequel (1989) took as their central thesis the possible disruption of the McFly family, should the alternative worlds briefly envisioned come to pass.

Back to the Future can also be described as a teen movie, one of the many of the eighties. Indeed in part, by the end of the decade, it was more sensible to talk of films like **Weird Science** (1985) and **Earth Girls Are Easy** (1988) as having Science Fiction elements than as being 'pure' Science Fiction. Of course there were pure Science Fiction outings, like the flawed **Blade Runner** (1982) with its chilling vision of the future, and **RoboCop** (1987) with its intriguing, if derivative, notions of the melding of man and the mechanical, but in the main such films were to be found in the exploitation strand of film-making. There **Mad Max II** (1981) and its grimy post-nuclear holocaust of a future was the most imitated film of the decade, closely followed by the still influential **Alien** (1977), whose sons and daughters continued to slash their way across America's screens. Another feature of many of these exploitation films was a growing self-consciousness with their in-references to fifties' films and retro chic.

By the end of the decade it was clear that Science Fiction films had lost the homogeneous feel they had at the beginning of the eighties: they were less escapist yet more derivative, more comic than pessimistic, but still questioning.

1895-1919

(1895) and Ferdinand Zecca's **A la Conquête de l'Air** (1901), were comic in intent and lasted only a minute or two, Georges Méliès' **Le Voyage dans la Lune** (1902) was a landmark in the history of the cinema, as much for its sophisticated narrative and epic length as for its subject matter which was derived from Jules Verne and H.G. Wells. Méliès' film marks the real beginnings of the Science Fiction cinema. Where other film-makers had been content to poke fun at the new and emergent technologies of the 20th century – X-rays, air flight, electricity, the motorcar – Méliès created a Science Fiction story and, in the process, identified the theme of space travel which became one of the abiding themes of the genre. Other directors isolated other themes and began to elaborate upon them, thus moulding the genre, but it was Méliès who laid its foundation.

After 1910, though trick films such as **La Ceinture Electrique** and **The Electric Leg** (both 1912 and both derived from earlier electricity films) continued to be made, film-makers and audiences took a more measured view of the 'impossibilities' they wished to make possible. Undoubtedly the most ironic illustration of this trend was the reception of **A la Conquête du Pôle** (1912), one of the last films Georges Méliès made before being forced to return to the stage as a magician. The film was quite simply too old-fashioned for the public: what had been revolutionary in 1902's *Le Voyage dans la Lune* was old hat a decade later. Méliès' fantastic voyages were supplanted by less imaginative but more directly compelling scenarios, such as those of the future-war sub-genre which made its first appearance with Walter Booth's **Airship Destroyer** (1909). Films of this type, which included **England's Menace, An Englishman's Home, Wake Up!** and **If England Were Invaded,** all of which were completed in 1914, when the possibility under imagination was a probability, touched real fears with their 'what if England were invaded' scenarios.

A la Conquête du Pôle was also old-fashioned in terms of its construction. Méliès' tableaux were undramatic and the film's characters stereotypes when compared to the faster paced American films of the day which featured more believable characters and situations. Films like **Frankenstein** (1910), the first version of Mary Shelley's classic novel – one that would reverberate through the history of both the Science Fiction and horror cinemas – **Without a Soul** (1916) and **Twenty Thousand Leagues Under the Sea** (1916) with its astounding underwater cinematography, were as fantastic as Méliès' film, but their emphasis was completely different. Similarly, serials and films like **The Exploits of Elaine** (1914), and its sequels, and those devoted to the cinema's first scientific detectives (such as **Lady Baffles and Detective Duck,** and **The Black Box,** both 1915, and **The Hand of Peril,** 1916) by their sheer speed and invention seemed to come from a different world from Méliès' 1912 film. It is also worth noting that the films devoted to the exploits of scientific detectives, which laid the foundations of a tradition that would flourish spectacularly in the thirties and again in the sixties in the wake of James Bond, included dramatically fashioned revisions of much of the content of the trick films of earlier years.

In America the new emphasis on narrative, speed and increased characterization transformed notions of the Science Fiction film, as well as film in general. In Europe too, the simple dramas of trick photography and fantastic happenings of earlier times developed along more sophisticated lines. Films like **Der Golem** (1914), **Verdens Undergang** and **Homunculus** (both 1916) were far more sombre than anything produced at the time in America. This is especially true of Fritz Lang's **Die Spinnen** (1919) which, though it remains one of the best *Boys' Own* adventure stories ever filmed, is far darker in tone than its American counterparts. It was this growing divergence of American and European notions of what cinema was and what it could do that shaped the Science Fiction cinema of the twenties.

Previous pages: *The wonderfully innocent world of early Science Fiction,* Le Voyage dans la Lune *(1902).*

Innocent Beginnings

If the cinema has its physical origins in a variety of scientific endeavours, on 28 December 1895, when Louis and Auguste Lumière held their first film show to paying customers in Paris, it entered the mainstream of the entertainment industry. Henceforth, the theatre, vaudeville and magic shows would be equally important elements in shaping its future. Accordingly the history of the early years of the cinema is a history of technical developments, of attempts to regularize film distribution and of the trickery by which the spectators' eyes were deceived by the hands of film-makers, who used undercranking and stop-motion techniques to make the impossible (moving pictures) possible. The description was later applied to the Science Fiction film itself.

Looking back to those days from the present, and literally excavating the beginnings of the Science Fiction film, it is easy to see Science Fiction elements in the numerous trick films of the period. But set against those simple films, most of which, like the Lumière brothers **Charcuterie Méchanique**

Right: *The founding fathers of the American Mutoscope and Biograph Company (left to right): H.N. Marvin, William Kennedy Laurie Dickson, Herman Casler and E.B. Koopman, photographed in 1895. Their company was founded to exploit the Biograph camera and projector with its sharper screen image when Edison refused to regularly supply them with films. The* Sausage Machine *was one of their early films.*

Charcuterie Méchanique: *It is fitting that mass production should be the subject of the first recorded example of a Science Fiction film. The film itself consists simply of the humorous transformation of a live pig into its processed products. The fear of standardization, also reflected in* Chirurgien Americain *(1897) – in Europe mass production was known as the 'American system' – was to be one of the most enduring themes of the Science Fiction cinema.*

1895

Charcuterie Méchanique *aka* The Mechanical Butcher
(LUMIERE; FR) b/w 1 min
The automated factory was predicted in this short film, in which one single machine converts a live animal into its processed products. The apparatus, similar to a standard sausage grinder, filled most of the single scene. A live pig was pushed by a butcher into one end of the machine, and moments later emerged from the other end as hams, spare ribs, bacon, strings of sausages, and other products. This film was catalogued under the heading 'Humorous Subjects'. Producer Lumière was the co-inventor of the cinématograph, and was mainly concerned with filming actualities. This film is a rare instance of his fictional work, and even rarer as a Science Fictional work. It inspired a great many imitations and variations by English and American producers, each of whom added their own interpretations to the theme.

co-d/p Louis Lumière *co-d* Auguste Lumière

1897

Chirurgien Americain *aka* A Twentieth Century Surgeon
(STAR; FR) b/w 2 min
This short film forecasts the whole present-day science of medical transplants in the humorous fashion of the period. Interestingly Méliès chose to call his film *Chirurgien Americain*. A beggar who has lost both his legs enters a doctor's surgery, and is swiftly supplied with a new pair of living limbs. The tramp is delighted, and the surgeon, clearly a filmic precursor of Baron Frankenstein, thinking that he might as well make a good job of the man, cuts off his rather unattractive head. This he replaces with a head of classic beauty, which registers distaste at his ragged raiment. So the surgeon changes the man's torso too and, handsomely clad, the totally renewed ex-tramp thanks the surgeon and departs in delight.

d/p/s Georges Méliès *lp* Georges Méliès

Gugusse et l' Automate *aka* The Clown and the Automaton (STAR; FR) b/w 1 min
Automatons, mechanical men, what after Karel Capek's play *R.U.R.* we came to call robots, were a 19th-century obsession, and indeed have their origins in the mists of alchemy. The invention of clockwork and its application to toys increased the interest, and fantasy writers like E.T.A. Hoffmann stirred the fascination with their tales, particularly *The Sandman*, 1815. Imitations of mechanical behaviour were popular on the vaudeville stage, and clearly this brief film is based on one such performance. We have to imagine the reaction of a typical French circus clown to the sudden mechanical movements of an automaton, for reportedly the film has been long lost. Even the descriptions of the day are all too brief and unhelpful as to content. The English catalogue simply says: 'Comic – good definition.' The film was the first to be produced by Méliès at his brand new studio in Montreuil-sous-Bois.

Gugusse was a professional clown from the Cirque d'Hiver in Paris.

d/p/s Georges Méliès *lp* Gugusse

Making Sausages *aka* The End of All Things
(G.A.S.; GB) b/w 1 min
This British film has basically the same plot as **The Sausage Machine,** made in the same year by the American Mutoscope and Biograph Company. The exact date of the New York film is not known, but George A. Smith, the producer of this film, recorded the sale of his first print to an Owen Brooks on 22 December 1897. It seems likely that Smith would have seen the Bioscope presentation on a visit to London, and devised his 'cover version' on returning to his Brighton studio. At the time, Bioscope films could only be shown on the huge and heavy Bioscope projectors, so their distribution potential was limited to one or two major theatres.

The original synopsis, published in the Warwick Trading Company's catalogue, is worth quoting in full, as it describes the film succinctly. 'Four men cooks at work in the kitchen. Live cats and dogs are put into the machine and come out as sausages. Incidentally a duck and an old boot is added to give flavour to the string.' And the writer added the comment, 'Always goes well.'

There were further variations on this fantastic machine theme, concluding in 1904 with Edison's **Dog Factory.** Details of the length of Smith's film vary. It is listed in contemporary sources as both 50 and 75 ft, both considerably shorter than the footage quoted in *A Reference Guide to American Science Fiction Films*, which makes it an impossible epic for the period: 1,250 ft!

d/p/s/c George A. Smith

Les Rayons Roentgen *aka* A Novice at X-Rays
(STAR; FR) b/w 1 min
Méliès, the great French pioneer of the trick film, devised and produced this satire on the recent discovery of the invisible penetrative rays by W.A. Roentgen. It was made three months after the British satire, **X-Rays** (1897), and whilst it may have been inspired by Smith's film, it makes a completely different and original comic point. The film is a single scene, which takes place in a scientific laboratory. The professor, played by Méliès himself, receives a client who desires to be X-rayed. The professor sits him in front of an apparatus and switches on. The patient's skeleton appears, then steps out of the

man's body, leaving the unsupported flesh to fall limply to the floor. A reversal of the switch restores the patient, who refuses to pay for the treatment, to normal. The professor insists, a scuffle ensues, and the table supporting the apparatus is overturned. The X-ray tube explodes and blows up the professor, whose remains are scattered all over the laboratory. A catalogue comment adds: 'A splendid subject, full of action and surprises!'

There are at least two special effects used in this short film: double exposure, to fade in the skeleton over the body, and stop action, to remove the professor and explode him into pieces. This was Méliès' second Science Fiction picture.

d/p/s Georges Méliès   *lp* Georges Méliès

The Sausage Machine

(AMERICAN MUTOSCOPE AND BIOGRAPH CO.)   b/w   1 min
The theory that lost and stray dogs were turned into sausagemeat was not a new one when this film was produced in New York. The popular slang term for a sausage in a roll was, of course, a 'hot dog'. What was new in this film was the creation of a complicated automatic machine capable of converting live dogs into strings of sausages in one single operation. This in itself was a satire on the conveyor belt systems currently being installed in American factories. Here derby-hatted operatives are seen feeding live dogs into one end of the great machine, which after much whirring of wheels delivers long strings of sausages through the outlet pipe. The film evidently remained in popular circulation for some years, for it was not copyrighted until 11 November 1902. It was also held up as an example of cinematic magic, frames from the film being reproduced in Albert E. Hopkins' treatise, *Magic*, published 1897.

Credits not available

X-Rays *aka* The X-Ray Fiend

(G.A.S.; GB)   b/w   1 min
In 1895 Louis Lumière patented his cinématograph and W. A. Roentgen demonstrated the penetrative qualities of the mysterious rays first discovered by Sir William Crookes. Small wonder, then, that the two most amazing discoveries of the decade should quickly link. In April 1897 Dr John McIntyre showed his X-ray cinematography of a frog's leg to the Glasgow Philosophical Society, and in October 1897 George Albert Smith, film-maker of Brighton, Sussex, made this humorous piece of Scientific Fiction, known to him as *X-Rays* and through later distributors' catalogues as the more commercial *The X-Ray Fiend*. To play the part of his eccentric professor, Smith hired Green, a comedian well-known in the area for his appearances in seaside summer

shows and Christmas pantomimes. For his two days' work on the one-minute film Green was paid 13s ($2). The only other expense listed in the G.A. Smith cashbook, preserved in London's National Film Archive, is the sum of 1s for a 'skeleton's shirt'. The idea for the film undoubtedly came to Smith from his neighbour and film-maker, James A. Williamson. Williamson was a chemist and had actually bought a Roentgen ray apparatus a month before (noted in *Amateur Photographer*, September 1897). Smith's synopsis is simple: Professor Green turns his X-ray machine onto a courting couple as a prank and exposes their embracing skeletons! As Smith's cashbook does not include a payment to the courting couple, we can assume amateur status. The film, made over 6 and 7 October, cost 14s, and the first copy was sold 21 days later to exhibitor David Devant for £2 10s. Even in 1897 movie-making was a profitable business!

d/p/s/c George A. Smith   *lp* Tom Green

La Lune à un Mètre *aka* A Trip to the Moon *aka* The Astronomer's Dream *aka* The Man in the Moon

(STAR/LUBIN; FR)   b/w   3 min
A Trip to the Moon might seem to be the first film to bear a title indicative of space travel. It contained nothing of the sort. It was the American release title of the Méliès fantasy, *La Lune à un Mètre*, which was given a less sensational, more truthful, title by the Frenchman's British releasing company, Warwick Trading: *The Astronomer's Dream*. Yet even they hinted at Science Fictional trimmings by adding an alternative title, *The Man in the Moon*. The film, entirely a Mélièsian whimsy, concerns an ancient astronomer who has a vision that his observatory is visited by a comically animated Moon which changes into a fairy maiden, would not warrant inclusion in this catalogue were it not for its American change of title, which has caused it to be considered by casual researchers the first American Science Fiction production. However, some deep research by George C. Pratt of George Eastman House has revealed the true story behind the title.

The film was copyrighted in the United States by film producer Sigmund Lubin, on 26 June 1899, some nine months after it was made. The change of title was not merely for box-office appeal: Lubin had pirated a French print and copyrighted it in his own name. It was actually shown earlier, in the programme of the Ninth and Arch Museum in Philadelphia, from 10 April 1899. On 10 June Lubin advertised the film in the *New York Clipper* as 'Absolutely new: *The Astronomer's Dream and Trip to the Moon*.' The following year Lubin advertised the film again, this time as *The Marvellous Trip to the Moon* (10 March 1900). The footage was given as 300ft, which is 105ft longer than Méliès' original. Either something extra had been added, or Lubin was exaggerating. Two years later Lubin advertised the film yet again, and again the footage had mysteriously increased. Now (11 October 1902) it was all of 1,200ft, a running time of 20 minutes!? In January 1903 Lubin published a new edition of his catalogue, which contains a detailed description of the film, now entitled *The Astronomer's Dream or the Trip to the Moon*. It begins with the complete Méliès *La Lune à un Mètre*, but after the astronomer has fallen asleep again at the end, Lubin adds these words: 'All the nursery rhymes are brought into play in this beautiful film. You see the old favourite rhyme "Hi Diddle Diddle". It is indeed a funny sight to see a cow jumping over the moon, but it is plainly shown in this marvellous moving picture.' Whether or not this additional film material was made by Lubin, or pirated from other productions, is not known: unfortunately whatever material Lubin deposited at the Copyright Office in Washington has disappeared. But it would seem from the evidence that the first American astronaut to make the trip to the Moon was a cow.

d/p/s Georges Méliès   *lp* Georges Méliès

Left: La Lune à un Mètre, *Georges Méliès' whimsical fantasy which was pirated and much extended by Sigmund Lubin.*

The cinema of Karl Knuebbel on Frankfurt station at the turn of the century.

1899

Un Bon Lit *aka* A Midnight Episode
(STAR; FR) b/w 1 min
The first film to feature an outsize insect and thus the forerunner of a genre that plagued the fifties and seventies. The single scene is the guest bedroom of an inn, where a guest retires for the night. The rays of the Moon shine on the bed through the open window. The sleeping man is suddenly awakened by a 'bug of gigantic proportions' which crawls over him. Jumping out of bed, he attacks the monstrosity and destroys it. As he is climbing back into bed he spots three more of the breed climbing the wall. He lights a candle and applies the flame to each bug 'causing them to explode with fine smoke effects'. After this mass slaughter he returns to bed and is soon sleeping.

Méliès, who made the film, had been a cartoonist, and the problem of bed-bugs was a typical one in the nineties. The fashioning of the several monstrous insects would not have presented many problems to him, although their means of movement must remain a mystery. The explosions would require careful stage-management, unless some stop-frame procedure was used. This film is an elaborated remake of a less Science Fictional film Méliès had produced three years earlier: *Une Nuit Terrible* (1896).

d/p/s Georges Méliès

La Pierre Philosophale *aka* The Philosopher's Stone
(STAR; FR) b/w 1 min
Charles Chaplin called Méliès 'a veritable alchemist of light', and, interestingly enough, Méliès played the leading role of the old alchemist in this early film. Alchemy could be considered the first Science Fictional science, for its students sought to create chemically a substance that would change base metal into gold, the so-called philosopher's stone. In this film, Méliès' philosopher succeeds, only to discover his triumph is nothing but a vision. The setting is the interior of a laboratory where a metallurgist is conducting his experiments. He puts various chemicals into a cauldron which is heating in a large open fireplace. Each new addition causes great clouds of smoke to ascend the chimney. Suddenly, out of the mists, evolves the distinct shape of a huge golden sovereign. This in turn dissolves into a beautiful woman offering the experimenter and his assistant a bag of gold. As they reach forth to grab it the apparition vanishes completely, and they realize the whole thing was a vision of their fevered

brains. The special effects required here were achieved by double exposure in the camera.

d/p/s Georges Méliès *lp* Georges Méliès

The X-Ray Mirror
(AMERICAN MUTOSCOPE AND BIOGRAPH CO.) b/w 2 min
X-rays, discovered in 1895 by W.A. Roentgen, were still a marvel to the public at large when the Biograph Company made this fantastical film only four years later. It was catalogued under the heading 'Trick Pictures' in the 1902 Advance Partial List, so evidently it was popular enough to warrant a longish life. The plot of Film No. 1179 is brief, as was the film (it is quoted as running '1½ lengths'). 'Girl goes to mirror to try on hat; sees ballet girl, and faints.' As the film was never deposited with the Library of Congress Copyright Office, no print has been preserved, so any elaboration on the above has to be conjecture. Whether there was an inventor of the mysterious X-ray mirror, as with the curious machine in the earlier British film, **X-Rays** (1897), we cannot know. Why the girl should see herself as a ballet dancer and not a skeleton, as the title leads one to suppose, is another mystery. Certainly the Biograph Company knew how to make such a transformation, for they had turned one of their actresses into a skeleton in both *The Cremation* and *The Startled Lover*, films numbered 908 and 909 and both made the previous year, 1898. The third mystery is why the sight of herself in a ballet skirt should have made the young lady faint – but it was a modest age!

d/c Wallace McCutcheon

1900

Coppélia ou la Poupée Animée *aka* Coppelia the Animated Doll (STAR; FR) b/w 2 min
Méliès' second venture into the subject of automata after **Gugusse et l'Automate** (1897). Unfortunately it is as sparsely dealt with in contemporary sources as the first. However, because of his frank titling we can deduce that this was a version, doubtless unauthorized, of *Coppélia*, the currently popular ballet by Délibes. This in turn derived from Edmond Audrian's opera, *La Poupée*, an 1896 adaptation to music of E.T.A. Hoffmann's 1815 story, *The Sandman*. The total film length of 130ft would not allow much plot development beyond the dollmaker's animation of his life-size dancing girl, but doubtless Méliès introduced one or more of his typical special effects. Unfortunately, all must be conjecture, as the film is long lost.

d/p Georges Méliès

A Jersey Skeeter
(AMERICAN MUTOSCOPE AND BIOGRAPH CO.) b/w 2 min
The first American film to feature an outsize insect. Although clearly made with the intention of burlesquing the notorious mosquitoes that plagued Jersey, the film can be seen as a forerunner of the enlarged ants of **Them!** (1954).

The original synopsis, as published in the Biograph Company's Advance Partial List of Spring 1902, in which the film carries the production number 1582, is short and to the point: 'Huge mosquito is annoying farmer, and finally carries him off in the air.' The film has since been restored from the paper print deposited for copyright on 16 April 1902, and the sparse details can now be filled out a little. The old farmer is found seated at a table, quaffing from a large barrel of Jersey applejack. The mosquito swoops in and flies around the rustic's head. He swats it with his broom, loses his balance, and falls. The skeeter picks him up by the seat of the pants and flies him out of frame. As the film is taken in one single shot, quite a clever bit of model construction was required, both to fly the monster mosquito, and to enable it to grab the actor, lift him and fly him up and away.

c Arthur Marvin

21

A la Conquête de l'Air *aka* The Flying Machine

(PATHE; FR) b/w 1 min

The new century, the twentieth, was very young when this prediction of the future of aviation was conceived. So, indeed, was the science of cinematography. Zecca, the ingenious director of most Pathé films of this period, created the earliest known use of the split screen for this brief excursion into Science Fiction. Devising a remarkable studio-built aircraft, a cigar-shaped vessel steered by a ship's-style capstan linked to a rudder, and powered by pedals linked to a single bicycle wheel, Zecca had an actor dressed as the inventor pedalling the prop whilst suspended against a blank backdrop. Then he rewound the film and the lower half of the lens was separately exposed whilst photographing an aerial panorama of Paris. The resultant combination amazed audiences of the day, who must have believed that the flying bicycle had truly been invented. In fact, the small, one-man aircraft was eventually developed in France, in the 1930s and called 'The Flying Flea'.

The film was copied in America by Edwin S. Porter, as **The Twentieth Century Tramp** (1902).

d/s Ferdinand Zecca

The Elixir of Life (WILLIAMSON; GB) b/w 1 min

Rejuvenation by means both fanciful (Ponce de Léon's *Fountain of Youth*) and scientific (monkey gland injections) were popular themes in fiction during this early period of cinema, and naturally this was reflected in subjects chosen for filming. This film opens with a decrepit old man sitting at a table bemoaning his infirmities. He takes out a bottle labelled 'Elixir of Life', sniffs it, and with shaking hand pours out a glassful. He drinks it quickly, causing a coughing fit, and gradually his face relaxes, his wrinkles disappear, and soon he is young once again. He lights a cigarette and beckons the audience to come up and have a drink of the elixir. The film, taken in a single semi-close-up, may have used special effects (dissolves) or, more likely, may have relied on the facial contortions of its actor, Dalton, a comedian of the period, in the manner of John Barrymore who in the 1920 version of **Dr Jekyll and Mr Hyde** accomplished the transformation without recourse to either makeup or stop-motion photography. At any rate it must have deceived its audience, for whom the camera, especially the new cinematographic camera, could not lie.

d/p James A. Williamson *lp* Sam Dalton

Fun in a Butcher Shop (EDISON) b/w 1 min

Piracy of ideas was rife in the early years of cinema, and the Biograph Company's success with their mechanical prediction, **The Sausage Machine** (1897) led to the Edison Company's production of *Fun in a Butcher Shop* some four years later. The premise was the popularly held belief that butchers made their sausages out of dogs found wandering in the streets of the city, but the fantasy element, of course, is that a machine that took live dogs in one end and produced links of sausage at the other could exist. In this version, a small boy brings his puppy into the butcher's shop, hands it to the operative, and has his pet turned into a pound of sausages. This is achieved by less of a scientific advance than the Biograph machine: the butcher simply turns a handle.

A much improved film **Dog Factory** (1904) was later made of the same subject.

d Edwin S. Porter *p* Thomas A. Edison

The Marvellous Hair Restorer

(WILLIAMSON; GB) b/w 1 min

The continuing problem of achieving a cure for the prematurely bald male head was first aired in this short fantasy. At the turn of the century when the film was made popular magazines were full of advertisements claiming that the long-sought cure had finally been achieved, and one such English 'cure' was actually sponsored by the popular author of dramatic monologues, George R. Sims. This substance, called 'Tatcho', was widely advertised and even had a popular song written in its praise (the first singing commercial?). In this film the bottle was apparently labelled '—', according to the catalogue decription. A bald man, dissatisfied with his appearance, tries '—' and is much gratified to find that the first application makes his one single hair grow both longer and curlier. A second application gives him quite a crop of short hair. He looks in a mirror and sees he has grown even more. A third application so improves the growth that he is unable to push a comb through it. In his excitement he knocks the bottle over and is startled to see hair grow all over the table top.

The entire film was shot in semi-close-up, featuring a comedian of the day, and presumably used a series of dissolves to achieve its effects. Like so many silent shorts, it was remade several times by various companies; the most notable version was **La Lotion Miraculeuse** (1903).

d/p James A. Williamson *lp* Sam Dalton

L'Omnibus des Toques *aka* Off to Bloomingdale Asylum *aka* Off to Bedlam (STAR; FR) b/w 1 min

The extraordinary concept of a mechanical horse was first featured in American dime novels, ten cent weeklies for boys, which were the forerunners of pulp magazines. The motive power was steam, and the robot creatures themselves stem from Edward S. Ellis and his *The Steam Man of the Prairies* (1865), which was the inspiration for *Frank Reade and His Steam Man*, which led to his *Steam Horse* and an entire *Steam Team*. These tales were translated for French boys and doubtless inspired Méliès, the inventive film producer. This film opens with an omnibus drawn by 'an extraordinary mechanical horse'. Sitting on top of the bus are four negroes. The horse makes a back kick and upsets the passengers, who turn white with the shock. They start slapping one another and this makes them turn black again. The four then merge into one large negro who refuses to pay the conductor his fare. The furious conductor sets fire to his bus and the giant bursts into a thousand fragments.

The alternative titles both feature asylums – Bloomingdale for the Americans, and Bedlam for the British.

d/p/s Georges Méliès

The ingenious Ferdinand Zecca's A la Conquête de l'Air, which features the earliest known example of split-screen technique.

The first Science Fiction epic, Georges Méliès' Le Voyage dans la Lune.

An Over-Incubated Baby (PAUL; GB) b/w 1 min
The incubator, which used heat to accelerate the hatching of eggs and the growth of young chicks, is given a Science Fiction advance in this film, which predicts its use on human beings. The scene is a professor's laboratory filled with chemical implements. A large machine bears the notice 'Professor Bakem's Baby Incubator – Two Year's Growth in Two Minutes!' The professor's boy assistant is cleaning the machine when a woman enters carrying an emaciated baby. The boy takes the required fee and puts the infant in the incubator. The mother departs and the boy lights the lamp under the machine, carefully testing the temperature with an enormous thermometer. He goes to lower the lamp but clumsily upsets it. Flames shoot up and the thermometer bursts. The professor returns, is horror-struck at the sight, and throws open the incubator cabinet. A very old man totters out. The Paul Animatographe Catalogue said: 'The expressions of the sorrow stricken mother are extremely humorous!'

d/s Walter R. Booth   *p* Robert W. Paul

1902

The Twentieth Century Tramp *aka* Happy Hooligan and His Airship (EDISON) b/w 1 min
Edwin S. Porter at this time was the one-man motion picture department of the Thomas A. Edison Company. A man with an inventive turn of mind, he was not above copying other countries' productions, particularly when some new development of cinematography was involved. He carefully examined an imported print of Pathé's **A la Conquête de l'Air** (1901) and discovered how director Ferdinand Zecca had combined two separate shots in a single print. The upper half, a studio shot, showed an inventor on his one-man aircraft, apparently flying over the rooftops of Paris. This was a continuing panoramic shot of the real thing, which filled the lower half of the picture. Porter duplicated the film by having an actor dressed as the currently popular tramp hero of Fred Opper's comic strip, 'Happy Hooligan', riding an airborne bicycle in the studio, combined with a panorama of New York City filmed from a convenient skyscraper. Presumably unable to build a realistic one-man airplane in his studio, Porter devised a simpler invention. He simply suspended a bicycle from an inflated gasbag, and had the hobo pedal furiously to simulate forward flight. The concept of a flying bicycle was common at this time and often featured in magazine cartoons.

d/s/c Edwin S. Porter   *p* Thomas A. Edison

Le Voyage dans la Lune *aka* **A Trip to the Moon** *aka* **A Trip to Mars** (STAR; FR) b/w 21 min
The world's first Science Fiction film epic, and the masterpiece of all cinema up to this point in time. Its epic length alone, 21 minutes in a day when films lasted little more than one or two minutes, would qualify it as a masterwork, even without consideration of its stunning content. Méliès, already acknowledged as the master manufacturer of 'trick films' and fantasies, indeed the creator of the whole genre, brought all his long experience as a stage magician and entertainer to fruition in this film, and although he equalled it in several later productions, he never surpassed it, or again produced a film which had so much impact on contemporary audiences.

For his plot he took inspiration from the two literary masters of Science Fiction, Jules Verne and his 1865 book, *From the Earth to the Moon*, and H.G. Wells with his *The First Men in the Moon*, published in 1901. Thus Wells' creation of the Selenites, crustaceous inhabitants of the Moon, was brand new when Méliès designed the costumes for his creatures. Verne supplied the concept of the great space gun, which more than 30 years later was used by Wells for his own journey into space, **Things to Come** (1936). Not content with scripting, designing, and constructing this epic, Méliès also played the leading role of Professor Barbenfouillis, whose great plan for the exploration of the Moon is accepted by the Scientific Congress of the Astronomic Club. First the master gun has to be cast at a vast foundry. Then the astronauts enter the space shell. The huge cannon is fired and the shell flies through space, landing right in the eye of the Man in the Moon. The explorers emerge and observe the appearance of the Earth from the Moon. A snowstorm starts, and the explorers descend into a crater for shelter, and thence into the interior of the Moon. In a grotto of giant mushrooms they are captured by the curious inhabitants, the Selenites, who take them before their King. The Earthmen manage to escape, and discover that when the pursuing Selenites are struck, they explode in puffs of smoke! The party find their shell again, and return to Earth, falling through the sky and splashing into the sea. After viewing the wonders of oceanic life, the explorers are rescued by a ship and returned to Paris. The city is *en fête*, and after a grand march past of marines and the French fire brigade, the heroes are decorated and a commemorative statue is unveiled by the Mayor.

The American producer Lubin pirated this film under the title *A Trip to Mars*.

d/p Georges Méliès   *lp* Georges Méliès, Victor André, Bleuette Bernon, Depierre, Farjaux, Corps de Ballet du Chatelet

1903

La Lotion Miraculeuse *aka* **The Miracle Notion** *aka* **A Wonderful Hair Restorer** (PATHE; FR) b/w 1 min
Another burlesque on the still unresolved restoration of hair to the bald by scientific means. A barber persuades a bald-headed customer to try an application of a new lotion. A vigorous massage ensues and the remedy is so successful that not only does the man's hair grow so fast that it is soon hanging down to his shoulders, but the barber also grows hair on his hands! Evidently inspired by the British film of two years' before, **The Marvellous Hair Restorer** (1901), this French variation uses trick photographic techniques notably point-of-view cutting and circular matte shots to simulate the look through a magnifying glass and, in addition, has a twist ending.

Credits not available

The Unclean World *aka* **The Suburban-Bunkum Microbe-Guyoscope** (HEPWORTH; GB) b/w 2 min
This is a burlesque of the first successful linking of the cinematograph and the microscope, which had been achieved by the scientific photographer, F. Martin Duncan and

released through Charles Urban's Urbanora Company as *The Unseen World:* the Urban-Duncan Micro-Bioscope. In this remarkable satire, Hepworth, formerly an employee of Charles Urban and now in charge of his own production company at Walton-on-Thames, plays the part of a 'quasi-scientific gentleman' who discovers something distasteful in his cheese sandwich. He places the offending stuff under his microscope, and a startling series of close-ups are seen on the screen. 'The unearthly looking swarming creatures are most grotesque and realistic!' claimed the Hepwix Films Catalogue, which also pointed out that this was 'the first time in the history of the cinematograph that the instrument has been used to burlesque a popular application of itself.' The magnified microbes created in the studio may have influenced the American **Love Microbe** (1907).

d Percy Stow   *p* Cecil M. Hepworth   *lp* Cecil M. Hepworth

The Voyage of the *Arctic* aka The Adventurous Voyage of the *Arctic* (PAUL; GB)   b/w   10 min

Although obviously inspired by the epic French fantasies of Georges Méliès, this British production not only manages to have a native flavour of its own, it also develops a storyline which Méliès himself followed years later in **A la Conquête du Pôle** (1912). For his hero, director Booth used, probably without permission, Captain Kettle, a fiery mariner featured in short stories by C.J. Cutcliffe-Hyne. Farren, who played Kettle on the vaudeville stage, did so again in this film, doubtless bringing his own costume and makeup. The film was subtitled 'How Captain Kettle Discovered the North Pole'.

There are 11 distinct scenes, following the Méliès formula for this type of film. The film opens in the captain's cabin on the good ship *Arctic*. The Queen of the polar region materializes and traces a chart of the northern hemisphere on the cabin panel. Up on deck icebergs are observed and a giant sea serpent rears up. The captain despatches it with his revolver. Frozen up against an iceberg, the captain, nonplussed, plays his melodeon. A polar bear hears the music and dances to it, until Kettle shoots it with his rifle. In the icefield they encounter an ice statue, which they melt by fire. It is the Queen, who had been frozen solid by the evil genius of the north. The aurora borealis appears, and changes into the gigantic evil genius. His breath freezes the crew solid, but the Queen restores them to life. The explorers then use dynamite on the wall of ice. This causes ice imps to rush out of the hole and capture them. They are taken to the castle of the evil genius. The mate dances a hornpipe on the giant's table, which evidently displeases the creature, for he picks the mate up and bites his head off, chewing it with relish! Under the table the Queen appears and frees Kettle from his chains.

The next scene is entitled 'The Vision of the Compass', which is seen oscillating, then pointing north (probably the term 'vision' is used to describe what we now know as a close-up). Kettle and his crew discover a lodestone cave under the North Pole. The magnetism attracts them into the air and they walk about upside-down on the cave roof. Finally emerging at the foot of the North Pole itself, Kettle uses a block and pulley to climb it and fly the Union Jack. The final shot of the film shows Kettle sitting on top of the Pole triumphantly puffing a cigar!

This film of an epic, imaginary journey to an unexplored region of the world is totally lost, save for an illustrated synopsis.

d Walter R. Booth   *p* Robert Paul   *lp* Fred Farren

Dog Factory aka Edison's Dog Factory
(EDISON)   b/w   4 min

A new and improved version of the same company's **Fun in a Butcher Shop** (1901). The same proposition, the existence of a single machine to convert live dogs into sausage links, is used but this time with a further scientific prediction, the process can be reversed. This was possibly to satisfy audience susceptibilities, which were becoming more refined as the new century progressed. The machine in the film is the size of a piano and carries the large label, 'Dog Transformer'. Behind it hang strings of sausages of varying sizes and, it seems, breeds, for they bear such labels as 'Bull Pups', 'Spaniels', etc. A customer enters, points to his selection of sausage, and the butcher unhooks a string and inserts it into the machine. The handle is cranked, and out of the other end leaps a live dog! Special requests are satisfied, too, such as the prize fighter who requires a particular brand of bulldog.

d Edwin S. Porter   *p* Thomas A. Edison

Le Raid Paris à Monte Carlo en Deux Heures aka An Adventurous Automobile Trip
(STAR; FR)   b/w   13 min

This film looks forward to the time when automobiles would be able to travel great distances at great speeds. Rather remarkably, the hero of the piece is supposed to be King Leopold of Belgium. The publicity made no mention that this was an impersonation, and added credence to the story by introducing a large gathering of genuine guest stars who were currently appearing at the Folies Bergères. The film, in fact, was originally produced for exhibition at the Folies during one of their revues, and only later allowed to be circulated as a film in its own right. King Leopold arrives in Paris to renew acquaintance with the pretty Parisiennes. He wants to visit the gambling resort of Monte Carlo, but cannot spare the 17 hours required for the express railway trip. He encounters an automobile manufacturer who says his new car can do the journey in three hours. (Note, the French time, by the title, was two hours, but perhaps this was thought just a little too unlikely for English-speaking audiences.) The King, delighted, takes the wheel and immediately reverses into a gendarme, flattening him! Then they are off, starting from the Grand Opera House in Paris, waved *bon voyage* by a gathering of friends (the guest stars). They drive speedily over the Alps, the car leaping into space from one summit. In Dijon they run over a tax collector and along the Mediterranean coast they collide with a woman selling oranges. They smash through a conservatory, a family's dining-room, and a wagon loaded with molten tar. At Monte Carlo, the car drives straight up the stairs of the Tribune of Honour, much to the delight of the assembled crowd.

The explorers crash-land on the sun in Voyage à Travers l'Impossible, *Georges Méliès' even more fantastical sequel to* Le Voyage dans la Lune *(1902). Even the carriage has a copyright notice on it.*

Above: A nickelodeon in a run-down area of New York and the attached promise of a daily change of programme.

the night sky the strange train travels, finally colliding with the Sun. Like the Moon in Méliès previous space outing, the Sun is a large and humorous face. Instead of landing in the eye, this time the explorers land in the mouth. From the wreck of their train, they observe the aurora borealis, and begin to sweat from the continual eruptions on the Sun's surface. To escape the heat they climb inside an icebox and are frozen solid. Thawed out by Mabouloff, they find their submarine undamaged in the wreckage and manage to launch it into space. The submarine's propellors steer it safely back to Earth, where a parachute emerges to float it down. Unfortunately it descends into the sea and drifts down to the bottom. The explorers use a searchlight to observe the denizens of the depths. Then a bursting steam pipe causes an explosion. The explorers are shot to the surface and cast safely ashore. Saved by sailors they are taken home in triumph.

The popularity of the film was so great that Méliès was called upon to produce three additional scenes, which were added to the end, bringing the total running time to an epic (for the period) half an hour. These extra scenes showed Mabouloff designing and constructing a gigantic electromagnet, which was mounted atop the tower of the Institute. Switched on, it attracted back the various vehicles lost during the expedition: the car, the train, etc.

d/p/s Georges Méliès *lp* Georges Méliès, Fernande Albany, May de Lavergne, Jehanne d'Alcy

1905

El Hotel Electrico *aka* The Electric Hotel

(HISPANOFILM; SP) b/w 8 min

Confusion reigns about the origins of this Science Fiction prediction of a hotel of the future. Reference books give the year as 1905, but all English language trade press reviews are late 1908. Bizarrely, *A Reference Guide to American Science Fiction Films* Vol.1 credits the production to the New York company, Vitagraph, and the direction to J. Stuart Blackton! The man who created it was the Catalan pioneer of cinematic animation Segundo de Chomon (1871-1929), who in 1906 moved briefly to Paris to work for Pathé, the parent company of Hispanofilm. De Chomon, considered the father of Spanish animation, would later make *La Maison Hantée* (released in the USA as *The Haunted House*) in Paris for Pathé in 1907. In this film, known to have influenced Blackton in New York to make *The Haunted Hotel* (1907), all the objects and furnishings in the house became mysteriously animated. In *La Maison Hantée*, the same mysterious animations occur, but are not given the rational explanation of the powers of electricity that underpin *El Hotel Electrico*.

In the hotel of the future, a visitor need only press a button to immediately have whatever he requires. First he has a brush-up. He presses a button and the brush comes up by itself and performs the work. Then he has a shave. Another button is pressed, and his face is lathered and shaved at high speed. And so everything is automated until the 'distribution boards' controlling the operations get out of order leading to extreme and comic confusion throughout the hotel. As a contemporary critic of the film concluded, 'One always has to pay the ransom of progress.'

d/s/c Segundo de Chomon

Twenty Thousand Leagues Under the Sea *aka* Amid the Wonders of the Deep (BIOGRAPH) b/w 18 min

The first film version of Jules Verne's classic fantasy novel of submarine adventure is something of a mystery. Unlisted in previous Science Fiction film researches (save for mention in Denis Gifford's *Science Fiction Film*), the film's origins are obscure. It was released in Britain via the French-owned Gaumont Company, but produced by Biograph, an American-owned company. However, it is unlisted in American Biograph records, and was not submitted for copyright at Washington. Biograph had licensed subsidiaries in England,

d/p Georges Méliès *s* Victor de Cottens *lp* Fernande Albany, Galipaux, Fragson, Jane Ivon, Little Tich, Antoni

Voyage à Travers l'Impossible *aka* Whirling the Worlds *aka* Voyage Across the Impossible *aka* An Impossible Voyage (STAR; FR) b/w 25 (30) min

'The most fantastic picture series ever conceived' was the advertising slogan for this remarkable cinematic excursion by Méliès, the French genius of illustrated imagination. The British distributors, at a loss for a suitable title for the show, held a public competition: *Whirling the Worlds* was an apt winner. Méliès wanted to produce a film that would not only follow the successful formula of his **Le Voyage dans la Lune** (1902) two years earlier, but which would leave that epic standing at the post. He succeeded spectacularly, although his science in this film is even less likely than that of the first.

Méliès plays the leading role of Engineer Mabouloff (Crazyloff in the USA), who proposes that the savants of the Institute of Incoherent Geography sponsor the greatest exploration expedition ever undertaken, for which he has designed a combination of railroad train, engine, automobile, airship and submarine, and soon the vehicles are under construction at a gigantic foundry. With much cheering, the special train sets out on its journey. The itinerary is Paris-Righi-Sun, and the party consists of 12 professors and their wives. They steam through snow-covered Switzerland and arrive at the Jungfrau station. They transfer to their special automobile, roar off at 500 mph, crash through the walls of the Righi Inn, and end up down a 2,000-ft precipice. Alpine guides climb to the rescue, and the team spends five weeks recovering in hospital. Then they set off again in their special train, up the side of the Jungfrau and away into space, assisted by airships attached to the carriage roofs. Through

Germany and elsewhere, so presumably it must originate with one of these. It is, however, too advanced a production for England.

The story introduces Captain Sam Whaler who, fishing off La Serena, encounters a strange sea monster. He tells his story to a naturalist who resides in the seaport of Coquimbo, where he studies marine flora and fauna. The professor is incredulous, but a further report in the local newspaper corroborates the claim. He decides to mount an expedition to harpoon the creature, and with his secretary and Captain Whaler sets sail aboard the *Discovery*. The monster appears and is revealed as a huge submarine. It sinks the ship, and the three survivors, Whaler, the professor and the secretary, clamber aboard the sub. Inside they meet the mysterious owner. The craft descends to the seabed and the owner takes the trio for an adventurous promenade. They fight and kill a strange fish, and the owner escorts them to his resting place, an undersea cave. They fall asleep and dream of fairy nymphs dancing, but awake suddenly to find to their horror that the fairy feet are the feelers of a giant squid! Fleeing, they encounter a great crab, which they blow to pieces. They return to the submarine with their trophies and the owner shows them photographs of the strange places he has visited. They choose to voyage to the South Pole. Here they receive an unwelcome reception so sail forthwith to an island in the Tropics. Here the three visitors try to escape, but are recaptured and imprisoned. Biting through their bonds they escape during the darkness of night, climb onto a log and float away. The log sinks and they drown. Under the sea Father Neptune takes pity and restores them to life and home.

Although touched with fantasy, the film is much closer to Verne than Méliès' later remake, **Deux Cent Mille Lieues sous les Mers** (1907).

Credits not available

1906

Le Dirigeable Fantastique *aka* **Inventor Crazybrains and His Wonderful Airship** *aka* **The Fantastical Airship**
(STAR; FR) b/w 3 min
The prediction here is that a motorized balloon will fly high enough to leave Earth's atmosphere and penetrate space. The inventor is labouring over this problem far into the night. Exhausted, he falls asleep in his laboratory and dreams that he has succeeded. The motors whirr and the balloon rises swiftly into space, taking the inventor, who is caught up in the net of the balloon, with it. In outer space he sees a comet with a fiery tail rushing towards him. They collide, there is a great explosion, and the inventor wakes up in his workshop. He immediately destroys his sheets of calculations and rolls of plans, and throws himself out of the window.

d/p/s Georges Méliès

The Doll Maker's Daughter
(HEPWORTH; GB) b/w 10 min
Yet another variation of the immensely popular ballet, *Coppélia*, this time made at the Hepworth studio at Walton-on-Thames. The film begins with the dollmaker's daughter encountering a mechanical model of herself, fashioned by her father. She winds it up and watches its jerky performance, imitating its actions in the manner of the popular robotic dance craze of the eighties. For a whim the girl puts on a dress identical to the doll's, and gets into the empty box just as her father comes into the workroom with a customer – a little princess in the company of her governess and an officer. Delighted with the life-like toy, she has it delivered to the palace. Her father, the Prince, watches his little daughter as she plays with the toy. However, the officer grows suspicious and tests the doll by putting a mouse at her feet. The girl is frightened out of her pose and leaps onto a chair. The Prince observes this and tries a little flirtation, sitting the girl on his knee. The dollmaker arrives with the real doll, makes the exchange, and sneaks off with his daughter. The officer, out to make trouble for the Prince, tells his wife. She rushes in a rage to catch the Prince making love to the girl, and all are surprised to discover the fake doll is a real doll after all. The idea of a live girl taking the place of a robot occurs again in Science Fiction cinema, most notably more than 40 years on in **The Perfect Woman** (1949).

d Lewin Fitzhamon *p* Cecil M. Hepworth *lp* Dolly Lupone

How to Make Time Fly *aka* **The Girl That Made the Time Fly** (PAUL; GB) b/w 5 min
One of a great number of trick films produced by the English pioneer Paul. The concept of altering the steady progress of time by some mechanical means became possible with the invention of photography. By means of a photograph, an instant of time could be captured for eternity. With the cinematograph, it became possible for a continuous length of time to be recorded, preserved, and played back in a future time. More, that moment of time could be extended or reduced, by changing the speed of the projector, or camera. This was the second 'trick' discovered by film-makers (the first was the reversal of time, made by showing a film backwards). This film combined normal cinematography with super-fast action, made by undercranking the camera.

This game with time commences with a little girl going up to the grandfather clock in her hall and removing the pendulum. This action causes the hands of the clock to whizz round the face in uncontrolled speed. Every natural action which takes place now accommodates itself to the speed of the clock. A party of paper-hangers working in the leisurely way traditional to their kind, are seized with a remarkable and ludicrous attack of energy. A number of visitors calling at the house find themselves scattering up the stairs at a great rate, while the girl's father eats his lunch at such a speed that apoplexy seems unavoidable. The power of the clock extends beyond the confines of the house and in the streets outside traffic is seen to increase its speed alarmingly.

d J. H. Martin(?) *p* Robert W. Paul

The Modern Pirates *aka* **The Raid of the Armoured Motor** (ALPHA; GB) b/w 9 min
The armoured car, which had come into use during the Boer War, is developed as a super-vehicle in the service of criminals in this 12-shot film. It was described in a contemporary account as 'a contrivance calculated to strike awe into the beholder, sheathed from front to back in grey-painted armour, even the wheels are protected, while the vehicle is steered in perfect safety from a kind of conning-tower'. The strange car makes its first appearance in a wild dash on a country village. Chickens pecking peacefully about the roadway are mysteriously swept into a receptacle in front of the car. Villagers who attempt to recapture their livestock are mercilessly shot down, and the village green is soon strewn with the bodies of wounded and dead countryfolk. A brave village constable boldly confronts the deadly invader, stepping into the middle of the road with both arms outstretched. A police car arrives to pursue the pirates, but soon suffers a breakdown. The daring raid ends suddenly when the speeding vehicle falls into the river and quickly sinks, drowning its unseen crew. Although made as early as 1906 this film was still advanced enough in concept to be re-released five years later, by Cosmopolitan Films, under the revised title, *The Raid of the Armoured Motor*.

Over half a century later, another more benevolent treatment of the same theme formed the basis of the Herbie and Dudu series, commencing with **The Love Bug** (1969) and **Ein Kaefer Geht Aufs Ganze** (1971).

d/p/s Arthur M. Cooper

The Pill Maker's Mistake

(HEPWORTH; GB) b/w 5 min

One of several burlesques dealing with the craze for extra energy, as promoted by patent medicines in the pages of popular magazines of the period. The film opens with a doctor and his assistant preparing pills. In the doctor's absence, a boy slips in through the window and adds an entire bottle of energizing liquid to the prepared pills. Outside the shop the doctor is advertising his new pills 'for invigorating and giving energy to all'. A buxom lady promptly purchases some pills and rushes home. She is a cook and has to prepare dinner for a large party. Exhausted, she goes to take a pill but in her agitated anxiety spills the entire boxful into the soup. They dissolve instantly, and the cook is too scared to inform the butler, who carries off the bowl. The soup is served to the assembly, who are soon thoroughly invigorated and energized! They rush forth to the doctor's shop and 'with more than neccessary violence illustrate that his goods have been much too effective'.

d Lewin Fitzhamon   *p* Cecil M. Hepworth

The '?' Motorist   (PAUL; GB) b/w 3 min

The increasing popularity of the motorcar and its seemingly unending powers of development in matters of design and speed, led to this tongue-in-cheek prediction of an Edwardian supercar half a century before Walt Disney took up the idea of a flying car in **The Absent-Minded Professor** (1961). It begins calmly enough, with a gentleman taking a lady for a spin in his shiny new auto. A careful policeman considers they are exceeding the lawful limit and waves for them to pull up.

They not only decline to do so, they drive right over him, severing several of his extremities! The constable gathers his spare parts and does running repairs while the car arrives at a public house. Instead of stopping, it runs straight up the wall, into the sky, through the clouds and lands on the Sun. Apparently impervious to heat, it tours the circumference of the Sun, flies off and lands on the ring of Saturn. A turn or two around this sky-high highway, and the car flies back to Earth, crashing through the roof of a building which turns out to be, appropriately enough, a magistrate's court.

The special effects are fairly primitive – the car in long shot is obviously a toy – but it was one of a great many trick and fantasy films produced by the English pioneer film-maker, Paul, very much on the pattern of the fantasy films made in France by Georges Méliès. There were no production credits on the film (a copy of which is preserved in the National Film Archive), but it is likely that Booth, a specialist in the genre, directed the film.

d Walter R. Booth   *p* Robert William Paul

Rescued in Mid-Air   (CLARENDON; GB) b/w 6 min

An unusual aircraft design – one which flies by means of flapping its wings – is introduced in this film. A young man and his lady friend are about to go for a bicycle ride when a motorbike, out of control, crashes into a trailer. The resulting explosion blows the girl into the air. Using her parasol as a parachute, she drifts down and alights on the top of a church steeple. Crowds gather to watch her as she is unable to climb down. Her father, an old professor, sees her plight and rushes to his garage. From it he wheels out his latest invention, an

The inventive Rescued in Mid-Air *and its wing-flapping airship.*

electrically powered airship with wings. He climbs aboard, flies into the air and makes good the girl's rescue. Unhappily they crash through the roof of a house and cause a final explosion.

The film is unusually sophisticated for the period, using superimposition for the enlargement of the plane, a revolving backdrop to suggest camera movements and cross-cutting to convey the drama of simultaneous actions.

d Percy Stow   *p* H.V. Lawley

Voyage Autour d'une Etoile *aka* Around a Star

(PATHE; FR)   b/w   8 min

This early excursion into outer space uses perhaps the most imaginary means of transport of all time: a soap bubble! An old astronomer has spent his life studying the stars and one, in particular, fascinates him. Baffled by being unable to conceive of a form of travel to cross space, he is idly observing some children blowing soap bubbles when the idea strikes him. He mixes a vast quantity of soapy liquid in a vat and creates a gigantic soap bubble. Thus one moonlit night he sails away in the bubble and duly arrives on the star. Here he is made welcome by the inhabitants, a royal lady and her dancing entourage. However Jupiter is enraged at his beloved's behaviour and flings the old professor out into space. He falls back to Earth and lands on a lightning conductor, where the shock and flash kill him.

d Gaston Velle

1907

La Ceinture Electrique *aka* The Wonderful Electric Belt

(GAUMONT; FR)   b/w   11 min

In the first decade of the 20th century, the powers of electricity were still mysterious enough to be considered the latest thing in cure-alls. Indeed, one reviewer of this film called it 'a skit on the craze for the cure anything nostrums which are one of the least desirable features of modern life'. Taking a contemporary fake into the realms of the possible, this film came up with an electric belt that really worked, shocking the wearer into super-vitality. A languid-looking person browsing through his morning paper comes across an advertisement for the electric belt. He promptly purchases one and is instantly energized into hyper-activity.

The special effect in this case was achieved by undercranking the camera.

d Romeo Rosetti   *s* Louis Feuillade

Deux Cent Milles Lieues sous les Mers ou le Cauchemar d'un Pêcheur *aka* Under the Seas

(STAR; FR)   b/w   18 min

The second screen version of Jules Verne's 1870 Science Fiction novel is a typical Méliès fantasy of the imagination, using the dream theme as an excuse to justify the impossible. Even his title exaggerates Verne's fantasy, increasing the voyage to 200,000 leagues under the sea. Méliès' hero is a humble fisherman who returns home tired from a trip. He falls asleep and dreams that the fairy of the ocean appears and escorts him to the port where a super-submarine awaits him. He is made captain of the vessel, and begins his voyage by sinking down to the seabed. Through the large windows he observes the wrecked hulks that litter the ocean floor, and the strange life around him. Giant shellfish open up to reveal beauteous sea nymphs, and giant starfish spin among the mermaids. Suddenly the submarine crashes into a wreck, and the captain finds himself fighting gigantic crabs, seahorses, and a huge octopus. He is saved by being caught in a large fishing net and hauled up to the surface. He then wakes up.

It is worth noting the number of similarities between the illustrations to Verne's novel, by Alphonse de Neuville, and the designs by Méliès in this film.

d/p/c Georges Méliès   *lp* Corps de Ballet du Chatelet

Dr Skinum

(AMERICAN MUTOSCOPE AND BIOGRAPH CO.)   b/w   10 min

Promoted as 'a scintillant satire of the physical culture fad' in *Biograph Bulletin* No.115 (14 December 1907), this remarkable film predicts the health farms of the eighties by elaborating on the latest craze of the first decade of the century. Dr Skinum is described as a learned professor of physiology, dermatology, biology, and all the other ologies. His claim is that 'Nature works wonders but Science goes one better', and in support his office is placarded with posters: 'We change Figures, Dispositions, Vocations, Characters, Complexions, Features'; 'Heroic Hypnotism and Hot Air'; 'Muddy Complexions Filtered'; 'Smallpox Pits Removed'. Skinum's first client is on the small side, a 3-foot female midget. Under treatment she is stretched to a 6-footer, but her clothes remain the same (a saucy joke betraying the production company's peep-show origins). The second client is an 8-foot beauty. The doctor hypnotizes her and places her under an apparatus best described as a 3,000-pound piledriver. A parade of ladies with oversize parts is next dealt with: huge feet, overlong nose, extreme elephantiasis. The latter lady receives an overdose of electrical current which reduces her – but to the size of a baby! 'Unquestionably an assured laughing hit!' concludes the synopsis.

Biograph failed to lodge a copy of the film for copyright purposes, so nothing remains beyond the illustrated leaflet.

d Wallace McCutcheon   *c* G.W. ('Billy') Bitzer *lp* Robert Harron

Hair Restorer

(WILLIAMS BROWN AND EARLE)   b/w   10 min

The search for a scientific specific certain to stimulate the barren follicles of the bald continues to this day. Eighty years ago makers of patent medicines advertised their phoney wares with unprosecuted confidence. Only in the realms of cinematic special effects was the cure seen to be possible. In this fantasy, the baldness is not a medical problem, but one caused by the violence of a furious wife who, catching her hirsute husband in the arms of the maid, pulls all his hair out in her fury. The plucked man flees to a local emporium and purchases a quantity of a new hair restorer. Back home in the bathroom a generous application results in an instant growth of fresh hair. The wife comes upon him and renews her frenzied plucking. In the struggle she falls into the bath, which is filled with the hair-grower. At once her own hair begins to lengthen and in moments she is completely covered in lengthening whiskers. The man locks her in the bathroom and returns armed with a pole, a muzzle, and a gang of men.

The dreaming fisherman caught up in a net in Georges Méliès' Deux Cent Milles Lieues Sous les Mers, a fantasy inspired by Jules Verne's more soberly titled novel.

The scene dissolves to a fairground, where the man and the maid are now on the payroll as wild animal trainer and assistant. They embrace much to the fury of the hairy bear behind them – the creature that once was the harridan wife!

Credits not available

Liquid Electricity *aka* The Inventor's Galvanic Fluid
(VITAGRAPH) b/w 8 min

J. Stuart Blackton, the creative cartoonist who had co-founded the Vitagraph Company in New York and shot it to success with a series of fantastic 'trick comedies' such as *The Haunted Hotel* earlier in the year, used the still mysterious powers of electricity as the basis of his first entry into Science Fiction. Although his basic trick effect here is achieved by simple undercranking of his camera, it is the application of the novel concept of liquid electricity that sets his story firmly in the possible impossible.

A chemist is labouring in his electrical laboratory, a set which predicts that created by Kenneth Strickfaden for **Frankenstein** (1931). He distils an electric fluid and sprays it on himself. Instantly his movements accelerate and, having dashed about his laboratory at lightning speed, he flops into his revolving chair and spins so rapidly he becomes a blur. The effect wears off and, returning to normal, he observes through the window some road cleaners at their leisurely work. He sprays them, and they clear the road at terrific speed. He decides to continue his experiments on the world at large and takes a walk. A girl struggling in a river is rescued by superfast swimmers, thanks to the fluid. A yawning clerk turns into a hustler, a gang of labourers hastily dig through a wood, a negro swiftly paints a fence, a slow shopkeeper becomes excessively brisk, an ancient cabhorse turns rapid circles with his cab, an idle messenger boy dashes about his business and a dozing policemen spins rapidly around a lamp-post before whizzing down the street. 'We have no hesitation in classing this film as one of the best issued for a long time' wrote the critic of *Kinematograph Weekly*. Indeed, it proved so popular that Blackton was obliged to produce a sequel, **Galvanic Fluid** (1908).

d/p J. Stuart Blackton

La Lotion Miraculeuse *aka* The Hair Restorer
(PATHE; FR) b/w 8 min

A French variation on the popular theme of a cure for baldness. This time it is a young man who is embarrassed by his totally bald head, especially when his young lady refuses to marry him. He purchases a new preparation guaranteed to raise hair, applies a liberal dose and is delighted to see a thick crop of hair develop at speed. He shows himself to his lady love, and she is so delighted she agrees to marry him. However, her mother is suspicious of the sudden growth. She and the girl examine the bottle of hair restorer and a little of the liquid spills onto their handkerchiefs. Later they wipe their warm faces with the infected cloths, and to their horror promptly grow beards. The man is aghast and applies another new fluid to their heads, a hair removing agent. This has more than the desired effect – it leaves the ladies totally bald!

Credits not available

Love Microbe
(AMERICAN MUTOSCOPE AND BIOGRAPH CO.) b/w 12 min

'The Tender Passion Microscopically Treated' was how the Biograph Company described this release in their *Bulletin* No.110 dated 19 October 1907. The theme of the film echoed the contemporary interest in microscopy, the cinematograph having already been linked to the microscope to show hitherto invisible microbes at enormous magnification upon the cinema screen. The comparatively new theory that much bodily behaviour could be traced to the unseen influences of micro-organisms is the basis for Professor Cupido's researches in this film. Creeping up behind a courting couple in a park, he uses his needle syringe to extract fluids from their entwined necks and hastens to his laboratory. Under his microscope he examines the male and female microbes (which in close-up are tinted bright red) and isolates the love bug. He develops a serum and uses his hypodermic for a series of experiments on humans obviously in need of a dose of love. His housekeeper, a 'virulent vixen' becomes an 'angelical Dulcinea' after a single jab. In the park a lethargic couple are soon passionately embracing. Dosing the beer jug of a passing urchin, Cupido is delighted to note that swigs of the mixture soon settle a violent fight between the lad's parents. Finally Cupido experiments on himself, and after an unfortunate interlude with a married patient, settles for a love-life with his housekeeper. A paper print of the film, deposited with the Library of Congress Copyright Department on 21 October 1907, has been restored, but without the red tint.

A year later Bitzer, one of the early cinema's most inventive and technically ingenious cameramen, began his 16-year-long association with D.W. Griffith, all of whose major films he photographed.

d Wallace McCutcheon   *c* G.W. ('Billy') Bitzer

The Mechanical Statue and the Ingenious Servant
(VITAGRAPH) b/w 7 min

The first use of the automaton, mechanical man, or robot in American cinema comes, not surprisingly, from the creative director/producer Blackton. Equally unsurprisingly, the development follows the formula of *Coppélia*, filmed so many times by European producers. Three boys are seen playing with their toys, and they break the ball of the smallest one. To pacify the infant, their father visits a toy shop to select a new toy for the lad. The proprietor first winds up a 2-foot-high clockwork mannikin, which proceeds to dance. Then he demonstrates a larger, life-size figure, a Roman gladiator. When wound up, the mechanical statue strikes a series of dramatic poses. Impressed, the father buys it and takes it home, leaving it in a servant's charge while he finds his little son. The inquisitive servant winds up the motor and is promptly whacked over the head by the gladiator's sword. The servant grapples with the automaton, throws it to the floor, then watches as the gladiator jumps up and rushes jerkily out of the door. Frightened of losing his job, the servant picks up the automaton's dropped sword and, dressing in a sheet, covers himself with flour to appear white. He stand on the statue's pedestal, posing stiffly as his employer returns. The father winds the key and the fake gladiator goes into a jerky dance, whacking his boss over the

Liquid Electricity, one of the many essays in trick photography by J. Stuart Blackton, the creative genius of the Vitagraph company.

head with his sword. The little boy laughs to see his father chase the gladiator around the room until it jumps through the window.

d/p J. Stuart Blackton

Le Tunnel sous La Manche *aka* Tunnelling the English Channel (STAR; FR) b/w 20 min

Finally a reality, the idea of a Channel tunnel has been with us for a century or more. Méliès gave a touch of authenticity to his remarkable vision by making the leading players lookalikes for President Fallières of France and King Edward VII of England. (In fact, he billed them as the genuine article, never revealing who his actors were.) The adventure begins in the staterooms of the French President's palace, where over a game of cards with King Edward, a discussion ensues concerning the proposed plan to link France and England by an underwater tunnel. The great leaders toast the project in wine, then retire to bed. Each dreams how the tunnel might be constructed, beginning with a fanciful linking of lengthening arms across the sea.

Then scenes from their dreams alternate. First we see the King taking up a pick to ceremoniously start the operation from the British side. He is aided by a large barrel of whisky. On the French side, the President decorates all the electric drilling team, assisted by his barrel of wine. The two ends of the tunnel proceed under the seabed, until a final charge of dynamite breaks through the final barrier and both ends meet.

Following suitable celebrations, the first train leaves Calais bearing the President across to Dover, then to Charing Cross Station, where he is greeted by King Edward and the band of the Salvation Army. The success is short-lived, for two trains collide in the middle of the tunnel. The awful crash scatters wounded and dead everywhere and then the sea floods in from above, drowning the survivors. The King and the President awake with the shock, and when the tunnel engineer arrives with his roll of plans, the rulers join in forcibly ejecting him.

The Channel tunnel theme reappeared in the Science Fiction cinema almost 30 years later with Curtis (Kurt) Bernhardt's **Der Tunnel** (1933), made in Germany, and a patriotic British remake of that film, **The Tunnel** (1935), by Maurice Elvey.

d/p/s Georges Méliès   *lp* Georges Méliès, Fernande Albany

Work Made Easy

(VITAGRAPH) b/w 8 min

Advertised as 'a picture for lazy people', this postulates the proposition that magnetic forces can be harnessed to relieve man of some of his hard labour in life. A professor of dynamics invents a machine which, by a mere turn of the handle, sends waves of magnetic force into inanimate objects. His intention is to have the objects perform their own tasks and thus relieve mankind of its most difficult and arduous labours. Taking his machine outdoors for a trial run, he sees piles of boxes and packing-cases in a factory yard. A turn of the handle and the boxes begin to move. Under magnetic direction they roll over, climb the fence, and clear the yard in seconds. Next he sees a building in the course of construction. He turns his handle and the boards fly off the ground and nail themselves to the framework. In a carpenters' shop he directs his rays to make a saw cut through wood, a hammer knock in nails, a chisel work itself, and so on. Unfortunately the men in the workshop object to this threat to their livelihood and mob him. The professor turns the machine on himself: he spins like a top until he is nothing but a blur, and flies out of sight.

It should be noted that a completely inaccurate synopsis of this film is given in *A Reference Guide to American Science Fiction Films*.

d/p J. Stuart Blackton

The Airship *aka* 100 Years Hence

(VITAGRAPH) b/w 7 min

The Vitagraph Company of America, under the direction of British born Blackton, specialized in the production of trick and fantasy films. Blackton had been a conjurer and had combined his lightning cartoon act with the sleight of hand of his partner, Albert E. Smith, before they had entered the cinematograph business. Small wonder, then, that the magical properties of cinema should so intrigue them. *The Airship* was publicized by the Company as 'A forecast of probable means of navigation in the coming century', although they were also careful to point out that the film was also 'a very novel comic', in case the production sounded too seriously scientific.

The story begins with a young lady and her gentleman friend entering the carriage of an airship. They take off and through the window observe a man as he flies past flapping a pair of wings fixed to his arms. The prankish passengers pass the time by throwing sand from the ballast bags and cabbages on those strolling below. In the traditions of the racist stereotypes of the period, a Jew, then a stock comic figure, receives most of the missiles and complains to a policeman. The constable mounts his aerocycle and pedals into the air in pursuit. The Jew borrows a pair of flying wings and takes off, too. However, he collides with the constable, crashes into the Moon, and falls down into the sea. Landing on the seabed he flirts with a mermaid before being swallowed by a whale. A passing ship catches the whale and pulls it onto the deck. Here sailors cut the animal open and much to their surprise, the Jew steps out. He is so delighted at his rescue that he dances the hornpipe.

d/p J. Stuart Blackton

An Animated Doll (ESSANAY) b/w 12 min

Robot stories continued to be inspired by the Délibes ballet *Coppélia*, founded on one of the tales of Hoffmann, and the incidence of dance routines in this version suggest that musical accompaniment was not uncommon in the nickelodeons of the 1900s.

A young boy is looking for a present for his little sister. He spots a life-size automated doll in the shop of an inventor and offers $5 for it. The inventor turns down the sum, and the frustrated youth hides on the premises until the inventor has left, then takes the doll, leaving his $5 as payment. He arrives

Le Tunnel sous La Manche, another of Georges Méliès' fantasies which was given an extra 'realistic' fillip by casting lookalikes in the roles of King Edward VII and President Fallières of France.

home, gives the doll to his sister, and winds it up. The doll then performs a short ballet dance. Suddenly the inventor bursts in and, after joining in the dance for a few moments, picks up the run-down doll and departs. The little girl is left weeping for her unusual toy.

p George Spoor, G.M. Anderson

La Cuisine Magnétique (PATHE; FR) b/w

Having discovered that the American Stuart Blackton succeeded in making objects move, apparently without any human assistance, without relying on 'invisible wires' but by exposing one frame at a time, de Chomon made a number of short fantasies using the same technique. In this picture, he brings to life a range of kitchen utensils ostensibly because of a magnetic force exerted on them. Other such fantasies included *La Table Magique, Les Jouets Vivants* and *La Liquéfaction des Corps Durs* (all 1908). These films foreshadowed the techniques later used with great success by animators such as Starewicz and Ray Harryhausen as well as in Norman MacLaren's pixillated films and Czech puppet movies.

De Chomon's best-known work includes his prediction of a hotel of the future **El Hotel Electrico** (1905) and his 'Chinese version' of **Voyage dans la Lune** (1909).

d/s/c/se Segundo de Chomon   *p* Ferdinand Zecca

Dr Jekyll and Mr Hyde (SELIG) b/w 16 min

The first of many film versions of Robert Louis Stevenson's classic 'shilling shocker', graphically describing a physician's self-experimentation in attempting to separate good from evil in the soul of man. The novel was so popular that it led to many adaptations for the theatrical stage, in both long and short form, and one of these is used in this Selig Polyscope version. It even includes long-shots of the theatre stage, and is divided into the four original acts, complete with rising and falling curtains. The unnamed actors taking part are evidently those of the theatrical performance, and the man who plays the double role of Jekyll and Hyde is described in *Moving Picture World* (7 March 1908) as 'so convincing that no greater display of ability to fulfil this role could be shown by any actor'. Act I is a vicarage garden, where the good doctor woos Alice, the vicar's daughter. Unfortunately he is addicted to a drug of his own mixing, and a quick quaff instantly releases his evil nature. He attacks Alice, and when her old father rushes to interfere, kills him with 'fiendish glee and demon strength'. Act II is the office of Utterson, lawyer of Chancery Lane. Jeykll visits him and suffers a vision of the gallows, a noose around his neck. Act III is the office of Dr Lanyon. A midnight caller is Hyde, who drinks his potion and changes into Jekyll, prostrating his old friend with astonishment. Act IV is Jekyll's laboratory where the remorseful doctor is visited by the loving Alice. He promises to see her on the morrow, but when she departs he drinks his drug yet again. As Hyde he poisons himself to kill the good Jekyll whom he hates. The evil experiment is over.

p William N. Selig

The Doctor's Experiment aka Reversing Darwin's Theory (GAUMONT; FR) b/w 8 min

Charles Darwin's theory of the origin of species was still very controversial at the time this film was made. A doctor has been trying to prove scientifically that man sprang from monkeys, and getting nowhere. Suddenly the reverse idea, to begin with a man and turn him into his ancestor, occurs to him. With his students he sets to work in his laboratory to discover a means of performing the necessary operation. At last he perfects a serum derived from monkeys, and inoculates a group of volunteers. One after the other they begin to leap and jump about like veritable simians. Curiously the influence proves contagious, and passers-by are soon joining in,

Right: A lazy tramp transformed into a man of speed and action courtesy of Energizer *in Wallace McCutcheon's burlesque on the boastful claims of breakfast cereal manufacturers.*

behaving like monkeys and performing all manner of apish tricks in the street! Public interest in the doctor's experiment grows apace, but try as he might he cannot discover an antidote to his serum. The victims of his experiment are rounded up, collected into a large cage, and put on exhibition. The doctor takes his pet ape, from whom he derived the serum, to visit the performing monkey-men, and the film ends on the monkey 'looking as much like a man as it is possible to do'.

Credits not available

Energizer

(AMERICAN MUTOSCOPE AND BIOGRAPH CO.)   b/w   12 min

A burlesque on the boastful claims of breakfast foods which, at this period of uncontrolled advertising, were competing on posters and in magazines with promises of boundless energy for all who ate them. Taking this theme to an advanced conclusion, the film presents yet another variety of crunchable corn flakes, actually called 'Energizer' and guaranteeing energy for the consumer. A housewife saddled with an indolent husband purchases a package and serves it to him. He is instantly transformed into a veritable hurricane, thanks to the fabulous flakes (and to undercranked camerawork). Meanwhile a sleepy hobo calls at the kitchen door in search of a leftover. The maid gives him the rest of the 'Energizer' and within moments the tramp is not only bursting with energy, he develops superhuman strength. Dashing into the street he loads heavy packing-cases onto a wagon with an ease and speed that leaves the carrier gasping. His feats 'would cause Hercules to turn green with jealousy' claimed *Biograph Bulletin* No.119, published 11 January 1908.

d Wallace McCutcheon   *c* F. A. Dobson

Galvanic Fluid *aka* More Fun with Liquid Electricity

(VITAGRAPH)   b/w   8 min

A sequel to Vitagraph's very successful production of the previous year, **Liquid Electricity** (1907). It continues the experiments of Professor Watt as he discovers a further property of his curious fluid – when applied to any object or person, it immediately gives it the power of flight. Watt goes for a stroll in the park, giving his discovery a first test on a passing nursemaid and her baby carriage. Instantly, they begin to fly around the park. The professor tries squirting a trolley car, and it too commences to fly. This attracts the attention of the police, but a quick squirt soon sends them flying. They return with reinforcements and Watt only escapes them by squirting himself and flying home. The angry crowd pursues him to his door, where he sprays the lot of them. As they fly rapidly into the sky, the professor drops the syringe. It explodes – and that is the end of Watt and his extraordinary experiments.

d J. Stuart Blackton

The Invisible Fluid

(AMERICAN MUTOSCOPE AND BIOGRAPH CO.) b/w 12 min
The first American film to be inspired by H.G. Wells' Science Fiction novel, *The Invisible Man*, published just ten years earlier. As with most films of this period, particularly those needing 'trick effects', the startling proposition of invisibility was played for laughs. An erudite scientist compounds a mysterious fluid which he loads into an atomizer. When sprayed onto an object, that object disappears, instantly and completely, for a period of ten minutes. The inventor mails the atomizer to his businessman brother in the hope that he can put it on the market. The brother, somewhat cynical, tries it out on himself and instantly vanishes, much to the amazement of the messenger boy who brought the package. The boy reads the covering letter and sees immediately the fun he can get out of the fluid. He tries it out on a girl walking her dog. One spray and the girl continues on her way, leading an empty chain. Next a fruit cart vanishes, followed by the irate Italian owner. Two delivery men are baffled when the heavy trunk they are lifting is made to disappear. Passing a church the boy squirts a groom, leaving the bride in hysterics! In a restaurant the youth has a meal, vanishes the lady cashier, and makes off with the till. Meanwhile those he has made invisible regain their visibility, one by one, track him down and give chase. He responds by making them vanish again but a policemen, creeping up from behind, manages to grab the atomizer. The youth is marched off to court, where in demonstrating his escapades he turns the spray onto himself and makes his invisible escape. All the disappearances were contrived by the simple stop-motion process.

d Wallace McCutcheon *c* G. W. ('Billy') Bitzer

The Man Who Learned to Fly

(HEPWORTH; GB) b/w 13 min
The rapidly developing science of aeronautics and its fascination in the public mind stimulated this fanciful prediction of the next step in the process. 'We have a peep into the future in the latest "Hepwix" comic number' wrote the trade reviewer of *Kinematograph Weekly* for 11 June 1908. The story opens in the study of an inventor. He is surrounded by numerous models of airships and airplanes of all shapes and sizes. While he is contemplating them, considering his next development in the young science of flying, he falls asleep and dreams. In his imagination he rises from his chair and goes out into the street, where the sight of a boy flying a kite suggests a new train of thought. He persuades the boy to push a garden roller over and over him until he is pressed flat. Then the boy is to tie a string to him and fly him as if he were a kite. The boy delightedly responds and soon the flattened inventor is rising and floating through the sky and, in the words of the reviewer, 'spreading terror on every hand'. The panicking populace flee from the floating flat man, who is finally brought to Earth by a timely rifle shot. The inventor crashes down, only to wake up with a start back in his study.

d Lewin Fitzhamon *p* Cecil M. Hepworth

The Monkey Man (PATHE; FR) b/w 11 min

One of the first films to illustrate brain transplants. As with many later productions of the thirties and forties, a human brain is exchanged with that of an ape. The results here are used primarily for laughs, however. The film opens in a doctor's surgery during an operation. While the surgeon is trepanning his unconscious patient an accident occurs to the man's exposed brain. The surgeon removes it and substitutes the brain of a monkey. After the man recovers he is dominated by the animal brain whose irresistible impulses force him to perform all manner of eccentric actions. The surgeon is fascinated by the results of his experiment, and leads his patient through the streets. The synopsis then adds a comment which illuminates the period in which the film was produced: 'To the great pleasure of all believers in Darwin's Theory!'

Credits not available

La Photographie Electrique à Distance *aka* Long Distance Wireless Photography (STAR; FR) b/w 6 min

An early prediction of large-screen television can be seen in this Méliès production, some 20 years before the first experiments of John Logie Baird, whose transmission of the face of a human (his earlier success had been the face of a ventriloquist's doll) was remarkably like the incident predicted by Méliès. Baird grabbed a neighbour's office boy, the nearest available human, and televised his face across his laboratory. Here Méliès' inventor transmits the faces of an old couple who chance upon his workshop. First Méliès persuades the old woman, who wears a poke bonnet, to sit beside his transmitter. Her face is promptly seen upon a nearby screen, her expressions much exaggerated through the enlargement. Then the bewhiskered husband takes her place, rather reluctantly, and sees his face so enlarged and distorted that he looks like an ugly monkey. The infuriated couple proceed to wreck the laboratory, and in the mêlée with Méliès the wife gets caught up in the flywheel of the wireless machine. Her husband rescues her and they make a hasty exit.

d/p/s Georges Méliès *lp* Georges Méliès, Fernande Albany

The Professor's Anti-Gravitational Fluid

(HEPWORTH; GB) b/w 6 min
Although the title refers to an anti-gravitational fluid, the synopsis (all that remains of this original work) refers to the material as a powder. The concept of anti-gravitational material had been postulated by H.G. Wells in his *First Men in the Moon* (1901). An old scientist manufactures a gravity-repellent powder and his first experiment is to sprinkle it on his breakfast egg, which floats into the air. A young boy observes this and steals the stuff, bent on mischief. He spoils a cricket match by floating away the stumps and then the batsman's bat. He makes a fish float off a monger's barrow, and a girl's hat float up into the sky. A crowd begins to collect and the boy tries to get rid of them by shaking the powder over them. Unfortunately he spills the rest of the powder and is chased back to the laboratory. He hides under the professor's table to watch as the mob wreck the laboratory.

d Lewin Fitzhamon *p* Cecil M. Hepworth *lp* Bertie Potter

Voyage à la Planète Jupiter (PATHE; FR) b/w 11 min

As well as filming a **Voyage dans la Lune** and *Mars* (both 1909), de Chomon, recruited by Pathé's artistic director Ferdinand Zecca, also provided this visit to Jupiter as competition for Méliès' successful films. Undoubtedly an extremely inventive special effects' man and a brilliant

The Invisible Fluid, *the first version of H.G. Wells' 1897 novel*, The Invisible Man.

cinematographer (he shot Pastrone's classic of the prewar Italian cinema, *Cabiria*, 1912-14), the wizard from Barcelona was not above copying the master, although he was always looking for ways to extend the technical repertoire of the camera, introducing daring superimpositions and even pioneering camera movements. Initially producing his films for Pathé's Spanish subsidiary, Hispanofilm, he emigrated to Paris in 1906 (where he was sometimes credited as de Chaumont), replacing Gaston Velle as the specialist for Pathé's trick films for four years before returning to Spain. His best-known work is **El Hotel Electrico** (1905).

A king contentedly surveys by telescope his realm, and scans the firmament, evidently with an eye to further enlarging his possessions. He dozes off and dreams that he goes flying up through the night sky, far beyond the Moon. He approaches the planet Saturn, where he is menaced by a pair of giant scissors, then flies on to Jupiter, where he disembarks. He gazes in wonderment at the strange scenery of the planet, and is suddenly surrounded by a mob of hostile inhabitants. They take him prisoner and lead him before the King of Jupiter, who reacts with anger, calling down the power of his mighty thunderbolts. The lightning flashes precipitate the traveller back into space. He flies about among the stars, then the clouds disperse and he tumbles back down to Earth. The shock of the fall wakes him up.

d/s/c/se Segundo de Chomon *p* Ferdinand Zecca

When the Man in the Moon Seeks a Wife

(CLARENDON; GB) b/w 15 min

The first British film to depict an alien from another world was made in Croydon, just outside London, by the Clarendon Company from one of a number of original screenplays written by the humorist Reed, whom Clarendon contracted to write exclusively for them for one year. Selected by the trade paper *Kinematograph Weekly* as No.20 in their series, 'Remarkable Film Subjects', the reviewer described the moon-man as follow: 'A personage appropriately clad from head to foot in white, but in other ways closely resembling the average citizen of this world more than the personages Mr H.G. Wells described as inhabiting the moon.'

The opening scenes are set in a lunar laboratory where the moonman surveys Earth through a giant telescope which he has just invented. By altering his focus he goes from a general survey of the planet to a view of England, then London, then St Paul's Cathedral, and finally the city's inhabitants. The moonman, lonely in his lunar world, decides he would like a London girl for a bride. Working feverishly in his laboratory he produces an anti-gravitational gas which enables him to float off the Moon and down to Earth. He passes through the clouds and lands on a chimney, which is on the roof of a girls' school. Clambering through the skylight he drops into the girls' dormitory, the ensuing shrieks sending him floating away again, thanks to his gas. He descends to the street and encounters a policeman. In a merry mood, the man takes the constable for a quick trip through the air. At last he encounters the lady he desires to marry, but has to overcome the reluctance of both the girl and her father. He gives her a quick dose of anti-gravity gas, and they float up to the ceiling where, crawling about like human flies, his proposal wins her agreement. The moonman puts paid to the girl's terrestrial lover by magically upsetting him into a river, and the couple float away to their lonely but lunar honeymoon. The film closes with the happy pair seated side by side on the horn of a crescent moon.

Interestingly, this first alien, like so many that were to follow (especially in the fifties), was in need of female companionship.

d Percy Stow *p* H. V. Lawley *s* Langford Reed

The Airship Destroyer *aka* The Battle in the Clouds *aka* The Aerial Torpedo (URBAN; GB) b/w 11 min

The first dramatic Science Fiction film from England was written and directed by Booth, who hitherto had confined his special effects' productions to comedy and fantasy (the *Professor Puddenhead's Patents* series). The film was given special promotion by its distributors, the Charles Urban Trading Company, who took a full page in the trade papers to proclaim: 'War in the Air! Possibilities of the Future! An actual motion picture prediction of the ideas of Rudyard Kipling, H.G. Wells, Jules Verne, and other powerful writers of imaginative fiction.' The promotion continued: 'Shows what might happen in the near future when aeroplanes have been perfected to the point of being practicable engines of war.' Film showmen were also reminded of the recent air meets that had taken place in Doncaster and Blackpool, newsreels of which had been released.

Booth split his story into three parts: one, Preparation; two, Attack and three, Defence. Part one showed supplies being landed at an 'aerocamp' and enemy airships starting on their journey. In sunny England an inventor proposes marriage to his sweetheart, but is rejected by her father. The announcement that England is under attack from an invading air armada gives the young man his great opportunity. Part two begins on the deck of an invading aircraft, from which shells are dropped on the countryside below. An armoured car pursues the airplane and discharges shells at it from its high-angled guns, but is quickly destroyed by one of the invaders' bombs. The aircraft bombs the railway line, derailing a train and killing a signal operator in his box. British airplanes take to the skies and an air battle takes place. The invaders shoot them down, and continue dropping bombs. The girl's house is hit and goes up in flames. She is

Thomas Alva Edison, one of the few inventors ever to become a successful businessman.

rescued by the inventor. Part three shows the inventor, assisted by his sweetheart, despatching his invention, the aerial torpedo. This device is controlled by wireless electricity, and thus can be directed at its moving target, the invaders' plane. A direct hit brings the aircraft crashing down in flames. It lands in a lake, and all that is left is a few floating pieces of wreckage. Victory is celebrated by the wedding of the inventor and his beloved with full parental approval. The film was sufficiently well made for it to be re-released six years later, during the Zeppelin attacks of World War I, under the revised title of *The Aerial Torpedo*.

d/s Walter R. Booth   *p* Charles Urban

An Apish Trick   (PATHE; FR)   b/w

The popular idea of rejuvenation through an injection of monkey gland serum gets another airing in this French film. A woman discovers her husband has been unfaithful, and for revenge gives him monkey gland treatment. This makes him behave like a monkey, and apparently the film did not treat the idea with taste. The English reviewer in the trade journal, *Bioscope*, complained, 'This is a film which repeats one of those occasional lapses into the vulgar which we have noticed before in Monsieur Pathé's productions. We cannot ourselves see any humour in situations of this sort.'

Credits not available

Aviation Has Its Surprises   (PATHE; FR)   b/w   8 min

The theme of aviation by inflation is burlesqued in this French film which, according to a contemporary review, formed 'a rousing comic skit replete with thrilling incidents'. A father tries to stop his daughter from meeting her sweetheart by locking her in her bedroom. Wringing her hands in despair at her open window she sees an airplane close by. She persuades the pilot to lend her the machine and flies off to her tryst. Her father sees this and makes up a mixture which, when swallowed, causes him to inflate like a balloon. He flies off in pursuit of the plane, sees his daughter meeting her lover at the top of the Eiffel Tower, and grabs the man by his collar. They fight in mid-air, and the struggle causes the father to suddenly deflate. The two men fall to the ground and are caught in a carpet. Meanwhile, the distraught damsel relieves her feelings by setting about an innocent sightseer.

Apart from its Science Fictional elements, the film is interesting as a reflection of the stirrings of independence among young women.

Credits not available

Bleary-Oh the Village Aviator
(GAUMONT; FR)   b/w   7 min
An interesting vision of aeronautics with an inventor living in a small French village where he has developed his own form of flying machine. In honour of his maiden flight the whole village has a holiday, and there is a great open air feast and much merrymaking. A stage is erected in the village square, and the inventor assembles his aircraft, a kind of motorcycle to which wings are attached. The keen aviator jumps in, turns the screw, the motor roars into life, and the airplane begins to take off. However, in taking its spring into the air, the engine breaks down and the machine speeds down the street. It knocks down lamp-posts, crashes through shop windows, brings down scaffoldings, then finally takes off. Flying over the village houses it explodes, and falls from roof to roof. The dazed inventor is found by the crowd sitting in the middle of the remains of his plane.

The English title, *Bleary-Oh*, is a pun on the name of the pioneer French aviator, Blériot.

Credits not available

The Earthquake Alarum
(SCHULTZE; G)   b/w   5 min
A nervous individual sees an advertisement for a marvellous automatic invention which is guaranteed to ring five minutes before an earthquake is about to occur. He purchases the device, hangs it on his bedroom wall, and goes to bed. Suddenly the telephone rings, and waking in fright, thinking it is his alarm bell, he rushes into the street in his nightgown. Embarrassed, he returns to bed and is fast asleep when visitors come ringing his doorbell. Out he rushes again, bowling them over. This time he is arrested for indecent behaviour. Finally getting home to bed again, he is just dozing off when the earthquake alarm really does ring. He ignores it and snuggles down in the bedclothes. Then the walls begin to rock, the ceiling falls in on the bed, and the poor man crawls out of the débris and hides under his bed.

Credits not available

The Electric Policeman   (GAUMONT; FR)   b/w   6 min
The imaginative application of electricity is once again the basis of a film combining comedy with trick effects. The hero is an overweight gendarme who is consistently knocked over by passing traffic and unable to give chase because of his bulk. Seeing an advertisement for the new 'electric boots' he buys a pair. As soon as they are on his feet he is unable to control himself, and finds himself rushing down the street at great speed. He bursts through brick walls, wooden gates, climbs up lamp-posts and splashes through canals. The entire local police force is called out to catch him but he races ahead of them all. Finally he comes into contact with some overhead tram wires and causes a massive fuse. A group of workmen bring him down to the ground, where he removes the boots and throws them away. Curiously, the obvious turn of plot – the gendarme using his amazing speed to pursue escaping crooks – seems not to have occurred to the Gaumont scenarist.

Credits not available

The Electric Servant   (URBAN; GB)   b/w   7 min
The third of the *Professor Puddenhead's Patents* series was not, in fact, issued as such by the distributor, Charles Urban Trading Company. Evidently the idea of a series of Science Fiction comedies had not caught on as planned. The plot followed the lines of the two previous episodes in that the professor's latest invention is sneakily appropriated and

A German cinema circa 1908. Note the sensationalist posters on the right.

humorously misused by his young son and daughter. According to the very brief synopsis published at the time of release, 'the apparatus is brought into touch with immovable objects, which perform astounding feats in consequence.'

d/s Walter R. Booth   p Charles Urban

Electric Transformations

(CLARENDON; GB)   b/w   7 min

The application of electrical power is taken to fanciful extremes in this comedy film, which uses the camera trick of dissolving one scene into another as its main special effect. The inventor is named Professor Bode, a pun on the music hall performer, Dr Walford Bodie, the Electrical Wizard, who claimed to be able to cure all kinds of sicknesses with his electrical apparatus. The professor is instructing a class of young ladies in the science of electrical transfusion of metals. He rapidly melts an iron horseshoe, then places an iron doorkey and a marble bust under the opposite poles of his instrument, and switches on the power. The metal dissolves and reforms into the shape of the marble bust. He performs a similar transformation with a flat-iron and a clock. His cook objects to this misuse of her kitchen clock and iron, so he forces her to take the place of the iron under the negative globe. Switching on, the current makes her face dissolve into that of the bearded Professor Bode, while he develops her face. The cook is furious, and only placated when the professor gives her the face of the prettiest girl in the class.

d Percy Stow   p H.V. Lawley

Electricity for Nervousness

(GAUMONT; FR)   b/w   5 min

Another film in which the application of electrotherapy is used as a cure. This time the sufferer of the nervous disease, St Vitus Dance, consults a doctor. Unable to control his spastic movements, he kicks the doctor around the surgery. The doctor decides to try an electric cure, and fits the patient with an electric belt plus electric pads at strategic anatomic points. The cure seems extreme to say the least, for the sufferer immediately begins to jump about jerkily in all directions. Leaping erratically down the street, he leans exhaustedly against the iron gates of a closed level-crossing. Immediately all the other folk leaning on the gates receive an electric shock and leap into the air. The man staggers off, and wherever he chances to catch hold of an object, whether it be a railing, a table, a chair, a bench, he causes severe shocks to whoever is in contact. Finally the poor fellow decides the disease is better than the cure and throws the belt and pads away, content to suffer simple twitches.

Credits not available

Percy Stow's Electric Transformations, *one of the many films of the period to play with the idea of electricity.*

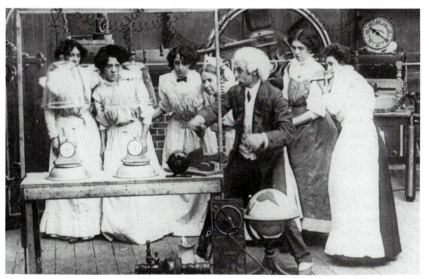

The Elixir of Strength   (PATHE; FR)   b/w   8 min

The theme of increased physical strength by the intake of some newly discovered mixture is a popular one, and lends itself to comedy laced with special effects. In this film the medium of press advertising is once again satirized in the promotion of Professor Rototo's elixir of strength. A henpecked husband, having been bullied by his wife and daughter, spots the ad and decides to try it. He obtains a dose from the professor himself, and finds himself so thoroughly invigorated that on the way home he tries out his new powers. He blows down a stone statue, juggles with a busking weight-lifter's equipment and stops a speeding car with an outstretched hand. After these feats, it is a simple matter to subdue his family into fetching him his slippers.

Credits not available

England Invaded   (STORMONT; GB)   b/w

The year 1909 saw an enormous upsurge of public concern about the possibility of the invasion of England by a European power. France, Germany, and even Russia were suspected of plotting this international takeover, and the popular press did little to cool these suspicions. The publications of Alfred Harmsworth, later Lord Northcliffe, particularly his string of boys' story papers and comics, were filled with alarming fiction. The most remarkable of the several cinematic excursions into the future-war theme was *England Invaded*. Today it would be called a 'multi-media' entertainment, for it consisted of a combination of motion pictures, both factual and fictional, recitation, song, and theatrical staging. It was created and conducted by an entertainer called Stormont, who wrote and scripted the scenario, had the film sequences enacted and photographed to his order, and who presented, narrated and sang the entire production on the stage (and screen) of the Coliseum Theatre in London's West End from 22 February 1909. 'Stroller', the pseudonymous commentator of the trade paper, *Kinematograph Weekly*, said Stormont's innovative turn 'brought down the house', but pointed out that the storyline plagiarized *An Englishman's Home*, the play by Guy du Maurier, which was filmed in 1914. The photography of the film sequences was carried out by Barker's Warwick Trading Company to Stormont's order. Stormont owned the production outright, and toured it personally through the Moss-Stoll and United County chains of theatres. On 18 March he took space in the trade press to point out that 'particular care has been taken to ensure that the uniform of the invaders should not resemble that of any European army'.

The years immediately before the outbreak of World War II saw a rush of similar film (eg **Q Planes** and **The Girl from Scotland Yard**, both 1937), which in an equally melodramatic way caught the fears of aerial invasion of the time.

d/p/s Leo Stormont   c William Barker

L'Homme Invisible *aka* An Invisible Thief

(PATHE; FR)   b/w   5 min

Like **The Invisible Fluid** (1908), this film was inspired by H.G. Wells' brilliant treatise on scientific invisibility, *The Invisible Man* (1897). It opens with a close-up of the book itself, the study of which inspires a young man to duplicate Wells' experiment. Apparently able to obtain the necessary drug, monocaine, he mixes the prescribed potion and drinks it. His body fades away, leaving only his clothing visible. He, taking off his clothes, goes into the street and robs a nearby house. He returns home with his spoils, dresses again, and puts on a face mask. Then he goes out again and robs a man and woman in the street. The police give chase but the thief removes his mask, strips off his clothing, and vanishes. The scared gendarmes flee in terror when they are attacked by their invisible quarry. This is a brilliantly worked out piece of cinematic trickery, the director here creating virtually all the special effects that were used by John P. Fulton in **The**

Invisible Man (1933) so many years later. Although there is a leaning towards comedy rather than thrills, particularly through the pranksterish activities of the young hero, the thirties version also had its quota of comedy, especially in the sequences featuring the invisible man and the police.

d Ferdinand Zecca

Hydrothérapie Fantastique *aka* The Doctor's Secret (STAR; FR) b/w 12 min

A mechanical means for reducing the obese is the subject of this Méliès fantasy, in which the producer/director plays the role of the bearded doctor. Several servants enter his medical consulting room, carrying their grossly overweight employer. The doctor carries out an examination, and has the patient placed in his complicated hydrotherapic machine. He switches it on, and the apparatus does its best, but the fat man proves too much for it and it explodes. The doctor and his assistants gather up the fragments of their patient, piece him together again, and the chap is overjoyed to discover that the experience has made him slim and elegant again.

d/p/c Georges Méliès *lp* Georges Méliès

The Invaders (CLARENDON; GB) b/w 10 min

One of several future-war fantasies that reflected the concern of the British over the threatened invasion of their islands during the first decade of the 20th century. This, the most thoroughly fictional and cinematic of the productions, was made by the Croydon-based Clarendon Films, who advertised it as 'The Most Exciting film story Ever Produced!' The critic of the *Kinematograph Weekly* was almost as enthusiastic: 'A remarkably well staged production, going with a swing from start to finish and illustrating what might be expected to happen if the dreaded invasion came about' (22 April 1909).

The film begins aboard ship off the coast of England. A foreign spy ingratiates himself with pretty Dora Smith (the actress is unnamed). Later, ashore and attending ladies night at a military club, Dora recognizes the foreigner again. He is next seen in the cellar of an East End tailor, where the tailors are revealed as trained soldiers in disguise. More foreign troops land in secret, disguised as civilians and women. The invaders use their machine-gun to attack a strategically placed house atop a hill. It is the home of Dora, and a bullet prostrates her lover. She writes a note and attaches it to the wing of her pet pigeon, then thrusts the bird up the chimney. It flies to a nearby Territorial Army camp and mounted men come galloping to the rescue. The spy carries Dora off to his East End hideout, but her wounded lover leads the Territorials to the rescue. The spy is shot, and the lovers embrace. The reviewer admired the way the heroine's house was reduced to a ruin by bombarding shells, but questioned the advisability of films which are not calculated to promote amity between nations.

d Percy Stow *p* H. V. Lawley

Invasion: Its Possibilities (URBAN; GB) b/w 18 min

The dreadful possibility of a foreign power invading the British Isles, a recurrent worry throughout history, was at a peak in the early years of the 20th century. The Harmsworth press, through its many popular publications ranging from the *Daily Mail* to *Boy's Friend*, was forever issuing dire warnings against France, Germany and Russia attacking the famous white cliffs of Dover, and each year an annual exercise of the armed forces helped quell public anxiety by showing the nation's preparedness. The Charles Urban Trading Company, leading producers and distributors of factual and educational films, used the manoeuvres of 1909 to construct an exciting and reassuring documentary showing the invasion of England and its successful repulse. 'A really attractive and soul-stirring set of pictures', wrote the critic of *Kinematograph Weekly* (4 March 1909), 'which will serve to still further accentuate the wave of patriotism that is stirring in our midst.' The film, one of the longest yet produced (1,055ft), is divided into two parts, 'As It Is' and 'As It Might Be'. The first, acting as a brief introduction, shows everyday life in the navy and army. In part two 'we see some most realistic scenes of what we might expect in the event of an invasion'. Beginning with a bird's-eye panorama of the camp, the alarm is sounded and the scouts set out. The naval brigade repels an attack, submarine mines explode and battleships open fire on the enemy. Invaders land, bringing horses and guns. Maxim-guns and new field-guns return their fire. The invaders land their heaviest weapon, the 4.7 gun, but the British win the day with their Maxim armour-clad train. The film closes with portrait views of Field-Marshal Earl Roberts, VC, Admiral Sir John Fisher, the Prince of Wales, and His Majesty King Edward VII. Appropriately, the code name for ordering a print of the film was 'Englishman'!

The film was premiered with enormous success at the Palace Theatre, London.

p Charles Urban

The Inventions of an Idiot (LUBIN) b/w 5 min
Inventors were considered creatures of ridicule by the popular media, who used them as eccentric caricatures in comic strips, insane protagonists in short stories, and in general responsible for most of the troubles of an age emerging reluctantly from the Victorian status quo. Seldom, however, has one of this scientific clan been so sneeringly labelled as the hero of this film. The 'idiot' of the title is a young inventor who demonstrates his latest series of devices to a friend. First comes a new kind of baby incubator which actually controls the environment without as well as within. Then an automated tonsorial cabinet, into which the friend steps for a demonstration. He emerges moments later in a bad temper, shorn of his hair and lengthy beard. Next they enter a new form of aerial transport and take off for a fast flight around the city. The machine reaches the unheard of speed of 200 mph and explodes. The inventor and his friend land unhurt, and the friend pleads that he be shown no more new inventions. The inventor grants his wish by pressing a button which promptly ejects his friend out of the aircraft. A fascinating parade of comic inventions, all of which are 'improvements' on devices of the time.

p Sigmund Lubin

Invisibility (HEPWORTH; GB) b/w 11 min
Picture-goers of this period must have come to believe that invisibility was a proven possibility by the time this film was released. So many films had been made appearing to prove the existence of invisibility, that it must surely have been accepted, at least by those of limited mentality. After all, there were no film magazines published for the public which could have carried articles explaining how these special effects' films were made.

In this film a man out for a stroll encounters an eccentric professor. The old man takes a small box from his pocket, and places a pinch of the powder in his mouth. As he swallows it, the professor fades from sight. The bewildered man puts his hands out to touch where the professor had been, and distinctly feels his body is still there, although it is completely invisible. Gradually the professor fades back into view. He offers to sell the box of powder to the man, who is delighted to buy it and hurries home. His late arrival is greeted with violent scolding by his bad-tempered wife. The man promptly swallows the powder and vanishes but not completely: his clothes remain visible. The next morning, while the now visible husband is still asleep, the wife silently steals his trousers. He wakes to find them missing, so dresses in shirt, collar, tie and boots, then takes a pinch of powder. Fading away, he walks downstairs and frightens his wife who sees nothing but a flapping shirt and boots. The invisible man then removes the shirt and his boots go walking out of the house and down the street. His wife follows them as they make their way to an outfitters' shop, frightening pedestrians and dogs as they go. The boots then come out of the shop, and above them, folded over an invisible arm, hang a new pair of trousers. The wife, the crowd, and the police all follow them as they walk home.

d Lewin Fitzhamon *p* Cecil M. Hepworth *lp* Lewin Fitzhamon

Life in the Next Century (LUX; FR) b/w 5 min
This film attempts to predict what the daily routine life of an average citizen will be like in 100 years' time from the film's release date, 1910. The man of AD 2010 awakens and presses a button. In the kitchen bread is sliced, travels by itself to the fire, and returns crisply toasted to the butterdish, where it spreads itself and soon arrives at the bedside with a pot of freshly brewed tea. The man presses another button and his morning post comes flying in. A third button brings his clothes to the bedside. Dressed, he proceeds about the house wearing motorized shoes, then goes to the office seated in his travelling chair. At the end of his easy day, the man of the future casts all his electrical appliances to the winds with an air of boredom and disgust. With everything automated, there is no interest left in life.

Significantly, this reassuring moral appeared at the conclusion of most of the electrical and mechanical gadget films of the period.

d Gerard Bourgeois *p* Leopold Lobel

The Magnetic Squirt (LE LION; FR) b/w 7 min
The magnetic fluid discovered by an old scientist in this short film is a substance which has wonderful properties, as his trial experiments prove. Taking his syringe out into the street, he presents it to a policeman who experiments by applying the fluid to a cripple. Instantly the man recovers the use of his legs and runs away in delight. They try the fluid on a porter who is struggling along the pavement carrying a heavy basket. One squirt, and the basket travels along of its own accord. They encounter a crowd of people fighting in the street, and the policeman squirts them all. He marches them off to prison, and has to give evidence against them in the magistrate's court. The Magistrate offends the policeman, so he gives the old man a squirt. His subsequent behaviour in the courtroom makes everybody laugh.

d Georges Hatot *p* Théophile Michaut

A Maker of Diamonds *aka* **The Diamond Maker** *aka* **Fortune or Misfortune** (VITAGRAPH) b/w 8 min
The manufacture of artificial diamonds was so often used in the fiction of this period that it seems to have superceded the earlier dream of the philosopher's stone, the much sought after way of turning base metal into gold. In this film the central character is a poverty-stricken old chemist called Mr Von Bellen, who is saddened by the unhappy home life of his wife and crippled daughter. Apparently inspired, he goes to his laboratory and creates a method of making artificial diamonds in a condenser. He takes the result home to show his wife, then takes it to the office of a diamond broker. The dealer examines the stone and buys it for a great sum. Suspicious at the old man's behaviour, the dealer sends his clerk after the man. He follows the old man to his home, and watches him giving the money to his delighted wife. Then he follows the old man as he returns to his laboratory and watches through the window as he proceeds to manufacture a second diamond. This time the stone is much larger. As the delighted chemist leaves the laboratory, the clerk climbs through the window and completely destroys the complicated equipment. The old man returns, sees his hopes of wealth in ruins, and goes mad.

d/p J. Stuart Blackton

Marvellous Fluid (LUX; FR) b/w 5 min
Another film based on the age-old concept of the 'fountain of youth', with the mythical becoming scientifically possible. A professor working in his laboratory discovers an elixir of life which has the power of rejuvenation. Delighted with his discovery, he sets forth jauntily on what he regards as an errand of mercy, bestowing his benefits upon all and sundry, good, bad and indifferent. The resulting rejuvenations were evidently comical, for a contemporary critic considered this film to be 'a sure cure for any fit of the blues we ever heard of!'

p Leopold Lobel

A Modern Dr Jekyll (SELIG) b/w 8 min
Although remarkably little can be traced in the way of contemporary reviews or published information of the actual content of this film, it would seem not to be a re-titled re-release of the same company's 1908 film, **Dr Jekyll and Mr Hyde,** as has previously been claimed by researchers. The

Selig original seems to have been set in the period of the novel and stage play, which would hardly allow the re-designation of 'Modern'. There are also contemporary references to this film as being a 'comedy'. The brief review given to the film in *Kinematograph Weekly* dated 17 February 1910 is as follows: 'An ingenious adaptation of Stevenson's classic replete with adventurous incident and sensation. Certain of general appreciation.' The review hardly supports the appellation 'Comedy'. By coincidence the film was reviewed and released in Britain in the same week as the British version of the Jekyll and Hyde story, **The Duality of Man** (1910).

p Williams N. Selig

Professor Puddenhead's Patents: The Aerocab and Vacuum Provider (URBAN; GB) b/w 6 min

The first of two Science Fiction comedies featuring the inventions of Professor Puddenhead, written and directed by Booth, Britain's early genius of special effects. The aerocab was described in a review as 'a weird contrivance with a remote connection to Wilbur Wright's aeroplane'. The professor has built his winged automobile in his garden, but is horrified to see it suddenly rise into the air under the control of his mischievous son and daughter. The children delight in their flight and are soon zooming over White City Exhibition, observing the famous flip-flap ride in action. Feeling hungry they decide to experiment with the vacuum provider, a tube-like attachment which they lower over a farmyard. The vacuum tube sucks up a live chicken, and delivers it to them cooked and ready to eat. They have fun with the tube, speedily clearing a table in a restaurant to the surprise of the diners. They lift a policeman off his feet, fly him through the sky, and let him drop. He falls in front of the professor, who is pursuing his aerocab on his bicycle. They proceed together, and suddenly an explosion above them sends the aerocab crashing to Earth. The disconsolate inventor sprinkles the burning wreckage with water from a garden watering-can while the policeman throws a pail of water over the boy's smouldering clothes.

d/s Walter R. Booth   *p* Charles Urban

Professor Puddenhead's Patents: The Electric Enlarger (URBAN; GB) b/w 5 min

The second of two Science Fiction comedies featuring the inventions of Professor Puddenhead, released two weeks after the first. The professor has invented an electric wand which gives off flashes when used. Anything touched with the wand grows to an immense size. His first experiment is upon a little moth which has invaded his laboratory. Immediately it grows into a gigantic insect filling the entire room. Everyone flees in terror, save the professor's brave manservant, who kills the creature. Then the man makes off with the wand, determined to enjoy himself. He first touches a fox-terrier, which grows to the size of a polar bear, then the head of a man sleeping in the park, and the head grows huge until it dwarfs the man's body. He enlarges a gardener's spade, and makes a caterpillar grow to the size of a snake. The professor and those he has annoyed pursue him, so he touches himself with the wand and grows into a giant. The professor draws his gun and fires, blowing his monstrous servant to pieces. Then he scares the crowd away for good by securing his wonderful wand and waving it at them.

d/s Walter R. Booth   *p* Charles Urban

Professor Weise's Brain Serum Injector

(LUBIN) b/w 5 min

The search for a way to increase intelligence by enlarging or developing the human brain, was a popular theme of this period, both in fiction and in real life: many advertisements in popular magazines claimed to be able to increase the reader's intelligence in return for an investment of their money. Patent medicines such as 'Brain Sparklers' were still advertised in the 1930s. In this film Professor Weise is researching into a fluid he calls his brain serum. Finalizing his experiments he loads a syringe and sallies forth into the streets to inject passers-by. He succeeds beyond all his expectations, but is finally set upon by the subjects of his experiments and forced to receive a dose of his own medicine.

p Sigmund Lubin

Professor Zanikoff's Experiences of Grafting

(LUX; FR) b/w 4 min

The advanced medical science of limb-grafting was used in this short film which centered around the eccentric experiments of a surgeon. The noble professor begins by demonstrating to his eager pupils his brand new method of curing the various physical defects to which the human race is subject. Whether genuine cases of deformity were used in the film is not clear, but the original critic commented that 'the results are extremely laughable and cleverly worked out'.

Credits not available

The Pulveriser (PATHE; FR) b/w 8 min

In their constant search for original ideas around which to build special effects productions, at the time referred to as 'trick films', the French company of Pathé Frères certainly found an original concept here. The central character is a scientist whose researches lead to the discovery of a pulverizing powder, which will not only reduce any object to dust, but any human being as well. Fortunately he also discovers an

The famous 1908 poster by Barrère caricaturing Emile and Charles Pathé. The Pulverizer was one of their many trick films of the period.

antidote which, when applied to the reduced matter, reverses the action and rebuilds it into its original form. Two youngsters snoop on the scientist's experiments and, inspired by the amazing actions of the pulverizer, steal it in order to terrorize the neighbourhood. They proceed to reduce all manner of objects to dust, which makes everyone think a band of thieves are at work stealing their possessions. Eventually the piles of powder are brought to the scientist's laboratory, where he uses his antidote to restore them to normal.

Credits not available

The Rubber Man (LUBIN) b/w 4 min

The first American film to devise a form of automaton or robot that owes more to pure Science Fiction than the European legends of mechanical dancing dolls. Here, an inventor fashions a humanoid out of rubber, powered by electricity. Unfortunately it gets its wires crossed and immediately goes out of control and throws the inventor and his family through the window. They summon the police, but it fights all three constables and goes rushing out into the street. It forces its way into an old spinster's house and promptly stuffs her up the chimney. While its pursuers pull the woman to safety the automaton wrecks a dry goods store, and crashes through the big drum of a German band. Caught at last the robot is ducked in a water trough, where the water infiltrates his rubber body and causes an electrical breakdown. The robot is rendered harmless. Although produced as a comedy, the idea of a robot/monster on the rampage is an intriguing filmic precursor of **Frankenstein** (1931).

p Sigmund Lubin

Up the Pole *aka* How I Cook-ed Peary's Record (URBAN; GB) b/w 6 min

Science Fiction satire on the real-life race between Peary and Cook to reach the Pole. Booth, who had made the science fantasy, **The Voyage of the *Arctic***, for R.W. Paul back in 1903, here used his earlier plot and format, shorn of much of its whimsy, for a harder-edged burlesque on the great achievement in polar exploration of the period. He replaced his former fictional hero, Captain Kettle, with another fictional hero, one more famous for his outrageous boastings, Baron Munchausen. The film took the form of a diary, starting on 1 April – All Fools' Day, of course. Munchausen sets out for the Pole: 'I go to victory or death!' Day 2 finds him in the ice wilderness where, by his personal hypnotic powers, he causes an igloo to be built. Day 3: He discovers the polar Queen entombed in a block of ice and dynamites her free. Day 4: Whilst he is asleep on his sled the Queen uses her polar star wand to tow him past his rival's ice-bound ship. Day 5: He arrives at the Pole and ascends it via magnetic attraction. Then he saws it down to take home as proof of his conquest. Attacked by a polar bear, he hynotizes the animal into helping him saw down the Pole. Then he makes the bear carry the Pole to his sled. The final entry is September 27: Munchausen reaches civilization in his motor-car, the Pole in the back seat and the bear steering.

d/s Walter R. Booth   *p* Charles Urban

Den Vidunderlige Haarelixir *aka* A Marvellous Cure (NORDISK; DEN) b/w 7 (6) min

The problem of curing the bald male head seems to have reached as far as Denmark, where this short film was produced. The hero is seen to be happy but bald; he objects to the fact that his little son should have more hair than he has. He spots an advertisement in his morning newspaper proclaiming that a cure for baldness has been discovered at last. He dashes out to buy a bottle, gives himself something of an overdose, and finds the results so effective that his new ambition is to return to his original bald state.

By coincidence, the film was released in Britain in the same week as the French version of this theme, **La Lotion Miraculeuse** (1907).

lp Petrine Sonne

Voyage au Centre de la Terre *aka* A Journey to the Middle of the Earth (PATHE; FR) b/w 9 min

This French film, created by the great Spanish director de Chomon, is the first to depict on screen the concept of a world inside the Earth. Unfortunately no detailed description was published, beyond a short review in the trade press. The storyline 'depicted the enthralling adventures of four intrepid individuals' who set forth from their homes with the curious ambition to walk to the middle of the Earth. The reviewer pointed out that 'as may be imagined there are innumerable openings for trick effects'. However, these were not, apparently, up to de Chomon's usual standard, for the critic, wrote 'the incidents on the way are not quite so astounding as they might be'. No print is known to exist, so we cannot know now what de Chomon's vision of life within the Earth was.

d/s/c/se Segundo de Chomon   *p* Ferdinand Zecca

Voyage dans la Lune *aka* Nuevo Viaje a la Luna (PATHE; FR) b/w

A short fantasy picture depicting scenes familiar from and similar to Méliès' **Le Voyage dans la Lune** (1902), except that de Chomon used Chinese actors and billed the film a 'Chinese fantasy'. Hailed as the Spanish Méliès, de Chomon had been recruited by the artistic director of the Pathé company, Ferdinand Zecca, on an inspection tour of Pathé's Spanish operations. An expert in trick photography, de Chomon was supposed to be Pathé's answer to the success garnered by Méliès. He made a number of fantasies in this vein, including **Voyage à la Planète Jupiter** (1908), **Voyage au Centre la Terre** and *Mars* (both 1909), mostly relying on stop-frame shooting techniques combined with superimpositions. His best-known work is **El Hotel Electrico** (1905), shot before Stuart Blackton's version of similar scenes. However, as de Chomon's collaborator, Rastelli, informed a group of historians later, he and de Chomon spent nights trying to figure out how Blackton had made the objects in *The Haunted House* (1907) move since they saw no evidence of the 'invisible wires' on which they had relied. After a while, they concluded that a special stop-frame technique must have been used, exposing one frame at a time. From then on, de Chomon abandoned his invisible wires as well (*La Table Magique*, **La Cuisine Magnétique**, *Les Jouets Vivants*, *La Liquéfaction des Corps Durs*, all 1908).

d/s/c/se Segundo de Chomon

The Wonderful Electro-Magnet (EDISON) b/w 7 min

The Science Fiction twist in this film is the improvement upon a standard electromagnet: instead of attracting only metal, it attracts human beings. The ingenious young inventor demonstrates his discovery to the manager of his local motion picture theatre, who at once recognizes it as a money-making proposition. He purchases the instrument from the inventor, and sets about attracting customers in this amazing new scientific way. One of the by-passers, unable to resist the magnetic rays, is the minister. The manager apologizes and explains the electromagnet. The minister laments his own lack of attendances of late, which gives the manager an idea. Next Sunday he takes the invention to the church and the visiting bishop is delighted to see a packed congregation. This film not only reflects contemporary interest in electromagnetism, it concerns itself with the schism between the church and the cinema. Seen as a threat to organized religion, cinemas were not, at this time, allowed to open on Sundays – in Great Britain. Whilst this was also true of some American cities and states, it was not a nationwide policy. Thus the film was devised as much as propaganda as for entertainment.

p Thomas Edison

1910

The Aerial Submarine (KINETO; GB) b/w 12 min

Booth, the British Georges Méliès, here makes his second Science Fiction prediction about the future of flight – the first was **The Airship Destroyer** (1909). This time, the popular concept of the all-purpose vehicle, long a favourite in the Science Fiction stories in such boys' weeklies as *Pluck* and *Halfpenny Marvel*, is used to great surprise effect. The film opens with a boy and girl playing at the seaside. They have a pair of field-glasses and through them spot a gang of pirates unloading their booty from a submarine. They clamber down the cliffs and use their hand camera to take snapshots of the pirates at work, but unfortunately are discovered. The pirates capture the children and take them prisoner aboard the submarine. Their father, searching for the children, finds the camera on the rocks and out of curiosity develops the exposed plate. It shows the pirates clearly and he takes it to the authorities for investigation.

Meanwhile, in the depths of the sea, the young prisoners are viewing the strange sights through a porthole. In the control cabin, the leader of the pirates turns out to be a woman. An ocean liner is sighted on the surface, and is promptly sunk by the pirates' torpedo. The pirates don divers suits and walk through a water-lock, across the ocean floor, to loot the wrecked liner now lying on the seabed. A naval submarine has been alerted and sails to the scene. Suddenly the lady pirate issues a new order and the submarine shoots to the surface, and goes flying into the air. It swoops over the naval sub and fires a shell at it, blowing it to fragments. Then the aerial submarine takes a course over mountainous terrain. A careless engineer, lighting a cigarette, drops a smouldering match near a tin of petrol. The resulting explosion wrecks the engines and the strange craft rapidly falls to Earth. The only solution is to take to the sea again, but they are trapped in the mountains. A series of explosions occur which destroy the pirate queen, her men, and their unique craft. Luckily the two children manage to escape in the confusion.

d/s Walter R. Booth *p* Charles Urban *c* Harold Bastick

The Aeroplanist's Secret
(COSMOPOLITAN; FR) b/w 12 min

A rare dramatic film for the period, dealing with an improvement in contemporary aviation techniques. An engineer has invented a new design of aircraft which will fly faster than anything yet manufactured. However, to complete his experiment he requires a light, high-speed motor. He hears of another engineer who has developed just such an engine, but when he tries to obtain it, he is refused. Determined to get the new engine, the inventor decides to force the engineer's wife to steal the plans for him. Compelled for the sake of her honour to accede to the inventor's demands, she steals the plans from her husband's studio but before handing them over she makes some small but vital alterations to the designs. The inventor builds the lightweight engine, and has it mounted into his plane. The result is a successful trial flight, then suddenly the plane goes out of control, crashes and the villainous inventor is killed.

Credits not available

Burglary by Airship (GAUMONT; FR) b/w 6 min

Another remarkable advance on contemporary aeronautics is demonstrated in this film. The hero is described as an up-to-date burglar who pursues his calling by means of an airship which has a huge magnet attached to the bottom of the cabin. His first victim is a wealthy financier, who is startled to

Charles Ogle as the monster in Frankenstein, *the first version of Mary Shelley's oft-filmed novel.*

see his steel safe suddenly whisked into the air, through the window, and annex itself to the airship. The burglar is not content with this major haul, however, and in his flight attracts the entire contents of an ironmonger's shop, a housekeeper's pails of water, a man riding his bicycle, a young woman in her iron bath, and a kitchen range together with its utensils. Lamp-posts fly into the sky, and a squad of brave firemen marching through the streets are astonished when their brass helmets fly off in unison. The baffled crowd of victims espy the sky-high culprit, fetch firearms, and shoot holes in the airship. It crashes to Earth, and the burglar is quickly and painfully captured. Remarked a reviewer, 'When flying machines become more popular they will not be an unmixed blessing if his film be any criterion.'

Credits not available

The Comet (KALEM) b/w 11 min

1910 was the year of Halley's comet, which reached its perehelion on 20 April. The world was well prepared for it, thanks to the newspapers and popular magazines, whose supplements contained prognostications galore by scientists and fictioneers. This remarkable and dramatic cinematic vision of Halley's comet breaking its orbit and crashing into the Earth was unique in early American cinema, and stands as a remarkable prediction, not of fact, but of films to come including **When Worlds Collide** (1951) and **Meteor** (1979). Kineto Films, releasing this Kalem production in Britain, called it 'An interesting example of what can be done by the kinematograph in depicting imaginary events in a realistic fashion: what might happen if the comet touched the Earth.'

The story opens in the dining-room of a rich man's mansion. The family are anxious at the news of the comet's approach and rush to a nearby observatory where the astronomer in charge explains the comet to them, and shows it to them through his giant telescope. The city is in a panic, and the inhabitants take to their cars and drive madly for safety. The comet is shown as it rushes through the sky towards Earth. In a miser's den the old man gathers his hoard, only to see it melt from the increasing heat. In a poor cottage an old widow suffers from the heat, growing thirsty. Then her cottage bursts into flames, and the Red Cross come rushing to the rescue. The countryside is burning: farms, cottages, the railway station and the grand mansion are all on fire. The people, seeking refuge from the great heat, find caves and rush underground. Soon they are down to the last drop of water. A man tries to steal it and is dealt summary justice. The crowds push deeper down until they come upon great stalactite caves, where they find some water pools at last. The comet passes the Earth and swings on its way. The final scene is a tragic panorama of the devastated surface of the Earth.

Other contemporary films with similar themes were **Himmelskibet** (1917) and **Verdens Undergang** (1916).

Credits not available

Dr Smith's Automaton   (PATHE; FR)   b/w   7 min
Another of several contemporary comedies based on the concept of the automaton. For once we have a useful description of the mechanical man: a critic calls him 'a man of buckram and hidden springs'. Dr Smith has invented an automaton, and his small son, bent on mischief, sneaks into the laboratory and sets the robot into motion. Once started, there is no way of stopping the mechanical man: men and woman go down like ninepins before his irresistible onward march. One by one the bruised victims join in the chase, running behind the distracted doctor. The automaton is finally brought to a palpitating halt by a 9-foot-high wall.

Credits not available

The Duality of Man   (WRENCH; GB)   b/w   9 min
This British version of Stephenson's *Dr Jekyll and Mr Hyde* was promoted as the story currently being exploited on the theatrical stage by H.B. Irving. The film begins with Dr Jekyll in his laboratory, experimenting upon himself by drinking a potion to separate good from evil in the human body. He changes into his evil persona, Hyde, and visits some public gardens nearby where gambling with playing cards is in progress. He snatches up a wad of banknotes and in the ensuing chase seriously assaults an old man. The police are called in and are hot on his trail when he returns to his chambers, drinks the potion, and changes back to Dr Jekyll. His pursuers depart, baffled. Jekyll's fiancée, Hilda, comes calling with her father. Suddenly Jekyll changes into Hyde and promptly murders his prospective father-in-law in the sight of the girl. Understandably horrified at the events, Hilda nevertheless undertakes not to divulge her fiancé's guilt. The police enter, having heard the commotion, and Hyde drinks a fatal dose of poison.

'A picture which will appeal to the lovers of the highly sensational' commented a critic at the time.

Credits not available

The Electric Insoles   (ESSANAY)   b/w   8 min
An American adaptation of the concept of electrified shoes and boots, as popularized by several European films. The idea of electric insoles was obviously an economic one, as it meant that no special prop boots had to be designed and built – the only trick effect was an undercranked camera. The hero suffers from his feet and a friend recommends that he try a pair of Dr Wright's electric insoles to cure their aching. He hobbles into a drugstore and purchases a pair, but discovers too late that they have been too heavily charged with electricity. Once he has them inside his shoes he is unable to make his feet behave. They rush him out of the shop and down the street. He grabs at a fence in order to stop, but tears along, ripping out the entire centre section. Two policemen leap to stop him, but like a human lightning streak he sends them sprawling. After several attempts to stop himself, he gives up and lets his feet take him where they will. His wild career comes to a screeching stop when his electrified shoes stick firmly to a manhole cover. His delight is short-lived, for now his many pursuers can catch up with him and take their painful revenge.

p George K. Spoor, G. M. Anderson

The Electric Vitaliser   (KINETO; GB)   b/w   9 min
The power of electricity, used in so many Science Fiction films of this early period, is given a slightly different twist in this film by the foremost British creator of trick films, Booth. Here his hero, the usual eccentric professor, discovers that electricity can restore life to the dead. His first experiment is conducted on his daughter's pet goldfish. The tear-stained child brings the bowl into his laboratory and a touch of the electric device recharges the fish with life. The second test follows immediately when outside a motorist runs over a dog. The dead animal is brought back to life, to the joy of its owner. The dramatic incidents now take a fanciful turn, as the professor conducts a new form of experiment: the installation of electric life force in objects that have never been alive. He begins with a draper's shop dummy. A touch of power and it goes walking jerkily into the park. The professor follows, and experiments on a statue of a Roman gladiator. This too jerks into life. Inspired, the professor visits a waxworks' emporium. Here he begins his experiments on a wax Scotsman. It promptly gives a spasmodic highland fling. Inside he revives dummies of Jem Mace, the boxing champion, Napoleon, Queen Elizabeth, Guy Fawkes, and the murderer Charlie Peace. Jem Mace promptly knocks them all down, Napoleon escorts the Queen away, Peace creeps off to commit a crime, and Guy Fawkes achieves his thwarted ambition by setting off a barrel of gunpowder. Meanwhile in the park, the tailor's dummy has inspired love in the waxen hearts of the gladiator and the Scotsman, who fight jerkily for her favours. All the animated figures follow the professor to his laboratory, where they perform a frenzied dance until the heat they generate melts them into a heap.

d/s Walter R. Booth   *p* Charles Urban   *c* Harold Bastick

The Elixir of Youth   (PATHE; FR)   b/w   9 min
One of several comedies built around the concept of a chemical cure for old age. This one is better than most, starring as it does the popular French film comedian, Wiffles. Wiffles is in love with a pretty young widow, but she rejects him as too old. He visits a chemist and buys a bottle of a newly advertised elixir of youth. He takes a draught and is transformed into a well-set-up young fellow. Not satisfied with this, he takes a few more swigs and passes through the stage of early manhood, youth, and childhood. Now he is far too young to marry, so the young widow sends him back to the chemist for a preparation to reverse his accelerating youth. Unfortunately the eager Wiffles takes an overdose and rapidly ages into his dotage. However, he finds consolation in flirting with the widow's maid. The maid makes the suggestion that Wiffles should try drinking a mixture of both elixirs. He does so, reverts to the age he was at the start of his experiments, and decides to abandon the widow in favour of marrying the maid.

lp Wiffles

Frankenstein   (EDISON)   b/w   16 min
The first attempt to capture Mary Wollstonecraft Shelley's brilliant novel, *Frankenstein or The Modern Prometheus*, on film, this is an extraordinary effort for the time. Although there had been many stage adaptations, this version for the screen, written and directed by Dawley, successfully reinterpreted, rather than condensed, the original material, into a totally new cinematic experience. It was billed as 'a liberal adaptation of Mrs Shelley's dramatic story' and claimed that 'in making the film the Edison Company has carefully tried to eliminate all the actually repulsive situations and to concentrate upon the mystic and psychological problems that are to be found in this weird tale'.

Frankenstein (Phillips), a young medical student, endeavours to create chemically a perfect human being. Unfortunately the result of his experiment is a misshapen monster (Ogle), who flees into the night. Frankenstein, sickened, is nursed back to health by his sweetheart, but on the eve of his wedding is visited by the monster. There is a struggle, and the monster sees himself reflected in the mirror. Horrified by the sight, he flees again. Later he breaks into the bride's room. Her shriek brings Frankenstein, and again there is a struggle and the monster flees. Finally the monster fades away ('The creature of an evil mind is overcome by love and disappears'), and the lovers embrace.

The curiously mystic finale spoils the otherwise dark mood which, after James Whale's classic **Frankenstein** (1931), was at the centre of, if not central to, all subsequent versions of the legend.

d/s J. Searle Dawley   *p* Thomas A. Edison   *lp* Charles Ogle, Augustus Phillips, Mary Fuller

Freezing Mixture   (KINETO; GB)   b/w   10 min

This production postulates a liquid preparation which would instantly deep-freeze live animals for transport across the world. It has apparently existed for some while, for the inventor of the fluid has already made his fortune with it when the film begins. The young man arrives in Australia to visit his uncle and is saddened to see how henpecked his favourite uncle has become. An idea strikes him, and he administers a dose of his freezing fluid to his aunt. The woman goes stiff and falls to the floor. The two men bundle her body behind a screen and depart to spend a little of the inventor's fortune. The maid has observed the incident, and proceeds to hide the bottle of antidote, before departing herself for a lover's tryst. When the roisterers return they are unable to find the antidote. Desperate to unfreeze the aunt, they carry her stiff body into the garden and pour pailsful of hot water over her. She remains obstinately solid. At last the maid returns, locates the missing antidote, and auntie is restored to life. By great good fortune only auntie's good qualities thaw out – her cross-grained temper remains frozen for ever. A remarkably similar film, **Freezing Auntie** (1912), was produced by the Edison Company two years later.

d Walter R. Booth   *p* Charles Urban   *c* Harold Bastick

The Invisible Thief   (GAUMONT; FR)   b/w   5 min

Today this film might be called the Gaumont Company's 'cover version' of Pathé's **L'Homme Invisible** (1909). It was accepted practice at this time for film companies to copy each other's successful productions, and although some vituperative agitation was expressed in the trade press of the period, no legal action appears to have been taken in the courts. Certainly, Continental companies do not seem to have had the benefit of a copyright office to register their films.

The anti-hero of this short film has the unexplained power of rendering himself invisible at will. He begins by borrowing a handy bicycle. Two gendarmes see the crime and give pursuit. They catch up with him and arrest him whereupon he vanishes. The stolen bicycle then goes sailing along the street, apparently of its own accord. The thief then reappears on the bicycle so the policemen immediately commandeer a passing car and drive after him. They soon overtake the bicycle but once again the thief makes himself invisible. The baffled gendarmes get out of the car to search for the crook, and while they do so he reappears in the car and drives cheerily away to freedom.

Credits not available

Un Matrimonio Interplanetario *aka* A Marriage in the Moon   (LATIUM; IT)   b/w   15 min

Italy's first entry into the space travel stakes is a remarkable combination of Science Fiction and operatic romance. The hero is a love-sick astronomer called Aldovino, who spends his time staring through his powerful telescope at the planet Mars. He has fallen in love with the daughter of a Martian astronomer, and with a powerful wireless telegraph transmits

a message of love to her. Yala, the Martian, receives the message and signals her love back to Earth. Her father agrees to the marriage, if the Earthman can meet them on the Moon in exactly one year's time. Working feverishly the scientist perfects a spaceship and is shot into space by a mortar. He lands safely on the Moon and greets the two Martians, who arrive by modern airship. The couple are promptly married, the astronomer having thoughtfully brought along a preacher as passenger. And there, on the Moon, they celebrate the first true 'honeymoon', while Moon maidens perform a ballet among the glistening rocks and grottoes.

d/s Enrico Novelli

The Police of the Future   (GAUMONT; FR)   b/w   8 min

According to this French prediction of the future, the police force will be airborne. They possess a special police airplane, in which they fly over the cities looking for criminals through their powerful telescope. The first crime of the day is quickly spotted: two thieves are seen robbing a man in the street. Instantly the sky police lower a large, tweezer-like instrument, which grasps the two crooks firmly about the waist. Struggling furiously, the men are hauled up into the plane. Many other evil-doers are observed and captured, including a dog stealing sausages from a butcher shop. At last the police plane descends and the day's bag is shot through a funnel into the station below. Here police seize the offenders and haul them off to jail.

Credits not available

Setting Back the Hands of Time
(PATHE; FR)   b/w   8 min

In this film a learned professor discovers yet another means of rejuvenation. This time it is a powder which has the power to make humans and animals young again. His method of application is, however, unique. He compresses the powder into the form of bullets and fires them from a special kind of pistol into the flesh of whoever requires rejuvenation. After various experiments, he decides to try the stuff out on his wife and assistant. Finding that she now prefers the company of the young and handsome assistant to his own, he commits self-rejuvenation. As he grows younger and more handsome, he has no difficulty in attracting his wife again.

Credits not available

Den Skaebnesv Angre Opfindelse *aka* Dr Jekyll and Mr Hyde *aka* Jekyll and Hyde   (NORDISK; DEN)   b/w   17 min

This Danish version of Robert Louis Stevenson's novel about

L'Homme Invisible (1909), Ferdinand Zecca's marvellous essay in invisibility, remade the following year by Gaumont as The Invisible Thief.

the separation of the good and evil nature of humankind was considered by the critics of the day to be far superior to Selig Polyscope's **Dr Jekyll and Mr Hyde** (1908). For one thing, the storyline followed the original book and not the theatrical version and for another, 'it is pleasing, if not actually amusing, to note the manner in which the Great Northern Company have sidestepped all the unpleasantness that might be expected'. The film was also praised for its light, detail, and surprising depth in studio work, as well naturalistic acting. The story itself was given a surprise twist in that it was shown as the scientist's dream of what might happen if he continued his experiments. He wakes at the end of the film, thus, thought the reviewer, the makers had found an ingenious way of putting their film before both children and the various boards of censorship.

The storyline has Jekyll as a rich young scientist and student of occult sciences. He demonstrates to a party of friends his new fluid which he hopes will change the mental, moral and physical makeup of man. They depart, and he sinks into a chair, dreaming of what will happen when he perfects the drug. He takes the medicine and changes into a hideous, debased creature who commits several public outrages. By means of an antidote, he changes back to Jekyll but the young scientist becomes horrified by the brutalities he has committed. Unfortunately, he begins to revert to his base self without recourse to the potion. As Jekyll he arranges with his solicitor for Hyde to be his heir, and causes much distress to his fiancée, Maud, with his sudden disappearances. As Hyde he commits further atrocities, and in presenting a cheque to pay for his sins, mistakenly signs it with Jekyll's signature. In a final scene of horror, Jekyll finds himself changing into Hyde in front of his fiancée – then awakens from his nightmare and takes the real Maud in his arms.

d Viggo Larsen   *p* de Olsen   *s* August Blom   *c* Axel Graatkjaer   *lp* Alwin Neuss, Oda Alstrup, August Blom, Einer Zangenberg, Viggo Larsen

A Trip to Mars (EDISON)   b/w   4 min
The motive force for this early American venture into outer space is chemical rather than mechanical or electrical. A celebrated professor labouring in his laboratory discovers two wonderful powders which, when combined, form a product which has the power to reverse the law of gravity. He experiments by sprinkling the substance on various objects in his laboratory and watches with delight as they float upwards into the air. Excited by his discovery, the professor rushes forth to tell the world, waving papers containing the powders, one in each hand, over his head. A little of each powder spills onto him, with the result that he goes sailing up into the clouds. He flies through the sky, finally falling down onto the surface of the planet Mars. Here he finds himself surrounded by giant trees, whose branches are alive and reach out to grasp him like gnarled arms. He scrambles clear but falls over a ridge and lands on the lower lip of a gigantic Martian. The sleeping giant wakes and blows out a cloud of steam, shooting the professor into the air. He catches the visitor in his hand, and blows him again. This time the air is the opposite of hot, and freezes the professor into a giant snowball. This grows, explodes, and propels the traveller back to Earth again. He crashes headlong into his laboratory, where he determines to destroy what remains of his strange discovery. He hurls the powders into the far corner of the room, where they combine, cause the side of the house to rise, and the professor is last seen sitting on the floor of his wildly spinning laboratory.

Credits not available

The Aerial Anarchists (KINETO; GB)   b/w   11 min
The third in Booth's astonishing trilogy of Science Fiction dramas about the future of aviation, following **The Airship Destroyer** (1909) and **The Aerial Submarine** (1910). Once again, Booth uses film to warn a complacent civilization of the horrors in store if the new power of manned flight is used by the wrong hands, as a means of making war. For the first time in cinema the destruction of famous buildings is shown, as the invaders rain bombs on London from the air. 'These exciting scenes are so magnificently and realistically staged that they will fill audiences with amazement and mystification.' The scenes, crude by today's standards, when contemplated with the eyes and minds of an audience of the period, are not only staggering, but predict accurately what actually came to pass, briefly in the World War I, then horrifically in World War II.

The film begins in a remote hut where anarchists are building an airplane. They take off and fly towards their objective, London. During the night a searchlight operating from an army fort picks them up. They answer with a well-placed bomb, destroying the fort. A second bomb is dropped on an important railway bridge, one train escapes the explosion, but a second crashes down into a chasm. The train bursts into flame, and firemen speed to rescue the trapped passengers. The airplane arrives over London and drops a bomb onto the dome of St Paul's Cathedral. Immediately the damaged building is engulfed in flames. Another church is bombed, and a wedding party narrowly escape with their lives. The bride and groom jump into their wedding car and pursue the plane. It fires on the car, which careers over an embankment and smashes. The bridegroom dashes to his own private plane and takes off. He catches up with the anarchists' machine and engages it in a gun battle. Damaged, the anarchists are forced to land, and flee to their hideout. They are pursued by soldiers and police and the fusillade of bullets explodes one of the bombs in the hut. Firemen arrive to quell the flames, but fail and the miscreants perish horribly in the same fiery death suffered by their victims.

The years immediately prior to World War II saw a rush of similar films (**Midnight Menace** and **Q Planes**, both 1937) which imagined aerial bombardment by anarchists/bolsheviks as central to any attack on Britain.

d/s Walter R. Booth   *p* Charles Urban   *c* Harold Bastick

The Automatic Motorist (KINETO; GB)   b/w   10 min
In this British film the pioneering 'trick film' director/producer Booth deals with the popular concept of the robot. The word was uncoined at this time, and the automatic motorist of the title is referred to in the original synopsis as 'the clockwork man'. For his plot, Booth goes back to his **The '?' Motorist** (1906) and *When the Devil Drives* (1907), replacing the basic fantasy of his earlier films with a scientific rationalization. A young couple, just married, set off for their honeymoon trip in an enclosed automobile. Their chauffeur is a clockwork man, newly completed by an aged inventor anxious to give his automaton a trial run. This proves instantly disastrous, for the car roars off at great speed, crashing into a policeman who tries to stop it, and dragging him behind. The car rushes through the city of London, up the side and dome of St Paul's Cathedral, and straight up into the sky. It lands on the Moon, then leaps across space to the ring of Saturn, where it drives round and round until it breaks through the planet's crust. Inside dwell a race of mysterious beings who, incensed by the invasion, prepare to fling the car back into space. Then a more beneficent being appears, waves her wand, and the car flies safely away, back to Earth. After a brief splash with a waterspout, the car drops into the sea. Still the robot drives implacably on, and the newly-weds are treated to the sight, through their sealed windows, of the monsters of the deep as they swim inquisitively by. The return to the surface is accomplished by the convenient eruption of an undersea volcano. As the car resumes its flight into space, the newly-weds manage to break their way out and parachute to Earth by means of their umbrellas. Leaving the car soaring on under the direction of the clockwork driver, they drift aimlessly through the air until a sportsman,

mistaking them for some new species of wildfowl, shoots at them, holing their improvised parachutes.

d/s Walter R. Booth   *p* Charles Urban   *c* Harold Bastick

Electric Boots   (PATHE; FR)   b/w   4 min

Pathé's variation on **The Electric Policeman** (1909) made by their rivals, the Gaumont Company. The same idea of electrified boots is used here, but instead of confining their use to one person, a policeman, the excitement comes from their use by a great number of people and interestingly and unusually the boots are seen as wholly beneficial. A surburban shoe store is promoting the latest thing in footwear, electric boots, and there are plenty of customers. Everyone who buys them rushes around at accelerated speed, completing their daily tasks in no time. A firm of builders buys the boots and the labourers promptly erect a new house at alarming speed. The film ends with the new owners moving in, thanks to furniture movers in their electric boots.

The main trick effect here was achieved through under-cranking the camera.

Credits not available

The Electric Villa   (PATHE; FR)   b/w   7 min

Another example of Science Fiction applied to the earlier ghost and fantasy concepts popularized at the turn of the century by Georges Méliès. Now, mysteriously moving household objects can be rationally explained by electricity instead of poltergeists and their relations. An enterprising house agent persuades a prospective client to view a newly-built house fitted with every electrical convenience. Insulated wires festoon every room, and there are various control knobs awaiting command by touch. The first knob causes the house-hunter to be thrust into a mobile chair and whisked into the dining-room, where a well-spread table awaits him. He prepares to dine, but the roast chicken somehow receives an overdose of electricity and comes to life. The man gets ready for bed and is suddenly tossed out of the sheets and locked away in the wardrobe. He breaks free but the carpet becomes electrified, rolls him up in it and flings him down the staircase and into the street. Either the electric villa is out of control, or it objects to human intrusion.

Credits not available

Hoffmanns Erzaehlungen *aka* Tales of Hoffmann

(ERSTE OESTERREICHISCHE/UNGARISCHE KINO-INDUSTRIE; HUN, AUSTRIA)   b/w   15 min

A filmed version of fragments of a theatrical performance of Offenbach's opera. The same three E.T.A. Hoffmann stories were later filmed in more cinematic adaptations by Oswald (1915), Neufeld (1923) and Powell (1951). The cast was the same as that of the Viennese troupe performing the opera, probably at the Burgtheater. The directors, especially Anton Kolm, initiated an art-film movement and production house in Vienna, Wiener Kunstfilm, to attract the middle-class audiences to the movies. At the time the film was made, Hungary didn't exist as a separate country and the Austrian Empire was ruled by the Habsburgs.

co-d/p/co-s Anton Kolm   *co-d/co-s* Luise Kolm, Jakob Fleck, Claudius Valtee

The Inventor's Secret   (BIOGRAPH)   b/w   8 min

This story of an automaton once again returns to the *Coppélia* theme of a toymaker and a life-like girl doll. The film begins with the old toymaker in his workshop, where he is putting the finishing touches to his automatic doll. Meanwhile a young girl is reported missing, and a reward of $500 is posted. A young policeman studies the poster and tells his sweetheart. She answers an advertisement for a cook required in the house of the toymaker, and is given the job. In the course of her work she spots the life-like doll as it walks about in the toymaker's workshop. She immediately mistakes it for the missing girl and tells her policeman sweetheart. The cop and the cook break into the workshop and grab the mechanical doll, planning to claim the reward. They immediately discover the truth, and are promptly expelled by the irate inventor.

This was one of the last one-reel films Griffith directed before starting to make two-reel length films during the period from 1911 to 1914, by which time he'd made some 450 films and become one of the most prolific directors of the early silent era. All this work was overshadowed, however, by his feature films commencing with *Birth of a Nation* (1915), probably the single most influential film in the history of the cinema, and certainly of the American cinema, for its astonishing combination of technical devices to dramatic effect. The film has been rightly attacked for its racist attitudes but its historical importance remains undiminished by such controversy.

d D. W. Griffith

The Magnetic Umbrella   (PATHE; FR)   b/w   10 min

Here a scientist creates a liquid which has magnetic properties. He experiments by pouring his potion over an umbrella, which immediately attracts everything around it. The scientist's small son observes this amazing effect and decides to further the experiment. He sneaks the umbrella out of the laboratory and is delighted to discover that it attracts people as well as objects. Inhabitants of the household come rushing uncontrollably from their rooms and down the stairs, drawn by the powerful magnet. The boy runs out of the house and tries it on passers-by with great effect. He arrives at a river and tries it on some swimmers, who whizz out of the water and give chase but the boy escapes them by opening the umbrella, which causes him to sail up into the sky.

Credits not available

A Marvellous Invention   (GAUMONT; FR)   b/w   5 min

A machine which has the power to accelerate motion far beyond the norm is the theme of this short film. Professor Boffo has perfected his device for increasing speed, and is preparing to give the first demonstration to the savants of the Scientific Institution. He gives careful instructions to his manservant as to the packing of the machine, but the clumsy fellow lets it drop as he struggles through the street. Instantly extraordinary events take place as the machine accidently switches itself on. It is as if a violent hurricane blows the whole town into a whirlwind of activity. Pedestrians, vehicles, dogs, bicyclists, even messenger-boys, are affected and begin to rush wildly and uncontrollably about the streets. The servant finally struggles the invention into the hall of the assembled professors. The ancient scientists are so affected by their massed acceleration that they have to hail Boffo as a genius.

Credits not available

The Motor Car of the Future

(MESSTER; G)   b/w   5 min

The automobile of tomorrow, as predicted in 1911. A motorist visits his local garage and selects one of the new models for a trial trip. He sets off at terrific speed, rushing through a forest and dodging the trees in an amazing way. He comes to a railway line and the car does not have to wait for a train to pass: it leaps right over it. The car speeds straight up a mountain and down the other side. Coming to the edge of the sea, it does not stop, but drives straight through it like a submarine. On land again, the car is quickly fitted with wings and flies into the air. The driver performs wonderful evolutions in the sky before flying back to the garage again. 'Startling trick effects', commented a contemporary critic.

Credits not available

The Philadelphia studio of Sigmund 'Pop' Lubin circa 1910 where The Rubber Man *(1909) was made.*

One Hundred Years After (PATHE; FR) b/w 13 min

This prediction of life in New York City a century ahead reflects the times in which it was made. The main preoccupation of men in the year 1911 was women's suffrage, and the main satire of this film is to suggest the awful fate in store if women are allowed the vote. The hero, Tom Editt (a pun on Thomas Edison, the great American inventor), has created a means of suspending life. Experimenting on himself, he leaves instructions that he is to be placed in the vaults of the Harvard safe deposit for 100 years. On 10 July 2011 the box containing his body is to be sent to the Mayor of New York with instructions on opening and revival. He is much surprised when he is revived by the Mayoress of New York. The world is now run by tall, lithe maidens wearing silk top-hats and knickerbockers. Men have been reduced to the second sex: they are undersized creatures wearing feathers in their hats, and skirts. The Mayoress herself is a charming lady, much impressed by Tom as a fine specimen of an inferior sex. She introduces Tom to her father, who reveals himself as a retrogressive male, secretly championing 'Votes For Men'. He invites Tom along to a meeting of male suffragists, where Tom speaks to the assembly, inspiring them with his suggestion that they should make a mass call on the Mayoress. She is not impressed, and quickly has her staff despatch the protesters through a radio-pneumatic tube. Then she makes love to Tom rather forcibly. He prefers the old-fashioned way. His courtly manners so impress the Mayoress that she resigns her office and decrees that men shall have the vote.

Credits not available

The Pirates of 1920 *aka* The Pirates of 19—

(CRICKS AND MARTIN; GB) b/w 15 min

A dramatic prediction of futuristic aeronautical piracy, advertised as 'The most startling film ever staged and a wonderful forecast of the wars in the future'. Lieutenant Jack Manley bids farewell to his sweetheart and sets sail aboard the first-class liner, *Minerva*, but the liner is marked down for capture by a gang of modern pirates who have their own high-powered airship. A shot from the airship as it hovers over the *Minerva* brings the liner to a standstill. The pirates lower rope-ladders and swarm down to the deck of the liner. In the struggle, the captain is killed and an officer is forced at revolver point to show the pirates where the bullion is kept. The boxes of gold are hoisted up into the airship but as the pirates prepare to depart, Jack and his men rush the ladders. Only Jack is able to hang on as the airship swings into space. The pirates drop a bomb onto the *Minerva*, and the explosion

sinks it with all hands. Jack climbs up into the airship's cabin, but is quickly overpowered and searched and a picture of his sweetheart is discovered. The pirate captain orders Jack to be slung over the side on a rope but Jack cuts himself free and falls into the sea. The pirate chief, attracted by Jack's sweetheart, diverts the airship to her home and abducts her. Meanwhile, Jack is rescued by passing fishermen, and goes for the police. His girl, repulsed by the pirate's evil intentions, manages to drop a note which is found by a policeman. She grabs a bomb from the airship's armoury and forces the pirates to land. She tries to escape on foot, and throws the bomb at the pursuers. It explodes, killing many of the pirates, but not the chief. He catches the girl, slings her over his shoulder, and is running for his airship when Jack and the police arrive. A quick skirmish, and the air pirates are killed.

The film was so popular that it was reissued in 1915 under the revised title of the *The Pirates of 19—*.

d/s Dave Aylott, A. E. Coleby *p* G. H. Cricks *c* J. H. Martin

Scroggins Goes in for Chemistry and Discovers a Marvellous Powder

(CRICKS AND MARTIN; GB) b/w 8 min

'Scroggins' was the star of a series of short comedies made in Mitcham by the Cricks and Martin Company. In this episode, Scroggins is a chemist, who in the course of his research comes up with a powder which has the power of shrinking whatever it comes into contact with. His first experiment is with his laboratory skeleton, which swiftly reduces in size to 18 inches high. Scroggins determines to experiment on living matter, and sallies forth into the streets. He first encounters a wedding party coming from the church. He sprinkles his powder on the young bride, who shrinks to a mere 2 feet, although her wedding dress remains full size. Leaving a much distraught bridegroom, Scroggins next encounters a policeman struggling to arrest a roughneck. Scroggins promptly sprinkles powder on the policeman, a rather unexpected move, which reduces the portly officer to the size of a three-year-old. A man is trying to climb a lamp-post to get a light for his pipe; Scroggins sprinkles the lamp-post, and the man puffs with pleasure. A coster is struggling to push his heavy barrow. A sprinkle from Scroggins, and the man strolls away with his barrow tucked beneath his arm. Scroggins concludes his experiments in a boxing hall, where a white man is about to be defeated by a Negro boxer. A sprinkle of powder, and the shrunken Negro is quickly knocked out.

The film can be considered the comic ancestor of **The Incredible Shrinking Man** (1957).

d A. E. Coleby *p* Georges H. Cricks *c* J.H. Martin

Vers l'Immortalité *aka* The Elixir of Life

(GAUMONT; FR) b/w 6 min

Once again, the traditional fantasy theme of the fountain of youth is given Science Fiction treatment. The venerable Dr Moyen, after long labours, has discovered a serum of immortality. News gets around and people, wanting to regain their youth, storm his laboratory to purchase a portion of potion. Disenchantment soon sets in, for with death abolished the population of the world increases and discomforts increase proportionately. The people decide that there is insufficient room on Earth for everybody. After hectic discussion, it is decreed that the first people to be destroyed en masse are the world's mothers-in-law. These are duly despatched, and then the populace turns its attention to the old doctor who caused all the trouble. The old man is killed, taking his secret of immortality to the grave with him. With the elixir lost for ever, life on Earth resumes its natural course.

The threat of an over-populated planet was a new concept at the time this film was made.

Credits not available

A la Conquête du Pôle aka The Conquest of the Pole

(STAR; FR) b/w 33 min

One of the last, and one of the longest, fantasy films produced, directed, designed, written, and starring the great French pioneer film-maker, Méliès. Although brilliantly conceived, as ever, by 1912 this type of excitable, imaginative adventure was no longer attractive to the picture-going public, who preferred the more straightforward excitements of American cowboys and Indians. The tableaux construction, where set-piece follows set-piece, had been superceded by D.W. Griffith's popularization of editorial techniques, which Méliès was either too old, or too staid, to adapt for his own films.

Professor Maboul has invented an aerobus, complete with a giant chicken's head. He intends to mount an air expedition to the North Pole, and assembles a team of six intrepid professors from six different nations: England, America, Germany, Spain, China, Japan. After due preparations, and despite a demonstration by suffragettes with their placards: 'The Pole for Women!', the international group sets forth. The great bronze and aluminium aircraft sails through the sky and crashes in the icy wastes of the Arctic. Despite an encounter with the monstrous giant of the north, they reach the Pole and return home in triumph in a dirigible.

d/p/s Georges Méliès lp Georges Méliès, Fernande Albany

La Ceinture Electrique aka The Electric Belt

(COSMOPOLITAN; FR) b/w 10 min

Electric belts, among other curious contrivances, were frequently advertised in popular magazines of this period, as patent cure-alls for lethargy, lassitude and the like. Few of them, one hopes, acted upon the human body in real life in the way they did in films. Here a mistress is annoyed by the lazy ways of her maidservant. Seeing an electric belt advertised she buys one and gives it to the maid to wear. Before the maid can tie it on, she is visited by her lover, a soldier. He insists on trying it on first, forgetting he is wearing a metal sword. This immediately begins to flash sparks, and the soldier finds himself lunging uncontrollably at everything within reach. He rushes down the street, threatening the populace with his flashing sword, until he is finally captured by a troop of brave boy scouts.

Credits not available

Dr Brompton-Watts' Age-Adjuster

(EDISON) b/w 5 min

The Edison Company's promotional material for this film referred to 'these days of cure-alls, quacks and new schools of medicine', and the film was designed as a satire on the elderly's hope for the restoration of youth. An old couple read Dr Brompton-Watts' alluring sign and visit his sanatorium. The husband, eager to be young again, takes an overdose of the chemical restorative and 60 years drop away from him so fast that he becomes an infant again. The baby drinks the remains of the drug and is transformed into a monkey – evident proof that Darwin was right. The doctor reverses his process and brings the patient forward in time to youthful manhood. However his wife, witness to these transformations, decides that she prefers to remain the age she is. She persuades her husband to take further treatment until he returns to his normal age. Together, the happy if aged pair leave the experimenter's curious clinic. Concluded the promo: 'The moral portrayed convinces us that things are better as they are.'

p Thomas A. Edison lp John Sturgeon, Edward Boulden, Mrs Wallace Erskine

Dr Jekyll and Mr Hyde

(THANHOUSER) b/w 15 min

Another American interpretation of Robert Louis Stevenson's novel concerning the chemically caused separation of man's inherent twin natures – good and evil. In this version, different actors portrayed the good physician, Dr Jekyll, and his wicked half, Mr Hyde, the camera being used to dissolve one upright personality into the other crooked and ill-formed personality. Jekyll experiments upon himself and is so repelled by his hideous evil side that he resolves never to experiment again. Unfortunately, once released, the evil in him continues to break unbidden to the surface, and he sets up in scruffy lodgings as Mr Hyde. While visiting his fiancée, the vicar's daughter, Jekyll begins to change and hurries away before she can see. As Hyde, he rushes back to the girl, intent on murdering her. Her father tries to help her but is swiftly despatched. Once Hyde has reverted to Jekyll, he is filled with remorse for his crime, but quickly changes back to Hyde, so that his manservant, not knowing Hyde's voice, fetches the police instead of the vital antidote. As the officers break down the laboratory door, Hyde takes poison and dies in agony.

One contemporary reviewer noted, 'The film is made with a finesse that is typical of the New Rochelle manufacturer.'

d Lucius Henderson p Edwin Thanhouser lp James Cruze, Harry Benham, Marguerite Snow

The Electric Leg

(CLARENDON; GB) b/w 8 min

Professor Bounds, seeking to aid unfortunate cripples, invents an electric leg. Mr Hoppit, a one-legged man, reads of the new invention, and much interested, visits the professor's laboratory. The professor gives a demonstration of how the powered limb works, and Hoppit buys it immediately. He straps it on and stumps off in delight. Unfortuately, however, an accidental movement of the switch sends Hoppit flying forth on a series of unfortunate adventures, his uncontrollable leg making him leap in directions he does not want to go. Finally the electrified leg carries him into the dormitory of a

Far left: *The plans of the giant of the North Pole for* A la Conquête du Pôle, *the longest of the, by now, old-fashioned fantasies of Georges Méliès and* left: *the giant in action.*

school for young ladies. The ensuing screams attract the local constable, who quickly arrests him and hops him off to prison.

d Percy Stow *p* H. V. Lawley

Freezing Auntie (EDISON) b/w 6 min
The process of deep-freezing carcase meat for preservation during transportation is taken a step further in this film which postulates a preparation which, when injected into a live cow, instantly freezes it solid, enabling it to be defrosted alive at a later date. A henpecked husband's nephew arrives in New York from Australia, bringing with him an amount of this new discovery. Disconcerted by the way his uncle is treated, he suggests to him that they end his miseries by injecting his wife. The uncle's prospective son-in-law overhears the plot and warns the woman. She substitutes tapwater for the serum, feigning interested innocence when they bring it to her pretending it is a new cure for rheumatism. They inject her and she pretends to freeze solid, observing the two men as they proceed to enjoy themselves, smoking cigars in the house and stealing her keys to the wine cellar. Whilst they are drinking merrily she goes down to the cellar disguised as her own ghost. They fall to their knees begging forgiveness.

lp William West, Alice Washburn, Harold M. Shaw, Marion Brooks, Edward Boulden, Bliss Milford

How Patrick's Eyes Were Opened
(EDISON) b/w 10 min
The concept of the visual telephone was cleverly used in this inventive drama. The *Edison Kinetogram* promotional piece is also interesting: 'All the imaginations of the great French writer Jules Verne were not in vain, for modern inventions have made most of them a reality.' The Edison Company made convincing reality of what they called the Projecto-Optican – 'the greatest invention of the age'. A wealthy Irish building contractor reads the advertisement: 'Attach this instrument to your telephone and see the person you talk with.' He phones for a demonstration in his office, and in due course tries it out by ringing the number of an attractive young lady he has met at a dance. He is shocked to see on his screen that she has a man with her, none other than a cardsharp of his acquaintance. He promptly buys the device in order to keep an eye on the girl. His hopes for marriage are dashed for further phone calls reveal her falseness: she is after his money. Armed with this knowledge, he is able to trick the tricksters and bow gracefully out.

lp Edward O'Connor, Alice Washburn, George Robinson, Harry Beaumont

The Invisible Cyclist (PATHE; FR) b/w 5 min
Pathé Frères, having made the original **L'Homme Invisible** (1909) and seen their concept pirated by their rivals, Gaumont, as **The Invisible Thief** (1910) evidently decided they would pirate the idea back again with *The Invisible Cyclist*, which is closer to the Gaumont version than their own original. The central character is a professional thief who has the unexplained power of being able to turn himself invisible at will. Whenever he is about to be caught in the act by the gendarmes, he vanishes. He steals a bicycle, the police pursue, and he disappears, but the bicycle continues on its way. The police continue their pursuit, so the thief abandons the bike for an automobile. As he drives away he loses his powers of invisibility. He drives wildly, crashing through houses, roaring over rooftops, and finally falls into the sea. Fully visible now, he is captured and thoroughly ducked.

Credits not available

Sammy's Flying Escapades (ECLIPSE; FR) b/w 7 min
'Sammy' was the British name for a comedian who starred in a series of comedies produced by the French Eclipse Company,

which was allied to Charles Urban's Trading Company. Here Sammy harks back to Happy Hooligan and others by inventing a flying bicycle. He mounts the winged machine and sets forth on his long flight back to his old homestead in a country village. He swoops elegantly to Earth, greeted by the awestruck peasants. Anxious to show off his invention, Sammy performs several aeronautical tricks on his aerocycle. At last he decides to fly back to Paris and waving profuse farewells, mounts his contraption. Unfortunately the machine now refuses to fly into the sky, and the furious inventor becomes the local laughing stock.

Credits not available

Dr Jekyll and Mr Hyde (IMP/U) b/w 30 min
By the time this version of Robert Louis Stevenson's well-known story was released, it was hardly necessary to make the public aware of the theme. Instead, publicity emphasis was placed upon the star, Baggott, whose dual role as both kindly doctor and evil monster was much praised by reviewers. George Blaisdell in *Moving Picture World* (1 March 1913) commented 'It is seldom that one man dominates a picture. In these two roles Baggott holds the centre of attention all the way . . . the leading man of the Imp Company outdoes himself. It is a forceful characterisation and shows much care and study. It may be said, and said in cold blood, that Mr Baggott has done nothing for the screen that will rank higher as an artistic piece of work than will his exposition of Mr Hyde.' In addition to the acting, the cinematography was also praised. 'It is through the means of the dissolving process that the transformation is made peculiarly effective. You see the change from the man of good to the man of evil right before your eyes.' Another review praised the cinematographic qualities of these changeover scenes as being far superior to 'the crude facial manipulations employed on the stage'.

The plot follows the concentrated versions of the novel used in most previous adaptations, but adds some preliminary scenes of Jekyll experimenting in a free clinic he operates in the London slums. Hyde's death is different: in his fury he spills the last remaining dose of antidote, and dies during a rage in which he attempts to destroy his laboratory. The police finally break in, and his friend, Dr Lanyon, covers the corpse with his cloak. When Alice (Gail), his fiancée, enters, she pulls back the cloak to see the man who killed her father – and sees Jekyll, her dead fiancé.

d/s Herbert Brenon *p* Carl Laemmle *lp* King Baggott, Jane Gail, Matt Snyder, Horace Crampton, William Sorrell

A Message from Mars
(UNITED KINGDOM FILMS; GB) b/w 60 (54) min
Perhaps the first Science Fiction stage play in modern theatre (*A Message from Mars* was first produced towards the end of 1899), Richard Ganthony's popular production (it had been revived several times in the West End before the film was made, and would be again) was filmed in a fairly straightforward adaptation with a cast of theatrical rather than cinema players. In a crystal ball the Martian Ramiel is shown the selfish actions of Earthling Horace Parlan (Hawtrey), and as punishment the Martian is ordered to go to Earth and reform the sinner. Initially he meets with rebuffs and hostility but eventually his mission is crowned with success as Parlan is transformed into a generous, kind-hearted man. Basically a religious fairy-tale that seems to have adapted *A Christmas Carol* to a somewhat more up-to-date and even outlandish setting, the Science Fiction elements that could have been introduced via the Martian fantasy are almost totally lacking. Even the opportunity to use some sort of 'screen' device that must surely have figured in the divine Martian technology is lacking, the picture shows events on Earth to the Martian by means of an ordinary fairground crystal ball.

The picture was remade in the US by Maxwell Karger for Metro in 1921 and some sources also mention a film entitled *A Message from Mars* as having been directed by Franklyn Barrett in New Zealand (possibly) in 1909. Metro's 1921 version had far better technical effects than this British picture but the acting was little improved.

d/s J. Wallett Waller   *p* Nicholson Ormsby-Scott
lp Charles Hawtrey, E. Holman Clark, Chrissie Bell, Frank Hector, Hubert Willis, Kate Tyndale, Evelyn Beaumont, Eileen Temple, Tonie Reith

1914

Dr Jekyll and Mr Hyde Done to a Frazzle
(CRYSTAL-SUPERBA)   b/w   10 min
This one-reel burlesque of the much-filmed Robert Louis Stevenson novel starred de Forrest in the double role of good Jekyll and evil Hyde. One of Warner Brothers' early releases, the film received little attention from contemporary reviewers, although one trade critic remarked that 'the sheer nonsense of it all is the reason of the fun'.

lp Charlie de Forrest

The Electrified Hump   (ALPHA; FR)   b/w   5 min
A hunchback visits a doctor in the hope that he may be rid of his deformity. The doctor is a 'quack' and applies electricity to the man's back. As a result, his hump is electrified. Exactly what effect this had can only be deduced from a contemporary account, which remarked that 'the humour arises from the effect of the electrified hump upon all persons and things with whom and which it is placed in contact.'

The black humour to be found in human deformities is typical of French comedies of this early period.

Credits not available

England's Menace   (LONDON; GB)   b/w   40 min
Of all those films which warned Great Britain that an invasion by a foreign power was a distinct possibility, this was the best made. It was produced by the well-financed London Film Company, directed by Shaw, who had had much experience in New York with the Edison Company, and written by Merwin, another Edison exile. The star was American, too, Flugrath – Shaw's wife. The film was made in May 1914, released in June 1914 – and World War I began in August. Although made so close to the brink of war, the enemy was not named. The film opens with the emperor of a foreign power planning the invasion of England. His chief spy, Clive, breaks into the house of Holmes-Gore, the Prime Minister's

secretary, and copies secret papers showing the movements of Britain's fleet and army. Flugrath, the Lord's daughter, has an amateur wireless rig in her playhouse. The spy uses it to receive messages, and one day the girl finds a discarded piece of paper upon which he has decoded a message. The wireless suddenly receives a message for the spy, which the girl writes down and is able to decode, thanks to the previous message she has found. It reads, 'The fleet is on its way toward the English coast'. The spy tries to stop her, but she manages to get to her father's motorcycle and ride madly to the Prime Minister's residence in Downing Street. Immediately the army is mobilized, and the fleet gets up steam. The Prime Minister uses the enemy's broken code to order their invasion fleet to turn back. The invasion of England is over before it could begin, and the people of England continue to go about their business never knowing of the great danger a young girl courageously averted.

d Harold Shaw   *s* Bannister Merwin   *lp* Edna Flugrath, Arthur Holmes-Gore, Vincent Clive, Charles Rock, Gerald Ames, Lewis Gilbert, George Bellamy

An Englishman's Home   (B. AND C.; GB)   b/w   45 min
This film, which belongs to the future-war category, depicts the invasion of England by a European power. It was adapted from a play, written in 1908 and produced in January 1909 at Wyndham's Theatre, at a time when all the popular media (novels, magazines, comics, the stage) were preoccupied with warning the country, and those who governed it, about the possibilities of such an invasion. The author, who called himself 'A. Patriot', was actually Major Guy Du Maurier. The film version went into production as the British nation prepared itself for World War I, but was not completed and shown until war had already been declared. Although war had become a reality, the dreaded invasion never did. The story concerns a typical English family, whose head strongly believes the principle that an Englishman's home is his castle. He treats with some scorn an enthusiastic volunteer who spends his spare time qualifying for a commission in the Territorial Regiment. Suddenly the German army lands in England and Mr Brown finds his 'castle' occupied by German officers who make it their headquarters. The invading army departs, but returns later and the house is besieged. Brown's son is shot before his eyes and his daughters placed in peril. He snatches up a rifle to keep the enemy at bay, but is overpowered by the enemy and shot before their firing squad. The young Territorial officer manages to warn the British army, and they come rushing to the rescue: too late to save Mr Brown. A contemporary critic found the production showed signs of hasty preparation, and condemned the acting as mediocre. What was worse, 'the Territorial forces are not shown to very great advantage'.

d Ernest G. Batley   *p* J.B. MacDowell   *lp* George Foley, Ernest G. Batley, Dorothy Batley

The Exploits of Elaine
(WHARTON PRODUCTION CO./PATHE EXCHANGE)
b/w   14 chaps
After the huge success of White's *The Perils of Pauline* (1914), Pathé had Gasnier supervise the direction of another major serial starring the athletic Serial Queen. The chapterplay's simple plot has White's Elaine Dodge attempting to find her father's killer, a villain called the Clutching Hand (Lewis, who later starred in Louis B. Mayer's version of **Dr Jekyll and Mr Hyde**, 1920). She is assisted by the most famous of the scientific detectives, Craig Kennedy (Daly) whose seemingly endless supply of gadgets rescues Elaine time and again from the predicament the Clutching Hand leaves her in. Although White's serials are often mentioned as examples of positive women's roles in cinema, it must be pointed out that, her athletic abilities notwithstanding, all she does is get herself into situations that the male detective has to save her from. In

Sheldon Lewis and Pearl White in the energetic The Exploits of Elaine.

fact, the main fantasy underpinning this and most subsequent serials is not that of the active woman but that of the ceaselessly repeated rescuing of damsels in distress.

For his part, Seitz, who acted in this picture, earned himself the title of Serial King after he completed the three Elaine serials, writing the last one as well. He often starred in his serials in addition to writing and directing them (eg **The Sky Ranger,** 1921) and became one of Hollywood's most prolific and anonymously professional directors.

This serial was followed by two sequels: **The New Exploits of Elaine** and **The Romance of Elaine** (both 1915).

d Louis Gasnier, Joseph A. Golden *p* Theodore W. Wharton, Leopold V. Wharton *s* Bertram Milhauser, Arthur B. Reeve, Charles L. Goddard *c* Joseph Dubray *lp* Pearl White, Creighton Hale, Arnold Daly, Sheldon Lewis, Floyd Buckley, William Riley Hatch, Raymond Owens, Robin Towney, Edwin Arden, G. B. Seitz

Der Golem *aka* The Golem *aka* The Monster of Fate
(DEUTSCHE BIOSCOP; G) b/w 55 min
The first of many films about the clay statue made and magically brought to life by Rabbi Loew in Prague of the 1580s to save the Jewish people. Wegener became fascinated with the legend while on location shooting *The Student of Prague* (1913), two years before G. Meyrink's famous novel about the golem was published. The story transposes the events to the 20th century as workers discover the massive figure (golem means shapeless mass) in the ruins of a synagogue and sell it to an antiquarian who animates it and uses it as a servant. In the end, the creature rebels as unrequited love causes it to go berserk until it falls to its death. Dissatisfied with the compromises imposed by the production company which forced him to update the story, Wegener remade the film in 1920 as he wanted to, with his wife Salmonova again as the female lead. The imposingly hulking makeup and costume were designed by the sculptor Belling and remained the classic image of the golem for decades. Wegener became so identified with the golem-figure that he permitted himself to parody his own role in *Der Golem und die Taenzerin* (1917), a comedy in which he plays the part of a man who dresses up as the golem in order to scare a dancer into loving him. The classic version, however, is that of 1920, clearly showing how many scenes of *Der Golem* were later to become standard situations in the Frankenstein series. In effect, this 1914 version could be seen as the continuation of the 1920 version. In turn, **Der Dorfsgolem** (1921) would then be the sequel, of sorts, to this 1914 film.

Paul Wegener as Der Golem which he remade to greater effect in 1920. The design of the monstrous figure, which greatly influenced that of the monster in Frankenstein *(1931), was by the sculptor Belling.*

Some sources cite a 'Golem' film directed by the Dane Urban Gad, the husband and 'creator' of Asta Nielsen. However, none of Gad's complete filmographies mention such a film and its existence is extremely doubtful.

d/co-s Heinrich (Henrik) Galeen *co-s* Paul Wegener *c* Guido Seeber *lp* Paul Wegener, Lyda Salmonova, Carl Ebert, Jacob Tiedtke, Rudolf Bluemner

The Great German North Sea Tunnel
(DREADNOUGHT; GB) b/w 40 min
The outbreak of what came to be called the Great War, in August 1914, brought back to public attention the much-mooted concept of a Channel Tunnel between England and France. One film-maker, a semi-professional whose work had mainly been confined to natural history subjects, wondered what would happen if the Germans had been working on an undersea tunnel of their own, with war-like rather than peaceable trade intentions. Thus Newman at his own Dreadnought Film Studios in Harlington, Hounslow, set about filming his 'war exclusive that will make history'. His double page advertisement in the trade press claimed his film would become 'the classic of the Great European War' in its 'depiction of a giant secret tunnel from Germany to England'. Unfortunately, little further information on the film has been traced.

d/p/s Frank S. Newman

If England Were Invaded *aka* The Raid of 1915
(GAUMONT; GB) b/w 45 min
This historic and mishandled epic of a future war could have been a landmark film, but due to cowardice on behalf of the distributor, failed in its timely prophecy. It began life as a warning novel entitled *The Invasion of 1910*, by the popular novelist William Le Qeuex. It was one of the first in a wave of warnings about the possibilities of England being invaded from the Continent, a national fear in the 1900s. When 1910 came and went without the forecast invasion, the title of the book was changed to *The Invasion of England*. The film suffered changes of title, too. It was originally made during the summer of 1913 under the title of *The Raid of 1915*, but the French-owned Gaumont Company, who financed the film, were nervous about the film and shelved it. However, when war broke out exactly a year later, in August 1914, the film was hurriedly completed, and re-titled *If England Were Invaded*, it was quickly trade shown and released by the end of September. The enemy was still heavily disguised under the name of the Nordeners, however, although the chief villain was given the Germanic name of Karl Kruse. The action takes place at a seaside village where the Nordeners land, aided by a number of their countrymen who have been posing as holidaymakers. Also on holiday is a Guards lieutenant, who leads a local counter-attack, aided by a brave Post Office girl. The film undoubtedly had a rousing patriotic effect on British cinema-goers, in the early days of 'war fever', but its impact would have been far greater had it been shown, as intended, a year earlier.

d Fred W. Durrant *lp* Leo Lilley, Diana Shaw, F. Dunn

In the Year 2014 (JOKER) b/w 10 min
This prediction of life exactly 100 years ahead (the film was released in January 1914) makes no pretence that travelling into the future, so that a person of the present may marvel at the advance of civilization, is possible. The entire film is set in the year 2014, and shows a time when women have not only attained 'the vote', but are generally in charge of the world of business. Mrs Jones and Daughter are stockbrokers. They advertise for a new stenographer, and hire the handsome young Charles. Mrs Jones promptly makes an improper advance on the young man, who is highly offended and rebuffs the middle-aged woman. The Daughter, who also

The diminutive (5ft 2in) Carl Laemmle at the highpoint of his career, the opening of Universal City, a 230-acre studio complex, which was attended by a crowd of 20,000 people in 1915.

works in the office, falls in love with Charles, but the young man is too shy to respond. Eventually the girl proposes, and the blushing man is led to the altar. The film is remarkably similar to the earlier **One Hundred Years After** (1911) and possibly is a remake of it.

p Carl Laemmle   *lp* Max Asher

The Magic Glass   (HEPWORTH; GB)   b/w   13 min
The application of the X-ray principle to optics, brilliantly realized many years later in Corman's **X: The Man with X-Ray Eyes** (1963) is forecast in this early British one-reeler. A professor (Desmond) is experimenting in his laboratory and, by chance, invents a substance which, when poured over his reading glass, enables him to see through solid objects. This gives him ample opportunity to observe the doings of his family without their knowledge. His activities arouse the suspicions of his young son, who treats his own reading glass with the liquid. Then he paints his mother's glass, too, and she is shocked to see her husband kissing the maid in the hall. The wife berates the professor, who in turn punishes his son.

d Hay Plumb   *p* Cecil M. Hepworth   *s* S.A. Screech
lp Eric Desmond

Percy Pimpernickel, Soubrette   (KALEM)   b/w   10 min
A prediction of life in 1950, 36 years after the film was made. As with most other prediction films of this early era, it forsees a time when the sex roles will be reversed, and is evidently intended as propaganda against female suffrage. Bess is the scion of the wealthy Rock family, the eldest daughter, but she is a wild one. She falls for the soubrette of a cabaret show, an effeminate fellow called Percy Pimpernickel. She proposes and they elope. As a result, the head of the family, Mrs Rock, ejects her daughter from the proverbial doorstep. Percy, upset, flees into hiding with his baby. The story forms a parody of the traditional melodramas of the period, and ends with the Rock family finding their long-lost son-in-law and grandchild, and taking them into their forgiving bosom.

d Albert Hale   *s* Edwin Ray Coffin   *lp* John E. Brennan

Sammy's Automaton   (ECLIPSE; FR)   b/w   6 min
Sammy, a continuing comedy character in a series of short films, turns scientist in this episode. He acquires a lay figure and endows it with a mechanism which turns it into a burlesque Frankenstein's monster. This creature gets out of control, breaking its way through brick walls. Sammy pursues it, attempting to bring it to a halt, but it marches implacably into the streets, scattering terror and destruction wherever it goes. It gives its creator a push, sending him flying through a wooden fence. Sammy eventually destroys his creation by throwing petrol over it, setting it on fire and reducing it to a pile of smouldering ashes. A contemporary critic wrote, 'The device by which the dummy is brought to life is most cleverly worked'.

Credits not available

Wake Up! *aka* **A Dream of Tomorrow**
(UNION JACK; GB)   b/w   70 min
Another of the several films of this period which were designed to warn Great Britain of the dangers of invasion by a European power. However, like others of this genre, it was produced and released too late to serve its purpose, war having been declared before the film could be completed and released. The film was the brainchild of Cowen, who wrote and directed, with support from the Boys Scouts Association and the War Office. The film was distributed by the French-owned Eclair Company. Field-Marshal Sir Robert Mars tries to arouse England to prepare for the imminence of war. He is opposed by Lord Pax, the Secretary of State for War, who argues for the reduction of armaments. Lord Pax, an ardent golfer, dreams that England is invaded by the Vaevictians as a result of his policy of compromise. War is consequently declared, and Pax's daughter, who loves a private in the army, is instrumental in regaining the stolen plans for the defence of the East coast. A contemporary critic found a scene showing the murder of three girls 'rather ludicrous'.

d/s Laurence Cowen   *lp* Bertram Burleigh

1915

Beneath the Sea   (LUBIN)   b/w   26 min
The story of an investor (Fowler) who constructs a high-speed submarine on behalf of the president (Mayo) and falls in love with the president's daughter (Whitman). The villain arranges for a mechanic (Routh) to sabotage the sub's test run but Fowler escapes and saves the boat into the bargain, which earns him the right to marry the president's daughter. A naïve adventure story which, although structured like a conventional fairytale, lacks the imagination of a Méliès to bring it alive.

p Sigmund Lubin   *s* Wilbert Melville, S. Rowland White
Jnr   *lp* Charles Fowler, Melvin Mayo, Velma Whitman,
W.E. Parsons, George Routh

The Black Box   (U)   b/w   15 chaps

A Feuillade-type serial in 15 episodes of about 25 minutes
each, starring Sanford Quest, the super science detective
(Rawlinson) who uses all kinds of gadgets, including an
elaborate electric mind-reading device, to do his detecting.
The plot involves an ape-like creature (Worthington) and a
suit which renders its wearer invisible when it is charged with
electricity, leaving only the hands visible. The serial was
extremely successful and proved a turning point in the careers
of both Rawlinson and Lloyd, who had appeared together
previously in *Won in the Clouds* (1914) and now saw their
careers getting a significant boost. Later that same year,
Universal launched another super science detective, but used
the gimmick less for suspense than for comedy, **Lady Baffles
and Detective Duck** (1915).

d/p/s Otis Turner   *lp* Herbert Rawlinson, Anna Little,
William Worthington, Mark Fenton, Laura Oakley, Frank
MacQuarrie, Frank Lloyd, Helen Wright, Beatrice Van

La Folie du Docteur Tube *aka* The Madness of Dr Tube   (LES FILMS D'ART; FR)   b/w   10 min

One of Gance's most interesting visual experiments. A
madman invents a system of crystal tubes that break up light
rays. This is the narrative excuse the director gave himself to
introduce lots of experiments with distorting lenses, mirrors
and changes in focus. A dispute with the producer kept the
film off the screens for a long time, allowing it to acquire an
undeserved underground reputation as a piece of avant garde
art.

Later efforts by Gance extended his experiments with
technology but the interest of his ventures was soon dwarfed
by the cliché-ridden sentimentality of the worlds he evoked in
his fictions. Occasionally, as in his *Napoleon* (1926, in which
Dieudonné took the title role) and **La Fin du Monde** (1930),
he even lapsed into the adoration of totalitarianism and in the
latter modestly cast himself as a misunderstood genius and
martyr to humanity. Gance's work can best be seen as the
French equivalent of such showpeople as Cecil B. DeMille or
Leni Riefenstahl.

*An example of the visual
trickery of* La Folie du
Docteur Tube, *a minor
but exhilarating essay in
the wonders of cinematic
effects from Abel Gance,
a director better known
for the grandiose*
Napoleon *(1926).*

d/s Abel Gance   *p* Louis Nalpas   *c* Léonce Henri Burel
lp Albert Dieudonné

Die Grosse Wette *aka* The Great Bet

(BAYERISCHE FILM/FETT UND WIESEL; G)   b/w   61 min

A comedy set in the year 2000 in the USA. The film offers a
satirical look at what life among the millionaires might be in
decadent 21st-century America. The plot, such as it is,
revolves around a wealthy businessman who bets his fortune
on his ability to live with a robot for three days. The story
involves a surfeit of comic domestic gadgetry in a palace filled
with all the 21st-century conveniences – an airline cab service,
an automated, push-button library, etc. Piel, who devised the
film, went on to make more Science Fiction comedies in the
early thirties (**Ein Unsichtbarer Geht Durch die Stadt**, 1933
and **Die Welt Ohne Maske**, 1934) after pursuing a successful
career in serials and adventure films, both in Germany and
France.

d/s Harry Piel   *lp* Ludwig Trautmann, Mizzi Wirth, Harry
Piel

Hoffmanns Erzaehlungen *aka* Tales of Hoffman

(RICHARD OSWALD FILM; G)   b/w

An early, pedestrian omnibus film, loosely knitting together
three stories. Closely modelled on Offenbach's opera, definitively filmed as **The Tales of Hoffman** by Michael Powell
(1951), the film combines the story of Olympia, the life-like
mechanical doll who becomes the erotic obsession of the hero,
with the stories of Schlemihl (a double story changed out of all
recognition) and Angela, the obsessive dancer who dances
herself to death (a theme also taken up by Powell in *The Red
Shoes*, 1948). The film, which is notable mainly for Manfred
Noa's sets, marked Krauss's screen début and was re-released
in 1921.

Oswald, a Viennese director who worked in many countries
and finished his career in Hollywood, was better known as a
specialist in sex education movies and costume dramas.

d/p/co-s Richard Oswald   *co-s* Fritz Friedmann-Frederich
c Ernst Krohn   *lp* Werner Krauss, Lupu Pick, Rely Ridon,
Friedrich Kuehne, Kurt Wolowsky, Erich Kaiser-Titz, Alice
Scheel-Hechy, Thea Sandten, Louis Neher, Ernst Ludwig

Lady Baffles and Detective Duck   (U)   b/w   11 chaps

Following on from their success with **The Black Box** (1915),
Universal launched another scientific detective serial starring
Asher as Duck, the inventor-detective who always manages to
outwit Lady Baffles (Peacock), the lovable lady crook. He has
a knack for coming up with outlandish contraptions which
help him get out of sticky situations and solve cases: these
include a rubberscope resembling a closed-circuit TV set-up
and a smellograph that functions like tear gas but can be sent
through walls. A witty serial relying on a seemingly endless
supply of *deus ex machinas* to allow Duck to triumph at the last
moment, the chapter headings tell a story in themselves: *The
Great Egg Robbery, The Sign of the Safety Pin, The 18 Carrot
Mystery, Baffles Aids Cupid, At the Sign of Three Socks, Saved
by a Scent, The Dread Society of the Sacred Sausage, The Ore
Mystery, When the Wets Went Dry, The Last Roll* and
Kidnapping the King's Kids.

That same year, Asher also appeared in *The Mechanical
Man* (1915), a variation on the mechanical doll story, best
filmed by Lubitsch (*Die Puppe*, 1919), in which an actor has
to take the place of an automat-figure until the automat itself
is ready or repaired. The scenarist, Badger, was promoted to
director in 1915. After working for Mack Sennett (where he
directed Gloria Swanson) he became something of a specialist
at making comedies starring women: Bebe Daniels in *Miss
Brewster's Millions* (1926), and, above all, Clara Bow whose
most successful films – *It* (1927), *The Campus Flirt* (1926) and
Hot News (1928) – he was responsible for.

d Allen Curtis   *p* Henry Gale   *s* Clarence C. Badger
lp Max Asher, Lillian Peacock, Henry Gale, William Henry,
Milburn Morante, William Franey

Life Without Soul (OCEAN) b/w 70 min

The first feature-length version of Mary Wollstonecraft Shelley's novel, *Frankenstein or The Modern Prometheus*, brought the story up-to-date (1915) and added a great deal of spectacle, which required location shooting in Florida, Georgia, Arizona, New York and the Atlantic Ocean. Frankenstein became Dr William Frawley and his monster 'the Creation'. Standing, the English-born actor who played the artifically created man, used little special makeup, but was highly acclaimed for his performance. 'His embodiment of the man without a soul adequately conveys the author's intent. He is awe-inspiring but never grotesque, and indicates the gradual unfolding of the creature's senses and understanding with convincing skill. At times he actually awakens sympathy for the monster's condition, cut off as he is from all human companionship' was the opinion of Edward Weitzel in *Moving Picture World*. Thus Standing would seem to have foretold Boris Karloff's classic interpretation of 1931. Despite much exciting advertising – 'A photoplay embracing a theme never before attempted in cinematography, and stupendous in its execution!' – the film failed to gain a decent release, and was re-edited and re-released by the Raver Film Corporation in May 1916, who added 'scientific films showing the reproduction of life in the fish world' plus a tinting and toning colour scheme throughout.

d Joseph W. Smiley *p* John L. Dudley *s* Jesse J. Goldburg
lp Percy Darrell Standing, William A. Cohill, Jack Hopkins, Lucy Cotton, Pauline Curley, David McCauley

The Mysterious Contragrav

(GOLD SEAL FILMS) b/w 26 min

An entertaining spy story with foreign agents trying to obtain the invention of Professor Coxheim (Stites): an anti-gravity device called a contragrav which can be used to make airplanes fly faster while using hardly any fuel at all. The final chase sequence as the Coxheim children (son and daughter) recover the contraption and fly away in their airplane pursued by the plane of the foreign agents is a fast and economically devised combination of stunts and thrills. The daughter escapes by strapping the contragrav to her body and jumping out of the plane, which gets shot down by the agents, killing her brother. Apparently, after this movie Stites gave up acting and became a stuntman instead, while McRae distinguished himself again directing **The Scarlet Streak** (1926).

d/s Henry McRae *lp* Frank Stites

The New Exploits of Elaine

(WHARTON PRODUCTION CO./PATHE EXCHANGE)
b/w 10 chaps

A sequel, or rather a ten episode extension, to **The Exploits of Elaine**, which had been released in December 1914. It again stars White as Elaine and Daly as the scientific detective Craig Kennedy who constantly has to rescue the energetic but luckless Elaine from the clutches of Wu Fang (Arden). He finds his search for the treasure of the Clutching Hand (the villain of *The Exploits of Elaine*) thwarted at every turn by Elaine and Craig, which leads him to attempt to dispose of them first, but to no avail as Kennedy keeps saving Elaine by resort to his array of scientific gadgets (including a computer, a sort of lie detector called a sphygmograph and various communication devices). After a number of adventures involving secret passageways, a mysterious ring, an explosive called trodite, a chair prone to spontaneous combustion and a new model torpedo, Kennedy and Fang fall into shark-infested waters. Fang's half-eaten body is washed up on shore but there is no trace of Kennedy, suggesting the next sequel may bring the solution, **The Romance of Elaine** (1915).

All three serials benefitted from a gigantic nationwide publicity campaign waged in William Randolph Hearst's newspapers and magazines. From a cinematic point of view,

the White serials were not out of the ordinary when compared to **The Black Box** or *The Diamond from the Sky* (both 1915). Compared to Léonce Perret's *L'X Noir* (1915), the White films were shoddily made and compared to **Lady Baffles and Detective Duck** (1915), they were unimaginatively scripted. Although White's role has been seen as emancipatory, the charming crook Lady Baffles, who constantly keeps her scientific detective on the defensive while White always has to be rescued by her protector, offers a far wittier and positive character for women to identify with. Although undoubtedly a fast-paced adventure story that thrives on making people and objects in the picture move, the suspicion must remain that the status of the White serials in film history has been bought by Hearst.

d Joseph A. Golden, Louis Gasnier *p* Theodore W. Wharton, Leopold V. Wharton *s* Bertram Milhauser, Arthur B. Reeve, Charles L. Goddard *c* Joseph Dubray
lp Pearl White, Creighton Hale, Arnold Daly, Edwin Arden, M.W. Rale

Pawns of Mars (BROADWAY STAR) b/w 40 min

An early, rather bellicose, version of the arms' race made during World War I, which makes it rather naïve. The story is set in Europe where two small countries, Cosmotania and Mapadonia, are engaged in an arms' race. The bad Mapadonians get hold of Dr Lefone's (Kent) new explosive and start a war but they are defeated by the invention of a death ray by the good Cosmotanian physicist John Temple (Morrison). The physicist marries the daughter (Kelly) of the doctor even though she has been accidentally blinded by her father's explosive device. Contemporary comments suggest the war scenes were spectacularly done.

d Theodore Marston *s* Donald I. Buchanan *lp* Dorothy Kelly, James Morrison, Charles Kent, George Cooper

The Return of Maurice Donnelly

(BROADWAY STAR) b/w 40 min

A propaganda film campaigning against capital punishment. A man (Delaney) has been electrocuted for a crime he didn't commit, but thanks to a special machine invented by a physician (Randolph) he is restored to life and is able to track down the real culprits. He is then happily reunited with his wife (Baird). The film had a commercial release but was also widely used by groups appealing for the abolition of the death penalty. It was made by the same company that had produced the moral tale warning against arms' races, **Pawns of Mars**

The Romance of Elaine, *the second sequel to* The Exploits of Elaine *(1914) in which Pearl White and Arnold Daly's scientific detective once more save America.*

(1915). Perhaps one irony involved in these highly moral pictures was the fact that they were released through Vitagraph, then locked in an intense competitive battle with the Edison Trust and presided over by Benjamin Hampton who was also the vice-president of the American Tobacco Company, not an organization noted for its high moral principles.

d William Humphrey *s* William Addison Lathrop
lp Leo Delaney, Leah Baird, Anders Randolph, Mary Maurice, Denton Vane, Garry McGarry, Josephine Earle

The Romance of Elaine (WHARTON PRODUCTION CO./ PATHE EXCHANGE) b/w 12 chaps
This second and final sequel to **The Exploits of Elaine** (1914) added another 12 episodes to the first extension of the adventures of Elaine Dodge (White) under the guardianship of the scientific detective Craig Kennedy (Daly), **The New Exploits of Elaine** (1915). By this time Seitz was writing and co-directing the picture without the official supervision of the Frenchman Louis Gasnier, who had learned his trade (not brilliantly) working with Max Linder in France before Pathé appointed him director-in-chief for its American subsidiary. The serial incorporated a great many plot ideas from the novels of Eugène Sue and relied on the fast-paced unfolding of a stream of incredible situations in order to deflect attention from the hasty and often very shoddy direction. Compared to the work of, say, Léonce Perret in France (*L'X Noir*, 1915) as well as in the USA (**The Empire of Diamonds**, 1920), American adventure serials such as the White movies, although far more famous, look like unimaginative potboilers which concentrate exclusively on the invention of incredible plot situations but fail to pay any attention to direction, editing or lighting. The films were nothing more than the frenetic movement of actors' bodies and objects. They were motion pictures in the most literal sense of the term: pictures of people and objects in motion.

This outing tells of a mysterious stranger, Dr X alias Marcus Del Mar (Barrymore, whose brother John played **Dr Jekyll and Mr Hyde** in 1920) who tries to obtain the torpedo designs or models left by the apparently dead Kennedy. Elaine and her faithful helper Jameson (Hale) discover that Dr X wants to mine all the East coast ports of the US. With the assistance and protection of Kennedy (revealed in the last episode), they foil the plan and save the country, although it isn't clear from what.

co-d/co-s George B. Seitz *co-d/p* Joseph A. Golden, Theodore Wharton, Leopold V. Wharton *co-s* Bertram Millhauser, Arthur B. Reeve, Charles W. Goddard *c* Joseph Dubray
lp Pearl White, Creighton Hale, Arnold Daly, Lionel Barrymore, G.B. Seitz

The War o'Dreams (SELIG) b/w 39 min
One of the many world-shaking-inventions movies of the period (**The Mysterious Contragrav, Beneath the Sea, Pawns of Mars** – all 1915). This time, Professor Ensign (Wallock) perfects a new explosive far more powerful than anything imagined so far. The US Secretary of War offers the impoverished chemist a vast amount of money for the invention, but the professor has a dream in which he sees the destruction his formula will cause, and he destroys it, deciding it is better to live in poverty than to be associated with the use of mass destruction weaponry.

The interesting part of such films is their combination of wealth, war and the launch of new products, as if the question of peaceful applications of scientific or technological progress didn't even enter into the picture. It was as if these films signalled that an aggressively expanding economy must inevitably be based on military technology and war. The Selig Company made other such 'invention movies', eg *The Five Franc Piece* (1916, directed by F.J. Grandon) about a 'wireless torpedo' contraption.

Bessie Love, star of The Flying Torpedo, *circa 1916.*

d E.A. Martin *p* William Selig *s* W.E. Wing
lp Edwin Wallock, Lillian Hayward, Bessie Eyton

The Comet's Comeback (BEAUTY) b/w 15 min
An elaborate comedy combining the fears of a comet-conscious world with Arthur Conan Doyle's novel, *The Poison Belt*, published three years earlier, in a plea against the current craze for speed. Sheehan plays a speed-loving motorist called Fuller Speed, who, ducking a speed cop, chances upon a lecture by Professor Peedeeque (a pun on PDQ, contemporary slang for Pretty Damn Quick). He claims that the world is speeding to its death, and unless it slows down, there will be no world by 1926. That night the professor, through his telescope, observes a strange comet approaching Earth. He checks his parchments and discovers an ancient Chinese astronomer, Ho Kem, predicted the return of the comet in 1,000 years, and that the gases from its trail would have the effect of slowing up the world. Studying it from his studio he realizes that indeed strange gases are emanating from it, and he brings into his sealed oxygen laboratory the bodies of his daughter and her two love-rivals, (one of whom is Sheehan), who lie gassed in the garden. They recover and observe through the sealed portholes the people of the city slowing down under the influence of the gas. A fight breaks out and the slow-motion struggle is highly humorous to observe, but the gas begins to creep into the studio, and there is only sufficient oxygen to keep two alive. They draw straws, and Sheehan loses. He is ejected through a porthole, and the last normal people wave a sad farewell as he slowly drifts into oblivion. 'One of the most original ideas that have been put in a comedy for many a day', remarked a critic.

lp John Steppling, John Sheehan, Carol Holloway, Dick Rosson

The Flying Torpedo (TRIANGLE) b/w 75 min
The concept of a wireless-controlled aerial torpedo to combat enemy aircraft was first proposed on film by the English director Walter Booth in his epic, **The Airship Destroyer** (1909). Seven years later, the American pioneer director

Griffith produced this feature-length depiction of the same concept, with all the technical advances that time had created.

Emerson, a wealthy novelist, helps finance his friend Aitken's invention of a radio-controlled flying torpedo. Unknowingly he is kept under observation by enemy agents who, as soon as he has perfected a model of his invention, gas him and steal it. The novelist, assisted by Love, his Swedish servant, applies his own storybook detection methods to tracking down the spies. She gives the alarm when he is captured by the spies, and the police save him from death at their hands. At that moment the Asians attack America, and 'an army of yellow men from the East' invade the West coast. The flying torpedo is quickly put into mass production and the invaders are driven back to their boats by a swarm of the exploding torpedoes, guided to their targets by wireless operators. The film's predictions came only too true: in World War II Germany perfected and directed flying bombs against Britain, and Japan attacked America at Pearl Harbor.

d Christy Cabanne, John O'Brien   *p* D.W. Griffith
s Robert Baker, John Emerson   *lp* John Emerson, Bessie Love, Spottiswoode Aitken, William Lawrence, Viola Barry, Fred Butler

The Hand of Peril

(PARAGON-WORLD PICTURES)   b/w   66 min
Together with D.W. Griffith, the French émigré Tourneur was the most innovative director working in Hollywood up to the early twenties. He pioneered film-making techniques which went far beyond the mechanics of story-telling, achieving a stylishness that pre-dated Caligarism (his *The Blue Bird* was made in 1918, a year before Wiene's *Caligari* film) and rivalled the best that was being done at the time in Sweden by Sjöstrom (Seastrom) and Stiller, leaving the rest of Europe far behind. For this film, he had his art director Ben Carré construct a set that allowed him to shoot in continuity what was happening in the nine rooms of a house, at one time even showing all nine rooms as so many separate spaces/frames in one image, a device later repeated by Jerry Lewis in *The Ladies Man* (1961).

The story is similar to that of many scientific detectives of the period (**Lady Baffles and Detective Duck** and **The Black Box**, both 1915). Adapted from a story by Arthur Stringer, it tells of James Kestner (Peters), a US Government secret agent, tracking down and exposing a gang of counterfeiters. Kestner appears to have an inexhaustible supply of scientific gadgets at his disposal for the task, including an X-ray device that makes walls transparent, like one-way mirrors (allowing Tourneur to construct his multi-imaged frame as if the outside wall of the house was removed).

Tourneur continued to make extraordinary fantasy films using camera, lighting and set design to create dreamily stylized pictures full of a visual wit and imagination that made his work unique in Hollywood (including *The Wishing Ring*, 1914; *Trilby*, 1915 and *Treasure Island*, 1920). Even MGM's **The Mysterious Island** (1929), although the work of three directors, bore the stamp of Tourneur's lyrically gothic style.

d/p/s Maurice Tourneur   *c* John van den Broek
lp House Peters, June Elvidge, Ralph Delmore, Doris Sawyer, Ray Pilcer, Madge Evans, George Cowl

Her Invisible Husband   (IMP/U)   b/w   14 min

This film treats the invisible-man theme as a domestic situation comedy. Moore, his wife Gail, and his mother-in-law pay a visit to see Delilah, the magic marvel, who has the power to make herself invisible at will. Much impressed, Moore returns the next day and asks for a keepsake. Delilah gives him a ring to wear, which turns Moore invisible without him realizing it. He is completely baffled, not to mention bruised, by people barging into him, stepping on his corns, and sitting down on him. His voice has become invisible too,

for he is unable to explain his predicament to his wife, who telephones the police. They have an unidentified male suicide, and the distraught wife recognizes the body as her missing husband. Moore sadly watches his own funeral pass by the window, then sees his wife responding to a sympathetic male friend. They fall in love, and the invisible husband watches them marry, then sees the happy pair retire behind locked doors. He decides to shoot himself to see if he is really dead, after all. The sound of the shot awakens him – he is sitting in his library, having experienced a vivid dream thanks to a late night whisky.

d Matt Moore   *p* Carl Laemmle   *s* Samuel Greiner
lp Matt Moore, Jane Gail, Frank Smith

Homunculus   (DEUTSCHE BIOSCOP; G)   b/w   6 chaps

Part of the artificial-creature series encompassing **Der Golem** (1914 and 1920), **Alraune** (1918, 1928, 1930) and **Metropolis** (1926), *Homunculus* was the most popular serial in Germany during World War I even influencing the dress of the fashionable set in Berlin. Foenss, a Danish star, is the 'perfect' creature manufactured in a laboratory by Kuehne. Having discovered his origins, that he has no 'soul' and is incapable of love, he revenges himself on mankind, instigating revolutions and becoming a monstrous but beautiful tyrant, relentlessly pursued by his creator-father who seeks to rectify his mistake. A bolt of lightning, life-giving for Frankenstein's creature, in the end destroys Homunculus. Slow-moving and slackly scripted, there are some expertly directed crowd scenes with geometrically arranged movements which inspired Lang, who used to be Rippert's assistant. The six chapters, listed as separate films in some sources, are: Part 1, *Homunculus* (70 minutes); Part 2, *Das Geheimnisvolle Buch* (76 minutes); Part 3, *Die Liebestragoedie des Homunculus* (65 minutes); Part 4, *Die Rache des Homunculus* (68 minutes); Part 5, *Die Vernichtung der Menschheit* (62 minutes); Part 6, *Das Ende des Homunculus* (60 minutes) – a total of 401 minutes. The serial was released in a condensed version of 275 minutes in 1920, by Decla-Bioscop, in three parts: Part 1, *Der Kuenstliche Mensch* (97 minutes); Part 2, *Die Vernichtung der Menschheit* (93 minutes) and Part 3, *Ein Titanenkampf* (85 minutes).

d Otto Rippert   *s* Robert Reinert   *c* Carl Hoffman
lp Olaf Foenss, Friedrich Kuehne, Ernst Ludwig, Albert Paul, Lore Rueckert, Max Ruhbeck, Lia Borre, Ernst Benzinger, Margarete Ferida, Ilse Lersen

Olaf Foenss as Homunculus, *the creature created by Frederich Kuehne as the perfect man who becomes a tyrant when he discovers he has no soul.*

An example of the astonishing underwater photography of the Williamson brothers for Twenty Thousand Leagues Under the Sea.

The Intrigue (PALLAS PICTURES/PAR) b/w 66 min

Another story about a young American inventor, Longstreet (Van Acker), who develops a new weapon: a sort of laser-ray gun that can electrocute people. But when the US government aren't interested, the ambitious entrepreneur tries his hand at the international arms' trade in Europe. Two warring countries try to get his weapon, one represented by the villainous Baron Rogniat (Davies), the other by the charming Countess Varnli (Ulrich), with predictable results, leading to the elevation of the amateur arms' dealer to the ranks of the nobility as he and the Countess provide the happy end.

The Irish director, Lloyd, had worked at the Lyric Stock Company in London before becoming a noted theatre director in the USA. After acting in films, including a role in the Science Fiction serial **The Black Box** (1915), he assumed the principal directorial responsibilities for the Pallas and Pallas-Morosco companies. His best work was *David Garrick* (1916), also scripted by Ivers and the first biopic, based on an original screenplay, glorifying the life and work of an actor.

d Frank Lloyd *p/s* Julia Crawford Ivers *lp* Lenore Ulrich, Cecil Van Acker, Howard Davies, Florence Vidor, Herbert Standing, Paul Weigel, Dustin Farnum, Winifred Kingston

Through Solid Walls (IMP/U) b/w 25 min

Belasco plays a young inventor and electrical genius who makes a machine that will permit the operator to see through opaque substances. He tries to interest Fenton, an eccentric financier, who tries out the device and becomes fascinated with something he sees in the house across the way. He keeps what he sees to himself, and when next morning, a ragged girl (Hunt) is found on the doorstep, he takes her in and gives her shelter. Soon she takes over the household, sacking the old butler and helping her friend, Short, take his place. Then Fenton's prize diamond is stolen and Belasco is accused. But Fenton calls the police and has Hunt and Short arrested. He had seen them conspiring in the house opposite, through the invention, and played along with their trick to steal the diamond. Having proved the device's worth, he agrees to finance its production.

d Walter Murton *p* Carl Laemmle *s* Elliott Clauson
lp Jay Belasco, Peggy Custer, Marc Fenton, Irene Hunt, Lou Short

Cecil Van Acker perfecting his laser ray in The Intrigue.

Twenty Thousand Leagues Under the Sea

(U) b/w 113 min

This epic combines the plots of Jules Verne's classic novels *Twenty Thousand Leagues Under the Sea* and *Mysterious Island*. Nemo (Hollubar) and his super submarine try to destroy all warships from whichever country. Having rammed and sunk an American ship he picks up some survivors who receive an education about life on the bottom of the ocean (which subsequently would be extended even farther in Richard Fleischer's 1954 film). Landing on a (mysterious) island, they discover a girl referred to as the child of nature (Gail) who could be Nemo's daughter. She is kidnapped by Arabs and rescued by Nemo and his *Nautilus* crew.

The main feature of the picture was the astonishing underwater photography shot in a specially built tank in a studio in Nassau. The Williamson Brothers (J. Ernest and George M.) developed a special camera for genuine underwater shooting, an experience that stood them in good stead later on when MGM made a version of **The Mysterious Island** (1929) and called on J. Ernest Williamson to take charge of the special effects.

d/s Stuart Paton *c* Eugene (Tony) Gaudio *se* J. Ernest Williamson, George M. Williamson *lp* Allen Hollubar, June Gail, Matt Moore, William Welsh, Lois Alexander, Dan Hamlon, Edna Pendleton, Curtis Benton, Howard Crampton, Wallace Clark

Verdens Undergang aka The End of the World

(NORDISK; DEN) b/w 65 min

Many fantasy film lists mention Blom's *Atlantis* (1913), which is an ordinary melodrama, but omit this film, an elaborate production foreshadowing Gance's **La Fin du Monde** (1930). Although Blom's depiction of the orgies that precede the collision of Earth with a comet do not match Gance's sense of eroticism, the Danish film is far more mature in its approach to social issues as it shows the poor, outraged at the excesses the bourgeoisie permits itself now that it no longer has to keep up the façade of human concern, taking up arms against the rich. The conflation of class war with the end of the world theme provides a good insight into the kind of fantasy the colliding comet motif actually represented at the time, and even why it was resurrected after World War II: it shows whose world was thought to be in danger of ending.

The effects are not very well done as bits of fireworks shower sparkles over a toy model of a city. And, considering Blom used to be an opera singer, his staging of a dancer's performance is remarkably inept, especially since he was Nordisk's top director and general artistic supervisor, in which capacity he worked on Holger Madsen's **Himmelskibet**

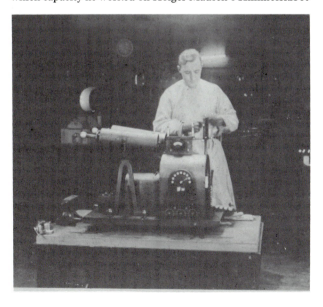

(1917), until 1918. This film was the last he personally directed for the company. The star of this fantasy also played the lead in the German serial **Homunculus** (1916) and was part of the contingent of Scandinavian film talent absorbed by the growing German film industry.

d/s August Blom   *p* Ole Olsen   *c* Axel Graatkjaer   *lp* Olaf Foenss, Ebba Thomsen, Carl Lauritzen, Johanne Fritz Peters, Frederik Jacobsen, Alf Bluetecher, Thorleif Lund

Without a Soul *aka* Lola

(WORLD/CLARA KIMBALL YOUNG CO.)   b/w   66 min

This film is adapted from a popular stage play by Owen Davis, which dealt with the revival of the dead by electrical machinery. Young, a popular star of the silent screen, played Lola 'with her usual discrimination and ease', in a screenplay written and directed by her husband, James Young. The story opens with the lovely Lola dramatically killed in a car crash. Her father, a doctor, lovingly places her corpse on a table in his laboratory and switches on his invention – an electric ray which he believes will restore life to the dead. As the current bathes her body in a pulsating glow, the muscles of her stony face relax, her eyelids temble, and she returns to life. But a vague shadow has hovered over her body: Death has come to claim her soul and bear it away. Lola is alive, but different. She casts aside her faithful fiancé in favour of a reckless lover, and destroys the lives of three other men. Small wonder her servant is heard to remark, 'Lola, how terribly you have changed!' But her soulless body is no longer healthy. She contracts disease of the heart. She falls to the laboratory floor, begging her father to restore her life for a second time. The doctor steadfastly refuses, destroying his invention for ever as his daughter finally dies. 'Unusual and very artistic' commented a contemporary critic.

The director, the star's husband, was then a major figure in the film industry, directing for a number of different companies the films which brought stardom to his talented wife. Young also made the extraordinary film, *Pups on a Rampage* (1900) which pioneered the technique of the photo-story in cinema, constructing a narrative by means of discontinuous still pictures, a procedure revived by Chris Marker for **La Jetée** (1963).

d/p/s James Young   *lp* Clara Kimball Young, Edward M. Kimball, Alec B. Francis, Irene Tams, Mary Moore, Naomi Childers

Himmelskibet *aka* The Airship *aka* The Sky Ship *aka* 400 Million Miles from the Earth

(NORDISK; DEN)   b/w   97 min

Probably the first real space adventure in film history and certainly the only one made in Denmark. The only other silent Danish Science Fiction film on record is Blom's **Verdens Undergang** (1916), since his *Atlantis* (1913) turned out to be a conventional melodrama and Gad's *Golem* non-existent. This is a pacifist tale of Professor Planetarios (Neiiendam) who takes his son (Tolnaes) to Mars where they find a vegetarian, white-robed, peace-loving people. The high priest's daughter agrees to return with them to Earth where their plea for peace is received enthusiastically by everybody except the villain on duty who is eliminated by a bolt of lightning. The film was an understandable call for peace in the third year of World War I, although it wasn't released until 1918. It was 'written' by the analphabet exhibitor and powerful boss of Nordisk, the main Danish production house, Olsen, who is often credited as director of Blom's *Atlantis*. The film is also notable for the brief appearance of Asther, the Swedish-born actor who became a star in Hollywood in the late twenties and thirties, playing the lead in a number of well-known films including Capra's *The Bitter Tea of General Yen* (1932). The next Danish Science Fiction film was **Reptilicus** (1962).

Alec Francis (left) and Edward Kimball set about reviving Clara Kimball Young from the dead, thus cheating death whose spectre vainly tries to lead her away, in Without a Soul.

d Holger Madsen   *p/co-s* Ole Olsen   *co-s* Sophus Michaelis   *c* Louis Larsen, Frederik Fuglsang   *lp* Nicolai Neiiendam, Gunnar Tolnaes, Zanny Petersen, Alf Bluetecher, Frederik Jacobsen, Svend Kornbeck, Birger von Cotta Schønberg, Harald Mortensen, Lilly Jacobsson, Nils Asther

The Inspirations of Harry Larrabee

(GENERAL FILM CO.)   b/w   53 min

A minor thriller based on a story by Howard Fielding and set in an apartment house which shelters, in separate flats, a playwright (Gray) and his lover (Landis) who are threatened by a ruthless jewel thief, the Wolf (Brownlee). When Landis gets herself killed defending her priceless possessions, Gray manages to have her recalled from the dead by means of a 'pulmoter', invented by a scientist friend of his. This makes the picture part of the batch of revival movies made between 1910 and 1920, together with **The Return of Maurice Donnelly** (1915), **Without a Soul** (1916) and **The Devil to Pay** (1920). This overly theatrical, woodenly acted and rather poorly directed effort functioned as a cheap filler for the distributor/producer which, together with the Edison Company, dominated the market at the time and could easily unload inferior movies on exhibitors dependent on the General Film Company for a regular supply of product.

d Bertrand Bracken   *lp* Clifford Gray, Margaret Landis, Winifred Greenwood, William Ehfe, Frank Brownlee

The Mystery Ship   (U)   b/w   18 chaps

The first serial starring the popular duo Wilson and Gerber. They teamed up for half a dozen pictures including **The Branded Four** and **The Screaming Shadow** (both 1920). Co-directed by John Ford's brother Francis, this serial recounts the adventures of Betty Lee and Miles Gaston (Gerber and Wilson), a relationship that starts in a hostile manner as he tries to sink her boat but ends with them as lovers. In the process, her fiancé (Worne) becomes a villain. He steals her father's map showing the location of a treasure and tries to murder her. A mysterious stranger, eventually revealed to be her father (De Bruillier), emerges to save Betty and Miles from various nasty situations – the phantom rescuer uses an armour-plated ship and other scientific marvels such as a laser-like energy ray and an electric spray gun that paralyzes people caught in its shower of sparks. The happy end restores wealth, a lover and a father to Gerber.

Moore, responsible for the special effects, was Universal's technical director. He designed and supervised the construction of the armour-clad cruiser which is so automated that one single person can handle all its functions from a gadget-ridden turret-cupola. Worne, the villain, later directed some of the Wilson and Gerber serials as well as **Nan of the North** (1921), which was produced by Wilson but didn't feature the two popular performers. Ford's career also remained entangled with that of the Wilson and Gerber team: he directed Worne in **The Craving** (1918) and also signed his name to the last of the duo's serials, **Officer 444** (1926).

d Francis Ford (O'Fearna), Harry Harvey *s* William Parker, Elaine Pearson *se* Milton Moore *lp* Ben Wilson, Neva Gerber, Duke Worne, Elsie Van Name, Kingsley Benedict, Nigel De Bruillier, Grace Cunard, Francis Ford

Az Osember *aka* The Prehistoric Man
(STAR; AUSTRIA) b/w
Technically Austrian since Hungary didn't become autonomous until 1918, this is the second Hungarian Science Fiction film of 1917 (with **A Tryton**). It tells of a scientist who develops a ray giving monkeys a human conscience. He succeeds with one ape, Dominiusz, who ends up as head of state. But when the ape turns on his benefactor, he is changed back to a simian condition and is last seen jumping from branch to branch as he disappears into the forest. Clearly a political film, it is difficult to assess, without more knowledge about the poet Somlyo and the novelist Gyori, who wrote the script, what or who is being lampooned.

d Cornelius Hinter *p* Alfred Deesy *s* Zoltan Somlyo, Ernoe Gyori *lp* Viktor Kurd, Myra Corthy, Richard Kornai, Turan Gusztav

A Tryton *aka* The Triton (STAR; AUSTRIA) b/w
The first Hungarian Science Fiction film of four, the others being **Az Osember** (1917), **Leleklato Sugar** (1918) and **Az Idoe Ablakaj** (1969). A hypersensitive sea monster (Huszar) falls in love with a pretty girl. Having tried to kidnap her, he then changes himself into a man and tries to buy her from her husband, who agrees. She proves to be unfaithful and the unfortunate sea monster returns to the deep.

Huszar was a very popular comic actor who, like many of his colleagues, designed much of his own film work. Since Hungary didn't become an autonomous republic until 1918, this film is technically Austrian.

d/p Alfred Deesy *s* Karloly 'Pufi' Huszar *lp* Karoly Huszar, Annie Goth, Viktor Kurd, Richard Kornai, Norbert Dan

1918

Alraune (NEUTRAT FILM; G) b/w 88 min
The first, apparently lost, film of Hanns Heinz Ewer's enormously popular novel about a mad scientist who artificially inseminates a prostitute with semen scooped from the ground beneath a freshly hanged man. The scientist's experiment produces the uncannily beautiful Alraune who becomes evil when she learns of her origins and turns on the doctor to wreak revenge. The theme is familiar from **Homunculus** (1916), Mary Shelley's *Frankenstein*, **Der Golem** (1914 and 1920) and the legends of alchemy. This version was subtitled *Die Henkerstochter, Genannt die Rote Hanne*, but released simply as *Alraune*. Most subsequent

Gunnar Tolnaes and an unknown actress in Himmelskibet, *the film that marked the beginning of the space opera sub-genre of Science Fiction.*

versions (1928, 1930, 1952) were based on Ewers' own adaptation of his book, the exception being the Kertesz (Curtiz) version of 1918.

d/c Eugen Illes *lp* Hilde Wolter, Gustav Adolf Semler, Friedrich Kuehne, Max Auzinger, Ernst Rennspies

Alraune (AUSTRIA, HUN) b/w 80 min
In this version, apparently no longer available, the Hungarian Kertesz (who later, as Michael Curtiz, directed some notable Errol Flynn movies) is said to have deviated from Ewers' original novel and differs from the classic film adaptations of 1928 and 1930. Instead of highlighting the artificial insemination of a prostitute with the semen of a hanged man causing Alraune to be born, Kertesz's version allegedly had the child fathered directly by a mandrake root copulating with a prostitute. Many sources list another version for 1919 entitled *Alraune und der Golem*. However, only a publicity poster announcing its production appears to be available and it is questionable whether the film was in fact ever made.

d Mihaly Kertesz (Michael Curtiz), Fritz Odon
s Richard Falk *lp* Guyla Gal, Rozsi Szollosi, Jeno Torzs, Margit Lux, Kalman Kormendy, Geza Erdelyi, Andor Kardos, Violetta Szlatenyi, Karoly Arnyai

The Craving *aka* **Delirium** (U) b/w 66 min
A minor film directed and written by John Ford's brother, Francis, then the more famous of the two. The story is similar to that of a great many Science Fiction plots of the time such as **The Intrigue** (1916), **The War o'Dreams** (1915), **Pawns of Mars** (1915). The scientist Carroll Wayles (Ford) invents a new powerful explosive which an Indian villain (Gerald) and an English officer's daughter (Gaston) try to obtain. The villain steals the invention but is killed as he tries to prepare the formula in his laboratory as Ford and Gaston get married. The twist to the story is that Ford plays the role of a scientist who becomes an alcoholic, and most of the plot centres on Gaston's efforts to help him kick the habit. Francis O'Fearna, who changed his name to Ford, directed, wrote and starred in the picture which had *Delirium* as its working title. Even though some sources credit John Ford as co-director, Universal's records attribute the picture to Francis, a fact confirmed by brother John in an interview with Peter Bogdanovich.

d/s Francis Ford *lp* Francis Ford, Mae Gaston, Peter Gerald, Duke Worne, Jean Hathaway

Leleklato Sugar *aka* **The Mind-Detecting Ray** (STAR; HUN) b/w
The last Hungarian Science Fiction film excluding shorts, until **Az Idoe Ablakaj** (1969). A mad scientist steals the mind-reading machine brought to him by a young man whom he then has locked up in an asylum. However, the machine unmasks the fraud. Deesy had also directed **A Tryton** and produced **Az Osember** (both 1917) and he went on to work as an actor and director in Vienna under the name Alfred Kempf Dezsi. Star's rival company, Corvin, founded by Alexander Korda, who produced **Things to Come** (1936) in Britain, in 1916, had made a fantasy film, *Magia* (1917), written by one of Hungary's foremost literary figures, Frigyes Karinthy, which was probably the first real Dracula movie, anticipating many aspects of *Nosferatu* (1922). But they never tried to compete in the area of Science Fiction.

d/p Alfred Deesy *s* Istvan Lazar *lp* Robert Fiath, Gusztav Turan, Annie Goth

The Master Mystery (OCTAGON FILMS) b/w 15 chaps
An unfortunate experience for the famous escapologist Houdini, who had counted on films to make him a lot of money and to immortalize his astounding escapes. The serial

A still from the first, lost, version of Hanns Heinz Ewers' novel Alraune.

achieved neither, partly because he didn't appear to understand cinema very well. He had assumed that audiences would notice that the escapes he performed in the movie had not been faked through cinematic means but were being performed 'live' on camera. However, the time when viewers naïvely thought that what they saw on the screen was 'real' had long since passed and Houdini's adventures seemed no more extraordinary than those of dozens of other serial characters. The plot concerns the wealthy inventor and boss of International Patents Inc. (possibly a reference to Thomas Edison), played by Pike, who develops all kinds of contraptions in his secret underground laboratory, located below his isolated castle. Locke (Houdini) is the agent of the department of justice charged with investigating the company. He falls in love with the tycoon's daughter (Marsh), but both are mercilessly persecuted by a creature called Robot Q (Buckley) which constantly sequesters Marsh in her father's palace, having disposed of the old man, and puts Houdini in apparently inescapable traps. In the end, it is revealed that the robot was in fact a man who managed to endow himself with supernatural strength through a mysterious device.

One of the writers, Reeve, did better work on **The Carter Case** (1919), a serial in which Marsh and Pike also performed. Houdini made two more major films, unfortunately equally unsuccessful: *The Grim Game* (1919) and **Terror Island** (1920).

d Burton King *p* Benjamin A. Rolfe *s* Arthur B. Reeve, Charles A. Logue *lp* Harry Houdini, Margaret (Marguerite) Marsh, William Pike, Ruth Stonehouse, Charles Graham, Floyd Buckley, Jack Burns, Edna Britton

Victory and Peace *aka* **The Invasion of Britain** (NATIONAL WAR AIMS COMMITTEE; GB) b/w 130 min
A future-war story made during the 1914-18 war, depicting the possible invasion of England by the German armed forces. Sponsored by the Ministry of Information, this expensive epic was so long in production that the war finished before the film did and in consequence it was never publicly shown. All that remains of it is a single reel of 978 ft, preserved in the

National Film Archive. The storyline centres around a nurse who saves an army captain from the invading Germans. Later he returns the compliment by saving her from capture when he leads the successful counter-attack. To direct the film the American Brenon, who had made the epic *Ivanhoe* (1913) in England before the war, was hired from Hollywood, and the original screenplay was written by Caine, an eminent author of the period. Many theatre stars of the period had cameo roles in the film.

d Herbert Brenon *s* Hall Caine *c* J. Roy Hunt
lp Matheson Lang, Marie Lohr, James Carew, Ellen Terry, Hayford Hobbs, Jose Collins

1919

The Carter Case (OLIVER FILMS INC.) b/w 15 chaps

By all accounts an exciting revival of the Craig Kennedy super scientific detective, the male lead in the most famous Pearl White serial **The Exploits of Elaine** (1914) and its sequels, **The New Exploits of Elaine** and **The Romance of Elaine** (both 1915). Here, Kennedy is played by Rawlinson, the star of another scientific sleuth serial, **The Black Box** (1915). The plot starts with the assassination of the owner and chief chemist of a giant chemical works (Hall) and the subsequent battles of his daughter (Marsh) and the detective against the villain, Avion (Marba), who stole and perfected the chemist's formula for a fluid that makes people invisible. Throughout, the detective and Marsh escape the traps and attacks of Avion by means of scientific gadgets such as a little cylinder hidden in Kennedy's shoe which turns out to be a powerful explosive, a special radar system, etc. The villain too uses gadgets such as a device that silences the motors of an airplane and radio-controlled missiles.

Each of the 15 chapters ran for about 25 minutes and, although launched with considerable publicity, it would appear that the production company lost faith in the serial and withdrew promotional support about halfway through, allowing the rather inventive picture to sink into oblivion. It was directed by Mackenzie, the man who under Louis Gasnier's supervision had helmed the first major success of Pearl White, *The Perils of Pauline* (1914).

Floyd Buckley as Robot Q menaces one of the cast in The Master Mystery.

d Donald Mackenzie *p* Harry Grossman *s* Arthur B. Reeve, John W. Grey *lp* Herbert Rawlinson, Margaret Marsh, Ethel Grey Terry, Coit Albertson, William Pike, Joseph Marba, Donald Hall, Kempton Greene, John Reinhardt, Gene Baker

Die Spinnen *aka* Die Abenteuer des Kay Hoog *aka* The Spiders (DECLA BIOSCOP; G) b/w 2 chaps

The best made and most inventive *Boys' Own* adventure story in cinema, unequalled until Steven Spielberg's *Raiders of the Lost Ark* (1981). Originally designed as a four-part story, only two chapters were made, nevertheless they form a coherent whole. The American adventurer Kay Hoog (de Vogt) battles it out with Lio-Sha (Orla) and her gang of Spiders led by John. The Spiders are based in Inca territory but their web spans across the world. The object of the battle, in which a series of damsels in distress are rescued by the hero, is a fabulous diamond able to bestow mastery of the world upon its possessor. Loosely inspired by the adventure stories of Karl May (and possibly a little by the Feuillade serials as well) the film is crammed full of astonishingly effective set-pieces in exotic locations, mostly recreated in a Hamburg studio. Highlights include a subterranean eruption and waterfalls, narrow escapes on a makeshift ark, a rescue by hot air balloon, mysterious criminal encounters in San Francisco's Chinatown, Inca temples and a grand climax in the Falklands involving a poisonous volcano. The omnipresent Spiders dwell in secret caves and cellars with sliding, armour-plated walls, a desk that descends into the floor, a circular mirror offering the villainess a controlling gaze at the goings-on in her conference rooms – anticipating the bank of TV monitors providing Mabuse with his 1,000 eyes (**Die Tausend Augen des Dr Mabuse**, 1960).

Part 1, *Der Goldene See* (80 minutes) is a little slow to get moving, but after the hesitant opening the pace doesn't slacken until the end of Part 2, *Das Brillianten Schiff* (97 minutes). Part 1 was later published as a book. Parts 3 and 4 (*The Secret of the Sphinx* and *For Asia's Imperial Crown*) were written but never filmed in spite of the huge success of the earlier episodes. After finishing Part 1, Lang had made a quickie, *Hara-kiri* (1919) based on *Madame Butterfly*, and the art directors Hermann Warm, Walter Reimann and Walter Roehrig asked Lang and Pommer to film the story called *Das Kabinett des Dr Caligari*. Pommer, however, insisted that Lang go and make Part 2 of *Die Spinnen* as quickly as possible. However, Lang's idea that the Caligari story should be framed by a 'normal' prologue and epilogue was retained for the final version of *Caligari* (1919), which was directed by Robert Wiene.

d/s Fritz Lang *p* Erich Pommer *c* (Part 1) Emil Schuemann, (Part 2) Karl Freund *lp* Carl de Vogt, Ressel Orla, Paul Morgan, Lil Dagover, Friedrich Kuehne, George John, Paul Biensfeldt, Rudolf Lettinger, Edgar Pauly, Meinhardt Maur

Unheimliche Geschichten *aka* Tales of the Uncanny (RICHARD OSWALD FILM; G) b/w 101 min

After adapting **Hoffmanns Erzaehlungen** (1915), Oswald made another omnibus film combining five stories framed by a narrative set in a bookshop, a technique Paul Leni later adapted to a waxworks' show for his *Das Wachsfigurenkabinett* (1924). For his uncanny tales, Oswald chose Poe's *Black Cat*, Stevenson's *The Suicide Club*, Anselma Heine's story *Die Erscheinung*, Liebmann's *Die Hand* and his own *Der Spuk*. No copy appears to have survived. Oswald remade one of these stories as a comedy, linking it with another Poe tale, in his sound film **Unheimliche Geschichten** (1932).

d/p/co-s Richard Oswald *co-s* Robert Liebmann
c Carl Hoffman *lp* Anita Berber, Reinhold Schuenzel, Conrad Veidt, Hugo Doeblin, Paul Morgan, Georg John

The 1920s

Dark Visions and Brash Adventure

The twenties saw a distinctive contrast between American and European approaches to the Science Fiction film. In Europe the imaginative possibilities of the genre were embraced wholeheartedly in a variety of ways. In Germany people like Paul Wegener (**Der Golem**, 1920), Henrik Galeen (**Alraune**, 1928) and above all Fritz Lang (most notably in **Metropolis,** 1926, and **Die Frau im Mond**, 1929) made searing use of the fantastic and predictive elements of the genre. In Russia, Jakov Protazanov and his designers in **Aelita** and Lev Kuleshov in **Luch Smerti** (both 1924) transformed the simple fast-paced adventure stories that were (and would continue to be) the mainstay of American cinema to produce stylish, innovative and witty films of social comment. And in France, films like René Clair's **Paris Qui Dort** (1923) and Jean Renoir's *jeu d'esprit* **Sur un Air de Charleston** (1927) testified to the continued strength of the experimental strand of film-making in Europe.

In America, with few exceptions such as the assured **Blake of Scotland Yard** (1927) and Jacques Tourneur's beautiful looking **The Mysterious Island** (1929), gadgetry, fast-paced action and melodrama held sway. In this, Hollywood, for possibly the only time in the history of the Science Fiction film, was suprisingly close to the mainstream Science Fiction literature of the day (as typified by writer and editor Hugo Gernsback). Serials like **The Flaming Disk** and **The Sky Ranger** (both 1920) anticipated those of the thirties, the golden age of the serial, while the string of rejuvenation films that included **Sinners in Silk** (the best of the cycle), **Black Oxen** and **Vanity's Price** (all 1924) and **One Way Street** (1925) were examples of the scientific melodrama at its most basic – films which reflected not the tensions within society, but simply the fads and fashions of their age.

In Britain a synthesis was attempted between the two traditions with little success. Thus a film like **High Treason** (1924), though it borrowed freely from *Metropolis* for its visual inspiration, lacked the power of Fritz Lang's film precisely because it ground its vision in a banal plot that was melodramatic even by the standards of Gernsback.

Significantly, such a comparison between American and European Science Fiction films is only possible before the arrival of sound. Its advent brought about the swift domination of American artistic, aesthetic and, above all, commercial practices in film-making. Henceforth, with only occasional but important exceptions, Science Fiction was to become the province of Hollywood film-makers. The irony of this was that in the thirties, Hollywood would all but abandon the genre and reduce it to little but a collection of discontinuous elements with which to enliven films of other genres.

Algol

(DEUTSCHE LICHTBILDGESELLSCHAFT; G)   b/w   93 min
A flatly directed oddity about the female spirit of the star Algol who leaves a mysterious machine bringing power and wealth to Jannings, a miner. But happiness decreases as power increases and familiar catastrophes follow one another. He finally destroys the infernal machine and dies in the process. Walter Reimann's set designs (sometimes erroneously attributed to the poet Paul Scheerbart, who died in 1915) are worth noting for their echoes of his collaboration on the designs for *Das Kabinett des Dr Caligari* (1919).

d Hans Werckmeister   *p* Richard Oswald   *s* Hans Brenert
c Axel Graatkjaer, Hermann Kricheldorff   *lp* Emil Jannings, John Gottowt, Hanna Ralph, Erna Morena, Ernst Hofman, Gertrud Welcker, Hans Adalbert von Schlettow, Kaethe Haack

The Branded Four   (SELECT PICTURES)   b/w   15 chaps
This chapterplay tells the story of the four daughters of a scientist, Dr Horatio Scraggs (Girard) who marked each one of them with a sign that would not appear to the naked eye until they came of age and were to inherit his vast fortune stored in gold in a secret hiding-place. The villain is the lawyer of the family (Dyer) while the daughters, especially Marion (Gerber), enlist the help of Alphabet Drake (Wilson) to trace the gold before Dyer can find it. An indication of the film's cheerful melodramatic excesses is the perfection by Dyer and a scientist (in episode ten) of a 'ray of destruction' that can wipe out the human race. But Drake shortcircuits the device. The happy end is provided by the death of the villain and the promise of a marriage between Drake and Marion. Wilson and Gerber starred together in a number of serials: *The Trail of the Octopus* (1919), **The Screaming Shadow** (1920), *The Mystery Box* (1925) and others. They proved a successful team at the box office, and when they split up, Wilson went on acting throughout the silent period while Gerber dropped out of the profession. Director Worne had played the villain in another Wilson and Gerber serial, **The Mystery Ship** (1917), directed by John Ford's brother Francis together with Harry Harvey. He also acted in Francis Ford's **The Craving** (1918), but from 1920 onwards was active mostly as a director: **The Screaming Shadow** (1920), **Nan of the North** (1921) and other serials. In their turn, Wilson, Gerber and Francis Ford teamed up again for their last serial, **Officer 444** (1926).

d Duke Worne   *s* Hope Loring, George W. Pyper
lp Ben Wilson, Neva Gerber, Joseph Girard, William Dyer, Ashton Dearholt, Pansy Porter, William Carroll

Previous pages: Dark visions of the future: Fritz Lang's Metropolis (1926).

An example of the marvellous sets of Walter Reimann for Algol.

John Barrymore in the most famous silent version of Dr Jekyll and Mr Hyde.

The Devil to Pay (BRUNTON FILMS) b/w 8o min

Like *The Surgeon's Experiment* (1914) and **The Return of Maurice Donnelly** (1915), this is another revival story about a man (Stewart) executed for something he didn't do and brought back to life by a doctor (Fenton). This allows the unfortunate fellow to track down the one who framed him, who turns out to be a wealthy banker. McKim was an experienced villain fresh from a successful career in Thomas H. Ince's films (*The Despoiler*, 1915, and *Honor's Altar*, 1916) and those of Ince's collaborator, Reginald Barker (*Between Men*, 1916). His best roles were in W.S. Hart vehicles such as *Blue Blazes Rawden* (1918) and *Wagon Tracks* (1919), although he will probably be best remembered for his participation in Douglas Fairbanks and Fred Niblo's *The Mark of Zorro* (1920).

It is tempting to speculate that the theme of 'revival' may have had something to do with the experience of war, as well as with the debates about capital punishment. In the twenties, the theme of 'rejuvenation' became more dominant, generating a series of pictures about people who resist growing old (**Black Oxen**, 1924; **Midstream**, 1929; **One Way Street**, 1925; **Vanity's Price**, 1924, and, the best of them, **Sinners in Silk**, 1924), a development that may be connected with the predominating atmosphere of the 'roaring twenties'. It is also interesting to note the difference between such 'youth' movies and the European, anxiety-ridden equivalent: the 'double' movies and their relation to the Faust myth – *Der Student von Prag* (1926) being the major example.

d Ernest C.Warde *s* Jack Cunningham, Frances Nimmo Green *lp* Roy Stewart, Robert McKim, Fritzi Brunette, George Fisher, Evelyn Selbie, Joseph J. Dowling, Richard Lapan, Mark Fenton, William Marion

Dr Jekyll and Mr Hyde

(FAMOUS PLAYERS LASKY) b/w 63 min
This, the most famous of the silent adaptations of Stevenson's novel, was the fifth version filmed in the USA. William Selig's company had started the series in 1908 translating a stage performance onto the screen; the 1912 version had starred James Cruze, later the celebrated director of *The Covered Wagon* (1923) and King Baggott, another actor who would turn director, starred in the 1913 adaptation. A comic version failed to impress in 1914. Besides this Robertson picture with Barrymore, two more Jekyll and Hyde movies were made in 1920, making a total of seven American versions in just 12 years. Although Baggott had attempted a transformation

Right: Ben Wilson as *the master criminologist Alphabet Drake in the cheerfully silly serial,* The Branded Four.

scene on the screen, Barrymore's *tour de force* of changing into Hyde on screen without makeup caused many critics to acclaim him the greatest screen actor yet. However, with hindsight, and comparing this picture to Wegener's **Der Golem** (1920) or to *Das Kabinett des Dr Caligari* and Veidt's performance (1919), not to mention Sjöstrom's films in Sweden, Barrymore's undoubtedly brilliant stagecraft, in the more intimate medium of cinema, comes across as excessive grimacing. In this respect, the American actor who appears to have understood the special aspects of cinematic acting best is Lon Chaney. Chaney's way of endowing his monstrous figures with an air of naturalness was far more effective than Barrymore's theatrical strategy of exaggerating facial and physical gesture to mime 'monstrosity'.

The script combines the novel with the structure of Richard Mansfield's stage adaptation (1897) and also borrows the character of Lord Henry from Wilde's *The Picture of Dorian Gray*, turning it into Sir George Carew (Hurst), the cynic who encourages Jekyll to persevere with his biochemical experiments trying to separate the good from the evil in people's personalities. The love interest is represented by Carew's daughter (Mansfield) who is attracted to Jekyll, while morality is incarnated by Dr Lanyon (Lane), the man who, at the end, lies to the police by claiming Hyde killed Jekyll and vanished, in order to preserve the memory of a 'good' man and, no doubt, to uphold the double standards characteristic of Victorian morality. Set roughly at the time Stevenson wrote the novel (1888), the movie also follows the tradition of Victorian melodramatic fiction which equates 'evil' with sexual desire which in turn is incarnated most unashamedly in the lower orders of society, the realm of the non-gentlemanly. The true star of the movie is the cinematographer, Struss, who ensured that every shot was at least atmospherically lit and well composed. Struss had learned his expertise working with Griffith and later photographed the brilliant images of Murnau's *Sunrise* (1927) together with Charles Rosher. Although a minor movie when seen in the context of the state of the art on an international level, the Robertson movie was still the best of the various Jekyll and Hyde adaptations in the USA, including the two other versions filmed in 1920: a short comedy which was no better than the equally dismal 1914 comedy, and Louis Mayer's contribution to the series which starred Sheldon Lewis. The classic sound versions are those of 1932 and 1941.

d John S. Robertson *p* Adolph Zukor *s* Clara S. Beranger *c* Karl Struss, Roy Overbough *lp* John Barrymore, Martha Mansfield, Brandon Hurst, Charles Lane, J. Malcolm Dunn, Cecil Clovelly, Nita Naldi, George Stevens, Louis Wolheim

Dr Jekyll and Mr Hyde

(LOUIS B. MAYER PRODUCTIONS) b/w 40 min

Together with the Robertson-Barrymore version and the short comedy starring Hank Mann, Mayer's was the third adaptation of the Stevenson novel that year. To avoid copyright problems, Mayer updated the setting, locating it in contemporary New York and changing the plot structure quite drastically. In this film, Jekyll dreams the tribulations that might ensue from his experiments and, having woken up, he abandons his attempts to develop a potion that might separate the good from the evil in an individual's personality. Apparently, the film was so quickly and cheaply made that the director withdrew his name from the credits. Lewis' acting of the Hyde character bears a marked similarity to the roles he played in a number of serials. He was the villain in *The Iron Claw* (1916) and in *The Hidden Hand* (1917), as well as incarnating the Clutching Hand in Pearl White's **The Exploits of Elaine** (1914). Mayer, who had made his first fortune distributing Griffith's *Birth of a Nation* (1915) on the East coast, went to Hollywood in 1917 and set up as a producer, with his own company, in 1920. With the foundation of MGM in 1924, he became one of the most powerful studio bosses in film history.

p Louis B. Mayer *lp* Sheldon Lewis, Alexander Shannon, Dora Mills Adams, Gladys Field, Harold Forshay, Leslie Austin

The Empire of Diamonds *aka* L'Empire du Diamant

(PATHE) b/w 80 min

An often-used plot about two scientists (Morlas and Mailly) who have invented a way of making artificial diamonds. As this would bring down the price of mined diamonds, the two are labelled crooks and pursued throughout France by the detective Matthew Versigny (Elliott), his sister (Fox) and his lover (Hunter). *Motion Picture News* commented that 'From a production point of view [this] is one of the best pictures we have ever seen.' Such a statement seems to bear out French historian Sadoul's judgement that Perret was technically in advance of Griffith. He had started making films for Gaumont in France, directed 'talking' pictures in Berlin in 1908, returned to Gaumont in 1909 where he made his most innovative films between 1912 and 1916 before working in the USA for Pathé America. Few of his films appear to have survived, but those few provide ample evidence of Perret's film-making genius, pioneering ways of editing and of using the frame which were unequalled anywhere in the world at the time (particularly in the serial *L'X Noir*, 1915, but also in the features *L'Enfant de Paris*, 1913, and *Le Roman d'un Mousse*, 1914). This American film was shot on location in France with a largely French cast. After finishing the movie, Perret remained in France but pursued his directing career in both countries. Largely because he happened to work at a time when the American industry established its dominance in the world's markets and Germany achieved prominence in Europe, Perret's cinema has remained badly under-valued. Even the generally held belief that his American work didn't match his extraordinarily advanced pictures in France is likely to be false, as both the comment cited earlier and Gloria Swanson's declaration that *Madame Sans Gêne* (1925) was her best film because of Perret's direction, seem to indicate.

d/p/s Léonce Perret *c* Rene Guissart *lp* Robert Elliott, Lucy Fox, Henry G. Sell, Leon Mathot, Jacques Volnys, L. Morlas, M. Mailly, Ruth Hunter

The Flaming Disk (GREAT WESTERN) b/w 18 chaps

This chapterplay stars Lincoln, the first screen Tarzan, a gigantic actor who was discovered and groomed by Griffith. In the publicity for this serial, Lincoln even had his name above the title, providing the main box-office attraction. The plot concerns Professor Wade (Kohlmar) who invents an

optical disk-lens that can concentrate the energy of the sun into a narrow beam able to vaporize steel. Secret agent Elmo Gray (Lincoln) is assigned to protect the professor and his invention, which could make a wonderful weapon for the government. The villain is Stanton (Watson) who, with a gang of crooks, steals the weapon and uses it to rob banks. Stanton even threatens to destroy a big city with his ray. One interesting twist to the story is that Elmo's brother, Jim (also played by Lincoln) is held under a hypnotic influence by the villain and participates in the evil-doing until he is finally shaken out of the trance in episode 17, in time to team up with his sibling, recover the weapon and kill the villain in the process. By the thirties such twists were commonplace. The classic example of this is **Dick Tracy** (1937).

Having appeared in *Tarzan of the Apes* and in *The Romance of Tarzan* (both 1918), Lincoln again teamed up with his co-star of *The Flaming Disk* (Lorraine) in *The Adventures of Tarzan* (1921).

d Robert F. Hill *s* Arthur Henry Gooden, Jerry Ash *lp* Lee Kohlmar, Elmo Lincoln, Louise Lorraine, Roy Watson, Fred Hamar, George Williams, Jenks Harris

Go and Get It

(MARSHALL NEILAN PRODUCTIONS) b/w 84 min

Taking its cue from Poe's *The Murders in the Rue Morgue*, this fast-paced action thriller tells of a mad surgeon who transplants the brain of a convict into the body of a powerful ape (Montana). The ape then proceeds to carry out the revenge murders the convict had planned. The plot also involves a corrupt newspaper publisher and a young journalist (O'Malley) who opposes, exposes and defeats the two villains and the ape. The romantic interest is provided by Ayres. Although full of the usual clichés about mad scientists and journalist heroes, the lively script and the accomplished acting, including a fine cameo performance by Beery, are skilfully orchestrated by Neilan, making this a more entertaining and exciting picture than most comparable efforts at the time. The atmospheric set designs by Maurice Tourneur's regular collaborator Ben Carré are particularly effective.

Neilan quickly became one of Hollywood's leading directors, supervising some of Mary Pickford's successes such as

Daddy Long Legs (1919) and *Dorothy Vernon of Haddon Hall* (1924). However, he just as suddenly faded into insignificance in the thirties. Montana's performance as the ape is vigorous and effective and earned him a similar role in the more prestigious fantasy picture based on Willis O'Brien's special effects, *The Lost World* (1925).

co-d/p Marshall Neilan   *co-d* Henry R. Symonds
s Marion Fairfax   *c* David Kesson   *lp* Pat O'Malley, Agnes Ayres, Wesley Barry, J. Barney Sherry, Noah Beery, Bull Montana, Walter Long

Der Golem: Wie Er in die Welt Kam *aka* **The Golem: How He Came into the World**   (PAGU; G)   b/w   84 min
The most famous, best made and truest to legend of the Golem films. After saving the Jews from Rudolf II of Habsburg's tyranny in Prague, Rabbi Loew (Steinrueck) removes the magic, life-giving scroll from the amulet on the Golem's chest (Wegener). However, the assistant Famulus (Deutsch) revives him to kidnap the beautiful Miriam (Salmonova). The creature rebels against the ignoble deeds he is made to perform, goes berserk and is eventually de-activated by a little girl who kindly offers him an apple. The Golem is moved by this act of gentleness and innocence, and as he bends over to receive the gift and to take the little girl in his arms, she snatches the star of David from his chest, making him a clay hulk again, lifeless. The film is an astounding piece of cinema, combining Wegener's best performance with Freund's virtuoso lighting camerawork, and Boese's special effects. The scenes of the invocation of the demon Astaroth, in particular, with the circles of fire and the ghostly appearance of the demon's face, the synagogue scenes and effects such as the dancing light of a seven branched candelabra stand out as moments of pure visual delight. Shot in a studio, the sets of old Prague were designed by the great architect Hanns Poelzig, using oblique lines, jagged contours and claustrophobic spaces creating an uncanny atmosphere. Many of the scenes first worked out here, including that of the encounter of the monster with the little girl, with catastrophic results for the creature, were later re-used in the Frankenstein films.

Der Golem is the first real example of a cinema in which acting, set design, photography and direction combine into an integral whole, signalling the beginning of a period no longer stagebound or relying almost exclusively on editing for its narrative and dramatic effects. The impetus for this new style was derived, ironically, from the stage experiments of Max Reinhardt (Wegener's mentor), Vsevolod Meyerhold and others, combined with the cinematic lyricism and atmospheric stylization used in the early Scandinavian cinema, which had been the world leader as far as the art of film was concerned, up to the rise of the German cinema.

Later versions have tended to imitate these notions of stylization rather than to look for their own creative syntheses of the trends of their time: Duvivier's **Le Golem** (1935) and Fric's **Cisaruv Pekar** (1951). These never matched the intensity of the Wegener-Boese-Freund-Poelzig collaboration, itself a great step forward from Wegener's own 1914 version.

co-d/s Paul Wegener   *co-d/se* Carl Boese   *c* Karl Freund
lp Paul Wegener, Albert Steinrueck, Ernst Deutsch, Lyda Salmonova, Otto Gebuehr, Hanns Sturm, Loni Nest, Greta Schroeder, Max Kronert

The Invisible Ray   (JOAN FILM SALES CO.)   b/w   15 chaps
This fast-moving chapterplay features Bracy as the minerologist who discovers a substance which emits a powerful radiation dangerous to human beings. He seals samples in a lead casket, sends one key to a friend, Professor Stone, and hangs another round his little daughter's neck. Her father having disappeared, presumed dead, she grows up in an orphanage with the name Mystery (Clifford). Later, she meets the professor and falls in love with his son (Sherrill). The two

are relentlessly pursued by a gang called the Crime Creators who are after the lethal substance hoping to fashion it into a weapon to threaten the world. The couple is protected and aided by an enigmatic figure called Deaux (who turns out to be Mystery's father, alive and well, played by Bracy) and a clairvoyant (Uzzell) who turns out to be her mother. Their friend John Haldane (Davis) is revealed to be the villain.

As an independent production, reviewers didn't pay much attention to the serial when it was released and it doesn't appear to have enjoyed the success it deserved although it was at least as good as the majority of product that emerged from the main companies. Pollard remained a minor director, achieving some box-office success with *The Leather Pushers* (1922), a boxing drama starring Reginald Denny.

d Harry Pollard   *p* Jesse J. Goldburg   *s* Guy McConnell
lp Jack Sherrill, Ruth Clifford, Sidney Bracy, Ed Davis, Corrine Uzzell, W.H. Tooker

The Screaming Shadow
(HALLMARK PICTURES)   b/w   15 chaps
In the early 1900s, a number of films had dealt with the fantasy of remaining young or of recovering youth, but in the twenties this wish-fulfilment scenario became a major theme with films such as **The Devil to Pay** (1920), **Black Oxen**, **Sinners in Silk** and **Vanity's Price** (all 1924), **One Way Street** (1925) and **Midstream** (1929). This serial combines the rejuvenation motif with *The Island of Dr Moreau* type of medical Science Fiction. John Rand (Wilson) witnesses a ritual in Africa involving monkey glands which seems to cause longevity. On his return to the US, he engages in similar experiments. However, Baron Velska of Burgonia (Girard) seems to have embarked on the same course with less moral scruples, using human guinea-pigs. Together with a wealthy journalist, Mary Landers (Gerber), Rand eventually exposes the Baron's evil procedures. Along the way, opposition has to be overcome from a rich backer of the Baron, the millionaire J.W. Russell (Crampton) and the high priestess of the virgins of eternal youth, Nadia (Terry).

Wilson and Gerber were a very successful team in a number of serials between 1917 (**The Mystery Ship**, co-directed by John Ford's brother Francis and with Worne as the villain) and 1926 (**Officer 444**, again directed by Francis Ford). Worne was closely associated with both the Wilson-Gerber team and Francis Ford as well. He had acted in Ford's **The Craving** (1918) and directed the Wilson-Gerber Science Fiction serial **The Branded Four** (1920).

d Duke Worne   *s* J. Grubb Alexander, Harvey Gates
lp Ben Wilson, Neva Gerber, Howard Crampton, William Dyer, William Carroll, Fred Gamble, Joseph Girard, Frances Terry, Pansy Porter, Claire Mille, Joseph Manning

Terror Island *aka* **Salvage**
(FAMOUS PLAYERS LASKY)   b/w   77 min
Houdini's third and last major movie was no more successful than the famous escapologist's two previous outings, **The Master Mystery** (1918) and *The Grim Game* (1919). Although directed by Cruze, a man with considerable experience of both acting and directing (who went on to make the classic western *The Covered Wagon*, 1923), the relatively expensive film barely broke even. The story involves Harry Harper (Houdini), the inventor of a special deep-sea submarine, and Beverly West (Lee) in a bid to rescue her father from natives on a South Sea island. They are impeded by Beverly's relatives (Theby, Taylor and Pallette) who are after a particularly valuable pearl in Beverly's possession. The happy ending is provided by Houdini and Lee getting married, her father having been rescued and the villains eliminated. The submarine features prominently in the narrative and bears a striking resemblance to Captain Nemo's *Nautilus* from **Twenty Thousand Leagues Under the Sea** (1916 and 1954). The action scenes are well conducted and the acting is

enhanced by the presence of the rotund Pallette as the principal villain. He started his career in 1913, and his credits include a performance under Griffith's direction in *Intolerance* (1916) and many other silent movies before his gravelly voice made him a familiar and distinctive presence in such classics as *Shanghai Express* (1932), *My Man Godfrey* (1936), *Topper* (1937), *Heaven Can Wait* (1943) and many others. Houdini's last film financed by Paramount was shot in the brand new Famous Players Lasky studio, the most modern and best-equipped film factory of all, providing room for ten directors to work on pictures simultaneously without interfering with each other.

d James Cruze *p* Adolph Zukor *s* John W. Grey, Arthur B. Reeve, Walter Woods *c* William Marshall
lp Harry Houdini, Lila Lee, Jack Brammall, Rosemary Theby, Wilton Taylor, Eugene Pallette, Edward Brady, Frank Bonner, Fred Turner

1921

The Diamond Queen (U) b/w 18 chaps

The familiar story of the artificial production of diamonds retold yet again (after *The Diamond Maker*, 1909 and 1914; *The Diamond Makers*, 1913 and the best of them all, **The Empire of Diamonds**, 1920). However, this serial adapted from Jacques Futrelle's novel *The Diamond Master*, added a new twist by setting most of the action in South Africa and centering the story on a heroine, Doris Harvey, played Pearl White style by vaudeville acrobat Sedgwick. The serial details Doris's adventures amongst cannibals (even becoming a cannibal queen herself) in an attempt to break the diamond cartel's power by flooding the market with artificial diamonds. Her motive is revenge for the death of her father, caused by his financial competitors. The artificial stones are prepared by Professor Ramsey (Smith) and the love interest is provided by a young millionaire on Safari, Mark Allen (Chesebro).

The serial was remade by Universal in 1929 as **The Diamond Master**. Futrelle, the promising young writer of detective stories who had died on the *Titanic* in 1912, provided the main plot ideas for most of these artificial diamond movies.

d Edward Kull *s* Robert F. Roden, George W. Pyer
lp Eileen Sedgwick, George Chesebro, Al Smith, Frank Clarke, Lou Short, Josephine Scott

Der Dorfsgolem *aka* Des Golems Letzte Abenteuer *aka* The Golem's Last Adventure

(SASCHA FILM; AUSTRIA) b/w

A broadly comic sequel to Wegener's first Golem film of 1914, rather than to his more successful 1920 version. In the typically Germanic manner of transposing classic stories into contemporary, inevitably comic, rustic settings, as in Lubitsch's *Romeo and Juliet in the Snow* (1920), the Golem is revived and used as cheap farm labour in a quaint village.

Director Szomogyi is not credited with ever having directed another film.

d Julius Szomogyi *p* Sascha Kolowrat-Krakowski

A Message from Mars (METRO) b/w 69 (63) min

A remake of the British film of the same title directed by J. Wallett Waller in 1913 (and, possibly, of a New Zealand adaptation of the same play by Richard Ganthony, also called *A Message from Mars* (1909) and directed by Franklyn Barrett). The story tells of a Martian (Ethier) who is sent to Earth by the God of Mars as a punishment. Before he is allowed to return he must change the egotistical Horace Parlan (Lytell) into a kind and generous man. The Martian succeeds by showing Parlan the results of his uncaring attitude, rather in the way Carol Reed's *The Third Man* (1949) had Joseph Cotten try to reform Orson Welles' Harry Lime

The model of the deep-sea submarine invented by Harry Houdini is about to be destroyed in the inept serial Terror Island.

by showing him the results of postwar black marketeering in medicines and drugs. Both appear to have taken their cue from Dickens' Scrooge character in *A Christmas Carol*. Parlan's conversion comes as he sees slum dwellings burning down and decides to make amends by offering a home to the woman he rescues from the flames. The photographic effects were extremely convincing at the time, with cunning superimpositions and a spectacular fire sequence. Lytell's acting, however, is way over the top and threatens to turn the stuffy moral tale into a farce, which is perhaps what it should have been from the start. The main change introduced by this version appears to be the use of a framing narrative in which Lytell is seen to dream the Martian sequence and the descent of the Martian to Earth. The effects of the dream experience become manifest as he wakes up and begins to lead a virtuous life.

d/p Maxwell Karger *s* Arthur Zellner, Arthur Maude
c Arthur Martinelli *lp* Bert Lytell, Raye Dean, Gordon Ash, Maud Milton, Alphonz Ethier, Leonard Mudie

Nan of the North (ARROW PICTURES) b/w 15 chaps

Like **The Invisible Ray** (1920) and other plots set in motion by the discovery of a powerful source of energy, this serial tells of a scientist who dies before he is able to tell the world about his extraordinary find: a meteor that struck the Earth contains titano, a substance containing unlimited energy. A woman, Nan (Little) travelling through the frozen north with her dogsled stumbles across the scientist's corpse and learns about the substance from his report. A copy of the report has fallen into the hands of a Yukon gang of thieves, and the heroine's adventures are triggered by the competition between her, assisted by the local constable (Clapham), and the villain (Girard) and his gang. Set in the snowy wastes around Dawson City, there are some spectacular location shots as well as an impressive blizzard sequence to liven up the action, making it as much a western as a Science Fiction movie.

The creative input for this serial was provided by the people responsible for the successful Wilson and Gerber serials (**The Branded Four** and **The Screaming Shadow**, both 1920 and directed by Worne) with Wilson producing instead of starring. Some of the actors encountered in their famous serials also appeared here: Girard again played the villain while Crampton, also a villain in previous outings, took the part of a shady store owner.

d Duke Worne *p* Ben Wilson *s* Karl R. Coolidge
lp Ann Little, Leonard Clapham, Joseph Girard, Hal Wilson, Howard Crampton, J. Morris Foster, Edith Stoyart

The Sky Ranger (PATHE EXCHANGE) b/w 15 chaps
Initially called *The Man Who Stole the Earth*, this serial pits
two inventors against each other. Santro (Semels), a Mabuse-
type mad scientist with hypnotic skills develops a noiseless
plane that can climb at a vertiginous rate and circle the Earth
in a matter of hours; Professor Elliot (Redman) discovers a
laser-type beam that can send signals to Mars and pick out
objects no matter how high they fly. Santro seeks to destroy
the ray since it constitutes the only thing on Earth that could
threaten his plane, but his daughter (Shanor) helps the other
inventor's daughter (Caprice) and her boyfriend (Seitz) to
overcome the megalomaniac plans of her father whose plane
ends up destroyed in the last instalment. The star of the show,
in all senses of the term, is Seitz, known as the Serial King
because he produced, directed and often starred in a number
of serials which were quite successful. He started as a
writer-director in 1916, collaborated on *The Perils of Pauline*
(1914) and on Pearl White's next smash hit, **The Exploits of
Elaine** (1914) under the supervision of Louis Gasnier. He
took a co-directing credit on **The Romance of Elaine** (1915).
Later on, he became one of the most prolific professional
directors in Hollywood, making nearly 40 movies between
1927 and 1933 before moving to MGM where he worked at an
even more rapid pace, taking responsibility for the popular
Andy Hardy series' most anodyne episodes. Few directors
equalled Seitz's professionalism. Many made better pictures.

d/p/co-s George B. Seitz *co-s* Frank Leon Smith
lp June Caprice, George B. Seitz, Harry Semels, Peggy
Shanon, Frank Redman, Joe Cuny, Charles Reveda,
Marguerite Courtot

1922

A Blind Bargain

(GOLDWYN PICTURES CORP.) b/w and col 60 min
Lon Chaney Snr was a veteran of nigh on 200 movies by the
time he starred in the dual role of a doctor and his misshapen
creature in this picture which remained his most famous
performance until his impersonation of *The Hunchback of
Notre Dame* (1923) earned him a worldwide following. The
story is similar to that used for the serial **The Screaming
Shadow** (1920). Dr Lamb (Chaney) is engaged in experiments

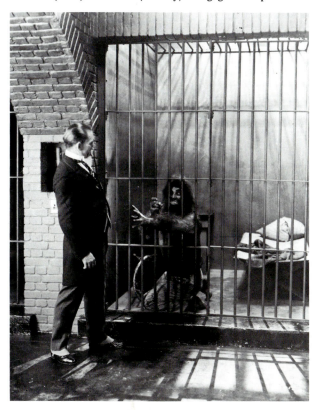

*Lon Chaney as the
doctor in* A Blind
Bargain, *one of
his most famous
performances. Director
Wallace Worsley
also directed* The
Hunchback of Notre
Dame (1923) *which
gave Chaney his best-
known role, that of
Quasimodo.*

with animal glands on human beings in the hope of
developing a rejuvenation serum. One of his less successful
experiments resulted in a hunchbacked, simian creature (also
Chaney). A down and out ex-soldier called Robert (McKee)
strikes the 'blind bargain' referred to in the title: he will allow
the doctor to experiment on him in exchange for a free
operation for his dying mother. The hunchback manages to
save Robert by releasing all the semi-human creatures locked
away in Lamb's cages. Lamb is killed in a horrible manner by
his former victims in an orgy of revenge that destroys the
entire laboratory and all its denizens. Robert escapes and is
reunited with his mother.

Chaney's performance as the hapless hunchback constituted a milestone in 'monstrous' acting, adopting the exact
opposite strategy from Barrymore's over-praised approach in
Dr Jekyll and Mr Hyde (1920): instead of grimacing and
gesticulating himself into monstrosity, as Barrymore had
done, Chaney tried to endow a monstrously contorted figure
with naturalness and humanity, which worked far better from
a cinematic point of view and was to provide the model for all
subsequent approaches to the problem of playing monsters
(eg Boris Karloff in **Frankenstein**, 1931, or Christopher Lee
in **The Curse of Frankenstein**, 1957). Director Worsley also
directed Chaney's performance in *The Hunchback of Notre
Dame*.

d Wallace Worsley *p* Samuel Goldwyn *s* J.G. Hawks
c Norbert Brodin *lp* Lon Chaney, Raymond McKee,
Jacqueline Logan, Fontaine LaRue, Virginia True
Boardman, Aggie Herring, Virginia Madison

La Cité Foudroyée

(PATHE/FILMS DE FRANCE; FR) b/w 72 min
After the play with distorting lenses in **La Folie du Docteur
Tube** (1915) and Méliès' trick films, this was France's first
real Science Fiction effort. The plot is rudimentary and
familiar. A mad scientist seeks to dominate the world by
means of the ray gun he has invented. As the destructive ray is
turned onto Paris, there are some spectacular scenes, including the collapse of the symbol of industrial France's virility,
the Eiffel Tower. Of the same order as Denmark's **Verdens
Undergang** (1916), these early Science Fiction spectacles
were soon superseded by the far more advanced products of
the USSR (**Aelita**, 1924) and Germany (**Die Spinnen**, 1919; **Dr
Mabuse, der Spieler**, 1922, and **Metropolis**, 1926). The
Swiss-born director Morat was a successful theatre actor
before being introduced to the cinema by Henri Fescourt who
cast him in a number of films, as did Feuillade. Morat went
on to become a director from 1919 until his death in 1929.

d Luitz Morat *s* Jean Louis Bouquet *c* Daniau Johnstone
lp Daniel Mendaille, Alexis Ghasne, Paul Journée,
Jeanne Maguenat, Armand Morris, George Cazalis,
Emilien Richaud

Dr Mabuse, der Spieler *aka* Dr Mabuse, the Gambler

(ULLSTEIN/UCO FILM/DECLA BIOSCOP/UFA; G) b/w 2 chaps
A far more accurate premonition of conditions in 1984 than
George Orwell's novel, Lang's film was originally received as
a realistic portrayal of the situation in a corrupt, inflation-
ridden Germany. The Spartakist rising of 1919 had been
defeated with the brutal murders of Rosa Luxemburg and
Karl Liebknecht, and political as well as entrepreneurial
gangsterism ruled virtually unchallenged. According to Lang,
the film was first shown with a prologue: a dynamic montage
of scenes of the socialist rising and the murderous right-wing
backlash, organized under state control, which eventually
triumphed. This would suggest that the world depicted in the
bulk of the film is a consequence of the Spartakists' defeat.
With the elimination of this introductory sequence from all
the surviving prints, the Mabuse film now stands as a negative
utopia: a total breakdown of law and order, ruthlessly
exploited by an evil genius combining in himself all human

knowledge, psychological and scientific, not so much for profit as for the sheer pleasure of wielding absolute power.

Loosely based on the novel by Norbert Jacques, serialized in the *Berliner Illustrierte*, and on newspaper items of the day, the figure of Mabuse has become one of the few film characters to have achieved the status of a cultural concept, as well known in his day as James Bond is today. Sequels were still being made more than 40 years later (**Scotland Yard Jaqt Dr Mabuse**, 1963; **Im Stahlnetz des Dr Mabuse**, 1961; **Die Unsichtbaren Krallen des Dr Mabuse**, 1961; Lang's own **Die Tausend Augen des Dr Mabuse**, 1960 and **Die Todesstrahlen des Dr Mabuse**, 1964).

Part 1 of *Dr Mabuse, der Spieler*, subtitled *Ein Bild der Zeit* (95 minutes) tells of how Mabuse (Klein-Rogge, also the mad scientist in Lang's **Metropolis**, 1926) amasses a fortune manipulating the stock market, ruining a weak count Told (Abel, the industrialist in *Metropolis*), mercilessly exploiting the Countess (Welcker) and his own girlfriend (Nissen), ruling by terror over his gang of forgers and murderers, able to strike anytime, anywhere at anybody, including his antagonist, the public prosecutor von Wenck (Goetzke, who played Death in Lang's *Der Muede Tod*, 1921). Having dominated a world of depravity, corruption, addiction, charlatanism and unrestrained 'free enterprise', gambling with human lives, Mabuse finishes totally mad and is carted off to an asylum at the end of Part 2 entitled *Inferno – Menschen der Zeit* (100 minutes).

As in all Lang's work, the exercise of power is signified, appropriately for a film-maker, in terms of the power to 'see' and to control through a technology as well as a mystique of vision. The *mise en scene* of looking, initiated in the monitors used in **Die Spinnen** (1919) and further elaborated in *Metropolis* and **Spione** (1928), culminates in the two Mabuse sequels Lang directed himself, **Das Testament des Dr Mabuse** (1933) and *Die Tausend Augen des Dr Mabuse* (1960), his last film. In his first Mabuse, Lang reserves most of the bravura sequences and effects around the theme of vision as Mabuse hypnotically influences or controls his victims, or conjures up visions for them. Lang was so pleased with his cinematographer, Hoffmann, that he used him again on his next project, the massive two-part epic *Die Nibelungen* (1924). Apparently, Eisenstein and Ester Shub learned their editing skills analyzing and attempting to re-edit the Mabuse film.

d Fritz Lang *s* Thea von Harbou *c* Carl Hoffman
lp Rudolf Klein-Rogge, Alfred Abel, Aud Egede Nissen, Gertrud Welcker, Bernhard Goetzke, Forster Larrinaga, Paul Richter, Georg John, Grete Berger, Hans Adalbert von Schlettow, Anita Berber, Paul Biensfeldt

The Radio King (U) b/w 10 chaps

Released barely two months after the first long-distance wireless tests in the USA, this short serial posits the possibility of instant worldwide communication via wireless/radio. As so often in these films revolving around a wonderful invention, it is the military aspect of its uses which is offered as the reason why we, the audience, should care what happens to the device and who controls it. The inventors of the super-radio, Brad and John (Stewart and Smith) present the device as a way for US military bases throughout the world to communicate with each other instantaneously, while the villain, Marnee (Bracey) wants the device to overthrow the US government. The conflict is fought out with the aid of numerous other electronic gadgets including remote-controlled doors which eventually trap the villain and his gang. Brad and a woman reporter (Lorraine) provide the happy ending as military domination of the world has been secured for the US establishment.

Stewart, the central character in **The Devil to Pay** (1920), was better known for his parts as a western hero and his healthy but somewhat dumb appearance didn't make for a convincing incarnation of a scientist and electronics' wizard.

Hill had directed Lorraine before in the far more exciting serial-thriller **The Flaming Disk** (1920), but his best work was his direction of **Blake of Scotland Yard** (1927).

d Robert F. Hill *s* Robert Dillon *lp* Roy Stewart, Louise Lorraine, Al Smith, Sidney Bracey, Clark Comstock, Ernest Butterworth Jnr

Alfred Abel as the weak count in Fritz Lang's magnificent Dr Mabuse, der Spieler.

The Young Diana (COSMOPOLITAN) b/w 90 min

Davies, the vivacious comedy actress and mistress of Randolph Hearst, the newspaper tycoon and model for *Citizen Kane* (1941), produced as well as starred in this picture, based on a Marie Corelli novel. The plot is a light-hearted version of *The Picture of Dorian Gray*, re-written for a woman. Davies plays the role of a jilted lover who is persuaded by a sinister doctor Dimitrius (Cordoba) to drink his youth elixir. Her body remains youthful as the years pass by but she dies of a heart attack because the elixir didn't prevent that vital organ from ageing. The lavish set-pieces such as an ice carnival in Montreux staged like a Busby Berkeley musical drown whatever interest the theme may have had. However, producer Davies did make every effort to get the best money could buy: the French pioneer director Capellani had worked with Max Linder and supervised the rise to stardom of Nazimova at MGM, while Vignola had directed Pauline Frederick's best melodramas and helmed the historical epic *When Knighthood Was in Flower* (1922), again starring Marion Davies.

d Albert Capellani, Robert G. Vignola *p* Marion Davies
s Luther Reed *c* Harold Wenstrom *lp* Marion Davies, Maclyn Arbuckle, Forest Stanley, Gypsy O'Brien, Pedro de Cordoba

Hoffmanns Erzaehlungen *aka* Tales of Hoffmann

(VITA/NEUFELD FILM; AUSTRIA) b/w 93 min
Like the 1911 and the 1915 versions, Neufeld's film is also based on Offenbach's opera and contains the same three stories. The main story has the narrator, Hoffmann himself, fall hopelessly in love with the mechanical doll Olympia, a theme parodied by Lubitsch in *Die Puppe* (1919) where it is a real woman who has to pass herself off as a mechanical doll instead of the other way round. In Lubitsch's film this gives rise to puns about having to oil her mechanism daily. The other two stories of the Offenbach opera have no Science

Fiction interest. The idea of introducing Hoffmann himself as the hero of the stories also stemmed from Offenbach's version and was adopted in all the films derived from that, including the most accomplished adaptation directed by Michael Powell, **The Tales of Hoffmann** (1951). Some of the actors of this 1923 version had previously been involved in the Kolm-Fleck-Veltée theatrical productions in Vienna, where Neufeld had worked with them.

d/p Max Neufeld *s* Josef Molina *lp* Dagny Servaes, Friedrich Feher, Eugen Neufeld, Max Neufeld, Karl Ehmann, Viktor Franz, Karl Forest, Paul Askonas, Lola Urban-Kneidlinger

Paris Qui Dort *aka* **Le Rayon Invisible** *aka* **The Crazy Ray** *aka* **At 3:25** (FILMS DIAMANT; FR) b/w 60 (29) min
Clair's first film is also France's best Science Fiction feature. Born René Chomette, he had assumed the name 'Clair' to star in a ballet film and in Feuillade serials (*L'Orpheline* and *Parisette*, both 1920). Although primarily interested in literature, he drifted into cinema as an actor and critic until, through his brother's connections (the experimental filmmaker Henri Chomette), Clair was given a small budget to make *Paris Qui Dort*. The film was intended as a return to the origins of cinema, exploiting the specifically filmic methods of creating fantasies, such as rhythm, movement, and the elasticity of film time, elements hotly debated at the time by French *cinéastes*: Jean Epstein, Marcel l'Herbier, Jacques Feyder and others.

Clair's film extended the experiments begun by Gance (**La Folie du Dr Tube**, 1915) and Louis Delluc's *La Femme de Nulle Part* (1922). The story tells of a mad scientist (Martinelli) who puts the whole of Paris to sleep with his invisible ray. A few people are left unaffected as they were out of reach in an airplane or on the Eiffel Tower. They wander through the city where time has stopped leaving everybody frozen into immobility. The comic aspects of the predicament – and of the positions in which people were frozen – are given free reign, as are the moral lessons to be learned: no man is an island; we all need each other to make life livable, etc. Eventually, Paris is allowed to come to life again, although with fits and starts as stop motion and slow motion are tried out in various permutations, adding more comedy. Whereas Gance's experiments had concentrated on the light aspects of the image, Clair, following Delluc, concentrated on the patterning of movement and temporal rhythms. Except for *Entr'acte* (1924), co-authored with the surrealist Picabia and shown before *Paris Qui Dort*, Clair's often visually striking films remained severely marred by a leaden and naïve moralism already in evidence in his first movie. A short version of the film was shown in the USA with the title *At 3:25*.

d/s René Clair *p* Henri Diamant Berger *c* Maurice Desfassiaux, Paul Guichard *lp* Henri Rollan, Madeleine Rodrigue, Albert Préjean, Marcel Vallée, Pré fils, Stacquet, Martinelli, Myla Seller

Radio Mania *aka* **M.A.R.S.** *aka* **Mars Calling** *aka* **The Man from Mars** (TELEVIEW CORP./HERMAN HOLLAND/W.W. HODKINSON CORP.) b/w 72 min
The first American attempt at a 3-D feature (in 1922 Bourgeois had made *Faust* in 3-D in Paris) required audiences to wear special glasses and proved a failure, prompting the producer to re-issue the film 'flat' under a number of different titles. In the fifties, in response to television, Hollywood returned to the idea of 3-D with renewed enthusiasm. The first of these films was *Bwana Devil* (1952) by Arch Oboler, a director almost as interesting for his obsessive hatred of TV as for his heavy-handed moralizing about social issues in such films as **Five** (1951).

Shot and set in the year when music was first transmitted from the USA to the UK, the film's hero (Mitchell) dreams of a two-way radio connection with Mars. In the dream sequence, the Martians are depicted with oversize heads signalling that they have 'a lot of brains' and with vaguely ancient-Egyptian looking clothes. However, when the starry-eyed inventor wakes up and finds that it was all a dream, he is so depressed that he is ready to abandon his research. The happy end is provided by his landlady's daughter (Irving) who manages to sell another of his inventions, a noiseless clock, for a princely sum of money, which spurs him on to continue work on the interplanetary radio project. The Irish-born director, whose real name was Roland de Gostrie, remained stuck at the cheaper end of B picture-making throughout his career but he managed to establish a respectable filmography that included **Frankenstein Meets the Wolf Man** (1943) and a number of Sherlock Holmes pictures starring Basil Rathbone between 1941 and 1946.

d Roy William Neill *p* Herman Holland *s* Lewis Allen Browne *c* George Folsey *lp* Grant Mitchell, Margaret Irving, Gertrude Hillman, W.H. Burton, Isabelle Vernon, J.D. Walsh, Peggy Smith, Betty Borders, Peggy Williams, Alice Effinger

The Unknown Purple
(CARLOS PRODUCTIONS) b/w and col 92 min
A well-acted thriller with a plot that would have been suitable for an interesting serial. The story concerns a scientist (Walthall) framed by his wife (Lake) and her lover (Holmes) for a crime so that she can obtain a divorce while he is in prison. On his release, he uses his invention, a device that produces a deep-purple glare while rendering its user invisible, to rob the adulterous pair and to frame them in return. The film was tinted in the appropriate colour for the scenes in which the purple light was to manifest itself, leaving only the hand of the otherwise invisible Walthall in frame. Played with considerable humour, the movie also managed to recapture some of the atmosphere of a Feuillade-type mystery, with disguises, daring robberies with mocking notes left by the perpetrator, a secret laboratory, etc. The picture

'Dreaming while the city sleeps': a scene from René Clair's delightful experimental film, Paris Qui Dort.

had been adapted from West's own play and already shows some of the characteristic blending of mystery, suspense and comedy that was the hallmark of West's later work such as *The Bat* (1926), *The Bat Whispers* (1931) and **The Monster** (1925).

d/co-s Roland West *p* A. Carlos *co-s* Paul Schofield
c Oliver T. Marsh *lp* Henry B. Walthall, Alice Lake, Stuart Holmes, Helen Ferguson, Frankie Lee, Ethel Grey Terry, James Morrison, Johnnie Arthur, Richard Wayne, Mike Donlin

1924

Aelita *aka* Aelita: The Revolt of the Robots
(MEZRAPBOM; USSR) b/w 120 (80) min

The futurist designs gracing *Aelita* decisively influenced all subsequent designers and illustrators of Science Fiction stories, especially the depiction of Mongo in **Flash Gordon** (1936). The dazzling beauty of the Queen of the Martians, Aelita (Solntseva, soon to marry Dovzhenko and become a noted director in her own right) is said to have caused hundreds of Soviet babies born that year to be named Aelita. The film is an eccentric comedy based on Alexei Tolstoy's story about an inventor (Tserételli) who shoots his wife and, together with a young soldier (Batalov) and the detective on the murder case (Illinsky), flees to Mars. He takes up with the Queen while Batalov foments a revolution with the help of a servant girl. The revolt fails but it all turns out to be a dream, and life on Earth isn't that bad anyway.

Accompanied by lots of pre-publicity, *Aelita* was intended to compete with the popular Western product at a time when the USSR was emerging out of a civil war, a defensive war and a famine. Soviet critics received it coolly but the audiences loved it. As in so many of the Soviet silent films, the comedy is fast and well-timed, poking good-humoured fun at the more uncomfortable sides of life in their own country while enthusiastically parodying the West's 'decadent' aspects. The acting is lively and drawn from a wide variety of competing acting styles in this most innovative period of world film history. The futurist and cubist designs (sets by Isaak Rabinovich, costumes by Aleksandra Ekster) were supplied by alumni of the famous Kamerny Theatre. According to Science Fiction writer Frederik Pohl, it was 'one of the best science fiction films from the days of the silents'. Only Kuleshov's **Luch Smerti** (1925) is as lively a film. The next Soviet space opera was made over a decade later, the stodgy **Komitchesky Reis** (1935).

d Jakov Protazanov *s* Fedor Ozep, Aleksey Fajko
c Yuri Zheliabovsky, Emil Schoenemann *lp* Yulia Solntseva, Nikolai Batalov, Igor Illinski, Nikolai Tserételli, Vera Orlova, Pavel Pol, Konstantin Eggert, Yuri Zavadski, Valentina Kuindzi, N. Tretyakova

Black Oxen
(FRANK LLOYD PRODUCTIONS) b/w 106 min

The fantasy of remaining young forever had been presented in films often before, but in the twenties it appears to have grown into a major neurosis. It underpinned the 'monkey gland' stories in the press at the time and in films such as **A Blind Bargain** (1922) and **The Screaming Shadow** (1920), as well as programming glossy melodramas such as **The Young Diana** (1922), **Vanity's Price** (1924), **One Way Street** (1925), **Midstream** (1929) and others. While most 'youth' films stressed the desire to arrest the ageing process, *Black Oxen* suggests a fantasy about turning back the clock by 30 years. Adapted from a Gertrude Atherton romance, the story rejuvenates the 58-year-old Madam Zattiany (Griffith) with the help of Dr Steinbach's (Nelson) X-ray operation, turning her into the 28-year-old Mary Ogden she was before marrying an Austrian Count who got killed in the war. However, some old acquaintances recognize her and she is forced to confess her secret, which turns her into an object of ridicule as well as envy. She leaves her lover, a drama critic (Tearle) to two

The influential futurist designs of Aelita, *one of the best Science Fiction films of the silent period.*

genuinely younger rivals (Bow and Lester), returning to Austria where she takes up with a prince (Hale) and devotes herself to the thankless task of restoring Austria to the great power status it used to have.

The fantasy was capably directed by the Irish émigré Lloyd, who had started off as a theatre director in London before becoming an actor (**The Black Box**, 1915) and eventually a minor but respected Hollywood director with pictures such as **The Intrigue** (1916) and *David Garrick* (1916) to his credit. The film is perhaps most notable for Bow's lively performance in a minor part. She was soon promoted to stardom as the young woman who had *It* (1927).

d/p Frank Lloyd *s* Mary O'Hara *c* Norbert F. Brodine
lp Corinne Griffith, Conway Tearle, Alan Hale, Otto Nelson, Otto Lederer, Clara Bow, Kate Lester, Thomas Ricketts, Thomas Guise, Harry Mestayer

The Last Man on Earth (FOX) b/w 88 min

An oddly misogynist comedy that proceeds from the premise than an epidemic wiped out all the males over 14 years of age except one, Elmer (Foxe), who is immune and lives the life of a recluse in a forest after his childhood sweetheart turned down his marriage proposal. The world, here equated with the USA, is run by women who behave either like men or in the way men have always pictured women. Thus, even though there are no men around, women are shown to be obsessed with trivia or with fashion, wearing transparent clothes and other 'sexy' garb. In either case, the women are presented as somewhat ridiculous. The female president allows the White House lawn to become overgrown with weeds and gives hordes of cats the run of the place. Gertie (Cunard) is a criminal who seeks refuge in the forest where Elmer dwells and even though he looks like the creature from boggy creek, she cannot help being attracted by his 'maleness'. She brings him to Washington where two female senators engage in an official boxing contest with Elmer as the winner's prize. Frightened, Elmer runs to his childhood sweetheart (Perdue) who is in the audience. The happy end is provided by her admission that she made a mistake and is now glad to accept him as her husband. Immediately, they produce twins who inherit Elmer's immunity from the male-killing disease and the human race is 'saved' as things return to the *status quo ante*. By 1924, Blystone was an experienced director who had made well over 40 films, mostly comedies. He had even collaborated with Keaton on *Our Hospitality* (1923) but that seems to have left no trace on his own solo work. The film was remade even more bizarrely as **It's Great to Be Alive** (1933).

d/p John G. Blystone *s* Donald W. Lee *c* Allen Davey
lp Earle Foxe, Grace Cunard, Derelys Perdue, Gladys Tennyson, Maryon Aye, Clarissa Selwynne, Pauline French, Marie Astaire, Fay Holderness, Jean Dumas

Laughing at Danger
(CARLOS PRODUCTIONS) b/w 70 min
A routine action story played with zest by Talmadge as the hero who prevents the destruction of the US navy by means of a deadly ray that has fallen into the hands of a gang of crooks led by Darwin Kershaw (Wheatcroft). He also rescues the professor who invented the ray (Girard) and his daughter (Novak) from the same gang of villains. A comparison between these US serials and the work of Kuleshov (**Luch Smerti**, 1925), Fritz Lang (**Die Spinnen**, 1919), Feuillade or Léonce Perret (*L'X Noir*, 1915) demonstrates the unimaginative conventionality of the American way of directing such pictures. It is as if all the creative energy went into the concoction of a script that would keep the actors as busy as possible, totally neglecting the ways in which lighting, camera movement, *mise en scene*, the use of the frame and editing could combine to produce far more powerful effects than simply filming people exuberantly dashing about, although that could at times also produce its own sense of abstract poetry (as in the White serials if looked at without attention to the story or characterization).

Horne later made his name as the director of Laurel and Hardy pictures, a job where his apparently non-existent sense of cinema was an advantage in that it put all the control of movement and timing into the hands of the two brilliant performers. Talmadge's film was independently produced and distributed by FBO, a company bought by Joseph P. Kennedy in 1922. Kennedy also presided over the Hayden-Stone Bank which was instrumental in buying Pathé's American operation and constituted a significant financial force in Hollywood.

d James W. Horne *p* A. Carlos *s* Frank Howard Clark
c William Marshall *lp* Richard Talmadge, Joe Girard, Joe Harrington, Eva Novak, Stanhope Wheatcroft

Sinners in Silk (MGM) b/w 69 min
One of three rejuvenation pictures released in 1924, together with **Black Oxen** and **Vanity's Price**. Arthur Merrill (Menjou) undergoes an operation in Europe, performed by Dr Eustace (Hersholt), which leaves him looking 20 years younger. He is also extremely wealthy, a combination that proves irresistible to most women, but Menjou comes to realize the juvenile aspects of his desire for everlasting youth when confronted with the 25-year-old son (Nagel) of a former, nearly forgotten, marriage. At this point the fantasy presented by the movie becomes a little more interesting: Menjou has to refuse the vivacious Boardman who throws herself at him even though she is also in love with Nagel. The incestuous overtones of the father's desire for the son's lover initiate quite a complex series of contradictory desires. By making Menjou the object of erotic desire and then mixing in incest motifs, the rejuvenation fantasy lands in more trouble than it can decently handle. The way out is provided by Menjou's elimination from the story: he leaves for Europe without the film containing any reference to what may happen to his ageing process (something all the other rejuvenation movies dwell on). Menjou's beautifully controlled comic acting manages to convey the presence of unspeakable desires

without ever letting them break through the thin veneer of social polish, except in the form of a (sometimes) corrosively cynical humour. The rest of the cast is also excellent, which, together with an excess of fantasy elements straining against the straightjacket of the plot structure, makes this by far the most interesting rejuvenation picture of the period.

d Hobart Henley *p* Louis B. Mayer *s* Carey Wilson
c John Arnold *lp* Adolphe Menjou, Eleanor Boardman, Conrad Nagel, Jean Hersholt, Edward Connelly, Jerome Patrick, John Patrick, Hedda Hopper, Virginia Lee Corbin, Dorothy Dwan

The Story Without a Name *aka* Without Warning
(FAMOUS PLAYERS LASKY) b/w 78 min
As in a great many movies at the time, the excuse for setting the plot in motion was provided by what Hitchcock would later call a McGuffin, which could be anything from a microfilm to photograph or any other object to which a 'special value' can be attributed. In these Science Fiction serials and features the McGuffin was usually a new explosive or, as here, a special ray. Moreno plays the inventor of an ultraviolet ray that can kill via radio as it is transmitted from one location to another. He gets kidnapped by the villains (Power and Wolheim) but manages to summon the US navy to his aid with an amateur radio he's rigged up. Ayres is the daughter of the top admiral but she too is kidnapped and handed over to a smuggler who intends to sell her as a white slave. The navy saves everybody and allows the two main actors to get married.

Adapted from a story by Arthur Stringer, the author who provided the story for **The Hand of Peril** (1916), brilliantly filmed by Maurice Tourneur, this picture appeared to lack a good title and the producers launched a competition to find one, achieving considerable publicity with their gimmick. The entry selected, but not used, was *Without Warning*. In spite of the many action scenes, there were also heavily melodramatic sequences which made the trade paper *Variety* comment that it might not please city audiences but would have the people 'in the wheat and corn belts . . . sit in open mouthed amazement.' Rosson, the cinematographer, soon became one of the world's leading cameramen, creating extraordinary images for von Sternberg's *The Docks of New York* (1928) and *The Case of Lena Smith* (1929). Willat's main achievement came a few years later with the fantasy film *The Isle of Lost Ships* (1929), although it didn't match Tourneur's marvellous version of that story filmed in 1923.

d Irvin Willat *p* Adolph Zukor, Jessy L. Lasky
s Victor Irvin *c* Hal Rosson *lp* Agnes Ayres, Antonio Moreno, Tyrone Power Snr, Louis Wolheim, Dagmar Godowaky, Jack Bohn, Maurice Costello, Frank Currier, Ivan Linow

Terreur *aka* The Perils of Paris
(EPINAY; FR) b/w 70 min
Between 1923 and 1925 Pearl White spent most of her time in Europe, acting in French films and appearing in shows in London and Paris. This picture was shot in Paris and offers a distilled version of typical White serial situations – which in their turn had been supervised by the French director Louis Gasnier and used Eugène Sue's novels as source material. The plot concerns a death ray invented by White's father (Baudin) which is stolen by crooks who kill the professor in the process. White sets out to recover the contraption and to avenge her father's death. The movie appears to consist of a formal play with the elements of the adventure serial, a format invented by French directors like Feuillade and Perret. In fact, it had been Feuillade's single-handed efforts, churning out serial after serial, which had prevented the US serials from totally destroying the French film industry at the time and the Pathé Company, responsible for White's pictures, had also allowed its directors to borrow liberally from Feuillade serials to

compete with them. The scenarist, Bourgeois, was also an experienced craftsman who had directed a *Faust* in 3-D (1922, a year earlier than the first US 3-D effort, **Radio Mania**, 1923). In some French sources, Bourgeois is credited as director of this feature while American sources credit another Frenchman, José, who had a minor acting role in *The Perils of Pauline* (1914), co-directed *The Iron Claw* and took sole credit for directing *Pearl of the Army*, both 1916 White vehicles. It is possible that different versions were prepared for the US and French markets, since French sources also suggest this was originally a six-part serial.

d/co-s Edward José *co-s* Gerard Bourgeois *lp* Pearl White, Robert Lee, Henry Baudin, Arlette Marchal, Martin Mitchell, Paul Vermoyal

Vanity's Price

(GOTHIC PICTURES) b/w 81 min
The third rejuvenation movie made in 1924, together with **Black Oxen** and **Sinners in Silk**. It tells of an ageing actress, Vanna (Nilsson) who bought an operation taking 20 years off her actual age. But the additional price she has to pay is a degree of amnesia, which proves embarrassing as she fails to recognize the man who proposed to her just before she had the operation (Standing) as well as her lecherous ex-husband (Holmes). Jealousies between the two rivals for a 'renovated' Nilsson culminate in a traumatic sequence of events: Holmes barges in on her and threatens her; her son, coming to her defence, is beaten up by his father whereupon her lover nearly kills his rival, all in one scene. This experience causes her rejuvenation operation to go into reverse and she puts on a few years but not enough to make the age difference unacceptable to Standing or to make her unsuitable for a conventional happy ending.

Nilsson repeated the ageing performance far more drastically the following year in **One Way Street** (1925). Neill, an Irish émigré, also directed **Radio Mania** (1923) and, later, **Frankenstein Meets the Wolf Man** (1943) and a series of Sherlock Homes movies starring Basil Rathbone, which suggests that if his directing skills didn't improve with the years, they were never less than professionally adequate.

d Roy William Neill *s* Paul Bern *c* Hal Mohr
lp Anna Q. Nilsson, Stuart Holmes, Wyndham Standing, Arthur Rankin, Lucille Bickson, Robert Bolder, Cissy Fitzgerald, Dot Farley, Charles Newton

1925

Luch Smerti *aka* Death Ray

(GOSKINO; USSR) b/w 125 min
One of the triumvirate that dominated the most brilliant and intelligent period in film history together with Eisenstein and Vertov, Kuleshov in particular was fascinated by Western forms of popular culture which he transformed and energized with an inventive creativity that has kept his best work as fresh today as the day it was made (eg *The Adventures of Mr West in the Land of the Bolsheviks*, 1924; *The Great Consoler*, 1933). *Luch Smerti* is made like an adventure serial, fast moving, funny and crammed full with amazing moments of pure cinematic delight. The script, which sometimes looks as if it was improvised on the spot, was signed by the famous director Pudovkin, who also helped design the sets and enthusiastically hammed it up as the villain, a bald-headed Jesuit called Revo. In the story, Lann (Komarov) needs the ray to make the revolutionary rising at the helium factory a success while an international gang of reactionaries, headed by Revo, try to get the deadly contraption for themselves. Highlights include a gunfight in a darkened room, Koklova (Kuleshov's wife) and her scarecrow way of moving, the acrobatic stunts which landed Pudovkin in hospital for a while and the incredibly fluid and energetic camera style. The first and last reels are missing from existing copies of the film.

After this *tour de force*, criticized for its 'lack of seriousness', Kuleshov was nearly dropped by his studio and came to be regarded as too exuberant a pioneer, and a liability in times less tolerant of his freewheeling experimental approach to cinema.

d Lev Kuleshov *s* Vsevolod Pudovkin *c* Aleksander Levisky *lp* Porfiri Podobed, Vsevolod Pudovkin, Sergei Komarov, Vladimir Fogel, Aleksandra Koklova, Leonid Obolensky, Sergei Hohlov, Andrei Gorshilin, Mikhail Doller, Lev Kuleshov

Madrid en el Año 2000 *aka* Madrid in the Year 2000

(MADRID FILMS; SP) b/w
A fantasy depicting Madrid in the distant (for 1925) future when the city has become a port thanks to the transformation of the Manzanares River into a Suez-type canal affording passage to the grandest of ocean liners. There are some spectacular scenes as ships glide through the city and past the Royal Palace, a sight that struck contemporary observers as both fantastic and slightly ridiculous. The special effects, particularly the superimpositions achieved by Blanco, elicited favourable responses.

The picture marked the début of Rey, who soon became a popular star in the Spanish talkies shot in the Paramount Studios in Joinville (France) and Hollywood since there were no sound facilities available in Spain until 1932. This movie remained the only known Spanish Science Fiction fantasy for about 20 years. In the sixties, with **Gritos en la Noche** (1962), Jesús Franco initiated the peculiarly gruesome sub-genre of medical-horror Science Fiction that became a Spanish speciality well into the seventies.

d/s Manuel Noriega *p* Luis Maurente *c* Agustin Macasoli *se* Enrique Blanco *lp* Roberto Rey (Iglesias), Javier Rivera, Amalia Sanz Cruzado, Juan Nadal

The Monster (MGM) b/w 71 min

This charming comedy thriller (which anticipates the basic premise of **The Cars That Ate Paris**, 1974) stars Arthur as the rustic graduate of a correspondence course in detection who foils the plans of mad scientist Chaney (guying his own performance in **A Blind Bargain**, 1922) to transfer a female soul into a male body, a project that requires a number of mutilated corpses. The bravura opening, the smoothly executed trapping of a car and its driver by Chaney and his mute servant (James), and sequences like Arthur's making good his escape by tightrope walking along telegraph lines, are mounted with a visual delicacy unusual in American films

Vsevolod Pudovkin as the bald-headed villain of Lev Kuleshov's gloriously fast-moving Luch Smerti.

Conrad Veidt considers his fate in Orlacs Haende, *one of the best versions of Maurice Renard's oft-filmed novel* Les Mains d'Orlac.

of this type. Similarly Arthur's constant recourse to his detective manual which provides instant solutions to the problems he's faced with, is handled, like Chaney's delicious performance, with a firm but humorous edge that makes the film so different from the dizzy-paced adventure movies that lay behind *The Monster*. West made better movies, notably *The Bat* (1926) and *The Bat Whispers* (1931), but in his short career he made nothing so wittily conceived and executed.

d/p Roland West   *s* Willard Mack, Albert G. Kenyon
c Hal Mohr   *lp* Lon Chaney, Johnny Arthur, Gertrude Olmsted, Hallam Cooley, Walter James, Knute Erickson, Charles A. Sellon

One Way Street   (FIRST NATIONAL)   b/w   74 min
Another rejuvenation movie, following **The Young Diana** (1922), **Black Oxen, Sinners in Silk** and **Vanity's Price** (all 1924). This picture, based on a story by Beale Davis, is set in an English diplomatic milieu. Austin (Lyon) is courted by Lady Sylvia Hutton (Nilsson) but gets involved with Kathleen (Kingsley), which costs him his job in the straightlaced diplomatic service. Having become a professional cardsharp, the former diplomat becomes involved with a young girl (Daw) and finds he again must refuse the advances of Lady Sylvia, who then publicly accuses him of cheating at cards, thus depriving the ex-diplomat of his only means of earning a living. Kathleen, who remained a good friend after their affair, defends Austin and angrily confronts Lady Sylvia in a stormy meeting. The emotional strain of the interview suddenly causes Sylvia to start ageing, whereupon it is disclosed that her youthful appearance was due to a surgical operation, the effects of which are reversed by the physiological changes that accompany intense emotional excitement. Ageing on screen was not a new challenge to Nilsson who had performed a similar feat in *Vanity's Price* (1924), although in that instance she wasn't required to age as drastically because she also had to provide the statutory happy end. In this picture, Austin and his young lover take care of that as he regains his position in the diplomatic corps and marries her.

As a specialist in comedies, Dillon wasn't the best possible choice to direct this awkward melodrama. He was more at ease with such movies as *The Perfect Flapper* (1924) starring Colleen Moore and at his best directing Mary Pickford's only comedy, *Suds* (1920).

d John Francis Dillon   *p/co-s* Earl Hudson
co-s Arthur Statter, Mary Alice Seully   *c* Arthur Edeson
lp Ben Lyon, Anna Q. Nilsson, Mona Kingsley, Lumsden Hare, Marjorie Daw, Dorothy Cumming, Thomas Holding, Jed Prouty, M. Gonzales

Orlacs Haende *aka* **The Hands of Orlac**
(PAN FILM; AUSTRIA)   b/w   109 min
The novel, *Les Mains d'Orlac* (1920) was written by Maurice Renard (1875-1939), one of the great under-estimated authors of Science Fiction in Europe. His best book, *Le Docteur Lerne-Sous-Dieu* (1908) is an extremely powerful version of the medical Science Fiction theme Wells had treated in *The Island of Dr Moreau* (1896), except that Renard's book has a far richer verbal and literary texture and revels more in the uncanny implications of such a story, enjoying the shudders of infringing moral taboos instead of being shocked by them. The consensus is that *Les Mains d'Orlac* is his weakest book.

The story is that of a piano player Orlac (Veidt) who loses his hands in a railway accident. A new pair of hands, formerly belonging to a murderer, is grafted into his arms. Although Wiene (who was also responsible for the expressionist classics *Das Kabinett des Dr Caligari*, 1919, and *Raskolnikov*, 1923) directs in a realistic style, leaving only the occasional expressionist echo during scenes of high psychological tension, it is the sensitive acting of Veidt as he conveys the agony of living with 'alien' hands that appear to have a will of their own, or, perhaps, that have a privileged relation with his own unconscious desires. Also Kortner, in the role of the hallucinatory figure of a blackmailer, is brilliant, making this one of the silent German cinema's best-acted fantasy films. The direction, however, except for a few flourishes, is a little flat. The misogyny of the film, a feature of so many of these fantasy films (as well as of the 'realist' ones) has become far harder to take now but it also provides a far more direct and obvious clue to the minds that generate these kinds of scenarios. The German cinematographer turned Hollywood director Karl Freund remade the film in 1935 as **Mad Love** (the best cinematic version of the story) and E.T. Greville remade it again in a Franco-British co-production in 1961 as *Les Mains d'Orlac*.

d Robert Wiene   *s* Louis Nerz   *c* Hans Androschin, Guenther Krampf   *lp* Conrad Veidt, Fritz Kortner, Carmen Cartellieri, Alexandra Sorina, Paul Askonas, Fritz Strassny

The Power God
(DAVIS DISTRIBUTING CO.)   b/w   15 chaps
After four popular serials between 1918 and 1921, including **The Screaming Shadow** and **The Branded Four** (both 1920), the successful Wilson and Gerber duo stopped performing for a few years. This serial marked their comeback and was followed by two more, *The Mystery Box* (1925) and **Officer 444** (1926), all directed by Ben Wilson, the latter in co-operation with John Ford's brother Francis, who also co-directed their first serial, **The Mystery Ship** (1917).

The plot of *The Power God* was set in motion by the invention developed by Professor Sturgess (Bahaglia): an atomically powered engine. After the professor is eliminated by the villains, his daughter is the only one to know the secret, but she (Gerber) suffers from amnesia. Together with her lover (Wilson), she escapes numerous attempts on their lives and somewhere along the line she bumps her head which restores her memory. The happy end is achieved when they manage to patent the engine, irrevocably marking it as their private property.

Wilson had tried his hand at producing (**Nan of the North**, 1921) and now embarked on a directing career, presumably because, aged 51, he was getting a bit old for such physically demanding roles as stars of action serials. This first effort was relatively successful but not because of the routine direction of the low-budget picture: the Wilson and Gerber names still proved a considerable box-office draw on the strength of their earlier movies.

d Ben Wilson   *s* Rex Taylor, Harry Haven
lp Ben Wilson, Neva Gerber, Mary Brooklyn, Mary Crane, John Bahaglia

Up the Ladder (U) b/w 79 min

An odd little movie about the link between sexual and financial power. James (Stanley) invents a television-scope, a combination of TV and telephone a year before John Logie Baird's first practical demonstration of television (1926). The vast amount of capital required to develop the invention commercially comes along in the shape of Jane (Valli), an attractive heiress. James marries the money and soon he is boss of a massive corporation. However, as he begins to squander his energies with another woman (Livingston) Jane leaves him, cutting off the flow of money and forcing him into a subordinate position in his own company. This lesson brings James to realize the true value of his feelings for his wife and the happy end sees him reunited with Jane and the cash in blissful wedlock, and once again back at the top of his corporation.

It is difficult to find a cruder apologia for the ruthless subordination of desire for money dressed up as a story of 'true love'. It is also interesting to speculate about the ways the script might have to be altered had the roles been reversed: an intelligent but sexually profligate woman who agrees to give the exclusive rights to her body in exchange for the presidency of a company. One is entitled to wonder what the happy end to that story would have been. In fact, the scientific invention would never have been attributed to a sexually promiscuous woman, which is what prevents this movie from becoming a straightforward advocation of male prostitution, which does constitute a novel use of the Science Fiction motif, to say the least.

d Edward Sloman *s* Grant Carpenter, Tom McNamara *c* Jackson Rose *lp* Virginia Valli, Forrest Stanley, Margaret Livingston, Holmes Herbert, George Fawcett, Priscilla Moran, Olive Ann Alcorn, Lydia Yeamans Titus

1926

Metropolis (UFA; G) b/w 182 (128,75) min

A monumental film, *Metropolis* is the classic of the genre, unparalleled in scope and ingenuity until Kubrick's **2001 – A Space Odyssey** (1968). Everything about it is gigantic, from the time it took to shoot (over 16 months when films were made in a few weeks) to the numbers involved: a cast of 37,383 people and a cost 7 million marks, which made it UFA's most expensive film ever (although they had just made the two-part epic *Die Nibelungen* (1924), also directed by Lang) and caused the merger of UFA with Decla Bioscop. The scale of the project was matched by Lang's directorial skills, by the inventiveness of one of the greatest special effects men in film history, Schuefftan and, unfortunately, by the stupidity of the script authored by Lang's wife, von Harbou, his constant scriptwriting companion at the time.

Set around the year 2000, a mammoth city is ruled by the super-efficient industrialist John Fredersen (called Masterson in some English/US versions) played by Abel, while his son Freder (Froehlich) frolics in paradisiacal gardens with his idle friends. The workers, a subhuman species of sluggish creatures, are under the sway of a 'saintly' Maria (Helm), who urges them not to rebel but to wait patiently for the arrival of a Mediator. While Froehlich gets captivated by the good Maria, his father has her kidnapped and gets mad scientist Rothwang (Klein-Rogge, who also took the lead in Lang's Dr Mabuse-films of 1922) to make a robot-replica of her as a substitute. However, the bad Maria then incites the workers to revolt and, mindless subhumans that they are, they dutifully do as she tells them, destroying machines, flooding their underground quarters and nearly killing everybody. Froehlich and the 'good' Helm save them and their children. In the end, the workers' foreman (George) shakes the industrialist by the hand as Labour and Capital are united via the great Mediator: Love. Reduced to this, its purely literary contents, H.G. Wells' comment that *Metropolis* was 'quite the silliest film' is justified, although he had seen only the severely cut English

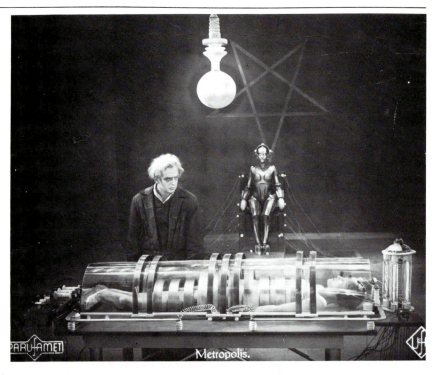

Metropolis.

version. Grierson called the conclusion 'silly and sentimental' and even Lang stated in 1959: 'I don't like *Metropolis*. The ending is false. I didn't like it even when I made the film.' Apparently Hitler, accompanied by Goebbels, saw the film in a small German town. They liked it as much as they had admired *Die Nibelungen* and when they came to power in 1933, Lang was asked to make their prestige pictures, in spite of them banning his 1933 film, **Das Testament des Dr Mabuse**. On the very day of that summons by the Nazi bosses, Lang packed his bags and left, eventually to reach the peak of his film career in Hollywood.

Hitler and Goebbels, however, were no more cine-literate than Wells or Grierson. Those who knew how to look beyond the literary aspects of film, such as Paul Rotha, in 1930 called it a 'wonderful exposition of cinematography' while a British picture such as **High Treason** (1929) 'with its arts-and-crafts design' showed 'how poorly England produces a film of this kind.' Reviewing the film in 1927, Buñuel wrote that *Metropolis* was 'two films glued together by their bellies', distinguishing between the silly script and the magnificently cinematic aspects: 'From the photographic angle, its emotive force, its unheard of and overwhelming beauty is unequalled.' More recently (1981), Frederik Pohl called it 'the first big budget and fully aware science fiction film.'

Inspired by his first glimpse of the Manhattan skyline in 1924, Lang achieved a visual intensity both in the filming of the dramatic, futurist sets and events, and in his skilful use of montage, at times even suggesting sound effects through the rhythmically arranged image patterns of throbbing pistons and light rays. The highpoints of the film are undoubtedly the doom-laden, underground city with its intricate, geometric choreography of groups and individual gestures as the workers move through the claustrophobic spaces and interact with oppressive machines; the Moloch machine at the top of a broad flight of stairs; the creation of the metallic Maria imbued with life through spectacular electrical charges (anticipating and providing the actual model for these scenes in the Frankenstein films); the cataclysmic destruction of the underground city and, above all, the torch-beam pursuit of Maria, a sequence of cinematic delirium summarizing the founding ambiguities of cinema as a machine for looking itself. Many of Lang's films hinge on the way looking itself has been woven into the very fabric of the film, from Haghi's cold, knowing stare in **Spione** (1928) to Mabuse's hypnotic

Rufolf Klein-Rogge, the mad scientist par excellence, at work in Metropolis.

gaze, multiplied to near infinity in Lang's third and last Mabuse film, **Die Tausend Augen des Dr Mabuse** (1960).

Lang was never that interested in 'depth of character', accepting the strengths and, as in this case, the weaknesses of his scripts. Instead, his films come alive almost against the grain of the script, on other, purely cinematic levels: holding shots longer, arranging visual echoes or allowing the visual to exceed the literary aspects of films (plot, character) to such a degree that the whole structure of the film is tilted out of balance, or rather in Buñuel's happy phrase, until the film becomes two films glued together by their bellies. In *Metropolis* Lang achieved this visual intensity with the assistance of the virtuoso cameraman and by Schuefftan's ingenious special effects, achieved through the combination of live scenes with scale models by means of mirrors, a procedure that became known as the Schuefftan (or Schuftan, as it was called in the USA) process. Lang also claimed that the scene where Abel sees George on a big screen was the first example of back projection, although similar effects had been achieved in Lang's own **Die Spinnen** (1919). Weigel, later to achieve world fame as Brecht's principle actress (and wife) appears as an anonymous worker.

At the box office, *Metropolis* flopped and nearly bankrupted UFA, causing it to be taken over by the financier Hugenberg, one of Hitler's major backers.

In 1984 the record producer Giorgio Moroder released an 83-minute, re-edited, tinted version of *Metropolis* with a disco score. Far from deforming the original, Moroder's film, though it has its critics, was a surprisingly faithful reconstruction of Lang's much mutilated classic.

d/co-s Fritz Lang   *p* Erich Pommer   *co-s* Thea von Harbou   *c* Karl Freund, Guenther Rittau   *se* Eugen Schuefftan (Shuftan)   *lp* Brigitte Helm, Alfred Abel, Gustav Froehlich, Rudolf Klein-Rogge, Fritz Rasp, Theodor Loos, Erwin Biswanger, Heinrich George, Olaf Storm, Grete Berger, Helene Weigel

Officer 444   (DAVIS DISTRIBUTING CO.)   b/w   10 chaps

This is the last of the successful Wilson and Gerber serials, directed by John Ford's brother Francis, who also co-directed their first success **The Mystery Ship** (1917). Most of their serials had relied on some scientific gadget to provide the motivation for displays of physical action (chases, fights). However, this serial referred to a bacteriological device that could be used either for good or ill (by 1928, in **Ransom**, the potential for 'good' chemical devices was dropped and attention was concentrated on military uses). The story tells of an inventor who confides his secret formula for a new gas to a nurse (Gerber) whom he charges to contact his son, a New York cop whose badge number is 444 (Wilson). The villain is the Frog (Ferguson), a master of disguises. The action is mostly set in Feuillade territory: sewers abounding with secret passageways, sliding panels and other hazards. The performance of the 52-year-old Wilson is not as energetic as that of most serial heroes and the action honours go mostly to his partner in the New York Police Department (Mower) as well as to Ferguson's masterly incarnation of the villainous Frog. Since **The Power God** (1925), Wilson had also taken some directorial responsibility, but that career was cut short by his death in 1930.

In another serial released that year, *The Radio Detective* (1926), Mower played the part of the legendary Craig Kennedy, the hero of the 36-part Elaine serials which began with **The Exploits of Elaine** (1914). But although based on a story by Reeve, the scenarist of the Elaine pictures, the scientific excuse was so ludicrous ('evansite' invented by a scout master called Evans), the plot so ramshackle, with hordes of boy scouts aiding the great detective, and the acting so poor that the film is best forgotten.

d Ben Wilson, Francis Ford   *lp* Ben Wilson, Neva Gerber, Al Ferguson, Phil Ford, August Vollmer, Jack Mower

The Scarlet Streak   (PATHE)   b/w   10 chaps

An energetic though conventionally plotted serial made by McRae, the director of the fast-paced adventure film **The Mysterious Contragrav** (1915). Based on Leigh Jacobson's story *Dangers of the Deep*, the action is set in motion by a laser-like red ray invented by Professor Crawford (Smith) and perfected together with his daughter, Mary (Todd). Daugherty plays the reporter whose articles may increase the market value of the contraption. The villain is Monk (Prisco), a foreign agent who kidnaps the professor, his gadget and his daughter, while Daugherty spends his time detecting and escaping until he secures the recovery of all three missing items. The action is capably conducted by McRae and the picture proved a successful accompaniment to the features released by Universal, which had bought half a dozen or so Pathé serials in 1926 purely for that purpose.

d Henry McRae   *lp* Jack Daugherty, Lola Todd, Al Smith, Albert Prisco, Virginia Ainsworth

Blake of Scotland Yard   (U)   b/w   12 chaps

An interesting departure from the standard formulas made by the best of the American silent serial directors whose credits include **The Flaming Disk** (1920) and **The Radio King** (1922). Instead of relying on the usual death ray or new explosive gimmick to initiate the action, this picture used the more exotic alchemist's dream of turning metals into gold, a motif best treated in Karl Hartl's **Gold** (1934). More importantly, Hill also departs from the adventure format by straying into Sherlock Holmes terrain, dispensing with the familiar all-American athletic hero or entrepreneur trying to preserve or increase US military power. Angus Blake (Stevenson), retired from the yard, is called in by Lady Blanton (Gray) for protection against the Spider (Montague) who is after her father's formula for the chemical production of gold. The serial chronicles the contest between Blake and the Spider in a mysterious and desolate castle filled with the spoils of empire. As a metaphor for the way the English aristocracy enriched itself, the image of transmuting raw materials into gold is quite apt, and naturally the Yard is there – unofficially, since Blake is not on active duty – to protect the wealth accumulated in that fashion. In addition, Blake is repeatedly rescued by a mysterious lady in white (Cunard), a suitable incarnation of a higher power or symbol (Britannia? Justice?) that can be called upon in the last resort. The picture distinguished itself in the creation of a suitably gothic atmosphere to enhance the suspense and heighten the emotional impact of the events at the remote castle, which made it one of the rare American serials not content merely to record the frenetic action but to use the basic resources of cinema in the way that French (Feuillade), German (Lang) and Russian (Kuleshov) directors had done. It would appear

A scene from Blake of Scotland Yard, *one of the sprightliest of silent serials.*

that in the USA only Maurice Tourneur in **The Hand of Peril**, 1916, *The Isle of Lost Ships*, 1923 and **The Mysterious Island**, 1929, and, to a lesser extent Hill, insisted on making film dramas instead of just filmed dramas.

d/co-s Robert F. Hill   *co-s/se* William Lord Wright
lp Hayden Stevenson, Gloria Gray, Monty Montague, Grace Cunard

Sur un Air de Charleston *aka* Charleston *aka* Charleston Parade *aka* Parade sur un Air de Charleston
(FILMS JEAN RENOIR; FR)   b/w   25 min
This, the last film made by Renoir's own company, was made with film stock left over from his commercially disastrous classic *Nana* (1926). Together with his trusted collaborators and family (the pictures starred his wife) he quickly shot his jazz fantasy on one single set at the Epinay Studios. The story tells of a scientist (Higgins, an American tap dancer appearing in Paris at the time) who lands on Earth in 2028 after an apocalyptic war has wiped out nearly all of civilization. In a desert he encounters a woman (Hessling) and finds they can only communicate through dance. As they perform the erotic rituals of the charleston, they fall in love and he takes her into his spaceship as they return to his planet.

Renoir shared the jazz craze that swept Paris at the time and his friend Jacques Becker, later also a noted director, introduced him to a pianist, Clement Doucet, who composed an original jazz score for the film which, unfortunately, appears to have been lost. The picture is a short, humorous and sensuous piece that looks more like a filmed show than a movie. Fantasy never was Renoir's strong point, but the sensual aspects of the performance were well arranged, even though a charleston adapted for white – even if European – audiences bore little resemblance to jazz. Renoir later claimed that this short film, shot in 1926 but released in March 1927, had originally been about twice as long but that he never bothered to finish it, suggesting the existing version consists of a number of edited sequences which were never meant to stand on their own as an autonomous picture.

d/p Jean Renoir   *s* Pierre Lestringuez   *c* Jean Bachelet
lp Catherine Hessling, Johnny Higgins, Pierre Braunberger, Pierre Lestringuez, Jean Renoir

The Wizard   (FOX)   b/w   75 min
The intuitive rejection of the popularized version of Darwin's theory of evolution, most infamously manifested in 1923 during the Scopes trial (an attempt to convict a teacher for having taught the theory), was matched by an equally intuitive acceptance of the theory, as demonstrated by the many stories and films in which apes acted out what men took to be their animal instincts: *The Missing Link* (1927), *Red Lights* (1923), *The Wizard* and, of course, *King Kong* (1933). The belief that the consumption of monkey glands would help

to keep one youthful testified to a similar intuition that simians represented men's unconscious past and source of vitality. *The Wizard*, taking its cue from Poe's *Murders in the Rue Morgue*, introduced an ape who carried out the homicidal fantasies of its human counterpart, Dr Paul Coriolos (von Seyffertitz). The doctor has the ape murder the people who condemned his son to the electric chair. He is found out by a journalist (Lowe) who thus saves a judge (Trevor) and his daughter (Hyams). In the end, the ape turns on its master and takes over completely before being killed by Hyams. An additional clarification of the fantasy underpinning such stories is provided by the doctor's gratuitous decision to graft a human face onto the ape, thus simultaneously confirming that the ape is just like a man and denying it by underlining the monstrosity of such a proposition.

The fantasy obviously struck a chord and the film was remade as **Dr Renault's Secret** (1942), while many other ape films later rehearsed the same motifs. Contemporary reviews commented on the humorous aspects of the story and singled out the suitably demonic performance of von Seyffertitz.

d Richard Rosson   *p* William Fox   *s* Harry O'Hoyt, Andrew Bennison   *c* Frank Good   *lp* Edmund Lowe, Leila Hyams, Gustav von Seyffertitz, E.H. Calvert, Barry Norton, Oscar Smith, Perle Marshall, Norman Trevor, George Kotsonaros

Alraune *aka* Unholy Love *aka* Daughter of Destiny
(AMA FILM; G)   b/w   125 min
Finished at the very end of 1927, this is the third and by far the best of the five adaptations of Hanns Heinz Ewers' immensely popular novel about a scientist (Wegener) who collects a hanged man's semen as it drops onto the earth underneath the gallows and artificially inseminates a prostitute with it. The daughter, Alraune (Helm, who also played the two Marias in **Metropolis**, 1926) is a pale, distant but, at least in this film, a very erotic beauty living in perpetual incestuous tension with her 'father', played by Wegener in the hulking and menacing way he played in **Der Golem** (1914 and 1920). When Helm discovers her origins and understands her lack of 'soul', her inability to love, as did **Homunculus** (1916) under similar circumstances, she turns on her creator in revenge.

The legend is also known as that of the mandrake root or the mandragora, the root that grows under the gallows, produced by the hanged man's semen and shaped like a

Brigitte Helm and Louis Ralph in the best, and most erotic, version of Alraune.

Left: Gustav von Seyffertitz as the evil doctor with his ape-creature in The Wizard.

humanoid creature. Throughout this film, the bond between Alraune and her root, the perverse relation between her and her little piece of man, vulnerable to destruction by fire, charges the atmosphere. In a way, Kertesz's version (1918) renders explicit what Galeen more successfully insinuates, allowing an obsessive sexuality to suffuse the whole texture of the film with an intensity rarely equalled in the silent cinema (except perhaps in Murnau's *Nosferatu*, 1922). Galeen had collaborated with Ewers before on the best version of *Der Student von Prag*, (1926), a sombrely romantic tale of a student who sells his mirror image. *Alraune* never quite reaches the shadowy magnificence of that film but more than makes up for that in the area of sensuality. Helm, who repeated her role two years later in a version directed by Oswald (1930), manages to convey a sense of extreme vulnerability and a coldly burning passion at the same time. Loder and Gert, soon to become a major star through her roles in Pabst's *Tagebuch einer Verlorenen* (1929) and *Dreigroschenoper* (1930), make brief appearances. Ewers went on to achieve considerable fame as an author. Apparently, in World War II, every German soldier was issued with a copy of the novel, *Alraune*. Ewers also wrote the 'Horst Wessel' song for the Nazis.

The 1952 version of *Alraune*, in spite of Kneff's presence in the title role, is a tame and awkwardly directed remake attempting to combine this black romantic story with the chief medical concerns of the fifties – abortion and artificial insemination.

d/s Henrik (Heinrich) Galeen   *c* Franz Planer   *lp* Brigitte Helm, Paul Wegener, Ivan Petrovich, Mia Pankau, Georg John, Valeska Gert, John Loder, Wolfgang Lilzer, Louis Ralph, Alexander Sascha

Code of the Air   (BISCHOFF PRODUCTIONS)   b/w   76 min
In an effort to cash in on the success of Rin Tin Tin, this independent production fielded Silverstreak, a dog accompanying Blair Thompson (Harlan), a secret agent on the track of the evil Professor Ross (Mong). With a device emitting kappa rays, Ross is shooting down airplanes and appropriating their cargo of stocks and bonds. The love interest is provided by Helen (Marlowe) as Silverstreak's rival for the secret agent's affections. By all accounts, the acting was acceptable but the technical credits poor, a judgement made credible by the director's track record which included *The Mad Ghoul* (1943), some very minor westerns and four Bulldog Drummond pictures. Mong was an experienced villain who was marginally better served by George B. Seitz in

An example of the surreal conflation of gimmickry and visual excess of Fritz Lang's Spione. *Beneath the greasepaint is Rudolf Klein-Rogge.*

Ransom (1928) as he impersonated the evil Wu Fang, the stereotyped villainous oriental whose name had served in **The New Exploits of Elaine** (1915) as well.

d James P. Hogan   *p* Samuel Bischoff   *s* Barry Barringer   *c* William Miller   *lp* Kenneth Harlan, June Marlowe, Arthur Rankin, William V. Mong, Paul Weigel, James Bradbury Jnr, Edna Mae Cooper, Silverstreak

The Kid's Clever   (U)   b/w   77 min
A routine yokel comedy about a mechanic called Bugs (Tryon) who concocts an amphibious car that doesn't need expensive fuel. The contraption looks like a junk heap, but the beautiful heiress Ruth Decker (Crawford), daughter of a wealthy car manufacturer (Simpson), is seduced by the car and its quaintly rustic inventor. Bugs' assistant sabotages the vehicle but Ruth and Bugs nevertheless manage to land a contract with her father, simultaneously tying him to the industrialist and to his daughter as entrepreneur and husband respectively. A minor part of the 'fun' is provided by Stepin Fetchit in his usual role of an idiotic blackman. It is worth recalling that, at the time, many counties in California operated an apartheid system requiring black people to obtain a special permit to be on the street after the curfew that was enforced for them. This also applied to black performers appearing in the Hollywood nightclubs.

d/p William James Craft   *s* Jack Foley   *c* Al Jones   *lp* Glenn Tryon, Kathryn Crawford, Russell Simpson, Lloyd Whitlock, George Chandler, Joan Standing, Max Asher, Florence Turner, Virginia Sale, Stepin Fetchit

Ransom   (COL)   b/w   73 min
Together with the Wilson and Gerber serial **Officer 444** (1926), this is one of the few pictures that refer to the irredeemably nasty side of scientific involvement with the military establishment: chemical warfare. The story concerns Burton Meredith (Burns), the inventor of a deadly nerve gas. The secret formula is wanted by an evil oriental called Wu Fang (Mong), whose name seems to indicate that he may be the reincarnation of the villain who battled with Craig Kennedy in **The New Exploits of Elaine** (1915). Fang abducts the son (Coombs) of Meredith's lover (Wilson), but she mistakenly hands the blackmailer the wrong chemical compound, angering Fang who threatens to torture her unless Meredith comes across with the goods. Meredith and a bevy of government agents rescue both his fiancée and her son. The ending has the hero receiving wide acclaim and expects the audience to join in the admiration for the inventor of a nerve gas that is designed to kill many more people than any of the existing chemical devices and to rejoice in the US army's possession of such a wonderful weapon. Mong's portrayal of the Chinese villain provides all that such a racist stereotype implied at the time. The contemporary trade journal *The Bioscope* condescendingly declared that 'the mother-love interest [is] strong and the acting quite good. The film should please working class audiences.' Director Seitz had worked on all three Elaine serials and gone on to earn the nickname of Serial King, often writing and directing as well as starring in his own movies, such as *The Sky Ranger* (1941). At the height of his extremely prolific career, he directed parts of the Andy Hardy saga at MGM. Seitz is the prototype of the anonymous Hollywood professional in the sense that his work is proficient but indistinguishable from that of all the other hack directors.

d George B Seitz   *p* Harry Cohn   *s* Elmer Harris   *c* Joseph Walker   *lp* Lois Wilson, Edmund Burns, William V. Mong, Blue Washington, James B. Leong, Jackie Coombs

Spione *aka* **The Spy**
(FRITZ LANG FILM/UFA; G)   b/w   186 min
Lang's fourth master-criminal thriller, after **Die Spinnen** (1919), **Dr Mabuse, der Spieler** (1922) and **Metropolis**

(1926). In fact, it would be more correct to describe Lang's films as depicting social structures that breed and legitimate criminality. His master-criminals merely go along with the logic of the social order they live in, turning its immense resources to their personal advantage, sometimes for profit, sometimes merely for the pleasure of playing 'the system'. In this sense, Lang's American film *The Big Heat* (1953) stands as the summation of the themes he broached in his German films, except that *The Big Heat* is less paranoid, better informed about the workings of society, and, therefore, far more pessimistic.

In *Spione*, Lang developed the prototype of all the master-spy films that flooded the market in the wake of **Doctor No** (1962). The mysterious Haghi (Klein-Rogge again, after playing Mabuse and the mad scientist in *Metropolis*) is director of the giant Haghi Bank. Made up to resemble Trotsky, he is in charge of an international spy ring. His agents Sonja (Maurus) and Kitty (Deyers) are his two main weapons, until Sonja falls for Tremaine (Fritsch), James Bond's predecessor. The film is a very fast-moving adventure story going all out for suspense, involving a spectacular train crash, a series of mysterious murders, coded telegrams, a buttonhole camera, a futuristic and labyrinthine underground spy centre, a mad car chase, anticipating a similar sequence in **Das Testament des Dr Mabuse** (1933), all of it shot with the brilliant sense of *mise en scene* and rhythm characteristic of all Lang's work, invariably getting the best out of his cinematographers and designers. The central figure, Haghi, is stripped of any human qualities, becoming a 'human computer' as Lang put it, deadlier than even Mabuse. This make the final unmasking of the evil genius as he appears in a cabaret as a clown, all the more poignant. Pick, later a director in his own right as well as the president of the German actors union until the Nazis took over, gives an outstanding performance as a Japanese spy. Rasp, better known for his roles in Pabst's films (*Die Buechse der Padora*, 1928) is a memorable aristocratic Russian spy, apparently modelled on a real-life figure of the Austrian General Redl. Hoerbiger, the immensely popular Viennese actor, makes an early appearance as a valet.

d/p/co-s Fritz Lang *co-s* Thea von Harbou *c* Fritz Arno Wagner *lp* Rudolf Klein-Rogge, Gerda Maurus, Willy Fritsch, Lien Deyers, Lupu Pick, Fritz Rasp, Craighall Sherry, Julius Falkenstein, Georg John, Paul Hoerbiger

Gerda Maurus

A futuristic looking car from the insipid High Treason, *a British attempt to ape* Metropolis *(1926).*

1929

The Diamond Master (U) b/w 10 chaps

A remake of the 18-episode serial **The Diamond Queen** (1921) based on the novel by Jacques Futrelle, a popular writer of detective fiction who was one of the victims of the *Titanic* disaster. The story tells of a group of diamond merchants who arrange the murder of Dr Harvey (Stern), the inventor of a process that can transmute dust into diamonds. His daughter, Doris (Lorraine) enlists the help of Mark (Stevenson) to track down the killers as well as to exploit the commercial potential of her father's invention. The rest of the serial is taken up with their detecting and constant escapes from the diamond merchants' heavies. This version, eight episodes shorter than the original, proceeds at a faster pace, packing more action into each instalment. One reason for the picture's success was the competent performances of the cast, some of whom had gained valuable experience in serials directed by the best of the American silent serial directors, Robert F. Hill. Lorraine had starred in **The Flaming Disk** (1920) and **The Radio King** (1922) while Montague had played the villain in **Blake of Scotland Yard** (1927).

d Jack Nelson *lp* Louise Lorraine, Hayden Stevenson, Al Hart, Monty Montague, Louis Stern, Walter Maly

Die Frau im Mond aka The Woman in the Moon aka The Girl in the Moon aka By Rocket to the Moon

(FRITZ LANG FILM/UFA; G) b/w 185 min

The film that invented the countdown – strictly for dramatic purposes. Made by the same team that had been responsible for **Metropolis** (1926), the strengths and weaknesses of the film are predictable: inventive direction weighed down by a leaden, sentimental and unintelligent script. A small group of people, including a woman (Maurus), two young men courting her (Fritsch and von Wangenheim), a professor (Pohl) and an unscrupulous American fortune-hunter (Rasp), financed by some industrialists, build a rocket in order to go and mine the gold that is supposed to be on the Moon. They also take a boy along (Gstettenbauer). Some are killed and the others are left stranded on the Moon. In effect, the first real space travel movie, significantly linking the opening up of the Moon as a territory with a goldrush. Lang appears only interested in the *mise en scene*, taking great care to make the details of this fantasy story as real and 'state of the art' as he can manage. As scientific advisors he got Willy Ley, who later escaped to the USA, and Hermann Oberth, who worked for the Nazis and, later, for George Pal on **Destination Moon** (1950). Lang insisted on documentary precision, anticipating the way a lunar rocket would have to be moved to its launch-pad. Although this is undoubtedly one of Lang's weakest films (the slow, ponderous business of moving rockets about didn't really suit his style), it was apparently inventive enough to

Left: *Gerda Maurus in* Die Frau im Mond, *the film in which Fritz Lang invented the countdown.*

scare members of the British Foreign Office witless and to cause the Nazis to withdraw the film from distribution while the Gestapo destroyed the spaceship model used in the film in order to keep their development of the VI and V2 rockets an absolute secret.

Fischinger, the famous experimental film-maker who eventually worked for Disney (*Fantasia*, 1939), assisted with the special effects.

d/p Fritz Lang *s* Thea von Harbou *c* Curt Courant, Otto Kanturek *se* Konstantin Tschetwerikoff, Oskar Fischinger *lp* Gerda Maurus, Willy Fritsch, Fritz Rasp, Gustav von Wangenheim, Klaus Pohl, Max Maximilian, Margarete Kupfer, Tilla Durieurx, Heinrich Gothe, Gustl Stark-Gstettenbauer

High Treason (GAUMONT; GB) b/w 95 (69) min
Based on a failed play by Noel Pemberton-Billing, who also financed the movie, this was a very poor British effort intended to match Lang's **Metropolis** (1926). Paul Rotha, the critic and film-maker, rightly used this Elvey picture as proof of 'how poorly England produces a film of this kind', dismissing the very things newspaper reviewers were raving about as drab 'arts-and-crafts design'. The story is set in 1940 and assumes London has become a concrete jungle with airplanes landing and taking off from the roofs of skyscrapers dwarfing St Paul's, with a fully operational channel tunnel linking England (the rest of the UK is supposed to feel itself included in that country) into a United Europe, and with broadcasting, including television, having replaced print journalism. The plot offers a mixture of political naïvety and downright silliness betraying a quite staggering ignorance about the historical processes at work in the inter-war period, although with hindsight, some amusing similarities with the situation in the eighties can be detected. The film tells of two powerblocks, a United Europe and a United America, confronting each other on the brink of war. A Peace League with millions of adherents tries to stop the two governments from destroying the world in a catastrophic war. The solution offered, in spite of the fine humanist sentiments voiced in the movie, is that a conflict between two power blocks can only be stopped by killing the leader of one of them, and the Peace League assassinates the leader of United Europe. It is also worth mentioning that the League is composed of 'Peace' women.

Released in the same year as Hitchcock's *Blackmail*, this movie was acclaimed as being equal to Hitchcock's work and making England the most advanced film nation in the world of the emerging sound era. The ludicrousness of comparing Hitchcock and Elvey shows how a blinkered chauvinism can lead critics to heap praise on mediocre products merely because they establish the presence of 'England' on the international market, a phenomenon that didn't die out after 1929; it was repeated regularly throughout postwar British film reviewing, reaching another depressing climax in the eighties with the adulation of *Gandhi* (1982) and the nostalgic academicism of *Chariots of Fire* (1980).

d Maurice Elvey *p/s* L'Estrange Fawcett *lp* Benita Hume, Jameson Thomas, Basil Gill, James Carew, Humberston Wright, Henry Vibart, Milton Rosmer, Wally Patch, Hayford Hobbs, Judd Green

Midstream
(TIFFANY-STAHL PRODUCTIONS) b/w 100 (70) min
The last of the twenties rejuvenation films. The series had included **The Young Diana** (1922), **Vanity's Price, Sinners in Silk, Black Oxen** (all 1924) and **One Way Street** (1925). This time, a Wall Street financier (Cortez) buys the special rejuvenation treatment available in a European spa in order to win Helen Craig (Windsor). On his return to the USA, he claims to be the nephew of the financier and quickly gets Helen to agree to a marriage. One evening they attend a performance of a *Faust* opera and drift into a violent quarrel over the show's merits, which causes the financier to revert back to his real age of 50. Helen, resenting both his duplicity and his age, leaves him. The happy end is provided by his discovery that his secretary (Eddy) loved him all along and is quite prepared to marry him. The picture was released in both silent and sound versions, but the silent print was withdrawn after it played unsuccessfully in a few minor theatres. The Viennese-born Cortez (whose real name was Jacob Krantz) had been groomed as a Latin lover but failed to impress. Most of his long career was spent appearing in second and third grade movies (**The Walking Dead,** 1936; *Mr Moto's Last Warning*, 1938), the highpoint being a minor role in John Ford's *The Last Hurrah* (1958). He also directed a few films, *City Girl* (1938), *Free Blonde and Twenty One* and *The Girl in 313* (both 1940).

d James Flood *s* Frances Guihan *c* Jackson Rose *lp* Ricardo Cortez, Claire Windsor, Montagu Love, Larry Kent, Helen Jerome Eddy, Leslie Brigham, Louis Alvarez, Florence Foyer, Genevieve Schrader

The Mysterious Island (MGM) 95 min
The first of five adaptations of Jules Verne's sequel to *20,000 Leagues Under the Sea*, this features the further adventures of Captain Nemo (here called Count Dakkar and played by Barrymore). Along with the name change Verne's novel was much altered and re-located in the fictitious country of Hetvia. Barrymore as the scientist ruler of Hetvia is seeking to prove the existence of a race of half-men, half-creatures living on the ocean floor. He invents a 'submersible' to travel to the bottom of the sea and finds the creatures, only to discover that in his absence Love has siezed control of his kingdom.

The film's lengthy production – it was three years in the making – was caused by a storm that wrecked the underwater film laboratory of writer/special effects man Williamson and MGM's decision to add sound to the film when Hubbard (who took over from Tourneur and Christensen) finally finished shooting. Though the plot is melodramatic and rambling, the special effects (especially the 'gill men' and the battle with the giant octopus) and underwater colour cinematography are marvellous.

The novel was filmed in 1941 (as **Tainstvenni Ostrov**), 1951, 1961 and 1972 (as **L'Isola Misteriosa e il Capitano Nemo**).

co-d/s Lucien Hubbard *co-d* Maurice Tourneur, Benjamin Christensen *p/se* J. Ernest Williamson *c* Percy Hilburn *lp* Lionel Barrymore, Jane Daly, Lloyd Hughes, Montagu Love, Harry Gribbon, Dolores Brinkman

The capture of one of the tiny half-men, half-fish creatures in the marvellous The Mysterious Island, *one of the most sumptuous-looking films ever.*

The
1930s

Mad Scientists and Comic Book Heroes

The thirties saw both Science Fiction literature and cinema in turmoil. But where Science Fiction writing, though it remained trapped in the ghetto of pulp magazines well into the forties, following the founding of *Astounding Stories* in 1930, swiftly developed beyond the naïve 'scientification' of Hugo Gernsback and earlier notions of 'scientific romance', the Science Fiction film saw no such steady development or process of clarification. Looking at the variety of films that were made during the decade it is clear that Science Fiction, in no sense, can be seen as an ongoing genre in the thirties.

In Europe, films like **La Fin du Monde** (1930), Abel Gance's overblown disaster epic, **F.P.1 Antwortet Nicht** (1932), a technological vision of the near future, and **Things to Come** (1936), a spectacular dressing up of H.G. Wells' austere vision of the far future, in their various ways continued the line of prophetic speculation of **Metropolis** (1926). Similarly, towards the end of the decade as the political climate grew decidedly colder in Europe, films as different as **Bila Nemoc** and **Q Planes** (both 1937), made use of Science Fiction elements to imagine the horrors of a second world war.

In America, however, after the false start of **Just Imagine** (1930) (which, though it drew its vision of the future from *Metropolis*, cast that vision in the most banal and melodramatic of plots) and the even odder **It's Great to Be Alive** (1933) there was no clear line of development. Instead, Science Fiction elements were seen as gimmicks (rather like sound) with which to enliven otherwise routine material, be it a melodrama (**Six Hours to Live**, 1932), thriller (**The Invisible Man**, 1933; **Television Spy**, 1939) or even a western (**The Phantom Empire**, 1935). But the most notable examples of this co-option of Science Fiction elements by another genre were **Frankenstein** (1931), **Doctor Jekyll and Mr Hyde** (1932) and **Mad Love** (1935). All these films dealt with important Science Fiction themes which later Science Fiction films would return to time and time again, yet all were presented as horror films. This was a reflection both of the success of the cycle of horror films (beginning with *Dracula*, 1930) that dominated the early years of the decade, a cycle which also led to the making of *King Kong* (1933), and of the atomization of Science Fiction into Science Fiction elements.

The culmination of this trend was Hollywood's consignment of Science Fiction to the Poverty Row world of the serials in the middle of the decade. There, a variety of criminals, mad scientists and larger than life figures sought world domination (and sometimes control of the whole galaxy) utilizing a series of bizarre gadgets and disguises in the course of their evil quest. Few of these serials retain their charm nowadays, but from such seemingly infertile ground sprang the one example of genuine pulp poetry that Science Fiction produced in the thirties, **Flash Gordon** (1936). Often dismissed as a mere 'space opera', which it undeniably was, *Flash Gordon* remains the most remarkable example of Science Fiction film-making of the decade and the one film that forms the link between the thirties and the seventies and the eighties and the phenomenon of **Star Wars** (1977).

Alraune *aka* Daughter of Evil

(UFA; G) b/w 103 min

This is the fourth version of Hanns Heinz Ewers' classic fantasy about the nature-nurture debates that accompanied the idea of a genetic-racial essence (others were made in 1918, twice, 1928 and again in 1952). Helm repeats the title role she had incarnated only two years before in Galeen's version (1928). This time, Bassermann is the scientist, Ten Brinken, who artificially inseminates a prostitute with a hanged man's semen, producing a beautiful but disturbingly cool and perverse daughter, Alraune. Bassermann, a fêted theatre actor trained by Max Reinhardt and film actor since 1913, cannot overcome the pedestrian direction of Oswald, better known for his sex education films and anodyne costume dramas. No doubt aware of the need to find a new angle so shortly after Galeen's version had achieved massive success, Oswald played this *Alraune* for 'realism', forgetting that this type of drama stands or falls on the creation of a perverse atmosphere, an uncanny and sexually charged mood in which what is repressed (barely) and suggested is far more important than the plot or the characters. By asking Helm to cease being a vamp and by inserting lots more lines for 'character development', Oswald in effect destroyed the basis of the story. The 1952 version makes a brave attempt to re-introduce a loaded, deathly sensuality, but also fails.

d Richard Oswald *p* Erich Pommer *s* Charlie Roellinghoff, Richard Weisbach *c* Guenther Krampf *lp* Brigitte Helm, Albert Bassermann, Agnes Straub, Kaethe Haack, Bernhard Goetzke, Martin Kosleck, Paul Westermeier, Liselott Schaak, Harald Paulsen, Henry Bender

Elstree Calling

(BRITISH INTERNATIONAL PICTURES; GB) b/w 95 min

A curiosity, this was a British response to the large-scale revue films which the major Hollywood studios made to put their stars through their talkie paces after the advent of sound. The ensemble numbers were directed by Charlot, Hulbert and Murray and the sketches by (a not very enthusiastic) Hitchcock. One of these makes a typically British joke about

Previous pages: H.G. Wells' bleak vision of life after World War II in Things to Come *(1936).*

Brigitte Helm, the robot of Metropolis *(1926), as the perverse* Alraune.

New York in 1980, as envisaged by David Butler in Just Imagine.

the advent of the television age (which would begin in Britain in 1935, though there had been experimental broadcasts as early as 1927). Harker and his family try unsuccessfully to watch the inaugural programme of British TV (in 1936, in reality) but are constantly interrupted by neighbours rushing in to tell the family how wonderful TV is.

d Alfred Hitchcock, André Charlot, Jack Hulbert, Paul Murray *p* Walter C. Mycroft *s* Val Valentine *c* Claude Freise Greene *lp* Gordon Harker, Anna May Wong, Donald Calthrop

La Fin du Monde *aka* The End of the World
(L'ECRAN D'ART; FR) b/w 91 min
The recent much publicized revival of Gance's *Napoleon* (1926) has turned that director into one of the most over-rated showmen in film history. Based on a story by the astronomer Camille Flammarion, this film tells of a comet that is about to collide with the Earth causing the end of the world, something Mary Pickford had effectively played for laughs in *Waking up the Town* (1925). The theme was used often, and usually better, by such directors as Rudolf Mate (**When Worlds Collide**, 1951) and Margheriti who made the masterpiece of this sub-genre, **Il Pianeta degli Uomini Spenti** (1961). In Gance's film, the Novalic brothers, one a religious maniac, Jean (Gance cast himself in this role of the martyred, misunderstood, Christ-like genius), the other a scientist, Martial (Francen), decide to save the world's moral fibre. Jean preaches the New Order – in decidedly fascist terms ('Humanity must cast aside those who are not born for victory. Only the strong shall remain.'). But as the end draws near, orgies and natural catastrophes proliferate.

Mercifully, a lot of Jean's role has been cut away by the producers who sacked Gance and issued their own version, edited without his blessing. The orgies were filmed with a flair for the erotic, a trait Gance shared with Cecil B. DeMille. Unfortunately, the re-editing also destroyed Gance's skilfully rhythmic montage, achieved with the help of his modernist and later fascist soulmate, Walter Ruttman, author of *Berlin – Die Symphonie einer Grosstadt* (1927). Shot as a silent film, Gance nevertheless experimented with sound effects, assisted by the directors Jean Epstein and E.T. Greville. A sonorized version was later issued, put together by Eugene Deslaw. The best thing about the film, its art direction, was due to Lazare

Meerson. Except for Francen, the acting is leaden, often becoming laughably overblown. The result is a hollow film, too silly for its advocacy of totalitarianism to be taken seriously. It is kinder to remember Gance for his technological comedy, **La Folie du Dr Tube** (1915).

d/co-s Abel Gance *p* Ivanoff *co-s* André Lang *c* Jules Krueger, Roger Hubert, Forster *se* Nicolas Roudakoff *lp* Abel Gance, Victor Francen, Georges Colin, Colette Darfeuil, Sylvie Grenade, Samson Fainsilber, Jean d'Yd, Wanda Vangen, Jeanne Brindeau, Philippe Hersent

Just Imagine (FOX) b/w 113 min
Made before Science Fiction, in Hollywood at least, was considered a subject matter only fit for serials and mad-scientist movies, this is a bizarre futuristic musical. Its greatest achievement is undoubtedly the miniature set of New York in 1980 which, built for a reported cost of $250,000 is almost as imaginative and lavish as that of **Metropolis** (1926) and later re-appeared as stock footage in numerous films, notably **Buck Rogers** (1939). Equally significant, however, the film (one of the flood of musicals that issued forth in the early thirties after the advent of sound), like so much of Hollywood's Science Fiction of the thirties, was representative, not of the Science Fiction writing of the time, but of a much earlier conception of the genre. Accordingly, it mixed intriguing speculation about the future with a melodramatic storyline that was already dated in 1930.

Created by De Sylva, Brown and Henderson as a sequel to their very successful musical *Sunnyside Up* (1929), the storyline follows the exploits of Brendel, as the man struck by lightning in 1930, when he wakes up in the strange world of 1980. Stephen Goosson and Ralph Hammeras' settings include many items that would become staples of later Science Fiction movies – automatic doors, food substitute pills, television phones – as well as an odd Martian landscape that looks like the wheatfields of Kansas. Once, however, we've been introduced to this world, the story soon descends into melodrama. Brendel helps Garrick's J-21 (numbers have replaced names in the world of 1980) to prove to the marriage tribunal that he's worthy of the hand of O'Sullivan's LN-18. This he does by accompanying and rescuing J-21 and others in the course of a trip to Mars. The cast, mostly of unknowns, are proficient enough but Butler, who'd also directed *Sunnyside Up*, is unable to animate the material. The film's failure, together with that of the even more bizarre **It's Great to Be Alive** (1933) did much to turn the major Hollywood studios against Science Fiction, a trend that was reinforced when, in the wake of Flash Gordon *et al*, the genre became associated with serials and comic strips.

d David Butler *p/s* Ray Henderson, B.G. De Sylva, Lew Brown *c* Ernest Palmer *lp* El Brendel, Maureen O'Sullivan, John Garrick, Marjorie White, Frank Albertson, Hobart Bosworth

Right: *Abel Gance as the misunderstood Christ-like genius in* La Fin du Monde.

The Last Hour

(NETTLEFORD PRODUCTIONS; GB) b/w 77 min

Briskly directed by Forde, a one-time British silent screen comic, this highly improbable piece of nonsense concerns the nefarious activities of Rome's prince of a mid-European state who steals a death ray, intending to force down planes and steal their cargoes, rather in the manner of the villains of **Ghost Patrol** (1936). Cooper is the stalwart member of the British Secret Service who brings him to book and Vaughan the plucky heroine.

d Walter Forde p Archibald Nettleford s H. Fowler Mear
c Geoffrey Faithfull lp Stewart Rome, Richard Cooper, Kathleen Vaughan, Alexander Field, Wilfred Shine, Billy Shine, James Raglan, George Bealby, Fred Arlton

Voice from the Sky

(G.Y.P. PRODUCTIONS) b/w 10 chaps

The first independent sound serial made in Hollywood, *Voice from the Sky* was directed and produced by one-time silent serial star Wilson. Wales, then a star of independent series westerns (and after a name change to Taliaferro a character actor) is the hero on the trail of a crazed scientist threatening to destroy the world. The title comes from the transmitter the villain builds to project his voice into the air so that whole cities can learn of his threats at the same time. Delores is the heroine.

By all accounts, no prints of this crudely mounted serial, which only achieved a limited release, have survived.

d/p Ben Wilson lp Wally Wales, Jean Delores

A Connecticut Yankee (FOX) b/w 97(78) min

The first sound version of Mark Twain's novel, *A Connecticut Yankee in King Arthur's Court* (which had been filmed as a pure fantasy in 1921 as *A Connecticut Yankee at King Arthur's Court*), this features Rogers as the blacksmith who after a blow on the head travels back to medieval England and out-performs Merlin (seen here as a villain) with his Yankee ingenuity. Rogers' interpretation of his role as a wise-cracking sage, replete with numerous anti-Depression jokes, has dated badly as has Butler's stolid direction, but several of the sequences (Rogers lassoing the knights of the Round Table in the middle of a tournament) retain their humour to this day. In retrospect, the same cannot be said of Conselman and Davis' interpolations concerning the vigour and essential correctness of democracy.

Twain's novel was subsequently filmed as **A Connecticut Yankee in King Arthur's Court** (1949) and **The Spaceman and King Arthur** (1979).

d David Butler s Owen Davis, William Conselman
c Ernest Palmer lp Will Rogers, Maureen O'Sullivan, William Farnum, Frank Albertson, Myrna Loy, Brandon Hurst

Frankenstein (U) b/w 71 (67) min

'It is one of the strangest stories ever told. It deals with the two great mysteries of creation, life and death. I think it will thrill you. It may even shock you. It might even horrify you...'

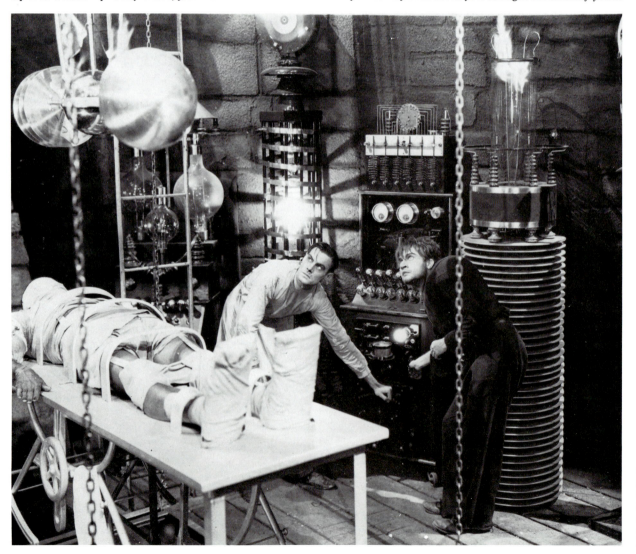

Colin Clive and Dwight Frye prepare to animate the monster amongst the elaborate electrical apparatus designed by Kenneth Strickfaden in Frankenstein.

loff, his height raised by wearing asphalt-spreader's boots and his head 'squared off' by putty and makeup, produced a lumbering figure struggling to achieve the humanity promised by his creator, Clive's Frankenstein. It is this mix of pathos and terror – as seen in the classic scene where the monster meets a little girl by the water's edge – that makes the film so enduring. Moreover, though Whale's conception of the film was clearly influenced by **Der Golem** (1920), which Whale screened before making Frankenstein, both in matters of content – the monster's encounter with the little girl being clearly 'borrowed' from the earlier film – and stylistically, the ironic, comic touches, the distinguishing feature of all his work, are clearly Whale's.

It is this sense of irony (in place of the gothic romanticism that Fisher would bring to the subject) that infects the whole film, making possible the bravura effects and preventing the stylized world and its inhabitants from collapsing into melodrama. At the same time, this irony limits the film's potential. In contrast to Rouben Mamoulian (**Doctor Jekyll and Mr Hyde,** 1932) and Karl Freund (**Mad Love**, 1935) who proceed by stripping the veneer of civilization from their central characters, Whale plays more of a game with both his characters and Mary Shelley's ideas (which he virtually abandons). The result is a more successful 'entertainment' (and one which could be repeated and repeated, as Universal did with their numerous sequels) but a film that is never quite as rich, resonant or ferocious as it might seem.

The plot features Clive as Baron Frankenstein who dreams of creating life and, with the assistance of Frye's hunchback dwarf, steals bodies from a cemetery in furtherance of his experiments. He finally succeeds (in probably the best sequence in the film with the help of Kenneth Strickfaden's marvellous electrical contraptions which would be aped in countless thirties serials) only for the monster, mistakenly given 'a criminal brain', to strangle the sadistic Frye. Like Mary Shelley's hero, Clive then turns his back on his creation only to have it escape and eventually return, pursued by the local villagers, and be burnt to death in Clive's laboratory after Clive has narrowly escaped death at the hands of the monster.

The film's importance rests less on the awkward shuffling of the characters through the story from effect to effect than on Whale's orchestration of those effects. Its success (made for only $250,000, it grossed over $25 million), following that of *Dracula* set in motion the horror cycle of the thirties and later, when it was sold to TV in 1957, a new wave of horror movies. A sequel followed in 1935, *The Bride of Frankenstein*.

d James Whale   *p* Carl Laemmle Jnr   *s* Garrett Fort, Robert Florey, Francis Edward Faragoh   *c* Arthur Edeson *se* John P. Fulton, Kenneth Strickfaden   *lp* Boris Karloff, Colin Clive, Mae Clarke, Lionel Belmore, Dwight Frye, John Boles, Edward Van Sloan

These words, spoken by Sloan in the character of the tutor to Clive's Frankenstein, form the prologue to Whale's classic version of Mary Shelley's novel. The novel had been filmed before (most notably in 1910 as **Frankenstein** and in 1915 as **Life Without Soul**) and would later be the source of countless (and all too often witless) films. None, however, with the sole exception of Terence Fisher's quartet of films for Hammer that began with **The Curse of Frankenstein** (1957) and ended with **Frankenstein Must Be Destroyed** (1969) have either the power or poetry of Whale's film.

Made in the wake of the enormously successful *Dracula* (1931), Universal initially cast Bela Lugosi (the star of *Dracula*) in the role of the monster. Promotional posters with Lugosi's name were distributed and the first adaptation of Peggy Webling's play, by John Balderston, with a much more romantic conception of the monster, was clearly written with Lugosi in mind. But after test footage of Lugosi was shot this romantic view of the monster (one truer to Mary Shelley's novel) was rejected in favour of a more threatening and macabre monster. Along with Lugosi, the film's original director, Robert Florey, dropped out to be replaced by Whale whose strong sense of the macabre and ability to create a stylized nightmare world (the result of 'a baroque form of expressionism' as one critic put it) was central to the film's success.

An Englishman, Whale was called to Hollywood to make *Journey's End* (1930) which he'd directed on the London stage. However, unlike the flood of stage directors who were imported by Hollywood's moguls in the wake of the coming of sound, Whale was no mere specialist in the problems of diction and matters of enunciation. Although his concept of the cinema was essentially theatrical, in contrast to the 'invisible' style of classic American directors like John Ford or Howard Hawks, Whale put that theatricality to work in the service of the camera. The result, in *Frankenstein* and even more so in **The Bride of Frankenstein** (1935), is films that are unique in the American cinema for their peculiar, almost European, blend of cinematic and theatrical virtues, seen in the lighting effects, tableaux and characterization.

Whale's other major contribution to the film lay in the selection of Karloff (whose career was henceforth stunted by his association with horror films) to play the monster. Together with Whale and makeup artist Jack B. Pierce (who worked on all the Universal Frankenstein films, except the last, **Abbott and Costello Meet Frankenstein**, 1948), Kar-

1932

Chandu the Magician   (FOX)   b/w   75 min
This was badly received at the time of its original release because the acting styles of Lowe in the title role and Lugosi as the arch-villain Roxnor were so different – Lowe under-acted while Lugosi gave one of his celebrated melodramatic performances, which led one critic to comment that they seemed to be in different films. In retrospect, the mix of magic and Lugosi's scientific gadgetry works well, even if the cliff-hanging action would have been better placed in a serial setting, which was exactly what happened when Lugosi took over the title role for *The Return of Chandu* (1934). Connors and Klein's script has Chandu (a yoga master as well as magician) given the task of ridding the world of Lugosi, who plans to make himself ruler of the Earth with the death ray he steals from Lowe's inventor brother-in-law, Walthall.

The careers of co-directors Menzies and Varnel subsequent-ly took radically different directions. Menzies became an

important art designer (on films like *Gone With the Wind*, 1939) and directed one of the most significant Science Fiction films of the thirties, **Things to Come** (1936), and the interesting **Invaders from Mars** (1953), while Varnel, after a brief career in Hollywood, went to Britain where he directed some of the best British comedies of the thirties and forties.

d Marcel Varnel, William Cameron Menzies *s* Barry Connors, Philip Klein *c* James Wong Howe *lp* Edmund Lowe, Bela Lugosi, Irene Ware, Henry B. Walthall, Herbert Mundin, Weldon Heyburn

Doctor Jekyll and Mr Hyde

(PAR) b/w 98 (90, 81) min

Made before the Production Code (a self-regulatory censoring body administered by the infamous Will H. Hays) came into operation in 1934, this is the most explicit of the film adaptations of Robert Louis Stevenson's classic novel. In place of the straightlaced evasions that normally figure in Hollywood treatments of such subjects, Mamoulian, and his writers Hoffenstein and Heath, make it clear that Hyde is more than the evil twin of March's Dr Jekyll. Rather, Mamoulian uses the tradition of Victorian melodramatic fiction, in which sexual activity is evil and only 'allowable' when a gentlemen leaves his class and enters the backstreets of the lower orders of society, to expose the repressions such a society is based upon. Thus Hyde's activities are not seen as merely monstrous (and therefore titillating) but as the logical conclusions of the frustrations of Jekyll's natural desires, as seen in the early scene where his wish to marry as soon as possible is viewed as being indecent by his fiancée's father (Hobbes). In short the film is less about good and evil and more about nature and civilization.

Similarly, Hopkins' prostitute is more than a body that Hyde (a marvellous performance by March, much better than his simpering impersonation of the good doctor) disports himself with. She is the constant reminder to Jekyll that his fiancée (Hobart) is sexually unavailable to him, by virtue of Hobbes' constant refusal to let go of his daughter. Given this explicit structure, it is not surprising that in place of the essentially decorative style for which Mamoulian is known, the film has a ferocity and fatalism about it, as the criss-cross patterns of shadows inexorably imprison March, that is

compelling. In this Mamoulian was greatly aided by cinematographer Struss (who had earlier worked on the best of the silent versions, that starring John Barrymore in 1920).

The centre of most versions of Stevenson's novel is the transformation scene, the moment good becomes evil. This is handled proficiently enough here by Mamoulian, but it no longer has such a central position in the film: in its place Mamoulian audaciously starts the film with a justly celebrated subjective sequence, seen from March's point of view, in which we see, by inference, the different Jekylls in terms of the various responses to him, from his manservant, coachman, students, etc. Thus Mamoulian has no need of the *grand guignol* melodramatics of Victor Fleming's 1941 film. Of all the versions of the novel, this can best be described as being about Jekyll/Hyde rather than Dr Jekyll *and* Mr Hyde.

March won an Oscar for his performance in the title role. Sadly, though the film was made before the Production Code, on its re-issue it was edited down. The most widely available print now, the 90-minute version, is such an edited version.

d/p Rouben Mamoulian *s* Samuel Hoffenstein, Percy Heath *c* Karl Struss *lp* Frederic March, Miriam Hopkins, Rose Hobart, Holmes Herbert, Edgar Norton, Halliwell Hobbes, Arnold Lucy

F.P.1 Antwortet Nicht *aka* Secrets of F.P.1 *aka* F.P.1 Doesn't Answer (UFA; G) b/w 115 (90) min

Reisch's screenplay is based on a novel by Robert Siodmak's brother Curt, a successful writer and scenarist also responsible for the original story of the classic *Menschen Am Sonntag* (1929) and the novels on which **Donovan's Brain** (1953) and **The Lady and the Monster** (1944) were based. F.P.1 is a giant platform (*Flugzeug Platform 1*) functioning as a mid-Atlantic airfield to allow planes to refuel on their regular Europe-American flights and the film is a flying ace's adventure story about the cut-throat competition in the airline business, especially on its most lucrative route. The idea was based on the proposals of the German engineer, A.B. Henninger, whose plans were considered at the time both in the USA and in Germany. At vast expense, a platform designed by Erich Kettlehut was constructed especially for the film on the island of Oie. It provided both the excuse for, and the highlight of, the film. Albers, a talented actor who was never allowed to transcend his image of the bland Aryan, is the flying ace, and Schmitz, fresh from her role in Dreyer's *Vampyr* (1932), is as inexpressive as ever. Lorre is excellent as the tragi-comic figure of a photographer

Left: *Frederic March finally, not to say literally, cornered in the definitive version of* Doctor Jekyll and Mr Hyde.

Conrad Veidt as the flying ace in the English version of F.P.1 Antwortet Nicht. *In the thirties big-budget productions were often made in different languages with different casts for different markets. There was also a French version of* F.P.1.

Charles Laughton as the demented Doctor Moreau and Kathleen Burke as his panther-woman creation in the superior Island of Lost Souls.

caught up in the flying adventures. Although a German film through and through, the English version with Veidt in the starring role and Esmond as the heroine provided at least a more interesting cast. The same German team of film-makers consisting of Hartl, Baecker, Rittau and Albers went on to produce the more impressive **Gold** (1934).

d Karl Hartl *p* Erich Pommer *s* Walter Reisch *c* Guenther Rittau, Otto Baecke *se* Konstantin Tschetwerikow *lp* Hans Albers, Paul Hartmann, Peter Lorre, Sybille Schmitz, Georg August Koch, Philipp Manning, Hermann Speelmans, Georg John, Rudolf Platte, Paul Westermeier, Arthur Pelsen
English version: co-s Robert Stevenson, Peter MacFarlane *lp* Conrad Veidt, Jill Esmond, Leslie Fenton, George Merritt, Donald Calthrop, Nicholas Nannen
French version: lp Charles Boyer, Daniela Parola, Jean Murat, Pierre Brasseur, Marcel Vallée

Die Herrin von Atlantis *aka* L'Atlantide *aka* Lost Atlantis *aka* The Mistress of Atlantis

(NERO FILM; G) b/w 87 min
The myth of the 'lost continent' destroyed at the height of its cultural life has led a tenacious life in literature and generated a respectable quantity of film scripts. There appear to be two basic trends. One tendency sublimates the Amazonian myth, as Rider Haggard did with his heroine Ayesha in *She*, published in 1887. The other ridicules the myth, as Pierre Benoît did with his Antinea, the female Bluebeard with her collection of mummified lovers, in *L'Atlantide*, published in 1919. Both tendencies have been merged, turned inside out, and have evoked lost continents on top of mountains, at the bottom of the sea or even at the centre of the Earth. Méliès' *La Dame du Feu* (1899) was probably the first film version in the Haggard tradition. Later versions of *She* (1916, 1917, 1926, 1935 and others) added little more than better special effects and, ultimately, more nudity (*She*, 1964 and *Slave Girls*, 1966). The Benoît tendency hasn't fared much better, starting with Feyder's *L'Atlantide* (1921) and Pabst's film, both set in the Sahara and with Angelo repeating his role in both films.

The story is told in flashback by de Saint-Avril (played by Klingenberg, Blanchar and McLaughlin respectively, in the German, French and English versions which were made simultaneously), the man who killed Morhange on Antinea's order. Helm plays Antinea, the cruel queen with her hall of 52 mummified lovers. Diessl, Angelo and Stuart are the intrepid Captain Morhange who tangles with Helm. The film seems

Right: *Brigitte Helm as the cruel Queen Antinea in* Die Herrin von Atlantis. *The marvellous sets were the work of Erno Metzner, who also designed* Westfront 1918 *(1930) and* Kameradschaft *(1931) for Pabst.*

much longer than it is, and in spite of the impressive list of talents that collaborated on it, including Erno Metzner as designer, it marks the beginning of Pabst's decline after a nearly unbroken string of classic films since 1925, from *Die Freudlose Gasse* to *Die Dreigroschenoper* and *Kameradschaft* (both 1931). The Danish *Atlantis* of 1913, directed by August Blom and not by Ole Olsen as is often claimed, is a straightforward melodrama that has nothing to do with Benoît's novel, which wasn't published until 1919. However, it is often forgotten that the Japanese also indulged in versions of the Atlantis story as in Honda's **Kaitei Gunkan** (1964).

d Georg Wilhelm Pabst *p* Seymour Nebenzahl *s* Ladislaus Vajda, Hermann Oberlaender *c* Eugen Schuefftan (Schuftan), Joseph Barth, Ernst Koerner *lp* Brigitte Helm, Gustav Diessl, Florelle Tela-Tchai, Odette Florelle, Vladimir Sokoloff, Heinz Klingenberg, Georges Tourreil, Mathias Wiemann
French version: s Alexandre Arnoux, Jacques Duval *lp* Brigitte Helm, Jean Angelo, Pierre Blanchar, Odette Florelle, Florelle Tela-Tchai, Vladimir Sokoloff, Georges Tourreil, Mathias Wiemann
English version: lp Brigitte Helm, John Stuart, Gibb McLaughlin, Gustav Diessl, Odette Florelle, Vladimir Sokoloff, Georges Tourreil, Mathias Wiemann

Island of Lost Souls   (PAR) b/w 72 min

A superior adaptation of H.G. Wells' novel of the same title. The script was co-authored by Wylie (his first), a Science Fiction writer whose seminal novel, *When Worlds Collide* (1932) was impressively filmed in 1951.

Laughton, who gives a magnificently chilling performance, is Moreau, a cool, rather than mad, scientist who is attempting to play God and speed up evolution by changing animals into humans. Arlen is the shipwrecked adventurer whom Laughton tries to mate with his panther-woman creation (Burke) and Hyams Arlen's fiancée who comes to his rescue. The dénouement has Laughton's ape-men rebel against him after they've tasted blood and take him to the 'house of pain' to conduct horrific surgery on him, just as he had on them, until the island is engulfed in fire.

The superb cinematography of Struss (who had shared the first Academy Award for photography with Charles Rosher for *Sunrise*, 1927) benefitted considerably from Kenton's persuading Paramount to shoot the film on location. The film was banned in several countries, including Britain for some time, and attacked by Wells for changing the central character from a kindly man to a sadistic monster.

A lurid remake followed in 1977, **The Island of Dr Moreau**.

d Erle C. Kenton   *s* Waldemar Young, Philip Wylie
c Karl Struss   *se* Gordon Jennings   *lp* Charles Laughton, Richard Arlen, Leila Hyams, Bela Lugosi, Kathleen Burke, Arthur Hohl

The Mask of Fu Manchu
(COSMOPOLITAN/MGM)   b/w   68 min
Fresh from his triumph as the monster in James Whale's **Frankenstein** (1931), Karloff was loaned by Universal to MGM for this, the definitive, Fu Manchu film. Christopher Lee's interpretation of the character in the irregular series of the sixties was more flamboyant but Karloff's is the more malevolent. Here he races Stone's Nayland Smith to the tomb of Ghengis Kahn to secure the scimitar and golden mask of the fabled warrior, possession of which will allow him to lead all Asia in an uprising against the whiteman. The script catches the imperial, racist, xenophobic fantasy of the Sax Rohmer novels perfectly and the direction by Vidor and Brabin (who replaced Vidor a few weeks into the shooting) is fast paced enough to paper over the patent silliness of the storyline. Most impressive is the laboratory in which Karloff and his daughtery Loy (whose performance was the model for that of Priscilla Lawson as Aura in **Flash Gordon**, 1936) ply the death ray that is eventually used against them. Morley is the much-threatened heroine and Starrett (who later achieved lasting fame as the Durango Kid in series westerns) her fiancé who suffers the sadistic admirations of Loy. All in all an engaging piece of claptrap.

d Charles Brabin, Charles Vidor   *p* Irving Thalberg   *s* Irene Kuhn, Edgar Allan Woolf, John Willard   *c* Tony Gaudio
se Kenneth Strickfaden   *lp* Boris Karloff, Lewis Stone, Myrna Loy, Karen Morley, Charles Starrett, Jean Hersholt

Six Hours to Live   (FOX)   b/w   78 min
A peculiar melodrama in which Baxter, a diplomat from Sylvaria attending an international trade conference at which he is assassinated for his views, is restored to life by Marion's eccentric scientist, but only for six hours. In his newly allotted lifespan, Baxter both saves Sylvaria from an iniquitous trade treaty its enemies have planned for it and redirects the affections of Jordan towards the stalwart Boles. Dieterle directs this farrago of nonsense with style, but the leaden melodramatics of the film though fully representative of their time, have lost much of their original charm.

d William Dieterle   *s* Bradley King   *c* John Seitz
lp Warner Baxter, Irene Ware, George Marion, John Boles, Edwin Maxwell, Miriam Jordan

Unheimliche Geschichten *aka* Tales of the Uncanny
(ROTO FILM; G)   b/w   89 min
Finished late in 1931, this is not a remake of Oswald's 1919 film of the same title. There is no framing narrative and Stevenson's *Suicide Club* has now been merged into a single story with Poe's *The System of Dr Tarr and Professor Feather*, producing a horror comedy revisiting many of the classic themes of the genre: Poe's black cat, Leni's *Waxworks* (1924), mad scientists etc, all wrapped up in a highly entertaining package. Leni's film, in particular, receives a merciless sending-up, possibly in retaliation for Leni's borrowing in 1924 of the framing gimmick Oswald had used in his original **Unheimliche Geschichten** (1919) (which Oswald himself had borrowed from Offenbach, whose **Hoffmanns Erzaehlungen** he had filmed in 1915).

The story of this film has Wegener, the original **Golem** (1914 and 1920) as well as **Alraune**'s 'father' (1928) as another mad scientist. He kills his wife and gets locked up in an asylum which he takes over and transforms into the premises of his suicide club. At last Wegener found a suitable vehicle in this, his first talkie, to send up himself and the whole 'expressionist' genre. It is worth noting that the idea of a mad genius taking over the asylum in which he is incarcerated was used again the following year in Lang's **Das Testament des Dr Mabuse** (1933). Indeed, considering the way **Dr Mabuse, der Spieler** (1922) had ended, it would have been difficult for Lang to start from any other premise.

d Richard Oswald   *p* Gabriel Pascal   *s* Heinz Goldberg, Eugen Szatmari   *c* Heinrich Gaertner   *lp* Paul Wegener, Bert Reisfeld, Harald Paulsen, Roma Bahm, Mary Parker, Paul Henkels, Eugen Kloepfer, John Gottowt, Blandine Ebinger, Maria Koppenhoefer

Eugen Kloepfer (left), Paul Wegener (centre) and Maria Koppenhoefer in Richard Oswald's comic parody of expressionism, Unheimliche Geschichten.

Left: Boris Karloff in the title role of The Mask of Fu Manchu.

Right: *The spectacular destruction of New York in* Deluge.

Deluge (RKO) b/w 70 min

This ambitious film imagines the destruction of New York by a combination of an earthquake and a tidal wave, following an eclipse of the sun. However, once the catastrophe is over, Goodrich and Duff's screenplay settles down into an easy soap opera with survivor Blackmer taking on Kohler's dyed-in-the-wool villain while (believing his wife to be dead) romancing Shannon, only to discover that his wife (Wilson) is alive. Whereupon Shannon does the proper thing and dives off into the sunset.

The spectacular special effects of the destruction of New York were bought by Republic and used by the studio in countless of its serials and series films.

d Felix E. Feist *p* Samuel Bischoff *s* John Goodrich, Warren B. Duff *c* Norbert Brodine *se* Ned Mann, William B. Williams *lp* Peggy Shannon, Sidney Blackmer, Lois Wilson, Matt Moore, Fred Kohler, Ralf Harolde

The Invisible Man (U) b/w 71 (56) min

This is co-scriped by Sheriff, the author of *Journey's End* which Whale directed with great success on the London stage. He was then called to Hollywood (along with the play's star, Colin Clive who played the Baron in the director's classic version of **Frankenstein,** 1931) to bring his stage success to the screen in 1930. In the course of his short career – he retired in his early forties to concentrate on painting – Whale was often associated with 'literary' films, but his reputation rests on his three forays into the field of Science Fiction and horror, *Frankenstein*, **The Bride of Frankenstein** (1935) and the witty black comedy, *The Invisible Man.*

Based on H.G.Wells' novel of the same title, the film features the expressive voice of Rains as the scientist driven mad by the side-effects of the invisibility serum he invents and imbibes. He becomes a scourge of the countryside, a malevolent Raffles figure, playing games with the police as he indulges in bank robbery for the sheer fun of it. Fulton's invisibility effects (which were utilized by Universal in various sequels and other films throughout the thirties and forties) have, deservedly, been widely praised. The scenes where Rains removes his glasses and bandages to reveal nothing at all (accomplished by dressing a stuntman in black velvet underneath the bandages and shooting the disrobing against a black velvet background) and Rains' final loss of invisibility as he dies (accomplished through elaborate stop

Claude Rains, the instruments of science and as fine a collection of English stereotypes as ever was found in Hollywood in James Whale's black comedy, The Invisible Man.

motion) still create a primitive sense of amazement and wonder that take us back to the origins of the cinema.

If the film is lightweight and Sheriff and Wylie's screenplay slow-moving, Whale's impish sense of black comedy remains a delight. The film made a star of Rains, just as *Frankenstein* had made one of Boris Karloff who turned down the role Rains subsequently took over.

A routine sequel followed in 1940, **The Invisible Man Returns** which in turn spawned a short-lived Invisible series that climaxed, like Universal's Frankenstein and Dracula series, in a confrontation between the Invisible Man and Abbott and Costello, **Abbott and Costello Meet the Invisible Man** (1951).

d James Whale *p* Carl Laemmle Jnr *s* R.C. Sheriff, Philip Wylie *c* Art Edeson, John Mescall *se* John P. Fulton *lp* Claude Rains, Gloria Stewart, Henry Travers, William Harrigan, Una O'Connor, Holmes Herbert, John Carradine, Walter Brennan

It's Great to Be Alive (FOX) b/w 69 min

This loose remake of **The Last Man on Earth** (1924), a surreal conflation of the musical and the Science Fiction genres, is undoubtedly one of the strangest Science Fiction movies ever made. A commercial disaster at the time, primarily because of its cast of relatively unknowns, in retrospect it is a compelling film. Directed by Werker who in the fifties made a series of hard-edged westerns beginning with *The Last Posse* (1953), it stars Roulien as a dapper man-about-town who after a disagreement with his fiancée (Stuart) sets out to attempt to fly the Pacific. He crash-lands on a deserted island and thereby survives when the entire male population is killed off by the strange disease 'masculitis'. Five years later, with the world populated entirely by female women and masculine (but not lesbian, though the implication is there) women carrying on business as usual, just after Oliver's attempts to create a synthetic man fail, Roulien is spotted. But before he can be brought back, 'for the good of womankind', he is kidnapped by Burgess' gangster who plans to auction him off to the wealthy dowagers of New York! Rescued by the police it is planned to distribute his favours around the world but he refuses, wanting only Stuart. Thus the lovers are re-united, but unlike the 1924 film which ends with them producing a pair of bouncing male twins immune from masculitis, there is no clear-cut happy ending.

The absurd storyline, fascinating in its own right, is matched by a directorial style which grows wilder as the plot develops from the ordinary to the extraordinary. Similarly, the performances, in particular that of the wiry (rather than muscular) Roulien as the saviour of womankind and Oliver as the doughty mistress of state, have a sprightliness about them that remains appealing. The net result is, even more than **Just Imagine** (1930), one of the most intriguing excesses in the history of Science Fiction film.

Roulien was a star in the Spanish cinema and accordingly a Spanish language version, *El Ultimo Varon sobre la Tierra*, was made simultaneously under the direction of James Tinling with Rositer Moreno, Mimi Aguglia, Romneldo Tirado and Carmen Rodriguez in the featured roles.

d Alfred Werker *s* Paul Perez, Arthur Kober *c* Robert Planck *lp* Raul Roulien, Gloria Stuart, Edna May Oliver, Herbert Mundin, Edward Van Sloan, Robert Greig, Emma Dunn, Amy Burgess

Men Must Fight (MGM) b/w 72 min
Like Maurice Elvey's earlier **High Treason** (1929), *Men Must Fight* is set in 1940 and climaxes in an air-raid on New York, in which the Empire State building is destroyed, as part of World War II. Clearly made in reaction to the events in Europe (though the enemy is described as a 'Confederation of Eurasian States') it's noticeable how sympathethic the film is to pacifism, in contrast to later British and American films. Wynyard, recently arrived in Hollywood from Britain, is the mother who leads a peace crusade, Holmes the son she can't convince not to fight and Selwyn (the director's wife who often starred in his films) Holmes' fiancée. A commercial and critical failure, both because of its theme and the plodding, earnest direction, the film is only memorable for the half accurate predictions of writer C. Gardner Sullivan.

d/p Edgar Selwyn *s* C. Gardner Sullivan *c* George Folsey *lp* Diana Wynyard, Lewis Stone, Phillips Holmes, May Robson, Ruth Selwyn, Hedda Hopper, Robert Young

Das Testament des Dr Mabuse *aka* The Testament of Dr Mabuse *aka* The Last Will of Dr Mabuse
(NERO FILM/CONSTANTIN/DEUTSCHE UNIVERSAL; G)
b/w 122 (95) min
The first sequel to Lang's own massively successful **Dr Mabuse, der Spieler** (1922). This has Mabuse, again played by Klein-Rogge (also the mad scientist in **Metropolis**, 1926 and the evil one in **Spione**, 1928) controlling an underworld criminal organization from his cell in the asylum where he was locked up at the end of the 1922 film. Before dying, he transfers his personality to Baum (Beregi), the director of the asylum, who continues as the reincarnation of Mabuse. Tracked down by the redoubtable Inspector Lohmann

(Wernicke), who had proved his ingenuity and tenacity in Lang's **M** (1931), Baum eventually flees into Mabuse's old cell where he too goes mad. Banned by Goebbels, although written by Lang's Nazi wife von Harbou, the film didn't achieve its impact until it was screened in a French version in New York in 1943. For this occasion, Lang issued a statement declaring that the film had been made to denounce Hitlerism: 'Slogans and doctrines of the Third Reich have been put into the mouths of criminals in the film.' Lang was nevertheless invited by Goebbels to become the Nazis' prestige director, whereupon Lang packed his bags and left Germany.

Das Testament is notable primarily for its breathtakingly suspenseful *mise en scene*, culminating in the night ride through the forest and along narrow roads at the end of the film, with the car's headlights echoing the torch-beam pursuit of Maria in *Metropolis*. However, this Mabuse film is dominated by the cop, Wernicke, an earthy but shrewd figure as obsessive as the evil genius he pursues.

When the film was banned, footage was smuggled out and edited in France by Lothar Wolff into a somewhat shorter German version running 95 minutes. It was remade, rather loosely, by Klinger in 1962.

d/p Fritz Lang *s* Thea von Harbou *c* Fritz Arno Wagner, Karl Vash *lp* Rudolf Klein-Rogge, Oskar Beregi, Otto Wernicke, Karl Meixner, Theodor Loos, Klaus Pohl, Wera Liessem, Gustav Diessl, Camilla Spira, Theo Lingen
French version: adapted by A. René-Sti *lp* Jim Gerald, Thomy Bourdelle, Maurice Maillot, Raymond Cordy, Monique Rolland, René Ferte, Daniel Mendaille, Georges Tourreil, Lily Rezillot, Ginette Gaubert

Der Tunnel *aka* The Tunnel
(VANDOR FILM/BAVARIA FILM; G) b/w 80 (73) min
Together with **Gold** (1934) and **F.P.1 Antwortet Nicht** (1932), *Der Tunnel* constitutes the trio of major German Science Fiction films in the sound period up to Lang's **Die Tausend Augen des Dr Mabuse** (1960). It was made by Bernhardt simultaneously in German and French versions before he fled the country and, after a brief career in France and in the UK, as Curtis Bernhardt in Hollywood, wrote some excellent *film noir* thrillers (*Conflict*, 1945, and *Possessed*, 1947). The story, based on a novel by Bernhard Kellermann published in 1913, has the engineer MacAllen (Hartmann/Gabin) construct a tunnel connecting Europe with the USA, a project backed by American financiers. His antagonist is the

Left: Raul Roulien nervously contemplates his fate in the bizarre It's Great to Be Alive.

Oskar Beregi and Rudolf Klein-Rogge in Fritz Lang's delirious Das Testament des Dr Mabuse.

Harry Piel preparing to become invisible in the hilarious Ein Unsichtbarer Geht Durch die Stadt.

speculator Woolf (Gruendgens in both versions) who causes an explosion followed by spectacular flood scenes and the death of hundreds of workers. In the end, the project is completed and Woolf commits suicide.

The film has a decidedly nationalistic and militaristic edge to it, preaching total dedication to the mammoth task for which lives, personal relations, family and happiness deserve to be sacrificed as the necessary price to be paid – and worth paying – for the realization of a grandiose national project. Schreck, best known for his incarnation of *Nosferatu* (1922) plays one of the money men. Two years later, possibly for the same nationalistic, militaristic and financial reasons (the original film had been a success), it was remade by Maurice Elvey in Britain (**The Tunnel**, 1935). Both the German version and the French one, which ran only 73 minutes, were banned by the Allies.

d/co-s Kurt (Curtis) Bernhardt *p* Ernst Garden
co-s Reinhart Steinbicker *c* Carl Hoffman *lp* Paul Hartmann, Olly von Flint, Gustaf Gruendgens, Attila Hoerbiger, Elga Brink, Max Weydner, Otto Wernicke, Will Dohm, Ferdinand Marian, Max Schreck
French version: co-s Alexandre Arnoux *lp* Jean Gabin, Madeleine Renaud, Raymonde Allain, Gustaf Gruendgens, André Nox, Edmond Van Daele, Pierre Nay, Robert Le Vigan, André Bertic, Alexandre Arnoux

Ein Unsichtbarer Geht Durch die Stadt *aka* Mein Ist die Welt *aka* An Invisible Man Goes Through the City *aka* The World Is Mine *aka* Master of the World

(ARIEL FILM; G) b/w 102 min
Whereas the bulk of German Science Fiction is on the edge of gothic-horror fantasy (**Alraune, Hoffmanns Erzaehlungen,** the Mabuse films), it would appear that only Lang (**Metropolis**, 1926; **Die Frau im Mond**, 1929) and Piel have plugged into the mainstream themes of the genre. Piel, a veteran of adventure serials, had made a Science Fiction comedy as early as 1915 (**Die Grosse Wette**) and returned to the genre in the early thirties. This film has Piel discover a weird contraption on the backseat of his cab. When he puts on the helmet-like thing and the battery backpack, he discovers that he becomes invisible. This advantage allows him to make a fortune at the races and to obtain a gold digging actress girlfriend (Arna). His best friend (Odemar) steals the contraption and robs a bank. After a chase involving an airship and various other adventure serial situations, Piel wakes up to discover the whole thing was a dream. The fast-paced action at the end

Right: The atomic reactor that transforms lead into gold in Gold.

doesn't make up for the triteness of the moral fable of riches not bringing happiness – and that, consequently, cab drivers shouldn't have aspirations above their social position.

Piel went on to make another such comedy the following year, **Die Welt Ohne Maske** (1934), also written by Rameau, and **Der Herr der Welt** (1934).

d Harry Piel *p* Alfred Greven *s* Hans Rameau *c* Ewald Daub *lp* Harry Piel, Lissy Arna, Fritz Odemar, Annemarie Soerensen, Olga Limburg, Gerhard Dammann, Eugen Rex, Ernst Behmer, Hans Ritter, Gina Falckenberg

Gold *aka* **L'Or** (UFA; G) b/w 120 min
The team that had been responsible for **F.P.1 Antwortet Nicht** (1932) also made *Gold*, a much better although rarely seen film. It updates the alchemist's dream of changing lead into gold by means of a sort of atomic reactor devised by Achenbach (Kayssler) and his collaborator Holk (Albers). The Scottish lead king, Wills (Bohnen) makes the German inventors an offer they can't refuse but after demonstrating that their invention works, they blow up their laboratory, abandoning the search for gold as unworthy of their talents. Apparently, when the Allies saw the film after World War II, they were sufficiently impressed by the sophisticated design of the reactor (by Otto Hunt) to have it examined by nuclear physicists in the USA in case it betrayed precocious knowledge of nuclear reactors the Germans weren't supposed to have. The photography was exceptionally evocative and the acting, for once in these German films, above par, especially that of Helm (the love interest) and Deyers, who had been the vamp in Lang's **Spione** (1928). The film's producer, Zeisler, was a good film-maker in his own right and later, in Hollywood, directed an atmospheric B picture re-working Lang's *The Woman in the Window* (1944) entitled *Fear* (1946).

The French version was made by the under-rated de Poligny, author of the extraordinary, deliriously romantic *La Fiancée des Ténèbres* (1944). In *L'Or*, Achenbach was called Lefevre (Gauthier) and the male lead, Holk, became Berthier (Blanchard). Wills was played by Karl and Helm, as usual, played in both versions.

d Karl Hartl *p* Alfred Zeisler *s* Rolf E. Vanloo
c Guenther Rittau, Otto Baecker, Werner Bohne *lp* Hans
Albers, Brigitte Helm, Friedrich Kayssler, Lien Deyers,
Michael Bohnen, Eberhard Leithoff, Rudolf Platte
French version: d Serge de Poligny *co-s* Jacques Thierry
lp Pierre Blanchard, Roger Karl, Brigitte Helm, Louis
Gauthier, Rosine Dereau, Line Noro, Jacques Dumnesil,
Marc Valbel, Henri Bosc, Robert Goupil

Der Herr der Welt *aka* **Master of the World** *aka*
Ruler of the World (ARIEL FILM; G) b/w 109 min
The fourth and last of Piel's Science Fiction movies (**Die
Grosse Wette**, 1915; **Ein Unsichtbarer Geht Durch die
Stadt**, 1933, and **Die Welt Ohne Maske**, 1934). The
semi-dramatic plot revolves around the creation of a robot
army of which a mad scientist is the sole master. The metal
contraptions are controlled by button-pushing workers who
are thus contributing to their own dehumanization and
redundancy. The crazy adventures of this latter-day Mabuse
also involve a death ray and assorted gadgets. Piel, who made
his reputation as a dare devil actor who never allowed himself
to be doubled in any scenes, did not act in this one. The bland
Schmitz, star of Dreyer's *Vampyr* and **F.P.1 Antwortet Nicht**
(both 1932) is as inexpressively photogenic as ever.

d Harry Piel *s* George Muehlen-Schulte *c* Ewald Daub
lp Sybille Schmitz, Siegfried Schuerenberg, Walter Franck,
Klaus Pohl, Aribert Waesher, Willi Schur, Otto Wernicke,
Walter Janssen, Karl Platen, Ernst Behmer

The Vanishing Shadow (U) b/w 12 chaps
In this engaging, if primitive, serial from Landers, Stevens is
the young hero intent on revenging his father who was
haunted to death by a smear campaign masterminded by
Miller and his political cronies. He's aided by Durkin's
scientist who provides him with a wide array of technological
gadgetry, including an invisibility vest and a destroying ray.
Ince is the charming heroine.

d Louis Friedlander (Lew Landers) *s* Het Manheim, Basil
Dickey, George Morgan *c* Richard Fryer *lp* Onslow
Stevens, Ada Ince, Walter Miller, James Durkin, Richard
Cramer, William Desmond

Die Welt Ohne Maske *aka* **The World Without a Mask**
(ARIEL FILM; G) b/w 109 min
After the Science Fiction comedy **Ein Unsichtbarer Geht
Durch die Stadt** (1933), Piel tried to repeat his success with
another comedy written by Rameau about two DIY enthusiasts
inventing a TV that can pick up images through walls. A
gadget that can look through walls gives rise to lots of gags
and chases as gangsters and other eager practitioners of

private enterprise try to get their hands on the invention.
Besides featuring Klein-Rogge, the star of most of Lang's
Science Fiction films (**Dr Mabuse, der Spieler,** 1922;
Metropolis, 1926 and **Spione,** 1928), the film also boasts the
presence of Tschechowa, the Reinhardt-trained German
movie vamp who became the darling of the Nazis.

d Harry Piel *s* Hans Rameau *c* Ewald Daub *lp* Harry
Piel, Kurt Vespermann, Annie Markart, Olga Tschechowa,
Rudolf Klein-Rogge, Hubert von Meyerinck, Philipp
Manning, Hermann Picha, Gerhard Dammann, Ernst
Behmer

Air Hawks (COL) b/w 69 (66) min
Just as variants of Frankenstein's monsters were used to inject
new twists into the cycle of gangster movies of the thirties in
films like **The Walking Dead** (1936), so this otherwise
routine outing in the concurrent cycle of airplane adventures
annexes the mad scientist and his death ray in an attempt to
give the film an extra gimmick. Bellamy is the small-time
operator trying to establish his own airline by securing a mail
contract whose chances look slim when a competitor turns a
death ray (which stops engines instantly) on his planes and
Kilian is the hard-bitten reporter who comes to his assistance.

d Albert Rogell *s* Griffin Jay, Grace Neville *c* Henry
Freulich *lp* Ralph Bellamy, Wiley Post, Tala Birell, Edward
Van Sloan, Douglas Dumbrille, Victor Kilian

The Big Broadcast of 1936 (PAR) b/w 105 (93) min
If in the thirties Science Fiction meant mostly gimmicks and
gadgetry, occasionally those gimmicks were put to hilarious
effect as in the amazing **It's Great to Be Alive** (1933) and this
farrago of appealing nonsense.

Oakie and Wadsworth jointly are 'The Singing Lochinvar'
(Oakie supplying the speaking voice, Wadsworth the singing
voice), the star of a near-bankrupt radio station. In the middle
of trying to raise money to purchase a revolutionary television
system, invented by Burns and Allen's uncle, which can
receive sight and sound from anywhere, broadcast or not,
they are kidnapped by millionaire countess Roberti who is in
love with their collective voice. In between their adventures,
courtesy of the invention, are a series of variety interludes
ranging from Bing Crosby to Amos 'n' Andy to the Vienna
Boys Choir to 25 performing elephants.

d Norman Taurog *p* Benjamin Glazer *s* Walter De Leon,
Francis Martin, Ralph Spence *c* Leo Tover *se* Farciot
Edouard, Gordon Jennings *lp* Jack Oakie, Henry
Wadsworth, George Burns, Gracie Allen, Lyda Roberti,
Wendy Barrie, Akim Tamiroff

Left: A scene from Die
Welt Ohne Maske, *one
of the four Science
Fiction films made by
Harry Piel, Germany's
Harold Lloyd.*

*Air Hawks. Frightened
scientist, death ray and
criminals, the
ingredients of so many
Science Fiction films of
the thirties.*

Elsa Lanchester looks aghast at Boris Karloff while Colin Clive (left) and Ernest Thesiger (right) look on apprehensively in The Bride of Frankenstein.

The Bride of Frankenstein (U) b/w 80 min

The sequel to Whale's **Frankenstein** (1931), *The Bride of Frankenstein* is even more impishly perverse than the earlier film. Where before Whale had used irony as a distancing effect and means of keeping at bay the gothic excesses of Mary Shelley's novel, excesses that Terence Fisher would excite in his Frankenstein films for Hammer commencing with **The Curse of Frankenstein** (1957), in *The Bride of Frankenstein* he indulges in a peculiar mix of morbidity and devastating black humour. Thus, for instance, the gown that Lanchester, in the title role, wears resembles both a burial shroud and a wedding dress, and the character of Thesiger's Dr Pretorious whose miniature *homunculi* include an amorous Henry VIII lookalike seem to come from a different film to the scene where Thesiger tells the monster confidentially, 'Gin is my only weakness', a line the actor also spoke in Whale's *The Old Dark House* (1932), and then offers Karloff a drop.

The movie has been widely praised as both Whale's best and the best of the thirties monster films. Certainly it is more stylishly mounted than the somewhat awkwardly constructed *Frankenstein* and the further sequels bear no comparison to it. However the cost of Whale's morbid playfulness is a further decrease in the primitive vigour of the material at his disposal. In short, what *Bride* represents is what can only be seen as the decisive step in the creation of the monster genre; as such, it marked a retreat from the ferocious, analytic quality of films like Karl Freund's **Mad Love** (1935) which represented a tradition that only re-surfaced in Roger Corman's cycle of films derived from the works of Edgar Allan Poe in the sixties.

On its own terms, however, the film was an undoubted success. Far more fluently organized than *Frankenstein*, the film follows the tribulations of Karloff's monster (who didn't die in the fire that ended *Frankenstein*, Mary Shelley – Lanchester again in another morbid touch – tells us in the film's prologue) until he meets Thesiger who promises to make him a mate. This Thesiger does with the reluctant help of Clive's Frankenstein, only for Lanchester to reject him, whereupon Karloff in his rage once more brings about a conflagration in which Lancaster, Thesiger and he die.

A further sequel, **Son of Frankenstein,** followed in 1939.

Right: Ferdinand Hart in the title role of Le Golem, *the most overtly erotic of the many versions of the legend.*

d James Whale *p* Carl Laemmle Jnr *s* John Balderston, William Hurlbut *c* John J. Mescall *se* John P. Fulton *lp* Boris Karloff, Colin Clive, Elsa Lanchester, Ernest Thesiger, Valerie Hobson, Dwight Frye

Gibel Sensaty *aka* Loss of Feeling

(MEZRAPBOM; USSR) b/w 85 min

Adapted from the novel *R.U.R.* (*Rossum's Universal Robots*, 1920) by the classic Czech writer Karel Capek, inventor of the term 'robot' (Czech for 'work'). The inventor Jim Riple manufactures robots to do all the work normally done by people. His creatures are extremely powerful and intelligent but they are devoid of feelings, which is a new twist to the Germanic version of artificial creatures lacking a 'soul' as in **Homunculus** (1916), **Metropolis** (1926) or **Alraune** (1928). A struggle ensues between the workers and the factory bosses over who is to control the uses and the direction of technological progress. Well made and humorous, this is an intelligent treatment of a story that had attracted the attention of French surrealists as early as 1924 when Artaud wanted to stage it. Little is known about Andreievsky except that he made the USSR's first colour-stereoscopic film, *Robinson Crusoe* (1946). Other Capek stories have been filmed in Eastern Europe, the most important being **Krakatit** (1948).

d Aleksander Andreievsky *s* G. Grebner *c* M. Magidson *lp* S. Vecheslov, V. Gardin, M. Volgina, A. Chekulaeva, V. Orlov, N. Ablov, N. Rybikov, P. Poltoratski

Le Golem *aka* The Golem, the Legend of Prague

(A-B BARRANDOV; FR, CZECH) b/w 100 (83) min

Whereas Wegener's original **Golem** films (1914 and 1920) had been based on the legend he had heard in Prague, Duvivier's version was based on Gustav Meyrink's novel, published in 1915. Rudolf II (Baur) wants to get rid of the constant threat posed by the Golem (Hart), now in the possession of Loew's successor, Rabbi Jakob (Dorat). Baur's mistress (Aussey), seeing her lover in the arms of two other ladies, allows the revived creature to destroy the palace and all its inhabitants. The plot also involves some Frenchmen at the court in various diverting scenes, putting the narrative structure under considerable stress. Shot in Prague with a mostly Czech crew, the film acquired a reputation for its overt eroticism in spite of the inappropriate vaudeville scenes introduced into this darkly romantic legend.

The only other French treatment of the story was made for TV by Jean Kerchbron (*Le Golem*, 1966), while the Czechs remade it as a comedy under the title **Cisaruv Pekar** (1951) and again as **Prazske Noci** (1968). The most recent version projects the story into the future: Szulkin's **Golem** (1979).

d/co-s Julien Duvivier *p* Jozef Stern *co-s* André-Paul Antoine *c* Jan Stallich, Vaclav Vich *lp* Harry Baur, Charles Dorat, Germaine Aussey, Ferdinand Hart, Jany Holt, Tania Doll, Roger Karl, Roger Duchesne, Marcel Dalio, Gaston Jacquet

Kosmitchesky Reis *aka* **The Space Ship** *aka* **The Cosmic Voyage** (MOSFILM; USSR) b/w 70 min
The first Science Fiction film in the USSR since **Aelita** (1924), this is a socialist-realist melodrama about a stubborn scientist who, in the face of official opposition, builds a spaceship and, together with his female assistant, flies to the Moon. The bureaucrats of the Moscow Institute for Interplanetary Travel are seen as hopelessly conformist and unsympathetic to the pioneering spirit of the heroic scientist, who is all smiles and white teeth but every bit as ambitiously individualist as his Hollywood counterparts. There are some impressive scenes against gigantic décor which reduces people to the size of ants. With rockets called 'Stalin' and 'Voroshilov' the political references are not exactly subtle. The Ukrainian director, Zhuravlev, was a minor figure in the Soviet cinema but Filimonov also wrote the interesting **Sieriebristaya Pyl** (1953).

d Vasili Zhuravlev   *s* A. Filimonov   *c* A. Galperin
lp Sergey Komarov, V. Kovrigin, Nicolai Feokistov, Vassili Gaponenko, K. Maskalenko

The Lost City (REGAL) b/w 12 chaps
Starring William 'Stage' Boyd, not to be confused with the William Boyd who assumed the mantle of Hopalong Cassidy, this is perhaps the most melodramatic serial ever. Boyd is the villainous Zolok, a mad scientist, who from his underground city in deepest Africa dreams of ruling the world. He announces his intentions by causing a worldwide series of electrical storms. Other technological marvels include a rejuvenation ray, a machine that makes giant zombies out of men and a death ray. Richmond is the engineer who tracks the sources of the electrical disturbances and finds Boyd's underground domain. But, if the film remains interesting for its technical inventiveness, its explicit racism – Boyd has a machine that turns blackmen into whitemen and reverses it as a punishment – is unpleasant.

d Henry Revier   *p* Sherman S. Krellberg   *s* Perley P. Sheehan, Eddie Graneman, Leon D'Usseau   *c* Roland Price, Eddie Linden   *lp* Kane Richmond, William 'Stage' Boyd, Claudia Dell, George 'Gabby' Hayes, William Bletcher

Mad Love *aka* **The Hands of Orlac**
(MGM) b/w 85 (67) min
This is indisputably the best version of Maurice Renard's oft-filmed novel, *Les Mains d'Orlac*. Shot through with Freudian imagery (ranging from the '*et fils*' crossed out on the sign above Orlac's father's jewellers' shop to the surrogate waxwork figure of Orlac's wife that Lorre serenades), like Rouben Mamoulian's **Doctor Jeckyll and Mr Hyde** (1932), the film's greatness rests on director Freund's refusal to treat the novel as merely a titillatory fantasy about a concert pianist (Clive) who is given the hands of a convicted knife-throwing murderer (Brophy). Accordingly, the centre of the film is not Clive's Orlac, as in **Orlacs Haende** (1925), but Lorre's Gogal, the man of science driven by his obsession to possess Clive's wife (Drake), seen first by us and Lorre, in the play within a play that opens the film, as the maiden branded on a medieval torture wheel, and later to become a waxwork image in Lorre's private museum. Moreover, Lorre is not a typical thirties mad scientist. The actual transplant (necessary because Clive's hands have been mangled in a railway crash) is shown as a triumph of medical technology and Lorre's assistants are professional men rather than the misshapen beings that cavort around Frankenstein. Lorre is a man deranged by his unrequited love, unrequited because he cannot articulate it in any but the most primitive fashion, for Drake who takes his revenge in the most sadistic means at his disposal. Thus having grafted a murderer's hands on the husband of the woman he lusts after and still finding her unresponsive, in a masterful scene, Lorre impersonates the

Above: *Peter Lorre as the doctor posing as his own victim to horrendous effect in the magisterial* Mad Love.

dead Brophy and summons Clive, now the chief suspect of the murder of his father with a knife, to a meeting. Revealing his metal gauntlets, Lorre (as Brophy) reveals the truth to Clive about the hands he now has the use of and, to prove he is the guillotined Brophy, shows the horrified Clive the steel brace that supports the head supposedly sewn back on by Lorre. As a piece of *grand guignol* the scene is chilling, especially as we don't know that the mysterious figure is Lorre until he returns home and removes the horrific disguise, almost having to tear himself free of the face-distorting mask. Thematically the sequence, which sees Lorre becoming a self-created image of another (rather like the waxwork of Drake he honours), is even more powerful. Like Frederic March's Jekyll/Hyde in Mamoulian's 1932 film, Lorre (who in his first American film gives one of the best performances of his career) is a man undone by his own desires, once the object of those desires has been 'stolen' from him by the cultured Clive who marries Drake.

The film is uneven in places (probably as a result of the different lighting styles of Toland and Lyons) and the pacing by Freund (a German cinematographer briefly turned director in Hollywood, here directing his last film before returning to cinematography) lacks the steady fatalism of Mamoulian's film. Similarly the end, Lorre knifed by Clive just as he is about to strangle Drake with her own hair, is pure melodrama, nonetheless, in its ferocious clarity the film remains one of the cinema's greatest celebrations and examinations of *amour fou*.

Right: One of the spectacular sets of The Tunnel, a British remake of Der Tunnel (1933).

d Karl Freund *p* John W. Considine Jnr *s* P.J. Wolfson, Guy Endore, John L. Balderston *c* Chester Lyons, Gregg Toland *lp* Peter Lorre, Frances Drake, Ted Healy, Colin Clive, Edgar Brophy, Henry Kolker, Sarah Haden

The Phantom Empire (MASCOT) b/w 12 chaps

Clearly based on James Churchward's series of 'factual' books about the lost continent of Lemuria, or Mu as he called it, that began with *The Lost Continent of Mu* (1926), this bizarre concoction of Science Fiction and the western gave birth to that strangest of creatures, the singing cowboy in all his glory. Ken Maynard had originally been slated for the lead, but after his conduct during the making of *Mystery Mountain* (1934) he lost the role to the young Autry.

Playing himself, as he henceforth would always do, Autry is the dude cowboy who runs a radio station from his ranch with himself as its singing star. A gang of crooks covet his radium mine and, while being pursued by Autry, they stumble upon the entrance to Murania, an underground civilization far in advance of ours but riven by similar tensions which are exacerbated by exposure to mankind. Both the crooks and Autry and his helpers are captured by the Muranians and their slave robots and only escape when conflict breaks out between the Muranians themselves, after Oakman's High Chancellor seeks Christie's throne for himself, which leads to the destruction of Murania.

Reviews attacked the mixing of Science Fiction and the western (which was soon repeated in **Ghost Patrol,** 1936), Autry's wooden performance and a dramatic structure which had Autry forever rushing back to his radio ranch to sing his songs, but the public, and especially the rural public, lapped it up.

The serial, which was far more influential in the development of the western than of Science Fiction, was edited down and re-issued as a feature in 1940 under the title of *Men With Steel Faces.*

Gene Autry amongst the oddities of the underground world of Murania in the serial The Phantom Empire.

d Otto Brower, B. Reeves Eason *p* Nat Levine *s* John Rathmell, Armand Schaefer *c* Ernest Miller, William Nobles *lp* Gene Autry, Wheeler Oakman, Frankie Darro, Betsy King Ross, Warner Richmond, Smiley Burnette, Dorothy Christie

The Tunnel *aka* Transatlantic Tunnel
(GAUMONT; GB) b/w 94 min

In this remake of Curtis Bernhardt's German film, **Der Tunnel** (1933), which was banned in Britain and America on the outbreak of war, Elvey interestingly and significantly changes the emphasis of the original film. Bernhardt's film centres on the dedication of all involved and the sacrifices necessary to achieve a task that is seen as both in the national interest and glorifying the nation. Elvey's film, for all its patriotic fervour – the tunnel is changed from linking Europe and America to linking Britain with America and Huston's President and Arliss' Prime Minister are brought on at the tunnel's completion to set their seal of approval on it – concentrates on the problems of engineer Dix and his family as the tunnel progresses. Accordingly, despite its spectacular modernist décor and superb special effects (such as a 50-foot 'radium drill' boring through the ocean bed), most of which were achieved through model work, and numerous conversations about the tunnel as an instrument of world peace, the grandeur of the project (or even the broad humour of Harry Harrison's later novel, *Transatlantic Tunnel, Hurrah!*, which sets the construction of such a tunnel in Victorian times) is lost. In its place is an elaborate romantic drama.

Elvey was a prolific director of routine British films, with the possible exception of **High Treason** (1929) which oddly enough has a plot based on the existence of a very similar tunnel to the one that this film celebrates the construction of.

d Maurice Elvey *p* Micheal Balcon *s* L.Du Garde Peach, Clemence Dane *c* G. Krampf *se* J. Whithead, B. Guidobaldi, A. Stroppa *lp* Richard Dix, Leslie Banks, Madge Evans, Walter Huston, George Arliss, Helen Vinson, C. Aubrey Smith

1936

Flash Gordon (U) b/w 13 chaps

This is the most enduring of the many Science Fiction serials of the thirties and forties. Alex Raymond, who'd earlier illustrated Dashiell Hammett's scripts for the Secret Agent X-9 comic strip, created the Flash Gordon strip for King Features as an answer to National Newspaper's Buck Rogers (who eventually followed Flash onto the silver screen with his own serial, **Buck Rogers,** in 1939). Raymond's strip has been hailed as the epitome of the American adventure comic strip for its elegance and style. Though the serial never catches the beauty of Raymond's idealized drawings, in Crabbe, Rogers' virginal Dale Arden, Middleton's Ming the Merciless and the fantastical décor of the planet Mongo, Stephani (who significantly had a hand in the scriptwriting, an unusual event in serial production) creates a *pot pourri* of mythologies that is still appealing today. Certainly the chapterplay looks better than its $500,000 ($350,000 according to some sources) budget suggests.

The storyline, drawn from Raymond's strip, is simple. Crabbe, Rogers and Shannon, their bewhiskered scientist friend, travel to Mongo when it appears that the gypsy planet is set on a collision course with Earth. There they find a bizarre world of floating cities and underground passages lorded over by Middleton, who has usurped the rightful ruler, Alexander's Prince Barin, and a complex romantic/sexual knot in which Ming lusts after the blonde Dale Arden who loves Flash who is lusted after by the dark Aura (Lawson as the daughter of Middleton) who in turn is loved from afar by Prince Barin. The result, however tatty the images occasionally look, is a fantastical world in which the characters are locked in an endless embrace.

The serial was followed by two sequels, **Flash Gordon's Trip to Mars** (1938) and **Flash Gordon Conquers the Universe** (1940) as well a sexploitation version, **Flesh Gordon** (1974) and a camp parody, **Flash Gordon** (1980).

d/co-s Frederick Stephani *co-s* George Plympton, Basil Dickey, Ella O'Neill *c* Jerry Ash, Richard Fryer *se* Norman Denes *lp* Larry 'Buster' Crabbe, Jean Rogers, Charles Middleton, Priscilla Lawson, Richard Alexander, Frank Shannon

Buster Crabbe in trouble in Flash Gordon, *the best of the Science Fiction serials of the thirties.*

Ghost Patrol (PURITAN) b/w 60 min

One of the several Science Fiction westerns made in the wake of the success of **The Phantom Empire** (1935), this is based on an original story by Mascot script editor, Wyndham Gittens. Ingraham is the inventor of a super ray that causes internal combustion engines to cease working. He is held captive by Miller and Oakman who use his ray machine to bring down mail planes. McCoy is the G-man, equally at home behind the controls of a plane as in the saddle of a horse, who investigates the crashes and brings the culprits to justice. A minor series western, it is of interest because it shows how in the thirties elements from different genres were grafted on to each other with such ease. Hence the decade produced Science Fiction gangster films, detective films, westerns and even Science Fiction musicals.

d Sam Newfield *p* Sigmund Neufeld, Leslie Simmonds *s* Joseph O'Donnell *c* John Greenhalgh *lp* Tim McCoy, Claudia Dell, Walter Miller, Wheeler Oakman, Slim Whitaker, Lloyd Ingraham

The Invisible Ray (U) b/w 82 min

In this amiable entry in the mad-scientist stakes, Karloff, after 'learning to capture light rays from the past', journeys to Africa in search of radium x he's located there. When he finds it and touches it he becomes contaminated and everything he touches dies. Lugosi gives an unusually restrained performance as a fellow scientist who discovers an antidote, but not before Karloff has become a crazed maniac. The superior

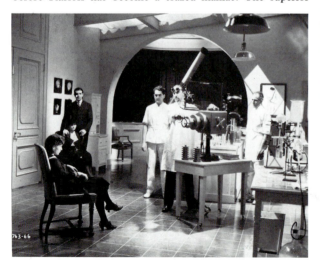

special effects are by Fulton who was also responsible for the process by which **The Invisible Man** (1933) remained invisible.

d Lambert Hillyer *p* Edmund Grainger *s* John Colton *c* George Robinson *se* John P. Fulton *lp* Boris Karloff, Bela Lugosi, Frances Drake, Frank Lawton, Walter Kingsford, Beulah Bondi

The Man Who Changed His Mind *aka* The Brainsnatchers *aka* Dr Maniac *aka* The Man Who Lived Again (GAINSBOROUGH; GB) b/w 68 min

This is one of a series of films Karloff made in Britain in the mid-thirties in an effort to avoid being typecast as either a mad scientist (as in **The Invisible Ray**, 1936) or the monster (as **Frankenstein**, 1931), roles which would haunt him throughout his lengthy career. The extent of his failure to secure other roles can be gauged from the storyline of this film in which he plays a doctor who perfects a machine capable of transferring the mind of one person into the body of another. When his fellow doctors laugh at him and his publisher backer (Cellier) deserts him, Karloff turns on his former backer with the idea of keeping alive his dying assistant, Calthrop. When this succeeds Karloff shares his secret of possible eternal youth (by changing bodies as he ages) with another assistant, Lee, with whom he falls in love, before eventually dying.

The storyline is over-complicated and Stevenson's direction only workmanlike. Indeed more interesting than the film was the ensuing court case in which the Vicomte de Maudit (who was shot for treason during World War II) brought an unsuccessful charge of plagiarism against Gainsborough.

d Robert Stevenson *p* Michael Balcon *s* L.du Garde Peach, Sidney Gilliat, John L. Balderstone *c* Jack Cox *lp* Boris Karloff, Anna Lee, John Loder, Frank Cellier, Donald Calthrop, Cecil Parker

The Man Who Could Work Miracles (LONDON; GB) b/w 90 min

A whimsical fantasy, this follow-up to **Things to Come** (1936) was only moderately successful at the box office. Young is the draper's assistant given superhuman powers as a test by three Gods who have been debating the future of humanity. At first he simply indulges himself, playing party tricks and sending a policeman 'to blazes', but soon, in the typical fashion of an H. G. Wells' character – the film is based on Wells' short story, *The Man Who Had to Sing* – Young sets his mind on the

Left: *Bela Lugosi as the good scientist in* The Invisible Ray.

betterment of mankind's lot. This he's singularly unable to do (he can't even make Gardner fall in love with him), and in exasperation he orders the planet to stop still, causing a near catastrophe until the Gods step in and set things to right. Director Mendes provides an appropriate light touch, but the film's whimsicality dates badly.

d Lothar Mendes   *p* Alexander Korda   *s* H.G.Wells
c Harold Rosson   *se* Ned Mann, Laurence Butler, Edward Cohen   *lp* Roland Young, Joan Gardner, Ralph Richardson, Ernest Thesiger, Robert Cochran, Wallace Lupino

Things to Come   (LONDON; GB)   b/w   130 (113) min
Though it was a failure at the box office and is slow moving to the point of boredom at times, *Things to Come* remains one of the most important Science Fiction films of all times. Its virtues are neither the philosophizing of Wells – under whose close supervision the film was made from his book, *The Shape of Things to Come* – nor the accuracy of the future history Wells and Biro produce, rather it is the vision of Menzies which brings to life Wells', now dated, ideas. Menzies, clearly a better art director than director of people, is unable to make much sense of the heavily pointed story but nevertheless he and art director Vincent Korda manage to animate Wells' blurry vision of the future.

The story begins in 1940 with the opening of World War II and then shifts to the desolation of 1970 where Everytown, now little but rubble, is ruled by Richardson's cruel 'Boss' before Massey's Cabal arrives and with his peace gas turns Richardson and the inhabitants of Everytown into good citizens. The scene then shifts to 2036 in which Everytown has become a peaceful, prosperous, technological Utopia marred only by the pomposity of its rulers and the lack of imagination of its populace. Against this background, Hard-

wicke's humanist sculptor argues for a return to less sterile ways with Everytown's ruler (Massey again). The film's compromise solution sees their son and daughter sent into space together with the hope that they will begin a more compassionate society. Stripped of the supporting structure of Menzies' images, Wells' ideas may seem banal, but the movie has a self-confidence about it that remains unbreakable.

d William Cameron Menzies   *p* Alexander Korda   *s* H. G. Wells, Lajos Biro   *c* George Perinal   *se* Ned Mann, Edward Cohen, Harry Zech   *lp* Raymond Massey, Cedric Hardwicke, Margaretta Scott, Ralph Richardson, Edward Chapman, Maurice Braddell

Undersea Kingdom (REP) b/w 12 chaps

This briskly mounted serial, Republic's second, boasted far more opulent sets than Levine's earlier Mascot productions. 'Crash' Corrigan stars as the naval hero who, when investigating mysterious earthquakes in his rocket-powered submarine, re-discovers the long-lost city of Atlantis. In company with Shaw's eccentric scientist and Wilde's sprightly newspaperwoman he finds that Atlantis is beset with warring factions, rather like Murania in **The Phantom Empire** (1935) on which the undersea kingdom is clearly modelled. Like that serial too, the plot features a wide range of scientific gadgetry – robots, death rays etc – which sits oddly side by side with the most traditional of sword battles and Roman-style gladiator costumes. Blue is the crazed tyrant planning to conquer the upper world and Chaney his menacing heavy.

d B. Reeves Eason, Joseph Kane p Nat Levine s John Rathmell, Maurice Geraghty, Oliver Drake c William Nobles, Edgar Lyons lp Ray 'Crash' Corrigan, Lois Wilde, Monte Blue, C. Montague Shaw, Lon Chaney Jnr, Smiley Burnette

The Walking Dead (WB) b/w 66 min

Though the plot is little but a clever variant on the revenge-inspired gangster films Warners were churning out, Curtiz's slick direction and Mohr's expressionistic lighting make this outing far superior to Karloff's other films of this period. Once again he plays 'the monster', this time a man wrongly convicted of murder, executed and brought back to life by Gwenn's benevolent scientist. But, if the plot is predictable, with Karloff turning on the real murderers and frightening them to death before expiring himself, Curtiz and Mohr create some suspenseful scenes.

d Michael Curtiz p Lou Edelman s Ewart Anderson, Peter Milne, Robert Andrews, Lillie Hayward c Hal Mohr lp Boris Karloff, Edmund Gwenn, Ricardo Cortez, Warren Hull, Robert Strange, Joseph King

Bila Nemoc aka The White Disease aka The White Sickness aka Skeleton on Horseback

(MOLDAVIA C.L.; CZECH) b/w 78 min

Haas, who later became a notable figure in the world of Hollywood B features, brought this film with him from Czechoslovakia after the Nazi invasion. The film's cinematographer, Heller, also fled Czechoslovakia, but to Britain where he eventually worked on such major productions as *The Ladykillers* (1955) and the influential *The Ipcress File* (1965).

Adapted from Karol Capek's play, the film paralleled events in Germany in describing the advance of a dictator to absolute power and his conflict with the idealist Dr Galen (Haas), who has invented a cure for the leprous disease (a

physical manifestation of fascism as it were) that is decimating the population. The dénouement, to which Capek strongly objected, features Haas' assistant saving mankind, but only after the death of the dictator.

For release in America the film was re-titled *Skeleton on Horseback* and given explanatory titles by Fanny Hurst.

d/p/s Hugo Haas c Otto Heller lp Hugo Haas, Bedrich Karen, Zdenek Stepanek, Karla Olicova, Vaclav Vydra Snr, Ladislav Bahac, Jaroslava Prucha

Bulldog Drummond at Bay

(BPI-WARDOUR; GB) b/w 78 (63) min

Lodge took over the title role from Ralph Richardson for this British addition to the Bulldog Drummond series which, oddly enough, were being made concurrently with Paramount's similar series starring Ray Milland. Even odder, in place of Phyllis Clavering, Drummond's long-suffering fiancée, the film features Mackaill as the British Secret Service agent Lodge proposes to at the close. Together the pair put paid to Jory's gang of international spies (who are masquerading as 'peace-workers' – a reflection of the popular view of pacifists at the time), trying to steal the plans of Britain's new 'robot plane'.

Lodge, Marlene Dietrich's leading man in *The Scarlet Empress* (1934), made a dashing Drummond. He later entered politics and was elected Governor of Connecticut in 1950.

d Norman Lee p Walter C. Mycroft s Patrick Kirwan, James Parrish c Walter Harvey lp Victor Jory, John Lodge, Dorothy Mackaill, Claude Allister, Richard Bird, Hugh Miller

Charlie Chan at the Olympics (FOX) b/w 71 min

While Bulldog Drummond was retrieving the stolen plans of a robot plane in **Bulldog Drummond at Bay** (1937), Oland's Charlie Chan was doing precisely the same thing en route to the infamous 1936 Berlin Olympics (footage of which is included in the film). Even stranger, in retrospect, the plot features Chan's No. 1 son (Luke) winning an Olympic gold medal in the swimming event, despite having been kidnapped by Gordon's armaments' adventurer and Wallace's spy.

d H. Bruce Humberstone p John Stone s Robert Ellis, Helen Logan, Paul Burger c Daniel B. Clark lp Warner Oland, Katherine De Mille, Pauline Moore, Allan Lane, Keye Luke, C. Henry Gordon, John Eldredge, Jonathan Hale, Morgan Wallace

Ray 'Crash' Corrigan interrogates C. Montague Shaw in Undersea Kingdom.

Left: Boris Karloff, once again 'the monster', in The Walking Dead.

Top right: *Ralph Byrd (right) is* Dick Tracy *in the first of Republic's quartet of cliffhangers devoted to the exploits of America's most famous detective.*

Dick Tracy (REP) b/w 15 chaps

This was the first of Republic's quartet of serials featuring Chester Gould's famous cartoon detective. Byrd lacked the angular jaw Gould gave his creation and the Tess Trueheart character was omitted in the interests of realism, but in the main the serial was faithful to the fantastic world the cartoonist wove around his detective. Stanley is the Lame One who with his Spider Armada and a panoply of gadgetry that includes a sound disintegrator and an impressive-looking futuristic aircraft, the flying wing, is finally foiled by Byrd. An inventive touch that gives a real dramatic edge to the proceedings is the transformation by Piccori's hunchback scientist of Tracy's brother into a zombie accomplice of Stanley. To make the change more effective, Tracy's brother is played by two actors, Dick Bench before and Young, with a sinister streak through his hair, after. Taylor and James direct forcefully, despite the serial's short (25-day) shooting schedule.

d Ray Taylor, Alan James *p* J. Laurence Wickland
s Barry Shipman, Winston Miller, Morgan Cox, George Morgan *c* William Nobles, Edgar Lyons *se* Howard Lydecker *lp* Ralph Byrd, Kay Hughes, Smiley Burnette, Lee Van Atta, John Piccori, Carleton Young, Edwin Stanley

Right: *John Loder hanging from the airliner while studio hands spray cloud effects around him during the making of* Non Stop New York.

The Girl from Scotland Yard (PAR) b/w 62 min

Morley is the spunky heroine on the trail of Cianelli's madman who has invented an airplane complete with death ray with which he intends to conquer Britain in this unintentionally humorous Paramount programmer. Baldwin is the square-jawed American who comes to her assistance and way down the cast list is Dennis O'Keefe, who was soon to become a leading man in B pictures, appearing for the last time under his real name of Bud Flanagan.

d Robert Vignola *p* Emanuel Cohen *s* Doris Anderson, Dore Schary *c* Robert Pittack *lp* Karen Morley, Eduardo Cianelli, Robert Baldwin, Katherine Alexander, Milli Monti

Midnight Menace (GROSVENOR; GB) b/w 78 min

This is one of the several British films made before World War II which imagined the bombing of Britain as a central element in any future war. Generally, as here, the idea was inserted into a melodramatic plot. Farrell is the newspaper cartoonist and Vyner the agony aunt who together foil the

Below: *Hugo Haas as the idealist Dr Galen in the political allegory* Bila Nemoc.

attempts by Kortner (as the minister of Grovinia) to launch a fleet of bomb-laden radio-controlled pilotless planes against an unsuspecting Britain while pleading the case for disarmament in public. This last point is very revealing of the mood of the times when pacifist views were associated with 'bolshevik' conspiracies.

d Sinclair Hill *s* G.H. Moresby-White *c* Cyril Bristow
lp Charles Farrell, Fritz Kortner, Margaret Vyner, Danny Green, Billy Bray

Non Stop New York (GAUMONT; GB) b/w 71 min

A curiosity, if only for its vision of transatlantic jet travel in the heady future of 1940, this film is directed by Stevenson who in 1939 moved to Hollywood where he had the odd distinction of a ten-year contract with David Selznick during which time he never directed a film for the Selznick studios but was loaned out by Selznick to other studios. The script follows attempts by gangsters to kill a stowaway chorus girl (Lee, then Stevenson's wife) who was a witness to a murder in London. Loder is the athletic hero.

d Robert Stevenson *s* Roland Pertwee, Derek Twist, Curt Siodmak, J.O.C. Orton *c* Mutz Greenbaum *lp* John Loder, Anna Lee, Francis L. Sullivan, Frank Cellier, Desmond Tester, William Dewhurst

Q Planes *aka* Clouds Over Europe
(HAREFIELD/LONDON; GB) b/w 82 min

In retrospect, notable for its prediction of the significance that the war in the air would play in World War II (which was also suggested in the same year in another British production,

Midnight Menace, 1937), this is a piece of routine hokum. Olivier is the test pilot who with Richardson's spiky detective puts paid to the plot of a gang of international spies to knock out Britain's new breed of bombers with a death ·ray. Conceived of as a comedy-mystery by its makers, the film was one of the numerous minor productions sponsored by Alexander Korda's London Films in the interest of greater utilization of his huge studio. With the exception of Richardson, whose performance is superb, the cast are colourless. Hobson is the pretty heroine.

d Tim Whelan, Arthur Woods *p* Irving Asher *s* Ian Dalrymple *c* Harry Stradling *lp* Laurence Olivier, Valerie Hobson, Ralph Richardson, George Curzon, Hay Petrie, John Longden

S.O.S. Coastguard (REP) b/w 12 chaps

Lugosi is the mad munitions inventor traitorously intent on supplying disintegrating gas to the war-like state of Moravania in this routine outing. Serialdom's Dick Tracy, Byrd, swaps his police uniform for that of a coastguard to stop Lugosi's attempts to smuggle the constituent parts of the gas out of America. The giant deaf-mute (Alexander) who finally turns on his master when Lugosi wounds him in the last reel is the chapterplay's most imaginative touch.

d William Witney, Alan James *p* Sol C. Siegel *s* Barry Shipmen, Franklyn Adreon *c* William Nobles *lp* Ralph Byrd, Bela Lugosi, Maxime Doyle, Carleton Young, John Piccori, Herbert Rawlinson, Richard Alexander

The Big Broadcast of 1938 (PAR) b/w 91 min

Yet another farce with interpolated songs and dances in the style of **The Big Broadcast of 1936** (1935). The excuse for the shenanigans this time is a transatlantic race between two liners, one of which receives extra assistance from 'a secret radio transmitter capable of producing a speed of 65 knots'. The gimmicks aside, the film is memorable as the screen debut of Hope, for Fields (in his last movie for Paramount) and his set-piece of a billiards' game in which he cheats outrageously, and for introducing the classic song 'Thanks for the Memory'.

d Mitchell Leisen *p* Harlan Thompson *s* Walter De Leon, Francis Martin, Ken England *c* Harry Fischbeck *lp* W. C. Fields, Martha Raye, Dorothy Lamour, Shirley Ross, Bob Hope, Lynn Overman, Ben Blue, Leif Erickson

Fighting Devil Dogs (REP) b/w 12 chaps

In this surprisingly effective serial marines Brix and Powell are engaged in defending democracy in a Far Eastern protectorate when they encounter the hooded and becloaked

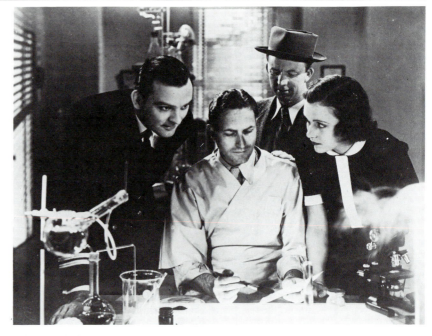

'Lightning' (Sothern), an evil dictator who decimates their platoon with his artificial thunderbolts. The serial has its origins in Republic's firm policy of honouring different branches of the military in one title a year. However, visually, the tin-hatted marines are no match for Lightning, a villain in the grand tradition, whose death in the final reel comes as a real let-down.

Seen in the eighties the serial has a disturbingly topical edge to it.

d William Witney, John English *p* Robert Beche *s* Barry Shipman, Franklyn Adreon, Ronald Davidson, Sol Shor *c* William Nobles *se* Howard Lydecker *lp* Lee Powell, Herman Brix (Bruce Bennett), Eleanor Stewart, Forrest Taylor, Hugh Sothern, Sam Flint

Flash Gordon's Trip to Mars

(U) b/w and tinted 15 chaps

This sequel to the phenomenally successful **Flash Gordon** (1936) serial sees Crabbe, Rogers (now sporting black hair) and Shannon on Mars from which Middleton's Ming the Merciless, in alliance with Roberts' evil queen, is stripping the Earth of nitrogen. Though it lacks both the budget and the pace of the original serial, it has its moments, especially in the clay people, humans turned to clay by Roberts. What is missing is the charming innocence of the original. It was planned to set the serial on Mongo, but after the success of Orson Welles' *War of the Worlds* broadcast of 1938, the studio changed the setting to cash in on things Martian.

d Ford Beebe, Robert F. Hill *p* Barney Sarecky *s* Ray Trampe, Norman S. Hall, Wyndham Gittens, Herbert Dolmas *c* Jerome Ash *lp* Larry 'Buster' Crabbe, Jean Rogers, Frank Shannon, Charles Middleton, Beatrice Roberts, Richard Alexander

Flight to Fame (COL) b/w 57 min

Robards is the madman who steals a death ray invented by Sothern in this routine airplane melodrama which is of interest as one of the earliest films of cinematographer Ballard. Farrell is the enthusiastic hero and Wells the sprightly heroine (and as per the formula, daughter of Sothern) who assists him.

d C. C. Coleman Jnr *s* Michael J. Simmons *c* Lucien Ballard *lp* Charles Farrell, Jacqueline Wells, Alexander d'Arcy, Jason Robards, Addison Richards, Hugh Sothern, Charles D. Brown

Ralph Byrd (left) examines the evidence in S.O.S. Coastguard

Left: *Eleanor Stewart held captive by a becloaked Hugh Sothern in* Fighting Devil Dogs.

Right: *Buster Crabbe (centre) with one of the clay people and Richard Alexander in the weak sequel to the delirious Flash Gordon (1936), Flash Gordon's Trip to Mars.*

The Gladiator (COL) b/w 72 min

Adapted from the first novel by Philip Wylie, a Science Fiction writer who later became a screenwriter and another of whose novels provided the basis of the classic **When Worlds Collide** (1951), *The Gladiator* was transformed by Melson and Sheckman from a study of a persecuted mutant into a vehicle for Brown's comic talents. He plays the weedy youth who becomes a superman after unknowingly taking a strength-inducing serum developed by Littlefield's experimenter. From then on it's crazy comedy all the way, with a strong sentimental undercurrent, as Brown (who gives a superb performance) leads the college team to victory on the football field and finally shows his strength of character by still defeating the wrestling champion when the effect of the serum has worn off. Travis is the girl who stands by.

d Edward Sedgwick *p* David L. Loew *s* Charlie Melson, Arthur Sheckman *c* George Schneiderman *lp* Joe E. Brown, June Travis, Dickie Moore, Lucien Littlefield, Robert Kent, Man Mountain Dean

Spy Ring *aka* International Spy (U) b/w 61 min

Hall is the polo-playing captain of artillery who lets down his side in the regimental championships in order to defeat a gang of international (polo-playing) spies who have stolen a revolutionary device that transforms a machine-gun into an effective anti-aircraft gun. The film is memorable for an early performance by Wyman as the brassy heroine; in the fifties she became a major star in melodramas like *Magnificent*

Below: *Joe E. Brown as the unlikely superman in a publicity pic for* The Gladiator.

Obsession (1954). Another plus is the forceful, if erratic, direction of Lewis who became a major director of B films in the forties and fifties.

d Joseph Lewis *p* Paul Malvern *s* George Waggner *c* Harry Neumann *lp* Jane Wyman, Leon Ames, William Hall, Ben Alexander, Jack Mulhall, Egon Brecher

Arrest Bulldog Drummond (PAR) b/w 60 (57) min

The first film in Paramount's uneven Bulldog Drummond series, this lacklustre adaptation of Sapper's *The Final Count* has Howard's Drummond suspected of stealing an 'atomic disintegrator' ray gun which can detonate explosives over half a mile away. To clear his name, Howard, his recently acquired wife (Angel) and his chums travel to a tropical island to do battle with Zucco who's murdered the inventor. Dull.

d James Hogan *p* William Le Baron *s* Stuart Palmer *c* Ted Tetzlaff *lp* John Howard, George Zucco, Heather Angel, H.B. Warner, Reginald Denny, E.E. Clive

Blake of Scotland Yard (VICTORY) b/w 15 chaps

This inept remake by Hill of his own 1927 silent serial stars Byrd (better known for his role as Dick Tracy) as Blake on the track of the claw-handed Scorpion who goes on the rampage with his combined death ray-television camera. Barclay is the plucky, much-threatened, heroine.

d/co-s Robert F. Hill *p* Sam Katzman *co-s* William Lord Wright *lp* Ralph Byrd, Joan Barclay, Herbert Rawlinson, Lloyd Hughes, Dickie Jones, Bob Terry

Buck Rogers (U) b/w 12 chaps

Based on America's first Science Fiction comic strip, Buck Rogers (created by Philip F. Nowlan in 1929) took to the skies in the wake of the huge success Universal had with their **Flash Gordon** (1936) serial. *Buck Rogers* lacked the mythological appeal of *Flash Gordon;* in its place was virtual non-stop action as Buck (Crabbe, who also played Flash) fights for democracy in the 25th century – in which he wakes up after a five-century snooze – against Killer Kane (Warde). The storyline consists of little but extended battles with Crabbe, and his companion Moore, dashing between Earth and Saturn in pursuit of Warde.

The serial was re-released in edited versions in 1953, as *Planet Outlaws* and 1965 as *Destination Saturn*. In the wake of **Star Wars** (1977), Universal produced an updated feature film **Buck Rogers in the 25th Century** (1979) and a teleseries.

d Ford Beebe, Saul A. Goodkind *p* Barney Sarecky *s* Norman S. Hall, Ray Trampe *c* Jerry Ash *lp* Larry 'Buster' Crabbe, Constance Moore, Jackie Moran, Jack Mulhall, Anthony Warde, C. Montague Shaw, Guy Usher

Dick Tracy's G-Men (REP) b/w 15 chaps
In the second of Republic's four serials devoted to the exploits of crime buster No. 1, *Dick Tracy Returns* (1938), Byrd's Tracy had been set against the evil Stark family (a pale imitation of Ma Baker and her sons), but for this outing Byrd was once more confronted with a fantastical villain, Pichel's evil Zarnoff, who starts the film by coming back from the dead courtesy of a mysterious 'life-giving' drug he's perfected. Fittingly, after causing mayhem for 14 episodes, in the last chapter he dies drinking from a well of pure arsenic.

Pichel later went on to become a director in which capacity he served on the landmark film **Destination Moon** (1950) while Byrd's girlfriend was played by Isley who achieved lasting fame as Jennifer Jones.

d William Witney, John English *p* Robert Beche, Sol Shor *s* Barry Shipman, Rex Taylor, Franklyn Adreon, Ronald Davidson *c* William Nobles *se* Howard Lydecker *lp* Ralph Byrd, Irving Pichel, Ted Pearson, Walter Miller, Phyllis Isley (Jennifer Jones)

The Man They Could Not Hang (COL) b/w 72 min
This is the first and best of a trio of medically inclined Science Fiction/horror films made by Grinde starring Karloff. The others are *The Man With Nine Lives* (1940), which features Karloff experimenting with cyrogenics, and *Before I Hang* (1940) in which Karloff is once more the conventional mad doctor, this time maddened by a rejuvenation serum derived from the blood of a homicidal maniac. All three films are essentially gothic tales of retribution in which the Science Fiction elements are merely decorative. Thus, *The Man They Could Not Hang* (which has a remarkably similar plot to **The Walking Dead**, 1936, which also starred Karloff) spends most of its time subjecting its characters – the judge, jury and key witnesses at the trial in which Karloff was sentenced to death (only to be revived by means of a mechanical heart) – to the various electronic horrors of a latterday equivalent of a haunted house.

The direction by Grinde, a much under-rated director, is both elegant and economic.

d Nick Grinde *p* Wallace MacDonald *s* Karl Brown *c* Benjamin Kline *lp* Boris Karloff, Lorna Gray, Robert Wilcox, Roger Pryor, Byron Fouger, Don Beddoe, Ann Doran

Le Monde Tremblera *aka* **La Révolte des Vivants** (CICC; FR) b/w 108 min
Based on the novel *La Machine à Prédire la Mort* by C.-R. Dumas and R.-F. Didelot, the story revolves around a young scientist whose invention accurately predicts people's moment of death. This causes consternation all round and provokes a riot which results in the inventor's death, just as the machine had predicted. The film is notable mainly for Leon Barsacq's

Buster Crabbe and Constance Moore held captive in Buck Rogers.

décors and as an early script by Clouzot, one of France's best postwar directors of social-conscience thrillers (*Le Salaire de la Peur*, 1953 and *Les Diaboliques*, 1955). Some sources cite Pottier as a pseudonym for the Czech born actor/director Ernst Deutsch, who played Famulus, the libidinous assistant who triggered off the aggravation in Wegener's **Der Golem** (1920).

The film was re-released in 1945 as *La Révolte des Vivants*.

d Richard Pottier *p* Leopold Schlosberg *s* Jean Villard, Henri-Georges Clouzot *c* Robert Le Febvre *lp* Madeleine Sologne, Mady Berry, Armand Bernard, Erich von Stroheim, Claude Dauphin, Roger Duchesne, Christiane Delyne, Sonia Bessis, Nina Sainclair, Julien Carette

The Phantom Creeps (U) b/w 12 chaps
Featuring Lugosi's last serial appearance, *The Phantom Creeps* is a decidedly melodramatic offering, and at a time when the serial was entering a more realistic phase. Lugosi plays Zorka, yet another mad scientist seeking world domination through the use of such gadgets as an 8-foot robot, a 'devisualizer belt' (which rendered him invisible and came courtesy of the invisibility effects Universal had developed for their Invisible Man series) and a deadly gas that induces suspended animation. Arnold is the plucky newspaperwoman and Kent the intelligence officer sent to investigate matters.

d Ford Beebe, Saul A. Goodkind *p* Henry MacRae *s* George Plympton, Basil Dickey, Mildred Barish *c* Jerome Ash, William Sickner *lp* Bela Lugosi, Robert Kent, Dorothy Arnold, Regis Toomey, Roy Barcroft, Edward Van Sloan

The Return of Dr X (WB) b/w 62 min
Bogart, his hair given a white streak for the occasion, plays the monster, a man restored to life through an injection of rare-group blood, who goes on the rampage in his search for blood in this twist on the Frankenstein legend. Morris is the hard-headed reporter and Morgan the doctor who follows the trail of bloodless corpses to Bogart's front door.

Though it had only a titular relationship, the film was promoted by Warners as a sequel to their surprising box-office success, *Dr X* (1932).

Left: Ted Pearson in action in Dick Tracy's G-Men.

Top right: A surreal moment from Son of Frankenstein.

d Vincent Sherman *p* Bryan Foy *s* Lee Katz *c* Sid Hickox *lp* Dennis Morgan, Wayne Morris, Rosemary Lane, Humphrey Bogart, John Litel, Olin Howard

S.O.S. Tidal Wave (REP) b/w 60 min
Boasting a marvellous climax, courtesy of **Deluge** (1933) from which it was borrowed, in which New York is engulfed simultaneously by a tidal wave and an earthquake, this is an interesting film less for its spectacular effects than for its use of television as a potentially powerful tool in the hands of the unscrupulous, a theme that was utilized far more in the fifties. Byrd is the television news reporter who exposes a corrupt candidate in a mayoral race. The screenplay by Shane and Kahn was based on a short story by James Webb who became a regular writer of scripts for Roy Rogers' series westerns and eventually won an Oscar for his script for *How the West Was Won* (1962).

Television Spy, Edward Dmytryk's second film.

d John H. Auer *p* Armand Schaefer *s* Maxwell Shane, Gordon Kahn *c* Jack Marta *lp* Ralph Byrd, George Barbier, Kay Sutton, Frank Jenks, Marc Lawrence

Son of Frankenstein (U) b/w 95 min
Universal's second sequel to **Frankenstein** (1931) is notable for the last performance by Karloff as the monster and the fine, possibly his finest, performance by Lugosi (the studio's original choice for the role of the monster in *Frankenstein*) as Ygor the shepherd hung for grave robbery who survives his ordeal and attempts to use the revived monster to kill those responsible for his conviction.

In place of the stark black and white of James Whale's *Frankenstein* with its sly comic touches, director Lee produces a more naturalistic, but still atmospheric, film complete with characters in place of the exaggerated stereotypes of the original. In Lee's hands, this re-interpretation works well enough, but despite the film's lavish budget, far bigger than that for *Frankenstein* or **The Bride of Frankenstein** (1935),

Below: The poster for S.O.S. Tidal Wave.

and some splendid sequences, it is noticeable that Karloff's monster has little to do once he is revived by Rathbone (as the Baron's son) and Lugosi, and that the character teeters on the edge of becoming a mere gimmick. Once the stylized world of James Whale's *Frankenstein* was disrupted, until the advent of Terence Fisher and his radical re-interpretation of the legend, the Frankenstein films, their developing naturalism notwithstanding, inevitably drifted into becoming mere horror outings, especially as after this film Universal set about milking the monster for all the character was worth.

d/p Rowland Lee *s* Willis Cooper *c* George Robinson
lp Boris Karloff, Bela Lugosi, Basil Rathbone, Lionel Atwill, Josephine Hutchinson, Lionel Belmore

Television Spy (PAR) b/w 58 min
This is the second film of director Dmytryk who made his mark in the forties with such thrillers as *Farewell My Lovely* (1944) and *Crossfire* (1947) before being branded as a communist by the House Committee on Un-American Activities and briefly blacklisted. That said, the film shows most of the vices of thirties Science Fiction-thrillers – an improbably melodramatic storyline and a minuscule budget. Quinn, then typecast as a baddie, is the international spy who steals the plans for a new long-range television system and Henry the hero who scuppers his plans. The film's one novel idea is the romance between Henry and Barrett which begins when he sees her on television and ends, quite bizarrely, with each of them gazing at each other's televised image in rapture.

d Edward Dmytryk *p* William Le Baron, Edward T. Lowe
s Horace McCoy, William R. Lipman, Lillie Hayward
c Harry Fischbeck *lp* William Henry, Judith Barrett, Anthony Quinn, William Collier Snr, Richard Denning, Dorothy Tree

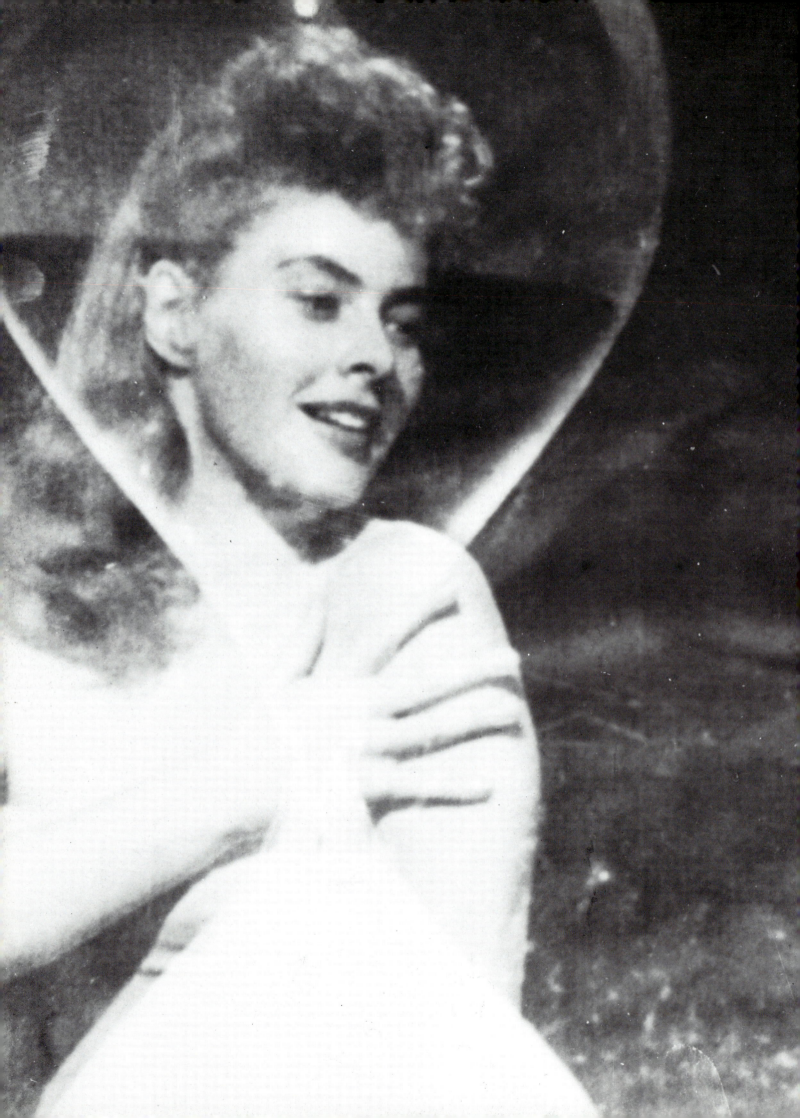

The
1940s

Science Fiction Eclipsed

The contrasting developments of Science Fiction literature and the Science Fiction film which were a feature of the thirties continued into the forties. In the magazines, still the genre's creative focus, the beginnings of modern Science Fiction were erected on the foundations laid down in the thirties, but in the cinema Science Fiction as such hardly existed. Various Science Fiction elements already existed, but they still awaited cohesive themes to form the centrepiece of the solid genre that would appear, as if from nowhere, in the fifties.

The few big productions of the decade such as **Dr Jekyll and Mr Hyde** and **Tainstvenni Ostrov** (both 1941) were, like their thirties predecessors, literary adaptations. Far more plentiful, however, were the heroes who had first appeared in America's comic books and strips. Like their comic brethren they too went to war in the forties to defend Democracy. Thus serials like **Captain Midnight** (1942), **Batman** (1943) and **Captain America** (1944) saw their heroes in action on the home front and, in a tired sequel to **The Invisible Man** (1933), **The Invisible Agent** (1942), Jon Hall donned the cloak of invisibility on behalf of the Allied cause. Even odder was **The Boogie Man Will Get You** (1942) in which Boris Karloff's eccentric scientist works on the creation of a superman as his contribution to the war effort. Karloff's performance is also notable as a parody on his mad scientist, a role he regularly essayed in the thirties. The film was thus an illustration of the fact that in the forties the horror cycle of the thirties (which had annexed many Science Fiction elements) turned to parody; indeed, it climaxed in the broad farce of **Abbott and Costello Meet Frankenstein** (1948).

If, in the main, Science Fiction films of the forties continued the trends of the thirties, a few pointed to the future. **Strange Holiday** (1945) and **Krakatit** (1948), each in their different ways, saw the revival of Science Fiction as a political allegory. The sprightly comedy **The Perfect Woman** (1949) marked a shift in interest from the likes of Franken-stein's flesh and blood creations to the creation of robots. Even more significantly, for all its serial breeziness, **The Purple Monster Strikes** (1945) introduced the twin themes of alien possession and the invasion of Earth from outer space which were to become central in the next decade. All that was needed to bind together these strands and create a genre out of the disparate fragments of Science Fiction in the forties was an over-riding theme, such as paranoia or fear. This was supplied by the new spectres unleashed by the dropping of the bombs on Hiroshima and Nagasaki that ended the Second World War and the rush of UFO sightings that began in earnest in 1947.

Dr Cyclops (PAR) 75 min

This marvellous film features Dekker as the mad scientist of the title who in the midst of the Peruvian jungle is conducting clandestine experiments in reducing humans to one fifth their normal size. Gloriously photographed in Technicolor by Hoch and Sharp and imaginatively directed by Schoedsack, best known for his production of *King Kong* (1933), the film stars Logan, Coley and Halton as the American explorers who are miniaturized by Dekker when they stumble on his jungle laboratory. In this form they are confronted with a series of terrifying monsters, a cat, a chicken and raindrops, in the same way as the legion of miniaturized people who would follow them in such films as **The Incredible Shrinking Man** (1957) and **Attack of the Puppet People** (1958) would be, before they are able to kill Dekker.

The special effects, mostly matts and back projection, are well executed – the film was made 'with a slide rule and blueprints' Schoedsack once told an interviewer – but it is the simple central idea that gives the movie its power.

d Ernest B. Schoedsack *p* Dale Van Every *s* Tom Kilpatrick *c* Winton C. Hoch, Henry Sharp *se* Farciot Edouard, Albert Hay *lp* Albert Dekker, Janice Logan, Thomas Coley, Charles Halton, Victor Kilian, Frank Yaconelli

Flash Gordon Conquers the Universe

(U) b/w 12 chaps

This is the weakest of the three serials devoted to the exploits of Flash Gordon; the other two are **Flash Gordon** (1936) and **Flash Gordon's Trip to Mars** (1938). Earth is being saturated by a deadly dust that spreads 'the purple death', so

Previous pages: *The dream sequence from* Dr Jekyll and Mr Hyde *(1941), the most naturalistic version of the story.*

Below: *Albert Dekker as* Dr Cyclops.

Buster Crabbe in all his finery in Flash Gordon Conquers the Universe.

Oscar Homulka (left) and a quizzical John Barrymore gaze at Virginia Bruce as The Invisible Woman.

once more Crabbe sets off in Shannon's rocket (with a new Dale Arden, Hughes replacing Jean Rogers) to do battle with Middleton's Ming the Merciless. Aware of the law of diminishing returns, Universal signalled the end of the Flash Gordon series by killing off Ming at the end of this chapterplay. Most of the footage of the dead planet of Frigea, on which Crabbe mines plante, 'the only known antidote to the purple death', was culled from the 1930 feature *The White Hell of Pitz Palu*.

d Ford Beebe, Ray Taylor *p* Henry MacRae *s* George H. Plympton, Basil Dickey, Barry Shipman *c* Jerome Ash *lp* Larry 'Buster' Crabbe, Carol Hughes, Charles Middleton, Frank Shannon, Beatrice Roberts, Anne Gwynne

The Invisible Man Returns (U) b/w 81 min
In place of the megalomaniac scientist, impersonated by Claude Rains in James Whale's classic **The Invisible Man** (1933), maddened by the side-effects of his experiments in invisibility, this sequel features the urbane Price (in his first starring role). No longer an anti-hero, Price is merely an honest man who uses the invisibility serum to clear himself of a murder he didn't commit. Fulton's special effects' work is as inventive as ever, but Siodmak and Cole's script has a predictability about it that even Price's mellifluous voice cannot overcome.

Bottom right: Vincent Price in action in the title role of The Invisible Man Returns.

d Joe May *p* Kenneth Goldsmith *s* Curt Siodmak, Lester Cole *c* Milton Krasner *se* John P. Fulton *lp* Vincent Price, Cedric Hardwicke, John Sutton, Nan Grey, Cecil Kellaway, Alan Napier

The Invisible Woman (U) b/w 72 min
Based on a story by Curt Siodmak and Joe May (writer and director respectively of **The Invisible Man Returns**, 1940), rather than on H.G. Wells' witty essay on the corrupting nature of power that served as the source of James Whale's classic **The Invisible Man** (1933), this is a would-be screwball comedy. Barrymore is fine as the mad scientist who turns model Bruce intermittently invisible and becomes the object of attention of foreign agents led by Homulka. Sutherland, best known for his comedies with W.C. Fields, directs in a workmanlike manner, but the film lacks the necessary frenetic pace to be wholly successful.

d A. Edward Sutherland *p* Burt Kelly *s* Robert Lees, Fred Rinaldo, Gertrude Purcell *c* Elwood Bredell *se* John P. Fulton *lp* John Barrymore, Virginia Bruce, John Howard, Charlie Ruggles, Oscar Homulka, Maria Montez, Donald MacBride

The Mysterious Dr Satan (REP) b/w 15 chaps
Best remembered for its charming, rather than frightening, robots, this gustily directed serial was greatly aided by the presence of the suave Cianelli, a veteran of many gangster films, in the title role. His plan, like most of serialdom's villains, is world domination. To do this he needs the remote control device that Shaw (by now typecast by Republic as the eccentric inventor) has perfected so as to be able to control his robots at a distance. Wilcox is the colourless masked hero, Copperhead, seeking to revenge his father's death at the

hands of Cianelli, who episode after episode stops Cianelli completing the construction of the device. Cianelli's prime robot is played by lanky stuntman Tom Steele.

d William Witney, John English *p* Hiram S. Brown
s Franklyn Adreon, Ronald Davidson, Norman S. Hall, Joseph Poland, Sol Shor *c* William Nobles *se* Howard Lydecker *lp* Eduardo Cianelli, Robert Wilcox, C. Montague Shaw, Ella Neal, Dorothy Herbert, Charles Trowbridge

The Sky Bandits (CRITERION/MON) b/w 62 min
The last in the Renfrew of the Mounties series, this lacklustre outing bears more than a family resemblance to the earlier *Yukon Flight* (1940). It features singing mountie Newill on the track of a gang hijacking gold-carrying planes from the Yukon with a death ray they've convinced a scientist he is perfecting as part of national defence work. Stanley, as ever, stands by.

d Ralph Staub *p* Phil Goldstone *s* Edward Halperin
c Eddie Linden *lp* James Newill, Louise Stanley, William Pawley, Jack Clifford, Dewey Robinson, Dwight Frye

1941

The Adventures of Captain Marvel
(REP) b/w 12 chaps
When Republic announced it would not be purchasing the rights to Superman, Fawcett Publications, the owners of the copyright to Captain Marvel who appeared in their *Whiz* comic book, offered the rights to Republic in exchange for the studio booking advertising space. The result was the first serial taken from a comic book (as opposed to a comic strip). Made during the golden years of Republic serials and directed with verve by serial veterans Witney and English, the outing greatly benefits from Tyler's athletic performance in the title role. The convoluted screenplay has the Captain on the track of Worth's master-criminal, the Scorpion, who is attempting to construct a matter-transformation device from ancient crystals found by a scientific expedition, as part of the necessary prelude to his plans for world domination. In the course of that expedition Coghlan's Billy Batson is given the gift of changing into the superhuman Captain Marvel on the utterance of 'Shazam'. The acronym stands for *S*olomon (wisdom), *H*ercules (strength), *A*tlas (stamina), *Z*eus (power), *A*chilles (courage) and *M*ercury (speed). The witty climax has the Scorpion, who has seen Billy Batson change into Captain Marvel, bind and gag him and demand to know how the transformation was achieved. Billy nods his assent, is ungagged, utters the magic word and saves the day.

The serial was re-issued in 1953 under the title *The Return of Captain Marvel*.

d William Witney, John English *p* Hiram S. Brown
s Sol Shor, Ronald Davidson, Norman S. Hall, Joseph Poland, Arch B. Heath *c* William Nobles
se Howard Lydecker *lp* Tom Tyler, Frank Coghlan Jnr, Harry Worth, Louise Currie, William Benedict, Bryant Washbourn

The Body Disappears (WB) b/w 72 min
In this would-be comedy the anodyne Lynn takes a serum invented by Horton and promptly turns invisible. Horton (who gives the best performance of the film) and heroine promptly follow suit. The invisibility special effects are vastly inferior to those pioneered by John P. Fulton for the series that began with **The Invisible Man** (1933).

d D. Ross Lederman *p* Brian Foy *s* Erna Lazerus, Scott Darling *c* Allen G. Siegler *se* Edwin B. Dupar
lp Jeffrey Lynn, Jane Wyman, Edward Everett Horton, Willie Best, Marguerite Chapman, Davis Bruce

Croisières Sidérales (FR) b/w 80 mins
This lacklustre love story features Sologne and Marchat as the young couple about to leave on the rocketship to the planets. He can't go and when she returns from her two-week trip she finds that the Earth (although it looks exactly the same) has aged 25 years, and Marchat with it. Whereupon he goes on the same trip so as to come back 25 years later and be the same age as his beloved.

d André Zwoboda *p/co-s* Pierre Gueriais *co-s* Pierre Bost
c Isnard *lp* Madeleine Sologne, Jean Marchat, Julien Carette, Suzanne Dehelly, Jean Daste, Maupi

Left: *The bland Robert Wilcox as the masked Copperhead in danger in* The Mysterious Dr Satan.

Tom Tyler in a publicity pic for The Adventures of Captain Marvel.

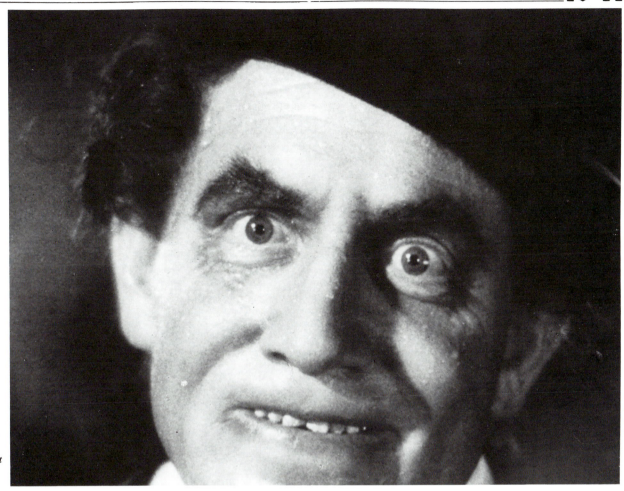

Right: *Spencer Tracy as Dr Jekyll and Mr Hyde in Victor Fleming's romantic version of Robert Louis Stevenson's classic tale.*

The Devil Commands (COL) b/w 66 min

In this intriguing re-working of the Frankenstein myth, Karloff is the scientist maddened by grief who, having perfected a machine that registers brain impulses and recorded those of his wife, desperately tries to make contact with her after her death. Working in conjunction with a spiritualist, he causes chaos and destruction all around him. Dmytryk, in the process of establishing himself as a B director of note, gives the images – a circle of metal suits each with a dead body inside, wired together to a living subject – a sadness that is unusual in such productions.

d Edward Dmytryk *p* Wallace MacDonald *s* Robert D. Andrews, Milton Gunzburg *c* Allen G. Siegler *se* Phil Faulkner *lp* Boris Karloff, Amanda Duff, Richard Fiske, Anne Revere, Ralph Penney, Dorathy Adams

Dick Tracy versus Crime Inc. (REP) b/w 15 chaps

This time out, Byrd, in his last film for Republic, is on the trail of the Ghost (Morgan, the younger brother of Frank Morgan, who was the wizard in *The Wizard of Oz*, 1939). The Ghost has the ability to make himself invisible through use of a ray machine devised by his tame scientist Lucifer (Davidson). In keeping with the fulsomely patriotic mood of the times, following America's entry into the war, the complicated plot has the Ghost undermining the war effort before being finally electrocuted by high tension power cables.

In 1952, the serial was re-issued as *Dick Tracy vs the Phantom Empire*.

d William Witney, John English *p* W.J. O'Sullivan *s* Ronald Davidson, Norman S. Hall, William Lively, Joseph O'Donnell, Joseph Poland *c* Reggie Lanning *se* Howard Lydecker *lp* Ralph Byrd, Ralph Morgan, Michael Owen, Jan Wiley, John Davidson, Kenneth Harlan

Right: *Boris Karloff, a mad scientist yet again, in the charming* The Devil Commands.

Dr Jekyll and Mr Hyde (MGM) b/w 127 (122) min

In the years between 1939 and 1941, Fleming made a trio of movies that it is hard to conceive of as being made by the same person: *The Wizard of Oz* (1939), *Gone With the Wind* (1939) and *Dr Jekyll and Mr Hyde*. The first, his masterpiece, magnificently mixes the surrealism that infuses the best of children's literature with Hollywood production values in a sympathetic fashion, the second (on which Fleming was assisted by Sam Wood and George Cukor, amongst others) shows Fleming the professional and the third, *Dr Jekyll and Mr Hyde*, is widely regarded as his best film.

Greatly sanitized, by comparison both to the superior 1932 version and John Barrymore's 1920 film, it certainly is the most naturalistic version of Robert Louis Stevenson's classic tale: Tracy, in the title roles foregoes excessive makeup for the

transformation so much so that when visiting the set Somerset Maugham reportedly asked, 'Which one is he playing now ?'. However the plush MGM version of Victorian England and Franz Waxman's lush score transform the dark novel into a love story. The result, the performances of Tracy and Bergman notwithstanding, is a typical Hollywood 'literary adaptation', all gloss and little substance.

d/p Victor Fleming *s* John Lee Mahin *c* Joseph Ruttenberg *se* Warren Newcombe *lp* Spencer Tracy, Ingrid Bergman, Lana Turner, Donald Crisp, Ian Hunter, Barton MacLane, C. Aubrey Smith

Tainstvenni Ostrov *aka* Mysterious Island
(GORKI; USSR) b/w 75 min
A faithful rendering of Verne's story published in 1875 and first filmed in Hollywood over a period of three years combining the talents of three directors, including the vastly under-rated Maurice Tourneur, as **Mysterious Island** (1929). Verne wrote the story to let his readers know what happened to the enigmatic Captain Nemo, as well as to Ayrton, the villain left behind by Captain Grant. More pedestrian than its American predecessor, the Soviet film sticks close to its source and concentrates on devising eye-catching design work for the *Nautilus* and efficient special effects, mainly attributable to Karyukov who later improved his skills and directed **Meshte Nastreshu** (1963). It is surprising that such care should have been taken over this fantasy film during the war. (The Germans cancelled their Science Fiction films leaving only a short remnant, presumably edited from scenes already shot by the time the cancellation came through, called *Weltraumschiff I Startet*, 1940.)

The Verne story was filmed again (1951, 1961 and 1972) but none of the versions constituted a major improvement. It took Zeman to render the world of Verne in all its gloriously imaginative aspects in his **Cesta do Praveku** (1955), **Vynalez Zkazy** (1958) and **Na Komete** (1970).

co-d E. A. Penzlin *co-d/co-s* B. M. Chelintsev
co-s M. P. Kalinin *c* M. B. Belskin *se* Mikhail Karyukov
lp M. V. Kommisarov, A. S. Krasnapolski, P. I. Klansky, R. Ross, A. A. Andrienkov, Yura Grammapykaty, A. K. Sona, I. C. Koslov

1942

The Boogie Man Will Get You (COL) b/w 66 min
This is the film that gave Lorre the 'Boogie Man' tag. Created to further exploit Karloff's stage success in *Arsenic and Old Lace*, the film features him as an eccentric scientist working on the creation of a superman (as his contribution to the war effort) from assorted limbs in his cellar laboratory. Lorre is the local policeman/real-estate agent/mayor and Karloff's partner in the enterprise. The comedy is fast and furious, if dated, with the two principals clearly enjoying poking fun at

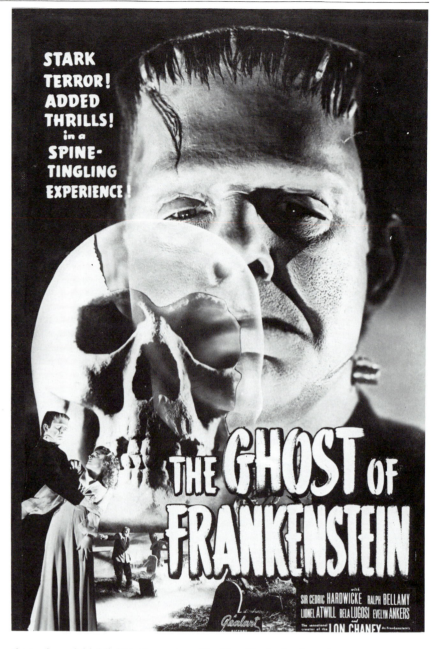

The publicity poster for The Ghost of Frankenstein.

themselves. A highlight is the portrayal by Pugelia of a fascist who, claiming he's a human bomb, arrives on the scene with the intention of stealing Karloff's secret formula for raising the dead.

d Lew Landers *p* Colbert Clark *s* Edwin Blum *c* Henry Freulich *lp* Boris Karloff, Peter Lorre, Maxie Rosenbloom, Frank Pugelia, Jeff Donnell, Larry Parks

Captain Midnight (COL) b/w 15 chaps
Weighed down with propaganda, this is a routine serial. Stuntman O'Brien, a regular co-star with Tex Ritter in his series westerns, has the title role as the black-costumed aviator on the trail of Craven's fifth columnist who has kidnapped scientist Washburn in order to obtain his secret range finder. Short, as Washburn's daughter (niece in the radio serial that gave birth to the Captain Midnight character), is the plucky heroine and Walter is Craven's similarly black-hearted daughter.

d James W. Horne *p* Larry Darmour *s* Basil Dickey, George H. Plympton, Jack Stanley, Wyndham Gittens
c James S. Brown *lp* Dave O'Brien, Dorothy Short, James Craven, Bryant Washburn, Luana Walters, Sam Edwards

Left: Maxie Rosenbloom *(left),* Peter Lorre *(centre) and* Boris Karloff, *this time parodying his mad scientist image, in the comic* The Boogie Man Will Get You.

Doctor Renault's Secret (FOX) b/w 58 min

This is the last film directed by Lachman, an American who, after making his name as a post-impressionist painter in France, gave up painting to begin a career as a film director in 1928, first in Britain then briefly in France before returning to America in 1933. His films, mostly routine second features, though workmanlike, were never as distinguished as his paintings. After a brief spell as a contract director with Fox, he quit film-making to return to painting in 1942.

This offering features Zucco as the conventional mad scientist who transforms Naish into an apeman as part of his experiments to speed up evolution. Better looking than most similar features (in great part thanks to the sympathetic art direction of Nathan Juran who was later to become a director of low-budget action and Science Fiction films himself, including **20 Million Miles to Earth** and **The Deadly Mantis**, both 1957, and **Attack of the 50-Foot Woman**, 1958), this is nonetheless an undistinguished film.

d Harry Lachman *p* Sol M. Wurtzel *s* William Bruckner, Robert F. Meztler *c* Virgil Miller *lp* J. Carrol Naish, George Zucco, John Shepperd (Shepperd Strudwick), Lynne Roberts, Mike Mazurki, Eugene Border, Jack Norton

The Ghost of Frankenstein (U) b/w 68 min

With this, the third sequel to James Whale's **Frankenstein** (1931), the character of the monster (played here by Chaney who appeared, in various roles, in all the subsequent Universal Frankenstein films) was radically changed. Henceforth, instead of the pathetic creature striving to achieve humanity, the monster became little but a lumbering killing machine imprisoned in the convoluted plots of Universal's writers (here Darling) until he was liberated by Terence Fisher in the innovative **The Curse of Frankenstein** (1957).

Here Chaney's monster is discovered in the sulphur pit he was thrown into at the end of **Son of Frankenstein** (1939) and, despite the efforts of Hardwicke (as 'the second son of Frankenstein'), Lugosi as Ygor (mysteriously returned from the dead – he was killed in *Son of Frankenstein*) and Atwill's sinister assistant revive him once more to terrify the villagers of Vasaria and turn on his masters. Kenton, who brought a real sense of dread to **Island of Lost Souls** (1932), directs in a workmanlike fashion but with little feeling for the material.

d Erle C. Kenton *p* George Waggner *s* W. Scott Darling *c* Milton Krasner, Woody Bredell *se* John P. Fulton *lp* Cedric Hardwicke, Ralph Bellamy, Lon Chaney Jnr, Lionel Atwill, Bela Lugosi, Evelyn Ankers

Invisible Agent (U) b/w 81 min

In this, the third sequel to **The Invisible Man** (1933), Hall, son of the inventor of the invisibility formula, volunteers to help the Allies as a spy. In company with Massey, who primly averts her eyes when he tells her he's naked as well as invisible, he outwits both the Germans and Japanese. Lorre plays a variant on his famous Mr Moto character as the sinister Japanese officer, even trying to catch his prey in a spider's web of transparent silken threads at one point. Marin directs in a lively enough style but the sudden shifts from thriller to melodrama to farce make for an erratic pace.

d Edwin L. Marin *p* Frank Lloyd *s* Curt Siodmak *c* Lester White *se* John P. Fulton *lp* Jon Hall, Ilona Massey, Peter Lorre, John Litel, Keye Luke, Holmes Herbert, Cedric Hardwicke

King of the Mounties (REP) b/w 12 chaps

In 1940, Republic released *King of the Royal Mounted*, a serial devoted to the patriotic exploits of Sergeant King (Lane). Though the impact of the chapterplay was much reduced by the villains not being clearly identified as Germans (which they were), because America was still at peace, it was a resounding success. Hence this sequel in which, America now being at war, the enemies are clearly identified as agents of Germany, Japan and Italy helping to prepare for an Axis invasion of Canada by bombing it from an undetectable plane. An inventor who comes up with a new kind of plane detector is killed, leaving Lane to protect the detector and rescue the inventor's daughter, Drake, when she's kidnapped by the enemy . . .

It's all thrilling stuff and, above all, *patriotic*, as Republic made clear in its promotion of the chapterplay: 'Unscrupulous plans for Western world conquest are shattered to bits when the hordes of yellow-bellied rats come to grips with the courage and cunning of Canada's Mounted Police!' Witney, directing on his own for a change, produced a stylish piece of nonsense, hindered only by the budgetary economies that war brought: to take just one example, blanks were rationed. More interestingly, a mark of the concern Republic's front office had over the name of the undetectable plane the villains operated from, the Falcon, can be gauged by the instruction sent down for the screenwriters to provide phonetic spellings of 'Falcon' whenever the word was used. Hence 'we cannot afford to lose the Falcon (fawlkn) plane'.

d William Witney *p* W.J. O'Sullivan *s* Taylor Cavan, Ronald Davidson William Lively, Joseph O'Donnell, Joseph Poland *c* Bud Thackery *lp* Allan Lane, Gilbert Emery, Russell Hicks, Peggy Drake, Douglass Dumbrille, Duncan Renaldo

Ne Le Criez Pas sur les Toits

(SNEG; FR) b/w 99 min

A routine, inoffensive comedy, made under Nazi occupation, built around the comic persona of Fernandel, the poetic and somewhat naïve 'simple soul'. He is the assistant of Professor Bontagues (Le Vigan) who has developed a formula to change seawater into gasoline. Vincent (Fernandel) for his part develops a liquid that will make flowers imperishable. When the professor dies, everybody assumes Vincent knows the formula and he has to deal with various violent threats to make him disclose what he doesn't know. Finally brought to trial by oil company representative Octave (Varennes) he is acquitted thanks to help from a woman journalist (Lemonnier), and the way is clear to a happy ending as he marries his guardian angel.

As with a number of Noel-Noel and Fernandel movies of the period, the script was slightly adapted and remade, with Cantinflas in the lead role, as a Mexican comedy (**El Supersabio,** 1948), and although Cantinflas is slightly more exuberant than Fernandel because he relies less on facial gestures and more on verbal and physical wit in the style of Jerry Lewis, there is very little to choose between the two performances. Both movies were designed for local consumption only, counting on the regular following of the national comedians.

d Jacques Daniel-Norman p Alexis Plumet s Jean Bernard-Luc, Alex Joffé, Jean Manse c Léonce-Henry Burel lp Fernandel, Meg Lemonnier, Robert Le Vigan, Thérèse Dorny, Marie-José Mafféi, Jacques Varennes, Paul Azaïs, Henri Arius, Madeleine Pagès, Georges Lannes

1943

Batman (COL) b/w 15 chaps

An unintentional farce, so melodramatic is Hillyer's direction, *Batman* was a surprise hit when released and has retained its popularity with audiences ever since, especially after its re-release as *An Evening with Batman and Robin* (1966) on the heels of the camp teleseries. The serial was based on the comic-book characters, created by Bill Finger and artist Bob Kane, who first appeared in Detective Comics in 1939. Wilson is the Caped Crusader and Crofts is the Boy Wonder, but it is Naish's evil Dr Daka who steals the show. With the aid of his zombie army and an over-the-top acting style he tries to steal America's radium for the Axis powers. A lacklustre sequel followed in 1949, **Batman and Robin**. 1989's **Batman** saw the character much changed.

d Lambert Hillyer p Rudolph C. Flothow s Victor McLeod, Leslie Swabacker, Harry Fraser c James Brown Jnr lp Lewis Wilson, Douglas Croft, J. Carrol Naish, William Austin, Shirley Patterson, Charles Middleton

Frankenstein Meets the Wolf Man (U) b/w 74 min

Although Siodmak's screenplay is ingenious in its melding of such disparate material and the direction by Neill (best known for his work on the long-running Sherlock Holmes series) is more than capable, nothing can conceal the fact that this sequel to both **Frankenstein** (1931) and *The Wolf Man* (1941) was simply intended to further milk the declining screen appeal of Universal's copyright monsters by combining them in different ways in different films.

The complex plot features Chaney as Lawrence Talbot searching for Baron Frankenstein who he's told can cure his lycanthrophy, being trailed by Knowles' doctor who's keen to read Frankenstein's diaries, and stumbling across Lugosi's monster. Lugosi, now ill, was doubled for much of the film (including his first close-up) by stuntman Eddie Parker, and his role was further reduced in the release prints of the film by numerous cuts, including the sequence that explains that he is blind. The inevitable climax has Chaney and Lugosi fighting amidst the wreckage of Frankenstein's laboratory only to be separated by the rush of waters from the dam dynamited by the ever restless villagers of Vasaria.

The film's success led the way for similar monster collections, the first of which was **House of Frankenstein** (1944).

d Roy William Neill p George Waggner s Curt Siodmak c George Robinson se John P. Fulton lp Lon Chaney Jnr, Bela Lugosi, Lionel Atwill, Patric Knowles, Ilona Massey, Maria Ouspenskaya

Lewis Wilson in a publicity pic for the (unintenionally) hilarious Batman.

Left: *Lon Chaney and stuntman Eddie Parker, doubling for Bela Lugosi, in* Frankenstein Meets the Wolf Man.

Top right: *Arthur Space shows his new bomb off to Laurel and Hardy's unlikely pair of private detectives in* The Big Noise.

The Big Noise (FOX) b/w 74 min

In this, one of their last feature films together, Laurel and Hardy play a pair of detectives sent to stand guard on the house of the inventor of a new bomb which a gang of jewel thieves have their eye on. The gags are more controlled than usual and the storyline is adhered to with few comic deviations, but nonetheless the film is only remembered for its odd moments – the array of gadgets in the scientist's home, for example and, best of all, Laurel and Hardy being chased by car, plane and boat.

Way down the castlist is Bobby Blake, then better known for his role as Little Beaver in the Red Ryder series westerns who subsequently had a great success in the title role of *Tell Them Willie Boy Is Here* (1969).

d Malcolm St Clair *p* Sol M. Wurtzel *s* W. Scott Darling *c* Joe MacDonald *lp* Stan Laurel, Oliver Hardy, Dorris Merrick, Veda Ann Borg, Frank Fenton, Arthur Space

Captain America (REP) b/w 15 chaps

This was both the last of Republic's cycle of wartime serials based on comic-book characters and the last serial to be directed by the energetic English at the studio. In the comic book Captain America was a GI who periodically went AWOL to battle Axis agents with his scientifically induced superpowers. But for the serial Republic changed the character to a battling DA who takes on the Scarab (a marvellous oily performance from veteran villain Atwill) and his 'dynamic vibrator'. Moreover, the action takes place on the home front.

Despite the patriotic atmosphere that suffused the serial, many of its plot devices, such as the torn treasure map, were as old as serialdom itself. Purcell, who gave a highly athletic performance in the title role, died of a heart attack shortly after completing work on the serial.

d John English, Elmer Clifton *p* W.J. O'Sullivan *s* Royal Cole, Ronald Davidson, Basil Dickey, Jesse Duffy, Harry Fraser, Joseph Poland, Grant Nelson *c* John MacBurnie *se* Howard Lydecker, Theodore Lydecker *lp* Dick Purcell, Lionel Atwill, Lorna Gray, Charles Trowbridge, Russell Hicks, George J. Lewis

Margaret Lockwood with Vic Oliver and Peter Graves in the delightful Give Us the Moon.

Dick Purcell captures a pair of heavies in Captain America.

Give Us the Moon (GAINSBOROUGH; GB) b/w 95 min

An interesting, albeit minor, futuristic comedy. Made during the war when drudgery and deprivation were the norm, it is set three years after the war and impishly imagines a time when it is possible to decide not to work. The hero, Graves,

stumbles across a group of people who call themselves 'the Elephants' and who have a healthy disregard for work, which leads to chaos when Graves and his newfound friends agree to manage Olivier's hotel and restaurant. Lockwood is the girl who tries to steady Graves and Simmons the precocious 11-year-old who, completely lacking in any inhibitions, keeps stirring the pot. Guest, directing from his own script, finds the right light touch.

d/s Val Guest *p* Edward Black *c* Phil Grindrod *lp* Margaret Lockwood, Vic Olivier, Peter Graves, Jean Simmons, Roland Culver, Irene Handl

The Great Alaskan Mystery (U) b/w 13 chaps

One of the cycle of patriotic serials made in America after her entry into World War II, this is an otherwise routine chapterplay. Scientist Morgan leads an expedition that includes hero Stone and his daughter, Weaver, to Alaska to mine the special ore that fuels his new invention, the Peragron (a ray gun). Once there, the party is attacked by a gang of Axis sympathizers until Stone is able to turn the tables on them. Taylor and Collins direct energetically enough but the script is too weak and predictable to keep one's attention.

d Ray Taylor, Lewis D. Collins *p* Henry MacRae *s* Maurice Tombragel, George H. Plympton *c* William Sickner *lp* Milburn Stone, Marjorie Weaver, Edgar Kennedy, Samuel J. Hinds, Martin Kosleck, Ralph Morgan

House of Frankenstein (U) b/w 71 min

Featuring an all-star cast of villains, Carradine as Dracula, Strange as Frankenstein's monster and Chaney as the Wolf Man, and slick direction from Kenton, *House of Frankenstein* bears so little resemblance to **Frankenstein** (1931) that it's hard to conceive of it (or its sequel, **House of Dracula**, 1945) in terms of either *Frankenstein* or *Dracula* (1930), the films that sparked off the thirties cycle of horror films. Produced by Malvern, a veteran of series westerns in which cost-cutting was the *sine qua non*, and scripted by Lowe from a draft screenplay by Curt Siodmak commissioned by Universal for the express purpose of bringing together as many of its copyright monsters as possible, the film's cheap-skate opportunism verges on surrealism at times as it moves from monster to monster with bewildering rapidity.

Karloff is the mad doctor who takes over Zucco's travelling horror show, briefly frees Carradine's Dracula (Zucco's prize exhibit) before letting him die in the sunlight and setting off in search of Frankenstein's diary and finding the preserved bodies of the monster (Strange, the fourth actor to play the role and a regular heavy/stuntman in Malvern's series westerns) and Chaney's Wolf Man. The resulting shenanigans (greeted by one critic as being 'only a little more terrifying than the house that Jack built') was a moderate box-office success and paved the way for an even more ludicrous outing, *House of Dracula*.

d Erle C. Kenton *p* Paul Malvern *s* Edward T. Lowe
c George Robinson *se* John P. Fulton *lp* Lon Chaney Jnr,
Boris Karloff, George Zucco, J. Carrol Naish, Glenn Strange,
Lionel Atwill, Anne Gwynne

The Invisible Man's Revenge (U) b/w 78 min
Hall, the patriotic spy of **The Invisible Agent** (1942), once more features in the title role, but as a killer seeking revenge on the men who framed him in this routine entry, one of the six films derived from H.G. Wells' novel *The Invisible Man*. Direction, by serial veteran Beebe, and script (which is virtually a rewrite of that for **The Walking Dead**, 1936) are workmanlike at best and the invisibility effects, once more provided by the ingenious Fulton, are clearly used as a gimmick to refresh an otherwise laboured film.

d/p Ford Beebe *s* Bertram Millhauser *c* Milton Krasner
se John P. Fulton *lp* Jon Hall, Lester Mathews, Gale
Sondergaard, John Carradine, Evelyn Ankers, Alan Curtis,
Leon Errol

Above: *Boris Karloff with the skeleton of Dracula in the bewildering* House of Frankenstein.

The Lady and the Monster (REP) b/w 86 min
This is the first version of the thrice-filmed novel, *Donovan's Brain* by Curt, brother of Robert, Siodmak, a German émigré who, on his arrival in Hollywood in 1938, wrote numerous scripts in the Science Fiction and fantasy vein and briefly turned director. The film was intended by Republic's owner, Herbert J. Yates, to be the first non-musical starring vehicle of his future wife, Ralston. However, Stroheim's strong performance as the deranged doctor completely overshadowed hers. Ralston and Arlen are the lovers and reluctant assistants of Stroheim who removes the brain from a dead criminal millionaire and keeps it alive. The brain grows in power and, assisted by Stroheim, schemes to revenge itself on those responsible for its death by using the weak-willed Arlen as an assassin. Alton's expressionistic lighting gives substance to the weak script and Sherman's routine direction.

The story was remade in 1953 as **Donovan's Brain** and in 1962 as **Vengeance**.

d/p George Sherman *s* Dane Lussier, Frederick Kohner
c John Alton *se* Theodore Lydecker *lp* Erich von
Stroheim, Vera Hruba Ralston, Richard Arlen, Mary Nash,
Sidney Blackmer, Lane Chandler

Return of the Ape Man (MON) b/w 60 min
Carradine and Lugosi give splendidly hammy performances as the scientists who revive a prehistoric ape in this old-fashioned film, especially in the sequences devoted to Lugosi's transplanting of Carradine's brain into the ape and the rampage that follows. The ape was played by Zucco and Moran at different times during the making of the film.

d Philip Rosen *p* Sam Katzman, Jack Dietz *s* Robert
Charles *c* Marcel Le Picard *lp* Bela Lugosi, John
Carradine, George Zucco, Frank Moran, Michael Ames,
Judith Gibson, Mary Currier

Vera Hruba Ralston, Richard Arlen and Eric von Stroheim in the atmospheric The Lady and the Monster.

Time Flies (GAINSBOROUGH; GB) b/w 88 min
This amiable comedy sends inventor Aylmer, his valet, Handley, and two businessmen silly enough to consider investing in Aylmer's time-machine, shooting back to Elizabethan times when the machine suddenly starts to work. The script is carefully structured and the comedy tightly controlled by one-time silent comic Forde. The film's main failing is Handley. It is worth noting that this is probably the first film to feature time travel via a machine.

d Walter Forde *p* Edward Black *s* J.O.C. Orton, Ted
Kavanagh, Howard Irving Young *c* Basil Emmott *se* Jack
Whitehead *lp* Tommy Handley, Evelyn Dall, George Moon,
Felix Aylmer, Graham Moffatt, Moore Marriott

Bottom left: *John Carradine and Jon Hall in* The Invisible Man's Revenge.

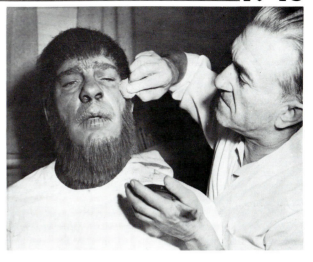

Right: *Jack Pierce, who created the makeup of the monster in the original* Frankenstein *(1931), applying makeup to Lon Chaney in* House of Dracula, *the last Frankenstein film Pierce worked on.*

House of Dracula (U) b/w 67 min

Clearly played for laughs rather than chills, *House of Dracula* opens bizarrely with Chaney's Wolf Man and Carradine's Dracula arriving at the home of mad doctor Stevens in search of cures. Stevens cures Chaney but in the process of giving blood to Dracula he receives the vampire's infected blood and, after disposing of Carradine who quickly reverts to type, he becomes a monster himself. He sets about reviving Frankenstein's monster (Strange, reprising his role from **House of Frankenstein,** 1944) and is only stopped by Chaney who once more slays the monster just as the villagers of Vasaria (here oddly called Visaria) arrive with their lighted brands. Kenton directs economically enough but Lowe's script is too clichéd to be either humorous or scary.

The film marked the end of the association of Jack B. Pierce, who created the makeup for the original **Frankenstein** (1931), with the creature. In the monster's next and last Universal outing, **Abbott and Costello Meet Frankenstein** (1948), the makeup was by Bud Westmore.

d Erle C. Kenton *p* Paul Malvern *s* Edward T. Lowe
c George Robinson *se* John P. Fulton *lp* Lon Chaney Jnr,
Onslow Stevens, John Carradine, Lionel Atwill, Glenn
Strange, Jane Adams

Manhunt of Mystery Island (REP) b/w 15 chaps

Stirling, fresh from her exploits as the whip-wielding heroine of *Zorro's Black Whip* (1944), here has the traditionally more passive role of the perpetually threatened heroine. With criminologist Bailey she searches for her missing father, Taylor. He's a scientist who has just invented a 'radiatomic power transmitter' and been captured by Barcroft's swaggering villain, a reincarnation of the infamous pirate Mephisto, courtesy of a transformation machine (a chair set in a room full of electrical gizmos which, with the aid of a dissolve, transforms anybody into the likeness of Barcroft). The film's middle section, which sees Bailey dividing his time between rescuing Stirling's imperilled heroine and trying to discover the identity of Mephisto, is overlong and relies on too many transformation scenes, but the enthusiastic fights, masterminded by action specialist Canutt, are in true serial style.

d Spencer Gordon Bennet, Wallace Grissell, Yakima Canutt
p Ronald Davidson *s* Albert DeMond, Basil Dickey, Jesse
Duffy, Alan James, Grant Nelson, Joseph Poland *c* Bud
Thackery *se* Howard Lydecker, Theodore Lydecker
lp Richard Bailey, Linda Stirling, Roy Barcroft, Keene
Duncan, Forrest Taylor, Jack Ingram

Roy Barcroft as the first of many would-be alien invaders of Earth in The Purple Monster Strikes.

The Monster and the Ape (COL) b/w 15 chaps

This is one of a pair of serials made by Bretherton, a director best known for his work on the Hopalong Cassidy series westerns. Morgan is the inventor of a robot that is powered by 'metalogen' and Macready the enemy agent out to get it and the formula for metalogen with the assistance of a killer ape called Thor (Ray 'Crash' Corrigan) and a variety of criminal accomplices. Lowery is the wide-grinned hero. Routine.

d Howard Bretherton *p* Rudolph C. Flothow *s* Sherman
Lowe, Royal K. Cole *c* C.W. O'Connell *lp* Robert
Lowery, George Macready, Ralph Morgan, Carole Mathews,
Jack Ingram, Anthony Warde

The Purple Monster Strikes (REP) b/w 15 chaps

'This is the proudest day in my life' says astronomer-inventor Craven, showing the construction plans of his rocketship to Barcroft's supposedly friendly Martian. 'Unfortunately,' replies Barcroft, 'it is also your last.' And so begins one of serialdom's most charming efforts. Barcroft kills the scientist, takes over his body and sets about laying the groundwork for an invasion from Mars with the help of assorted criminals. Moore puts paid to such ideas while rescuing the ever-threatened Stirling.

The serial was the first to deal with an invasion from outer space, previous serials having devoted themselves to Earthbound mad scientists, and one of the first films to treat the theme of alien possession which became one of the most important themes in the genre in the fifties.

d Spencer Gordon Bennet, Fred Brannon *p* Ronald
Davidson *s* Royal Cole, Albert DeMond, Basil Dickey,
Barney Sarecky, Lynn Perkins, Joseph Poland *c* Bud
Thackery *se* Howard Lydecker, Theodore Lydecker
lp Roy Barcroft, Dennis Moore, Linda Stirling, James
Craven, Roy Barcroft, Bud Geary, Mary Moore

Strange Holiday aka The Day After Tomorrow

(SOUND MASTERS INC./ELITE PICTURES) b/w 61 (54) min

This strange political fable was made by Oboler in 1942, when its tale of America transformed into a fascist police state was far more topical, but not released until 1945. Rains is the businessman who, on his return from a lengthy hunting trip, finds the constitution overthrown, a police state and an apathetic populace. Oboler directs in his usual unsophisticated, hectoring style but the vision of America he presents remains powerful today, in great part because it has become such a central theme of the modern Science Fiction film.

d/s Arch Oboler *p* A.W. Hackel, Edward Finney
c Robert Surtees *se* Howard Anderson, Ray Mercer
lp Claude Rains, Barbara Bates, Paul Hilton, Gloria Holden,
Milton Kibbee, Martin Kosleck

1946

The Crimson Ghost (REP) b/w 12 chaps

This routine serial was touted by Republic as stemming from the headlines of the day: 'an amazing answer to the atomic bomb explodes in a blaze of serial super action'. But if the chapterplay's origins were contemporary, those ideas were cast in the most traditional of formulas. Thus Serial Queen Stirling, as the heroine, was in constant danger and the main plot device was the identity of the villain. To make this even more difficult, Republic had Bud Geary play the Ghost in his skull and cloak disguise and I. Stanford Jolley provide the voice (and when the Ghost in disguise spoke to Jolley, who had another role in the film, another actor dubbed the voice of Jolley in character). The Ghost's plans for world domination required the possession of the cyclotrode, a counter-atomic device that shortcircuited all electrical currents in its vicinity when switched on. To this purpose he kidnaps the machine's inventor (Duncan) only to be foiled at the last minute by criminologist Quigley. Television's Lone Ranger, Moore, then alternating between playing goodies and baddies, plays the Ghost's principal heavy.

A condensed version of the chapterplay was released in 1966 as *Cyclotrode X*.

d William Witney, Fred Brannon *p* Ronald Davidson
s Albert DeMond, Basil Dickey, Jesse Duffy, Sol Shor
c Bud Thackery *lp* Charles Quigley, Linda Stirling, Clayton Moore, Keene Duncan, Joe Forte, Rex Lease

1947

Brick Bradford (COL) b/w 15 chaps

For all producer Katzman's corner cutting and penny pinching, this remains one of the most enjoyable 'cheapo' serials. Richmond is hired by the UN to protect an anti-missile device perfected by Merton from the implacably evil Quigley. He travels first to the Moon (via a 'crystal door', courtesy of Katzman's budgetary meanness) to rescue Merton and then back into the 18th century to recover part of the formula. The plot's unevenness is countered by Bennet's tongue-in-cheek direction, especially when special effects are being used.

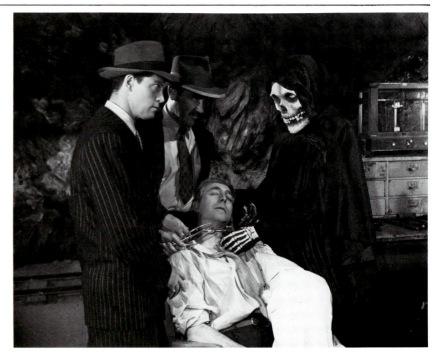

Bud Geary as The Crimson Ghost.

d Spencer Gordon Bennet *p* Sam Katzman *s* George H. Plympton, Arthur Hoerl, Lewis Clay *c* Ira H. Morgan
lp Kane Richmond, Rick Vallin, Linda Johnson, Charles Quigley, John Merton, Pierre Watkin

Jack Armstrong (COL) b/w 15 chaps

This time it's Oakman (an actor better known for his villains in series westerns) who's the mad scientist threatening the world with a ray gun mounted on an orbiting spaceship in this chapterplay from quickie producer Katzman. Hart is the All-American high school student who with his chums, La Planche and Brown, traces Oakman to Grood Island and puts an end to his plans for world domination. Fox's direction is basic, but far worse is the unimaginative script.

d Wallace Fox *p* Sam Katzman *s* Arthur Hoerl, Lewis Clay, Royal K. Cole, Leslie Swabacker *c* Ira H. Morgan
lp John Hart, Rosemary La Planche, Joe Brown Jnr, Wheeler Oakman, Claire James, Pierre Watkin

1948

Abbott and Costello Meet Frankenstein
(U) b/w 92 (83) min

Probably Abbott and Costello's best film, this was the first of the *Abbott and Costello Meet . . .* series; subsequently they would meet, *Boris Karloff* (1949), **The Invisible Man** (1951), *Captain Kidd* (1952) and **Dr Jekyll and Mr Hyde** (1953), amongst others. Made by Universal in an attempt to prolong the flagging careers of both Abbott and Costello and its monster series of movies, the film marked the end of the studio's association with both Frankenstein and Dracula.

The rudimentary plot has the duo chasing a re-animated Lugosi (in his only screen portrayal of the vampire, apart from *Dracula*, 1930) and Frankenstein's monster (Strange) for whom Lugosi is seeking a new brain. Costello is the unlikely choice. Made with a bigger budget than the two previous Frankenstein outings, **House of Frankenstein** (1944) and **House of Dracula** (1945) and with better special effects, the film has an honest, if juvenile, vulgarity about it that is preferable to Universal's recent efforts in the series.

Left: Abbott and Costello Meet Frankenstein, a new lease of life for the comic duo but the kiss of death for Universal's already tired re-workings of the Frankenstein legend. Glenn Strange is the monster.

d Charles T. Barton *p* Robert Arthur *s* John Grant, Frederic I. Renaldo, Robert Lees *c* Charles Van Enger
se David S. Horsley, Jerome H. Ash *lp* Bud Abbott, Lou Costello, Bela Lugosi, Lon Chaney Jnr, Glenn Strange, Leonore Aubert

Bruce Gentry – Daredevil of the Skies

(COL) b/w 15 chaps

Despite the poor animation of the flying discs (similar to that utilized in the Katzman-produced **Superman**, 1948) which hero Neal is on the track of, this is one of the better of Columbia's serials. The stunting by Tom Steele and Dale Van Sickel, who'd fought each other countless times, is superior and Bennet and Carr's direction is fast and furious. Taylor has the double role of scientist and villain (the Recorder, so called for his fondness of communicating through recorded messages) whose plans to destroy the Panama Canal are foiled by Neal and Clark.

d Spencer Gordon Bennet, Thomas Carr *p* Sam Katzman *s* George H. Plympton, Joseph F. Poland, Lewis Clay *c* Ira H. Morgan *lp* Tom Neal, Judy Clark, Ralph Hodges, Forrest Taylor, Hugh Prosser, Jack Ingram

Counterblast *aka* The Devil's Plot

(BRITISH NATIONAL; GB) b/w 100 (90) min

In marked contrast to the straightforward patriotism of the American films made and set around wartime, British treatments of the war were more reflective. Hence this suspenseful thriller has for its hero and villain the same character, Johns' German scientist. On escaping from a POW camp, Johns impersonates an Australian doctor that he's murdered in order to continue his bacteriological experiments with a deadly serum that the Germans plan to introduce into Britain. Pilbeam gives an assured performance as the assistant he falls for while Beatty is the suspicious lab assistant who finally exposes Johns. Oddly when it was finally released in America in 1953, it was thought to be too violent, a testament to the disturbing plausibility of Whittingham's script.

d Paul L. Stein *s* Jack Whittingham *c* James Wilson *lp* Mervyn Johns, Nora Pilbeam, Karel Stepanek, Robert Beatty, Margaretta Scott, Sybilla Binders

Dick Barton – Special Agent

(HAMMER/MARYLEBONE; GB) b/w 70 min

Stannard makes an effective, athletic Dick Barton in this adaptation of the famous radio serial (in which Noel Johnson had played Barton) by Edward A. Mason, who went on to create Britain's longest running radio serial, *The Archers*. The script by Stranks and Goulding follows the comic-strip adventure style of the radio series well enough but the cramped sets and Goulding's heavy-handed direction make for an awkwardly slow-moving film. Wincott is the sinister

Don Stannard in danger in Dick Barton – Special Agent.

villain, planning to bring England to its knees with germ bombs and Shaw and Ford are suitably dizzy as Barton's henchman, Jock and Snowey. So powerful was the mystique of Dick Barton that two sequels followed in swift succession, **Dick Barton Strikes Back** (1949) and **Dick Barton at Bay** (1950). In retrospect, the film's real significance lies in it being the first production of Hammer Films, the newly formed production arm of Exclusive Films, the company that would make most of the best (and some of the worst) British Science Fiction and horror films of the fifties and sixties.

d/co-s Alf D. Goulding   *p* Henry Halstead   *co-s* Alan Stranks   *c* Stanley Clinton   *lp* Don Stannard, George Ford, Jack Shaw, Gillian Maude, Geoffrey Wincott, Beatrice Kane

Krakatit (CZECHOSLOVENSKY FILM; CZECH) b/w 106 min
Like Andreievsky's **Gibel Sensaty** (1935), this is an adaptation from a story by the classic Czech author Karel Capek. Less well made and more stodgily scripted, the film recounts the moral fable of the scientist Prokop (Hoeger) who discovers a new explosive which he calls Krakatit. It is a potentially more controllable equivalent of nuclear power and could put an end to the insane notion of atomic warfare. As such, the Capek story is a political version of Verne's *Face au Drapeau* filmed by Karel Zeman in 1958 as **Vynalez Zkazy**. This film is a timely reminder, made shortly after the US dropped the Hiroshima and Nagasaki bombs, concentrating on the mental aberrations that become acute problems when politicians and financiers become involved in decisions about the exploitation of inventions, and the problems scientists have in facing up to the real reasons why they were encouraged to make grandiose inventions in the first place. The overall pacifist sentiment, conveyed with sardonic humour at times, continues and confirms the dominant tone of all Eastern bloc Science Fiction movies, with the exception of **Aelita** (1924), which advocates revolution.

Vavra, a lecturer and experimental film-maker as well as a prolific director of features, gained international recognition fairly late with his *Romance pro Kridlovku* (1966). Recently, he has remade this story under the title **Cerne Slunce** (1979).

d/co-s Otakar Vavra   *co-s* Frantisek Milic   *c* Vaclav Hanus *lp* Karel Hoeger, Florence Marly, Frantisek Smolik, Eduard Linkers, Jiri Plachy, Jaroslav Prucha, Natasha Tanska, Miroslav Homolka, Bedrich Vrbsky, Karel Dostal

Superman (COL) b/w 15 chaps
The creation of Jerome Siegel and Joel Schuster was the perfect amalgam of three of the themes that dominated American pulp magazines in the second quarter of the 20th century – the alien visitor from another planet, the superhuman being and dual identity. First brought to life in National Comics' *Action* in June 1938, Superman had the misfortune to be acquired by quickie producer Katzman who, after failing to interest either Republic or Universal in a big-budget package deal, finally secured a low-budget deal with Columbia. Whereupon Katzman set about slashing the budget until it was virtually impossible to believe in the character. Director Bennet later recounted the story of the artist who offered Katzman really effective animation to show Superman flying at $64 a foot and 'not so effective' animation at $32 a foot; Katzman naturally chose the cheaper. Yet, if compared to the cartoon shorts of Max Fleischer, Katzman's Superman was awful, the serial astonished its creators by turning out to be the highest grossing serial of all time, so powerful was Superman's mystique.

Above: *Ex-dancer Kirk Alyn, the cinema's first Man of Steel, in* Superman.

118

Like the 1978 film, **Superman – the Movie,** the serial opens with an extended account of Superman's origins, before setting the Man of Steel (former dancer Alyn) against the evil Spider Woman (Forman) who, with her deadly piece of kryptonite and a deadly reducer ray, seeks Superman's death and world domination. The chapterplay was followed by two equally low-budgeted sequels, **Atom Man versus Superman** (1950) and **Superman and the Mole Men** (1951) before finally all doubts that a man could fly were dispelled in a trio of big-budgeted extravaganzas, *Superman – the Movie* and its sequels, **Superman II** (1980) and **Superman III** (1983).

Neill is Lois Lane, Bond, Jimmy Olson and Watkin, Perry White.

d Spencer Gordon Bennet, Thomas Carr *p* Sam Katzman *s* Arthur Hoerl, Lewis Clay, Royal K. Cole *c* Ira H. Morgan *lp* Kirk Alyn, Noel Neill, Tommy Bond, Carol Forman, George Meeker, Jack Ingram, Pierre Watkin

El Supersabio (POSA FILMS; MEX) b/w 100 min
A Mexican remake of the French Fernandel comedy **Ne Le Criez Pas sur les Toits** (1942), which offers the grossly naïve moral cliché that poetic and scientific mentalities are diametrically opposed to each other. The story concerns a scientist, Arquimides Monteagudo (Baena), who develops a formula to transform seawater into gasoline while his assistant, Cantinflas, invents a liquid that will make flowers imperishable. When the professor dies, everybody suspects that Cantinflas possesses the secret formula, including the agents of a rapacious oil company who send Octavio (Cobo) to extract the secret from the naïve Cantinflas. Finally, after several attempts have been made on his life, Cantinflas is framed but a woman journalist Marisa (Aguiar), helps him get acquitted and the happy couple plan their wedding.

Cantinflas is best known in Anglo-Saxon territories for his role as the canny but uncouth comic sidekick of David Niven in *Around the World in Eighty Days* (1956). A number of his Mexican films are in fact adaptations of French scripts written for Fernandel or Noel-Noel.

d Miguel M. Delgado *p* Jacques Gerlman, Santiago Reachi *s* Jaime Salvador, Inigo de Martino, Alex Joffé, Jean Bernard-Luc *c* Raul Martinez Solares *lp* Mario Moreno Cantinflas, Perla Aguiar, Carlos Martinez Baena, Alejandro Cobo, Aurora Walker, Alfredo Varela Jnr, Jose Pidal, Edouardo Casado, Carmen Novelty

1949

Batman and Robin *aka* **The New Adventures of Batman and Robin** *aka* **The Return of Batman**
(COL) b/w 15 chaps
For this inferior sequel to **Batman** (1943), Lowery took over the role of the playboy millionaire/Caped Crusader first essayed by Lewis Wilson and Duncan replaced Douglas Croft as Robin, the Boy Wonder. This time they're confronted with the Wizard, a criminal genius on the loose in Gotham City

Robert Lowery and Johnny Duncan as Batman and Robin.

Mae Clark in danger in the lively King of the Rocket Men.

Below: *Pamela Devis as* The Perfect Woman, *a comic fantasy in which lingerie and underwear play an unusually prominent role.*

with a remote control ray gun. The slim budget, short shooting schedule and the obvious lack of concern by all make for a tiresome serial.

d Spencer Gordon Bennet *p* Sam Katzman *s* George H. Plympton, Joseph F. Poland, Royal K. Cole *c* Ira H. Morgan *lp* Robert Lowery, Johnny Duncan, Jane Adams, Lyle Talbot, Ralph Graves, Don C. Harvey

A Connecticut Yankee in King Arthur's Court *aka* A Yankee in King Arthur's Court (PAR) 107 min

This fluffy musical musical version of Mark Twain's classic novel (which had previously been filmed by David Butler in 1931 as **A Connecticut Yankee**) features Crosby offering a song-and-dance interpretation of the title role. In place of the ironies of Twain's novel and the anti-Depression philosophizing of Butler's film, Crosby and director Garnett generate a freewheeling farce in which any sense of contrast between Arthurian England and the present is lost. The result (best remembered for introducing the song *Busy Doin' Nothin'*) is pure escapism and a film in marked contrast to the Science Fiction films that followed in the fifties.

Twain's novel was filmed again, in an even more light-hearted manner by the Disney studio, in 1979 as **The Spaceman and King Arthur**.

d Tay Garnett *p* Robert Fellows *s* Edmund Beloin *c* Ray Rennahan *se* Gordon Jennings *lp* Bing Crosby, Rhonda Fleming, William Bendix, Cedric Hardwicke, Murvyn Vye, Alan Napier, Richard Webb

Dick Barton Strikes Back

(EXCLUSIVE; GB) b/w 73 min

The second and best of Dick Barton's trio of screen adventures (the first was **Dick Barton – Special Agent**, 1948 and the last **Dick Barton at Bay**, 1950). This time Stannard in the title role takes on Cabot and Raglan's pair of international

Right: *Maria Montez as the* Siren of Atlantis.

criminals who are in possession of an atomic device capable of devastating whole towns. The film's justly remembered climax has Stannard first escape from a cage of poisonous snakes in Blackpool Zoo and then fight his way to the top of the Blackpool Tower to stop Cabot turning the ray onto the city. Grayson directs at such a pace that there is little time to question the creaky dramatics of the story.

d Godfrey Grayson *p* Henry Halstead *s* Ambrose Grayson *c* Cedric Williams *lp* Don Stannard, George Ford, Sebastian Cabot, Bruce Ealker, James Raglan

It Happens Every Spring

(FOX) b/w 89 (87) min

Milland is the penniless scientist who invents a coating that when painted on a baseball repels wood and goes on (briefly) to fame and fortune as a baseball pitcher in this lightweight comedy. Peters is the fiancée suspicious of his new-found sporting prowess. Bacon directs his slight material in a workmanlike fashion.

d Lloyd Bacon *p* William Perlberg *s* Valentine Davis *c* Joe MacDonald *se* Fred Serson *lp* Ray Milland, Jean Peters, Paul Douglas, Ted de Corsia, Ray Collins, Ed Begley

King of the Rocket Men (REP) b/w 12 chaps

As the days of the serial drew to a close, Republic (and Columbia) turned increasingly to Science Fiction for inspiration. However, such modern concerns sat uneasily with the very traditional plots Republic's screenwriters kept (re-) writing. Thus, although *King of the Rocket Men* features a rocket-suited hero (Coffin) on the trail of the masked Dr Vulcan (Jolley), the storyline has him spending vast amounts of time trying to puzzle out which of the scientists at Science Associates (Republic's writer's block standing in for the scientific foundation) is Dr Vulcan. That said, the flying sequences are amongst the best mounted by Republic while Coffin's twisting of the three control knobs of his suit to 'on', 'up' and 'fast' before taking off are fondly remembered by many for their camp charm.

Clarke, the inveterate newspaperwoman on the trail of the identity of the mysterious Rocketman, is best remembered as the girl who got a grapefruit shoved into her face by James Cagney in *Public Enemy* (1931).

d Fred C. Brannon *p* Franklyn Adreon *s* Royal Cole, William Lively, Sol Shor *c* Ellis W. Carter *se* Howard Lydecker, Theodore Lydecker *lp* Tristram Coffin, Mae Clarke, Don Haggerty, I. Stanford Jolley, James Craven, House Peters Jnr

The Perfect Woman (TWO CITIES; GB) b/w 89 min

A stylishly mounted light comedy, but nothing more. Roc is the niece of eccentric scientist (Malleson) who pretends to be the robot he has invented when he declares that it is indistinguishable from a human. Patrick, as the young man who falls for her, and Roc play off each other nicely and Devis provides a wonderful creaky impersonation of the robot while Knowles directs with the necessary light touch.

d/co-s Bernard Knowles *co-p/co-s* George Black *co-p* Alfred Black *c* Jack Hilyard *lp* Patricia Roc, Nigel Patrick, Miles Malleson, Irene Handl, Pamela Devis, Constance Smith

Siren of Atlantis *aka* Atlantis *aka* Queen of Atlantis

(UA) b/w 75 min

This is a remake by producer Nebenzal of his earlier version of Pierre Benoît's novel, *L'Atlantide* **Die Herrin von Atlantis** (1932). O'Keefe and Aumont are the two Foreign Legionnaires who stumble upon a secret passage in the desert that leads to the fabled lost continent of Atlantis which is ruled over with ruthless efficiency by Montez's Queen Antinea. Surprisingly, considering Nebenzal's involvement with Pabst's 1932 film, this is a camp outing full of posturing and little else; even the set-piece where Montez shows O'Keefe and Aumont her collection of mummified lovers is thrown away. One reason for the film's mediocrity was the number of directors who worked on it: it was begun by Arthur Ripley who was supplanted by John Brahm before finally editor Tallas was brought in to re-shoot certain sequences and interpolate material from Pabst's film.

The film has secured for itself a certain cult reputation due to the presence of Montez.

d Gregg Tallas *p* Seymour Nebenzal *s* Roland Leigh, Robert Lax *c* Karl Struss *lp* Maria Montez, Jean-Pierre Aumont, Dennis O'Keefe, Henry Daniel, Morris Carnovsky, Alexis Minotis

The 1950s

Science Fiction Reborn

The fifties was the decade in which anxiety, paranoia and complacency marched hand in hand. On the threshold of space, man had discovered and used a force so frightening that it could mean the extinction of the species. The world only so recently saved for democracy was once again divided, this time by an Iron Curtain and in America subversion from within became a prevalent fear. These anxieties, expressed and explored in a variety of ways created the Science Fiction film genre. Few of the movies were masterpieces, yet a surprising number of fifties Science Fiction films retain their power and resonance to this day, however banal they stand revealed in retrospect.

Films as diverse as **The Thing** (1951), **Them!** (1954), **The Quatermass Xperiment** (1955), **Invasion of the Body Snatchers** (1956), **The Incredible Shrinking Man** (1957) and **I Married a Monster from Outer Space** (1958) reflect the paranoia of the period. It was films in this mould, rather than the landmark **Destination Moon** (1950) and its sober celebration of man's imminent conquest of space, that dominated the decade. Monsters from without and within – Hollywood itself was investigated by the House Committee on UnAmerican Activities – threatened America, as often as not created or awakened by the Bomb (as in **The Beast from 20,000 Fathoms**, 1953). Nature rebelled (most notably in those films by Jack Arnold set on the fringes of the desert) and a variety of aliens, many of whom, like **The Man from Planet X** (1951), had peaceful intentions, were received with hostility. A few films, like **The Day the Earth Stood Still** (1951) and **The 27th Day** (1957) addressed themselves directly to the political implications of such anxieties, while others, notably **War of the Worlds** (1953) and **When Worlds Collide** (1951), had a religious dimension that saw as a punishment the catastrophes that befell man.

Outside America, countries which subsequently became major producers of Science Fiction films – Britain, Japan, Italy and Mexico – turned to the genre in their own distinctive ways. Even when the films seemed to parallel the concerns of their American counterparts (as in **Gojira** (1954), which saw the beginnings of the complex and fascinating Japanese monster movie tradition), further examination reveals that, though the initial situation – a monster awakened by an atomic test – seems similar, the concerns are in fact very different. Similarly, when Eastern European film-makers turned to the genre, their films – like **Niebo Zowiet** (1959) – were, for the most part, remarkably free of the paranoia that infected American films.

By the end of the decade when the concerns of the early fifties had shifted and the anxieties lifted, the Science Fiction film had (temporarily) lost ground. The creature-features – the films devoted to monsters and monstrous aliens – increasingly took on the characteristics of the horror film. Following the success of Hammer's **The Curse of Frankenstein** (1957) and the successful issuing of the Universal horror films of the thirties to television, the revival of the horror film was at the expense of the Science Fiction film. But the fifties had proved that there was both a market and a place for Science Fiction films. After the fifties Science Fiction was no longer unusual.

Atom Man versus Superman (COL) b/w 15 chaps
An intriguing sequel to **Superman** (1948) introduced Superman's arch-enemy Lex Luthor (Talbot), the Atom Man of the title, to the screen. With his synthetic kryptonite he keeps Superman (Alyn) at bay while he sets his henchmen to sack Metropolis. When Superman recovers, Luthor responds by kidnapping Neill's Lois Lane and sending her into outer space. Needless to say, Talbot as Luthor acts Alyn off the screen before ending up in prison. Ironically, the flying sequences are even better than those of the 1948 serial though the budget was far smaller.

d Spencer Gordon Bennet *p* Sam Katzman *s* George H. Plympton, Joseph Poland, David Mathews *c* Ira H. Morgan *lp* Kirk Alyn, Noel Neill, Lyle Talbot, Tommy Bond, Pierre Watkin, Jack Ingram

Destination Moon (GEORGE PAL PRODUCTIONS) 91 min
It's fitting that the first Science Fiction film of the fifties should have been *Destination Moon*, the critical success of which was to revive a stultifying genre. Henceforth, though the genre would remain, in America and Britain at least, trapped in the province of Poverty Row, Science Fiction would be an important strand in the history of the cinema. The reasons for this were complex: the advent of the Cold War (present in *Destination Moon* in the America general's comment to the effect that the Moon is a strategic military location and if America doesn't get there first someone else will); the growing interest in technology (which could be seen as either a 'good' or 'bad' thing); and the UFO phenomenon which continued unabated into the fifties despite government agencies attempts to explain the sightings, which began in earnest in 1947. The net effect, however 'unscientific' many of the films were, was that in the first half of the decade Science Fiction became the medium in which the various responses to the facts of the first atomic age were played out in the cinema. In short, Science Fiction briefly supplanted horror as the genre that dealt in fear and paranoia.

Turning from the genre to the film, what is most noticeable is how Science Fiction's taking the place of horror was literalized in *Destination Moon*, even though the movie hardly touches any of what were to become the main themes of the genre in the fifties. In place of the shadowy, expressionistic lighting of the horror genre, director Pichel and producer Pal attempted a steadfast documentary approach. Their immediate concern was to distance their film from the space-opera concept of the genre that was the legacy of **Flash Gordon**

Previous pages: *Science Fiction taking off in the fifties:* When Worlds Collide *(1951).*

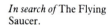

In search of The Flying Saucer.

Destination Moon, the film that marked the late arrival, in Science Fiction cinema, of documentary realism.

(1936), the effects of their stylistic revolution were far more far reaching. Accordingly, when Pal was approached by Heinlein (on whose decidedly juvenile novel, *Rocketship Galileo* his and Ronkel's original screenplay was based) his concern was to further documentize the screenplay. He consulted physicists and astronomers, as well as technicians, before shooting began and employed astronomical painter Chesley Bonestell (whose illustrations for Willy Ley's imagined history of space flight, *Conquest of Space*, won him international recognition) and designer Ernest Fegte to create a realistic cratered Moon surface. It took 100 men two months to build the moonscape Bonestell had designed into a 2-foot-high, 20-foot-long lunar panorama. Scientific information was supplied by German rocket expert Hermann Oberth, who had earlier, with Ley, performed the same function for Fritz Lang on his **Die Frau im Mond** (1929) and makeup artist Webster Phillips fitted each actor with a device that would stretch his features to simulate an increase in velocity.

The film itself details the first Moon landings and, although the flight is hazardous, the script is colourless and wooden; the dominant concern of those involved was to make the journey to the Moon realistic rather than dramatic, and for the most part its predictions were remarkably accurate. Indeed, in retrospect, the one concession to popular tastes of the times – Wesson's joky electronics' technician – is painfully forced. Eventually the rocket lands on the Moon, but so much fuel has been consumed in landing that the crew (led by Archer) have no chance of leaving. They jettison everything that is inessential and find they are still overweight until Archer quick-wittedly discovers a means by which Wesson – who has gloriously decided to sacrifice himself that the others might survive – can re-enter the ship without his 100-pound plus pressure suit. The ship then successfully takes off back to Earth.

Shooting was marred by script quarrels with backers who were terrified the film would flop in the same way that *The*

Great Rupert (1949), Pal's first essay in production (which was also directed by Pichel), had, but Pal fought against the script changes and won. If, in retrospect, the end result is a curiously flat film, at the time its sobriety marked an important step in the genre's evolution.

The film won the 1950 Oscar for special effects.

d Irving Pichel *p* George Pal *s* Robert Heinlein, Rip Van Ronkel, James O'Hanlon *c* Lionel Lindon *se* Lee Zavitz *lp* John Archer, Warner Anderson, Tom Powers, Dick Wesson, Erin O'Brien Moore, Ted Warde

Dick Barton at Bay (HAMMER; GB) b/w 68 min
This was the last of the short-lived Dick Barton series of films that ended with the death of Stannard, who'd played Barton in all three films, in a car crash. Just as in **Dick Barton Strikes Back** (1949), also scripted and directed by the Grayson brothers, this outing sees Barton on the trail of international criminals who are threatening to destroy Britain with a death ray. Walsh is the inventor and Desni his daughter, both of whom are held captive by the villains in their aptly located hideout in the Beachy Head lighthouse. The direction stresses simple adventure at the expense of character to great effect.

d Godfrey Grayson *p* Henry Halstead *s* Ambrose Grayson *c* Stanley Clinton *lp* Don Stannard, Meinhart Muir, Tamara Desni, George Ford, Percy Walsh

The Flying Saucer (COLONIAL) b/w 69 min
Early fifties paranoia tended to link the Russians and flying saucers and numerous UFO sightings were imagined to be Russian spy ships or, worse, carrying Russsian weapons. Conrad and Young's screenplay clearly links the fear of invasion from Russia and outer space together.

Secret agent Conrad (who also directed, produced and co-wrote the screenplay) tracks a flying saucer to Alaska and discovers it has been built by scientist Engel who hopes to sell it to the Americans. The Russians capture Conrad and Engel's treacherous assistant (Pyle) steals the saucer, only to have it explode in mid-air since Engel's planted a bomb on board. The film's climax has Engel giving the secret of the saucer to the US government.

Little seen and too often promoted as a 'lost classic' the film is of interest more for its title than anything else. The film saw the term flying saucer supplanting 'flying disc' – though in the film itself both phrases are used – which had previously been in vogue.

d/p/co-s Mikel Conrad   *co-s* Howard Irving Young
c Philip Tannura   *lp* Mikel Conrad, Pat Garrison, Hantz Von Teuffen, Denver Pyle, Lee Langley, Roy Engel

Garou Garou le Passe Muraille

(CITE FILMS; FR)   b/w   90 min
In between *Kind Hearts and Coronets* (1949) and **The Man in the White Suit** (1951), Britain's sexiest voice, Greenwood's, was used in this subversive comedy based on Marcel Aymé's novel. Unfortunately, it had to be dubbed into French and Boyer's film remained Greenwood's only French movie. Bourvil plays the shy clerk who discovers that he can walk through walls. In an effort to impress Greenwood, he pretends to be a super-gangster and gets himself arrested but keeps escaping, making fools of the police. In the end, he is acquitted of any crimes, but, returning to his drab job, he also finds he has lost his special ability.

The German adaptation of this story, **Ein Mann Geht Durch die Wand** (1959) advocated a voluntary abandonment of the ability to transgress boundaries in order to promote acquiescence in the grey and servile life of the petty clerk, a long way from Bourvil's naïve but cheerful anti-authoritarianism. The direction is light-hearted and Oury, later to become a noted comedy director himself, contributes an entertaining comic performance. An English version was prepared but that lost all the French voices and doesn't appear to have been released.

d/co-s Jean Boyer   *p* Walter Rupp   *co-s* Michel Audiard
c Charles Suin   *se* Paul Raibaud   *lp* Bourvil, Joan Greenwood, Marcelle Arnold, Raymond Souplex, Gerard Oury, O'Brady

Rocketship X-M *aka* Expedition Moon

(LIPPERT)   b/w and red   78 min
Director Neumann, a German who came to Hollywood in 1925, is best known for **The Fly** (1958). He rushed *Rocketship X-M* into production while **Destination Moon** (1950) was still being photographed and succeeded in having it released first.

The film features the first manned rocketship expedition to the Moon that veers off course and lands on Mars. Once there, the expedition (led by Emery) discover a desolate

surface with a dome-shaped building and an enormous metallic mask and deduce that a technically superior race had lived on the planet, but had been the victims of an atomic holocaust, an idea that has served numerous Science Fiction writers and film-makers henceforth. When blind Stone-Age Martian survivors attack the crew, killing Emery and Beery and wounding O'Brien, Bridges and Massen run for their lives. They eventually make it back to the ship and take off but then run out of fuel and, in a surprisingly down-beat ending, crash on Earth and are killed.

Although in contrast to *Destination Moon*, *Rocketship X-M* is clearly more space-opera inclined, Neumann and cinematographer Struss combine to create a sense of pulp poetry that is far more memorable than Pal's attempt at documentary realism. The Mars sequences (shot in Red Rock Canyon and tinted red for effect) are particularly successful.

d/p/s Kurt Neumann   *c* Karl Struss   *se* Jack Rabin, I.A. Block   *lp* Lloyd Bridges, Osa Massen, John Emery, Noah Beery Jnr, Hugh O'Brien, Morris Ankrum

Gene Roth (with microphone) as the evil Vultura in Captain Video, *the only serial based on a TV programme.*

Abbott and Costello Meet the Invisible Man

(U)   b/w   82 min
By the early fifties, Abbott and Costello's popularity was beginning to fade and their producers went out of their way to dream up gimmicks to enliven their films. Here they meet the Invisible Man in a patchily amusing offering in which the duo are new (and very green) private eyes hired by boxer Franz to prove he is innocent of murdering his manager. Franz takes scientist Guild's invisibility serum (the same as Claude Rains took in the original **The Invisible Man** (1933) – his picture hangs portentiously on Guild's wall). Eventually, after Costello has posed as a brilliant boxer with invisible Franz doing the slugging, the duo find the real killer.

Later outings saw them go to Mars (1953) and meet Jekyll and Hyde (1953); they had already met Frankenstein (1948).

d Charles Lamont   *p* Howard Christie   *s* Robert Lees, Frederic Rinaldo, John Grant   *c* George Robinson
se David S. Horsley   *lp* Bud Abbott, Lou Costello, Arthur Franz, Sheldon Leonard, Nancy Guild, William Frawley

Captain Video   (COL)   b/w   15 chaps

With this offering, the only theatrically released serial to be based on a TV programme, Hollywood acknowledged the growing power of television. Holdren took over the title role

Left: Lloyd Bridges and Osa Massen en route to Mars in Rocketship X-M.

from TV's Al Hodge to do battle with Roth's Vultura on the planet Atoma. Made on a shoestring budget by Grissell and Bennet who, with 52 chapterplays to his credit, was the undisputed King of the Serials, it was, like the robots Roth sends against Holdren, crude in the extreme.

d Spencer Gordon Bennet, Wallace A. Grissell *p* Sam Katzman *s* Royal K. Cole, Sherman A. Lowe, Joseph F. Poland *c* Fayte Brown *se* Jack Erickson *lp* Judd Holdren, Larry Stewart, George Eldredge, Gene Roth, Don C. Harvey, William Fawcett

Cisaruv Pekar *aka* **The Emperor's Baker** *aka* **The Return of the Golem** (CZECHOSLOVENSKY FILM; CZECH) 87 min
This film shows there are two types of Golem story. In one the clay hulk stands for someone's spiritual powers, in the other for an unbounded source of natural energy such as nuclear power, a difficult to control but very potent force the use of which depends on moral and political considerations. The former type tends towards magic and psycho fiction (eg **Der Golem** of 1914, 1920, 1935 and 1979). The latter links the Golem with films such **Sieriesbristaya Pyl** (1953), **Gibel Sensaty** (1935), **The War Game** (1965) or **Dr Strangelove** (1964). This Czech version is a comic variant on the latter type and works as a nuclear power parable. Fric, a pioneer of both the Czech and the Slovak cinemas, sets the story again around 1610 in Prague. Rudolf II uses the state treasury to finance lots of charlatans working in laboratories searching for ways of turning lead into gold or looking for the Golem while the population starves. A baker, who is also a lookalike for the emperor (Werich in both parts), discovers 'the force' and, taking the emperor's place, sets the Golem to work making bread for the nation. Although rather flatly directed, the film proved very successful and received wide distribution.

d/co-s Martin Fric *p/co-s* Jan Werich *co-s* Jiri Brdecka *c* Jan Stallich *lp* Jan Werich, Marie Vasova, Natasha Gollova, Bohuslav Zahorsky, Frantisek Filipovsky, Vaclav Tregl, Zdenek Stepanek, Jiri Plachy, Frantisek Cerny

The Day the Earth Stood Still (FOX) b/w 92 min
One of the best American Science Fiction films of the fifties. The theme mirrors the birth, death and resurrection of Christ and has an allegorical flavour that Hollywood normally shunned. Based on the short story *Farewell to the Master* by Harry Bates, it is intelligently directed by Wise (who later directed **The Andromeda Strain**, 1970, and **Star Trek: The Motion Picture**, 1979) from North's literate script.

An alien planetary federation, disapproving of Earth's policy of atom-bomb testing, despatches Rennie and his robot, Gort, to warn Earth to stop its aggression or be blown apart. The duo land in Washington DC in an impressive flying saucer (which cost some $100,000 to build) with this awesome message. Rennie, naturally enough, is gunned down as a false prophet but a revengeful Gort kills the soldiers and re-activates him. He places Gort and a number of counterparts in society as police robots then leaves in his saucer, ascending Christlike to his federation, warning Earthlings that they must either live in peace or be destroyed by Gort and his kind.

What makes the film so successful is Wise's balancing of his ominous allegory with the sub-plot of Rennie's attempts to discover what humans are really like by taking a room in a boarding house where he meets Neal (who gives a superb, restrained performance) and her young son (Gray). Fittingly, it is Neal who saves the day, uttering the immortal phrase: 'Gort! Klaatu barada nikto' and so stopping the robot from destroying Earth after Rennie's 'death'.

d Robert Wise *p* Julian Blaustein *s* Edmund H. North *c* Leo Tover *se* Fred Sersen *lp* Michael Rennie, Patricia Neal, Hugh Marlowe, Billy Gray, Sam Jaffe, Lock Martin

Five (LOBO PRODUCTIONS) b/w 93 min
Oboler produced, directed and wrote the screenplay for this film, which features five survivors of a nuclear holocaust (Phipps, Douglas, Anderson, Lampkin and Lee) bickering in a Frank Lloyd Wright-designed cliff-top mansion (which in fact was Oboler's own home). Clearly intended seriously (and treated as such by the trade), the film in retrospect is more interesting for the gaps in Oboler's conception of a post-nuclear-holocaust future, gaps which are revealing of fifties notions of nuclear warfare. Thus, in contrast to Peter Watkins' **The War Game** (1965) or even Nicholas Meyer's

more popularistic telefilm, *The Day After* (1983), Oboler's film is little but a filmed debate about humanity regenerating rather than an account of the inevitable destruction of humanity that atomic warfare must entail. The result is a simplistic film, made even more so by Oboler's arch moralizing about his survivors and which, unlike the similarly intentioned **The World, the Flesh and the Devil** (1959), is weighed down by its liberal framework. Accordingly, in contrast to Roger Corman's far more exploitative visions of the end of the world (for example, **The Day the World Ended**, 1956 or **The Last Woman on Earth**, 1960), the film, despite its seriousness, wears its hearts too much on its sleeve to animate an audience. In short, the film's arguments are too pat and its characters too stereotyped to penetrate the prejudices of its intended audience.

The plot is equally rudimentary. Lee dies early from atomic poisoning and Anderson quarrels with Lampkin with an eye to winning Douglas, although Phipps is also interested in her. Anderson eventually kills Lampkin and takes a pregnant Douglas to the city to search (fruitlessly) for her husband. Anderson gets radiation poisoning and, when Douglas' baby dies, she returns to Phipps to start a new world.

A prolific writer of radio plays in the thirties, Oboler made his film début in 1945 with *Bewitched*, which was based on his own radio play *Alter Ego*. He was an interesting, albeit strangely uncinematic, film director, best remembered for his hatred for television, the rival to his beloved radio, which led him to experiment with 3-D – he made the movie which sparked off the fifties cycle of films in the format, *Bwana Devil* (1952) – and later with Space Vision, in which he shot **The Bubble** (1966), and for his constant attempts to moralize about the state of mankind in his films. **The Twonky** (1953) is probably the oddest of his films.

d/p/s Arch Oboler *c* Louis Clyde Stoumen, Sid Lubow
lp William Phipps, James Anderson, Susan Douglas, Charles Lampkin, Earl Lee

Flight to Mars (MON) 72 min
Following the success of **Destination Moon** and **Rocketship X-M** (both 1950), Monogram produced this low-budget offering. It was a failure, mainly because of Strawn's clichéd screenplay, poor characterization and unlikely Martians. Shot in 11 days, *Flight to Mars* is an unimaginatively directed (by Selander), dull space opera involving four men and the statutory woman crash-landing in front of Block's backdrop painting of Mars. The schematic plot involves the Earthmen and Martians clashing after one of their number falls for Mitchell's newsman and the Earthmen foiling a planned invasion of Earth.

Although the humanoid Martians wear *Destination Moon* pressure suits, there are some impressive effects, particularly when the ship flies over the surface and strange dark monolithic towers reach high into a bright orange sky.

d Lesley Selander *p* Walter Mirisch *s* Arthur Strawn
c Harry Neumann *se* Irving Block, Jack Cosgrove (Rabin)
lp Marguerite Chapman, Cameron Mitchell, Arthur Franz, Virginia Huston, John Litel, Richard Gaines

Flying Disc Man from Mars (REP) b/w 12 chaps
Virtually a remake of **The Purple Monster Strikes** (1945), this sprightly serial features Gay as the Martian (dressed in the same outfit as Roy Barcroft in the earlier chapterplay so as to be able to use footage from it) who arrives on Earth to prepare for its invasion by Mars. To achieve this Mota (atom spelt backwards), as the Martian is called, has first to rebuild his disc-shaped rocketship – a flying saucer in everything but name – with the enforced aid of scientist Craven (reprising his role from the earlier serial). From his spacecraft he intends to bomb Earth into submission. Reed is the young scientist who becomes suspicious. The well-mounted climax has Gay, Craven and their criminal associates engulfed in molten lava when Reed diverts an atomic bomb so that it falls on Gay's hideout in the interior of a volcano.

In addition to that from *The Purple Monster Strikes*, the serial featured stock footage from such diverse serials as **King of the Mounties** (1942), *G-Men versus the Black Dragon* (1943), *Secret Service of Darkest Africa* (1943) and **King of the Rocket Men** (1949). In 1958 the serial was re-edited and issued as a feature entitled *Missile Monsters*.

d Fred C. Brannon *p* Franklyn Adreon *s* Ronald Davidson *c* Walter Strenge *se* Howard Lydecker, Theodore Lydecker *lp* Walter Reed, Lois Collier, Gregory Gay, James Craven, Harry Lauter, Richard Irving

El Hombre y la Bestia *aka* **The Man and the Beast** *aka* **El Extraño Caso del Hombre y la Bestia** *aka* **The Strange Case of the Man and the Beast** *aka* **El Sensacional y Extraño Caso del Hombre y la Bestia**
(SONO; ARG) b/w 80 min
An effective remake of Robert Louis Stevenson's classic tale *Dr Jekyll and Mr Hyde* starring Soffici, who also directed, produced and co-wrote the picture. A straightforward adaptation of Stevenson's story, it emphasizes the pathetic aspects of Jekyll's 'other' personality. Interestingly, this undercuts the

Above: *A scene from* Five, *Arch Oboler's serious, if naïve, allegory about life in a post-nuclear-holocaust world.*

Left: Flight to Mars, *one of the dullest space operas of the fifties.*

schematicism of the original story which was premised on a split between undiluted good and equally monolithic evil, a split repeated in the Hollywood versions of the story, best filmed by Rouben Mamoulian as **Doctor Jekyll and Mr Hyde** (1932). In this Argentinian version, Hyde does not appear as a cousin to the Wolf Man but more as an up-to-date vampiric figure with long fingernails and large teeth. Filmed in stark black and white, it contains some memorable scenes such as when the windows of a passing train light up, in flashes, the face of the fleeing Dr Jekyll, in an underground tunnel, and, with each flash, the demonic features of Mr Hyde take over more and more.

A lacklustre Mexican remake, by Julian Soler, used the same title in 1972.

d/p/co-s Mario Soffici   *co-s* Ulises Petit de Murat, Carlos Marin   *c* Antonio Merayo, Alberto Muñoz   *lp* Mario Soffici, Olga Zubarry, Jose Cibrian, Rafael Frontura

Lost Continent   (LIPPERT)   b/w and green   83 (79) min
For the first time in America dinosaurs and a rocketship are combined in Newfield's workmanlike handling of the story of an atomic-powered rocket (borrowing footage from **Rocketship X-M,** 1950), which disappears in the South Pacific. The rocket has a secret device on board so Romero, Chandler, Beaumont, Hoyt and Bissell are sent on a rescue mission, only to have their plane crash-land on an island in the same area. They discover uranium fields, which cause the radioactivity which drew the rocket and the plane down, and a number of prehistoric animals which have been preserved in the freak environment.

Interestingly, when they discover the lost continent, the black-and-white print turns green. 'Look,' says one of the characters, 'someone must have put a green bulb in the sun.' In fact a simple green tint was applied directly to the film for the sequence.

Producer Neufeld and his brother director Sam Newfield (who anglicized his name) as a team were responsible for numerous Poverty Row productions for PRC in the forties.

d Samuel Newfield   *p* Sigmund Neufeld   *s* Richard H. Landau   *c* Jack Greenhalgh   *se* Augie Lohman   *lp* Cesar Romero, John Hoyt, Hugh Beaumont, Chick Chandler, Sid Melton, Whit Bissell

The Man from Planet X

(MID-CENTURY FILMS)   b/w   70 min
A triumph of the pulp imagination, *The Man from Planet X* was shot by Ulmer in only six days on sets left over from *Joan of Arc* (1948). The story is a conventional conflation of the melodramatic – an evil scientist (Schallert) battles with an honest reporter (Clarke) for the love of Field – and the cosmic – an alien arrives on Earth in search of assistance for his freezing planet – but director Ulmer binds his material together in a wholly unusual fashion, choosing odd camera angles and creating a real sense of suspense that the erratic fog machine can't obscure. Most interesting of all is Ulmer's depiction of humanity as heartless and as cold as the planet of the aliens who are condemned to extinction when the humans refuse to help and the army bombard the lonely alien and his ship with bazookas. The end, the passage of Planet X through the sky, marked by rushing winds and flashing lights, is accordingly far more sombre than that of most invasion films.

d Edgar G. Ulmer   *p/s* Aubrey Wisberg, Jack Pollexfen *c* John L. Russell   *se* Andy Anderson, Howard Weeks, Jack Rabin   *lp* Robert Clarke, Margaret Field, Raymond Bond, William Schallert, Roy Engel, Charles Davis

The Man in the White Suit

(EALING STUDIOS; GB)   b/w   85(81) min
One of the few British films to treat seriously the problems of industrial relations (and far tougher than *I'm All Right Jack,* 1960), *The Man in the White Suit* is both a searing indictment of British conservatism in which the preservation of the *status quo* is the be all and end all of activity and a gentle reminder, in the person of Guinness' naïf idealist, of the social implications of scientific research.

Guinness is the scientist who invents an everlasting cloth only for his invention to be ruthlessly suppressed by the mill owners (under the leadership of Thesiger). Greenwood (who

gives a superb performance) is the boss's daughter who frees him when he's imprisoned and Martin the washer-woman who poses the awkward question, 'What becomes of me when there's no washing to do?' Intricately plotted (as in the sequence where Guinness, desperate to explain his invention to his boss, Parker, cannot get to see him because Parker is trying to find the whereabouts of the man responsible for overspending the research budget, Guinness) and full of images resonant with meaning (as in the shining white suit made of the everlasting material that Guinness wears for much of the film), the film has an acerbity about it that few other Ealing comedies possess. A marvellous movie.

d/co-s Alexander Mackendrick   *p* Sidney Cole
co-s Roger MacDougall, John Dighton   *c* Douglas Slocombe
lp Alec Guinness, Joan Greenwood, Cecil Parker, Michael Gough, Ernest Thesiger, Howard Marion Crawford, Miles Malleson, Edie Martin

Mr Drake's Duck
(DOUGLAS FAIRBANKS JNR PRODUCTIONS; GB)
b/w   85(71) min
Based on a story by Ian Messiter, this is a typically jolly British caper about a duck that lays radioactive, explosive eggs. Honeymooners (Fairbanks and Donlan) on a farm discover the phenomenon and the armed forces move in to cope. A variation on the fairy-story theme of the goose that laid the golden egg, this lacks the charm necessary to bring off such an idea.

Twenty years later Vincent McEveety made the remarkably similar **Million Dollar Duck** (1971) for the Disney studios.

d/s Val Guest   *p* Daniel M. Angel   *c* Jack Cox   *lp* Douglas Fairbanks Jnr, Wilfred Hyde-White, Yolande Donlan, Howard Marion Crawford, Jon Pertwee, Peter Butterworth

Mysterious Island (COL) b/w 15 chaps
Though, in typical serial fashion, this loose adaptation of Jules Verne's novel introduced a vast amount of new material, including Randle as a beautiful visitor from Mercury seeking to mine radioactive ore with which to blow up the Earth, it actually contains more of the original novel than any of the other four film versions (made in 1929, 1941, 1961 and 1972). Crane leads the Confederate troops who escape from a Union prison camp in 1865 and arrive on the mysterious island. There, with Penn's Captain Nemo, they put paid to Randle's schemes. Predictably plotted and cheaply made, the serial remains quaintly appealing.

d Spencer G. Bennett   *p* Sam Katzman   *s* Lewis Clay, Royal K. Cole, George H. Plympton   *c* Fayte Brown
lp Richard Crane, Marshall Reed, Karen Randle, Ralph Hodges, Gene Roth, Leonard Penn

George Reeves as mild-mannered reporter Clark Kent in Superman and the Mole Men.

Superman and the Mole Men *aka* Superman and the Strange People (LIPPERT) b/w 67 min
A real exploitation quickie, as was befitting for someone following in the footsteps of Sam Katzman, the producer of the first two Superman serials, **Superman** (1948) and **Atom Man versus Superman** (1950), this feature was made to promote the *Superman* teleseries that followed swiftly in its wake. Reeves takes over from Kirk Alyn as Superman and Coates takes over the Lois Lane role. Sent to Silsby to cover a story about the sinking of the world's deepest oilwell, they encounter the luminous Mole people of the title who are driven upwards by the drilling. The populace of Silsby under the leadership of Benson take up arms against the Mole Men, 'because they're different' before Reeves sorts things out with a grin and a lot of liberal philosophizing. Ineptly made, the film is oddly charming, if only for co-producer Maxwell's script which wore its liberal heart on its sleeve, probably because talk was cheaper than special effects.

d Lee Sholem   *p* Robert Maxwell, Barney A. Sarecky
s Richard Fielding (Robert Maxwell)   *se* Ray Mercer
lp George Reeves, Phyllis Coates, Luke Benson, Billy Curtis, Tony Baris, Jack Banbury

The Tales of Hoffmann
(THE ARCHERS/LONDON; GB)   127 (115) min
After the success of the amazing colour film, *The Red Shoes* (1948), he had made with Powell and Pressburger, the famous conductor and composer Thomas Beecham suggested they make Offenbach's often-filmed opera into a classical musical, again in glorious Technicolor and with top class dancers. None of the previous film versions (**Hoffmanns Erzaehlungen** of 1911, 1915 and 1923) had even attempted to convey the spectacular aspects of a well-photographed operatic ballet. Financed by Korda, designed by Hein Heckroth and choreographed by Frederick Ashton, Powell and Pressburger's film offers a fairytale rendering of the stories with Helpmann as the central figure in each and Shearer as the mechanical doll Olympia who steals his heart. Made relatively cheaply and quickly (shot in nine weeks), it might have received first prize in Cannes if the film-makers had agreed to

Left: Douglas Fairbanks Jnr and Yolande Donlan as the honeymooners who find a goose that lays radioactive eggs in the weak fantasy Mr Drake's Duck.

Right: *Leonid Massine in The Tales of Hoffman, Michael Powell's glorious Technicolor extravaganza.*

cut the last episode. They didn't, but the section was removed from the British distribution copy anyway. Made by the same team that had produced *The Red Shoes*, this film didn't quite achieve the same cinematic standards, although there are some memorable moments when dance, décor, colour and camera movement combine to magnificent effect.

d/p/s Michael Powell, Emeric Pressburger   *c* Christopher Challis   *lp* Robert Helpmann, Moira Shearer, Robert Rounseville, Ludmilla Tscherina, Leonid Massine, Ann Ayers, Frederick Ashton, Pamela Brown, Meinhard Maur, Edmond Audran

The Thing *aka* The Thing (from Another World)
(WINCHESTER PICTURES)   b/w   86 min

The Thing, *one of the most influential Science Fiction films of the fifties and one of the few acknowledged classics of the decade. Above* the poster *and below* the alien spores start to grow.

A marvellous film, *The Thing*'s virtues, though celebrated by some (including writer/director Michael Crichton who has called it 'the best Science Fiction film ever made'), have been partially obscured by two controversies, one major, one minor, that have surrounded it since its initial release. The minor one – who directed it, its credited director, Nyby, or its producer Hawks? – is easily cleared up. Hawks bought the rights to the story by John W. Campbell (better known as the legendary editor of *Astounding Science Fiction*) in the forties, commissioned the script, mapped out the film, rehearsed the actors and supervised the actual shooting as well as acting as the film's producer. The film's credited director, Nyby (who didn't direct again until 1957 and the mediocre *Hell on Devil's Island*) had edited several of Hawks' films and, as a favour, to enable him to get his director's ticket, Hawks allowed Nyby to direct the film under his close control. But more revealing

than these 'facts' are the style, look and themes of the film which are undoubtedly Hawksian. In particular, the overlapping dialogue and the relaxed performances of the actors confirm that the film was 'made' by Hawks.

Far more interesting, and revealing of the vast gap between Science Fiction and Science Fiction cinema, was its reception by Science Fiction critics and practitioners. In contrast to the generally favourable reception the film received, they savaged it as, as one critic put it, 'a radical betrayal of its source', for transforming Campbell's shape-changing alien into a *monster* and for its attitude to science in general. The response of journalist Spencer after listening to Cornthwaite's professor explain what the creature is, 'an intellectual carrot, the mind boggles', was widely quoted as exemplifying Hawks/Nyby's crude concept of science and the film was blamed by many for initiating the monster cycle of Science Fiction films which rapidly supplanted the documentary/realist approach of **Destination Moon** (1950) which was generally admired by the Science Fiction fraternity. This argument is misplaced – Spencer is, after all, a journalist whose comments, notably the closing injunction to 'Watch the skies' which has passed into legend, are clearly indicted by Hawks as being clichés, quick and crude descriptions of the situation. Moreover, although Cornthwaite's scientist is presented as misguided in his commitment to pure knowledge, he is depicted by Hawks with sympathy as a professional. More imporantly, in comparison to, say, Frederick Pohl and Cyril Kornbluth's *The Space Merchants* (1952), one of the best novels of the period and representative of the interests of the writers of the time, as Science Fiction, *The Thing* is undeniably old-fashioned. What the reception of the Science Fiction fraternity to *The Thing* represented was the fear that just as the genre was becoming respectable, the cinema was resurrecting the dreaded bug-eyed-monster syndrome of yesteryear. In this they were correct but, in choosing *The Thing* to blame, they seriously misread the film.

Needless to say, the movie is far more interesting than the debates which have surrounded it. Hawks' only other venture into the genre, **Monkey Business** (1952) reveals the dangers of man's anarchic tendencies when unleashed by the drug B-4, *The Thing*, described by Cornthwaite as feeling 'No pleasure, no pain . . . no emotion . . . Our superior in every way', represents those dangers *in extremis*. Like the creature in **Alien** (1979), the thing wants nothing more than to survive and procreate at whatever cost to those around it. B-4 removes the necessary inhibitions that are the mark of social existence, the creature in *The Thing* has no such inhibitions from the start. This view is imbedded in the very structure of the film which perpetually contrasts the group working in unison to a common purpose, as in the marvellous sequence where the individual members of the group of scientists and soldiers sent to investigate the sighting of a mysterious aircraft in Antarctica slowly spread themselves round the shape of the frozen UFO until they form a circle around the spaceship. As individuals they create danger for the group when they act independently, like the soldier who accidentally unfreezes the creature and Cornthwaite who tries to grow more creatures when he discovers that it is a plant. Only the individual actions of Tobey, the natural group leader, who represents concerned instinctive behaviour, as when he quickly slams shut the door to the greenhouse after opening it to reveal Arness' creature, and Sheridan (who has the charming, if unscientific, idea that, if the creature is a vegetable, then 'cooking' it might kill it) are underwritten by Hawks.

Hawks' assumptions about extra-terrestrial life are undeniably conservative (compared to those of Steven Spielberg in **Close Encounters of the Third Kind**, 1977, for example), but their articulation results in one of the best Science Fiction movies of all times.

d Christian Nyby   *p* Howard Hawks   *s* Charles Lederer
c Russell Harlan   *e* Linwood Dunn, Donald Stewart
lp Kenneth Tobey, Margaret Sheridan, Robert Cornthwaite, Douglas Spencer, James Arness, Dewey Martin

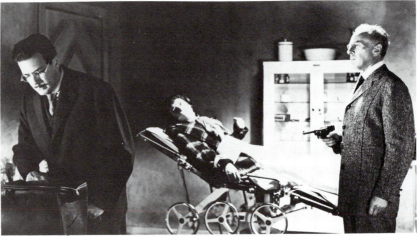

A scene from The Whip Hand, *one of the decade's oddest examples of anti-communism.*

Unknown World

(J.A. RABIN-I.A. BLOCK PRODUCTIONS)   b/w   73 min
Scientist Kilian desperately searches for the solution to impending nuclear devastation in a ploddingly directed film derivative of **Rocketship X-M** (1950), on which producers Rabin and Block had collaborated on the special effects. Backed by playboy Kellogg, a team drills down in a 'cyclotram' to investigate the possibilities of using the centre of the Earth as an atomic fallout shelter. Eventually they find a cavern but a volcanic eruption forces the machine back to the surface.

The screenplay by Kaufman (who later wrote *Bad Day at Black Rock*, 1955, amongst other films) deserved a better director than Morse to tense out its contrast between the

Left: The remnants of mankind take off for Zyra in Rudolph Maté's impressive spectacle, When Worlds Collide.

fruitful, but threatened, surface and the literally sterile, but safe, world to be found below the Earth.

d Terrell O. Morse   *p/se* Jack Rabin, Irving Block
s Millard Kaufman   *c* Allen G. Siegler, Henry Freulich
lp Victor Kilian, Bruce Kellogg, Otto Waldis, Jim Bannon, Tom Handley, Dick Cogan

When Worlds Collide
(GEORGE PAL PRODUCTIONS/PAR)   83 min

Artist Chesley Bonestell (who later created the Martian landscape for **Conquest of Space**, 1955) was responsible for the epic visions of Earth and the planet Zyra for this Pal film scripted by Boehm from the novel of the same name by Edwin Balmer and Philip Wylie, which Cecil B. DeMille had planned to film in 1934. The slow build-up to the passing over Earth of the planet Zyra is well conceived by the Oscar-winning special effects team of Jennings and Barndollar (despite considerable use of stock footage), with erupting volcanoes, tidal waves and eventual destruction. There are classic scenes of weird shapes floating around the skyscrapers of New York, and a giant tidal wave devastating Times Square.

Eventually the Earth collides with the star Bellus and is destroyed. But just before this traumatic conclusion to Earth's history, a rocket-load of survivors, headed by Derr and chosen by lottery, blast off to Zyra. At first the planet looks inhospitable with mountains and snow, but when the apprehensive party land, they find a paradise with water meadows, flowers and lush countryside. They settle thankfully in their new world. The film's unsettling conclusion has the survivors glimpse a futuristic city on the far horizon.

In retrospect the film seems peculiarly old-fashioned, less for the melodramatic sub-plot constructed around the affair of Derr and Rush, than for its initial premise, that a natural cosmic disaster would bring about the end of the world, which side-stepped the fears of a nuclear holocaust of the time.

d Rudolph Mate   *p* George Pal   *s* Sydney Boehm   *c* John F. Seitz, W. Howard Greene   *se* Gordon Jennings, Harry Barndollar   *lp* Richard Derr, Barbara Rush, Peter Hanson, John Hoyt, Larry Keating, Judith Ames

The Whip Hand   (RKO)   b/w   82 min

A Science fiction thriller, full of suspense, ingeniously made from an unreleased film, *The Man He Found*, directed and designed by Menzies, which centred on the discovery of Adolf Hitler, hiding out in Minnesota and once more plotting world domination. Howard Hughes, then head of RKO, got cold feet when the film was completed and accordingly asked writers Bricker and Moss to use the footage in a new way. Out went Hitler and in came the communists, operating with a German biologist who is using a small American town for germ-warfare experiments. In place of Hitler, Waldis is the ex-Nazi communist sympathizer plotting full-scale American destruction. Although a rarity nowadays, it was one of the best received anti-communist films of the fifties, probably because of the skilful way Menzies put together Bricker and Moss' re-workings of the old material. The communist message is unsubtle – 'Like clockwork every May Day, the Iron Curtain is lifted just long enough to impress the rest of the world that communism is on the march!' says the narrator over shots of a May Day parade – but otherwise the film is highly atmospheric, in particular the scenes in the mansion that is the Nazi headquarters in the pine forest.

d William Cameron Menzies   *p* Lewis J. Rachmil
s Stanley Rubin (*The Man He Found*), George Bricker, Frank L. Moss (*The Whip Hand*)   *c* Nicholas Musuraca
lp Elliott Reid, Carla Balenda, Raymond Burr, Otto Waldis, Edgar Barrier, Michael Steele

Alraune *aka* Unnatural *aka* Vengeance *aka* Mandragore   (CARLTON; WG)   b/w   92 min

A clumsy attempt to link topical medical and journalistic concern with artificial insemination with the gothic fantasy about the creation of life and individuality, this is the last version to date of the bestseller by Hanns Heinz Ewers, published in 1913, filmed twice in 1918, then by Galeen in 1928 (the best version), and by Oswald two years later. The title role played by Helm in 1928 and in 1930, is here taken by Knef. Von Stroheim (over)acts the part of the scientist, Ten Brinken, who collects a hanged man's semen from under the gallows and artificially inseminates a prostitute, thus achieving a daughter incapable of 'love', Alraune. The Viennese director Rabenalt, better known for his Nazi propaganda films and for countless operettas, *lederhosen* and *heimat-schmalz*, was obviously totally unsuitable for this darkly romantic story of obsessive, intensely perverse, sexuality. Knef uses her husky voice to good effect, and von Stroheim trades on his established image, but both are left to their own devices by a director who appears to have strayed onto the wrong set. Boehm, in his second screen appearance, is the bland and blond Teuton who later achieved fame as Romy Schneider's partner in the *Sissi* series, until Michael Powell cast him, appropriately, as the psychopathic killer in *Peeping Tom* (1960).

d Arthur Maria Rabenalt   *p* O. Lehmann   *s* Fritz Rotter
c Friedl Behn-Grund   *lp* Hildegard Knef (Neff), Erich von Stroheim, Karl Boehm, Jula Koschka, Trude Hesterberg

Bela Lugosi Meets a Brooklyn Gorilla *aka* The Boys From Brooklyn *aka* The Monster Meets the Gorilla
(JACK BRODER PRODUCTIONS)   b/w   75 min

Lugosi, his career already bedevilled by management, money, marital and drug problems, is the star of this awful piece. He's partnered by Mitchell and Petrillo, faded nightclub performers who made a living out of impersonating Dean Martin and Jerry Lewis – which they do here.

Falling out of a plane on their return from entertaining troops in Guam, the duo are rescued by South Sea natives and meet Dr Zabor (Lugosi), who specializes in a serum which can turn people into gorillas and with whom Mitchell vies for the love of native girl, Charlita. The film is neither funny, nor even unintentionally funny, like Edward D. Wood's **Plan 9 from Outer Space** (1956).

d William Beaudine   *p* Maurice Duke   *s* Tim Ryan
c Charles Van Enger   *lp* Bela Lugosi, Duke Mitchell, Sammy Petrillo, Charlita, Muriel Landers, Al Kikume

Below: Eric von Stroheim with Hildegard Knef as his perverse daughter Alraune.

1952

Captive Women *aka* **3,000 AD** *aka* **1,000 Years from Now**
(WISBERG-POLLEXFEN PRODUCTIONS) b/w 65 (64) min
Pleased with the success of **The Man from Planet X** (1951),
Wisberg and Pollexfen went on to film this piece. In
atom-bomb-devastated New York, human beings have split
into three warring factions – the Norms (good), the Mutates
(indifferent) and the Upriver people (bad) – who hunt each
other in the ruins of Manhattan. The Mutates (led by Randell)
have suffered radiation sickness and raid the Norms (led by
Clarke) to carry off untainted women for breeding purposes.
But both the Norms and the Mutates are at war with the
Upriver people (led by Randall) who worship the Devil. After
much strife the evil Uprivers are drowned in a flooded tunnel
under the Hudson River and Mutate Randell falls in love with
Norm Field. There are some interesting special effects with
New York as an overgrown jungle, shooting out tentacles
underneath the Hudson river, but Gilmore's direction is limp.

The theme is one that re-appeared in the seventies.

d Stuart Gilmore *p/s* Aubrey Wisberg, Jack Pollexfen
c Paul Ivano *lp* Robert Clarke, Margaret Field, Gloria
Saunders, Ron Randell, Stuart Randall, William Schallert

George Wallace (in the rocket suit first worn by Tristram Coffin in King of the Rocket Men, 1949) as Captain Cody, 'Sky Marshal of the Universe' in the cheap and intermittently cheerful serial, Radar Men from the Moon.

1 April 2000 *aka* April 1st, 2000
(WIEN FILM; AUSTRIA) b/w 105 min
This was commissioned by the Austrian government as a
gentle plea to the Allied forces occupying Austria to grant
them self-determination. According to the story, everything
in the country is running smoothly and harmoniously right up
to April fools' day of the year 2000, when the Allied forces
have decided to grant Austria independence, at long last.
Contemporary opinion thought the film a small variety turn
blown up into a blockbuster feature with a cast of thousands.
It was screened at a few European and Latin American
festivals before disappearing back into oblivion. One point of
interest is an appearance by Curt Jurgens before he became an
international star. Wagner of *Caligari* fame photographed the
proceedings as dramatically as he could, but the leaden weight
of both Liebeneiner's direction and the Austrian government's interest in the film proved too much for him.

d Wolfgang Liebeneiner *p* Karl Ehrlich *s* Ernst Maboe,
Rudolf Brunngraber *c* Fritz Arno Wagner *lp* Josef
Meinrad, Hilde Krahl, Judith Holzmeister, Otto Tressler,
Paul Hoerbiger, Hans Moser

Hilfe Ich Bin Unsichtbar *aka* Help I'm Invisible *aka* Alas I'm Invisible
(JUNGE FILM UNION; WG) b/w 88 min
A sentimental domestic comedy even tamer than the Piel
comedies of the thirties (**Die Welt Ohne Maske**, 1934) and as
fulsome in its praise for priggish mediocrity as **Ein Mann
Geht Durch die Wand** (1959). Lingen is the small-minded

husband who toys with electric gadgetry and accidentally
makes himself invisible, disrupting his own life as well as that
of his equally grey family. The direction fails to overcome
such unpromising material and even destroys what little
comedy there could be by playing down the farcical elements
in favour of 'human' touches, ruining the possibility of
making this into a genuine grotesque representation of a
thoroughly stunted social group.

d E.W. Emo *p* Karl Junge *s* Herbert Tjadens, Erwin
Kreker, Kurt Werner *c* Hans Schneeberger *lp* Theo
Lingen, Inge Landgut, Fita Benkhoff, Grethe Weiser,
Margarethe Haagen, Kaete Pontow, Arno Aszmann

Invasion U.S.A.
(AMERICAN PICTURES CORP.) b/w 74 (70) min
The influence of Arch Oboler's **Five** (1951) on director Green
is clear in this interesting piece about atomic war. Its release
was largely ignored and, consequently, today it's practically
forgotten.

Basically an all-out assault on communism, preying on the
fears of its audiences, the film features O'Herlihy as a
mysterious stranger hypnotizing a group of people in a New
York bar into thinking that the Cold War is over and the
Russians have launched a full-scale atomic attack. Members
of the group die horrible deaths, the last plunging from the
top of a skyscraper, before they realize they have been
hypnotized and, with some relief, continue to discuss the
anti-communist war they see as inevitable. Though its
low-budget over-reliance on stock footage from World War II
and army training films diminishes its impact, it remains an
evocative film. It was the first film that producer Zugsmith,
best known for the melodramas he made with director
Douglas Sirk (*Written on the Wind*, 1956 and *The Tarnished
Angels*, 1957) had any creative control over.

d Alfred E. Green *co-p* Albert Zugsmith *co-p/s* Robert
Smith *c* John L. Russell *lp* Dan O'Herlihy, Gerald Mohr,
Peggie Castle, Robert Bice, Erik Blythe, Wade Crosby

Monkey Business (FOX) b/w 97 min
This classic comedy from the (uncredited) director of **The
Thing** (1951) treats the rejuvenation theme so popular in the
twenties with a madcap frenzy. Stable and stolid married
couple Grant and Rogers revert to frantic adolescent behaviour under the influence of an elixir discovered by Grant
and taken by the pair by mistake. Like *Bringing Up Baby*
(1938), the film is an essay on responsibility in which the

Left: Cary Grant, Ginger Rogers and Marilyn Monroe in Howard Hawks' screwball comedy about rejuvenation, Monkey Business.

elixir, B-4, opens up the frighteningly anarchic world (seen at its most disturbing in the movie's conclusion in which all the major characters revert to childish behaviour, swinging around the laboratory like chimpanzees) that lies just beneath the surface of civilized life. However, where in the earlier film, Katharine Hepburn's zany irresponsibility forced Grant's stiff professor to see how sterile his life was, *Monkey Business* highlights the dangers of such action on a larger scale.

The result, elegantly scripted and directed with his customary authority by Hawks, the most 'invisible' of Hollywood directors, is one of the finest American comedies ever. Monroe, who co-starred with Jane Russell in Hawks' next film, *Gentlemen Prefer Blondes* (1953) gives a marvellous performance as the secretary Grant attempts to live it up with.

d Howard Hawks *p* Sol C. Siegel *s* Ben Hecht, Charles Lederer, I.A.L. Diamond *c* Milton Krasner *lp* Cary Grant, Ginger Rogers, Charles Coburn, Marilyn Monroe, Hugh Marlowe, Henri Letondal, Larry Keating

Radar Men from the Moon (REP) b/w 12 chaps
Wallace, wearing the rocket suit from Republic's earlier **King of the Rocket Men** (1949), is Captain Cody, 'Sky Marshal of the Universe' in this cheap, very cheap, and cheerful chapterplay who puts paid to Moon monarch Barcroft's plans of invading Earth. The storyline was made even more complicated than it might have been by the studio's insistence on using stock footage and, wherever possible, props from previous outings. More charming was screenwriter Davidson's total disregard for scientific truth. Thus, on the Moon, where most of the action takes place, Wallace needs no spacesuit and is unaffected by the reduced gravity – and this two years after **Destination Moon** (1950).

In 1966, the serial was condensed into a feature, *Retik, the Moon Menace*.

d Fred C. Brannon *p* Franklyn Adreon *s* Ronald Davidson *c* John MacBurnie *se* Howard Lydecker, Theodore Lydecker *lp* George Wallace, Aline Towne, Roy Barcroft, William Bakewell, Clayton Moore, Peter Brocco

Red Planet Mars (MELABY PICTURES) b/w 87 min
Based on the play *Red Planet* by screenwriter Balderston (whose plays had formed the basis for the scripts of both *Dracula*, 1930 and **Frankenstein**, 1931) and John Hoare, *Red Planet Mars* deals more explicitly with the reds-under-the-beds fears of America in the early fifties than any other Science Fiction film of the decade.

A husband and wife scientist team (Graves and King) pick up television transmissions from Mars, in which Mars is described as a utopian planet, ruled over by a god-like supreme authority. On Earth, the news is received badly by both Western governments and the communists – in one sequence aged peasants become revolutionaries and topple the Russian government, replacing it with a priestly monarchy. An ex-Nazi scientist (Berghof), the inventor of the 'hydrogen tube' with which Graves made contact with Mars, claims that the Martian messages are fakes – he knows because he sent them in the hope of bringing about the collapse of capitalism. Then, in a ludicrous climax, as Graves and Berghof argue, a further message comes from Mars, in which a Martian says that the supreme authority on Mars is God himself. Graves, Berghof and King die in a 'hydrogen explosion' caused by the maddened Berghof shooting at the transmitter and, in an epilogue, Bouchey's kindly President of the USA commends Graves and speaks with pleasure about the new world order.

Religious crusades, most of which included strong anti-communist messages (such as those run by Billy Graham), swept America in the early fifties and several Science Fiction movies of the decade, notably **The Day the Earth Stood Still** (1951) had a strong religious element to them. *Red Planet*

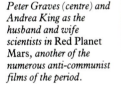
Peter Graves (centre) and Andrea King as the husband and wife scientists in Red Planet Mars, *another of the numerous anti-communist films of the period.*

Mars, Veiller's first independent production, however, displays its religiosity and 'message' with such disregard for narrative or character that it is virtually unwatchable.

d Harry Horner *p/co-s* Anthony Veiller *co-s* John L. Balderston *c* Joseph Biroc *lp* Peter Graves, Andrea King, Herbert Berghof, Marvin Miller, Morris Ankrum, Walter Sande, Willis Bouchey

Untamed Women

(JEWELL ENTERPRISE PRODUCTIONS) b/w 70 min
Shot in under a week and using footage from *One Million BC* (1940), *Untamed Women* is, quite simply, awful. Frantically directed by Connell, the film stars Conrad (who directed **The Flying Saucer**, 1950) as a World War II bomber pilot, picked up alone from a liferaft. Under sodium pentathol, he tells his doctor (Talbot) that he was washed ashore with his crew on an island full of beautiful, if savage, women and dinosaurs. The women (who are apparently descended from the Druids) fear the 'hairy men' from the sea who pillage them at will. The bomber crew give the girls a helping hand and in the climax to end all climaxes, a volcano erupts killing the dinosaurs, the girls and the hairy men, leaving only Conrad alive, to be picked up alone from a liferaft.

d W. Merle Connell *p* Richard Kay *s* George W. Sayre *c* Glen Gano *se* Paul Sprunk, Alfred Schmid *lp* Mikel Conrad, Doris Merrick, Richard Monqhan, Mark Lowell, Lyle Talbot, Morgan Jones

Zombies of the Stratosphere (REP) b/w 12 chaps
This time out it's Holdren who wears the mask and flying suit that did such sterling service in **King of the Rocket Men** (1949) and **Radar Men from the Moon** (1952). He plays a sort of star ranger who uncovers and foils a complicated plot whereby the Martians plan to blow the Earth up with an H-bomb and then shift Mars into Earth's orbit to get the benefit of Earth's superior climate (?!). Bradford is the villain, Nimoy (later to achieve lasting fame as Mr Spock) his zombie henchman and Waxman the treacherous scientist who helps them. The script, by Davidson who, single-handed, wrote the last 13 Republic serials, is crude as is Brannon's direction. But then in 1952, the serial was a thing of the past.

A year later Holdren took over the role of Commander Cody, sky marshal of the Universe, first essayed by George Wallace in *Radar Men from the Moon* (1952) but the serial was a false one culled from episodes of Republic's Commander Cody teleseries.

In 1958, an edited down version of this serial was re-issued as *Satan's Satellites*.

d Fred C. Brannon *p* Franklyn Adreon *s* Ronald Davidson *c* John MacBurnie *se* Howard Lydecker, Theodore Lydecker *lp* Judd Holdren, Aline Towne, Lane Bradford, Leonard Nimoy, Wilson Wood, John Crawford, Stanley Waxman

Abbott and Costello Go to Mars *aka* On to Mars
(U) b/w 77 min
Abbott and Costello slapstick and double-talk their way through the crash-landing of their rocketship on Venus, while headed for Mars. The all-female population (all entries from the Miss Universe contest) hate men and Venus itself is depicted by director Lamont as a mountainous and fog-enshrouded planet with vast underground caves ruled over by Queen Alura (Blanchard). Pursued by the Queen and her horde, the duo reach their rocketship in the nick of time and blast off back to Earth, where they arrive in Manhattan, making the Statue of Liberty duck. A dreary offering, this is one of the worst of Abbott and Costello's films.

d Charles Lamont *p* Howard Christie *s* John Grant, D.D. Beauchamp *c* Clifford Stine *se* David S. Horsley
lp Bud Abbott, Lou Costello, Mari Blanchard, Robert Paige, Martha Hyer, Jack Kruschen

Abbott and Costello Meet Dr Jekyll and Mr Hyde
(U) b/w 76 min
Having met Frankenstein (1948) and the Invisible Man (1951) and travelled to Mars (1953), this just had to happen when producers, using every gimmick they could think of, were trying to revive the (fading) popularity of the comedy duo. Working from a story by Sid Fields and Grant Garrett, scriptwriters Loeb and Grant have Bud and Lou as US detectives tangling with the Jekyll and Hyde legend in Edwardian London. The transformation scenes are particularly effective and Karloff plays Jekyll with great brooding enthusiasm but the movie did little to help regain the duo's popularity.

d Charles Lamont *p* Howard Christie *s* Leo Loeb, John Grant *c* George Robinson *se* David S. Horsley *lp* Bud Abbott, Lou Costello, Boris Karloff, Eddie Parker, Craig Stevens, Helen Westcott

Alérte au Sud *aka* Alert in the South
(NEPTUNE/SIRIUS/FONORAMA; FR) 110 min
A desert adventure story to the glory of the French army and its secret service one year before the Algerian war of independence officially broke out. The idea was furnished by André-Paul Antoine and the script by Le Chanois, himself an

Left: *The charming robot from* Undersea Kingdom *(1936) and* The Mysterious Dr Satan *(1940) makes a welcome return to the cinema in the silly* Zombies of the Stratosphere.

Bud Abbott (plus Miss USA, 1952, Jackie Loughery) and Lou Costello on Venus in Abbott and Costello Go to Mars.

Above: *The Beast from 20,000 Fathoms* menaces *New York.*

unremarkable director at the time. Mad scientist Nagel (von Stroheim) has established an atomic plant in the Sahara from where he can direct a death ray. The French agent Jean Pasquier (Pascal) and his boss (Murat) locate the base and with the help of the troops, destroy the plant killing Nagel. Van Eyck plays a sinister but debonnaire spy while the love interest is represented by the dancer Nathalie (Canale). There are lots of desert action scenes, shot in Morocco, with effective musical accompaniment by Joseph Kosma. Sorano and Tissier provide the comic relief.

d Jean Devaivre *s* Jean-Paul Le Chanois *c* Lucien Joulin
lp Jean-Claude Pascal, Erich von Stroheim, Peter van Eyck, Daniel Sorano, Jean Murat, Jean Tissier, Gianna-Maria Canale, Lia Amanda, D. Lecourtois, R. Francoeur

The Beast from 20,000 Fathoms (WB) b/w 80 min
The first of the awakening-giant-monster films of the fifties, which established the basic formula which many other films then followed. Director Lourié was Renoir's principal designer in France during the thirties, but this was his first Science Fiction work. He went on to make **The Colossus of New York** (1958), **Behemoth, the Sea Monster** (1959) and **Gorgo** (1961).

Based on the short story *The Fog Horn* by Ray Bradbury, *The Beast* was animator Harryhausen's first project. Although here the special effects are not particularly original, with better budgets and greater maturity, Harryhausen's work became far more interesting.

A dinosaur is awakened from a deep sleep in the Arctic by an atomic explosion. Defrosted by the blast, the bewildered dinosaur returns to its original ancestral home, which is now covered by New York City. Having created havoc, traditional style, in New York in an atmospheric ending, the dinosaur is lured into an amusement park and killed, amongst ferris wheels and roller-coasters. Morheim and Freiberger's script is stilted and the film suffers from long periods of inaction but Lourié's direction is surprisingly atmospheric and he makes his low budget look much more expensive by adroit use of lighting and shadow.

The Beast reportedly cost less than $200,000 to make and grossed more than $5 million, which set the financial precedent for the run of monster pictures to follow.

Right: *Lew Ayres as the scientist who falls under the sway of the brain he keeps alive in* Donovan's Brain, *the best version of Curt Siodmak's thrice-filmed novel.*

d Eugène Lourié *p* Hal Chester, Jack Dietz *s* Lou Morheim, Fred Freiberger *c* Jack Russell *se* Ray Harryhausen, Willis Cook *lp* Paul Christian, Paula Raymond, Cecil Kellaway, Kenneth Tobey, Lee Van Cleef, Donald Woods

Cat Women of the Moon *aka* **Rocket to the Moon**
(ASTOR/2-M PRODUCTIONS) b/w 64 min
Hilton's direction and Hamilton's screenplay are never dull but as a combination they are very bad. A crew from an American air-base land on the Moon, steered to a certain spot by Windsor who is telepathically dominated by the leader of the cat women (Brewster) who inhabit caves between the dark and light sides of the Moon. Tufts leads the expedition, arriving in a spaceship whose control room belonged to a previous submarine film – you can still see the periscope.

Having killed a couple of giant horned spiders, Tufts and crew arrive at a Greek-looking Moon city (reportedly left over from a Marco Polo film) where they confront the cat women, who are dressed in black leotards and don't look like cats at all. They are anxious to hitch a lift to Earth and use their telepathy to try to dominate the crew but are weakened by wrangling amongst themselves. Hurriedly the crew return to their submarine control room and take off back to Earth.

The film was made in 3-D which made the antics – some of which were performed in front of crumpled backdrops, one of them showing Monument Valley – even more hilarious. Astor remade the film in 1958 as **Missile to the Moon**.

d Arthur Hilton *co-p/se* Jack Rabin *co-p* Al Zimbalist *s* Roy Hamilton *c* William F. Whitley
lp Sonny Tufts, Marie Windsor, Victor Jory, Susan Morrow, Douglas Fowley, Carol Brewster

Donovan's Brain
(DOWLING PRODUCTIONS) b/w 83 min
Two other Hollywood films, **The Lady and the Monster** (1944) and **Vengeance** (1962) were based on Siodmak's book *Donovan's Brain* but this version by vintage director Feist is the closest to the original novel. Ayres as brain scientist Cory

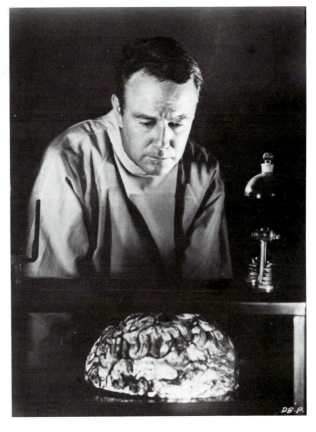

(played with real conviction) tries to save the life of millionaire Donovan (Colgan) but fails. Seizing his opportunity for the advancement of science, he removes Donovan's brain and secretly keeps it alive in his laboratory only to have the brain take over his mind. The take-over sequences are brilliantly portrayed with Ayres altering the expression on his face without any help from the makeup department. Donovan's brain has evil intent, and apart from making the scientist continue his tax-dodging scene it tries to kill Ayres' assistant Evans (a fine performance) and wife Davis (Nancy Reagan to be). But as Ayres begins to strangle her, a lightning bolt strikes the brain and the menace is no more.

d/s Felix Feist *p* Tom Gries *c* Joseph Biroc *se* Harry Redmond Jnr *lp* Lew Ayres, Gene Evans, Nancy Davis, Steve Brodie, Lisa K. Howard, Michael Colgan

Four-Sided Triangle
(HAMMER; GB) b/w 81 (74) min
Based on William F. Temple's novel, director Fisher winds up the film with a massive conflagration – an ending he used on the many Frankenstein films he subsequently directed. A low-budget film, it relies on invention rather than special effects when a scientist (Murray) constructs a machine that can duplicate human beings. This ambitious idea comes unstuck when he duplicates the woman he loves (Payton), who has in fact fallen for another man (Van Eyssen). The irony is that the clone also falls for Van Eyssen. Tabori and Fisher's script is interesting but the tiny budget restricts any potential the film might have had.

d/co-s Terence Fisher *p* Alexander Paal, Michael CCarreras *co-s* Paul Tabori *c* Reginald Wyer *lp* Barbara Payton, Stephen Murray, John van Eyssen, James Hayter, Percy Marmont, Glyn Dearman

Invaders from Mars
(NATIONAL PICTURES CORP.) 82 (78) min
One of the most unusual films of the fifties. Menzies – who directed **Things to Come** (1936) – making his last film as a director, achieves a brilliant nightmarish quality by brooding atmosphere and imagery. A youngster (Hunt) is awakened by the sound of a flying saucer. His father (Erickson) investigates and disappears to return a changed man. The boy's mother (Brooke) seems different too, whereupon Hunt finds a couple of radios buried in his parents' necks. He seeks the professional help of a psychologist (Carter) and an astronomer (Franz), and they find that the flying saucer is operated by green creatures and captained by a tentacled Martian head

(played by midget actress Luce Potter) who controls his Earth slaves. Hunt and Carter are captured by the aliens but rescued by a colonel of the militia (Ankrum), and the Martian spaceship is destroyed by explosives.

The American version ended with Hunt waking up having dreamt it all, then hearing a flying saucer land. The longer European version retains the story as it stands, eliminates the nightmare of waking up and adds a section in an observatory. The whole film is seen through a child's eyes and the menacing alien adults not only emphasize the isolation of the child's world but also underline the reds-under-the-bed paranoia of the fifties.

The film was originally designed for the 3-D process but the idea was dropped before shooting began. Nevertheless, in spite of the low budget, this is the first 'invasion' film to be shot in colour.

d William Cameron Menzies *p* Edward L. Alperson *s* Richard Blake *c* John Seitz *se* Jack Cosgrove (and, uncredited, Jack Rabin, Irving Block, Howard Lydecker) *lp* Helena Carter, Arthur Franz, Jimmy Hunt, Leif Erickson, Hillary Brooke, Morris Ankrum

It Came from Outer Space: *man dwarfed by the vastness of a construction not of his own making.*

Left: *Jimmy Hunt (right) and Helena Carter taken captive by the Martians in* Invaders from Mars, *the first of the many invasion films of the fifties to be made in colour.*

Right: *Judd Holdren (centre) examines serialdom's last secret laboratory in company with Fred Berest and Nick Stuart in* The Lost Planet.

It Came from Outer Space (U) b/w 80 min

This is the first Science Fiction film by Arnold who later became a striking, often brilliant, fantasy director. Producer Alland, who was Orson Welles' protégé at the Mercury Theatre, played the newsreel reporter in *Citizen Kane*. Based on a screen treatment, *The Meteor* by Ray Bradbury, Essex's script features aliens crash-landing on Earth in a ship that looks like a meteorite. The familiar figure of the unworldly astronomer (Carlson) witnesses the event in true H.G. Wells' style, but when he tries to tell his fellow human beings about the appearance of the aliens no-one will believe him. The aliens are helped by the fact that they are invisible and are able to replace local people with alien doubles, who behave in a similar manner to the originals with some slight differences, including a zombie-like stare when the doubles are not in the company of other human beings. The aliens have merely stopped off on Earth because their spaceship has broken down and they need human beings as mechanics. The repair work is slow and the aliens need more and more humans to help them and, as a result, the doubles proliferate. Eventually the locals decide to take direct action against the stranded aliens and attempt to destroy them but Carlson, having discovered that the aliens mean no harm to the world, protects them in the final confrontation. When the spaceship is repaired the aliens take off for outer space, having returned the missing citizens and reclaimed their doubles. From this perspective the film can be seen as an optimistic version of **The Man from Planet X** (1951).

Dark desert roads and sudden moments of fear underline Arnold's ability as a director of Science Fiction films, and Essex's/Bradbury's lines match his images superbly. 'You see lakes and rivers that aren't really there, and sometimes you think the wind gets into the wires and sings to itself.' The film was shot in 3-D but still works when shown 'flat'. One of the art directors, Robert Boyle, was a Hitchcock 'regular' and worked on **The Birds** (1963).

d Jack Arnold *p* William Alland *s* Harry Essex
c Clifford Stine *se* David S. Horsley *lp* Richard Carlson, Barbara Rush, Charles Drake, Russell Johnson, Joseph Sawyer, Alan Dexter

Below: *Richard Carlson desperately trying to re-assert control of the new atomic technology that has created an energy eating radioactive isotope in the imaginative* The Magnetic Monster.

Killer Ape (SAM KATZMAN) b/w 68 min

One of a series of Jungle Jim films, based on Alex Raymond's strip cartoon. Here scientist Paiva is experimenting on apes with a new drug, which takes away their will to fight. Once he has perfected the drug, Paiva intends to sell it to the highest

bidding warlike nation. One-time Tarzan Weissmuller comes to the rescue, after the man-ape (Palmer) kills Paiva, and burns the creature alive in a cave. The budget was so small, a consistent feature of Katzman's productions, that Palmer only wore a fur waistcoat and a set of false teeth.

d Spencer L. Bennet *p* Sam Katzman *s* Carroll Young, Arthur Hoerl *c* William Whitley *lp* Johnny Weissmuller, Carol Thurston, Nestor Paiva, Max Palmer, Burt Wenland, Paul Manon

The Lost Planet (COL) b/w 15 chaps

This was the last of Hollywood's theatrically released Science Fiction serials. Holdren, who had starred in both Columbia and Republic's last batch of such films, is the reporter and saviour of the galaxy – the aim of world domination which had satisfied most of the villains of the thirties and forties being inflated in almost the same proportion as the budgets of the later serials were deflated. Fox is the mad scientist and Taylor the eccentric scientist he kidnaps. The end was a fitting one: seeking to escape, Fox boards his 'cosmojet' and orders his robot to set course for deep space, only to have the robot miscalculate and set a course for infinity.

d Spencer Gordon Bennet *p* Sam Katzman *s* George H. Plympton, Arthur Hoerl *c* William Whitley *lp* Judd Holdren, Vivian Mason, Ted Thorpe, Forrest Taylor, Michael Fox, Gene Roth, Fred Berest, Nick Taylor

The Magnetic Monster

(A-MEN PRODUCTIONS) b/w 76 min

Using stock footage from **Gold** (1934) for its climax, this is an excellent, low-budget Science Fiction drama involving a new radioactive isotope which eats energy – and doubles its size every 12 hours by converting the energy into matter. A nearby town is threatened but the isotope is eventually rendered harmless by feeding it a 900,000,000-volt electric charge.

Siodmak (whose best film as a director this is) and Tors wrote their original script with the hope of creating a teleseries around Carlson's character as a member of the Office of Scientific Investigations. Mudie is the scientist finally consumed by his creation – whereupon Carlson delivers the film's moral, 'in nuclear research, there is no place for lone wolves' – and Bryon Carlson's dedicated wife.

d/co-s Curt Siodmak *p/co-s* Ivan Tors *c* Charles Van Enger *se* Jack Glass *lp* Richard Carlson, King Donovan, Jean Bryon, Harry Ellerbe, Leo Britt, Leonard Mudie

The Maze (AA) b/w 80 min

A highly original, flawed piece, based on the novel by Maurice Sandoz. Carlson, about to be married to Hurst who is still chaperoned by her aunt (Emery), is summoned back to his old Scots ancestral home just before the wedding and does not return. Following him, Hurst and Emery arrive at the castle only to find that Carlson is prematurely aged and will not see them. In a maze with a pond at its centre, Hurst can see mysterious people circulating and Emery sees something that turns out to be a man-frog. Shot in 3-D (and replete with numerous extraneous 'pelt and burns' effects), this is a very strange, grotesquely fascinating, piece competently directed by Menzies and full of suspense, yet almost ruined by a small budget. Eventually the frog turns out to be one of Carlson's ancestors – the true laird – who has lived for 200 years as a man-frog, and is taken to bathe freely at night in the middle of the maze by his servants.

d William Cameron Menzies   *p* Richard Heermance
s Dan Ullman   *c* Harry Neumann   *lp* Richard Carlson, Veronica Hurst, Katherine Emery, Michael Pate, Hillary Brooke, John Dodsworth

The Mesa of Lost Women *aka* Lost Women *aka* Lost Women of Zarpa

(A.J FRANCES WHITE-JOY HOUCK PRODUCTIONS)   b/w 70 min
There are overtones of **Cat Women of the Moon** (1953) in this piece directed by Tevos and Ormond. Coogan is Dr Araña (Spanish for spider), a crazy scientist conducting experiments on dwarfs, giant spiders and women in an attempt to make women more ferocious. Travis is briefed by Coogan's deposed partner (Stevens) to fly to Mexico to stop the project. After a conflict with Coogan's victims the *mesa* is finally blown up but one of the women survives, presumably for a sequel that never came. The special effects are grim and the film is a pale shadow of *Cat Women*.

co-d/s Herbert Tevos   *co-d* Ron Ormond   *p* Melvin Gordon, William Perkins   *c* Gil Warrenton, Karl Struss   *lp* Jackie Coogan, Richard Travis, Allan Nixon, Mary Hill, Robert Knapp, Tandia Quinn, Harmon Stevens

El Monstruo Resucitado *aka* Doctor Crimen

(INTERNATIONAL CINEMATOGRAFICA; MEX)   b/w 85 min
The first major medical Science Fiction movie in Mexico, loosely based on the Frankenstein story but injecting gory surgical motifs into it, laying the foundations of the genre that came to dominate Hispanic Science Fiction in the sixties and seventies, as exemplified by the work of Jesús Franco from **Gritos en la Noche** (1962) onwards. Set in the Balkans, this story concerns a bored journalist, Nora (Miroslava) who is ordered by her boss (Wagner) to follow up a mysterious advertisement placed by Dr Ling (Linares Rivas). Ling turns out to be a misshapen creature who, rejected by his peers, has become the stereotypical mad scientist, here specializing in plastic surgery. He falls in love with Nora but fearing she will betray him he resuscitates a young man who committed suicide, Ariel (Navarro) by transplanting a new brain into him, and orders him to fetch Nora so that he can kill her. However, Nora and Ariel fall in love and the zombiesque youth rebels against the orders of his master, turning on him and killing him, whereupon Wagner saves Nora from the beautiful young zombie. The picture closes as Nora holds the now definitely dead Ariel's body in her arms. The movie inverts the usual Frankenstein roles, making the monster attractive and the doctor a monster. The role of the servant, played by Lugosi in **Son of Frankenstein** (1939) and **The Ghost of Frankenstein** (1942), is here allotted to an ape-like creature called Crommer (Berne). The somewhat perverse overtones of necrophilia and beauty-and-the-beast motifs make this a more interesting picture than Urueta's more immediately sexploitative work such as *La Ilegitima* (1955), the film that showed Ana Luisa Peluffo in the nude and launched her career in Mexican sex-and-fantasy pictures such as **El Hombre Que Logro Ser Invisible** (1958) and **Los Astronautas** (1960).

d/co-s Chano Urueta   *p* Sergio Kogan   *co-s* Andrino Maiuri
c Victor Herrera   *se* Jorge Benavides   *lp* Miroslava, Carlos Navarro, Jose Maria Linares Rivas, Fernando Wagner, Alberto Mariscal, Stefan Berne

The Neanderthal Man

(WISBERG-POLLEXFEN PRODUCTIONS)   b/w   77 min
Wisberg and Pollexfen made the successful **The Man from Planet X** (1951), directed by Edgar Ulmer and the not-so-successful **Captive Women** (1952). That film's direction had been a major factor in its failure and so, in an attempt to restore their reputation, they hired DuPont, once Germany's leading film critic and later a film-maker.

The clichéd script centres on Shayne, a mad scientist who tries out a serum on his housekeeper, sees her regress to an ape-woman and then tries it out on himself. DuPont, a minor talent in the best of circumstances, could bring no innovation to such a leaden Jekyll and Hyde idea and Shayne blunders on woodenly, turning himself from man to menacing ape-monster, wearing an equally wooden mask that doesn't flex with his facial movements. He eventually dies at the claws of a sabre-toothed tiger he has also created.

d E. A. DuPont   *p/s* Aubrey Wisberg, Jack Pollexfen
c Stanley Cortez   *se* Jack Rabin, David Commons
lp Robert Shayne, Richard Crane, Doris Merrick, Joyce Terry, Robert Long, Dick Rich

Phantom from Space

(PLANET FILMWAYS INC.)   b/w   72 min
Producer/director Wilder (brother of Billy) made this humorless but workmanlike low-budget quickie with ambitious special effects from Weldon and Anderson. It is probably his best film, his later work degenerated to the utter silliness of **Killers from Space** (1954).

An invisible alien (Sands) crash-lands on Earth in a flying saucer near a large US observatory and kills two men and some innocent picnickers. The killings alert cop Landers and scientists Anders and Nelson, who find the fatal flaw in the alien's makeup: to breathe Earth's atmosphere he has to wear a helmet containing air from his own world. Anders and

Below: *Robert Shayne as* The Neanderthal Man, *one of the many monsters unleashed by scientific experimentation in the fifties.*

Phantom from Space, *the best of W. Lee Wilder's Science Fiction films.*

Right: George Barrows in his gorilla suit plus diving helmet with Claudia Barrett and George Nader in Robot Monster, *probably the most famous bad movie of all time.*

Nelson lure the alien into their observatory and put him in an infra-red light machine, which makes him visible. They then remove his helmet and in the ensuing chase he falls to his death from a ladder.

d/p W. Lee Wilder *s* Bill Raynor, Myles Wilder *c* William Clothier *se* Alex Weldon, Howard Anderson *lp* Ted Cooper, Rudolph Anders, Noreen Nash, James Seay, Dick Sands, Lela Nelson, Harry Landers

Project Moonbase (GALAXY PICTURES) b/w 63 min
This rarely seen film, constructed from the first episodes of an unsold teleseries, *Ring Around the Moon*, was co-scripted by Heinlein (his last involvement in film-making) who'd earlier co-written the script for the influential **Destination Moon** (1950). The melodramatic plot contains everything that the makers of *Destination Moon* tried to avoid. Johns is the spy who causes the first moonshot (from an orbiting space station already established by the Americans) to crash, leaving Martell and Ford stranded on the Moon. Whereupon they are promptly married by satellite! Slackly scripted and unimaginatively directed by former stuntman Talmadge, the film is only of interest for a few of the odd quirks that Heinlein introduced. Thus, in typical Heinlein fashion, the Martell

character is called Colonel Breiteis (ie bright eyes) and the president of America is a woman.

The special effects by Fresco are better than one would expect from a television production but the film lacks the sense of confidence that even Heinlein's worst novels have in abundance.

d Richard Talmadge *p* Jack Seaman *s* Robert A. Heinlein, Jack Seaman *c* Willard Thompson *se* Jacques Fresco *lp* Donna Martell, Ross Ford, Hayden Rorke, James Craven, Larry Johns, Herb Jacobs, Ernestine Barrier

Robot Monster
(THREE DIMENSIONAL PICTURE PRODUCTIONS)
b/w 63(62) min
Probably the best known 'bad movie' of the genre, as much for the ludicrous mix of naïvety and banality of Ordung's screenplay as for Tucker's repetitive slow-moving direction, *Robot Monster*, for all its silliness, is a remarkably conventional Science Fiction movie, as a synopsis makes clear. Set in the form of a dream of Moffett's space-crazy ten-year-old, Ordung's script features a family of six led by scientist Mylong (whose mittel-European accent gives the film an extra, odd *frisson*) as the last survivors on Earth after the Ro-Mans have decimated the rest of the population with their 'calcinator ray'. The reason behind the invasion is that Earth is on the threshold of space travel and the rational Ro-Mans fear competition. Mylong and company are immune to the effects of the calcinator ray because Mylong has just invented total immunization serum and, accordingly, the single Ro-Man invader has to track them down and physically kill them. Just as he is about to do this, Moffett wakes up and the dream is over.

But if the film is conventional, touching on many of the themes of American Science Fiction of the early fifties, Tucker's unimaginative articulation of his material makes the movie quite extraordinary. The Ro-Man, played by Barrows in his oft-seen gorilla suit with a diving helmet complete with wavering antennae, agonizes over his mission in dialogue that seems to be an unconscious parody of logical positivism at its most inane: 'I cannot, yet I must. How do you calculate that? At what point on the graph do "must" and "cannot" meet? Yet I must – but I cannot!' The conjunction of such earnest dialogue (spoken by John Brown), Barrows' ridiculous outfit, inept special effects (such as the Ro-Man's intergalactic bubble-blowing communications table) and Tucker's flat direction – the film's structure consists of alternating between the Ro-Man either walking about or communicating with his

leader, 'the great one' (also played by Barrows) and the Mylong family continually recapitulating the plot to each other – is simply tedious. Even the Ro-Man's abduction of Barrett and his growing attraction to her lacks any dramatic edge.

The film's faults, as usual, were the result of woefully inadequate finances – shot in an experimental 3-D format, the film reportedly cost less than $16,000 – and Tucker and Ordung's lack of imagination. Footage from *One Million BC* (1940) and **Flight to Mars** (1951) is included in the film. Director Tucker, who attempted suicide after a dispute with the production company, was also responsible for **Cape Canaveral Monsters** (1960). More surprisingly, the score is by Elmer Bernstein (who also scored **Cat Women of the Moon**, 1953) who later moved on to bigger budget films such as *Thoroughly Modern Millie* (1967), for which he won an Oscar.

d/p Phil Tucker   *s* Wyott Ordung   *c* Jack Greenhalgh   *se* Jack Rabin, David Commons   *lp* George Barrows, Gregory Moffett, George Nader, Claudia Barrett, John Mylong, Selena Royle

Sieriebristaya Pyl *aka* Silver Dust
(MOSFILM; USSR)   102 min

In the middle of the first Cold War, a reporter from *Life* magazine saw this film and angrily accused it of being 'red propaganda' totally misrepresenting the USA. The story has an American scientist, Sam Stil (Bolduman) invent a ghastly radioactive dust and try to find human guinea pigs for tests (in the USA, troops and prisoners were used for such tests). Two competing businessmen, aided by a hawkish general and an ex-Nazi scientist (Werner von Braun?) are after the stuff. The *Life* reporter objected to the film's inclusion of anti-American scenes such as someone being falsely arrested, the kicking of a negro maid, an attempted lynching. . . . In the end, Stil is killed by hired guns in the pay of big business. The acting was no more true to life than the usual Cold War portrayals of the opposition (see, for example, the representations of 'communists' in Hollywood). None of the incidents nor the characters seem in themselves improbable, although Room, the director of such classics as *Bed and Sofa* (1927) and *The Ghost That Will Not Return* (1929), always liked a degree of stylization to make clear that film characters always represent far more than just 'individuals', a stylistic honesty not often manifested in the West. The scenarist, Filimonov, had also co-written the more pedestrian **Kosmitchesky Reis** (1935), which suggests that Room dominated the film, ably assisted by the USSR's top cameraman, Tissé, who had shot all Eisenstein's classic films. The result is an interesting, amusing and not at all far-fetched piece of work.

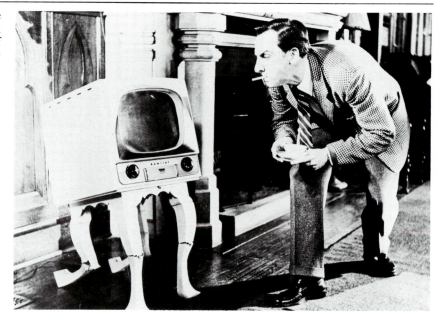

Above: *Hans Conried argues with his TV set in Arch Oboler's extraordinary assault on television,* The Twonky.

d Abram Room   *s* August Jakobson, A. Filimonov   *c* Edouard Tissé   *se* P. Malaniksev   *lp* M. Bolduman, Valentina Utchakova, Vladimir Larionov, A. Chanov, S. Pilyavskaya

Spaceways   (HAMMER; GB)   b/w   76 min
Fisher later became a major British director in the horror genre, largely for Hammer, but this, with its slow-moving script by Tabori and Landau from Charles Eric Maine's original radio play, is only in a minor film.

Duff is an American scientist working on a new British rocket whilst his wife (Chevreau) has an affaire with Osborn, another scientist who is also a Russian spy. Suddenly they disappear and investigator Wheatley assumes that Duff has despatched the corpses of Chevreau and Osborn into outer space – the perfect murder. To prove his innocence, Duff takes his lover (Bartok) in a rocket to the satellite where Wheatley has suggested the bodies probably lurk. Too late, Wheatley discovers Chevreau and Osborn hiding out on Earth, and in chagrin Osborn kills Chevreau; no doubt Duff and Bartok live happily ever after.

Fisher directs inventively, choosing odd camera angles to heighten the tension but the poor dialogue, static scenes and the unimaginative rocket sets (V2 rockets in long shots and a brief sequence from **Rocketship X-M**, 1950) make for a routine outing.

d Terence Fisher   *p* Michael Carreras   *s* Paul Tabori, Richard Landau   *c* Reginald Wyer   *lp* Howard Duff, Eva Bartok, Alan Wheatley, Cécile Chevreau, Andrew Osborn, Michael Medwin

The Twonky   (ARCH OBOLER PRODUCTIONS)   b/w   72 min
Director, producer, screenplay writer and inventor of the single projector 3-D system, Space Vision, which he used when making **The Bubble** (1966), Oboler was originally a radio producer whose hatred of television veered towards paranoia. He discovered *The Twonky* (written by Henry Kuttner under the pseudonym Lewis Padget) in the forties magazine *Unknown*, which published stories in a light but gruesome vein. Like most of his films, this is a very heavy-handed piece of moralizing.

Conried plays a philosophy professor who is given a new TV by his wife (Warren). Like Oboler, Conried hates TV, particularly this one which is a Twonky, a robot that is concerned to change Conried's life. The Twonky lights Conried's pipe, tells him what he should read and is able to alter the thoughts of those around him. Conried hits back,

Eva Bartok surrounded by the bakelite verities of British Science Fiction of the early fifties in Spaceways.

Mickey Rooney as The Atomic Kid. *In retrospect the movie reveals just how unaware of the real dangers of radiation poisoning people were in the fifties.*

determined to preserve his own will, his own free speech and in the end he destroys the Twonky.

Despite the essential whimsicality of the central idea, especially when compared to Oboler's more committed films, notably **Strange Holiday** (1945) and **Five** (1951), Oboler is unable to invest the project with any leavening humour. United Artists grudgingly gave it a limited release 17 months after the film had been completed.

d/p/s Arch Oboler   *c* Joseph Biroc   *lp* Hans Conried, Billy Lynn, Gloria Blondell, Janet Warren, Ed Max, Al Jarvis

War of the Worlds

(GEORGE PAL PRODUCTIONS/PAR)   85 min
Although Pal's film is flawed it remains a landmark in the history of Science Fiction cinema. He altered the location of the original Wells' novel from London in 1890 to California in 1953 and made several other changes – the famous Martian war machines in the shape of walking tripods have been replaced by sinister flying saucer-like craft, for instance. Even less effective is the love interest which is placed awkwardly in the path of the plot. Nevertheless Lyndon's script is strong and Haskin's direction is well-paced and stylish (he later directed **Conquest of Space** (1955) and **The Power** (1967) for Pal), although not all Jennings' spectacular special effects work well – on their first appearance the Martian war machines have an obvious network of wires surrounding them.

When a meteor falls near a small community in southern California, a large orb emerges. A death ray disintegrates the

Below: The Martians attack in War of the Worlds.

first investigators and scientist Barry guesses that the meteor is a pioneer Martian spaceship. He then discovers that meteors have been landing all over the world. Soon flying machines with attached death rays arise from the meteors, and no matter how much armament is gathered against them (including an A-bomb), the death-dealing flying machines are invincible. The machines are not robots, but controlled from within by Martians, who raid Los Angeles but eventually succumb to Earth's bacteria. The ruined buildings, the deserted city, the death rays and the Martians themselves come together in a stunning special effects' climax.

With the exception of **Earth versus the Flying Saucers** (1956), *War of the Worlds* is the only American Science Fiction film to feature a mass invasion of aliens (a commonplace in Japanese Science Fiction) which gives the film a deeper resonance than normal, especially when allied to Haskin's dwelling on religious symbols and the prologue which suggests, equally unusually, that the Earth is merely one of many planets. The result, the sub-plot of Barry and Robinson's developing romance notwithstanding, is that *War of the Worlds* remains watchable to this day, a film that is less a simple mirror of American attitudes and fears of the fifties and more a reflection of man's conservative responses to the idea of other life-forms before the possibility of such contact was seen as possible. In this respect, despite the updating, the film is true to H.G. Wells' novel.

d Byron Haskin   *p* George Pal   *s* Barre Lyndon   *c* George Barnes   *se* Gordon Jennings, Wallace Kelley, Paul Lerpae, Ivyl Burks, Jan Domela, Irmin Roberts   *lp* Gene Barry, Ann Robinson, Les Tremayne, Lewis Martin, Robert Cornthwaite, Sandro Giglio, Cedric Hardwicke (narrator)

The Atomic Kid

(MICKEY ROONEY PRODUCTIONS)   b/w   86 min
Freeman and Murphy's script (based on a story by Blake Edwards) has Rooney survive an atomic test glowing with radioactivity. In retrospect, like the scene in **War of the Worlds** (1953) where the military simply brush off the radiation dust that falls on their clothes after they've dropped an A-bomb on the Martians, *The Atomic Kid* reveals just how unaware of the real dangers of radiation people were in the fifties, even at the height of fears about 'the bomb'. Thus when Rooney is put into hospital to be decontaminated, his sharp buddy (Strauss) tries to make a quick buck out of the accident. He gets mixed up with a spy (Keane) but Rooney, when released, is able to bust the spy ring before, after marrying his nurse (Davis), he picks another house which is due for an atomic test. Martinson, making his début feature, directs in the camp style that reached its apotheosis in **Batman** (1966).

d Leslie H. Martinson *p* Mickey Rooney *s* Benedict
Freeman, John Fenton Murphy *c* John L. Russell Jnr
se Howard Lydecker, Theodore Lydecker *lp* Mickey
Rooney, Robert Strauss, Elaine Davis, Bill Goodwin, Whit
Bissell, Robert Emmett Keane

The Bowery Boys Meet the Monster

(AA) b/w 66 min

The Boys, intent on creating a playground for local kids,
approach the Gravesend family who have an old house that
seems ideal. They then discover that Dehner wants to put a
brain in Cosmos, his gorilla and his brother, Corrigan, has
invented a robot called Gorog. Other members of the family
show equal initiative with Mason, a vampire, searching for
necks, and Corby trying to satisfy the insatiable needs of her
man-eating plant. The result is a farcical vehicle for the
Bowery Boys that is only spasmodically funny.

Bernds, a regular on the Bowery Boys and Blondie series,
directed a number of low-budget Science Fiction movies
including **Space Master X-7** and **Queen of Outer Space**
(both 1958), and **Return of the Fly** (1959).

d/co-s Edward Bernds *p* Ben Schwalb *co-s* Elwood Ullman
c Harry Neumann *se* Augie Lohmann *lp* Leo Gorcey,
Huntz Hall, Lloyd Corrigan, Ellen Corby, John Dehner,
Laura Mason

The Creature from the Black Lagoon

(U) b/w 79 min

Half-man, half-fish, the amphibious creature from the black
lagoon is as threatening as the shark in *Jaws* (1975), with
which it has strong links. Director Arnold was an early
pioneer of the art of playing on the fears of the average human
being – as Spielberg did in the seventies and Spielberg was
reportedly heavily influenced by the brooding, menacing style
of Arnold's atmospheric film.

Denning, accompanied by Carlson and his fiancée Adams,
leads the expedition to capture the gill-man. They drug the
creature but he breaks loose forcing them to track him
through his underwater lairs – some of the best sequences,
with sunlight slanting through on to the surface whilst below
the creature lurks amongst sunken logs and weeds – where
Denning is killed and Adams kidnapped. Carlson tries to
rescue Adams, and in the final confrontation other members
of the expedition shoot the creature and it plunges deep into
the lagoon. The creature was played out of the water by
Chapman and underwater by Browning, who had to hold his
breath for five minutes at a time as there was no room for an
aqualung in the tightly fitting costume.

Strong on atmosphere (it was filmed in 3-D) and plot, but
with a low budget, the film is an excellent example of how to
make a good monster movie. Talking of *Creature*, Arnold
said, 'it plays upon a basic fear that people have about what
might be lurking below the surface of any body of water. You
know the feeling when you are swimming and something
brushes your legs down below – it scares the hell out of you if
you don't know what it is. It's the fear of the unknown. I
decided to exploit this fear as much as possible in filming *The
Creature from the Black Lagoon* but I also wanted to create
sympathy for the creature. . .'. The film was a financial
success and two sequels followed: **Revenge of the Creature**
(1955) and **The Creature Walks Among Us** (1956).

d Jack Arnold *p* William Alland *s* Harry Essex, Arthur
Ross *c* William E. Snyder *se* Charles S. Wellbourne
lp Richard Carlson, Julia Adams, Richard Denning,
Ben Chapman, Ricou Browning, Antonio Moreno

Devil Girl from Mars

(DANZIGER PRODUCTIONS; GB) b/w 77 (76) min

Written by Mather and Eastwood from their play of the same
name, the setting of this British revision of **The Day the
Earth Stood Still** (1951), a film that would be 'revised' yet

again by Burt Balaban in Britain as **The Stranger from Venus**
(1954), is a remote Scottish inn in which escaped killer
Reynolds takes shelter only to find an exhilarating mixture of
British stereotypes – the barmaid (Corri), the newspaperman
(McDermott), the unhappy model (Court) and the scientist
(Tomelty). Laffan's Nyah arrives from Mars in her spaceship,
dressed in a leather jumpsuit and miniskirt, intoning the
script to explain that Mars has been taken over by women and

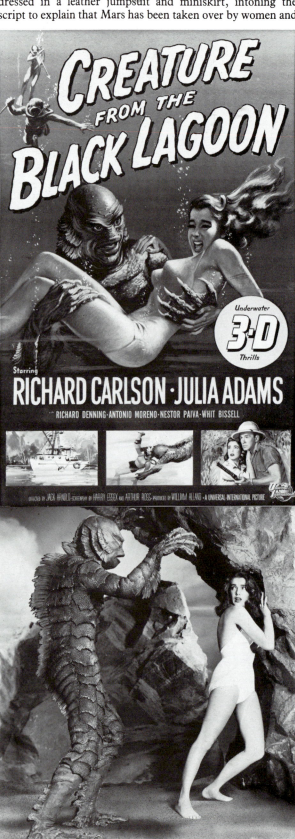

Left: The Creature from
the Black Lagoon.
*Beneath the suit of the
fifties best-loved creature
was Ricou Browning.*

Hazel Court menaced by Martian invader Patricia Laffan in one of the silliest examples of British Science Fiction, Devil Girl from Mars.

dominated by the Honda-Tsuburaya team at Toho. Unlike most Western contributions to the genre, the Japanese creatures were generally played by actors in rubber suits (here Godzilla is played by the producer, Tanaka) who would trample all over scale models of cities, usually culminating in the destruction of Tokyo. Godzilla himself (with only one or two exceptions, all monsters were male) is a 400-foot-tall reptile inspired by the tyrannosaurus rex that fights the giant ape in *King Kong* (1933). He is awakened by an A-bomb explosion and emerges fully grown from the sea to attack Japan. In the end, a weakness is identified by clever Japanese scientists and the monster is killed – usually with a possibility for revival. Here, oxygen is removed from the sea to defeat the monster when all the world's weaponry has failed.

Many aspects of this ritualistic pattern, based on an original story credited to Shigeru Kayama, became standard features of the genre, including the breathing of fire (occasionally ice – Baragon – or a laser – Ghidorah – or fire-extinguisher – Gaos). There is virtually no amorous intrigue in these films: the monster is the star and people are victims. The violence is impersonal and massive but not represented as personal, detailed cruelty. The monsters do not eat people. In fact they rarely eat at all. They are amphibian, until the appearance of Gappa (**Daikyoju Gappa**, 1967), the triphibian monster. The major exception to these generic conventions is **Mosura** (1961): she is female, flies and is a contraption manipulated with wires, not a rubber-suited actor. Other variations came into play as the genre developed its own dynamic.

The great character actor Shimura, familiar from many Kurosawa movies, appeared in this immensely successful film and made various guest appearances in subsequent Honda monster movies, including **Chikyu Boeigun** (1957). Made at a boom time in Japanese production – the country was overtaking the USA as world leader in film production – the smash hit was bought by Joseph E. Levine who initiated the practice of inserting newly shot American footage into foreign films, an example followed with Russian Science Fiction by Corman and others (**Planeta Burg**, 1962; **Meshte Nastreshu**, 1963; etc). Terry Morse was employed to shoot scenes with Raymond Burr as a reporter witnessing the events. Some Japanese footage was eliminated, but the US version still ran 17 minutes longer than the original. It was released in 1956 and proved almost as big a box-office success as Honda's film. Except for *Gigantis*, Godzilla's subsequent performances were all in colour: **Gigantis** (1955), **King Kong Tai Gojira** (1963), **Mosura Tai Gojira** (1964), **Kaiju Daisenso** (1965), **Ghidorah Sandai Kaiju Chikyu Saidai No Kessan** (1965), **Nankai No Daiketto** (1966), **Gojira No Musuko** (1967), **Kaiju Soshingeki** (1968), **Oru Kaiju Daishingeki** (1969), **Gojira Tai Hedora** (1971), **Gojira Tai Gaigan** (1972), **Gojira Tai Megalon** (1973), **Gojira Tai Mekagojira** (1974) and **Mekagojira No Gyakushu** (1975).

the result is 'an intransigent matriarchy'. Aided by Chani, her robot, she circles the inn with an invisible electronic shield and demands healthy Earthmen to take back to Mars for breeding purposes. Eventually Reynolds heads for London in her spacecraft but manages (mysteriously) to blow it up from the inside, gloriously sacrificing himself and killing po-faced Nyah.

The film has a cult reputation in America.

d David Macdonald *p* Edward J. Danziger, Harry Lee Danziger *s* John C. Mather, James Eastwood *c* Jack Cox *se* Jack Whitehead *lp* Patricia Laffan, Hazel Court, Hugh McDermott, Peter Reynolds, Joseph Tomelty, Adrienne Corri

Gog (IVAN TORS PRODUCTIONS) 85 min

Although few colour prints now exist, Tors' slow-moving and over-explanatory offering was originally made in colour and 3-D – although little advantage was taken of the process. Gog and Magog are non-humanoid robots dominated by a convincing computer called NOVAC (*N*uclear *O*perated *V*ariable *A*utomatic *C*omputer) at a laboratory in New Mexico which is developing the first space station. Investigator Egan arrives to check sabotage allegations and discovers that a chain of murders is being carried out – the most visually effective of which involves a man trapped in a low temperature unit who freezes and then shatters as he hits the floor. Eventually it is discovered that the computer is controlled by a high-flying jet and is being programmed to sabotage its own base, with the help of the robots. Director Strock proceeds at a creaking pace, pausing to explain every scientific device – of which there are many – a feature that was *de rigueur* in all Tors' productions.

d Herbert L. Strock *p* Ivan Tors *s* Tom Taggart *c* Lathrop B. Worth *se* Harry Redmond Jnr *lp* Richard Egan, Constance Dowling, Herbert Marshall, John Wengraf, Philip Van Zandt, Valerie Vernon

Right: Death stalks a New Mexico Space laboratory when the master computer, NOVAC, is sabotaged in Herbert Strock's slow-moving Gog.

Gojira *aka* Godzilla King of the Monsters
(TOHO; JAP) b/w 81 (98) min
Together with King Kong and Frankenstein's monster – both later reincarnated in the Japanese Kaiju Eiga or monster movies – Godzilla is the most popular screen monster ever, appearing in more than 15 films and spawning a whole genre

Left: *The first appearance of Godzilla, the most famous Japanese monster of all*, in Gojira.

After this unexpected box-office smash, Honda's next major creation was **Rodan** (1956), followed by Baran (**Daikaiju Baran**, 1958) and *Mosura* (1961). Other companies later developed their rival beasts: the children's film studio, Daiei, created Gamera (**Daikaiju Gamera**, 1966); Nikkatsu created the *Gappa* family (1967) and Shochiku Guilala (**Uchu Daikaiju Guilala**, 1967).

d/co-s Inoshiro Honda   *p* Tomoyuki Tanaka   *co-s* Takeo Murata   *c* Masao Tamai   *se* Eiji Tsuburaya, Akira Watanabe, Hiroshi Mukoyama   *lp* Takashi Shimura, Momoko Kochi, Akira Takarada, Akihiko Hirata, Fuyuki Murakami, Sachio Sakai, Ren Yamamoto, Frank Iwanaga
US version: lp Raymond Burr

Killers from Space

(PLANET FILMWAYS INC.)   b/w   71 min
Graves is the scientist survivor of a plane crash who is captured and brainwashed – during which he sees his heart suspended in the air above his body in a cave – by aliens from Astron Delta to be sent out as their representative to Earth. His wife (Bestar) and assistant (Gerstle) note that Graves has turned to espionage and, although he's given a sodium pentathol injection in order to establish the truth, the explanation is so bizarre that no-one will believe him. The simple climax has Graves, when the brainwashing wear off, returning to the aliens' cave, shutting off the dynamo from which they are gaining power and stepping out of harm's way as the aliens are decimated in an atomic explosion. A cheaply made, cheap film.

d/p W. Lee Wilder   *s* Myles Wilder   *c* William Clothier
lp Peter Graves, Barbara Bestar, James Seay, Frank Gerstle, Steve Pendleton, John Merrick

William Lundigan and Martha Hyer in a bizarre publicity pic for Riders to the Stars.

The plot centres on Marshall's endeavours to catch a meteor to discover why it is meteors don't burn up in the 'cosmic rays' outside the Earth's atmosphere, which he's sure will destroy rocketships. At each step in the training of the astronauts (Carlson, Lundigan and Karnes), the script dutifully explains every point while director Carlson (a regular actor in Science Fiction films and occasional director) dutifully stops the action. The result is not merely an awful film, but the classic example of how not to make Science Fiction on a small budget, the proof (as if it were needed) that Science Fiction is more a matter of fiction than science (however good or bad the science might be).

d Richard Carlson *p* Ivan Tors *s* Curt Siodmak *c* Stanley Cortez *se* Harry Redmond Jnr, Jack Glass *lp* William Lundigan, Herbert Marshall, Richard Carlson, Martha Hyer, Dawn Adams, Robert Karnes

Rocket Man (PANORAMIC PRODUCTIONS) b/w 79 min
Bruce, the celebrated satirist, co-scripted this uninspired film. Orphan Winslow receives a ray gun from an anonymous spaceman which makes people tell the truth when it's fired. Justice of the peace Byington adopts him and the little town faces up to the effects of the ray gun which in the end is used to stop the villain (Parnell) taking over the orphanage. A minor point of interest is that the spaceman is wearing Klaatu's impressive spacesuit from **The Day the Earth Stood Still** (1951).

d Oscar Rudolph *p* Leonard Goldstein *s* Lenny Bruce, Jack Henley *c* John Seitz *lp* George Winslow, Spring Byington, Charles Coburn, Anne Francis, John Agar, Emory Parnell

The Snow Creature
(PLANET FILMWAYS INC.) b/w 80 min
The first fifties film about the Abominable Snowman involving the discovery of the creature by expedition leader Langton. The Yeti is sent to Los Angeles where he breaks out of his cage, goes on the rampage and is eventually chased into the sewers where he is killed. Sands, who played the **Phantom from Space** (1953), is the Yeti whose totally inadequate furry suit results in most of his scenes being played in the half-light. Billy Wilder's brother Lee directed in the gloom.

d/p W. Lee Wilder *s* Myles Wilder *c* Floyd D. Crosby *se* Lee Zavitz *lp* Paul Langton, Leslie Denison, Teru Shimada, Rollin Moriyama, Robert Kino, Dick Sands

The Stranger from Venus *aka* **Immediate Disaster** *aka* **The Venusian** (RICH AND RICH PRODUCTIONS/PRINCESS PICTURES; GB) b/w 75 min
This low-budget remake of **The Day the Earth Stood Still** (1951), featuring the same female lead, Neal, was filmed in England. She crashes her car and is approached by a stranger (Dantine), who tells her that he is from Venus. He and Neal fall in love and Dantine reveals that he has been sent to Earth because the Venusians are concerned about our misuse of atomic power. Neal's fiancé (Bond) gets help to set up an electronic trap for the alien spaceship but, when Dantine threatens retribution from his mothership, Bond gives up and Dantine sends his back-up fleet away – a heroic gesture as the Earth's atmosphere is killing him. In a melodramatic death scene with Neal he disappears, leaving only a scarf as a keepsake.

Most of the action is confined to one limited set, an inn, a central location for so much English low-budget drama, be it Shakespeare or *Coronation Street*. For all its ineptness, the film is quaintly moving, perhaps the result of its American director, Austrian star and German writer's total misunderstanding of English matters, which gives the pub conversations in particular an edge of surrealism.

Above: *Three of the aliens from Astron Delta in the unimaginative* Killers from Space.

Monster from the Ocean Floor *aka* **It Stalked the Ocean Floor** *aka* **Monster Maker**
(PALO ALTO) b/w 64 min
The feature début of Ordung (best remembered for the awful script for **Robot Monster**, 1953), this film is only of note as Corman's first production.

Ordung directs at a funereal pace this tale of Kimbell's lady illustrator, on holiday in Mexico, seeing a sea monster (a one-eyed octopus) but being unable get marine biologist Wade to believe her. Determined to prove herself right, she pursues the monster underwater where it attacks her before she's rescued, in the nick of time, by Wade in a mini-sub which rams the monster. Made for less than $12,000, the most imaginative thing about the film was the way Corman acquired the mini-sub: manufacturers Aerojet General gave it free in return for the publicity.

d Wyott Ordung *p* Roger Corman *s* William Danch *c* Floyd Crosby *lp* Anne Kimbell, Stuart Wade, Dick Pinner, Jack Hayes, Wyott Ordung, Inez Palange

Riders to the Stars (A-MEN PRODUCTIONS) 82 min
American Science Fiction of the fifties can be divided into two groups, best contrasted by the work of Roger Corman and George Pal respectively. Corman, by far the more inventive director/producer of the two, working with far smaller budgets manages to invest his films with a genuine sense of drama. The characters are stereotypes and the monsters ludicrous, but the films, even when they are as patently silly as **It Conquered the World** (1956), have a degree of wit about them that comes from taking the characters and their situations seriously and imaginatively. In complete contrast, Pal's work as a producer is underpinned by an almost documentary approach to his material. From **Destination Moon** (1950) onwards, his films have a concern with scientific realism, often at the expense of drama. It is this, above all, that both made the films so important at the time and so stilted nowadays. Tors, one of the most prolific producers of Science Fiction in the early fifties, even more than Pal, is concerned with scientific verisimilitude. Indeed the constant feature of his films is the detailed explanation of technical and scientific matters at the expense of drama. *Riders to the Stars* is the perfect example of this.

d/co-p Burt Balaban   *co-p* Gene Martel   *s* Hans Jacoby
c Kenneth Talbot   *lp* Patricia Neal, Helmut Dantine, Derek
Bond, Cyril Luckham, Marigold Russell, Arthur Young

Target Earth (ABTCON PICTURES INC.)   b/w   75 min
Based on the novella *Deadly City* by Ivar Jorgenson, this
features Crowley as the girl who discovers a nearly deserted
city menaced by robots and watches in horror whilst they kill
most of the remaining population with death rays which are
built into their heads (a testament to the influence of Klaatu
from **The Day the Earth Stood Still**, 1951). Denning rounds
up the survivors and creates a defence committee and,
eventually, scientist Bissell finds the robots' achilles' heel by
using ultrasonic waves to crack the faceplates in their armour.
In the process he destroys himself and the other survivors,
except Crowley and Denning. The robots are disappointing,
poorly designed and lumbering, but the initial scenes of the
characters alone in the deserted city are surprisingly compelling. Director Rose only made two other films.

d Sherman A. Rose   *p* Herman Cohen   *s* William Raynor
c Guy Roe   *se* Dave Koehler   *lp* Richard Denning, Virginia
Grey, Kathleen Crowley, Richard Reeves, Robert Roark,
Whit Bissell

Them! (WB)   b/w   93 min
Directed by Douglas in semi-documentary style *Them!* is one
of the best American Science Fiction films of the fifties. So
confident were Warners of its success that its content was kept
secret during production and even the posters did not give
much away. A child (Descher) is discovered wandering in the
desert in a state of deep shock by two policemen (Whitmore
and Drake). Nearby they find a wrecked trailer and a single
track in the sand, then hear a chilling cry on the horizon. Back
in town, Drake hears the cry again, steps out of a building –

Tobor, the emotional robot, comes to the rescue in Tobor the Great.

and is never seen again. FBI agent Arness investigates and
discovers that atomic tests in the desert have produced a giant
species of ant. Special effects man Ayers built only two
principal ants – one complete and the other mounted on a
boom, with only a head and forequarters. The production
crew used this model for close-ups and a series of levers
operated the ant's moving parts. Other inanimate insects were
built for 'crowd scenes' and a wind machine moved their

Left: *The discovery of the queen and her brood in* Them!. *The film's success spawned numerous imitations.*

antennae to and fro. On the rampage the ants are eventually destroyed by poison gas – except for a queen, who escapes and lays her eggs in a Los Angeles drain. The eggs spawn more giant ants but these are burnt alive in the catacomb of drains before they can do more damage.

Although the film has been described by some commentators as an anti-communist tract, with the ants as communists and Arness as the FBI man cleaning up America, it lacks the paranoia of such films. In contrast to **I Married a Monster from Outer Space** (1958), for instance, which dwells on the take-over of normal middle American townspeople by aliens to create its sense of paranoia, *Them!* places its characters on the fringes of the hostile world of the desert. The fear of *I Married a Monster from Outer Space* is of being sapped from within, the fear of *Them!* is wholly external; they, the ants, are finally on the march. In short, the film contrasts the artificial havens of man's cities with the hostile world of the desert where nature reigns supreme.

Them! was the largest-grossing Warner film of 1954 and was quickly imitated by films like **Tarantula** (1955), **The Black Scorpion** (1959) and **The Deadly Mantis** (1957).

d Gorden Douglas *p* David Weisbart *s* Ted Sherdemann *c* Sid Hickox *se* Ralph Ayers *lp* Edmund Gwenn, James Whitmore, James Arness, Joan Weldon, Sandy Descher, Chris Drake

Tobor the Great (DUDLEY PICTURES) b/w 77 min
An inventor (Holmes) creates a large robot Tobor (Smith) with emotions, who can also receive telepathic impulses. Gadge (Chapin) an 11-year-old scientific genius and Holmes' grandson forms the closest relationship with Tobor (robot spelt backwards). The first child/robot film to be made in America in the sound era, robots having been the playthings of countless kids in the silent era (eg **Dr Smith's Automaton**, 1910), it was followed by **The Invisible Boy** (1957) and **The Colossus of New York** (1958).

Communist spies capture Holmes and Chapin but Holmes summons Tobor (by means of a secret transmitter hidden in a mechanical pencil) and Tobor comes to the rescue. The ending is oddly brutal for a children's film with Holmes blasting Tobor off into space.

Sholem's direction is trite and sentimental, a feature of so many juvenile-oriented Science Fiction outings of both the Disney studios and the British Children's Film Foundation.

d Lee Sholem *p/co-s* Richard Goldstone *co-s* Phillip Macdonald *c* John L. Russell *se* Howard Lydecker, Theodore Lydecker *lp* Charles Drake, Karen Booth, Billy Chapin, Taylor Holmes, Lyle Talbot, Lew Smith

20,000 Leagues Under the Sea
(WALT DISNEY) scope 127 min
This is one of Disney's best action films. Fleischer (ironically enough the son of Disney's only major competitor in the animation field in the thirties, Max Fleischer) directs Fenton's straightforward script with obvious enjoyment.

Mason gives a wonderfully measured performance as the cultured yet fanatical Nemo (called Dakkar in the Verne novel) who uses his 'submersible', the *Nautilus*, to sink the warships of all nations in a frenzied attempt to end warfare on Earth, giving the film a topical edge which climaxes in the mushroom cloud that hangs over Nemo's island base when it is destroyed in the finale. Such concerns, however, were clearly secondary to Fleischer (who also made **Fantastic Voyage**, 1966 and the awkward **Soylent Green**, 1973). He treats the story as an adventure, pure and simple, in which Nemo's principles take second place to the much-praised fight with a giant squid. The result is an energetically mounted movie that has become the model for all subsequent treatments of Nemo's emperor of the ocean floor. Douglas is suitably vulgar as the rough diamond of a harpoonist who, in company with Lukas' humanitarian scientist and Lorre's nicely comic valet, is rescued by Nemo. All three become Nemo's reluctant passengers whose continued attempts to escape form the basis of the film's plot.

The film, which won Oscars for its special effects and art direction, more significantly was the first to be distributed by

Right: *The* Nautilus *from* 20,000 Leagues Under the Sea.

the Disney company's newly established distribution arm, Buena Vista.

d Richard Fleischer *p* Walt Disney *s* Earl Fenton
c Franz Planer *se* John Hench, Josh Meadow, Ub Iwerks
lp Kirk Douglas, James Mason, Paul Lukas, Peter Lorre, Robert J. Wilke, Carleton Young

1955

Cesta do Praveku *aka* Journey to the Beginning of Time *aka* Voyage to Prehistory

(STUDIO GOTTWALDOW; CZECH) 92 (87) min

Zeman is one of the few genuine successors of Méliès. His marvellously inventive and often stunningly beautiful combinations of live action, puppets, animation, uncannily precise models and painted sets, are unrivalled. This film, typical of his work – mostly Jules Verne type stories aimed primarily at children – has four boys who voyage down an underground river until they come upon a land where prehistoric monsters still roam. The animals were electronically controlled puppets animated with stop-frame techniques and multiple exposures, anticipating methods developed later by Harryhausen and the **Star Wars** (1977) type of special effects.

As happened with **Planeta Burg** (1962), an American producer, Cayton, picked up the film, shot additional scenes with four American kids discovering a secret cave as they are rowing in Central Park, dubbed the lot and released it in 1966 as *Journey to the Beginning of Time*, possibly cashing in on the success of *One Million Years BC* (1965, which starred Raquel Welch). The extra shooting was by Huston. Cayton credited himself as co-author with Zeman. The boys were called James Lukas, Victor Betjal, Peter Hermann and Charles Goldsmith.

Zeman's next project was not merely inspired by Verne, he began translating Verne's stories directly to the screen, combining a number of them for his **Vynalez Zkazy** (1958).

d/s Karel Zeman *c* Vaclav Pazdernik, Antonin Horak
lp Vladimir Bejval, Petr Herrman, Zdenek Hustak, Josef Lukas
US version: p/co-s William Cayton *c* Anthony Huston

Conquest of Space (PAR) 81 min

Based on the book *The Mars Project* by Werner von Braun, Pal saw this as a sequel to **Destination Moon** (1950), which he had made independently. When Paramount saw the script they objected to the expense and, as a result, the original concept was scaled down, very much to the detriment of the project. Pal had originally conceived a manned exploration of

Left: *Phil Foster in conversation with Joan Shawlee in George Pal's uninspired sequel to* Destination Moon *(1950),* Conquest of Space.

Two of Karel Zeman's electronically controlled puppets in the charming Cesta do Praveku.

Gigantis and Angurus in mid-battle in Gigantis.

financed by mobster Granger. Gay's experiments in removing the top of the victim's skull, taking out the brain and replacing it with atomic energy, result in the creation of an atomic zombie. The giant goes on the rampage, destroying buildings and railways, and is only stopped when Granger, realizing that Denning is on to him and he has nothing to lose, sends out all his zombies *en masse,* to be shot up in gruesome style by the police.

Far worse films have been made and indeed achieved a cult following of sorts but few others have assembled so many elements – gangsters, atomic power, zombies, Nazis – and simply placed them together side by side in such an unconscious fashion.

d Edward L. Cahn   *p* Sam Katzman   *s* Curt Siodmak
c Fred Jackman Jnr   *lp* Richard Denning, Angela Stevens, John Launer, Michael Granger, Gregory Gay, Karl Davis

Gigantis *aka* **Gojira No Gyakushu** *aka* **The Fire Monster** *aka* **The Volcano Monster** *aka* **Godzilla Raids Again** *aka* **The Return of Godzilla** *aka* **Godzilla's Counterattack** *aka* **Counterattack of the Monster** (TOHO; JAP) b/w 78 min
The second appearance of Godzilla (**Gojira,** 1954), although in a slightly modified form and under an assumed name. In this story devised by Shigeru Kayama, he is discovered on a remote island fighting another monster, Angurus (who reappeared later teamed up with Godzilla in **Gojira Tai Gaigan,** 1972, and in **Gojira Tai Mekagojira,** 1974). Both were awakened by A-bomb blasts. Gigantis kills his rival and moves towards Tokyo, destroying Osaka en route, until he is buried by an avalanche of ice on a snow-covered island. The rubber-suited actors enthusiastically stomp across delicately made toy models of cities and crash through high tension wires (an effect that occurs in nearly all Kaiju Eiga). The lack of success of this effort may have persuaded Toho to reunite Honda with the Godzilla team for their next major creation, **Rodan** (1956).

An American version of *Gigantis* was produced by Paul Schreibman and directed by Hugo Grimaldi in 1959.

d Motoyoshi Oda   *p* Tomoyuki Tanaka   *s* Takeo Murata, Sugeaki Hidaka   *c* Seichi Endo   *se* Eiji Tsuburaya, Akira Watanabe, Hiroshi Mukoyama, Masao Shirota   *lp* Hiroshi Koizumi, Setsuko Wakayama, Minoru Chiaki

Venus, Mars and Jupiter, but he ended up with only the Mars journey and an insipid father-son relationship worked into the storyline. The aerial reconstructions of the planet Mars are prophetically accurate, but the film suffers heavily from Paramount's cheese-paring.

In the near future a massive space station orbits the Earth and an equally vast spaceship is being built. At the last minute the ship is ordered on an arduous journey to Mars but the captain (Brooke), seeing the flight as an attempt to reach God, considers it blasphemous and tries to stop the ship from landing. Fleming is Brooke's son and the film's nominal hero.

The most successful aspect of the film is the view of the planet itself, created by astronomical painter, Chesley Bonestell. The red sandy world with its chunky black rock looks extraordinary, as does the darker hue of the Earth-like sky. The final script by O'Hanlon (after versions by Barré Lyndon, Philip Yordan, and George Worthington Yates were rejected by Paramount) is even more religous in tone than that of **War of the Worlds** (1953) as when Brooke defends his decision not to go to Mars with the immortal words: 'There are some things that man is not meant to do.'

The film, which was a financial disaster ending Pal's uneasy relationship with Paramount, marked the end of the cycle of 'realist' space films until they were revived following the spectacular success of **2001 – A Space Odyssey** (1968). For the moment, invasions of Earth and monsters would take the place of space exploration as the dominant themes of American Science Fiction.

d Byron Haskin   *p* George Pal   *s* James O'Hanlon
c Lionel Lindon   *se* John P. Fulton, Irmin Roberts, Paul Lerpae, Ivyl Burke, Jan Domela   *lp* Walter Brooke, Eric Fleming, Mickey Shaughnessy, William Hopper, Phil Foster, Benson Fong, Joan Shawlee

The Creature with the Atom Brain
(CLOVER) b/w 69 min
This is an absolutely atrocious film: Siodmak's screenplay is disjointed, Cahn's direction leaden and the production values non-existent. Needless to say, it has its surreal charms as the baldest of plot synopses makes clear. Davis is the giant who seriously injures his boss in a fit of pique. Denning is the investigating police doctor who discovers that the giant has mysteriously been atom-powered by ex-Nazi scientist Gay,

It Came from Beneath the Sea (CLOVER) b/w 77 min
This was the first of a dozen films which Schneer produced with special effects by Harryhausen who'd done the animation effects on the atmospheric **The Beast from 20,000 Fathoms** (1953). Harryhausen was given an extremely small budget and accordingly his animated octopus only has six tentacles but, more importantly, it works effectively, rising from the sea in a rage after being contaminated by radiation and spectacularly attacking a ship by clambering up on the bows and dragging it

Right: John Launer (left), complete with low-budget evidence of his operation, as The Creature with the Atom Brain. *Richard Denning (right) is the investigator who discovers Davis has been atom-powered by ex-Nazi scientist Gregory Gay.*

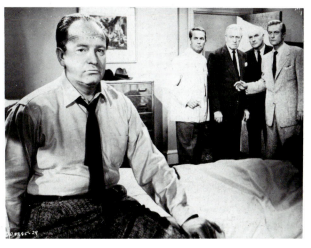

down to the seabed. When the creature invades San Francisco submarine captain Tobey with scientists Curtis and Domergue attempt to defend the city by setting bombs off at the entrance to the harbour. But these only drive the monster octopus onto the Golden Gate Bridge, where it severs the span. Tobey and Curtis electrify the bridge and drive the creature onto the city streets until it is forced back into the water by flame-throwers and Tobey finally destroys it with an atomic torpedo.

Shot in the realist manner that dominated American Science Fiction after the success of **Them!** (1954), despite the refusal of the City Fathers of San Francisco to allow location filming, it's noticable that the underwater atomic test that unleashes the monster is merely used as a plot device and little is made of it in comparison to either earlier films or the slew of Japanese monster movies that followed **Gojira** (1954).

d Robert Gordon *p* Charles H. Schneer *s* George Worthington Yates, Hal Smith *c* Henry Freulich *se* Ray Harryhausen, Jack Erickson *lp* Kenneth Tobey, Faith Domergue, Donald Curtis, Ian Keith, Dean Maddox

King Dinosaur (ZIMGOR) b/w 63 min

Shot in little over a weekend, *King Dinosaur* has none of the delirium of Roger Corman's 'weekend film' **Little Shop of Horrors** (1960). In its place is the tired hokum Gordon specialized in, stock footage (from *One Million BC*, 1940) and enlarged photographs of sleepy lizards for dinosaurs. The plot is equally rudimentary. Bryant leads an expedition to a newly arrived planet in our solar system and discovers various primitive life-forms which are blown up with an A-bomb.

d/co-p Bert I. Gordon *co-p* Al Zimbalist *s* Tom Gries *c* Gordon Anvil *se* Howard A. Anderson Co. *lp* Bill Bryant, Wanda Curtis, Douglas Henderson, Patricia Gallagher, Marvin Miller (narrator)

Kiss Me Deadly (PARKLANE) b/w 105 min

Mickey Spillane's 1952 novel *Kiss Me Deadly* is concerned with a search for stolen narcotics. Aldrich and writer Bezzerides significantly altered this to a box of radioactive material being sought after by foreign agents which explodes at the film's climax when Rogers, unaware of what the box contains, opens it. This transformation and Aldrich's concomitant interrogation of Meeker's Mike Hammer (whose misogynistic violence was unabashedly celebrated by Spillane) marks *Kiss Me Deadly* as one of the few examples of a screen adaptation that so alters its source material as to be unrecognizable when film and book are placed side by side.

The thirties and post James Bond sixties are full of films with bizarre devices and inventions that were essentially McGuffins – Alfred Hitchcock's word for a gimmick, unimportant in itself but which hero and villain seek. But in *Kiss Me Deadly*, the mysterious box that will unleash total death and destruction if opened is no McGuffin; rather it is the touchstone of all the film's characters. Meeker's strutting, empty arrogance, Rogers' unalloyed greed and Dekker's tired cynicism are all rendered redundant by the cataclysmic explosion that ends the film. (Some versions of the film end with Meeker and Cooper escaping from the beach house and stumbling into the sea, but the effect remains the same; once the box is opened, just as once the children are set free in **The Damned**, 1961, which ends on a similar image, there is no hope of safety.)

But, if the end renders meaningless the mystery and quest for the truth that precede it, an appropriate enough image for the first nuclear age, the film retains its power. Aldrich, Bezzerides and cinematographer Laszlo portray a series of lost characters: the doomed Christina (Leachman) whose 'remember me' plea sets Meeker in motion after he has briefly rescued her only to witness her death at Dekker's hands; Rogers with her leech-like fascination with the box she opens in defiance of

all rational considerations; and the cheerfully innocent 'va, va voom' mechanic Dennis (one of the film's and the fifties most memorable characters).

At the centre of the movie is Meeker's brutish, repressed Hammer who delights in voyeurism (he's a divorce investigator who uses his faithful secretary, Cooper, to provide the necessary evidence when required) and whose determination takes us through the complex threads of the frantic narrative. It is this double view that makes the role of Hammer (who, as it were, stands in for so many of *film noir*'s detectives) so fascinating. His callousness is a mask, the cost of getting through life in a society in which 'feeling' is considered dangerous, just as the cost of Cooper's obvious feelings for Meeker are the repeated travesties of her play-acting out her feelings for him with other men for his sake. Aldrich binds together this web of self deceit (that, typically of films of the period, even extends to culture, the representatives of which – poetry, painting, opera, etc – are seen as tainted and powerless rather than as liberating) with some of the most visceral images seen in the cinema and a breathless, excessive directorial style that is compelling.

The result is one of the great American films of the fifties and one of the few films to live up to its (prophetic) title.

d/p Robert Aldrich *s* A.I. Bezzerides *c* Ernest Laszlo *lp* Ralph Meeker, Albert Dekker, Paul Stewart, Maxine Cooper, Gaby Rogers, Cloris Leachman, Nick Dennis, Wesley Addy, Jack Lambert, Jack Elam

Below: *Gaby Rogers opens Pandora's Box in the marvellous* Kiss Me Deadly.

d Julian Soler   p Felipe Mier, Oscar J. Brooks   s Carlos Leon, Carlos Orellana, Pedro de Urdimales   c Agustin Martinez Solares   lp Adalberto Martinez Resortes, Evangelina Elizondo, Andres Soler, Famie Kaufman Vitola, Jose Bronco Venegas, Bertha Lehar, Amalia Aguilar

The Quatermass Xperiment *aka* **The Creeping Unknown** (HAMMER FILMS; GB) b/w 82(78) min
Based on Kneale's ground-breaking teleseries – Hammer had a tradition stretching back to its first production, **Dick Barton – Special Agent** (1948) of adapting radio and television material for the large screen – the phenomenal success of this film in both Britain and America transformed Hammer's fortunes. The company quietly dropped its planned next production, a costume drama, *King Charles and the Round-heads*, and put into immediate production a sequel, **Quatermass II** (1957), the similar **X the Unknown** (1956) and began negotiating for the rights to the Frankenstein character. Thus began the British boom in Science Fiction (and horror) films.

Broadly speaking, the film is a condensation of the teleseries (though the character of Quatermass himself is considerably altered from Kneale's cultured intellectual to become, in Donlevy's fine performance, a tetchy, dominating man of science).

The sole survivor (Wordsworth, who with the assistance of Phil Leakey's makeup gives a marvellous performance as the pitiful man literally decomposing before our eyes) of a rocketship crash starts behaving strangely and a fungus-like growth appears on his hand. He escapes from the hospital and the growth creeps all over this body until he is nothing but a living fungus. The organism spreads around London, killing everybody in its wake and threatening to grow larger by the hour, until finally Quatermass corners it in Westminster Cathedral and electrocutes it.

In retrospect, what is most revealing about the film is the surprising confidence in space exploration (and science in the figure of Donlevy's Quatermass) that underpins it. After the alien is killed, the film climaxes with a second rocket launch. This is in marked contrast to the next instalment of the series, the bleak and far superior *Quatermass II*.

d/co-s Val Guest   p Anthony Hinds   co-s Richard Landau   c Walter Harvey   se Leslie Bowie   lp Brian Donlevy, Margia Dean, Jack Warner, Richard Wordsworth, David King Wood, Harold Lang, Lionel Jeffries

Revenge of the Creature (U) b/w 82 min
Few sequels are as successful as their predecessors, but Arnold's follow-up to **The Creature from the Black Lagoon** (1954) is better than most, though the atmosphere and sinister overtones of the original are dissipated by too much footage being devoted to the gill-man creature. In place of that Arnold emphasizes the creature's sexual interest in Nelson as he

Richard Wordsworth, made up by Phil Leakey, as the astronaut taken over in the landmark film, The Quatermass Xperiment.

Los Platillos Voladores *aka* **Los Platos Voladores** (MIER Y BROOKS; MEX) b/w 95 min
An inane musical comedy starring Marciano (Resortes) and his fiancée Saturnina (Elizondo). With his latest invention, a car with an airplane engine, Marciano plans to participate in a race to win enough money to get married. An accident sees them stranded in a village where they are mistaken for Martians. A professor, Saldaña (Soler), and his colleagues perform intelligence tests on them and they play the game while winning the affection of the local poor through charitable actions. When they confess the truth to Saldaña, he admits that he knew of their imposture but had not spoken out because they were doing so much good for the local people. As they leave the village to go on a honeymoon, they meet real Martians and disappear. According to a contemporary Mexican critic, the pacifist message of the movie is: if everybody were as idiotic as the characters in the movie, there would be no more problems in the world.

Soler made a number of the cheap Mexican fantasy pictures, including **El Castillo de los Monstruos** (1958), *La Locura del Terror* (1960) and a Jekyll and Hyde film, *El Hombre y la Bestia* (1972). He also contributed to the masked wrestler series with titles such as **Santo Contra Blue Demon en la Atlantida** (1968). His assistant director on this movie, Alfonso Corona Blake, became one of the five most prolific contributors to the fantasy genre together with Soler, Alfredo Crevenna, Federico Curiel and René Cardona.

Right: Ricou Browning wreaking havoc in Revenge of the Creature.

watches her swimming with her lover. They kiss enthusiastically on the surface, whilst down below, hidden amongst the weeds, the creature looks on with growing interest.

The plot follows the capture of the creature by Bromfield and Williams who take him to an oceanarium in Florida where Agar and Nelson, two ichthyologists, try to teach him to speak. Eventually he breaks out, kills Bromfield and returns to the ocean.

Although made in 3-D, *Revenge* was mainly shown 'flat'. Another sequel, **The Creature Walks Among Us** followed in 1956.

d Jack Arnold   *p* William Alland   *s* Martin Berkeley
c Charles S. Welbourne   *lp* John Agar, Lori Nelson, John Bromfield, Nestor Paiva, Grandon Rhodes, Robert B. Williams

Tarantula   (U)   b/w   80 min

One of the many children of **Them!** (1954), *Tarantula* is a compelling film, less for the subject matter – a giant tarantula on the rampage – than for director Arnold's eerie use of the desert landscapes, a feature of his best work (with the obvious exception of **The Incredible Shrinking Man,** 1957). The stillness is haunting and allows the tension to mount. 'Every beast that crawled or swam or flew began there,' comments one of the characters. Undoubtedly, Arnold used the desert for budgetary reasons but the use to which he puts his locations is far more effective than most similarly cost-conscious directors.

The plot is crude but straightforward. A tiny spider, which Carroll has injected with special nutrients, escapes into the desert and becomes gigantic. Its first attacks are on cattle but it quickly turns to people until it becomes the size of an office block, and can grab cars in its jaws and reduce them to scrap iron. Finally, a swarm of air force jets pour napalm on the monster and it burns to death.

The destruction of the cars – the symbol of advanced technology in America – introduced what soon became a potent, if over-used, symbol in the American cinema.

d Jack Arnold   *p* William Alland   *s* R.M. Fresco, Martin Berkeley   *c* George Robinson   *se* Clifford Stine   *lp* John Agar, Mara Corday, Leo G. Carroll, Nestor Paiva, Ross Elliott, Ed Rand

This Island Earth   (U)   86 min

On the surface a full-blooded space opera complete with interplanetary warfare and bug-eyed monsters, *This Island Earth*, like **Forbidden Planet** (1956) has a deeply disturbing undercurrent running through it. Though its narrative line is unclear at times, its basic plot is simple enough. Aliens from Metaluna, who are at war with the Zahgons, kidnap a group of Earth scientists and ask, then order, them to help repair the

failing planetary shield that protects Metaluna. But, before they can do this, the Zahgons disintegrate the shield. The remaining scientists (Reason and Domergue), with the help of Morrow's friendly Metalunian, escape just in time.

Several elements make it unusual compared to most Science Fiction films of the period: the essentially friendly aliens; the idea that man's prowess with atomic power can be used beneficially; its vivid and imaginative use of colour (it was one of the last films to be made in the three-strip Technicolor process) and its extravagant special effects. But more interesting is the fact that the film reflects the interests of Science Fiction writers of the time. Like *Forbidden Planet* (with which it also shares one of the best titles of any Science Fiction film), its premises and arguments are, in pulp form, real examples of speculative thinking. And indeed, (again with *Forbidden Planet*) it is one of the few Science Fiction films of the fifties to have been written seriously about at any length (notably by Raymond Durgnat in his long essay, 'The Wedding of Poetry and Pulp' in *Films and Feelings*).

The direction and acting are bland but Cohen and O'Callaghan's script, though it's undeniably over-talkative, has a primitive grandeur about it that is reflected in Stine's glowing cinematography and marvellous special effects. The film's debates are complex, contrasting the intellectual but passive Metalunians with the limited but effective technological know-how of mankind as the scientists try to save Metaluna, for example. Accordingly, the film's space operatics are given a dreamlike quality (which Durgnat examines at length) and a moral dimension that makes the dramatic situation far more interesting. The result is a film rather like the vastly inferior **Plan 9 from Outer Space** (1956) that seems to work almost wholly at an unconscious level, a film that becomes more and more interesting as you dig into it and expose the contradictions its surface (like that of the planet Metaluna itself) can hardly contain.

The final sequences of the destruction of Metaluna were directed by Jack Arnold.

d Joseph Newman   *p* William Alland   *s* Franklin Cohen, Edward G. O'Callaghan   *c/co-se* Clifford Stine
co-se Stanley Horsley   *lp* Jeff Morrow, Faith Domergue, Rex Reason, Russell Johnson, Douglas Spencer, Reg Parton, Ed Parker

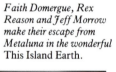

Left: *Leo G. Carroll and tarantula in* Tarantula, *one of the many children of* Them! *(1954).*

Faith Domergue, Rex Reason and Jeff Morrow make their escape from Metaluna in the wonderful This Island Earth.

Above: *The wonderful Attack of the Crab Monsters, the most commercially successful of Roger Corman's early films.*

Attack of the Crab Monsters

(LOS ALTOS) b/w 70(63) min

The most commercially successful of his early features, *Attack of the Crab Monsters* saw Corman refining his directorial style to produce a film in which a shock or the fear that a shocking event would take place immediately occurs in virtually every scene. As a result, in contrast to other creature-features of the period in which there were long barren periods, usually filled up with speechifying, between the attacks of the monsters, Corman's films have a speed and directness about them that remains appealing to this day, however tatty the films look. A further result of this strategy is an intensifying of the sense of disequilibrium that lies behind the films.

A would-be rescue party (including Garland, Duncan, Johnson and Bradley) arrives on a tiny desert island to find that the scientists they've come to pick up have vanished and the island is slowly slipping into the sea, as a result of the tunnelling beneath it of 25-foot mutated crabs. Once out of the sea, the monsters take over the minds of those they kill and the survivors hear the voices of their dead compatriots calling to them from the crabs. The climax has Garland, Duncan and Johnson left on the island, now a tiny outcrop, with the last remaining crab.

d/p Roger Corman *s* Charles B. Griffith *c* Floyd Crosby
lp Richard Garland, Pamela Duncan, Russell Johnson, Leslie Bradley, Mel Welles, Richard Cutting, Tony Miller

The Beast with a Million Eyes

(SAN MATEO PRODUCTIONS) b/w 78 min

This flawed, but interesting, piece features a transferable force enclosed within the body of an alien being. The force lands in the American countryside and, by telepathy, transfers itself at will to animals and a mentally defective farm-hand (Tarver). The force's war-like intentions are clear when humans are attacked by thousands of suicidal birds, savaged by possessed dogs and battered by lowing cows under its control, before it's destroyed by an intelligent family (Birch, Thayer and Cole) who show it love – something the force can't abide.

Clearly intended as an allegory about a malevolent God – 'Hate and malice are the keys to power' is the creature's only message for mankind – the film (Kramarsky's only one)

remains interesting, for all its flaws, if only for its unusual central idea. Equally fascinating are its production circumstances, as revealed by Bert Gordon, then associated with AIP who distributed the film, which give a sense of the bizarre world of independent production in the fifties. 'Most of the movies were made around titles that James [Nicholson, the co-founder of AIP with Samuel Arkoff] would dream up and sell in advance. We had a terrible experience with *The Beast with a Million Eyes*. Nicholson created a tremendous ad and poster featuring this monster with a million eyes. There was no script, no picture, no nothing ... they finally shot this movie out in the middle of the desert, non-union for $23,000. But the monster they used looked like a coffee percolator buried in the sand ... The exhibitors, meanwhile, were so excited by the lavish ad campaign that they all flew out ... to see the movie. When it was screened for them, they went into shock. There was no beast. There were no million eyes. There was nothing but a coffee percolator. One of the exhibitors, Joe Levine, pulled out a checkbook and said "How much money do you need to reshoot this movie? We can burn this one." Undaunted, Jim Nicholson went into the editing room, took a knife and scratched all over the emulsion of the film during the monster footage – all over the percolator. I don't know how he did it, but when they rescreened the climax there were these wonderfully eerie lightning flashes coming out of this object. All of a sudden our coffee percolator was a dangerous spaceship shooting rays. The movie got by. Boy we were really innovative in those days.' In fact the effects were generated by spiral designs being optically laid over the images.

d/p David Kramarsky *s* Tom Filer *c* Everett Baker
se Paul Blaisdell *lp* Paul Birch, Lorna Thayer, Chester Conklin, Donna Cole, Richard Sargent, Leonard Tarver

The Black Sleep *aka* Dr Cadman's Secret

(BEL-AIR) b/w 82 min

Rathbone is the mad scientist conducting experiments into suspended animation on another scientist, Rudley, who he has set up on a murder charge. He gives him a swig of the Black Sleep, in order to gain Rudley's knowledge to help him operate on his wife's brain tumour. Rathbone's other experiments involve slicing up his victims' brains and leaving them as hideously deformed freaks, like Chaney. LeBorg's direction is pedestrian and the script by Higgins is surprisingly plodding.

Rathbone gives an evocative performance, as does Lugosi who is silent throughout. This was his first and last full-scale part after his de-addiction from morphine and he died soon after the film's release.

d Reginald LeBorg *p* Howard W. Koch *s* John C. Higgins *c* Gordon Avil *lp* Basil Rathbone, Herbert Rudley, Laurie Munroe, Akim Tamiroff, Bela Lugosi, Lon Chaney Jnr

Bride of the Monster *aka* Bride of the Atom

(ROLLING M PRODUCTIONS/BANNER FILMS) b/w 69 (67) min

Bride of the Monster, another of Wood's mediocre films, has mad scientist Lugosi, aided by Johnson, working on an atomic-ray machine in a swamp, with the aim of creating a race of super beings. The victims invariably die, with the sole exception of one who has turned into a monster octopus (for which Wood borrowed the prop from Paramount) and lives in a nearby pond. Reporter King, a graduate of the Lois Lane school of journalism, enters the swamp to track down the missing citizens and, naturally, is captured. The climax, after Johnson has turned the atomic ray on Lugosi, has Lugosi turn into an atom-powered monster before finally exploding in a mushroom cloud.

Like so many of Wood's inept films, the main faults of this one are those of the home movie. Many of the cast were amateurs whose presence was determined by other factors. Thus McCoy was the son of one of the film's financiers and Dunn plays the police captain with a parakeet in continual attendance because he was a clown who specialized in children's parties and the parakeet was part of his act. Similarly, there was a six-month hiatus in the production when the money ran out. In short, what distinguishes it from other tawdry Hollywood failures is precisely its amateur conception.

Wood was also responsible for the equally dire, but far better known, **Plan 9 from Outer Space** (1956).

d/p/co-s Edward D. Wood Jnr *co-s* Alex Gordon *c* William Thompson *se* Pat Dinga *lp* Bela Lugosi, Loretta King, Tony McCoy, Harvey Dunn, George Becwar, Tor Johnson

The Creature Walks Among Us (U) b/w 78 min
The second sequel to **The Creature from the Black Lagoon** (1954), the first of which was **Revenge of the Creature** (1955). The first two films were made in 3-D and directed by Jack Arnold. The greater loss in this case was Arnold for Sherwood's direction, although competent, changes the monster from the interesting amphibian man to an unsympathetic, conventional, lumbering monster.

Scientist Morrow sets out for the swamps, intent on capturing the creature and experimenting on his red corpuscle count in an attempt to start a new species. He traps the creature who, after a burning incident, loses his gills, whereupon Morrow discovers human flesh and lungs under his scales. Eventually the creature is taken to San Francisco, but escapes and, although it appears that his burnt gills will cause him to drown, the ending is left open for another sequel which was never made.

d John Sherwood *p* William Alland *s* Arthur Ross *c* Maury Gertsman *lp* Jeff Morrow, Rex Reason, Leigh Snowden, Gregg Palmer, Ricou Browning (the creature before the burning), Don Megowan (the creature after the burning)

The Day the World Ended
(GOLDEN STATE) b/w scope 81 min
Corman's first Science Fiction film, *The Day the World Ended* is a bleak variant on Arch Oboler's **Five** (1951). A group of survivors of a nuclear holocaust, Birch, his daughter Nelson, geologist Denning, gangster Connors, his girlfriend Jergens,

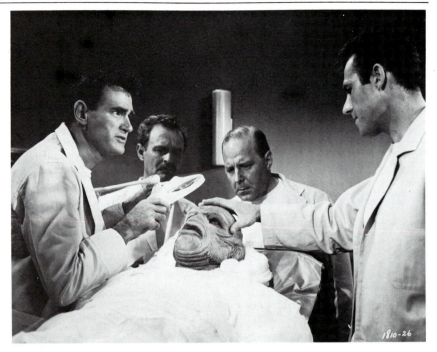

Man the cruel experimenter in The Creature Walks Among Us.

scientist Hatton and Dubov's terminal radiation case, make their way to a mountain retreat. Rusoff's script is melodramatic in the extreme with the group squabbling in the most obvious ways while outside the shelter the creatures of the forest mutate wildly and inside Dubov does the same. However, Corman pushes the material, almost forces it, into significance by taking his characters seriously and by associating the situation with the Garden of Eden myth. Thus the retreat is a paradise, a paradise under threat, the struggle between Denning and Connors parallels that of Cain and Abel, the mutant that Dubov becomes (portrayed by Blaisdell) is the serpent and Denning and Nelson, Adam and Eve. In short, a triumph of the pulp imagination.

d/p Roger Corman *s* Lou Rusoff *c* Jock Feindel *se* Paul Blaisdell *lp* Richard Denning, Adele Jergens, Lori Nelson, Touch (Mike) Connors, Paul Birch, Raymond Hatton, Paul Dubov, Paul Blaisdell

Earth versus the Flying Saucers *aka* Invasion of the Flying Saucers (COL) b/w 81 min
Best remembered for Harryhausen's superior stop-motion special effects, that make the flying saucers look very convincing, and its fine title, this is an otherwise routine outing from Sears, a director who was clearly more at home in the western. The script is closely influenced by **War of the Worlds** (1953) but lacks the naïve grandeur of that film. In its place is an awkward plot that needed only the presence of Roy Barcroft for the film to be mistaken for **The Purple Monster Strikes** (1945).

The leathery inhabitants of a dying planet arrive at a US base where, although not hostile, they're greeted with gunfire. The aliens declare war, knock out the soldiers at the base with death rays and their fleet of life-like flying saucers launch a large-scale attack on Earth. Victory seems certain within 60 days until one of the aliens dies mysteriously and scientist Marlowe discovers that they are sensitive to high-frequency sound, beams up at the flying saucers, and the fleet falls spectacularly into a number of famous Washington landmarks.

d Fred F. Sears *p* Charles H. Schneer *s* George Worthington Yates, Raymond T. Marcus (Bernard Gordon) *c* Fred Jackman Jnr *se* Ray Harryhausen, Russ Kelley *lp* Joan Taylor, Hugh Marlowe, Harry Lauter, Morris Ankrum, Donald Curtis

Left: *One of the mutants in* The Day the World Ended, *the first Science Fiction film directed by Roger Corman.*

Right: *Robby the robot warning Walter Pidgeon (centre), Leslie Nielson and Anne Francis of the approach of the monster from Pidgeon's own subconscious in the glorious* Forbidden Planet.

Fire Maidens from Outer Space

(CRITERION; GB)   b/w   80 min

A bottom-of-the barrel piece of British Science Fiction, this begins with the arrival of a spaceship (captained by Dexter) on the 13th moon of Jupiter. Guided to a safe landing by a mysterious voice, the crew discover a lost civilization – descendants of the lost continent of Atlantis. All are women, except for an old man (Berry). Their plan is to return to Earth to create a new Atlantis but this is hampered by a monster who kills Berry and steals one of the fire maidens. The crew rescue her, casting the monster into a fiery pit and return to Earth with a senior fire maiden, promising to go back for the others.

The film's one claim to fame is its extensive use of classical music (mostly Borodin) as background music, a trick that

Hugh Marlowe and Joan Taylor (inset) in Earth versus the Flying Saucers *which includes the classic line, 'If they land in our nation's capital uninvited, we won't meet them with tea and cookies'.*

Stanley Kubrick deployed with far more aplomb in **2001 – A Space Odyssey** (1968).

d/s Cy Roth   *p* George Fowler   *c* Ian Struthers
lp Anthony Dexter, Susan Shaw, Paul Carpenter, Harry Fowler, Sydney Tafler, Owen Berry

Forbidden Planet   (MGM)   scope   98 min

One of the most charming works in the Science Fiction genre, *Forbidden Planet* is nothing less than an updated version of Shakespeare's *The Tempest*. It takes as its Prospero a scientist called Morbeus (Pidgeon) who lives with his daughter (Francis) who, like Shakespeare's Miranda has never seen men, on a planet named Altair IV, while the role of Ariel is played by Robby the Robot, the first robot to become a popular hero in its own right.

Wilcox, whose best known film is his first, the efficient, if sentimental, *Lassie Come Home* (1943), directs with surprising flair and sophistication. Almost as interesting as the re-working of *The Tempest* are the sumptuous sets depicting Altair IV with its two suns and green skies and the underground cities of steel and porcelain of the Krel, the long-dead race whose dangerous secrets Pidgeon has partially unravelled. The film is clearly mounted as a juvenile offering, hence the robot and flying saucers, which was presumably why Wilcox was assigned to direct. However, Wilcox (whose subsequent *I Passed for White*, 1960, which he also produced and wrote, is a remarkably tough film for its time) had other ideas and delicately, step by step, set about subverting the fairy story and transforming it into a nightmare.

The Krels died because in the course of their development they reached the point where they not only freed themselves of material restrictions, they also made material their nightmares which killed them. Although unaware of the power he has tapped, Pidgeon has similarly unleashed the power of his own Id, first to kill his fellow explorers when they want to return home: he spares only his daughter. The significance of this becomes clearer when another group of explorers, led by Nielson, arrive to investigate. First Pidgeon tries to warn them off and when they land the previous attacks are repeated, this time because Pidgeon is clearly jealous of the

157

attentions paid by Nielson to his innocent daughter for whom he clearly has incestuous feelings.

After the climactic battle against the monster, the literalization of Pidgeon's jealousies and unspeakable desires, Pidgeon finally understands what he has created and dies fighting his own creation thus leaving Francis free to leave her home with Nielson.

Although the film is charmingly mounted for the most part, some of the details, notably the comic interludes, are intrusive and some of the acting wooden, but in the manner of films as diverse as **This Island Earth** (1955) and *The Wizard of Oz* (1939), *Forbidden Planet*, a simply marvellous title, has an adventurousness about it that is wholly compelling.

Robby the robot proved so popular that producer Nayfack revived him for the less successful **The Invisible Boy** (1957).

d Fred M. Wilcox   *p* Nicholas Nayfack   *s* Cyril Hume
c George Folsey   *se* A. Arnold Gillespie, Warren Newcombe, Irving G. Reis, Joshua Meador   *lp* Walter Pidgeon, Anne Francis, Leslie Nielson, Warren Stevens, Jack Kelly, Richard Anderson, Earl Holliman, James Drury

The Gamma People

(WARWICK FILMS; GB)   b/w   79 (76) min
A minor oddity. On a European trip, newsman Douglas and photographer Phillips find their railway carriage detached in a quiet siding. They emerge to discover they're in Eastern bloc Gudavia. Director Gilling, who later made the classic *Plague of the Zombies* (1966), blends an uneasy but not uninteresting mixture of comic opera and drama when, jailed as spies, Douglas and Phillips are released by Rilla's dictator who does not want the press to focus attention on Gudavia. The reason is that he's experimenting with gamma rays, turning out few geniuses but a superfluity of idiots (known as Goons). Considering the plot's possibilities, its anti-communist propaganda is surprisingly muted, as Phillips and Douglas battle for Gudavia's sanity.

d/co-s John Gilling   *p/co-s* John Gossage   *c* Ted Moore
se Tom Howard   *lp* Paul Douglas, Eva Bartok, Leslie Phillips, Walter Rilla, Philip Leaver, Martin Miller

Der Ideale Untermieter *aka* The Ideal Lodger

(WOLF SCHMIDT FILM; WG)   b/w   98 min
In keeping with fifties fantasies about automation, this is a children's film about a domestic robot befriended by a child and threatened by politicians, scientists and military men. According to its publicity made as a protest against creeping standardization, the robot is meant to prove that there is no real difference between the average conversation between ordinary people and the conversational skills of an electronically programmed automaton. Troubles only begin when the

daughter (Schindler) strikes up a friendship with the metal box and brings it home. The film is utterly tasteless and rather dim-witted – it even manages to use electric shock treatment in a mental hospital as one of those 'hilarious' things people do in harmless comedies.

Schmidt is best known for a series of broad comedies about the fictional family Hesselbach. This film was released in 1957.

d/p/s Wolf Schmidt   *c* Heino Koenig   *lp* Wolf Schmidt, Sibylle Schindler, Lia Woehr, Holger Hagen, Susi Jera

The Indestructible Man

(C.G.K. PRODUCTIONS)   b/w   70 min
A decidedly routine outing. Chaney plays a dead killer who is brought back to life via electricity by scientist Shayne. No longer partnered by Wisberg, with whom he made **Captive Women** (1952) and **The Neanderthal Man** (1953), Pollexfen directs woodenly. The resuscitated Chaney (originally known as 'the Butcher') murders several of his former associates who had doublecrossed him and then turns on Shayne. Impervious to bullets, Chaney has been made mute by the re-animation and he eventually takes shelter in the Los Angeles drains, a favourite location of low-budget film-makers, where he is finally trapped and killed. The film is an unofficial remake of **The Walking Dead** (1936).

d/p Jack Pollexfen   *s* Sue Bradford, Vy Russell   *c* John Russell Jnr   *lp* Lon Chaney Jnr, Marion Carr, Robert Shayne, Ross Elliott, Stuart Randall, Kenneth Terrell

Invasion of the Body Snatchers

(WALTER WANGER PRODUCTIONS)   b/w   scope   80 min
One of the best (and best known) Science Fiction films of the fifties, *Invasion of the Body Snatchers*, though it has been read by many as an anti-Senator McCarthy tract (and by others as the classic example of an anti-communist film of the period for its handling of the take-over from within theme), is far better and far more complex than such crude reductions suggest. Indeed, the film, with its attack on conformity and lack of feelings and its defence of emotions, highlights the fact that at such a generalized level anti-McCarthy and anti-communist films are remarkably similar. Of course, it's

Above: *Kevin McCarthy trying to warn the world of the coming of the pods in the classic* Invasion of the Body Snatchers.

Left: *Paul Douglas and Eva Bartok in* The Gamma People, *a peculiar blend of Science Fiction and the spy film.*

possible to read the movie along these lines but to do so is to omit consideration of the film's more pertinent concerns. In short, the strengths of Siegel's film are that it centres not on the social and generalizeable, but on the specific mystery of the difference between a human and an automaton-like existence. Rather than merely reflect America's paranoid fears of the times, in the manner of Philip Kaufman's 1978 remake which is best seen as a witty assault on the 'me' generation, Siegel interrogates those fears.

McCarthy is the doctor who, on his return from a medical convention, finds his hometown disturbingly different and quickly discovers the cause, an invasion of parasite aliens (pods) that have the power to replace humans with soulless simulacra. Shot in Siegel's sober yet energetic style and using real locations for the fictional Californian town of Santa Mira, the opening sequence creates a strong sense of unease that turns to terror in the second half as the good citizens of Santa Mira start to send out the pods across America. The horror of the situation is all the more chilling for being so understated: a mother, holding a pod, to a nurse, 'Shall I put this in with the baby?', 'Yes, then there'll be no more crying'.

At the heart of the film is the terrible mystery of the process of the take-over, marvellously realized in the sequence where McCarthy and his girlfriend (Wynter) are shown by Belice (Donovan) and his wife the 'blank' pod that will become him, if he goes to sleep. McCarthy's instinctive reaction is equally revealing of Siegel's vision of otherness: with assistance from Donovan McCarthy frantically attacks the pods with a pitchfork, a scene made even more gruesome by the creatures' immobility and their closeness to humanity.

The result is one of Siegel's best films, despite studio interference. Against his wishes, in order to make the film more positive, a prologue and epilogue were added and much of the humorous dialogue of the first half of the movie (written by Sam Peckinpah who worked on the film uncredited) was excised. These alterations, however, don't diminish the power of Siegel's own ending, McCarthy staring wild-eyed into the camera shouting 'You're next' as the cars and trucks with blank-faced drivers pass him by, taking no notice of his warning.

d Don Siegel   *p* Walter Wanger   *s* Daniel Mainwaring
c Ellsworth Fredricks   *se* Milt Rice   *lp* Kevin McCarthy, Dana Wynter, King Donovan, Carolyn Jones, Larry Gates, Jean Willes, Whit Bissell

The bat-mites attack in Roger Corman's It Conquered the World.

It Conquered the World

(SUNSET PRODUCTIONS)   b/w   71 min

Flippantly dismissed by Corman as demonstrating 'a central axiom of Science Fiction films [is that] the monster should always be bigger than the leading lady' – the original monster had been created as low and bulky in conformity with Venus' heavy gravity – this is a far better film than Corman suggests.

Van Cleef is the idealist who guides the cucumber-shaped, fanged Venusian (portrayed as ever by Blaisdell) to Earth, in the hope than a Venusian-ruled Earth will be a better place, only to discover that the Venusians intend to transform mankind into zombie slaves with the aid of their electronic 'bat-mites', and Graves is the scientist who foils the invasion. Emphatically directed and surprisingly well acted (especially by Garland, the film's emperilled heroine), the movie survives its silly monster.

An inferior remake followed in 1966, **Zontar, the Thing from Venus,** directed by the unimaginative, if prolific, Larry Buchanan.

d/p Roger Corman   *s* Lou Rusoff   *c* Frederick E. West
se Paul Blaisdell   *lp* Peter Graves, Beverly Garland, Lee Van Cleef, Sally Fraser, Russ Bender, Jonathan Haze, Charles B. Griffith

Kotetsu No Kyojin *aka* Supergiant

(SHIN TOHO; JAP)   b/w and col   scope   9 (11) chaps

Japanese Superman series with episodes of varying lengths, starring Utsui as the stoic and invulnerable hero fighting evil aliens from various planets. He is usually either aided by children or busy rescuing them. Plots involve Utsui saving the world from flying saucers, nuclear rockets, malignant satellites, germ warfare, death-ray-spewing synthetic monsters sent by enemy space stations, etc. Many of the episodes were paired and, slightly cut, released as features.

Chap. 1 **Supah Jaianto** *aka* **The Steel Man from Outer Space**   (1956)   scope   49 min
d Teruo Ishii   *p* Mitsugi Okura   *s* Ishiro Miyagawa
c Takashi Watanabe   *lp* Ken Utsui, Minako Yamada, Junko Ikeuchi, Minoru Takada, Ryo Iwashita, Utako Mitsuya

Chap. 2 **Supah Jaianto** *aka* **Rescue from Outer Space**   (1956)   scope   52 min
Credits as for Chap. 1, with which it was combined and released, cut to 85 minutes, as **Supergiant I** *aka* **The Appearance of Supergiant.**

Chap. 3 **Kotetsu No Kyojin – Kaiseijin No Mayo** *aka* **Devils from the Planet** *aka* **Invaders from the Planets**   (1957)   scope   49 min
d Teruo Ishii, Akira Mitsuwa, Koreyoshi Akasaka
p Mitsugi Okura   *s* Ishiro Miyagawa   *c* Akira Watanabe
lp Ken Utsui, Minako Yamada, Junko Ikeuchi, Minoru Takada, Kan Hayashi, Reiko Seto, Chisako Tahara, Akira Tamura

Chap. 4 **Kotetsu No Kyojin – Chikyu Metzubo Sunzen** *aka* **The Earth in Danger**   (1957)   scope   40 min
Credits as for Chap. 3, with which it was combined and released, cut to 83 minutes, as **Supergiant II** *aka* **The Atomic Rulers of the World** *aka* **Attack of the Flying Saucers.**

Chap. 5 **Jinko Eisen To Jinrui No Hametsu** *aka* **Spaceship of Human Destruction**   (1958)   b/w and col   scope   40 min
d Teruo Ishii   *p* Mitsugi Okura   *s* Shinsuke Niegishi, Ishiro Miyagawa   *c* Hiroshi Suzuki, Nobu Boshi   *lp* Ken Utsui, Utako Motsuya, Ken Hayashi, Hiroshi Asami, Teruhisha Ikeda, Junko Ikeuchi, Minoru Takada

Chap. 6 **Uchutei To Jinko Eisen No Gekitotsu** *aka* **The Destruction of the Space Fleet**   (1958)   b/w and col   scope   39 min
Credits as for Chap. 5, with which it was combined and

released in 1964, running time 79 minutes, as **Supergiant Against the Satellites** *aka* **Attack from Space** *aka* **Invaders from Space.**

Chap. 7 **Uchu Kaijin Shutsugen** *aka* **Spacemen Appear**
(1958) 44 min
d Akira Miwa   *p* Mitsugi Okura   *lp* Ken Utsui, Chisako Tawara

Chap. 8 **Akuma No Keshiin** *aka* **The Devil Incarnate** (1959)
d Chogi Akasaka   *lp* Ken Utsui, Reiko Seto

Chap. 9 **Dokuga Okoku** *aka* **Kingdom of the Poison Moth**
(1959)
d Chogi Akasaka   *lp* Ken Utsui, Terumi Hoshi
Chapters 7, 8 and 9 apparently were combined and released as
The Brain from Outer Space, running time 146 minutes.

Three further instalments may have been made in 1959 but it is not certain that these films were, in fact, part of the same series: **Araumi No Oja,**   *d* Tetsu Taguchi;   *lp* Ken Utsui, Naoko Kubo; **Gonin No Hanzaisha,**   *d* Teruo Ishii;   *lp* Ken Utsui, Yoko Mihara and **Jotai Sambashi** *aka* **Red Piers,**   *d* Teruo Ishii;   *lp* Ken Utsui, Akemi Tsukushi.

El Ladron de Cadaveres

(INTERNATIONAL CINEMATOGRAFICA; MEX)   b/w   80 min
The most successful Mexican horror-Science Fiction film of the period, widely acclaimed in France and foreshadowing aspects of Terence Fisher's interpretation of the creature in **Frankenstein Must Be Destroyed** (1969). It mixes the Frankenstein story with that of King Kong in a wrestler setting, the whole imbued with a classic expressionist mad-doctor atmosphere and shot in a deliriously romantic style. Starting out with foggy graveyard scenes as Ogden (Riquelme) seeks corpses into which animal brains can be transplanted, the movie ends with a powerful evocation of King Kong as a wrestler (Ruvinskis) endowed with the brains of an ape seeking out his former lover (Dominguez) as he climbs up the outside of a building and gets shot by the police. Highlights include the scenes in which the wrestler-ape, losing control during a bout, tears off his mask to reveal the hairy face underneath, and the moments where he goes berserk in a rage, desperately struggling to fix onto memories of his life before he died and was revived by the transplanted monkey brain.

The result is a bizarre and impressive picture from a director who started out with imitations of John Ford (*Tres Hombres Malos*, 1948) and Hollywood gothic movies. Although no John Ford, his ability to combine intense physicality (surgery and wrestling) with the more metaphysical sides of horror imbued his fantasy pictures with a genuinely unsettling tonality, as in *Misterios de Ultretumba* and *El Grito de la Muerte* (both 1958), foreshadowing not just Terence Fisher's later films but also the best of the Italian horror movies by Mario Bava, Antonio Margheriti and Riccardo Freda. The wrestler Ruvinskis, here playing the ape-man, made his name with this picture and eventually achieved national fame as Neutron, the central character in the most interesting of the masked wrestler series. He also parodies his own persona in the comedy **El Superflaco** (1967).

d/co-s Fernando Mendez   *p* Sergio Kogan
co-s Alejandro Verlitsky   *c* Victor Herrera   *lp* Columba Dominguez, Crox Alvarado, Wolf Ruvinskis, Carlos Riquelme, Arturo Martinez, Edouardo Alcaraz, Guillermo Hernandez-Lobo Negro, Alejandro Cruz, Lee Morgan

Man Beast

(FAVOURITE FILMS OF CALIFORNIA)   b/w   67 min
This Abominable Snowman movie has Maynor and Nelson mounting an expedition to the Himalayas to search for Maynor's missing brother. Local guide Maruzzi takes them to Lewis who believes the Yeti are a form of primitive man. The Yeti attack and the entire cast, with the exception of Maynor and Nelson, die. The film was cobbled together by producer/director Warren, and even includes some Mexican footage, nevertheless he does succeed in achieving some interestingly bestial Yetis.

d/p Jerry Warren   *s* B. Arthur Cassidy   *c* Victor Fisler
lp Tom Maruzzi, Virginia Maynor, George Skoff, George Wells Lewis, Lloyd Nelson, Rock Madison

The Mole People   (U)   b/w   77 min

An unimaginative film in which Agar (blandly) plays the leader of an anthropological expedition to the Middle East in search of a lost tribe, the Sumerians who live underground, served by their slaves the Mole People. The lost tribe practise the usual sacrifices and rituals, with an added twist that only some of them can stand the sunlight – the albinos are charred instantly. Agar and his expedition are captured and eventually escape, leaving the Mole People rising up in revenge.

Patrick is the traditionally much-threatened heroine.

d Virgil Vogel   *p* William Alland   *s* Laszlo Gorog
c Ellis Carter   *se* Clifford Stine   *lp* John Agar, Cynthia Patrick, Hugh Beaumont, Alan Napier, Nestor Paiva, Robin Hughes

El Monstruo de la Montana Hueca *aka* The Beast of Hollow Mountain   (NASSOUR BROTHERS – PELICULAS RODRIGUEZ; US, MEX)   scope   81 min

Madison, a Mexican rancher, hears of a marauding giant lizard which lives in a swamp near Hollow Mountain and goes off in search of it. Nassour and Rodriguez direct in a workmanlike manner but Stahl's photography is superb. However it's the monster itself that steals the show: Nassour invented a new process by which, he claimed, he could electronically control the 'lizard'. In fact, he used the technique of 'replacement animation' in which a series of models was made, each different from the other for each frame of film, thus making the monster's movements far more realistic because all its details could be altered from frame to frame. The result, as so often in Science Fiction, was a monster far more prepossessing than the film it was in.

co-d/co-p Edward Nassour   *co-d/co-s* Ismael Rodriguez
co-p William Nassour   *co-s* Robert Hill, Carlos Orellana
c Jorge Stahl Jnr   *se* Jack Rabin, Louis DeWitt   *lp* Guy Madison, Patricia Medina, Eduardo Noriega, Carlos Rivas, Mano Navarro, Pascual Gargia Peña

Beverly Garland as the imperilled heroine in Roger Corman's marvellous Not of This Earth.

Above: 1984, *George Orwell's bleak vision of the future, much softened by director Michael Anderson.*

1984 (HOLIDAY FILM PRODUCTIONS; GB) b/w 91 min

In 1954 Nigel Kneale, the originator of the Quatermass trilogy, adapted George Orwell's novel, *1984*, for BBC television with Peter Cushing as Winston Smith. The teleplay, which caused a furore when it was broadcast, was a success because it both took Orwell's novel seriously and had the confidence to recast the material for the (small) screen. A year later John Halas and Joy Batchelor used Orwell's *Animal Farm* as the basis of an equally ferocious animated feature.

In contrast to these brave efforts, this film directed by Anderson (who was later responsible for **Doc Savage – The Man of Bronze**, 1975 and **Logan's Run**, 1976) stands revealed as a hymn to caution, a simplified version of the book that pays little heed to the ideas that make it so significant a work. Indeed the prevarication of those concerned even extended to the filming of two different endings. The British release print has O'Brien's Winston Smith defying Big Brother and dying while the American print ends with the lovers O'Brien and Sterling brainwashed into submission and parting of their own 'free will'. Thus, in place of Orwell's savage satire on the rise of the authoritarian state (and specifically Stalinism), producer Rathvon and Anderson mount a vapid romance in which beefy O'Brien and mousey Sterling are clearly intended to represent the undying spirit of rebellion. Even the drabness of life in Oceania that Orwell creates so convincingly, is lost in the film which, like so many literary adaptations, centres on the slim storyline of the novel.

O'Brien is the clerk in the Ministry of Truth who refuses to accept the totalitarian state of 1984, where each citizen is watched at all times, and creates his own free state with his lover (Sterling), only to be betrayed by party member Redgrave. Only Redgrave, who brings an arrogance and dynamism to his role, is at all compelling, suggesting momentarily the delight with which Orwell's state functionaries applied themselves to their repressive work.

d Michael Anderson   *p* N. Peter Rathvon   *s* William P. Templeton, Ralph Bettinson   *c* C. Pennington Richards *se* B. Langley, G. Blackwell, N. Warwick   *lp* Edmond O'Brien, Michael Redgrave, Jan Sterling, David Kossoff, Mervyn Johns, Donald Pleasence, Kenneth Griffith

Not of This Earth (LOS ALTOS) b/w 67(65) min

The best of Corman's Science Fiction films of the fifties, this elegant thriller anticipates many of the themes the director would explore more fully in his better-known Edgar Allan Poe adaptations. Birch is the alien in a grey flannel suit collecting human blood (and leaving drained corpses behind) for shipment back to his home planet of Davana. However, he is more than merely conventionally menacing. Rather, like the heroes of Corman's Poe inspired films, he is a rarified figure, fragile – he finally dies because the high pitch of a motorbike siren causes him so much pain he crashes his car – yet powerful – when he removes his dark glasses anyone who gazes into his pupil-less eyes, dies – the representative of a dying race desperately seeking sustenance on Earth.

The film also introduced Corman's unique brand of suspense-horror-comedy (notably in the encounter between Birch and Miller's eager vacuum cleaner salesman) that he would later hone to perfection in films like **The Little Shop of Horrors** (1960). But, more importantly, the film marked Corman's difference from his contemporary Science Fiction

161

film-makers. In other hands the film would have been undoubtedly full of reds-under-the-beds implications which Corman eschews in favour of an other-worldly nightmare in brittle shades of grey.

d/p Roger Corman   *s* Charles B. Griffith, Mark Hanna
c John Mesall   *se* Paul Blaisdell   *lp* Paul Birch, Beverly Garland, Morgan Jones, William Roderick, Jonathan Haze, Richard Miller

Phantom from 10,000 Leagues

(MILNER BROTHERS PRODUCTIONS)   b/w   81 (72) min
Like Bert I. Gordon, the Milner brothers also used the crudest, most sensational posters to attract the public in – and then produced the limpest possible images on the screen.

Oceanographer Taylor arrives at a beach to investigate mysterious deaths caused by a sea phantom which turns out to be a mutated monster guarding underwater deposits of uranium ore. The mutant has been created by Whalen in an experiment and is powered by atomic light. Eventually it turns on its master whereupon both are killed in a dynamite explosion.

The film was one of the first releases of the American Releasing Corporation which within a year mutated into AIP and distributed the flood of independent Science Fiction and horror movies aimed, like this, at the growing drive-in youth audience, the one growth area in the American film-market.

d/co-p Dan Milner   *co-p* Jack Milner   *s* Lou Rusoff
c Bryden Baker   *lp* Kent Taylor, Cathy Downs, Michael Whalen, Rodney Bell, Helene Stanton, Philip Pine

Plan 9 from Outer Space *aka* Grave Robbers from Outer Space   (J. EDWARD REYNOLDS PRODUCTIONS)   b/w   79 min

Too often celebrated as the worst Science Fiction film ever, a claim made by some for **Bride of the Monster** (1956) which Wood also directed, though it certainly *is* a bad film, this is undeserving of either the attention its cult status has brought it or of the denigration heaped upon it.

Essentially an amateur production mounted in the most trying circumstances in which, to match the two minutes of film Wood acquired featuring a silent Lugosi (probably from the uncompleted *Tomb of the Vampire*), Wood hired his wife's homeopathic healer and because he didn't look in the least like Lugosi had him carry a cloak in front of him at all times, the film's failings are obvious. More interestingly, the film, with its predictable plot of aliens trying to conquer Earth by reviving the dead as zombies, is revealing of just how deep-seated the fear of being taken over from within (by communists) was in America in the fifties. Other films, such as **Invasion of the Body Snatchers** (1956) and **I Married a Monster from Outer Space** (1958) dealt with that fear as well but in far more complex ways, articulating it with imagination and exploring the paranoia that lay beneath it, in short interrogating the fear to produce significant films about conformity and sexuality. What Wood does is simply express the fear in a wholly unconscious manner that bizarrely shows how insubstantial such fears are in isolation. To be activated in an audience those fears need to be structured. Thus it is entirely fitting that *Plan 9 from Outer Space* should make little sense as a film and be barely watchable. It literally 'says' nothing, it has no characters, no story, no direction, no whatever; it's a completely unstructured dream produced with no interference from the conscious mind at all.

What, finally, a film like *Plan 9 from Outer Space* reveals is just how much art and artifice go to make up the 'realism' that Hollywood films take for granted. In Wood's case, such a realist aesthetic is simply unattainable.

d/p/s Edward D. Wood Jnr   *c* William Thompson
lp Bela Lugosi, Vampira, Tor Johnson, Lyle Talbot, Joanne Lee, Gregory Walcott, Duke Moore, Tom Keene

Rodan *aka* Radon *aka* Radon the Flying Monster

(TOHO; JAP)   79 (74) min
The first monster in glorious Eastmancolor and Honda-Tsuburaya's second major success for Toho after the relative failure of Honda's *Jujin Yukiotoko* (1955) and Oda's awkward resurrection of Godzilla in **Gigantis** (1955). Rodan is a pterodactyl that can fly at supersonic speed, causing shock waves analogous to those following an atomic explosion. The bird emerges from a coalmine where it was hatched and ate a swarm of mammoth dragonflies called Meganuron. The destruction of Japan is accompanied by the monster's shrill screams as it is traced to Mount Aso, a volcano, where its mate has laid some eggs. The volcano's eruption incinerates them both, although Rodan did reappear later on as a 'good' monster, teaming up with Godzilla and Mothra against Ghidorah in **Ghidorah Sandai Kaiju Chikyu Saidai No Kessan**, 1965). The special effects are impressive, especially the volcanic eruption and the death of the monsters in the gushing lava. Scenes of military attacks on the bird are similar to shots in **Them!** (1954).

The American version added no scenes to the original, only a hectoring voice-over by David Duncan. Rodan's other appearances are in **Kaiju Daisenso** (1965) and **Kaiju Soshingeki** (1968).

d Inoshiro Honda   *p* Tomoyuki Tanaka   *s* Takeshi Kimura, Takeo Murata   *c* Isamu Ashida   *se* Eiji Tsuburaya
lp Kenji Sahara, Yumi Shirakawa, Akihiko Hirata, Akio Kobori, Yasuko Nakata, Minosuke Yamada, Yoshibumi Tajima, Kiyoharu Ohnaka

Satellite in the Sky

(TRIDELTA PRODUCTIONS; GB)   scope   85 min
A predictable mix of British stiff-upper-lip heroics and melodrama, *Satellite in the Sky* is a lacklustre film. A rocket is sent up into space to explode an experimental tritonium bomb above the stratosphere. Moore, the captain, is joined on board by the bomb's inventor, Wolfit (who hams it up outrageously). The bomb becomes attached to the ship and the crew struggle desperately to dislodge it until Wolfit climbs out onto the outside of the ship, grabs the bomb and pushes it off into space – with himself on board. It explodes harmlessly but kills him.

The outer-space special effects are effective as is the model work which includes a huge underground modern space

Below: *Donald Wolfit (centre) as the wonderfully eccentric scientist in the decidedly minor* Satellite in the Sky.

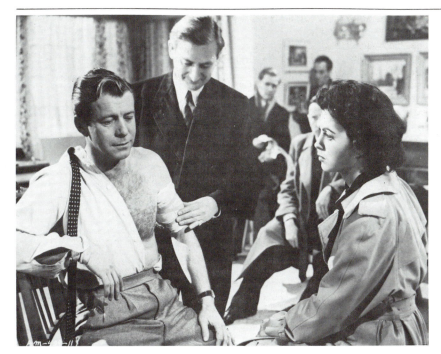

Gene Nelson (left) as the man 7½ seconds into the future in Timeslip. *Faith Domergue looks on.*

complex and a rocket launch which runs on a track over a mountain, an idea borrowed from **When Worlds Collide** (1951). Veevars, who provided the special effects, later worked on **2001 – A Space Odyssey** (1968).

d Paul Dickson *p* Edward J. Danziger, Harry Lee Danziger *s* John Mather, J.T. McIntosh, Edith Dell *c* Georges Perinal, Jimmy Wilson *se* Wally Veevers *lp* Kieron Moore, Lois Maxwell, Donald Wolfit, Brian Forbes, Jimmy Hanley, Thea Gregory

Timeslip *aka* The Atomic Man

(MERTON PARK PRODUCTIONS; GB) b/w 93 (76) min
Like **Spaceways** (1953), this Science Fiction thriller is based on a novel (*The Isotope Man*) by Charles Eric Maine. Dragged from the Thames with a bullet in his back, Arne dies clinically on the operating table for a few seconds and then recovers. American reporter Nelson interviews him and finds that not only are his answers odd but he has a strange resemblance to atomic scientist Rayner (Arne again) who is alive and well in his laboratory. From here on the plotlines multiply confusingly and in the process Maine's novel idea of a man 7½ seconds in the future is quickly reduced to predictable skullduggery, in which scientist Arne is a spy. Hughes directs breezily in the American manner he perfected until graduating to the big budgets of *Cromwell* (1970) and the like.

d Ken Hughes *p* Alec C. Snowden *s* Charles Eric Maine *c* A.T. Dinsdale *lp* Gene Nelson, Faith Domergue, Joseph Tomelty, Peter Arne, Vic Perry, Donald Grey

Uchujin Tokyo ni Arawaru *aka* The Mysterious Satellite *aka* The Cosmic Man Appears in Tokyo *aka* Space Men Appear in Tokyo *aka* Warning from Space *aka* Unknown Satellite over Tokyo (DAIEI; JAP) 87 min

Exploiting the A-bomb and flying-saucer themes prevalent at the time, this film based on Gentaro Nakajima's novel is one of Japan's first serious Science Fiction efforts outside the Kaiju Eiga (monster movies) genre, although monsters do appear in it. Here the creatures stem from an alien planet (a theme that became widespread in the late sixties) called Paira. The aliens are giant starfish with an eye in the middle of their body. As they are friendly, they change into human shapes in order not to frighten people. Their leader, Ginko (Karita) admonishes the people on Earth not to use their nuclear weapons against each other but to join forces with Paira to destroy the fiery planet that is on a collision course with the

Right: Rodan, *the first Japanese monster movie in colour.*

Earth. After the Earth has heated up disastrously, causing tidal waves (another commonplace of the genre), a Japanese scientist (Yamagata) develops a special bomb which is fired by the Pairans from their spacecraft, destroying the menacing planet. For once, aliens are depicted as friendly, a refreshing change from the usual Cold War mentality suffusing Science Fiction material at the time.

Good special effects and fine colour photography add to the interest of this prolific Daiei house director's work.

d Koji Shima *p* Masaichi Nagata *s* Hideo Oguni *c* Kimio Watanabe *se* Kenmei Yuasa *lp* Toyomi Karita, Keizo Kawasaki, Isao Yamagata, Shozo Nanbu, Buntaro Miake, Mieko Nagai, Kiyoko Hirai

The Werewolf (CLOVER) b/w 83(78) min

A typical Katzman quickie, this silly chiller is only of interest for what it represents in the development of the Science Fiction and horror genres. It marks precisely the point at which horror, which had been a dormant genre in the early fifties, began to take over from Science Fiction. This trend was confirmed within a year when, in the wake of the sale of the Universal Frankenstein films (which although milestones in the development of the Science Fiction genre were structured as horror films and were expressionistic rather than realistic in tone) to American TV and the success of British Hammer's romantic/gothic versions of *Dracula* (1957) and Frankenstein (**The Curse of Frankenstein**, 1957), both of which were in colour, producers started actively looking for horror rather than Science Fiction stories to film. Finally, in the sixties, Roger Corman, a prolific producer/director of Science Fiction in the mid-fifties, abandoned the genre for horror after the phenomenal success of the Edgar Allan Poe inspired *The House of Usher* (1960).

What makes Sears' film so interesting is its attempt to combine the radically different styles of the two genres in one film. Thus, Launer and Lynn are Science Fiction scientists and the serum which turns Ritch into a werewolf is intended to cure radiation but the film is shot in a (would-be) expressionistic style that suggests a gothic rather than scientific universe. Needless to say, the film cannot contain these strains in equilibrium.

d Fred F. Sears *p* Sam Katzman *s* Robert E. Kent, James B. Gordon *c* Edwin Linden *lp* Steven Ritch, Don Megowan, Joyce Holden, Eleanore Tanin, S. John Launer, George M. Lynn

World Without End (AA) scope 80 min

Produced by Allied Artists, who usually bought in independent productions for distribution, this re-working of H.G. Wells' novel *The Time Machine* (which was filmed officially in 1960) had a bigger budget and better special effects than most of Bernds' other films, including **Return of the Fly** (1959).

Breaking through a time-warp, four astronauts (led by Marlowe) land on Earth in AD 2508 only to discover that a nuclear war has devasted the planet. Mutants and giant spiders roam the surface whilst the remnants of humanity live underground in a world composed of connecting tunnels. Hydroponic gardens provide food and air whilst the somewhat listless inhabitants (led by Gates) wear elf-like tunics and tights, designed by *Esquire* illustrator Vargas. The atmosphere is peaceful as weapons are now banned and there is a democratically elected ruler. But the men are impotent, the race is dying out slowly and the surface mutants are becoming more daring until Marlowe and his companions inspire the survivors to fight the mutants and spiders with home-made bazookas for what is left of Earth's surface. Ironically the money spent on the film's special effects only serves to highlight the weak melodramatics of Bernds' script and the stodginess of his direction.

d/s Edward Bernds *p* Richard Heermance *c* Ellsworth Fredricks *se* Milton Rice, Jack Rabin, Irving Block *lp* Hugh Marlowe, Nancy Gates, Rod Taylor, Lisa Montell, Christopher Dark, Shawn Smith

X the Unknown (HAMMER; GB) b/w 86(80) min

This is a superior example of the sober, realist tradition of British Science Fiction. Directed by Ealing regular Norman (who replaced Walton when he fell ill in the middle of shooting) as a thriller with only a few gothic inflections – the setting is the Scottish moors – the film takes for its central situation the discovery, during a routine army training exercise, of a primeval mud creature, formed at the time of the original cooling of the Earth's crust, that has adapted itself to live off radiation. The opening is superb: a tracking shot of a soldier crossing a desolate gravel pit with an ominously clacking geiger counter, then the camera pulls back to reveal he's taking part in a training programme before a further soldier sets off only to find, not the object hidden by his commanding officer but a new source of immense radioactivity and for the ground to literally open up at his feet.

Left: *One of the Pairans (giant starfish-like aliens) that come to Earth to warn mankind of a planet on collision course with the world in* Uchujin Tokyo ni Arawaru.

The descent into the monster's pit in the superior X the Unknown.

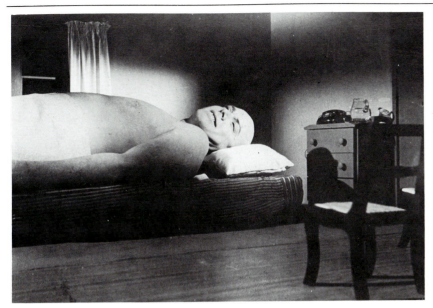

The Amazing Colossal Man, *probably Bert I. Gordon's finest film.*

Jagger, the film's fading American star and Quatermass lookalike, is suitably authoritative as the scientist who convinces everyone something serious is afoot and, after a thrilling descent into the monster's abyss (from which it has periodically emerged and killed in its search for further radiation), disposes of it with 'electronic waves'. Although the film's middle section drags somewhat and is occasionally too flippant (as when a doctor and nurse's lovers' tryst in the radiation room of the nearby hospital ends with the pair punished for their lovemaking by the monster), Gibbs' austere black and white cinematography (in which the night scenes were, unusually, shot at night) and Jagger's performance create a strong sense of atmosphere.

An interestingly, but not fully developed, sub-plot that looks forward to the magnificent **Quatermass II** (1957) centres on the conflict between the scientific establishment and the military about what to do and between Jagger's boss (Chapman) and Jagger about the role of science. Equally interesting, the film, in marked contrast to most American Science Fiction films, presents Jagger as a humanist (rather than as an obsessed genius).

Sangster, whose first script this is, subsequently wrote the scripts for Fisher's radical reinterpretation of the Frankenstein myth, **The Curse of Frankenstein** (1957) and **The Revenge of Frankenstein** (1958).

d Leslie Norman, Joseph Walton *p* Anthony Hinds
s Jimmy Sangster *c* Gerald Gibbs *se* Les Bowie, Jack Curtis *lp* Dean Jagger, Leo McKern, William Lucas, Edward Chapman, John Harvey, Anthony Newley, Norman Macowan

1957

The Abominable Snowman *aka* The Abominable Snowman of the Himalayas

(HAMMER; GB) b/w scope 91 (85) min
Based on Nigel Kneale's teleplay *The Creature*, this is the last Abominable Snowman movie of the fifties (the others were **The Snow Creature**, 1954 and **Man Beast**, 1956). Kneale had written the successful *Quatermass* series and Hammer were anxious to repeat the earlier success but this effort lacked subtlety, despite the fact they hired *Quatermass* director, Guest, to bolster the project.

Cushing, a botanist leading an expedition to the Himalayas, joins Tucker, who is searching for the Yeti. When the couple spot, and Tucker kills a Yeti, Cushing discovers Tucker only has exploitation in mind. En route back to England a number of disasters occur, Tucker is killed in an avalanche and Cushing confronts the Yeti who, knowing him to be a

Right: *Peter Cushing (left) and Forrest Tucker with the captured Yeti in* The Abominable Snowman.

'goodie', disappear into the night, leaving him unharmed. Kneale's teleplay was far stronger than this rather weak, but well photographed, offering.

d Val Guest *p* Aubrey Baring *s* Nigel Kneale
c Arthur Grant *lp* Forrest Tucker, Peter Cushing, Maureen Connell, Richard Wattis, Robert Brown, Michael Brill

The Amazing Colossal Man

(MALIBU) b/w 81 (80) min
Considered to be director Gordon's best film, this clumsy would-be epic tries to capitalize on Arnold's far superior **The Incredible Shrinking Man** (1957). Langan stars as an army officer caught up in an atomic explosion who becomes a 60-foot giant as a result of radiation poisoning. He becomes insane, breaks out of captivity and destroys people and cardboard cutouts of various national landmarks. Scientist Hudson goes after him with an enormous hypodermic – one of the film's (unintentionally) hilarious scenes involves Langan pulling the needle out of his foot with an expression of dazed surprise. The climax, derived from *King Kong* (1933) has him plunge to his death off Hoover Dam after putting down his fiancée Downs. A sequel, **War of the Colossal Beast**, arrived in 1958.

d/p/co-s/se Bert I. Gordon *co-s* Mark Hanna *c* Joseph Biroc *lp* Glenn Langan, Cathy Downs, William Hudson, James Seay, Larry Thor, Russ Bender

Un Amour de Poche

(MADELEINE FILMS/SNEG/CONTACT ORGANISATION; FR)
b/w 85 min
A comedy version of **The Incredible Shrinking Man** (1957) motif. Marais plays a biologist whose formula N734 can shrink matter. Threatened with discovery by a jealous fiancée (Page), Marais' lab assistant and lover (Laurant) takes the formula and is reduced to a 16-cm statuette which fits into her lover's pocket. However, Page discovers the mini-rival and takes her on board for a cruise to America, pursued by Marais in a motorboat. Page accidentally drops Laurant overboard but the contact with saltwater restores Laurant to her normal size and she is fished out of the sea by Marais.

Kast, a critic for both *Cahiers du Cinéma* and *Positif*, was a noted documentarist in the fifties. This was the first of an uneven series of features which included *Le Bel Age* (1960) and *La Morte Saison des Amours* (1961), two archetypal New Wave movies. Kast can be seen as a more commercial (and often funnier) Eric Rohmer, a director more at home filming conversation and witty lines, in the tradition of Sacha Guitry's filmed theatre, rather than making movies. His short film *La*

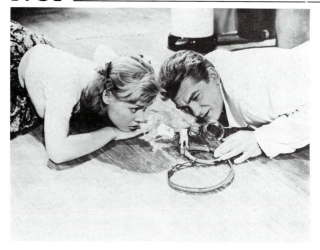

Brûlure de Mille Soleils (1965), with drawings by Edouardo Luis, and this Science Fiction comedy are arguably his best work, the former for its intelligence, this for its light-hearted, tongue-in-cheek approach to Science Fiction.

d Pierre Kast *p* Gilbert de Goldschmidt *s* France Roche
c Ghislain Cloquet *lp* Jean Marais, Geneviève Page, Agnès Laurant, Régine Lovi, Amédée, Pasquali, Joëlle Janin, Jean-Claude Brialy, Flip

The Beginning of the End

(AMERICAN BROADCAST-PARAMOUNT THEATRES PRODUCTIONS) b/w 74 min
Gordon, the celebrated showman of Science Fiction, produces, directs and supplies the appalling special effects for this outing which, derived from **Them!** (1954), features giant locusts (grasshoppers) on the rampage. Their stick-like bodies and bulbous eyes make for a dramatic first appearance as they come stumbling over the horizon, but after this they become merely risible. Journalist Castle and scientist Graves do battle with the flesh-hungry locusts when they swarm on Chicago. Finally Graves comes up with a maniacal idea – he records the locusts' mating calls, rows out into a lake, puts the calls on a PA system and the insects rush into the lake, lemming-like, where they drown.

One of the last to be released under the Republic banner, the film was the first made by AB-PT, the short-lived production company established by the ABC-TV network and the Paramount Chain of Theatres.

Gordon returned to this theme two decades later with **The Food of the Gods** (1976).

d/p/co-se Bert I. Gordon *s* Fred Freiberger, Lester Gorn *c* Jack Marta *co-se* Flora Gordon *lp* Peggie Castle, Peter Graves, Morris Ankrum, Richard Benedict, James Seay, Thomas Browne

Chikyu Boeigun *aka* The Mysterians *aka* Earth Defence Force (TOHO; JAP) scope 89 (85) min

Having created two durable monsters, **Gojira** (1954) and **Rodan** (1956), Honda, Tsuburaya and the Toho team, including cameraman Koizumi and composer Akira Ikufube, both regular collaborators for years to come, turned to a combination of space opera and monsters of a different sort.

This story has aliens coming to Earth in flying saucers and dispatching a robot bird, Mogella, which shoots death rays out of its eyes. The aim of the visit is to find women to breed with the aliens whose planet was destroyed by a nuclear explosion. In the seventies, this type of story would be repeated with two major variants: the monsters would be integrated into the Kaiju Eiga genre and battle with Earth monsters, while the destruction of the alien planet would no longer be attributed to nuclear mishaps but to pollution as in **Gamera Tai Shinkai Kaiju Jigura** (1971).

Here, the Mysterians are split into good and bad ones, landing in Japan because the Japanese are supposed to represent the best qualities of humanity, except that they object to miscegenation. The best scenes involve the interaction between the aliens and those with the fabulous metallic bird, especially its destruction as it walks across a bridge that collapses, causing the device to shortcircuit and the aliens to admit defeat.

This film does reveal some of the fantasy elements underpinning the whole genre. Initially, the monsters represented an attempt to mythify and thus to absorb somehow the cultural experience of having been victims of nuclear aggression. This element is present in this film in the form of aliens sending a contraption to Japan which will steal its vital, life-giving forces. As the genre developed, however, this changed and the force that threatened to destroy the country evolved into forces defending the country, in parallel with a changed attitude in official circles towards the rearmament of Japan. By the mid-seventies, militarist nationalism had become overt enough no longer to need cloaking in monstrous disguises. This sent the monster movie genre into decline and drastically reshaped its thematic construction, shifting the theme of the nuclear-generated monsters towards the theme of alien-generated monsters coping with the ravages of pollution. This scenario would allow the monster forces to become friendly and beneficial (though still causing massive destruction, as all massive military action must), even necessary for the survival of Japan. This change in the ritualistic enactment of a relationship towards military force represented in the shape of monsters pushed the genre into space opera territory on TV as well, spawning a myriad of Science Fiction teleseries, some of which were directed by Fukasaku and are said to have inspired the **Star Wars** (1977) films, which in turn elicited new imitations in Japan.

d Inoshiro Honda *p* Tomoyuki Tanaka *s* Shigeru Kayama, Takashi Kimura *c* Hajime Koizumi *se* Eiji Tsuburaya, Hidesaburo Araki, Sadamasa Arikawa, Akira Watanabe *lp* Kenji Sahara, Yumi Shirakawa, Takashi Shimura, Akihiko Hirata, Momoko Koichi, Susumu Fujita, Hisayo Ito, Fuyuki Murakami, Minosuke Yamada, Yoshio Kosugi

The Curse of Frankenstein (HAMMER; GB) 83 min

Greeted with critical revulsion when first released – one critic suggested a new film certificate, SO (for sadists only) – *The Curse of Frankenstein* marked a radical departure from James Whale's classic interpretation of the legend in **Frankenstein**

Left: *Agnès Laurant and Jean Marais discover the shrinking properties of formula N734 in the comic Un Amour de Poche.*

Below: *Science and the military, in co-operation as they invariably were in the fifties, here momentarily powerless in the face of the giant locusts of The Beginning of the End.*

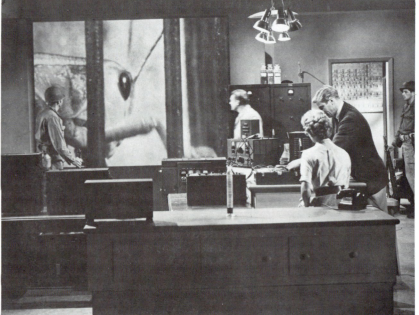

Mogella, the robot bird, on the warpath in Chikyu Boeigun.

(1931). In part this was motivated by the fact that, though the story was in the public domain, Jack Pierce's makeup for the monster was Universal's copyright. Accordingly, Phil Leakey (who'd previously handled the makeup of Richard Wordsworth's mutating spaceman in **The Quatermass Xperiment**, 1955) was instructed to create a new creature. Another significant change was from black and white to colour. Far more important, however, was director Fisher and writer Sangster's re-structuring of the legend to concentrate not on the monster but his creator, Cushing's Baron Frankenstein who, unlike Colin Clive's bland scientist, is a full-blown over-reacher.

Accordingly, Fisher's Frankenstein is no longer the conventional (mad) scientist, but the human personification of Robert Cornthwaite's description of the alien in Howard Hawks' classic **The Thing** (1951), 'No pleasure, no pain . . . no emotions . . . Our superior in every way'. The result is a film whose comfortable brass and mahogany Victorian world, unlike that of the numerous Jules Verne adaptations of the time such as **20,000 Leagues Under the Sea** (1954), is perpetually undercut by the cold steel of the scalpel with which Cushing clears his path to knowledge. Elegantly structured by Sangster, the story is told by Cushing while awaiting execution for the murder of his servant, killed by mistake while he did battle with the monster (Lee) which then conveniently falls into a bath of acid; the narrative line consists of little but Cushing gathering the necessary organs and attempting to give life to his creation (which he does twice).

An even more impressive sequel, also scripted by Sangster, **The Revenge of Frankenstein**, followed in 1958. As well as setting the tone of Hammer's subsequent sorties into the gothic, such as *Dracula* (1957), also made by Sangster and Fisher, the film was influential on the emerging medical-horror genre of the Latin cinema that reached its highpoint with the gruesome **Gritos en la Noche** (1962).

Right: *Peter Cushing's Baron Frankenstein confronted by his creation, Christopher Lee, in* The Curse of Frankenstein.

d Terence Fisher *p* Anthony Hinds *s* Jimmy Sangster
c Jack Asher *lp* Peter Cushing, Robert Urquhart, Hazel Court, Christopher Lee, Valerie Gaunt, Noel Hood, Sally Walsh

The Cyclops (AB & H) b/w 75 (65) min

Bert I. Gordon, the showman who lured his audiences in to a tame screen via sensational posters, was responsible for *The Cyclops*. The sheer hamminess of the acting and the paucity of the Cyclops itself make for some memorable moments when Talbot, aided by Craig, mounts an expedition in the Mexican mountains in search of her missing fiancé (Parkin). They arrive in a valley where radiation has resulted in monster-sized animals and a 25-foot-high human being, with tissue distorting one side of his face and a huge swollen eye, lurks in vengeful misery. The expedition eventually escape the creature's malicious intentions but as they leave the valley Talbot realizes the wretched Cyclops is her own fiancé. Gordon enlarged a considerable number of animals, including a gopher, but the monsters, appearing on a split screen, appear to have no connection with the actors at all. The

Cyclops is barely more credible. Gordon's other films include **The Amazing Colossal Man** (1957), probably his finest movie, and **Empire of the Ants** (1977).

d/p/s/se Bert I. Gordon   *c* Ira Morgan   *lp* Gloria Talbot, James Craig, Lou Chaney Jnr, Tom Drake, Duncan Parkin

The Deadly Mantis *aka* The Incredible Preying Mantis (U) b/w 79 min

The reputation of **Them!** (1954), which was by far the best American giant insect film, was much tarnished by its successors. *The Deadly Mantis*, which features a huge praying mantis living on an iceberg, is a case in point. After it has devasted most of the Arctic, US colonel Stevens mounts an expedition to track it down. His clumsy handling of the situation, however, only drives the mantis south, where it creates havoc in Washington DC before finally being gassed in Manhattan.

Juran, who directed the first script filmed by Roger Corman, *Highway Dragnet* (1954), directs in a perfunctory manner. His best work as a director is undoubtedly the fantasy film, *The Seventh Voyage of Sinbad* (1958).

d Nathan Juran   *p* William Alland   *s* Martin Berkeley   *c* Ellis Carter   *se* Fred Knoth   *lp* Craig Stevens, William Hopper, Alix Talton, Donald Randolph, Pat Conway, Florenz Ames

Escapement *aka* The Electronic Monster

(ALEC C. SNOWDEN PRODUCTIONS/ANGLO-AMALGAMATED; GB) b/w 80(72) min

Based on Charles Eric Maine's novel of the same title, *Escapement* is one of the first Science Fiction films to examine the possibility of a manmade machine becoming a monster and a precursor of later and more sophisticated films such as **Brainstorm** (1983) and **Videodrome** (1982). Insurance investigator Cameron is sent to look into the death of a matinée idol in Europe. He sleuths his way into a clinic whose inmates are hypnotized, then filed away to dream. Their dreams are changed into sexual nightmares and murderous fantasies by the Nazi-inspired doctor (Illing) and his electronic machine, and then projected back to the patients to act them out.

Tully's direction is sprightly enough but the screenplay is laboured and fails to develop the central premise at all.

d Montgomery Tully   *p* Alec C. Snowden   *s* Charles Eric Maine, J. Maclaren-Ross   *c* Bert Mason   *lp* Rod Cameron, Mary Murphy, Meredith Edwards, Peter Illing, Kay Callard, Larry Cross, Carl Duering

Fiend Without a Face (EROS; GB) b/w 75 min

This is one of several Science Fiction movies, mounted by small British companies to cash in on the success of **The Quatermass Xperiment** (1955), clearly intended for the American market, hence the presence of Thompson, a fading Hollywood actor and the pseudo-American location (a US army base in a remote corner of Canada). The film is directed by Crabtree (a cinematographer turned director of Gainsborough melodramas who is best remembered for the exotic *Horrors of the Black Museum*, 1958) in the sombre realistic style of such British films. A minor effort, it remains interesting if only for Leder's intelligent cannibalization of the central idea of **Forbidden Planet** (1956) that features Reeves as a scientist who invents a machine that turns thoughts to energy and accidentally projects his dislikes in physical form. The resulting 'brains', propelled by the whip of their spinal cords, suck their victims dry. The first half, with investigator Thompson discovering numerous corpses, is rather plodding, but the climax is unusually graphic for the period.

d Arthur Crabtree   *p* John Croydon   *s* Herbert J. Leder   *c* Lionel Banes   *se* Puppel Nordhoff, Peter Nielsen   *lp* Kyanston Reeves, Marshall Thompson, Terry Kilburn, Kim Parker, Peter Madden, Michael Balfour

From Hell It Came

(MILNER BROTHERS PRODUCTIONS) b/w 73(70) min

The most notable feature of this pedestrian offering from the Milner Brothers is the endearing scowling monster that looks like a walking tree stump. When Palmer is condemned to death on the evidence of his wife (Ridgeway), a witch-doctor (Swan) and a tribal chief (Barron) on a Pacific island, he ends up with a knife in his heart, buried upright in a coffin, swearing eternal vengeance. Whereupon radiation causes a plague and mutancy on the island and Palmer is revived as a walking tree stump to secure his revenge before once more being killed by scientist Andrews. The monster was designed by Paul Blaisdell, the designer of several monsters for Roger Corman.

d Dan Milner   *p* Jack Milner   *s* Richard Bernstein   *c* Brydon Baker   *lp* Tod Andrews, Tina Carver, Suzanne Ridgeway, Gregg Palmer, Robert Swan, Baynes Barron

Left: *The death throes of The Deadly Mantis.*

Below: *A thought monster attacks in the graphic* Fiend Without a Face.

Above: *Grant Williams battles a spider in the marvellous* The Incredible Shrinking Man.

Examining the evidence: a scene from The Giant Claw, *one of the silliest Science Fiction movies of the decade.*

Adapted from his second novel (the film rights to which he only sold on the condition he could do the screenplay after the debacle of the sale of his first novel, *I Am Legend*, which, when it eventually reached the screen in 1964 as **L'Ultimo Uomo della Terra**, was not from his screenplay), Matheson and director Arnold brilliantly articulate the transformation of the familiar into the malevolent. Affected by radiation, Williams begins to shrink, and as he does so the safe and comforting aspects of his home become menacing. He does battle with his own cat and then later fights a spider for survival before disappearing into the grass forest of his lawn.

The film's power rests upon the fact that, unlike other miniaturization films such as **Dr Cyclops** (1940), it is not merely an exotic adventure story. Moreover, unlike the inferior 1981 remake, **The Incredible Shrinking Woman**, it forces us to see life from the perspective of the ever-diminishing central character.

d Jack Arnold   *p* Albert Zugsmith   *s* Richard Matheson
c Ellis W. Carter   *se* Clifford Stine, Alexander Golitzin, Robert Clatworthy, Roswell A. Hoffmann, Everett A. Broussard   *lp* Grant Williams, Randy Stuart, April Kent, Paul Langton, Raymond Bailey, William Schallert, Frank Scannell, Billy Curtis

The Giant Claw   (CLOVER)   b/w   76 min

Shot in just under two weeks, this is probably the best unintentionally funny monster movie of the fifties, featuring an inept buzzard-like bird with huge feet, turkey feathers on its wings, a long neck and glassy eyes. The clumsy bird arrives from outer space to hatch an egg. It is first seen by Morrow whose friends are unconvinced until the bird grabs a train and flies off with it dangling from its beak. Radioactive as well as large, the bird has an anti-matter shield which ensures it does not show up on radar. Finally Morrow comes up with a device to pierce the shield and kills the monster which sinks into the sea, leaving one claw upraised.

What makes the movie so hilarious is the combination of atrocious special effects, farmed out by Katzman to a laboratory in Mexico, and the sheer silliness of the design of the giant bird.

d Fred F. Sears   *p* Sam Katzman   *s* Samuel Newman, Paul Gangelin   *c* Benjamin H. Kline   *lp* Jeff Morrow, Mara Corday, Morris Ankrum, Louis D. Merrill, Edgar Barrier, Robert Shayne

I Was a Teenage Werewolf

(SUNSET PRODUCTIONS)   b/w   76 min

One of the most famous movie titles of all time, this was the first feature of Fowler, who went on to make the highly original **I Married a Monster from Outer Space** (1958). Raw-meat-loving teenager Landon is sent to psychiatrist Bissell in an attempt to cure his psychotic rages. Bissell, however, is crazy and believes that mankind can only be saved from atomic war by an enforced return to primitive times. To this end, he injects Landon with a mysterious serum, hypnotizes him and sits back to watch the startling results. Thornton's script and Fowler's suprisingly witty direction have Landon behaving outlandishly as a fully fledged werewolf, butchering those he comes into contact with, including Bissell, before being killed by Phillips' friendly cop.

d Gene Fowler Jnr   *p* Herman Cohen   *s* Ralph Thornton
c Joseph La Shelle   *lp* Michael Landon, Yvonne Lime, Whit Bissell, Tony Marshall, Dawn Richard, Barney Phillips

The Incredible Shrinking Man   (U)   b/w   81 min

One of the great anxiety movies of the fifties, *The Incredible Shrinking Man*, is far more than a collection of superb special effects. Matheson's script perfectly captures the paranoia rampant in Cold War America as the hero's life, marriage and prospects literally collapse around him as he shrinks to oblivion.

Right: *Michael Landon as the all-American youngster in* I Was a Teenage Werewolf.

Eyer is the son of computer expert Abbott, transformed into a genius by his father's super computer, who rebuilds Robby only to have the robot taken over by the super computer, which is bent on world domination. In effect, Hume neatly parallels the relationship of Robby and the computer to that of Eyer and his father: both 'parents' are megalomaniacal in their own way and both 'sons' have to defy their parents to first create disorder (when Robby makes him invisible Eyer takes his revenge on his parents by playing pranks on them) and then restore order (Robby smashes the computer that Abbott can't bear to destroy).

Hoffman's direction is routine and the acting of the principals (Eyer excluded) is bland, but Hume's sympathetic script and the film's unusual perspective remain engaging to this day.

d Herman Hoffman   *p* Nicholas Nayfack   *s* Cyril Hume
c Harold Wellman   *se* Jack Rabin, Irving Block, Louis DeWitt   *lp* Richard Eyer, Philip Abbott, Diane Brewster, Harold J. Stone, Robert H. Harris, Denise McCarthy

Kronos (REGAL) b/w scope 78 min
Kronos is the 100-foot-high energy-accumulating alien robot who comes to Earth to steal as much energy as possible. He arrives on a California beach and proceeds to march inland, sucking up energy as he goes. Meanwhile, to the alarm of scientist Morrow, a ball of electricity invades and takes over the body of his colleague Emery. Directed unimaginatively by Neumann, the potential of Goldman's script is missed, but there are some interesting ideas, particularly when the military try to H-bomb Kronos and the robot merely absorbs the enormous energy, becoming even bigger as a result. Eventually Morrow finds a way of shortcircuiting Kronos, the robot absorbs its own energy – and disappears. The special effects are superb, despite the low budget, and Struss' cinematography gives the impression of a far bigger budget than the $160,000 *Kronos* cost to make.

d/p Kurt Neumann   *s* Lawrence Louis Goldman   *c* Karl Struss   *se* Jack Rabin, Irving Block, Gene Warren   *lp* Jeff Morrow, Barbara Lawrence, Eliot John Emery, George O'Hanlon, Morris Ankrum, Kenneth Alton

Invasion of the Saucermen *aka* **Invasion of the Hell Creatures** *aka* **The Hell Creatures** *aka* **Spacemen Saturday Night** (MALIBU) b/w 69 min
Clearly intended as a comedy, in itself a mark that the invasion cycle of fifties Science Fiction films was coming to an end, this dismal offering features Terrell and Castillo as the unlikely teenage lovers' lane habituées turned defenders of middle America from an invasion of 'little green men'. When they accidentally run over one of the aliens, Gurney and Martin's confusing plot has the aliens frame them for the murder of Gorshin's drunk (murdered by the little green men by injecting him with alcohol which they excrete from needles in their fingertips) in an attempt to conceal their presence on Earth.

However, Cahn's attempts to invert the accepted verities of teenage-parent relationships of the fifties and to satirize the idea of an invasion from outer space are only half-hearted at best. Moreover, the sequences like Hatton driving off the aliens with a pitchfork, the military blowing up the spaceship by mistake and the aliens' encounter with an enraged Bramah bull, are so weakly mounted it's hard to find them convincing, let alone humorous. Similarly, the climax which has the teenagers turning their headlights on the aliens and evaporating them palls in contrast to the silly but remarkably charming **The Blob** (1958), another film that shows teenagers in an unusually heroic light.

The film, which was remade as **The Eye Creatures** (1965) was the last by Osborn, who is best remembered for his role as Cadet Happy in the *Space Patrol* teleseries.

d Edward L. Cahn   *co-p* James H. Nicholson   *co-p/co-s* Robert J. Gurney Jnr   *co-s* Al Martin   *c* Frederick E. West   *se* Paul Blaisdell, Howard A. Anderson   *lp* Steve Terrell, Gloria Castillo, Frank Gorshin, Raymond Hatton, Russ Bender, Douglas Henderson, Lyn Osborn

The Invisible Boy (PAN PRODUCTIONS) b/w 90 min
Following the success of **Forbidden Planet** (1956) producer Nayfack quit MGM and set up his own company, Pan Productions, and persuaded that film's writer, Hume, to fashion a screenplay from Edmund Cooper's short story *The Invisible Boy* (which had no robot in it) that featured *Forbidden Planet*'s Robby the Robot in a central role. The charming result, which was not a sequel to *Forbidden Planet* (though it has always, understandably, been overshadowed by that film) is unique amongst American Science Fiction of the fifties in being constructed from the viewpoint of its ten-year-old hero (Eyer) who makes friends with Robby. In Eastern Europe and Japan such a perspective was quite common, but American juvenile-oriented films, even those of the Disney studio, rarely took the point of view of their young heroes, before Steven Spielberg's **E.T.** (1982).

Left: *The 'little green men' of* Invasion of the Saucermen *as devised by Paul Blaisdell, a master of low-budget special effects.*

The giant crystals on the march in The Monolith Monsters.

Right: *Robby the robot and Richard Eyer in the engaging* The Invisible Boy.

The Man Who Turned to Stone

(CLOVER) b/w 71 min

Scientist Jory has the secret of eternal youth and is determined to preserve it in this Katzman quickie written by the blacklisted Gordon under the pseudonym of 'Raymond T. Marcus'. Jory, Ledebur and others steal the youth of young women via an electric apparatus (that wouldn't look out of place in a forties, or even thirties, film) placed in the bath tub. As their youth needs continuously topping up (they turn to stone if uncharged), Jory starts a reformatory for young women who keep having heart attacks when required for topping-up purposes. Eventually psychiatrist Hudson exposes the system, the reformatory is burnt down, Jory and Ledebur turn to stone and stalwart heroine Austin is rescued. A silly, charmless film, it lacks even the intelligence to let Jory ham up his part.

d Leslie Kardos *p* Sam Katzman *s* Raymond T. Marcus (Bernard Gordon) *c* Benjamin H. Kline *lp* Victor Jory, Charlotte Austin, William Hudson, Frederick Ledebur, Jean Willes, Ann Doran

Man Without a Body

(EROS/BRITISH FILMPLAYS LTD; GB) b/w 80 min

Coulouris is the financier with a brain tumour who hits on the novel idea of resurrecting the head of Nostradamus with a view to using Nostradamus' powers of prediction to first assist in the running of his business and eventually to take over the reins of power from him. The highpoint of the film, before it collapses into a predictable climax with Golden's Nostradamus (his head now attached to a body in the interests of greater efficiency) turning on Coulouris and bringing about both their deaths, is an extended debate between Coulouris and Nostradamus' head in which the pair harangue each other, Nostradamus finding the purpose for which he's been re-animated too petty.

The direction by Sanders and Wilder (the brother of Billy) is decidedly pedestrian but the delirium of the central idea survives even its awkward articulation. Interestingly, the film, though not a great financial success, sparked off a number of similar re-animated head films, including **Die Nackte und der Satan** (1959) and the fantasy, *The Thing That Couldn't Die* (1958).

d M. Lee Wilder, Charles Sanders *p* Guido Coen *s* William Grote *c* Brendan Stafford *lp* Robert Hutton, George Coulouris, Julia Arnall, Nadje Regin, Michael Golden, Kim Parker, Tony Quinn

The Monolith Monsters (u) b/w 77 min

Based on a story by Jack Arnold and Fresco, this simple but effective minor film has some extraordinarily good special effects by Stine. Set in and around Arnold's favourite location – a small town on the edge of the desert – the film interestingly concentrates on creating the ethos of small-town life rather than on a few colourful (not to say clichéd) characters. The result, with its strong storyline, is one of the more interesting of the realist American Science Fiction movies of the fifties. Williams is the geologist who discovers a meteor shower whose crystal fragments absorb silicon from anything (turning those who touch them to stone) and expand when exposed to water and Albright the local schoolteacher who helps him evacuate the town when the now huge crystals advance on it.

As a result *The Monolith Monsters* is a superior B movie, no more but certainly no less.

171

d John Sherwood   *p* Howard Christie   *s* Norman Jolley, Robert M. Fresco   *c* Ellis W. Carter   *se* Clifford Stine   *lp* Grant Williams, Lola Albright, Les Tremayne, Trevor Bardette, Linda Scheley, Phil Harvey

The Monster That Challenged the World

(GRAMERCY PRODUCTIONS) b/w 83 min

An excellent low-budget Science Fiction thriller, briskly directed by Laven, who generates a suspenseful, often eerie, atmosphere. An underwater earthquake throws up the eggs of a prehistoric sea snail. When hatched, its monster progeny – enormous caterpillar-like creatures – attack naval bases and suck all the liquids from the bodies of their victims. They are eventually destroyed by local commander Holt (who, looking far fatter than in his days as a series western star, gives an assured performance), who rescues victim Dalton and her daughter from certain death when he unleashes a steam line and scalds the last of the snails to death. Lohman's monsters are ingeniously made and the whole enterprise is suprisingly compelling.

d Arnold Laven   *p* Jules V. Levy, Arthur Gardner   *s* Patricia Fielder   *c* Lester White, Maurice Vaccarino, *se* Augie Lohman   *lp* Tim Holt, Audrey Dalton, Hans Conried, Harlan Warde, Casey Adams

The Night the World Exploded

(CLOVER) b/w 64 min

Seismologist Leslie invents a device that will predict changes in the Earth's crust in this conventional offering directed by Sears. Predicting a nearby earthquake, Leslie, fellow scientist Coffin and assistant Grant discover there is a fault at the Earth's core, causing an alarming increase in the number of earthquakes. The team discover E-112, a new element found in black stones at the centre of the Earth. Once the stones are in water they are neutralized but if exposed to the air they absorb nitrogen and explode – causing the earthquakes. Similar to John Sherwood's imaginative **The Monolith Monsters** (1957), this pedestrian offering has the scientists advocating the flooding of all low-lying areas of the world – a radical solution which halts production of E-112.

d Fred F. Sears   *p* Sam Katzman   *s* Luci Ward, Jack Natteford   *c* Benjamin H. Kline   *lp* Kathryn Grant, William Leslie, Tristram Coffin, Raymond Greenleaf, Charles Evans, Frank Scannell

Quatermass II *aka* Enemy from Space

(HAMMER; GB) b/w 85 min

The bleakest and best of the trilogy of films (the others are **The Quatermass Xperiment**, 1955 and **Quatermass and the Pit**, 1967) adapted from Kneale's teleseries, *Quatermass II* sets Donlevy's determined scientist against alien invaders who have all but taken over the British government and are on the verge of world conquest. Clearly influenced by George Orwell's *1984*, which Kneale had adapted for British television to great effect in 1954, the film is a chilling political allegory in the manner of Don Siegel's **Invasion of the Body Snatchers** (1956) but with the significant difference that Kneale stresses not the process of the alien takeover but the connivance of those in authority. Thus, although the film has a conventional happy ending, its conspiratorial edge remains intact.

Kneale objected to Guest's rewrite of his screenplay as a coarsening of the original teleseries and to Donlevy's brusque performance, but the film's power is undeniable. What is particularly impressive is the way the story develops from a few seemingly odd occurrences to an enveloping sense of nightmare in which nothing and no-one is what and who he seems to be, a feature it shares with both Siegel's film and Robert Aldrich's similarly apocalyptic thriller, **Kiss Me Deadly** (1955). The film opens with Donlevy, angry that

funds for his Moon rocket project have been cut off, meeting a couple who gabble about strange goings-on at Wynnerton Flats. When he later learns of a strange meteorite shower landing in that vicinity he investigates, only to discover that the surrounding area is cordonned off and at its centre are a collection of pressure domes which look remarkably like his moonbase life-support system. It soon transpires that the (artificial) meteorites contain tiny living organisms that have the ability to take over humans and that the life-support system is being prepared for the waiting aliens by the zombies they have taken over to provide them with a habitable environment, Earth's atmosphere being unsuitable for them. The manner of Donlevy's unravelling of the conspiracy (which ranges to the upper reaches of government and includes the Commissioner of Scotland Yard) is marvellously handled by Guest and cinematographer Gibbs, as are some of the details, such as Donlevy encouraging the local villagers, done out of work by the zombies, to pump air into the domes to kill the aliens and the authorities responding by blocking the pipes with the bodies of those workers they've bought off. With **The Damned** (1961), this is the highpoint of the British Science Fiction film.

The third of the series, *Quatermass and the Pit*, was not filmed by Hammer until 1967.

d/co-s Val Guest   *p* Anthony Hinds   *co-s* Nigel Kneale   *c* Gerald Gibbs   *se* Les Bowie   *lp* Brian Donlevy, William Franklyn, Tom Chatto, John Longden, Percy Herbert, Sidney James, Bryan Forbes

Below: *Brian Donlevy as Dr Quatermass beside one of the pressure domes at Wynnerton Flats in the bleak* Quatermass II. *On the right is one of the human mutations created by the aliens.*

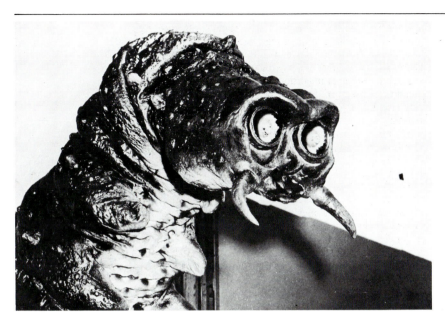

The Monster That Challenged the World, *one of the more beguiling creature-features of the fifties.*

El Robot Humano *aka* La Momia Azteca contra el Robot Humano *aka* The Aztec Mummy vs the Human Robot *aka* The Robot vs the Aztec Mummy

(CINEMATOGRAFICA CALDERON; MEX) b/w 80 (65) min
The last of three movies featuring the Aztec Mummy. The series included *La Momia Azteca* and *La Madicion de la Momia Azteca*, both directed by Portillo in 1957. This film has the evil Dr Krupp (Castañeda) in pursuit of the sacred jewels guarded by the mummy of Popoca. First he hypnotizes Flor (Arenas) in order to blackmail her lover (Gay) into revealing the location of the treasure, and then he constructs a robot out of metal and bits of corpses, giving it life in a scene reminiscent of the Frankenstein movies. However, the mummy proves too strong for the robot and at the end of the picture the robot is reduced to a heap of scrap. Nevertheless, the metal suit was used again in **La Nave de los Monstruos** (1959).

An American version of this movie was released in 1965, produced by K. Gordon Murray and using the pseudonym William C. Stell to disguise the name of Calderon in the production and script credits. Portillo was simply a commercial director, mostly stringing musical numbers together into a feature-length movie. His *La Isla de los Dinosauros* (1966) consists for the most part of shots lifted from Don Chaffey's *One Million Years BC* (1965).

d Rafael Portillo *p/co-s* Guillermo Calderon *co-s* Alfredo Salazar *c* Enrique Wallace *lp* Ramon Gay, Rosita Arenas, Crox Alvarado, Luis Aceves Castañeda, Arturo Martinez, Salvador Lozano, Guillermo Hernandez-Lobo Negro, Jesus Murcielago Velazquez, Alejandro Cruz

She Devil (REGAL) b/w scope 77 min

Neumann's other fifties films in the genre – **Rocketship X-M** (1950), **Kronos** (1957) and **The Fly** (1958) – all had interesting moments although none achieved any great imaginative heights. *She Devil* is the worst of his work, because lack of suspense combined with poor characterization renders an already ludicrous plot and far too talkative screenplay unworkable. Another reworking of the Jekyll and Hyde situation, the film is based on John Jessel's short story *The Adaptive Ultimate*. Kelly is seeking a cure for disease by extracting the serum from fruitflies, and with Dekker's assistance he finds a guinea-pig (Blanchard) who is suffering from TB. The serum is successful but the side-effects give Blanchard criminal tendencies. She murders the wife (Baker) of a wealthy man (Archer), marries him and then kills him in a car crash in which she is unhurt (resistance to injury being another side-effect of the serum), benefitting by millions from

his will. Kelly and Dekker eventually pounce on her, give her the antidote and she dies. Another side-effect is a dramatic change in Blanchard's hair colour – from blonde to brunette, masterminded by cinematographer Struss who had been responsible for stage-managing Frederic March's on-camera transformation in Rouben Mamoulian's classic version of Stevenson's tale **Doctor Jekyll and Mr Hyde** (1932) – Neumann's clumsy way of signalling her personality change.

d/p/co-s Kurt Neumann *co-s* Caroll Young *c* Karl Struss *lp* Mari Blanchard, Jack Kelly, Albert Dekker, John Archer, Fay Baker, Blossom Rock

The Strange World of Planet X *aka* The Cosmic Monsters *aka* The Crawling Terror

(EROS; GB) b/w 75 min
Based on the British TV serial and novel by René Ray, this features Tucker as a scientist whose experiments upset cosmic rays which blast a hole in the Earth's ionosphere. The hole damages the atmosphere, turning a tramp into a homicidal maniac and blowing up insects to huge proportions. The film's poor effects make the insects look ludicrous and set the seal on an already plodding screenplay. Eventually, having noticed the problem from afar, friendly alien Benson appears, anxious to help. With his special powers he is able to restore order.

d Gilbert Gunn *p* George Maynard *co-s/c* Joe Ambor *co-s* Paul Ryder *lp* Forrest Tucker, Gaby André, Martin Benson, Wyndham Goldie

Teenage Monster *aka* Meteor Monster

(MARQUETTE PRODUCTIONS) b/w 65 min
After the commercial success of **I Was a Teenage Werewolf** (1957), which grossed over $2 million in North America, producers quickly jumped on the 'teenage' bandwagon. A case in point is this film which began production as *Meteor Monster* but was completed as *Teenage Monster*. Others in the teenage mini-cycle were **I Was a Teenage Frankenstein** (1958), **Teenage Caveman** (1958) and **Teenagers from Outer Space** (1959).

Rays from a mysterious meteor turn Perkins into a murderous hairy monster who sets out on a rampage of killings. Gwynne, his loving mother, conceals him in the cellar, but suspicion grows as his killings continue. Marquette directs with evident relish, but to little effect.

d/p Jacques Marquette *s* Ray Buffum *c* Taylor Byars *lp* Anne Gwynne, Gloria Castillo, Stuart Wade, Gilbert Perkins, Steven Parker, Charles Courtney

Toto nella Luna *aka* Toto in the Moon

(MAXIMA FILMS/VARIETY FILMS/MONTFLUOR FILMS; IT,SP) b/w 90 min
One of the series of films dealing with the comic adventures of Toto. The initial situation would seem to be modelled on Jean Renoir's classic *Le Crime de M. Lange* (1936) but once would-be Science Fiction writer and clerk to Toto's dictatorial magazine publisher Achille (Tognazzi) is (mistakenly) revealed to be the only person whose blood will withstand the pressure of space flight the film descends into broad farce. Various nations, space rockets at the ready, compete for Tognazzi's participation in their respective space programmes while space creatures create doubles of both Toto and Tognazzi to prevent man from reaching the Moon. The film includes an early performance by Koscina, as Tognazzi's fiancée, who later became a leading lady in numerous European co-productions before moving, briefly, to Hollywood.

d/co-s Stafano Steno *p* Mario Cecchi Gori *co-s* Alessandro Continenza, Scuola *c* Marco Scarpelli *lp* Toto, Sylvia Koscina, Ugo Tognazzi, Luciano Salce, Sandro Milo, Giancamo Furia

The Ymir and elephant fight it out in 20 Million Miles from Earth, *a film best remembered as Ray Harryhausen's first attempt at monster-making.*

20 Million Miles to Earth

(MORNINGSIDE PRODUCTIONS) b/w 84 (82) min
Special-effects master Harryhausen's first attempts at monster-making are only partially successful in this low-budget, poorly scripted would-be epic. When the first mission to Venus crashes into the sea off the coast of Italy, sole survivor Calder (Hopper) is desperately concerned that the canister containing a specimen of Venusian life has been lost. Eventually a child discovers the canister and removes a jelly-like substance, which hatches into a tailed creature which local zoologist (Puglia) puts in a cage. Twenty-four hours later, already 4 feet tall, the creature escapes and kills a dog and a farmer, but is recaptured and taken to a laboratory, where it keeps growing. Puglia calls it an Ymir – the Norse word for the mythological father of all the giants. Electrical sedation is tried, and when this breaks down the sulphur-eating Ymir escapes for the second time, batters an elephant to death, and heads for the top of the Colosseum where in the predictable finale the military kill the Ymir with mortar and bazooka fire.

Director Juran, later to direct **First Men in the Moon** (1964) builds flatly around the effects of Harryhausen, who has a cameo appearance as the man feeding elephants in the zoo.

d Nathan Juran *p* Charles H. Schneer *s* Bob Williams, Christopher Knopf *c* Irving Lippman, Carlos Ventigmillia *se* Ray Harryhausen *lp* William Hopper, Joan Taylor, Frank Puglia, John Zaremba, Thomas Browne Henry, Titu Vuolo

The 27th Day (ROMSON PRODUCTIONS) b/w 75 (64) min

This is one of the most blatantly anti-communist films of the fifties, a film on a par with John Wayne's *Big Jim McLain* (1952). Mantley's original novel had clearly been an allegory, but in the hands of director Asher (better known as the director of the first beach-party movie, *Beach Party*, 1963), Mantley's own script is cheapened in the interest of zeroing in on anti-communism.

An alien (Moss) gives five different people in five different countries a box of capsules capable of destroying life on any continent because his own planet is dying and his people want to make Earth their home. It is against his race's ethics to destroy intelligent life, he explains, but as mankind seems intent on destroying itself, he is giving human beings a chance to kill themselves in a dignified manner. When opened, the capsules will kill instantly but they become harmless after 27 days or on the death of one of the five – they respond to the telepathic commands of their owners. French throws her box into the sea, Tsien commits suicide and her capsules turn to dust and Barry and Voskovec keep silent until (after Moss

broadcasts to the world, naming the five) Janti is summoned by Soviet leader Schnabel who wants to use his capsules to destroy the Western world. Just as Janti is about to crack he is shot by an over-zealous Russian guard and, once again, the capsules turn to dust.

Barry and Voskovec join French and, when Schnabel declares (nuclear) war, the three release the remaining capsules and every 'enemy of peace and freedom' dies. The aliens are invited to Earth to found a new society based on peace and love; Barry and French get each other and the Russians – from an American point of view – get what they deserve.

The film's naïvety is matched by Asher's pedestrian direction. It nonetheless remains interesting, if one forgets the anti-communist additions, as an example of the idealist strain in Science Fiction cinema that reached its apogee in **2001 – A Space Odyssey** (1968).

d William Asher *p* Helen Ainsworth *s* John Mantley *c* Henry Freulich *lp* Gene Barry, Valerie French, George Voskovec, Arnold Moss, Stefan Schnabel, Ralph Clanton, Azenath Janti, Marie Tsien

Below: Arnold Moss (arms on hip) as the alien dispenses the five boxes of capsules in The 27th Day.

resultant 'perfect being', played by Blaisdell (in the same suit he wore for the Cahn-directed *The She Creature*, 1956) is ridiculous: with its stringy hair and staring eyes it looks more like a walking carpet than a man/woman/beast. However, Conway decides that his creations are not perfect enough in that they will not kill on his telepathic command. He meets the murderous English and turns her into a monster. Predictably she rounds on her creator in a conclusion that's as ludicrous as the rest of the film. This is undoubtedly Cahn's worst film as director.

d Edward L. Cahn   *p* Alex Gordon   *s* Russell Bender, V.I. Voss   *c* Frederick E. West   *lp* Marla English, Tom Conway, Touch Connors, Mary Ellen Kaye, Lance Fuller, Paul Blaisdell

1958

A Pied, à Chevel et en Spoutnik *aka* A Dog, a Mouse and a Sputnik *aka* Sputnik

(FILMS AROUND THE WORLD; FR)   b/w   94(92) min
In this uneasy mixture of Science Fiction and French bourgeois comedy, Noel-Noel befriends a mouse and a dog who, unknown to him, have landed from a Russian satellite. French and Russian scientists try to persuade him to part with the animals by inviting him to Moscow where he is allowed to visit the rocket launch site. By accident Noel-Noel finds himself inside a rocket as it is launched, but, resourcefully, he takes over the controls when the scientist on board becomes ill. He makes a safe landing, becomes a hero in Moscow and returns happily to France with the dog.

d Jean Dréville   *p* Louis De Masure   *s* Jean-Jacques Vital   *c* André Bac   *lp* Noel-Noel, Denise Gray, Mischa Auer, Darry Cowl, Noel Roquevert

The Astounding She-Monster
aka The Mysterious Invader

(HOLLYWOOD INTERNATIONAL PRODUCTIONS)   b/w   60 min
A female alien (Kilpatrick) makes a clandestine landing in a forest. Surrounded by a radioactive force field, she kills by touch and unwittingly frees heiress Harvey and geologist Clarke, held captive by Duncan's gangster, before Clarke disposes of her with a homemade acid bomb which eats through her protective metal suit just as it transpires that Kilpatrick is a benign visitor. The only point of interest in this clumsily directed, silly film is its misogynistic attitude to women in its association of female beauty with evil and unconventional independence with male fears of castration. The point is even more forceful for being so unself-consciously expressed in Hall's wooden screenplay.

d/p Ronnie Ashcroft   *s* Frank Hall   *c* William C. Thomas   *lp* Robert Clarke, Keene Duncan, Marilyn Harvey, Jeanne Tatum, Shirley Kilpatrick, Ewing Brown

Attack of the 50 Foot Woman

(WOOLNER/AA)   b/w   65 min
A bald humanoid alien giant lands on Earth in the desert, and hijacks a young woman driver (Hayes). He accidentally alters her genetic balance and she begins to grow – to the consternation of a clutch of doctors who are unable to help her. Despite the corniness of Hanna's screenplay and Juran's plodding direction her size does have a curious fascination but her accelerating growth-rate does little for her mental balance and, when she finds her husband carrying on with another woman (Vickers), she squeezes them to death. Her jealousy and size cannot go unchecked and the sheriff arrives to kill her with a riot gun. The special effects are dire – for the most part the 50-foot woman is represented by her oversized hand.

d Nathan Hertz (Juran)   *p* Bernard Woolner   *s* Mark Hanna   *c* Jacques Marquette   *lp* Allison Hayes, William Hudson, Yvette Vickers, Roy Gordon, George Douglas, Otto Waldis

Above: *Allison Hayes about to squeeze her erstwhile husband William Hudson to death in* Attack of the 50 Foot Woman.

The Unearthly   (AMERICAN BROADCAST – PARAMOUNT THEATRES PRODUCTIONS)   b/w   73 (68) min

Carradine is the forties-style mad scientist seeking to achieve immortality who is partnered by researcher Buferd in this drab offering. Hayes, who has had a nervous breakdown, is sent by her doctor (Gordon) to Carradine for him to experiment on. At this point, the script becomes confused with police officer Healey arriving on the scene posing as an escaped criminal, Carradine (who overacts so much it's hard not to read his contempt for the screenplay into his performance) lusting after Hayes and finally the 'failures', patients made immortal but grotesquely cut about in the process, taking their revenge on Carradine. Peters' direction is equally crude.

Hayes was the 50-foot woman in **Attack of the 50-Foot Woman** (1958) and the bald giant Johnson appeared in the best forgotten **Plan 9 from Outer Space** (1956).

d/p Brooke L. Peters   *s* Geoffrey Dennis, Jane Mann
c Merle Connell   *lp* John Carradine, Allison Hayes, Myron Healey, Roy Gordon, Tor Johnson, Marilyn Buferd

The Unknown Terror

(EMIRAU PRODUCTIONS)   b/w   76 min
Searching for her brother in a South American jungle, Powers, her unsympathetic husband, Howard, and crippled friend, Richards, arrive at the Cave of Death, where crazed scientist Milton and Indian wife Wynn subject local natives to experiments with a strange fungus that grows in the cave and turns people into fungoid monsters. Warren directs briskly enough but the monsters are unintentionally hilariously funny – they are simply actors entirely covered in soap suds. The ending features the traditional explosion that decimates the fungus – and some of the cast – and leaves Powers and Richards to mouth sweet nothings to each other.

After this film Warren, a screenwriter turned director, specialized almost exclusively in westerns before quitting the cinema to work full-time in television.

d Charles Marquis Warren   *p* Robert Stabler   *s* Kenneth Higgins   *c* Joseph Biroc   *lp* John Howard, Mala Powers, Paul Richards, Gerald Milton, May Wynn, Duane Gray

Voodoo Woman   (CARMEL)   b/w   77 min

Conway, the older brother of actor George Sanders in one of his last roles, is a power-mad doctor determined to create the perfect human being. Using a combination of science and voodoo ('the white man's science and the black voodoo') he creates a new species – a cross between man and beast. The

Attack of the Puppet People (AIP) b/w 79 min

Gordon produced, directed and wrote the original story for this film, as well as handling the special effects. He specialized in monsters who were usually oversized (rather than undersized) men or women double-exposed against a pre-filmed background. Like so many Poverty Row hucksters, he believed in 'pulling 'em in' with flamboyant posters – leaving the audience, once in their seats, to howl at the fake images on the screen.

Dollmaker Hoyt miniaturizes human beings to a tenth of their normal size but Gordon is unable to further develop his motivation for this – loneliness. Similarly, an attempted love story between miniaturized Agar and Kenny soon peters out – as does the suspense inherent in the idea of the doll people's desperate attempts to return to their normal size.

d/p/se Bert I. Gordon   *s* George W. Yates   *c* Ernest Laszlo   *lp* John Agar, John Hoyt, June Kenny, Michael Mark, Marlene Willis, Ken Miller

Bijo to Ekitai Ningen *aka* The H Man *aka* Beautiful Women and the Hydrogen Man

(TOHO; JAP)   scope   87 (79) min

Taking a different approach to the imaginary aftermath of nuclear explosions, Honda and Tsuburaya temporarily abandoned their monsters (**Gojira**, 1954, and **Rodan**, 1956) to offer a story set in the contemporary drug-trafficking gangster milieu. A ship that has passed through a nuclear test zone oozes radioactive liquid that can turn people into blobs (**The Blob** was also made in 1958). As they drip onto other human beings, they also get liquefied. Rain washes them into the sewers where they proliferate. In the end, they are destroyed by flame throwers which set the entire sewage system of Tokyo alight. The plot appears merely as an excuse to string together extraordinary scenes of hallucinatory images as bodies liquify, enclosed within gelatinous blobs. Such scenes, together with the *film noir* aspects of the gangster plot, make this Honda's most sensual film, a quality not usually associated with his work. He tried to repeat this success in **Gas Ningen Daiichigo** (1960) but to no avail.

Based on an original idea of Hideo Kaijo, this is one of Honda's best movies.

d Inoshiro Honda   *p* Tomoyuki Tanaka   *s* Takeshi Kimura   *c* Hajime Koizumi   *se* Eiji Tsuburaya   *lp* Kenji Sahara, Akihiko Hirata, Yumi Shirakawa, Koreya Senda, Eitaro Ozawa, Mitsuru Sato

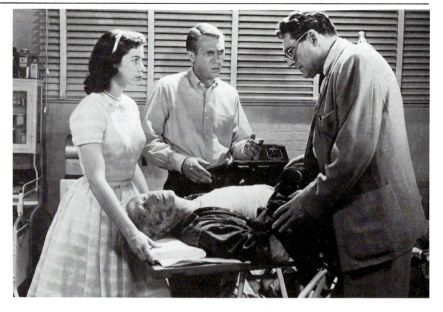

Steve McQueen (centre) and Aneta Corseaut as the teenage saviours of Middle America in The Blob.

The Blob (TONYLYN PRODUCTIONS/PAR) 85 min

A meteor brings a blob of space protoplasm back to Earth. The blob grows until it consumes some of the inhabitants of a small American town and becomes elephant-sized. McQueen (in his third screen role) and Corseaut see the blob and report that it has eaten the town's doctor and his nurse – but no-one is prepared to believe them. McQueen rallies a group of hatred-obsessed teenagers who have also seen the blob, and together they try to warn the police, only to be dismissed as fantasy merchants.

Sloane's special effects are authentic – the blob grows bigger in a supermarket and even bigger in a cinema – but both direction and script are lacklustre. Nonetheless, the blob itself and the idea of teenagers saving (rather than destroying) small-town America results in a strangely appealing, if camp, movie.

Finally, the teenagers discover that the blob does not like being cold and, whilst stunned by electricity, it is squeezed into a transport plane and dropped into the Antarctic. A sequel followed in 1971, **Beware! the Blob**.

The film's title song, 'The Blob', written by Burt Bacharach and Hal David, was an American Top 40 hit for the Five Blobs.

d Irvin S. Yeaworth Jnr   *p* Jack H. Harris   *s* Theodore Simonson, Kate Phillips   *c* Thomas Spalding   *se* Barton Sloane   *lp* Steve McQueen, Aneta Corseaut, Earl Rowe, Olin Howlin

The Brain Eaters (CORINTHIAN) b/w 60 min

Robert Heinlein's forceful novel *The Puppet Masters* (1953) dealt with an invasion of symbiotes from Titan, a satellite of Saturn. In the book the symbiotes are shapeless blobs of protoplasm that attach themselves to the back of human beings in order to dominate their minds. Director Ve Sota and writer Urquhart, however, substitute monsters from the Earth's core for the blobs of protoplasm. In the course of this substitution, the paranoia of possession from within, the transformation of people into aliens, which was one of the richest themes of American Science Fiction films of the fifties, as seen in such films as **Invasion of the Body Snatchers** (1956) and **I Married a Monster from Outer Space** (1958), is replaced by the more traditional, and less resonant, invasion by space monsters theme. Even this is erratically handled at best.

Four of the cast later achieved a fame of sorts: Nelson became a regular on the *Peyton Place* teleseries, Nimoy a member of the *Star Trek* team, Lee a prominent TV producer and Hill a producer/director of minor horror movies.

Left: John Hoyt as the dollmaker with his miniaturized humans in Attack of the Puppet People.

Right: *The mysteries of science:* Brain from Planet Arous.

d Bruno Ve Sota   *p* Edwin Nelson   *s* Gordon Urquhart
c Larry Raimond   *lp* Edwin Nelson, Leonard Nimoy, Alan
Frost, Jack Hill, Jody Fair, Joanna Lee

Brain from Planet Arous

(MARQUETTE PRODUCTIONS)   b/w   71 min
Scientist Agar is overpowered by a large flying superbrain
called Gor that arrives on Earth from another planet in this
silly film that remains oddly charming for its sheer literalism.
Brisk direction and efficient camerawork help the brain to
enter Agar's body effectively, much to the consternation of his
girlfriend Meadows, who becomes alarmed by Agar's strange
new behaviour. Whereupon another flying brain, called Vol,
arrives in pursuit of Gor, takes temporary possession of Agar's
dog and tells Meadows how to kill the evil brain by landing a
well-aimed blow on the side of its head. Once this is done
Agar returns to normal and to Meadows.

d Nathan H. Juran   *p/c* Jacques Marquette   *s* Ray
Buffum   *lp* John Agar, Joyce Meadows, Robert Fuller,
Thomas B. Henry, Ken Terrell

El Castillo de los Monstruos *aka* Noche de Terror *aka* Castle of the Monsters

(PRODUCCIONES SOTOMAYOR; MEX)   b/w   90 min
A haunted-house comedy from the author of the abyssmal
musical comedy **Los Platillos Voladores** (1955), which also
starred the able comedienne Elizondo. Parodying in a rather
broad manner the horror pictures churned out by William
Castle and American International in the USA, Soler's film
deploys the old cliché of the couple whose car breaks down,
forcing them to spend the night in a deserted castle. This
framework provides the excuse to stage the appearance of
virtually the entire range of monster characters available at
the time: a gorilla, a werewolf, a creature (from the Black

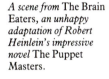

Lagoon), a mummy, a Frankenstein monster called Frente-
stein, a vampire incarnated by Mexico's leading vampire
performer, Robles, and assorted effects. The madly exaggerated gallery of monsters lends the picture the charm that can
come from excess, but Soler's career remained firmly stuck at
the cheap end of Mexican fantasy movies, except perhaps for
his Jekyll and Hyde remake, *El Hombre y la Bestia* (1972).

Sotomayor became one of Mexico's most prolific producers
and continued to make frequent excursions into fantasy-
comedy mixtures such as the amateurish **La Nave de los
Monstruos** (1959). After Cantinflas, Clavillazo was the
principal Mexican comic, starring in a great many musical
comedies as well as in the comic space opera **El Conquistador
de la Luna** (1960).

A scene from The Brain Eaters, *an unhappy adaptation of Robert Heinlein's impressive novel* The Puppet Masters.

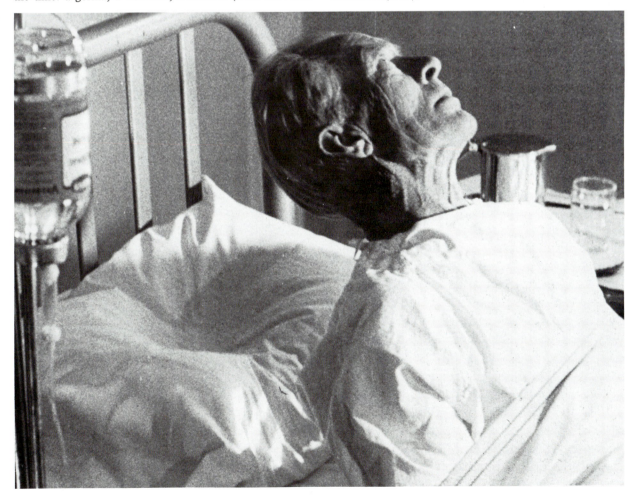

d Julian Soler *p* Jesús Sotomayer, Alberto Hernandez Curiel *s* Fernando Galiana, Carlos Orellana *c* Victor Herrera *lp* Antonio Espino Clavillazo, Evangelina Elizondo, German Robles, Carlos Orellana, Guillermo Orea

The Colossus of New York

(WILLIAM ALLAND PRODUCTIONS) b/w 70 min

In this re-working of the Frankenstein theme, surgeon Kruger transplants his dying son's (Martin's) brain into the body of a mechanical monster. Wolff plays the colossus with great enthusiasm, projecting lethal rays from the creature's eyes when it runs amok in the United Nations. Lourié's direction is juvenile, particularly when the monster is eventually subdued by Martin's son, but the initial scenes of their meeting after the transplant have moments of pathos.

Lourié had dealt with the theme of a monster (here manmade) returning to its breeding place or trying to protect its own in **The Beast from 20,000 Fathoms** (1953) and returned to it in **Gorgo** (1961).

d Eugène Lourié *p* William Alland *s* Thelma Schnee *c* John F. Warren *se* John P. Fulton *lp* John Baragrey, Mala Powers, Otto Kruger, Robert Hutton, Ed Wolff, Ross Martin, Charles Herbert

Daikaiju Baran *aka* Varan the Unbelievable *aka* The Monster Baran

(TOHO; JAP) scope 87 (70, 62) min

After the brief excursions into other aspects of Science Fiction (**Chikyu Boeigun**, 1957, and **Bijo to Ekitai Ningen**, 1958), Honda and the Toho team, including composer Akira Ifukube, returned to the mainstream Kaiju Eiga genre with their third monster, adding Varan to **Gojira** (1954) and **Rodan** (1956). Varan is a scaly reptilian patterned on Godzilla. He is disturbed by the US navy's Commander Bradley (Healey) who is trying to change saltwater into freshwater by means of chemical experiments. Varan proceeds on the customary journey towards Tokyo destroying the island where Bradley and his Japanese wife (Kobayashi) blithely performed their poisonous work in spite of the local inhabitants' resistance. Eventually, Varan is killed by chemical weapons shot into his underbelly. The story was devised by

Vincent Price watches a spider head for his (literally) half brother in The Fly, *one of the most extraordinary monster pics of the fifties.*

Koizumi, Honda's regular cameraman, and scripted by Sekizawa who became the director's trusted scenarist for years to come. The film has a ragged look about it and there are far too many scenes of Varan emerging from the water and being bombarded with explosives.

The American version, severely cut and released in 1961, was produced by Baerwitz who had extra scenes featuring Healey inserted. Such US versions, often the only ones available in the West, were also drastically re-edited, making it virtually impossible to assess what the films subjected to such cannibalization actually looked like.

d Inoshiro Honda *p* Tomoyuki Tanaka *s* Shinichi Sekizawa *c* Hajime Koizumi *se* Eiji Tsuburaya *lp* Myron Healey, Tsuruko Kobayashi, Clifford Kawada, Derrick Shimazu, Kozo Nomura, Ayumi Sonoda, Koreya Senda, Akihiko Hirata
US version: p Jerry A. Baerwitz *s* Sid Harris *c* Jack Marquette

Earth v the Spider *aka* The Spider

(SANTA ROSA PRODUCTIONS) b/w 73 (72) min

A giant spider, the result of radiation from an atom-bomb test, goes on the rampage in Gordon's cheapskate version of Jack Arnold's **Tarantula** (1955). Hungry for human flesh, it causes mayhem before being captured and put on display as a tourist attraction, whereupon the loud rock 'n' roll music played at a teenage dance briefly brings it back to life. The special effects, a crude mix of homemade miniature sets and clumsy split-screen work, are typical of Gordon, a director whose posters were invariably better than the films they advertised.

d/p/co-se Bert I. Gordon *s* Laszlo Gorog, George Worthing Yates *c* Jack Marta *co-se* Flora Gordon *lp* Ed Kemmer, June Kenney, Gene Persson, Gene Roth, Hal Torey, Mickey Finn

The Flame Barrier

(GRAMERCY PRODUCTIONS) b/w 70 min

After the successful launch of a satellite by the Soviet Union in 1957, there was considerable public agitation about trespassing into the unknown. In exploitation of that fear, this

Left: The artwork for the poster for The Colossus of New York.

Right: *Boris Karloff as Baron Frankenstein in Frankenstein 1970.*

film features a missing satellite discovered by Franz in the Yucatan jungle and covered in strange alien protoplasm that, on investigation, emits a deadly heat. The mass continues to grow, spewing out deadly rays that separate flesh from bone by extreme heat. The jungle sequences are full of suspense but the protoplasm has the look of a sub-standard, low-budget special effects' department. Brown and Padula are the adventurers hired by Franz's wife (Rowley) to rescue him.

d Paul Landres   *p* Arthur Gardner, Jules V. Levy   *s* Pat Fielder, George W. Yates   *c* Jack McKenzie   *lp* Arthur Franz, Kathleen Crowley, Robert Brown, Vincent Padula, Rodd Redwing, Kaz Oran

The Fly (FOX) scope 94 min
A great deal of money was spent on this extraordinary matter-transmitter film and Clavell (later to become a director and author of the bestselling novel *Shogun*) was hired by director/producer Neumann expressly to bring realistic dialogue to an unrealistic idea.

Hedison is the scientist who experiments with his own matter-transmitter and becomes mixed up with a fly – he takes the head and wing of the fly and the fly takes the scientist's head and arm. The idea is utterly ridiculous but the fly-man image has a morbid attraction to this day and Neumann handles his strong cast well. (He also demanded that they play the material straight.) With the aid of his wife (Owens), Hedison attempts to reverse the procedure but the fly proves elusive. Eventually the scientist goes mad and pleads with Owen to kill him by putting his head in a steam press. The fly suffers a less immediate fate by becoming trapped in a spider's web. The fly appears to have human vocal chords if not a brain, and vigorously shouts for help whilst the spider bears down on him, only to be hit with a rock by Marshall's police inspector. Such an unhappy ending is unusual in Hollywood films.

Neumann, who died soon after the film's completion, also made **Rocketship X-M** (1950) and **Kronos** (1957).

The Fly (adapted from a short story by George Langelaan) was a surprising financial success and two sequels, **Return of the Fly** (1959) and **Curse of the Fly** (1965), followed.

d/p Kurt Neumann   *s* James Clavell   *c* Karl Struss   *se* Lyle B. Abbott   *lp* Al (David) Hedison, Patricia Owens, Vincent Price, Herbert Marshall, Charles Herbert

George Sanders (left) and Joseph Cotten (centre) in the workmanlike Jules Verne adaptation, From the Earth to the Moon.

Frankenstein 1970 (AA) scope 83 min
Frankenstein 1970 was made by Allied Artists in the wake of the extraordinary success of Hammer's Frankenstein films in America. But where Hammer reinterpreted the Frankenstein legend, this film merely adds new gimmicks to the story (as Hammer themselves would do in the seventies). Frankenstein (Karloff, the monster in James Whale's classic **Frankenstein**, 1931) tries to revive his original monster (Lane) with a blast of atomic energy from a reactor which he buys by renting the castle to a TV crew. He also uses parts of their bodies to reassemble his monster. Karloff's interpretation of the Baron is traditional but the storyline which has the Baron a victim of Nazi torturers and the monster attacking crew and starlet (Lund) is an indication of what was in store for Mary Shelley's creation.

d Howard Koch   *p* Aubrey Schenck   *s* Richard Landau, George W. Yates   *c* Carl E. Guthrie   *lp* Boris Karloff, Tom Duggan, Jana Lund, Charlotte Austin, Don 'Red' Barry, Mike Lane

From the Earth to the Moon (WAVERLY) 100 min
This extremely slow-moving adaptation of Jules Verne's novel stars the ubiquitous Cotten as a munitions manufacturer and sponsor, like the industrialists in **Destination Moon** (1950), of the first manned rocket to the Moon. The special effects are workmanlike but the pace is slow and the script slack. Though it is set in Victorian times, the film, unlike, for example, another adaptation from Verne, **Captain Nemo and the Underwater City** (1969), makes nothing of its period setting. Thus, even the firing of the rocket from a huge cannon is not fully exploited. Paget and Dubbins are the lovers who return to Earth when the rocket explodes, leaving Sanders and Cotten to crash on the Moon's surface. An interesting touch is the presence of Verne himself, played by Carl Esmond.

d Byron Haskin   *p* Benedict Bogeaus   *s* Robert Blees, James Leicester   *c* Edwin DuPar   *se* Lee Zavitz   *lp* Joseph Cotten, George Sanders, Debra Paget, Don Dubbins, Patric Knowles, Morris Ankrum

Gekko Kamen *aka* The Man in the Moonlight Mask *aka* The Moonbeam Man
(TOEI; JAP) b/w scope 102 min
A combination of two comic-strip-style superhero stories, *Daiichibu* (85 minutes) and *Dainibu* (51 minutes), cut to feature length. The movie pits the evil Skull Mask against the good Moonlight Mask as they struggle over the blueprints of a formidable new weapon called Ho-Joe Bomb, poetically

indicating something about the postwar Japanese relationship to the US, in the realm of popular culture at least. The good masked figure is revealed to be the policeman investigating the theft of the plans and the evil one the inventor's assistant. As so often in Japanese films, even the most perfunctory plot in the cheapest of films is enhanced by a striking sense of graphic design and pictorial values far superior to anything in comparable Western products, except perhaps some Italian movies by Bava (for example, **Diabolik**, 1967).

The film appears to have spawned sequels with the same characters although there is some confusion as to the status of these further adventures of the Moonlight Mask. Shoichi Shimazu is credited with two different films called *Gekko Kamen* (both 1959). Satoru Ainodu is credited with *Gekko Kamen* (1959) and Eijiro Wakabayashi with *Gekko Kamen – Satan No Tsume* (1959), all of which starred Omura. Some of these titles may refer to the same film or to different episodes or to combinations of episodes.

d Tsuneo Kobayashi *s* Yarunori Kawauchi *c* Ichiro Hoshijima *lp* Fumitake Omura, Junya Usami, Hiroko Mine, Mitsue Komiya, Yaeko Wakamizu, Yasushi Nagata

Giant from the Unknown

(SCREENCRAFT ENTERPRISES PRODUCTIONS) b/w 77 min
The superstitious inhabitants of a remote Californian mountain village imagine that a spirit from the past is haunting them. The spirit in question turns out to be a gigantic Spanish conquistador (Baer) brought to life by 20th-century lightning. Taussig and Brooke's plodding and predictable script is made even more so by Cuhna's listless direction and the inept special effects.

d/c Richard E. Cuhna *p* Arthur A. Jacobs *s* Frank Hart Taussig, Ralph Brooke *se* Harold Banks *lp* Edward Kemmer, Sally Fraser, Buddy Baer, Morris Ankrum, Bob Steele

Gary Conway as the reluctant monster and Whit Bissell as his creator in the engaging I Was a Teenage Frankenstein.

El Hombre Que Logro Ser Invisible *aka* El Hombre Invisible *aka* The Invisible Man

(CINEMATOGRAFICA CALDERON; MEX) b/w 95 min
A very free adaptation indeed from H.G.Wells' novel best filmed by James Whale as **The Invisible Man** (1933). The plot, seriously bent toward the melodramatic aspects of the story, concerns a scientist, Luis (Benedico) who invents a formula for invisibility and administers it to his imprisoned brother, Carlos (de Cordova), locked away for having killed his partner. Free again, Carlos meets with his lover, Beatriz (Peluffo, one of the sexy starlets launched by Urueta's *La Ilegitima*, 1955). However, the drug also causes madness, and Carlos starts fancying himself as master of the world. He kills Luis and becomes a terrorist until Beatriz sets a trap for him. The police shoot him and he expires in the arms of the sad Beatriz who betrayed him to the authorities.

Crevenna, together with Alfonso Cardona Blake, Julian Soler, Federico Curiel and Rene Cardona became one of the handful of film-makers responsible for most of the cheap Mexican fantasy pictures. His best known work includes *La Huella Macabra* (1962), *Aventura al Centro de la Tierra* (1965), *La Mujer del Diablo* (1972) and contributions to the masked wrestler series such as **Santo Contra la Invasion de los Marcianos** (1966).

d Alfredo B. Crevenna *p* Guillermo Calderon *s* Alfredo Salazar, Julio Alejandro *c* Raul Martinez Solares *lp* Arturo de Cordova, Ana Luisa Peluffo, Raul Meraz, Augusto Benedico, Nestor Barbosa, Jorge Mondragon, Roberto G. Rivera, Roy Fletcher

I Married a Monster from Outer Space

(PAR) b/w 78 min
Best remembered for its emphatic title, this is a stylish piece of fifties reds-under-the-beds paranoia. On the eve of his wedding Tryon is kidnapped by aliens and linked to a machine which gives an alien lookalike his memory. The many tendrilled aliens, who are able to take on human shape, have travelled to Earth for the most traditional of reasons in the genre: their planet is dying and they need women to mother their young. Talbott marries her alien lookalike fiancé but quickly becomes suspicious. Tryon breaks down, says he loves her and then, to prove his love, confesses all to her. Talbott seeks official help only to find that the alien lookalikes are now in power, whereupon, in an act of genius, she goes to the nearest hospital and collects together the expectant fathers and 'real men'. These form an anti-alien squad, discover the

Left: *An alien, without his protective human disguise, in the magnificent* I Married a Monster from Outer Space.

creature's flying saucer and free the hostages, thus once more saving the day for American and freedom.

While the film was clearly fuelled by the Cold War mentality of the fifties, in retrospect it is its sexual politics that are more interesting, and disturbing.

Director/producer Fowler worked with Fritz Lang as an editor and Lang's influence shows in the dark, brooding, shadowy interiors. A marvellous example of this has Tryon standing on a balcony in a thunderstorm. Momentarily thrown by the intensity of the storm, he drops his guard and his face dissolves into his true alien features before, just as quickly, becoming human again.

Tryon graduated briefly to A features where his inexpressivity as an actor was even more marked, before quitting acting for a successful career as a novelist.

d/p Gene Fowler Jnr *s* Louis Vittes *c* Haskell Boggs *se* John P. Fulton *lp* Tom Tryon, Gloria Talbott, Ken Lynch, John Eldredge, Valerie Allen, Maxie Rosenbloom

I Was a Teenage Frankenstein

(SANTA ROSA PRODUCTIONS) b/w and col 74 (72) min
In this quickly mounted follow-up to **I Was a Teenage Werewolf** (1957) Bissell as the versatile scientist assembles a human body from an assortment of different cadavers. Kandel's quirky screenplay is surprisingly effective, particularly when the young face of a kidnapped teenager is grafted on to the monstrous head. Bizarrely the body is then dismantled before crating for shipment to England, whereupon the monster (Conway) naturally protests, kills Bissell and goes on the rampage. The excellent makeup helps the

Below: Ray 'Crash' Corrigan as the monster taken on board by a spaceship returning from Mars in It! The Terror from Beyond Space.

credibility of the sewn-together cadavers and the film bursts into glorious colour for the climax when the monster is electrocuted by a power board.

One of the mini-series of teenage Science Fiction films that followed in the wake of *I Was a Teenage Warewolf*, it remains watchable because Kandel's script, though sadly not Strock's direction which is pedestrian, has an element of parody about it.

d Herbert L. Strock *p* Herman Cohen *s* Kenneth Langtry (Aben Kandel) *c* Lothrop Worth *lp* Whit Bissell, Phyllis Coates, Robert Burton, Gary Conway, George Lynn, John Cliff

It! The Terror from Beyond Space *aka* It! The Vampire from Beyond Space (VOGUE PICTURES) b/w 69 min

This film reputedly inspired the basic storyline of **Alien** (1979). A space expedition returning from Mars discovers it has taken on board a blood-drinking monster (Corrigan). Skilfully the monster stalks the crew through the corridors of the ship and kills them one by one. Under the leadership of Thompson the remaining survivors try to seal off the creature in the bottom section of the ship but the monster has enormous powers and soon beats its way through and moves towards the bridge where the remaining crew members are gathered. Sadly when the monster finally emerges from the shadows it loses all credibility for it's clearly a man dressed in an ill-fitting rubber suit. Nonetheless, Cahn's forceful direction brings the intriguing script (if not the monster) to life.

In 1966 the story was loosely remade by Curtis Harrington as **Queen of Blood**.

d Edward L. Cahn *p* Robert E. Kent *s* Jerome Bixby *c* Kenneth Peach Snr *lp* Marshall Thompson, Shawn Smith, Kim Spalding, Ann Doran, Ray 'Crash' Corrigan, Dabbs Greer

The Lost Missile

(WILLIAM BERKE PRODUCTIONS; US, CAN) b/w 70 min
This slackly scripted and weakly directed offering has an alien missile circling the Earth at 4000 miles an hour. The heat generated by its speed destroys Ottawa and threatens New York City. Young scientist Loggia battles against time but devises a minute hydrogen war-head inside a nuclear missile, which destroys the weapon just before it arrives at New York.

The film was the last to be directed by Berke, a one-time cinematographer turned director/producer in the early forties, who specialized, for the most part, in series westerns.

d Lester W. Berke *p* Lee Gordon *s* John McPartland, Jerome Bixby *c* Kenneth Peach *lp* Robert Loggia, Ellen Parker, Larry Kerr, Philip Pire, Marilee Earle, Joe Hyams

Missile to the Moon (ASTOR) b/w 78 min

An inferior remake of **Cat Women of the Moon** (1953), *Missile to the Moon* is best remembered for its extraordinarily inept plot, set and props. An expedition led by Travis lands on the Moon (in fact California's Red Rock Canyon) in company with a pair of reform school escapees (Cook and Clarke). In subterranean Moon caves they discover a group of Moon women living in fear of a deadly giant spider. The Moon women (an assortment of beauty contest winners) wear mesh stockings and a continuous air of harassment.

When the group of assorted women, gangsters, scientists and young lovers break through to the surface of the Moon, they have to do battle with rock creatures who are male and therefore rivals for the favours of the Moon women, before reaching the safety of their spaceship and blasting off for Earth.

d Richard Cuhna *p* Marc Frederic *s* H. E. Barrie, Vincent Fotre *c* Meredith Nicholson *se* Ira Anderson, Harold Banks *lp* Richard Travis, Cathy Downs, K.T. Stevens, Tommy Cook, Gary Clarke, Nina Bara

The Monster from the Green Hell

(GROSSE – KRASNE PRODUCTIONS)   b/w   71 min

In this silly offering Davis leads an expedition of scientists into the African jungle in search of an experimental rocket-ship and its cargo of wasps which have been exposed to radiation. The wasps emerge as monsters, but, enlarged as they are, they are unable to fly. However, Davis fails to prevent them going on a trail of destruction, but after a murderous foray they stumble into an erupting volcano. Inept special effects, a charmless script and Crane's routine direction waste the surprisingly strong cast of Davis, Cianelli and Sokoloff.

d Kenneth Crane   p Al Zimbalist   s Louis Vittes, Endre Boehm   c Ray Flin   se Jess Davison, Jack Rabin, Louis DeWitt   lp Jim Davis, Robert E. Griffin, Barbara Turner, Eduardo Cianelli, Vladimir Sokoloff, Joel Fluellen

Monster on the Campus   (U)   b/w   77 min

This is perhaps the least interesting of Arnold's films in the genre. Franz is the college professor who is transformed into a prehistoric ape-man (Parker) in the course of experiments he conducts on a million-year-old fish. Cinematographer Metty and special effects' man Stine make the most of the ape-man's path of devastation through the campus but the script lacks any sparkle.

d Jack Arnold   p Joseph Gershenson   s David Duncan   c Russell Metty   se Clifford Stine   lp Arthur Franz, Joanna Moore, Judson Pratt, Nancy Walters, Troy Donahue, Eddie Parker

La Morte Viene Dalla Spazio aka Le Danger Vient de l'Espace aka Death from Outer Space aka The Day the Sky Exploded

(LUX/C.C.F.LUX/ROYAL FILM; IT, FR)   b/w   85 (80) min

A comet story beginning with the launch of a joint US, USSR and UK atomically powered rocket from Australia. However, something goes wrong and astronaut MacLaren (Hubschmid) is forced to abort his part of the mission and return to Earth while the rest of the rocket proceeds to hit the Sun, triggering a mammoth explosion that sends a shower of asteroids towards the earth and causes massive changes in the climate. Tidal waves, typhoons and other catastrophes accompanying sudden changes in climatic conditions cause widespread panic. MacLaren gathers an international group of scientists and persuades governments to use their atomic weaponry in a common effort to save the planet by shooting the bombs at the asteroids, pulverizing them. The picture's main asset is Bava's excellent cinematography; both acting and direction fail to transcend a poor script.

Heusch's film initiated the Italian genre of horror Science Fiction which produced one of the most visually striking sixties Science Fiction movies, Margheriti's **Il Pianeta degli Uomini Spenti** (1961). An English language version of Heusch's picture was prepared by William DeLane Lee.

d Paolo Heusch   p Guido Gianbartolomei   s Marcello Coscia, Alessandro Continenza   c Mario Bava   lp Paul Hubschmid, Madeleine Fischer, Fiorella Mari, Ivo Garrani, Dario Michaelis, Sam Galter, Jean-Jacques Delbo, Peter Meersman, Massimo Zeppieri

The Most Dangerous Man Alive

(TRANS-GLOBAL FILMS INC.)   82 (76) min

The last film of veteran director Dwan, this is a farrago of nonsense made even more so by the minuscule budget producer Bogeaus made available to his director. Randall is the convict who in the course of his prison break is exposed to a cobalt bomb explosion. He survives, only to discover that he's rapidly turning into a man of steel. He goes after the men who framed him and wreaks a path of destruction until he's 'dissolved' by massed flame throwers.

The film, which was shot in Mexico, was not released until 1961. More interestingly, it is this film that is being remade by the film crew in *The State of Things* (1982), Wim Wenders' bitter essay on the politics of film-making.

d Allan Dwan   p Benedict Bogeaus   s James Leicester, Philip Rock   c Carl Carvahal   lp Ron Randall, Debra Paget, Elaine Stewart, Anthony Caruso, Gregg Palmer, Morris Ankrum

Queen of Outer Space   (AA)   scope   80 min

This bizarre essay in sexual politics stars Mitchell as the Queen of Venus who, having wiped out the male Venusians, is set on destroying Earth with her disintegrator ray. Fleming is the leader of an expedition that crash-lands on Venus (looking like a cross between a tropical garden and a studio mock-up of a South American jungle).

The affair between Fleming and Gabor (her 'darlink' Hungarian accent still strongly to the fore), who turns against Mitchell, is less interesting than the antecedents of the majority of the film's props. The ray guns, costumes and bits of the forest are from **Forbidden Planet** (1956), most of the special effects are from **World Without End** (1956) and the main body of the spacecraft is from **Flight to Mars** (1951).

Ron Randall and Elaine Stewart in The Most Dangerous Man Alive, *the last film of veteran Allan Dwan.*

Left: *The million-year-old fish that causes all the trouble in Jack Arnold's curious* Monster on the Campus.

d Edward Bernds   *p* Ben Schwalb   *s* Charles Beaumont
c William Whitley   *lp* Zsa Zsa Gabor, Eric Fleming, Laurie
Mitchell, Paul Birch, Barbara Darrow, Dave Willock

Top right: The
Revenge of
Frankenstein: *the
perfect body which
fittingly enough will be
inhabited by its creator,
the perfect mind, Baron
Frankenstein, at the
film's climax.*

d Edward Bernds   *p* Ben Schwalb   *s* Charles Beaumont
c William Whitley   *lp* Zsa Zsa Gabor, Eric Fleming, Laurie
Mitchell, Paul Birch, Barbara Darrow, Dave Willock

The Revenge of Frankenstein   (HAMMER; GB)   91 min

In this, the first of Hammer's numerous sequels to the phenomenally successful **The Curse of Frankenstein** (1957), Fisher once again took for his central character the monster's creator, Cushing's Baron Frankenstein, rather than the monster (played here by Gwynn, replacing Christopher Lee), even to the point, in the extraordinary climax, of Frankenstein actually inhabiting the body he has created. However, where in the earlier film Frankenstein was merely an over-reacher, *The Revenge of Frankenstein* sees Cushing's Baron, who has escaped the guillotine with the assistance of Gwynn's crippled warder (to whom he promises a new body) as rather more merciful and humane, more the victim of the prejudices his work inspires than of his sadistic inclinations. Thus, it is others who transform his creation into a murderous animal. This heroizing of Frankenstein, seen both in Fisher's presentation of the character and in the plot as Cushing seduces Matthews (who later transplants Frankenstein's brain into a new body that he might live again) to his side, and transformation of him into a scourge of the bourgeoisie is Fisher's greatest contribution to the Frankenstein myth.

Right: *Carrying the
'space brain' to safety in
Jack Arnold's assured*
The Space Children.

d Terence Fisher   *p* Anthony Hinds   *s* Jimmy Sangster
c Jack Asher   *lp* Peter Cushing, Michael Gwynn, Francis
Matthews, Eunice Grayson, John Welsh, Lionel Jeffries,
Richard Wordsworth, Michael Ripper

The Space Children

(WILLIAM ALLAND PRODUCTIONS)   b/w   69 min

Director Arnold has often used landscape to tremendous effect and here he makes imaginative, haunting use of a desolate beach. Schoenfeld's script features a peace-seeking 'space brain' which controls the children of technicians and space scientists on a US base, compelling them to sabotage the launch of a rocket that will place a hydrogen bomb in outer space. The film's pacifist stance is unusual for the fifties, when such films weren't considered good box office. The film is also notable for Laszlo's assured cinematography, which suggests a far bigger budget than was available.

Below: *Zsa Zsa Gabor
(without mask) held
captive after rebelling
against her sisters in the
weak* Queen of Outer
Space.

d Jack Arnold   *p* William Alland   *s* Bernard C. Schoenfeld
c Ernest Laszlo   *se* John P. Fulton   *lp* Adam Williams,
Peggy Weber, Michael Ray, Jackie Coogan, John Crawford

Space Master X-7 *aka* Mutiny in Outer Space

(REGAL)   b/w   scope   71 min

Told in semi-documentary style, this routine film, clearly influenced by **The Quatermass Xperiment** (1955), features Williams and Ellis as the security agents sent to investigate a space probe that returns to Earth covered in fungus. When mixed with blood, the fungus grows to enormous proportions and consumes everything in its path, killing the scientist in charge (Frees) and then taking over the body of his fiancée (Thomas). She becomes anti-social, to say the least, until Williams finds a decontamination antidote which destroys the creeping menace and restores Thomas to her former pristine state. Director Bernds finds himself running out of story before the film is over and has to set up a lengthy hunt for Thomas, to pad out the film.

The movie featured the first 'solo' appearance of Moe Howard, one of the Three Stooges.

d Edward Bernds   *p* Bernard Glasser   *s* George Worthington
Yates, Daniel Mainwaring   *c* Brydon Baker
lp Bill Williams, Lyn Thomas, Robert Ellis, Paul Frees, Joan
Barry, Thomas B. Henry

Teenage Caveman aka Out of the Darkness

(MALIBU) b/w 65 min

Described by its star Vaughn as 'one of the best-worst films of all times' this is a masterpiece of the pulp imagination. Its dinosaurs first trampled the Earth in *One Million BC* (1940) and *Unknown Island* (1948) and its special effects and sets are ludicrous, to say the least, yet the film is mounted with a seriousness that is compelling.

Vaughn is the caveman of the title who chafes at the self-imposed restrictions that govern the activities of his tribe. His father, the 'symbol maker', tells Vaughn never to cross the river, because on the other side lies the land of 'the monster that kills with a touch'. But Vaughn crosses nonetheless, so strong is his desire for knowledge, and soon discovers that the monster is nothing but an old man (Bradley), dressed to look as frightening as possible, rather like the tinpot showman who was behind the mighty effects of *The Wizard of Oz* (1939). After the old man dies Vaughn finds inside his suit (in fact a radiation suit) a book that reveals that the time is not the prehistoric past but the post-nuclear-holocaust future.

The optimistic ending which suggests that a better world will be constructed out of the old, is unusual for Corman who in most of his films in the genre depicts a world on the verge of destruction.

d/p Roger Corman   *s* R. Wright Campbell   *c* Floyd Crosby
lp Robert Vaughn, Leslie Bradley, Darrah Marshall, Frank De Corva, Joseph Hamilton, Marshall Bradford

Terror From the Year 5,000 aka Cage of Doom

(AIP) b/w 74 min

Downs and Stratton invent a machine that can bring objects from the future into the present in this intriguing, if clumsily mounted, Science Fiction thriller. Jens (in her screen début) is materialized from the year 5000. Horribly disfigured and sinisterly disguised as a nurse, she is looking for men to take back with her to revitalize the human race, which has virtually

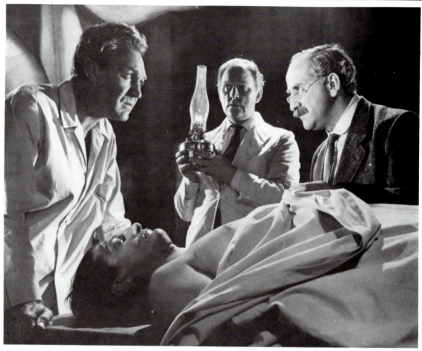

destroyed itself. She hypnotizes Stratton into going back with her but is finally killed by archaeologist Costello, who realizes that she is contaminating the present with virulent radio-activity.

d/p/s Robert Gurney Jnr   *c* Arthur Florman   *lp* Ward Costello, Joyce Holden, John Stratton, Frederick Downs, Fred Herrick, Beatrice Furdeaux, Salome Jens

The Trollenberg Terror aka The Crawling Eye aka The Creature from Another World

(TEMPEAN FILMS; GB) b/w 85 min

This atmospheric, low-budget film was adapted by Sangster from Peter Key's successful British teleserial. Mitchell, a professor in the Swiss town of Trollenberg, discovers a strange cloud that, due to the film's small budget, is all too obviously a piece of cottonwool attached to a photograph. He explains his fears to Tucker, a visiting UN science investigator but, a few days after his warning, a number of mountain climbers are discovered decapitated.

Soon the cloud descends from the mountains and encloses the village. Some residents escape but Mitchell, Tucker and Munro (who gives an excellent performance as a girl with extrasensory perception who can communicate with aliens) stay to battle with the aliens, when they finally appear, Cyclops-like, with long, waving and menacing tentacles. Both direction and screenplay create considerable tension, notably in Tucker's rescue of a young girl from the monster, and although the resolution is simplistic – the RAF drop firebombs on the aliens – the general tone of the film is surprisingly sombre, anticipating the more complex treatment of the same theme in **Quatermass and the Pit** (1967).

d Quentin Lawrence   *co-p* Robert S. Baker   *co-p/c* Monty Berman   *s* Jimmy Sangster   *se* Les Bowie   *lp* Forrest Tucker, Laurence Payne, Janet Munro, Jennifer Jayne, Warren Mitchell, Andrew Faulds

Vynalez Zkazy aka The Diabolical Invention aka The Fabulous World of Jules Verne aka Weapons of Destruction aka Invention of Destruction aka The Deadly Invention

(STUDIO GOTTWALDOW; CZECH) b/w 87 (83) min

A marvellously poetic evocation of Jules Verne's world achieved through a combination of live action, animation, puppets and glass painting. Zeman managed to create images

Warren Mitchell (right) examines the body of Andrew Faulds while Forrest Tucker looks on in The Trollenberg Terror.

Left: *Robert Vaughn as the* Teenage Caveman *in Roger Corman's masterpiece of the pulp imagination.*

Right: *The beast and the miniature sets of* War of the Colossal Beast.

that were like Benette and Riou's etchings that had illustrated the Hetzel edition of Verne's works. At the end of the 19th century, the inventor Professor Roch (Navratil) and his assistant, Hart (Tokos) develop an explosive strong enough to replace the energy to be had from oil and coal. The plot involves the rich villain, Artigas (Holub), who seeks to acquire the substance, a *Nautilus*-type submarine, a deserted volcanic island harbouring a pirate city built in a crater, a hidden lake with a super sophisticated laboratory on its shore, a rocket-firing cannon, etc. Mostly derived from Verne's *Face au Drapeau*, the script introduces elements from **20,000 Leagues Under the Sea**, filmed by Fleischer in 1954, and **Mysterious Island** (filmed in 1929, 1941, 1951, 1961 and 1972). The art director, Zdenek Rozkopal also deserves a special mention.

Zeman went on to direct an astoundingly beautiful version of the Muenchhausen story, *Baron Prasil* (1961), far superior to the celebrated Nazi extravaganza, *Muenchhausen*, produced to celebrate ten years of the Third Reich in 1943. Zeman also modelled his Muenchhausen images on the illustrations, by Doré and Burger that had appeared in the book. Other Zeman-Verne films were **Cesta do Praveku** (1955), **Ukradena Vzducholod** (1966) and **Na Komete** (1970).

Capek's story about a powerful explosive and source of energy, **Krakatit**, was filmed in 1948 and in 1979 as **Cerne Slunce**.

d/co-s Karel Zeman   *co-s* Frantisek Hrubin   *c/se* Jiri Tarantik   *lp* Arnost Navratil, Lubor Tokos, Miloslaw Holub, Frantisek Slegr, Vaclav Kyzlink, Jana Zatlukalova

War of the Colossal Beast *aka* The Terror Strikes

(CARMEL)   b/w and col   74 (68) min
Director/producer Gordon is best remembered for the spectacular posters that announced his films and the decidedly unspectacular special effects of the films themselves. Here, Parkin is the 60-foot man with the mind of a wild beast, discovered in Mexico. Horribly disfigured, he is captured and brought to Los Angeles, but escapes and goes on the rampage. The sequel to Gordon's **The Amazing Colossal Man** (1975), the film has its moments of pathos, particularly when the colossal man is told by his sister (Fraser) that he is doing wrong, in a scene repeated virtually intact from the earlier film. Full of regret, he kills himself on high tension telephone

Below: Vynalez Zkazy: *Karel Zeman's poetic evocation of the fabulous world of Jules Verne.*

wires. At this emotive point the film bursts into full colour – a melodramatic trick already used by Herbert L. Strock in **I Was a Teenage Frankenstein** (1958).

d/p/co-se Bert I. Gordon   *s* George Worthing Yates   *c* Jack Marta   *co-se* Flora Gordon   *lp* Sally Fraser, Roger Pace, Dean Parkin, Russ Bender

War of the Satellites

(ROGER CORMAN PRODUCTIONS)   b/w   66 min
Corman seized the publicity surrounding the Russian's first Sputnik, shot this in eight days and had it in the cinemas only a couple of months after the event. The signs of swift making are all too evident, especially in the over-talkative script and the mis-match between the special effects (which were shot separately) and the action.

The UN attempts to send a manned spaceship into orbit. To prevent this, anonymous alien minds create an impenetrable barrier in space and warn Earth that if the project goes ahead the planet will be destroyed. When scientist in charge Devon is killed in a car crash, the aliens restore him to life to help prevent the expedition but the rocket takes off anyway and when Devon tries to crash it into the barrier, he's overpowered by the crew.

A comparison between this and Corman's other films of the period show how uncommitted to the project Corman clearly was. The result is a conventional film, in which the aliens clearly represent the Russians, from America's most unconventional director of Science Fiction.

d/p Roger Corman   *s* Lawrence Louis Goldman   *c* Floyd Crosby   *se* Jack Rabin, Irving Block, Louis DeWitt   *lp* Susan Cabot, Dick Miller, Richard Devon, Robert Shayne, Jerry Barclay, Eric Sinclair, Jay Sayer

The Alligator People

(ASSOCIATED PRODUCERS) b/w scope 74 min

This mediocre offering was made at the end of his career by Del Ruth, a former gagman for Mack Sennett and director best remembered for his lavish, if anonymous, musicals of the forties, during an attempted comeback after a five-year absence from film-making. He shows himself decidedly ill-at-ease in the new, to him, world of low-budget productions. Even sadder, the film is the last one made by one of Hollywood's most imaginative cinematographers who, as well as sharing the Oscar for cinematography with Charles Rosher for *Sunrise* in 1927, was the photographer of Rouben Mamoulian's classic version of **Doctor Jekyll and Mr Hyde** (1932). The result is an ineptly mounted creature-feature with Macready as the scientist experimenting with an alligator serum intended to help disabled people grow new limbs. Crane is the wounded man who takes the serum and discovers himself growing scales and hungry for human and animal flesh. Garland is the imperilled heroine.

d Roy Del Ruth *p* Jack Leewood *s* O.H. Hampton, Charles O'Neal *c* Karl Struss *lp* George Macready, Bruce Bennett, Lon Chaney Jnr, Beverly Garland, Freda Inescort, Douglas Kennedy

Arzt Ohne Gewissen *aka* Das Letzte Geheimnis *aka* Privatklinik Prof. Lund

(DIVINA FILM; WG) b/w 95 min

Another gory example of German medical Science Fiction, the highpoint of which must be the bizarre **Die Nackte und der Satan** made in the same year and using some of the same motifs, eg heart transplants with equipment that looked impressive but wasn't quite as professional as that used in real life a few years later.

In Harnack's film, Dr Lund (Preiss) does his medical experiments on what in this genre are regarded as worthless women – prostitutes and club singers. Preiss, who went on to make his name playing Dr Mabuse from Lang's **Die Tausend Augen des Dr Mabuse** (1960) onwards, plays the role of the latter day Dr Frankenstein with manic as well as melodramatic gusto. Harnack may have made this film as personal therapy after contributing to the genre of bigot-pornography with his *Roman eines Frauenarztes* (1954) and before making *Ein Frauenarzt Klagt An* (1964). Baal is a young actress introduced to the screen by Georg Tressler, head of the film department within the Marshall Plan for Austria and director of the film often cited as the first example of 'new German cinema', *Die Halbstarken* (1956), starring Baal. However, her career remained stuck at the lower end of the market in sexploitation horror thrillers and prostitute-krimis such as **Die Toten Augen von London** (1961).

The giant dinosaur, awakened by an atomic test, on the rampage in London in Behemoth, the Sea Monster.

d Falk Harnack *p* Ilse Kubaschewski *s* Werner Zibaso *c* Helmut Ashley *lp* Wolfgang Preiss, Karin Baal (Blauermel), Ewald Balser, Barbara Ruetting, Cornell Borchers, Wolfgang Kieling, Erica Beer, Walter Jacob, Emmerich Schrenk, Agnes Windeck

Behemoth, the Sea Monster *aka* The Giant Behemoth

(EROS; GB) b/w 80 min

Like the equally insipid **Gorgo** (1961), this borrows extensively from Lourié's **The Beast from 20,000 Fathoms** (1953) for its basic plot, a prehistoric monster (here a dinosaur) revived in the aftermath of an atomic explosion and travelling to and terrorizing a city (here London). The original film, Lourié's first as a director, was highly influential: its success and that of **Them!** (1954) initiated the fifties monster cycle in American Science Fiction. Equally important, though the film looks primitive nowadays, it reveals Lourié as a master at creating suspense through mood and evocative lighting. Some of this quality is present in *Behemoth, the Sea Monster*, notably the scene in the darkened laboratory illuminated by the phosphorescent glow of an irradiated fish, but, for the most part, despite the monster being created by O'Brien of *King Kong* (1933) fame, the film is at best routine.

Evans is the American scientist who saves London when the dinosaur appears by firing a radium-filled torpedo at it, whereupon, in its death throes, the monster brings down London Bridge.

co-d/s Eugène Lourié *co-d* Douglas Hickox *p* Ted Lloyd *c* Ken Hodges *se* Jack Rabin, Irving Block, Louis DeWitt, Willis O'Brien, Pete Peterson *lp* Gene Evans, Andre Morell, Jack MacGowran, Leigh Madison, Henry Vidon

The Black Scorpion

(AMEX PRODUCTIONS) b/w 88 (80) min

Inspired by Gordon Douglas' **Them!** (1954), Ludwig's surprisingly bleak offering features giant scorpions, large spiders, giant worms with claws and other unfriendly monsters appearing as a result of atomic radiation. They fight amongst themselves at length until only one giant scorpion is left. This emerges from a cave beneath the Mexican desert and sets out on the rampage. Denning is the wooden-headed hero who kills the remaining scorpion with an electrified harpoon.

Left: *Beverly Garland is befriended by a gruesome-looking Richard Crane in* The Alligator People.

Inferior to the more imaginative *Them!*, the film comes complete with numerous scenes whch are purposely dimly lit to cover up the inept special effects. Only the stop-motion sequences are successful. These were created by Willis O'Brien (the animator on *King Kong*, 1933) in 1953, for a film about prehistoric life that was never finished.

d Edward Ludwig   *p* Frank Melford, Jack Dietz
s David Duncan, Robert Blees   *c* Lionel Lindon
se Willis O'Brien, Peter Peterson   *lp* Richard Denning, Mara Corday, Carlos Rivas, Mario Navarro

The Brain That Wouldn't Die

(STERLING PRODUCTIONS/CARLTON)   b/w   81 min
Clearly derivative of Curt Siodmak's **Donovan's Brain** (1953), Green's attempts to mix horror and Science Fiction fail because script and direction are all too obvious. Evers is the modern Frankenstein, a surgeon experimenting with transplants, whose creation is so horrible to look at he keeps it in a locked dungeon. When his fiancée (Leith) is decapitated in a road accident, he keeps the head alive and sets about looking for a new body for her. Predictably, just as he's about to operate on model Lamont his monster escapes, sets fire to the laboratory and kills Evers before departing à la King Kong with the still unconscious Lamont cradled in his arms.

d/s Joseph Green   *p* Rex Carlton   *c* Stephen Hajnal
se Byron Baer   *lp* Herb Evers, Virginia Leith, Adele Lamont, Paula Maurice, Bruce Brighton, Doris Brent

Caltiki, il Monstro Immortale *aka* Caltiki, the Immortal Monster   (GALATEA FILMS/

CLIMAX PRESENTATIONS; IT, US)   b/w   76 min
A minor outing, this was one of the earliest Italian films to be aimed at the American market, hence the Mexican setting and the 'American' pseudonyms (later to become one of the oddest features of the Spaghetti western) of most of the cast and crew. The film's other point of interest is that it was completed by cinematographer Bava who in the sixties became Italy's premier horror director and made several stylish Science Fiction films, including **Terrore nello Spazio** (1965) and **Diabolik** (1967).

Led by Merivale's professor, a group of scientists find a blob-like monster, Caltiki (in fact a huge quantity of cows' entrails with a man inside to make it move), while excavating a Mayan tomb. They kill it, but back in the laboratory the

specimen they take comes back to life and then goes on the rampage until it is burned to death. Though the acting is routine and the script leaden, Bava injects a few stylish flourishes.

d Robert Hampton (Ricardo Freda), (uncredited) Mario Bava
p Samuel Schneider   *s* Philip Just (Filippano Sanjust)
c/se John Foam (Mario Bava)   *lp* John Merivale, Didi Sullivan (Didi Perego), Gerard Herter, Daniela Rocca, Giacomo Rossi-Stuart, Gay Pearl, Daniele Pitani

The Cosmic Man   (FUTURA)   b/w   72 min

One of a series of films of the fifties infected with the general fear of nuclear war, this engaging, low-budget oddity, like Robert Wise's far more assured **The Day the Earth Stood Still** (1951), explores the idea of a benevolent alien trying to set Earth to rights. Thus Carradine's Cosmic Man arrives on Earth, anxious to spread the word of love, but is greeted with suspicion and hostility for he is different. The Cosmic Man has a negative human image, ie a black skin with a white shadow (the film's only real special effect), which he conceals by wearing black clothes and dark glasses. Scientist Bennett and his girlfriend, Greene, discover the truth about the lurking stranger who is still intent on good work. To prove this, he restores a crippled child to health, but even his miracles are initially hostilely received. The film's optimistic ending has a certain naïve power.

d Herbert Greene   *p* Robert A. Terry   *s* Arthur C. Pierce
c John F. Warren   *se* Charles Duncan   *lp* Bruce Bennett, John Carradine, Angela Greene, Paul Langton, Scotty Morrow, Lyn Osborn

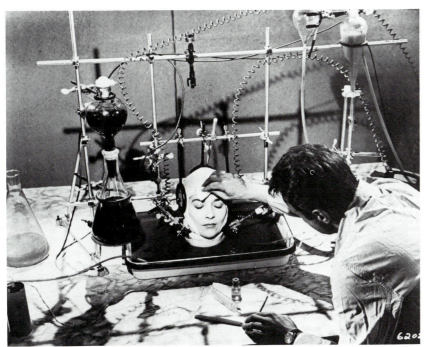

Demons of the Swamp *aka* The Giant Leeches

(BALBOA) b/w 62 min

Clark and Vickers battle giant leeches when they go on the rampage in the Florida swamps, creating havoc. Like the film, its credits have an also-ran quality about them. Gordon, a regular heavy in westerns and often to be found in the films of Roger Corman, is a better actor than writer; producer Corman's career has always been overshadowed by that of his brother, producer/director Roger, while Kowalski's career in television is more interesting than his film career.

d Bernard L. Kowalski *p* Gene Corman *s* Leo Gordon *c* John M. Nickolaus Jnr *lp* Ken Clark, Yvette Vickers, Michael Emmet, Bruno ye Sola

First Man into Space *aka* Satellite of Blood

(ANGLO-AMALGAMATED; GB) b/w 77 min

One of the numerous films derived from **The Quatermass Xperiment** (1955), this lacklustre outing features an astronaut (Edwards) who returns from space covered in a strange type of slime, collected whilst flying through meteor dust. Eventually the organism kills Edwards but still inhabits his corpse. To survive, it must have human blood and, after several vampirish murders and a break-in at a blood bank, Edwards' brother, scientist Thompson, manages to manoeuvre Edwards into a decompression chamber and kill the organism and Edwards. Landi is the heroine who screams every time Edwards appears.

d Robert Day *p* John Croydon, Charles F. Vetter Jnr *s* John C. Cooper, Lance Z. Hargreaves *c* Geoffrey Faithfull *lp* Marshall Thompson, Marla Landi, Robert Ayres, Bill Edwards, Bill Nagy, Carl Jaffe

4D Man *aka* Master of Terror *aka* The Evil Force

(FAIRVIEW PRODUCTIONS) 85 min

Yeaworth frantically directs this fantastic but interesting film about a scientist, Congdon, who develops a method of penetrating solid matter. He does this with the assistance of his brother, Lansing, by using an electric motor to stir up his brain waves, but this uses up his life-force and causes him to age rapidly. To prevent this, he starts drawing life-force from others, killing them in the process. The unusual ending has his fiancée Meriwether first persuade him to temporarily abandon his power and then shoot him.

d/co-p Irvin Shortess Yeaworth Jnr *co-p* Jack H. Harris *s* Theodore Simonson, Cy Chermak *c* Theodore J. Pahle *se* Barton Sloan *lp* Robert Lansing, Lee Meriwether, James Congdon, Robert Strauss, Patty Duke

The Giant Gila Monster

(HOLLYWOOD PICTURES CORP.) b/w 74 min

Cline's slick photography and the passable special effects of Hammeras and Risser result in this, the feature début of Kellogg, a veteran cinematographer and second unit director, being a far better film than it might appear. A monster (apparently from nowhere) feeds on trees, wrecks trains and breaks into a teenage dance hall, until it meets up with Graham's grizzly sheriff who acts everyone else off the screen.

d/co-s Ray Kellogg *p* Ken Curtis *co-s* Jay Sims *c* Wilfred Cline *se* Ralph Hammeras, Wee Risser *lp* Don Sullivan, Lisa Simone, Shug Fisher, Jerry Cortwright, Fred Graham, Beverly Thurman

Have Rocket Will Travel (COL) b/w 76 min

A juvenile musical romp with the Three Stooges (Howard, Fine and De Rita, who replaced Joe Besser, who in turn had replaced Shemp Howard on his death in 1955). The cleaners at a rocket base, the Three accidentally launch themselves into space and land on Venus where they meet a unicorn which talks, a thinking machine and a giant spider which clutches a flame thrower. The film climaxes, in traditional style, in a lengthy pie fight after which the trio return home as heroes.

Cheaply made and harshly received by the critics, the film, their first feature for over five years, was a phenomenal success and revived their careers at a time when Columbia had chosen not to renew their contract to appear in shorts and the team was on the verge of breaking up after Howard had appeared on his own in **Space Master X-7** (1958).

Director Rich subsequently had a successful career in American television as well as directing such melodramas as *Madame X* (1966).

d David Lowell Rich *p* Harry Romm *s* Raphael Hayes *c* Ray Cory *lp* The Three Stooges (Moe Howard, Larry Fine, Joe De Rita), Jerome Cowan, Anna-Lisa, Bob Colbert

Herrin der Welt *aka* Il Mistero dei Tre Continenti *aka* Les Mystères d'Angkor *aka* Mistress of the World

(CCC FILM/FRANCO-LONDON-FILM/CONTINENTAL FILM/UFA; IT,FR,WG) b/w 2 parts (100 min, 90 min)

The last movie made by Dieterle before he retired, *Herrin der Welt* is also the only Science Fiction film made by the German-born director who, like Fritz Lang, left Germany for Hollywood in the thirties and subsequently returned at the end of his career. Best known for *A Midsummer Night's Dream* (1935) which he co-directed with Max Reinhardt in whose theatrical troupe he'd acted in Germany, *The Hunchback of Notre Dame* (1939) and a number of ponderous biopics for Warners in the thirties and early forties, Dieterle had a feel for

As ever in the fifties the military (far right) stand in discreet attendance upon the scientists: First Man into Space.

Left: *Robert Lansing as* The 4D Man.

Right: *The Three Stooges in orbit in* Have Rocket Will Travel.

atmosphere that only frequently surfaced in his Hollywood films.

Sadly this two-part European co-production, a cocktail of Science Fiction and thriller elements, is a dull offering which is far more interesting for its credits than anything else. Presle is the master spy dashing around the world chasing after a secret formula for a new source of energy discovered by Cervi and his daughter Hyer and in turn being chased by Ventura and Thompson as the good guys, here working for the Swedish Intelligence Service. Sabu, the original *Elephant Boy* (1937) is Cervi's double-dealing assistant.

d/p William Dieterle *s* Jo Esinger, M.G. Petersson
c Richard Angst, Richard Oelers, Peter Homfield
lp Martha Hyer, Carlos Thompson, Micheline Presle, Gino Cervi, Lino Ventura, Sabu

The Hideous Sun Demon *aka* Blood on His Lips *aka* Terror from the Sun *Aka* The Sun Demon

(PACIFIC-INTERNATIONAL) b/w 74 min
Director/producer Clarke is the physicist contaminated by radiation at an atom plant which causes him to regress in evolutionary terms and become a giant lizard in this routine outing. When exposed to sunlight Clarke turns into a killer lizard and goes on the rampage until he is finally trapped on the roof of a huge gas tank from which he predictably falls to his death.

Clarke, an actor since the forties, was a regular in low-budget Science Fiction movies of the fifties (notably in Edgar Ulmer's **The Man from Planet X**, 1951) before turning producer with this film. He subsequently produced **Beyond the Time Barrier** (1960), also directed by Ulmer, amongst others.

The direction here is rudimentary.

co-d/p Robert Clarke *co-d* Thomas Bontross, Gianbatista Cassarino *se* E.S. Seeley Jnr, Doane Houg *c* John Morrill, Vilis Lapenieks Jnr, Stan Follis *lp* Robert Clarke, Patricia Manning, Nan Peterson, Patrick Whyte, Fred La Porta

Invisible Invaders (PREMIUM) b/w 67 min

One of the many dangers encountered in Journey to the Centre of the Earth.

Invisible invaders arrive from the Moon, take over human corpses and then embark on the conquest of Earth in this lacklustre precursor of **Night of the Living Dead** (1968). Under the leadership of once-dead scientist Carradine, the corpses march over the countryside, looking suitably grisly, and cause havoc, taking over the bodies they kill en route. Agar finally saves the day by using a special high-frequency sound which drives the aliens out of the corpses. Cahn's direction is routine at best and his over-reliance on shoddily matched stock footage destroys what credibility Newman's screenplay might have had.

d Edward L. Cahn *p* Robert E. Kent *s* Samuel Newman
c Maury Gertsman *se* Roger George lp John Agar, Jean Byron, Robert Hutton, John Carradine, Paul Langton, Eden Hartford

Journey to the Centre of the Earth

(FOX) scope 132 min
First filmed, under the novel's original title, in 1909 by the 'Spanish Méliès', Segundo de Chomon, Jules Verne's *Voyage au Centre de la Terre* was resurrected by Fox to capitalize on Disney's success with **20,000 Leagues Under the Sea** (1954), which also featured Mason (as Nemo), as a vehicle for their new teenage star Boone. Accordingly, the screenplay was fashioned by Brackett and Reisch to leave space for Boone to sing four songs.

Shot in the Carlsbad Caverns, New Mexico, the film follows the expedition of Mason, Dahl, Ronson, Boone and Baker (whose high-heel shoes look decidedly out of place) to find the lost civilization that once existed at the centre of the Earth. David is the evil count Saknussemm who follows them but Levin concentrates more on the expedition's natural obstacles, which include prehistoric monsters, a field of giant mushrooms and a magnetic storm on the interglobal ocean which beaches Mason's party on the shores of the lost city of Atlantis, than human treachery. The result is a firmly juvenile offering with little of the real sense of wonder of Verne's novel. The end, with Mason and Dahl and Boone and Baker declaring their love for each other after being catapulted to safety throught the Stromboli volcano, is particularly sickly.

d Henry Levin   *p/co-s* Charles Brackett   *co-s* Walter Reisch *c* Leo Tover   *se* L.B. Abbott, James B. Gordon, Emil Kosa Jnr   *lp* Pat Boone, James Mason, Arlene Dahl, Diane Baker, Alan Napier, Thayer David, Peter Ronson

The Killer Shrews

(HOLLYWOOD PICTURES CORP.)   b/w   69 min
Produced by one-time singing cowboy Curtis, who also stars in the film (along with executive producer and the film's distributor, McLendon), this was shot back to back, using the same production crew, with **The Giant Gila Monster** (1959). Lumet is the scientist experimenting with shrews (small mouse-like insectivorous mammals) who develops a serum that transforms them into wolf-sized flesh-eaters. In the course of a storm, they escape Lumet's island laboratory and attack riverboat captain Best and Lumet's daughter Goude. A lacklustre creature-feature, it suffers badly from the inept special effect: the shrews are nothing more than greyhounds in shaggy coats and false teeth.

d Ray Kellogg   *p* Ken Curtis   *s* Jay Simms   *c* Wilfred Cline *lp* James Best, Ingrid Goude, Baruch Lumet, Ken Curtis, Gordon McLendon

Ein Mann Geht Durch die Wand *aka* The Man Who Could Walk Through Walls

(DEUTSCHE FILM HANSA; WG)   b/w   99 min
A light comedy in the Harry Piel tradition (**Ein Unsichtbarer Geht Durch die Stadt**, 1933) with Germany's king of the lower middle-class fantasies, Ruehmann. Based on Marcel Aymé's novel, *Le Passe-Muraille*, the story has Ruehmann as a tax office clerk who is given the power to walk through walls. For a while, this produces some funny situations but in the end, the clerk realizes one doesn't need extraordinary abilities to be happy and he cheerfully resigns himself to his drab life. The comedy received the Lubitsch prize for the best humorous film of 1960; Lubitsch must have turned in his grave!

The same story was filmed by Jean Boyer as **Garou Garou le Passe Muraille** (1950) with Bourvil and Joan Greenwood.

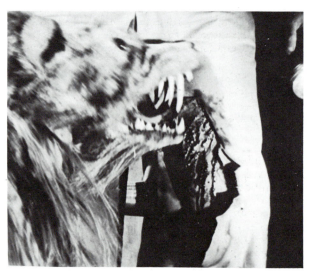

d Ladislao Vajda   *p* Kurt Ulrich   *s* Istvan Bekeffi, Hans Jacoby   *c* Bruno Mondi   *lp* Heinz Ruehmann, Nicole Courcel, Rudolf Rhomberg, Rudolf Vogel, Hans Leibelt, Hubert von Meyerinck, Lina Carstens, Karl Michael Vogler, Anita von Ow

Die Nackte und der Satan *aka* The Head

(RAPID FILM/WOLFGANG HARTWIG/PRISMA FILM/TRANSLUX; WG)   92 min
A genuinely bizarre case of medical Science Fiction by Trivas, the Russian director who had collaborated with the arch-realist Pabst in the twenties. After working in the USA and France, he celebrated his return to Germany by collaborating with his old friends, the multi-chinned Simon and Hermann Warm, one of the principal expressionist set designers, including for *Das Kabinett des Dr Caligari* (1919).

Professor Abel (Simon) invents a serum that keeps a dog's severed head alive. The mad Dr Ood (Frank) performs a heart transplant on Simon, and then keeps Simon's severed head alive on a glass slab, wired up with electrodes and pleading to be allowed to die. Frank also grafts the head of a hunchbacked nurse (Kernke) onto the body of a stripper (Maybach) and thus creates his ideal woman. The plot gets even more complicated before the good doctor eventually burns the lab down and Simon's head is allowed to rest in peace. The scenes with Simon, who kept a pair of hands in a pickle jar in Vigo's classic *L'Atalante* (1934), reduced to his admittedly extra-ordinary head are collectors' items. Trivas, whose best-known film was the widely respected pacifist movie *Niemandsland* (1931), never directed another film.

The theme of the severed head, although not unique (eg *The Thing That Couldn't Die*, 1958, **Man without a Body**, 1957, and **Dark Star**, 1974) was never the same again after Simon's performance.

d/s Victor Trivas   *p* Wolfgang Hartwig   *c* Georg Krause *se* Theo Nishwitz   *lp* Michel Simon, Horst Frank, Paul Dahlke, Karin Kernke, Christiane Maybach, Helmut Schmid, Dieter Eppler, Kurt Mueller-Graf, Maria Stadler, Otto Storr

La Nave de los Monstruos

(PRODUCCIONES SOTOMAYOR; MEX)   82 min
A childish and badly made comic-strip fantasy starring Piporro dressed as a cowboy confronting the denizens of a spaceship. The craft has travelled from planet to planet collecting specimens from the local fauna such as a cyclops, a

Michel Simon's severed head pleads in vain for death while Horst Frank looks on in the intriguing Die Nackte und der Satan.

Left: The Killer Shrews *in action.*

fish-man, etc. The crew is also a motley collection of horrors called Uk, Zak Utir, Taguel the Prince of Mars, Espectro of the Planet Death and Tor the robot, modelled on the metal contraptions familiar from Republic serials. The women are a vampire (Velazquez) and the sexy captain (Lepe) of the spaceship who decides to stay on Earth with Piporro while the rest continue on their travels. By all accounts, a bizarre but ill-mounted production mixing elements from sexploitation, Science Fiction (a heat ray and all kinds of electronic gadgetry is used) and songs. The movie was Sotomayor's follow-up to the previous childish parody production he had financed, **El Castillo de los Monstruos** (1958).

Like everything else about the film, the metal robot costume of Tor was secondhand, having been used previously in a Calderon production, **El Robot Humano** (1957), where it was dismantled by the Aztec Mummy. Director Gonzalez is best known for his comedies starring the popular heart-throb Pedro Infante, including that performer's most successful outing, a remake of Gregory La Cava's *My Man Godfrey* (1936) entitled *Escuela de Vagabundos* (1954).

d Rogelio A. Gonzalez *p* Jesús Sotomayor *s* Jose Maria Fernandez Unsain, Alfredo Varela Jnr *c* Raul Martinez Solares *lp* Eulalio Gonzalez Piporro, Ann Bertha Lepe, Lorena Velazquez, Consuelo Frank, Manuel Lopez, Jesús Rodriguez, Jose Pardave

Niebo Zowiet *aka* The Sky Calls *aka* The Heavens Call
(DOVZHENKO STUDIO; USSR) 77 min

Celebrating the Sputniks (1953 and 1957), as well as their rocket to the Moon (1959), this is the first major Soviet space travel movie since **Kosmitchesky Reis** (1935). It was followed by the Polish/East German **Der Schweigende Stern** (1960) and the brilliantly designed Russian space movies of the early sixties (**Planeta Burg**, 1962, and **Meshte Nastreshu**, 1963). Like the latter two, *Niebo Zowiet* was also cannibalized by an American producer, who used the excellent footage of alien worlds and space flights, combined this with newly shot plot material and issued the whole thing as **Battle Beyond the Sun** (1963). A graduate from the special effects' department (**Tainstvenni Ostrov**, 1941), Karyukov co-directed here and eventually became principal director on *Meshte Nastreshu*.

The story here involves two manned space rockets, one to the Moon and one to Mars, making a stopover on a gigantic artificial satellite equipped with laboratories, gardens and comfortable dwellings, anticipating similar staging posts in **Silent Running** (1971) and **Android** (1982).

d Aleksander Kozyr, Mikhail Karyukov *s* A. Sazonov, Yevgeny Pomeshchikov *c* Nikolai Kulchitsky *se* F. Syemyannikov, N. Ilushin *lp* Ivan Perevertsev, Alexander Shvorin, Konstantin Bartashevich, Taisa Litvinenko, G. Tonunts, V. Cheriyak, V. Dobrovolski, A. Popova, L. Borisenko, S. Filimonov

On the Beach (LOMITAS) b/w 134 min

On the Beach is the most celebrated of the anti-nuclear-war films of the fifties, a reputation that reflects more accurately Kramer's success in publicizing the film, than the film itself. For all its good intentions (and the majestic cinematography of Rotunno), the film is ill-served by Kramer's heavy-handed, dull direction and Paxton's overwrought script which transform the tragedy of the end of mankind brought about by his own hand into a series of personal melodramas: the hardheaded sailor, Peck, and the cynical socialite, Gardner, who don't have time to work things out; the young married couple (Perkins and Anderson) confronted with the problem of giving a suicide pill to their child and Astaire's racing driver who prefers to gas himself rather than take a pill. Moreover, unlike Nevil Shute's novel which is notable for its narrative clarity, Kramer's film merely drifts along.

Significantly, Kramer puts his faith not in the power of the central situation – in 1964 an atomic war has destroyed life in every part of the world but Australia and slowly but surely the winds are bringing the radioactive fallout to Melbourne – but in his star cast. The result is a film about issues in which the issues quickly get buried. Only in the extended sequence in which Peck takes his submarine to California, from where they have received a radio signal suggesting that there are survivors only to find the message is the result of a window blind pull cord wrapped around a morse key and blowing in the wind, does Kramer show the rising hopes followed by bitter disillusionment of his characters as they confront something more than merely their own deaths.

d/p Stanley Kramer *s* John Paxton *c* Giuseppe Rotunno *se* Lee Zavitz *lp* Gregory Peck, Ava Gardner, Fred Astaire, Anthony Perkins, Donna Anderson, Guy Doleman, John Tate

Return of the Fly
(ASSOCIATED PRODUCERS) b/w 78 min

In this often (unintentionally) hilarious sequel to **The Fly** (1958) Halsey, the late inventor's son, re-assembles his father's matter-transference equipment, despite the dire warnings of Price (reprising his role as the brother of the inventor from the earlier film). Once again, this time due to the activities of his assistant Frankham, who is a spy, things go wrong and Halsey becomes part-man, part-fly, before

Price is able to reconstruct him as a normal human being. Although Bernds' script is overly episodic and his direction flat, the film was a commercial success and a further sequel, **The Curse of the Fly**, followed in 1965.

d/s Edward L. Bernds *p* Bernard Glasser *c* Brydon Baker *lp* Vincent Price, Brett Halsey, David Frankham, John Sutton, Danielle DeMezt, Pat O'Hara

Teenagers from Outer Space *aka* The Gargon Terror

(TOPOR CORP.) b/w 87 (85) min

A virtual one-man production by Graeff, this silly piece of hokum involves an invasion of teenage aliens who land on Earth in their flying saucers. Their aims are to breed and graze their space cattle, lobster-like monsters called Gargons. Due to the film's minuscule budget the monsters are gloriously absurd, blown-up photographs of lobsters, seen mostly in shadow form. Leader of the teenage star pilots Love makes the fatal mistake of falling for Anderson and, despondent, guides his companions' saucers into a mountainside, killing himself and all of them.

Dunn, a clown specializing in children's parties who appeared in **Bride of the Monster** (1956) complete with his parakeet, this time left the bird behind.

d/p/s/c Tom Graeff *lp* David Love, Dawn Anderson, Harvey B. Dunn, Bryan Grant, Tom Lockyear

The 30-Foot Bride of Candy Rock

(COL) b/w 75 min

In this, his only film without Bud Abbott, Costello is a meek handyman whose girlfriend, Provine, is turned into a 30-foot giant by scientist Conlin. Conlin also invents a time displacer, which sends Costello back to prehistoric times and to the Civil War period, and a device which enables Costello to fly. The result is an ill-paced movie, but one that, for once, lacks the stridency of Abbott and Costello's outings together. Costello died shortly after completing the film.

d Sidney Miller *p* Edward Sherman *s* Rowland Barber, Arthur Ross *c* Frank G. Carson *se* J. Rabin, I. Block, Louis DeWitt *lp* Lou Costello, Dorothy Provine, Gale Gordon, Jimmy Conlin, Charles Lane, Will Wright, Doodles Wenver

Ein Toter Hing im Netz *aka* It's Hot in Paradise *aka* Body in the Web *aka* The Spider's Web *aka* Girls of Spider Island *aka* Horrors of Spider Island (INTERNATIONAL FILM/ RAPID FILM; WG, AUSTRIA) b/w 82 min

A group of eight young women, victims of an air crash, are stranded on a desolate island. They find the corpse of an explorer caught in the web of a monster (d'Arcy) – their manager who has been transformed into a spider after being bitten by a poisonous insect. The film rather arbitrarily inserts shots of a hairy, wheezing spider into footage of the women, scantily dressed, taking showers, doing their hair and tugging at each other's breasts. Plump blonde Valentin also added extra sensuality to the bizarre **Die Nackte und der Satan** (1959) while former matinée idol d'Arcy made up as a hairy monster may be a case of poetic justice. The image of the explorer in the web is inserted occasionally, without any plot motivation, rather like a found object. This could qualify as one of the worst films ever made.

d/s Fritz Boettger *p* Gaston Hakim *c* Georg Krause *lp* Helga Frank, Barbara Valentin, Alex d'Arcy, Harald Maresch, Helga Neuner, Reiner Brand, Eva Schauland, Dorothee Gloecklen

Uchu Daisenso *aka* Battle in Outer Space *aka* The World of Space (TOHO; JAP) scope 93 (90) min

Honda's second space opera, the first being **Chikyu Boeigun** (1957). Starting with a series of catastrophes that befall the Earth in 1965, including the emptying of Venice's lagoon followed by the dumping of all the water onto the city itself, the burning of New York and the destruction of the Golden Gate bridge by a space torpedo, it becomes clear that the Earth is under attack from an alien planet. Two spaceships are sent out to do battle with the enemy. After a land-based encounter on the Moon there follows a clash in space, filmed with spectacular effects and a very effective use of colour for the futuristic toy landscapes. The dubbing is atrocious, as usual mismatching completely the voice and the physique of the actors. Although the scenery does look a bit tatty now and then, this doesn't really detract from the playful entertainment which never set out to be realistic anyway. The original story is credited to Jotaro Okami, and the crew is the familiar Honda team, including composer Akira Ifukube.

By this time, Toho was making its Science Fiction movies with the American market firmly in mind, producing films ready for dubbing, either shooting in two versions simultaneously or beefing up the 'American interest' themselves, usually by featuring a few minor US guest stars.

d Inoshiro Honda *p* Tomoyuki Tanaka *s* Shinichi Sekizawa *c* Hajime Koizumi *se* Eiji Tsuburaya *lp* Ryo Ikebe, Kyoko Anzai, Minoru Takada, Koreya Senda, Leonard Stanford, Harold Conway, George Whitman, Elise Richter, Hisaya Ito, Yoshio Tsuchiya

Und Immer Ruft das Herz (ALFU; WG) b/w 86 min

A story no doubt partly inspired by the Sputnik II flight with the dog Laika (1957). The plot is similar to that of countless Disney features: a lover of wildlife (Moehner) goes to the thick forests of Finland where he meets a dog who leads him to a girl (Savo) he can save from drowning. However, the lovers separate and the interesting feature of the film is the way contact is re-established: the zoologist bundles his dog into a rocket and shoots it into space – only to land on his love-lorn lady's lawn.

d/s George Freedland *c* Esko Toeryi, Herbert Koerner *lp* Ann Savo, Carl Moehner, Paul Dahlke, Helmut Schmid, Richard Haussler

The World, the Flesh and the Devil

(SOL C. SIEGEL/HARBEL PRODUCTIONS) b/w scope 95 min Suggested by M.P. Shiel's novel *The Purple Cloud*, Mac-Dougall's vision of post-nuclear America was clearly influenced by Arch Oboler's **Five** (1951). However, where Oboler's concerns were the possibility of such a holocaust,

Below: *A surreal moment from* Uchu Daisenso.

Harry Belafonte takes to the streets in the impressive The World, the Flesh and the Devil

before embarking on a successful career directing short films (*Le Sang des Bêtes*, 1949; *Hôtel des Invalides*, 1951), Franju had co-founded the celebrated Cinématheque Française with Henri Langlois. His love of cinema was firmly rooted in the intellectual climate that spawned his soulmate, Luis Buñuel, and profoundly marked the French New Wave directors who were, in fact, a generation younger. By an odd coincidence, Franju's classic of medical Science Fiction was made in the same year as Victor Trivas' bizarre **Die Nackte und der Satan** (1959). The two films set the terms for nearly all future mad-surgeon movies: Trivas with his gleeful indulgence in the bizarre for its own sake and Franju with a highly stylized, lyrical work playing on the anxieties that accompany the voyeuristic pleasures that underpin our desire for cinema. A few years later, in **Gritos en la Noche** (1962), Jesús Franco combined both approaches and added both nudity and sadism of a directly sexual kind, thus achieving the commercially successful formula that thrived, most notably in the Latin cinema, for the next two decades.

A pale copy of Franju's surrealist classic was furnished by Michael Pataki entitled **Mansion of the Doomed** (1975).

d/co-s Georges Franju   *p* Jules Borkon   *co-s* Jean Redon, Claude Sautet, Pierre Boileau, Thomas Narcejac, Pierre Gascar   *c* Eugene Schuftan (Eugen Schuefftan)   *se* Assola, Georges Klein   *lp* Pierre Brasseur, Edith Scob, Alida Valli, François Guerin, Juliette Mayniel, Beatrice Altariba, Alexandre Rignault, Claude Brasseur, René Genin, Michel Etcheverry

screenwriter turned director (and later producer) MacDougall was clearly more interested in mounting a blunt allegory about race relations. Thus, the three survivors, representing the human condition, are a black man (Belafonte), an innocent girl (Stevens) and a bigoted adventurer (Ferrer). MacDougall and cinematographer Marzorati brilliantly capture the sense of desolation that a deserted New York implies, and, although the debates between Belafonte and Ferrer (who, when he comes across Belafonte and Stevens, is horrified by their union) are far too wordy, the finale, the two men stalking New York, rifles in hand in search of each other, is impressively mounted. The climax is highly unusual for a fifties film. Belafonte, after reading the biblical injunction about beating swords with ploughshares on the side of the United Nations' building, throws down his rifle and, in the final shot, the three walk off arm in arm. As one critic has written, the end marks the disappearance of two cherished ideals of Western society – monogamy and racial purity.

d/s Ranald MacDougall   *p* George Englund   *c* Harold J. Marzorati   *se* Lee LeBlanc   *lp* Harry Belafonte, Inger Stevens, Mel Ferrer

Les Yeux Sans Visage *aka* Eyes Without a Face *aka* The Horror Chamber of Dr Faustus

(CHAMPS ELYSEES/LUX FILM; FR, IT)   b/w   90(88) min
A virtually unanimous chorus of British reviewers bayed their revulsion when Franju's sombrely poetic masterpiece was released, in a slightly softened version, after a controversial premiere at the Edinburgh Festival where seven viewers fainted during the performance.

The plot, adapted from his own novel by Redon, draws on stock situations from pulp fiction, always a prized source of inspiration for the French surrealists. Dr Genessier (Brasseur), responsible for the accident that disfigured his daughter Christiane (Scob), steals the faces of young women and tries to graft them onto his daughter's. In the end, the dogs he kept for experimental purposes attack him and tear off his face as the demented Christiane, still faceless, slowly disappears into the night. The first images of a car's headlights gliding over the restless trees of a wooden lane, the work of Germany's brilliant cinematographer, Schuftan, establishes an eerie atmosphere that is maintained throughout the movie, perfectly serving Franju's unnervingly intense direction.

Although this was the director's second film, it reached both Britain and America before *La Tête Contre les Murs* (1958), a powerful picture hailed by Godard in terms that could equally well apply to *Les Yeux Sans Visage*: 'A crazy film on madmen, thus a film of insane beauty.' In 1936,

Right: Les Yeux Sans Visage: the most poetic and mysterious of the films of Georges Franju.

Yusei Oji *aka* The Prince of Space *aka* Invaders from the Spaceship *aka* The Star Prince *aka* Invaders from Space

(TOEI; JAP)   b/w   scope   2 chaps (57 min, 64 min)
Cheap children's superhero picture in which the Planet Prince (Umemiya), disguised as a bootblack, arrives in a flying saucer to defend liberty and justice. He defeats Phantom Mission, a character seeking world domination and master of magic tricks. In chapter 1, Phantom Mission steals the secret of a new rocket fuel and sets off into space where the good guy catches up with him and wins the ensuing contest. However, the baddie returns in chapter 2, assisted by giants who kidnap a physicist and send him into orbit. Planet Prince rescues the marooned inventor and once more defeats the bad guy. The film was made with uncharacteristically crude designs for the spaceship and the suits. Compared to Kobayashi's **Gekko Kamen** (1958), the comic-strip effects are singularly unimaginative.

Wakabayashi had also contributed one episode to the *Gekko Kamen* series: *Satan No Tsume* (1959).

d Eijiro Wakabayashi   *s* Shin Morita   *c* Masahiko Iimura   *lp* Tatsuo Umemiya, Joji Oda, Hiroko Mine, Takashi Kanda, Ushui Skashi, Nobu Yatsuna

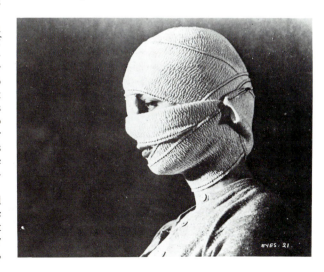

The 1960s

Science Fiction Becomes Respectable

Following the rebirth of Science Fiction in the anxious fifties, at the beginning of the sixties it seemed that the genre would once more be reduced to a mere collection of decorative elements used to enliven the films of other genres. Thus Fritz Lang's **Die Tausend Augen des Dr Mabuse** (1960) sparked off a revival of Mabuse thrillers and Jesús Franco's **Gritos en la Noche** (1962) initiated a stream of medically inclined Science Fiction-horror films from the Latin cinema. The classic example of this grafting of Science Fiction elements on to another genre was the James Bond series of films that commenced with **Doctor No** (1962). The success of these films inspired countless imitations, each, despite their frantic search for new wrinkles, firmly in the Bond mould.

However, whereas in the thirties such films (and serials) almost completely dominated the genre, in the sixties they were only one of its strands. In Italy, for example, where numerous Bond lookalikes were produced, Antonio Margheriti's **Space Men** (1960) introduced a series of visually exciting mainstream Science Fiction films. More significant than the internationalization of the genre this represented was the new-found respectability of Science Fiction in Europe. Films like **The War Game** (1965), **Alphaville** (1965), **Fahrenheit 451** (1966) and **Je T'Aime, Je T'Aime** (1967) used the speculative possibilities of Science Fiction to intriguing purpose. Similarly in Japan, the once simple movies about radiation-induced monsters developed until by the end of the decade the sub-genre had become a fascinating mirror of postwar Japanese political history.

In America, although fewer films were being made than during the mid-fifties, Science Fiction finally emerged from the bottom half of the double bill. Following the success of **The Absent-Minded Professor** (1961), the Disney Studio committed itself to a series of influential, if juvenile, Science Fiction outings. More importantly, the success of **On the Beach** (1959) encouraged established stars and directors to turn to Science Fiction. The bigger budgets they brought with them resulted in films as diverse as **The Birds** (1963), **Dr Strangelove** (1964) and **Seconds** (1966). The culmination of this trend came in 1968 with the release of **2001 – A Space Odyssey** and **Planet of the Apes**. *Apes*, which generated four sequels and a teleseries, gave added weight to the questioning tendency of big-budget Science Fiction while *2001* transformed both the look and the budgets of Science Fiction films. Equally influential, though not as celebrated at the time, was George Romero's **Night of the Living Dead** (1968) which created a sub-genre which would be mined throughout the seventies in countless exploitation pictures, by Romero as well as others.

The net result was that by the seventies, Science Fiction, like any other film genre, came in all shapes and sizes. In the era of spaceflight, in the decade man first stepped on the Moon, Science Fiction's fantasies, far from being exhausted as they were translated into reality, were renewed.

The Amazing Transparent Man

(MILLER CONSOLIDATED PICTURES)   b/w   60(56) min
This is the companion piece to the superior **Beyond the Time Barrier** (1960), which was also distributed by American International Pictures. Clearly inspired by **The Invisible Man** (1933), Lewis's routine script features Triesault as the scientist who develops an invisibility serum and administers it to Kennedy's convict who uses it as an aid to bank robbery until he is hunted down by the police and rival gansters. Ulmer, generally able to make moody, atmospheric pictures on the slimmest of budgets, here is unable to do more than decorate this low-low-budget outing with the occasional stylistic flourish.

d Edgar G. Ulmer   *p* Lester D. Guthrie   *s* Jack Lewis
c Meredith M. Nicholson   *se* Roger George   *lp* Marguerite Chapman, Douglas Kennedy, James Griffith, Ivan Triesault, Red Morgan, Carmel Daniel, Edward Erwin

The Angry Red Planet *aka* Invasion of Mars

(SINO)   94 min
Director Melchior created a genuinely interesting vision of Mars with the use of the pinkish tinting process of Cinemagic for this otherwise routine film. Although the desert regions have conventional craters and rocks, the planet also has dense jungles, pulsating with extraordinary tentacled plants, cities whose buildings strike out into the clouds and, because there is no wind, a lake which is a perfect mirror. Four astronauts from Earth land on Mars and do battle with enormous animals (which look like a cross between rats, bats, spiders and crabs) and the Martians themselves, who are three-eyed giants, before the three men are killed and Hayden returns to Earth.

d/co-s Ib Melchior   *co-p/co-s* Sid Pink   *co-p* Norman Maurer   *c* Stanley Cortez   *se* Herman Townsley, Michael Sternlight, Art Wasson   *lp* Gerald Mohr, Nora Hayden, Les Tremayne, Jack Kruschen

Los Astronautas *aka* Turistas Interplanetarios *aka* Dos Viajeros del Espacio

(PRODUCCIONES ZACARIAS; MEX)   85 min
An Abbott and Costello-type comedy starring the slapstick couple of clowns, Viruta and Capulina (Campos and Henaine). On a Venus ruled by women, the men demand a share of power because, although there is no more strife, there is no 'fun' anymore either. x7 (Romand) and x8 (Mora) are despatched to Earth to find two men who can be held up as

Previous pages: *Science Fiction goes into the mystic in the sixties: 2001 – A Space Odyssey (1968).*

Edgar G. Ulmer's disappointing The Amazing Transparent Man.

Nora Hayden returns to Earth after her ordeal on The Angry Red Planet.

The past as the future, George Pal's eccentric Atlantis, the Lost Continent.

ousness and crudity, sometimes, as in this picture, mixing both.

d/co-s Miguel Zacarias *p* Mario A. Zacarias
co-s Roberto Gomez Bolaños *c* Manuel Gomez Urquiza
lp Marco Antonio Campos, Gaspar Henaine, Gina Romand, Norma Mora, Erna Martha Bauman, Antonio Raxel, Armando Saenz, Tito Novaro, Jorge Casanova, Rica Osorio

Atlantis, the Lost Continent

(GALAXY PRODUCTIONS/MGM) 90 min
With two solid box-office hits – *Tom Thumb* (1958) and **The Time Machine** (1960) – and the confidence of MGM boss Sol Siegel behind him, Pal started on the film about the lost continent he had long wanted to make. Based on the play *Atlanta* by Sir Gerald Hargreaves, the movie has young Greek fisherman Hall rescue Taylor, the Princess of Atlantis and journey with her to the underwater world in a submarine. On arrival, however, Hall finds Atlantis is guarded by death rays and dominated by mad scientists, who try to turn him into an animal. The film is set in the days of the Roman Empire and Pal was able to borrow footage from *Quo Vadis* (1951) to pep up the fantasy world. Eventually Hall leads an escape just as Atlantis suffers a volcanic eruption. Although the special effects (the submarine, the death ray and the devastation of Atlantis) are acceptable, Pal's comic-strip approach was clearly at odds with that of scriptwriter Mainwaring, a fact made more problematic when MGM rushed the film into production during a writers' strike without a finished script. The result is a film more in the style of the Republic serial **Undersea Kingdom** (1936) than G.W. Pabst's definitive version of the Atlantis myth **Die Herren von Atlantis** (1932).

d/p George Pal *s* Daniel Mainwaring *c* Harold E. Wellman
se A. Arnold Gillespie, Lee LeBlanc, Robert R. Hoag
lp Anthony Hall, Joyce Taylor, John Dall, Bill Smith, Edward Platt, Frank de Kova

The Atomic Submarine

(GORHAM PRODUCTIONS/AA) b/w 72 min
This is probably the best of producer Gordon's low-budget films of the fifties and sixties, thanks in great part to the no-nonsense direction of Bennet, a man schooled in the lower than low-budget productions of Sam Katzman such as

examples to the obstreperous Venusian males. They bring back the two comics who succeed, largely involuntarily, in making them laugh, thus proving that only men know how to bring 'fun' into the world. The plot also involves a fight between the Venusians and the Martians, cast in the role of villains, and the transformation of Capulina into a champion boxer. The happy end sees the two Venusian women and the two comics leave for a honeymoon on the Moon.

The basic plot situation of a society ruled by women, presented as the height of absurdity, is similar to Emilio Gomez Muriel's *El Sexo Fuerte* (1945), Mexico's first major 'utopian' film presenting an alternative social order. The humour in both these intensely misogynistic fantasies is extremely basic and the sets appear to be adaptations of Disneyworld. Although shooting started in November 1960, the picture was not released until 1964, after the same comic duo's **Los Invisibles** (1961). Zacarias started his career making musical comedies in the early thirties and achieved some notoriety in the forties, particularly with the début film of Maria Felix, *El Peñon de las Animas* (1942), starring Jorge Negrete. However, his later work oscillated between ponder-

The submersible flying saucer and The Atomic Submarine.

Superman (1948), **Batman and Robin** (1949) and numerous series Westerns.

Franz is the commander of a US atomic-powered submarine sent to investigate a number of undersea disasters around the North Pole. There they find a cyclops-like monster in a submersible flying saucer intent on taking over the world. Even the extensive use of newsreel clips can't dent the film's charm.

d Spencer G. Bennet *p* Alex Gordon *s* Orville H. Hampton *c* Gilbert Warrenton *se* Jack Rabin, Irving Block, Louis DeWitt *lp* Arthur Franz, Dick Foran, Brett Halsey, Tim Conway, Paul Dubov, Bob Steele, Sid Melton

Los Automatas de la Muerte

(ESTUDIOS AMERICA/PRODUCCIONES CORSA; MEX) 80 min
The final part of the trilogy that introduced Neutron the Black Masked wrestler (Ruvinskis) to the cinema. The confrontation between Caronte (Aleman) and Neutron climaxes with the wrestler pitted against the army of robots manufactured by the evil doctor to do his dirty work while he gets on with blackmailing the world into submitting to his domination under the threat of his neutron bomb. As in the previous two titles in the series, **Neutron el Enmascarado Negro** and **Neutron Contra el Dr Caronte** (both 1960) the story is liberally interspersed with musical interludes.

d Federico Curiel *p* Emilio Gomez Muriel *s* Alfredo Ruanova *c* Fernando Alvarez Garces Colin *lp* Wolf Ruvinskis, Julio Aleman, Armando Silvestre, Roberto Ramirez, Rodolfo Landa, Grek Martin, Ernesto Finance, David Lama, Los Tres Ases, Trio Los Diamantes

Beyond the Time Barrier

(ROBERT CLARKE PRODUCTIONS) b/w 75 min
Despite its routine script, this remains one of Ulmer's best Science Fiction films. Clarke (the star of Ulmer's marvellous **The Man from Planet X**, 1951) is the pilot catapulted into the future while testing a new hypersonic aircraft. There he finds the Earth desolate and its few inhabitants living a subterranean existence after the 'cosmic nuclear plague of 1971' and at war with the mutants who roam the surface. Sokoloff, the ruler of the remaining humans, wants to mate Clarke with his deaf-mute daughter (Tompkins) as all the humans are sterile. However, Clarke (who also produced the film and **The Hideous Sun Demon**, 1959), after helping defeat the mutants, manages to escape back to 1960 by using the 'reverse relativity paradox'.

Put as baldly as that, and remembering the tatty sets and special effects of the film, *Beyond the Time Barrier*, is at best a low-budget outing. What lifts it is Ulmer's atmospheric direction, in which the subterranean world of the future is visualized as a series of seemingly endless catacombs, and the static conception of the Clarke character, trapped and virtually powerless in a world not of his own choosing. It is this fatalistic view which makes the ending, like that of *The Man from Planet X*, far less positive than it appears to be.

d Edgar G. Ulmer *p* Robert Clarke *s* Arthur C. Pierce *c* Meredith M. Nicholson *se* Roger George *lp* Robert Clarke, Darlene Tompkins, Arianne Arden, Vladimir Sokoloff, John van Dreelen, Red Morgan

Cape Canaveral Monsters (CCM) b/w 69 min

This belated entry in the reds-under-the-beds cycle of films features alien life-forces which arrive in Florida to interfere with the US space programme at Cape Canaveral by taking over the bodies of humans and turning them into zombies. The film is directed by Tucker, best remembered for the awful **Robot Monster** (1953). He publicly blamed the failure of that film on Wyatt Ordung's laboured script, and so wrote this one himself. Peters is the wooden-headed hero.

d/s Phil Tucker *p* Richard Greer *c* Merle Connell *lp* Scott Peters, Linda Connell, Jason Johnson, Katherine Victor, Frank Smith

El Conquistador de la Luna aka Clavillazo en la Luna
(PRODUCCIONES SOTOMAYOR; MEX) 90 min

A broad comedy starring Clavillazo, star of the slapstick **El Castillo de los Monstruos** (1958) which was also made by the team responsible for the childish space opera **La Nave de los Monstruos** (1959). Here Clavillazo plays Bartolo, a mechanic who lives in an automated house and courts the daughter (Peluffo) of the absent-minded professor don Abundio (Soler), the inventor of a spaceship that runs on cheap new fuel. While playing around with the professor's invention, the lovers trigger off the rocket and travel to the Moon where people live under the ground, communicate telepathically and can become invisible at will. An evil Martian rules and sends an atomic bomb to destroy the Earth, but the young couple destroy the flying saucer carrying it. There are the customary misogynistic jokes such as a four-armed Martian women who used to be a beauty queen and is intent on snaring Clavillazo.

Contemporary comments indicate that the effects were more primitive than those achieved by Méliès while the script was lathered with cloying sentimentality and maudlin nationalism, with dreamily uttered phrases about claiming the Moon for Mexico – which didn't prevent all the inscriptions in the spacecraft from being in English. A liberal use of TV stock shots and vaudeville costumes show that the production values were on a par with the script's intelligence and humour. Gonzalez must be regarded as a director who tried hard to make better films than the average Mexican potboiler, but he simply was not capable of doing so, not even when he was handed a good script like that of Buñuel's frequent collaborator Luis Alcoriza for *El Esqueleto de la Señora Morales* (1959).

d Rogelio A. Gonzalez p Jesús Sotomayor s José Maria Fernandez Unsain, Alfredo Varela Jnr c Raul Martinez Solares lp Antonio Espino Clavillazo, Ana Luisa Peluffo, Andres Soler, Oscar Ortiz de Pinedo, Victoria Blanco, Ramiro Gamboa

Dai Sanji Sekai Taisen – Yonju-Ichi Jikan no Kyofu
aka **The Final War** aka **World War III Breaks Out** aka **Jikan No Kyofu**
(NEW TOEI; JAP) b/w scope 77 min

Not to be confused with **Sekai Daisenso** (1962), also referred to as *The Final War* or *The Last War*, but made by Toho; the eminently plausible thesis of Hidaka's film is that the US accidentally explodes a nuclear bomb. In this instance, they do so over South Korea, triggering off recriminations between North and South Korea followed by US-USSR confrontation, fought out first over Tokyo and then the rest of the world until the only country left is Argentina.

Although the film follows on from the success of **On the Beach** (1959), Hiroshima was still fresh in Japanese memory, which allowed the film to represent more of the point of view of the victims than Kramer's film, made from the standpoint of the perpetrators of the nuclear holocaust, had. The sub-plot of a journalist (Umemiya, the superhero of **Yusei Oji**, 1959) who finds his loved one dead in Tokyo before dying himself is played in the grand style of high melodrama. The ending is both traditional and appropriate: heavy rain is falling as a memorial service is held for most of humanity.

d Shigeaki Hidaka s Hisataka Kai c Tadashi Aramaki
lp Tatsuo Umemiya, Yoshiko Mita, Yajoi Furusato, Noribumi Fujishima, Yukiko Nikaido, Michiko Hoshi

Denso Ningen aka The Secret of the Telegian aka The Telegian
(TOHO; JAP) scope 85(75) min

An interesting story of a man who can teleport himself to different locations. The plot concerns the revenge of a soldier who was doublecrossed at the end of the war by his friends and left for dead in a cave, together with a scientist they were supposed to hide from the advancing Americans. However, he survived the ordeal and the scientist eventually perfected his invention, working in an underground laboratory. The soldier uses it to kill his former colleagues. The device itself, a tubular glass box, works with clariotrons, small coils which the script claims will replace transistors. They can do for bodies what television does for images. Tsuburaya's special effects are as good as any achieved in the world at the time and the cinematography achieves respectable *noir*-ish overtones. After the surreal **Bijo to Ekitai Ningen** (1958) and the failure of **Gas Ningen Daiichigo** (1960), this was one of Toho's last transformation movies. Fukuda, who rounded off the series started by Honda, was called upon to take over again from Honda to continue Toho's monster movies series.

d Jun Fukuda p Tomoyuki Tanaka s Schinichi Sekizawa
c Kazuo Yamada se Eiji Tsuburaya lp Koji Tsuruta, Akihiko Hirata, Yumi Shirakawa, Tadao Nakamura, Seizaburo Kawazu

Gas Ningen Daiichigo aka The Human Vapor
(TOHO; JAP) scope 92(80) min

A re-working of Honda's marvellous **Bijo to Ekitai Ningen** (1958). This time, the central character is a convict (Tsuchiya) who, as a result of his participation in experiments, finds he can transform himself into a cloudy substance. This enables him to perpetrate crimes with impunity. This is not as visually impressive as the previous movie, probably because invisibility and gaseous substances are not notably photogenic material.

The film was one of the Toho team's last serious attempts at a transformation movie. Henceforth they would concentrate on the mainstream of the monster movies which the company had made its own.

d Inoshiro Honda p Tomoyuki Tanaka s Shinichi Sekizawa c Hajime Koizumi se Eiji Tsuburaya
lp Yoshio Tsuchiya, Kaoru Yachgusa, Tatsuya Mihashi, Keiko Sata, Bokuzen Hidari

Invasion of the Animal People aka Terror in the Midnight Sun aka Space Invasion from Lapland
(GUSTAF UNGER FILMS/A.B. FORTUNA; US,SW) 73(55) min

This Swedish-American co-production was shot on location in Lapland and benefits from the compulsively eerie landscape of the territory. A spaceship lands and releases a giant stone-age monster, which goes on the rampage. After much carnage, it's recaptured by the aliens who then return to their distant planet. The film was severely cut for its American

The low-budget sets of Edgar G. Ulmer's impressive Beyond the Time Barrier.

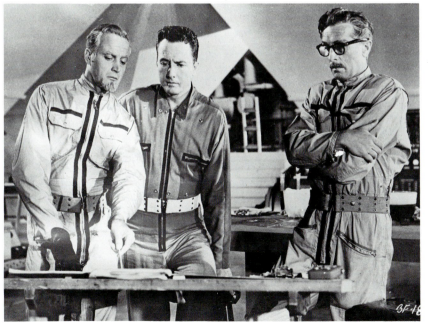

release and new footage (of Carradine as both performer and narrator) inserted. This had the effect of transforming what was clearly originally a mysterious film into one that is all too predictable in which a geologist and his niece Wilson foil an invasion from outer space.

d Virgil Vogel, Jerry Warren   *p* Bertil Jernberg, (*US version*) Jerry Warren   *s* Arthur C. Pierce   *c* Hilding Bladh   *lp* John Carradine, Bengt Blomgren, Ake Grönberg, Barbara Wilson, Robert Burton, Sten Gester, Jack Heffner

Konga   (MERTON PARK/HERMAN COHEN; GB, US)   90 min
Cohen had made **I Was a Teenage Werewolf** (1957) and originally intended to call this silly film *I Was a Teenage Gorilla*. The film features Gough as the university professor who brings back a special enzyme-producing plant that is capable of transforming animals into giants and a little chimpanzee called Konga from his travels in the African jungle. Konga receives some of the enzyme and, in a particularly inept special effect, shoots through the roof to become a giant ape. Johns is Gough's girlfriend and one-time British pop star Conrad the earnest student who helps track down the marauding giant ape.

d John Lemont   *p/co-s* Herman Cohen   *co-s* Aben Kandel (Kenneth Langtry)   *c* Desmond Dickinson   *lp* Michael Gough, Margo Johns, Jess Conrad, Claire Gordon, Austin Trevor, Jack Watson

The Last Woman on Earth

(FILMGROUP)   scope   71 min
A fascinating minimalist film – three characters in an apocalyptic story about the end of the world! – *The Last Woman on Earth* survives its low low budget and terrible acting (the budget only extended to ferrying the crew and actors to Puerto Rico so, to finish the script, writer Towne became actor Wain) through Corman's transformation of the slight material through his, almost ritualistic, directorial style which makes resonant even the corniest of images such as a climax in a deserted church.

A small-time gangster (Carbone), his wife (Jones-Moreland) and a young lawyer (Towne) flee to an isolated island off Puerto Rico and unwittingly escape the nuclear

Michael Gough and the chimpanzee he transforms into a giant ape in Konga.

conflagration that destroys the rest of humanity. The clichéd romantic triangle that follows as the men struggle for possession of Jones-Moreland and the future is treated allegorically, rather than melodramatically, by Corman. Carbone wants to rebuild the world (almost in the image of the old) while Towne wants to simply live out his days as pleasurably as possible. The result is a film that, despite its tacky surface, has the vision of the best of Science Fiction writing, a rare occurence in American Science Fiction films of the period.

d/p Roger Corman   *s* Robert Towne   *c* Jack Marquette
lp Anthony Carbone, Betsy Jones-Moreland, Edward Wain (Robert Towne)

The Leech Woman

(JOSEPH GERSCHENSON PRODUCTIONS)   b/w   77 min
Bud Westmore's striking makeup is the most notable feature of this workmanlike offering, the last to be directed by Dein, a Poverty Row regular. Deep in the jungle, the unloved wife (Gray) of scientist Terry discovers he's about to try out a youth serum on her. She decides she'd rather experiment on him and has Terry killed according to a local tribal ritual, which allows the murder of the husband to resurrect a wife's beauty. The secret ingredient of the transformation is the pineal gland of a live human male, so not only is the killing drawn out, it is also continual – the glands only last a short time. Her murderous foray is finally halted by Williams, whereupon she turns to dust.

d Edward Dein   *p* Joseph Gerschenson   *s* David Duncan
c Francis Rosenwald   *lp* Coleen Gray, Grant Williams, Phillip Terry, Gloria Talbot, John Van Dreelen, Estelle Hemsley

The Little Shop of Horrors

(SANTA CLARA)   b/w   70 min
Undoubtedly the best movie ever made in two days, *The Little Shop of Horrors* is possibly also the funniest Science Fiction horror film ever. Directed with gusto by Corman and acted with aching delight by its cast (which includes an early performance by Nicholson as the masochist who turns down all offers of pain relief from a sadistic dentist), the movie has a verve about it that its slim budget cannot suppress. Thus, once Haze's anaemic flower assistant has discovered that the new species of plant he has accidentally created has a liking for blood, and the film has established its own level, however

Left: Coleen Gray as The Leech Woman, *one of the several low-budget rejuvenation films of the early sixties.*

Right: *A smiling Kenneth More watched by Michael Hordern (left) in the weak British farce*, Man in the Moon.

tatty the sets are, however silly the plant's angry cries of 'feed me, feed me' are on further reflection, our commitment to the film has been secured. Unlike many of the really bad Science Fiction films (such as the infamous **Plan 9 from Outer Space**, 1956) that have become cult classics in recent years because their ineptitude and total lack of imagination invite laughter, *The Little Shop of Horrors* invites us to laugh with it, as in the sequences where various bodies are fed to the plant, *and* to care for Haze's down-trodden little man desperately trying to extend his stay in the sun just a little longer. Hence the end is both appropriate and dramatically satisfying. At the ceremony in Haze's honour mounted by the horticutural world, the plant's leaves open to reveal the faces of its victims reflected on its leaves whereupon Haze commits suicide by diving into it, taking a knife along with him to kill it.

An amazing film.

d/p Roger Corman   *s* Charles B. Griffith   *c* Arch Dalzell
lp Jonathan Haze, Jackie Joseph, Mel Welles, Dick Miller, Jack Nicholson, Myrtle Vail

Man in the Moon

(ALLIED FILM MAKERS/EXCALIBUR; GB)   b/w   99 min
This dated British spoof stars More as Mr Normal, who earns his living as a medical guinea-pig. When prize money is offered for an astronaut to take part in a pioneering moonshot, More volunteers. The film begins promisingly enough, with a satiric edge to its humour, but soon descends to the level of a Norman Wisdom-like farce.

d Basil Dearden   *p/co-s* Michael Relph   *co-s* Bryan Forbes
c Harry Waxman   *lp* Kenneth More, Shirley Ann Field, Michael Hordern, Noel Purcell, Charles Gray, John Phillips, Norman Bird

Neutron Contra el Dr Caronte

(ESTUDIOS AMERICA/PRODUCCIONES CORSA; MEX)   80 min
The sequel to **Neutron el Enmascarado Negro** (1960), also shot at the America Studios in three parts with the same production team and cast. In spite of the end of *Neutron el Enmascarado Negro*, Dr Caronte (Aleman) wasn't dead after all. A new figure emerges, Marchik, who seeks to obtain Caronte's secret formula for the neutron bomb. Since Caronte's robots have eliminated Marchik's pistoleros, the latter invokes the help of Neutron, the Black Masked wrestler (Ruvinskis) and his friends. Nevertheless, the evil doctor manages to kill Marchik and abduct the good Dr Thomas and Nora (Arenas). Neutron succeeds in turning the automatons

against their creator and rescuing Nora, who finds that her masked hero is none other than her fiancé, Carlos. The third picture in the series, **Los Automatas de la Muerte** (1960), sees the final confrontation between Caronte's robots and Neutron. Shot with the other two titles in 1960 to constitute a challenge to the status of Santo, the Silver Masked wrestler, the pictures were released together in 1962.

d Federico Curiel   *p* Emilio Gomez Muriel   *s* Alfredo Ruanova   *c* Fernando Alvarez Garces Colin   *lp* Wolf Ruvinskis, Julio Aleman, Armando Silvestre, Rosita Arenas, Roberto Ramirez, Rodolfo Landa, Trio Los Diamantes, Los Tres Ases

Neutron el Enmascarado Negro

(ESTUDIOS AMERICA/PRODUCCIONES CORSA; MEX)   80 min
Shot in the America Studios, which was only allowed to make short films, this picture was made in three parts designed to be joined later into a feature. The same process applied to the other two titles, shot immediately afterwards, continuing the adventures of Neutron, the Black Masked wrestler (Ruvinskis), **Neutron Contra el Doctor Caronte** and **Los Automatas de la Muerte** (both 1960). This first instalment introduces the main characters: Neutron, Dr Caronte, the good Dr Thomas and a group of Neutron's friends including Nora (Arenas) and a TV reporter. The plot has Dr Caronte (Aleman), the leader of a group of scientists who invent a neutron bomb with which he plans to achieve world domination. In the end, the bomb is neutralized and the evil doctor, it seems, eliminated. However, at the beginning of the next feature, he is alive and well. The three Neutron movies were shot back to back starting in September 1960, but they weren't released until the spring of 1962.

d Federico Curiel   *p* Emilio Gomez Muriel   *s* Alfredo Ruanova   *c* Fernando Alvarez Garces Colin   *lp* Wolf Ruvinskis, Julio Aleman, Armando Silvestre, Rosita Arenas, Roberto Ramirez, Claudio Brook, David Lama, Trio Los Diamantes, Los Tres Ases

Orlak, el Infierno de Frankenstein *aka* Orlak, the Hell of Frankenstein

(FILMADORA INDEPENDIENTE; MEX)   103 min
The Frankenstein monster appeared in a number of Mexican fantasy pictures including **El Castillo de los Monstruos** (1958), **Frankenstein, el Vampiro y Compania** (1961), **El Monstruo Resucitado** (1953) and **Santo Contra la Hija de Frankenstein** (1971) but Orlak remains the main Mexican incarnation of the creature. The plot has ex-convict Jaime (Cordero) liberate Frankenstein (Soler) from jail. The doctor introduces his benefactor to his creature, Orlak (also played by Cordero): a remote-controlled body with a metal skeleton, who is able to speak, survives on blood, is afraid of fire and

Jonathan Haze (left) and the plant with a difference he breeds in the marvellous The Little Shop of Horrors.

walks the streets dressed in black, with a black cape and a sombrero. Jaime uses Orlak to destroy those who sent him to prison and to take revenge on his unfaithful lover, the third-rate singer Estela (de Castilla). His new love is Elvira (Dorantes), the daughter of a judge, whose beauty also attracts Orlak. In one of the more impressive sequences, Orlak walks off with Elvira in his arms in a classic beauty-and-the-beast image. Another scene offers an interesting variation on the celebrated passage in Whale's **Frankenstein** (1931) where the creature meets a child. Here, the monster is seen struggling against his overwhelming desire to kill the infant, which seems a more logical plot situation than the Victorian motif used in the original.

Director Baledon was a matinée idol in the forties and graduated to direction with *Amor de Locura* (1952). He acquired the reputation of being an extremely fast worker, which made him the darling of the fast-buck producers. He dabbled in all the Mexican genres, including a remake of Ford's *My Darling Clementine* (*Mi Adorada Clementina*, 1953). His best-known work was *Los Salvajes* (1957), starring Pedro Armendariz. *Orlak* was shot in the America Studios, licensed only to make shorts and newsreels, feature film production being reserved for the rival union based at the Churubusco-Azteca studios. America Studio *cinéastes* often got around this restriction by making their films in instalments designed to be edited together later as a feature. *Orlak* was such a product, made in four episodes.

d/p Rafael Baledon   *s* Alfredo Ruanova, Carlos Enrique Taboada   *c* Fernando Alvarez Garces Colin   *lp* Joaquin Cordero, Armando Calvo, Andres Soler, Rosa de Castilla, Irma Dorantes, Pedro de Aguillon, David Reynoso, Carlos Ancira, Carlos Nieto

Rat *aka* **War**   (JADRAN FILM; YUG)   b/w   84 min
The godfather of Italian neo-realism wrote this post-atomic-war parable as his contribution to the ban the bomb campaigns of the period. In Zavattini's characteristically melodramatic way, the film tells of a marriage interrupted by the outbreak of war and the couple finding themselves, marriage still unconsummated, amongst the few survivors of an A-bomb explosion. As they roam through devastated cityscapes reminiscent of Hiroshima, it emerges that the strain has proved too much for the woman and she goes mad. The Italian trained (Centro Sperimentale) director succeeds in creating some harrowing scenes of desolation although the actual effects of such a war appear curiously under-estimated. The finger of blame is squarely pointed towards politicians irresponsible enough to conceive of nuclear war as an option. Shot on location with a decidedly documentary flavour, the photography is rough and stark. Bulajic became best known for his features dealing with national history but his international reputation is based on the documentary account he provided of the earthquake-stricken *Skopje 63* (1964).

The next Yugoslav Science Fiction fantasy was their answer to England's **Lord of the Flies** (1963), **Sedmi Kontinent** (1966).

d Velko Bulajic   *s* Cesare Zavattini   *c* Kresko Grcevic
lp Anton Vrdoljak, Eva Krzyzewski, Ita Rina, Tana Mascarelli, Janez Vrhovic, Lyubisa Jovanovic, Velimir (Bata) Zivojinovic

Der Schweigende Stern, *the first influential postwar space opera from Eastern Europe.*

Der Schweigende Stern *aka* Raumschiff Venus Antwortet Nicht *aka* The Silent Star *aka* First Spaceship on Venus *aka* Milczaca Gwiazda *aka* The Astronauts

(DEFA/ILLUZJON FILM UNIT; EG, POL)   scope   94(109, 78) min
Echoing the title of the well-known **F.P.1 Antwortet Nicht** (1932), this film inaugurated a series of Eastern European space operas (**Planeta Burg**, 1962; **Meshte Nastreshu**, 1963; **Ikarie XB-1**, 1963) no doubt following the flights of Sputnik (1957) and Gagarin (1961). This primarily East German film was shot in 1959-60, set in 1970 (English and US versions moved that forward to 1985) and based on Poland's most famous Science Fiction writer's first novel, Stanislaw Lem's *The Astronauts* published in 1951.

All peoples on Earth are living in harmony. Scientists discover a magnetic spool containing a message from Venus that refers to an attack. An international commission sends an expedition to Venus in Kosmokrator 1 (in English Cosmostrator), with a crew which includes a chess-playing robot. On Venus, they discover the ruins of a very advanced civilization that fell victim to its own destructive impulses. The pacifist message dovetails with US films on the same theme (supporting ban the bomb campaigns), such as **On the Beach** (1959) or **Beyond the Time Barrier** (1960).

Lem's later work veered more towards interplanetary paranoia, as in **Solaris**, published in 1961 and filmed in 1971, and **Test Pilota Pirxa** (1978). The director, Maetzig, was co-founder of the post-war film industry in East Germany and remained its most prestigious exponent well into the sixties. The cast is notable mainly for its international character and unknown in the West except for Tani, the female lead in *The Quiet American* (1958), *The Savage Innocents* (1959), **Invasion** (1966) and many other films. The sets, especially those representing the dead Venusian city, the weird landscapes and angry volcanoes are Anatol Radzinowicz's best work, excelling his designs for the children's fairytale *O Dwoch Takich Co

Left: Seddok, l'Ereda di Sarona, *another in the cycle of rejuvenation movies and, more significantly, one of the first Italian Science Fiction films.*

Ukradli Ksiezyc (1962). Released in the US in a dubbed version in 1963, the film apparently ran 15 minutes longer than the original, while the English copy was 31 minutes shorter than the American. This version was produced by Hugo Grimaldi, the producer of a number of fantasy films including **The Human Duplicators** (1965), a film he also directed.

d/co-s Kurt Maetzig   *co-s* Jan Fethke, Wolfgang Kohlaase, Guenther Reisch, Guenther Ruecker, Alexander Graf Stenbock-Fermor   *c* Joachim Hasler   *se* Ernst Kunstmann, Vera Kunstmann, Jan Olejniczale, Helmut Grewald, Martin Sonnabend   *lp* Yoko Tani, Oldrich Lukes, Ignacy Machowski, Julius Ongewe, Michail Postnikow, Kurt Rackelmann, Guenther Simon, Tan Hua-ta, Lucinna Winnicka, Ruth-Maria Kubitschek

Seddok, l'Erede di Santana *aka* Atom Age Vampire
(TOPAZ; IT)   b/w   105(87) min

Similar in theme to Roger Corman's **The Wasp Woman** (1960), this routine Italian offering is noteworthy as the only essay in production of Bava, Italy's best-known director of horror and Science Fiction whose credits include such films as **Diabolik** (1967) and **Terrore nello Spazio** (1965). Hideously scarred singer Loret's beauty is temporarily restored by scientist Lupo's serum which has to be taken from dead women. The serum's effects don't last long and a continuous supply of dead women has to be found before Loret is finally eliminated by Fantoni.

co-d/co-s Anton Guilio Majano   *co-d* Richard McNamara   *p* Mario Bava   *co-s* Piero Monviso, Gino de Sanctis, Alberto Bevilacqua, John Hart   *c* Aldo Giordano   *se* Ugo Amadoro   *lp* Alberto Lupo, Susanne Loret, Sergio Fantoni, Roberto Berta, Franca Paridi Strahl

Space Men *aka* Assignment Outer Space
(TITANUS/ULTRA FILM; IT)   73 min

One of the strengths of even the worst of Italian Science Fiction is the visual sense of its designers and set decorators. In contrast to the angular predictability of most British and American Science Fiction, the space stations, moons and asteroids of Italian Science Fiction have an imaginative vibrancy about them that connects as much with fantasy as with the sober, however pulp inspired, Anglo-American predictions of the look of the future. When, in addition, such films are directed by the likes of Bava (whose **Terrore nello Spazio**, 1965, is the masterpiece of the genre) or, as here, Margheriti, a director with an equally keen visual style, the results can be superb.

This, his first film, is not one of Margheriti's best, the narrative line is unclear and jerky (a common fault in the director's work), but its visual splendours are ample compensation. Von Nutter is the reporter who, while visiting an orbiting space station, stops a runaway rocket under the control of its electronic brain and Farinon is the romantic interest.

Margheriti's other Science Fiction films include **Il Pianeta degli Uomini Spenti** (1961), his best work, **I Diavolo della Spazio**, **I Diafanoidi Portano la Morte** and the superior **I Criminali della Galassia** (all 1965) and **Il Pianeta Errante** (1966).

d Antonio Margheriti   *s* Vassily Petrov   *c* Marcello Maciocchi   *se* Caesar Peace   *lp* Rik von Nutter, Gabriella Farinon, David Montressor, Archie Savage, Alain Dijon, Franco Fantasia

Die Tausend Augen des Dr Mabuse *aka* The Thousand Eyes of Dr Mabuse *aka* The Diabolical Dr Mabuse
(CCC-FILM/CRITERION/CEI-INCOM; WG, FR, IT)   b/w   103 min

After a successful career in the USA, Lang accepted an offer to film in Germany again, where he made his last two films, gloriously crowning a long and distinguished filmography with this sequel to his own prewar Mabuse films (**Dr Mabuse, der Spieler**, 1922, and **Das Testament des Dr Mabuse**, 1933). The spirit of Mabuse, who died in an asylum in the 1933 film, was kept alive by the Third Reich mentality, ready for a reincarnation. Inspired by a Nazi blueprint for bugging a hotel, Lang invented the Hotel Luxor with its two-way mirrors and TV cameras hidden in every ornament, transmitting images down to the basement where Mabuse's successor, Professor Jordan (Preiss) presides over his worldwide criminal organization, keeping tabs on everybody via an enormous bank of monitors. The story has Travers (Van Eyck) about to acquire an atomic plant and becoming involved in mysterious events with a blind clairvoyant, Dr Cornelius, and Marion (Addams). The climax in the basement of the hotel Luxor and the car chase that ends with the apparent drowning of Mabuse's executioner (Vernon), offer some of Lang's most deliriously cinematic sequences, as light pierces pools of darkness and the power of *mise en scene*, of vision, is multiplied a thousandfold in the realm of the blind seer. In addition, the film's relentless suspense hinges on a 'blind spot' assumed amongst the viewers: Cornelius and Jordan are played by the same actor who also disguised his name on the credits so as not to give the game away too soon. The result is a breathless, complex and awesome piece of cinema meditating on the imbrication of looking and power, with its myriad possibilities of masquerades, disguises, pretenses, false appearances etc, all giving the lie to the proverb that seeing is believing. Lang proposes instead: seeing is believing the wrong thing because you never see what you believe you are seeing. The film was so powerful it spawned another five sequels, merely trading on Lang's achievement: **Im Stahlnetz des Dr Mabuse** (1961), **Die Unsichtbaren Krallen des Dr Mabuse** (1961), **Das Testament des Dr Mabuse** (1962), **Scotland Yard Jagt Dr Mabuse** (1963) and **Die Todesstrahlen des Dr Mabuse** (1964).

d/p/co-s Fritz Lang   *co-s* Heinz Oskar Wuttig   *c* Karl Loeb   *lp* Peter Van Eyck, Dawn Addams, Gert Froebe, Wolfgang Preiss (Lupo Prezzo), Werner Peters, Andrea Cecchi, Reinhard Koldehoff, Christiane Maybach, Howard Vernon, Nico Pepe

The Time Machine   (GALAXY FILMS/MGM)   103 min
Although Pal didn't update H.G. Wells' novel, as he had done **The War of the Worlds** (1953), he and writer Duncan emasculated it in the interests of simplicity to such an extent that little of Wells' original vision remains. The novel reflected the class divisions of Victorian society and cast them into the future where the Eloi and Morlocks were crude caricatures of the effete aristocrats and brutalized working class of Wells' times. The film also omits Wells' pessimistic view of the evolutionary process that concludes the novel. In their place, Pal mounts a glossy, all too cosy, confection, best remembered for its Oscar-winning special effects, in which Taylor's time traveller rouses the gentle Eloi (rather in the manner of the hero of Mark Twain's *A Connecticut Yankee in King Arthur's Court*, another novel of social criticism of the time, filmed in 1931 as **A Connecticut Yankee**) with his hearty brand of individualism to do battle against the troglodyte-like Morlocks. Accordingly, though the opening section with its Victorian bric-à-brac and William Ferrar's charming time machine, is promising, once Taylor sets forth on his voyages through time the film quickly loses the disturbing possibilities that made Wells' novel so exciting.

The Time Machine, which was one of MGM's biggest grossing films of 1960, was also Pal's most financially successful production.

d/p George Pal   *s* David Duncan   *c* Paul C. Vogel   *se* Gene Warren, Tim Barr, Wah Chang   *lp* Rod Taylor, Alan Young, Yvette Mimieux, Whit Bissell, Sebastian Cabot, Tom Helmore

Above: *Barbara Shelley confronts the fact that Martin Stephens is not quite her son in* Village of the Damned.

Rod Taylor takes on the Morlocks in George Pal's indifferent The Time Machine.

12 to the Moon (LUNA) b/w 74 min
A companion piece to Gebhardt's **The Phantom Planet** (1961), this is a decidedly minor offering, the presence of Bodeen (writer of *Cat People*, 1942) and Alton, one of Hollywood's unsung cinematographic geniuses, notwithstanding. The Lunar Eagle 1 is on a voyage to the Moon with a democratically international crew of 12. First, one of the spacemen dies from a stream of molten silver and then lunar dust kills another while the rest of the crew are continuously pelted with meteors on an inhospitable landscape. There is no sign of a population initially but air-pockets in caves lead to a subterranean world where the Moon men lurk. Anxious to teach man the error of his ways, they threaten to freeze Earth unless mankind stops making war. Suitably chastened, the expedition returns home.

d David Bradley   *p* Fred Gebhardt   *s* DeWitt Bodeen
c John Alton   *se* Howard A. Anderson, E. Nicholson
lp Ken Clark, Anthony Dexter, Francis X. Bushman, Tom Conway, Robert Montgomery Jnr, John Wengraf

Village of the Damned (MGM; GB) b/w 77 min
John Wyndham, who died in 1969, was one of the most widely read Science Fiction writers of the fifties and this film is based on *The Midwich Cuckoos*, one of his best works. The film is remarkably faithful to the novel, but Rilla's direction is surprisingly pedestrian, failing to make enough of the enigmatic world Wyndham creates.

The inhabitants of an English village fall into a trance-like sleep for 24 hours, at the end of which time every woman in the community discovers she is pregnant. All the highly intelligent offspring are of similar appearance, have telepathic powers and one-group minds. Sanders (who gives a calculatingly icy performance) and his wife Shelley, parents of one of the children David (Stephens) realize that the children are aliens, sent from another planet to invade Earth. Sanders' suspicions are detected by the children and, by now sure that the 'children's' intentions are malevolent, he sets out for the school with a bomb. He creates a mental brick wall between himself and the advanced minds of the children but, in the film's best sequence, they literally tear down the mental bricks one by one. Eventually the bomb explodes and they are all killed.

A superior remake followed in 1963 **Children of the Damned**, which used an urban setting to much greater effect. Both films make for a fascinating comparison, especially in terms of the radically different views parents take of 'foreign' offspring, with Larry Cohen's **It's Alive** (1973) and its sequel **It Lives Again** (1978).

d/co-s Wolf Rilla   *p* Ronald Kinnoch   *co-s* Stirling Silliphant, George Barclay   *c* Geoffrey Faithfull
se Tom Howard   *lp* George Sanders, Barbara Shelley, Martin Stephens, Michael Gwynne, Laurence Naismith, Richard Vernon, John Phillips

Visit to a Small Planet
(PAR/WALLIS-HAZEN PRODUCTIONS) b/w 85 min
Made just before Lewis made the switch from acting to directing (as well as acting) with *The Bellboy* (1960), *Visit to a Small Planet* is as much Lewis' film as it is Taurog's. However, the film's origins (Gore Vidal's 1957 satirical Broadway play) and its subject matter (the confrontation of Lewis' rational visitor from outer space with emotional humans) are too limiting for Lewis' immensely individualistic humour. Vidal, needless to say, was decidedly unhappy with the result.

Blackman is the girl Lewis falls for and Clark the opinionated TV newscaster and firm disbeliever in flying saucers and the ilk in whose garden Lewis lands.

d Norman Taurog   *p* Hal B. Wallis   *s* Edmund Beloin, Henry Garson   *c* Loyal Griggs   *se* John P. Fulton   *lp* Jerry Lewis, Joan Blackman, Earl Holliman, Fred Clark, Lee Patrick, Gale Gordon

The Wasp Woman
(FILMGROUP/SANTA CLARA) b/w 73 (66) min
A minor entry from Corman, *The Wasp Woman* was the first production of his Filmgroup company. Like so many of the rejuvenation films of the twenties (**Black Oxen, Sinners in Silk, Vanity's Price**, all 1924), it takes for its premise the

Susan Cabot as The Wasp Woman.

search for eternal youth and its costs. Cabot is fine as the cosmetic queen who, worried about her wrinkles, turns to demented scientist Marks and his wasp enzymes. The predictable result sees Cabot beautiful again until after-effects turn her into a wasp at night. She murders some of her employees and is eventually bundled through a window, only to discover that she can't fly. Gordon's script is intelligent but Corman fails to make the wasp-woman's activities sufficiently frightening.

d/p Roger Corman *s* Leo Gordon *c* Harry Newman
lp Susan Cabot, Fred Eisley, Barboura Morris, Michael Marks, William Roerick, Frank Gerstle

1961

The Absent-Minded Professor
(WALT DISNEY) b/w 97 min
MacMurray is the absent-minded professor of the title – he missed his own wedding twice – who invents an anti-gravity flying rubber, Flubber, and Olson his long-suffering fiancée in this sprightly directed Disney offering. He uses it to enhance a losing kids' basketball game and plants it into his model T Ford engine and flies off into the clouds – he even gets as far as Washington, where he's at first treated as a UFO, and tries to convince Congress of the importance of his discovery. The deft direction of Stevenson, MacMurray's fine performance and excellent special effects are under-pinned by Walsh's anti-authoritarian screenplay which mocks red tape and official mumbo-jumbo in a surprisingly successful manner. The film's enormous success led to a sequel, **Son of Flubber** (1963).

d Robert Stevenson *p* Walt Disney *s* Bill Walsh
c Edward Colman *se* Peter Ellenshaw, Eustace Lycett, Robert A. Malley, Joshua Meador *lp* Fred MacMurray, Nancy Olson, Keenan Wynn, Tommy Kirk, Ed Wynn, Leon Ames, Wally Brown, Alan Carney

L'Atlantide – Antinée l'Amante della Citta Sepolta
aka **Journey Beneath the Desert**
(CCM/FIDES; FR, IT) 100 (89) min
This is one of the many versions of Pierre Benoît's fantasy novel *L'Atlantide*, which include **Die Herren von Atlantis** (1932) and **Siren of Atlantis** (1949). Ulmer, whose best Science Fiction film is **The Man from Planet X** (1951), despondently directs a dull plot which has three lost helicopter pilots (Trintignant, Fulton and Riviere) find the entrance to Atlantis near a desert H-bomb test site. Despite some stunning visual sequences (notably those in the shadowy tunnels that lead to Atlantis and its cruel queen, Harareet), the film is slow-moving and both dubbing and voice synchronization poor.

d Edgar G. Ulmer, Giuseppe Masini (uncredited Frank Borzage) *p* Nat Watchberger *s* Ugo Liberatore, Remigio des Grosso, André Tabet, Armedo Nazzari *c* Enzo Serafin *se* Giovanni Ventimiglia *lp* Jean-Louis Trintignant, Haya Harareet, Georges Riviere, Rad Fulton, Armedo Nazzari, Gabriella Tinti, Gianmaria Volonte

Le Avventure di Topo Gigio *aka* The Magic World of Topo Gigio *aka* The Italian Mouse
(JOLLY FILM/CINECIDI/COMPAGNIA PEREGO TELECAST; IT) 85(75) min
An animated puppet film in which Topo Gigio, the mouse created and animated by Perego, joins with his friends Rosy and the cowardly worm Giovannino in building a rocket to the Moon. However, the flight goes wrong and they land in an amusement park where they perform with a friendly puppeteer to the children's delight. A jealous magician kidnaps Rosy but Topo Gigio manages to humiliate the magician and liberate his friend. The picture then provided two alternative endings. In one, they defeat the magician and make their escape from the fairground, in the other they get the nasty magician to reform and to join up with the friendly puppeteer. An English-language version was produced by Richard Davis and directed by Luca de Rico. The effects are not particularly striking nor the characters particularly seductive, but the technical side of the puppet animation is competently handled.

d/co-s Federico Caldura *p/co-s* Mario Perego *c* Giorgio Battilana *se* Ettore Catalucca

The Beast of Yucca Flats
(CARDOZA-FRANCIS FILMS) b/w 60 min
Francis wrote and directed this crudely made piece about a Russian scientist (Johnson, once better known as a wrestler than an actor but now a cult star following the re-release of films like this and the infamous **Plan 9 from Outer Space**, 1956), who is chased into an A-bomb test area by communist agents when he defects to America. Narration takes over from sparse dialogue (an indication of the film's low, low budget) when Johnson is turned into a fiend who goes on the rampage, as a result of exposure to radiation. After kidnapping and murdering several local residents, he is eventually killed by Mellor's intrepid policeman.

d/s Coleman Francis *p* Anthony Cardoza *c* John Cagle
lp Tor Johnson, Douglas Mellor, Larry Afen, Barbara Francis, Bing Stafford, Tony Cardoza

Chelovek Amfibia *aka* The Amphibious Man
(LENFILM; USSR) 96 min
A combination of *Aquaman* and **The Creature from the Black Lagoon** (1954). Ichtiandr (Korenev) is the son of Dr Salvator (Simonov), a marine biologist who managed to make his boy a perfectly amphibious creature. The sea devil, as he is known locally, saves the beautiful Guttiera (Vertinskaya) from the sea and they fall in love, but as she is forced to marry the rich owner of the fishing fleet, Korenev loses her, looks for her in cities far and wide, gets imprisoned and generally maltreated. This eventually impairs his amphibious abilities, forcing him to return to the sea for good. This aquatic *Love Story* (1970) proved an unexpected popular success with sentimental teenagers throughout the USSR and received the Silver Spaceship at the 1963 Trieste Festival for its 'poetic qualities'. The story was taken from a novel by Aleksander Bielajew. Vertinskaya, the very pretty heroine, went on to become one

It's a bird, it's a plane, it's . . . The Absent-Minded Professor.

Shirley Anne Field is contaminated as she tries to rescue one of the children in The Damned, *one of the highpoints of the British Science Fiction film.*

of the USSR's outstanding young actresses, appearing as Ophelia opposite Smoktunovsky's Hamlet in Kozintsev's famous *Gamlet* (1964).

d Guennadi Kazansky, Vladimir Chebotarev   *s* Akiba Golburt, Aleksander Ksenofontov, Aleksei Kapler   *c* Edouard Rasovski   *lp* Vladimir Korenev, Anastasia Vertinskaya, Nikolai Simonov, Mikhail Kozakov, Anatoli Smiranin, Vladen Davidov

The Damned *aka* These Are the Damned

(HAMMER/SWALLOW; GB)   b/w   scope   96 (87, 77) min
Despite being butchered by its producers (and its release being delayed for some two years), *The Damned* remains, with the Quatermass trilogy, the highpoint of the first wave of the British postwar Science Fiction film. Jones' script (written in close collaboration with Losey) neatly twists and turns its way from the most unlikely of openings – Carey attacked by Reed (who, in true Losey style, has hardly repressed incestuous designs on his sister, Field) and his gang of leather-clad motor bikers with sadistic glee in dingy Weymouth – to a compelling ending – a helicopter hovering above Carey and Field, now lovers and dying, poisoned by the irradiated children they have set free, drifting out to sea, as if to finally cleanse themselves, while behind them they leave the wailing children who can't survive outside the protected environment they've been prised from.

The film's starting point, scientist Knox's attempts to deal with the awesome effects of radiation that will follow a nuclear war, is hardly new in Science Fiction, but Losey brings to his plan to rear a gaggle of irradiated children, who will be able to live after the (inevitable) nuclear holocaust, a chilling intensity that is wholly fresh. Moreover, the power of the central image, the isolated children being prepared for a world in which their silver-suited keepers cannot survive and only able to communicate with their 'father' by TV, is reflected throughout the film in numerous ways, all of which deepen the disturbing sense of self-delusion that the major characters share. Thus Knox's girlfriend, Lindfors, who thinks the secret establishment is where Knox keeps his new mistress, is a sculptress of bird-like figures (actually made by Elizabeth Frink) that look like the charred corpses a nuclear war will produce in abundance and her one 'bird of freedom' sculpture is ironically transmuted in the climax to the helicopter hovering over the doomed lovers – an image Losey would

Right: The deserted newsroom of the Daily Express *in* The Day the Earth Caught Fire.

return to and extend in *Figures in a Landscape* (1970). Similarly the children, who Carey and Field discover by accident, represent the children their escapist romance will not produce and they set them free as much as a token of commitment to each other than out of misplaced righteous indignation. Yet another strand of the film's imagery equates Reed and Knox, gangleaders both.

It is this, the richness of Losey's images, caught in the brittle grey cinematography of Grant in which sea and sky are omnipresent, rather than the shock content of the story that makes the film so powerful. The film won the Golden Asteroid at the 1964 Trieste festival of Science Fiction films.

d Joseph Losey   *p* Anthony Hinds   *s* Evan Jones
c Arthur Grant   *lp* Macdonald Carey, Shirley Anne Field, Viveca Lindfors, Alexander Knox, Oliver Reed, James Villiers, Walter Gotell

The Day the Earth Caught Fire

(BRITISH LION/PAR; GB)   b/w   scope   99 (90) min
In marked contrast to **The Quatermass Xperiment** (1955), which was also directed by Guest, this is a slickly made confection, its documentary style notwithstanding. Two simultaneous nuclear tests at the North and South Poles disturb the Earth's orbit and send the planet shooting towards the Sun. Bizarrely enough, the salvation of mankind is found in the release of four atomic bombs which push the Earth back into its proper orbit. The film's sense of drama is best captured in the central sequence in the composing room of the *Daily Express* (where much of the action takes place with its former editor, Arthur Christiansen, gleefully playing himself). After two of the bombs have been detonated the camera pans between two pre-set front pages: one reads 'World Saved', the other 'World Doomed'.

Bowie's special effects are convincing – in particular the sequence in which the Thames dries up – suggesting a far bigger budget than Guest had available.

d/p/co-s Val Guest   *co-s* Wolf Mankowitz   *c* Harry Waxman
se Les Bowie   *lp* Edward Judd, Janet Munro, Leo McKern, Michael Goodliffe, Bernard Braden, Reginald Beckwith

The Flight That Disappeared *aka* The Flight That Vanished

(HARVARD PRODUCTIONS)   b/w   73 (71) min
Nuclear physicist Lummis, research assistant Raymond and rocket propulsion expert Hill are en route by plane to a vital Pentagon meeting about a newly developed superbomb. The plane reaches a fantastic altitude and everyone blacks out,

regaining consciousness on a mysterious plateau in space where the trio of scientists are tried by a jury of future generations. Having been told to stop trying to destroy the future, the three destroy their notes on the superbomb and the plane is returned to Earth.

One of the last films of LeBorg, who spent most of his career on Poverty Row making B pictures for the likes of Monogram and Universal, this is an interesting, if minor, addition to the list of pacifist-inclined Science Fiction movies.

d Reginald LeBorg *p* Robert E. Kent *s* Ralph Hart, Judith Hart, Owen Harris *c* Gilbert Warrenton *se* Barney Wolff *lp* Craig Hill, Paula Raymond, Dayton Lummis, Gregory Morton, John Bryant, Addison Richards, Nancy Hale

Frankenstein, el Vampiro y Compania *aka* Frankenstein, the Vampire and Co.
(CINEMATOGRAFIA CALDERON; MEX) 80 min

A Mexican remake of **Abbott and Costello Meet Frankenstein** (1948) starring Agapito (Loco Valdes) and Paco (Jasso). The duo are to deliver the bodies of a vampire (Bulnes) and of Frankenstein's creature to a deserted castle, but the bodies come alive. The vampire plans for Dr Sofia (Veryan) to transplant the dim-witted Agapito's brain into the Frankenstein creature's body and then to send it on a mission to conquer the USA. The plan is foiled by the wolf man who interrupts the crucial operation. In the ensuing fight, the castle burns down killing both the werewolf and the vampire while the creature sinks into quicksand.

This was the fourth appearance of the Frankenstein monster in Mexican movies after **El Monstruo Resucitado** (1953), **Orlak, el Infierno de Frankenstein** (1960) and the comedy **El Castillo de los Monstruos** (1958) and surfaced again a number of times in the Santo series, wrestling with the Silver Masked hulk. Alazraki is best known as the director of *Raices* (1953), a neo-realist Mexican classic as stylized as any of the Italian neo-realist melodramas. However, the credit for *Raices* was probably due more to the input of the adventurous producer Manuel Barbachano Ponce and the extraordinary cameraman Walther Reuther. After some excellent productions, including one of the very few Mexican movies with Dolores del Rio (*¿Adonde Van Nuestros Hijos?*, 1956), Alazraki reverted to his own level of directing, contributing to the masked wrestler movies with *Santo Contra los Monstruos* (1961), the first of the long-running series.

d Benito Alazraki *p* Guillermo Calderon *s* Alfredo Salazar *c* Enrique Wallace *lp* Manuel Loco Valdes, José Jasso, Joaquin Garcia Vargas Borolas, Quintin Bulnes, Antonio Bravo, Jorge Mondragon, Martha Elena Cervantes, Nora Veryan, Roberto G. Rivera

Gorgo (KING BROTHERS; GB) 79 min

Director Lourié handles his scenes of crowd panic convincingly and Howard's special effects of the destruction of London are superb in this monster-rescues-its-young entry. A 250-foot mama monster comes to rescue her 65-foot son Gorgo from the circus he's been put on show in after his capture in the Irish Sea. She makes short work of most London landmarks before rescuing her baby and returning to the ocean depths. Lourié, originally Renoir's art designer, directed a number of monster films including the influential **The Beast from 20,000 Fathoms** (1953) and **Behemoth, the Sea Monster** (1959), both of which deal with monsters either returning to their old hunting grounds or seeking to rescue their young. This is the least interesting of his Science Fiction films.

d Eugène Lourié *p* Wilfred Eades *s* John Loring, Daniel Hyatt *c* F.A. Young *se* Tom Howard *lp* Bill Travers, William Sylvester, Vincent Winter, Christopher Rhodes, Joseph O'Connor, Bruce Seton

Mum to the rescue in Gorgo.

Los Invisibles (FILMADORA CHAPULTEPEC; MEX) 90 min

Following on from **Los Astronautas** (made in 1960 but not released until 1964), the Viruta and Capulina duo (Campos and Henaine) are on the trail of a jewel thief (Fajardo) with the aid of a paint invented by don Alberto (Chino Herrera) which can make people and objects invisible. However, the effects are only temporary and this flaw leads to the uncovering of the villain. The romantic interest of this silly farce is provided by don Alberto's daughters, Susana and Patricia (Cervantes and Gallardo), the lovers of the Abbott and Costello-type pair.

Salvador, a director of Spanish origin, began his career as the scenarist for the popular comedian Cantinflas before graduating to direction with some adaptations of French stories and comedies exclusively for local audiences. He became one of Mexico's most prolific directors and was responsible for Buster Keaton's saddest experience in cinema, the abysmal *El Moderno Barba Azul* (1946), as well as for the Abominable Snowman pictures *El Monstruo de los Volcanes* and *El Terrible Gigante de las Nieves* (both 1962). *Los Invisibles* was made in 1961 but not released until 1963, preceding by one year the release of the duo's *Los Astronautas* (1960).

d Jaime Salvador *p* Pedro Galindo *s* Roberto Gomez Bolaños *c* Jose Ortiz Ramos *lp* Marco Antonio Campos, Gaspar Henaine, Edouardo Fajardo, Martha Elena Cervantes, Rosa Maria Gallardo, Daniel Chino Herrera, Jose Jasso, Chucho Salinas, Lucila de Cordova

Journey to the Seventh Planet
(CINEMAGIC; DEN, US) 83 min

Featuring virtually the same cast and crew as Pink's **Reptilicus** (1962), this Danish-American co-production starts promisingly but quickly heads into all too predictable territory. In 2001, a United Nations exploration team, led by Agar, lands on Uranus and finds it protected by a 'brain' that feeds the team members images from their own consciousness. Thus, a homesick Swede finds a replica of his village, a man scared of rats is attacked by a giant rodent and all the crew meet duplicates of their girlfriends. By offering them this mix of seductive and frightening images the 'brain' hopes to scare them off the planet. However, too quickly this odd blend of **Forbidden Planet** (1956) and **Solaris** (1971) degenerates into silliness with the explorers defeating the brain when it materializes (by subjecting it to low temperatures) and so claiming Uranus for mankind.

d/p/co-s Sidney Pink   *co-s* Ib Melchior   *c* Aage Wiltrup *se* Bent Barford Films   *lp* John Agar, Greta Thyssen, Ann Smyrner, Mimi Heinrich, Carl Ottosen, Ove Sprogoe

La Marca del Muerto
(ALAMEDA FILMS; MEX)   b/w   80 min
This odd movie from the writers of **La Nave de los Monstruos** (1959) features Casanova as a Doctor Malthus. Searching for a compound that will bestow immortality upon him, Malthus' experiments with the blood of youthful victims lead him to the gallows in 1890. Swearing vengeance, he also discovers that his formula doesn't quite work: before dying, he sees himself ageing by 100 years. Apparently, the only way for the formula to work is to mix it with young blood and inject it directly into the heart. Seventy years later, a young doctor Malthus returns to Mexico from his medical studies in Europe, discovers his ancestor's laboratory and becomes fascinated by the record of the old doctor's experiments. He manages to locate the mummified corpse of the old man and to revive it with a young woman's blood. But he finds that his identical forefather (Casanova again) starts demanding more victims, including the young Malthus' fiancée, Rosa (Furio). At this, he balks and rebels against the old tyrant. In the end, the laboratory and Malthus burn while young Malthus and Rosa provide the happy resolution. It is interesting to speculate why the name of the most celebrated proponent of population control was used in this picture: perhaps as a form of resisting the theory of population control which expects third world people to accept draconian measures in order to safeguard the supply of food for the overfed first world.

Cortes is a Puerto Rican actor who graduated to directing with *La Picara Susanna* (1944), a comedy starring his wife Mapy Cortes. In Mexico, he remained a prolific director of vaudeville type pictures, often starring his wife, and fantasy and sexploitation films.

d/co-s Fernando Cortes   *p* Cesar Santos Galindo, Alfredo Ripstein Jnr   *co-s* Jose Maria Fernandez Unsain, Alfredo Varela Jnr   *c* Jose Ortiz Ramos   *lp* Fernando Casanova, Sonia Furio, Pedro de Aguillon, Aurora Alvarado, Rosa Maria Gallardo, Hortensia Santoveña, Edmundo Espino

Un Martien à Paris *aka* A Martian in Paris
(LES FILMS UNIVERS; FR)   b/w   87 min
Subtitled 'The Martian Letters' in an obvious pun on Pascal's *The Provincial Letters*, a satirical attack on the Jesuits, a film satirizing the inhabitants of Earth and their odd customs may be expected from the title. But Cowl, France's popular precursor of Marty Feldman, delivers only a manic solo of verbal and facial contortions. The Martians send Cowl to find out about the mysterious Earth disease called 'love' so that an antidote may be developed. But he catches the malady from Mirel in spite of her irascible father (Vilbert). The cheaply made farce starts well as the Martians watch the Earth on a large screen, expressing their incomprehension and concern at the behaviour they witness. The rest of the movie has Cowl as an incompetent seducer ogling women and indulging in his peculiar adaptations and imitations of Jerry Lewis. The scenarist Vilfrid, a regular collaborator of Cowl's, also penned material for that comic's even more manic successor, Louis de Funes, including **Le Gendarme et les Extraterrestres** (1978).

d/co-s Jean-Daniel Daninos   *p/co-s* Jacques Vilfrid *c* Marcel Combes   *lp* Darry Cowl, Nicole Mirel, Henri Vilbert, Gisèle Segur, Michele Verez, Pierre Louis

Master of the World   (AIP)   104 min
Based on Jules Verne's novel *Clipper of the Clouds* and its sequel *Master of the World*, this was one of AIP's earliest excursions into big-budget film-making. In 1848 mad scientist Robur (Price) creates a flying machine and holds the world to ransom: either the world outlaws war or he will destroy it. In effect, this film is an aerial version of *20,000 Leagues Under the Sea* (the successful filming of which in 1954 by Richard Fleischer had set in motion a Jules Verne bandwagon), complete with the Victorian notions of science of that novel (the *Albatross*, as Robur calls his ship, is a vast clippership made into a plane by the addition of huge rotor blades to the masts). Bronson is the government agent captured by Price in company with munitions' manufacturer Hull, his daughter Webster and her fiancé, Frankham. After witnessing the destruction of the Egyptian and Austrian armies, Bronson succeeds in destroying the *Albatross* and freeing its captives.

Script and direction are both surprisingly lightweight, perhaps because the problem of unifying the mood of the two novels was so great. The first (published in 1886) sees Robur as a visionary and idealist, the second (published in 1904) marks Verne's growing disenchantment and conceives of its hero as a clumsy, power-hungry megalomaniac. These tensions are repressed in the film in favour of an atmosphere in which adventure dominates.

d William Witney *p* James H. Nicholson *s* Richard
Matheson *c* Gil Warrenton *se* Ray Mercer, Tim Barr, Wah
Chang, Gene Warren *lp* Vincent Price, Charles Bronson,
Henry Hull, Mary Webster, Wally Campo, Vito Scotti, David
Frankham

Mosura *aka* **Mothra** (TOHO; JAP) scope 100 min
Unlike **Gojira** (1954) or **Rodan** (1956), or indeed the vast
majority of the creatures invented later on, Mothra is basically
a friendly creature. Its destructiveness is a result of being
wronged and of its awkward size. Mothra is also the only
major creature in the Kaiju Eiga genre which is female and, its
third distinctive mark, it is not played by a rubber-suited
actor. Instead, it is a contraption manipulated with strings.
All this makes Mothra one of the most interesting monsters in
the genre. The drama, based on a story by Shinichiro
Nakamura, is initiated with the theft of a huge egg and the
kidnapping of minuscule female twins called the Peanuts
Sisters (played by the Itoh Sisters) from an island that had
been used for H-bomb tests. The egg hatches and an
enormous larva creeps out. Mothra, angered by the theft of its
offspring and by the abduction of its two tiny guardians, sets
out to recover them, destroying much of Japan in the process,
although a great deal of the damage is caused unintentionally,
out of clumsiness. The movie ends happily with the reunifica-
tion of the giant moth and the miniature twins. They all
return to their island where henceforth the Peanuts Sisters
will control the enlarged symbol of femininity. Technically,
the operation of the moth contraption is awkward at times,
but this doesn't interfere with the mythical and ritualistic
aspects of monster scenarios, and Mothra became a popular
figure very quickly. It reappeared in **Mosura Tai Gojira**
(1964) where it was defeated by the titanic reptile, still a
'baddie' at the time, and then it joined forces with both Rodan
and Godzilla against Ghidorah in **Ghidorah Sandai Kaiju
Chikyu Sandai No Kessan** (1965). It also participated in the
all-star monster movie **Kaiju Soshingeki** (1968).

d Inoshiro Honda *p* Tomoyuki Tanaka *s* Shinichi
Sekizawa *c* Hajime Koizumi *se* Eiji Tsuburaya
lp Frankie Sakai, Hiroshi Koizumi, Kyoko Katawa, the Itoh
Sisters
US version: *d* Lee Kresel *p* David Horne *s* Robert
Myerson

Muz z Prvniho Stoleti *aka* **The Man from the First
Century** *aka* **The Man from the Past** *aka* **Man in Outer
Space** (CZECHOSLOVENSKY FILM; CZECH) b/w 95 min
A leaden space comedy offering a variation on the Rip Van
Winkle theme. Joseph (Kopecky), an upholsterer, accidentally launches a spaceship with himself inside it. In 2447, he
returns to Earth with a companion from another planet,
Adam (Lukavsky). They find a world ruled by automation.
Aided by his friend, Joseph tries to adjust and even becomes
famous thanks to his amazing scientific knowledge – largely
prompted by Adam. In the end, he is allowed to return to
1962 with Adam's warning against excessive mechanization
ringing in his ears. The sets are pleasing but laboured humour
and bad acting spoil the film.

Better known for his rather heavy-handed satire on western
movies, *Lemonadovy Joe* (1964), Lipsky was one of the less
subtle Czech directors who made their mark in the early
sixties, although his **Adele Jeste Nevecerela** (1978) is
genuinely inventive and funny.

*Radovan Lukavsky and
Milos Kopecky in the
weak satire* Muz z
Prvniho Stoleti.

d/s Oldrich Lipsky *c* Vladimir Novotny *lp* Milos
Kopecky, Radovan Lukavsky, Anita Kajlichova, Otomar
Krejca, Vit Olmer, Lubomir Lipsky, Vladimir Hlavaty, Josef
Hlinomatz, Zdenek Rehor, Anna Pitasova

The Mysterious Island
(CHARLES H. SCHNEER PRODUCTIONS; GB,US) 100 min
This is the best known, but by no means the best, of the
numerous versions of Jules Verne's novel *L'Ile Mystérieuse*.
The first was by MGM in 1929; there was a Russian version
made for the Children's Film Studio in 1941, Columbia
produced a 15-part serial in 1951 and Omar Sharif starred in a
French/Italian/Spanish co-production made in 1972.

In this version, Jules Verne's original concept has been
updated. The plot has a group of prisoners, headed by Craig,
escape from a Confederate prison by balloon, which collapses
gently into the sea. They are eventually washed up on the
shores of the mysterious island, where they immediately
plunge into Harryhausen's special effects, which are undoubtedly the best thing in the movie. These include a giant
hen, giant bees and a giant crab, all created by Lom's Captain
Nemo, who has been mutating animals in an attempt to
answer the world's food needs. Greenwood and Rogan are the
shipwrecked survivors Craig and company protect from
marauding pirates. Endfield directs energetically enough but
the script is too predictable to be engrossing.

Left: Ray Harryhausen
*with some of the special
effects' designs for* The
Mysterious Island.

d Cy Endfield *p* Charles H. Schneer *s* John Prebble, Daniel Ullman, Crane Wilbur *c* Wilkie Cooper *se* Ray Harryhausen *lp* Michael Craig, Joan Greenwood, Michael Callan, Gary Merrill, Herbert Lom, Beth Rogan, Nigel Green

The Phantom Planet

(FOUR CROWN PRODUCTIONS) b/w 82 min

Despite its silly plot, this remains an entertaining minor movie, if only for its intriguing cast and Marshall's energetic direction. The *Pegasus IV* survives a meteorite storm, but is badly damaged and begins to drift in space. Astronaut Fredericks attempts repairs but is forced to land on a nearby asteroid. There, once he breathes the atmosphere, he shrinks to the same size as the population, led by Dexter, who have utilized the asteroid as a spaceship. The aliens are friendly but slow-moving and menaced by the asteroid's other inhabitant – a cannibalistic, fast-moving monster played by Richard Kiel, later to achieve fame as Jaws in the Bond movies. Fredericks elects to throw in his lot with the aliens in his journey through space and fight off the monster in a predictable amateurish climax.

d William Marshall *p/co-s* Fred Gebhardt
co-s William Telaak, Fred De Gorter *c* Elwood J. Nicholson
lp Dean Fredericks, Coleen Gray, Dolores Faith, Anthony Dexter, Francis X. Bushman, Richard Weber, Dick Haynes

Il Pianeta degli Uomini Spenti *aka* Battle of the Worlds *aka* Planet of the Lifeless Men *aka* Guerre Planetari

(ULTRA FILM/SICILIA CINEMATOGRAFICA; IT) 95(84) min

This is one of Margheriti's most humorous, inventive and stylish films, effortlessly transcending the crudities of the script, the acting and the special effects. Professor Benson (Rains) ridicules the claims of his colleagues that a meteorite is about to collide with the Earth. He is proved right when the thing stops and appears to launch flying saucers against the Earth. Rains finds that the meteor has been sent by an alien planet, the inhabitants of which have died, leaving the computers on board to carry out mechanically what they have been programmed to do. Fascinated by the wealth of knowledge the central computer must contain, he gains access to it but is blown up together with the contraption as the military leaders on Earth send their hardware to destroy the meteor. The film is too wordy and Rains appears to be the only one capable of enjoying his role; its success lies less in Margheriti's intelligently ironic treatment of clichés, politicians and military pundits, than in the deliriously stylized setting, uncannily beautiful and garish at the same time, culminating in the images of the dead alien world which is all swirling colours, weird machines, insanely fantastic spaces and lines. The film is an object lesson in how to let cinema triumph over both script and acting, allowing visual style and imagination to carry their own corrosively fascinating meanings. The result is an astonishing piece of cinema which dwarfs all pseudo-philosophic moralizing about Mankind and the World.

d Anthony Dawson (Antonio Margheriti) *p* Thomas Sagone *s* Vassily Petrov *c* Raffaello Masciocchi
lp Claude Rains, Bill Carter, Umberto Orsini, Maya Brent, Jacqueline Derval, Maria Mustari, Guiliano Gemma, Carlo D'Angelo, Carol Danell, Renzo Palmer

I Pianeti contro di Noi *aka* The Planets Against Us *aka* Hands of a Killer (PC PRODUZIONE CINEMATOGRAFICA/ COMPTOIR FRANCAIS DU FILM/VANGUARD FILMS; IT, FR) 85(68) min

As usual savaged by British and American distributors, this nonetheless remains a striking looking film. Lemoine is the runaway humanoid robot from a distant planet whose very touch means death who is finally exterminated (outside the Cinecitta studios, interestingly enough) when the army and an alien spaceship turn assorted ray guns on him. Far more impressive than the narrative's incongruities is Ferrara and Pavoni's handling of individual sequences: the explosion of the world's telecommunications centres at the film's beginning and the melting of Clair after she kisses Lemoine, which testify to the strong visual sense of the film-makers.

d/co-s Romano Ferrara *p* Alberto Chimenz, Vico Pavoni
co-s Piero Pierotti *c* Pier Ludovico Pavoni *lp* Michael Lemoine, Maria Pia Luzi, Jany Clair, Marco Guglielmi, Ottello Toso, Peter Dane

Im Stahlnetz des Dr Mabuse *aka* The Return of Dr Mabuse (CCC-FILM/SPA CINEMATOGRAFICA/ CRITERION; WG,IT,FR) b/w 88 min

This is a lacklustre outing compared to the brilliance of Fritz Lang's films devoted to the title character, **Dr Mabuse, der Spieler** (1922), **Das Testament des Dr Mabuse** (1933) and **Die Tausend Augen des Dr Mabuse** (1960), to the last of which this is an unofficial sequel made by the same production companies and directed by Reinl when Lang turned the project down. Reinl, a director whose style is far better suited to the open plains of the Winnetou westerns than the claustrophobic world of Dr Mabuse, directs woodenly from a script which has little of the élan of the earlier films. The plot features Mabuse (Preiss) planning to subjugate Munich with an army of zombies created at the local prison with a drug invented by Forster. Froebe and Barker (who was soon to assume the role of Old Shatterhand in Reinl's Winnetou films) are the detectives on Mabuse's trail in company with reporter Lavi (who also just happens to be Forster's daughter).

d Harald Reinl *p* Wolf Brauner *s* Ladislas Foder, Marc Behm *c* Karl Lob *lp* Gert Froebe, Lex Barker, Daliah Lavi, Wolfgang Preiss, Rudolf Forster, Joachim Mock

Die Toten Augen von London *aka* The Dark Eyes of London *aka* The Dead Eyes of London

(RIALTO FILM; WG) b/w 95 min

Based on *The Testament of Gordon Stuart*, this film belongs to the immensely successful series of Edgar Wallace thrillers made in Germany in the early sixties. The story was filmed by Walter Summers as *The Dark Eyes of London* (1939), starring Bela Lugosi as the doctor in charge of an institute for the

Below: *The climactic battle of* Im Stahlnetz des Dr Mabuse, *an inferior sequel to Fritz Lang's masterful* Die Tausend Augen des Dr Mabuse (1960).

blind. Following on from Lang's **Die Tausend Augen des Dr Mabuse** (1960), the film further elaborates the highly cinematic theme of blindness, generating suspense by showing what characters cannot see and playing upon the vulnerability of eyes, a particularly sensitive point for dedicated film viewers. It features an early performance as a menacing villain by the Berlin-theatre trained Kinski and the imposing Berber as a human robot. As in **Arzt Ohne Gewissan** (1959), Blauermel is the heroine threatened by the lunatic fringe of the medical profession.

d Alfred Vohrer   *s* Trygve Larsen   *c* Karl Loeb
lp Joachim Fuchsberger, Karin Baal (Blauermel), Dieter Borsche, Ady Berber, Klaus Kinski (Claus Nakszynski), Eddi Arent, Wolfgang Lukschy

Die Unsichtbaren Krallen des Dr Mabuse *aka* The Invisible Dr Mabuse   (CCC-FILM; WG)   b/w   89 min
Preiss here repeats the title role he performed so well in Lang's **Die Tausend Augen des Dr Mabuse** (1960) but, this time, he acquires the means to make himself invisible. Barker is Joe Como, the FBI agent on his trail and Dor (Reinl's wife) is Liane, the sexy dancer who is the object of desire for both men. At the end, Mabuse is locked up in an asylum, where he will be refound in **Das Testament des Dr Mabuse** (1962) – and where he died in Lang's **Das Testament des Dr Mabuse** (1933). Some scenes are reminiscent of Lang, such as the Metropol Theatre and its cellar doubling for the Hotel Luxor of the 1960 Mabuse film, and the performing clown refers back to Haghi's end in **Spione** (1928). But ex-Tarzan Barker lacks the edgily neurotic presence of Van Eyck, while Dor spends most of her time either terrified or drugged out of her wits. Barker and Dor appeared together again in another Reinl film, *Die Schlangengrube und das Pendel* (1967).

The film was released in 1962 and many sources locate it after **Im Stahlnetz des Dr Mabuse** (1961) whereas it probably preceded it. Brauner, the man who had invited Lang back to Germany and who was executive producer on *Die Tausend Augen des Dr Mabuse* produced all the sequels, usually employing Fodor to write them.

d Harald Reinl   *p* Artur Brauner   *s* Ladislas Fodor
c Ernst Kalinke   *lp* Lex Barker, Karin Dor, Wolfgang Preiss, Siegfried Lowitz, Rudolf Fernau, Kurt Pieritz, Werner Peters, Heinrich Gies, Hans Schwartz, Carl de Voigt

Voyage to the Bottom of the Sea
(WINDSOR)   scope   105 min
When the experimental submarine, *Seaview*, surfaces after its trial run, the crew (headed by Pidgeon) find the sky alight and the polar ice caps about to melt. Despite opposition from Fontaine, Pidgeon manages to save the Earth by firing a missile into the Van Allen belt. Allen and Bennett's screenplay is far too wordy but Abbott's special effects (at their best in a fight against a giant octopus) are lively enough.

The glass-nosed nuclear submarine cost $400,000 to build and was later used in the successful TV series Allen made from the film.

d/p/co-s Irwin Allen   *co-s* Charles Bennett   *c* Winton Hoch
se L.B. Abbott   *lp* Walter Pidgeon, Robert Sterling, Joan Fontaine, Barbara Eden, Peter Lorre, Michael Ansara, Frankie Avalon, Regis Toomey

The *Seaview, the star of Irwin Allen's pedestrian* Voyage to the Bottom of the Sea.

Lex Barker as the FBI agent Joe Como, *hot on the trail of Dr Mabuse in* Die Unsichtbaren Krallen des Dr Mabuse.

Above: *Joseph Wiseman is* Doctor No.

d/co-p Wesley E. Barry   co-p Edward J. Kay   s Jay Simms
c Hal Mohr   lp Don Megowan, Frances McCann, Erica
Elliott, Don Dolittle

The Day Mars Invaded Earth

(API)   b/w   scope   70 min

Clearly derived from **Invasion of the Body Snatchers** (1956),
this film features a couple of holidaymakers (Taylor and
Windsor), who begin seeing doubles of their friends and
family. In fact, the doubles are Martians who are quietly
killing off humans and replacing them with alien minds and
resurrected humanoid bodies in order to prevent the exploration and colonization of Mars by Earth. Director Dexter ends
his film with the Martians triumphant, which is against the
Hollywood rule, but the mediocre script drains the film of
much of its intended shock effect.

d/p Maury Dexter   s Harry Spalding   c John Nickolaus
Jnr   lp Kent Taylor, Marie Windsor, William Mims, Betty
Beall, Lowell Brown, Greg Shank

Doctor No   (EON; GB)   b/w   105 min

Based on the novel by Ian Fleming, *Doctor No* was the first in
the long-running James Bond series. Connery is Bond battling
against the oriental Doctor No (Wiseman) who has invented
an atomic device to deflect US missiles and tries to blackmail
America from a remote island fortress/laboratory in the
Caribbean. Eventually Wiseman is boiled alive by Connery in
a pool of water which contains an atomic reactor.

Subsequent Bond films became progressively more elaborate and more fantastic, populated by cyphers rather than
characters but *Doctor No* is notable for Connery's bully-boy
sadistic interpretation of Bond, clipped in speech and quick in
action. Similarly, Young's direction strikes exactly the right
note of flamboyant excitement.

The film's phenomenal international success produced a
gaggle of imitations around the world and several sequels
which eventually made Bond (who would later be impersonated by George Lazenby and Roger Moore before Connery
returned to the role in **Never Say Never Again**, 1983), one of
the longest running series characters in film history.

d Terence Young   p Harry Saltzman, Albert R. Broccoli
s Richard Maibaum, Johanna Harwood, Berkely Mather
c Ted Moore   se Frank George   lp Sean Connery, Ursula
Andress, Joseph Wiseman, Jack Lord, Anthony Dawson,
Bernard Lee, Lois Maxwell

La Cara del Terror *aka* Face of Terror *aka* Face of Fear   (DOCUMENTO FILMS; SP)   b/w   83(81) min

Following the success of Jesús Franco's **Gritos en la Noche**
(1962), this movie extends the particular mixture of thriller,
horror and medical Science Fiction which, until the eighties
video gore movies, appeared to be a peculiarly Spanish genre.
The film tells of a plastic surgeon (Rey) who tries out a new
process on the disfigured face of a mentally disturbed woman
(Gaye), endowing her with a serenely beautiful face. She
escapes, taking with her a lotion needed to prevent a reversal
of the treatment. She succeeds in marrying a well-to-do man
but on their return from honeymoon, in the car, she discovers
she has run out of lotion and changes back into her former
unsightly appearance. Her husband stops the car and flees but
she runs him over before going back to the doctor's house for
more lotion. The surgeon's assistant (Cuetos) fights with Gaye
and the latter falls to her death, her face lying in the
remainder of the desired liquid. The combination of melodrama and horror is not handled particularly well and the
actors appear to take themselves a little too seriously.

An American version was produced by Jack Leroy Miles
and directed by William J. Hole.

d Isidoro Martinez Ferry   p Gustavo Quintana
s Monroe Manning   c Jose F. Aguayo   lp Lisa Gaye
Fernando Rey, Virgilio Teixeira, Conschita Cuetos, Gerard
Tichy, Carlos Casaravilla, Emilio Rodrigiuez, Angel
Menendez

Creation of the Humanoids

(GENIE PRODUCTIONS INC.)   75 min

This interesting film, one of the first to deal sympathetically
with machines being mistreated by humans, is badly let down
by Simms' over-talkative script. In the post World War III
world, man has rebuilt his cities with the help of sophisticated
robots called Clickers, who appear human and have electronic
brains and stable emotions. Their increasing demands for
equality are given added weight by the fact that the majority
of the human race were killed in the war and most of the
remaining survivors were sterile. Scientist Megowan, who is
sympathetic to the robots' demands, gives them blood
transfusions in the hope of making them fertile. The climax
has Megowan failing but then discovering that he too is a
robot, but an advanced model that is capable of procreation.

Right: *A moment of truth in* The Day Mars Invaded Earth.

Il Gigante di Metropolis *aka* Giant of Metropolis

(CENTRO; IT) scope 92 min

Mitchell is the bare-chested muscleman who travels to the advanced civilization of the city of Atlantis before it was lost to the sea in this sword-and-sandal epic. There he finds Cortez's King and his team of scientists possess the secret of immortality and such advanced science (fiction) hardware as a magnetic death ray. They plan to impose their rule over the inhabitants of Atlantis in perpetuity but Mitchell stops them and, in the resulting destruction, Atlantis sinks to the bottom of the ocean. Script and direction are cheerfully tongue-in-cheek.

d Umberto Scarpelli *p/co-s* Emmino Salvi *co-s* Sabatino Ciuffino, Oreste Palellea, Ambrogio Molteni, Gino Stafford *c* Mario Sensi *lp* Gordon Mitchell, Bella Cortez, Roldano Lupi, Liani Orfei, Furio Meniconi

Gritos en la Noche *aka* The Awful Dr Orloff *aka* Cries in the Night

(HISPAMER; SP) b/w 88(80) min

The initiator of an entire sub-genre mixing horror and medical Science Fiction in a gory way bordering on the pornographic, exacerbating a tradition started in the fifties Mexican Science Fiction stories and codifying it into a generic formula. Based on the novel by David Kuhne, the film tells of a Dr Orloff (Vernon) who compulsively drains young women of blood and attempts to graft new skin onto his daughter's disfigured face. He is assisted by a lecherous, blind hunchback, Morpho (Valle) who matches his master's sadism and disposes of the corpses. The film lingers on the denuded bodies of women as Vernon uses his scalpel on them and as the blind Morpho explores their figures, lying chained in the doctor's dungeon. This is a sick combination of Jack the Ripper stories, set at the turn of the century, with Vernon stalking the foggy backstreets in search of victims, with elements from Terence Fisher's horror movies made for Hammer in the late fifties. The mixture of eroticism and sadistic surgery must have struck a chord in its audiences for this film spawned not only a number of sequels but also set the tone for a peculiarly Hispanic type of Science Fiction that flourished for more than a decade, dominated by the visually surreal, excessively visceral but often lazily filmed (relying on a surfeit of zooms) movies of Franco, usually starring Vernon or Christopher Lee, occasionally Klaus Kinski: *El Secreto del Dr Orloff* (1964), *Besame Monstruo* (1967), *Los Ojos del Dr Orloff* (1973) and many more. Even the less gruesome examples of Hispanic Science Fiction veered towards the motifs that had proved successful at the box office, such as brain transplants and other forms of physical horror (**Las Ratas No Duermen de Noche**, 1974 and **Odio Mi Cuerpo**, 1975).

d/s Jesús Franco *p* Serge Newman, Leo Lax *c* Godofredo Pacheco *lp* Howard Vernon, Conrado San Martin, Perla Cristal, Diana Lorys, Riccardo Valle, Maria Silva, Mara Laso, Felix Dafauce, Faustino Comejo

Invasion of the Star Creatures

(AMERICAN INTERNATIONAL) b/w 81 min

The screenplay, by Haze (who appeared in many of Roger Corman's films) tries – sometimes successfully – to make fun of the limitations of low-budget Science Fiction. Two American soldiers (Ball and Ray) on army manoeuvres encounter two Amazon women (Victor and Reed) who, under the control of vegetable aliens (who look like scarecrows and are called Star Creatures), plan to conquer the Earth. The Star Creatures invade the army base, but when the Amazons fall in love with the soldiers their hostile war plans are cancelled and the monsters and the Star Creatures are firmly despatched back to outer space. The film's best sequence is the attack on Ball and Victor by a star creature hiding on the back seat of Ball's car.

d Bruno DeSoto *p* Merj Hagopian *s* Jonathan Haze *c* Basil Bradbury *lp* Bob Ball, Frankie Ray, Gloria Victor, Dolores Reed, Mark Ferris

Klaun Ferdinand a Raketa *aka* Rocket to Nowhere *aka* Clown Ferdinand and the Rocket

(STUDIO BARRANDOV; CZECH) b/w 73 min

Before making the internationally respected, although somewhat cerebral, **Ikarie XB-1** (1963), Polak directed this light-hearted children's film about a robot(Smrz)-controlled spaceship that rescues three kids and a clown (Vrstala) from a devastated city. Polak handled the story with flair avoiding most of the maudlin sentimentality and naïveté that usually spoils children's films involving a robot, clowns or, as in this case, both (a case in point is Schmidt's **Der Ideale Untermiester**, 1956).

Made in the same year as **Wielka Wielksza Najwielksza** (1962), the Polish children's film, it shows that, at the time, Eastern European film-makers were tending to take more care creating a marvellous atmosphere in their work by evolving a fantasy world with children, rather than simply filming stories with kids or supposedly seen through their eyes, as in Western Europe. Czech films in particular (although Polish and Russian films too), such as Zeman's work, construct the whole movie as a children's film instead of simply providing access to the stories through identification with children in the story itself.

Left: Il *Gigante di Metropolis.*

Gritos en la Noche, *a landmark in the evolution of the medical sub-genre of Science Fiction.*

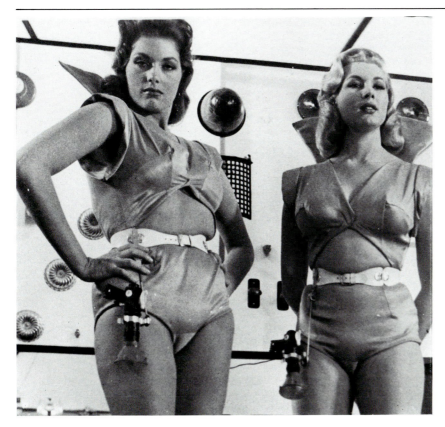

Gloria Victor and Dolores Reed as the Amazonian women under the control of aliens in Invasion of the Star Creatures.

d/co-s Jindrich Polak   *co-s* Ota Hofman   *c/co-se* Jan Kallis   *co-se* Milan Nejedly, Jiri Hlupy, Pavel Necesal, Karel Cisarovsky, Frantisek Zerslicka   *lp* Jiri Vrstala, Eva Hrabetova, Hanus Bor, Vladimir Horka, Vaclav Stekl, Jaroslav Valek, Ludek Kindermann, Jan Kurcik, Karel Smrz

Moon Pilot   (WALT DISNEY)   98 min

Unwilling astronaut Tryon has three days to go before blasting off to the Moon. During this time he is assailed by Saval's sexy alien, who arrives on Earth to warn him to beware of 'proton rays' in space, and O'Brien, a security agent convinced Saval is a spy. Tombragel's screenplay, which gets bogged down in the romance, is at its best when broadly comic. Keith is excellent as an irate airforce general. The film was director Neilson's first for the Disney studios, for whom he regularly worked in the sixties.

d James Neilson   *p* Walt Disney   *s* Maurice Tombragel   *c* William Snyder   *se* Eustace Lycett   *lp* Tom Tryon, Brian Keith, Edmond O'Brien, Dany Saval, Bob Sweeney, Kent Smith

Panic in Year Zero *aka* End of the World

(LOU RUSOFF-ARNOLD HOUGHLAND)   b/w   92 min

Effectively directed by Milland, an occasional director since the engrossing *A Man Alone* (1955), *Panic in the Year Zero*, despite its rather lurid story, is noteworthy for the ruthlessness Milland and writers Simms and Morton suggest will be required to survive. Milland, wife Hagen and two teenage kids Avalon and Mitchell flee the nuclear blast that has devasted Los Angeles and go to an isolated cave in the hills. His family are horrified by Milland's seeming change in personality but after Mitchell is raped and Avalon unhesitatingly kills the violators they come to accept the change as the cost of survival. The film makes for an interesting comparison with **No Blade of Grass** (1970).

Right: Jean Hagen, Ray Milland, Frankie Avalon and Mary Mitchell (left to right) as the post-nuclear-holocaust family in Panic in Year Zero.

d Ray Milland   *p* Arnold Houghland, Lou Rusoff   *s* Jay Simms, John Morton   *c* Gil Warrenton   *se* Pat Dinga, Larry Butler   *lp* Ray Milland, Jean Hagen, Frankie Avalon, Mary Mitchell, Joan Freeman, Richard Garland, Rex Holman

Planeta Burg *aka* Storm Planet *aka* Cosmonauts on Venus *aka* Planet of Storms

(LENINGRAD STUDIO OF POPULAR SCIENCE FILMS; USSR)
85(74) min

Discounting **Kosmitchesky Reis** (1935) for its heavy socialist-realism and Stalinism, *Planeta Burg* is the only truly well made and visually exciting Russian space travel film between **Aelita** (1924) and **Solaris** (1971), far better than the stodgy version of Efremov's classic story **Tumannost Andromedy** (1968). Three spacecraft set out for Venus, two arrive, one commanded by Captain Masha (Ignatova) which remains in orbit and one that lands on the planet. The rest is a fast-paced adventure story, told with considerable humour, involving volcanic eruptions, giant animals and hostile plants. The sets are stunningly designed with outlandish colour schemes rendering the uncanny alienness of the Venusian landscapes as well as the spectacular aspects of space travel itself. The appearance of a Venusian is wisely delayed to the very end, and even then only suggested as being 'just like us'. As in all popular space operas, there is a robot (called John) who occasionally goes out of control. Here he is given to talking gibberish and playing forties dance music, a more appropriate musical accompaniment to space fantasies than the monumentally majestic waltz of **2001 – A Space Odyssey** (1968). The result is the best straightforward, unpretentious Science Fiction space travel movie made in the USSR.

As happened with Zeman's **Cesta do Praveku** (1955), an American producer, in this case Roger Corman, bought the film. Curtis Harrington and Peter Bogdanovich were hired to cannibalize large chunks of the Soviet film, which were dubbed and combined with newly shot material starring Basil Rathbone and Faith Domergue. The results were released directly to TV as **Voyage to a Prehistoric Planet** (1965). Bogdanovich also used the Soviet footage for his TV film, **Voyage to the Planet of Prehistoric Women** (1966), which had additional scenes with Mamie Van Doren and assorted bathing beauties.

d/co-s Pavel Klushantsev   *co-s* Alexander Kazantsev   *c* Arkady Klimov   *lp* Gennadi Vernov, Vladimir Temelianov, Yuri Sarantsev, Georgi Zhonov, Kyunna Ignatova

La Poupée *aka* The Doll *aka* He, She or It

(FILMS FRANCO-AFRICAINS; FR)   scope   95 min

A French variation on themes used in Lang's **Metropolis** (1926). Set in a Latin American banana republic run by banker Moren (Gora) and governed by Colonel Roth (Cybulski), the plot concerns a revolutionary (Cybulski again) who would have assassinated the colonel if someone hadn't beaten him to it. This unforeseen event causes the revolution, inspired by the figure of the banker's wife (Teal) – a clear

reference to Eva Peron. Teal plays a woman who, as a result of experiments with molecular multiplication, has become an automaton rather like the robot Maria in Lang's film, hailed as the 'angel' of the revolution. In the end, the revolutionary replaces the slain colonel while the 'doll' leads the rebels into an ambush, restoring the initial situation to the great satisfaction of the string-pulling banker. Only the faces will have changed, ever so slightly.

Wittily written by Audiberti from his own play, and shot by Coutard using colour and format to dramatic effect, the film is a neglected jewel of political Science Fiction with an intelligent performance by Cybulski (better known for his performances in the films of Andrzej Wajda) in the double role, and even more trenchant than Buñuel's treatment of a similar theme, *La Fièvre Monte à el Pao* (1959).

d/p Jacques Baratier *s* Jacques Audiberti *c* Raoul Coutard *lp* Zbigniew Cybulski, Sonne Teal, Catherine Milinaire, Claudio Gora, Sacha Pitoëff, Daniel Emilfork, Laszlo Zabo, Jacques Dufilho

Reptilicus (CINEMAGIC; DEN, US) 90 min

Made in Denmark by Pink this is a mediocre film, badly let down by its weak special effects, about a prehistoric reptile, the tail of which is found by an oil expedition and taken back to a laboratory where it regenerates itself and then goes on the rampage. The one startling sequence is the moment when the oil explorers find their drill bringing up mangled flesh and blood and exhume the creature's tail from the bog it's been lying in, comatose, for centuries.

The film features virtually the same cast and crew as Pink's earlier **Journey to the Seventh Planet** (1961).

d/p/co-s Sidney Pink *co-s* Ib Melchior *c* Aage Wiltrup *lp* Carl Ottosen, Ann Smyrner, Mimi Heinrich, Poul Wildaker, Asbjorn Andersen, Marla Bregens

Road to Hong Kong (MELNOR; GB) b/w 91 min

The last Road picture, this lacklustre outing involves Hope accidentally memorizing the formula for a super rocket fuel after taking a drug which gives him a photographic memory. The complex plot then has Crosby and Hope despatched to the planet Plutonium. Few of the wisecracks and gags are funny, let alone in the Road tradition. Shot in Britain, the film features guests appearances from the likes of Frank Sinatra, Dean Martin and Peter Sellers, who was slowly establishing himself as an international star.

d/co-s Norman Panama *p/co-s* Melvin Frank *c* Jack Hildyard *se* Wally Veevers, Ted Samuels *lp* Bing Crosby, Bob Hope, Dorothy Lamour, Joan Collins, Robert Morley, Felix Aylmer, Walter Gotell

Santo Contra el Cerebro Diabolico
(PELICULAS RODRIGUEZ; MEX) 85 min

Nine years elapsed between the Silver Masked wrestler's first appearance, *El Enmascarado de Plata* (1952) and the beginning of a series that eventually numbered about 30 titles. Benito Alazraki and Alfonso Corona Blake started the ball rolling with *Santo Contra los Monstruos* and *Santo Contra las Mujeres Vampiras* respectively (both 1961). Three more titles, started in 1961 but finished and released in 1962, were quickly added by Curiel, *Santo Contra el Rey del Crimen*, *Santo en el Hotel de la Muerte* and *Santo Contra el Cerebro Diabolico*, each designed to show off the masked wrestler in a different context, from a western to an urban setting by way of a mad scientist's laboratory, all interspersed with the usual musical numbers.

The diabolical brain of the title is that of a mad scientist who conducts experiments with corpses and constructs Frankenstein-type monsters which eventually kill him. However, before coming to grips with the mad doctor, Santo has to eliminate a mysterious character called La Sombra Negra who killed his sister in order to obtain the gold mine located on her hacienda. The movie came in three parts, as did the other two titles filmed at the same time, partly to circumvent the legislation and union agreements which restricted America Studios and its union to making newsreels and shorts, features being reserved for the rival union at the Churubusco-Azteca Studios. This often led to America Studio based film-makers producing features in instalments which could then be edited into a single feature later. Although scripted as a children's picture, like the singing cowboy movies or the Republic serials in the USA, this instalment was deemed to be for adults only, introducing an ambiguity that would be exacerbated later with the introduction of sex scenes into the Santo films while the rest of the film remained on the level of a Tarzan series. This suggests the films were less for children than for an audience conceptualized as being 'infantile'.

d/co-s Federico Curiel *p* J. Rodriguez *co-s* Antonio Orellana, Fernando Oses *c* Fernando Alvarez Carces Colin *lp* Santo, Fernando Casanova, Ana Bertha Lepe, Roberto Ramirez, Luis Aceves Castañeda, Celia Viberos, Augustino Benedico

Left: Sonne Teal as the erotic automaton in the witty La Poupée.

A scene from The Underwater City, *one of the worst examples of American Science Fiction of the sixties.*

It's a bird, it's a plane, it's . . . The Three Stooges in Orbit.

Sekai Daisenso *aka* The Last War *aka* The Final War
(TOHO; JAP) scope 110(80) min

Like **Dai Sanji Sekai Taisen – Yonju-Ichi Jikan No Kyofu** (1960), this film was conceived in the wake of the success of **On the Beach** (1959). It was made by one of Toho's routine house directors better known for his *Playboy President* comedies of 1961. The story is very topical: the two superpowers have nuclear missiles targeted on each other's cities and could wipe out the world at the push of a button. Accidents and false alarms in nuclear bases, together with an increase in tension and crises in various contentious areas of the world, make World War III seem imminent. An uprising along the 38th Parallel in Korea is narrowly defused by peace initiatives but the collision of two superpower aircraft over the Arctic causes a misunderstanding and the final holocaust ensues. In blinding flashes all the world's cities are destroyed and the people in rural areas die slowly and agonizingly of radiation poisoning. Again, told from the point of view of the victims of nuclear aggression as opposed to that of the perpetrators of the monstrous 'error', the film's premise is a totally believable, and even probable, scenario. The effects achieved by Toho's master Tsuburaya are memorable and the acting makes the relevant points, although it is difficult to assess the performances: what would constitute 'appropriate behaviour' in such circumstances is anybody's guess.

d Shue Matsubayashi *p* Tomoyuki Tanaka *s* Toshio Yasumi, Takeshi Kimura *c* Rokuro Nishigaki *se* Eiji Tsuburaya *lp* Frankie Sakai, Nobuko Otowa, Akira Takarada, Yuriko Hoshi, Yumi Shirakawa

Das Testament des Dr Mabuse *aka* The Testament of Dr Mabuse (CCC-FILM; WG) b/w 88 min

A somewhat updated remake of Lang's identically titled film of 1933. Mabuse, played again by Preiss who had made the role his own since **Die Tausend Augen des Dr Mabuse** (1960), lives in an asylum where he re-forms his criminal organization and takes over the place by hypnotizing its director (Rilla). After Mabuse's death during brain surgery, Rilla is thus compelled to carry out Mabuse's 'will'. The inspector (Froebe, also in a role he started playing in *Die Tausend Augen*) became the sixties incarnation of the fascinating Lohmann figure of Lang's 1933 film and also of his *M* (1931). Lohmann indeed is now the main character through

Right: Das Testament des Dr Mabuse, Werner Klinger's inferior remake of Fritz Lang's 1933 film.

whose eyes and special knowledge of the evil genius the audience gets a sense of the Mabuse menace. The Mabuse/Lohmann tandem has become as closely connected as the Dracula/Van Helsing one. The film is notable mainly for the presence of Berger, the Viennese actress who entered cinema through Brauner, the mastermind behind all the Mabuse films of this period as well as the producer of a sizeable proportion of the trashier sector of German cinema in the sixties. Preiss' performance is the only link with Lang's Mabuse figure as he manages to capture some of the manic qualities Rudolf Klein-Rogge used to bring to the part (**Dr Mabuse, der Spieler**, 1922, and **Das Testament des Dr Mabuse**, 1933).

The next sequel, **Scotland Yard Jagt Dr Mabuse** (1963) was more interesting.

d Werner Klinger *p* Artur Brauner *s* Ladislas Fodor, Robert Adolf Stemmle *c* Albert Benitz *lp* Gert Froebe, Senta Berger, Helmut Schmid, Wolfgang Preiss, Charles Regnier, Walter Rilla, Harald Juhnke, Leon Askin, Ann Savo, Claus Tinney

The Three Stooges in Orbit
(NORMANDY PRODUCTIONS) b/w 87 min

In this lacklustre outing Stooges Howard, Fine and De Rita defeat the plans of Martians Og and Zog to steal the secret plans of a vehicle that can be tank, helicopter and submarine from an eccentric inventor (Sitka).

Bernds was one of the Stooges' regular writer/directors. His other credits include **The Bowery Boys Meet the Monsters** (1954), **World Without End** (1956), **Space-Master X-7** (1958), in which Howard appeared on his own, **Queen of Outer Space** (1958) and **Return of the Fly** (1959).

d Edward Bernds *p* Norman Maurer *s* Elwood Ullman *c* William F. Whitley *lp* The Three Stooges (Moe Howard, Larry Fine, Joe De Rita), Carol Christensen, Edson Stoll, Emil Sitka

The Underwater City
(NEPTUNE PRODUCTIONS) b/w scope 78 min

Although filmed in Eastmancolor, Columbia considered this film so bad it was printed in black and white and released as the bottom half of a double bill. Harris' muzzy screenplay

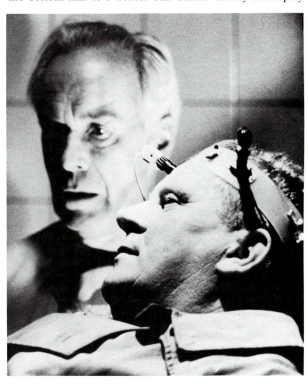

centres on man's first attempts to live underwater in a giant shelter. Eventually, the ocean floor caves in and only a small part of the shelter remains. Lundigan and Adams are the honeymooning couple who survive.

d Frank McDonald *p* Alex Gordon *s* Owen Harris
c Gordon Avil *se* Howard C. Lydecker, Howard A. Anderson *lp* William Lundigan, Julie Adams, Roy Roberts, Carl Benton Reid, Chet Douglas, Paul Dubov

Vengeance *aka* Ein Toter Sucht Seiner Moerder *aka* The Brain

(CCC/GOVERNOR PRODUCTIONS; GB, WG) b/w 83 min
The last version to date of Curt Siodmak's novel, *Donovan's Brain* (previously filmed as **The Lady and the Monster**, 1944 and **Donovan's Brain**, 1953), this is a routine outing, only notable for its stress on blood and gore (in the manner of Hammer's Frankenstein films). Van Eyck is the doctor who saves the brain of an industrialist only to fall under its power and (temporarily) become its instrument in the revenge it seeks on those responsible for the industrialist's death and Heywood is the industrialist's daughter and murderer he falls for. Francis, always a better director of horror than of Science Fiction, plods through Mackie and Stewart's well-thumbed script.

d Freddie Francis *p* Raymond Stross *s* Phil Mackie, Robert Stewart *c* Bob Hulke *lp* Peter Van Eyck, Anne Heywood, Cecil Parker, Bernard Lee, Jack MacGowran, Ellen Schwiers, Miles Malleson

Wielka Wielksza Najwielksza *aka* The Great Big World and Little Children

(START UNIT; POL) b/w 102 min
Excluding Jan Batory's children's fairytale *O Dwoch Takich Co Ukradeli Ksiezyc* (1962), which is close to *Finian's Rainbow* (1968) and *The Wizard of Oz* (1939), this film appears to be the first all-Polish Science Fiction feature. Even so, it is another children's fantasy film combining three different stories. Two are about kids and their relation with a world of objects that come alive to help them. Only the third one belongs to the genre as it shows two children, Ika and Groszek (Sienko and Purzynski) who enter a silver sphere and find themselves on a distant planet called Vega where they learn what the world would be like after an atomic war. The tales were adapted, by the author, from Broszkiewicz's book, and the sets as well as the costumes contribute a great deal to the film's effectiveness. The celebrated Wanda Jakubowska,

production manager of the Start Unit and director of the powerful autobiographical Auschwitz movie *Ostatni Etap* (1948), supervised Sokolowska's film.

d/co-s Anna Sokolowska *co-s* Jerzy Broszkiewicz
c Kazimierz Vavrzyniak, Jacik Korcelli *lp* Kinja Sienko, Woychiech Purzynski, B. Bilewski, Zbigniew Josefowicz, J. Klosinski, Z. Kucowna, Z. Malowski, E.B. Mickus, B. Pawlik

Yosei Gorasu *aka* **Gorath** (TOHO; JAP) scope 89 min
Foreshadowing a plot device used again in **Kyuketsuki Gokemidoro** (1968), **Kessen Nankai No Daikaiju** (1970) and **Uchu Daikaiju Guilala** (1967), Gorath is generated by the organic material picked up by a spaceship as it moved through a cloudy substance. The cells brought back multiply and reconstitute the rest of the monster's body. The plot involves a red hot planet on a collision course with the Earth. To avoid disaster, scientists decide to shift Earth out of its orbit, setting off massive explosions in Antarctica, but these merely cause a huge monster to loom forth which interferes with the scientific efforts to save the world. Eventually, the creature is killed, and after tidal waves and the heating up of the Earth,

Left: *Peter Van Eyck as the doctor who falls under the sway of the brain he saves in* Vengeance.

The red hot planet on collision course with Earth in Yosei Gorasu, *one of the first Japanese space operas.*

Right: *Rod Taylor, Veronica Cartwright (left) and Tippi Hedren under attack in* The Birds.

the collision is narrowly averted as the Earth is indeed shifted into a different orbit. The movie also features a convincingly executed space walk three years before Leonov became the first man to leave his spacecraft in flight and boasts a guest performance of the brilliant character actor Shimura, who starred in many Kurosawa films including the extraordinary *Ikiru* (1952), and was also one of the performers in the original **Gojira** (1954).

d Inoshiro Honda *p* Tomoyuki Tanaka *s* Takeshi Kimura *c* Hajime Koizumi *se* Eiji Tsuburaya *lp* Ryo Ikebe, Akihiko Hirata, Jun Tazaki, Yumi Shirakawa, Takashi Shimura, Kumi Mizuno

1963

Battle Beyond the Sun (FILMGROUP) 75 min
Roger Corman took an executive producer credit for this film which uses a great deal of footage from the Russian film **Niebo Zowiet** (1959). That film featured the northern and southern hemispheres (clearly the USA and USSR) racing to land on Mars and the Americans being rescued by the Russians, when they found themselves in difficulties. Corman neatly removed the Russian propaganda and the Americans were no longer the greedy capitalists out to win the space race. Colchart, a pseudonymous Francis Ford Coppola, shot additional scenes on the cheap in Hollywood to replace these. The special effects' footage from the Russians is superb but like Corman's other 'Russian' films (**Voyage to the Prehistoric Planet**, 1965 and **Voyage to the Planet of Prehistoric Women**, 1966, both of which were culled from **Planeta Burg**, 1962) one remains more impressed with Corman's cheek and financial astuteness than with the finished film.

US footage: d/p Thomas Colchart *s* Nicholas Colbert, Edwin Palmer *lp* Edd Perry, Arla Powell, Andy Stewart, Bruce Hunter

The Birds (U) 119 min
Although no explanation, scientific or otherwise, is offered for the birds' attacks on the inhabitants of Bodega Bay, *The Birds* belongs in this volume because of its enormous influence on subsequent Science Fiction films: its success led to the stream of revenge-of-nature films of the seventies, all of which are inferior to Hitchcock's film. The culmination of Hitchcock's use of bird imagery (that stretches back to the swooping birdlike camera movement of *Young and Innocent*, 1937, and is most marked in *Psycho*, 1960), *The Birds* begins with Taylor catching and re-imprisoning the bird in the pet shop where he meets Hedren and climaxes with the twin attacks on Hedren (in the phone box and the attic) in which she literally becomes a bird in a cage. It is Hitchcock's darkest film, depicting as it does the sudden eruption into the seemingly calm ordered lives of its principal characters the hidden, forbidden (and repressed) passions they have hitherto avoided expressing. Indeed, as Donald Spoto's account of its filming in his revealing biography of Hitchcock demonstrates, it would seem that the film also represents the first spilling over into the director's own life of those passions he's previously serviced through his art: the two-minute sequence where the birds attack Hedren in the attic (which took a week to film) by all accounts consisted virtually of the displaced rape of the actress by Hitchcock. Certainly the technical complexity of the film's special effects (masterminded by Hitchcock and created by Hampton and Iwerks) in their formal perfection

produce a coldness that is quite chilling. From this perspective, the birds are best seen as an objective correlative of the arbitrariness of life, held at bay by civilized behaviour – virtually all the secondary characters are emotionally dead – until Hedren, on a whim, arrives in Bodega Bay and begins the lengthy teasing of Pleshette, Taylor and Tandy that unleashes the chaos of human emotions on the town and special punishment on herself by the gruesome personal attacks.

d/p Alfred Hitchcock *s* Evan Hunter *c* Robert Burks *se* Lawrence A. Hampton, Ub Iwerks *lp* Tippi Hedren, Rod Taylor, Jessica Tandy, Suzanne Pleshette, Ethel Griffies, Veronica Cartwright, Charles McGraw, Ruth McDevitt

Der Chef Wuenscht Keine Zeugen *aka* No Survivors Please (HANS ALBIN FILMS; WG) b/w 93(91) min

An attempt to cash in on the fear of nuclear warfare, the film offers a variation on the theme best presented in **Invasion of the Body Snatchers** (1956): aliens take over the bodies of leading politicians and military men in order to create a war that will kill off all people on Earth, vacating the planet for the inhabitants of a planet of a sun in Orion. Although the body-snatching gimmick does allow savings to be made in the special effects and costume departments, the portrayal of world leaders and generals as nasty warmongers does have its attractions. The Hungarian-born writer/director Szekely had a long career in his own country before working in Hollywood where he made *Miracle on Main Street* (1939), *Revenge of the Zombies* (1943) and a dozen other films. He is best known for directing **The Day of the Triffids** (1963). His script for this German film, also made in 1963, has all the earmarks of having been drafted on the back of an envelope. Most problems in plot development appear to be solved by the simple expedient of changing location, thus the action jumps all over the world, although keeps mostly to attractive tourist areas.

co-d/p Hans Albin *co-d/co-s* Peter Berneis *co-s* Istvan (Steve) Szekely *c* Heinz Schnackertz *lp* Maria Perschy, Uwe Friedrichsen, Robert Cunnigham, Karen Blanguernon, Gustavo Rojo, Ted Turner, Stefan Schabel, Burr Jerger, Wolfgang Zilzer, Dirk Hansen

Children of the Damned *aka* Horror!
(MGM; GB) b/w 90 min

A remake of, rather than a sequel to, **Village of the Damned** (1960) and, unlike most second workings, this version of John Wyndham's *The Midwich Cuckoos* is more interesting than the original film. This time the six supernatural children are discovered around the world, brought together by UNESCO investigators Badel and Hendry and eventually destroyed by fear and ignorance, rather than by calculated effort. No longer malevolent, the powers of the children achieve new dimensions. Moreover, unlike their precursors in *Village of the Damned*, they remain *children* and, as such, become pawns in the love-hate relationship between Hendry and Badel in which Badel seeks to destroy them almost in revenge for Hendry's rejection of him for Ferris. The climax, the children hiding in a ruined church and being blown up accidentally, is chillingly staged.

Of all the films derived from Wyndham's work, *Village of the Damned*, **The Day of the Triffids** (1963) and **Quest for Love** (1971), this is the best.

Barbara Ferris (centre) with the Children of the Damned, *a superior remake of* Village of the Damned *(1960).*

Above: *Janette Scott in danger in the horrendous* The Day of the Triffids.

The Crawling Hand

(JOSEPH F. ROBERTSON) b/w 89 min

Breck and Taylor, clearly embarrassed by their roles, are the scientists investigating the disappearance of an astronaut after his craft has exploded on entering Earth's atmosphere in this terrible film. They discover that, except for his hand which is found by medical student Lauren, the astronaut was blown to pieces. The severed limb, infected by an alien force, strangles Lauren's landlady, before turning (unsuccessfully) on Lauren himself. Possession of the hand makes Lauren into a Jekyll and Hyde character, with his own hands infected with a desire to kill, which Strock signals by having Lauren wear black makeup around his eyes.

Strock, best known for **I Was a Teenage Frankenstein** (1958), did not make another film in the sixties.

d/co-s Herbert L. Strock *p* Joseph F. Robertson
co-s William Edelson *c* Willard Van der Veer *lp* Peter Breck, Kent Taylor, Rod Lauren, Sirry Steffen, Arline Judge, Alan Hale

The Day of the Triffids

(SECURITY PICTURES; GB) scope 94 min

The most lavish of the adaptations of the works of John Wyndham (which include **Village of the Damned**, 1960 and **Children of the Damned**, 1963, both derived from *The Midwich Cuckoos*, and **Quest for Love**, 1971), this is an overblown, turgid film, full of heavy moralizing and out-of-place romantic interludes. Matters were made even worse by the film's stop-start production: it was only completed a year after major filming was finished. Accordingly, in place of Wyndham's typically British response to the notion of an invasion from outer space, replete with echoes of the Battle of Britain and a concern with the imminent collapse of a certain (rather prim middle-class) way of life, the film transforms the novel into a simplistic adventure story.

Keel (who rewrote his own dialogue, he thought Yordan's was so bad) is the American naval officer (whose eyes are bandaged when a shower of meteorites blinds most of humanity) who leads an ill-assorted group of sighted people (including Scott, Maurey and Faye's little girl) against the Triffids. The Triffids, 7-foot-high galloping broccoli (an English monster, if ever there was one) are simply ludicrous and the climax, Keel, having discovered the giant vegetables are attracted by sound, luring them to a saltwater grave over a cliff top, is remarkably similar to that of **The Beginning of the End** (1957).

This was the penultimate film of Hungarian-born Sekely, who had fled to America in the thirties.

d Steve Sekely, (uncredited) Freddie Francis
p George Pitcher *s* Philip Yordan *c* Ted Moore
se Wally Veevers *lp* Howard Keel, Nicole Maurey, Janette Scott, Kieron Moore, Mervyn Johns, Alison Leggatt, Ewan Roberts, Janina Faye

The Evil of Frankenstein (HAMMER; GB) 84 min

Leadenly directed by Francis, this is the third of Hammer's Frankenstein offerings. In marked contrast to the first two, **The Curse of Frankenstein** (1957) and **The Revenge of Frankenstein** (1958), it concentrates on the monster (played by ex-wrestler Kingston in makeup that resembles that worn by Boris Karloff for the Universal films, a reflection, no doubt, of Universal's financial involvement in the production). Even worse, Hinds' pseudonymously written script re-works the worst clichés of the later Universal films in the series. Thus, once again, the villagers of Karlstaad go hunting the monster and Frankenstein (Cushing) has to seek help from Woodthorpe's hypnotist to revive the frozen monster only for Woodthorpe to use the monster to kill and rob for him. The result, complete with the predictable climax in which Frankenstein and the monster are engulfed in flames while the villagers look on, is a decidedly lacklustre film.

The version shown on American television has some scenes deleted and new ones (shot in America) added.

d Freddie Francis *p* Anthony Hinds *s* John Elder (Anthony Hinds) *c* John Wilcox *se* Les Bowie *lp* Peter Cushing, Kiwi Kingston, Sandor Eles, Peter Woodthorpe, Duncan Lamont

Ikarie XB-1 *aka* Icarus XB-1 *aka* Voyage to the End of the Universe

(STUDIO BARRANDOV; CZECH) b/w scope 81(65) min

Following on from his own children's film **Klaun Ferdinand a Raketa** (1962) and, no doubt, from the Soviet success **Planeta Burg** (1962), Polak made this somewhat clinical acount of an international group who leave their automated, 25th-century world in a spaceship, commanded by Abajev (Stepanek), in search of a 'green' world according to the English version, a 'white' world according to the original. They run into an abandoned spacecraft with the corpses of crew and passengers, dead for hundreds of years – an event

d Anton M. Leader *p* Ben Arbeid *s* Jack Briley
c David Boulton *se* Tom Howard *lp* Ian Hendry, Alan Badel, Barbara Ferris, Alfred Burke, Sheila Allen, Clive Powell, Bessie Love

repeated to more eerie effect in **Alien** (1979). The film is cool and detached, as if the characters and their world are seen from a totally uninvolved position. The American reporter who angrily dismissed **Sieriebristaya Pyl** (1953) as 'red propaganda' for its possibly too accurate portrayal of aspects of US society, would have noted with interest that the US version of this Czech film, dubbed, cut to 65 minutes and titled *Voyage to the End of the Universe*, added a scene at the end of the film, possibly explaining why the English version mentions the search for a 'green' planet instead of a white one: as the spacecraft nears its destination, the occupants look out and are made to see . . . the Statue of Liberty. The detached tone of the film, in spite of the emphasis on constant physical movement and some gruesome deaths by radiation, may be due to the involvement of the scenarist Juracek who wrote *Josef Kilian* (1963) for director Jan Schmidt and went on to direct the heavily moralistic tale about a post-nuclear-holocaust world, **Konec Sprna v Hotelu Ozon** (1966).

d/co-s Jindrich Polak   *p* Rudolph Wohl   *co-s* Pavel Juracek   *c* Jan Kallis   *lp* Zdenek Stepanek, Radovan Lukavski, Dana Medriska, Otto Laskovic, Jiri Vrstala, Frantisek Smolik

La Jetée *aka* The Pier *aka* The Jetty
(ARGOS FILMS; FR)   b/w   29 (27) min

Marker, a novelist, photographer and *cinéaste*, is one of the rare artists whose every film allows us to discover what a marvellous cinema we could have. Alain Resnais described him as 'The prototype of 21st century Man ... He appears human but he may well be from the future or from another planet. I'd rather think he is from the future because then we can believe that a couple of centuries from now, all earthlings will resemble Marker.' *La Jetée* was released on *the* bill of the sixties as the short accompanying Godard's **Alphaville** (1965). It is a short, unique and fragile masterpiece exploring the very edges of cinema itself. With an explicit nod towards Hitchcock's *Vertigo* (1958), Marker proposes a central character, H (Hanich) living in a post-nuclear-war Paris where survivors are trapped in subterranean vaults. The logic of cause and effect, and therefore of sequentiality, has been disturbed, locking the survivors in a timeless present. H, however, is obsessed by a memory image of a woman's face, possibly glimpsed on the pier at Orly airport. This tenuous link with the past, and thus with time, provides an enigmatic, somewhat menacing scientist (Ledoux) with a chance to reconnect with history through H's imagination. Subjected to experiments, H extends his memory and is also projected into the future where he finds that the scene he remembered is that of a woman witnessing his own violent death. Except for one brief moment, the entire film consists of still images accompanied by a voice-over narration spoken by Jean Negroni. With this photo-novel technique, Marker explores the links between memory, time and vision. Like much of his work, the movie is deeply paradoxical. Ostensibly marking the borderline between a cinematic past (Lang, Hitchcock) and a future best exemplified by Michael Snow's *Wavelength* (1967), it can equally well be seen as remembering *Wavelength* and anticipating the post-modernist cinema of a Marguerite Duras; the paradox is that wherever or however one cares to

Below: La Jetée: *the moment of truth as the moment of death.*

King Kong and Godzilla do battle amidst a swarm of helicopters in King Kong Tai Gojira.

draw a dividing line between a past and a future of cinema, that is where *La Jetée* seems to belong. It seems to live on the fixed, yet constantly shifting, edge between the cinema we have and the one we could have, or between cinema and not-cinema. In philosophical terms, the film's position is undecidable. Pointing to possible futures, it also reorganizes our understanding of what must have gone before, making it a movie in the future anterior tense, which is, strictly speaking, impossible. Marker's photo-novel technique was used previously in James Young's *Pups on a Rampage* (1900), but it took Marker to make the device historically meaningful. The picture was awarded first prize at the Trieste festival in 1963.

d/p/s Chris Marker *c* Jean Chiabaud *se* C.S. Olaf
lp Davos Hanich, Hélène Chatelain, Jacques Ledoux, André Heinrich, Ligeia Borowczyk, Pierre Joffroy, William Klein, Etienne Becker

King Kong Tai Gojira *aka* King Kong Versus Godzilla

(TOHO; JAP) b/w 99(91) min
A fascinating pop culture representation of US-Japanese relations. The spectre unleashed by the US's nuclear aggression, Godzilla, is once more activated as an American atomic submarine causes an iceberg to explode, liberating the monster. King Kong is represented as a *nisei* deity: a god living on the Solomon Islands occupied by the Japanese but captured by the US making this Kong into a representative of the mixture of both countries' military culture, a mythical theme later rendered even more explicit in the shape of the Japanese version of Frankenstein's monster (**Frankenshutain Tai Baragon**, 1965). Kong starts out as a defender of Japanese fishermen as he defeats a giant octopus. The conflict between the internalized form of US culture, Kong, and the representation of American aggression in the form of a mythical beast, Godzilla, is fought out over Mount Fuji. The

wholesale destruction of Tokyo is almost taken for granted in such a context and the film dwells more on the comic side of the contest, which includes scenes where the two monsters play ball with an enormous rock. In the end, the unresolvable struggle overtly staged as a boxing match is terminated by an earthquake throwing both into the sea. Kong wades back on shore but Godzilla disappears from sight until, in his next picture, **Mosura Tai Gojira** (1964) he again does battle with a 'good', indigenous monster, Mothra.

The US version, which was produced by Beck, directed by Montgomery and written by Mason and Howard, cut some Japanese footage and inserted scenes starring Keith. Apparently, the script of the movie was based on an old Willis O'Brien treatment first called *King Kong Versus Frankenstein*, then *King Kong Versus the Ginko* and finally *Prometheus Versus King Kong*. After passing through a number of hands in Hollywood, the idea was sold to Toho who substituted Godzilla for Prometheus.

d Inoshiro Honda *p* Tomoyuki Tanaka *s* Shinichi Sekizawa *c* Hajime Koizumi *se* Eiji Tsuburaya
lp Tadao Takashima, Yu Fujiki, Akiko Wakabayashi, Mie Hama, Kenji Sahara, Akihiko Hirata, Ichiro Arishima
US version: d Thomas Montgomery *p* John Beck *s* Paul Mason, Bruce Howard *lp* Michael Keith, James Yogi, Harry Holcombe

Lord of the Flies

(ALLEN-HOGDON PROD./TWO ARTS; GB) b/w 91 min
Set in the near future, this adaptation of William Golding's novel follows the speedy descent into primitivism of a group of public schoolboys when the plane that's taking them to safety from an unseen nuclear catastrophe crashes on a remote desert island. Brook, all of whose films are scarred by an excessive theatricality, highlights Golding's themes (the fact

of original sin and the slimness of the barrier between civilization and savagery) strongly enough but both his script and direction are far too respectful to their very literary source. Thus, in place of the frenzy of guilt that the novel throws up as the children preserve and deform the empty rituals of public school that result in the murder/sacrifice of one of their number, Brook offers a crude and amateurish reading of the novel rather than a cinematic interpretation of Golding's allegory.

d/s Peter Brook   *p* Lewis M. Allen   *c* Tom Hollyman, Gerald Feil   *lp* James Aubrey, Tom Chapin, Hugh Edwards, Roger Elwin, Tom Gaman

Matango *aka* **Matango Fungus of Terror** *aka* **Attack of the Mushroom People**
(TOHO; JAP)   b/w   89(84, 70) min
A revealing variation on the theme of drugs in Science Fiction films: a shipwrecked group of holidaymakers, stranded on a desolate island, eat an exotic, multicoloured fungus and turn into mushrooms themselves. The film offers itself as an extended metaphor on desire. The isolated and deprived group, frustrated of their fantasy escape holiday, succumb to the temptation of the plant, initially described as a powerful narcotic. This indulgence causes their desires to take over their entire being and they become walking vegetables in rubbery phallic shapes, signifying nothing but desire. The ones to resist longest are a young couple, who have other ways of satisfying their desires, even on a desolate island. However, in keeping with the conventional depiction of women, the female of the couple wants 'more' than she gets and she too becomes a sign of her desire writ large. The young man escapes and recounts his story to unbelieving hospital doctors. Remembering the woman now lost to him, he too begins to sprout mushroomy growths on his face. Illogical on any level except that of fantasy, where it is glaringly consistent, this is a picture that, like Honda's **Chikyu Boeigun** (1957), allows us to glimpse something of the nature of the dream logic that structures the monster movie scenarios.

d Inoshiro Honda   *p* Tomoyuki Tanaka   *s* Takeshi Kimura   *c* Hajime Koizumi   *se* Eiji Tsuburaya   *lp* Akira Kubo, Yoshio Tsuchiya, Kenji Sahara, Hiroshi Koizumi, Kumi Mizuno, Miki Yashiro

Meshte Nastreshu *aka* **A Dream Come True**
(ODESSA STUDIOS; USSR)   68 min
A follow-up to the successful **Planeta Burg** (1962) with equally impressive settings and landscape designs but extremely weak on plot, almost as if the film were designed to be cannibalized by an American producer who would shoot his own narrative footage and combine it with the 'ready made' bits of lyrical, weird and visually stunning sets. This is in fact what happened to *Planeta Burg* and **Cesta do Praveku** (1955), earning valuable foreign currency even though the films were destroyed in the process.

The plot of this Russian film concerns the inhabitants of the planet Centurius who, attracted by a (Russian) song emanating from the Earth, send a spacecraft to investigate, but the craft is diverted to Mars. The three planets are characterized by three different design styles. On Centurius, red and green dominate while the architecture is all curves and soft edges; Earth has simply designed sets and monumental architecture while Mars is an endless sandy desert. The graphic lyricism strongly evokes prewar American magazine covers suggesting the makers may have had the possibility in mind that sections of their film might be used in American contexts. Karyukov had previously made an account of the space race rivalry between the USSR and the USA, **Niebo Zowiet** (1959). He also did the special effects for the Russian version of *Mysterious Island*, **Tainstvenni Ostrov** (1941).

co-d/co-s Mikhail Karyukov   *co-d* Otar Koberidze   *co-s* Alexander Berdink, Ivan Bondin   *c* Aleksei Gerasimov   *lp* Larissa Gordeichik, Otar Koberidze, Boris Borisenko, N. Timofeev, P. Shmakov, A. Genesin, N. Volkov, T. Pockena, L. Chinidzhanei, S. Krupnik

Dirk Bogarde (centre) prepares for immersion while John Clements (left) and Michael Bryant look on in The Mind Benders.

Left: *Tommy Kirk in the title role of* The Misadventures of Merlin Jones.

The Mind Benders (NOVUS; GB) b/w 113 (99) min

In this fascinating, if flawed, film, Clements is the MI5 agent investigating the death of an elderly scientist whom he suspects of turning traitor and Bogarde the dead man's assistant, convinced that he died as a result of brainwashing experiments being carried out in his laboratory. Bogarde demonstrates the experiment to Clements and then repeats it with himself as the subject, proving that feelings can be drained from a subject's mind – in this case his love for his pregnant wife (Ure) – and leave him mentally unstable enough to commit suicide. The final traumatic childbirth scenes shake off the brainwashing. The duel of wits between Bogarde and Clements, with Bogarde so eager to be tested it's clear he's already slightly unbalanced, is skilfully scripted by Kennaway while Dearden, an erratic director, manages to endow the sensory deprivation tank in which Bogarde immerses himself with a macabre quality simply by presenting it to us soberly.

d Basil Dearden p Michael Relph s James Kennaway c Denys Coop lp Dirk Bogarde, Mary Ure, John Clements, Michael Bryant, Wendy Craig, Harold Goldblatt

The Misadventures of Merlin Jones (WALT DISNEY) 88 min

This turgid Disney romp, which looks suspiciously like two segments of The Disney TV Hour joined together, stars Kirk as the college student who invents an electrical brain with which he can read other people's thoughts. Kirk is partnered by Funicello (soon to be a regular in Beach Party movies) who sings the film's awkward title song. The Augusts' screenplay is decidedly routine but despite poor reviews the film grossed some $4 million on its domestic release.

d Robert Stevenson p Walt Disney s Tom August, Helen August c Edward Colman lp Tommy Kirk, Annette Funicello, Leon Ames, Stuart Erwin, Alan Hewitt, Connie Gilchrist

Mouse on the Moon

(WALTER SHENSON PRODUCTIONS; GB) 85 min

This is a sequel to The Mouse That Roared (1959), a surprise international success.

Rutherford is the Grand Duchess of Fenwick, the smallest country in the world, whose wine-powered rocket (the brainwave of scientist Kossoff) races the Russians and Americans to the Moon, and not only wins the race but rescues the American and Russian astronauts. Lester's direction is spirited enough but Pertwee's script is leaden and the film sorely misses Peter Sellers, the star of The Mouse That Roared. That said, Moody plays the Prime Minister with great panache and Thomas is a gloriously silly-ass spy.

d Richard Lester p Walter Shenson s Michael Pertwee c Wilkie Cooper lp Margaret Rutherford, Bernard Cribbins, Terry-Thomas, Ron Moody, David Kossoff, June Ritchie, John Le Mesurier

The Nutty Professor

(JERRY LEWIS PRODUCTIONS/PAR) 107 min.

This re-working of Robert Louis Stevenson's Dr Jekyll and Mr Hyde, which features Lewis as an eccentric academic who swallows a mysterious potion and becomes an ultra-cool swinger, is one of the comedian's best films. Lewis' comedy has always been intensely physical and gestural – it's as though the excessive emotions of his characters take over direct control of his body – and it's equally notable that so many of his best films involve the hero splitting himself into several roles (as in The Family Jewels, 1965) and killing off alternative identities (The Patsy, 1964). Understandably such a notion of comedy, if only because of its childish excessiveness (not to mention Lewis' obsession with his erstwhile partner, Dean Martin, who figures here as Buddy Love, the crooner Lewis becomes after taking the potion) has been generally received with hostility by critics. This film, probably because the Stevenson story acts as both a structur-

Right: *David Kossoff as the absent-minded professor and hero of* Mouse on the Moon.

Left: *Klaus Kinski (right), in wonderful form as a villain, in* Scotland Yard Jagt Dr Mabuse.

ing device and 'explains' Lewis excessive mannerisms, is one of the few to have been well received. The first half is brilliantly imaginative, only towards the end does Lewis succumb to the sentimentality that scars even his best work. Stevens is the college student bewildered by events.

d/co-s Jerry Lewis   *p* Ernest D. Glucksman   *co-s* Bill Richmond   *c* Wallace Kelley   *se* Paul K. Lerpae
lp Jerry Lewis, Stella Stevens, Del Moore, Kathleen Freeman, Howard Morris, Elvia Allman, Buddy Lester

Omicron   (LUX/ULTRA/VIDES; IT)   b/w   102 min
An omicron, a creature from another planet, re-animates the corpse of an Italian worker (Salvatori) in this sporadically funny comedy. Gregoretti's direction is intelligent and the re-animation sequences are excellent, but too much of the humour falls flat as when the alien works machines with amazing rapidity, becomes involved with a strike and falls in love. The film's conclusion has Salvatori convince the alien parasite that Venus would make a far more hospitable environment.

d/s Ugo Gregoretti   *p* Franco Cristaldi   *c* Carlo di Palma
lp Renato Salvatori, Rosemary Dexter, Gaetano Quartaro, Mara Carisi, Ida Serasini, Calisto Calisti

Pasi Spre Luna *aka* **Steps to the Moon**
(BUCURESTI FILM; ROM)   b/w   60 min
A crazy comedy extending a single gag into a short children's feature. The opening sets the tone: a superlative airport with a spaceship ready for take-off; the hero plugs in his electric razor and the whole place is plunged into darkness. It is the story of a man (Beligan) who, while waiting to embark on a voyage to the Moon, dreams of meeting all the famous names

that in one way or another signposted the road to space travel. The list goes from mythological figures such as Prometheus, Artemis (Petrescu) and Mercury (Vasiliu-Birlic) via the Caliph of Baghdad (Teodorescu) to Leonardo da Vinci (Botta), Galileo (Demetru), Cyrano de Bergerac, H.G. Wells and Jules Verne. Popescu-Gopo, best known for his widely respected animation work, thus continues the popular Zeman-type of children's fantasy films evoking Verne's world (**Cesta do Praveku**, 1955, and especially **Vynalez Zkazy**, 1958) although the Romanian film is surprisingly conventional: one would have expected an animator to construct more sophisticated images instead of unimaginative sets for realistically staged events.

Popescu-Gopo later made another children's introduction to the great mythical figures of Western culture, updating the Faust myth in his *Faust XX* (1966), and went on to make an uneasy comedy, **Comedia Fantastica** (1975).

d/s Ion Popescu-Gopo   *c* Stefan Horvath   *se* Alexandru Popescu   *lp* Radu Beligan, Grigori Vasiliu-Birlic, Emil Botta, George Demetru, Ovidiu Teodorescu, Irina Petrescu

Santo en el Museo de Cera *aka* **Samson in the Wax Museum**
(FILMADORA PANAMERICANA; MEX)   92 min
The Enmascarado de Plata (The Silver Mask) encounters Frankenstein's monster in a wax museum, which turns out to be a front for the mad doctor Karol's (Brook) experiments with cell tissue. After a woman photographer (Bellini) fails to return from the museum, the masked wrestler is called in by her sister (Mora) and her lover (Rojo). The figures created by Dr Karol come alive and, after Santo has rescued Bellini, turn on their evil master. Combining elements from the later Universal Frankenstein movies with Andre De Toth's *House*

of Wax (1953), the effects are amateurish and the whole thing remains on the level of a children's serial. Santo later met the creature again and even wrestled with it in **Arañas Infernales** (1966) and in **Santo Contra la Hija de Frankenstein** (1971).

This was Blake's second Santo picture but he had already established his reputation as a fantasy director with *La Mujer y la Bestia* (1958) and *El Mundo de Vampiros* (1960). He had started directing with a melodramatic variation on Buñuel's *Los Olvidados* (1950) entitled *El Camino de la Vida* (1956) before concentrating on sexy movies starring Ana Luisa Peluffo or Kitty de Hoyos, starlets launched by their nude appearances in *La Ilegitima* (1955). Although Blake's scripts were never very interesting, he has a tendency to stylize his images and to concentrate on photogenic sequences, totally neglecting all the literary or psychological aspects of the plot. This gives his movies a visual poetry often lacking in more prestigious productions.

d Alfonso Corona Blake   *p* Alberto Lopez   *s* Fernando Galiana, Julio Porter   *c* Jose Ortiz Ramos   *lp* Santo, Claudio Brook, Ruben Rojo, Norma Mora, Roxana Bellini, Fernando Oses, Jose Luis Jimenez, Jorge Mondragon, Conception Martinez

Scotland Yard Jagt Dr Mabuse *aka* Scotland Yard Hunts Dr Mabuse

(CCC-FILM; WG)   b/w   90 min
The fourth sequel to Lang's **Die Tausend Augen des Dr Mabuse** (1960) has Mabuse's spirit in control of the psychiatrist Dr Pohland, who is able to impose his will on anybody by means of an electronic hypnotizing machine. He is opposed by Van Eyck, while Kinski appears in one of his familiar villainous roles. This attempt to combine Mabuse with material from Edgar Wallace, whose work was used for a large number of popular *krimi* films in Germany at the time, was an interesting idea that failed to work. The main quality of the film is that it combines the acting talents of Van Eyck and Kinski, both actors able to endow their performance with an intensely neurotic edge. The direction is uninspiring, no doubt because Ostrmayer had started his career amongst the Nazis and was far more at home with *Heimat* schmalz and phony 'social concern' movies than with any genuinely critical understanding of the darker sides of either film-making or the desire for other sorts of power.

d Paul May (Ostrmayer)   *p* Artur Brauner   *s* Ladislas Fodor   *c* Nenad Jovicic   *lp* Peter Van Eyck, Werner Peters, Sabine Bethmann, Dieter Borsche, Walter Rilla, Klaus Kinski (Claus Guenther Nakszynski), Agnes Windeck, Hans Nielsen, Ruth Wilbert

The Slime People

(JOSEPH F. ROBERTSON/HANSEN ENTERPRISES)   b/w   60 min
Nuclear tests awaken slippery, scaly monsters near Los Angeles in this quickie. The revitalized humanoid prehistorics erect a fog dome over the city so that the temperature is more akin to their usual slimy environment. Hutton, a one-time forties heart-throb directing his only film, also has the lead as the man who lifts the fog around LA – if only it could be done in reality – and destroys the monsters.

d Robert Hutton   *p* Joseph F. Robertson   *s* Vance Skarstedt   *c* William Troiano   *se* Charles Duncan   *lp* Robert Hutton, Les Tremayne, Robert Burton, Judee Morton, Susan Hart, John Close

Son of Flubber   (WALT DISNEY)   b/w   103(100) min

A comedy sequel, the first ever mounted by the Disney studios, to **The Absent-Minded Professor** (1961), *Son of Flubber* has the usual mawkish moral overtones. 'Even if they fall flat on their faces, they're still going forward' says MacMurray, commenting on why he teaches America's youth. A comparison of the two films is interesting; it's clear that *Son of Flubber* has exactly the same structure and rhythms as *The Absent-Minded Professor* (and many of the supporting cast of the earlier film). Thus, the basketball game of *Professor* is replaced with the football game of *Flubber*, complete with Alan Carney and Gordon Jones as coach and referee respectively. The net result of this duplicating of an earlier film is a sense of aimlessness (a common feature of sequels) because the reasons for action lie outside the storyline.

MacMurray is the inventor of 'dry rain', which he hopes will earn enough money to prevent his college being repossessed by Wynn's financier and Kirk, Wynn's son, the inventor of 'flubbergas' with the aid of which the college's football team win the day. Stevenson directs in his usual vigorous style.

d Robert Stevenson   *co-p/co-s* Bill Walsh   *co-p* Ron Miller   *co-s* Don DaGradi   *c* Edward Colman   *se* Peter Ellenshaw, Eustace Lycett, Robert A. Mattey, Jack Boyd, Jim Fetherolf   *lp* Fred MacMurray, Nancy Olson, Keenan Wynn, Tommy Kirk, Ed Wynn, Charles Ruggles, Leon Ames, William Demarest

Unearthly Stranger

(INDEPENDENT ARTISTS. A JULIAN WINTEL-LESLIE PARKYN PRODUCTION; GB)   b/w   74 min
This chilling film has scientist Neville, who's working on a secret space-time project, discover his wife (Licudi) is an alien, partly because she sleeps with her eyes open. When several space scientists are murdered, Licudi confesses to Neville that she's spearheading an alien invasion and that he should die next but she finds she can't kill him because she's fallen in love with him. This seals her fate with her alien controls and, in a haunting final image, Krish has the alien cry and the tears leaving tracks down her cheeks, like acid burning her face. Reversing the roles of **I Married a Monster from Outer Space** (1958), Krish and screenplay writer Carlton produced an unusually thoughtful British Science Fiction movie.

The football game, one of the highlights of Son of Flubber.

d John Krish   *p* Albert Fennell   *s* Rex Carlton   *c* Reg Wyer   *lp* John Neville, Gabriella Licudi, Philip Stone, Patrick Newell, Jean Marsh, Warren Mitchell

Der Unsichtbare *aka* The Invisible Man
(AERO FILM; WG)   b/w   94 min

This is loosely based on H.G. Wells' classic novel, filmed by James Whale as **The Invisible Man** (1933), but sstylistically derived from the wave of Edgar Wallace thrillers and the Mabuse films then swamping Germany with high-contrast black-and-white *krimis*, as they were called. Mostly indebted to the derivative **Die Unsichtbaren Krallen des Dr Mabuse** (1961), this story revolves around an evil maniac (Desny), a professor (von Borsody) who has disappeared, and his brother (Regnier) who, together with his girlfriend (Schwiers), does the suspecting and the detecting. A fairly anodyne thriller, routinely scripted and directed, it's most interesting aspect is the way it associates gangsters, scientists and industrialists at the height of Germany's postwar economic 'miracle'.

d/p/co-s Raphael Nussbaum   *co-s* Vladimir Semitjof   *c* Michael Marszalek   *lp* Ivan Desny, Ellen Schwiers, Charles Regnier, Ilse Steppat, Hannes Schmidhauser, Hans von Borsody, Herbert Stass, Harry Fuss, Christiane Nielsen, Joachim Hansen

X – The Man with X-Ray Eyes *aka* The Man with X-Ray Eyes   (ALTA VISTA)   88 (80) min

The basic opposition between vision and blindness (as seen in **Not of This Earth**, 1956 and in the numerous heroes who wear dark glasses in his films) is a central strand of Corman's work. Generally he uses the eyes as a metaphor for consciousness with the character's power of vision providing the key to his state of consciousness. Milland's Dr Xavier, who can literally see through things, is the extreme example of this. But, as so often in Corman, such increased powers of knowledge and perception bring him neither power nor happiness but transform him into a rarified figure, one who sees too much and trembles on the brink of another world from which he retreats (literally here, the film's conclusion has him tearing out his own eyes in biblical fashion) in fear.

Cast in the form of a thriller with Milland in his thirst for knowledge experimenting on himself and then taking flight when he accidentally kills his boss who intends to cut off his funds for further research, Corman's achievement in *X – The Man with X-Ray Eyes* is, as it were invisibly, to have bent the genre to his own ends. The result is one of his undisputed masterpieces, the weak special effects notwithstanding.

The film won the Golden Asteroid in the Trieste festival of Science Fiction films in 1963.

d/p Roger Corman   *s* Robert Dillon, Robert Russell   *c* Floyd Crosby   *se* Butler-Grover Inc.   *lp* Ray Milland, Dana Van Der Vlis, John Hoyt, Don Rickles, Harold J. Stone, Lorie Summers, Vicki Lee

El Asesino Invisible
(FILMADORA PANAMERICANA; MEX)   85 min

The stars of Crevenna's two space operas, **Gigantes Planetarios** and **El Planeta de los Mujeres Invasoras** (both 1965) had a trial run in this picture by Cardona, one of Mexico's most prolific directors. Here, Murray plays Inspector Martinez and Roel the unfortunate daughter of a scientist who, together with her lover (Agosti), invents a machine that can make people invisible. Their first experiment succeeds in making a rabbit disappear before the disbelieving eyes of a Golden Masked wrestler (Rivero). But the professor is killed, his apparatus stolen and the boy who looked after the laboratory along with it, apparently. After a spate of daring bank robberies committed by an invisible person, inspector Martinez discovers that Roel's lover and the boy are in fact the

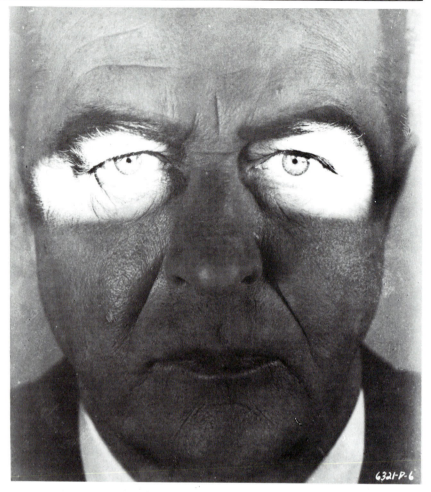

Above: *Ray Milland as X – The Man with X-Ray Eyes.*

culprits, betrayed by the fact that the invisibility effect only lasts for a couple of hours.

The script, which echoes the plot of **Los Invisibles** (1961), was co-written by Cardona's son, who had acted in his father's movies before becoming a scenarist and eventually a director as well. Cardona Senior was a veteran director of routinely commercial fare often mixing elements of established genres into kaleidoscopic pictures offering whatever were assumed to be the most successful ingredients of the current money-spinners. However, he did make a few interesting movies in the forties, such as *El Espectro de la Novia, El As Negro* and *La Mujer sin Cabeza* (all 1943) for which the poet Xavier Villaurrutia wrote the dialogue. David T. Bamberg, who starred in all three films, as well as in *El Museo del Crimen* (1944) in the role of Fu Man Chu, the super detective and magician, wrote the scripts.

d/co-s Rene Cardona   *p* Alberto Lopez   *co-s* Rene Cardona Jnr   *c* Raul Martinez Solares   *lp* Guillermo Murray, Adriana Roel, Ana Bertha Lepe, Carlos Agosti, Jorge Rivero, Miguel Arenas, Karloff Lagarde, Los Sinners

Le Ciel sur la Tête *aka* Sky Above Heaven *aka* Stade Zero *aka* Il Cielo sulla Testa *aka* Skies Above *aka* Sky Beyond Heaven
(GAUMONT/GALATEA; FR, IT)   scope   107 min

Made after **Doctor Strangelove** (1964), this lavishly produced fantasy, actively assisted by the French airforce and navy, which lent its prestigious aircraft carrier the *Clemenceau* as the principal set, is an understandably tame warning against nuclear war. A radioactive satellite suddenly appears over the US, triggering an escalation of suspicions, errors and actions between the superpowers but a nuclear holocaust is avoided as the Russians and the Americans join forces to attack the satellite which disappears as suddenly as it appeared. The result is a pacifist film that suceeds in turning itself into a glamorization, if not a glorification, of the armed forces and their photogenic weaponry (critics wrote about the *Clemenceau* as 'a splendid steel monster'). Séchan and Tabary's colour photography is dramatic and sharp, generating the necessary sense of adventure. A cast of unknowns underlines the ordinariness of the people involved in the emergency and reinforces the audience's identification with the armed forces. Nevertheless, the film is a poor effort when compared to other films produced in France at the time such as **La Jetée** (1963), **Alphaville** (1965) or *La Brûlure de Mille Soleils* (1965).

d/co-s Yves Ciampi *p* Irenée Leriche *co-s* Alain Satou, Jean Chapot *c* Edmond Séchan, Guy Tabary *lp* André Smagghe, Jacques Monod, Marcel Bozuffi, Yves Brainville, Guy Tréjean, Henri Piegay, Bernard Fresson, Beatrice Cenci

Creeping Terror

(TELEDYN/METROPOLITAN INTERNATIONAL PICTURES) 75 min
Special effects' man Lackey deserves to be as well known as directors Edward D. Wood (**Plan 9 from Outer Space**, 1956) and Bert I. Gordon (**The Amazing Colossal Man**, 1957) for his ability to create ludicrous monsters. He is responsible for the strange-looking alien monster, constructed of foam with five men inside to make it crawl, who lumbers out of a crashed spaceship in the Colorado desert. Savage and O'Neill battle the man-eating creature who is threatening world domination while Sherwood directs at a wooden pace.

d John Sherwood *p* William Alland *s* Arthur Ross
c Maury Gertsman *se* Clifford Stine, John Lackey
lp Vic Savage, Shannon O'Neill

The war room in Dr Strangelove.

Il Disco Volante *aka* The Flying Saucer

(DINO DE LAURENTIIS; IT) b/w 93 min
This routine outing is one of the numerous films made by comedian Sordi (once described as Italy's Peter Sellers) who, soon afterwards, further extended his range of activities by writing and/or directing the majority of his subsequent films. Here he plays several characters, all of whom see Martians land on Earth and are locked up in a lunatic asylum when they persist in claiming they've seen flying saucers. Although made for domestic consumption, the comedy is more restrained than usual in reflection of the strong supporting cast which includes Vitti (better known internationally for her work with Antonioni) and Mangano, then married to producer De Laurentiis. Director Brass later achieved a fame of sorts as the (uncredited) director of the softcore pornographic epic, *Caligula* (1979) produced by *Penthouse*'s Bob Guccione.

d Tinto Brass *p* Dino De Laurentiis *s* Rudolfo Sonego
c Bruno Barcarol *lp* Alberto Sordi, Monica Vitti, Silvano Mangano, Eleonora Rossi Drago, Guido Celano, Alberto Fogliani

Doctor Strangelove, or How I Learned to Stop Worrying and Love the Bomb

(HAWK FILMS; GB) b/w 94 min
Originally conceived by Kubrick as a straight drama, he later decided that the only way to tell the story of an accidental nuclear war was as a black comedy. The resulting film, with its delicious mix of polished realism and bleak, despairing satire, remains the funniest work about nuclear war yet with the possible exception of the *Whoops Apocalypse* teleseries. Indeed, with excess written into the film in the form of

and destroys the transmitter station that is controlled by aliens from a distant planet.

Fisher does his best with Cross's muddled script.

d Terence Fisher *p* Robert L. Lippert, Jack Parsons *s* Henry Cross *c* Arthur Lowis *lp* Willard Parker, Virginia Field, Dennis Price, Thorley Walters, Vanda Godsell, David Spencer, Anna Falk

Fail Safe

(MAX E. YOUNGSTEIN-SIDNEY LUMET PRODUCTIONS/PAR) b/w 111 min
Released soon after **Doctor Strangelove** (1964), this offering covers much the same ground far less successfully. The result is a film reminiscent of the work of Arch Oboler, though better made, a meretricious film that wears its heart too openly on its liberal sleeve in its story of an accidental nuclear attack made on Russia by the USA. To avert a world war and appease the Russians, Fonda's American President is forced to bomb New York. Lumet's doggedly realist direction only serves to further blunt the film's message.

d Sidney Lumet *p* Max E. Youngstein *s* Walter Bernstein *c* Gerald Hirschfeld *se* Storyboard Inc. *lp* Henry Fonda, Dan O'Herlihy, Walter Matthau, Frank Overton, Edward Binns, Fritz Weaver, Larry Hagman

First Men in the Moon

(COL; GB, US) scope 107 (104) min
Co-scripted by Kneale, better known as the creator of the *Quatermass* teleseries which was later successfully filmed by Hammer (**The Quatermass Xperiment**, 1955; **Quatermass II**, 1957 and **Quatermass and the Pit**, 1967), this is a jolly version of H.G. Wells' 1901 visionary novel which was the inspiration for Georges Méliès' **Le Voyage dans la Lune** (1902). A hugely enjoyable piece of fluff, greatly aided by Harryhausen's special effects, it closely follows Wells' fantasy about an 1899 British moon landing. Jeffries, Judd and Hyer are the brave astronauts.

Director Juran (who oddly signed several of his films, such as **Attack of the 50-foot Woman**, 1958, Nathan Hertz) shared an Oscar for his design of John Ford's *How Green Was My Valley* (1941).

The film was released in Cinerama in West Germany.

Left: Henry Fonda as the beleaguered President of the United States in Fail Safe.

First Men in the Moon, Nathan Juran's engaging version of H.G. Wells' visionary novel of the Victorian conquest of space.

Sellers' three roles (he plays the ex-Nazi scientist Dr Strangelove, the American President and a stiff-upper-lipped British officer) and Pickens' 'Ride 'em Cowboy' attitude to Doomsday, the net effect is strangely comforting. From this perspective it is significant that the film was made in the sixties rather than the fifties when the bomb was a far more undefined object of social concern. Thus, though Hayden's maniacal right-wing airforce general who makes a pre-emptive strike against Russia because he thinks fluoridization to be a communist-inspired means of 'sapping our vital bodily fluids', may connect with the fear of a takeover from within, a staple of American Science Fiction films of the fifties, the real fear the film expresses is a concern with technology (the Doomsday machine) which, it suggests, cannot be trusted. This is a fear explored in other notable films of the sixties, such as **Seconds** (1966), **The Forbin Project** (1969) and, of course, the HAL sequence in Kubrick's own **2001 – A Space Odyssey** (1968).

The film is undoubtedly funny, but in retrospect it also seems to strain for effects, as in the sequence where Vera Lynn's *We'll Meet Again* is juxtaposed with the falling of the nuclear missile on Russia (a sequence that anticipates that in *2001* in which *The Blue Danube* is played over the gracefully, gently turning spacewheel). Interestingly, Kubrick himself seems to have been aware of this, for he shot but deleted from the film a climactic custard-pie fight amongst those present in the war room after the dropping of the bomb on Russia.

But, if the film, which was wildly over-praised at the time of its release, is flawed it remains, with *Lolita* (1962), the most robust of Kubrick's films, poised as it is between the technical ingenuity of his earlier films and the ornate, mannered excesses of his later work.

d/p/co-s Stanley Kubrick *co-s* Terry Southern, Peter George *c* Gilbert Taylor *se* Wally Veevers *lp* Peter Sellers, George C. Scott, Sterling Hayden, Keenan Wynn, Slim Pickens, Peter Bull

The Earth Dies Screaming

(LIPPERT/PLANET; GB) b/w 62 min
This is the first of Fisher's workmanlike trio of Science Fiction films for Planet (the others are **Island of Terror**, 1966, and **The Night of the Big Heat**, 1967), all of which deal with isolated communities under threat of extra-terrestrial invasion. American test pilot Nolan (Parker) returns from a flight to discover that England has been devastated. He joins up with other survivors (including Price, Field and Walters) and travels to London, where they are attacked by robots who kill by touch and resurrect the corpses as mindless zombies. Eventually Parker discovers the power source of the robots,

Above: *Sean Connery in extremis in Goldfinger.*

d Nathan Juran   p Charles H. Schneer   s Nigel Kneale, Jan Read   c Wilkie Cooper, Harry Gillam   se Ray Harryhausen   lp Edward Judd, Martha Hyer, Lionel Jeffries, Peter Finch (uncredited), Miles Malleson, Betty McDowall, Erik Chitty, Hugh McDermott

Flesh Eaters (VULCAN PRODUCTIONS)   b/w   92(88) min
A lacklustre low-budget shocker. Wilkin, Morley, Tudor and Sanders are shipwrecked off a desert island but, before they can climb out of the water, they discover a flesh-eating bacteria in the sea. They elude this (just!) only to be confronted by crazed scientist, Kosleck, who is conducting anti-social experiments on this remote island and is anxious to try out some of his discoveries on his guests. Curtis directs with enthusiasm but little imagination.

d/co-p Jack Curtis   co-p Terry Curtis   co-p/s Arnold Drake   c Carson Davidson   se Roy Benson   lp Martin Kosleck, Barbara Wilkin, Rita Morley, Ray Tudor, Byron Sanders

Goldfinger (EON; GB)   109 min
This large-scale, very glossy entry in the Bond series revolves around villain Goldfinger's (Froebe) attempts to plant an atomic bomb in Fort Knox, in order to contaminate the world's gold deposits and put up the value of his own hoards, earned through international smuggling. Bond (Connery) and Pussy Galore (Blackman) foil the plan with three minutes to spare. The special effects are innovative and Hamilton's direction professional.

Like the *Carry On* series, the Bond films are more interesting as sociocultural phenomena than as individual pictures. What is noticeable about this outing, the comic delights of Sakata's Oddjob and Blackman's tamed lesbian aide, is the film's increasing dependence on technology and Ken Adam's baroque (almost Busby Berkeley-like) sets for its comic-strip appeal.

d Guy Hamilton   p Albert R. Broccoli, Harry Saltzman s Richard Maibaum, Paul Dehn   c Ted Moore se John Stears, Frank George   lp Sean Connery, Gert Froebe, Honor Blackman, Shirley Eaton, Tania Mallet, Harold Sakata, Bernard Lee, Lois Maxwell

Kaitei Gunkan aka **Atoragon, the Flying Supersub** aka **Atragon** aka **Ataragon**
(TOHO; JAP)   scope   96(88) min
A Japanese version of the Atlantis myth, combined with monster and space movie elements, this picture marks a major development in the Japanese Science Fiction genre. Previously, militarism had been represented explicitly as impotent against foreign invasions or implicitly as responsible for the disasters that befall Japan in the shape of monsters unleashed by thermonuclear explosions. *Kaitei Gunkan*, on the other hand, has a 'good' atomically powered submarine-airship-mole (the mechanical equivalent of a triphibian being) commanded by an admiral who refused to surrender at the end of the war. He now is seen as the only possible saviour of

The flying-super-submarine Ataragon in danger in Kaitei Gunkan, *a Japanese version of the Atlantis myth, which in its celebration of atomic power (the super-sub is atomic powered) marked a significant shift in the Japanese cycle of monster movies.*

Right: *Russ Meyer's* Kiss Me Quick!, *one of the first of many sexploitation essays in Science Fiction.*

Japan. The evil underwater empire of Mu, with its eel-like monster goddess Wenda, threatens Earth with destruction unless the supersub, its only real opponent, is surrendered. The symbol of Japanese national pride does not surrender but defeats the threat to its country without resorting to nuclear weapons, apparently on humanitarian grounds. The acting, the dubbing and the effects' work show signs of carelessness and are disappointing.

Subsequent monster movies began to see a wholesale shift away from the depiction of monsters as threats to Japan. Instead a more ambivalent attitude towards the military force they incarnate became more manifest, including a positive evaluation of nuclear weapons, especially in **Kaiju Daisenso** (1965). Significantly, the film was made in the year that the Liberal-Democratic Party, which represented the military-industrial complex in Japan, won a significant electoral victory, temporarily ending the extremely militant opposition to its régime and cautiously embarking on a campaign to revive militarist nationalism in Japan.

d Inoshiro Honda *p* Tomoyuki Tanaka *s* Shinichi Sekizawa *c* Hajime Koizumi *se* Eiji Tsuburaya *lp* Tadao Takashima, Yoko Fujiyama, Hiroshi Koizumi, Jun Tazaki, Ken Uehara, Kenji Sahara, Tetsuko Kobayashi, Akemi Kita, Akihiko Hirata

Kisses for My President *aka* Kisses for the President

(PEARLAYNE/WB) b/w 113 min
A one joke film – in the near future a female President of the United States is elected and her husband ponders his role as the first lady – *Kisses for My President* lacks the manic charms of a movie like *It's Great to Be Alive* (1933) or the satiric edge of **Wild in the Streets** (1968). In their place writers Binyon and Kane supply an abundance of corn with MacMurray, at his domesticated best, grinning and grizzling as the put-upon first lady to Bergen's manly woman president and Wallach as

the visiting dictator with an eye for the pleasures of the flesh. The result is a flat film, one far more revealing of the mores of its times than its makers realized.

Director/producer Bernhardt started his career in the theatre before turning to the cinema in 1926. He directed several films, including UFA's first talking picture and **Der Tunnel** (1933), before, like so many German film-makers of the time, emigrating to America via France and England. *Kisses for My President*, his last film, was made after an attempted return to film production in Germany in 1960.

d/p Curtis Bernhardt *s* Claude Binyon, Robert G. Kane *c* Robert Surtees *lp* Polly Bergen, Fred MacMurray, Arlene Dahl, Eli Wallach, Edward Andrews, Donald May

Kiss Me Quick! *aka* Dr Breedlove

(FANTASY PRODUCTIONS) 80 min
This is one of the numerous skin-flicks produced and directed by former amateur film-maker Meyer. A one-time newsreel cameraman turned photographer of nudes for *Playboy* magazine, in 1959 he began making self-produced soft-porn movies and quickly won himself the title of 'King of the Nudies'. It was his films that paved the way for the sexploitation explosion of the seventies. After the phenomenal success of *Vixen* (1968), he briefly entered the Hollywood mainstream with *Beyond the Valley of the Dolls* (1970) and *The Seven Minutes* (1971) before returning to what he once called 'the more honest world of sexploitation'.

This, one of his wittier films, features Coe as the alien, Sterilox, who comes to Earth in search of female partners (the women of his planet are barren). After briefly falling in love with a vending machine, he visits Dr Breedlove (a parody of Peter Sellers' Dr Strangelove), an expert at creating artificial women, one of whose creations he takes back with him. Coe also plays Frankenstein's monster, one of Breedlove's first experiments in creation.

d/p/s Russ Meyer   c Lester Kovac (Laszlo Kovacs?)
lp Jackie DeWitt, Fred Coe, Althea Currier, Claudia Banks

I Marziani Hanno Dodici Mani *aka* Llegaron los Marcianos *aka* The Twelve Handed Men of Mars

(PRODUZIONE D.S./EPOCA FILMS; IT, SP)   b/w   95 min

A broad comedy, *I Marziani Hanno Dodici Mani* features Panelli, Croccola, Garinei and Landa as the four Martians (X1, X2, X3 and X4 respectively) who come to Earth in human form to prepare for an eventual invasion only to find Earth more congenial than Mars. One becomes a real-estate developer, one a politician, one falls in love and Croccola, most charming of all, becomes a Science Fiction writer. The score is by Ennio Morricone, better known for his music for the Dollar trilogy and numerous other Italian Westerns.

d/s Franco Castellano, G. Pipola   p Dario Sabatello
c Alfio Contini   lp Paolo Panelli, Carlo Croccola, Enzo Garinei, Alfredo Landa, Magali Noel, Cristini Gajonia

Mosura Tai Gojira *aka* Gojira Tai Mosura *aka* Godzilla Versus Mothra *aka* Godzilla Versus the Thing *aka* Godzilla Versus the Giant Moth *aka* Mothra Versus Godzilla *aka* Godzilla Fights the Giant Moth

(TOHO; JAP)   scope   94(90, 87) min

Godzilla's fourth appearance and Mothra's second in a movie that quickly overshadowed the previous box-office hit **King Kong Tai Gojira** (1963). The story has Mothra's giant egg, washed ashore by a hurricane, stolen and exploited by carnival promoters. The Peanuts Sisters, the tiny twins guarding the moth on the island where it is regarded as a deity, come to plead for the return of the egg but to no avail. However, when Godzilla again embarks on an attack of Japan, the sisters are persuaded to try and invoke the help of Mothra, who is getting a bit too old for such tasks and is defeated by Godzilla. However, the two larva that emerge from Mothra's egg entangle the reptile in a web of silky, sticky threads, making it topple over a cliff. The introduction of little monsters, to appeal to the children's market and solicit the audience's sympathies, was to prove a successful gimmick

employed time and again, most effectively in Nikkatsu's affectionate parody of the genre, **Daikyoju Gappa** (1967) and in **Gojira No Musuko** (1967).

d Inoshiro Honda   p Tomoyuki Tanaka   s Shinichi Sekizawa   c Hajime Koizumi   se Eiji Tsuburaya, Sadamasa Arikawa, Akira Watanabe, Motoyoshi Tomioka, Kuichiro Kishida   lp Akira Takarada, Yuriko Hoshi, Hiroshi Koizumi, Yu Fujiki, the Itoh Sisters

Pajama Party *aka* The Maid and the Martian

(AIP)   scope   85 min

One-time Disney star Kirk plays the Martian pioneer who arrives at Lanchester's swimming-pool party in this youth-market musical caper, a role he would repeat in the hilarious **Mars Needs Women** (1966). He falls in love with Funicello, another Disney regular (the pair had played opposite each other in **The Misadventures of Merlin Jones,** 1963) who graduated to AIP's endless stream of Beach Party movies, the girlfriend of Lanchester's nephew. Two con-men trying to rob the household of a hoard of money are continuously interrupted by Kirk and Funicello's songs and Keaton makes a surprise appearance as Chief Rotton Eagle.

Heyward's slack script is tightened by Weis' competent direction.

d Don Weis   p James H. Nicholson, Samuel Z. Arkoff
s Louis M. Heyward   c Floyd Crosby   se Roger George
lp Tommy Kirk, Annette Funicello, Elsa Lanchester, Buster Keaton, Harvey Lembeck, Jesse White, Dorothy Lamour, Frankie Avalon

Robinson Crusoe on Mars

(A SCHENCK-ZABEL PRODUCTION)   scope   109 min

Haskin, the director of **Destination Moon** (1950) and **War of the Worlds** (1953), made this interesting film that hides behind an absurd title. Only very loosely based on Daniel Defoe's novel, Melchior and Higgins' script starts with a spaceship crash-landing on Mars and Mantee's survivor desperately struggling to live in an alien landscape with only a small monkey to keep him company. He inhabits a cave,

The discovery of Mothra's giant egg in a scene reminiscent of The Thing *(1951) from* Mosura Tai Gojira.

manages to replenish his air supply by heating rocks to provide oxygen and is haunted by images of his dead colleague. The loneliness starts to drive him mad and his convincing fight for survival begins. Eventually alien spaceships arrive with a complement of slaves and Mantee rescues Lundin to be his Man Friday. Death Valley provided the Martian landscape and effects' man Butler (who later worked on **Marooned**, 1969, also shot in Death Valley) matted the valley's blue stones orange. Oddly enough, the Martian ships resemble the death ships of *War of the Worlds*.

d Byron Haskin   *p* Aubrey Schenck   *s* Ib J. Melchior, John C. Higgins   *c* Winton C. Hoch   *se* Lary Butler
lp Paul Mantee, Vic Lundin, Adam West

Santa Claus Conquers the Martians
(JALOR PRODUCTIONS)   82 min
Although the title is one of the most wonderful in the genre, this film is cloying. Familiar folk-hero (Call) is kidnapped by the Martians to brighten the lives of their deprived children. After some depressingly twee adventures, which Webster directs with saccharine aplomb, patronizingly playing down to his young audience, the old gentleman manages to turn the tables on the Martians and make his escape.

In recent years, the film's amateurish performances and production have garnered it a cult reputation as one of the worst films ever made.

d Nicholas Webster   *p* Paul Jacobson   *s* Glenville Mareth
c David Quaid   *lp* John Call, Leonard Hicks, Vincent Back, Victor Stiles, Donna Conforth, Bill McCutcheon

The Time Travelers   (DOBIL/AIP)   85 min
Conceived by Melchior and Hewitt (who co-authored the original story) as a sequel to **The Time Machine** (1960), this is undoubtedly Melchior's best film as director and writer.

Earth is totally devastated by a nuclear war and the survivors, living in a labyrinth and protected from the mutants who roam the surface by an army of android robots, build a spaceship to carry them to the new world of Alpha Centauri. They are joined by a group of scientists, led by Foster, who, in 1964, accidentally created a time-portal and are now trapped in the future. Melchior's vision of the future is fascinating and Hewitt's excellent special effects give his inventions – a matter-transfer chamber, hydroponic gardens where flowers emerge from seeds in seconds, the time-portal itself, inter-planetary satellites, a colour music machine, a laser which cuts holes in the rock face – even greater credibility. Eventually the scientists are briefly able to return to 1964 but they cannot alter the course of history. The bleak ending has the time travelers caught in a time loop, forever cycling from 1964 back to the future over and over again.

The Time Travelers was re-made as **Journey to the Centre of Time** (1967).

d/s Ib Melchior   *p* William Redlin   *c* William Zsigmond
se David Hewitt   *lp* Preston Foster, Merry Anders, John Hoyt, Dennis Patrick, Carol White, Joan Woodbury

Die Todesstrahlen des Dr Mabuse *aka* Dr Mabuse's Rays of Death   (CCC-FILM/FRANCO-LONDON-FILM/ SERENA FILM; WG, FR, IT)   b/w   95 min
In this film, the last in the series to date, Mabuse (again played by Preiss) wants to blitz the world to death with a gigantic concave mirror condensing energy into a death ray. His plans are foiled, yet again, by Van Eyck. By this time, Spectre had monopolized the world domination stakes with the James Bond films and Mabuse had to acknowledge defeat in the face of the flood of Bond and Bond imitations saturating the market, each one outdoing the other in production values, gadgets and special effects. A cheapo German producer such as Brauner, who had the rights to the Mabuse character and had produced all the sixties Mabuse films from **Die Tausend Augen des Dr Mabuse** (1960) onwards, either directly or as executive producer, could no longer compete with the American money flooding Europe's film industry. Besides, the obsessive black-and-white world of Mabuse would not have translated well into the glossy world of Bond, Helm or Flint.

The Argentinian director Fregonese had made interesting movies in America (*Blowing Wild*, 1953, *Black Tuesday*, 1954, among others), and had a knack for filming violence which is all too rarely manifested in this Mabuse effort. Beatty and Genn appear in entertaining cameo parts designed for the British and American markets.

d Hugo Fregonese   *p* Artur Brauner   *s* Ladislas Fodor
c Ricardo Pallottini   *lp* Peter Van Eyck, O.E. Hasse, Yvonne Furneaux, Wolfgang Preiss, Rika Dialina, Yoko Tani, Charles Fawcett, Gustavo Rojo, Robert Beatty, Leo Genn

Uchudai Dogora *aka* Dogora the Space Monster *aka* Dagora *aka* Space Monster Dogora
(TOHO; JAP)   scope   83(80) min
The Dogora were odd creatures. Unlike their predecessors, they starred in a film but weren't used again, thus sharing the fate of the many incidental monsters that populated the genre. As such, this film is closer to the **Matango** (1963) type movie than to the Kaiju Eiga proper. As a fantasy, *Uchudai Dogora* offers a representation of a sense of victimization, of being preyed upon on an international scale. The monsters are cells

Left: John Call as Santa spreads good cheer in the truly awful Santa Claus Conquers the Martians.

Mutants and androids do battle in Ib Melchior's engaging low-budget production The Time Travelers.

Above: *Vincent Price as L'Ultimo Uomo della Terra, Sidney Salkow and Ubalda Ragona's cheapskate version of Richard Matheson's classic novel, I Am Legend.*

screenplay drastically rewritten by Leicester. Unhappy with the result, Matheson put his pen-name, Swanson, to the collaboration.

Price is the only survivor of a plague that killed most of the Earth's population and turned the remainder into mutant monsters who besiege him each night. By day, he journeys through the city, staking as many of the mutants – who, terrified of the light, lurk in dark ruins, waiting for darkness to attack the man whose normality they detest – as he can. Gradually, Price becomes weary of his nightly sieges and eventually the mutants kill him.

I Am Legend is one of Matheson's most compelling novels, but his heavily atmospheric style is not well translated here, where the crude repetitive violence is as unsatisfactory as Price's oddly low-key performance.

d Sidney Salkow, Ubalda Ragona   *p* Robert L. Lippert
s Logan Swanson (Richard Matheson), William P.
Leicester   *c* Franco Delli Colli   *lp* Vincent Price, Franca
Bettoia, Emma Danieli, Giacomo Rossi-Stuart, Umberto Rau

1965

Agent 505 - Todesfalle Beirut *aka* Agent 505
(RAPID FILM/METHEUS FILMS/COMPAGNIE LYONNAISE DE
CINEMA; WG, IT, FR)   scope   93 min
Stafford and Howland are the secret agents who save Beirut from destruction by Leipnitz's diabolical villain in this would-be James Bond lookalike Science Fiction thriller. The film is elaborately staged with touches of humour but the script is entirely predictable, as is Ennio Morricone's harsh score.

d/s Manfred R. Koehler   *p* Wold C. Hartwig   *c* Knut
Seedorf, Klaus Werner   *lp* Frederic Stafford, Chris
Howland, Harald Leipnitz, Geneviève Cluny, Gisella Arden,
Pierre Richard

Alphaville *aka* Une Etrange Adventure de Lemmy Caution
(CHAUMIANE/FILMSTUDIO; FR, IT)   b/w   98 min
Godard's fascination with the forms and conventions of popular culture, especially its American manifestations, is well known. *Alphaville*, originally titled *Tarzan versus IBM*, is the most glorious example of this obsession. Before embarking on this Science Fiction *film noir*, he tried out some of the ideas in a contribution to the omnibus film *RoGoPag* (1962). His episode, entitled *Le Nouveau Monde*, told of a man who becomes an alien in his own city, Paris, after an atomic explosion has changed the psychic structure of all his fellow Parisians. A few years later, he contributed an episode called *Anticipation* to another omnibus film, *Le Plus Vieux Métier du Monde* (1967). This time a man from another planet arrives at Orly airport and is escorted to the local hotel where he finds that prostitution has become extremely specialized: one girl mutely performs the gestures of love only, while another only speaks of love without doing anything. The happy ending occurs when he teaches the 'courtly love' girl that the mouth can be used both for speaking and for performing love: they kiss.

Alphaville is a far more complex work. It was made in the same year as *Pierrot le Fou* (1965), when Godard was at the height of his commercial success and was both reviled and revered as a major innovative force in French (and world) cinema. The film is classic 'first phase' Godard, before he turned his lucid intelligence to more directly political issues. The idiosyncratic mix – popular and high culture, myth, fairy tales and realism, linguistics and philosophy, sex and violence – is as might be expected from a film of this period in his career. The plot intertwines the myth of Orpheus and Eurydice with the Oedipus legend. Lemmy Caution (Constantine) is the intergalactic agent who arrives in Alphaville in search of Dr von Braun (Vernon), the evil genius who left the Outer Countries and is now in charge of the central computer

that mutated after being exposed to radiation and have become huge octopus-like creatures. They hover over Japan, feeding on its raw materials as well as on its riches: they eat carbon, extracted through their tentacles. First they appear as competition for a gang of diamond robbers, melting the safe with their fiery breath and gobbling up the precious stones. Then they devour trains, ships and even the famous Wakato bridge. They behave like a global force of exploitation, appropriating the country's wealth on a scale far beyond that of the local small entrepreneurs such as thieves. The monsters are defeated when a Japanese scientist discovers they are vulnerable to wasp's venom and the whole of Japan, in a massive national effort, bands together to provide the required stuff to eliminate the threat. Made in the same year as **Kaitei Gunkan** (1964), an ambivalent but unmistakable evocation of a glorious, undefeated Japan, *Uchudai Dogora* sketches in some of the fantasy elements that were available to be exploited by unsavoury forms of nationalism. The effects are entertaining and the scope and colour format is skilfully utilized, creating some impressive, dreamlike scenes.

d Inoshiro Honda   *p* Tomoyuki Tanaka   *s* Shinichi
Sekizawa   *c* Hajime Koizumi   *se* Eiji Tsuburaya
lp Yosuke Natsuki, Yoko Fujiyama, Akiko Wakabayashi,
Hiroshi Koizumi

L'Ultimo Uomo della Terra *aka* The Last Man on Earth
(LA REGINA/ALTA VISTA; IT, US)   86 min
The first of two films based on Matheson's novel *I Am Legend* – the second is **The Omega Man** (1971). Matheson wrote the original screenplay for *The Last Man on Earth* for Hammer in 1957 but they sold the project to Lippert who had Matheson's

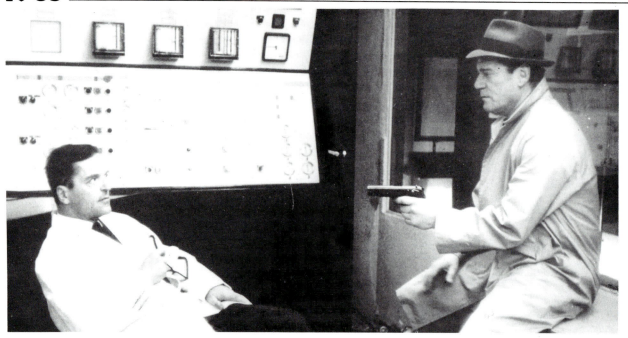

The slippery Howard Vernon (left) and the granite-faced Eddie Constantine debate ethics in Jean-Luc Godard's masterful Alphaville.

Alpha 60. Karina plays von Braun's daughter, Natasha, an employee at the Institute of General Semantics, assigned to Caution as his official guide. After witnessing the death of his contact and predecessor, Henry Dickson (Tamiroff) and numerous adventures, Caution eventually confronts the computer and confuses it by providing poetic answers to schematic questions. He kills von Braun, destroys Alpha 60 and drives out of the city accompanied by Natasha who has learned some of the long-forgotten words such as 'conscience'. He tells her not to look back while she slowly mouthes the phrase 'I love you'.

The picture's originality is not to be found in the clichéd opposition between emotion and science. The conventions of the Science Fiction thriller merely provide the framework for a film which mobilizes, enthusiastically, the themes and images of the genre as a sort of magnetic field within which to release a myriad of philosophical and aesthetic ideas while maintaining an overall shape to the thing. Such a freewheeling approach affords the viewer an uncommonly wide and liberating range of pleasures. In this sense, *Alphaville*, together with *Pierrot le Fou*, is Godard's most romantically anarchic movie. The intricate gestural and iconic rhythms as men in trenchcoats and hats move through shadowy or harshly lit spaces, enacting stock situations of the hard-boiled thriller in appropriately seedy locations, often surrounded by surfaces reflecting bright neon light or naked bulbs; the multilayered mesh of classic mythology, Perrault's tales, comic strips, Hollywood movies and cheap detective stories; Constantine's performance as a parody or an extension of his own roles in previous Lemmy Caution films derived from Peter Cheyney's character (*Les Femmes s'en Balancent*, 1953; *Lemmy pour les Dames*, 1961; *Ça Va Barder*, 1954; *Je Suis un Sentimental*, 1955, and many others) are all hugely enjoyable. Further pleasures can be derived from Godard's parody of Parisian intellectuals (Comolli and Fieschi, two critics of *Cahiers du Cinéma* appear as Jekel and Eckel, two white-coated semanticians) or by tracing the director's gradual move towards a more directly political consideration of the relations between ideology and artistic production, between images and sounds.

Godard's own characteristically polemical comment on the film's plot is that it isn't set in the future at all: Caution is a man from the forties suddenly catapulted into the Paris of the sixties. But perhaps the best approach to the movie is simply to engage with it as a tissue of intellectual and sensual pleasures, a feast for *cinéphiles*.

d/s Jean-Luc Godard *p* André Michelin *c* Raoul Coutard *lp* Eddie Constantine, Anna Karina, Akim Tamiroff, Howard Vernon, Laszlo Szabo, Michel Delahaye, Jean-André Fieschi, Jean-Louis Comolli, Christa Lang, Jean-Pierre Léaud

Amanti d'Oltretomba *aka* The Faceless Monsters *aka* Nightmare Castle

(PRODUZIONE CINEMATOGRAFICA EMMECI; IT) 105(73) min
A sadistic mélange of Science Fiction and horror – it begins with the brutal disfiguration of one of a pair of lovers with a hot poker and the pouring of acid on the other – this is a pedestrian film. Miller is the Victorian scientist, experimenting with the regeneration of blood through electricity, who turns on first his wife (Steele) and then on her sister (Steele again) who inherits the property. Steele is in fine form as the avenging sister and some of the sequences are powerful but the distributors' cuts and the all too predictable plotline make for a weak film.

d/co-s Allan Grunewald (Mario Caiano) *p* Carlo Caiano *co-s* Fabio De Agostini *c* Enzo Barboni *lp* Barbara Steele, Paul Miller, Helga Liné, Lawrence Clift, John McDouglas (Giuseppe Addobbati), Rik Battaglia

Berlino Appuntamento per le Spie *aka* Spy in Your Eye

(ITALIAN INTERNATIONAL FILM/PUBLI ITALIA; IT) 105(84) min
A rather interesting voyeuristic spy movie in which the Russians implant a mini-telecamera in the eye of American spy Bert Morris (Halsey) during an operation to cure his blindness. With this advantage they manage to see through the eye of their opponent and kidnap Paula (Krauss), the daughter of a deceased Nobel Prize winning scientist who had developed a death ray. The general suspicion is that he somehow communicated the secret formula to his daughter, which makes her sought after by both the US and USSR. In the end, the spy in the eye is discovered and used to feed false information to the Russians while Bert and Paula escape to safety, where it is established that the canny scientist had the formula tattooed on his daughter's scalp, allowing the hair to hide it. The voyeuristic gimmick is quite effective and would suggest the script contains interesting devices and cinematically effective ideas: unfortunately, the rest of the movie is boringly routine, indifferently directed, spy action stuff. It is sad to see Andrews, the fascinating performer in Lang's *Beyond a Reasonable Doubt* (1956) and Jacques Tourneur's

Right: *Dana Andrews causes a* Crack in the World.

Night of the Demon (1957) failing to overcome the weaknesses of a picture, unlike Claude Rains who managed to turn clichéd situations to his advantage in the extraordinary **Il Pianeta degli Uomini Spenti** (1961).

d Vittorio Sala   *p* Fulvio Lucisano, Lucio Marcuzzo
s Romano Ferrera, Adriano Baracco, Adriano Bolzoni
c Fausto Zuccoli   *lp* Brett Halsey, Paula Krauss, Dana Andrews, Gastone Moschin, Tania Beryl, Alessandro Sperli, Mario Valdemarin, Tino Bianchi, Renato Baldini

City Under the Sea *aka* War Gods of the Deep
(BRUTON/AIP; GB, US)   scope   83 min
This minor film was the last directed by Tourneur, the son of director Maurice Tourneur and best known for his forties horror films, such as *Cat People* (1942), and his marvellous *film noir, Out of the Past* (1947).

A weird blend of Jules Verne (Price is the Nemo-like ruler of a subterranean city off the Cornish coast) and Edgar Allan Poe (Price kidnaps Hart, believing her to be the reincarnation of his dead wife), the film is nonetheless mounted as an adventure film, replete with feeble comic interludes. The result is all too predictable with Hunter and Tomlinson rescuing Hart just as the city explodes.

d Jacques Tourneur   *p* Daniel Haller   *s* Charles Bennett, Louis M. Heyward   *c* Stephen Dade   *se* Frank George, Les Bowie   *lp* Vincent Price, Tab Hunter, David Tomlinson, Susan Hart, John Le Mesurier, Henry Oscar, Derek Newark

Crack in the World   (SECURITY PICTURES)   98(96) min
An experiment to tap the energy at the Earth's core goes horribly wrong in this well-mounted disaster epic. Giant earthquakes and tidal waves cause havoc as an immense crack spreads on the Earth's surface. Scientists blow a hole in its path with a nuclear bomb, but this only serves to send the débris off in another direction and Earth gains a new moon. Andrews is the scientist responsible for the disaster, dying of cancer and trying to come up with a solution fast and Moore his doubting assistant. Director Marton creates a real sense of tension, especially at the climax when Andrews supervises the lowering of a second bomb into the crack.

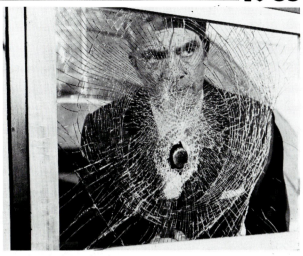

d Andrew Marton   *p* Bernard Glasser, Lester A. Sansom
s Jon Manchip White, Julian Halevy   *c* Manuel Berenguer
se Alec Weldon   *lp* Dana Andrews, Janette Scott, Kieron Moore, Alexander Knox, Peter Damon, Gary Lasdun, Mike Steen

I Criminali della Galassia *aka* The Wild, Wild Planet
(MERCURY FILM INTERNATIONAL/SOUTHERN CROSS PRODUCTIONS; IT)   93(85) min
Full of marvellous ideas, some of which are borrowed from other films (such as the hall of mirrors sequence which is remarkably similar to that in Orson Welles' *The Lady from Shanghai*, 1948), this is one of the best of Margheriti's films. Set in AD 2015, when the planetary system is ruled by rival factions, Reiner and Moretti's script features Serato as the evil scientist who is miniaturizing and then kidnapping the leaders of the United Democracies with the assistance of a legion of artificial, inflatable women (!). Russell is the wooden hero who leads the cavalry to the rescue in the last reel.

The film is a sequel to **I Diafanoidi Portano la Morte** (1965) with which it shares virtually the same cast and production team.

I Criminali della Galassia, *a marvellous example of the visual excitement of Italian Science Fiction.*

d/co-p Anthony Dawson (Antonio Margheriti)
co-p Joseph Fryd s Ivan Reiner, Renato Moretti c Riccardo
Pallottini lp Tony Russell, Lisa Gastoni, Massimo Serato,
Franco Nero, Charles Justin (Carlo Guistini)

Curse of the Fly (LIPPERT) b/w scope 86 min
The third, last and least, film in the Fly series (the others were
The Fly, 1958, and **Return of the Fly**, 1959), this was shot in
England. Scientist Donlevy (who played the professor in **The
Quatermass Xperiment**, 1955 and **Quatermass II**, 1957)
experiments with the matter-transmitting machine and physically distorts the people he transmits. The victims (headed by
Baker) are horrified, particularly when one of them ages to a
skeleton in a few seconds. Donlevy fares little better. He is
transmitted to London only to find that his son has destroyed
the remaining booth there.

d Don Sharp p Robert L. Lippert, Jack Parsons s Harry
Spalding c Basil Emmott se Harold Fletcher lp Brian
Donlevy, George Baker, Carole Gray, Michael Graham,
Jeremy Wilkins, Rachel Kempson

La Decima Vittima aka **The Tenth Victim**
(C.C. CHAMPION/LES FILMS CONCORDIA; IT, SP) 92 min
This disappointing version of Robert Sheckley's witty short
story, *The Seventh Victim*, features Mastroianni and Andress
as the competing killers in the 21st century where legalized
murder has taken the place of birth control and war. As an
added edge each plans to kill the other before TV cameras. The
futuristic settings are convincing and there are many fine
touches (at one point a character pulls out a first edition of
Flash Gordon and Andress' secret weapon is a double-
barrelled bra), but Petri's satirical intentions quickly collapse
in the face of the jarring acting styles of the two leads and the
weak script which lacks a cohesive narrative line.

d/co-s Elio Petri p Carlo Ponti co-s Tonino Guerra, Giorgio
Salvioni, Ennio Flaiano c Gianni Di Venanzo
lp Marcello Mastroianni, Ursula Andress, Elsa Martinelli,
Massimo Serato, Salvo Randone, Luce Bonifassy, Mickey
Knox

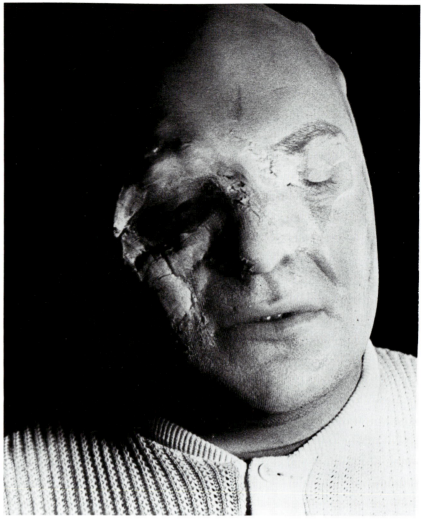

Curse of the Fly,
the last of the Fly trilogy
of films.

I Diafanoidi Portano la Morte aka **I Diafanoidi Vengono
da Morte** aka **War of the Planets**
(MERCURY FILM INTERNATIONAL/SOUTHERN CROSS
PRODUCTIONS; IT, SP) 99 min
Shot back to back with **I Criminali della Galassia** (1965)
which is an informal sequel to it, this features not only the
same production team as *I Criminali*, but virtually the same
cast in the same roles. The Diaphanois of the title are
incorporeal beings from Mars who attack Earth and its ring of
defensive satellites by taking over humans. Plot and acting are
rudimentary but the direction is full of the visual splendours
one expects of Margheriti. His other Science Fiction films
include: **Space Men** (1960), **Il Pianeta degli Uomini Spenti**
(1961), **I Diavolo della Spazio** (1965) and **Il Pianeta Errante**
(1966).

d/co-p Antonio Margheriti co-p Joseph Fryd, Walter
Manley s Ivan Reiner, Renato Moretti c Riccardo
Pallottini lp Tony Russell, Lisa Gastoni, Carlo Giustini,
Massimo Serato, Michel Lemoine, Franco Nero

I Diavoli della Spazio aka **The Snow Devils** aka **Space
Devils** (MERCURY FILM INTERNATIONAL/
SOUTHERN CROSS PRODUCTIONS; IT) 78 min
A minor entry from Margheriti, who with Mario Bava is
undoubtedly Italy's best director of Science Fiction. The plot
combines the Abominable Snowman with an errant planet, a
regular feature in Margheriti's work, from which the Snow-
men, the only survivors of the planet Aytia, are intending to
disturb the meteorological balance of the Earth. Stuart is the
hero who, like Tony Russell in **Il Pianeta Errante** (1966),
manages to destroy the wandering planet. Though the film's

Left: *Ursula Andress as
the 21st-century assassin
in Elio Petri's flawed
satire,* La Decima
Vittima.

narrative is jerky and contains too many bizarre plot elements, Margheriti's direction is as visually imaginative as ever.

d/co-p Antonio Margheriti   *co-p* Joseph Fryd   *s* Charles Sinclair, William Finger, Ivan Reiner, Moretti   *c* Riccardo Pallotini   *se* Victor Sontolda   *lp* Giacomo Rossi-Stuart, Ombretta Colli, Renato Baldini, Archie Savage

Die Monster Die *aka* Monster of Terror

(AIP)   80 min

Karloff (a marvellous performance) is the puzzled scientist confronting a radioactive meteorite which makes plants grow to an enormous height and humans mutate in a grisly fashion in this film based on H.P. Lovecraft's classic short story *The Colour Out of Space*. Adams is the brash young man puzzled by Karloff's hostile behaviour when he comes to visit Farmer, his fiancée and Karloff's daughter. The direction of Haller (who had worked regularly with Roger Corman as art director), making his feature début, is stylish but slow-moving, remarkably similar in feel to that of his *The Dunwich Horror* (1970), also derived from a Lovecraft story.

d Daniel Haller   *p* Pat Green   *s* Jerry Sohl   *c* Paul Beeson   *lp* Boris Karloff, Nick Adams, Freda Jackson, Suzan Farmer, Terence de Marney, Patrick Magee

Dr Goldfoot and the Bikini Machine

(AIP)   pv   88 min

Price is enjoyably self-indulgent as the manic Goldfoot who builds beautiful bikini-clad robots to seduce the world's playboys into financial disaster. The result is a lacklustre farce in which intelligence officer, Avalon, investigates, is tortured, escapes and foils Price's plans.

The sequel, **Dr Goldfoot and the Girl Bombs** (1966), is far more stylish.

d Norman Taurog   *p* Anthony Carras   *s* Elwood Ullman, Robert Kaufman   *c* Sam Leavitt   *se* Roger George   *lp* Vincent Price, Frankie Avalon, Susan Hart, Dwayne Hickman, Fred Clark, Jack Mullaney

Dr Who and the Daleks   (AARU; GB)   scope   85 min

Cushing plays Dr Who in the first screen adaptation of the highly successful teleseries written by Terry Nation. His bumbling assistant Castle accidentally switches on the Tardis (the telephone-box-like time-machine) and transports himself, Cushing and his two spirited granddaughters (Linden and Tovey) through space to future planet Skaro which is

being laid waste by a neutron war. There Cushing and company become involved in the conflict between the evil Daleks and the good Thals. The Daleks, mutated aliens sitting inside mobile transporters and projecting lethal death rays, are vanquished before they can detonate another bomb.

Nation's serial was, and still is, extremely popular with both adults and children. Like the American *Star Trek* teleseries, at its best it featured interesting ideas rather than action, which this film fails to do.

A sequel, **Daleks – Invasion Earth 2150 AD**, followed in 1966.

d Gordon Flemyng   *co-p/s* Milton Subotsky   *co-p* Max J. Rosenberg   *c* John Wilcox   *se* Ted Samuels   *lp* Peter Cushing, Roy Castle, Jennie Linden, Roberta Tovey, Michael Coles, Geoffrey Toone

The Eye Creatures   (AZALEA)   80 min

An uncredited remake of **Invasion of the Saucermen** (1957), this is one of the several films AIP commissioned from Buchanan's Azalea productions to complete a package about to be sold to television, rather in the manner that major studios in the thirties and forties commissioned independent producers to complete the second half of their double bills.

Made at a frantic speed with little care (in contrast to the low, low budget films Roger Corman made for distribution by AIP in the fifties), it closely follows the storyline of *Invasion of the Saucermen*. Ashley is the mature teenager who saves America from invasion.

d/p Larry Buchanan   *c* Ralph K. Johnson   *lp* John Ashley, Cynthia Hull, Warren Hammack, Chet Davis

The Face of Fu Manchu   (HALLAM; GB)   scope   96 min

The first film based on the character created by Sax Rohmer since the lacklustre 1940 serial, *Drums of Fu Manchu*, this initiated an irregular series of films devoted to the exploits of the oriental master criminal who, though regularly defeated by Nayland Smith (here Green), always had the last word in the form of his prophecy of doom: 'The world has not heard the last of Fu Manchu.'

Here, Lee is excellently sinister as Fu Manchu who goes to Tibet to gather bunches of poisonous flowers from which to make a gas, the effectiveness of which he demonstrates by destroying all human life in a remote English village. Sharp directs (in Ireland, with Dublin standing in for London of the 1920s) with great style, capturing the atmosphere of excess that Rohmer specialized in.

A sequel followed in 1966, **Brides of Fu Manchu**, also directed by Sharp.

d Don Sharp   *p/s* Harry Alan Towers   *c* Ernest Steward   *lp* Christopher Lee, Tsai Chin, Nigel Green, Howard Marion-Crawford, James Robertson Justice, Walter Rilla, Karin Dor

Fantômas Se Déchaîne *aka* Fantômas Strikes Back

(SNEG/PAC/VICTORY; FR, IT) scope 94(88) min

This is a tedious addition to the series of films devoted to the master criminal Fantômas. Whereas Louis Feuillade conceived of the character as the scourge of the bourgoisie, director Hunebelle here simply sees his 'hero' as yet another supervillain. Marais in the title role kidnaps a group of scientists and puts them to work developing a mind-controlling ray. Funès is the pompous police commissioner who stops him almost accidentally but cannot prevent his escape at the end in an 'aerial car'. The best thing in the film is Fantômas' stylish, elaborate volcano hideout.

d André Hunebelle *p* Alain Poire, Paul Cadeac *s* Jean Halain, Pierre Foucaud *c* Raymond Lemoigne *se* Gil Delamre, Gérard Cogan *lp* Jean Marais, Louis de Funès, Mylène Demongeot, Jacques Dynam, Robert Dalban, Albert Dagnat

Frankenstein Meets the Space Monster *aka* Duel of the Space Monsters

(VERNON-SENECA FILMS) b/w 78(75) min

Android space pilot Saunders (Reilly), a precursor of sorts to television's *Six Million Dollar Man*, is attacked by laser-gun-wielding alien Princess Marcuzan (Hanold) and Nadir (Cutell), her dwarf acolyte, when they land on Earth in search of humans to replenish their dying planet. Shortcircuited, Reilly goes temporarily haywire while Hanold and Cutell start their kidnapping mission. The highpoints of the crudely made film consist of the Princess's pet, a ferocious space monster called Mull terrorizing her victims, before Reilly, rewired but limping, frees them, defeats Mull and destroys Hanold, Cutell and their spaceship. The film, which has nothing to do with either Mary Shelley's *Frankenstein* or the Frankenstein legend, its title nothwithstanding, was shot in Puerto Rico.

d Robert Gaffney *p* Robert McCarty *s* George Garret *c* Saul Midwall *lp* James Karen, David Kerman, Nancy Marshall, Robert Reilly, Marilyn Hanold, Lou Cutell

Frankenstein Meets the Space Monster, *one of several films, its title notwithstanding, to bear no relation to the Frankenstein legend.*

Furankenshutain Tai Baragon *aka* Frankenstein Conquers the World *aka* Frankenstein Versus the Giant Devil Fish *aka* Frankenstein and the Giant Lizard

(TOHO; JAP) scope 95(87) min

Having revived King Kong in **King Kong Tai Gojira** (1963), Honda added his own interpretation of Frankenstein's monster to the Toho monster gallery, immediately inscribing it as a sympathetic creature prepared to fight 'evil' non-Japanese such as the scaly Godzilla-variant Baragon ('borrowed' a year later by the rival Daiei company and re-christened Barugon in a bid to recapture the children's market for monster movies). According to the script, the Nazis had shipped the heart of Frankenstein's monster to Hiroshima where its box was opened just as the bomb dropped. A boy eats the exposed heart and grows into a 30-ft-tall horror with a high forehead and unsightly teeth. Baptized Frankenstein by the locals, he represents a Japan that has ingested two of Western culture's most lethal products: the Nazi heart and the US A-bomb. The deformed result is a Japanoid hybrid living on the slopes of Mount Fuji and vaguely controlled by the 'friendly' American scientist, played by Adams, who is there to help rebuild Hiroshima. Initially planned as a fight between Frankenstein and a giant octopus (an echo of **Uchudai Dogora**, 1964), only a few scenes were shot before the project was changed into a contest with the lizardy Baragon. The octopus scenes surfaced later in **Furankenshutain No Kaiju – Sanda Tai Gailah** (1966). This picture was made in collaboration with American International producers Henry Saperstein and Reuben Bercovitch, and officially co-starred Adams in the original Japanese version, instead of the usual practice of buying the Japanese film and adding scenes later for the US release.

d Inoshiro Honda *p* Tomoyuki Tanaka *s* Kaoru Mabuchi *c* Hajime Koizumi *se* Eiji Tsuburaya *lp* Tadao Takashima, Nick Adams, Kumi Mizuno, Yoshio Tsuchiya, Takashi Shimura

Ghidorah Sandai Kaiju Chikyu Saidai No Kessan *aka* Ghidora the Three Headed Monster *aka* Ghidrah *aka* Chikyu Saidai No Kessan *aka* The Biggest Battle on Earth *aka* The Biggest Fight on Earth *aka* Monster of Monsters

(TOHO; JAP) scope 85 min

Ghidorah, the three-headed dragon from outer space which first appeared in **Kaiju Daisenso** (1965), is probably the nastiest of Honda's monsters. In this, its second outing, it threatens the Earth, which is defended by Godzilla (sixth film), Rodan and Mothra (third films). In fact, when Mothra

Left: Furankenshutain Tai Baragon, *one of the most inventive re-workings of the Frankenstein myth.*

finds she cannot do the job alone, the other two who have had previous experience of the dragon (in *Kaiju Daisenso*, 1965) are called in. The anthropomorphization of the Earth monsters is now complete and their positive character is underlined as they defeat the nasty Ghidorah in a spectacular fight on Mount Fuji (again). The end allows for a re-match (which materialized in **Kaiju Soshingeki**, 1968): Mothra envelops the baddie in a silky web, echoing the way Godzilla was defeated by the Mothra-larvae in **Mosura Tai Gojira** (1964), and the others throw him into the sea. The visual effects are better than usual and the cast includes Okada, best known for his performance in Resnais' *Hiroshima Mon Amour* (1959), as well as the brilliant Shimura, star of Kurosawa's *Ikiru* (1952) and veteran from Godzilla's first picture **Gojira** (1954).

d Inoshiro Honda *p* Tomoyuki Tanaka *s* Shinichi Sekizawa *c* Hajime Koizumi *se* Eiji Tsuburaya *lp* Yosuke Natsuki, Yurihiko Hoshi, Hiroshi Koizumi, Takashi Shimura, Eiji Okada, the Itoh Sisters

Gigantes Planetarios *aka* Gigantes Interplanetarios
(ESTUDIOS AMERICA/PRODUCCIONES CORSA; MEX) 80 min
A routine children's adventure story about a young scientist Daniel (Murray) in love with Silvia (Roel), the assistant of a professor who has constructed a spaceship. Daniel and Silvia together with a boxer (Guerra) and his comic manager (Ferrusquilla) journey to the planet of Eternal Night in the Galaxy of Rumania. The planet's inhabitants live under the ground to escape the blinding light scorching its surface and are ruled by a protector (Galvez) intent on destroying the Earth with a death ray. The heroes manage to use the ray against the Protector and to hand over the planet's government to its good people before returning to Earth, leaving behind the boxer and his manager who have fallen for two extra-terrestrial beauties. The picture was followed immediately by another adventure of the same four characters, **El Planeta de los Mujeres Invasoras** (1965), also directed by Crevenna. Both were released in 1966.

Crevenna had made his name as a fantasy director with melodramatic stories such as **El Hombre Que Logro Ser**

Ghidorah, the three-headed dragon from outer space, on the rampage in Ghidorah Sandai Kaiju Chikyu Saidai No Kessan.

Invisible (1958), *La Huella Macabra* (1962) and *Aventura al Centro de la Tierra* (1965). However, none of his pictures ever transcended the level of children's serials, and the sets and costumes for his space operas, which continued with **Santo Contra la Invasion de los Marcianos** (1966), appeared constructed from DIY children's toy kits.

d Alfredo B. Crevenna *p* Emilio Gomez Muriel *s* Alfredo Ruanova *lp* Guillermo Murray, Adriana Roel, Rogelio Guerra, Jose Angel Espinosa Ferrusquilla, Jose Galvez, Jacqueline Fellay, Evita Muñoz, Irma Lozano, Nathanael Leon Frankenstein, Carlos Nieto

Giperboloid Ingenera Garina *aka* The Hyperboloid of Engineer Garin *aka* Engineer Garin's Death Ray
(GORKI; USSR) b/w scope 96 min
Set in 1925, the year of Kuleshov's **Luch Smerti**, this film tells of a mad scientist who wants to conquer the world with a death ray. It could be a pessimistic sequel to Kuleshov's classic adventure story in that it shows how eventually the coveted death ray falls into the hands of the reactionaries, not an unreasonable suggestion to make with the wisdom of hindsight. Based on Alexei Tolstoy's novel, Garin (Yevstigneev) is the villain who steals the blueprints for the device from his teacher and seeks to use it for his own benefit, but a capitalist chemical concern is after it as well. The moral is that artisanal individualism such as Garin's must be taken over by evil multinationals unless the state intervenes through its security apparatus to ensure that the nation's talents are used for the common good instead of for private gain. A slow-moving adventure story, routinely directed and designed, it does not live up to the standards set by **Planeta Burg** (1962) although, at times, attention is diverted to incidental details such as the code number 001 on a security officer's uniform.

Some sources give M. Berdishevski as director, but Soviet catalogues credit Gintsburg with that role.

d/co-s Alexander Gintsburg *co-s* Joseph Manevich *c* Alexander Rybin *lp* Yevgeny Yevstigneev, Vsevolod Safonov, Mikhail Astangov, Natalya Klimova

The Human Duplicators *aka* Spaziale K.1
(WOOLNER BROS/INDEPENDENTI REGIONALI; US, IT) 82 min
Although the villain of this entry is an alien, the film marks the beginnings of a return to the technical gimmickry of the thirties. Thus, fittingly, it stars Kiel who became one of the more bizarre jokes in the later James Bond films, which were the ultimate in technological gadgetry.

Kolos (Kiel) is a giant alien invader who takes over Macready's laboratory, in which he's created a race of androids, in this confused and over-ambitious offering from Grimaldi. Kolos plans to produce a series of look-alikes of Western leaders so that a blanket alien takeover can be arranged. Martin (Nader) and Wilson (Nichols) fight back and eventually succeed in destroying Kolos and his robots with a laser beam.

d/co-p Hugo Grimaldi *co-p/s* Arthur C. Pierce *c* Monroe Askins *lp* George Nader, Barbara Nichols, George Macready, Dolores Faith, Richard Kiel, Richard Arlen

Kaiju Daisenso *aka* Invasion of the Astro Monster *aka* Battle of the Astros *aka* Monster Zero *aka* Invasion of Planet X (TOHO; JAP) scope 96 min
Godzilla's fifth and Rodan's second appearances in a new twist to the Kaiju Eiga genre: the monsters that so recently threatened the world have now been changed into the Earth's most powerful weapons, confirming a drastic shift in attitude towards military force, signalled in **Kaitei Gunkan** and **Uchudai Dogora** (both 1964). Here, an alien planet requests the aid of Godzilla and Rodan to fight the three-headed Ghidorah, a dragon able to fly at supersonic speed, shooting

death rays out of its eyes and spitting a laser beam. Rodan and Godzilla are transported to the planet, cocooned in an energy cell that looks like a soap bubble. But the evil planet people wish to combine the three monsters to conquer the Earth. A space mission led by Adams is despatched to help the Earth monsters and fetch the heroes back home. Their assistance takes the form of sophisticated hi-fi equipment, made in Japan, that emits a high frequency wave too powerful for the monsters to bear.

While *Uchudai Dogora* (1964) was called a 'space monster', it was in fact a mutated cell. The first real space monster originated on another planet is Ghidorah, the most vicious of the creatures that populate the genre, possibly because it had no connection with tensions within Japan and represented a pure and hostile 'outside'. It returned to do battle with Godzilla and Rodan, reinforced by Mothra, in **Ghidorah Sandai Kaiju Chikyu Saidai No Kessan** (1965) and participated in the all-star **Kaiju Soshingeki** (1968) as the enemy of just about everyone. In the American version, extra scenes beefing up Adams' part were added. From this film onwards, Godzilla became a loved national institution.

d Inoshiro Honda *p* Tomoyuki Tanaka *s* Shinichi Sekizawa *c* Hajime Koizumi *se* Eiji Tsuburaya *lp* Nick Adams, Akira Takarada, Akira Kubo, Keiko Sawai, Kumo Mizuno, Jun Tazaki, Yoshio Tsuchiya

Kdo Chce Zabit Jessu? *aka* **Who Killed Jessie?** *aka* **Who Would Kill Jessie?** *aka* **Who Wants to Kill Jessie?**
(CZECHOSLOVENSKY FILM; CZECH) b/w 80 min
One of the loveliest comic-strip stories around, together with Bava's **Diabolik** (1967), and winner of the first prize at the Trieste Festival of 1966, this started out as a children's film but developed into a full-blown crazy comedy. A woman scientist (Medricka) develops a somnigraph which can materialize dream images on a screen and then manipulate nightmarish dreams to change them into peaceful ones. When she uses it on her husband (Sovak), she discovers his dreams about a luscious comic-strip heroine, Jessie (Shoberova) dressed à la Li'l Abner, always chased by an evil cowboy (Effa) and an equally overbearing superman (Visny). When the straight-laced wife attempts to improve her husband's dreamworld, the machine malfunctions and, instead of disappearing, the comic-strip characters appear live in the

Kaiju Daisenso *which features the first appearance of a monster from outer space in the Japanese cycle of monster movies.*

couple's flat, causing chaos in their lives. Full of wonderfully inventive gags and effects, the film would have gained by being in colour.

Vorlicek went on to make a series of fantasy comedies about contraptions that turn desires into reality (**Coz Takhle Dat Si Spenat**, 1976, and **Pane Vy Jste Vdova**, 1971, also featuring Shoberova). The acting by Vorlicek regular, Sovak, and by Medricka, as well as the beautiful Shoberova, who was subsequently signed by Hammer to star in *The Vengeance of She* (1968) under the name Olinka Berova, is absolutely delightful. The photography is by the expert Nemecek, who also collaborated with Milos Forman. From this success onwards, Vorlicek and Makourek collaborated on the best Czech crazy comedies.

d Vaclav Vorlicek *s* Milos Makourek *c* Jan Nemecek
lp Jiri Sovak, Dana Medricka, Olga Shoberova (Olinka Berova), Karel Effa, Juraj Visny

Maciste e la Regina di Samar *aka* **Hercules Against the Moon Men** (NIKE CINEMATOGRAFICA/COMPTOIR FRANCAIS DU FILM; IT, FR) scope 88 min
Maciste (here portrayed by Ciani), one of the Italian cinema's longest serving heroes is called upon by the people of Samar to liberate them from their evil queen (Clair) and the race of stone-like Moonmen who keep her in power, in this routine Italian sword and Science Fiction entry. The resulting story of good princesses (D'Alberti) and princes (Honore) and sacrificial victims through the use of which the Moonmen hope to raise their own queen from the dead is a crudely mounted fantasy. Ciani flexes his biceps at the appropriate moments but the deadpan direction of Gentilomo (whose *Maciste Contro il Vampiro*, 1961, is far superior) fails to animate a story that trembles on the edge of fable.

d/co-s Giacomo Gentilomo *p* Luigi Mondello *co-s* Arpad De Riso, Nino Scolaro, Angelo Sangarmano *c* Oberdan Tyojani *lp* Sergio Ciani, Jany Clair, Anna-Maria Polani, Nando Tamberlani, Jean-Pierre Honore, Delia D'Alberti

Mutiny in Outer Space *aka* **Ammutinamento nello Spazio** *aka* **Invasion from the Moon**
(WOOLNER BROTHERS/A HUGO GRIMALDI PRODUCTION; US, IT)
b/w 85(82) min
One of a pair of international co-productions directed in 1965 by Grimaldi (the other being **The Human Duplicators**), who is better known for his American versions of foreign films, such as **Der Schweigende Stern** (1960).

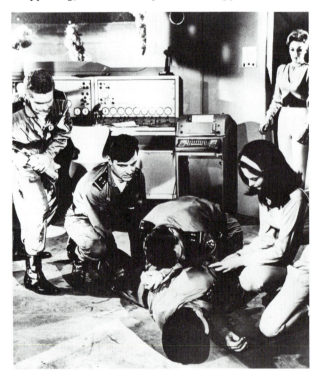

Left: *Another death from the mysterious fungus in* Mutiny in Outer Space, *made by Hugo Grimaldi, better known for his American versions of foreign films.*

Astronauts, led by Leslie, return to their orbiting space station after an expedition to the ice caves of the Moon, with a strange fungus which begins to take over the station, killing all in its wake. It thrives on heat and continues to grow before Leslie, aided by Faith and Langan, discovers that the growth has every intention of reaching Earth. The crew destroy it by saturating the station with frozen particles, thus removing its source of heat. Routine fare.

d/co-p Hugo Grimaldi   *co-p/s* Arthur C. Pierce   *c* Archie Dalzell   *lp* William Leslie, Dolores Faith, Pamela Curran, James Dobson, Glen Langan, Richard Garland

The Navy vs the Night Monsters *aka* The Night Crawlers
(STANDARD CLUB OF CALIFORNIA)   90(87) min
Based on the novel *Monster from the Earth's End* by Murray Leinster, this is the only film directed by screenwriter Hoey. Man-eating plants are discovered in Antarctica and are transferred to a US naval base in the South Seas, where they get hungry and go on the rampage. Hoey directs imaginatively, greatly aided by Cortez's inventive camerawork, as the plants threaten the lives of the islanders and biologist Sande watches his assistant Mason being devoured.

The presence of Van Doren as the imperilled heroine (in her penultimate film) has led to the film achieving a certain cult reputation in recent years.

d/s Michael Hoey   *p* George Edwards   *c* Stanley Cortez *se* Edwin Tillman   *lp* Mamie Van Doren, Anthony Eisley, Pamela Mason, Bill Gray, Bobby Van, Walter Sande

The Night Caller *aka* Blood Beast from Outer Space
(ARMITAGE FILMS; GB)   b/w   84(82) min
An intelligent low-budget Science Fiction thriller from Gilling, a director better known for his work in the horror genre. Scientists Saxon and Haines (who brings real conviction to her part) discover an alien energy transmitter only to lose it when its inhabitant emerges. Sent to Earth to provide women for 'genetic experiments' on his home planet of Ganymede, the alien hits on the well tried idea of advertising for models and then shipping them home. Saxon in company with Burke's police inspector finally catches him but not before the, otherwise surprisingly friendly, alien has strangled Haines after she has discovered his whereabouts.

d John Gilling   *p* Ronald Liles   *s* Jim O'Connolly *c* Stephen Dade   *lp* John Saxon, Maurice Denham, Patricia Haines, Alfred Burke, John Carson, Jack Watson

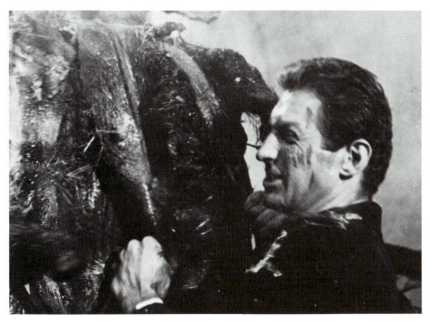

Operazione Goldman *aka* Lightning Bolt
(SEVEN FILMS/BGA/BALCAZAR; IT, SP)   scope   96(94) min
This is one of the better pieces of Italian hokum that have their origin in the operatic technology of the James Bond series of films. Montalban is the shadowy brewery magnate – he's principally photographed from below through a beer glass – and latterday Captain Nemo who dreams of world domination in his underwater city. He deflects American Moon rockets with laser guns stationed in beer trucks (!?) in the vicinity of Cape Kennedy only to have his plans foiled at the last minute by secret agents Eisley and Lorys. The sets, especially the underwater city, and the apocalyptic conflagration at the end are wittily engineered.

d Anthony Dawson (Antonio Margheriti)   *p* Cleto Fontini, Joseph De Blasio   *s* Alfred (Alfonso) Balcazar, Jose Antonio de la Loma   *c* Richard Paton (Riccardo Pallotini) *lp* Anthony Eisley, Wandisa Leigh (Guida), Diana Lorys, Ursula Parker (Luisa Rivelli), Paco Sanz, Rene Montalban

Our Man Flint   (FOX)   scope   108 (107) min
The first of a pair of would-be parodies of the James Bond films (the other being the tiresome **In Like Flint** 1967), *Our Man Flint* is a weak film, best remembered as the suave Coburn's first starring role. With his bevy of girls and an all-purpose cigarette lighter (that deals out 82 different kinds of death), super-scientist, super-stud, super-spy Flint foils the plans of a trio of scientists seeking world domination by controlling the weather.

d Daniel Mann   *p* Saul David   *s* Hal Fimber, Ben Starr *c* Daniel L. Fapp   *se* L.B. Abbott, Howard Lydecker, Emil Kosa Jnr   *lp* James Coburn, Lee J. Cobb, Gila Golan, Edward Mulhare, Benson Fong, Shelby Grant, Rhys Williams, Russ Conway

Pinnochio in Outer Space
(SWALLOW/BELVISION; US, BEL)   71 min
Wooden doll Pinnochio blasts off in a rocketship with his friend Nurtle the Turtle in this animated feature. They land on Mars and are confronted by Astro the Flying Whale who plans to invade Earth. Goosens intended to make the puppet more boy than wood but, unfortunately, he is unable to bring any imagination to this concept and loses many fanciful opportunities. Eventually Pinnochio, with the help of Nurtle, triumphs and stops the Space Whale's ambitions by grounding him on Mars.

d/c Ray Goosens   *p* Norman Prescott, Fred Ladd   *s* Fred Laderman   *Voices* Arnold Stang, Conrad Jameson, Minerva Pious

El Planeta de las Mujeres Invasoras

(ESTUDIOS AMERICA/PRODUCCIONES CORSA; MEX) 80 min
A follow-up to **Gigantes Planetarios** (1965), made by the same crew and with the same central characters. This time Daniel (Murray) and Silvia (Roel) come to grips with the inhabitants of the planet Sibila, a world dominated by women and ruled by a contrasting pair of twins, the cruel Adastrea (Campbell) and the sweet Alburnia (Velazquez). The women seek to conquer the Earth but their lungs are not suited for the Earth's atmosphere, so they perform surgical experiments on humans to try and find the right lungs to enable them to mount their flying saucer invasion. The heroes prevent the Sibilan women's efforts to engage in wholesale kidnapping of children for their cruel experiments. In the end, the ruling twins are killed and the terrestrial four (including the boxer and his comic manager, Guerra and Ferrusquilla) return home.

Although the film is a little sexier than the team's previous space adventure, the narrative, sets and costumes all remain stuck in the world of pre-teen comic-strips. Crevenna attempted to repeat the formula of combining nursery school comics with more sexy scenes in his next space opera **Santo Contra la Invasion de los Marcianos** (1966).

d Alfredo B. Crevenna *p* Emilio Gomez Muriel
s Alfredo Ruanova *lp* Guillermo Murray, Adriana Roel, Rogelio Guerra, Jose Angel Espinosa Ferrusquilla, Lorena Velazquez, Elizabeth Campbell, Maura Monti

El Rayo Disintegrador *aka* Aventuras de Quinque y Arturo el Robot (PETRUKA FILMS; SP) b/w 80 min

This juvenile film features a ten-year-old boy (Solis) and a robot called Arturo that looks more like the Tin Man from *The Wizard of Oz* (1939) than anything else – his joints even need oiling – on the trail of a band of criminals who've stolen a disintegrator ray. The resulting adventures of the pair are sentimentally mounted, the odd references to Dr Mabuse notwithstanding.

d/p/co-s Pascual Cervera *co-s* Jose E. Arangueron
c Manuel Rojas *lp* Peter Solis, Maria Jesús Balenciaga, Joaquin Nieto, Sergio Mendizabal, Jose Luis Coll, Maria Hevia

The Satan Bug (MIRISCH/KAPPA) 114 min

An uneven Science Fiction thriller from Sturges, a director more at home in the western (*Bad Day at Black Rock*, 1955; *The Law and Jake Wade*, 1958; *The Magnificent Seven*, 1960 and *Hour of the Gun*, 1967) than Science Fiction (**Marooned**, 1969). Clavell and Anhalt's adaptation of Alistair MacLean's novel is intelligent enough but Sturges' direction depends too much on action clichés to work.

A scientist is murdered after producing a deadly virus (the satan bug) at Space Three, an American top-security research station in the desert, and the flasks containing the virus stolen. Maharis and Andrews investigate and find that Basehart, a paranoid millionaire, has seized the virus and is holding the US to ransom in a bid to stop the government's experiments in germ warfare. He plants several of the flasks in and around Los Angeles but Maharis saves the day, and America's germ-warfare programme.

d/p John Sturges *s* James Clavell, Edward Anhalt
c Robert Surtees *se* Paul Pollard *lp* George Maharis, Richard Basehart, Anne Francis, Dana Andrews, Edward Asner, Frank Sutton, Simon Oakland

Sergeant Deadhead, the Astronut (AIP) 89 min

Taurog directs, as if asleep, this lightest of light comedies which features pop singer turned actor Avalon as the bumbling girl-shy airman who takes shelter in a missile just before it takes off during a guardhouse breakout and becomes an extrovert hero as a result of a personality change during the

flight. Arden is the ever-patient girlfriend and Buster Keaton has a walk-on part as a fireman.

Above: *George Maharis in danger in* The Satan Bug.

d Norman Taurog *p* James H. Nicholson, Samuel Z. Arkoff *s* Louis M. Heyward *c* Floyd Crosby *se* Roger George *lp* Frankie Avalon, Eve Arden, Cesar Romero, Fred Clark, Gale Gordon

The Silencers (MEADWAY-CLAUDE/COL) 104 min

This is the first and best of the four-strong series devoted to the exploits of superspy Matt Helm (all of which starred Martin), mounted by Columbia in an attempt to cash in on the phenomenal success of the James Bond films. Intended as parodies, though not as gross as **Batman** (1966), the films, for the most part, lacked either the confidence of the Bond movies or the naïvety of the serials of the thirties and forties – their spiritual forebears. Even odder was Columbia's choice of Donald Hamilton's Matt Helm character as their facsimile Bond. Though his later books were clearly influenced by Ian Fleming's Bond novels, the first ones (commencing with *Death of a Citizen*, 1960, from which this film is partially derived) were, if anything, the complete antithesis of Bond. Their plots were fantastical but the novels had a firm realistic edge that was completely missing from Fleming's work.

This outing sees Helm putting an end to plans to reprogram an American atomic missile to fall back on the New Mexico testing grounds. Adams is his assistant (called Lovey Kravezit, an indication of the level of wit on display), Gregory, Helm's 'M' and Charisse, Stevens and Lavi amongst the distractions Martin faces. Three sequels followed, **Murderer's Row** (1966), **The Ambushers** (1967) and the non Science Fiction *The Wrecking Crew* (1968).

d Phil Karlson *p* Irving Allen *s* Oscar Saul
c Burnett Guffey *lp* Dean Martin, Beverly Adams, Stella Stevens, Daliah Lavi, Cyd Charisse, Victor Buono, James Gregory, Robert Webber

Sins of the Fleshapoids (MIKE KUCHAR) 40 min

The feature film début of Kuchar who had been making experimental 8mm movies with his brother George (here the villain) for over a decade, *Sins of the Fleshapoids* is a glorious simultaneous parody and celebration of Hollywood Science Fiction B features and their comic-strip mentality. The movie is set in the far distant future in which the survivors of a nuclear holocaust lead lives of exquisite beauty and boredom, their every whim catered for by humanoid robots called fleshapoids. One of these, Zar (Cowan) starts feeling human emotions and seeks a mate (Thomas) who in the film's hilarious conclusion produces a baby, a miniature robot. The plot is beautifully rudimentary and the sets have no pretence to be anything but backrooms but the combination of Kuchar's pulp imagination and the over-saturated colour of the film combine to give the movie the feel and look of the comics that clearly inspired it. This is further intensified by Kuchar's decision to use speech bubbles when he found his budget didn't run to synchronous sound.

d/p/s/c Mike Kuchar *lp* Bob Cowan, Donna Kerness, George Kuchar, Maren Thomas, Julius Mittleman, Gina Zuckerman

Space Monster *aka* First Woman into Space
(AIP-TV) 80 min

A workmanlike low-budget offering. The first woman astronaut (York) blasts off from Earth with a male crew and lands on the ocean floor of a mysterious anonymous planet, where the natural hazards include underwater mountain ranges, giant crabs and sea monsters. York, Bender, Brown and Barron battle against routine effects before returning home after meeting one of the planet's minute aliens in a miniature spaceship.

d/s Leonard Katzman *p* Burt Topper *c* Robert Tobey
lp Russ Bender, Francine York, James B. Brown, Baynes Barron

Spaceflight IC 1 (LIPPERT; GB) b/w 65(63) min

Spalding's weak script and Knowles' poor direction don't help this tale of a spaceship which heads out, some 50 years into the future, to start a new colony. The occupants are selected on the basis of health, blood and technical knowledge and are only allowed to procreate on a regulated birth control

Sins of the Fleshapoids, Mike Kuchar's experimental essay in Science Fiction.

plan. Williams is the authoritarian captain who provokes a predictable internal crisis when doctor's wife Marlowe is discovered to be seriously ill. After seven of the crew mutiny, democracy re-asserts itself and the colonists resume their search for a suitable planet.

d Bernard Knowles *p* Robert L. Lippert, Jack Parsons
s Harry Spalding *c* Geoffrey Faithfull *lp* Bill Williams, Norma West, John Cairney, Linda Marlowe, Jeremy Longhurst, Kathleen Breck

The Spy with My Face (ARENA PRODUCTIONS) 88 min

Based on the teleplay *The Double Affair* by Clyde Ware from the teleseries *The Man from Uncle*, this gadget-ridden TV spin-off features Berger as the villain. With her fleet of miniature robots and her secret weapon, a robot replica of Vaughn's Napoleon Solo, she plans to either win control of the world or destroy it. Vaughn and McCallum are briskly put through their paces by Newland, whose direction is as gimmicky as that of the TV series.

Unlike other Uncle films, such as *The Spy in the Green Hat* (1966), this was not compiled from episodes of the teleseries.

d John Newland *p* Sam Rolfe *s* Clyde Ware, Joseph Calvelli *c* Fred Koenekamp *lp* Robert Vaughn, David McCallum, Senta Berger, Leo G. Carroll, Sharon Farrell, Paula Raymond, Michael Evans

Terrore nello Spazio *aka* Planet of the Vampires
(ITALIAN INTERNATIONAL FILM/CASTILLA CINEMATOGRAFICA;
IT, SP) 86(85) min

A gorgeous atmospheric confection from Bava who was Italy's leading cinematographer in the fifties and in the sixties made a series of elegant horror films. Surveying the planet Aura, Sullivan first has one of his spaceships vanish and then his own is forced to land by a strange gravitational pull. It transpires that the disembodied inhabitants of the planet have willed the spaceships there in order to take over the astronauts' bodies and thus leave the planet. The script is banal but Bava's direction is compelling and the alien landscape is wonderfully conjured up out of little but pastel-shaded fog and cardboard rocks. Similarly, in sequences like the resurrection of three dead astronauts, from beneath their futuristic headstones, in their polythene shrouds, Bava's ever-moving camera creates a chilling sense of menace. The result is a triumph of the pulp imagination.

d/co-s Mario Bava *p* Fulvio Lucisano *co-s* Callisto Cosulich, Antonio Roman, Alberto Bevilacqua, Raphael J. Salvia *c* Antonio Rinaldi *lp* Barry Sullivan, Norma Bengell, Angel Aranda, Evi Morandi, Fernando Villena, Franco Andrei

Thunderball (EON; GB) scope 132 min

The fourth outing for Connery's James Bond, *Thunderball* was produced by McClory only after a protracted legal struggle with Harry Saltzman and Albert Broccoli, the producers of the other Bond films who claimed they owned the rights to the Bond character as well as the Bond stories. One of the most commercially successful of the Bond series, it was remade by McClory with Connery once more back in the role he'd vacated as **Never Say Never Again** (1983) which soon outgrossed the contemporary Roger Moore Bond outing, *Octopussy* (1983). Young's direction is efficient enough but *Thunderball* is a decidedly creaky affair, Celi's magnificent arch-villain who attempts to hold Miami to ransom with a pair of hijacked atomic bombs apart. Script and direction rely too much on vulgar displays of flesh and not enough on the action set-pieces that had sustained the earlier entries in the series. The best sequence is the climactic underwater fight which was masterminded by Ricou Browning, best known for the underwater sequences of **The Creature from the Black Lagoon** (1954), who would repeat them for *Never Say Never Again*.

d Terence Young *p* Kevin McClory *s* Richard Maibaum, John Hopkins *c* Ted Moore *se* John Stears *lp* Sean Connery, Claudine Auger, Adolfo Celi, Rik Von Nutter, Bernard Lee, Luciana Paluzzi, Lois Maxwell

Village of the Giants (BERKELEY PRODUCTIONS) 81 min

Gordon, who usually seduced his audiences into the cinema with sensational posters and then let them down with awful films, here produces some excellent special effects. A group of teenagers go to a small town for help after their car is wrecked. Howard, something of an inventor, creates a food for giants which the teenagers steal. They grow to enormous proportions and terrorize the town, but are eventually subdued by young lovers Kirk and Doherty who discover an antidote. Sadly, the plot is weak and the climax, accordingly, comes sluggishly. The story is based on *The Food of the Gods* by H.G. Wells, which Gordon filmed in 1976.

The score was the first by rock musician Jack Nitzsche who later wrote the music for several major films, including *Performance* (1970).

d/p/co-se Bert I. Gordon *s* Alan Caillou *c* Paul C. Vogel *co-se* Flora Gordon *lp* Tommy Kirk, Johnny Crawford, Beara Bridge, Bob Random, Charla Doherty, Ronny Howard

Voyage to the Prehistoric Planet
(FILMGROUP) 80 min

The first of a pair of films (the other being **Voyage to the Planet of Prehistoric Women**, 1966) Roger Corman created by cannibalizing footage from the Russian **Planeta Burg** (1962). To make matters even more confusing, Harrington shot extra footage of Rathbone (wearing the same costume and on the same set) and with cannibalized footage from yet another Russian film (probably **Meshte Nastreshu**, 1963, which Corman had already plundered for **Battle Beyond the Sun**, 1963) to make **Queen of Blood** (1966). Undoubtedly the behind-the-scenes wheeling and dealing that went into these films is more interesting than the films themselves, although they were very useful exercises for the likes of Harrington, Peter Bogdanovitch (the pseudonymous director of *Voyage to the Planet of Prehistoric Women*) and Stephanie Rothman who worked in a production capacity on most of these films (including this one). The rudimentary plot features the crew

Mario Bava's Terrore nello Spazio, *Italian Science Fiction at its most stylish.*

Above: The War Game, *the best of Peter Watkins' 'documentaries of the future'.*

of a spaceship crash-landing on a planet (mostly footage from *Planeta Burg*) and relaying their adventures (Russian footage again) to Domergue on a space platform (Russian footage) orbiting above them. Rathbone is the scientist in charge who never leaves the one new set Harrington had constructed for the film.

US footage: d/s John Sebastian (Curtis Harrington) *p* George Edwards *c* Vilis Lapenieks *lp* Basil Rathbone, Faith Domergue, Marc Shannon, Christopher Brand, John Bix, Lewis Keane, Robert Chanta

The War Game (BBC; GB) b/w 50(47) min

Originally made for television, this is the first (and best) of Watkins' 'documentaries of the future'. It was banned by the BBC as being too realistic. Using simulated newsreels and street interviews, Watkins focuses on the appalling results of a nuclear attack on a small Kent town.

The film is full of sharp, penetrating images (the mass cremations and buckets of wedding rings taken from the dead and the execution squads, composed of solid English Bobbies, for example) that are very disturbing, pinpointing concussion, disfigurement, slow death by radiation poisoning and civil disorder in an immediate way. Certainly compared to the widely seen and well-received telefilm *The Day After* (1983), made nearly 20 years later, *The War Game* retains its power to shock and anger an audience.

d/p/s Peter Watkins *c* Peter Bartlett *Narrators* Michael Aspel, Dick Graham

Ztracena Tvar *aka* The Lost Face

(SVABIK-PROCHAZKA; CZECH) b/w 85 min

Czech medical Science Fiction – the country's dominant sub-genre – played as a broad comedy. The basic idea is that a doctor (Brodsky) can successfully transfer organs from one body to another as well as change his own face. Lack of money and recognition from official clinics prompt his involvement with a gangster who killed a priest: his role is to put on the face of the victim. His face-changing skill makes him a rich man but eventually, after quite a few changes, he sticks to his original frontage. The moral appears to be that we may wear

different faces but being a decent idealist in a corrupt environment can be difficult and create the wrong impressions. The film is well acted and fast paced, but the moral points are rather heavily underlined and the bits of social symbolism over-emphasized.

Medical Science Fiction was better treated in comic form by the crazy comedy team of Vorlicek and Makourek in films such as **Kdo Chce Zabit Jessu?** (1965) and **Coz Takhle Dat Si Spenat** (1976).

d/co-s Pavel Hobl *co-s* Josef Nesvadba *c* Jiri Vojta *lp* Vlastimil Brodsky, Fred Demare, Jana Brezkova, Frantisek Filipovsky, Marie Vasova, Martin Rurek, Nina Popelikova, Jiri Vala, Zdenka Prochazkova

1966

Agent for HARM (DIMENSION IV) 84 min

Enquiry agent Richman is assigned by the security chief of HARM to investigate the murder of a scientist Corey's assistant. Corey is working on an antidote to a spore which converts human flesh into fungus and is found in meteoric fragments. Corey is kidnapped and dies from contact with the spores, but Richman foils Russian plans to grab the formula and infect American crops with the spore.

On the surface, this would seem to be merely one of the many derivatives of the Bond films in which a cast of relative unknowns do battle with an inevitable array of gadgets. But, if the script and acting are routine, Oswald's direction is a *tour de force*. The result is an entertaining, if empty, film.

d Gerd Oswald *p* Joseph F. Robertson *s* Blair Robertson *c* James Crab *se* Harry S. Wollman *lp* Mark Richman, Wendell Corey, Carl Esmond, Barbara Bouchet, Martin Kosleck, Rafael Campos

Arañas Infernales *aka* Cerebros Diabolicos

(FILMICA VERGARA; MEX) 85 min

Competing with Santo for the title of the most popular freestyle masked wrestler, the Blue Demon always remained a second ranker. He started his film career late, in 1963, after Santo had been going for 11 years and Neutron had built up a following as well. To catch up with Santo, Blue Demon was paired with him in a number of double acts such as **Santo Contra Blue Demon en la Atlantida** and **Santo y Blue Demon Contra los Monstruos** (both 1968), in which the blue-trousered hulk was played by Cruz. In this picture he is still going solo against the spidery invaders from another planet who can change their appearance to that of human beings but whose hands have a tendency to revert back to spidery aspects. Blue Demon wrestles an opponent called Frankenstein while the erotic interest is provided by Sanchez and Cervantes, the latter playing a spidery woman. The film was released in 1968 together with the two immediate follow-up Blue Demon pictures: **Blue Demon Contra Cerebros Infernales** and *Blue Demon Contra las Diabolicas* (both 1967).

Curiel, along with Alfredo Crevenna, Alfonso Corona Blake, Julian Soler and Rene Cardona, was responsible for a large proportion of Mexico's fantasy production during the sixties and seventies. Never a distinguished director, his work included **Santo Contra El Cerebro Diabolico** (1962), **Los Automatas de la Muerte** (1960) and a number of other Neutron movies starring Wolf Ruvinskis.

d/s Federico Curiel   *p* Luis Enrique Vergara
c Alfredo Vribe   *lp* Alejandro Cruz, Blanca Sanchez, Martha Elena Cervantes, Nathanael Leon Frankenstein

Around the World Under the Sea
(IVAN TORS PRODUCTIONS)   120 min
Ricou Browning, the amphibian-man from **The Creature from the Black Lagoon** (1954) directed the underwater sequences, the best, of this dull film, clearly derived from Jules Verne's novels. When mysterious tidal waves suddenly appear as the result of a fissure in the Earth's crust, Bridges and his crew of scientists are sent in a futuristic submarine to place earthquake warning devices along a fault on the ocean floor that encircles the globe. The submarine's crew face the traditional hazards of such films, sexism (half the scientists object to the presence of Eaton), a near mutiny and a giant moray eel, before completing their mission.

d/p Andrew Marton   *s* Arthur Weiss, Art Arthur   *c* Clifford Poland   *se* Project Unlimited   *lp* Lloyd Bridges, Shirley Eaton, Brian Kelly, David McCallum, Keenan Wynn, Marshall Thompson

Batman   (FOX)   105 min
The Batman serials of the forties (**Batman**, 1943 and **Batman and Robin**, 1949) played the material straight, at least intentionally so, for the most part. But, following the extraordinary success of the camp *Batman* teleseries of 1966, Batman returned to the silver screen a changed man. Thus, in Semple's excessive script, West (the Caped Crusader), and Ward (the Boy Wonder), both reprising their TV roles, indulge in as much verbal buffoonery as fisticuffs with their quartet of villains, the Joker, Penguin, Riddler and Cat Woman (Romero, Meredith, Gorshin and Meriwether, all repeating their TV roles). Similarly Martinson, who had been at the helm of several of the television episodes, repeats the flat look and garish colours for which the series had become noted. As a result, the film, though initially very successful – it grossed nearly $2 million in North America on its release – soon palls.

The storyline follows the attempts of the villainous quartet to steal a dehydrator machine that turns people into dust as a necessary step in their plans of world domination.

d Leslie Martinson   *p* William Dozier   *s* Lorenzo Semple Jnr   *c* Howard Schwartz   *se* L.B. Abbott   *lp* Adam West, Burt Ward, Lee Meriwether, Cesar Romero, Burgess Meredith, Frank Gorshin

Rupert Davies (left) is unable to help in Brides of Fu Manchu.

however inelegantly, with serious social issues, are not the type of films which benefit from 3-D.

This film, which utilizes Oboler's Space Vision, is a case in point. The film was clearly intended as an indictment of the small town mentality which demands conformity and inhibits free expression, but the supporting structure for this is a peculiar mix of extensive dialogue sequences and crude special effects that simply don't gel. Cole, Walley and Desmond are the trio forced to land their plane when they run into an electrical storm. They discover that the small town they land near is populated by mindless zombies and once they enter they are stopped from leaving by an invisible energy field. After much talk they realize that extra-terrestrials have lowered a giant bubble (which led to the 3-D system being called 'Bubblevision' by some) over the town, and smash their way out. The resulting film has a certain naïve charm but is decidedly overlong, especially in view of the slim characterization of the three principals.

d/p/s/se Arch Oboler *c* Charles Wheeler *lp* Michael Cole, Deborah Walley, Johnny Desmond, Kassie McMahon, Barbara Eiler, Viginia Gregg

Castle of Evil (NATIONAL TELEFILM ASSOCIATES) 81 min

A murderous robot (Thourlby) menaces Mayo, Brian and Brady as they gather on a remote island to learn how they may or may not benefit from a crazed scientist's will in this tedious film. The robot is programmed to kill the member of the trio responsible for disfiguring the scientist before his death. Agatha Christie-style it is revealed that if any one of the trio dies, then the other two will share his or her portion. Doctor Brian dies first and it is shown that the robot's programming has been altered by one of the heirs to kill the other. The climax sees Brady gunning down the robot with a laser gun found in the laboratory.

d Francis D. Lyon *p* Earle Lyon *s* Charles A. Wallace
c Brick Marquard *se* Roger George *lp* Scott Brady, Virginia Mayo, Lisa Gaye, David Brian, Hugh Marlowe, William Thourlby

Cyborg 2087 (FEATURE FILM CORP.) 86 min

Planned for television but released theatrically, this is an interesting, if minor, film. Professor Marx (Franz) develops a machine to control human minds but, by 2087, the invention has been perverted by aspiring scientists and cyborgs – human beings whose abilities are controlled by surgically implanted devices and who are used in the creation of a totalitarian state – have been created. Cyborg Garth (Rennie) achieves temporary mental freedom, steals a time machine and returns to 1966 with the aim of persuading Franz not to disclose his secret, thereby altering the course of history. Sadly, this fascinating concept is let down by some poor performances (especially that of Rennie). The predictable conclusion sees Franz destroy his machine and thus eliminate Rennie and his pursuers who will now not exist.

d Franklin Adreon *p* Earle Lyon *s* Arthur C. Pierce
lp Michael Rennie, Karen Steele, Wendell Corey, Warren Stevens, Eduard Franz, Harry Carey Jnr

Daikaiju Gamera *aka* Gamera *aka* Gammera *aka* Gamera the Invincible

(DAIEI; JAP) scope 88 min

The first serious Daiei monster film since **Uchujin Tokyo ni Arawaru** (1956). Gamera was pressed into service as a rival to Godzilla after the latter's change from a 'nasty' monster to a national children's hero in Toho's **Kaiju Daisenso** and **Ghidorah Sandai Kaiju Chikyu Saidai No Kessan** (both 1965). This change had proved massively successful, especially in Daiei's specific market: children and teenagers. Gamera is a giant turtle awakened by an atomic blast. It heads for Tokyo eating everything along the way. Finally, the creature

Above: *Adam West as the camp* Batman.

Brides of Fu Manchu (HAMMER; GB) 94 min

This is the second of the two movies the talented Sharp made for producer Towers in the Fu Manchu series based on Sax Rohmer's novels about the oriental bogeyman. Although by no means as stylish as its predecessor, **The Face of Fu Manchu** (1965), it contains more genuine *frissons* than the Bond films which sparked the revival of the characters. Lee, a delightfully evil villain, kidnaps the daughters of government leaders so as to accumulate a sufficiently large ransom to build a huge ray gun and take over the world. Wilmer, replacing Nigel Green as Nayland Smith, foils him at the last minute.

d/co-s Don Sharp *p* Oliver A. Unger, Harry Alan Towers
co-s/c Ernest Steward *lp* Christopher Lee, Douglas Wilmer, Howard Marion-Crawford, Marie Versini, Rupert Davies, Tsai Chin

The Bubble (MIDWESTER MAGIC-VUERS) 112(94) min

A successful radio dramatist of the thirties and forties, Oboler went to Hollywood in 1945 and in 1951 wrote, directed and produced **Five** which is generally regarded as the first of the cycle of fifties anti-bomb films. Then in 1952, he launched the cycle of 3-D movies with his *Bwana Devil*. However, while Hollywood quickly tired of the 3-D gimmick (especially as it did little to halt falling ticket sales) Oboler persisted. A decade later he perfected Space Vision, his own 3-D system which required a specially ground lens but not the cumbersome second camera and projector of earlier 3-D systems. What makes Oboler's persistence all the more remarkable is that his own films, which are talkative in the extreme and deal, is captured, bundled into a rocket and fired into space. However, it returned quickly enough to star in another movie that same year, **Gamera Tai Barugon** (1966). Subsequent appearances included: **Gamera Tai Gaos** (1967), **Gamera Tai Viras** (1968), **Gamera Tai Guiron** (1969) and **Gamera Tai Daimaju Jaiga** (1970).

The American version of the movie contained extra footage starring Brian Donlevy, Albert Dekker and Diane Findlay. A revised script, by Richard Kraft, made the Americans into the saviours of the world by having them discover the way to get rid of the pest.

d Noriaki Yuasa *p* Yonejiro Saito *s* Fumi Takahashi *c* Nobuo Munekawa *se* Yonesaburo Tsukiji *lp* Eiji Funakoshi, Harumi Kiritachi, Junichiro Yamashita, Yoshiro Kitahara, Michiko Sugata

Daleks – Invasion Earth 2150 AD *aka*
Invasion Earth 2150 AD

(AARU;GB) scope 84 min
In this sequel to **Dr Who and the Daleks** (1965) Cushing once again plays the eccentric Doctor, once again confronted by the Daleks (mutated aliens sitting inside mobile transporters), still anxious to take their revenge on Earth. Cribbins is the London Bobby who mistakes the Tardis for a police-box and is transported with Cushing and his granddaughters (Tovey and Curzon) to the desolated future Earth. There they find that the Daleks have not only conquered Earth but are planning to rip out its core with a huge bomb and use the planet as a spaceship. Cushing and Co join the underground resistance movement and manage to divert the bomb by creating a magnetic forcefield which destroys the Daleks who are sucked into the Earth's core.

Flemyng directs carelessly and the result, like the earlier film, is far inferior to the BBC's teleseries.

d Gordon Flemyng *co-p/s* Milton Subotsky *co-p* Max J. Rosenberg *c* John Wilcox *se* Ted Samuels *lp* Peter Cushing, Bernard Cribbins, Ray Brooks, Andrew Keir, Jill Curzon, Roberta Tovey

Destination Inner Space

(UNITED PICTURES/HAROLD GOLDMAN ASSOCIATES) 83 min
A failed attempt to give an extra fillip to yet another low-budget monster-from-the-depths offering, by making the monster an amphibian alien. Brady and North (making her return to the screen after an absence of nearly ten years) are the scuba-suited scientists who discover an alien spaceship at the bottom of the sea and do battle with the monster when, back in the laboratory, it emerges from its pod. Ron Burke is the alien, which was clearly modelled on **The Creature from the Black Lagoon** (1954).

d Francis D. Lyon *p* Earle Lyon *s* Arthur C. Pierce *c* Brick Marquard *lp* Scott Brady, Sheree North, Gary Merrill, John Howard, Mike Road, Wende Wagner

The Destructors

(UNITED PICTURES/HAROLD GOLDMAN ASSOCIATES) 96 min
A dire thriller replete with Science Fiction gadgetry that became an essential element in such films in the wake of the success of the James Bond movies. Egan is hero on the trail of a gang of spies who are trying to steal the Cyclops disintegrator ray. There follows a complex plot full of cross and doublecross, including Blackman and Owens who compete for Egan's attentions.

d Francis D. Lyon *p* Earle Lyon *s* Arthur C. Pierce, Larry E. Jackson *c* Alan Stensvold *se* Roger George *lp* Richard Egan, Patricia Owens, Joan Blackman, John Ericson, Michael Ansara, David Brian

Daleks – Invasion Earth 2150 AD, *the second film derived from the* Dr Who *teleseries.*

Searching for the books in Fahrenheit 451.

Dimension 5 *aka* Dimension 4
(UNITED PICTURES/HAROLD GOLDMAN ASSOCIATES) 92(88) min
Made by the same team as the more interesting **Cyborg 2087**
(1966) this low-budget production, ineptly directed by
Adreon, has Chinese communist agents hiding an H-bomb in
a shipment of rice with the aim of decimating Los Angeles.
Hunter and Woods are rival US agents, equipped with
time-travel belts to propel themselves into the future. Against
this advantage, the communist agents don't stand a chance.
Sakata, the most villainous of the communists, is better
known for his impersonation of Oddjob in **Goldfinger** (1964).

d Franklin Adreon   *p* Earle Lyon   *s* Arthur C. Pierce
c Alan Stensvold   *se* Roger George   *lp* Jeffrey Hunter,
France Nuyen, Harold Sakata, Donald Woods, Linda Ho,
Robert Ito

Dr Coppelius   (CHILDHOOD PRODUCTIONS; US, SP) 97 min
Based on the ballet by Délibes and Nuitter, this is a late
addition to the robot ballet film cycle. Coppelius (Slezak)
creates Coppélia (Corday), a beautiful dancing doll robot.
Village youth Selling falls in love with the robot and his
girlfriend (played by Corday again) disguises herself as the
robot whilst Dr Coppelius imprisons Selling and tries to
implant his spirit into the doll to give her humanity.
Girlfriend Corday sneaks Selling out, leaving the doll and her
creator heartbroken – although Slezak then decides that lusty
life with the village barmaid is preferable to mechanical
beauty.
Director/writer Kneeland succeeds in creating a delightful
children's film from the *Coppélia* ballet, itself derived from
one of the tales of Hoffman, which were filmed in 1911, 1915
and 1923 as **Hoffmanns Erzaehlungen** and in 1951 as **Tales
of Hoffmann**.
In 1976, an inferior sequel, *The Mysterious House of Dr C*,
was made, again starring Slezak.

d/s Ted Kneeland   *p* Frank J. Hale   *c* Cecilo Paniagua
lp Walter Slezak, Claudia Corday, Eileen Elliott, Caj Selling,
Carman Rojas

Dr Goldfoot and the Girl Bombs *aka* Le Spie Vengono
dal Semifreddo *aka* I Due Mafiosi dell FBI
(ITALIAN INTERNATIONAL FILM/AIP; US, IT) 85(80) min
This Italian sequel to **Dr Goldfoot and the Bikini Machine**
(1965) sees Bava taking over from Taurog as director, but
Price again plays over-the-top Goldfoot, this time building a

force of sexy robot women to assassinate NATO generals in an
attempt to foment war between the United States and Russia.
Goldfoot builds fuses into the robot's navels, so directly the
generals make love to them, they explode. One-time rock
'n'roller Fabian is the American agent who foils the Doctor's
plot. The original was much funnier, but looked far less
stylish and was far less erotic. Nonetheless, this remains the
least interesting of Bava's films.

d Mario Bava   *co-p/co-s* Louis M. Heyward   *co-p* Fulvio
Luciano   *co-s* Robert Kaufman, Castellano Pipolo   *c* A.
Rinaldi   *lp* Vincent Price, Fabian, Franco Franchi, Ciccio
Ingrassia, Laura Antonelli, Movana Tahi

2+5 : Missione Hydra
(GOLDEN MOTION PICTURES; IT) 95 min
This routine Italian offering, notable only for its acceptance as
commonplace the idea that a nuclear war might destroy Earth,
follows the adventures of a group of humans kidnapped by
aliens in a spaceship that seems all too familiar, having
appeared in nearly all the Italian Science Fiction films of the
mid-sixties. The two races learn co-existence as they battle an
array of space monsters.

d/co-s Pietro Francisci   *p/co-s* Aldo Calamara, Ermano
Curti   *c* Silvano Ippoliti   *lp* Leanora Ruffo, Anthony
Freeman, Kirk Morris, Roland Lesaffre, Leontine Snell,
Gordon Mitchel

Fahrenheit 451   (ANGLO-ENTERPRISE/RANK/
VINEYARD PRODUCTIONS; GB) 112 min
Undoubtedly Truffaut's worst film, *Fahrenheit 451*, adapted
from Ray Bradbury's first and most successful novel of the
same title, suffers from its director's commitment to character
(which momentarily transforms Cusack's burner of books,
which burn at 451°F, into a genuinely sympathetic person) at
the expense of the novel's vision of life. Bradbury's novel is
simplistic in its espousal of the 'book people' (people who
learn books off by heart and thereby keep alive the spirit of
free thought in a society that has banned books in an effort to
stamp out any opposition to it and has transformed the once
proud putters out of fires into the burners of books) but it
retains a polemical sharpness that is wholly absent in the film.
The difference between the two is nowhere more apparent
than in the closing images of the novel and film. In the
former, the book people's transformation of themselves into a
living library and arsenal for future revolutionaries is celebrated. In the latter, as they circle in the snow endlessly
intoning the world's literature, Truffaut's camera sees them as
zombies; they have become as brainwashed in their commitment to that which they don't understand as their book-
burning persecutors.
But, if the film makes little sense of the ideas it plays with,
Truffaut's lingering shots of the books aflame apart, as an
essay in loneliness, a perpetual fear of Truffaut's characters, it

Right: *Vincent Price
camps it up in* Dr
Goldfoot and the Girl
Bombs.

is more successful. From this perspective, Christie's naïve literateuse represents, not the danger of knowledge which Werner's fireman is meant to combat, but simple companionship. Similarly, Werner's journey is not from reading to revolution, but from isolation to a sense of belonging. Hence Cusack's fire chief cannot win back Werner because he can't offer the same degree of companionship. But, by the same token, he is a rounded, sympathetic character rather than a mere functionary, because he represents belonging, if only at the level of professional camaraderie.

That said, as it stands, the film, Truffaut's first in colour, is considerably less interesting than the diaries Truffaut kept during its making which, like Lillian Ross' *Picture* (about the making of *The Red Badge of Courage*, 1951), but on a more personal level, are a fascinating document about film-making. Equally it would seem, on the evidence of **The Man Who Fell to Earth** (1976), that much of the credit for the visual splendour of the film must go to cinematographer Roeg. Truffaut's only other involvement with Science Fiction was as an actor: he plays the French scientist in **Close Encounters of the Third Kind** (1977).

d/co-s Francois Truffaut   *p* Lewis M. Allen
co-s Jean-Louis Richard   *c* Nicolas Roeg   *se* Charles Staffel, Bowie Films   *lp* Julie Christie, Oskar Werner, Cyril Cusack, Anton Diffring, Jeremy Spenser, Bee Duffell

Fantastic Voyage (FOX) scope 100 min

A silly but fascinating film, the action of *Fantastic Voyage* consists of a dangerous trip around the body of a top scientist who has a blood clot for which there is no known medical cure. A medical team (led by Boyd with Welch and O'Brien in support) and submarine are miniaturized and injected into the scientist's bloodstream. The heart and lungs become monster obstacles, the sub passes through the brain and watches as a saboteur is ingested by hungry white corpuscles. The mini-sub, *Proteus*, was created by Harper Goff, who was also responsible for the *Nautilus* in Disney's **20,000 Leagues Under the Sea** (1954). The special effects are convincing and Laszlo bathed the sets – giant reproductions of the heart, lungs and brain – with a pulsating light to give them greater reality and movement.

Fleischer said of his reasons for wanting to do the film: 'What also attracted me was the possibility of being able to inspire young people to some understanding of the incredible complexity of the human body and the sheer wonder of it.' Doctors inspected his sets – including the largest working model of the heart ever made, 40 feet by 30 feet – for accuracy, all the actors 'flew' on wires, and the year-long shooting was slow and fraught with difficulty. Although the film is a visual delight, in the psychedelic tradition, it lacks sufficient drama to sustain the narrative.

d Richard Fleischer   *p* Saul David   *s* Harry Kleiner
c Ernest Laszlo   *se* L.B. Abbott, Art Cruickshank, Emil Kosa Jnr   *lp* Stephen Boyd, Raquel Welch, Edmond O'Brien, Donald Pleasance, Arthur Kennedy, Arthur O'Connell

Frankenstein Created Woman
(HAMMER/WB; GB, US) 92 min
As the title suggests, this offering saw Hammer introducing the sexual themes of their Dracula films (such as *Kiss of the Vampire*, 1962) into their equally long-running Frankenstein series. The result is an intermittently powerful but erratically scripted mix of poetic images, visceral shocks and para-science in which Cushing's Frankenstein revives the dead Denberg (a former Playboy centrefold in her only major film role) and gives her the soul of her dead lover (Morris) only for her to set about seducing and then murdering the three men responsible for the death of her father and Morris. The most beautiful looking of Fisher's Frankenstein films (which include **The Curse of Frankenstein**, 1957, **The Revenge of**

Frankenstein, 1958 and **Frankenstein Must Be Destroyed**, 1969), it nonetheless fails because Cushing's role is so minor and the Denberg character clearly belongs to the world of Dracula rather than Frankenstein.

Above: *Science Fiction turns inwards, the journey into the human body in* Fantastic Voyage.

d Terence Fisher   *p* Anthony Nelson Keys   *s* John Elder (Anthony Hinds)   *c* Arthur Grant   *se* Les Bowie   *lp* Peter Cushing, Susan Denberg, Robert Morris, Thorley Walters, Peter Blythe, Duncan Lamont, Barry Warren

The Frozen Dead
(GOLDSTAR PRODUCTIONS/SEVEN ARTS; GB, US) 95 min
This outlandish offering is far superior to **It!** (1966), Leger's companion piece, a lacklustre modern version of the Golem legend. Andrews is the latterday Baron Frankenstein experimenting on reviving deep-frozen Nazi corpses that have been in suspended animation since World War II and Stepanek the Nazi general who dreams of re-animating whole battalions of frozen Nazis (of which it seems he has an endless supply kept in suspended animation) to do battle for the glory of the Third Reich. Set against the bizarre grandeur of these dreams are the budgetary verities of the film (which curtails its action to Andrews' suitably gloomy country mansion) and the conventional central situation of Palk as the emperilled heroine (and Andrews' niece). Breck is Palk's girlfriend who soon becomes the centrepiece of the film, the head that Andrews needs to refine his animation technique, and Gilbert the good scientist who saves the day.

Even Leger's pedestrian direction cannot remove the delirium from images such as the rack of human arms ready for use and Breck's soulful boxed-in head. An equally bizarre film along the same lines is **Shock Waves** (1970).

The articulated arms of The Frozen Dead, one of the most charmingly bizarre films of the sixties, in action.

d/p/s Herbert J. Leger   c David Boulton   lp Dana Andrews, Anna Palk, Philip Gilbert, Karel Stepanek, Kathleen Breck, Alan Tilvern, Tom Chatto, Basil Henson

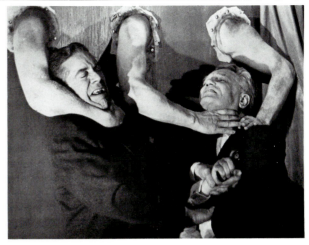

Furankenshutain No Kaiju – Sanda Tai Gailah *aka* The War of the Gargantuas *aka* Duel of the Gargantuas
(TOHO; JAP)   scope   88 min

A sequel to **Furankenshutain Tai Baragon** (1965), again made in cooperation with American International's producer Henry Saperstein, who decided the creatures looked more like Kong than Frankenstein's monster and arranged for all references to the previous Frankenstein film to be dropped, including the flashback that explained how a 'brother' of the monster had emerged. In the original movie, Furankenshutain had lost a hand which apparently generated a new body for itself. The Japanese brother, Sanda, is brown and friendly while the 'outsider' is green and mean. Significantly, Japan's Self Defence Force vanquishes the 'green' brother, the first time military force succeeds against a monster in this genre. But the brown one takes pity on him and nurses him back to health. The irredeemable outsider then turns on his

Frankenstein's revived monster fights his brother in Furankenshutain No Kaiju – Sanda Tai Gailah, *one of the most interesting Japanese monster movies.*

kind brother as well. After a fight that destroys Tokyo (as usual) both are caught in a volcanic eruption leaving the ending open enough for possible sequels. The role of the US scientist on duty (Tamblyn) is also interesting: the Japanese military had disobeyed his orders when they attacked the green monster, and their success only proved their increasing autonomy as well as professionalism. Mizuno recreates her *Furankenshutain Tai Baragon* role as the pretty Japanese assistant of the clever US scientist. The effects are spectacular and extremely well done, especially the scenes where the brothers tramp across crowded motorways, with cars bumping into their toes. The initial appearance of Gailah, as he emerges out of the sea, is accompanied by shots of a giant octopus's attack on a ship, which come from a discarded sequence of *Furankenshutain Tai Baragon*.

d/co-s Inoshiro Honda   p Tomoyuki Tanaka   co-s Kaoru Mabuchi   c Hajime Koizumi   se Eiji Tsuburaya   lp Russ Tamblyn, Kumi Mizuno, Kenji Sahara, Kipp Hamilton, Jun Tazaki

Gamera Tai Barugon *aka* Gamera Versus Barugon *aka* Gambara Versus Barugon *aka* The War of the Monsters
(DAIEI; JAP)   scope   101 min

At the end of its first movie, **Daikaiju Gamera** (1966), the giant turtle was shot into space. It now emerges that a meteorite hit the rocket and diverted it back to Earth and Gamera now also appears to have jet propulsion as it flies, trailing exhaust fumes. An opal egg, found in a cave in New Guinea, hatches and reveals Barugon, soon a 130-ft-long lizardy thing with horny spikes on its back and a unicorn on its snout. The spikes create a deadly energy field in the form of a rainbow that melts everything it touches. Gamera is drawn to Barugon's energy and fights the lizard, dragging it into Lake Biwa and defeating it after Tokyo and Osaka have been devastated. The effects, achieved by Yuasa, the director of all the other Gamera movies, are better than in the previous Gamera film, and Barugon's blue blood colouring the lake is a stylish innovation. Gamera too is a friendly monster able to compete with Godzilla for the affection of children. Barugon seems to be the only instance when a company imitated another company's monster (Toho's **Furankenshutain Tai Baragon**, 1965). Toho was quick to respond to the challenge by developing 'Frankenstein' into a popular hero along with Godzilla and also by multiplying its pictures featuring more than one of the familiar Toho monster stable, even celebrating its 20th monster movie (**Kaiju Soshingeki**, 1968) by mobilizing almost the whole range of Toho monsters in one picture, an array no other studio could match.

d Shigeo Tanaka   p Hidemasa Nagata   s Fumi Takahashi   c Michio Takahashi   se Noriaki Yuasa   lp Kojiro Hondo, Kyoko Enami, Akira Natsuki, Koji Fujiyama, Yuzo Hayakawa, Ichiro Sugai

Garibah no Uchu Ryoko *aka* Gulliver's Travels Beyond the Moon (TOEI; JAP) 85 min

A charmless animated feature. Drawn in the style of early Disney (but completely lacking any real sense of perspective) the film follows the exploits of a waif who sets sail for the star of Hope in company with a toy soldier and Gulliver and along the way saves a planet over-run by robots who have revolted. The film is one of the earliest in the cycle of Japanese animated Science Fiction films for children that followed in the wake of the Japanese monster movies, and one of the few to be distributed in the West.

d Yoshio Kuroda *p* Hiroshi Okawa *s* Shinichi Sekizawa

In the Year 2889 (AZALEA) 80 min

This uncredited remake of **The Day the World Ended** (1956) features Petersen and O'Hara, amongst others, as the survivors of an atomic war menaced by cannibalistic human mutants who have telepathic powers. Buchanan directs in the naïve style of his best-known film **Mars Needs Women** (1966). His other films include **Zontar, the Thing from Venus** (1966), an uncredited remake of **It Conquered the World** (1956) and **It's Alive** (1968), which is not to be confused with the marvellous Larry Cohen 1973 film of the same title.

d/p Larry Buchanan *s* Harold Hoffman *c* Robert C. Jessup *se* Jack Bennett *lp* Paul Petersen, Quinn O'Hara, Charla Doherty, Neil Fletcher, Billy Thurman

Invasion (MERTON PARK; GB) b/w 82 min

Made on a very small budget but imaginatively photographed by Wilson, the setting of this highly atmospheric film is an English hospital outside which two humanoid aliens, a police official (Tani), and his prisoner (Young) crash-land. Dr Vernon (Judd) protects the prisoner but other aliens arrive and demand that Young should be handed over to them immediately. When Judd turns down this request they surround the hospital with an impenetrable forcefield before he outmanoeuvres the aliens in a tense, well-paced climax.

Tani is best remembered for her performance in the visually striking **Der Schweigende Stern** (1960).

d Alan Bridges *p* Jack Greenwood *s* Roger Marshall *c* James Wilson *se* Ronnie Whitehouse, Jack Kline, Stan Shields *lp* Edward Judd, Valerie Gearon, Yoko Tani, Lyndon Brook, Tsai Chin, Eric Young

Island of Terror *aka* Night of the Silicates (PLANET; GB) 89 min

This is the second, and best, of Fisher's trio of Science Fiction films for Planet. Cushing is the scientist experimenting with a new cure for cancer who, when his research goes awry, produces giant mutated viruses that can suck the bones out of their victims. Fisher, better known for his Hammer horror films, creates some effective, if nasty, images.

d Terence Fisher *p* Tom Blakeley *s* Alan Ramsen, Edward Andrew Mann *c* Reg Wyer *se* John St John Earl *lp* Peter Cushing, Edward Hudd, Carole Gray, Eddie Byrne, Sam Kydd, Niall MacGinnis

It! (GOLDSTAR PRODUCTIONS/SEVEN ARTS; GB, US) 97 min

This tired re-working of the Golem myth, best filmed by Paul Wegener in 1920 as **Der Golem**, features McDowall as the mad museum curator – he keeps the mummified body of his mother at home – who discovers and animates the legendary statue of the Golem (Sellers). The one interesting departure from the legend is that at the end, after the Golem has destroyed London Bridge on McDowall's telepathically transmitted directions as a test of his powers, although McDowall dies when the authorities drop an atomic bomb, the Golem itself goes free, walking into the sea.

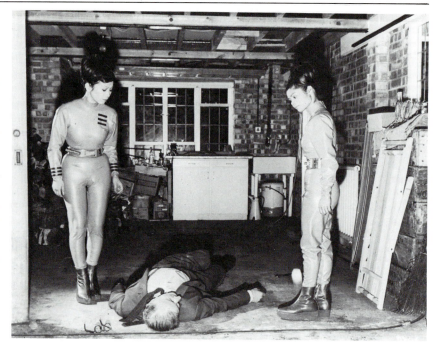

Leger directs leadenly and McDowall produces his usual mannered performance, all nervous ticks and little motivation. Accordingly, the film has none of the delirium of the same director's **The Frozen Dead** (1966) with which it was originally released on a double bill.

Above: *The atmospheric Invasion.*

d/p/s Herbert J. Leger *c* David Bolton *lp* Roddy McDowall, Jill Haworth, Paul Maxwell, Aubrey Richards, Ernest Clark, Oliver Johnston, Alan Sellers, Noel Trevarthen

Jesse James Meets Frankenstein's Daughter (CIRCLE PRODUCTIONS) 82 min

The last film to be directed by Beaudine who entered the cinema as a property boy for D.W. Griffith in 1909, this, sadly, is an ineptly made exploitation quickie. Onyx is the descendant of Baron Frankenstein who settles in Mexico and starts experimenting on kidnapped schoolchildren. When Lupton's Jesse James gets wise to Onyx, who attacks her role with real glee, she transforms a wounded friend of his into a robot and sets it on him. Like its companion piece, *Billy the Kid versus Dracula* (1965), the film has achieved cult status in recent years.

d William Beaudine *p* Carroll Case *s* Carl K. Hittleman *c* Lothrop Worth *lp* John Lupton, Carl Bolder, Narda Onyx, Steven Geray, Raymond Barnes, Jim Davis, Felipe Turich

Kaitei Daiseno *aka* Terror Beneath the Sea *aka* Water Cyborgs (TOEI; JAP) scope 95(87) min

An unpretentious but energetically directed mixture of comic strips, Science Fiction and monster movies. A mad scientist rules a vast futuristic city under water. With a colleague, he succeeds in devising a machine that changes people into amphibious creatures under his control ie cyborgs looking like the **Creature from the Black Lagoon** (1954). The plot also involves atomic waste as a power source for the devilish contraption, surgical interventions to facilitate the change from person to cyborg, moral control, etc. The photography takes full advantage of the opportunities to achieve striking images in bold colours and with sophisticated compositions, worthy of the best in comic strips.

An American version was made at the same time as the Japanese film, using mostly English-speaking performers. Neal, Gruber and Daning also appeared in Shochiku's **Uchu**

Daikaiju Guilala (1967), where their acting was equally wooden. Sato, a young director, used the pseudonym Terence Ford for the US version, to suggest that the largely American cast had not, in fact, been directed by a Japanese.

d Hajime Sato (Terence Ford) *p* Masafumi Soga
s M. Fukuishima *c* K. Shimomura *se* Nobuo Yajima
lp Shinichi Chiba, Peggy Neal, Franz Gruber, Gunther Braun, Andrew Hughes, Erik Nielson, Mike Daning, Hideo Murata

Konec Sprna v Hotelu Ozon *aka* **The End of August at the Hotel Ozone**

(STUDIO BARRANDOV; CZECH) b/w 87 min
Set 15 years after the atomic holocaust, the atmosphere and plot of this film are close to that of Carpenter's **Escape from New York** (1981) or to one of Corman's exploitation films. A gang of women, brutalized by having to survive in a devastated world, go around ruthlessly and callously scavenging, primitively killing animals for food and eventually coolly murdering the aged owner of a deserted hotel (Jariabek) in order to steal his gramophone. The women behave like a gang of Wild Angels might, except that the deliberate pace, the modernist electronic music by Jan Klusak and the photography all combine to signal 'art movie' status. Seidlerova, as the second in command, and Ponicanova as the elderly leader of the gang, turn in impressive performances, while the others merge into a collective animalistic identity. Schmidt and Juracek had collaborated before on an art house movie, *Josef Kilian* (1963) which was equally pregnant with existential anxiety, the very antithesis of Vorlicek and Makourek's crazy comedies (**Kdo Chce Zabit Jessu?**, 1965, and **Pane Vy Jste Vdova**, 1971).

Schmidt has recently completed a trilogy of films about primeval times, *Trilogie Z Praveku* (1977).

d Jan Schmidt *s* Pavel Juracek *c* Jiri Macak *lp* Beta Ponicanova, Magda Seidlerova, Hana Vikotva, Natalie Maslovova, Jana Novakova, Ondrei Jariabek, Vanda Kalinova, Irina Lzicarova, Jitka Horejsi, Alena Lippertova

Mars Needs Women (AZALEA) 80 min
This lacklustre offering from the prolific Buchanan is one of the many films offered, like lambs to the slaughter, by Michael Medved and other 'bad-movie' cultists as examples of Hollywood film-making at its worst. Low low-budget Science Fiction films with their virtually unconscious direct reflection of the concerns of their times (which make them so interesting as socio-cultural items) and ineptly mounted special effects only too often take pride of place in such 'bad-movie' pantheons. Generally made by independent companies with near amateur casts, such films are too easy a target. Moreover, to invite us to laugh at them is also to ask us to accept certain professional standards of film-making as absolutes. A better target would be films like **The Day of the Triffids** (1963), a film made by 'professional' film-makers with a lavish budget which was an unmitigated disaster. Thus, while *Mars Needs Women* is indeed a bad movie, it's no more than that. Produced, directed, scripted and edited by Buchanan, it features Disney regular Kirk as the leader of a group of Martians who come to Earth in search of women with which to repopulate Mars. Their arrival is viewed by the military as a prelude to an invasion while Kirk romances space geneticist Craig in the guise of a science reporter. Interestingly, the Martians' view of women as purely beautiful breeding machines is considered horrendous by the military – 'They're kidnapping our women!' – but is actively supported by the film: the women the Martians attempt to kidnap include a burlesque dancer, a geneticist and an airline stewardess.

Filmed in catch as catch can locations, including a disused ice factory, the film is oddly overbalanced in favour of the

John Lupton in danger in Jesse James Meets Frankenstein's Daughter.

Martians. Their final defeat – they escape without any women – like that of the interplanetary visitor in Edgar Ulmer's far superior **The Man from Planet X** (1951), is more an indictment of mankind than a victory.

d/p/s Larry Buchanan *c* Robert C. Jessup
lp Tommy Kirk, Yvonne Craig, Byron Lord, Roger Ready, Warren Hammack, Pat Delany, Bill Thurman

Murderer's Row (MEADWAY-CLAUDE/COL) 108 min

The second of Columbia's Matt Helm series, mounted in an attempt to cash in on the success of the Bond films, this is decidedly inferior to the first, the Phil Karlson directed **The Silencers** (1965). Baker's limp screenplay which, minus the sexual games the characters play with each other, wouldn't be out of place in a thirties serial, has Martin's Helm, his assistant Adams and Ann-Margret on the trail of her scientist father. He's been kidnapped by Malden's would-be dictator of the world who, with the scientist's 'helio-ray', threatens to destroy Washington DC.

Not only is the film dull and, like those that were to follow (**The Ambushers**, 1967 and *The Wrecking Crew*, 1968), wholly derivative of the Bond films, but unlike its similarly derivative Italian counterparts, it lacks any sense of style.

d Henry Levin *p* Irving Allen *s* Herbert Baker
c Sam Leavitt *se* Danny Lee *lp* Dean Martin, Ann-Margret, Beverly Adams, James Gregory, Karl Malden, Camilla Sparv, Tom Reese

Nankai No Daiketto *aka* Ebirah Terror of the Deep *aka* Godzilla Versus the Sea Monster *aka* Big Duel in the North Sea (TOHO; JAP) scope 87 min

Godzilla's seventh film, while Mothra makes a guest appearance in its fourth movie (although this creature must be the original Mothra's daughter, if not granddaughter). As for Ebirah, the giant crab or lobster, this remained its only star turn: it was torn limb from limb by Godzilla in the film's climactic fight. However, as it could regenerate itself from any detached part of its anatomy, Ebirah returned briefly in **Kaiju Soshingeki** (1968). The positive valuation of Godzilla, the monster representing the force unleashed at Hiroshima and Nagasaki against Japan, is enhanced by associating the bad monster in this movie with a totalitarian organization seeking world domination: Red Bamboo. While Godzilla engages Ebirah in battle, Mothra saves those who have been subjugated by the Reds, organizing an airlift to evacuate people from an island before it explodes. The film has its humorous moments as Godzilla, who learned to play ball in **King Kong Tai Gojira** (1963) reveals himself far more adept

Florence Marley as the Queen of Blood, one of the several American films made by cannibalizing Russian movies.

at football as he and Ebirah play with an enormous rock at the start of their fight.

Godzilla's next performance was directed by Fukuda, another Toho house director who had finished off Honda's transformation movies in the late fifties, and who took over from Honda again in the early seventies. Honda later used footage from Fukuda's film in **Oru Kaiju Daishingeki** (1969).

d Jun Fukuda *p* Tomoyuki Tanaka *s* Shinichi Sekizawa
c Kazuo Yamada *se* Eiji Tsuburaya *lp* Akira Takarada, Toru Watanabe, Hideo Sunazuka, Kumi Mizuno, Jun Tazaki

Il Pianeta Errante *aka* War Between the Planets

(MERCURY FILM INTERNATIONAL; IT) 77 min
A surprisingly ugly-looking film with a naïve plot to match this has none of the wit or invention of Margheriti's earlier **I Criminali della Galassia** (1965). The story is the old one of a wandering asteroid on a collision course with Earth and the team of brave men, led by Stuart, who detonate it in the nick of time. Characterization, dialogue and plot are uniformly bad, only the asteroid itself, visualized as a living being into whose heart the heroes must travel, is at all impressive.

d/co-p Anthony Dawson (Antonio Margheriti) *co-p* Joseph Fryd *s* Ivan Reiner, Renato Moretti *c* Riccardo Pallottini *lp* Jack Stuart, Amber Collins (Ombretta Colli), John Bartha, Enzo Fiermonte, Alina Zalewska, Freddy Urger

The Projected Man

(MCL/PROTELCO FILMS; GB) scope 90(77) min
Matter-transmitting machines, as **The Fly** (1958) and its two sequels revealed, are fraught with problems. In this mediocre British offering the machine is sabotaged and disfigures its creator, Halliday (who is acting as the guinea-pig), turning him into a monster who can kill at a touch with an electric force. He goes on the rampage before, in a moment of clarity, he realizes what he's become and destroys himself and his equipment. Woolland is the doubting Thomas of a scientist and Peach the blonde scientist girlfriend in Cooper and Bryan's traditional screenplay.

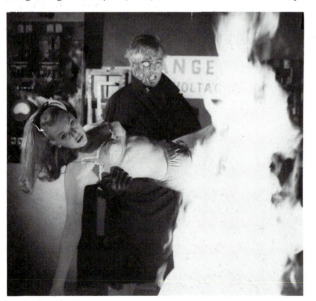

Left: Bryan Halliday as the disfigured scientist with Tracey Crisp in The Projected Man.

d Ian Curteis *p* Maurice Foster, John Croydon *s* John C. Cooper, Peter Bryan *c* Stanley Davey *se* Flo Nordhoff, Robert Hedges, Mike Hope *lp* Bryan Halliday, Mary Peach, Norman Woolland, Roland Allen, Derek Farr, Tracey Crisp, Sam Kydd

Queen of Blood *aka* Planet of Blood

(GEORGE EDWARDS PRODUCTIONS/AIP) 81 min

This is one of the several films made by AIP, at the time Roger Corman was working for them, by cannibalizing Russian films with their superior (big-budget) special effects (in this case, by all accounts **Meshte Nastreshu**, 1963) and shooting additional, more action-oriented, footage around it. Other films made in this manner include **Battle Beyond the Sun** (1963), **Voyage to the Prehistoric Planet** (1965) and **Voyage to the Planet of Prehistoric Women** (1966).

The crude plot features three astronauts, Saxon, Hopper and Meredith encountering a crashed spaceship and its sole survivor – the green-tinted Marley. She, it quickly transpires, is a haemophiliac vampire who, after being transported to the mother ship, sets about killing the crew one by one (a plot reminiscent of **It! The Terror from Beyond Space**, 1958 and one that was revived with far greater success in **Alien**, 1979). Finally in a struggle with Meredith she is cut and bleeds to death, leaving behind a nest of eggs which Rathbone, the mission commander, takes back to Earth to study.

The film was shot in eight days for less than $50,000 – the largest single item being $1,000 for the space helmets which had to match those in the Russian footage. But if the plot is rudimentary, Harrington's direction is effectively atmospheric, generating a real sense of menace.

d/s Curtis Harrington *p* George Edwards *c* Vilis Lapenieks *lp* John Saxon, Basil Rathbone, Judi Meredith, Dennis Hopper, Florence Marley, Forrest J. Ackerman

Santo Contra la Invasion de los Marcianos *aka* Santo Versus the Martian Invasion

(PRODUCCIONES CINEMATOGRAFICAS; MEX) 85 min

Made at the height of Mexico's flying-saucer craze, this was Crevenna's third space opera in two years; he had just finished

Gigantes Planetarios and **El Planeta de los Mujeres Invasoras** (both made in 1965 but released in 1966). The movie opens with stock shots from TV showing a rocket launch and a space walk. On TV, Santo then witnesses the appearance of Martians on Earth demanding an end to nuclear testing and space shots. But in contrast to the alien in **The Day the Earth Stood Still** (1951), the Martians, led by Argos (played by the wrestler Ruvinskis), threaten to and in fact do disintegrate people with a ray emanating from their 'astral' eye. They can also disappear simply by pressing a button on their belt. In addition to killing people they also kidnap a number of them to study their physiological construction, which suggests that their mission of 'peace' was no more than a scenarist's gimmick to set a plot about alien invasion in motion without bothering with details such as logic or consistency in the stringing together of plot-events.

Santo succeeds in rescuing the kidnapped Earthlings before he blows up the spaceship killing all the aliens who had chosen Mexico as a landing place because, they say in the picture, it was such a peaceful country. The sex interest introduced for the more adult members of the audience is provided by two female Martian wrestlers (Norvind and Monti) who strike up a decidedly physical relationship with the Silver Masked hulk. The actor called 'Frankenstein', who also appeared in *Gigantes Planetarios* (1965), is yet another wrestler making regular guest appearances in the wrestler-fantasy movies built around Santo, Neutron and Blue Demon.

d Alfredo B. Crevenna *p* Alfonso Rosas Priego *s* Rafael Garcia Traversi *c* Jorge Stahl Jnr *lp* Santo, Maura Monti, Eva Norvind, Wolf Ruvinskis, Belinda Corell, Gilda Miros, El Nazi, Benny Galan, Natanael Leon Frankenstein

Seconds (PAR/JOEL/GIBRALTER) b/w 106 min

A compelling study in paranoia, *Seconds* charts director Frankenheimer's growing disillusionment with technology, a theme first expressed in *The Manchurian Candidate* (1962) and *Seven Days in May* (1964). Where those films, however, dealt with the public misuse of modern technology (brainwashing and media manipulation) *Seconds*, like **Coma** (1978), deals

Right: Seconds, *John Frankenheimer's chilling study in paranoia.*

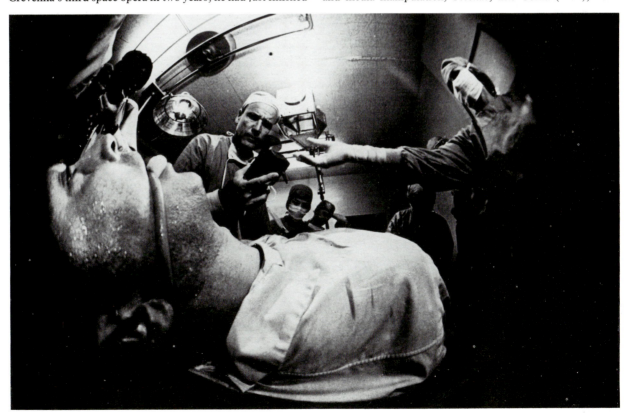

Jerry Lewis is Way . . . Way Out.

with its private misuse as a man discovers that the costs of rejuvenation and a new life are being trapped in the wrong body.

Randolph is the middle-aged businessman who pays a mysterious organization to return him to his youth by faking his death and making surgical alterations. The transformation soon turns sour when Hudson (playing Randolph's new identity) tires of the exhaustion of youth and becomes nostalgic for middle age and his family. When he discovers he is not allowed to return, he becomes desperate and starts making a nuisance of himself to the organization. The chilling conclusion has Hudson prefer death rather than continue to deny his real identity. So the organization kill him and prepare to recycle his body organs for use by other aspirants for a 'new life'. Howe's superb cinematography gives an eerie feel to Frankenheimer's desolate images.

d John Frankenheimer *p* Edward Lewis *s* Lewis John Carlino *c* James Wong Howe *lp* Rock Hudson, Salome Jens, John Randolph, Will Geer, Jeff Corey, Richard Anderson, Murray Hamilton

Sedmi Kontinent *aka* Siedma Pevnina *aka* The Seventh Continent

(JADRAN FILM/KOLIBA FILM; YUG, CZECH) scope 80 min
A distinguished animator's first feature, aimed at children but casting its net wider than that. Whereas the English **Lord of the Flies** (1963) showed how children conditioned by English society and education would inevitably and 'spontaneously' resort to an extremely nasty and authoritarian form of social organization, this Yugoslav-Czech co-production gives a socialist reply to such fantasies. A white boy and a yellow girl slip away from a car-crowded ferry and establish a profoundly egalitarian, non-racist world on a deserted island, using their imagination to recreate their environment. Many children of all races and nationalities are attracted to the place until in the end everybody is seen eagerly swimming to reach the new seventh continent. Although a little naïve about the beneficial aspects of the way Eastern Europe educates children, the film at least shows that kids' fantasies have their own dynamic and

that the deformations inflicted upon children's mental lives by the divisive and bullying rituals of English public schools should not be passed off as somehow more 'natural' than any other form of social conditioning. The film's combination of animation and live action shows the extent to which Vukotic, the founder of the celebrated Zagreb school in the fifties, had broken with the Disney style that had dominated animation throughout the world.

d/co-s Dusan Vukotic *co-s* Andro Lusicic *c* Karel Krska
lp Iris Vrus, Tomica Pasaric, Andulaj Seck, Hermina Pipinic, Demetar Bitnec

Sting of Death (ESSEN PRODUCTIONS) 75 min

In this unimaginative piece of low-budget Science Fiction Vella is the disfigured marine biologist who breeds giant jellyfish electrically in an underwater cave and has developed a technique for transforming himself into a monster, half jellyfish, half human. Hawkins is the wooden heroine he loves in vain and Morrison the hard-headed hero. Interspersed amongst the killings are several songs by Neil Sedaka.

d William Grefe *p* Richard S. Flink *s* Al Dempsey
c Julio C. Chavez *se* Harry Kerwin *lp* Joe Morrison, Valerie Hawkins, John Vella, Jack Nagle, Sandy Lee Kane, Deanna Dund

Superago Contro Diabolicus *aka* Superago versus Diabolicus

(LIBER FILM/SEC FILM/BALCAZAR; IT, SP) scope 87 min
With only a bullet-proof leotard and his strength to defend himself with, Cianfriglia is Superago, a wrestler turned crime fighter, one of the legion of superheroes who populated the Italian cinema from the time of Hercules onwards. Few of the films were distributed outside Spain and Latin America because outside of the cultural traditions that nourished them they made little sense.

Here the muscular Superago takes on mad scientist Diabolicus who has been stealing uranium so as to produce a radioactive gold isotope that will guarantee him domination of the world. The finale has Diabolicus attempt to flee into outer space only to have his rocket blown up by a malfunctioning computer.

As usual the narrative is clumsily handled and the acting rudimentary but the design of Diabolicus' subterranean headquarters is imaginatively conceived.

d Nick Nostro   *co-p/co-s* J.J. Balcazar   *co-p* Ottavio Poggi   *co-s* F. Giarda   *c* Francisco Marin   *lp* Ken Wood (Giovanni Cianfriglia), Gerard Tichy, Loredna Nusciak, Monica Randal, Francisco Castillo Escalona, Emilio Messina, Geoffrey Copleston

Thunderbirds Are Go   (AP FILMS; GB)   scope   94 min

This is the first, and best, of the pair of films (the other being **Thunderbird 6**, 1968) developed by the Andersons from their successful teleseries *Thunderbirds* which was devoted to the exploits of a group of puppets who, under the collective title of International Rescue, saved the 21st century from a variety of evils. Here, the team lead the first manned expedition to Mars and foil would-be saboteurs. The special effects, as ever, are superb but Jeff Tracey, Lady Penelope (whose impeccable English voice is that of Sylvia Anderson), Brains and company are far too bland to retain one's interest for any length of time.

The film's title song is by the Shadows while the title itself is one of the teleseries' most famous catchphrases.

d David Lane   *p/co-s* Sylvia Anderson   *co-s* Gerry Anderson   *c* Paddy Seale   *se* Derek Meddings, Shaun Whittacker-Cook

Ukradena Vzducholod *aka* The Stolen Dirigible *aka* Two Years Holiday

(STUDIO BARRANDOV; CZECH)   88 min

After **Cesta do Praveku** (1955), a Vernesque story, and **Vynalez Zkazy** (1958), directly adapting Verne's stories, this time Zeman elaborates on a theme often used in Verne's books: a voyage in a technologically extremely advanced, by 19th-century standards, contraption. During the great exhibition of 1889 in Paris (the inauguration of the Eiffel Tower) five children steal the dirigible constructed by Professor Findejs (Randa). They travel across Europe and wind up on a deserted island where they experience the adventures one expects in a Verne novel. Zeman's next Verne adaptation was more successful, **Na Komete** (1970), showing how a simple children's film could be infinitely superior to the mess Gance had made of the comet-colliding-with-the-Earth theme in his **La Fin du Monde** (1930).

Ukradena Vzducholod, Karel Zeman's imaginative Science Fiction fantasy for children.

d/co-s Karel Zeman   *co-s* Radovan Kraty   *c* Josef Novotny, Bohuslav Pikhart   *lp* Cestmir Randa, Michal Pospisil, Hanus Bor, Jan Malat, Jitka Zelenohorska, Josef Hauvic, Josef Vetrovec

Voyage to the Planet of Prehistoric Women *aka* Gill Woman *aka* Gill Women of Venus

(FILMGROUP)   78 min

Unable to resist a bargain, Corman often bought footage, especially if it contained spectacular special effects, with the idea of building a film around the bought footage. In the case of **Planeta Burg** (1962), Corman managed to get two films from the material, **Voyage to a Prehistoric Planet** (1965), made with additional scenes directed by Curtis Harrington, and this, the additional sequences of which were the (pseudonymous) directorial début of film critic Bogdanovich.

Astronauts crash on Venus and face the hazards of an alien world, which include Russian lizard-men, robots and dinosaurs. Telepathic women led by Van Doren transport them back to the safety of Earth when the astronauts kill their god – a pterodactyl. Like *Voyage to a Prehistoric Planet*, the film was issued directly to television.

US footage: d Derek Thomas (Peter Bogdanovich)
p Norman D. Wells, Roger Corman   *s* Henry Ney
lp Mamie Van Doren, Mary Mark, Paige Lee

Way … Way Out

(COLDWATER/JERRY LEWIS/FOX)   scope   106 min

Set in 1994, with Lewis as a lunar-based weather expert this is a weak comedy from Douglas who, though he began his career as a gagman for the Hal Roach studios in the twenties and intermittently returned to the genre, was clearly happier making action movies such as *Rio Conchos* (1964) and *The Detective* (1968). The romantic complications which follow from Lewis' falling for Stevens (a far better actress than this and her earlier, mostly *ingénue*, roles allowed her to show) lead to conflict between the American and Russian moonbases. Neither script nor direction leave sufficient space for Lewis' highly mannered brand of comedy.

d Gordon Douglas   *p* Malcolm Stuart   *s* William Bowers, Laslo Vadnay   *c* William H. Clothier   *se* L.B. Abbott, Emil Kosa Jnr, Howard Lydecker   *lp* Jerry Lewis, Connie Stevens, Robert Morley, Dick Shawn, Anita Ekberg, Dennis Weaver, Sig Ruman

Women of the Prehistoric Planet

(STANDARD CLUB OF CALIFORNIA)   91 min

Despite its intriguing conclusion, in which Adam and Eve are revealed to be alien astronauts, this is a mediocre film. Corey is the Centaurian leader of a mission searching for survivors from one of his spaceships which crashed on an unknown planet on which giant lizards and dinosaurs roam. On its arrival, the expedition (which includes Agar and Larsen) find that the sole survivor is a child grown to adulthood with no memories of Centaurus who promptly kidnaps Tsu. Just as she convinces him of who he is volcanic explosions cause the expedition to leave. Later, safe in space, Corey names the planet 'Earth'. The film is amateurishly made and the effects are hardly special.

d/s Arthur C. Pierce   *p* George Gilbert   *c* Archie Dalzell
se Howard A. Anderson   *lp* Wendell Corey, Keith Larsen, John Agar, Irene Tsu, Paul Gilbert, Stuart Margolin, Merry Anders

Zontar, the Thing from Venus

(AZALEA)   80 min

This is an uncredited remake of **It Conquered the World** (1956). Alien monster Zontar – looking like a large blundering bat – arrives on Earth and sets about conquering the world by shutting off all its power sources.

Agar is the stolid hero. Producer/director/writer Buchanan (best known for **Mars Needs Women**, 1966) creates some (unintentionally) hilarious scenes, including his small, low-budget crowds hysterically panicking in the wake of Zontar's creaking, flapping wings.

d/p/co-s Larry Buchanan   *co-s* H. Taylor   *c* Robert B. Alcott   *lp* John Agar, Susan Bjorman, Anthony Houston, Patricia DeLaney, Warren Hammack

The Ambushers (MEADWAY/CLAUDE/COL)   102 min
Slackly directed by Levin (who had also overseen the second in the four-strong Matt Helm series, **Murderer's Row**, 1966), this tiresome Bond parody sends Martin in search of an experimental flying saucer that mysteriously crash-lands in Mexico where, posing as a photographer, he puts paid to the various representatives of foreign governments seeking its secrets. Rule and Berger are amongst the decorations on view, Adams (in her last outing in the series) is his assistant and Gregory his 'M'.

A non Science Fiction sequel, the last in the series, followed in 1968, *The Wrecking Crew*, and, in 1975, Helm (played by Tony Franciosa) was brought out of retirement for a lacklustre telefilm, *Matt Helm*.

d Henry Levin   *p* Irving Allen   *s* Herbert Baker   *c* Burnett Guffey, Edward Colman   *se* Danny Lee   *lp* Dean Martin, Senta Berger, Janice Rule, James Gregory, Beverly Adams, Albert Salami, Kurt Krasznar

Automat Na Prani *aka* The Wishing Machine
(STUDIO GOTTWALDOW; CZECH)   83(75) min
A children's film warning against mistaking fantasies for reality, which makes it an antidote to the vast majority of American children's fiction, particularly the films of the Disney studio. Two boys build a machine that can make wishes come true. As this is the time when space flights are all over the media and Leonov has just become the first man to do a 'space walk' (1965), they naturally want to go to the Moon, although they don't have a clue about the dangers of such a journey and are totally unprepared for it. In the end, the military intervenes and they are reminded of the way things work in reality. The film succeeds by avoiding the condescendingly adult view of children as lovable cuties so prevalent in this type of fiction.

Robert Braverman produced an English language version (1971) for which he wrote a new script.

d/s Josef Pinkava   *c* Jiri Kolin   *lp* Vit Weingaertner, Milan Zeman, Frantisek Filipovsky, Josef Hlinomaz, Miloslav Holub, Rudolf Deyl Jnr, Karel Effa, Jana Rendlova, Marketa Rauschgoldova

Barbarella (MARIANNE PRODUCTIONS/
DINO DE LAURENTIIS; FR, IT)   pv 98 min
This piece of interplanetary titillation is based on Jean-Claud Forest's risqué French comic strip which achieved international notoriety in the early sixties. The tone of the film is set by its opening sequence, a free fall striptease by Fonda in the title role, in which director Vadim clearly demonstrates that his aim was to make his (then) wife an international sex star in the mould of his previous wives (Brigitte Bardot and Annette Stroyberg). But, if the resulting adolescent voyeurism has all the passion of a masturbatory fantasy and suggests a deep-seated hostility to women on Vadim's part, Fonda's wide-eyed innocence remains appealing. The film's most revealing failing is its lack of narrative drive, necessitated by Vadim's need to stop the action and present his scantily clad wife for the audience to ogle.

The story is little but Flash Gordon in drag with Barbarella saving the 40th century from destruction at the hands of the

John Phillip Law and Jane Fonda in Barbarella.

demented O'Shea (who gives a wickedly larger than life performance in the grand tradition of serialdom's villains) and his positronic ray. In this she gets erratic and erotic support from Hemmings (who turns in an effective comic performance), Law's statuesque blind angel and Pallenberg's lesbian Black Queen. The script (co-authored by Southern) has a humorous and cutting edge to it that no other Vadim film possesses. This is supported by Renoir's ravishing cinematography and a number of gloriously decadent sets of designer Mario Garbuglia, which are remarkably faithful to Forest's drawings. The result is a confectionary delight that surprisingly survives its cynical centre.

d/co-s Roger Vadim   *p* Dino De Laurentiis   *co-s* Terry Southern, Claude Brûle, Vittorio Bonicelli, Clement Biddle Wood, Brian Degas, Tudor Gates, Jean-Claude Forest   *c* Claude Renoir   *se* August Lohman   *lp* Jane Fonda, John Phillip Law, Anita Pallenberg, Milo O'Shea, David Hemmings, Marcel Marceau

Battle Beneath the Earth
(REYNOLDS VETTER PRODUCTIONS; GB)   91(83) min
This naïve offering takes for its premise the notion that Chinese troops are burrowing their way under America as part of their plan to take over the free world, a literalization of the reds-under-the-bed cliché if ever there was one. Sadly, though the idea is a charming one, its execution is less so, the deadpan acting styles of those involved notwithstanding. Mathews is the defender of democracy and Benson the Chinese commander, a character who wouldn't be out of place in a thirties serial so stereotyped is he as 'the Oriental villain'.

d Montgomery Tully   *p* Charles Reynolds   *s* L.Z. Hargreaves   *c* Kenneth Talbot   *se* Tom Howard   *lp* Kerwin Mathews, Viviane Ventura, Robert Ayres, Peter Arne, Martin Benson, Peter Elliott

Billion Dollar Brain
(LOWNDES PRODUCTIONS; GB)   pv   111 min
This is thought by many to be the best of Russell's films because his tendency to excess was held in check by the strong narrative line supplied by McGrath's witty scenario. The third film to be adapted from Len Deighton's spy novels, *Billion Dollar Brain* sets Caine (who gives a neatly calculated deadpan performance) with assistance from Homulka's KGB colonel against Begley's crazed Texan millionaire who plans a private invasion of Russia which he mistakenly thinks is ripe for revolution. Clearly happier in the set-pieces, notably the invasion, constructed as a parody of the famous ice-breaking

sequence in Eisenstein's *Alexander Nevsky* (1938), Russell fails to give any dramatic edge to his characters, especially Malden's doublecrossing agent feeding false information into Begley's super-computer.

d Ken Russell *p* Harry Saltzman *s* John McGrath *c* Billy Williams *lp* Michael Caine, Karl Malden, Françoise Dorléac, Oscar Homulka, Ed Begley, Guy Doleman, Vladek Scheybal

The Blood Beast Terror *aka* The Vampire-Beast Craves Blood

(TIGON BRITISH; GB) 88 min
A minor shocker from Sewell, a director better known for his work in the fantasy field. Flemyng is the mad professor who creates a giant moth for his daughter (Ventham), who has the unfortunate ability to metamorphoze herself into a monster death's head moth, in the hope of stopping her murderous assaults on all and sundry, only to discover that his creation too needs blood. However, even Cushing's authoritative Victorian detective on the trail of the gruesome murders can't overcome the weak script, slack direction and dire special effects.

d Vernon Sewell *p* Tony Tensor *s* Peter Bryan *c* Stanley A. Long *se* Roger Dicken *lp* Peter Cushing, Robert Flemyng, Wanda Ventham, Vanessa Howard, David Griffen, Kevin Stoney

Blue Demon Contra Cerebros Infernales *aka* Blue Demon Vs el Crimen *aka* Cerebro Infernal *aka* Blue Demon Versus the Infernal Brains

(ESTUDIOS AMERICA/CINEMATOGRAFICA RA; MEX) 85 min
Following on from **Arañas Infernales** (1966) and released only one month after that picture in 1968, this adventure of

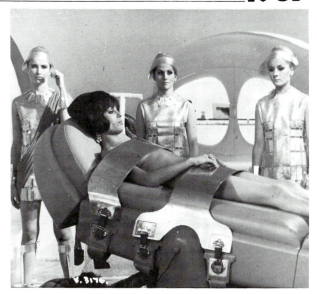

the grotesquely masked wrestler with the blue trousers (Cruz) pits him against a Dr Sanders who kills scientists and other people such as wrestlers in order to extract the phenomenal intelligence and knowledge from their brains. He is assisted by a group of obedient female zombies he has created. After Blue Demon had disposed of all these nasties, the masked wrestler teamed up with the popular Silver Masked hulk, Santo, in **Santo y Blue Demon Contra los Monstruos** and **Santo Contra Blue Demon en la Atlantida** (both 1968).

Urueta, the director of Mexico's first major medical Science Fiction picture, **El Monstruo Resucitado** (1953), became an extremely prolific *cinéaste*, launching the careers of such sex and fantasy film stars as Kitty de Hoyos and Ana Luisa Peluffo in his *La Ilegitima* (1955), a film about a painter which provided an excuse to show the starlets in the nude as models. He also launched the film career of the wrestler Wolf Ruvinskis in *La Bestia Magnifica* (1952) before becoming a specialist in fantasy pictures in a wide variety of settings ranging from the West (*La Cabeza de Pancho Villa*, 1957) to gothic horror (*El Baron del Terror*, 1961). He was also responsible for a number of Blue Demon movies of the sixties, including the wrestler's next picture, *Blue Demon Contra las Diabolicas* (1967).

d Chano Urueta *p* Rafael Perez Grovas *s* Antonio Orellana, Fernando Oses *c* Alfredo Uribe *lp* Alejandro Cruz, David Reynoso, Ana Martin, Victor Junco, Noe Murayama, Dagoberto Rodriguez, Barbara Angely

Casino Royale (FAMOUS ARTISTS/COL; GB) pv 131 min
Despite a substantial budget, glittering stars and effective set-pieces, this would-be stylish and ever so confused piece, which uses five directors and numerous Bond spoofs (including Niven, Sellers and Welles), has its tongue far too firmly in its cheek to succeed. Sellers gives the most interesting performance, but even he can't transcend the frantic plot which sends Bond hurtling from flying saucers to heaven's pearly gates and has space for Frankenstein's monster to make a guest appearance. Intended as *the* parody that would stem the flood of Bond movies, it fell flat on its face and sadly only speeded up the Bond production line.

d John Huston, Ken Hughes, Val Guest, Robert Parrish, Joe McGrath *p* Charles K. Feldman, Jerry Bresler *s* Wolf Mankowitz, John Law, Michael Sayers *c* Jack Hildyard, John Wilcox, Nicolas Roeg *se* Cliff Richardson, Roy Whybrow, Les Bowie *lp* David Niven, Peter Sellers, Ursula Andress, Orson Welles, Joanna Pettet, Woody Allen, William Holden, Charles Boyer, George Raft, Peter O'Toole, Jacqueline Bisset, John Huston, Daliah Lavi

Dai Koesu Yongkari *aka* **Monster Yongkari** *aka* **Great Monster Yongkari** *aka* **Yongkari, Monster from the Deep**
(KUK DONG FILM CO.; S. KOREA) scope 100(79) min

A South Korean contribution to the anti-communist propaganda that monster movies at times were used for in the mid-sixties (eg **Nankai No Daiketto**, 1966). This was after the monsters had been seen as resulting from American nuclear policies and before they came to be depicted as controlled by aliens out to dominate the world and to escape pollution. Yongkari is released by an atomic blast that caused an earthquake in China. It first surfaces at the border post of Panmunjom where it causes the destruction of 'Freedom House' before invading South Korea and destroying Seoul. It drinks gasoline and devours an ice-making plant before an ingenious Korean scientist identifies its weakness: it is vulnerable to an ingredient of ammonia called $X2$. This substance is sprayed onto the creature which collapses, no doubt ready for a resurrection in a sequel, although this appears to be its only recorded foray. Yongkari's appearance is remarkably similar to the Godzilla suit worn in Japan, although its tail seems considerably longer, incorporating aspects of Baragon. The Korean landscape is used to good effect and the overall impression is more favourable than the other South Korean contribution to the genre, **Wang Ma Gwi** (1967).

d Kiduck Kim *s* Yunsung Suh *c* Kenichi Nakagawa, Inchib Byon *lp* Yungil Oh, Chungim Nam, Soonjai Lee, Moon Kang, Kwang Ho Lee

Daikyoju Gappa *aka* **Gappa the Trifibian Monster** *aka* **Monster from a Prehistoric Planet**
(NIKKATSU; JAP) scope 90(81) min

The Nikkatsu Corporation's only contribution to the Kaiju Eiga (monster movie genre). As a studio, it specialized in adult films and gangster thrillers, and this tongue-in-check movie can be seen as a conscious but affectionate parody of the whole genre. The profit-seeking actions of a Japanese magnate trigger the destruction of Tokyo: the monsters attack because their baby has been kidnapped to be put in a freak show. Ma and Pa Gappa go to Japan to recover their offspring and wreak havoc until their baby is returned to them. The tearful reunion scene is played at Tokyo airport, where the proud parents teach their young one to fly before taking off back to their island. The creatures look like a cross between **Gorgo** (1961) and **Gojira** (1954) and their itinerary through Japan is a joke in itself: they visit the standard tourist spots, taking in the Atami holiday resort, the Mount Fuji-Hakone area and, of course, Tokyo's Haneda Airport. Additional entertainment is provided by the standard earthquake, tidal wave and volcanic eruption, as well as a quote from **Furankenshutain No Kaiju – Sanda Tai Gailah** (1966) – the octopus scenes shot for an earlier Frankenstein film but not used until *Furankenshutain No Kaiju*. The effects are excellent and the script worthy of a witty children's comedy.

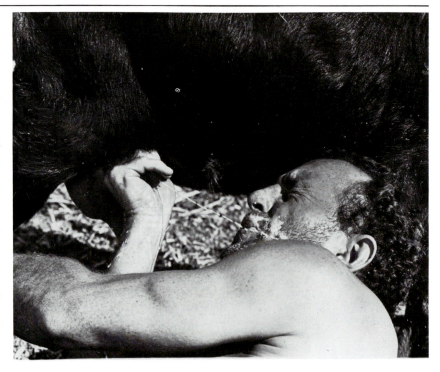

d Haruyasu Noguchi *p* Hideo Koi *s* Iwao Yamazaki, Ryuzo Nakanishi *c* Muneo Keda *se* Akira Watanabe *lp* Tamio Kawaji, Yoko Yamamoto, Yuji Okada, Koji Wada, Tatsuya Fuji

Colin Blakely in Michael Cacoyannis' uneven The Day the Fish Came Out.

The Day the Fish Came Out
(MICHAEL CACOYANNIS PRODUCTIONS; GB, GR) 109 min

An interesting, but flawed, offering from Cacoyannis whose *Zorba the Greek* (1964) was a huge international success.

A NATO bomber with two H-bombs and a new kind of doomsday weapon on board crashes into the sea. Pilot Blakely and navigator Courtenay manage to reach a nearby Greek island, which becomes the centre of a tourist boom when a NATO recovery team arrives, disguised as holidaymakers. The clumsy satire blackens when the islanders contract deadly viral infections from the plane's cargo. Dead fish float on a blackened sea, whilst the tourists, knowing they are soon to die, dance frantically on the beach. The film fails because Cacoyannis is unable to integrate the different styles – farce, satire, slapstick and reality – with any coherence.

d/p/s Michael Cacoyannis *c* Walter Lassally *lp* Tom Courtenay, Sam Wanamaker, Colin Blakely, Candice Bergen, Ian Ogilvy, Patricia Burke

Devilman Story *aka* The Devil's Man
(GV-SEC FILM/LION INTERNATIONAL; IT) scope 85(80) min

One of the numerous films Madison made in Italy in the sixties, this is a routine mad-scientist offering. The plot is so traditional that it wouldn't have been out of place in a thirties serial, but the sets (especially Devilman's secret laboratory), as is so often the case in Italian Science Fiction films of the sixties, are delightfully futuristic. Madison and Baratto (in accordance with the formula of such films, the daughter of the missing scientist) trace her father to an abandoned fortress in the North African desert where the silver helmeted Devilman (Sambrell) is planning with the scientist's enforced help to transplant a superbrain into his own head. The elaborately staged finale has nomadic Moors riding to the rescue of all concerned, cavalry style.

d Paul Maxwell (Paolo Binachini) *p* Gabrielle Cristani *c* Aldo Greci *lp* Guy Madison, Liz Barrett (Luisa Baratto), Aldo Sambrell, Alan Collins (Luciano Picozzi), Diana Lorys, Ken Wood (Giovanni Cianfriglia)

The primitive but fascinating Dai Koesu Yongkari, an example of South Korea's annexation of the Japanese monster movie genre in the service of anti-communist propaganda.

Diabolik *aka* **Danger: Diabolik**

(DINO DE LAURENTIIS/MARIANNE PRODUCTIONS; IT,FR)
105(88) min
This stylish Science Fiction thriller decorated by one-time cinematographer Bava with his usual visual panache features Law as a latter-day Fantômas who at one point, to the joy of the populace, destroys Italy's tax records. If the film is slight and sags badly in the middle, the sets and set-pieces are memorable. The finale is particularly fine. After stealing a 20-ton radioactive gold ingot, Law melts it down in his high-tech hideout only to have it explode and shower him with molten gold, thus turning him into a living statue.

d/co-s Mario Bava   *p* Dino De Laurentiis   *co-s* Dino Maiuri, Adriano Baracco   *c* Antonio Rinaldi   *lp* John Phillip Law, Marisa Mell, Michel Piccoli, Adolfo Celi, Terry-Thomas, Claudio Gora

Dos Cosmonautas a la Fuerza

(AGGATA FILMS/IMA FILMS; SP,IT)   b/w   89 min
A would-be farce this film, which anticipates much of the plot of **Capricorn One** (1977), features Ingrassia and Franchi as a pair of Russian astronauts believed lost in space just before they reach the Moon. To cover up matters the Russian authorities send a pair of identical astronauts (Ingrassia and Franchi again) into space for a short trip, intending to greet them on their return as the first travellers to the Moon. However, it transpires that the original ship was not lost and accordingly, four astronauts return. Clearly intended as a displaced satire on Spanish bureaucracy, Fulci's film is too insular to be enjoyed outside the broad notions of comedy that fathered it.

d Lucio Fulci   *s* Vittorio Metz, José Luis Dibildos, Amedeo Sollazzo   *c* Tino Santoni   *lp* Franco Franchi, Ciccio Ingrassia, Emilio Rodriguez, Monica Randal, Maria Silva, Linda Sini, Chiro Bermejo

I Fantastici Tre Supermen *aka* **The Fantastic Three**

(CINESECOLO/PARNASS FILM/FFP/AVALA FILM; IT,WG,FR,YUG)
94 min
Acrobatics and clowning play a large part in this routine comic strip of a film, as one would expect from a work by Parolini. Stella and Jordan are the pair of bullet-proof Superman-suited robbers who, along with FBI agent Harris, are in pursuit of master criminal Golem (Brockmann). Golem's secret weapon is a universal reproducer which, in the highpoint of the film, he uses to produce an army of Harris lookalike robots.

A lacklustre sequel followed in 1970, *Che Fanno I Nostri Supermen tra la Vergini*.

d/co-s Frank Kramer (Gianfranco Parolini)   *p* Italo Martinenghi, Aldo Addobbati   *co-s* Marcello Coscia   *c* Francesco Izzarelli   *lp* Tony Kendal (Luciano Stella), Brad Harris, Nick Jordan, Joscen Brockmann, Sabine Sun, Bettina Busch

Flick *aka* **Dr Frankenstein on Campus**

(AGINCOURT; CAN)   81 min
A modern variant on the Frankenstein legend, *Flick* is energetically directed by Taylor and benefits from a carefully pitched performance from Ward as the student, newly arrived on campus from Europe, who is ridiculed by his fellow students for his name, Viktor Frankenstein IV. He turns out to be not a distant relation of Baron Frankenstein but the creation of Sullivan's professor of computer studies. Shot through with references to student protest and drugs (Ward's fellow students try to get him expelled by photographing him with a marijuana cigarette) and slackly plotted, the film survives by dint of its jaunty attitude to its material. Interestingly, Ward's creature stands midway between Boris Karloff's monster and the robot androids of **Westworld** (1973) and the like who would soon take over from mere monsters as the most important menacers of mankind.

d/co-s Gil Taylor   *p/co-s* Bill Marshall   *co-s* David Cobb   *c* Jackson Samuels   *lp* Robin Ward, Kathleen Sawyer, Austin Willis, Sean Sullivan, Ty Haller, Tony Moffat-Lynch

Le Fou du Labo 4 *aka* **The Madman of Lab 4**

(GAUMONT; FR)   90 min
Lefebvre invents a gas which makes people love each other in this lacklustre French comedy and is immediately pursued by spies, gangsters, the police and his own boss, all of whom are anxious to learn the secret formula. The highlight of Besnard's alternately heavy-handed and whimsical direction is a western parody, set in a Wild West town just outside Paris, where the gangster boss comes to seek the gas.

d/p Jacques Besnard   *s* Jean Halain   *c* Raymond Lemoigne   *lp* Jean Lefebvre, Maria Latour, Bernard Blier, Pierre Brasseur, Margo Lion, Michel Serrault

Gamera Tai Gaos *aka* **Gamera Versus Gaos** *aka* **Gamera Versus Gyaos** *aka* **The Return of the Giant Monsters** *aka* **Boyichi and the Supermonster** *aka* **Daikaiju Kuchusen**

(DAIEI; JAP)   scope   87(85) min
Gamera's third performance, again directed by Yuasa, pits him against a scaly fox-like creature, Gaos, which is the opposite of the turtle in almost every way: Gaos flies faster, hates fire, cannot bear sunlight, launches a yellow fire-extinguishing smog from its breast (although a male creature, its breast evokes female characteristics) and eats humans. Gamera loves water, spits fire, flies slower and eats A-bombs while being the children's friend. Accordingly, Gamera spends a lot of time either rescuing kids or being assisted by them. The strategy seems to have worked: Gamera became the most popular monster after Godzilla and allowed Daiei to recapture some of its special markets. The effects and the models are of professional standard, on a par with those achieved by the Toho pictures and, although the acting may not be very impressive, acting was never what such movies were about anyway. Gamera wins by getting Gaos to be burned by the sun.

d Noriyaki Yuasa   *p* Hidemasa Nagata   *s* Fumi Takahashi   *c* Akira Uehara   *se* Kazufumi Fujii, Yuzo Kaneko   *lp* Kojiro Hongo, Kichijiro Ueda, Naoyuki Abe, Reiko Kasahara, Taro Marui, Yukitaro Hotaru, Yoshio Kitahara

John Phillip Law as Diabolik.

Gojira No Musuko aka Son of Godzilla
(TOHO; JAP) scope 86(71) min

Godzilla's eighth appearance and the second directed by Honda's successor, Fukuda, backed by the Honda team members Sekizawa and Tsuburaya. In response to competition for the children's market from Daiei with Gamera and Nikkatsu's successful introduction of lovable baby monster Gappa in **Daikyoju Gappa** (1967), Toho also launched a baby monster. Weather experiments conducted by Dr Kasumi (Takashima) make the island of Zorgel's temperature soar with the result that all plants and animals, including insects, grow to giant proportions. The heat also causes an egg to be hatched, revealing the little Godzilla who is soon joined by his father. The baby, blowing smoke rings under the tender gaze of his dad, becomes friendly with Reiko (Maeda) and when she is attacked by Spigon, a giant spider, father and son come and kill the hairy thing. As the fauna of the island is getting too dangerous, the scientists freeze the place by causing the temperature to drop, leaving the one-parent Godzilla family to go into hibernation as the humans leave the place. This film is made with considerable humour and features probably the best special effects in the series.

d Jun Fukuda *p* Tomoyuki Tanaka *s* Shinichi Sekizawa, Kazue Shiba *c* Kazuo Yamada *se* Eiji Tsuburaya, Sadamasa Arikawa *lp* Tadao Takashima, Akira Kubo, Beverly Maeda, Akihiko Hirata, Yoshio Tsuchiya, Kenji Sahara, Susumu Kurobe

In Like Flint (FOX) scope 114(107) min
Like its title (a weary pun on 'in like Flynn'), this sequel to **Our Man Flint** (1965) is an awful movie. Despite the presence of Coburn in the title role, it is, if anything, even worse than the similarly Bond-inspired Dean Martin quartet of Matt Helm films that commenced with **The Silencers** (1965). Douglas' direction is leaden and Fimberg's script, which wouldn't be out of place as a *Man from Uncle* teleplay, is equally dire. A group of female villains, based in the Virgin Islands, substitute members of their gang for the astronauts aboard America's newly launched orbiting space platform and then arm them with nuclear missiles in a bid for world domination. Coburn (as super-spy/super-stud Flint), Cobb, as the bewildered space official and Duggan as the president turn in possibly the worst performances of their careers.

A lacklustre telefilm with Ray Danton as Flint followed in 1976, *Dead on Target*.

d Gordon Douglas *p* Saul David *s* Hal Fimberg *c* William Daniels *se* L.B Abbott, Emil Kosa Jnr, Art Cruikshank *lp* James Coburn, Lee J. Cobb, Andrew Duggan, Jean Hale, Hanns Landry, Steve Inhat, Herb Edelman, Yvonne Craig

L'Inconnu de Shandigor aka The Unknown Man of Shandigor (FRAJEA FILMS; SWITZ) 90 min
A minor film, this is one of the better of the numerous Bond lookalikes of the sixties. Emilfork is the villainous scientist whose discovery of a means of stopping atomic weapons working makes him the target of the world's secret agents, including Vernon and Dufilho (American and Russian agents respectively). Boyer is Emilfork's innocent daughter and Carruthers the mysterious stranger who rescues her when her father is devoured by the sea monster he keeps in his pool in a bizarre climax.

The film's saving graces are its tongue-in-cheek attitude to its material and Roy's surprisingly witty direction, both of which mark it out from the more obvious contemporary Bond imitations.

d/co-s Jean-Louis Roy *p/co-s* Gabriel Arout *c* Roger Bimpage *lp* Marie-France Boyer, Ben Carruthers, Daniel Emilfork, Howard Vernon, Jacques Dufilho, Serge Gainsbourg

Je T'Aime, Je T'Aime
(PARC FILM/FOX EUROPA; FR) 91 min

Repetition (as in the title of this film), time and memory have been constant themes in Resnais' films from *Hiroshima Mon Amour* (1958) onwards. However, Resnais has rarely needed the supporting structure of Science Fiction. In *L'Année Dernière à Marienbad* (1961), for example, he simply contrasts the memories of the central character with other versions of the past and present, refusing to signal which of the several versions of 'reality' is the 'right' one. But here, as if attempting to defeat rational views of Time by tackling them head on, Resnais explicity includes the technological para-phernalia of the Science Fiction film.

Rich is the man recovering from a suicide attempt who, feeling that his life is pointless, agrees to assist a research team investigating the nature of time. He goes back in time (in a machine that looks like a giant pear) first for a few minutes and then for random periods of time. Soon he gets caught up in living once more through the bitter-sweet love affair that led to his attempted suicide, while feeling guilty for Georges-Picot's death. Although finally Rich is released from his literal entrapment in time it is only into a present in which he has only the past to contemplate. The result is a complex, yet surprisingly accessible, film.

d/co-s Alain Resnais *p* Mag Bodard *co-s* Jacques Sternberg *c* Jean Boffety *lp* Claude Rich, Olga Georges-Picot, Anouk Ferjac, Annie Fargue, Bernard Fresson, Yvette Etievant

Journey to the Centre of Time
(BOREALIS/DORAD) 82 min

Directed by Hewitt, a regular collaborator of Ib Melchior, another specialist in low-budget Science Fiction, this is a mediocre film. Made with a minuscule budget and a woeful lack of imagination, it features Sofaer, Eisley and Perreau as the scientists who, in company with the villainous Brady, are hurtled far into the future by their time-machine where they have a series of improbable adventures, watching Earth being destroyed by aliens in the future, battling a prehistoric monster in the past and meeting themselves in the present.

d/co-p David L. Hewitt *co-p* Ray Dorn *s* David Prentiss *c* Robert Caramico *se* Modern Film Effects *lp* Scott Brady, Anthony Eisley, Gigi Perreau, Abraham Sofaer, Austin Green, Tracey Olsen

Ben Carruthers and Marie-France Boyer caught amongst the weird shapes of the rooftops of the Gaudi-designed flats in L'Inconnu de Shandigor.

Right: *Mechni-Kong, the robot version of King Kong, in the bizarre* King Kong No Gyakushu.

Jules Verne's Rocket to the Moon *aka* Those Fantastic Flying Fools

(JULES VERNE FILMS; GB)   scope   101(95) min

Director Sharp's third film for producer Towers (who wrote the original story under his Peter Welbeck pseudonym), despite its title, has little connection with Jules Verne. Rather, it simply seeks to make use of Verne's name to give extra appeal to a routine Science Fiction fantasy.

Donahue, Froebe and Thomas frolic in Victorian England where P. T. Barnum (Ives) struggles to finance sending one of his own circus midgets by rocket to the Moon. The rocket is sabotaged, the ship lands in Tsarist Russia, and the film descends to weak comedy.

d Don Sharp   *p* Harry Alan Towers   *s* Dave Freeman *c* Reg Wyer   *se* Les Bowie, Pat Moore   *lp* Burl Ives, Troy Donahue, Gert Froebe, Terry-Thomas, Lionel Jeffries, Hermione Gingold, Klaus Kinski, Daliah Lavi

King Kong No Gyakushu *aka* The Revenge of King Kong *aka* King Kong's Counterattack *aka* King Kong Escapes (TOHO; JAP)   scope   104(96) min

Having been knocked out by Godzilla in **King Kong Tai Gojira** (1963), the gorilla starts his return engagement by defeating a dinosaur. He also falls in love with Miller, the woman member of an expedition led by Reason and Takarada. The plot involves an evil Dr Who (Amamoto) acting on behalf of a Madame Piranha (Hama). He is mining a radioactive substance with the help of a specially designed robot-Kong, Mechni-Kong. However, the robot goes on the blink necessitating the abduction of the real Kong to proceed with the mining operation. This also requires the kidnapping of the expedition members Kong has taken up with. Eventually, Kong breaks out of his mine and defeats his mechanical replica in a fight on top of Tokyo Tower. Some familiar set-pieces, such as a sea monster's attack on a submarine, Kong's boxing match with one of Godzilla's poor relations and the climactic battle with his metallic sibling are impressively staged with good effects, although the model work shows signs of the deadening effects of routine production activities.

The American version contains more dialogue scenes with American members of the cast.

d Inoshiro Honda   *p* Tomoyuki Tanaka   *s* Kaoru Mabuchi   *c* Hajime Koizumi   *se* Eiji Tsuburaya *lp* Rhodes Reason, Mie Hama, Linda Miller, Akira Takarada, Eisei Amamoto
US version: d/p Arthur Rankin Jnr   *s* William Keenan

Claude Rich is dragged back in time in Alain Resnais' impressive Je T'Aime, Je T'Aime.

Ne Jouez Pas avec les Martiens *aka* Don't Play with Martians *aka* Comme Mars en Carême

(FILDEBROC/LES PRODUCTIONS ARTISTES ASSOCIES; FR)
100(85) min

A farcical tale of Martians landing on a small island off the coast of Brittany in the presence of two incompetent reporters (Rochefort and Vallardy) and a social worker with extra-sensory perception (Méril). The Martians eventually leave, taking with them a newly born set of sextuplets because, it emerges, one of them was the father. Based on a trivial book by Michel Labry, this inconsequential film was Lanoë's first feature, for which he also wrote the music and the script. Rochefort plays in a cabaret style while his sidekick, Vallardy, opts for the grotesque. There is no possible justification for this film being awarded the critic's prize at the Trieste festival of 1968, but it happened nevertheless. De Broca, later to become one of France's most commercial directors, collaborated on the script.

d/co-s Henri Lanoë   *p* Georges Casati   *co-s* Johanna Harwood, Philippe de Broca   *c* René Mathelin   *lp* Jean Rochefort, Macha Méril, André Vallardy, Haydée Politoff, Pierre Dac, Frédéric de Pasquale

Night of the Big Heat *aka* Island of the Burning Damned *aka* Island of the Burning Doomed

(PLANET; GB)   97(94) min

Based on the novel *Night of the Big Heat* by John Lymington, this, the third of Fisher's trilogy of films for Planet, concerns alien protoplasm that takes over a British island and causes a winter heatwave so fierce that most of the island's inhabitants are burnt to death. Cushing and Lee are amongst the survivors who discover the energy-starved aliens, desperate for any heat source. When all seems lost, they are melted by a storm caused by the heat-saturated atmosphere. Fisher's leisurely, atmospheric style does little to dramatize events.

d Terence Fisher   *p* Tom Blakeley   *s* Ronald Liles, Pip Baker, Jane Baker   *c* Reg Wyer   *lp* Christopher Lee, Peter Cushing, Patrick Allen, Sarah Lawson, Jane Merrow, William Lucas, Jack Bligh

OK Connery *aka* **Operation Kid Brother**
(DARIO SABATELLO PRODUCCIONES; IT) 104 min
Sean Connery's brother, Neil, is the cosmetic surgeon thrust
into espionage when he is described as 'James Bond's
brother'. Another camp touch is the presence of Lee, M in the
Bond films, and Celi, the villain of **Thunderball** (1965) as the
master criminal intent on world domination from his futuristic atomic underground city, complete with such gadgetry as a
truth-compelling hypnosis machine and a radiation device
that can de-activate weapons. That said, though it's stylishly
mounted, the result is a routine Italian spy romp.

d Alberto de Martino *p* Dario Sabatello *s* Paul Levi, Frank
Walker, Canzio *c* Alejo Ulloa *se* Gagliano
lp Neil Connery, Daniela Bianchi, Adolfo Celi, Agata Flori,
Bernard Lee, Anthony Dawson (Antonio Margheriti)

Perry Rhodan – SOS aus dem Weltall *aka* **Alarm im
Weltall** *aka* **Quatro Tre Due Uno Morte**
(TEFI FILM/PEA/ATTOR FILM; WG,IT,SP) scope 79 min
The popular German series of Perry Rhodan novels written by
Walter Ernsting under the pseudonym Clark Dalton has been
translated into many languages and could have been used for
dozens of scripts for undemanding children's space adventure
stories but this and its sequel, **Orbito Mortal** (1968), seem to
be the only film adaptations on record. It has Rhodan
(Jeffries) come to Earth, accompanied by some extra-
terrestrial friends he picked up on the Moon. They sort out
groups of politicians and criminals doing nasty things to the
world at large. The result is a trivial film recycling familiar
Bond-type situations with a Science Fiction twist, co-written
by one of the regular collaborators of Ernsting on the novels,
Scheer. The only notable thing about the movie is that the
uneven, but at times visually very exciting, director Margheriti was responsible for the special effects.

d Primo Zeglio *p* E. von Theumer *s* K.H. Scheer, K.H.
Vogelmann *c* Ricardo Pallottini *se* Anthony Dawson
(Antonio Margheriti) *lp* Lang Jeffries, Essy Persson,
Joachim Hansen, Ann Smyrner, Luis Davila, Danièle
Martin, Pinkas Braun, Stefano Sibaldi

The Power (MGM/GALAXY) pv 108(99) min
A taut para-psychological thriller, *The Power* neatly updates
the traditional serial formula of having its hero trying to find
out which one of an élite group of scientists is the villian, and,
in this case, alien. Rennie is the suave scientist bent on world
domination who with his superbrain can kill by merely
focussing his willpower on an individual and Hamilton is the
hero. Gay's script ends in cliché, with Hamilton suddenly
discovering that he too has a superbrain, but, until the
dénouement, Haskin keeps the story bubbling away to good
effect. The plot's twists and turns – at one point following the
clue of the name left by the first murder victim, Hamilton is
left in the desert to die, he finds what he thinks is the safety of
a water-hole only to discover it's a target area for US airforce
bombers – and the unnerving visualization of Rennie's
telekinetic powers give the movie an authority that belies its
slim budget.

The film was badly received when first released but since
then has developed a growing reputation.

d Byron Haskin *p* George Pal *s* John Gay *c* Ellsworth
Fredricks *se* J. McMillan Johnson, Gene Warren
lp George Hamilton, Suzanne Pleshette, Nehemiah Persoff,
Michael Rennie, Earl Holliman, Aldo Ray

The President's Analyst (PANPIPER/PAR) pv 104 min
Coburn (who gives a marvellous performance) is the
psychoanalyst who breaks down under the strain of listening
to the President's problems in this clever amalgam of spy
spoof and youth movie. Faced with his home being bugged,
telephone tapped and girlfriend working for the FBI, Coburn

*Paul Jones as the much
manipulated rock star in
Peter Watkins' bleak
Privilege.*

Left: *A bewildered
James Coburn as* The
President's Analyst.

Right: *The discovery of the alien spaceship in* Quatermass and the Pit.

takes refuge in a middle-class American home, where the family describe themselves as 'militant liberals'. Father (Darden) collects guns, mother (Delaney) takes karate lessons and Junior is into wire-tapping.

Flicker's direction and screenplay are genuinely witty – the Canadian secret service disguised as a Liverpool beat group, for example – but the growing sense of absurdity as the FBI, CIA, the Russians and the Chinese all pursue Coburn gives the film a developing sense of purposelessness. The climax has Coburn discover who really runs America – the Telephone Company with its bland collection of robots (headed by Harrington) who are out to control the world by planting miniature telephones in the brain of every human being. If, like **Wild in the Streets** (1968) and **Privilege** (1967), *The President's Analyst* is an uneven film, like them it has retained its power to shock and amuse as the years pass.

d/s Theodore J. Flicker   *p* Stanley Rubin   *c* William A. Fraker   *se* Westheimer Co.   *lp* James Coburn, Godfrey Cambridge, Severn Darden, Joan Delaney, Pat Harrington, Barry McGuire, Will Geer

Privilege
(WORLDFILM SERVICES/MEMORIAL ENTERPRISES; GB)   103 min
Based on a story by Johnny Speight (creator of Alf Garnett), *Privilege* stars Jones as the rock star, Shorter, who becomes a tool of the state and the church when he is used to control and manipulate the minds of the young. Watkins, the maker of **The War Game** (1965), making his feature début, modelled Shorter on the success of the Beatles. For a while, Jones complies with the state's demands, but he soon rebels, under the influence of his girlfriend (Shrimpton), only to be murdered by his adoring fans. Watkins directs in a heightened documentary style and the result is bizarrely disturbing, very much in the manner of Stanley Kubrick's **A Clockwork Orange** (1971). Terribly received at the time – it was attacked as amateurish – in retrospect, the film's theme of the ability of government to defuse the more radical implications of youth revolt and co-opt youth culture is all the more powerful for having been shown to be correct numerous times since *Privilege*.

d Peter Watkins   *p* John Heyman   *s* Norman Bogner   *c* Peter Suschitsky   *lp* Paul Jones, Jean Shrimpton, Mark London, Max Bacon, Jeremy Child, William Job

Below: Project X, *one of the most imaginative examples of low-budget film-making to come out of America in the sixties.*

Project X   (WILLIAM CASTLE ENTERPRISES)   97 min
This is an imaginative piece of low-budget Science Fiction from veteran B director and producer Castle. It survives the flimsy characterization of Morris' script through the commitment of all concerned to the plot's strong ideas and Castle's emphatic direction which keeps the story in constant motion. George's secret agent returns to America in 2118 with a blank memory after delivering his last message that Sino-Asia will destroy the West in two weeks. In an attempt to restore his memory Jones freezes George, gives him the identity of a 1968 bank robber on the run and materializes his dreams. The intricate developments that follow are unusually imaginative. Even better is the film's resolution which has the West saved (George was carrying a virulent strain of the bubonic plague) but George, its saviour, unaware of his momentous role.

d/p William Castle   *s* Edmund Morris   *c* Harold Stine   *se* Paul K. Lerpae   *lp* Christopher George, Greta Baldwin, Henry Jones, Monte Markham, Harold Gould, Phillip E. Pine

Quatermass and the Pit *aka* Five Million Years to Earth
(HAMMER; GB)   97 min
Delayed by Hammer for several years, this is the concluding chapter in the trilogy of films (the others being **The Quatermass Xperiment**, 1955 and **Quatermass II**, 1957) adapted from Kneale's *Quatermass* teleseries. A fourth instalment, *The Quatermass Conclusion* was shown on British television in 1979.

The first of the films to be scripted by Kneale without any interference, it lacks the intensity of *Quatermass II*; in its place Kneale offers a mix of scientific and occult speculation that needed more screen time than was available. Moreover, Baker's direction is limp, over-relying on close-ups for dramatic effect. Accordingly, the definitive version remains the 1959 teleseries.

While constructing a new underground subway, workers discover an ancient Martian spaceship. Quatermass (played this time by Keir) investigates and discovers dead insect men in the hull. This, however, is no ancient relic – the ship is alive, exuding deadly electricity, heat rays and telepathy. Through an energy force contained in the ship, Quatermass learns that the Martians landed at the dawn of Earth's time in search of slaves and speeded up the process of evolution by advancing the apes to men before dying out.

The film's glossy production values diminish the impact of Kneale's genuinely exciting speculations (in which, for example, significant occult beliefs are explained by reference to the satanic Martians who, it is also suggested, are the sources of much of man's culture as well as his genetic development). Nonetheless, some of the individual sequences are impressive: the drill operator driven off the spaceship he is

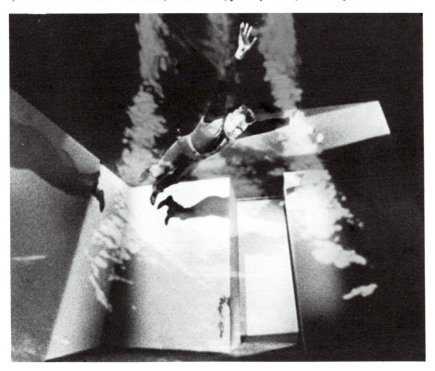

trying to penetrate and sent spinning in a whirlwind of paper and dust and the sudden burst of energy from the ship that projects huge Martian landscapes across the skies of London.

If the film is badly flawed, Kneale's speculations (which parallel, though in a malevolent fashion, those of **2001 – A Space Odyssey**, 1968, and anticipate the physical horror of **Alien**, 1979) remain intriguing, if only because they are so different from those of his contemporaries.

d Roy Ward Baker   *p* Anthony Nelson Keys   *s* Nigel Kneale   *c* Arthur Grant   *se* Bowie Films   *lp* Andrew Keir, Barbara Shelley, James Donald, Julian Glover, Duncan Lamont, Bryan Marshall

The Reluctant Astronaut (U) 101 min
In this weak comedy Knotts is the vertigo sufferer who becomes unwittingly involved in manned space flight, thanks to his war-veteran father (O'Connell, who gives the film's best performance). The script is routine and too much of the comedy is over-emphatic, neither slapstick nor witty enough.

d/p Edward J. Montaigne   *s* James Fritzell, Everett Greenbaum   *c* Rexford Wimpey   *lp* Don Knotts, Arthur O'Connell, Leslie Nielsen, Joan Freeman, Jesse White, Jeanette Nolan, Frank McGrath

El Superflaco *aka* Chiquito pero Picoso
(ALFA FILMS; MEX) 90 min
A Harold Lloyd-type comedy parodying the wrestler genre, immensely popular in Mexico since *Santo – El Enmascarado de Plata* (1952). This picture has a weedy character (Pompin) receiving a hormone injection from a doctor (Herrera) which makes him an invincible wrestler. But his strength evaporates just before his bout with the champion, Rudy (played by Ruvinskis, who went on to portray the masked wrestler Neutron in a whole series of pictures). The love interest is provided by Elizondo, a regular in these films, who ably plays the dual role of Rebecca, a worker secretly in love with Pompin, and Brigida, an artist ostensibly infatuated with Rudy the wrestler. In the end it is revealed she impersonated Brigida in order to excite Pompin's jealousy and the couple get together for the happy finale.

Elizondo also appeared in a number of fantasy comedies opposite Clavillazo (**El Castillo de los Monstruos**, 1958) and Resortes (**Los Platillos Voladores**, 1955). Pompin could have become Lloyd's equal and a major star had he been better served by his material and directors. Instead, this picture was made by Delgado, a thoroughly indifferent director of many vaudevillesque comedies incuding **El Supersabio** (1948). As usual, a number of musical interludes interrupt the action, reducing a potentially Lloyd-ish comedy to the level of an anodyne cabaret act.

d Miguel M. Delgado   *p* Fidel Pizarro   *s* Gunther Gerszo, Carlos Orellana   *c* Jose Ortiz Ramos   *lp* Evangelina Elizondo, Alfonso Pompin Iglesias, Wolf Ruvinskis, Daniel Chino Herrera, Jose Jasso, Alfredo Varela Jnr, Nacho Contla, Arturo Bigoton Castro, Luis Manuel Pelayo

The Terrornauts (AMICUS; GB) 75(62) min
A companion piece to **They Came from Beyond Space** (1967), this juvenile film, though adapted from Murray Leinster's novel, *The Wailing Asteriods*, is clearly inspired by the *Dr Who* teleseries. Hence, the unlikely defenders of Earth include Oates' astronomer who's been seeking contact with other life-forms, Hayes' tealady, a secretary (Marshall), a visiting accountant (Hawtrey) and Oates' assistant (Meadows). An alien spaceship takes them to a strange fortress constructed as a warning to future generations by man's alien forebears, just before they were defeated by their old (alien) enemies. As soon as man leaves his planet and starts exploring the solar system, the ancient enemy forces (or so the fortress warns) will resume hostilities. The result is a lacklustre affair.

d Montgomery Tully   *p* Max J. Rosenberg   *s* John Brunner   *c* Geoffrey Faithfull   *se* Bowie Films, Ernest Fletcher   *lp* Simon Oates, Zena Marshall, Charles Hawtrey, Patricia Hayes, Stanley Meadows, Max Adrian

They Came from Beyond Space (AMICUS; GB) 85 min
Based on Joseph Millard's marvellously titled novel, *The Gods Hate Kansas*, this inferior piece of Science Fiction features alien invaders from another planetary system who arrive on Earth amidst a meteorite shower and set about transporting humans to the Moon to work on their crippled fleet of spaceships. Hutton is the scientist who first rescues his girlfriend (Jayne) from their clutches and finally establishes friendy contact with the aliens. The leaden script and erratic direction notwithstanding, the film is of interest for its optimistic ending.

d Freddie Francis   *co-p/s* Milton Subotsky   *co-p* Max J. Rosenberg   *c* Norman Warwick   *se* Bowie Films   *lp* Robert Hutton, Jennifer Jayne, Zia Moyyeddin, Bernard Kay, Michael Gough, Geoffrey Wallace

Uchu Daikaiju Guilala *aka* Girara *aka* The X from Outer Space *aka* Guirara *aka* Guilala
(SHOCHIKU; JAP) scope 89 min
Shochiku's first monster movie re-deploys the plot device pioneered in **Yosei Gorasu** (1962) and used again by Shochiku in **Kyuketsuki Gokemidoro** (1968). Guilala is generated from a substance that sticks to a spacecraft travelling from the Moon to Mars. It grows and absorbs all the

Below: *Don Knotts as* The Reluctant Astronaut, *a feeble space comedy.*

The leaden They Came from Beyond Space.

tool of a human brain he keeps alive in his laboratory. Vieyra's direction is more thrillerish than most offerings in the sub-genre (such as the gruesome **Gritos en la Noche**, 1962) which have tended to centre on physical (and sexual) horror to the exclusion of almost anything else. Thus the film's conclusion is a traditional shoot-out between the police and Barbero.

d/s Emilio Vieyra   *p* Orestes Trucco   *c* Anibal Gonzalez   *lp* Richard Bauleo, Gloria Prat, Aldo Barbero, Susan Beltrán, Justin Martin, Michel Angel, Mary Albano, Al Bugatti, Alex Klapp

Wang Ma Gwi *aka* Monster Wangmagwi

(CENTURY CO.; S. KOREA)   scope   80 min
The first all-Korean Science Fiction movie offers a space variation on *King Kong* (1933), about a rubber-clad giant with pointed claws, flapping ears and a facemask reminiscent of Corman's monster in **It Conquered the World** (1956). The creature is launched via flying saucers by advanced aliens seeking world domination. First it tramples on Seoul and then burns it down by spewing a death ray onto the city in a very poor imitation of the Japanese monster movies, although allegedly made with considerable production resources. The carefully constructed miniature models were photographed by S. Byun, South Korea's expert and pioneer in this type of work. He also designed the monster. That same year, South Korea also produced **Dai Koesu Yongkari** but this was done with the assistance of a Japanese cameraman and cannot be counted an all-Korean production. However, the result was a better imitation of the Japanese monster movies.

d Hyukjin Kwon   *s* Hayong Byun   *c* Changyong Ham   *se* Soojai Byun   *lp* Kungwon Nam, Haekyung Kim, Unjin Hahn, Hikap Kim

Yevo Zovut Robert *aka* They Call Me Robert *aka* His Name Is Robert *aka* He Was Called Robert *aka* Call Me Robert   (LENFILM; USSR)   scope   91 min

Pursuing a theme outlined by Karel Capek and filmed as **Gibel Sensaty** (1935), this film confirms in an entertaining manner that people cannot be replaced by robots, not even on distant planets. In this version of the theme, the robot Robert is let loose on society only to find out that he doesn't understand how it works or how people negotiate its complexities, often irrationally, in their daily lives. Many more films would feature robots taking off under their own power in order to make a similar point, although they do so more menacingly and often more humorously as well: from **2001 – A Space Odyssey** (1968) to **Alien** (1979) via **The Forbin Project** (1969), **Westworld** (1973) and **Dark Star** (1974). The most recent, and perhaps the best treatment of the subject for a long time, is **Android** (1982). The twist to this story is that the robot, biochemically created, looks exactly like its creator, allowing for many comic situations.

d Ilya Olshvanger   *s* Lev Kuklin, Yuri Printsev   *c* Edgar Shtyrtskober   *lp* Oleg Strizhenov, Marianna Vertinskaya, Vladimir Pobol, Mikhail Pugovkin, Yuri Tolubeyev, D. Dranizin, N. Mamaeva

You Only Live Twice

(EON/DANJAG; GB)   scope   116 min
Loosely based on the novel by Ian Fleming, this Bond movie has Connery as authentic and sophisticated as ever. Despite Gilbert's clumsy direction, Dahl's script in which Spectre tries to start World War III by creating a spaceship that will swallow American and Russian space capsules, makes *You Only Live Twice* one of the wittiest Bond movies.

However, by this stage in James Bond's screen career, designer Ken Adam and his sets had virtually taken control of the films. As a result, the actors became, for the most part, little more than mannequins attached to the sets in various

energy of the weapons used against it, growing bigger still, until anti-matter, Guilalalium, is collected from the outer universe and showered over the beast as it attacks the Astroflying Centre at the base of Mount Fuji. The creature shrinks back to cell size and is sent into space.

At this stage of the genre, the thematic construction shifts away from representations of the way Japan mythologizes its relation to the US and to its own militarism. These issues appear to have been settled, quite openly, in the public sphere where they require different forms of representation, but this leaves the monster movie genre up in the air, with nothing left but to repeat itself or to find a new set of issues to be mythologically and ritually worked through. Eventually, such a new but far more innocuous thematic would be found in pollution and its links with rapid technological/industrial development, programming a change towards pollution monsters in conjunction with space opera settings which also permit a more direct us/them set of confrontations.

Guilala is well designed, as are the sets and the models, but there is an unfortunate tendency to film the creature frontally with the camera at 'normal' human height, as opposed to the usual low angle shots required to endow the monster with an imposing stature and a sense of menace.

d/co-s Kazui Nihonmatsu   *p* Akihiko Shimada   *co-s* Hidemi Motomochi, Moriyoshi Ishida   *c* Shizuo Hirase   *se* Hiroshi Ikeda   *lp* Eiji Okada, Toshiya Wazaki, Peggy Neal, Itoko Harada, Shinichi Yanagisawa, Franz Gruber, Keisuke Sonoi, Mike Daning, Torahiko Hamada

La Venganza del Sexo *aka* The Curious Dr Humpp

(PRODUCTORES ARGENTINOS ASOCIADOS; ARG)   85(80) min
An interesting addition to the medical strand of Science Fiction that is so strong in the Latin cinema, this Argentinian film anticipates some of the themes that David Cronenberg later developed with far greater intensity in films like **The Parasite Murders** (1974). Bauleo is the reporter who discovers that a sadistic, sex-crazed scientist (Barbera) is responsible for the rash of kidnappings in the city. He eventually tracks down Barbero, by following him when he buys huge quantities of aphrodisiacs with which he is experimenting upon his captives, and discovers that he is the

ways. Similarly Gilbert's job as director was to simply show off Adam's work, which includes a rocket launching base in a volcano along with a heliport and monorail, to its best advantage. Surprisingly, considering this emphasis on décor, the film and subsequent entries in the series lack the simple sense of delight of the far cheaper sets of the numerous Italian derivatives of Bond.

d Lewis Gilbert   *p* Albert R. Broccoli, Harry Saltzman
s Roald Dahl   *c* Freddie Young   *se* John Stears
lp Sean Connery, Donald Pleasance, Akiko Wakabayashi, Tetsuro Tamba, Mie Hama, Karin Dor

1968

The Astro-Zombies

(A. RAM LTD/T.V. MIKELS PRODUCTION)   90 min
Made by Mikels, who later directed the equally awful, *The Corpse Grinders* (1972), with a budget that only stretched to the construction of one set, this ridiculous Poverty Row outing features Carradine (an actor whose appetite for work led him into all kinds of odd movies in the sixties and seventies) as the sinister Dr De Marco who, in order to build himself a race of all-powerful artificial men (the astro-zombies of the title), needs a constant supply of vital organs. Corey is the FBI man on his trail and Campos the cheerful Mexican cut-throat. A terrible film.

d/p/co-s Ted V. Mikels   *co-s* Wayne Rogers   *c* Robert Maxwell   *lp* Wendell Corey, John Carradine, Rafael Campos, Tom Pace, Joan Patrick, Wally Moon

The Bamboo Saucer

(NTA/HARRIS ASSOCIATES/JERRY FAIRBANKS)   100 min
This low-budget quickie starts from the interesting premise that the Americans and Russians unite in a hunt for a flying saucer in Red China. Duryea, whose last film this was, leads the US team to a Chinese village. En route, they meet a Russian team, which includes Nettleton, on the same mission. The uneasy alliance is the result of both groups' fear of being

discovered by the Chinese. Eventually Duryea, Ericson and Nettleton escape in the saucer (whose origin is never revealed) and head into outer space. The result is an unusual thriller with a fantastical Science Fiction conclusion tacked on at the end.

The film was reportedly based on an incident in the fifties when the shell of a supposedly alien craft was located on an island near Sweden.

d/s Frank Telford   *p* Jerry Fairbanks   *c* Hal Mohr
se J. Fulton, Glen Robinson   *lp* Dan Duryea, John Ericson, Lois Nettleton, Bob Hastings, Vincent Beck, Bernard Fox

Cliff Robertson as the moron who briefly becomes a genius in Charly.

The Blood of Fu Manchu

(UDASTEX FILMS; GB)   91 (61) min
A feeble offering in the irregular series of films devoted to the repeated attempts of Sax Rohmer's dastardly villain (here impersonated, as he was throughout the sixties, by Lee) to take over the world. His plan this time is to send ten beautiful girls, injected with a deadly poison, to deliver the kiss of death to the world's leaders. Greene's Nayland Smith is Fu Manchu's first victim but, as ever, he recovers to save himself and the world in the nick of time. The lacklustre script and direction are made even more incomprehensible by the substantial cuts made in most release prints, leaving one hoping, and not for the first time, that Fu Manchu's end promise, 'The world will hear from me again', will not be fulfilled.

d Jess (Jesús) Franco   *p* Harry Alan Towers   *s* Peter Welbeck   *c* Manuel Merino   *lp* Christopher Lee, Goetz George, Richard Greene, Howard Marion Crawford, Tsai Chin, Shirley Eaton

Left: The rocket launch base in You Only Live Twice.

Right: Brasil Anno 2,000, *Walter Lima's political allegory.*

Brasil Anno 2,000 (MAPA FILM; BRAZIL) 95 min

A muted political allegory, *Brasil Anno 2,000* apes the style of Glauber Rocha (whose sister Annecy is the film's star). Set in the year after World War III, Lima's script follows the wanderings of Rocha and her mother (Alencar) amidst the desolation of the Brazilian countryside. Goncalves is the reporter who exposes the burgeoning hypocrisy of the new state: at one point, to get food, Rocha and Alencar have to pretend to be Indians, the oppressed peasants of contemporary Brazil, who have become a privileged minority in the new country.

d/p/s Walter Lima Jnr *c* Guido Cosulich *lp* Annecy Rocha, Enio Goncalves, Iracema de Alencar, Ziembinsky, Manfredo Colasanti, Helio Fernandez

Brides of Blood

(HEMISPHERE PRODUCTIONS; US, PHIL) 92 (90) min
One of the first American-Philippine co-productions, *Brides of Blood* anticipates one of the major themes of the sexploitation horror/Science Fiction films that would follow: the desire of a victim (here Hills as the wife of scientist Taylor sent to investigate reported sightings of mutants) to enjoy sex with a monster (Montenegro who mutates after exposure to nuclear radiation) to her cost. That said, the film, its retinue of well-conceived grotesqueries aside, lacks the necessary narrative drive to truly shock. Romero subsequently directed a number of films for the Philippines' branch of Roger Corman's New World Productions.

co-d Gerardo de Leon *co-d/p* Eddie Romero *lp* John Ashley, Kent Taylor, Beverly Hills, Eva Darren, Mario Montenegro, Oscar Keesee

Charly

(SELMUR/ROBERTSON ASSOCIATES) scope 106 (103) min
The good intentions of all concerned (particularly Robertson who formed his own production company to make the film and supplies an excellently modulated performance in the title role) notwithstanding, this confused film is marred by director Nelson's continual recourse to heart-tugging sentimentality. Robertson plays the 30-year-old assistant in a bakery with an IQ of 68 who becomes the guinea-pig of neurosurgeon Janney and psychiatrist Skala. From their successful experiments on mice they believe they can cure his mental retardation through surgery. They are successful and overnight Robertson becomes a genius and finds emotional maturity in an affair with his teacher Bloom. Far less successful is the diatribe against modern civilization in which

Below: Countdown, *an uneasy combination of soap opera and Science Fiction from Robert Altman.*

screenwriter Silliphant and Nelson indulge. Accordingly the film's best moments come when it centres on Robertson, bemoaning being beaten by a super-mouse called Algernon in an intelligence test or simply waiting for the day when he once more will become a moron when Algernon starts regressing.

The film has its origins in Daniel Keyes' short story and later novel, *Flowers For Algernon*. In 1980, the subject was, briefly, transformed into a Broadway musical.

d/p Ralph Nelson *s* Stirling Silliphant *c* Arthur J. Ornitz *lp* Cliff Robertson, Claire Bloom, Leon Janney, Lilia Skala, Dick Van Patten, William Dwyer

Countdown

(WILLIAM CONRAD PRODUCTIONS) pv 101 (73) min
Based on Hank Serles' novel *The Pilgrim Project*, this film remains an uneasy combination of soap opera and Science Fiction, in great part because the production circumstances were almost as fraught as the race to the Moon between the Russians and the Americans that Mandel's script details. Altman's camera, however, concentrates on the behind-the-scenes dramatics in which civilian scientist Caan replaces Duvall as the man for the American moonshot while, behind the bland US propaganda that is issued to the public, project boss Ihnat and flight surgeon Aidman argue over safety precautions and the need to beat the Russians and Duvall's wife (Baxley) takes to drink because of her husband's total immersion in his work.

Altman's emphasis on such quirky personal relationships is hard to follow – the film was re-edited against his wishes – but enough remains to reveal the highly individual sense of character that would make *M.A.S.H.* (1970) such a success.

d Robert Altman *p* William Conrad *s* Loring Mandel *c* William W. Spencer *lp* Robert Duvall, James Caan, Barbara Baxley, Steve Ihnat, Charles Aidman, Joanna Moore

Le Dernier Homme aka The Last Man

(FR) 85 (82) min

Set in a post-nuclear-holocaust world, this variant on Arch Oboler's **Five** (1951) is a weak satire on French sexual attitudes. When Bouillon, his wife (Torkeli) and their companion (Brill) emerge from a caving expedition, they discover that they are the only people left alive in the world. Bouillon promptly reverts to type, mistreats his wife and sets about seducing Brill, only for his pregnant wife to run away and, on her return, find them dying of radiation poisoning. The film's best sequence is the sight of a dead town which the rats have taken over. For the most part, however, this film is melodramatically conceived and the acting and direction uniformly wooden.

Surprisingly, the film won Bitsch the Golden Asteroid at the 1969 Trieste festival of Science Fiction films.

d/s Charles Bitsch *p* Dovidas Annouchka *c* Pierre Lhomme *lp* Sofia Torkeli, Corinne Brill, Jean-Claude Bouillon

Die Folterkammer des Dr Fu Manchu aka The Castle of Fu Manchu

(TERRA FILMKUNST/BALCAZAR/ITALIAN INTERNATIONAL FILM/ TOWER OF LONDON FILMS; WG, SP, IT, GB) 92 min

Another lacklustre offering in the irregular Fu Manchu series. This time Lee's Fu Manchu has developed an invention that freezes water instantly. To perfect it (and thus threaten the world again) he kidnaps a scientist with a heart disease and, to keep him alive, a doctor (Stoll) to perform a heart transplant.

Against such a script Lee and Greene (as Nayland Smith) have no chance.

d Jess (Jesús) Franco *p* Harry Alan Towers *s* Peter Welbeck *c* Manuel Merino *lp* Christopher Lee, Richard Greene, Howard Marion Crawford, Gunther Stoll, Tsai Chin, Rosalba Neri

Gamera Tai Viras aka Gamera Tai Uchukaiju Bairasu aka Gamera Versus Viras aka Gamera Versus Outer Space Monster Viras aka Destroy All Planets

(DAIEI; JAP) scope 75 min

Gamera's fourth appearance, this time in a straightforward children's film. Having defeated one spaceship about to attack the Earth, Gamera captures two boy scouts who, while messing about with a submarine, caused it to submerge. But since Gamera is known to be a lover of children, the boys soon realize that their monster is being controlled by aliens. They release the creature from the alien force and get it to attack the enemy spaceship and its ally, the monster Viras, a beast with three tentacles and six legs. The film continues the shift of the monster genre towards a space opera context, as had Shochhiku's **Uchu Daikaiju Guilala** (1967), diminishing the thematic interest of the genre. The next appearances of Gamera, again directed by Yuasa, would be **Gamera Tai Guiron** (1969) and **Gamera Tai Daimaju Jaiga** (1970).

d Noriyaki Yuasa *p* Hidemasa Nagata *s* Fumi Takahashi *c* Akira Kitazaki *se* Kazafumi Fujii, Yuso Kaneko *lp* Kojiro Hongo, Toru Takatsuka, Carl Crane, Michiko Yaegaki, Mari Atsumi, Junko Yashiro, Peter Williams

Gamma Sango Uchu Daisakusen aka The Green Slime aka Battle Beyond the Stars aka Death and the Green Slime

(TOEI/SOUTHERN CROSS FILMS; JAP,US) 90 (77) min

The first official Japanese-American co-production, with, for the most part, a Western cast and Japanese crew. The story concerns a mission to destroy an asteroid on a collision course with the Earth. This is successful but a green slime from the asteroid is taken back to the space station Gamma III, commanded by Jaeckel. There, the slimy cells proliferate and form serpent-like creatures. The astral triffids kill most of the Gamma crew with electric shocks until the station is

Above: Gamma Sango Uchu Daisakusen, *the first Japanese-American co-production.*

evacuated and exploded, killing Jaeckel in the process and leaving a rocket commander (Horton) with Jaeckel's girl (Paluzzi) to provide the happy ending. Not a very convincing entry in the vegetable monster movie sub-genre, which includes **Matango** (1963), **From Hell It Came** (1957), *The Land Unknown* (1957) and **Day of the Triffids** (1963). Paluzzi looks uncomfortable and is unconvincing as a space scientist while Jaeckel plays the role as he does sergeants in war movies.

Fukasaku is better known for his direction of *Tora Tora Tora* (1970) and **Fukkatsu No Hi** (1980), both with international casts. He started directing in 1961 and achieved popularity with Yakuza and Samurai films in the seventies. He returned to the space opera with the inventive **Uchu Kara No Messeji** (1978). His TV Science Fiction is said to have influenced George Lucas' **Star Wars** (1977).

d Kinji Fukasaku *p* Ivan Reiner, Walter Manley *s* Charles Sinclair, William Finger, Tom Rowe *c* Yoshikazu Yamasawa *se* Akira Watanabe *lp* Robert Horton, Richard Jaeckel, Luciana Paluzzi, Bud Widom, Ted Gunther, Robert Dunham, David Yorston, William Ross

Hello Down There

(IVAN TORS PRODUCTIONS) 98 (88) min

This would-be comedy, a sort of underwater version of *Swiss Family Robinson*, features Randall as the designer of an underwater house who agrees to test it out with his wife (Leigh) and children who comprise half a rock group, The Hang-Ups. The stream of generation gap jokes (a tycoon of Teen called Nate Ashbury) are the weakest part of the film. Even odder is the presence of Arnold, a director who in the fifties with films like **Tarantula** (1955) and **The Incredible Shrinking Man** (1957) showed himself a master of paranoia. Certainly this comfortable aquatic fantasy is as far removed from **The Creature from the Black Lagoon** (1954) as one can imagine.

d Jack Arnold *p* George Sherman *s* Frank Telford, John McGreevey *c* Cliff Poland *lp* Tony Randall, Janet Leigh, Jim Backus, Roddy McDowall, Ken Berry, Richard Dreyfuss

Right: Kaiju
Soshingeki, *Toho's
20th monster movie.*

Janet Leigh in Hello
Down There, *Jack
Arnold's lacklustre
underwater comedy.*

The Illustrated Man
(SKM PRODUCTIONS/WB)   pv   103 min
Steiger gives a wonderful interpretation in the title role as the
Cassandra-like figure whose visions, the living tattoos that
cover his body and over which he has no control, cause angry
soul-searching in the wanderer who meets Steiger. Sadly,
however, Smight's direction forcefully separates reality from
fantasy, a meeting point Ray Bradbury (on three of whose
interconnecting stories the film is loosely based) was keen to
blur. Nonetheless, the film remains interesting, for its
literalization of the power and fascination dreams have for us
in the form of Drivas' wanderer who quickly becomes
obsessed with the living illustrations Steiger wears. The
theme of all three stories that Steiger 'tells' – a couple eaten by
the fantasy figures their children conjure up; astronauts

seeking shelter on a rain-sodden Venus; and a couple giving
their child a suicide pill the day before the world is due to end,
only to be told that there was an error in the calculations and
the world will survive – is betrayal.
   Drivas is the wanderer and Bloom (then married to Steiger)
the mysterious illustrator responsible for the tattoos.

d Jack Smight   *co-p/s* Howard B. Kreitsek   *co-p* Ted Mann
c Philip Lathrop   *se* Ralph Webb   *lp* Rod Steiger, Claire
Bloom, Robert Drivas, Don Dubbins, Tim Weldon, Jason
Evers, Christine Matchet

It's Alive   (AZALEA)   80 min
Director/producer/writer Buchanan (who did the same all-
round job on **Zontar, the Thing from Venus**, 1966) got his
ideas for this film from Richard Matheson's novel *Being*. A
crazy farmer (Osterhouse) discovers a prehistoric monster
near his farm and imprisons three people, Kirk (the star of
Mars Needs Women, 1966, the best known of Buchanan's
films), Bonne, and Thurman in a cave to provide food for his
pet. They try various way of escaping before Kirk finally
manages to turn the tables on Osterhouse.

d/p/s Larry Buchanan   *c* Robert Alcott   *se* Jack Bennett
lp Tommy Kirk, Shirley Bonne, Billy Thurman, Corveth
Osterhouse, Annabelle Macadams

Kaiju Soshingeki *aka* Destroy All Monsters *aka*
Operation Monsterland *aka* The March of the
Monsters   (TOHO; JAP)   scope   89 min
To celebrate their 20th monster movie (although that depends
a little on which ones count as monster movies) Toho fielded
the Honda-Tsuburaya team with the entire range of their
major monsters, eleven in all. The plot, set in 1999 in keeping
with the genre's shift towards space opera settings, involves
the monsters breaking out of the island where they are held
captive, destroying most of the world's capitals (or at least
postcards of them) and running amok in a most uncharacteristic fashion. The scientists who guarded them had been taken
over by aliens called Kilaaks who had planted transmitters
into the scientists' necks as well as into the monsters. The
female aliens operate from a base on the Moon, as well as from
an underground headquarters on Earth, and their final
weapon is the unleashing of the dreaded Ghidorah against the
Japanese monsters. The titanic battle that follows, located as
usual on Mount Fuji, is witnessed from a safe distance by
baby Godzilla who cheers and applauds his elders. The battle
over and won, the creatures do a little victory dance before
retreating back to monster island. By this time, it seems that
Godzilla (in his eighth outing), Rodan, Anzilla (from **Gigantis**, 1955), Mothra, Varan, Ebirah, Baragon, Wenda (from

Kaitei Gunkan, 1964) and company have degenerated into vaudeville characters. The effects are perfunctory, all effort having been concentrated on the finale.

d/co-s Inoshiro Honda   *p* Tomoyuki Tanaka   *co-s* Kaoru Mabuchi   *c* Taiichi Kankura   *se* Eiji Tsuburaya, Sadamasa Arikawa   *lp* Akira Kubo, Jun Tazaki, Yoshio Tsuchiya, Kyoko Ai, Yukihiko Kobayashi, Kenji Sahara, Andrew Hughes, Nadao Kirino, the Itoh Sisters

Kyuketsuki Gokenidoro *aka* **Goke Bodysnatcher from Hell** *aka* **Goke the Vampire**
(SHOCHIKU; JAP)   scope   84 min
After Daiei's bid for the monster movie market with **Gamera Tai Barugon** (1966) and Nikkatsu's **Daikyoju Gappa** (1967), Shochiku, a studio more oriented towards thrillers and horror, also entered the fray with this Science Fiction story developed from a plot device similar to that of **Yosei Gorasu** (1962). Instead of a spaceship, Sato's film has an ordinary airliner pass through a cloudy substance. It crash-lands in the desert and a passenger (Ko) is taken over by the mysterious alien influence encountered in the sky: he becomes a vampire. Soon everybody is a vampire except the captain (Yoshida) and the stewardess (Sato). But when they reach a highway at the end of their ordeal, they make the same discovery that Kevin McCarthy made at the end of **Invasion of the Body Snatchers** (1956); the aliens have already taken over – and more flying saucers are on the way. One interesting aspect of this movie is that, whereas the US film proceeds by means of cloning, the Japanese film posits a vampiric relation in which the parasite takes over the body and transforms an ordinary person into a bloodsucking maniac. This suggests a notion of colonization rather than substitution, which is the American film's fear.

Indeed, the Japanese victims are forever scarred by the process of colonization while the US version presents its victims as ordinary people with 'alien' ideologies. In spite of these points of interest, the film is over-written, awkwardly directed and badly acted. Sato had made horror films for Toei and eventually directed Science Fiction episodes for the teleserial *Captain Vrutura*. Shochiku's other entry in the Kaiju Eiga genre was the more successful **Uchu Daikaiju Guilala** (1967).

d Hajime Sato   *p* Takashi Inomata   *s* Susumu Takaku, Kyuzo Kobayashi   *c* Shizuo Hirase   *lp* Hideo Ko, Teruo Yoshida, Tomomi Sato, Eizo Kitamura, Masaya Takahashi, Cathy Horlan, Kazuo Kato, Yuko Kusunoki

The Lost Continent   (HAMMER; GB)   98 min
Carreras' forceful direction and Arthur Lawson's imaginative sets are the driving forces behind this wonderfully silly story (derived from Dennis Wheatley's novel, *Uncharted Seas*) about an old tramp-steamer with a cargo of explosives that blunders off course and into a pocket of time in which the Spanish Inquisition is still in progress. The movie is decidedly uneven but some of the scenes, such as our first view of the Spanish inhabitants of the nightmare world of the Sargasso Sea crossing the killer seaweed on gas-filled balloons, are breathtaking. The strong cast, which includes Porter as the steamer's captain, Read as El Diabolo and Knef and Stock, gives weight to an otherwise ludicrous script. A sublime folly.

d/p Michael Carreras   *s* Michael Nash   *c* Paul Beeson *se* Robert A. Mattey, Cliff Richardson   *lp* Eric Porter, Hildegard Knef, Suzanna Leigh, Tony Beckley, Nigel Stock, Benito Carruthers, Darryl Read

Mission Mars

(SAGITTARIUS/RED RAM PRODUCTIONS) 77 min

This absurd, yet appealing, piece of low-budget Science Fiction interestingly parallels **2001 – A Space Odyssey** (1968) in its use of the idea of a presence waiting for man to reach it, but with the central difference that it wraps this up in a highly melodramatic plot. McGavin, Adams and DeVries are the astronauts who encounter two drifting dead Russian spacemen on their way to Mars and the frozen body of a third on the planet. They fight off the alien presence, powered by mysterious polarites that gather the sun's energy, and McGavin and the revived Russian return to Earth. Webster, who is better known for the awful **Santa Claus Conquers the Martians** (1964), directs far better than that film would suggest.

d Nick Webster *p* Everette Rosenthal *s* Mike St Clair *c* Cliff Poland *lp* Darren McGavin, Nick Adams, George DeVries

Mister Freedom

(OPERA/LES FILMS DU RONDPOINT; FR) 110 (94) min

An enjoyable, if heavy-handed, satire on all things American and its handling of the Vietnam war in particular, *Mister Freedom* was made by former fashion photographer Klein. Rather like the anti-Superman in the *Superman* comics who with the best of intentions perpetually causes havoc by mis-applying his superpowers, Abbey's Mister Freedom, in trying to save France for democracy against an assortment of supervillains, finds he has to destroy the country. However, Klein's unabashedly comic-strip style direction is interposed with too much speechifying to be wholly successful. Thus a few nice touches aside (the American Embassy in Paris is a giant supermarket, a witty commercial for an aerosol defoliant and Seyrig's delicious impersonation of a drum-majorette-

whore), the film remains an historical, rather than compelling, oddity. Klein's subsequent films have all been documentaries.

d/s William Klein *p* Guy Belfond, Michael Zemer, Christian Thivat *c* Pierre Lhomme *lp* John Abbey, Delphine Seyrig, Jean-Claude Drouot, Philippe Noiret, Donald Pleasance, Yves Montand

The Monitors (BELL AND HOWELL PRODUCTIONS-CUE/WILDING/SECOND CITY PRODUCTIONS) 92 min

This is noteworthy as the first film to be financed by film-equipment manufacturers Bell and Howell whose plan to make Chicago a leading theatrical film-making centre soon collapsed. The film is an erratic, unsuccessful attempt at 'flower power' satire by the Second City Cabaret Group. The basic plot features the attempts by the monitors of the title, who are good-intentioned aliens determined to foist love and peace on unruly humans, to invade Earth, only to fail like so many would-be invaders before them. The movie is constructed as a series of sketches, some of which – like the TV campaign for peace which features guest appearances from the likes of Senator Everett Dirkson and Xiaviar Cougat (!) that the monitors mount – are wickedly funny, but sadly director Shea and writer Gold fail to integrate their material at all.

Accordingly, the scrappy film remains, at best, an evocation of the hippy movement of the late sixties. The cinematography of Zsigmond, who later graduated to features such as **Close Encounters of the Third Kind** (1977) and *Heaven's Gate* (1980), makes the film look far better than it, in fact, is.

d Jack Shea *p* Bernard Sahlins *s* Myron J. Gold *c* William (Vilmos) Zsigmond *lp* Guy Stockwell, Susan Oliver, Avery Schreiber, Sherry Jackson, Shepperd Strudwick, Keenan Wynn

John Abbey in the title role of William Klein's freewheeling satire Mister Freedom.

Night of the Living Dead, *George Romero's stunning movie début and one of the most influential Science Fiction films of recent years.*

Night of the Living Dead (IMAGE TEN) b/w 96 min
An astoundingly assured début, this independently financed movie was made over a number of weekends by Romero and a group of film-makers in Pittsburg. The minuscule budget and erratic shooting schedule in no way diminish the power of the film, the best 'invasion' movie since the seminal **Invasion of the Body Snatchers** (1956). Like that movie, it proceeds towards its ironic end with a ruthless logic and on the way deflates virtually every cliché it throws up. Thus, to take just two examples, the resourceful hero (Jones) does everything right but to no avail and the heroine (O'Dea), once immobilized by shock, remains so throughout the film.

Romero's genius lies in following through what at first seems to be a wholly contrived idea, that radiation fallout from an abortive launch of a rocket to Venus should revive and 'zombieize' corpses into mindless killers, until as the zombies grow in number the film's sense of terror becomes all-consuming. Romero further intensifies this by showing how quickly his characters collapse under the stress of their new-found situation. The film's final irony, the shooting of Jones in mistake for a zombie by a gun-crazy member of the public, is similar in tone to that of *Easy Rider* (1969).

d/c George A. Romero   *p* Russell Streiner, Karl Hardman   *s* John A. Russo   *lp* Judith O'Dea, Duane Jones, Karl Hardman, Keith Wayne, Judith Ridley, Marilyn Eastman

N.P. *aka* **N.P. – The Secret**
(ZETA-A-ELLE PRODUCCIONES; IT)   106 min
A political fable, *N.P.* fails because its targets are too diffuse and Agosti's direction is too bland. Rabal is the industrial tycoon who, just before he can implement his plan of total industrial automation and so abolish work, is kidnapped and brainwashed. He loses his memory and becomes first a social refugee and then a worker, like those he'd threatened to 'liberate' from work. Together with other workers he demands the right to work. For all its weaknesses the film is interesting because, unlike most visions of the future in which unlimited leisure is a fact, it centres on the human cost of such leisure.

d/s Silvano Agosti   *p* Enrico Zaccaria   *c* Nicola Dimitri   *lp* Francesco Rabal, Ingrid Thulin, Irene Papas

Orbito Mortal *aka* **Mission Stardust**
(AITOR/PEA/THEUMER; SP, IT, WG)   95 min
This sequel to **Perry Rhodan – SOS aus dem Weltall** (1967) is the only other film based on the series of novels begun by Walter Enstine (under the pseudonym Clark Dalton) but taken over by a writing team, which became a European cult. Limply directed by Zeglio, it features Rhodan (Jeffries) joining an expedition that is forced to land on the Moon. There they find a spaceship in which there are two aliens, Persson and Karelson, members of a dying race who have telepathically engineered the expedition's landing. Rhodan first defends the pair from their renegade robots and then brings them back to Earth to cure them of the disease they're suffering from.

Compared to the delirious pulp poetry of the novels the film, like *SOS aus dem Weltall*, is strangely pedestrian.

d Primo Zeglio   *p* E. Von Theumer   *s* K.H. Vogelmann, Frederico Urrutia   *c* Manuel Merino   *lp* Lang Jeffries, Essy Persson, Luis Davila, Daniel Martin, Gianni Rizzo, John Karelson

Planet of the Apes (APJAC)   pv   102 min
An impressive film, *Planet of the Apes* was one of the most successful Science Fiction films of the sixties. It spawned four (inferior) sequels, **Beneath the Planet of the Apes** (1969), **Escape from the Planet of the Apes** (1971), **Conquest of the Planet of the Apes** (1972) and **Battle for the Planet of the Apes** (1973) and a TV series, and won itself a cult following.

The literate script by Serling and the once-blacklisted Wilson faithfully follows Pierre Boulle's novel, *Monkey Planet*, in pointedly contrasting the ordered, almost medieval, society of the apes with the violent arrogance of Heston's human astronaut transported through a time-slip to a post-nuclear-catastrophe Earth on which the apes have taken upon themselves the role of defenders of 'humanity'. Moreover, the central section of the film, in which Heston is held captive by friendly ape scientists (Hunter and McDowall) and examined with a mind to the possibility that he might be 'the missing link' in simean evolution, is full of delicate comedy in which rational ape confronts irrational man. But the film's success depends less on its argument than on Schaffner and cinematographer Shamroy's breathtaking visuals. Mostly shot in and around the national parks of Utah and Arizona, Schaffner uses the futuristic rock formations there to create a real sense of an alien landscape. Similarly the famous end in which Heston finds the ruined remains of the Statue of Liberty (and with it the bitter realization that he is on Earth after all) works as a marvellous visual conceit rather than as a message.

The wonderfully flexible ape makeup, which allowed the actors playing the apes to create characters rather than stereotypes, was created by John Chambers.

d Franklin J. Schaffner   *p* Arthur P. Jacobs   *s* Michael Wilson, Rod Serling   *c* Leon Shamroy   *se* L.B. Abbott, Art Cruickshank, Emil Kosa Jnr   *lp* Charlton Heston, Roddy McDowall, Kim Hunter, Maurice Evans, James Whitmore, Linda Harrison

Popdown (FREMAR PRODUCTIONS; GB)   98 (54) min

A real oddity, this exploitation quickie features a panorama of 'Swingin' London' 1968-style (and appearances from several cult rock groups such as Dantalion's Chariot, the Brian Auger Trinity and Blossom Toes). The excuse for this is the visit of two aliens, sent to observe Earth life, who become fascinated with pop music. The result is an indulgent but pleasing pop-culture collage.

d/p/s Fred Marshall   *c* Oliver Wood   *lp* Diane Keen, Jane Bates, Zoot Money, Carol Rachell, Debbie Slater, Bill Aaron

Charlton Heston with scientists Roddy McDowall and Kim Hunter in the landmark Planet of the Apes.

Prazske Noci *aka* Prague Nights *aka* The Nights of Prague (FELIX BROZ UNIT; CZECH)   92 min

An omnibus movie combining three tales of Prague by three different film-makers. Two are set in the Middle Ages: *The Bread Shoes* directed by Schorm and *The Poisoned Poisoner* directed by Makovek, who also directed the framing story called *Fabricius*. The third legend, made as a live action film by the noted animator Brdecka, tells the story of the golem, but with a different twist. Rabbi Loew learns that Rudolph II asked a Polish rabbi, Chaim (Klusak) to make a golem. Loew arranges for Chaim to be seduced by a mute girl (Brezkova) who manages to wipe the magic formula off the golem's forehead, making it crumble into pieces that smother the libidinous rabbi. Then it is revealed that the girl herself was an artificial creature manufactured by Loew. The episode is lovingly shot by Kallis, who also photographed **Klaun Ferdinand a Raketa** (1962). The atmosphere occasionally echoes the sensual aspects of Duvivier's **Le Golem** (1935) while the décors are closer to Wegener's classic **Der Golem: Wie Er in die Welt Kam** (1920).

co-d/s Jiri Brdecka   *co-d* Evald Schorm, Milos Makovek   *c* Jan Kallis, Frantisek Uldrych   *lp* Jana Brezkova, Jan Klusak, Teresa Tuszynska, Josef Somr, Josef Abrham, Lucie Novot, Jan Libicek, Milos Kopecky, Milena Dvorska, Vaclav Kotva

Il Re dei Criminali *aka* Superago

(GV-SEC FILM/IZARO FILM; IT, SP)   scope   95 (87) min

This is one of the numerous films devoted to the exploits of Cianfriglia's Superago, an Italian series hero who normally takes on routine criminals but occasionally (as here and in **Superago Contro Diabolicus**, 1966) ventures into the realms of Science Fiction. As a character, Superago, a wrestler turned defender of justice, and his bulletproof leotard only makes sense in the context of the Italian popular cinema. A meld of the muscular heroes of the 'sword and sandal' epics that dominated the Italian cinema in the early sixties with the numerous Bond lookalikes that followed, seen in isolation, both the character and his films are simply ridiculous.

Here he foils the plans of Madison's mad scientist who has been kidnapping the world's top athletes and replacing their hearts with electronic circuits so as to keep them under his control.

d Paul Maxwell (Paolo Bianchini)   *p* Oliver Wells   *s* Richard Lovelace (Julio Buchs)   *c* Geoffrey Packett (Godofredo Pacheco)   *lp* Guy Madison, Ken Wood (Giovanni Cianfriglia), Liz Barrett (Luisa Baratto), Diana Loris, Harold Sambrel (Aldo Sambrell), Thomas Blank (Blanco)

Santo Contra Blue Demon en la Atlantida

(PRODUCCIONES SOTOMAYOR; MEX)   89 min

The first encounter between the popular Santo and the relative newcomer Blue Demon (Cruz) who made his first screen appearance in 1963. This picture sees the two masked wrestlers in Atlantis where they grapple with an ex-Nazi (Rado) who has discovered the secret of eternal youth and dreams of ruling the world. Proceeding mostly by means of mind-control techniques, which allows him to pit one wrestler against the other for a while, the Nazi lives in a setting of stock shots mostly borrowed from Inoshiro Honda's **Kaiju Daisenso** (1965). Honesty would dictate the inclusion of Eiji Tsuburaya in the credits as responsible for the special effects instead of the Mexican cinematographer listed.

Soler's work, except perhaps for his 1972 remake of the Argentinian version of Jekyll and Hyde, **El Hombre y la Bestia** (1951), remained firmly stuck in the nether regions of the cheapest sector of Mexican fantasy pictures and comedies such as **El Castillo de los Monstruos** (1958) and **Los Platillos Voladores** (1955).

d/co-s Julian Soler   *p* Jesús Sotomayer   *co-s* Rafael Garcia Traversi   *c/se* Raul Martinez Solares   *lp* Santo, Alejandro Cruz, Jorge Rado, Rafael Banquella, Silvia Pasquel, Magda Giner, Rosa Maria Piñeiro, Griselda Mejia

Santo y Blue Demon Contra los Monstruos *aka* **Santo Contra los Monstruos de Frankenstein** *aka* **Santo and the Blue Demon Vs the Monsters**
(PRODUCCIONES SOTOMAYOR; MEX) 84 min
Like **El Castillo de los Monstruos** (1958), also a Sotomayor production, and Honda's **Kaiju Soshingeki** (1968), this is an all-star monster film offering a general contest between the two masked wrestlers and an array of monsters including a vampire (Alvizu), two vampire women (Tako and Ponce), a werewolf (Lara), a mummy (Rosales), a cyclops (Cepeda) and Frankenstein's creature, here called Franquestein (Leal). The assumption that quantity is synonymous with entertainment value even causes the Blue Demon to be provided with a double as the mad Dr Halder (Ancira) creates a robot double of the blue-trousered hulk in a distant reminder of the doubling of Maria in Fritz Lang's **Metropolis** (1926). Eventually, the Silver Masked hero releases the good Blue Demon and together they defeat the villains created by Halder and his misshapen assistant (Martinez). Highlights include a Frankenstein creature with a moustache and a beard driving a car and a chaotic freestyle wrestling bout in which the monsters invade the ring to battle with Santo, causing some raised eyebrows amongst the spectators in the stadium.

The veteran Martinez, who started directing in 1938, had made a few ambitious social melodramas but in the main he specialized in farcical comedies before joining the ranks of routine fantasy picture directors with *La Casa del Terror* (1959) starring Lon Chaney Jnr.

Martinez followed this movie with the witchcraft/zombie picture *Santo y Blue Demon en el Mundo de los Muertos* (1969).

d Gilberto Martinez Solares *p* Jesús Sotomayor *s* Rafael Garcia Traversi *c/se* Raul Martinez Solares *lp* Santo, Alejandro Cruz, Hedy Blue, Jorge Rado, Carlos Ancira, Adalberto Martinez, Vicente Lara, David Alvizu, Gerardo Cepeda, Manuel Leal, Fernando Rosales, Elsa Maria Tako, Yolanda Ponce

La Señora Muerte *aka* **Madame Death**
(FILMICA VERGARA; MEX) 85 min
After starring in Frederico Curiel's potboiler *Las Vampiras* (1967), Carradine went on to play the lead in this surgical Science Fiction piece about a disfigured woman (Torne) desperately trying to regain her beauty by means of skin transplants and blood transfusions from forcibly recruited victims subjected to gruesome experiments. Carradine is left to ham it up as he pleases in the role of Dr Diabolo, the surgeon who keeps failing to achieve lasting results and forces Torne to kill even more victims. The plot echoes Jesús Franco's **Gritos en la Noche** (1962) but in spite of an opening sequence clearly indicating what is at stake in these fantasies (a couple having sex when, at the climactic moment, the man is seized by violent convulsions and rushed to hospital, only to die under the surgeon's knife), Salvador never achieves the sick surreality nor the warped, catholic sense of guilty fascination with physicality and sex so characteristic of Franco's medical Science Fiction.

Salvador's undistinguished career included the most embarrassing film Buster Keaton was ever associated with, *El Moderno Barba Azul* (1946) and comedies for local consumption such as **Los Invisibles** (1961) with the Mexican equivalents of Abbott and Costello, Viruta and Capulina.

d Jaime Salvador *p* Luis Enrique Vergara *s* Ramon Obal Jnr *lp* Regina Torne, John Carradine, Elsa Cardenas, Miguel Angel Alvarez, Victor Junco, Nathanael Leon Frankenstein, Isela Vega, Alicia Ravel, Patricia Ferrer

Shirley Thompson versus the Aliens
(KOLOSSAL FILMS; AUST) 104 min
Featuring Haddrick as a wax model of the Duke of Edinburgh brought to life by aliens and used by them as their spokesperson, this is a self-indulgent, but surprisingly funny, movie in the style of Sharman's other cult film, **The Rocky Horror Picture Show** (1975). Like that film it was adapted from a stage show. Told in flashback by Shirley Thompson (Harders) to her psychiatrist, the film follows her story of meeting with aliens (in the guise of a motorcycle gang) in an amusement park and her attempts to tell the world what she saw, only to have everybody, from her nagging mother (Johns) down, disbelieve her. As a result she goes mad.

Amongst the tricks deployed by Sharman is a clever use of colour: the flashback scenes are in black and white, the asylum scenes are under-exposed and the 'fantasy' scenes are in colour.

d/p/co-s Jim Sharman *co-s* Helmut Bakaitis *c* David Sanderson *lp* Jane Harders, John Likoxitch, Helmut Bakaitis, Tim Eliott, June Collins, Marion Johns, Ronn Haddrick

Swiss Made
(YVES YERSIN PRODUCTIONS; SWITZ) 100 min
Backed by the Swiss national bank as part of the country's celebrations of its 100th anniversary, this compendium film alternately pokes fun at and glorifies the Swiss character, which it sees as typified by complacency and an absolute belief in efficiency, in a trio of futuristic episodes. The first of these concerns the return from Brazil of an ageing revolutionary who, on finding his dreams have come true, yearns for the old days. The best episode is about a robot film crew who make a documentary about modern Switzerland, all the while bemoaning that the country is run by unfeeling computers.

The film is amateurishly made and has never been exhibited outside Switzerland.

co-d/p/co-s Yves Yersin *co-d* Fritz Maeder, Fredy Murer *co-s* Michel Contat *c* W. Lesiewicz *lp* Henri Noverraz, Elsa Shorecka, Herbert Herrman

Thunderbird 6 (AP FILMS; GB) scope 90 min
This is the second film derived from American producer Anderson's teleseries, *Thunderbirds*, devoted to the exploits of a group of puppets who under the collective title of International Rescue save the 21st century from a variety of evil, but bland, villains. In this offering, the team, with the aid of their new spaceship of the title, take on the Black Phantom. The model work and special effects are good but the clichéd characters (especially their monotonous voices) make the film far too long at 90 minutes.

d David Lane *p/co-s* Sylvia Anderson *co-s* Gerry Anderson *c* Harry Oakes *se* Derek Meddings

Alan Tracey, puppet defender of the universe extraordinary, in the Thunderbirds teleseries from which Thunderbirds Are Go and Thunderbird 6 are derived.

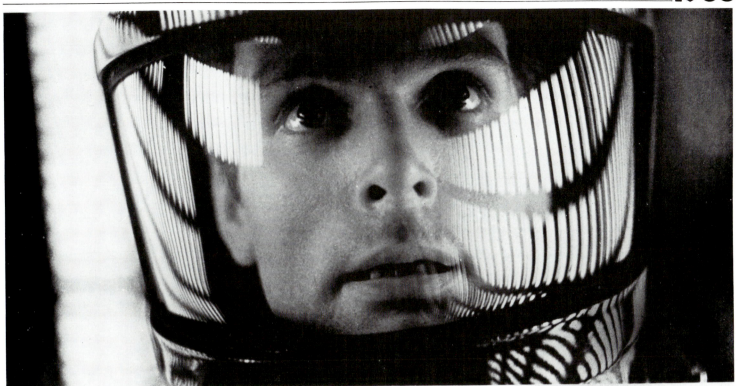

Kier Dullea in 2001 – A Space Odyssey, *the most influential Science Fiction film of the sixties.*

Tumannost Andromedy *aka* **The Andromeda Nebula** *aka* **Andromeda the Mysterious** *aka* **The Cloud of Andromeda** (DOVZHENKO STUDIO; USSR) scope 77 min
The Pole Stanislaw Lem, author of **Solaris** (published in 1961 and filmed in 1971) and the Russian Ivan Efremov are regarded as the main exponents of Science Fiction literature in Eastern Europe. Efremov's *The Andromeda Nebula*, a highly lyrical and quietly humanist novel published in 1957, was adapted far too reverently for this film, although the author had consented to some alterations to bring the technological aspects of the fantasy more up-to-date. The central character, an introspective figure in the novel, is a man born on a spaceship halfway towards the star MNI9026+7AL. But the film's characters suggest that everybody living in *Star Trek*-times is uniformly nice and smiling, acting like over-weight scoutmasters. The adventure, premissed on the possibility of interplanetary communication, is devoid of any drama, the script is grossly overwritten, dialogues are declaimed and the whole thing reeks of timid academicism. In short, a very disappointing adapation of an interesting book.

d/co-s Yevgeny Sherstobitov *co-s* Vladimir Dimitriyevski
c Nikolay Yefremov *lp* Viya Artmane, Sergey Stolyarov, Nikolay Kryukov, Tatyana Voloshina, Lado Tskhvariashvili

2001 – A Space Odyssey
(MGM) Super pv 161 (141) min
2001 – A Space Odyssey was undoubtedly the most influential Science Fiction film of the sixties. Henceforth, for better or worse, Science Fiction cinema would have a truly speculative aspect to it, in the manner of Science Fiction writing. Significantly, Clarke, on whose novella *The Sentinel* it was based, is like Robert Heinlein who co-scripted the landmark film **Destination Moon** (1950), a noted Science Fiction writer. Henceforth good special effects and big budgets became the norm. Moreover, the film quite literally changed our concept of space and spaceships. Where before the pencil-shaped rocketships of *Destination Moon* formed the grid of our assumptions about the look of a spaceship, henceforth the building blocks of spaceships would be more akin to the angularity of Lego pieces and their size more commensurate with the vastness of deep space, as in the sequence where the *Discovery* slowly crosses the Cinerama screen for what seems an eternity (a scene that quickly became one of the cliché shots of post-*2001* Science Fiction).

It's worth stressing these features of *2001*, for, though in retrospect it was the film that re-introduced a sense of spectacle to Science Fiction, it has been usually celebrated in terms of its (ambiguous) meanings and attacked for the pretentiousness and sterility of its views; in short, it has been hailed as a film of ideas rather than the visual conceit it is. For above all, *2001* is a matter of logistics, the giant space station being matched by the most minor details of costume and décor (including such notables as the space toilet), the purpose of which Kubrick has often stated was to show the everyday nature (or ordinaryness) of space travel in a near future when it was possible. Similarly the 'star gate' sequence (also called the 'cosmic ride') which precedes astronaut Dullea's rebirth as a 'transcended man' was celebrated for its hallucinogenic-like effects long before the film was re-issued, billed as 'The Ultimate Trip'.

This is not to say the film has no ideas, merely to momentarily sidestep the statements the film makes. A comparison of a single frame of *2001* with ones from **Dark Star** (1974) and/or **Solaris** (1971) clearly reveals very different views of the future, space travel and man: the simple mess of *Dark Star*'s spaceship compared to the sterility of Kubrick's *Discovery* speaks volumes. However, the more telling comparison is with Steven Spielberg's **Close Encounters of the Third Kind** (1977). Kubrick's film explains man's development in terms of the monolith, most explicitly in the adventurous jump cut that takes us from primitive man to space-age man. For Kubrick, man, though ingenious (as in the sequence where Dullea outwits the murderous super-computer, HAL), is essentially led by the mysterious force that the monolith represents. This passive view of man's role explains both the view of space travel of the film's décor and the formal qualities of the narrative which constantly opposes inhuman circles and rectangles. In Kubrick's film, the never-seen aliens are clearly man's superiors, indulgently helping him along; in Spielberg's man meets the aliens on equal terms. For Kubrick, man is little more than the property of the unseen aliens, for Spielberg man achieves his own destiny.

In 1983, a sequel to be directed by Peter Hyams was announced, *2010 – Odyssey II* for release in 1984/5.

d/p/co-s Stanley Kubrick   *co-s* Arthur C. Clarke
c Geoffrey Unsworth   *se* Wally Veevers, Douglas Trumball·
Con Pederson, Tom Howard   *lp* Keir Dullea, Gary
Lockwood, William Sylvester, Daniel Richter, Leonard
Rossiter, Douglas Rain (voice of HAL), Robert Beatty,
Margaret Tyzack

The Vengeance of Fu Manchu
(BABASDAVE FILMS, GB)   89 min
A lacklustre continuation of Towers' Fu Manchu series
(especially when compared to the first two, **The Face of Fu
Manchu**, 1965 and **Brides of Fu Manchu**, 1966, both
directed with verve and invention by Don Sharp), this
contrasts Wilmer's Nayland Smith's setting-up of Interpol
with Lee's Fu Manchu's creating of an equally international
syndicate of crime. The heart of the plot has Lee subsitute
Wilmer with a double who is then convicted of murder. Only
Chin as Lee's venomous daughter plays her part with any real
conviction.

d Jeremy Summers   *p* Harry Alan Towers   *s* Peter Welbeck
(Towers)   *c* John von Kotze   *lp* Christopher Lee, Douglas
Wilmer, Tsai Chin, Horst Frank, Noel Trevarthen, Maria
Rohm, Tony Ferrer

Wild in the Streets   (AIP)   96 min
For all its excesses, many of which date badly, this is a
wickedly funny movie. Thom's inventive script, set in the
near future, imagines an America with over 50 per cent of the
population under 25 and Jones' pop star becoming president
(after the voting age has been reduced to 14) and retiring
everybody over 35 to rest homes where they are force-fed LSD.
Although the movie leans heavily on the dreams of an
alternative society of America's first generation of hippies
(encapsulated in the famous slogan of the times, 'don't trust
anyone over 30') on a deeper level the film is yet another
satirical study of the American family. Jones' political
ambitions (first raised by Holbrook's opportunistic senator
out to get the youth vote) are simply an attempt to get back at
his domineering mother (Winters). The end wittily has Jones
a contented family man and the ten-year-olds calling for a
revolution.

At the time of its release the movie seemed pure fantasy.
Now after a number of presidential campaigns have made
extensive use of rock stars, the idea of a rock star (rather than
an elderly actor) in the White House seems less surprising.

d Barry Shear   *p* James H. Nicholson, Samuel Z. Arkoff
s Robert Thom   *c* Richard Moore   *lp* Christopher Jones,
Shelley Winters, Diane Varsi, Hal Holbrook, Millie Perkins,
Richard Pryor

The Bed Sitting Room
(OSCAR LEWENSTEIN PRODUCTIONS; GB)   91 min
A charming failure, this adaptation of Antrobus and Spike
Milligan's surreal farce about life after World War III is full of
brilliant ideas presented in an unsettling hit-and-miss manner
by Lester. The characters mutate into bed-sitting rooms,
wardrobes and parrots with terrifying ease but the film, its
quirky humour notwithstanding, lacks any coherent sense of
development. Given heroic support by his actors, particularly
Richardson in the title role, Lester is still unable to make
anything of his post-nuclear-holocaust world other than a
string of, often hilarious, jokes. The film shows, more than
any other of the director's, Lester's need for a strong narrative
line against which he can set his absurd, inconsequential sense
of humour, as in **Superman III** (1983).

d/p Richard Lester   *s* John Antrobus   *c* David Watkin
se Phil Stokes   *lp* Ralph Richardson, Rita Tushingham,
Michael Hordern, Arthur Lowe, Mona Washbourne, Spike
Milligan

Beneath the Planet of the Apes   (APJAC)   pv   94 min
This is the best of the four sequels to the enormously
successful **Planet of the Apes** (1968), despite the fact that the
script coarsens the original conception. In place of the
exhilarating landscapes of the earlier film and its portrait of a
complex society, director Post and his writers offer a stark
contrast between militaristic apes and mutant, telepathic
humans living in the subterranean remains of New York.
Nonetheless, some of the details are imaginative – such as the
mutants worshipping a doomsday bomb (an echo of Walter
M. Miller's fine Science Fiction novel, *A Canticle For
Leibowitz*) – and Buono (as one of the mutants) and Heston
(now a psychotic) give fine performances. Despite the
annihilation of Earth by Franciscus in the last reel further Ape
films followed in the wake of the phenomenal success of this
one.

The sets were originally built for *Hello Dolly* (1969).

d Ted Post   *p* Arthur Jacobs   *s* Paul Dehn, Mort
Abrahams   *c* Milton Krasner   *se* L.B. Abbott, Art
Cruickshank   *lp* James Franciscus, Charlton Heston, Kim
Hunter, Victor Buono, Maurice Evans, Jeff Corey

The Body Stealers *aka* Invasion of the Body Snatchers
aka **Thin Air**   (TIGON BRITISH/SAGITTARIUS; GB, US)   91 min
A inept re-working of **Invasion of the Body Snatchers** (1956)
in which aliens take over the bodies of men testing a

*Richard Lester's surreal
vision of life after a
nuclear holocaust,* The
Bed Sitting Room.

Left: *Youth takes over,
Diane Varsi in* Wild in
the Streets.

Beneath the Planet of the Apes, *the best of the sequels to* Planet of the Apes *(1968).*

drama when the first case St Jacques is given is a racial murder and ends in total cliché with a surprise courtroom twist in which the white bigot (Nielsen) is found innocent of the murder of his black mistress. In the circumstances St Jacques' performance is a model of circumspection. Needless to say, the film has none of the bite of Melvin Van Peebles' treatment of a similar subject, *Watermelon Man* (1970).

d Robert Stevens   p/s Seeleg Lester, Richard Wesson
c Arthur J. Ornitz   lp Raymond St Jacques, Susan Oliver, Janet MacLachlan, Leslie Nielsen, Donnelly Rhodes, David Bailey

The Computer Wore Tennis Shoes
(WALT DISNEY)   90 min
A witless Disney comedy with Russell (who would later become John Carpenter's regular leading man in films like **Escape From New York**, 1981 and **The Thing,** 1982) as the college student who transfers into his brain the entire contents of the computer owned by Romero's amiable racketeer.
    A sequel, **Now You See Him, Now You Don't,** followed in 1972.

d Robert Butler   p Bill Anderson   s Joseph L. McEveety
c Frank Phillips   lp Kurt Russell, Cesar Romero, Joe Flynn, William Schallert, Alan Hewitt, Debbie Paine

Curious Female   (FANFARE FILMS)   75 min
The feature début of Rapp, *Curious Female* is little but an extended joke. In the year 2117, the world is controlled by a master computer and permissiveness is rife but romance frowned upon, so groups of movie buffs gather together to show old movies. Sadly the film Allister and Westberg watch is hardly the stuff of romance, as its title, *The Three Virgins,* makes clear. Nonetheless, the idea of contrasting contemporary and future notions of censorship remains appealing, even if its execution is less so.

d/p Paul Rapp   s Winston R. Paul   c Don Birnkrant
lp Angélique Pettyjohn, Charlene Jones, Bunny Allister, David Westberg, Julie Connors, Michael Greer

Doppelganger *aka* Journey to the Far Side of the Sun
(CENTURY 21 PRODUCTIONS; GB)   101 min
Produced by the Andersons, whose major claim to fame is the

revolutionary new parachute as they pass through a red mist. Connery and Allen are the investigators called in who soon come across mysterious goings-on in a top secret space research laboratory. The overly talkative script ends bizarrely with the men returned and Allen agreeing to help Wilde's alien to find 'volunteers' to help repopulate her planet.

d Gerry Levy   p Tony Tenser   s Mike St Clair   c Johnny Coquillon   lp George Sanders, Maurice Evans, Patrick Allen, Neil Connery, Lorna Wilde, Hilary Dwyer

Captain Nemo and the Underwater City
(OMNIA FILMS; GB)   pv   106 min
An engaging return to the underwater world of Captain Nemo (played with authority by Ryan). The script is routine and Hill's direction only workmanlike but the ornate Victorian décor of Nemo's underwater city of Templemer is charmingly conceived. Connors is the American senator who with a clutch of passengers is saved by Nemo when their ship is sunk in mid-Atlantic and taken to Templemer in the *Nautilus*. Once there, in a plot device that wouldn't have been out of place in **Undersea Kingdom** (1936), the greed of some of the rescuees at the sight of Nemo's oxygen-making plant which turns rocks to gold as a side-effect ferments rebellion in the underwater city which is only settled when the remaining visitors return to the surface promising to keep the secret of Templemer's existence to themselves.

d James Hill   p Bertram Ostrer   s Pip Baker, Jane Baker, R. Wright Campbell   c Alan Hume, Egil Woxholt
lp Robert Ryan, Chuck Connors, Nanette Newman, John Turner, Luciana Paluzzi, Bill Fraser

Change of Mind   (SAGITTARIUS)   98 min
This is yet another liberal treatment of the race problem, made in the wake of *Guess Who's Coming to Dinner?* (1967), but cast in the bizarre world of brain transplants in which a white DA is saved by having his brain transplanted into the body of a dead blackman, St Jacques. The script starts interestingly enough with St Jacques rejected by both his wife (Oliver) and the wife (MacLachlan) of the blackman whose body he's inherited. However, it soon plummets into melo-

Right: *The golden dome of Templemer in* Captain Nemo and the Underwater City.

Thunderbirds TV series, this is a lacklustre piece of Science Fiction. The initial idea is intriguing, a tenth planet is found on the far side of the Sun, only for it to turn out to be a parallel world, a mirror image of Earth. Similarly, Medding's special effects are as impressive as ever. But the wooden, over-talkative script and erratic storyline (suggesting the film was much altered in the course of production) drains the movie of all possible drama. Hendry and Thinnes are the astronauts who voyage to the parallel world and Wymark the scientist driven mad by their discovery.

d Robert Parrish   *p/co-s* Gerry Anderson, Sylvia Anderson
co-s Donald James   *c* John Read   *se* Derek Meddings, Harry Oakes   *lp* Ian Hendry, Roy Thinnes, Lynn Loring, Herbert Lom, George Sewell, Patrick Wymark

Erinnerungen an die Zukunft *aka* Chariots of the Gods
(TERRA FILMKUNST; WG)   92(56) min
Included here because it's decidedly fiction not fact, this documentary, one of several in recent times to propose bizarre views about man's development, takes for its premise Erich von Daeniken's theories (to use the word loosely) that evolution on Earth was speeded up by the arrival of extra-terrestrial beings (ie Gods) who left traces of their visits. Like von Daeniken's books, the film as assembled by Reinl poses 'scientific' questions and presents its evidence in such a provocative way as to demand either the audience's complete belief or such total rejection that, like the scientists who have treated von Daeniken's theories as utter rubbish, one's 'objectivity' is called into question. Perhaps the wittiest use von Daeniken's ideas have been put to comes in Steven Spielberg's *Raiders of the Lost Ark* (1981). A positive thirties adventure film, it borrows for its central gimmick von Daeniken's idea of the Ark of the Covenant as an otherworldly weapon and then treats the idea with all the due solemnity of the serial.

Reinl is best known for his interesting series of westerns devoted to Winnetou, the creation of German romantic novelist Karl May.

d/s Harald Reinl   *c* Ernst Wild, Claus Riedel, Richard R. Rimmel

The Forbin Project *aka* Colossus – The Forbin Project
(U)   pv   100(88) min
A chilling Science Fiction thriller, this movie had its release delayed by Universal for some two years because they were unsure how to promote it in the wake of the phenomenal success of **2001 – A Space Odyssey** (1968). Bridges' uncluttered script imagines a near future in which Western defences are turned over to the vast Colossus computer (the brainchild of Braeden), sealed deep in the Rocky Mountains. In response, the Russians turn over their defences to a similar computer, Guardian. Whereupon the two computers link up and make a bid for world domination and Braeden is given the job of switching them off.

Unlike Robert Wise's **The Andromeda Strain** (1970) which spent too much time on technological gadgetry, director Sargent cleverly plays up the thriller element in which Colossus, like *2001*'s HAL, becomes a central character. Even the comic interlude in which Colossus, like a son, measures its father (the strength of Braeden's drinks and the manner of his lovemaking with Clark) is relatively successful.

d Joseph Sargent   *p* Stanley Chase   *s* James Bridges
c Gene Polito   *se* Albert Whitlock   *lp* Eric Braeden, Susan Clark, Gordon Pinsent, William Schallert, Leonid Rostoff, George Stanford Brown

Frankenstein Must Be Destroyed
(HAMMER; GB)   97 min
This is the only one of Fisher's impressive series of Frankenstein films to end traditionally with the monster

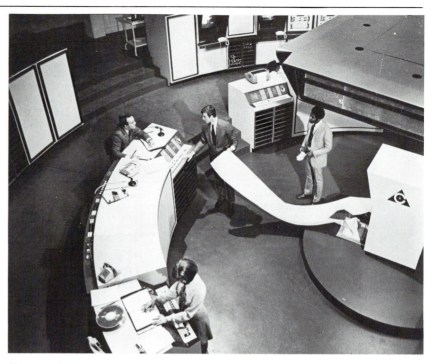

Feeding information to Colossus in The Forbin Project.

(Jones, who gives the most sympathetic portrait of the monster in its long screen history) returning to destroy its creator, Cushing. More significantly, the film marked the culmination of Fisher and Cushing's interpretation of Baron Frankenstein as a romantic rebel hemmed in by the restrictions of his time rather than the simple mad scientist of the Universal films of the thirties. Frankenstein's downfall, as always, is his unswerving search for knowledge but Batt's intelligent screenplay brings about that downfall, not through the Baron's pride but through the emotional and intellectual incomprehension of those who surround him. Thus the centre of the film is not the creation of the monster (which is truncated to a mere brain transplant) but the inability of Jones' 'monster' to live in his new body after his wife (Audley) has fled from terror at the familiar/unfamiliar sight of him.

The result, with its flamboyant details, a dead body sent shooting into the air as the result of a burst watermain, Jones desperately trying to explain the situation to his wife, is the most romantic version of the Frankenstein myth and one of Fisher's major works.

d Terence Fisher   *p* Anthony Nelson Keys   *s* Bert Batt
c Arthur Grant   *lp* Peter Cushing, Veronica Carlson, Simon Ward, Freddie Jones, Thorley Walters, Maxine Audley

Gamera Tai Guiron *aka* Gamera Versus Guiron *aka* Attack of the Monsters   (DAIEI; JAP)   scope   88 min
By this time, Yuasa's series of Gamera movies, which had started with **Daikaiju Gamera** and **Gamera Tai Barugon** (both 1966) had established him as the most prolific Kaiju Eiga director, next to Toho's Honda who contributed more than 20 titles. This fifth instalment has Gamera once more rescuing the world through his devotion to children, saving them from the enemy monster. On a planet on the other side of the Sun, the kiddie-loving turtle fights the knife-headed Guiron to release two children from the clutches of the beautiful women aliens whose speciality is eating people's brains. The film appears to be marking time, as do all the other monster movies of the period, merely repeating hollow patterns. Pollution did not emerge as the new central, cohesive theme until **Gojira Tai Hedora** (1971).

d Noriyaki Yuasa   *p* Hidemasa Nagata   *s* Fumi Takahashi
c Akira Kitazaki   *se* Kazafum Fujii   *lp* Nobuhiro Kashima, Christopher Murphy, Miyuki Akiyama, Yuko Hamada, Eiji Funakoshi, Kon Omura

Gladiatorerna *aka* The Peace Game *aka* The Gladiators

(SANDREWS; SW)   105(91) min

An uneven follow-up to Watkins' famous TV pseudo-documentary **The War Game** (1965), which was banned by the BBC, *Gladiatorerna* substitutes for the moral outrage of that film a clumsy collection of clichés that wouldn't be out of place in a routine Hollywood B production. Thus at one moment in the games a British general tells his Chinese counterpart: 'In our country we always let the away team kick off first.' The film is set in the near future where war has been reduced to a gladiatorial contest between different teams, each representing one of the nations of the world, in the annual Peace Games. In the midst of a contest between China and the West a student tries to disrupt the games and so prove they are being used to control the world's population, but the inconsequential and confused plot deprives the film of any argument Watkins presumably intended to raise.

d/co-s Peter Watkins   *p* Göran Lindgren   *co-s* Nicholas Gosling   *c* Peter Suschitzky   *se* Stig Lindberg   *lp* Arthur Pentelow, Frederick Danner, Kenneth Lo, Björn Franzen, Hans Bendrik, Tim Yum

Ido Zero Daisakusen *aka* Latitude Zero

(TOHO; JAP)   scope   106(95) min

This absurd film, loosely modelled on Jules Verne's novels about the exploits of Captain Nemo, takes for its central premise the idea of a colony of scientists living on the bottom of the ocean floor to which they've been ferried by a seemingly ageless Cotten in his 1805-built *Nautilus* lookalike, *Alpha*. Japanese oceanographer Takarada, physicist Okada and journalist Jaeckel are rescued by Cotten and taken to the scientific colony when their bathesphere is injured in an underwater volcano explosion. There they do battle with a

cheerfully evil Romero (who gives the film's best performance) before he's killed by one of his more bizarre creations, a flying lion with the brain of his former mistress. The film's charm is sadly punctured by its inept special effects.

d Inoshiro Honda   *s* Shinichi Sekizawa, Ted Sherdeman   *c* Taiichi Kankura   *se* Eiji Tsuburaya   *lp* Joseph Cotten, Cesar Romero, Akira Takarada, Richard Jaeckel, Masumi Okada, Patricia Medina

Az Idoe Ablakaj *aka* The Windows of Time

(STUDIO 4-MAFILM; HUN)   85 min

The first Hungarian Science Fiction feature since **Leleklato Sugar** (1918). Unlike Western films that use cryogenics or hibernation for the purposes of space travel (**Alien**, 1979) or horror (*Die Schlangengrube und das Pendel*, 1967), Eastern European films tend to use projection into the future as a device to comment on the present and the political or moral options available to us now (as in **Muz z Prvniho Stoleti**, 1961). In Fejer's film, five people wake up, after a period of hibernation, in the distant future. Eva (Tyszkiewicz) was a famous singer whose husband committed suicide; Beryl (Wenzel) had horrible concentration camp experiences; Maguy (Mikolajewska) has an incurable disease contracted during the first quark war; Avram (Andonov) wanted to find out whether his pioneering theory of quarks would prove correct and Sinis (Gabor) turns out to have been the President who ordered the dropping of the quark bombs that destroyed the world. All had a reason for wanting to be put in hibernation and when they wake up, the problem is to establish to what extent each was complicit in causing the cataclysmic war. Each protagonist is played by someone from a different nationality. Tyszkiewicz is the very beautiful Polish star of some W. Has films including *The Saragossa Manuscript* (1964); Andonov is a well-known Bulgarian director/actor; the others are German, Russian and Hungarian. Sadly, although it's impressively photographed, the direction can't overcome the slow and unimaginatively constructed script.

d Tamas Fejer   *s* Peter Kuczka   *c* Miklos Herczenik   *lp* Beata Tyszkiewicz, Ian Andonov, Krystina Mikolajewska, Heidemarie Wenzel, Miklos Gabor

The Love Bug   (WALT DISNEY)   107 min

The first in a series of films devoted to Herbie, the Volkswagen Beetle with a mind of its own, *The Love Bug* was the most successful live action film of the Disney studios for some years. Directed with gusto by Stevenson, the film is a judicious mix of farce, wild chases and special effects. If the coating is undeniably sugary, the principals (Jones, Lee, Tomlinson and Hackett) go at their material with a glee that is charming. Jones is the unsuccessful racing driver and Lee his scatterbrained girlfriend who discovers the beat-up Beetle he's bought has magical powers. Similarly, Tomlinson as the personification of greed is quite superb.

Several sequels followed, including **Herbie Rides Again** (1974) and **Herbie Goes to Monte Carlo** (1977), while in Germany *The Love Bug*'s success encouraged Rudolph Zehetgruber to produce a vastly inferior four-strong series devoted to the antics of a Beetle called Dudu, beginning with **Ein Kaefer Geht aufs Ganze** (1971).

d Robert Stevenson   *p/co-s* Bill Walsh   *co-s* Don Da Gradi   *c* Edward Colman   *se* Eustace Lycett, Alan Mayley, Peter Ellenshaw   *lp* Dean Jones, Michele Lee, David Tomlinson, Buddy Hackett, Joe Flynn, Benson Fong

Manden Der Taenkte Ting *aka* The Man Who Thought Life   (ASA FILM; DEN)   b/w   96 min

One of the few Danish Science Fiction films since **Himmelskibet** (1917). Steinmetz (Price) makes things materialize through mental power. With the help of a surgeon (Neergaard), he wants to create an artificial human being through thought. When the surgeon refuses, Steinmetz 'thinks' a duplicate of the surgeon who gradually takes the place of the original one. Shot in starkly contrasted black and white, neither script nor direction ever overcome the problem that there isn't much excitement in showing a man who sits somewhere thinking. The art direction by Helge Refn and the photographic techniques provide the main points of interest.

d/co-s Jens Ravn   *co-s* Henrik Stangerup   *c* Witold Leszczynski   *lp* Preben Neergaard, John Price, Lotte Tarp

Marooned
(FRANKOVICH-STURGES PRODUCTIONS)   pv70   133 min

Like so many Science Fiction films of the sixties (and later) this film suffers from too much effort being spent on special effects and technical gadgetry, to convince us of the plausibility of its situation – the rescue of astronauts marooned in space by a joint Russian-American expedition – and not enough on the dramatics of the situation. Accordingly, the almost documentary approach of Sturges (a director far more

Terence Stamp in the title role of The Mind of Mr Soames.

at home on the plains of the old West than in the void of space) is completely at odds with the clichéd storyline in which events like Crenna's suicide (that his companions might live) are presented in such a melodramatic fashion as to be laughable. Peck, as the head of Mission Control, Hackman and Janssen (the pilot of the American rescue ship) turn in personable performances, but to no avail.

d John Sturges   *p* M.J. Frankovich   *s* Mayo Simon   *c* Daniel Fapp   *se* Lawrence W. Butler, Donald C. Glouner, Robbie Robertson   *lp* Gregory Peck, Richard Crenna, David Janssen, Gene Hackman, James Franciscus, Lee Grant

The Mind of Mr Soames   (AMICUS; GB)   98 min

Based on the novel by Charles Eric Maine (who'd had **Spaceways**, 1953 and **Escapement**, 1957 made from earlier novels of his) this is an intelligent Science Fiction thriller. Stamp plays Mr Soames, the innocent 30-year-old released from a coma by Vaughn's surgeon. After only an elementary education, he escapes into the terrifying outside world where like the hero of **Charly** (1988) his childish manner provokes instant hostility. The second half of the film is less successful. Stamp's descent into violence is coupled with his being seen by the script as a clichéd victim figure, exploited by the mass media.

d Alan Cooke   *p* Max J. Rosenberg, Milton Subotsky   *s* John Hale, Edward Simpson   *c* Billy Williams   *lp* Terence Stamp, Robert Vaughn, Nigel Davenport, Donal Donnelly, Christian Roberts, Judy Parfitt

Moon Zero Two   (HAMMER; GB)   100 min

This Science Fiction western, the first of a string of such films that includes **Battle Beyond the Stars** (1980), an unofficial remake of *The Magnificent Seven* (1960), and **Outland** (1981), which was closely modelled upon *High Noon* (1952), is a decidedly juvenile affair. Olson is the lone gunslinger, once remembered as the first man to set foot on Mars, Schell the girl in distress and Mitchell the claim-jumping Moon magnate of a villain whose plans they scupper. The only new wrinkle in the formula-ridden plot is Corri's all to brief role as the female sheriff gunned down by Bresslaw's heavy.

d Roy Ward Baker   *p/s* Michael Carreras   *c* Paul Beeson   *se* Kit West, Nick Allder, Les Bowie   *lp* James Olson, Catherina von Schell, Warren Mitchell, Adrienne Corri, Bernard Bresslaw, Dudley Foster

Left: Marooned, John Sturges' lightweight space opera.

Right: *George Lazenby in his only outing as James Bond,* On Her Majesty's Secret Service.

The Most Dangerous Man in the World *aka* The Chairman (APJAC/FOX) pv 99 min

Peck is the Nobel prizewinner who visits China in order to steal from his former teacher the formula for a new enzyme that will enable crops to be grown anywhere in this weak spy-thriller which borrows its central plot device from Hitchcock's *Torn Curtain* (1966) and its gadgetry (Peck has a transmitter and an explosive device implanted in his skull) from James Bond. Sadly, Thompson quickly forsakes the possible moral dimension of his storyline in favour of Bond heroics. Indeed the cynicism of Peck's paymasters is so much taken for granted that it comes as no real surprise when the Red army, in a (then) highly topical climax, ride to Peck's rescue, 7th Cavalry style, in the final reel.

d J. Lee Thompson *p* Mort Abrahams *s* Ben Maddow *c* Ted Moore *lp* Gregory Peck, Anne Heywood, Arthur Hill, Conrad Yama, Alan Dobie, Francisca Tu

On Her Majesty's Secret Service

(EON PRODUCTIONS/DANILAQ; GB) pv 140 min

Though it grossed over $9 million in North America alone ($3 million more than **Doctor No**, 1962), this is undoubtedly the least interesting of the series of films devoted to Ian Fleming's superspy, James Bond. The film's failure was the result of two factors, the flaccid direction of Hunt, the editor of the earlier Bond films, and the lifeless characterization offered by Lazenby in the title role. In place of Sean Connery's menacing school bully (and later Roger Moore's debonnaire man about town) Lazenby offers little but good looks. Accordingly, with no centre to the film, the absurd and over-complex plot is revealed for what it is, the excuse for a collection of set-pieces in exotic locations supported by dialogue that was clichéd when it appeared in the serials of the thirties and forties. Savalas is Bloefeld, seeking world domination and a place in

Burke's peerage, by threatening to destroy the world's flora and fauna and Ferzetti (best remembered for his role as the railway magnate in *Once Upon a Time in the West*, 1968) the gangster who offers Lazenby assistance and his daughter (Rigg) in marriage. Even the film's ending which sees Lazenby and Rigg married after Savalas' plans have been foiled only for Rigg to be killed by gangsters in his pay seems no more than a last minute gimmick.

d Peter Hunt *p* Harry Saltzman, Albert R. Broccoli *s* Richard Maibaum *c* Michael Reed *se* John Stears *lp* George Lazenby, Diana Rigg, Telly Savalas, Gabriele Ferzetti, Ilse Steppat, Yuri Borienko

Moon Zero Two, *the first space opera western.*

Oru Kaiju Daishingeki *aka* **Godzilla's Revenge**
(TOHO; JAP) scope 92(70) min
The Honda-Tsuburaya team's last Godzilla film (the monster's tenth) is a sad occasion. The plot concerns a boy who dreams of going to monster island, having adventures and even conversing with the Godzillas, father and son. The sad part is that a good deal of the movie merely replays footage from **Nankai No Daiketto** (1966) and **Gojira No Musuko** (1967). With the death of Tsuburaya in 1970 and Honda's last major film, **Kessen Nankai No Daikaiju** (1970), an era had passed in the Japanese Kaiju Eiga, although many more monster movies would be made. At Toho, Fukuda took over from Honda, although the latter did return briefly with the impressively crafted **Mekagojira No Gyakushu** (1975), to celebrate 20 years of Godzilla films. The genre appeared to have run out of steam at this period, awaiting another 'issue' to take over from the nuclear war/US occupation concerns that had underpinned most of the fantasy scenarios of the previous 15 years' monster movies.

d Inoshiro Honda *p* Tomoyuki Tanaka *s* Shinichi Sekizawa *c* Mototaka Tomioka *se* Eiji Tsuburaya
lp Kenji Sahara, Tomonori Yazaki, Machiko Naka, Sachio Sakai, Chotaro Togin, Yoshibumi Tajima

Ruusujen Aika *aka* **Time of Roses**
(FILMINOR; FIN) b/w 106 min
The only Finnish Science Fiction feature on record. Set in the 21st century, in a Finland that considers itself egalitarian, humane and democratic, a researcher in the official history department (Tuominen) prepares a TV programme documenting the life of a shopgirl (Vepsa) who committed suicide in 1976. The film then concentrates on showing what today may look like to a well-meaning media liberal 50 years hence. As the researcher begins to mix up the past and the present – his current girlfriend is also played by Vepsa – the film shifts into another gear as the main theme becomes the power of the media to shape our understanding of the world we live in and its history: we have no option but to experience life through falsifying representations selected by media hacks. Well acted, scripted by Jarva's regular collaborators, the film is part of Jarva's continuing critical examination of contemporary Finland, and one of the few examples, together with **Der Grosse Verhau** (1970), of politically literate Science Fiction. Jarva can be regarded as the director who started off the Finnish 'new wave' with his film *Night and Day* (1962) and he continued to be that country's leading film-maker for two decades.

d/p/co-s Risto Jarva *co-s* Peter von Bagh, Jakko Pakkasvirta *c* Antti Peippo *se* Anssi Blomstedt, Erkki Kurenniemi *lp* Arto Tuominen, Ritva Vepsa, Tarja Markus, Eero Keskitalo, Kalle Holmberg, Eila Pelikonen, Unto Salminen

Santo en la Venganza de las Mujeres Vampiro *aka* **La Venganza de las Mujeres Vampiro** *aka* **The Vengeance of the Vampire Women** (CINEMATOGRAFICA FLAMA/
PELICULAS LATINOAMERICANAS; MEX) 90 min
A sequel of sorts to Alfonso Corona Blake's *Santo Contra las Mujeres Vampiro* (1962). Here the Silver Masked wrestler is confronted by Mayra (Romand), a female vampire who has gathered an army of fellow creatures of both sexes to destroy the bulky and presumably blood-rich wrestler. According to Mayra, Santo is the last descendant of the man who destroyed her ancestors in 1630 in Transylvania. She is assisted by Dr Brancor (Junco), the man who revived her and also manages to create a synthetic person made from bits of corpses. The direction by Curiel is routine, but is is worth noting that by this time the Santo series had become a decidedly 'adult' entertainment with lots of sex and sadism, a long way from the initial conception of the masked wrestler on the model of

Oru Kaiju Daishingeki, *one of the worst of the Godzilla series.*

the Phantom, the popular American comic-strip hero. As usual, the credits do not give the name of the actor playing the role of the beefy wrestler, but it is likely to have been Eric del Castillo, the man who played the part in **Santo Contra la Hija de Frankenstein** (1971).

d Federico Curiel *p/co-s* Jose Garcia Besne
co-s Fernando Oses *c* Jose Ortiz Ramos *lp* Santo, Aldo Monti, Norma Lazareno, Gina Romand, Victor Junco, Patricia Ferrer, Carlos Suarez, Alfonso Munguia, Yolanda Ponce, Fernando Oses

Scream and Scream Again (AIP/AMICUS; GB) 95 min
A chilling film, though it was ridiculed at the time of its release (primarily for its silly title), *Scream and Scream Again* is now widely acknowledged as being one of the best Science Fiction films made in Britain. The chase sequence in which Gothard (a humanoid created by Price as part of his plans for a new super-race) is cornered by the police after a murder, escapes and after a lengthy car chase is captured again only to break free – he tears his handcuffed arm off – before plunging into a vat of acid, has been justly celebrated as a directorial *tour de force*. Nevertheless, the fragmented structure of the film which creates a world in which paranoia is a natural reaction is equally impressive. From the film's disorienting opening, a man in bed gazing with horror at his limbless trunk, Wicking's superb script masterfully juggles the strands of his story: Price's clinic whose patients provide assorted limbs for the super-race; Jones as the representative of an East European state planning to conquer Britain by substituting the supermen for members of the government; the solid, comfortable world of the British police investigating what at first seems to be merely a bizarre series of murders. The film's marvellous climax is similar in tone to that of **Invasion of the Body Snatchers** (1956): Lee's head of the secret service (a superman) stops the investigation (the death of Price and Jones providing a solution to the affair) proceeding any further, to the ironic relief of the police.

d Gordon Hessler *p* Max J. Rosenberg, Milton Subotsky
s Christopher Wicking *c* John Coquillon *lp* Vincent Price, Christopher Lee, Peter Cushing, Michael Gothard, Marshall Jones, Alfred Marks

Il Seme dell'Uomo *aka* **The Seed of Man**
(POLIFILM; IT) 114(101) min
Ferreri's grotesquely misogynist fantasies about men's loss of control over women and over life in general has produced

many confused and objectionable but nevertheless memorable movies, such as *Dillinger Is Dead* (1969), *La Grande Bouffe* (1973) and *Why? Why Not?* (1978). The fear of impotence and castration, graphically portrayed in *The Last Woman* (1976), here takes on a global dimension, elevating an adolescent anxiety into a cosmic fear of the end of the world. A succession of catastrophes and epidemics destroy civilization as we witness, on TV monitors, the end of London and the Pope's death. Two survivors, Ciro (Margine) and Dora (Wiazemsky) live in a house by a deserted beach. They collect objects for their makeshift museum of 'past civilization'. He wants a son. She refuses on the grounds that it is pointless and that they do not have the right to inflict that world on a new human being. Some horsemen, also survivors, come along and, taking the role of 'the authorities', order them to procreate. In the face of Dora's stubbornly rational refusal, Ciro drugs her and rapes her in her sleep. The pregnancy, however, is terminated as both are accidentally blown up. As an anticipation of the destruction of the world and what may happen afterwards if anybody is left alive, the film is absurd rather than tragic or grotesque. However, as a projection of male anxieties into a concretized dreamworld, the film achieves a poignancy and sadness, underlining the ludicrous mismatch of an apocalyptic vision that turns out to be merely a deep-seated fear of women as sexual beings. But taken on this level, the film does succeed in presenting uncanny, almost surreal, imagery laced with a coolly sardonic humour.

d/co-s Marco Ferreri *p* Roberto Giussani *co-s* Sergio Bazzini *c* Mario Vulpiani *lp* Anne Wiazemsky, Marco Margine, Annie Girardot, Rada Rassimov, Maria Teresa Piaggio, Angela Pagano, Deanna Frosini

Some Girls Do

(ASHDOWN FILM PRODUCTIONS; GB) 93 min
A sequel to *Deadlier Than the Male* (1967), this lacklustre outing pits Johnson's Bulldog Drummond, a pale imitation of Sean Connery's James Bond let alone Sapper's original character on whom he's theoretically based, against his old enemy Carl Peterson (here Villiers who at one point, highly inappropriately, appears dressed up as the Duke of Wellington). The plot, which is as confused as the numerous mini-skirted would-be assassins who are forever making attempts on Drummond's life, centres on Peterson's attempt to destroy a new British supersonic aircraft.

d Ralph Thomas *p* Betty E. Box *s* David Osborn, Liz Charles-Williams *c* Ernest Steward *se* Kit West
lp Richard Johnson, Daliah Lavi, Beba Loncar, James Villiers, Sydne Rome, Robert Morley

Vincent Price operates in Scream and Scream Again.

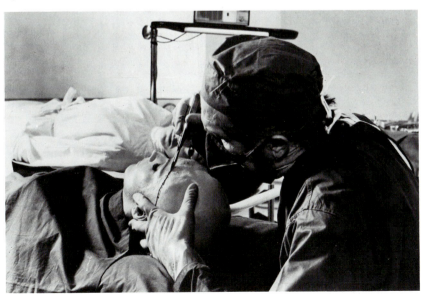

Stereo

(EMERGENT FILMS; CAN) b/w 65 min
The directorial début of Cronenberg, *Stereo* introduces the themes of voyeurism, a vengeful (almost puritanical) view of sexuality and an interest in telepathy that dominate his subsequent films, notably, **The Parasite Murders** (1974) and **Scanners** (1980). In the near future, a group of youngsters volunteer for an experiment to be conducted under the auspices of the Canadian Academy for Erotic Enquiry to attempt to break down conventional repressions and expose sexuality for what it is, a sort of 'polymorphus perversity'. To this effect the volunteers submit to surgery to remove their power of speech and increase any latent telepathic powers they may have. The resulting film is confused but disturbing in the manner of the more assured *The Parasite Murders*.

d/p/s/c David Cronenberg *lp* Ronald Mlodzik, Iain Ewing. Jack Messinger, Clara Mayer, Paul Mulholland, Arlene Mlodzik

Le Temps de Mourir *aka* Twice Upon a Time

(FILMS DE LA LICORNE/FILMSKY; FR) 92(90) min
This French futuristic thriller stars Karina as the mysterious girl who brings Cremer's banker a video of his own death and Rochefort as the man who unwittingly kills Cremer as foretold in the video. Though the film won a special prize at Trieste in 1970, Farwagi's direction is bland, making little of the play of time and space his script explores. Of the principals only Karina (adopting the little girl lost persona she first put to use in the films of Jean-Luc Godard) and Rochefort as the bewildered killer bring any conviction to their parts.

d/p/co-s André Farwagi *co-s* Alain Morineau *c* Willy Kurant *lp* Anna Karina, Bruno Cremer, Jean Rochefort, Billy Kearns, Catherine Rich, Daniel Moosman

When Dinosaurs Ruled the Earth

(HAMMER; GB) 100 min
Sadly only an echo of what might have been – Hammer commissioned a treatment from J.G. Ballard, one of Britain's foremost Science Fiction writers and then allowed director Guest to re-write it so that most of the highly original ideas were left out – this remains, nonetheless, the best of Hammer's cycle of exotic films set in prehistoric times that began with *One Million Years B.C.* (1964). Ballard's original treatment sought to explain the creation of the Moon as part of a violent cosmic upheaval, but in Guest's hands the cataclysmic events are merely excuses for placing his bikini-clad prehistoric women in a series of threatening situations. Vetri and Hawdon are the star-crossed lovers who survive their hostile environment (at one point courtesy of a dinosaur that fosters Vetri!) and persecution by the chief of Vetri's tribe, Allen.

d/s Val Guest *p* Aida Young *c* Dick Bush
se Jim Danforth, Allan Bryce, Roger Dicken, Brian Johncock *lp* Victoria Vetri, Robin Hawdon, Patrick Allen, Drewe Henley, Imogen Hassall, Sean Caffrey

Zeta One

(TIGON BRITISH; GB) 82 min
Adapted from a comic strip in the short-lived *Zeta* magazine, this is a piece of soft-core Science Fiction pornography. Set against a minimum of backdrops, secret agent Hawdon recounts to his fellow poker players the events of his last mission in which he foiled the plans of the Angvians (an extra-terrestrial race of super-women) in their attempts to take over Earth. The film is filled with soft-core sex couplings which have little relevance to the storyline. Among the (surprised) actors are Robertson Justice, Hawtrey and Addams.

d/co-s Michael Cort *p* George Maynard *co-s* Alastair McKenzie *c* Jack Atchelor *lp* Robin Hawdon, Yutte Stensgaard, James Robertson Justice, Charles Hawtrey, Dawn Addams, Lionel Murton

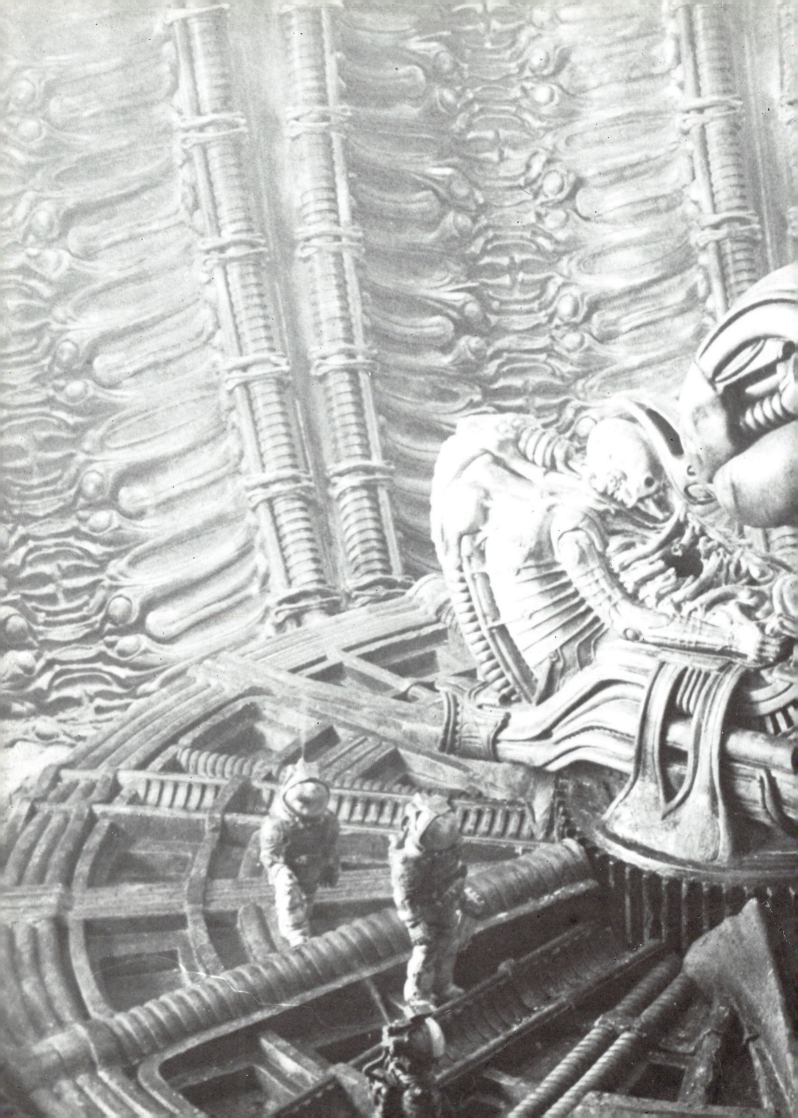

The
1970s

The Seventies

Big Budgets and Big Bucks

The Science Fiction film entered the seventies in a healthier state than at any time in its past. The success of films like **Barbarella** (1967), **2001 – A Space Odyssey** and **Planet of the Apes** (both 1968) made the genre attractive to producers. Equally significant, however, at a time when the costs of movie-making were spiralling and the number of films being made in Hollywood was falling almost as fast as cinema attendances, Science Fiction fulfilled one important criterion for film producers. They could see what the money was being spent on: special effects. Thus, ironically, the very high costs of special effects which in the past had militated against Science Fiction became a point in its favour in an era when big budgets became the norm of mainstream film production. Accordingly, throughout the decade those films requiring extensive special effects – disaster and, especially, Science Fiction films – were suddenly pushed to the fore. These big budgets were not necessarily beneficial. Films like **Earth II** (1971), **Slaughterhouse-Five** (1972), **Rollerball** (1975) and **Logan's Run** (1976) are all examples of films in which all the creative energy seems to have emanated from the special effect's department.

The climax of this trend was the series of mega-hits of the late seventies, **Star Wars, Close Encounters of the Third Kind** (both 1977), **Superman – The Movie** (1978) and **Star Trek – The Motion Picture** (1979). These same movies also testified to a radical shift in the tone of the Science Fiction film from the bittersweet questioning of tendencies within modern society to an unabashed celebration of escapism, gee-whizz heroics and innocence. With few exceptions and only in Europe, in films like **Der Grosse Verhau** (1970), **A Clockwork Orange** (1971), **The Man Who Fell to Earth** (1976) and **Stalker** (1979), did Science Fiction retain the questioning attitude which had made it such a forceful genre in the past.

The other notable trends of the period were the upsurge of sexploitation Science Fiction, of which **Flesh Gordon** (1974) is the best example, and the revenge-of-nature cycle of films which produced such oddities as **Night of the Lepus** (1972). In part both these trends reflected the wholesale upsurge of the exploitation film (for example **The Cars That Ate Paris,** 1974, and **Death Race 2000,** 1975) and climaxed at the end of the decade when Roger Corman financed a *Star Wars* lookalike, **Battle Beyond the Stars** (1980) at a cost which would have paid for virtually all his productions of the fifties.

In retrospect what is remarkable about Science Fiction in the seventies is that so many of the decade's best films – **Glen and Randa** (1971), **It's Alive** (1973), **Dark Star** (1974) and **Blue Sunshine** (1977) – were oddball films, out of synch with their times and as often as not financed independently. By the same token, with the obvious exception of *Close Encounters of the Third Kind* and *Star Wars*, the mega-hits of the decade were far less interesting as examples of the possibilities of the genre and, as their phenomenal success confirms, far more interesting as examples of the new Hollywood at work.

The Andromeda Strain

(U/ROBERT WISE PRODUCTIONS) pv 131 min

Based on the best-selling novel by Michael Crichton, this film shares many of the preoccupations of **Westworld** (1973) which Crichton himself wrote and directed. Gidding's screenplay, which is very faithful to the novel, follows a government research team that is trying to isolate and destroy an alien micro-organism that arrives on Earth on board a space satellite that crashed in New Mexico. Wise, who termed the project 'science fact' (rather than fiction), spent most of his $6.5 million budget on making believable both the massive Wildfire Research Establishment and the attempts by the scientists (Olson, Hill, Wayne and Reid) to stop the alien micro-organism spreading. Ironically, however, it is the opening and closing sequences, the retrieval of the two living humans from the ghost town in New Mexico, shot to look like another but eerily familiar world, and Olson's attempt to defuse the research centre's fail-safe system when the organism has mutated into a benign strain on its own, that are the most successful. Thus, though Wise, with the capable assistance of Trumbull's special effects, holds true to the central vision of Crichton's novel, that technology must not be trusted, much of the irony of the story, the organism mutating on its own and the research team's sudden new task of defeating their own computers if they are to survive, is lost through Wise's visual commitment to technology.

Previous pages: *Science Fiction in the seventies: big bucks and big budgets* – Alien *(1979).*

George Mitchell (with meat cleaver) attacks his would-be rescuer in Robert Wise's The Andromeda Strain.

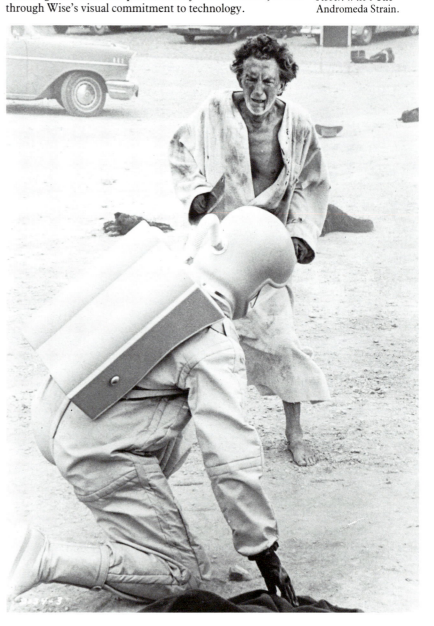

Right: City Beneath the Sea, *one of the silliest of Irwin Allen's many disaster films.*

Right: City Beneath the Sea, *one of the silliest of Irwin Allen's many disaster films.*

d/p Robert Wise   *s* Nelson Gidding   *c* Richard H. Kline   *se* Douglas Trumbull, James Shourt   *lp* Arthur Hill, David Wayne, James Olson, Kate Reid, Paula Kelly, George Mitchell

Blood of Frankenstein

(INDEPENDENT – INTERNATIONAL)   91 min

Boasting a guest appearance by Forrest J. Ackerman, a noted Science Fiction collector and historian, a story which begins with Chaney's 'Groton the mad zombie' decapitating a girl and a plot which features Naish's Frankenstein running a museum of horror from his wheelchair, *Blood of Frankenstein* is a gleeful film, not least for the way in which Pugsley and Sherman's script stumbles cheerfully from corpse to corpse. Carrol is the sister of the decapitated girl who, with assistance from Eisley, ends the complex plans of revenge Frankenstein and Vorkov's Dracula set in motion. Adamson, one of the most active directors of exploitation quickies of the seventies, directs with crude vigour.

d/co-p Al Adamson   *co-p* John Vandom   *s* William Pugsley, Samuel M. Sherman   *c* Gary Graver, Paul Glickman   *lp* J. Carroll Naish, Lon Chaney Jnr, Regina Carrol, John Bloom, Anthony Eisley, Zandor Vorkov

City Beneath the Sea *aka* One Hour to Doomsday

(KENT PRODUCTIONS/MOTION PICTURES INTERNATIONAL)   120 (93) min

This silly concoction from Allen, who subsequently specialized in 'disaster' films, unsurely melds together the possibility of the destruction of the Earth (a planetoid is on collision course with Earth) with an attempted hijack of American gold reserves from the underwater city they are transferred to for safekeeping (!). Whitman is the admiral in charge of the underwater city who deflects the planetoid by firing missiles at it and in his spare time puts paid to the attempts by his brother (Wagner) to steal the gold.

d/p Irwin Allen   *s* John Meredyth Lucas   *c* Kenneth Peach   *se* L.B. Abbott, John C. Caldwell   *lp* Stuart Whitman, Robert Wagner, Rosemary Forsyth, Robert Colbert, Richard Basehart, Joseph Cotten

Crimes of the Future   (CRONENBERG; CAN)   b/w   65 min

A follow-up and close companion piece to **Stereo** (1969), Croneberg's second cross-over movie from the Canadian 'underground', perhaps predictably, mirrors and magnifies its predecessor's audacity in terms of quirky, visceral aesthetics and conceptual focus, though its seminal status as a cornerstone of the unique Cronenberg *oeuvre* up to and including **Videodrome** (1982) has only become apparent in retrospect. Characteristically working with matters of genetic engineering and the scientific shortcircuiting of evolution, Cronenberg here presents us with a world where deadly cosmetics have wiped out all post-pubertal females and are responsible for mutating men back towards primeval stages of the species' biological development; and where Antoine Rouge, the mad dermatologist who has lent his name to the malignant epidemic malady, may just have been reincarnated in the body of a young girl. The plot's eccentric twists spring from the disparity (seen as inevitable by Cronenberg) between abstract theory and the unintended effects of experimental practice: a split visualized neatly in the fact that all the radically 'inefficient' institutions of genetic and psychic production are housed in showcases of architectural sterility. As the academics of the House of Skin, led by Rouge's disciple Adrian Tripod (Mlodzik), struggle to come to terms with new mysteries of the organism (and in some cases, new organs), high on the list of the future's potential crimes appears paedophilia for procreation. A stylized, balletic acting mode and a disembodied soundtrack mixing marine-life sounds with meaningless technological babble add to both the blacker-than-black humour and the sense of a microcosmic world viewed with perverse scientific detachment.

d/p/s/c David Cronenberg   *lp* Ronald Mlodzik, Jon Lidolt, Tania Zolty, Jack Messinger, Paul Mulholland, William Haslam, Willem Poolman

Egghead's Robot
(INTERFILM/FILM PRODUCERS' GUILD/
CHILDREN'S FILM FOUNDATION; GB)   56 min
Chegwin is the egghead of the title who programs a robot (wittily played by his brother, Jeffrey), invented by his father (Wattis) to double for him in situations where brawn rather than brain is required. The result is a jolly, juvenile piece of Science Fiction and one of the better productions sponsored by the Children's Film Foundation. Kinnear is the ill-tempered park keeper and butt of the Chegwins' jokes.

d Milo Lewis   *p* Cecil Musk   *s* Leif Saxon   *c* Johnny Coquillon   *lp* Keith Chegwin, Jeffrey Chegwin, Kathryn Dawe, Roy Kinnear, Richard Wattis, Patricia Routledge

Gamera Tai Daimaju Jaiga *aka* Gamera Versus Jiger *aka* Gamera Versus Monster X *aka* Monsters Invade Expo 70
(DAIEI; JAP)   scope   83 min
The giant turtle's sixth film, again directed by Yuasa who established Gamera as Daiei's answer to Toho's Godzilla and a firm favourite on the children and teenage markets as it defended Japan from one monstrous attacker after another. In this one, the iguana-like Jiger, released from beneath a talismanic statue removed from its sacred site to figure in the world exhibition, threatens to invade Expo 70. In the fight between Gamera and the uninvited visitor, Gamera's breast is pierced by Jiger's tail. The bad monster then proceeds to lay an egg in the wound. The egg hatches inside Gamera's body and a little Jiger sucks his host's blood, draining the children's hero. Two kids use a mini-submarine to penetrate into the turtle's veins, identify the parasitical monster and effect a cure, after which the restored Gamera eliminates Jiger in time for Expo 70 to open without further mishap. The result is a routine film with mawkish children combining Science Fiction with rather more melodrama than usual, although the idea of introducing one monster into another one is an interesting gimmick, allowing for an adaptation of the **Fantastic Voyage** (1966) theme to the Kaiju Eiga.

d Noriyaki Yuasa   *p* Hidemasu Nagata   *s* Fumi Takahashi   *c* Akira Kitazaki   *lp* Tsutomu Takakuwa, Kelly Varis, Katherine Murphy, Kon Omura, Junko Yashiro

Gas-s-s-s, Or It Became Necessary to Destroy the World in Order to Save It *aka* Gas! Or It Became Necessary to Destroy the World in Order to Save It
(SAN JACINTO/AIP)   79 (77) min
This sprawling film, confused and confusing, was made by Corman after two decades of making films to specific briefs and bringing them in on schedule. The result is a personal film, one full of references back to his previous work, which terminated his long-standing relationship with AIP (who thoroughly disliked it) and led to Corman setting up his own production (and later distribution) company, New World Pictures. Accordingly, it's tempting to see this indulgent offering and his last film, *The Red Baron* (1970) as Corman's envoi, if not to the cinema, then to directing; he hasn't directed a film since.

Much influenced, like **Wild in the Streets** (1968), by notions of an alternative society, Armitage's script (written in close collaboration with Corman) follows the travels of Corff and Giftos who, after a poisonous gas has killed off everyone over the age of 25 (only to have the under-25s immediately resume the political squabbling of their elders), head out for the desert. Guided by a mysterious Edgar Allan Poe figure (complete with raven), they meet a grotesque collection of characters as they search for a hippy commune and freedom in New Mexico. What makes the film so exhilarating is Corman's playful transformations (in which Hells Angels become the conservative guardians of the golf links, for example) and his willingness to parody his material as he goes. If the resulting film is too excessive to be accessible, in the process Corman produces a welter of vignettes that never fail to amuse.

d/p Roger Corman   *s* George Armitage   *c* Ron Dexter
lp Robert Corff, Elaine Giftos, Pat Patterson, George Armitage, Alex Wilson, Alan Braunstein

Der Grosse Verhau *aka* The Big Mess
(KAIROS FILM; WG)   b/w and col   86 min
Besides being a withering critique of the costly pretentiousness of **2001 – A Space Odyssey** (1968), Kluge's film is also a straightfaced comedy, unique in the genre because instead of focusing on adventure or individual heroics, it provides an uncommonly intelligent picture of the type of society we will have in 2034 if current trends are allowed to continue unchecked. The Milky Way is in a mess. After seven failed galactic revolutions and six lost wars, the Suez Canal Company is in total control of all means of transport and communication and, therefore, of all commerce and, consequently, of the social order. Some small entrepreneurs still work the more dangerous trade routes with aged spaceships and a few smugglers do good business wrecking other spaceships and selling them for scrap or making deals with insurance companies. Everybody is at war, the sharpest form of competition, with everyone else, but on the terms of the monopoly, which is also planning intergalactic military campaigns to acquire more raw materials and power. The film is marvellously acted, especially by Graue whose idiosyncratic way of rolling and biting the sounds of the German language is

Below: *Edgar Allan Poe and his Eleanore complete with raven and modern transport in Roger Corman's introspective masterpiece* Gas-s-s-s, Or It Became Necessary to Destroy the World in Order to Save It.

Peter Cushing in I, Monster, *Stephen Weeks' bravura re-working of Robert Louis Stevenson's oft-filmed classic tale,* Dr Jekyll and Mr Hyde.

dying scientist, Hauser, in an effort to retain the scientific secrets he hasn't yet written down, and who discovers that along with scientific information come the ghosts of the dead man's life. Siodmak's contrasting of Nazi Germany (Hauser was a committed Nazi) with the present (McCallum is an apolitical Jewish intellectual) is somewhat melodramatized by writer Spies and director Sagal. Thus, the conclusion, which sees McCallum reject Hauser's wife (Palmer), who has remained a loyal Nazi, and set off in search of the SS guard who punished Hauser for his defection from the Nazi party, is little but a petty act of vengeance.

Nonetheless, the initial perplexity that McCallum feels as Hauser's memories flood over him, disturbing his grip on his own life, is well captured. Strasberg, as McCallum's wife, and Webber, as his boss, provide strong support. The film won the Golden Asteroid at Trieste in 1971.

d Boris Sagal *p* Jack Laird *s* Adrian Spies *c* Petrus Schloemp *lp* David McCallum, Susan Strasberg, Lili Palmer, Leslie Nielsen, Helmut Kautner, Herbert Fleischmann, Hans Elwenspoek

La Horriplante Bestia Humana *aka* Night of the Bloody Apes (UNISTAR; MEX) 82 (81) min

Directed with quaint disregard for continuity by Cardona (who is best known for his exploitation quickie, *Survive*, 1976), this is a strange melding of the Frankenstein theme – Moreno transplants a gorilla's heart into his dying son (Silvestre) only to have him mutate into an ape – and the wrestler films that were a speciality of the Mexican cinema. Here the wrestler, in an unusual twist, is the much-threatened, cat-suited heroine (Lazareno). A nice touch has Moreno, after he's recaptured Silvestre and replaced the gorilla's heart with a human one, lost him and recaptured him again, collapse from a heart attack and so once more the rapidly mutating Silvestre escapes before being shot.

d/co-s René Cardona *p* Alfredo Salazar *co-s* René Cardona Jnr *c* Raúl Martinez Solares *se* Javier Torres Torija *lp* José Elias Moreno, Carlos López Moctezuma, Armando Silvestre, Norma Lazareno, Agustín Martinez Solares

The Horror of Frankenstein

(HAMMER/EMI; GB) 95 min
Based on an early script by Sangster, this is a decidedly routine affair and compares unfavourably to Hammer's previous Frankenstein outing, Terence Fisher's magisterial **Frankenstein Must Be Destroyed** (1969). Sangster who scripted both **The Curse of Frankenstein** (1957) and **The Revenge of Frankenstein** (1958) here offers nothing more than a camp version of the Frankenstein legend, transforming Bates' Frankenstein from a man obsessed with the acquisition of knowledge into a sexual athlete who uses the monster to eliminate the witnesses to the various murders he commits. This demythologizing of Hammer's original conception and Sangster's listless direction only remind one of the power of Fisher's Frankenstein movies.

d/p/co-s Jimmy Sangster *co-s* Jeremy Burnham *c* Moray Grant *lp* Ralph Bates, Kate O'Mara, Graham James, Veronica Carlson, Dennis Price, Bernard Archard

I, Monster (AMICUS; GB) 75 min

Made on a minuscule budget, this film is notable for the stylistic bravura of Weeks (making his feature début) which brings some life to Subotsky's inept, yet faithful, adaptation of Robert Louis Stevenson's oft-filmed story, *Dr Jekyll and Mr Hyde*. Lee is the doctor and Cushing his solicitor suspicious of Lee's double identity.

d Stephen Weeks *co-p* Max J. Rosenberg *co-p/s* Milton Subotsky *c* Moray Grant *lp* Christopher Lee, Peter Cushing, Mike Raven, Richard Hurndall, George Merritt

perfect for conveying the image of an ordinary bully (Douglas, the trigger-happy auxiliary pilot, trained in the air force), whose brain processes more scientific information than Einstein ever dreamt of but whose intelligence is that of the normal 'company man'. This combination of extreme technological competence and stunted intelligence offers a telling portrait of technocratic officials (astro/cosmonauts and the like) in the making. The space technology used is the exact opposite of that idealized in *2001*: spaceships are computers housed in ramshackle contraptions that look as if they were designed by cowboy plumbers. At last a film that puts the space heroes in their place: neither robots nor adventurous geniuses but people who realize that the values of shady shopkeepers, administered by military and other bureaucrats of social control – people who are the slightly dim-witted but competent servants of a system that exploits and ultimately destroys them – are those that rule the world. In the meantime, life goes on...

d/p/co-s Alexander Kluge *co-s* Wolfgang Mai *c* Thomas Mauch, Alfred Tichawsky *se* Guenther Hoermann, Hannelore Hoger, Joachim Heimbucher *lp* Siegfried Graue, Vincenz Sterr, Maria Sterr, Silvia Forsthofer, Henrike Fuerst, Claus-Dieter Reents, Hajo von Zuendt, Hark Bohm

Hauser's Memory (U) 104 min

A telefilm released theatrically in Europe, this is based on the sequel to Curt Siodmak's thrice-filmed novel, *Donovan's Brain*. Like that novel, its theme is the takeover of a living person by a dead one. McCallum is the scientist who volunteers to receive an injection of fluid from the brain of a

L'Inafferrabile Invincible Mr Invisible *aka* **Mr Superinvisible** (EDO CINEMATOGRAFICA/PRODUCCIONES CINEMATOGRAFICA DIA/PETER CARSTEN PRODUKTION; IT,SP,WG) scope 93 (90) min

This unimaginative would-be Disney-like comedy thriller (hence the presence of Jones, a regular in Disney films, and the sheepdog) has invisibility as its tired gimmick. Jones is the scientist who thinks he's invented a new virus that could be used in germ warfare, promptly loses it and then after (mistakenly) drinking an invisibility potion retrieves it. De Isaura is the stylish villain and Schoener the plucky heroine.

d Anthony M. Dawson (Antonio Margheriti) *p* Peter Carsten *s* Mary Eller, Oscar Saul (Luis Marquina) *c* Allejandro Ulloa *lp* Dean Jones, Gastone Moschin, Ingeborg Schoener, Peter Carsten, Amalia de Isaura, Roberto Camardiel

The Incredible Two-Headed Transplant

(MUTUAL GENERAL CORPORATION/TRIDENT ENTERPRISES) 88 min

The presence of Dern as the ever-twitching mad scientist notwithstanding, this is a terrible, albeit intermittently funny, film. Directed by former editor Lanza at a breakneck pace, the film has Dern graft the head of a homicidal maniac (Cole), who unsuccessfully attacks Dern and his wife (Priest), onto a moron (Bloom). The two-headed monster predictably goes on the rampage (the film's worst sequences) before returning to Dern's ranch laboratory to menace Priest once more and once more be killed, this time in company with Dern.

d Anthony M. Lanza *p/co-s* John Lawrence *co-s* James Gordon White *c* John Steely, Glen Gano, Paul Hipp *se* Ray Dorn *lp* Bruce Dern, Pat Priest, Albert Cole, John Bloom, Casey Kasem, Berry Kroeger

Iron Bread (THAI) scope 80 min

This joyously iconoclastic anti-**Metropolis** (1926) was made by Peï, a Thai director who spent some time in France before returning to his country, with non-professional actors. The film starts with a world of robots at work, producing gadgets the only purpose of which is to keep the robots occupied in producing them. The automatons rebel and free themselves (with lots of parody images poking fun at the conventions of socialist realism and workers breaking their chains) in a luddite orgy of destruction. They then construct a new society geared towards pleasure rather than work. At the end of the movie, another rebellion is brewing: the revolution shall be permanent or it shall die. The film rushes from gag to gag anticipating the outrageously accurate exaggerations characteristic of the Monty Python sketches: a mad scientist mistakes a human for a robot in disguise and proceeds to dismember him to prove his point in spite of the screamed protests of the victim. Grotesque parody combined with an astute cinematic intelligence make *Iron Bread* a genuinely exuberant crazy comedy in the tradition of *The Extraordinary Adventures of Mr West in the Land of the Bolsheviks* (1924).

d/p/s Vivian Peï *c* To Kaminoki *lp* non-professionals

Junket 89

(BALFOUR FILMS/CHILDREN'S FILM FOUNDATION; GB) 56 min

Steeped in the tradition of Billy Bunter *et al* this is an engaging outing from the Children's Film Foundation, not least because it's so militantly English – it even features a guest appearance from cricketer Gary Sobers – at a time when British films were either American financed or firmly targeted on the American market. Thoroughly juvenile in conception, it stars Brassett as the Just William/Jennings lookalike schoolboy who first fixes up Wilson's experimental instant transportation machine with judiciously placed chewing gum and then sets off to distant parts. Plummer directs with his eyes on drama and comedy rather than sentiment.

d Peter Plummer *p* Carole K. Smith *s* David Ash *c* Tony Imi *lp* Stephen Brassett, John Blundell, Linda Robson, Richard Wilson, Mario Renzullo, Freddy Foote

Kessen Nankai No Daikaiju *aka* The Space Amoeba *aka* Yog-Monster from Space *aka* Nankai No Daikaiju

(TOHO; JAP) scope 84 (81) min

After **Kaiju Soshingeki** (1968), **Oru Kaiju Daishingeki** (1969) and the unexpectedly engaging return to the Atlantis myth with **Ido Zero Daisakusen** (1969), previously treated by Honda in **Kaitei Gunkan** (1964), Toho lost the services of Tsuburaya who died in 1970. The genre, however, had become tired, increasingly repeating the same hollow patterns rather than adapting to the changing preoccupations of its audiences. This film is no exception. It combines the 'monster island' idea (*Kaiju Soshingeki*, 1968) with the 'spaceship traverses a mist picking up an alien substance' device (**Yosei Gorasu**, 1962; **Kyuketsuki Gokemidoro**, 1968 and **Uchu Daikaiju Guilala**, 1967).

On the island, a group which includes a photographer (Takahashi), a reporter (Kubo) and an industrial spy (Sahara) are terrorized by Gezoras (giant squids), Ganimes (crabs) and Kamoebas (turtles) before Sahara is also taken over by the alien force that caused these creatures to develop. The alien thing had been brought to Earth by a spaceship that passed through a mysterious blue mist. Sahara and all his fellow monsters are destroyed by a volcano. The below-standard effects and less than impressive camerawork make the film a poor ending to Honda's career. He only made a brief return to directing to celebrate two decades of Godzilla movies with **Mekagojira No Gyakushu** (1975), a film which recaptures some of his old sparkle.

d Inoshiro Honda *p* Tomoyuki Tanaka, Fumio Tanaka *s* El Ogawa *c* Taiichi Kankura *se* Sadamasa Arikawa, Yoichi Manoda *lp* Akira Kubo, Atsuko Takahashi, Toshio Tsuchiya, Kenji Sahara, Noritake Saito, Yukihiko Kobayashi, Satoshi Nakamura, Yuko Sugihara

Na Komete *aka* On the Comet *aka* Hector Servadac's Ark (STUDIO BARRANDOV; CZECH) scope 88 min

The fourth of Zeman's expeditions into Verne territory (**Cesta do Praveku**, 1955; **Vynalez Zkazy**, 1958 and **Ukradena Vzducholod**, 1966). This film is an adaptation of Verne's novel *Hector Servadac*, published in 1877, and recounts an outlandish story, set in 1888, of how a piece of the Earth became a comet floating through space with all the

John Bloom and Albert Cole are The Incredible Two-Headed Transplant.

Nigel Davenport (right) leads his family in search of safety in Cornel Wilde's powerful No Blade of Grass.

inhabitants of the area still on it, like a latter-day Noah's ark. In the end, the comet threatens to collide with Earth. Shot with extraordinary visual flair and an uncanny sense of detail, characteristics of Zeman's work, the film is a spectacular yet charming piece of work with memorable scenes of meteorological phenomena. It makes all the points, simply and often humorously, that Gance's **La Fin du Monde** (1930) tried to hammer home.

d/co-s Karel Zeman *co-s* Jan Prochazka *c* Rudolf Stahl *lp* Emil Horvath Jnr, Magda Vasayova, Frantisek Filipovsky, Josef Vetrovec, Cestmir Randa

No Blade of Grass (MGM;GB) pv 96(80) min

As an actor, Wilde, a one-time member of the American Olympic fencing team, starred in numerous swashbuckling films of the forties and fifties and was the unlikely impersonator of the sickly Chopin in *A Song to Remember* (1945). His acting style has been accurately summed up by David Thomson as 'cheerfully flat'. The same could be said of his work as a producer/director. A genuine primitive, in films like *The Naked Prey* (1966) and *Beach Red* (1967), Wilde offered accounts of man as an animal clothed in civilized trappings that could only too easily be slipped off. *No Blade of Grass*, based on John Christopher's novel, *The Death of Grass*, is perhaps marginally less powerful, but equally naïve in its account of a family's struggles to survive in the new world created by a virus that has destroyed virtually all the Earth's crops. The breakdown of society is detailed with some glee, deserted towns with corpses strewn everywhere, polluted rivers and parched land, and the characters who assault the Constance family, a psychopath (May) and bikers are equally stereotypes, but Wilde's vision, as demonstrated in the heightened style he adopts, is genuinely frightening. Davenport is the father and Wallace (Wilde's wife and the star of many of his films as director) the mother who survives against all odds.

Right: A montage of monsters and disaster from Kessen Nankai No Daikaiju, *one of Inoshiro Honda's lesser films.*

d/p Cornel Wilde *s* Sean Forestal *c* H.A.R. Thompson *se* Terry Witherington *lp* Nigel Davenport, Jean Wallace, John Hamill, Anthony May, Lynne Frederick, George Coulouris

La Ragazza di Latta *aka* The Tin Girl *aka* The Girl of Tin (SCETR FILMS; IT) 95 min

Set in a near future in which the Smack Corporation is all powerful, *La Ragazza di Latta* stars Antonelli as the bored executive who withdraws into his own fantasies. These fantasies centre on a mysterious girl (Rome) he sees one day but cannot trace. Just as the fantasies begin to take over his life Antonelli sees Rome again and discovers she is an android manufactured by the Smack Corporation. Aliprandi and cinematographer de Giovanni create a disorientating sterile environment in the peculiar blend of past and future, but the film is too slow-moving and Antonelli's rebelliousness too calculated to impress.

d/p/co-s Marcello Aliprandi *co-s* Fernando Imbert *c* Gastone de Giovanni *lp* Roberto Antonelli, Sydne Rome, Elena Persiani, Umberto D'Orsi, Adriano Amidei Migliano

Signale – Ein Weltraumabenteuer *aka* Signals – An Adventure in Space

(DEFA/ZESPOLY FILMOWE; EG, POL) scope 70mm 91 min

Like **Der Schweigende Stern** (1960), this is an East German-Polish collaboration which puts the emphasis on space adventure in a picture primarily aimed towards a youthful audience. Based on Carlos Rasch's novel *Asteroidenjaeger*, it is set in the middle of the 21st century and tells the story of a spaceship that has lost its bearings and of another craft seemingly on a routine patrol which investigates the problem. Shot in 70mm, the spaceship designs were manifestly derivative of **2001 – A Space Odyssey** (1968), but they at least managed to create a convincing sense of 'space', that is of the dimensions of the craft as well as of the dimensions of the environment within which the crafts evolve. But as so often in

uninspired space opera, the plot structure and the characters are simply those of war, western or other adventure stories transplanted into a space-opera setting.

d/co-s Gottfried Kolditz *co-s* Claus-Ulrich Wiesner
c/co-se Otto Hainisch *co-se* Kurt Marks, Stanislaw Duelz
lp Piotr Pavlikovsky, Yevgeny Sharikov, Gojko Mitic, Yuri Darie, Helmut Schreiber, Alfred Mueller, Irena Karel, Soheir Morshedy, Karin Schroeder, Wolfgang Kieling

THX 1138 (AMERICAN ZOETROPE) scope 95 min

This is the directorial début of Lucas who seven years later transformed the genre with **Star Wars** (1977). The film was developed from *THX 2238 4EB*, a 20-minute film he made while a student a UCLA's film department. In contrast to the gee-whizz dramatics of *Star Wars*, *THX 1138* offers a sombre view of the future, akin to that of **1984** (1956). Few of the details of Lucas' film are original – in **Just Imagine** (1930), for example, numbers had replaced names – but the look of the film is marvellous. With his mobile camera, which rarely moves into close-up on the disturbingly sterile white cocoon of underground tunnels, and the minimum of sets, Lucas presents us with a bleakly pessimistic portrait of the future.

Duvall in the title role is the individual who aches for freedom and after an illegal affair – love is outlawed – with McOmie and a period of detention sets off on a desperate search for the outside world. The storyline is confusing, the role of Pleasance for example is unclear, but the film's images, Duvall caught in an ominous blood-red sunset at the end, or the gleaming chrome robot policeman that is malfunctioning and walks repeatedly into a wall, remain powerful. Similarly, if things like the continued exhortations to consume and the police's offer of assistance to the people they are pursuing, are commonplaces in the mainstream of Science Fiction writing, Lucas' presentation makes them all the more powerful. One marvellous jest concludes the film; just as Duvall is about to be caught, the search for him is called off because it has already exceeded its budget.

The film was made with minimal studio interference during the actual shooting and was drastically re-edited by Warners. It has since become a cult film.

d/co-s George Lucas *p* Lawrence Sturhahn *co-s* Walter Murch *c* Dave Meyers, Albert Kihn *lp* Robert Duvall, Donald Pleasance, Don Pedro Colley, Maggie McOmie, Ian Wolfe, Marshall Efron

Toomorrow

(SWEET MUSIC/LOWNDES PRODUCTIONS; GB) pv 95 min
Toomorrow is a lightweight musical fantasy, blandly directed by Guest, clearly (and understandably) out of sympathy with his own script. Newton-John, Thomas, Cooper and Chambers are the Chelsea art students who form a group, Toomorrow. Their gimmick is a 'tonalizer' which sets up

vibrations that the Alphoids, whose own music has become soulless, believe can re-invigorate astral music. Dotrice is the chief Alphoid who kidnaps the group only to find that they can't perform in unsympathetic surroundings. The film's silly climax has the Alphoids record the group's performance at a benefit concert at the Roundhouse (!?) and beam it to outer space, as if the puppy love sentiments of the music could restore the harmony of the spheres.

Far more interesting than the glossy, soulless story and sad performances of the principals is the mismatching of the talents of writer/director Guest and producers Saltzman and Kirshner who dominate the film. Saltzman, better known as the co-producer of the James Bond films, is presumably the source of the film's awkward but extravagant design while music publisher Kirshner (best known as the creator of the Monkees) is responsible for the vapid cuteness of Toomorrow. Newton-John went on to make *Grease* (1978).

d/s Val Guest *p* Harry Saltzman, Don Kirshner *c* Dick Bush *se* Ray Caple, Cliff Culley *lp* Olivia Newton-John, Benny Thomas, Vic Cooper, Karl Chambers, Roy Dotrice, Imogen Hassall, Tracey Crisp, Roy Marsden

Zabil Jsem Einsteina, Panove *aka* I Killed Einstein, Gentlemen (CZECHOSLOVENSKY FILM; CZECH) 95 min

A broad comedy from the author of **Muz z Prvniho Stoleti** (1961) but whose fame in the West rests mainly on his western spoof *Lemonadovy Joe* (1964). In fact, his best work and the only film that justifies his reputation as a comedy director is **Adele Jeste Nevecerela** (1978).

The storyline of this laboured film is that after the nuclear holocaust, women are discovered to have been rendered sterile by radiation so scientists despatch a team in a time machine to kill Einstein. The silly premise that Einstein would be responsible for any nuclear explosion that might occur betrays the profound lack of satirical intelligence that robs the film of any cutting edge. The pace of the proceedings is not controlled well enough to gloss over the many unfunny and misogynist gags. Even Makourek, the regular contributor to Vorlicek's marvellously witty comedies (**Kdo Chce Zabit Jessu?** 1965, or **Pane Vy Jste Vdova**, 1971) couldn't rescue this predictable farce. The comic talents of excellent actors like Sovak and Janzurova are wasted.

d/co-s Oldrich Lipsky *co-s* Josef Nesvadba, Milos Makourek *c* Ivan Slapeta *lp* Jiri Sovak, Jana Brezhova, Iva Janzurova, L. Lipsky

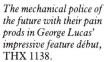

Left: *Olivia Newton-John in the lightweight fantasy* Toomorrow.

The mechanical police of the future with their pain prods in George Lucas' impressive feature début, THX 1138.

Malcolm McDowell and his fellow droogs about to begin their evening of violence in A Clockwork Orange.

1971

Beware! the Blob *aka* Son of Blob
(JACK H. HARRIS ENTERPRISES) 88(81) min

The only film to date directed by Hagman, an actor best known for his portrayal of the infamous J.R. in the *Dallas* teleseries, this is a dull sequel to **The Blob** (1958). Whereas the earlier film had a certain charm about it, this offering, though it attempts to duplicate the sense of menace of the original as the blob stalks (or rather wobbles) along a mid-western town in search of victims, is both too camp – the film starts with the blob's first victim being devoured while watching a re-run of *The Blob* on television – and too laboured. Cambridge, Lynley, Berman and Meredith are amongst the guest stars called up to 'do a turn' before meeting their sticky ends in this would-be comedy.

d Larry Hagman *p/cop-s* Anthony Harris *co-s* Jack Woods *c* Al Hamm *se* Tim Barr *lp* Robert Walker, Gwynne Gilford, Godfrey Cambridge, Carol Lynley, Shelley Berman, Burgess Meredith, Gerrit Graham

Blinker's Spy-Spotter
(EYELINE/CHILDREN'S FILM FOUNDATION; GB) 58 min

A quaint British version of **It Happens Every Spring** (1949) with the difference that Spooner's Blinker invents not a wood-repelling substance but a 'goal-repeller' which gains him a place in the Strikers football team. Directed by Stephens with an eye to gadgetry, the film lacks the necessary narrative pace to give its old-fashioned story of boys versus spies the charm it requires.

d Jack Stephens *p/co-s* Harold Orton *co-s* David Ash *c* Mark MacDonald *lp* David Spooner, Sally-Ann Marlowe, Brent Oldfield, Edward Kemp, Martin Beaumont

Right: The quiet before the storm in Larry Hagman's inept Beware! the Blob.

A Clockwork Orange (POLARIS PROD./WB; GB) 136 min

Though **2001 – A Space Odyssey** (1968), its Homeric title notwithstanding, clearly sees man as not in control of his destiny, it nevertheless remains an affirmative film; *A Clockwork Orange*, though it celebrates free will, is a far more pessimistic offering. The earlier film ends with the birth of the new 'transcended' man, *A Clockwork Orange* opens (and closes) with the frightening image of McDowell's young thug about to go on the rampage and then follows his rehabilitation, by the horrendous Ludovico technique, which leaves him unable to cope with the violence he once meted out; whereupon, as part of an electioneering ploy, he is restored to his former self, his murderous instincts again intact.

Both Kubrick and Anthony Burgess, on whose novel Kubrick's screenplay is based, have said the message of the film is the need for (and the price of) free will. Though the

film was attacked both for the violence McDowell metes out and then suffers, it should be stressed that the film's violence is more stylized than realistic, more shadowplay than blood and gore. Indeed the violence is more shocking than physical with its intertwining of such valued and varied cultural products as 'Singing in the Rain' (which McDowell sings and dances as he and his 'droogs' beat up Magee and rape Corri) and Beethoven's 9th Symphony (McDowell's favourite piece of music) with the omnipresent violence of Kubrick's near future. That said, if the film's argument demands, as one critic has put it, that as we watch 'we shed out humanity that McDowell may acquire it', the film's bravura sense of style has a coldness about it that smacks of cynicism, especially when compared to the more modestly conceived **Terminal Man** (1974) in which society also tries to restructure an individual to save him from himself. In Mike Hodges' film the scientists are misguided, in Kubrick's they are merely, like McDowell, the products of their society.

d/p/s Stanley Kubrick *c* John Alcott *lp* Malcolm McDowell, Patrick Magee, Michael Bates, Adrienne Corri, Miriam Karlin, Warren Clarke, John Clive, Carl Duering

Diamonds Are Forever
(EON PRODUCTIONS/DANJAQ; GB) pv 120 min
This film marked Connery's brief return to the role of James Bond, a role he eventually returned to once more in **Never Say Never Again** (1983). Gray as Bloefeld is smuggling diamonds from South Africa in order to construct a laser gun which he plans to send into space, point at Washington and demand world disarmament (!?) or else. Director Hamilton uses the thin plot as the springboard for a collection of set-pieces set in exotic locations and against Ken Adam's baroque sets. The film has little real drama (its makers' attitude is too tongue-in-cheek for that), rather it marks the beginnings of the take-over of the series by technological gadgetry. The result is a film with some of the charm, but little of the innocence, of the serials of the thirties into whose traditions Bond and Bloefeld as hero and villain fit perfectly.

d Guy Hamilton *p* Harry Saltzman, Albert R. Broccoli
s Richard Maibaum, Tom Mankiewicz *c* Ted Moore
se Albert Whitlock, Wally Veevers, Leslie Hillman, Whitey McMahon *lp* Sean Connery, Jill St John, Charles Gray, Lana Wood, Jimmy Dean, Bruce Cabot

Earth II (WABE/MGM) 97(75) min
An awful film. On board the independent orbiting space station dedicated to peace, the crew (Lockwood, Hylands, Franciosa and Rhodes) argue over whether the station should be armed and then set out to disarm a Chinese space station when that arrives in orbit. The end is horribly predictable with Earth and Earth II saved, and a baby born. Gries, whose western *Will Penny* (1967) suggested real talent, directs aimlessly.

d Tom Gries *p/s* William Read Woodfield, Allan Balter
c Michel Hugo *se* Howard Anderson Co, Howard Anderson Jnr, Art Cruickshank, Robert Ryder, J. McMillan Johnson
lp Gary Lockwood, Scott Hylands, Hari Rhodes, Anthony Franciosa, Mariette Hartley, Gary Merrill

Escape from the Planet of the Apes
(APJAC) pv 97 min
The second sequel to **Planet of the Apes** (1968), this transforms the bold conception of the earlier film into a crude and painfully sentimental story. Dehn's script takes up where that for **Beneath the Planet of the Apes** (1969) ended and follows Hunter and McDowall back through the time-warp to today's Earth. At first they are welcomed (by Dillman's scientist) and then hunted, when they escape after Hunter becomes pregnant, by Braedon who, fearing that it is their offspring that will later dominate man, wants to terminate the pregnancy. From this point on the clichés fly thick and fast.

d Don Taylor *p* Arthur P. Jacobs *s* Paul Dehn
c Joseph Biroc *se* Howard A. Anderson Co.
lp Roddy McDowall, Kim Hunter, Ricardo Montalban, Bradford Dillman, Eric Braeden, Natalie Trundy

La Figlia di Frankenstein *aka* Lady Frankenstein
(CONDOR INTERNATIONAL; IT) 99 min
A typically Italian sensationalist twist to the Frankenstein myth, this offering sees Bay as the daughter of Frankenstein (Cotten, who in the sixties and seventies was possibly the world's most travelled actor) first assisting him create a

Left: *Kim Hunter as Zira discovers the pleasures of champagne while Bradford Dillman looks on, in* Escape from the Planet of the Apes *the third in the Ape series of films.*

Earth II, *a lacklustre space opera from Tom Gries.*

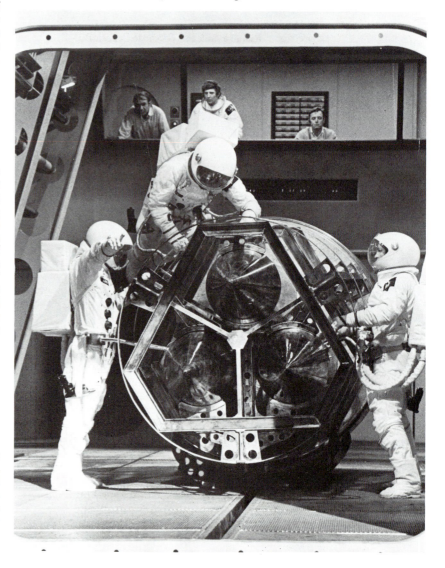

Above: La Figlia di Frankenstein, *monster and stake.*

monster and then taking over from him, when the monster turns on him, and creating another to fight it. Von Theumer directs with an eye to grotesque detail (Bay is strangled by the monster she creates as she makes love to it) but with little wit or invention.

d/p Mel Welles (Ernst von Theumer) *s* Edward Di Lorenzo *c* Richard Pallotin (Riccardo Pallotini) *se* Cipa *lp* Joseph Cotten, Sara Bay, Mickey Hargitay, Paul Whiteman, Herbert Fux, Paul Muller

Gamera Tai Shinkai Kaiju Jigura *aka* Gamera Versus Zigra *aka* Gamera Versus the Deep Sea Monster Zigra
(DAIEI; JAP) scope 87 min

Yuasa's seventh Gamera film, six of which he directed, starting with **Daikaiju Gamera** (1966), and one of which he arranged the special effects for, **Gamera Tai Baragon** (1966). The others that established Gamera as Godzilla's rival for children's affections were **Gamera Tai Gaos** (1967), **Gamera Tai Viras** (1968), **Gamera Tai Guiron** (1969) and **Gamera Tai Daimaju Jaiga** (1970).

The Zigra star having become polluted, the Zigrans come to Earth's seas and plan to take over before the Earth's inhabitants pollute their own planet beyond remedy. To demonstrate their power, the female alien who appears to direct operations causes earthquakes and thus destroys some cities. The spaceship she came in turns into a monster which kills Gamera who has come to defend the children from the alien invaders. However, the kids revive the dead turtle which is lying on the bottom of the ocean by sending an enormous electric charge up its body. It then revives, kills the Zigrans and flies away. The film is marred by bad special effects and a worse script. The notion of aliens taking control of the monsters reduced the creatures to mere pawns in us/them games, emptying them of their own mythic qualities and their ability to incarnate complex social fantasies. However, the introduction of 'pollution' as a theme restored some thematic pertinence to the genre and nearly all monster movies in the seventies would make references to the devastating effects of pollution in the same way that the earlier movies had referred to atomic explosions.

d Noriyaki Yuasa *p* Yoshihiko Manabe *s* Fumi Takahashi *c* Akira Uehara *se* Kozufumi Fujii *lp* Reiko Kasahara, Mikiko Tsubouchi, Koji Fujiyama, Isamu Saeki, Yasushi Sakagami, Arlene Zoellner, Gloria Zoellner

Glen and Randa (SIDNEY GLAZIER PRODUCTIONS) 94 min

McBride's first feature, *David Holzman's Diary* (1967) which was a fictional portrait (its title and the fact that it won first prize in the Mannheim Documentary festival, notwithstanding) of an auto-voyeur, announced his obsession with the cinema of Jean-Luc Godard which would finally lead to his strangely effective remake of Godard's first feature, *A Bout de Souffle* (1959), as *Breathless* (1983). In between these films he made two strikingly experimental movies, *My Girlfriend's Wedding* (1968) and *Glen and Randa* which were far more documentary, indeed almost ethnological, in form and style. The first was, as its title suggests, the odd story of the marriage of McBride's girlfriend (to avoid deportation from America) to a hippie friend and the second the most innocent vision of post-nuclear-holocaust America.

In contrast to, say, Mike Kuchar's experimental **Sins of the Fleshapoids** (1965) which glorified the trash aesthetics of the American B movie, *Glen and Randa* highlights the innocent sense of wonder that is an equally significant element of American popular culture. The film follows the travails of Glen (Curry) and Randa (Plimpton), two noble savages who leave their private garden of Eden at Curry's prompting in search of civilization, the City of Metropolis, proof of the existence of which they find along the way in the shape of an old *Wonder Woman* comic book. Much of the film's power comes from ex-editor McBride's decision to observe his characters. Thus, rather than highlight their quest by concentrating of the drama of their journey through the desolate post-nuclear-holocaust landscapes, McBride pinpoints the bizarre ordinaryness of their journey, often (as in the fishing scene or the lengthy sequence in which Curry sits, empty pipe in mouth, gazing at a broken-down television set because that is what leading a civilized life means) equating real time and screen time and reducing editing and camera movements to a minimum. The result is a charming evocation of both innocence and the costs of Curry's quest for knowledge – Plimpton dies in childbirth because they've quit their Eden – as he, their newborn child, Chambliss' old man (and guardian of knowledge in the shape of the artifacts of the past) and a goat set off in a small boat across the sea, still in search of Metropolis.

d/co-s Jim McBride *p* Sidney Glazier *co-s* Rudolph Wurlitzer, Lorenzo Mans *c* Alan Raymond *lp* Steven Curry, Shelley Plimpton, Woodrow Chambliss, Garry Goodrow, Roy Rox, Robert Holmer, Hubert Powers

Gojira Tai Hedora *aka* Godzilla Versus the Smog Monster *aka* Godzilla Versus Hedora
(TOHO; JAP) scope 85 min

An ecological monster movie provides the setting for Godzilla's eleventh screen performance, although the star has changed beyond recognition: from the death-ray-spewing horror of 1954 to the clownish figure prancing about under Banno's direction for the benefit of undemanding children, his change seems to indicate that the energy and the mythical quality have gone from the Godzilla series, although the subsequent **Gojira Tai Mekagojira** (1974) does have its entertaining moments. The story is edifying: industrial waste and pollution pumped into the sea produces a living sludge, activated by particles of a monstrous substance that arrived on Earth attached to a comet. Hedora feeds on pollution. It also emits a crimson death ray from its eyes and can turn itself into a flying saucer as well. Godzilla turns up to save the day, aided by the military's giant electricity generators. The central human figure is a boy (Kawase) who provides his eminent scientist father (Yamauchi) with the clue as to how to get rid of the monstrous sludge. The picture is interrupted by psychedelically staged pop songs and explanatory animation sequences, considerably slowing down the action and betraying a total lack of any sense of continuity, although that defect may be due to the US version's slapdash adaptation of the original movie. The acting, especially that of the mawkish child and the earnest father, is very affected, and together with an execrable soundtrack, this makes the picture painful to watch at times. Nevertheless, it signalled a fundamental shift in the monster movie genre, introducing (with **Gamera Tai Shinkai Kaiju Jigura**, 1971) the theme of global pollution which became the thematic mainstay of the series for the next ten years, replacing the traditional atomic radiation motif as the main cause for the disasters befalling Japan.

d/co-s Yoshimitsu Banno   *p* Tomoyuki Tanaka
co-s Kaoru Mabuchi   *c* Yoichi Manoda   *se* Shokei Nakano
lp Akira Yamauchi, Hiroyuki Kawase, Toshie Kimura

El Hombre Que Vino de Ummo *aka* Dracula versus Frankenstein *aka* Assignment Terror
(PRODUCCIONES JAIME PRADES/EICHBERG FILM/INTERNATIONAL JAGUAR; SP,WG,IT)   scope   87 min
Despite its charming idea, alien invaders led by Rennie set about terrorizing mankind by reviving the monsters of the popular imagination, Dracula, the Werewolf, the Mummy, the Reptile and Frankenstein's monster, this is a mediocre film. Even the witty idea of having the aliens in monster form succumb to the emotions of their bodies' previous owners falls flat. The English language title makes no sense: it is Rennie's assistant, Dor, and the Werewolf (Naschi) who save Earth from invasion.

d Tulio Demichelli   *p* Jaime Prades   *s* Jacinto Molina Alvarez   *c* Godofredo Pacheco   *se* Antonio Molna
lp Michael Rennie, Karin Dor, Craig Hill, Paul Naschi, Patty Sheppard, Peter Damon

Horror of the Blood Monsters *aka* Creatures of the Red Planet *aka* Flesh Creatures of the Red Planet *aka* The Flesh Creatures *aka* Vampire Men of the Lost Planet
(INDEPENDENT INTERNATIONAL)   85 min
This is one of the better of the numerous exploitation films (including the awful **Cinderella 2000**, 1977) directed by Adamson in the late sixties and seventies. Although Adamson never graduated from the world of low-low-budget film-making to even the heights of the small budgets of the likes of Roger Corman's New World pictures, his films, especially when Zsigmond was his cinematographer (even his sexploitation ones) are generally characterized by a commitment to narrative clarity that is unusual.

Horror of the Blood Monsters (scripted by a woman, McNair, another unusual occurence in low-budget film-making) features an invasion of Earth by a colony of extra-terrestrial vampires. In the manner of **Flash Gordon** (1936), Carradine, Dix (both regulars in Adamson's films) and Volante blast off from Earth to a latterday Mongo to destroy the vampire's home base. After doing battle with cat-men, claw demons, snake people and the like they finally emerge victorious and return to Earth as saviours. Shot mostly in the Philippines and utilizing footage from *One Million BC* (1940) and *Unknown Island* (1948), the film is energetically, if unimaginatively, mounted.

d/p Al Adamson   *s* Sue McNair   *c* William (Vilmos) Zsigmond, William G. Troiano   *se* David L. Hewitt
lp John Carradine, Robert Dix, Vicki Volante, Joey Benson, Jennifer Bishop, Bruce Powers

Ich Liebe Dich Ich Toete Dich *aka* I Love You I Kill You   (UWE BRANDER FILMPRODUKTION; WG)   94 min
In the late sixties, some *cinéastes* tried to re-invent what is perhaps the only genuinely German film genre, the *Heimat*-film. Usually set in picturesque rural areas, these films provide an idealized view of cosy provincialism, presenting village mediocrity as the very foundation of German values, as the home (*Heimat*) of Teutondom. The genre was very popular during the Nazi era and retained its popularity after the war. A new generation of *cinéastes* tried to turn the genre upsidedown by making negative, often paranoid 'village' films depicting the locals as malevolent pod-people. Brandner's film deviates from the conventions by setting the story in the near future. The inhabitants of a village are kept happy with pills and games while nearby there is a hunting area for the privileged rulers who arrive once a year, descending onto the village in helicopters. Guards keep order and ensure that the pleasure ground of the powerful remains inviolate. A new teacher begins poaching, largely out of boredom. A sub-human gamekeeper falls in love with him and the two deviants are pushed further into the margins, eventually into conscious rebellion and defeat. This paranoid fantasy gives some indication about the state of mind which helped produce anarchic terrorism as a viable and relatively popular political programme among the German left at the time. Shot in cold colour at a slow, deliberate pace, the film quickly tips over into a bleak schematism in which power is in 'their' hands and the people are cowed, happy vegetables. Only homosexuals and rejects, the male marginals – marginal women are depicted as anonymous prostitutes – are left as positive misfits. The political lessons inherent in such a parable are obvious and unsavoury. As a document of its time, the film shows the limitations of a politics of paranoia but also that it isn't as easy as all that to subvert an established and popular genre.

d/p/s Uwe Brandner   *c* Andre Dubreuil   *lp* Rolf Becker, Hannes Fuchs, Helmut Brasch, Nicolaus Dutsch, Monika Hansen, Thomas Eckelman, Marianne Blomquist, Wolfgang Ebert, Stefen Moses

La Invasion Siniestra *aka* The Incredible Invasion
(FILMICA VERGARA; MEX)   90 min
Just before his death in 1969, Karloff acted in scenes of four films produced by Vergara: *The Fear Chamber* and *House of Evil* (both of which remain unreleased), *Isle of the Snake People* (1971) and this inept mixture of horror, sexploitation and Science Fiction. The story concerns Professor Mayer (Karloff) who invents a radioactive power source. An alien in a flying saucer comes to destroy the contraption lest it be used as a weapon. He takes over the body of a homicidal sex maniac

The intriguing, if disappointing, Ich Liebe Dich Ich Toete Dich.

Above: *Charlton Heston as* The Omega Man.

(Beirute) whose crimes, including the murder of a local girl (Monti), upset the villagers. As the villagers attack and destroy the laboratory in the tradition of **Frankenstein** (1931), Mayer and his assistant (Guzman) manage to defeat the alien, leaving Guzman and Linder, who plays Karloff's daughter, to provide the happy ending.

According to Hill, the production circumstances of these pictures were disastrous. Karloff had rejected the four scripts sent to him by Vergara, and Hill, who shared the services of Karloff's lawyer, was asked to rewrite them. Karloff then agreed to do them provided all scenes involving him would be shot in Hollywood because it was exceedingly painful for him to move about. The scenes were shot in 1968. Shortly afterwards, Karloff died, but so did Vergara. All the remaining scenes were shot later in Mexico without Hill's knowledge and the finished products, released in 1971, bore little relation to the scripts Hill had used to do the Karloff scenes back in 1968. Apparently American International tried to buy the shots with Karloff in order to make other films with them, possibly to be arranged by Corman, but the legal and copyright problems due to Vergara's death made this impracticable. This Mexican episode put a sad end to Karloff's long and distinguished career. Some credits list the name of Ibañez as being responsible for the scenes added after Karloff's death, but since many of these credits contain pseudonyms, it may be an injustice to Ibañez to include his name as co-director.

co-d/s Jack Hill   *co-d* Juan Ibañez   *p* Enrique Vergara *c* Austin McKinney, Raul Dominguez   *se* Jack Tannenbaum   *lp* Boris Karloff, Enrique Guzman, Christa Linder, Maura Monti, Yerye Beirute, Tito Novaro, Mariela Flores, Griselda Mejia, Rosangela Balbo

Ein Kaefer Geht Aufs Ganze

(BARBARA FILM; WG)   91 min
It was only natural that Germany should make its own tribute to the Volkswagen Beetle, affectionately known as Dudu in this film, although Disney had beaten them to it with the Herbie series (beginning with **The Love Bug**, 1969). The gimmick of a custom-made car with extraordinary powers and outlandish fittings was pioneered in the silent cinema (**The Modern Pirates**, 1906) but brought to the fore in the James Bond movies before becoming a popular US teleseries (*Knight Rider*). In this film, Dudu wins the Kalahari rally in East Africa, the most demanding endurance test on the rally calendar. Three more instalments, in the same uninspiring vein, followed. All were made by Zehetgruber for the Munich-based Barbara Film and all mercifully were restricted to the domestic German language market: **Ein Kaefer Gibt Vollgas** (1972), **Ein Kaefer auf Extratour** (1973) and **Das Verrueckteste Auto der Welt** (1974). All the films were scripted, produced and directed by Zehetgruber, who sometimes starred in them as well, under the pseudonym Robert Mark.

d/p/s Robert Mark (Rudolph Zehetgruber)   *c* Alexandra Posch   *lp* Richard Lynn, Gerd Duwner, Katharina Oginski, Jim Brown, Constanze Sieck, Lex County, Bob Mackay

Million Dollar Duck   (WALT DISNEY)   92 min

A Science Fiction variant of the goose-that-laid-the-golden-eggs fairytale, this is one of the better of the Disney studios family comedies. The duck in question has been exposed to radiation. Jones, Duncan and Montgomery are the family who try to cash in on their good fortune, only to cause a worldwide economic crisis when the price of gold falls and Flyn the treasury department official, who happens to live next door, on their trail. The result is a lightweight comedy, which is very similar to **Mr Drake's Duck** (1951).

d Vincent McEveety   *p* Bill Anderson   *s* Roswell Rogers *c* William Snyder   *se* Eustace Lycett   *lp* Dean Jones, Sandy Duncan, Lee Harcourt Montgomery, Joe Flynn, Tony Roberts, James Gregory

The Omega Man

(WALTER SELTZER PRODUCTIONS)   pv   98 min
Like the first version of Richard Matheson's superb novel, *I Am Legend* (the inept **L'Ultimo Uomo della Terra**, 1964) *The Omega Man* radically transforms the thrust of the novel. Where the novel is full of paranoia and takes for its last man a nervous victim besieged by vampires (caused by a Sino-Russian war), Sagal's over-emphatically directed film features a muscular Heston as the gun-toting last man, sipping fine wines as he watches his favourite film, *Woodstock* (1970) in preparation for hunting down the zombies led by Zerbe's fanatic. The erratic plotline follows Heston's running battle with the zombies in the course of which he discovers other untainted human beings to whom he passes on a serum that might save mankind.

The project needed someone like George Romero, whose **Night of the Living Dead** (1968) has a chilling vision more in keeping with that of Matheson's novel.

d Boris Sagal   *p* Walter Seltzer   *s* John William Corrington, Joyce H. Corrington   *c* Russell Metty   *lp* Charlton Heston, Anthony Zerbe, Rosalind Cash, Paul Koslo, Lincoln Kilpatrick, Eric Laneuville

Pane Vy Jste Vdova *aka* Sir, You Are a Widower *aka* Mister, You Are a Widower

(STUDIO BARRANDOV; CZECH)   90 min
Like **Kdo Chce Zabit Jessu?** (1965) and, later, **Coz Takhle Dat Si Spenat** (1976), this is one of the Vorlicek-Makourek team's medically based Science Fiction comedies. This one involves transplants and artificial limbs of all kinds (arms,

brains) and even a completely artificial person, Mrs Stub, played by Janzurova, who also plays two more characters, an actress and a murderess. She deservedly obtained the best actress prize for the three roles at the Trieste festival. The plot also mobilizes a king whose right arm is inadvertently cut off by a guard, but a good replacement limb is attached, allowing him to salute quite effectively. There is a fortune-teller who always gets things wrong and an exuberant ending with fireworks and other festive happenings to celebrate the complete disbanding of the army. The film features the beautiful Shoberova, fresh from her disappointing stint at the Hammer studios (*The Vengeance of She*, 1968), where she was billed as Olinka Berova, and the brilliant comedian Sovak, a regular in the Vorlicek-Makourek crazy comedies. The result is a piece of gloriously black and at times gory humour about people changing bits of themselves, far outclassing a previous Czech effort along these lines, **Ztracena Tvar** (1965).

d/co-s Vaclav Vorlicek   *co-s* Milos Makourek   *c* Vaclav Hanus   *lp* Iva Janzurova, Olga Shoberova, Jiri Sovak, Jiri Hrzan, Jan Libieck, Eduard Cupak, Frantisek Filipovsky, Milos Kopecky

Percy   (ANGLO-EMI/WELBECK; GB) 103 min

A silly infantile film about the world's first penis transplant, *Percy*, though it interestingly reverses the idea that whereas blood donors wonder where their blood has gone the recipient of a penis would wonder who its previous owner was and to what use he had put it, sacrifices everything for a series of crude jokes, mostly of a barrack-room nature. Accordingly, both the direction, by Thomas, and script, by Leonard, are so full of innuendo as to deprive all concerned of any chance of shining. Bennett is the recipient of 'Percy', Elliott his doctor and Sommer and Ekland two of Percy's temporary residences. The score, by Ray Davies, is performed by the Kinks. A sequel, **Percy's Progress**, followed in 1974.

d Ralph Thomas   *p* Betty E. Box   *s* Hugh Leonard
c Ernest Steward   *lp* Hywel Bennett, Denholm Elliott, Elke Sommer, Britt Ekland, Cyd Hayman, Patrick Mower

Punishment Park
(CHARTWELL FILMS/FRANÇOIS FILMS) 89 min

With **The War Game** (1965), this is the most successful of Watkins' interrogations of the present through reconstructions of the future. Set in a not too distant future where America's Indo-China war has spread wider and opposition to it has led to the setting up of detention camps throughout America to hold draft-resisters, the film follows a British documentary film unit, led by Watkins himself, as it observes a group who chose the three-day ordeal in a 'punishment

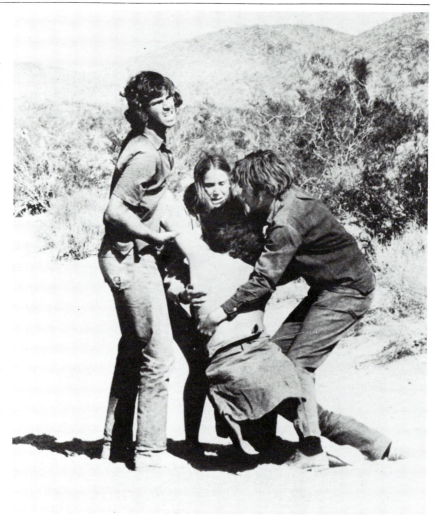

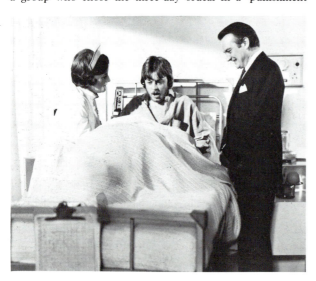

park' rather than a three-year jail sentence. In effect a re-staging of the Vietnam War in the heartland of America (Bear Mountain), the film is a powerful and despairing, if occasionally muddled, indictment of the possibilities of repression in America.

Punishment Park, *Peter Watkins' re-staging of the Vietnam War in the heartland of America.*

d/s Peter Watkins   *p* Susan Martin   *c* Joan Churchill
lp Carmen Argenziano, Stan Armsted, Jim Bohan, Frederick Franklyn, Gladys Golden, Sanford Golden

Quest for Love
(PETER ROGERS PRODUCTIONS; GB) 91 min

Although superficially similar to **Je T'Aime, Je T'Aime** (1967) and **Hu-Man** (1975), this is decidedly inferior to either film. Adapted from the short story *Random Quest* by John Wyndham, neither director Thomas nor writer Feely make imaginative use of the parallel world idea that is the film's central premise; instead they prefer to mount a traditional romance.

Bell is nicely surprised as the physicist who wakes up in a parallel world (where John Kennedy is still alive, there's no war in Vietnam and Everest is still unconquered). He finds himself to be a successful, if vainglorious, playwright and falls in love with his wife (Collins) only to have her die just when he's convinced her that he really isn't who he seems to be. The shock of her death returns him to his own world to embark on a frantic search for her before she dies in this world as well.

d Ralph Thomas   *p* Peter Eton   *s* Terence Feely   *c* Ernest Steward   *lp* Joan Collins, Tom Bell, Denholm Elliott, Laurence Naismith, Lyn Ashley, Juliet Harmer, Trudy van Doorn

Left: *Hywel Bennett gets his first sight of Percy while Denholm Elliott looks proudly on in Ralph Thomas' infantile film.*

The Resurrection of Zachary Wheeler

(GOLD KEY ENTERTAINMENTS/VIDTRONICS COMPANY/MADISON
PRODUCTIONS/NEW MEXICO FILM INDUSTRY COMMISSION)
100 min

The feature début of Wynn, *The Resurrection of Zachary
Wheeler* anticipates the territory mined so explosively by
Michael Crichton in **Coma** (1978), only to collapse into Cold
War rhetoric for its conclusion. Dillman is the playboy
senator resurrected from the dead by organ transplants from
zombies (called somas) bred for the purpose by Daly's sinister
doctor and Nielsen the reporter who uncovers Daly's plot
only to supress his story, convinced that Daly's plans are for
America's good when he learns that the next patient is to be
Chou En-Lai, a change in whose politics is to be the price of
eternity. Efficiently mounted for the most part, the film sags
sadly when Daly begins expounding at length his philosophies
about power to Dillman and Nielsen.

d Bob Wynn   *p* Bob Stabler   *s* Jay Simms, Tom Rolf
c Bob Boatman   *lp* Leslie Nielsen, Bradford Dillman, James
Daly, Angie Dickinson, Robert J. Wilke, Jack Carter

Santo Contra la Hija de Frankenstein *aka* La Hija de Frankenstein *aka* Santo vs Frankenstein's Daughter *aka* The Daughter of Frankenstein

(CINEMATOGRAFICA CALDERON; MEX)   97 min

Credits rarely give the real name of the Silver Masked wrestler
who starred in more than 30 films. Since he never removed his
mask, not even in the obligatory nude love scenes introduced
in the late sixties, it is likely that different hulks played the
part, especially as Santo's first appearance dated back to 1952.
In another contemporary Santo picture, *Santo en la Venganza
de la Momia* (1971), the role was played by Eric del Castillo,
which suggests that del Castillo may well have played the role
in a number of Santo pictures in the late sixties and early
seventies. Here he destroys the Frankenstein monster – called
Ursus – at the beginning of the picture before going on to
oppose the daughter of the mad scientist because she conducts
medical-type experiments on unwilling victims in an effort to
concoct an elixir of eternal youth extracted from the blood of
young women. Her punishment is that, at the end of the film,
she turns old and ugly. The creature's name, Ursus, is a
distant echo of the silent Italian superhero/villain, revived in
the sixties as a sort of Hercules.

Delgado's indifferently made films included the unfunny
parody of wrestler movies **El Superflaco** (1967) and the
equally dismal **El Supersabio** (1948).

d Miguel M. Delgado   *p* Guillermo Calderon   *s* Fernando
Oses   *c* Raul Martinez Solares   *lp* Santo, Gina Romand,
Roberto Cañedo, Carlos Agosti, Sonia Fuentes, Lucy
Gallardo, Jorge Casanova

Silent Running   (U/MICHAEL GRUSKOFF PRODUCTIONS/
DOUGLAS TRUMBULL PRODUCTIONS)   89 min

A wonderful film. The message of **2001 – A Space Odyssey**
(1968), for which Trumbull masterminded the special effects,
was that man needed guidance from beyond. The message of
Silent Running, significantly set in the year 2001, is that man
(and his creations, the film's robots) must be his own saviour,
even at the risk of madness. Thus, adrift in space in a literal
Garden of Eden that was intended to refurbish an Earth
devastated by nuclear war, Dern (who gives a compelling
performance) refuses to destroy his private world when
ordered to. Instead with the help of his robots he tends his
garden and then sends it out into deep space to seed a possible

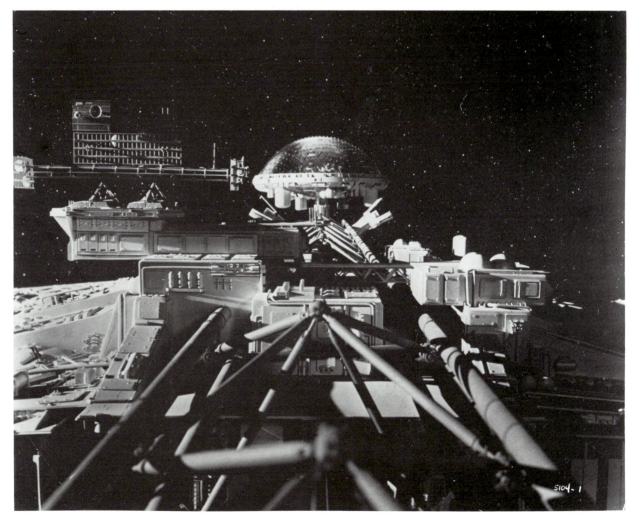

Right: *The spaceship
Valley Forge in Douglas
Trumbull's* Silent
Running, *one of the few
Science Fiction films of
recent years to retain a
human dimension in the
face of the technological
hardware and special
effects that have
increasingly come to
dominate the genre.*

second chance for mankind. In keeping with this theme, Trumbull gives his film a human dimension. Thus even the flight through Saturn's rings is presented not as spectacle, as was the 'stargate' sequence in *2001*, but as an essential part of Dern's escape: by chance he has been found by Earth's authorities who want to mount a rescue attempt. The final images, of the forest tended with a battered watering can by the remaining robot, is one of the most powerful images, both sad and optimistic at the same time, in the modern Science Fiction film.

d/co-se Douglas Trumbull *p* Michael Gruskoff *s* Deric Washburn, Mike Cimino, Steve Bocho *c* Charles F. Wheeler *co-se* John Dykstra, Richard Yuricich, Richard O. Helmer, James Rugg, Marlin Jones, R.L. Helmer, Vernon Archer *lp* Bruce Dern, Cliff Potts, Ron Rifkin, Jesse Vint, Mark Persons, Steven Brown, Cheryl Sparks

Solaris (MOSFILM; USSR) scope 167 min
The classic Soviet Science Fiction counterpart to **2001 – A Space Odyssey** (1968). Like the American film, it offers the kind of confused humanist philosophy which Kluge's **Der Grosse Verhau** (1970) so corrosively castigates. Tarkovsky's epic is based on the Polish writer Stanislaw Lem's novel, published in 1961. But whereas the novel is entirely set on the planet Solaris, Tarkovsky frames the story by two visions of Earth: the first is an ordinary, realist one before the psychologist Kelvin (Banionis) sets off to investigate what is happening with the crew on the Solaris station. The second one is an idyllic vision of a rural, family cottage, possibly formed on the oceanic substance of the planet itself. This encapsulation suggests that the most extraordinary thing man can think coincides with a nostalgic fantasy image of our origins. Man may go to Solaris but his spirit is eternal and unchangeable. Solaris itself is presented as a giant brain, or rather an intelligent substance (God?) that communicates with its visitors by materializing, in human form, a figure

representing a trauma or obsessive dream or memory that haunts them. As such, it functions as a conscience is said to function, and any attempt to understand its mysteries is doomed to come up against the limits of man's own mind. If it were not for the intensely cinematic and fascinating *mise en scene*, the intellectual content of the film would be seen as a set of very antiquated romantic clichés. However, the cinematic power of the representations is such that the brilliance of the imagery and the skilfully controlled rhythm is all absorbing, making the content merely a minor irritant.

It is interesting to note that both *2001* and *Solaris* offer intellectual banalities cloaked in cinematic splendour while *Der Grosse Verhau* ridicules such operatic grandeur and provides an intensely intelligent, and therefore infinitely more disturbing, vision of human development in the space age and beyond.

d/co-s Andrei Tarkovsky *co-s* Friedrich Gorenstein *c* Vadim Jusov *lp* Natalya Bondarchuk, Donatas Banionis, Nikolai Grinko, Yuri Jarvet, Vladislav Dvorzetsky, Anatoly Solonitsyn

The Troublesome Double

(INTERFILM/CHILDREN'S FILM FOUNDATION; GB) 57 min
In this sequel to **Egghead's Robot** (1970), Chegwin's young inventor builds and programs a robot double for his sister (Collins) so that she can win the local swimming meet. Though it lacks the vigour of the earlier film (a common failing of sequels), it remains a sprightly juvenile film thanks to the performance of Chegwin and sisters Julie and Tracy Collins as the girl and robot respectively.

d Milo Lewis *p* Cecil Musk *s* Leif Saxon *c* Alfred Hicks *lp* Keith Chegwin, Julie Collins, Tracy Collins, Richard Wattis, Josephine Tewson, Larry Martyn

Zero Population Growth *aka* Z.P.G.

(SAGITTARIUS) 96 min
Set in the 21st century, Ehrlich and de Felitta's script imagines a future in which, due to over-population and pollution, the world's government decrees that no children are to be born for 30 years. Campus creates a disturbing sense of a future in which walkie-talkie dolls have supplanted babies, people queue for hours to see synthetic grass and a trip to a computer enquiry terminal can lead to a sudden grilling

Oliver Reed and Geraldine Chaplin with their child in the weak Zero Population Growth.

Left: *Donatas Banionis as the psychologist sent to investigate the peculiar goings-on on the* Solaris *space station in Tarkovsky's breathtaking film.*

from the master computer, but once Reed and Chaplin decide to have a baby both script and direction collapse into panegyrics about motherhood and family life.

d Michael Campus *p* Thomas F. Madigan *s* Max Ehrlich, Frank De Felitta *c* Michael Reed *se* Derek Meddings *lp* Oliver Reed, Geraldine Chaplin, Diane Cilento, Don Gordon, Bill Nagy, Aubrey Woods

1972 ———————————————————————

The Boy Who Turned Yellow
(ROGER CHERRILL LTD/CHILDREN'S FILM FOUNDATION; GB)
55 min
A fascinating failure, this film reunites the Powell-Pressburger team with Challis, their regular cinematographer in the fifties. The plot, a meld of Science Fiction and fantasy, in the mould of the pair's masterpiece *A Matter of Life and Death* (1946), follows the adventures of Dightam's youth when he suddenly turns yellow. The adventures are slight (a search for a missing pet mouse at the Tower of London) and Eddison's alien has little to do but the film remains engaging for all that. The colour effects are a model of the 'a little is enough' rule that far too few Science Fiction films follow.

d Michael Powell *s* Emeric Pressburger *c* Christopher Challis *lp* Mark Dightam, Robert Eddison, Helen Weir, Brian Worth, Esmond Knight, Laurence Carter

Conquest of the Planet of the Apes
(APJAC/FOX) Todd-AO 35 85 min
This further vulgarization of **Planet of the Apes** (1968) is set in the period just before the destruction of mankind in a nuclear holocaust after which the apes will reign supreme. Hemmed in by his previous scripts (**Beneath the Planet of**

Below: *Vincent Price at his camp best in search of the waters of life in Robert Fuest's elegant, if empty,* Dr Phibes Rises Again.

the Apes, 1969 and **Escape from the Planet of the Apes**, 1971), Dehn can do no more than attempt to tie up the loose ends of the Apes saga. Accordingly, the film's plot is only inventive in so far as it edges the story towards the situation found in the first (and best) of the series. McDowall plays Caesar, in a cheapened version of John Chamber's ape makeup, who leads a revolution of the ape pets (dogs and cats have been wiped out by a mysterious disease and apes have taken their place) against their increasingly oppressive human masters, and Rhodes is the sympathetic black who helps him. The climactic descent into violence, luridly directed by Thompson, with ape versus man fighting for control of the Earth shows just how far the copyright owners have travelled from *Planet of the Apes*.

d J. Lee Thompson *p* Arthur P. Jacobs *s* Paul Dehn *c* Bruce Surtees *lp* Roddy McDowall, Don Murray, Natalie Trundy, Ricardo Montalban, Hari Rhodes, Severn Darden

Death Line (K-L PRODUCTIONS; GB) 87 min
Unlike most exploitation quickies which, however promising their initial premises are, generally collapse into a predictable dénouement, *Death Line*, like the equally impressive **Scream and Scream Again** (1969), has the courage to follow its central premise through to the end and confront its characters (and the audience) with their worst possible fears as reality. The film's central idea is that since a cave-in in 1892 during the construction of a proposed underground station beneath the British Museum which buried alive a number of men and women, those people have carved out a horrific existence for themselves in an interconnected series of rat-infested, disused tunnels. But if the idea is as fanciful as it's powerful, Sherman (making his feature début) directs with such élan that questions concerning the plausibility of the situation simply evaporate. Moreover the structure of the film, which contrasts policeman Pleasance's lonely, isolated existence above ground with the obvious humanity of the last of the descendants of the tunnel people, Armstrong (whose strong performance recalls that of the doomed Richard Wordsworth in **The Quatermass Xperiment**, 1955) as seen in his care and concern for his dying mate, is elegantly worked out. We are introduced to the film's horrific underground world through a marvellous red herring: two students find a man unconscious on a tube platform, when they return with the police he's gone and it transpires that he's a highly placed government official. But his disappearance has nothing to do with his job; he's been taken by Armstrong in a desperate attempt to keep his pregnant wife alive. An impressive film.

d Gary Sherman *p* Paul Maslansky *s* Ceri Jones *c* Alex Thomson *se* John Horton *lp* Donald Pleasance, Norman Rossington, Hugh Armstrong, Christopher Lee, David Ladd, Sharon Gurney, James Cossins

Doomwatch (TIGON BRITISH; GB) 92 min
Derived from the British teleseries, but with the TV characters taking a back seat to movie stars Geeson and Bannen, this is an interesting film, despite director Sasdy's over-reliance on horror film clichés. The doomwatch team are investigating the effects of oil pollution off the Cornish coast when they find the islanders of Balfe are strangely disfigured as a result of the illegal dumping of chemical and radioactive waste which have combined to form a virulent new disease.

d Peter Sasdy *p* Tony Tenser *s* Clive Exton *c* Kenneth Talbot *lp* Ian Bannen, Judy Geeson, John Paul, Simon Oates, George Sanders, Geoffrey Keen

Dr Phibes Rises Again (AIP; GB) 89 min
A superior sequel to *The Abominable Dr Phibes* (1971), this is directed with real zest by Fuest (a veteran of *The Avengers* TV series, which was noted for its camp excesses). Having been revived automatically at a preordained conjunction of the

planets, Price, in the title role, sets off in search of the river of life, the waters of which he intends to revive his wife with. To achieve this he first must secure the map showing its location which has come into the possession of Quarry's suave antiquarian. The two, pursued by a pair of inept policemen (Jeffrey and Cater) handle the resulting shenanigans and arch dialogue with great aplomb. The end suggests a further sequel which didn't materialize.

d/co-s Robert Fuest *p* Louis M. Heyward *co-s* Robert Blees *c* Alex Thomson *lp* Vincent Price, Robert Quarry, Peter Cushing, Peter Jeffrey, John Cater, Fiona Lewis

Frogs (AMERICAN INTERNATIONAL) 90 min
This is one of the best of the revenge-of-nature cycle of films that erupted in the seventies in the wake of a renewed interest in ecology. The film's success lies in great part in the decision by director McGowan (making his feature début) and his producers to simply film frogs, turtles, lizards and so forth in their natural habitat and interleave these sequences with life-size (not blown up) shots of them encroaching upon the isolated house of Milland, frogs hopping onto a birthday cake, butterflies luring Irving into the swamp where leeches are waiting to suck her dry, and so forth. Moreover, rather than attempt to explain the creature's strange behaviour the film simply states that the frogs are on the warpath. The result is a film that is compelling both as a horrifying vision of what might happen and as an allegory in the manner of **The Birds** (1963).

d George McCowan *p* George Edwards, Peter Thomas *s* Robert Hutchison, Robert Blees *c* Mario Tosi *lp* Ray Milland, Sam Elliott, Joan Van Ark, Lynn Borden, Adam Roarke, Judy Pace, Holly Irving

Gojira Tai Gaigan *aka* **Gojira Tai Gigan** *aka* **War of the Monsters** (TOHO; JAP) scope 89 min
After some decidedly pallid Godzilla films (**Gojira Tai Hedora**, 1971, and **Oru Kaiju Daishingeki**, 1969), the monster's twelfth appearance is more worthy of his reputation. A cartoonist (Ichikawa) designs a Godzilla Tower for a children's park but finds out that his employers are aliens trying to take over the Earth because their own planet is dying due to pollution. The aliens – large black cockroaches in human form – summon Ghidorah (in his fourth performance) and Gaigan, a new creation with one crimson eye and a chainsaw built into his chest. Against them are the combined forces of Godzilla and Anzilla (first seen in **Gigantis**, 1955). After their victory, the good 'Japanese' monsters return to monster island, their home since **Kaiju Soshingeki** (1968). Again exploiting the pollution theme, the most inventive aspect of this movie is the depiction of the aliens' dying planet: the shots are all taken from contemporary Tokyo. Fukuda managed to revive the series by linking the monster genre with current preoccupations and fantasies, although the introduction of a 'hippy' figure seems decidedly out of place in this context. The monsters are played by Haruo Nakajima (Godzilla), Yukietsu Omiya (Angurus), Kanta Ina (Ghidorah) and Kengo Nakayama (Gaigan).

d Jun Fukuda *p* Tomoyuki Tanaka *s* Shinichi Sekizawa *c* Kiyoshi Hasegawa *se* Shokei Nakano *lp* Hiroshi Ichikawa, Yuriko Hishimi, Tomoko Umeda, Minoru Takashima, Kunio Murai, Susumu Fujita, Toshiaki Nishizawa

The Groundstar Conspiracy
(U/HAL ROACH INTERNATIONAL) pv 95 min
A slick thriller variant on the Frankenstein theme with Sarrazin (who gives a carefully calculated performance) as the monster and Peppard standing in for the doctor. After an explosion at a top secret American space project in which he is horribly mutilated, Sarrazin is rebuilt by Peppard and used as bait to find the persons responsible. The plot's double structure, Sarrazin has no memory and is trying to discover who he is and Peppard is trying to solve the mystery, is well handled by Johnson and even the obligatory romantic sub-plot is less irritating than one would expect.

d Lamont Johnson *p* Trevor Wallace *s* Mathew Howard *c* Michael Reed *se* Herbert Ewing *lp* George Peppard, Michael Sarrazin, Christine Belford, Cliff Potts, James Olson, Tim O'Connor

L'Homme au Cerveau Greffé *aka* **The Man with the Transplanted Brain**
(PARC FILM/MAG BODARD/MARIANNE PRODUCTIONS/UGC/MARS PRODUZIONE/PARAMOUNT ORION FILM; FR,IT,WG) 72 min
An extended reverie by one of the co-founders of the prestigious *Cahiers du Cinéma*, on a theme initiated by Terence Fisher in **Frankenstein Must Be Destroyed** (1969). The plot contrives to have the brain of a noted surgeon (Aumont) suffering from a fatal heart disease transplanted into the body of a young man (Carrière) dying of brain injuries. This extends the mental life of one and the physical existence of the other. Complications set in when it emerges that the surgeon's daughter (Machiavelli) was the lover of the young man and is now in the position of desiring the body within which her father's brain is housed. The desirability of that body is signalled to the audience by making Carrière a German racing driver, thus not only evoking Lelouch's fashionable *Un Homme et une Femme* (1966) but also justifying the tapping of German production sources. The picture underplays the medical and the horror aspects of the plot in order to concentrate on the incestual and moral implications of the situation. Within those limits, the elegantly shot picture is effective, although the plot doesn't seem able to make up its mind whether to tell the story from the point of view of the hybrid or to present the issues through the way the other characters relate to the somewhat bland central figure. The script was based on a book by Victor Vicas and Alain Franck.

d/s Jacques Doniol-Valcroze *p* Philippe Dussart, Maurice Urban *c* Etienne Becker *lp* Mathieu Carrière, Jean-Pierre Aumont, Nicoletta Machiavelli, Michel Duchaussoy, Marianne Eggerikx, Martine Sarcey

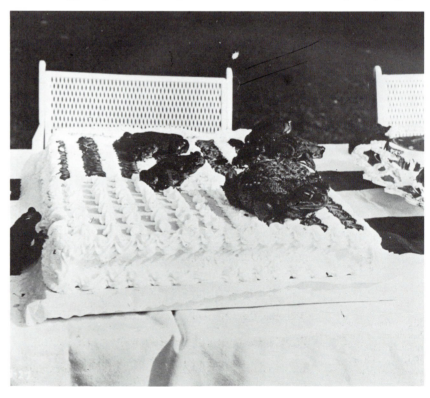

Below: *The American flag despoiled in George McCowan's superior début feature,* Frogs.

Michael Sarrazin (right) as the monster with George Peppard as Frankenstein in The Groundstar Conspiracy, *a thriller variant on the Frankenstein myth.*

L'Isola Misteriosa e il Capitano Nemo *aka* The Mysterious Island *aka* The Mysterious Island of Captain Nemo
(CITE FILMS/COPPERCINES; IT,FR,SP) 96 min
Filmed mostly in Africa this is a lifeless version of the oft-filmed Jules Verne novel. Showing all the signs of being hastily mounted, the film retains much of the plot of Verne's novel about Confederates who, after escaping from Richmond in a balloon, are stranded on a deserted island, but little of the flavour. Sharif is a colourless Nemo, the mysterious stranger also stranded on the island with his submarine, the *Nautilus*, who comes to the Confederates' assistance.

d/co-s Juan Antonio Bardem *p* Jaques Bar *co-s* Jaques Champreus *c* Enzo Serafin, Guy Deecluze, Julio Ortaz *lp* Omar Sharif, Philippe Nicaud, Gerald Tichy, Jess Hann, Rafael Bardem, Gabriele Tinti

Kadoyng
(SHAND PICTURES/CHILDREN'S FILM FOUNDATION; GB) 60 min
Whereas Hollywood's commitment to Science Fiction before the phenomenal success of **Star Wars** (1977) oscillated wildly between occasional big-budget extravaganzas such as **2001 – A Space Odyssey** (1968) and exploitation quickies, in Britain the Children's Film Foundation regularly produced moderately budgeted juvenile Science Fiction films. In doing this the normally conservative organization showed itself well in advance of Hollywood's film moguls in its realization that children would be the target audience for Science Fiction.

One of the Foundation's best efforts, this gentle comedy features a trio of children who find an alien (Maguire) from a planet of 'brainy people', only he's not quite so brainy. Accordingly, their joint efforts at stopping a planned motorway, though finally successful, are not without their difficulties. The scene where the children's family politely don't question Maguire's odd appearance (he has a pair of antennae) is charming.

d Ian Shand *p* Roy Simpson *s* Leo Maguire *c* Mark McDonald *lp* Teresa Codling, Adrian Hall, David Williams, Stephen Bone, Leo Maguire, Bill Owen

Ein Kaefer Gibt Vollgas *aka* A Beetle Goes Flat Out
(BARBARA FILM/COORDINATOR FILM; WG,SWITZ) 91 min
The second film starring Dudu the Volkswagen Beetle. Zehetgruber, the writer of **Ein Kaefer Geht aufs Ganze**

Right: 'Shock Horror Sensation . . . Bunny rabbits attack man': William Claxton's appealing Night of the Lepus.

(1971) also directed this one, by all accounts two undemanding tasks. Here, Dudu has been programmed as a crime fighter and totally obeys its master, wittily called Jimmy Bondi (Fuchsberger). Working for a Lisbon-based 'security organization' – which provides the opportunity to use cheap but touristically attractive locations, courtesy of the Portuguese government in need of foreign currency – Dudu and Jimmy eliminate a gang forging $5 bills. Two more Kaefer films were to follow, easily matching this one's total lack of interest: **Ein Kaefer auf Extratour** (1973) and **Das Verreuck-teste Auto der Welt** (1974).

d/p/s Rudolf Zehetgruber *c* Hannes Staudinger *lp* Joachim Fuchsberger, Robert Mark (Rudolf Zehetgruber), Kathrin Oginski, Heinz Reincke, Heidi Hansen, George Goodman, Arturo Duarte, Ottorino Polentini

Night of the Lepus (MGM) 88 min
Full of incidental delights, such as monster rabbits galloping in slow motion while thundering hooves play on the soundtrack, this production is far superior to Lyles' series of low-budget westerns featuring elderly actors and actresses. The plot is predictable enough, but Claxton creates enough *frissons* to make the idea of monster rabbits (created when a new serum is used by pest control officers) to be more than humorous. Whitman is the rancher who, when all seems lost, drives the rabbits onto an electrified section of railway track.

d William F. Claxton *p* A.C. Lyles *s* Don Holliday, Gene R. Kearney *c* Ted Voigtlander *se* Howard.A. Anderson Company *lp* Stuart Whitman, Janet Leigh, Rory Calhoun, DeForest Kelley, Paul Fix, Melanie Fullerton

Now You See Him, Now You Don't
(WALT DISNEY) 88 min
A sequel to **The Computer Wore Tennis Shoes** (1969), but with more humour than the original, this family comedy sees Russell discovering an invisibility serum and foiling Romero's charming gangster from taking over the near-bankrupt college Russell is a student at. Both plot and direction are old-fashioned but the actors and the Disney Studio's special effects make for an engaging, if lightweight, film.

d Robert Butler *p* Ron Miller *s* Joseph L. McEveety *c* Frank Phillips *se* Eustace Lycett, Danny Lee *lp* Kurt Russell, Cesar Romero, Joe Flynn, Jim Backus, William Windom, Edward Andrews

Panico en el Transiberiano *aka* Horror Express
(GRANADA FILMS/BENMAR; SP, GB) 90(88) min
Despite Martin's all too obvious direction with its over-reliance on shock effects, this remains an intriguing film. Its audacious central idea is that an alien with the ability to take

control of its victims arrived on Earth at the dawn of mankind, only to be trapped in what anthropologist Lee thinks is the 'missing link' when he unearths it in China in 1906, with the coming of the Ice Age. On the way back to civilization with his specimen on the Trans-Siberian express, the alien 'wakes up' and, using the information it gains by draining the minds of its victims, it kills its way to knowledge in a desperate attempt to build a spaceship to get back home, re-animate the corpses of his race and further the invasion plan.

D'Usseau and Halvey's intricate script is cleverly paced (leaving us to guess the extent of the alien's powers rather than telling us, for example), some of the characters (such as Mendoza's Russian priest who worships the alien) are well thought out and the train setting is well used, even if the exteriors are palpably models. The result is a suprisingly adventurous script that deserved a better director than it got.

d Eugenio Martin *p* Bernard Gordon *s* Arnaud d'Usseau, Julian Halvey *c* Alejandro Ulloa *se* Pablo Perez *lp* Christopher Lee, Peter Cushing, Telly Savalas, Silvia Tortosa, Jorge Rigaud, Albert de Mendoza

Slaughterhouse-Five

(U/VANADAS PRODUCTIONS) 103 min

This is big-budget Science Fiction at its worst. In place of the absurd view of life in which the horror of the bombing of Dresden is paralleled by the nightmarish existence of the central character who becomes 'unstuck in time' and flits endlessly from moment to moment which Vonnegut made the centre of his novel, Hill offers a traditional (if relatively unconventionally structured) indictment of the insanity of war. Sacks is the middle-aged optometrist who, unable emotionally to come to terms with the bombing of Dresden (for which newsreel footage of the razing of Prague was used), becomes dislocated in time and is taught by the benign Tralfamadorians (whose main enjoyment in life seems to be watching Earthmen sleep, eat and procreate) to concentrate on the good moments in his life. Hence Sacks is rewarded by the Tralfamadorians by the gift of sex-film star Montana Wildhack (exuberantly played by Perrine) to keep him company in the one-man zoo they create for him on Tralfamador. The result is a sugar-coated version of a novel which, although it isn't its writer's best work, has a nightmarish quality entirely lacking in the film.

d George Roy Hill *p* Paul Monash *s* Stephen Geller *c* Miroslav Ondricek *lp* Michael Sacks, Ron Leibman, Eugene Roche, Valerie Perrine, Sharon Gans, Robert Blossom

Superzan y el Niño del Espacio *aka* Superzan and the Space Boy (TIKAL INTERNACIONAL; MEX) 130 min

A genuine children's space opera adapting many of the usual motifs of Mexican fantasy pictures for a young, instead of an infantile, audience. A golden boy from the planet Arminia, Silio (Lanuza), observed by Beto and his daughter Carmen, lands in a field with his spaceship. He is on a mission to inform Dr Bertini of all the wonderful inventions his planet can give to the people of Earth to improve life and to contribute to a happy, peaceful social existence. However, Bertini only wants the information to help him rule the world. He captures Silio and Carmen, making her into a robot. Silio telepathically summons Beto for help but he is attacked by Bertini's robots. Finally, Silio calls in Superzan, the man with supernatural powers, but Bertini calls on another superman, Sartillo. In the ensuing fight, the laboratory is destroyed and the children escape, pursued by the robots. In the end Silio's father, the king of the planet Arminia, asks the boy to come home and acknowledge that his humanitarian mission has been defeated – temporarily. Constructed like a serial, the picture's excessive running time is mainly due to too many

moral interludes and sentimental scenes, but compared to the other Mexican movies supposedly designed for children, this offering is ably directed and quite entertaining.

d/s Rafael Lanuza *c* Antonio Ruiz *lp* Superzan, Giovanni Lanuza, Caro Laniesti, Claudio Lanuza, Freddy Pecherelly

The Thing with Two Heads (SABER) 86 min

Clearly modelled on **The Incredible Two-Headed Transplant** (1970), on which several of the people associated with this film worked, *The Thing with Two Heads* has the saving grace of humour.

Milland is the scientist (and racist to boot) who's been planning to transplant his head onto a healthy body only to have it grafted onto a blackman wrongly convicted of murder (Grier) when he slips into a coma. From here on the jokes flow fast and furious as each head seeks control of Grier's body and to have the other head removed. The film is slackly directed but the tongue-in-cheek acting of Milland and Grier survives all.

d/s Lee Frost *p* Wes Bishop *c* Jack Steely *lp* Ray Milland, 'Rosey' Grier, Don Marshall, Roger Perry, Chelsea Brown, Kathy Bauman

Tomb of the Undead

(MILLENIUM PRODUCTIONS) 59 min

An exploitation quickie made to cash in on the success of **Night of the Living Dead** (1968), *Tomb of the Undead* has none of the morbid wit or invention of George Romero's film. The inept script by director Hayes has prisoners, killed in an attempted prison break, transformed into zombies when formaldehyde (!?) is spilled over their mass grave and launching an attack on the prison. Hayes' direction is equally clichéd, especially the climax where the zombies are first transfixed by the beauty of Charney and then shot.

d/s John Hayes *p* H.A. Milton *c* Phil Kenneally *se* Richard Helmer *lp* Duncan McLeod, John Dennis, John Dullaghan, Lee Frost, Lewis Sterling, Marland Procktor, Susan Charney

Above: *Michael Sacks as the man 'unstuck in time' and Valerie Perrine as sex star Montana Wildhack on Tralfamador in George Roy Hill's leaden Slaughterhouse-Five.*

Right: *The apes take a prisoner (Noah Keen) in* Battle for the Planet of the Apes, *the last of the five-strong* Ape *series.*

Ach Jodel Mir Noch Einen – Stosztrupp Venus Blaest zum Angriff *aka* 2069: A Space Odyssey *aka* Sex Charge
(TRANSOCEAN INTERNATIONAL FILM/VICTORIA FILM; WG,AUSTRIA) 82 min

A silly comedy in which women from Venus come to Earth to find men prepared to help them ensure the survival of the Venusian race. A cheap sexploitation effort in which the Venusian women's space suits consist of a motorbike helmet (plus visor) and some brightly coloured plastic belts, the humour is execrable, the women pleasant to look at and the men they mate with uniformly repulsive.

d Hans Sternbeck   *s* Willy Pribil   *c* Michael Marszalek
lp Nina Frederic, Heidrun Hankammer, Catherina Conti, Gerti Schneider, Alena Penz

Battle for the Planet of the Apes
(APJAC)   pv   86 min

With their unimaginative script the Corringtons (who also scripted **The Omega Man**, 1971) at least manage to tie up the loose ends left by Dehn in his screenplay for **Conquest of the Planet of the Apes** (1972) and bring the story full circle to the beginning of **Planet of the Apes** (1968), the film that begat this five-strong series. McDowall (who originally played the ape scientist Cornelius) reprises his role as Caesar (Cornelius' son) and fights off the challenge to the apes by gorillas (led by Akins) and mutant humans (led by Darden) to lay the groundwork for the ape society that flourishes in *Planet of the Apes*. Even the brief appearance of Huston (a director given to making guest appearances as an actor in the most unlikely of films) fails to relieve the tedium.

d J. Lee Thompson   *p* Arthur P. Jacobs   *s* John William Corrington, Joyce Hooper Corrington   *c* Richard H. Kline
se Gerald Endler   *lp* Roddy McDowall, Claude Akins, Natalie Trundy, Severn Darden, Lew Ayres, John Huston

Carne per Frankenstein *aka* Flesh for Frankenstein
(C.C. CHAMPION & I/JEAN YANNE-JEAN-PIERRE RASSAM; IT,FR)   95(87) min

In place of the simple 'pelt and burn' effects that 3-D was usually put to, Morrissey here uses Arch Oboler's Space Vision 3-D system (developed by Oboler for **The Bubble**,

Paul Morrissey's Carne per Frankenstein, *a film that literalizes the blood-and-guts clichés of the Frankenstein legend through its use of Arch Oboler's Space Vision 3-D system.*

1966) to literalize the 'blood and guts' clichés that lie at the heart of so many of the Frankenstein films. Accordingly the recurrent motif of the film is the disembowelling of numerous characters in glorious 3-D. The rudimentary plot has Frankenstein (Kier) attempting to create a Serbian master-race and his wife/sister (Van Vooren) competing for their sexual favours. The result is an ugly looking would-be Jacobean tragedy in which the corpses pile up in a suitable enough fashion but to little purpose.

d/s Paul Morrissey   *p* Andrew Braunsberg   *c* Luigi Kuveiller   *se* Carlo Rambaldi   *lp* Joe Dallesandro, Monique Van Vooren, Udo Kier, Arno Juerging, Carla Mancini, Srdjan Zelenovic

The Clones *aka* Clones
(HUNT-CARD PRODUCTIONS)   94 min

An exploitation quickie, *The Clones* veers uneasily between self-parody and ponderous action. Greene is the research scientist who flees from a malfunctioning secret laboratory to discover that he's been cloned as part of a plot by Adams to take over the world. The initial confrontation of Greene and his double is appropriately chilling and the discovery by Greene's clone that he doesn't like being Greene is equally imaginatively handled. However, once the plot proper gets underway, the film goes steadily downhill to a predictably joky end in a disused funfair (complete with a 'See the Real You' sign hanging above a mirror maze).

co-d/p Paul Hunt   *co-d* Lamar Card   *s* Steve Fisher
c Gary Graver   *lp* Michael Greene, Otis Young, Gregory Sierra, Susan Hunt, Stanley Adams, Alex Nicol

The Crazies   (PITTSBURGH FILMS)   103 min
A far slicker film than Romero's début, **Night of the Living Dead** (1968) which this is virtually a remake of, *The Crazies* suffers from looking too calculated. In place of the rugged, disturbing atmosphere of his first film, this (like David Cronenberg's similarly infected remake of his classic, **The Parasite Murders**, 1974, **Rabid**, 1976) sees Romero over-striving for effects.

The story is simple. A plane carrying an untested vaccine intended for bacteriological warfare to which there is no known antidote crashes and the population of Evans City is infected. Into the area come the military with instructions to either kill or cure the crazed inhabitants. McMillan and Carroll are the couple on the run from both military and the Crazies. The movie's one point of departure from *Night of the Living Dead* is Romero's pointed contrast between the military, who, as they follow orders, are revealed to be as crazed as the Crazies, and the care and concern shown each other by the members of the group they hunt. Thus, Jones, after realizing that he's infected, sacrifices himself that

McMillan and the pregnant Carroll can escape, only for Carroll, like the hero of *Night of the Living Dead*, to be pointlessly shot by the military.

d/s George A. Romero *p* A.C. Croft *c* S. William Hinzman *se* Regis Survinski, Tony Pantanello *lp* Lane Carroll, W.G. McMillan, Harold Wayne Jones, Lloyd Hollar, Richard Liberty, Lynn Lowry

The Day of the Dolphin
(ICARUS PRODUCTIONS/AVCO EMBASSY) pv 104 min
Generally considered purely as a political thriller, this is a routine affair in which trained dolphins are kidnapped by a right-wing extremist group which plans to use them to plant mines on the presidential yacht. What lifts the film is the commitment of Nichols and screenwriter Henry to the growing relationship between the dolphins and their trainer (Scott), a relationship that is neither clinically detached nor gooey and sentimental. The film's central irony is that having taught the dolphins to speak and relate to humans, Scott is unable to also teach them to discriminate between humans.

d Mike Nichols *p* Robert E. Relyea *s* Buck Henry *c* William A. Fraker *se* Albert Whitlock, Jim White *lp* George C. Scott, Trish Van Devere, Paul Sorvino, Fritz Weaver, Jon Korkes, Edward Herrmann

Digby – The Biggest Dog in the World
(WALTER SHENSON FILMS; GB) 88 min
Digby, fed on a chemical intended to increase the protein yield of vegetables destined for use in space flight by mistake, evacuates centre stage too often for this juvenile fantasy to work. His place is taken by a stream of British comics, ranging from Milligan to Norman Rossington and beyond, whose antics soon pale. Beaumont is fine as Digby's owner who rescues his dog with a shrinking mixture just before the army put into operation their plan to bomb Digby into submission, but McGrath doesn't give the necessary screen time to either boy or dog for the dramatics to be anything but false.

d Joseph McGrath *p* Walter Shenson *s* Michael Pertwee *c* Harry Waxman *se* Tom Howard *lp* Jim Dale, Spike Milligan, Angela Douglas, Richard Beaumont, Milo O'Shea, John Bluthal

The Final Programme *aka* The Last Days of Man on Earth
(GOODTIMES ENTERPRISES/GALDIOLE FILMS; GB) 89 min
A stylish attempt to bring the terrifying future world of Michael Moorcock to the screen, *The Final Programme* is a seriously flawed film. The main reason for this is that Fuest (whose **Dr Phibes Rises Again**, 1972, was a camp success)

Above: *George Scott and friend in Mike Nichols' moving, if confusing,* The Day of the Dolphin.

puts all his energies into the film's elegant sets rather than into structuring and restraining Moorcock's manic, sprawling vision. In short, Fuest reduces the elemental to the merely decorative. Thus Finch's Jerry Cornelius becomes, in Fuest's hands, merely a cynical variant on the Flash Gordon character. Given the task of rescuing the world, he prefers instead to rescue his sister and when he fails in that to seek revenge on his brother (O'Connor). Almost unintentionally, he secures the missing 'final programme' of his father with which his father's acolytes (Magee, Crowden and Coulouris, a terrifying threesome, if ever there was one) intend to rescue mankind from the famine and wars it is suffering. Whereupon the new messiah, born of the coupling of Finch and Runacre, turns out to be a misshapen monster. The end works as a cruel jest at the expense of **2001 – A Space Odyssey** (1968), but it makes no sense in the pattern of the film, being just one more inversion of the heroic rescues attempted by Flash Gordon, Buck Rogers and the like.

d/s Robert Fuest *p* John Goldstone, Sandy Lieberson *c* Norman Warwick *lp* Jon Finch, Jenny Runacre, Sterling Hayden, Patrick Magee, Graham Crowden, Derrick O'Connor, George Coulouris

Frankenstein and the Monster from Hell
(HAMMER; GB) 99 min
A routine film from Fisher who, in his previous Frankenstein film, **The Revenge of Frankenstein** (1958), had transformed the essentially Gothic figure that Frankenstein had become back to the romantic character that lies at the heart of Mary Shelley's original novel.

Briant is the would-be Frankenstein who is committed to an asylum for the criminally insane only to discover that it is run by Cushing's Baron Frankenstein himself. The opening is atmospheric enough, but once the experiments (to give a new brain to one of the inmates) gets underway, Fisher seems unable to stop Hinds' screenplay from descending into melodrama as it searches for shock effect after shock effect. Like Hammer's attempts to bring Dracula up-to-date, the film shows the studio as out of step with the seventies as it was in step with the fifties and sixties.

d Terence Fisher *p* Roy Skeggs *s* John Elder (Anthony Hinds) *c* Brian Probyn *lp* Peter Cushing, Shane Briant, Madeline Smith, John Stratton, Bernard Lee, Patrick Troughton

Left: Digby – the Biggest Dog in the World.

Frankenstein: The True Story

(U; GB) 123 min

This is a digest of the two-part telefilm first shown on
American television in 1973. Its title notwithstanding, the
film is no truer than the countless adaptations of Mary
Shelley's novel. Rather, writers Isherwood and Bachardy,
clearly the prime movers in the endeavour, seek to re-define
and articulate an aspect of Shelley's novel that is missing from
so many of the films derived from it, the relationship between
Frankenstein (here Whiting) and the creature (here Sarrazin),
which is further intensified by the facial similarities of the two
actors. Thus Sarrazin becomes not the 'other' – Frankenstein's dreams writ large – but his shadowy double whose
physical disintegration after his 'birth' – he is born not as a
mangled mass of humanity but as a beautiful innocent –
parallels the emotional collapse of his master who, disgusted
with his creation, rejects it. It is this, rather than the
suggested parallels between the characters of the novel and
those present while Mary Shelley was writing it (Byron,
Shelley, Dr Polidori) which is made in the prologue, that is
the driving force of the film. Thus, despite his rejection of the
monster, Frankenstein finds himself tied to his creation. He is
blackmailed by Mason's Dr Polidori into creating a mate for it
(Seymour) and finally he finds the monster on board the ship
when he flees. Whereupon, after the monster has killed his
wife (Paget), he finally accepts his responsibilities and
amongst the Arctic wastes brings down an avalanche that
buries them both.

d Jack Smight *p* Hunt Stromberg Jnr *s* Christopher
Isherwood, Don Bachardy *c* Arthur Ibbetson *se* Roy
Whybrow *lp* James Mason, Leonard Whiting, David
McCallum, Jane Seymour, Nicola Paget, Michael Sarrazin

Gojira Tai Megalon *aka* Godzilla Versus Megalon

(TOHO-EIZO; JAP) scope 74 min

Another response to Daiei's challenge. **Gamera Tai Daimaju
Jaiga** (1970) was answered by **Gojira Tai Gaigan** (1972), and
Gamera Tai Shinkai Kaiju Jigura (1971) is countered by this
film, which goes underground instead of underwater. Godzilla's 13th star-turn has him pitted against Megalon, an
enormous cockroach with a death ray emanating from the top
of its head, and Borodan, a big black chicken. Both the
baddies are in the service of the Seatopians who wish to take
revenge on the surface people for the damage they inflicted on
the Seatopian civilization by underground nuclear tests. The

plot also deploys a robot, sent to fetch Godzilla from monster
island, and together they save Japan once more. The effects
are expertly done and it looked as if the series was beginning
to revive under the guidance of Fukuda and with the new
energizing theme of pollution, here combined with the old
theme of nuclear experiments. The promise of revival was
fulfilled by the next two instalments, **Gojira Tai Mekagojira**
(1974) and **Mekagojira No Gyakushu** (1975), putting Toho
firmly back in command of the monster movie (Kaiju Eiga)
genre.

d/co-s Jun Fukuda *p* Tomoyuki Tanaka *co-s* Shinichi
Sekizawa *c* Yuzuru Aizawa *lp* Katsuhiko Sasaki, Hiroyuki
Kawase, Yutaka Hayashi, Kotaro Tomita

Horror Hospital

(NOTEWORTHY FILMS; GB) 91 min

An enjoyable parody of the Frankenstein story, *Horror
Hospital* has the simple virtue, absent in so many Science
Fiction and horror exploitation quickies, of humour. Askwith
is the pop star who goes to holiday with Shaw at Gough's

health farm only to discover that Gough is the mad scientist *par excellence* and that the 'hotel' is staffed by his monstrous creations, one of which (Martin) eventually sets them free. Gough is in fine form and some of the details, a tap that drips blood for example, are handled with an assurance that goes beyond a mere poking fun at the genre.

d/s Antony Balch   *p* Richard Gordon   *c* David McDonald
lp Michael Gough, Robin Askwith, Vanessa Shaw, Ellen Pollock, Skip Martin, Dennis Price

House of the Living Dead *aka* Doctor Maniac
(ASSOCIATED FILM PRODUCERS; S. AFRICA)   87(83) min
This is a bizarre conflation of Mary Shelley's *Frankenstein* and Edgar Allan Poe's *The Fall of the House of Usher*. Burns is the would-be Frankenstein who, having separated from their dead bodies and kept alive the souls of a variety of animals, sets about experimenting on his family in the middle of the South African veldt in the first half of the 19th century. Field is the fluttering heroine and fiancée of his brother (killed earlier by Burns who now masquerades as him) and Oxley is the middle-aged doctor and man of rational science who finally comes to her rescue, literally riding a white horse, at the climax. Over the doom-laden family rules Inglis' cold matriarch.

Sadly, director Austin and writer Marais are unable to either unite the disparate influences behind the film or animate the story. Thus, despite the large number of killings and an ending which has Burns driven to his death by the menagerie of souls unloosed from their containers, the film lacks any drama at all.

d Ray Austin   *p* Matt Druker, Basil Rubin   *s* Marc De V. Marais   *c* Lionel Friedberg   *se* Protea Holdings   *lp* Mark Burns, Shirley Ann Field, David Oxley, Margaret Inglis, Dia Sydow, Lynne Maree

It's Alive   (LARCO)   91 min
Written, produced and directed by Cohen and featuring a magnificent performance from Ryan, *It's Alive* is a masterful essay in paranoia and dissection of the ties that bind in family life. Cohen neatly inverts the normal 'invasion' (from without) by having the invasion come from within when Ryan's wife Farrell (who has been taking a new drug) gives birth to a malevolent mutant that kills four doctors and nurses on its entry into the world. This gives the film a powerful double structure; out on the streets the mutant is hunted down while at home Ryan and Farrell's solid family relationship is shattered as both try to come to terms with what they've produced. Ryan at first, out of desperate guilt feelings, joins the hunt for his son but eventually, like Farrell for whom motherhood explains all, he attempts to defend his terrifying offspring. Alongside this interrogation of family life, which

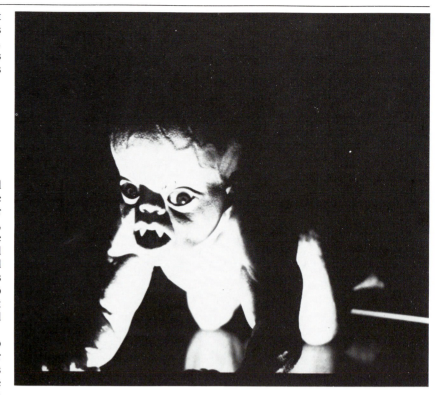

The mutant baby in Larry Cohen's magnificent It's Alive.

Cohen suggests is able to come to terms with anything (as in the scene where a horrified Ryan watches his older son trying to make friends with the scared mutant), Cohen mounts a taut thriller. Both strands are finally united in the storm drains of LA where Ryan fails to save his son.

Cohen made a sequel, **It Lives Again**, in 1978.

d/p/s Larry Cohen   *c* Fenton Hamilton   *lp* John Ryan, Sharon Farrell, Andrew Duggan, Guy Stockwell, James Dixon, Michael Ansara

Ein Kaefer Auf Extratour *aka* A Beetle in Overdrive
(BARBARA FILM; WG)   95 min
The third in the series of Dudu films starring a Volkswagen Beetle with lots of extra powers, gadgets and futuristic fittings. Written and directed by Zehetgruber, who must also take the blame for **Ein Kaefer Geht aufs Ganze** (1971) and **Ein Kaefer Gibt Vollgas** (1972). As with the others, this is one Beetle that was kept strictly for domestic German consumption. One more Beetle ordeal followed, **Das Ver-rueckteste Auto der Welt** (1974).

d/p/s Rudolf Zehetgruber   *c* Ruediger Meichsner
lp Robert Mark (Rudolf Zehetgruber), Sal Borgese, Kathrin Oginski, Walter Giller, Carl Moehner

Molchaniye Doktora Ivens *aka* The Silence of Dr Evans
(MOSFILM; USSR)   90 min
Vaguely reminiscent of the theme broached in **The Day the Earth Stood Still** (1951), although nowhere near Wise's film from a cinematic point of view, *Molchaniye Doktora Ivens* tells of three aliens from the peaceful planet Oraina who come to Earth and find nothing but violence, injustice and grief. Their experiences open the eyes of Dr Ivens (Bondarchuk) who begins to doubt the wisdom of his researches into longevity as there seems little point in prolonging life unless its quality can be improved first. The doctor dies and the female alien is killed, causing the others to realize that their visit was premature – the Earth is still far too primitive a civilization – and to leave.

The film makes a reasonable point and it is refreshing to find such a film amongst the routinely optimistic Soviet fantasy films, but the script over-emphasizes its moral lessons

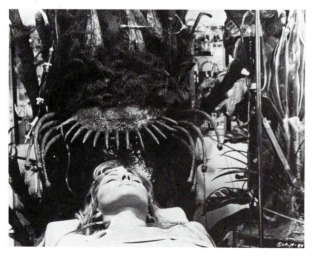

Left: Julie Ege in danger in Jack Cardiff's The Mutations.

and the direction is only average. The main points of interest are in the casting: Obolenski is a survivor from Kuleshov's film *The Extraordinary Adventures of Mr West in the Land of the Bolsheviks* (1924) and Bondarchuk, a respected actor in the USSR, is better known in the West for his somewhat overblown direction of the East-West co-productions *War and Peace* (1967) and *Waterloo* (1969).

d/s Budimir Metalnikov   *c* Yuri Sokol, Vladimir Bondarev *lp* Sergey Bondarchuk, Zhanna Bolotova, I. Kuznetsov, Leonid Obolenski, Irina Skobtseva

The Mutations

(GETTY PICTURE CORP.; GB)   92 min

Another variant on the Frankenstein theme, *The Mutations* features Pleasence as the conventionally mad scientist this time trying to synthesize plant and animal life-forms and creating a series of circus sideshow freaks in the process, including a lizard woman and a human Venus fly trap for example. In comparison to Todd Browning's *Freaks* (1932) which treated its characters with compassion, *The Mutations*, in the manner of *Terror of Tiny Town* (1938), a western with a cast of midgets, invites us to leer at Pleasence's misshapen creations and his deformed assistants (Baker and Dunn).

d Jack Cardiff   *p/co-s* Robert D. Weinbach   *co-s* Edward Mann   *c* Paul Beeson   *se* Ken Middleham, Mike Hope *lp* Donald Pleasence, Tom Baker, Brad Harris, Michael Dunn, Julie Ege, Scott Antony

Nippon Chiubotsu *aka* The Submersion of Japan

(TOHO; JAP)   104 min

The central premise of this spectacular disaster film is the sinking of Japan into the sea due to a fault in the deep sea trench that runs beneath its islands. At first the warnings of oceanographer Kobayashi aren't heeded and, when they are taken seriously by the Japanese authorities, the government's pleas for help are rejected by the governments of the Western world until Mount Fuji, the old stomping ground of numerous Japanese monsters, erupts and Japan starts slipping into the sea.

The film seems to be a parable about Japan's relationship with the West, which is willing to buy Japanese goods but unwilling to receive the Japanese as citizens; interestingly, the one country that immediately accepts Japan's new 'exports' is Switzerland, the one European country dependent on the continuance of free trade for its own survival. Moritani directs vigorously, eliding and compressing whenever possible the tragic love sub-plot about the separation of Ishida and Tanba, in favour of Nakano's spectacular special effects.

d/p Shiro Moritani   *s* Shinobu Hashimoto   *c* Hiroshi Murai, Daisaku Kimura   *se* Tereyoshi Nakano   *lp* Keiji Kobayashi, Tetsuro Tanba, Hiroshi Fujioka, Ayumi Ishida

Nuits Rouges *aka* Shadowman

(TERRA FILMS/SOAT; FR,IT)   105(88) min

Made concurrently with, and featuring the same cast as, Franju's teleseries *L'Homme Sans Visage*, this is a wholly charming descent into the world of diabolic invention and bloody murder of Pierre Souvestre and Marcel Allain whose novels formed the basis for Louis Feuillade's memorable silent serial *Fantômas* (1913). In *Judex* (1963), Franju recreated the romantic, fantasy world of Feuillade and took as his hero an avenger and administrator of justice, here Franju takes for his hero an arch-criminal (played ironically enough by screenwriter Champreux, who is Feuillade's grandson). *Judex* is a magical film in which even the creatures of the natural world (dogs, birds) come to the hero's assistance; *Nuits Rouges* is a claustrophobic film ruled over by the shadowman whose tentacles spread everywhere and who himself pops up in the most unlikely disguises to defeat the ineffectual representatives of law and order time and time again. But if the shadowman is a character clearly in the tradition of Fritz Lang's Dr Mabuse (as celebrated in **Dr Mabuse, der Spieler**, 1922; **Das Testament des Dr Mabuse**, 1933 and **Die Tausend Augen des Dr Mabuse**, 1960), Franju's treatment of him is far more playful than Lang's, more charming than frightening. Accordingly, the plot is fantastical (but not in the manner of American serials of the thirties) with Champreux, assisted by Hunnicutt and the evil Harrari and his army of zombies on the trail of the fabled treasure of the Knights Templar. Pagliai is the weak hero, Chaplin his girlfriend and Froebe the tireless policeman. Most impressive are the film's set-pieces, Harrari's laboratory-cum-torture chamber, the roof-top chases and the ornate rituals of the Knights Templar.

The German version differs from the original in that it shows the demise of shadowman.

d Georges Franju   *p* Raymond Froment   *s* Jacques Champreux   *c* Guido Renzo Bertoni   *lp* Jacques Champreux, Gayle Hunnicutt, Gert Froebe, Clement Harrari, Ugo Pagliai, Josephine Chaplin

Phase IV

(ALCED/PAR/PBR PRODUCTIONS; GB)   84 min

Directed by Bass whose animated titles introduced many a Hollywood film, this is one of the revenge-of-nature cycle of films of the seventies. The revengers this time are the ant population of Arizona which, having destroyed its natural enemies, unites and marches on the experimental dome in which (mad) scientist Davenport takes refuge with Frederick and Murphy. Action, dialogue and characterization are stilted and the film borrows too many clichés from other films, notably the opening shots which recall the world of **2001 – A Space Odyssey** (1968), but nevertheless Bass assembles the elements of his film to great effect. In this he is greatly aided by the documentary footage of the ants shot by Ken Middleton (who later did the same for **Bug**, 1975), which is interleaved throughout the film. Some of the scenes are striking, the attempts at communication with the ants, for example, even if the final confrontation of man and ant relies on too much cross-cutting to be effective and the climax – Murphy and Frederick join the ants – is ridiculously implausible.

The film won the Grand Prix at the 1975 Trieste festival of Science Fiction films.

Below: Phase IV, *Saul Bass' ambitious evolutionary essay.*

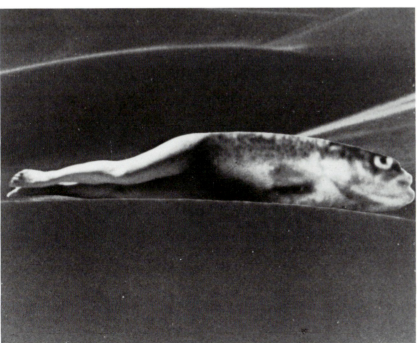

d Saul Bass *p* Paul B. Radin *s* Mayo Simon *c* Dick Bush *se* John Richardson *lp* Nigel Davenport, Lynne Frederick, Michael Murphy, Alan Gifford, Helen Horton, Robert Henderson

La Planète Sauvage *aka* Fantastic Planet
(LES FILMS ARMORIAL/SERVICE DE RECHERCHE ORTF/ CESKOSLOVENSKY FILMEXPORT; FR,CZECH) 71 min

This animated feature, an adaptation of Stefan Wul's novel, *Oms en Série*, is essentially a re-telling of the David and Goliath story in Science Fiction guise. On the planet Yagam the 39-foot-tall Draags see the tiny, short-lived Oms (the descendents of humans who travelled to Yagam in the distant past) as fit only to be pets until one, Terr, accidentally is educated by the Draags, unites the Oms in resistance to the Draags and wins equality for his race. If the plot is simplistic, the animation and sculptured landscapes are impressive.

d/co-s René Laloux *p* Simon Damiani, Andre Valio-Cavaglione *co-s* Roland Topor *c* Lubomir Rejthar, Boris Baromykin

Schlock (GAZOTSKI FILMS) 80 min
The feature début of former 20th Century Fox mailboy Landis who later graduated to the likes of *National Lampoon's Animal House* (1978) and *The Blues Brothers* (1980), this is the most successful creature-feature spoof of the seventies. Unlike the similarly intentioned **Attack of the Killer Tomatoes** (1978), it manages for the most part to both play homage to – as in the sequence where the ape-like schlockthropus, played by Landis himself, goes to the cinema to see **The Blob**, 1958, and goes berserk because it doesn't like the ending – and parody the monster films of the fifties – after going on the rampage and, despite leaving a trail of banana skins, not being caught by the ineffectual police, the schlockthropus becomes a public hero and a TV programme offers a prize to the viewer who correctly guesses how many people he'll kill before being captured. Other bizarre plot details include the monster's brief love affair with a blind girl who rejects him after regaining her eyesight and discovering he isn't the dog she thought he was.

The film, which features a guest appearance by makeup artist John Chambers (best known for his work on **Planet of the Apes**, 1968), won the Golden Asteroid at the 1973 Trieste festival of Science Fiction films.

René Laloux's *imaginative* La Planète Sauvage.

d/s John Landis *p* James C. O'Rourke *c* Bob Collins *lp* John Landis, Saul Kahn, Joseph Piantodosi, Richard Gillis, Alvici, Eliza Garrett

Sleeper
(JACK ROLLINS AND CHARLES JOFFE PRODUCTIONS) 88 min

Allen is the unlikely Buck Rogers who wakes up in the 21st century to find himself pressganged into the service of the revolution in this sly comedy. A health food neurotic who has been frozen when a minor operation on a peptic ulcer went wrong, he is revived by doctors into a totalitarian world where the gratification of pleasure (always an impossibility for an Allen character) is all. Structured like a silent comedy (but more Keatonesque than Chaplinesque), although the film leaves plenty of breathing space for Allen's paranoid humour (Allen as an inefficient robot and the world ruled by a leader whose nose is all that remains and from which scientists propose to clone him, for example), the film is one of the few of Allen's movies to integrate his comic turns into the straitjacket of a strong plot.

Two episodes of Allen's previous film, *Everything You Wanted to Know About Sex but Were Afraid to Ask* (1972) were inventive parodies of Science Fiction. The first, which satirized fifties creature-features, saw Allen menaced by a gigantic female breast (which he eventually trapped in a huge brassière) while the second was a delicious re-working of **Metropolis** (1926) in terms of the workings of the human body with the brain, intent on achieving the perfect orgasm, readying his troops, which include spermatozoa decidedly worried about their eventual destination, for action.

d/co-s Woody Allen *p* Jack Grossberg *co-s* Marshall Brickman *c* David M. Walsh *se* Ralph Rosenblum, A.D Flowers, Gerald Endler *lp* Woody Allen, Diane Keaton, John Beck, Mary Gregory, Don Keefer, Don McLiam

Soylent Green (MGM) pv 97 min
The last film by Robinson, who died before it was released, *Soylent Green* stars Heston as the future's lone honest cop and searcher for truth. Set in a highly implausible future (the MGM backlot with the minimum of futuristic touches), Greenberg's script deforms Harry Harrison's anti-utopian novel *Make Room, Make Room* to little purpose. The year is 2022, the place an over-populated New York whose inhabitants depend on synthetic foods manufactured by the Soylent Corporation and Heston the cop who, in the course of a murder investigation, discovers that the corporation's new synthetic food is manufactured from human corpses. Fleischer directs

Left: *Woody Allen as an inefficient robot butler in the hugely enjoyable* Sleeper.

Right: *A food riot in the ineptly mounted* Soylent Green.

in an unusually plodding manner, as though weary of the project, with the result that Heston's growing disillusionment as he approaches the truth has no dramatic edge to it at all. Nonetheless, the film won a Nebula award as the best Science Fiction film of the year.

d Richard Fleischer   *p* Walter Seltzer, Russell Thatcher
s Stanley R. Greenberg   *c* Richard H. Kline
se Braverman Productions   *lp* Charlton Heston, Leigh Taylor-Young, Edward G. Robinson, Chuck Connors, Joseph Cotten, Brock Peters, Paula Kelly

Sssssss *aka* **Ssssnake**   (ZANUCK-BROWN/U)   99 min
Martin (who gives a wonderful hammy performance in the manner of John Carradine) is the ophiologist obsessed with the idea that cold-blooded creatures will inherit the Earth and sets about transforming Benedict into a snake-man in preparation. But once Benedict begins mutating into a giant cobra and Martin takes to killing everyone who suspects Benedict to be the mysterious snake-man with a variety of snakes, the film swiftly settles into a predictable rut to climax, as one might expect, with Benedict, now a cobra, fighting a mongoose.

The makeup is by John Chambers whose flexible ape makeup was an important element in the success of **Planet of the Apes** (1968).

d Bernard L. Kowalski   *p* Dan Striepeke   *s* Hal Dresner
c Gerald Perry Finnerman   *se* Elkin/Universal
lp Strother Martin, Dirk Benedict, Heather Menzies, Richard B. Shull, Tim O'Connor, Jack Ging

Traumstadt *aka* **Dream Town** *aka* **City of Dreams**
(INDEPENDENT FILM/MARAN FILM PRODUKTION; WG)   124 min
Schaaf belongs to the first generation of new German *cinéastes* who achieved an international reputation in the late sixties.

His best-known work was *Taetowierung* (1967), the story of a boy rebelling against his stepfather. Schaaf distinguished himself by the care he took with his décors and a well-developed sense of design but, in this film, ornamentalism has taken over, making the movie an overlong series of loosely connected set-pieces repetitiously cataloguing the fashionable 'youth' designs characteristic of the sixties, psychedelic body painting and all, rendering the film hopelessly old-fashioned even while it was being made.

The story, extremely freely adapted from Kubin's classic expressionist novel *The Other Side* (1909), tells of a couple

Sssssss, one of the numerous seventies mutation movies.

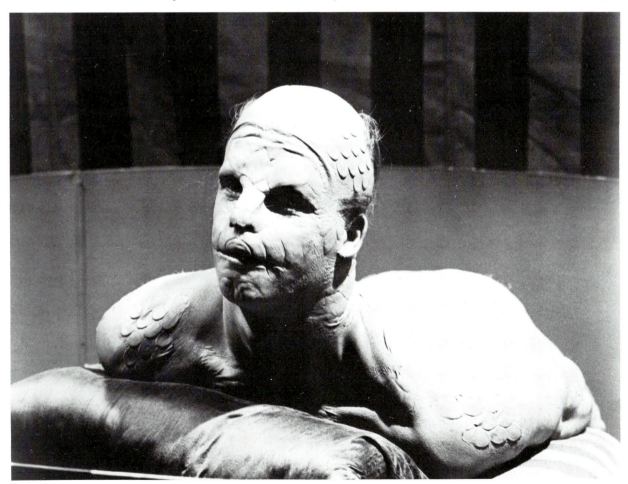

(Oscarsson and Fendel) who travel to a small, isolated city state, rather like that of **Westworld** (1973), where people can live out all their fantasies and wishes. The predictable result is chaos, mirrored in the meandering succession of scenes eventually leading to the destruction of the city. Apparently Schaaf's cameras were on hand as a small Austrian city was blown up to make way for a dam, allowing for realistically filmed destruction scenes which form the highlight of the film. Schaaf's heavy moralizing (people's fantasies are beastly and boringly routine at the same time and should never be translated into reality) only helps to increase the tedium.

Oscarsson gives his usual competent performance as the neurotic lead but the rest of the cast fight a losing battle against the décor.

d/s Johannes Schaaf   *p* Heinz Angermeyer   *c* Gerard Vanderberg   *lp* Per Oscarsson, Rosemarie Fendel, Eva Maria Meineke, Alexander May, Helen Vita, Herbert Boettcher, Rony Williams, Heinrich Schweiger, Louis Waldon

Westworld (MGM) pv 89(79) min
Crichton here neatly inserts the classic Science Fiction theme of the robot as man's slave on the verge of self-emancipation at whatever the cost to mankind into the thriller/western format. Benjamin is suitably wooden as the holidaymaker exploring the delights of the Wild West in a futuristic Disneyland, Delos, who is suddenly confronted with a 'real' gunman to draw against rather than a slave robot to kill at will. Brynner – a marvellous piece of casting – is superb as the cold, cold robot turned killer.

Crichton, making his feature film début, directs a little aimlessly and the central theme of man's creations turning on him is handled in a rather one-dimensional manner compared to the treatment of the theme in the work of Science Fiction writer Philip K. Dick (where, for example, a robot's desire to

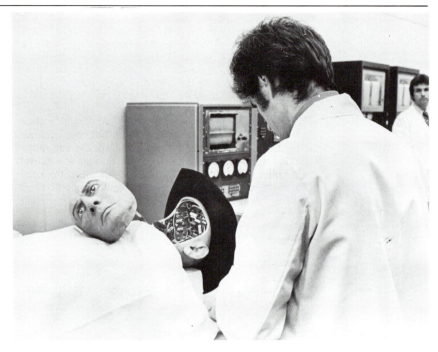

become a freelance writer is stated matter-of-factly). But the climactic chase through the underground corridors of Delos, mirroring that of **The Andromeda Strain** (1970) which was based on a novel by Crichton, is chillingly mounted. An inferior sequel, **Futureworld**, followed in 1976.

d/s Michael Crichton   *p* Paul N. Lazarus   *c* Gene Polito   *se* Charles Schulthies   *lp* Yul Brynner, Richard Benjamin, James Brolin, Norman Bartold, Victoria Shaw, Alan Oppenheimer

Above: *Yul Brynner undergoes repairs in* Westworld.

The God Zardoz *in John Boorman's ambitious film.*

Zardoz

(JOHN BOORMAN PRODUCTIONS/FOX; GB) pv 105(104) min

Inspired as much by his interests in magic (which Boorman would later give full rein to in *Excalibur*, 1981), as in Science Fiction, *Zardoz*, like the director's earlier magnificent *Point Blank* (1967) is a film that destroys the genre to which it belongs to recreate it anew. Thus, seen from one perspective, it is the most conventional of films. The post-atomic world of 2293 is divided into two zones, the Outlands, a polluted wasteland populated by brutals who do little but procreate and fight, and the Vortex in which live a mixed community of thinkers who keep the brutals in check through a selectively bred police force of exterminators. One of these, Connery's Zed, crosses from the Outlands to the Vortex and brings about the demise of its eternal inhabitants. In parallel with this energetically mounted revolt-of-the-masses movie, Boorman attempts a philosophical disquisition in which freedom and death are interlocked and science (which breaks this link, by making eternal life possible) represents unfreedom, as opposed to magic (by which Connery gains access to the life support system of the 'eternals' which he then destroys). Accordingly, when Connery arrives at the Vortex he finds a community whose members long for death which they see as salvation. If the two strands of the film never quite balance (in great part due to the energy of Connery's performance which transforms Zed into a moral, rather than philosophical, rebel), the attempt remains impressive. Moreover, Unsworth's extraordinary cinematography of the Irish landscape gives the images a hypnotic opulence that even Boorman's in-jokes (like the reference to Frank Baum's *Wizard of Oz* novel) cannot disturb.

d/p/s John Boorman *c* Geoffrey Unsworth *se* Gerry Johnston *lp* Sean Connery, Charlotte Rampling, Sara Kestelman, Sally Anne Newton, John Alderton, Niall Buggy

1974

The Cars That Ate Paris

(SALT PAN FILMS/AUSTRALIAN FILM DEVELOPMENT CORP./ROYCE SMEAL PRODUCTIONS; AUST) pv 88 min

In place of the benign Volkswagen Herbie, the star of a string of Disney-produced comedies that began with **The Love Bug** (1969), Australian writer/director Weir transforms his VW into a terrifying metal porcupine and harbinger of death. The central situation, a cross between that of *High Noon* (1952)

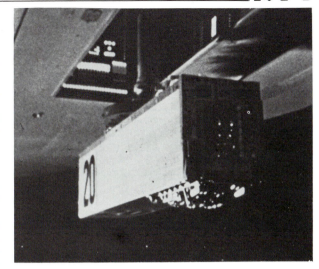

and *The Wild One* (1954), has the town of Paris in the Australian outback terrorized by its tearaway adolescents who patrol the streets in vehicles encrusted with the wreckage of cars they've lured there and cannibalized. The car's passengers have been experimented upon by the town doctor (Miles) and reduced to living vegetables. Against this backdrop, Meillon's impotent mayor tries to encourage crash victim Camilleri to bring law and order back to Paris, only to have Camilleri, once he's killed his first teenager and the town has been reduced to rubble, speed off into the night in search of fresh adventure. Weir, making his feature début, directs cleverly, rejecting conventional narrative logic in favour of a schematic view of his exploitation material.

d/s Peter Weir *p* Jim McElroy, Howard McElroy *c* John McLean *lp* Terry Camilleri, John Meillon, Peter Armstrong, Kevin Miles, Max Gillies

Damnation Alley

(LANDERS-ROBERTS/ZEITMAN/FOX) pv 95 (91) min

Based on Roger Zelazny's nightmarish novel of the same title about the last surviving Hell's Angel who takes a convoy of anti-plague serum through a post-nuclear-holocaust America from California to New York, *Damnation Alley* substitutes four conventional heroes for Zelazny's one (reluctant) hero. In the process, Sharp and Heller (writers more at home in the western) consistently tone down the novel while the penny-pinching special effects replace the novel's images of a devastated America with a mix of ill-painted cycloramas and ineptly enlarged 'killer cockroaches'. Peppard is suitably wooden as the commander and Sanda the inexpressive romantic interest.

d Jack Smight *p* Jerome M. Zeitman, Paul Maslansky *s* Alan Sharp, Lukas Heller *c* Harry Stradling Jnr *se* Milt Rice *lp* Jan-Michael Vincent, George Peppard, Dominique Sanda, Paul Winfield, Jackie Earle Haley, Kip Niven

Dark Star (JACK H. HARRIS ENTERPRISES) 83 min

Carpenter's feature film début was conceived as a reply to Stanley Kubrick's **2001 – A Space Odyssey** (1968). In place of the metaphysical pretensions and over-riding sense of sterility of that film, Carpenter, whose film was made with a ludicrously small budget ($60,000) over a three-year period, posits litter – the ship looks more like a school locker room than the acme of high technology – boredom and a malfunctioning (rather than menacing) computer as the realities of space travel. Moreover, in contrast to the solemnity of Kubrick's film, Carpenter produces a sly comedy in the style of Howard Hawks (the director of **The Thing**, 1951, which Carpenter remade in 1982) whose benign influence suffuses the project. Two sequences, the hilarious chase led co-screenwriter O'Bannon by the crews' alien pet (which resembles nothing more threatening than a beachball) that ends with O'Bannon caught in a liftshaft with the lift in motion and Narelle's attempts to convince a talking bomb not to detonate on board by recourse to phenomenological philosophy, are amongst the most remarkable and memorable of the modern Science Fiction cinema.

However, the film is far more than the sum of its parts. Carpenter's vision is of men, literally leaderless (their captain, Saunders, is dead and kept in a cyrogenic freezer and animated when his advice, which he gives complainingly, is needed), succumbing to their deepest fantasies in the loneliness of space. Accordingly, when the talking bomb finally tires of philosophy and opts for achieving its identity as a bomb and explodes, it gives Pahich the opportunity to become part of the Phoenix asteroids he's obsessed with and surf-obsessed Narelle to ride the last big wave.

Like Carpenter, O'Bannon continued to work in the Science Fiction field: he scripted **Alien** (1979) and wrote the first draft of what eventually became **Blade Runner** (1982).

d/p/co-s John Carpenter   *co-s/se* Dan O'Bannon
c Douglas Knapp   *lp* Brian Narelle, Dre Pahich, Cal Kuniholm, Dan O'Bannon, Joe Saunders, Miles Watkins

Escape to Witch Mountain (WALT DISNEY) 97 min

Richards and Eisenmann are the teenagers from outer space with superhuman powers but no memory of who they are in this workmanlike Disney offering that, Hough's deft direction notwithstanding, suffers from an excess of corn. Milland is the villainous ogre who kidnaps them, intending to profit from their powers of telepathy, Pleasance his henchman and Albert their tetchy saviour. The unimpressive special effects make a nonsense of what might have been a cheerful conclusion to the film when Albert's camper takes to the skies to escape Milland.

A sequel, **Return from Witch Mountain,** followed in 1978.

d John Hough   *p* Jerome Courtland   *s* Robert Malcolm Young   *c* Frank Phillips   *se* Art Cruickshank, Danny Lee *lp* Eddie Albert, Ray Milland, Donald Pleasance, Kim Richards, Ike Eisenmann, Denver Pyle

Fin de Semana para los Muertos *aka* The Living Dead at the Manchester Morgue

(STAR FILMS/FLAMINIA PRODUZIONI; SP,IT) 93 min
A suprisingly effective variant on George Romero's classic **Night of the Living Dead** (1968), Grau's film, for all its borrowings, has an urgency about it that is compelling. Shot in the Lake District of Britain, Continenza and Coscia's script

takes for its starting point the idea that a new chemical which attacks the nervous system of insects when sprayed over crops has the unfortunate side-effect of bringing the dead back to life as cannibals. Lovelock is the hero, thought by Kennedy's ineffectual policeman investigating the murders that quickly follow the raising of the dead to be a member of a Satanic sect, who sets things temporarily to rights. The ironic climax has Lovelock shot by Kennedy only to be revived as a zombie when the crop-dusting is resumed. Grau makes little of the implications of his story, instead he fragments it to produce *frisson* after *frisson* with his angled camera and ominous framing. A stylish film.

d Jorge Grau   *p* Edmondo Amati   *s* Sandro Continenza, Marcello Coscia   *c* Francisco Sempere   *se* Giannetto De Rossi, Luciano Bird   *lp* Ray Lovelock, Christine Galbo, Arthur Kennedy, Aldo Massasso, Giorgio Trestini, Roberto Posse

Flesh Gordon (GRAFFITI PRODUCTIONS) 90 (84,78) min

Begun as a simple piece of hard-core pornography which guyed the **Flash Gordon** (1936) serial and shot on 16 mm, midway through filming the budget was revised upwards and the film's sex scenes softened for general distribution. The end result, the superior special effects notwithstanding, is a film that, for all its sexual innuendo, is as naïvely mounted as the original. Thus Flash becomes Flesh (Williams), Zarkoff, Jerkoff (Hudgins), their spaceship phallus-shaped and the destructor ray of Ming (here Wang and played by Hunt), ruler of Mongo (here Porno), instead of threatening the destruction of the Earth turns its inhabitants into copulating fiends. A surprising success at the box office, it was followed by another camp remake, **Flash Gordon** (1980), which was also full of sexual innuendo.

co-d/s Michael Benveniste   *co-d/co-p/c* Howard Ziehm *co-p* William Osco   *se* Tom Scherman, Cinema Research, Ray Mercer, Howard Ziehm, Lynn Rogers, Walter R. Cichy   *lp* Jason Williams, Suzanne Fields, Joseph Hudgins, William Hunt, John Hoyt, Mycle Brandy

The Flying Sorcerer

(ANVIL/CHILDREN'S FILM FOUNDATION; GB) 52 min
This simple-minded fantasy from the Children's Film Foundation lacks any bite. Even worse it sees the Foundation leaving the wholesome world of *Boy's Own,* which at least had

Flesh Gordon, *the sexploitation version of* Flash Gordon (1936) *and a surprising box-office success.*

Left: *Ike Eisenmann and Kim Richards as the teenagers from outer space in the juvenile offering,* Escape to Witch Mountain.

a definite British edge to it, for the even more sugary world as created by the Disney studios. Burfield is the youngster transported back to the Middle Ages who, on his return, brings a troublesome dragon with him.

d/co-s Harry Booth   *p* Hugh Stewart   *co-s* Leo Maguire
c Leslie Dear   *se* John Poyner   *lp* Kim Burfield, Debbie Russ, John Bluthal, Tim Barrett, Bob Todd, Erik Chitty

Gojira Tai Mekagojira *aka* Godzilla Versus the Bionic Monster (TOHO-EIZO; JAP) scope 80 min

Godzilla's 14th performance sees him fight his own double, which is revealed to be a cyborg, ie a mechanical replica, controlled by alien invaders. It emerges that the good Godzilla can only defeat his rival with the help of King Seeser, a legendary monster god embodying the spirit of Okinawa. The film then veers between space opera, monster movie and sorcery, culminating in a Sergio Leone-inspired face-off between the two Godzillas and Seeser. Along the way, the Godzilla twin has attacked Anzilla, the hero's recent ally in **Gojira Tai Gaigan** (1972) but old antagonist in **Gigantis** (1955). The final fight is suitably impressive although the tongue-in-cheek reference to Leone slows the action down too much. The script, based on an idea from Sekizawa, suggests interesting connections between Science Fiction and sorcery, as well as between Japan and the long-standing hostility felt by Okinawans towards Japan. But, unfortunately, it doesn't succeed in knitting these suggestions together in a productive manner.

d/co-s Jun Fukuda   *p* Tomoyuki Tanaka   *co-s* Hiroyasu Yamamura   *c* Yuzuru Aizawa   *se* Shokei Nakano
lp Masaki Daimon, Kazuya Aoyama, Akihiko Hirata, Hiroshi Koizumi, Masao Imafuku, Beru-Bera Lin, Mori Kishida, Kenji Sahara

Herbie Rides Again (WALT DISNEY) 88 min

A sequel to **The Love Bug** (1969), this was one of the most successful of the Disney studio's live action films of the seventies. Directed with panache by Stevenson (who'd also helmed the original film), the movie follows the further exploits of Herbie, the anthropomorphized Volkswagen Beetle, which comes to the assistance of Powers and Hayes in their fight against dyed-in-the-wool villain, property director McIntire who wants to erect the tallest office building in the world on their land. The script is predictable and the characters stereotyped but some of the scenes show real comic invention, as in the climax when Herbie leads a 7th Cavalry

composed of all the VWs in San Francisco to the rescue of Hayes, beseiged by an army of monstrous bulldozers shrouded in menacing fog.

A similar, though inferior, series of films with a VW called Dudu as their hero was made in Germany, commencing with **Ein Kaefer Geht aufs Ganze** (1971).

d Robert Stevenson   *p/s* Bill Walsh   *c* Frank Phillips
se Art Cruickshank, Alan Maley, Eustace Lycett, Danny Lee   *lp* Helen Hayes, Ken Berry, Stefanie Powers, John McIntire, Keenan Wynn, Huntz Hall

The Man with the Golden Gun
(EON PRODUCTIONS; GB) 125 min

This tepid Bond outing sets Moore (in the role Sean Connery made his own) against Lee's Scaramanga, an assassin who uses golden bullets. Hamilton, making his fourth Bond movie, directs listlessly, only rising to the occasion in the climactic set-piece in Lee's hall of mirrors where Moore and Lee shoot it out. Ekland is Bond's unlikely assistant who rescues the missing solex (a device for 'harnessing the sun's energy') and Villechaize, Lee's midget assistant. Suprisingly there isn't a joke about the Lone Ranger in the whole film.

d Guy Hamilton   *p* Harry Saltzman, Albert R. Broccoli
s Richard Maibaum, Tom Mankiewicz   *c* Ted Moore, Oswald Morris   *se* John Stears   *lp* Roger Moore, Christopher Lee, Britt Ekland, Maud Adams, Herve Villechaize, Clifton James

Moskva – Kassiopeia *aka* Moscow – Cassiopeia
(GORKI; USSR) scope 83 min

A children's version of **2001 – A Space Odyssey** (1968), especially as far as the spaceship designed by Konstantin Zagorski and Vladimir Chernyshev is concerned. Smoktunovsky, who achieved international recognition for his performance as the prince in Kozintsev's version of *Hamlet*, *Gamlet* (1964), plays the special duties officer who arranges for a team of scientists under 15 years of age to be sent on a mission to a star in the Cassiopeia constellation. They will have to travel for so long that they will be adults by the time of their arrival – or at least, that is the plan. A stowaway, Lob (Basov, the son of actress, Fateyeva, who also has a cameo part) acts as the disturbing element in this routine adventure story with humorous interludes. As expected, the unexpected happens and the teenagers have to take command of the situation, confronting real danger as they approach their destination. Basov and Popova, playing Katya, the girl who inspires romantic feelings in her male crew-colleagues, in particular, perform well. The film was conceived in two parts, with the arrival on Alpha in Cassiopeia providing the starting point for Part 2, called **Otroki vo Vselennoi** (1975).

d Richard Viktorov   *s* Avenir Zak, Isai Kuznetsov
c Andrei Kirillov   *lp* Innokenty Smoktunovsky, Volodya Basov, Ira Popova, Vasili Merkureyev, Natalya Fateyeva, Sasha Grigoriev

Nostradamus no Daiyogen *aka* Prophecies of Nostradamus *aka* Catastrophy 1999

(TOHO; JAP) scope 90 min

The trend of pollution movies initiated by **Gojira Tai Hedora** (1971) is here combined with the disaster movie wave of the period. The result is the pollution movie to end them all. A bay lined with heavy industry produces some giant blood-sucking slugs. Dr Nishiyama (Tamba) sees them as the result of toxic waste and warns the nations of the world against the massive build-up of pollution in the seas as well as in the atmosphere, but his warnings are dismissed. One night the sea turns red, killing all marine life. In addition, infant mortality soars, plant life either shrivels or grows to enormous proportions and, as new, lethally poisonous carnivorous forms of flora and fauna emerge, the polar ice melts, the sun turns green, climates change and radioactive mutants roam the Earth. Crowds panic and raid food stores while governments automatically resort to military means to solve the situation. The film ends with a horrifying vision of what eventual survivors may look like. A brilliant array of special effects and a deliriously imaginative concatenation of surreal images make this an impressive firework display of all elements of disaster, pollution and monster movies rolled into one giant spectacle. The title evokes the alleged prophecies of the French mystic and astrologer Michel de Nostradamus that the world would end in July 1999 and the film chronicles the events that might precede such a catastrophe. As a fantasy of the end of the world, few are more captivatingly realized.

d Toshio Masuda *p* Tomoyuki Tanaka, Osamu Tanaka *s* Toshio Yasumi *c* Rokuro Nishigaki *se* Teruyoshi Nakano *lp* Tetsuro Tamba, Toshio Kurosawa, So Yamamura, Kaoru Yumi, Takashi Shimura, Yoko Tsukasa

The Parasite Murders *aka* They Came from Within *aka* Shivers

(CINEPIX/CANADIAN FILM DEVELOPMENT CORP.; CAN) 87 min

In contrast to Cronenberg's earlier films (**Stereo**, 1969 and **Crimes of the Future**, 1970) which were conceived of and executed as experimental films, this disturbing exploitation movie sees the director entering the mainstream of commercial cinema. It was badly received, especially in Canada, for its calculated orchestration of gory special effects, the most graphic in the cinema until that of the remarkably similar **Alien** (1979). But, if the film's visceral style marks it off from Cronenberg's earlier work, thematically *The Parasite Murders* is at one with the earlier films with its obsessive mix of Puritan revulsion at sexual activity that runs hand in hand with the concern that man has lost contact with his physical nature. These twin concerns are perfectly imbedded in the parasite research doctor (Fred Doerderlein) creates and implants in his patients in place of the organ transplants they ask for: a living organism that is an aphrodisiac crossed with venereal disease. This shocking concept is realized starkly in the fits the inhabitants of the self-sufficient Starliner complex suffer as the parasites emerge. The contrast between the clinical world of the Starliner complex and its casually promiscuous inhabitants turned into sex fiends by the rapidly spreading parasites is brilliantly captured by Cronenberg. The special effects as the parasites emerge and jump from person to person are unusually shocking, not for their goriness in particular, but because they make visible and concretize the sense of uncleanness associated with the transmission of venereal disease. This feeling is further intensified in the film's most celebrated sequence, the entrance of a parasite which crawls up through the plughole and then between the legs of a woman relaxing in the bath, glass of wine in hand, by casting Steele, *the femme fatale* of horror pictures of the sixties and seventies as the woman.

The film's structure is remarkably similar to that of George Romero's **Night of the Living Dead** (1968), a couple (Hampton and Lowry) try to stop the spread of the plague

before finally succumbing, but Cronenberg's is the far more disturbing vision and far closer to reality.

d/s David Cronenberg *p* Ivan Reitman *c* Robert Saad *se* Joe Blasco *lp* Paul Hampton, Joe Silver, Lynn Lowry, Barbara Steele, Allan Migicovsky, Susan Petrie

The Stepford Wives with Katharine Ross at the centre and Paula Prentiss behind her.

Percy's Progress

(BETTY E. BOX – RALPH THOMAS PRODUCTIONS; GB) 101 min

Though it touches on several of the themes broached in the delightful **It's Great to Be Alive** (1933) – Lawson, the recipient of the world's first penis transplant, as the only potent man in the world after a sudden contamination of the world's drinking water, for example – *Percy's Progress* lacks any of the ambition of Alfred Werker's film. Instead director Thomas and his writer Colin seem content to simply string together a seemingly endless series of flaccid jokes about impotence. Moreover, the film lacks the honest vulgarity of Donald McGill's famous seaside postcards; in its place Thomas proffers breast and buttock in profusion but to no erotic effect.

d Ralph Thomas *p* Betty E. Box *s* Sid Colin *c* Tony Imi *lp* Leigh Lawson, Elke Sommer, Denholm Elliott, Judy Geeson, Harry H. Corbett, Vincent Price

Las Ratas no Duermen de Noche

(PRODUCCIONES MEZQUIRIZ/EUROCINE-EUROPRODIS; SP, FR) scope 93 min

In keeping with the dominant tradition of Science Fiction in Spain, this film falls squarely within the sub-genre of medical fiction, started off by the prolific Jesús Franco in 1962 with his gruesome **Gritos en la Noche**. Fortuny, a young and decidedly minor director, plays it straight, combining a crime thriller with the brain transplant gimmick much in use at the time (eg **Odio Mi Cuerpo**, 1975). Naschy plays the gangleader who receives a serious head wound while escaping from the police. A professor (Palmer) is compelled to transplant the brain of a decapitated rival gangleader nicknamed El Sadico into Naschy's head with predictable results as the 'normal' thief's personality is gradually taken over by that of his sadistic competitor. The medical angle gives this mainly routine thriller a touch of physical horror as an added ingredient. However, direction and acting, not to mention the technical credits, are poor. Fortuny's career wasn't helped by this effort, and his films veered between soft sexploitation movies (with some violence added) and a Dracula spoof, *El Pobre Dracula* (1976).

d/s Juan Fortuny *c* Raymond Heil *lp* Paul Naschy, Richard Palmer, Carlos Otero, Oliver Mathot, Silvia Solar, Victor Israel, Evelyn Scott, Richard Kolin, Gilda Anderson

Santo Contra el Doctor Muerte

(CINEMATOGRAFIA PELIMEX; SP, MEX) scope 96 min
A decidedly minor instalment in the long-running Santo series, started by Benito Alazraki with *Santo contra los Monstruos* (1961). The primarily Mexican series accumulated over 20 titles, and from 1968 onwards, Santo, the masked wrestler, even teamed up regularly with his box-office rival, El Demonio Azul, after an initial confrontation in **Santo Contra Blue Demon en la Atlantida** (1968), directed by Julian Soler. This Spanish co-production is well integrated into the dominant 'medical' Spanish Science Fiction tradition initiated by Jesus Franco in 1962 with **Gritos en la Noche**. Here, the villain (Rigaud) restores paintings by means of an unusual process: he injects his models with a tumour-producing virus which, once removed from their dead bodies, yields a chemical substance that allows him to achieve perfect reproductions of famous paintings. Santo is the one who breaks up the traffic in forgeries. The rationale for the gimmick remains unclear, unless it is supposed to represent a sick version of procreation: a man injects something into a woman and the subsequent growth is, quite literally, the basis of a reproduction. But the elaboration of such dream logic into the script is perfunctory, as is the direction. Perhaps the most questionable aspect of the movie is that an interest in art and science is associated with a warped personality while everything that is healthy and admirable is symbolized by the bulky shape of an overweight masked wrestler.

d/co-s Rafael Romero Marchent *co-s* Jose Luis Merino *c* Godofredo Pacheco *lp* Carlos Romero Marchent, Helga Line, George Rigaud, Antonio Pica, Mirta Miller

The Stepford Wives

(FADSIN CINEMA ASSOCIATES) 115 min
Despite the slow pace of Goldman's script and Forbes' solemn direction, *The Stepford Wives* remains an intriguing film, as much for the central performances of Ross and Prentiss, in her best role for several years, as for its subject. They play the newly arrived wives in the Connecticut village of Stepford whose attempts to animate the strangely contented women of the community fail before it's revealed that the wives are in fact robot replicas programmed by O'Neal's sinister scientist and one-time Disneyland employee. The chilling climax, the local supermarket full of zombie wives, including Prentiss and Ross, cheerlessly exchanging small talk and recipes, is overlong in coming and the film's satirical intentions too deeply buried in the melodramatic execution of the plot. In short, a film, which was mistakenly attacked as anti-feminist, that lacks the bite of Ira Levin's original novel.

A telefilm sequel followed in 1980, *Revenge of the Stepford Wives*.

d Bryan Forbes *p* Edgar J. Scherick *s* William Goldman *c* Owen Roizman *lp* Katharine Ross, Paula Prentiss, Peter Masterson, Nanette Newman, Patrick O'Neal, Tina Louise

George Segal in the title role of Mike Hodges' stylish and haunting Terminal Man.

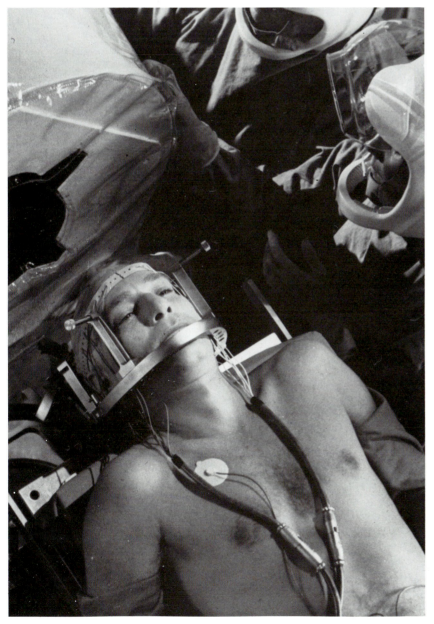

Terminal Man (WB) pv 107 (104) min

Badly received at the time of its original American release (and yet to be distributed in Britain) for its self-consciousness, which was thought to be out of place in an 'action' movie, this is a superior thriller. Former television director Hodges and cinematographer Kline brilliantly capture the flavour of Michael Crichton's pessimistic novel.

Segal is the psychotic who has a tiny computer implanted in his brain to control his violent tendencies, only to discover that the process of being 'calmed down' by the computer is so pleasurable that he goes on a murder spree simply for the pleasure of being restrained. In contrast to **Westworld** (1973), written and directed by Crichton himself, in which man is threatened by his creations, robots, or **Coma** (1978), another of Crichton's films, in which human bodies are broken down into spare parts to be used by those who can afford to pay for them, *Terminal Man* examines the frightening prospect of man and machine locked in a symbiotic relationship that is mutually destructive. The result is a film that covers much of the same ground as **A Clockwork Orange** (1971) but with the difference that whereas Stanley Kubrick celebrates Malcolm McDowell's violence as the mark of free will in a totalitarian society, Segal, after being operated on by the well-meaning doctors, is just the same as before. Thus Hodges' film ends with the scientists, seen throughout in black and white (though the film is in colour), killing their creation (the film opens with a magnificent extended sequence of Segal's (re)birth on the operating table) and recoiling in horror from the monster they cannot change.

If in the film's big scene – the murder of Clayburgh, Segal's one-time girlfriend (who is even called Angela *Black* and whose last act, in keeping with the film's colour coding, is to paint her nails black) – Hodges is unable to restrain himself, for the most part he lets the camera (and Segal's worried eyes) leisurely pan over the banks of equipment and monitors that, despite their shiny promise, can do nothing for Segal.

d/p/s Mike Hodges   *c* Richard H. Kline   *lp* George Segal, Joan Hackett, Richard A. Dysart, Jill Clayburgh, Donald Moffat, Matt Clarke, Michael C. Gwynne, James Sikking

Das Verrueckteste Auto der Welt *aka* The Maddest Car in the World   (BARBARA FILM; WG)   93 min

The fourth and last of the Kaefer films starring Dudu the Volkswagen Beetle. As in the first one of the series, **Ein Kaefer Geht aufs Ganze** (1971), the narrative excuse for putting Dudu through its paces is a rally. Racing through Europe, the Beetle, equipped with incredible gadgets, including helicopter blades, climbs up vertical cliffs, overcomes glaciers, crosses rivers, lakes and the Alps and generally does things to impress the audience with the inventiveness of writer/director Zehetgruber's imagination. It fails to do so.

d/p/co-s Rudolf Zehetgruber   *co-s* G. von Nazzani
c Ruediger Meichsner   *lp* Robert Mark (Rudolf Zehetgruber), Kathrin Oginski, Sal Borgese, Evelyne Kraft, Walter Giller, Walter Roderer, Ruth Jecklin, Gerhard Frickhoefer, Walter Feuchtenberg

Who ?

(LION INTERNATIONAL/HEMISPHERE PRODUCTIONS/MACLEAN & CO; GB)   93(91) min

Based on Algis Budry's taut thriller, this is a modest offering. Bova plays the American scientist who, after a near-fatal accident near the Russian border, is returned by the Russians after extensive surgery that has transformed him into a cyborg, part-man part-machine. Before he can be allowed to resume his urgent top-secret research, the American authorities have to ascertain whether Bova is Bova, a plant or what. Gould is the enthusiastic investigator and Howard the cynical Russian spy trainer, both of whose hopes are dashed when Bova decides to return, not to his secret work, but to the farm his dead parents worked. Gold directs as though unimpressed by his own script, spending too much time on chases rather than concentrating on the impassive Bova who gives the film's best performance as the listless cyborg.

d Jack Gold   *p* Barry Levinson   *s* John Gould (Jack Gold)
c Petrus Schloemp   *se* Richard Richtsfeld   *lp* Elliott Gould, Trevor Howard, Joseph Bova, Ed Grover, James Noble, John Lehne

Young Frankenstein

(GRUSKOFF/VENTURE FILMS/CROSSBOW PRODUCTIONS/ JOUER)   b/w   108 (106) min

In contrast to *Blazing Saddles* (1974) which saw Brooks gloriously sending up the West and all things Western with broad brushstrokes, *Young Frankenstein* is a far more restrained offering, less surreal and far more unified in tone, a pastiche rather than a parody. Using some of the sets from James Whale's **Frankenstein** (1931) and the original designs for Frankenstein's laboratory, Brooks and cinematographer Hirschfeld successfully recreate the mood and looks of the original. The anarchic jokes are still there – Wilder as Frankenstein's inept grandson asking 'Pardon me boy is this the Transylvania station?' and receiving the reply, 'Ja, Ja track 29, can I give you a shine?' and the amiable monster (Boyle, who gives a superb performance) lighting up two cigarettes after ravishing a willing Kahn, for example – but Brooks' treatment of the material is far more reverential than one might expect. Interestingly, like Paul Morrissey (in **Carne per Frankenstein**, 1973), though in a far more witty and delicate manner, Brooks chooses to update the legend by centering on the character's sexual proclivities. Thus having created the monster, Wilder swaps bodies with it on Kahn's prompting. Only Feldman's hunchbacked Igor seems out of place with his constant mugging.

d/co-s Mel Brooks   *p* Michael Gruskoff   *co-s* Gene Wilder
c Gerald Hirschfeld   *se* Hal Millar, Henry Miller Jnr
lp Gene Wilder, Peter Boyle, Marty Feldman, Madeline Kahn, Cloris Leachman, Gene Hackman

Black Moon   (NEF; FR)   100 min

Strikingly photographed by Nykvist (who later worked on Malle's first American film, the controversial *Pretty Baby*, 1978) this strange film envisages a future in which men and women are at war with each other. In anticipation of David Gladwell's **Memoirs of a Survivor** (1981), Malle's film features Harrison (the grand-daughter of Rex Harrison) as the mysterious young girl who flees the present into a fantasy world populated by unicorns and the likes of Dallesandro (still, as in Paul Morrisey's series of films for Andy Warhol, treated very much as a sex object). Malle creates both worlds with great economy – women being lined-up, kissed lightly on the cheek and then shot, representing the present, for example, but the point of the fantasy world Harrison immerses herself in remains a puzzle and the conclusion, which sees her offering her breast to the unicorn, as though to keep it and the world it represents alive, seems simply to be tacked on to the film.

The film, which was inspired in part by Lewis Carroll's *Alice in Wonderland*, was shot in and around Malle's own farmhouse.

d/p/co-s Louis Malle   *co-s* Ghislain Uhry, Joyce Bunuel
c Sven Nykvist   *lp* Cathryn Harrison, Thérèse Hiehse, Joe Dallesandro, Alexandra Stewart

Blumen fuer den Mann im Mond *aka* Flowers for the Man in the Moon   (DEFA; EG)   83 min

A leaden moral fable dripping with lofty sentiments, this maudlin children's film was made with a socialist-realist mentality at least 40 years out-of-date. A famous vegetable grower and chairman of an agricultural co-operative has a son with ambition: the boy wants to grow flowers on the Moon to make working life there a bit more jolly. A test pilot helps him with this laudable project, together with a professor of biology quaintly called Professor Vitamin. After complicated tests and a lot of hard work the wonder boy succeeds in developing a flower that will grow on the inhospitable Moon.

Young Frankenstein, *Mel Brooks' affectionate send-up of the Frankenstein story.*

Don Johnson in the powerful A Boy and His Dog.

with his investigation into a new kind of fire-producing bug which feeds on carbon that is thrown up in the wake of an earthquake. But once he's crossed the mysterious insect with a cockroach to produce a flesh-eating insect, the script and Szwarc's direction collapse into predictability and implausibility. The insect sequences were shot by Ken Middleton who served in the same capacity on *The Hellstrom Chronicles* (1971) and **Phase IV** (1973).

d Jeannot Szwarc   *p/co-s* William Castle   *co-s* Thomas Page
c Michel Hugo   *se* Phil Cory, Walter Dion   *lp* Bradford
Dillman, Joanne Miles, Richard Gilliland, Jamie Smith
Jackson, Alan Fudge, Jesse Vint

Comedia Fantastica *aka* **A Fantastic Comedy**
(CASA DE FILME CINCI; ROM)   90 min
An odd mixture of morality play, comedy and psycho-drama from the skilful animator turned feature director, Popescu-Gopo, who had previously made **Pasi Spre Luna** (1963) in this children's cinema genre. The plot combines two stories: one of a robot sent by extra-terrestrials to look for new sources of energy on Earth; the other about a boy isolated in a space craft orbiting Earth, victim of an experiment to make him grow up into a perfect human specimen. The highly disturbing scenes of the boy desperately trying to escape from the nightmarish experiment totally destroys the light-hearted humour of the robot story. The production is very professional and the script marks a step forward from the usual East European space travel fantasies for children although the result is an interesting idea that has gone wrong.

d/s Ion Popescu-Gopo   *c* Grigore Ionescu, Stefan Horvath
lp Dem Radulescu, Cornel Coman, Vasilia Tastaman, George
Mihaita, Horea Popescu

Death Race 2000   (NEW WORLD)   79 min
Adapted from an original story by Ib Melchior, a veteran of Science Fiction quickies, co-written by Thom (the writer of the impressive **Wild in the Streets**, 1968) and Corman-alumnus Griffith and directed by Bartel in bravura comic-book style, *Death Race 2000* is a hugely enjoyable movie. Rushed into production by Corman to cash in on the projected success of **Rollerball** (1975), it is vastly superior to Norman Jewison's flaccid film.

d/co-s Rolf Losansky   *co-s* Irmgard Speitel, Ulrich Speitel
c Helmut Grewald   *lp* Jutta Wachowiak, Stefan Lisewski,
Dieter Franke, Sven Grothe, Astrid Heinz, Dirk Foerster,
Yvonne Diessner

A Boy and His Dog
(THIRD LQJ INC./JAF PRODUCTIONS)   89 min
A Boy and His Dog is based on the novella by Harlan Ellison, the 'wild man' of modern Science Fiction whose controversial collection of stories *Dangerous Visions* was highly influential in both broadening the market for Science Fiction and stimulating the genre's practitioners. The directorial début of Jones, a regular character actor in westerns (particularly those of Sam Peckinpah), the film broaches the by now traditional theme of life in a post-nuclear-holocaust America in an entirely untraditional manner. At the heart of Jones' rambling narrative lies the relationship between Johnson's scavenger and his dog, Blood, with whom he can communicate telepathically. But in place of the usual sentimentality that underpins such relationships, Jones substitutes a heady and cynical pragmatism. Hence the film's climax has Johnson reject the idea of a loving relationship with Benton in order to kill her and feed her to the starving Blood before the pair walk off into a troubled sunset.

The second half of the film, in which Johnson descends from the ravaged surface to discover the life-style of Middle America preserved as if in aspic, but in need of new blood unless it is to collapse, is less successful, if only because its targets are more obvious and the plot convolutions required to get Johnson back to the surface too forced. The film is at its impressive best in Jones' visualization of the devastation that is the year 2024 and when he simply lets Johnson and Blood meander on, each comment of the dog brutally undercutting our every expectation of a canine's perception of life.

d/s L.Q. Jones   *p* Alvy Moore   *c* John Arthur Morrill
se Frank Rowe   *lp* Don Johnson, Susanne Benton, Jason
Robards, Tim McIntire, Alvy Moore, Helene Winston

Bug   (PAR)   101 min
Seeming at first to be yet another revenge-of-nature film, *Bug*, produced by Castle, a veteran in the field of low-budget horror and Science Fiction, suddenly changes course in the middle to become a routine mad-scientist movie. Dillman is fine in the central role of the scientist who becomes obsessed

Right: Joanne Miles in danger in Bug.

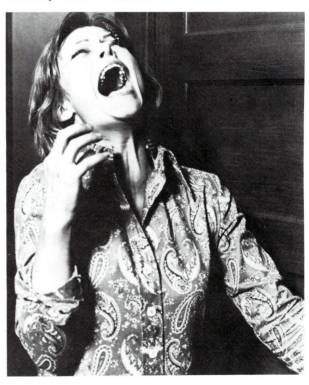

Mary Woronov ejects an unwelcome passenger in Paul Bartel's enjoyable Death Race 2000.

Set against the background of a crudely but deftly sketched 1984-ish society, the film features loner Carradine and Stallone (as the wonderfully manic hoodlum, a role he would further refine into international stardom) as the major contenders in the Transcontinental Death Race, the blood and circuses of the year 2000. The film is pulp, and often purple prose pulp at that, from start to finish (when Carradine finally sides with the good guys, runs over Mr President and declares an end to violence!) but Bartel, in mosaic fashion, dots the fast-moving film with enough comic conceits and satirical interludes to distance himself from the project's exploitation origins.

d Paul Bartel *p* Roger Corman *s* Robert Thom, Charles Griffith *c* Tak Fujimoto *se* Jack Rabin and Associates, Richard MacLean *lp* David Carradine, Simone Griffeth, Sylvester Stallone, Mary Woronov, Roberta Collins, Martin Kove

Doc Savage – The Man of Bronze (WB) 100 min

Doc Savage, created by Lester Dent (who used the pen-name Kenneth Robeson), was one of the major pulp heroes of the thirties. In the sixties a selection of the 181 stories featuring the 'Man of Bronze' and his 'Amazing Five' were reprinted by Bantam and sold remarkably well. Veteran Science Fiction film-maker Pal secured the rights to the character he once enthusiastically described as a 'thirties James Bond'. Sadly the resulting film has neither the innocence of the thirties serials nor even the minimal wit of the Bond movies. Ely (a one-time Tarzan) is the wooden Savage and Wexler the ill-conceived villain who, having murdered Savage's father, has taken over the secret goldmine deep in the South American jungle. Anderson's direction is pedestrian and the special effects (a robot plane and the green death) rudimentary.

Director Anderson was also responsible for **1984** (1956), the dire adaptation of George Orwell's novel.

d Michael Anderson *p/co-s* George Pal *co-s* Joe Morhaim *c* Fred Koenekamp *se* Howard A. Anderson, Sass Bedig, Robert MacDonald *lp* Ron Ely, Paul Gleason, Paul Wexler, Bill Lucking, Michael Miller, Eldon Quick

The Giant Spider Invasion

(CINEMA GROUP 75/TRANSCENTURY PICTURES) 76 min

Despite the joky reference to *Jaws* (1975) this film is clearly a displaced item from the fifties cycle of radiation (and such like) mutation movies. It even comes complete with Brodie and Hale as the boy-meets-girl couple who save the day. But, whereas the fifties films were at least a direct reflection of their times, this ineptly mounted offering has no such backdrop. Co-writer Easton is the greedy farmer who stumbles upon radiation-soaked spiders' eggs and, thinking them diamonds, refuses to divulge their location to investigators Brodie and Hale. Whereupon he's gobbled up by an unconvincing giant queen spider which, in a pale imitation of Jack Arnold's **Tarantula** (1955), sets out to menace a small mid-western town.

d/co-p Bill Rebane *co-p/co-s* Richard L. Huff *co-s* Robert Easton *c* Jack Willoughby *se* Richard Albain, Robert Millay *lp* Barbara Hale, Steve Brodie, Leslie Parrish, Alan Hale, Robert Easton, Kevin Brodie

Hu-Man

(ROMANTIQUE FILMS/ORTF/YVES PAUTHE/M.F.MASCARO PRODUCTIONS; FR) 105 min

Strangely similar to Alain Resnais' **Je T'Aime, Je T'Aime** (1967), *Hu-Man* stars Stamp as an actor called Terence Stamp who, depressed after the death of his young wife, agrees to become the first voyager in time when he's approached by an old flame (Moreau) acting on behalf of a mysterious organization. He makes one journey back into the past, fuelled by emotional power which the organization is able to collect and transform into matter. But, after once more witnessing the death of his wife, he tries to quit, only to be sent to the distant future. There he learns how to manipulate time himself and returns to join his wife and face death with her. Laperrousaz, a one-time documentary film-maker, directs with a penchant for psychedelic effects reminiscent of Roger Corman's *The Trip* (1967), but at far too slow a pace.

The film won the Golden Asteroid at the 1976 Trieste festival of Science Fiction films.

d/co-s Jerome Laperrousaz   p Yves Pauthe, M.F. Mascaro
co-s Guillaume Laperrousaz, André Ruellan, Francis Guilbert
c Jimmy Glasberg   lp Terence Stamp, Jeanne Moreau,
Agnes Stevenin, Frederick Van Pallandt, Franck Schwacke,
Gabriella Rysted

Invasion of the Love Drones
(A SENSORY MAN PRODUCTION)   72 min

This sexploitation offering was shot over a period of two
years, which explains the mismatch between the footage set
on Earth and that on board the spaceship (where most of the
erotic action takes place). A very loose remake of Jack
Arnold's **It Came from Outer Space** (1953), *Invasion of the
Love Drones* features Ash as the alien Dr Femme whose
spaceship runs on sexual energy. Accordingly she has first to
create a race of love drones with which to cause a worldwide
orgy which in turn will fuel the invasion of the Earth. The
film is as amateurishly made as most of the soft-core porn of
the time.

d/p/co-s/c Jerome Hamlin   co-s Dr Conrad Baunz, Michael
Gury   lp Eric Edwards, Viveca Ash, Bree Anthony, Tony
Blue, Sarah Nicholson, Jamie Gills

Mansion of the Doomed aka The Terror of Dr Chaney
(CHARLES BAND)   89 (86) min

An inept re-working of George Franju's classic **Les Yeux
Sans Visage** (1959). Basehart is the surgeon obsessed with
restoring the eyesight of his daughter (Stewart), lost in a car
crash when he was driving. He goes on the rampage removing
the eyes from an ever-growing number of people he then
keeps caged in his underground laboratory. The predictable
climax has the victims, led by a distraught Stewart, tearing
out Basehart's eyes.

*Ron Ely in the title role
of Michael Anderson's
dire* Doc Savage – The
Man of Bronze.

d Michael Pataki   p Charles Band   s Frank Ray Perilli
c Andrew Davis   lp Richard Basehart, Trish Stewart, Gloria
Grahame, Lance Henriksen, Al Ferrara, Libbie Chase

Mekagojira No Gyakushu aka Terror of Mechagodzilla aka The Escape of Megagodzilla aka Monsters from the Unknown Planet
(TOHO-EIZO; JAP)   scope   83 min

A sequel to **Gojira Tai Mekagojira** (1974) provided Honda
with the opportunity to direct the monster he launched in
1954 in its 20th birthday performance, in the 15th film
starring the tyrannosaurus rex lookalike. The director seemed
to have recovered from his fallow spell since **Kaiju Soshingeki**
(1968). Here, the bad monsters are once more controlled by
aliens who are served by an embittered scientist and his
daughter. The aliens repaired her after a fatal accident and she
now survives as a cyborg. The aliens also launch their cyborg
Godzilla, Mekagojira (Mori) against the Earth, in tandem
with Titanosaurus (Fuyamoto). Both of them are supervised
and encouraged by the cyborg woman. Godzilla (Kawane),
with the help of an enormous supersonic machine reminiscent
of the hi-fi equipment used in **Kaiju Daisenso** (1965) defeats
the invasion. As in the previous Godzilla film, it is the
Mekagojira who steals the show and provides the best visual
moments in the picture.

d Inoshiro Honda   p Tomoyuki Tanaka   s Yukiko
Takayama   c Motoyoshi Tomioka   se Teruyoshi Nakano
lp Katsuhiko Sasaki, Tomoko Ai, Akihiko Hirata, Tadao
Nakamura, Katsumasu Uchida, Goro Mutsu, Kenji Sahara,
Toru Kawane, Kazunari Mori, Tatsumi Fuyamoto

Odio Mi Cuerpo aka I Hate My Body
(GALAXIA FILMS/ANDRE KUHN; SP, SWITZ)   97 min

A confused and misogynist exploitation of the brain transplant gimmick (a popular theme at the time, see for example,
Las Ratas No Duermen de Noche, 1974). An engineer's
brain is transplanted into the body of a woman (Bastedo) who
then finds that she cannot get the engineering jobs the same
brain with a male body would have been able to obtain quite
easily. The problems start when Bastedo's sexual identity,
which the film presents in totally stereotyped ways, comes
into question: lack of femininity is signified in terms of a
butch lesbian tendency as well as the conventional images of
'mannish' women such as leather and whips. As Terence
Fisher showed in **Frankenstein Created Woman** (1966), the
notions of sexual difference and socially determined gender
difference can be mobilized in very complex ways in these
cross-sex brain transplant movies. However, Klimovsky's
film merely replays the tritest of conventions in a muddled
script. In the end, Bastedo expiates her guilt of not being
enough of a woman by dying, killed by a would-be rapist. The
suggestion the film leaves is that it is Bastedo's 'mannish'
aspects which prevented the rape and caused her death as an
'impossible' creature.

The prolific Klimovsky felt far more at home with less
challenging subjects such as routine Italian westerns and sexy
horror movies like *La Noche de los Vampiros* (1975) or *La
Noche de Walpurgis* (1971).

d/co-s Leon Klimovsky   p Juan Ramon Jimenez, André
Kuhn   co-s Solly Wollodarski   c Francisco Sanchez
lp Alexandra Bastedo, Byron Mabe, Narciso Ibañez Menta,
Gemma Cuervo, Manuel Zarzo, Eva Leon, Maria Silva

Otroki vo Vselennoi aka Teenagers in Space
(GORKI; USSR)   scope   85 min

The second part of **Moskva – Kassiopeia** (1974) which ended
when the young scientists cum space crew, all under 15 years
of age, reached Alpha in the constellation of Cassiopeia. There
they discover a planet much like Earth – which saves on
design costs – ruled by robots who maintain their human
subjects in a state of permanent, vegetable-like happiness.
The children manage to free the people by shortcircuiting the
robots, thus restoring everybody to their normal neurotic
selves. As a political parable, the message is transparent and
wittily castigates a ruling elite for its authoritarian paternal-

ism, however benevolent. There are even a few first generation robots who dogmatically stick to their assigned roles, relentlessly blocked into a single pattern, such as the Iron Mum, with pram and all. Smoktunovsky again plays the mission controller who finally orders the kids back to Earth. On the whole, this second part is more entertaining than the first, wasting less time convincing us of the lovability of the children.

d Richard Viktorov *s* Avenir Zak, Isai Kuznetsov *c* Andrei Kirillov *lp* Misha Yershov, Sasha Grigoriev, Volodya Savin, Volodya Basov, Innokenty Smoktunovsky, Olya Bityukova

The Rocky Horror Picture Show (FOX; GB) 101 min
This camp version of O'Brien's huge stage success has over the years become a cult classic, more because of the people it's played to in the course of its lengthy New York run, many of whom came dressed as their favourite characters and would mouth the lines on cue, than for the film itself which, its inconsequential tacky delights notwithstanding, is ill-conceived.

O'Brien and Sharman's screenplay crosses the Franken-stein legend – Curry's transvestite alien, Frank-N-Furter, plans to create the perfect male sex object – with nostalgic memories of rock 'n' roll and fifties B movies, which provide the structuring context for all that follows. Bostwick and Sarandon are the engaged couple who, when their car breaks down, enter the decadent world of Frank-N-Furter, a magnificent performance by Curry. Sharman retains the parodic edge of the stage play but opens up the action needlessly, dissipating the energy of the original.

d/co-s Jim Sharman *p* Michael White *co-s* Richard O'Brien *c* Peter Suschitzky *se* Wally Veevers *lp* Tim Curry, Susan Sarandon, Barry Bostwick, Richard O'Brien, Jonathan Adams, Nell Campbell

Rollerball (UA) scope 129 (125) min
Rollerball takes for its central premise an idea common in Science Fiction novels of the fifties and which reached its climax in the work of Philip K. Dick, that in the future the world will be controlled not by governments but by corporations who offer the populace bread and circuses while their executives lead lives of luxury. That said, the film was a (deserved) commercial and critical disaster, with only a few redeeming features (notably Richardson's dotty computer librarian and some of the actual rollerball sequences). Set in 2018, Harrison's story imagines rollerball, a combination of football, hockey, motor derby and motorbike racing, as the perfect spectator sport to both dissipate the population's anti-social feelings and inculcate a sense of sameness. Caan is the loner, ordered to quit playing because he's so successful and is thus bucking the system in which star players are meant to rise and fall regularly, and Houseman the cynical patriarch.

The conclusion, after an overly complicated plot that mixes political intrigue and romance to no purpose, is predictable with Caan and the system surviving against all odds.

d/p Norman Jewison *s* William Harrison *c* Douglas Slocombe *se* Sass Bedig, John Richardson, Joe Fitt *lp* James Caan, John Houseman, Maud Adams, Ralph Richardson, John Beck, Moses Gunn

Shock Waves *aka* **Death Corps** *aka* **Almost Human**
(LAWRENCE FRIEDRICKS ENTERPRISES) 86(85) min
A fascinating oddity, *Shock Waves* almost survives the minuscule budget at its disposal by dint of Wiederhorn's imaginative direction. The film's absurd premise is that a German battalion of dead troops, resuscitated zombies, when found to be uncontrollable, were sunk, together with their ship, in the Caribbean. They re-surface in the wake of an underwater explosion and attack the passengers of a pleasure

Above: Rollerball, *big-budget Science Fiction at its worst.*

cruiser stranded on a desert island. Some of the imagery, like the zombies emerging from the sea, is compelling but the film quickly settles into yet another version of **Night of the Living Dead** (1968) with Adams (the heroine of **Invasion of the Body Snatchers,** 1978, and a regular member of the cast of the *Flipper* teleseries), Buch and Halpin (another *Flipper* regular) besieged by the zombies. Cushing is the battalion's one-time commander who is unable to reassert any control over them and Carradine the old sea captain whose boat is stranded on the desert island. Director Wiederhorn later made the minor Horror outing *Eyes of a Stranger* (1980).

That said, the movie's rental figures ($34,200,000 by 1990) testify to its enduring appeal and confirm it, in terms of the ratio between budget and profits, as one of the most successful Science Fiction films ever.

d/co-s Ken Wiederhorn *p/c* Rueben Trane *co-s* John Harrison *lp* Peter Cushing, John Carradine, Brooke Adams, Fred Buch, Luke Halpin, Jack Davidson

The Super Inframan *aka* **The Infra Superman**
(SHAW BROTHERS; HONG KONG) scope 90 min
One of the rare Hong Kong fantasy films resorting to scientific knowledge instead of mystic or magical lore, although there is plenty of that here as well. After their disappointing collaboration with the Hammer Studio on *The Legend of the Seven Golden Vampires* (1974), the Shaw Brothers turned to the Superman story for further inspiration. An evil queen, decked out with skulls and snakeskins to embody the stereotype of the phallic mother fantasy, rules an

Right: *Yul Brynner as The Ultimate Warrior, the first film to mix Science Fiction with Kung Fu.*

underground realm and threatens to unleash natural catastrophes on the world in a bid for world domination. A kung fu fighter is transformed, with the help of a scientific laboratory and electronic gadgets reminiscent of 'sick bay' in the *Star Trek* teleseries, into an invincible hero and triumphs over the bad mother and her minions. The film relies almost totally on the impact of isolated fragments, without much overall structure other than its dream logic, mixing horror, martial arts, Science Fiction and comic strips into a kaleidoscopically organized exploitation movie. The lack of soul-searching moralism is refreshing, but the *mise en scene* is too haphazard for the juxtaposed fragments to clash in interesting ways. Li Hsiu-Hsien also played the hero in the Hong Kong monster movie *The Mighty Peking Man* (1977), a dream-like and delirious compendium of all the colonial motifs and sexual fantasies, awkwardly cloaked in Western versions of Tarzan, King Kong and other 'exotic' jungle movies. Indeed, *The Mighty Peking Man* is one of the most exciting and intelligent treatment of the King Kong/Tarzan myths in cinema.

d Hua Shan *lp* Li Hsiu-Hsien, Terry Liu, Wang Hsieh, Lu Sheng, Yuan Man-Tzu

The Ultimate Warrior (WB) 94 min

Promoted as the first 'Kung Fu Science Fiction' movie, *The Ultimate Warrior*, for all its ridiculous excesses (Brynner in the title role disposing of heavy after heavy and still having time to help deliver a baby in the finale, for example) is interesting as the forerunner of the cycle of gang movies of the eighties that includes **Escape from New York** (1981) and **1990: I Guerrieri del Bronx** (1982). Set in 2012, von Sydow is the leader of a beleaguered community struggling for survival in the ruins of a New York that is beset by marauding street gangs. Kelton is his horticulturist son-in-law who's developing plant strains resistant to the poisons in the atmosphere, Miles his pregnant daughter and Brynner the stranger who comes to their aid. Clouse directs with a strong preference for action, as in the long and bloody fight between Smith's gangleader and Brynner. The result is a cheap-looking actioneer with little atmosphere to support its comic-strip plot.

One of the more entertaining creatures who live At the Earth's Core.

d/s Robert Clouse *p* Fred Weintraub, Paul Heller *c* Gerald Hirschfeld *se* Van der Veer Photo Effects, Gene Griggs *lp* Yul Brynner, Max von Sydow, Joanna Miles, Richard Kelton, William Smith, Stephen McHattie

At the Earth's Core (AMICUS; GB) 90 min

Based on Edgar Rice Burroughs' fantastical novel of the same title, this is a well-mounted, if essentially frivolous, film. Cushing and McClure are the scientists who discover the enclosed world of Pellucidor when their geological excavator, the 'iron mole' goes out of control during its tests. There they fight dinosaurs and save the inhabitants from the Mahars, a race of female pterodactyls, with great gusto, if not quite the rugged charm of the original novel. Munro, better known for her role as Stella Star in the bizarre **Starcrash** (1979), is the princess in distress.

The film was a sequel to *The Land that Time Forgot* (1974) in which the Antarctic stood in for the Earth's core.

d Kevin Connor *p* John Dark *s* Milton Subotsky *c* Alan Hume *se* Ian Wingrove *lp* Doug McClure, Peter Cushing, Caroline Munro, Cy Grant, Keith Barron, Godfrey James

Behind Locked Doors

(BOX OFFICE INTERNATIONAL; S. AFRICA) 90 (80) min

An updated sexploitation version of **Frankenstein** (1931), this crudely mounted shocker features Denner and Reeves as the young girls punished for their promiscuity for the voyeuristic delectation of its audience. Garth is the knight errant who offers them sanctuary when their car runs out of petrol and swiftly turns into their tormentor. After imprisoning them, he reveals his plans for making the perfect love object. Far less visceral than Latin offerings in the medical Science Fiction sub-genre, such as the gruesome **Gritos en la Noche** (1962), the film's centre of interest is sexual, rather than physical, horror. The predictable climax has Garth destroyed by his previous attempts at female perfection animated by the fire Denner and Reeves start as they make their escape.

d/p/co-s Charles Romine *co-s* Stanley H. Brasloff *lp* Eve Reeves, Joyce Denner, Daniel Garth, Irene Lawrence, Ivan Hager

The Big Bus

(COHEN AND FREEMAN/PHILLIPS/PAR) pv 89 min

Containing as spirited a collection of disaster gags as one could hope for, this is a totally charming movie. The bus of the title is the world's first nuclear-powered bus under constant threat from oil interests and its drivers and crew in the course of its first transcontinental trip. Sprightly mounted and with a cast of delightfully crazy characters (including Auberjonois as a

priest who has lost God and Ferrer as the villain directing his inefficient saboteurs from an iron lung), the film manages to straddle the line between parody and celebration with real finesse. Bologna, in particular, gives a strong performance as the driver given one last chance after being boycotted by his fellow drivers because one night he lost all his passengers in a cannibalistic orgy.

d James Frawley *p/s* Fred Freeman, Lawrence J. Cohen *c* Harry Stradling Jnr *se* Lee Vasque, Gail Brown, Bob Dawson *lp* Joseph Bologna, Stockard Channing, René Auberjonois, José Ferrer, Ned Beatty, Lynn Redgrave

Coz Takhle Dat si Spenat *aka* A Nice Plate of Spinach *aka* What Would You Say to Some Spinach

(STUDIO BARRANDOV; CZECH)   90 min

Vorlicek, again working in tandem with his usual collaborator Makourek, has become the principal and the most brilliant Science Fiction comedy specialist around. His best movie to date, **Kdo Chce Zabit Jessu?** (1965) received a Golden Asteroid at the Trieste festival, as did Iva Janzurova for her performance in Vorlicek's **Pane Vy Jste Vdova** (1971). After a few straight fantasy comedies, this film marks the team's return to the terrain of medical Science Fiction with a hilarious but astute treatment of the rejuvenation motif. A scientist develops a machine which has two peculiarities: if badly adjusted, it causes miniaturization instead of rejuvenation, and it works twice as well if the candidate-patient has eaten spinach. The contraption is stolen by the boss of a beauty parlour and as incompetents start handling the machine, the results are varied and unpredictable. The film is wittily directed with a well-paced dosage of gags, and, on this occasion, Makourek's contribution to the comedies was recognized – he shares a full directorial credit.

d/s Vaclav Vorlicek, Milos Makourek *c* Frantisek Uldrich *lp* Vladimir Mensik, Jiri Sovak, Josef Somr, Peter Kostka, Eva Treytnorova

Dogs

(MAR VISTA/LA QUINTA FILM PARTNERS/BRUCE COHN PRODUCTIONS)   90 min

Like **Day of the Animals** (1977) clearly derived from Alfred Hitchcock's **The Birds** (1963), *Dogs* is a decidedly cut-price entry in the seventies cycle of revenge-of-nature films. McCabe is the emperilled heroine caught in various locations when the domestic dogs of a south-western farming community turn on their owners and start hunting in packs, and McCallum the biology professor who comes to her rescue. Cheaply made – the 'killer' dogs consist of half a dozen or so ragged animals at most – and unimaginatively directed by Brinckerhoff, the film is routine at best. The movie's highlight is the oddest homage to the famous shower sequence of *Psycho* (1960), with a dog taking over the Anthony Perkins' role.

d Bruce Brinckerhoff *p* Allan F. Bodoh, Bruce Cohn *s* O'Brian Tomalin *c* Bob Steadman *lp* David McCallum, George Wyner, Sandra McCabe, Sterling Swanson, Holly Harris, Fred Hice, Lance Hool, Debbie Davis

Dr Black, Mr Hyde *aka* The Watts Monster

(CHARLES WALKER-MANFRED BERNHARD PRODUCTIONS) 87 min

A blaxploitation version of Robert Louis Stevenson's classic tale, directed with glee by Crain (who'd earlier made *Blacula*, 1972), this is one of the better blaxploitation pictures of the seventies. Writer LeBron switches the locale from London and the 19th century to the present and the Watts ghetto of Los Angeles and makes Casey's doctor (wittily called Pride) a leading member of the black community who is deeply involved in good works. Casey's performance is well judged and Crain's direction emphasizes the action (which climaxes

in a chase up and around the Watts Towers) without reducing the characters to mere cyphers. The result is a minor, but enjoyable, film.

d William Crain *p* Charles Walker *s* Larry LeBron *c* Tak Fujimoto *lp* Bernie Casey, Rosalind Cash, Marie O'Henry, Ji-Tu Combuka, Milt Kogan, Stu Gilliam

Embryo   (SANDY HOWARD PRODUCTIONS)   108 min

Hudson is the scientist turned would-be Pygmalion to the beautiful, icy woman (Carrera) he grows in his laboratory in this uninspired film from Nelson. The relationship between the two leads is well set up, but once Hudson sets about launching her in society, the film moves inexorably in an all too predictable direction, and ends with Hudson destroying Carrera after they begin a sexual relationship. Ladd as Hudson's jealous housekeeper helps generate the sexual tension that is essential and which Nelson only too quickly allows to dissipate in the second half of the film.

d Ralph Nelson *co-p/co-s* Anita Doohan *co-p* Arnold H. Orgolini *co-s* Jack W. Thomas *c* Fred Koenekamp *lp* Rock Hudson, Diane Ladd, Barbara Carrera, Roddy McDowall, Ann Schedeen, John Elerick, Jack Colvin, Vincent Bagetta

The Food of the Gods   (AIP)   88 min

Of all the low-budget film-makers of the fifties, Gordon is probably best remembered for his provocative posters for films like **The Amazing Colossal Man** (1957) and **Attack of the Puppet People** (1958) which singularly failed to deliver the promises his posters blazoningly made. In this, his first Science Fiction film in nearly a decade, and based on, as the credits are careful to explain, 'a portion of the novel by H.G. Wells', Gordon remains true to form. Promising a revenge-of-nature film he delivers instead a concoction that would have seemed old-fashioned in his heyday of the fifties when at least his films reflected something of the mood of the times.

The manic Gortner is the football pro who saves Franklin and her family from a series of giant creatures (mostly either crudely manipulated models or optically enlarged real rats) and Meeker (who gives the film's best performance) the evil industrialist who wants to exploit the strange new food that causes the creatures to grow to such alarming proportions.

d/p/s/co-se Bert I. Gordon *c* Reginald Morris *co-se* Tom Fisher, John Thomas, Keith Wardlow *lp* Marjoe Gortner, Pamela Franklin, Ralph Meeker, Ida Lupino, John Cypher, Belinda Balaski

Frankenstein all'Italiana *aka* Frankenstein Italian Style
(RPA; IT) 93 min

With a monster that looks more like pop singer Gary Glitter, so high are his platform shoes, than Boris Karloff who played the part in James Whale's classic **Frankenstein** (1931), this, like **Carne per Frankenstein** (1973) is a sexploitation version of the legend. The monster first disrupts the marriage ceremony of his creator, then dies and, after being comically revived, satisfies the desires of its creator's assistant, wife and servant (Davoll, Tann and Mazzemauro respectively) before, in repetition of **Young Frankenstein** (1974), the professor (Maccione) revives the idea first introduced into the cinema in **Percy** (1971) of transplanting the monster's penis onto himself. The humorous and sex scenes are equally crude.

d Armando Crispino *p* Filberto Bandini *s* M. Franciosa, M.L. Montagnana *c* Giuseppe Aquari *lp* Aldo Maccione, Glanrico Tedeschi, Ninetto Davoll, Jenny Tann, Anna Mazzemauro, Lorenzo Guerrieri

Futureworld
(AUBREY CO./PAUL N. LAZARUS III/AIP) 107 (104) min

A sequel to **Westworld** (1973), *Futureworld* reduces the impact of its central situation – robots turning against their masters – with an explanation that wouldn't be out of place in a thirties serial: Hill is the administrator of Delos, planning to take over the world by substituting his robots for world leaders. By the time, in a would-be chilling twist, it's revealed that Hill too is a robot, it's too late, for the film has rejected the cold purity of the robots, as essayed in the earlier film, in favour of seeing them as lumbering tin-cans.

Fonda is the dashing reporter and Danner his more than competent Girl Friday. A teleseries followed in 1980 – *Beyond Westworld*.

d Richard T. Heffron *p* Paul N. Lazarus III, James T. Aubrey *s* Mayo Simon, George Schenck *c* Howard Schwartz, Gene Polito *se* Gene Griggs, Brian Sellstrom *lp* Peter Fonda, Blythe Danner, Yul Brynner, Arthur Hill, John Ryan, Stuart Margolin

God Told Me To *aka* Demon (LARCO) 89 min

Though dubiously blessed with an intrusive snippet of conventionally tacky UFO effects' work (in fact a belated addition demanded by the film's American distributors), Cohen's typically resonant and audacious thriller is anything but mainstream Science Fiction. Taking up the motif of

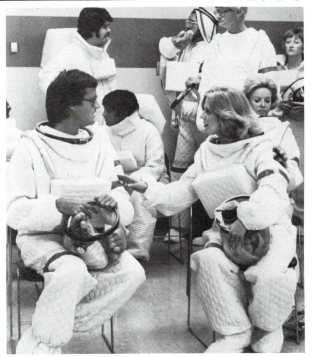

manifest monstrousness common to all his provocative genre movies from *Bone* (1972) to *Q – The Winged Serpent* (1982) – a motif usually linked thematically to the pursuit, possession or exercise of power, as in the figures of the gangster of *Black Caesar* and *Hell Up in Harlem* (both 1973), or the FBI boss himself in *The Private Files of J. Edgar Hoover* (1977) – Cohen here mounts an inspired speculation on a skewed Second Coming, pitting the virgin-born sons of a wrathful deity against each other on the streets of New York. By surrounding his densely plotted crime narrative (mass murderers claiming divine guidance for their carnage) with a tantalizing appraisal of contemporary religion and a network of telling allusions to the ramifications of superstition, Cohen intriguingly develops material that might have come from Von Daeniken's *Chariots of the Gods* (with its God-as-alien theme) into a brilliantly repercussive investigation of individual and social repression, sexuality, guilt and faith. Lo Bianco is the closet Catholic cop coming towards traumatic self-knowledge, Lynch the explicitly hermaphrodite antagonist and the UFO their 'angelic' father.

d/p/s Larry Cohen *c* Paul Glickman *se* Steve Neill *lp* Tony Lo Bianco, Deborah Raffin, Sandy Dennis, Sylvia Sidney, Richard Lynch, Sam Levene

Logan's Run (MGM) Todd-AO35 118 min

This film was initially set up by producer George Pal with Anderson (who had directed the awful **Doc Savage – The Man of Bronze** for Pal in 1975) scheduled to direct only to have one change of MGM executives throw out the project and another reinstate it but without Pal. Like **The Final Programme** (1973), *Logan's Run* is more a matter of décor than anything else, but unlike Robert Fuest's film, which was drenched in cynicism, Anderson's is a cheerfully told tale of young rebels set in a Disneyland conception of the future. The year is 2274 and everyone lives a beautifully ordered sterile life in huge geodesic domes until the age of 30 when they are 'renewed' (ie killed). York is the 'runner' whose job it is to stop those due for renewal escaping who, in company with Agutter, leaves the dome and finds Ustinov, the living proof that life is possible beyond 30 and so ends the benevolent tyranny of dome life.

The film spawned an equally anodyne teleseries, *Logan's Run*, in which Gregory Harrison and Heather Menzies took the principal roles.

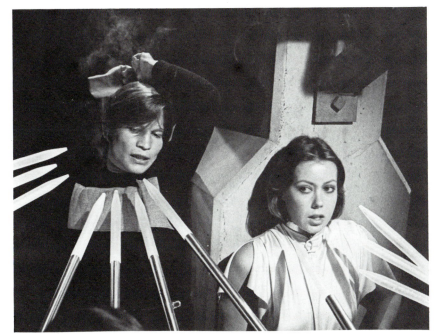

d Michael Anderson *p* Saul David *s* David Zelag
Goodman *c* Ernest Laszlo *se* L.B. Abbot, Glen
Robinson *lp* Michael York, Richard Jordan, Jenny Agutter,
Roscoe Lee Browne, Peter Ustinov, Farrah Fawcett-Majors

The Man Who Fell to Earth

(BRITISH LION; GB) pv 138 min
Bowie's extraordinary extra-terrestrial persona, Mayersberg's
elliptical script and Roeg's mosaic approach combine to
produce an extravagant film whose plot confusions only serve
to intensify the doomed transformation of Bowie from alien to
human. Like James Fox in *Performance* (1970), Bowie first
thinks he's found a safe refuge in Earth, a place literally to
recharge and refuel himself. But as the optimistic first half,
dominated by images of travel, of going somewhere, ends,
images of enclosure begin to take over and we see Bowie's
Thomas Newton finally crushed by the force of (emotional)
gravity whose laws his human namesake discovered.

Arriving on Earth from his drought-stricken planet, Bowie
builds an industrial empire with the assistance of patent
lawyer Henry, with the idea of funding the building of a
spaceship to rescue his race (and family), only to become the
obscure object of desire of the government (who blind him
unthinkingly), Clark (who makes a sad human of the once
proud alien) and scientist Torn who betrays him, Judas-like,
when Bowie won't explain himself. A beautiful-looking
movie, full of marvellous, intricate images, Roeg plots the
descent of Bowie into humanity with an inevitability that is
compelling. The end with Torn and Clark huddling together
for comfort while Bowie wanders America, a shadow of his
former self, while his world slowly dies has much of the anger
of Edgar Ulmer's Poverty Row classic **The Man from Planet
X** (1951).

d Nicolas Roeg *p* Michael Deeley, Barry Spikings *s* Paul
Mayersberg *c* Anthony Richmond *se* P.S.Ellenshaw,
Camera Effects *lp* David Bowie, Rip Torn, Candy Clark,
Buck Henry, Bernie Casey, Jackson D. Kane

Rabid

(CINEPIX/DIBAR SYNDICATE/CANADIAN FILM DEVELOPMENT
CORP./FAMOUS PLAYERS; CAN) 91 min
Virtually a remake of Cronenberg's **The Parasite Murders**
(1974), *Rabid* lacks the power of the earlier movie, its
similarly apocalyptic ending notwithstanding. In place of the
sexual parasites of the earlier movie, Cronenberg here opts for
the simpler image of a horde of rabid vampires created by
accident when a plastic surgeon 're-structures' a badly

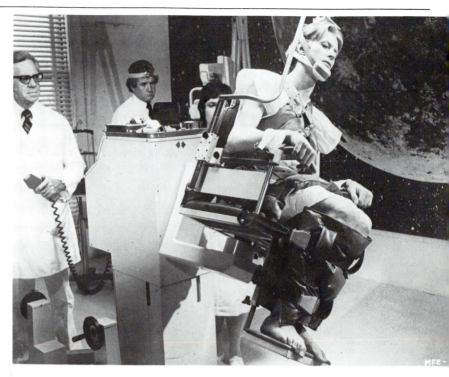

mutilated Chambers (a star of hard-core porn movies) and
leaves her with an uncontrollable lust for blood and a 'phallus'
under her arm to satisfy it. The result is a film full of shocks as
Cronenberg twists his supple narrative first this way then that
in a surprisingly playful fashion. But if *Rabid* is a better-made
film than *The Parasite Murders*, it is also a far safer film.

d/s David Cronenberg *p* John Dunning *c* René Verzier
se Al Griswold *lp* Marilyn Chambers, Frank Moore, Joe
Silver, Howard Ryshpan, Patricia Gage, Susan Roman

Rollerbabies (CLASSIC) 84 min

A sexploitation film as dire as the film that inspired it
(Norman Jewison's overwrought **Rollerball**, 1975), like
Cinderella 2000 (1977), *Rollerbabies* takes for its starting
premise a future in which 'love' (and procreation) is illegal for
reasons of over-population. In its place, love-making has
become a major form of entertainment on television where it
is performed only by licensed artists and is overseen by the
Federal Exhibitionism Commission (the film's one original
idea). Random is the TV producer whose career is in decline
who, with the aid of De Hat's scientist, comes up with the
idea of a roller-derby mass orgy. The film's satiric intentions
are undercut by Stevens' heavy-handed exploitative direction
and the inexpressive cast.

d/p Carter Stevens *s* Wesson Smith *lp* Robert Random,
Suzanne McBain, Yolanda Savalas, Terri Hall, A.
Chameleon, Philip De Hat, Jerry Schneiderman

Spermula (FILM AN CO./PARLAFRANCE; FR) 105 min

A superior piece of eroticism in the French style, *Spermula*
boasts lavish art deco sets as well as numerous couplings. A
suggestive melding of the real and the surreal, it features
Haddon as the leader of a race of virgin vampire women in
thirties dress from a distant planet who live on sperm (which
they consume via fellatio) rather than blood. Once on Earth
they set about making slaves of mankind until Haddon falls in
love with Kier. The plot notwithstanding, the various
couplings are shot in such a way as to show the women rather
than the men as submissive.

d/p/s Charles Matton *c* Jean-Jacques Flori *lp* Dayle
Haddon, Udo Kier, Georges Geret, Ginnette Leclerc,
Joycelyne Boisseau, François Dunoyer, Isabelle Mercanton

*David Bowie, the
cinema's most
convincing and
disturbing alien in* The
Man Who Fell to
Earth.

*Left: Danger threatens
in* Rabid, *David
Cronenberg's virtual
remake of his own* The
Parasite Murders
(1974).

Squirm (THE SQUIRM CO.) 92 min

This revenge-of-nature film features man-eating worms besieging an isolated farmhouse after a fallen power cable has transformed them into flesh-eaters. Writer Lieberman directs neatly, with enough black humour (MacLean's sheriff eating a plate of spaghetti as he listens in disbelief to the story of the worms' turning, a tap being turned on and worms, not water, emerging) to paper over the cracks of his preposterous plot. Scardino is the intelligent hero and Pearcy the much-threatened heroine, but the film's real stars are the worms themselves whose simple presence is charmingly frightening.

d/s Jeff Lieberman *p* George Manasse *c* Joseph Mangine
se Bill Milling, Don Farnsworth, Lee Howard *lp* John
Scardino, Patricia Pearcy, R.A. Dow, Peter MacLean, Fran
Higgins, Jean Sullivan

Vandaag of Morgen *aka* Any Day Now

(R. KERBOSCH; NETH) 82 min
Following the pattern set by **1984** (1956) and **Doctor Strangelove** (1964), this Dutch film offers a version of the state of the world a few decades into the future. The idea is that the Third World countries have united into a single block monopolizing all the raw materials in the world; the USA has withdrawn from Europe and the European countries have formed the US of Europe, governed in a totalitarian manner and indoctrinating the people via TV. In the course of the film, a group of arbitrarily chosen people have to decide on a Third World request to exchange one million skilled workers for raw materials. The group finds out that all they are required to do is rubberstamp a decision that has already been made elsewhere, and that their decision is needed only to provide a democratic gloss to the event. That part of the story is reasonable enough, but the depiction of a Third World which is everywhere except the USA or Europe and which doesn't have skilled workers, while Europe – the 'big brother' world of TV manipulation – seems to be working perfectly, pertains more to the realm of Sunday paper paranoia than to any analytically informed extrapolation of current trends into the future, as is achieved so masterfully in Kluge's **Der Grosse Verhau** (1970).

Below: Mission control at Houston in Capricorn One.

d/p/co-s Roeland Kerbosch *co-s* Ton van Duinhoven
c Hein Groot *lp* Ton van Duinhoven, Wim de Haas, Cees
Linnebank, Huib Roos

The Bionic Boy

(BAS FILM PRODUCTION/RJR FILMS; HONG KONG, PHIL) 95 min
Cashing in on the well-promoted American teleseries *The Six Million Dollar Man*, this film combines the bionic gimmick with Korean-style martial arts. It stars an 11-year-old boy from Singapore, Suarez (Yap), well known locally for his precocious expertise in *taekwondo*, karate and judo. In the movie, Yap is the son of an Interpol agent who gallantly saves the life of a wealthy industrialist and is killed for his action by gangsters who want to take control of the south-east Asian economy away from the decent people who, with the help of the USA, control it now. Surviving a car crash that kills the rest of his family, Yap is taken to a friendly neighbourhood US airforce hospital where he is fitted with artificial limbs. He then proceeds, still with the kind assistance of Interpol, to wipe out the competition as revenge for his dad. However the rival boss escapes in time for a sequel to be possible. Totally lacking in humour and imagination, the film turns the athletic Yap into an uppity little brat. By the standards set in Hong Kong for martial arts movies, this film lacks style and intelligence in all possible departments.

Yap's next outing was the equally dire **Dynamite Johnson** (1978).

d Leody M. Diaz *p* Bobby A. Suarez *s* Romeo N.
Galang *c* Arnold Alvaro *lp* Johnson Yap, Ron Rogers,
Susan Beacher, Carole King, Clem Parsons, David McCoy,
Steve Nicholson, Kerry Chandler, Debbie Rogers, Kathleen
Scherini

Blue Sunshine

(ELLANBY FILMS/THE BLUE SUNSHINE CO.) 95 min
Squirm (1976), Lieberman's début feature, was one of the best examples of the revenge-of-nature cycle of films of the seventies and revealed a concern with sexuality (as opposed to the mere display of sex) akin to that of David Cronenberg (as seen in films like **The Parasite Murders**, 1974, and **Rabid**, 1976). In this, his second film, Lieberman edges even closer to Cronenberg territory, but treats his material with a manic freneticism and sense of humour (as in the opening party sequence where a finger-snapping Sinatra imitator suddenly goes berserk or in the hilarious conversation in which Rodin the artist and Rodan the monster are momentarily confused) that is wholly his own.

King is the reluctant hero, sought after the murder of Richard Crystal (who he's killed in self-defence), who discovers a link between a rash of murders and the premature hair loss of the murderers. He traces this back to ex-professor turned politician Goddard, the inventor of Blue Sunshine, a form of LSD that leaves its takers with a delayed chromosonal imbalance which is triggered by sudden hair loss and then transforms them into psychotic killers.

Directed with real panache by Lieberman, as various examples of middle America turn into crazed killers, *Blue Sunshine* is undoubtedly one of the best Science Fiction thrillers of the seventies.

d/s Jeff Lieberman *p* George Manasse *c* Don Knight
lp Zalman King, Deborah Winters, Mark Goddard, Robert
Walden, Charles Siebert, Ann Cooper

Capricorn One

(CAPRICORN ONE ASSOCIATES/ASSOCIATED GENERAL FILMS)
pv 127 (124) min
Sadly, the intriguing premise of Hyams' script, that the astronauts scheduled for the first manned space flight to Mars (Brolin, Waterston and Simpson) should be removed from the ship which is unsafe and asked to fake the trip on a specially constructed studio set, is let down by Hyams' scattershot direction. Rather than concentrate on the dilemma of the astronauts, who quickly realize that their lives are in danger, Hyams spends too much time poking fun at NASA and the media. Accordingly, the film slowly fizzles out, until Gould's

investigative reporter and Savalas' eccentric crop-duster appear on the scene in a bi-plane as Brolin's unlikely rescuers from NASA's assassins. The wittily staged 'Mars landing' is the best thing in the film.

d/s Peter Hyams   *p* Paul N. Lazarus III   *c* Bill Butler
se Henry Millar Jnr, Henry Millar Snr, Bob Spurlock, Bruce Mattock   *lp* Elliott Gould, James Brolin, Brenda Vaccaro, Sam Waterston, O.J. Simpson, Telly Savalas, Karen Black

Cinderella 2000

(INDEPENDENT INTERNATIONAL)   Todd-AO 35   95 min
Promoted as a sexploitation version of **Star Wars** (1977) – 'From the *Stars and Worlds* of Another Galaxy, a *Futuristic Fantasy* for Adults' – *Cinderella 2000* is a decidedly Earth-bound affair. Essentially a would-be musical parody of the fairy story, it is set in the year 2047 in a world ruled over by Fuller's Controller and his computers in which 'love' is outlawed, a common premise in sexploitation Science Fiction (for example **Rollerbabies**, 1976). Erhardt has the title role and Ross and Cowans are the wicked sisters. After being transformed into a (literally) ravishing beauty, Erhardt attends Fuller's masked ball and several couplings later has 'liberated' the Earth.

Adamson, a prolific (s)exploitation director of the late sixties and seventies with a surprising penchant for the western (for example, *Five Bloody Graves* and *The Gun Riders*, both 1969 and both made with the benefit of cinematography by Vilmos Zsigmond), also made the superior **Horror of the Blood Monsters** (1971). This offering, despite its marginally higher budget than normal, is one of the least of his generally energetic films.

d/p Al Adamson   *s* Bud Donnelly   *c* Louis Horvath
lp Catherine Erhardt, Jay B. Larson, Vaughn Armstrong, Erwin Fuller, Bhurni Cowans, Adina Ross, Rena Harmon

Close Encounters of the Third Kind

(COL/EMI)   pv   135 min
Unlike **Star Wars** (1977) which revitalized the genre by investing the traditional hokum of thirties serials with a wholly modern mix of special effects, or **2001 – A Space Odyssey** (1968) which mixed its special effects with bland overbearing philosophical speculation, *Close Encounters* sees Spielberg magnificently deploying a vast array of cinematic effects to create the most primitive responses in his audience, one that takes us back to the origins of the moving image that is the cinema: a sense of wonder.

Quite simply, Spielberg's success, demonstrated earlier in *Jaws* (1975) and later in **E.T.** (1982), lies in his ability to deflect any preconceptions an audience might have about aliens or Science Fiction in general and leave it simply watching the skies in awe. Accordingly, the film has none of the paranoia that infects so much of Science Fiction, in print or on celluloid. Even the representatives of authority who try to stop Dreyfuss and Dillon reaching the landing place agreed between Truffaut and the extra-terrestrials, turn out to be friendly, and when Dreyfuss breaks through the security cordon he is welcomed by both. In place of paranoia Spielberg substitutes obsession, seen equally in Truffaut's scientist who has travelled the world examining the physical evidence left by the aliens in their attempts to communicate with us, and in Dreyfuss' unstructured attempts to make sense of his own close encounter. All this leads remorsely to the climactic encounter with the aliens (greatly expanded, but less effective in the re-edited *Special Edition* of the film), in which the audience is allowed a degree of emotional participation rarely seen in the cinema as Spielberg stage-manages the most benign possible meeting of man and alien.

This benevolent view of life beyond the stratosphere is carefully prepared by Spielberg who divides the responses to the idea of kindly aliens between his three major characters. Dillon travels towards the Devil's Tower in Wyoming because she cares for the child she's lost to the aliens (in one of the most thrilling deployments of special effects in the history of the cinema) while Truffaut, whose Gallic charm is used by Spielberg as a shorthand for liberal humanism, cares scientifically. But most impressive of all is Dreyfuss, a typical Spielberg hero, a man at odds with himself because he has no great role to play. He is the tetchy employee of the power company given a chance to amount to something by following through his obsession. It is his performance and his domestic environment (in which miracles like the parting of the Red Sea, glimpsed in a sequence from *The Ten Commandments*, 1956, on his television, are a commonplace) that, above all, prepare the audience for the most gloriously optimistic ending in the history of the Science Fiction film.

Although, like *Citizen Kane* (1941), the origins of *Close Encounters* in no way determine its meanings, its roots are of

'Watch the skies', Steven Spielberg's celebration of innocence: Close Encounters of the Third Kind.

interest, especially as the movie is the climax of the flying-saucer films of the fifties which were directly inspired by the UFO sightings that began in earnest in 1947. The film's title is derived from *The UFO Experience* (1972) by Dr J. Allen Hynek (who was also a technical advisor on the movie and appears as the pipe-smoking observer at the climactic meeting with the aliens). Similarly, the Truffaut character is based on Jacques Vallée, a French UFO-logist (and one-time collaborator of Dr Hynek) and many of the details of the film are based on actual reports of UFO sightings. Not surprisingly, the film has been hailed by UFO-logists as sympathetic to their views. However, whether Spielberg is or isn't a 'true believer' and the fact that the origins of much of the film lie in UFO-logy, though they provide fuel for interesting speculations in their own right, are finally irrelevant to the film itself. The movie's success lies not in its sources but in Spielberg's majestic transformation of his diverse material.

In 1980, Spielberg re-edited his material, adding new footage, deleting some of the sequences in Dreyfuss' home and extending the encounter with the aliens, for release as *Close Encounters of the Third Kind – The Special Edition.*

d/s Steven Spielberg   *p* Julia Phillips, Michael Phillips
c Vilmos Zsigmond; (additional American scenes) William A. Fraker, (Indian sequence) Douglas Slocombe
se Richard Yuricich, Douglas Trumbull, Roy Arbogast, George Polkinghorne   *lp* Richard Dreyfuss, François Truffaut, Teri Garr, Melinda Dillon, Bob Balaban, J. Patrick McNamara

Day of the Animals

(FILM VENTURES INTERNATIONAL)   95 min
An hilariously inept entry in the revenge-of-nature cycle of films of the seventies, this offering from Girdler who'd previously re-worked *The Exorcist* (1973) as *Abby* (1974) and *Jaws* (1975) as *Grizzley* (1976) sees him attacking **The Birds** (1963) with a similar lack of success. The woodland animals turn on the humans, according to the unsophisticated screenplay, because of a breakdown in the Earth's ozone layer caused by excessive use of aerosols. But once the ill-assorted group (led by George and including such unlikely people as Roman and Jaeckel's professor) enter the woods, Girdler and Norton abandon all attempts at either explanation or narrative clarification in favour of an all out assault on the humans by the unconvincing animals.

d William Girdler   *p* Edward L. Montoro   *s* William Norton, Eleanor E. Norton   *c* Bob Sorrentino
lp Christopher George, Leslie Nielsen, Lynda Day George, Richard Jaeckel, Ruth Roman, Michael Ansara, Paul Mantee

Demon Seed   (MGM)   pv   95 min

Christie is the separated wife of computer programmer Weaver by whom his creation, the super-computer Phase IV, decides to have a child in this silly technological melodrama. Like **The Forbin Project** (1969), the film takes for its central idea that a computer might think itself superior to its creators. But whereas in that film the computer remains rational, here Phase IV quickly succumbs to the human vices of pride and venality. Accordingly, the scenes in which Christie is held prisoner by Phase IV (which has taken control of her automated house) are totally lacking in drama and even the twist in the tale which has the computer's 'baby' be the spitting image of the child Christie and Weaver lost, seems more melodramatic than telling.

d Donald Cammell   *p* Herb Jaffe   *s* Robert Jaffe, Roger O. Hirson   *c* Bill Butler   *se* Tom Fisher, Glen Robinson
lp Julie Christie, Fritz Weaver, Gerrit Graham, Berry Kroeger, Lisa Lu, Larry J. Blake

Empire of the Ants   (CINEMA 77/AIP)   89 min

Producer/director Gordon is best known for the posters advertising his films than for the films themselves. Here he revives, in the age of special effects no less, his favourite trick of photographically enlarging his monsters (here ants) and awkwardly superimposing them on footage, including humans. The result is a charmless, silly film about an unlikely group of real-estate developers (led by an even more unlikely Collins) who are beseiged by giant killer ants mutated by contact with radioactive waste. Lansing is the adaptable hero.

d/p/co-se Bert I. Gordon   *s* Jack Turley   *c* Reginald Morris   *co-se* Roy Downey   *lp* Joan Collins, Robert Lansing, John David Carson, Albert Salmi, Jacqueline Scott, Robert Pine

The End of the World

(IRWIN YABLANS CO./CHARLES BAND)   86 min
An irresistibly silly movie, if only for the casting of Lee as the catholic priest replaced by an alien lookalike who, in company with the nuns of St Catherine's convent (also aliens), is intent on destroying the Earth because it is irredeemably polluted. They then intend to return to their own planet of Utopia by means of a time-machine constructed of little more than decoratively arranged pieces of sticky tape and cardboard. Lyon and Scott are the scientists who discover the plot, but not in time to save the world, and, in a surprising end, decide to voyage to Utopia with Lee and company.

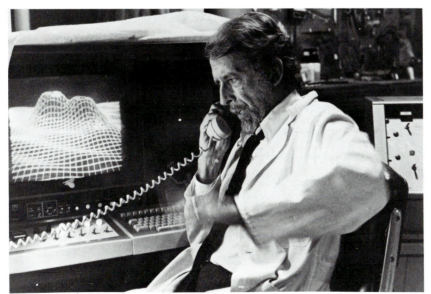

d John Hayes   *p* Charles Band   *s* Frank Ray Perilli   *c* John Huneck   *se* Harry Woolman, Sunrise Canyon Video
lp Christopher Lee, Sue Lyon, Kirk Scott, Dean Jagger, Lew Ayres, MacDonald Carey

Foes (COATS-ALEXANDER-COATS) 90 min
Heavily influenced by **Close Encounters of the Third Kind** (1977), this is a spotty and one-dimensional film. Carey is the UFO expert whose actions while tracking a flying saucer (which looks like a hubcap thrown in the air) are intercut with those of Wiley, Blanchard and Clemens as the inhabitants of the island that the saucer descends on. Coats, who appears in the film as the aliens' first victim, directs in a workmanlike fashion.

d/s/co-se John Coats   *p* Robert D.E. Alexander, Richard Coats   *c* Michael Sabo   *co-se* Scott Farrar, Christopher George, Cinema Research, Film Effects of Hollywood
lp MacDonald Carey, Jerry Hardin, Jane Wiley, Alan Blanchard, Gregory Clemens, John Coats

The Glitterball
(MARK FORSTATER PRODUCTIONS/CHILDREN'S FILM FOUNDATION; GB) 56 min
This is undoubtedly one of the best of the Children's Film Foundation productions. Cockliss, who later made the energetic **Battletruck** (1982), directs with great economy and at a fast pace, sidestepping the usually treacly treatment of children to be found in the CFF's films. In this, he is greatly aided by Johnson and Page's special effects which bring the glitterball alien to life with total mobility. Buckton and Jayne are the boys who, in anticipation of Steven Spielberg's **E.T.**

(1982), find an alien and help it phone home. The climax in which the mothership returns to rescue the glitterball from Pember's small-town thief is mounted with real panache.

d Harley Cockliss   *p* Mark Forstater   *s* Howard Thompson   *c* Alan Hall   *se* Brian Johnson, Charles Page
lp Ben Buckton, Keith Jayne, Ron Pember, Marjorie Yates, Barry Jackson, Andrew Jackson

Herbie Goes to Monte Carlo (WALT DISNEY) 105 min
This is a sequel to **The Love Bug** (1969) and **Herbie Rides Again** (1974), respectively the top and fifth box-office successes in North America in their years of release. Both these films were directed by Robert Stevenson, who deftly captured the comic possibilities of Herbie, a Volkswagen with a mind of its own. In the hands of McEveety, the slapstick is less sure and the narrative line erratic. Re-united with Jones, his driver in *The Love Bug*, Herbie falls in love with a Lancia, wins the Paris–Monte Carlo rally and foils would-be diamond thief Marin.

d Vincent McEveety   *p* Ron Miller   *s* Arthur Alsberg, Don Nelson   *c* Leonard J. South   *se* Eustace Lycett, Art Cruickshank, Danny Lee   *lp* Dean Jones, Don Knotts, Julie Sommars, Jacques Marin, Roy Kinnear, Bernard Fox

The Incredible Melting Man
(QUARTET PRODUCTIONS/AIP) 86 (84) min
Similar in theme to the magnificent **The Quatermass Xperiment** (1955), this spotty but interesting film by Sachs features Rebar as the sole survivor of a disastrous space mission to Saturn. Back on Earth, his flesh melting from a mysterious infection that also transforms him into a flesh-

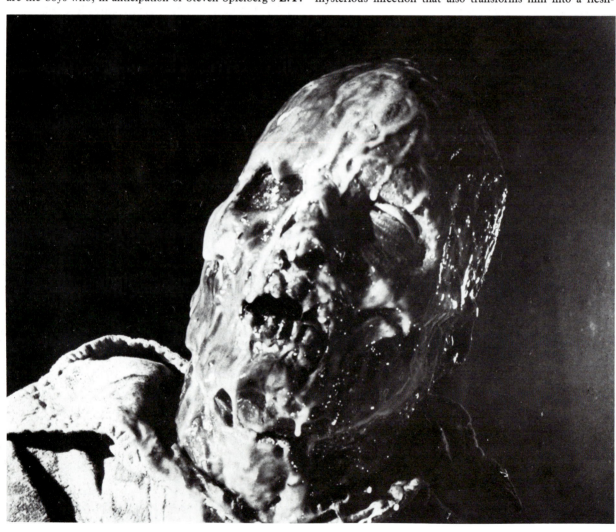

Alex Rebar, with makeup by Rick Baker, in the title role of The Incredible Melting Man.

Don Taylor's The Island of Dr Moreau, *an inferior remake of* The Island of Lost Souls *(1932).*

eating ghoul, he is tracked by DeBenning's scientist and Aldredge's sheriff (who thinks at first he's on the trail of a wild animal). Though the special effects are only routine, Rebar inspiring laughter rather than the terror and pity we are clearly intended to feel for him, Sachs injects the film with a grisly humour, two elderly pensioners billing and cooing while Rebar looks on and the children's game of hide and seek that Rebar interrupts in a clear homage to James Whale's **Frankenstein** (1931). The result is a better than average monster-on-the-rampage outing.

d/s William Sachs   *p* Samuel W. Gelfman   *c* Willy Curtis
se Rick Baker, Harry Woolman   *lp* Alex Rebar, Burr
DeBenning, Myron Healey, Michael Aldredge, Ann Sweeny,
Lisle Wilson

The Island of Dr Moreau   (CINEMA 77/AIP)   98 min
This inferior remake of **Island of Lost Souls** (1932) features the square-jawed Lancaster in the role previously essayed by Charles Laughton. Where Laughton was a sadistic experimenter, Lancaster is simply a mad scientist, seeking to speed up evolution and transform animals into humans. Shot in brilliant colour in the Virgin Islands, the film has none of the brooding intensity of Erle C. Kenton's sombre movie. Similarly the confrontation between York's castaway and Lancaster's Dr Moreau lacks any depth; York is simply the handsome hero and Lancaster the black villain. The best thing in the film is the makeup, created by John Chambers (who served in a similar capacity on **Planet of the Apes**, 1968), of the 'humanimals'.

d Don Taylor   *p* John Temple-Smith, Skip Steloff   *s* John
Herman Shaner, Al Ramrus   *c* Gerry Fisher   *se* Cliff
Wenger   *lp* Burt Lancaster, Michael York, Nigel Davenport,
Barbara Carrera, Richard Basehart, Nick Cravat

Izbavitelj *aka* The Rat Saviour *aka* The Redeemer
(JADRAN FILM/CROATIA FILM; YUG)   87 min
Based on a Science Fiction story by Alexander Greene, a Soviet writer who died in Stalin's purges, *Izbavitelj* is a powerful political allegory, which in many ways foreshadows Ionesco's much better known *Rhinocéros*. Set in Zagreb in the thirties, the plot is a variant on that of **Invasion of the Body Snatchers** (1956). Vidovic is the vagrant writer who discovers that a new breed of rats, with the ability to change their shape, are taking over the city by killing and then impersonating their victims. He eliminates the rats with a chemical provided by Sovagovic's scientist but not before he's killed the girl he loves (Majurec), thinking her to be a rat-person.

Right: Kingdom of the Spiders, one of the better revolt-of-nature films of the seventies.

The allegorical character of the film is somewhat confusing – the rats seeem to represent a too generalized form of fascism – but Papic's direction (which won the film a Golden Asteroid at the 1977 Trieste festival of Science Fiction films) is dramatic and several of the sequences quite graphic and visceral in a manner that is unusual in Eastern European film-making.

d/co-s Krsto Papic   *co-s* Ivo Brexan   *c* Iveca Rajkovic
lp Ivica Vidovic, Mirjana Majurec, Relja Basic, Fabijan
Sovagovic, Ilija Ivezic

Kingdom of the Spiders
(ARACHNID PRODUCTIONS/DIMENSION PICTURES)   95 (90) min
A superior revolt-of-nature film, *Kingdom of the Spiders* scores over so many other films in the sub-genre through its commitment to character rather than stereotypes, Cardos' inventive direction and the sly, humorous script of Robinson and Caillou. Aiming for an escalating sense of fear rather than mere sudden shock effects, the film follows Shatner's vet as he investigates the change in habits of the normally solitary tarantulas that suddenly appear in Arizona and begin working together and seeking larger prey than usual following the introduction of a new crop-dusting spray.

The story is predictable enough but the images that accompany it are both surprisingly powerful – a town full of cocooned corpses – and witty – heroine Bolling stalked by a tarantula in the shower only for her to squash it just when its about to bite her. Certainly the end, with the town and its inhabitants preserved for future food as the spiders set off in search of pastures new, comes closer to the tone of Hitchcock's **The Birds** (1963) than most variations on this theme.

d John 'Bud' Cardos   *p* Igo Kantor, Jeffrey M. Sneller
s Richard Robinson, Alan Caillou   *c* John Morrill
se Greg Auer   *lp* William Shatner, Tiffany Bolling, Woody
Strode, Lieux Dressler, David McLean, Natasha Ryan,
Marcy Lafferty

Nakusei Daisenso *aka* War of the Planets *aka* War in Space
(TOHO; JAP)   scope   86 min
An unfortunate, because far too literal, attempt to cash in on the success of **Star Wars** (1977) by Fukuda, Inoshiro Honda's successor at Toho. In 1980, the OVNI attack Earth in the first interplanetary world war. A spaceship, designed as an equivalent of the ship in a popular animation series, **Uchusenkan Yamato** (1977), is launched to Venus by a secret organization. There, an aerial battle decides the fate of the galaxy. Lacking in inventiveness, the film doesn't match up to Fukasaku's **Uchu Kara No Messeji** (1978) which also mobilizes sorcery and gimmicks, such as the recruitment system employed in *The Magnificent Seven* (1960), from Hollywood westerns. Fukuda's effort remains a pale, though entertaining, secondhand version of the Lucas film rather

than an enjoyable elaboration of the Japanese teleserials which are said to have partly inspired Lucas' film in the first place. The original story, if that term can be used in this context, for Fukuda's film was by Hachiro Jingui.

d Jun Fukuda   *p* Tomoyuki Tanaka, Fumio Tanaka *s* Ryuzo Nakanishi   *c* Jo(yuzuru) Aizawa   *se* Shokei Nakano   *lp* Kensaku Morita, Yuke Asano, Ryo Ikebe, William Ross, Masaya Oki

Operation Ganymed

(PENTAGRAMMA/ZWEITES DEUTSCHES FERNSEHEN; WG) 126 (120) min

A black film, impressively shot and well written although a little on the long side from Erler, Germany's leading contemporary Science Fiction director, whose work has been virtually confined to TV. He contributed many excellent Science Fiction films to the series *Das Blaue Palais*, including *Das Genie* (1974) and, recently, together with his regular cameraman Grasshoff, he shot the excellent *Fleisch* (1979), also for ZDF, the TV station that co-produced *Operation Ganymed*. Winner of the first prize at Trieste's Science Fiction festival in 1978, the film's story is ingenious. A UN-sponsored mission to Ganymed has been given up for lost, but against all odds and after 1,585 days in space, mostly without any communication with the Earth, one of the spacecraft returns to Earth with five surviving crew members. They also bring sensational evidence of life on the planet they visited. They land in a desert in Mexico and, unaccustomed to the hardships of surviving in a desert on Earth, they start quarrelling, go mad with thirst, murder each other and commit cannibalism until one lone exhausted, crazed survivor reaches a village.

Erler and Grasshoff went on to make *Plutonium* (1978), also for ZDF. However, that last effort is disappointingly racist: it starts from the proposition that a Third World country could

trigger off a nuclear war by irresponsibly using its capacity to manufacture the weapons required, as if the 'superpowers' could be relied on to act responsibly . . .

d/p/s Rainer Erler   *c* Wolfgang Grasshoff   *lp* Horst Frank, Dieter Laser, Uwe Friedrichsen, Juergen Prochnoww, Claus Theo Gaestner, Vicky Roskilly, Wolf Mittler

Spider-Man   (DANCHUCK PRODUCTIONS)   92 min

Overseen by Stan Lee, the mastermind of *Marvel* comics on whose Spiderman character this is based, Swackhamer's film is wholly charmless. Made as the pilot for the teleseries and theatrically released in Europe, it follows the attempts by Hammond, a science student turned into spiderman when bitten by a radioactive spider, to foil monstrous villain David's plans of world domination. In place of the neurosis that lay at the centre of the comic-book character, Swackhamer and writer Boretz have substituted the simple problem of Peter Parker/Spiderman being, like so many superheroes of the past, sought after by the police as a suspicious character.

d E.W. Swackhamer   *p* Edward J.Montagne   *s* Alvin Boretz   *c* Fred Jackman   *se* Don Courtney   *lp* Nicholas Hammond, Lisa Eilbacher, Michael Pataki, Thayer David, David White, Ivor Francis

The Spy Who Loved Me

(EON PRODUCTIONS; GB   pv   125 min

Probably best remembered for Carly Simon's scorching rendition of the theme song, 'Nobody Does It Better' and for the introduction of Kiel's 'Jaws' character, this is a weak entry in the Bond saga.

Jurgens is the latterday Captain Nemo dreaming of destroying all life on the surface of Earth (starting with Moscow and New York, which he plans to blow up with nuclear missiles) and creating a private undersea kingdom and

Bach is the voluptuous Russian detailed to assist Bond track down the missing nuclear submarines and save civilization as we know it. Renoir's visuals are pretty enough, especially when the elaborate sets (such as Jurgens' undersea headquarters) and comic-book stunts don't intrude.

d Lewis Gilbert *p* Albert R. Broccoli *s* Christopher Wood, Richard Maibaum *c* Claude Renoir *se* Alan Maley
lp Roger Moore, Barbara Bach, Caroline Munro, Richard Kiel, Curt Jurgens, Walter Gotell, Geoffrey Keen, Bernard Lee, Lois Maxwell

Star Wars (LUCASFILM/FOX) pv 121 min

How to begin?

With worldwide rentals of almost $400 million to 1984, *Star Wars* isn't quite the biggest grossing film of all time to date; that privilege belongs to **E.T. The Extra-Terrestrial** (1982) which has grossed some $30 million more, though the *Star Wars* trilogy – *Star Wars*, **The Empire Strikes Back** (1980) and **Return of the Jedi** (1983) – has earned some $700 million in worldwide rentals. What these suitably astronomical figures represent – and as any parent knows they are nothing compared to the merchandising revenue the *Star Wars* toys have meant to Lucasfilm – is far more than a mere upsurge of interest in Science Fiction similar, albeit on a vastly grander plane, to that which followed **Destination Moon** (1950) and **2001 – A Space Odyssey** (1968). *Star Wars* was carefully planned by Lucas and producer Kurtz as 'a real gee-whizz movie' for children and adults and the merchandising rights were secured in advance (a response to Universal's virtually giving them away to help promote Lucas' previous film, *American Graffiti*, 1973). And the film (which was made for a modest $11 million, as opposed to the $32 million apiece the sequels cost), once its try-outs suggested that it had the potential to be *very* popular, was the subject of the most carefully mounted attempt to mould and stimulate the public appetite. With *Star Wars* both Science Fiction and Hollywood came of age.

In retrospect, it's easy to see the flaws in *Star Wars*, to see that it's naïve rather than innocent and that its borrowings are simply other people's ideas put to work rather than allusions. It doesn't increase the meanings present in the film to know that C-3PO is based on the robot in **Metropolis** (1926); that the bombing raid on the Death Star has its origins in both *The Dam Busters* (1954) and *633 Squadron* (1964); that the victory celebrations at the end are borrowed from *Triumph of the Will* (1936) or that Luke's return to the burnt-out homestead of his uncle and aunt is a quotation from *The Searchers* (1956). In short, *Star Wars* is a self-consciously manufactured fairy

Robert Vaughn as the ufologist and defender of Earth in the sprightly Starship Invasions.

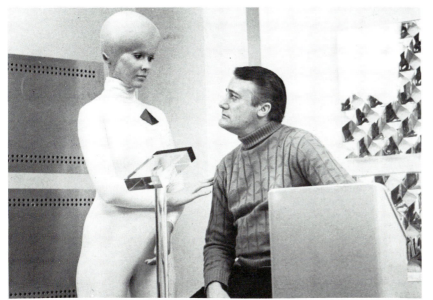

story, carefully put together from bits of **Flash Gordon** (1936), its main inspiration, and numerous other serials which, for all their glorious lunacy, with few exceptions (of which *Flash Gordon* is the paramount example), cloaked their bizarre plots in a morality that was far more inflexible than the fairy stories of old. It is this sense of pastiche which runs through the whole film that limits it, just as Steven Spielberg's far more inventive imagination was curtailed in *Raiders of the Lost Ark* (1982) by the requirement to film not an adventure story but the adventure *genre*, circa 1936.

Lucas' one addition to the world of the serial, of course, is the stunning special effects. Interestingly, in comparison to *2001 – A Space Odyssey* for which Stanley Kubrick went back to silent film techniques to generate a sense of spectacle in which still cameras watched seemingly impossible objects move in space, Lucas' special effects (which were only possible due to the computer-controlled camera developed by Dykstra, Douglas Trumbull's assistant on *2001*), like early American cinema, stress motion and movement above all. They invite not amazement but excitement, just as the plot invites us to cheer for the good guys, smile at the antics of their various anthropomorphized companions and hiss the black-hearted villain. Seen from this perspective, Lucas' tale of 'a long time ago in a galaxy far away' may seem, like 'the Force', a marvellous con trick signifying nothing but Lucas' ability to manipulate his audience; and yet the film works. *Star Wars* is an exhilarating film. More interestingly, the rough grid of relationships Lucas puts to work – spunky heroine (Fisher), wise old man (Guinness), pretend cynic (Ford), earnest young man (Hamill) and their various assistants set against the evil Darth Vader (Prowse) with his endless supply of cannon fodder and the ultimate secret weapon, the Death Star – has proved capable of refinement and intensification until by the time of *Return of the Jedi* the storyline is as interesting (and suddenly the stuff myths are made of) as the special effects.

Like Richard Donner's equally knowing revision of the Superman legend, **Superman – The Movie** (1978), Lucas, for all the shallowness of the ideas that went to make the film, in *Star Wars* lays the foundation for what has become, like Joel Schuster and Jerry Siegel's original *Superman*, a myth for our times. In *Star Wars* itself that myth is hardly articulated but the phenomenal success of the film made possible the characters' eventual entry into legend.

Although the film was nominated for several major Oscars, perhaps fittingly it only won awards in the technical categories: art direction, sound, editing and visual effects.

d/s George Lucas *p* Gary Kurtz *c* Gilbert Taylor
se John Dykstra, John Stears, Richard Edlund, Grant McCune, Robert Blalack *lp* Mark Hamill, Harrison Ford, Carrie Fisher, Alec Guinness, Peter Cushing, David Prowse, Anthony Daniels, Kenny Baker, Peter Mayhew, James Earl Jones (uncredited voice of Darth Vader)

Starship Invasions *aka* Alien Encounter

(HAL ROACH INTERNATIONAL; CAN) 89 min

The début feature of Hunt, this is a surprisingly traditional film: not only does it dress its heroes in white and its villains in black but it features fifties-type flying saucers rather than spaceships à la **2001 – A Space Odyssey** (1968), let alone those of **Star Wars** (1977). Lee is the leader of a group of rebels from another planet who want to settle on Earth and Vaughn the UFO-logist who, with support from friendly representatives of the Intergalactic League who have already established themselves on the ocean floor, does battle with them. Made on a tiny budget that seemingly didn't stretch to synchronized sound – hence the characters communicate by means of mental telepathy – the film stands up well when compared to the Republic films it apes, less well against the Science Fiction of the day, even though the special effects are well mounted.

d/*co-p*/*s* Ed Hunt   *co-p* Norman Glick, Ken Cord   *c* Mark Irwin   *se* Warren Keillor   *lp* Robert Vaughn, Christopher Lee, Daniel Pilon, Tiiu Leek, Helen Shaver, Henry Ramer

Uchusenkan *Yamato* aka Space Cruiser
(ACADEMY; JAP)   101 min

This is one of the series of animated films derived from the popular Japanese TV serial. It features the adventures of a refurbished World War II battleship, the *Yamato*, transformed into a space cruiser and captained by the moralizing Okida. The film's premise, the world is suffering from radiation poisoning created by the Gorgons as a preliminary to colonizing the Earth, and the presence of the startling-looking battleship, suggests a deeper concern on the behalf of the film's Japanese makers. However, the film swiftly degenerates into crude melodramatics supported by at best indifferent animation and numerous borrowings from **Star Wars** (1977), notably the brave little robot that saves the day when the Gorgons lodge a gigantic missile in the prow of the *Yamato*.

Two sequels followed, *Saraba Uchu Senkan* Yamato (1978) and Yamato *Yo Towano* (1979).

d/*p*/*co-s* Yoshinobu Nishizaki   *co-s* Keisuke Fujikawa, Eiichi Yamamoto   *se* Mitsuru Kashiwabara

Wizards   (BAKSHI PRODUCTIONS/FOX)   81 min

This animated feature is influenced equally by the spectacular landscapes of modern Science Fiction illustrators and the anthropomorphic style of Walt Disney's cartoons. However, Bakshi is unable to satisfactorily unite his diverse sources and the result is a simplistic, if occasionally impressive, film. The action is set several million years into a post-nuclear-holocaust future in which radiation and mutation have transformed humans into dwarves and goblins, two of which, the good wizard Avatar and his brother the evil Blackwolf do battle for control of the Goodlands. The presence of dwarves and goblins notwithstanding, the film is predictable, especially when Blackwolf (who's discovered a horde of Nazi propaganda films) sets about uniting his forces with a revamped Nazi ideology and starts building long-outlawed weapons. Similarly, the film's animation style veers erratically between the cutesy-pie of Disney and the rather more erotic vision of *Playboy*'s Vargas (especially in the drawing of the heroine Elinore).

d/*p*/*s* Ralph Bakshi   *c* Ted C. Bemiller   *voices* Bob Holt (Avatar), Jesse Wells (Elinore), Richard Romanus (Weehawk), Steve Gravers (Blackwolf), David Proval (Peace), James Connell (President)

Adele Jeste Nevecerela *aka* Adele Hasn't Eaten Yet
(STUDIO BARRANDOV; CZECH)   scope   90 min

Lipsky's comedies are not known for their lightness of touch nor for their inventiveness (**Muz z Prvniho Stoleti**, 1961; **Zabil Jsem Einsteina, Panove**, 1970). However, this film has both qualities in abundance. A parody of the Nick Carter stories, it has the famous detective called to Prague and solving the mystery of the carnivorous plant, Adela, raised by the villain of the piece. Carter survives the most improbable attempts on his life and flies around with a portable flying kit which allows him to land on the balcony of the villain's beautiful daughter – no doubt with a nod at a similar exploit in **Superman – The Movie** (1978). Carter also has exploding cigars (brand name: Alfred Nobel) able to dynamite steel doors, and a flying bicycle foreshadowing the BMXs of **E.T.** (1982). Set in a lovingly recreated turn-of-the-century Prague, the visual style of the film freely uses quotes from comics, postcard images, Feuillade movies, etc. It is difficult to believe this is the same director who made the thoroughly mediocre films upon which his reputation is based. The lovely Shoberova, star of **Kdo Chce Zabit Jessu?** (1965) and *The Vengeance of She* (1968) confirms her status as a very fine comedienne.

d/*s* Oldrich Lipsky   *c* Jaroslav Kucera
lp M.Docolomanski, R. Jrusinski, Olga Shoberova (Olinka Berova), Nadia Konvalinkova, L. Pesek

The Amazing Captain Nemo   (WB)   103 min

Replete with cut-price special effects and a hand-me-down version of Darth Vader from **Star Wars** (1977), this is a lacklustre addition to the adventures of Jules Verne's Captain Nemo (here briskly impersonated by José Ferrer). Revived from suspended animation when American divers Hallick and DeBenning find the crippled *Nautilus*, Ferrer is persuaded to help them find Meredith's evil genius who is holding Washington to ransom from his own super-submarine. Along the way they save Atlantis from Meredith's plans of conquest. Meredith is the suitably hammy villain and George the mandatory beautiful blonde scientist.

The villainous Necron 99 leaving Scorth in Ralph Bakshi's animated feature Wizards.

Left: Evil genius Burgess Meredith and his Darth Vader clone in the cut-price The Amazing Captain Nemo.

Right: *Gregory Peck cast against type as the sinister Dr Mengele in* The Boys from Brazil.

d Alex March *s* Norman Katkov, Preston Wood, Robert C. Dennis, William Keys, Mann Rubin, Robert Bloch, Larry Alexander *c* Lamar Boren *se* L.B. Abbott, Van Der Veer Photo Effects *lp* José Ferrer, Burgess Meredith, Tom Hallick, Burr DeBenning, Lynda Day George, Mel Ferrer

Attack of the Killer Tomatoes
(NAI ENTERTAINMENT) 87 min
Clearly intended as a spoof on the creature-features of the fifties – and as such similar in conception to the fondly remembered Dr West's Medicine Show and Junk Band's surprise 1966 American Top Ten record, 'The Eggplant That Ate Chicago' – *Attack of the Killer Tomatoes*, for all the delirium of its title, is a sadly inept film.

De Bello's only feature to date, the film imagines San Diego menaced by a group of mutant tomatoes and comes complete with pastiche fifties songs to edge the action along. Miller is the teenage descendent of the heroes of **The Blob** (1958) who saves the day.

d/co-p/co-s John De Bello *co-p/co-s* Steve Peace
co-s Costa Dillon *c* John K. Culley *se* Greg Auer
lp David Miller, George Wilson, Sharon Taylor, Jack Riley, Rock Peace

Battlestar Galactica (U) 122 (117) min
Originally titled *Star Worlds*, as if it wasn't clear enough how derivative of **Star Wars** (1977) it was, *Battlestar Galactica* was the pilot for the teleseries of the same name which, like the same producer's **Buck Rogers in the 25th Century** (1979), was released theatrically in Europe. Greene is the patriarchal commander of the Battlestar Galactica, leading a wagontrain of some 200 spaceships containing the survivors of the human race and searching the voids for the haven of Earth. The film is accordingly a strange mix of the flight of the Israelites from Egypt, the *Wagon Train* teleseries and the views of Von Daeniken whose 'God was an Astronaut' slogan the film literalizes.

Hatch and Benedict are the Luke Skywalker lookalikes, Jenson the Princess Leia clone and Muffit the bland version of the chirpy R2-D2. Larson's screenplay follows the destruction of the 12 colonies of mankind by the Cylon robots of Dick Durock's imperious leader and the first attempts by the travel-weary wagontrain to pitch camp on the planet Carilla, home of the seemingly peaceful Ovions who, in fact, are in league with the Cylons.

Dirk Benedict (left) and Richard Hatch, the bland heroes of Battlestar Galactica.

A surprise success, both on its theatrical release and on television, in retrospect its juvenile orientation and the restrictions imposed on the project by its being on television, the superior special effects (masterminded by producer Dykstra of *Star Wars* fame) notwithstanding, make for a charmless clone of George Lucas' paen to the innocent delights of gee-whizz heroics.

d Richard A. Colla *p* John Dykstra *s* Glen A. Larson
c Ben Colman *se* Richard Edlund, Dennis Muren, Karl Miller, Joe Goss *lp* Lorne Greene, Richard L. Hatch, Dirk Benedict, Jane Seymour, Ray Milland, Lew Ayres, Maren Jenson

The Bees
(BEE ONE/PANORAMA FILMS PRODUCTION) 85 (83) min
A New World quickie version of **The Swarm** (1978). The storyline is more in keeping with the post-Watergate mood of America – a mutant strain of killer bees is captured by a giant American corporation who then set about marketing the huge amounts of honey the bees make before the bees escape and set about devastating America as a preliminary to securing an agreement from the United Nations to take more care of the Earth's environment – but the execution is primitive compared to most of New World's outings. Tompkins and Saxon head the cast but it is Carradine, playing his role as the famous bee scientist with an atrocious German accent simply for the fun of it, who steals the show.

d/p/s Alfredo Zacharias *c* Leon Sanchez *lp* John Saxon, Angel Tompkins, John Carradine, Claudio Brook, Alicia Encinias

The Boys from Brazil
(PRODUCER CIRCLE) pv 125 min
Ira Levin's absurd, but still gripping, novel about the plan to establish the Fourth Reich through clones of Hitler prepared by Peck's sinister geneticist, Dr Mengele, which is only stopped at the last minute by Olivier's elderly Nazi-hunter, is transformed by director Schaffner and cinematographer Decaë into a lavish travelogue in which the action shifts James Bond-like from the Alps, to the jungle of Brazil and the autumn forests of Connecticut at the drop of a hat. The plot mechanism itself, the murder of elderly men so that their

Hitler clones of adopted sons will grow up in the 'right' environment, is well worked out by screenwriter Gould, but the conflicting acting styles of Olivier, whose ticks and mannerisms were based on those of real-life Nazi-hunter Simon Wiesenthal, and Peck, who produces an unusually restrained performance, as the matched obsessives has the effect of reducing the film to a tasteless *Boy's Own* adventure.

d Franklin J. Schaffner *p* Martin Richards, Stanley O'Toole *s* Heywood Gould *c* Henri Decaë *se* Roy Whybrow *lp* Gregory Peck, Laurence Olivier, James Mason, Lilli Palmer, Uta Hagen, Denholm Elliott

The Cat from Outer Space

(WALT DISNEY) 103 (98) min

Scripted by cartoonist Key, this is an engaging Disney outing. Dubbed *Close Encounters of a Furred Kind* by several critics, the film displays its technical trickery with aplomb, especially in the climactic aerial chase. Zunar J5/90 Doric 4-7 (quickly renamed Jake) is the extra-terrestrial cat stranded on Earth when his spaceship breaks down. From this pleasing premise, Tokar and Key develop three neatly entwined strands: the comic attempts by Morgan to find the supposed spaceman from the spaceship; the attempts by the evil McDowall (who overplays his role in the tradition of Disney villains) to steal Jake's collar (the source of his superpowers); and Berry's attempts to raise the $120,000 in gold needed to repair the spaceship. Only the end, with Jake (who was played by Rumpler, an Abyssinian cat and his sister Amber) becoming an American citizen, jars.

d/co-p Norman Tokar *co-p* Ron Miller *s* Ted Key *c* Charles F. Wheeler *se* Eustace Lycett, Art Cruickshank, Danny Lee, *lp* Ken Berry, Sandy Duncan, Harry Morgan, Roddy McDowall, McLean Stevenson, Jesse White

Coma (MGM) 113 min

Coma, the second film directed by former doctor Crichton – the first was **Westworld** (1973) – is a taut medical thriller. The opening, setting up the hospital routine, is clumsy, but once Bujold's suspicions that healthy patients are having comas induced for some obscure reason are raised, Crichton handles the inventive, disturbing plot with panache and assurance. The film's sense of paranoia is further enhanced by

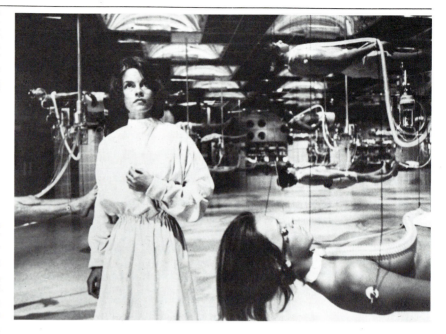

Crichton's concentration on his characters in preference to the welter of medical technology on show. In Hitchcock fashion, Crichton forces us into identification with Bujold (who gives a splendid performance) by numerous point-of-view shots as she uncovers Widmark's private organ transplant operations for which the coma-induced hospital patients are providing the organs. This identification with Bujold brings real tension to what might otherwise have been a collection of imperilled heroine sequences that rises to a crescendo of a climax when the originally disbelieving Douglas finally stops the minor operation on Bujold in the course of which Widmark intends to kill her.

d/s Michael Crichton *p* Martin Erlichman *c* Victor J. Kemper *se* Joe Day, Ernie Smith *lp* Genevieve Bujold, Michael Douglas, Elizabeth Ashley, Rip Torn, Richard Widmark, Lois Chiles

Genevieve Bujold discovers the truth in the splendid Coma.

Dawn of the Dead *aka* Zombies

(LAUREL GROUP PRODUCTIONS/DAWN ASSOCIATES)
127 (125) min

Romero has suggested that his *Dawn of the Dead* is more than merely a sequel to **Night of the Living Dead** (1968), that it is the second film in a projected trilogy that was to show the zombies taking over control of the world. Seen from that perspective, the film, which ends with the undead still rampant, is a failure, simply because they are totally characterless as individuals and represent nothing more than a continuous threat to the established order as a group. Certainly they are never conceived of as representing any kind of new social order. Thus even the symbolism of the four main characters (Emge, Foree, Reininger and Ross) taking refuge in a civil-defence shelter amidst a huge shopping mall in which, like Charlton Heston before them in **The Omega Man** (1971), they live like kings, is lost through Romero's over-emphasis on the possible parallels between zombieism and consumerism.

Yet seen as the 'straight ahead horror film' that Romero has also claimed *Dawn of the Dead* to be, like *Halloween* (1979) with its equally indestructible boogieman, the film is a remarkable example of pacing and visual design, created solely to cause shock after shock. In this respect, the special makeup effects of Savini are particularly well done.

d/s George A. Romero *p* Richard P. Rubinstein *c* Michael Gornick *se* Tom Savini *lp* David Emge, Ken Foree, Scott H. Reininger, Gaylen Ross, David Crawford, David Early

Left: Zunar J5/90 Doric 4-7 is The Cat from Outer Space.

Right: *Lou Ferrigno is The Incredible Hulk.*

Deathsport (NEW WORLD) 83 min

Though it is set in the future ('a thousand years hence in the aftermath of the Great Neutron Wars') and borrows extensively from Paul Bartel's **Death Race 2000** (1975), the true progenitor of this New World piece of fluff is Carradine's *Kung Fu* teleseries. Carradine plays the mystic range guide captured by McLean's petty tyrant for the purpose of a gladiatorial contest against his motorbike riding heavies. The action is well mounted and the narrative pace swift – the film begins in mid-battle, for example – in the fast cutting style of so many New World movies, but the mystic interludes (which are taken unusually seriously by directors Suso and Arkush) are given an inordinate amount of screen time. Similarly Suso and Stewart's script lacks the saving grace of humour that characterizes the best New World product. The result is a routine exploitation pic.

co-d/co-s Henry Suso *co-d* Allan Arkush *p* Roger Corman *co-s* Donald Stewart *c* Gary Graver *se* Hank Stockert, Philip Huff, Jack Rabin *lp* David Carradine, Claudia Jennings, Richard Lynch, William Smithers, David McLean, Will Walker, Brenda Venus

Dynamite Johnson *aka* The 12 Million Dollar Boy *aka* The New Adventures of the Bionic Boy

(BAS FILM PRODUCTION/COSMOPOLIS FILMS; PHIL) 95 min

This sequel to **The Bionic Boy** (1977) pits little Suarez (Yap) against an ex-Nazi who, from a base amongst an enslaved Northern Filipino tribe, plans to take over the world, beginning with the destruction of Hong Kong by means of a laser beam. The tribe, used as forced labour in a uranium mine, is kept in line by a fire-breathing iron dragon operated by the villain. The boy, with bionic legs, is aided by the authorities as he saves the natives and the world. The disturbing part of the film, made without any humour, is that it appears to have been made for an adult audience. In a children's film, the notion that the world's troubles can be sorted out by a 12-year-old boy with strong legs might have been understandable as an attempt to exploit the megalomaniac fantasies of little boys who are not too bright at school, but in a film for adults . . . The acting is inept and the directing could have been done by someone with a bionic head.

d/p Bobby A. Suarez *s* Ken Metcalfe, Joseph Zucchero *c* Baby Cabrales *lp* Johnson Yap, Marie Lee, Ken Metcalfe, Joseph Zucchero, Johnny Wilson, Joe Sison, Alex Pecate, Chito Guerrero, Pete Cooper

Dawn of the Dead, *George Romero's sequel to the marvellous* Night of the Living Dead *(1968).*

Le Gendarme et les Extraterrestres (SNC; FR) 91 min

A routine instalment in the long-running series of farces starring de Funes, a popular actor with grotesque facial contortions, hysterical speech and manic gestures. Plugging into the wave of Science Fiction movies, police sergeant Cruchot (de Funes) is confronted by occupants of a flying saucer that has landed in St Tropez. The aliens look exactly like human beings but when someone knocks on them, they sound hollow, like empty petrol cans. Also, they drink oil. A few good comedy routines are repeated mercilessly to extend this material for a brief sketch into a feature-length movie. If the screen persona of de Funes doesn't appeal, the picture is unbearably boring.

d Jean Girault *s* Jacques Vilfrid *c* Marcel Grignon, Didier Tarot *lp* Louis de Funes, Michel Galabru, Maurice Risch, Jean-Pierre Rambal, Maria Mauban, Guy Grosso, Michel Modo, Jacques François

A Hitch in Time

(EYELINE/CHILDREN'S FILM FOUNDATION; GB) 57 min

Scripted by Ealing veteran Clarke (who was responsible for the scripts for *Hue and Cry*, 1947, *The Lavender Hill Mob*, 1951 and *The Titfield Thunderbolt*, 1953, amongst others) this is a whimsical, if decidedly old-fashioned, outing from the Children's Film Foundation. Troughton (a one-time Dr Who) is the dotty scientist whose erratic time-machine sends teenagers McVey and McLellan back and forth in time where they save various of their ancestors.

d Jan Darnley-Smith *p* Harold Orton *s* T.E.B. Clarke *c* Tommy Fletcher *lp* Michael McVey, Pheona McLellan, Patrick Troughton, Jeff Rawle, Sorcha Cusack, Ronnie Brody

The Incredible Hulk (U) 104 min

Like Spiderman, the Incredible Hulk has his origins in *Marvel* comics and like him, the Hulk was much softened in the course of the move from comic book to television, which this was made for and then released theatrically in Europe. The practice of adapting comic characters for the screen stretches back to the thirties, many of whose serial heroes first breathed in the comic strips and books of that innocent era. The Hulk as created by Stan Lee was a neurotic Jekyll and Hyde figure whose rage couldn't be constrained in his human personality. In the hands of producer Johnson and his fellow writers, the Hulk is just another gimmicky hero (and indeed one who owes as much to the teleseries *Fugative* as to *Marvel* comics) encased in a glossy production. The film explains the origins of the Hulk (Ferrigno) as the alter-ego of Bixby's David Banner, created when Banner subjected himself to a high dosage of gamma rays, and sets him on the run (he's accused of his own murder) in search of a cure.

co-d/co-p/co-s Kenneth Johnson   *co-d* Sigmund Neufeld Jnr   *co-p* Chuck Bowman   *co-s* Thomas E. Szollosi, Richard Christian Matheson   *c* Howard Schwartz, John McPherson *lp* Bill Bixby, Susan Sullivan, Jack Colvin, Lou Ferrigno, Susan Batson, Mario Gallo

Invasion of the Body Snatchers
(SOLOFILM CO.)   115 min

This is one of the more interesting of the cycle of remakes that emerged in Hollywood in the seventies. Kaufman and writer Richter wittily update Don Siegel's 1956 classic by replacing the simple contrast between rational 'pod' people and emotional humans with the more complex idea that urban alienation makes it virtually impossible to distinguish between pods and people. From this perspective, the film becomes an assault on the 'Me Generation' of the seventies, a literalization of psychiatrist Nimoy's words in the film, 'People are changing, they're becoming less human', a point neatly underscored as plants from outer space (whose arrival is masterfully shown in the pre-credit sequence devised by Ron Dexter and Howard Preston) take control of the chic houseplant world of San Francisco.

But, although Richter's screenplay is a radical re-statement of Siegel's original theme, Kaufman's direction is less sure, with the result that the paranoia of the earlier film is far less prevalent. In its place are numerous shock effects intended to create menace but which dissipate the mood and tone of Richter's literate screenplay. Similarly Sutherland, as the public health inspector who finds the people around him are strangely changing and is then given the runaround by the city authorities after he's found out about the pods, is too earnest and not instinctive enough in his defence of humanity pure and simple against the improved life the human pods claim is theirs.

Adams is effective as Sutherland's assistant and, in a playful homage to the original film, Kevin McCarthy reprises his role as the hero of that film, still desperately trying to inform the world of the danger of the pods. Even more ironically, Siegel himself has a cameo role as the cabbie (and pod) who takes the fleeing Sutherland and Adams out of the city.

Donald Sutherland finds that there's more than plants in the garden in Invasion of the Body Snatchers.

d Philip Kaufman   *p* Robert H. Solo   *s* W. D. Richter *c* Michael Chapman   *se* Dell Rheaume, Russ Hessey *lp* Donald Sutherland, Brooke Adams, Leonard Nimoy, Veronica Cartwright, Jeff Goldblum, Art Hindle

L' Isola degli Uomini Pesce *aka* The Island of the Fish Men   (DANIA FILMS/MEDUSA; IT)   91 min

This combination of **The Creature from the Black Lagoon** (1954) and H.G. Wells' *The Island of Dr Moreau* tells of a megalomaniac biologist (Cotten) living on a deserted island and holding his beautiful daughter (Bach) captive there. His *chef d'oeuvre* in biological experimentation is the creation of fish-men whom he employs as slave labour, salvaging treasure from the ruins of Atlantis at the bottom of the ocean. There are plenty of shots of Bach scantily dressed, in wet clothes or being mauled by the fishy creatures in a somewhat sexploitative approach to the whole subject. As with most of Martino's films, the direction is thoroughly average.

d/p/co-s Sergio Martino   *co-s* Sergio Donati, Cesare Frugoni *c* Giancarlo Ferrando   *lp* Joseph Cotten, Barbara Bach, Richard Johnson, Claudio Cassinelli, Beryl Cunningham

It Lives Again   (LARCO/WB)   91 min

A marvellous sequel to Cohen's **It's Alive** (1973), *It Lives Again* intensifies the central situation of the earlier film by the simple process of centering, not on the confused reactions of the parents of the mutant babies, but on their determination to save them at all costs from the authorities who are systematically terminating the pregnancies of all mothers who might produce abnormal babies. This is signalled in the imaginatively staged opening sequence in which Ryan, reprising his role as the guilt-ridden father of *It's Alive*, is the intruder at the party given by Forrest in honour of his pregnant wife Lloyd and obsessively details first his guilt and then his growing realization that the mutants respond to affection. Contrasted to Ryan and Forrest, who slowly undergoes a change of heart like Ryan before him, is Marley's cop, also the father of a mutant, who is determined to wipe out the mutant babies.

Left: *Frederic Forrest and Kathleen Lloyd, as the anguished parents of* It Lives Again, *confront their offspring.*

Wisely, Cohen only hints at why and how the mutants have come into being. Instead, in the manner, if not the style, of Steven Spielberg, the American cinema's other great contemporary explorer of family life, Cohen merely observes the emotional agonies of his characters as they seek to overcome the contradiction between their quiet family lives and the horrors they have brought forth and learn to love in opposition to all around them.

d/p/s Larry Cohen   *c* Fenton Hamilton   *lp* Frederic Forrest, Kathleen Lloyd, John P. Ryan, John Marley, Andrew Duggan, Eddie Constantine

Der Junge Moench *aka* The Young Monk
(HERBERT ACHTERNBUSCH; WG)   84 min

Achternbusch, a Bavarian eccentric, is a respected literary figure in both Germany and France who occasionally makes highly idiosyncratic films packed with extremely broad Bavarian humour and surreal fantasy elements. At times, his films come close to some of the more outrageous *Monty Python* sketches that work simply by enlarging slightly the sorts of everyday stupidity and obnoxiousness one normally finds mildly annoying. As a result, Achternbusch's films tend to be addressed to a very specific audience familiar with the attitudes and modes of speech he puts on the stage while precisely risking to upset that audience as they feel targeted. An example of this is his most recent film, a Bavarian version of *The Life of Brian* (1979), *Das Gespenst* (1983). The film so incensed the authorities that efforts were made to stop its production.

Der Junge Moench is set after a global catastrophe in which the Earth has become one enormous desert. One of the few survivors is seeking God and finds an Easter bunny in a cemetery. Another one puts himself in a trance and tries to remember what 'Nation' meant. Later on, having made themselves Pope and Cardinal, with Bunny as God, they plan to go to Italy with a woman, but Italy has sunk into the sea. One strangely commonplace notion and situation follows another in totally uncommon ways.

d/p/s Herbert Achternbusch   *c* Joerg Jeshel   *lp* Herbert Achternbusch, Karolina Herbig, Brank Samarovski, Heinz Braun, Barbara Gass, Luisa Francia

Kiss Meets the Phantom *aka* Attack of the Phantoms
(HANNA-BARBERA/KISS-AUCOIN PRODUCTIONS)   86 min

Planned as part of the promotion for the four solo albums by the members of the rock group Kiss and consisting mostly of footage of the group's concerts at the Magic Mountain amusement park, this telefilm (released theatrically in Europe), like the group's own Kiss Marvell comic-book

Piranha, a witty exploitation film from director Joe Dante and writer John Sayles.

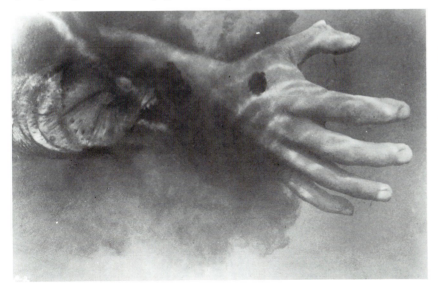

series, is best viewed as part of the slickest marketing strategy ever mounted by a rock 'n' roll group. The slim plotline sees Zerbe's deranged cybernetics' wizard creating robot versions of the group in an attempt to cause a riot and so destroy the amusement park when he's dismissed. Some of the sequences, the group's fight against cybernetic Hanna-Barbera cartoon characters, for instance, are well mounted but the comic-strip characterization of the group and Hessler's tired direction make for a lacklustre film for all but the most committed Kiss fan.

d Gordon Hessler   *p* Joseph Barbera, William M. Aucoin   *s* Jan Michael Sherman, Don Buday   *c* Robert Carmanico   *se* Westheimer Company   *lp* Kiss (Peter Criss, Ace Frehley, Gene Simmons, Paul Stanley), Anthony Zerbe, Deborah Ryan, John Dennis Johnston, Lisa Jane Perksy

Laserblast   (IRWIN YABLANS CO.)   80 min

Rejoicing in one pure moment of cinema, when its hero, Milford, shoots a poster for **Star Wars** (1977) to bits with his newly acquired laser gun left behind by an alien, *Laserblast* is an otherwise wholly unimaginative film. Milford is the loner who finds the gun and a mysterious pendant left by a fleeing lizard-like alien, only to be taken over by the alien when he wears the pendant. In this guise he revenges himself on everyone who's mistreated him, before being eliminated by kindly (but equally monstrous-looking) aliens who have been searching for the original owner of the laser gun. Even the non-stop series of exploding cars becomes monotonous in the hands of director Rae. Accordingly, the film lacks the cult appeal of its companion piece, the Band-produced **The End of the World** (1977).

d Michael Rae   *p* Charles Band   *s* Franne Schacht, Frank Ray Perilli   *c* Terry Bowen   *se* Harry Woolman, Paul Gentry, Dave Allen   *lp* Kim Milford, Cheryl Smith, Gianni Russo, Ron Masak, Dennis Burkley, Barry Cutler

Piranha   (NEW WORLD/PIRANHA PRODUCTIONS)   94 min

A witty exploitation picture, *Piranha* survives its awkward moments by dint of director Dante (a former contributor to American fan magazine *Castle of Frankenstein*) and writer Sayles' decision to play their material for laughs rather than chills. Menzies is the private eye, looking for a pair of missing hitch-hikers, who, in company with Dillman, stumbles on a secret army base at which a strain of man-eating piranha has been developed for use in the Vietnam war. For further testing the piranhas are to be let loose in a closed section of a local river. Skipping deftly over the larger issues, Dante produces a mounting crescendo of cinematic homages (notably to *Jaws*, 1975, much of the central situation of which, the holiday resort worried more about lost revenue than danger, Sayles adapts) and shock effects.

Sayles later scripted Roger Corman's most expensive production to date, **Battle Beyond the Stars** (1980) and wrote and directed *The Return of the Secaucus Seven* (1979), a marvellously inconsequential examination of the promises of the sixties from the standpoint of the cold realities of the seventies.

d Joe Dante   *p* Jon Davison, Chako Van Leeuwen   *s* John Sayles   *c* Jamie Anderson   *se* Peter Kuran, Bill Hedge, Rick Taylor, Pat O'Neill, Doug Barnett, Dave Morton, Jon Berg   *lp* Bradford Dillman, Heather Menzies, Kevin McCarthy, Keenan Wynn, Dick Miller, Barbara Steele

Return from Witch Mountain   (WALT DISNEY)   93 min

A routine sequel to **Escape to Witch Mountain** (1974) which was also directed by British émigré Hough, this features the further adventures of Richards and Eisenmann as the two alien children with superhuman powers. This time Eisenmann is kidnapped by villains Lee and Davis when Lee turns his mind-control ray on the boy until Richards and an

unlikely quartet of tearaways rescue him. Hough handles the predictably coy script with a surprising degree of invention, but the colourless characterization of the alien children drains the film of the charm it so desperately needs to succeed.

d John Hough *p* Ron Miller, Jerome Courtland
s Malcolm Marmorstein *c* Frank Phillips *se* Eustace
Lycett, Art Cruickshank, Danny Lee *lp* Kim Richards, Ike
Eisenmann, Bette Davis, Christopher Lee, Jack Soo,
Anthony James

Spider-Man Strikes Back

(CHARLES FRIES PRODUCTIONS/DAN GOODMAN PRODUCTIONS/
DANCHUK PRODUCTIONS) 93 (92) min
A sequel to **Spider-Man** (1977) and, like that, derived from the teleseries of the same name, *Spider-Man Strikes Back* is a lacklustre offering. Hammond is once again Peter Parker (a pale imitation of the *Marvel* comic-book character), the clumsy student who turns into Spider-Man, here on the trail of students who've made their own makeshift atomic bomb, who foils master criminal Alda (who gives the film's best performance) when he steals it from them.

d/co-p Ron Satlof *co-p/s* Robert Janes *c* Jack Whitman
se Don Courtney *lp* Nicholas Hammond, Robert F. Simon,
Michael Pataki, Robert Alda, Chip Fields, Joanna Cameron

Superman – The Movie (DOVEMEAD/

INTERNATIONAL FILM PRODUCTIONS; GB) pv 143 min
Fittingly for a character that first took to the celluloid skies in human guise under the aegis of penny-pinching producer Sam Katzman (in **Superman**, 1948), *Superman* (a movie that at one time seemed headed for the history books as the most publicized project in preparation that never reached the screen, let alone the skies) was promoted when it was finally completed with the slogan 'You'll believe a man can fly'. It was a promise that director Donner and his special effects' team fulfilled to the letter. More surprisingly, the film treads a delicate line between gently guying Joel Schuster and Jerome Siegel's original character – Reeve's Superman having difficulty finding a phone booth to change in and his constant stream of mock earnest advice to Lois Lane – and idealizing the man of steel as the saviour the modern world so clearly needs. This last point is further underlined in the most

beautiful section of the film, devoted to Superman's youth, in which the wheatfields of the Mid-West are transformed into a veritable Eden, a theme made even more pressing by the film's references to the work of such diverse American artists as Norman Rockwell and Andrew Wyeth. Their respectively sentimental and austere visions are conflated in the magnificent cinematography of Unsworth, whose last film it was although some of the footage he shot for the movie was later used in **Superman II** (1980).

Less successful are the film's opening sequences of the destruction of the planet Krypton. Brando (whose reported $2.5 million for 13 days' shooting was a stroke of genius, garnering the film almost as much publicity as David O. Selznick's search for his Scarlett O'Hara prior to the shooting of *Gone With the Wind*, 1939) and York are more than satisfactory as Superman's parents, but the death throes of Krypton are too sudden to generate any real sadness or sense of concern for the child who will become mankind's saviour. Far more successful is the confrontation with Hackman's Lex Luthor, assisted by the sexy Perrine and the incompetent Beatty (a marvellous performance). Avoiding the camp clichés of **Batman** (1966), the writers and actors manage to create a broadly comic yet still dramatic work, akin to the neat bantering that Reeve as Clark Kent suffers at the hands of his colleagues in the *Daily Planet* office.

Donner, directing with accomplished broad brushstrokes to maintain the sense of wonder so essential to the film's success, only fails when the special effects become too intrusive, as in the oddly ineptly mounted collapse of the dam with its faint echoes of Sam Katzman's attitude to quality, which drain the sequence of all drama. However, the film's successes, central to which is Reeve's charmingly innocent performance, far outweigh its occasional lapses.

Co-writers Benton and Newman, previously best known for their script for Arthur Penn's *Bonnie and Clyde* (1967), had previously co-authored the Broadway musical, *It's a Bird . . . It's a Plane . . . It's Superman* (1966). Sequels followed in 1980 and 1983.

d Richard Donner *p* Pierre Spengler *s* Mario Puzo, David
Newman, Leslie Newman, Robert Benton *c* Geoffrey
Unsworth *se* Colin Chilvers, Roy Field, Derek Meddings,
Brian Smithies, Denis Rich, Zoran Perisic, John Richardson,
Bob MacDonald, Derek Botell, Bob Harman
lp Christopher Reeve, Margot Kidder, Gene Hackman,
Valerie Perrine, Ned Beatty, Marlon Brando, Susannah York

Left: Trash cans fly magically to the rescue of the teenage defenders of the alien children stranded on Earth in Walt Disney's Return from Witch Mountain.

'You'll believe a man can fly': Superman – The Movie.

Above: Warlords of Atlantis, *Kevin Connor's skimpy re-working of the Atlantis myth.*

The Swarm (WB) pv 116 min

A dull plodding disaster pic from Allen who (in company with Jerry Jameson) made the genre his own in the seventies with films like *The Towering Inferno* (1974) and *The Day the World Ended* (1979). Based, like **The Killer Bees** (1976), which also features Johnson, on newspaper headlines about a new strain of bees that first made its appearance in America in the seventies, the film follows the attempts of etymologist Caine to put paid to a swarm of African 'killer' bees. The rudimentary plot, fleshed out with cameos from Widmark, Chamberlain, de Havilland and the like, sees Caine dashing here and there and finally saving Houston. In recent years the film has developed a certain cult notoriety, akin to that of **Plan 9 from Outer Space** (1956).

d/p Irwin Allen *s* Stirling Silliphant *c* Fred J. Koenekamp *se* L.B. Abbott, Van Der Veer Photo Effects, Howard Jensen *lp* Michael Caine, Katharine Ross, Richard Widmark, Richard Chamberlain, Ben Johnson, Olivia de Havilland

Test Pilota Pirxa *aka* Test Pilot Pirx *aka* Doznaniye Pilota Pirksa *aka* The Test of Pilot Pirx

(ZESPOLY FILMOWE/TALLINNFILM; POL, USSR)
scope 104 min

Winner of the Golden Asteroid at Trieste's festival (1979), this is another film based on a story (*Inquiry*) by Poland's best-known Science Fiction author, Stanislaw Lem, who wrote a number of Pirx stories as well as **Solaris** (filmed in 1971) and the novel that inspired **Der Schweigende Stern** (1960). This time, Pirx is sent on a mission to Saturn with a crew of people and robots, the ones hardly distinguishable from the others, as in **Alien** (1979). A big electronics concern manufactures 'perfect' robots and is keen to prove their superiority over human space crews. Consequently, they programmed the craft's computer to escalate the negative aspects of operational commands made in a moment of human weakness until the situation is so catastrophic that only one of the robots can save the day. The twist comes when, out of human weakness, Pirx refuses to give operational commands, prompting his second-in-command, a robot, into rash action which destroys him. Back on Earth, Pirx is hauled into court, accused of neglecting his duties to the point of causing a robot to be destroyed . . .

The ingenious storyline is unfortunately impaired by a script which constantly veers off into James Bond-type

adventures. Cheaply made, repeating the same few set-ups time and again for the interior of the spaceship, the film is disappointing.

d/co-s Marek Piestrak *co-s* Vladimir Valutski *c* Janusz Pavlovski *lp* Sergiusz Desnitsky, Boleslaw Abart, Vladimir Ivashov, Alexandr Kaidanovsky, Tyno Saar, Zbigniew Lesien

Uchu Kara No Messeji *aka* Uchu No Messeji *aka* Message from Space

(TOEI/TOHOKUSHINSHA EIGA; JAP) scope 105 (90) min
Received as a variation on **Star Wars** (1977), as was Fukuda's **Nakusei Daisenso** (1977), this film borrows many of the US film's gimmicks, including a funny robot, chases through narrow canyons and a host of bizarre creatures. However, it has been suggested that it was Fukasaku's Science Fiction films for Japanese TV which partly inspired the Lucas film in the first place. Further back, the basic plot devices for this movie echo *The Magnificent Seven* (1960), now with one extra outlaw hero, making it eight.

The story concerns the planet Jilluca which is about to be obliterated by the Gavanas empire. Eight non-conformist heroes are summoned to the planet's aid and defeat the empire. Combining sorcery with Jules Verne imagery (a spaceship that looks like a real 19th-century sailing ship on its way to some Mysterious Island) and *Star Wars* electronics, the picture is brimful of ideas playing fast and loose with the treasury of popular culture. The picture is equally exciting visually, often reminiscent of the great Czech interpreter of Verne, Karel Zeman. The fast-paced action is conducted by Fukasaku with uncharacteristic expertise and the special effects were supervised by a pupil of Tsuburaya. A superior space opera-fantasy picture – the only sadness is that the superb talents of Vic Morrow were thrown away in only a few scenes, in spite of his starring credit.

Budgeted at $5 million, it was the most expensive Japanese film until **Fukkatsu No Hi** (1980), also directed by Fukasaku.

d Kinji Fukasaku *p* Banjiro Vemura, Yoshinoru Watanabe, Tan Takaiwa, Ryo Hirayama, Yusuke Okada, Simon Tse, Naoyuki Sugimoto, Akira Ito *s* Hiro Matsuda *c* Toro Nakajima *se* Nobuo Yajima, Masahiro Noda, Shotaro Ishinori, Minoru Nakano, Noboru Takanashi *lp* Vic Morrow, Shinichi Chiba, Phily Casnoff, Peggy Lee Brennan, Sue Shiomi, Tetsuro Tamba, Mikio Narita, Makoto Sato, Isamu Shimizu

Right: *Olivia de Havilland, one of the many cameo roles in Irwin Allen's* The Swarm, *undoubtedly the silliest of Allen's many silly films.*

Warlords of Atlantis *aka* Seven Cities to Atlantis

(EMI/JOHN DARK – KEVIN CONNOR PRODUCTIONS; GB)
96 (78) min

This skimpy re-working of the Atlantis myth sees McClure, a regular in such adventures, and Gilmore as the Victorian antiquarians who descend to the lost civilization, do battle with an octopus and a bizarre mutant dinosaur and foil Massey's plans to conquer the upper world. Hayles' script piles incident upon incident ingeniously enough, including an elaborate genealogy for the Atlanteans (they came from Mars) but Connors' routine direction and the poor special effects undercut the cheerful excesses of the screenplay. Charisse provides a cameo as an unlikely inquisitor.

d Kevin Connor *p* John Dark *s* Brian Hayles *c* Alan Hume *se* John Richardson, George Gibbs, Roger Dicken *lp* Doug McClure, Peter Gilmore, Shane Rimmer, Lea Brodie, Daniel Massey, Cyd Charisse

1979

Alien

(FOX/BRANDYWINE-RONALD SHUSETT PRODUCTIONS; GB)
pv 117 min

Constructed as craftily as the commercials Scott first made his name with – the film opens, for example, with the crew of the *Nostromo* awakening and ends with the sole survivor, Weaver, returning to sleep after her literal nightmare – *Alien* is nothing less than a gigantic 'Boo!', set in outer space, where, as the film's advertising slogan goes, 'No-one can hear you scream'. At the heart of the movie lies H.R. Giger's alien (or rather aliens, as the prawn-like creature that bursts forth from Hurt's chest grows and grows) and its ferocious will to live and procreate at whatever cost to those around it.

Although the film can be seen as an inversion of **Star Wars** (1977), which supplied the hardware, and **Close Encounters of the Third Kind** (1977), which offered us a benign alien (rather than a remake of Edward L. Cahn's **It! The Terror from Beyond Space**, 1958, which it closely resembles), in fact Ridley's movie is far closer to the tradition of H.P. Lovecraft. His turn-of-the-century tales about the 'Necronomism' provided Giger, who illustrated the collected tales of Lovecraft, with his vision of the 'biomechanoid' being, a mixture of human and mechanical elements fused together. Thus, it was entirely fitting that *Alien* was shot at Bray studios, the long-time production base of Hammer Films, the company that made the best (and some of the worst) horror (and Science Fiction) films in Britain, and that the imagery of the film should be sexual rather than high tech.

The film, which deservedly won its design team an Oscar for special effects, is a stunningly mounted series of visceral shocks. Yet strangely, the film's psychological overtones notwithstanding, unlike **The Parasite Murders** (1974), *Alien* remains just another, superior, horror outing.

d Ridley Scott *p* Gordon Carroll, David Giler, Walter Hill *s* Dan O'Bannon *c* Derek Vanlint, Denys Ayling *se* Filmfex Animation Services, Carlo Rambaldi, Clinton Cavers, Bernard Lodge, Brian Johnson, Nick Allder, Allan Bryce *lp* Tom Skerritt, Sigourney Weaver, Veronica Cartwright, Harry Dean Stanton, John Hurt, Ian Holm

Americathon (LORIMAR) pv 85 min

Directed by Israel whose *Tunnelvision* (1976) was an uneven but enjoyable parody of the media at work, *Americathon* mines the same territory far less successfully. Set in the near future it imagines America, where jogging is mandatory and automobiles are used as gardens, on the verge of bankruptcy when Chief Dan George decides to call in its vast debt to him. President Ritter takes a puff on his (marijuana) cigarette and comes up with the idea of staging a mammoth telethon to raise the money. Reigert (who would later star in Bill Forsythe's charming comedy, *Local Hero*, 1983) is the aide in the pay of

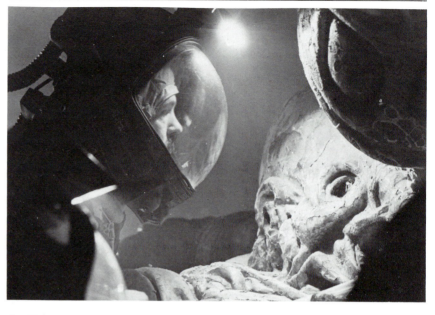

Tom Skerritt examines the remains of a long-dead Alien in Ridley Scott's gigantic 'boo' of a film.

the Herab Republic (an unlikely alliance of Israel and her Arab neighbours) who attempts to sabotage the telethon so the Herab Republic can take over America.

Israel's scattershot approach produces a few laughs but far more puzzling are the credits which, due to extensive re-editing in a desperate attempt to rescue the film, list a number of performers (including Elvis Costello and the Beach Boys) whose scenes have been eliminated.

d/co-s Neil Israel *p* Joe Roth *co-s* Michael Mislove, Monica Johnson *c* Gerald Hirschfield *lp* Peter Reigert, Harvey Korman, Fred Willard, Chief Dan George, John Ritter, Meatloaf, Nancy Morgan, Richard Schaal

The Black Hole (WALT DISNEY) 98 min

The Disney studio's response to **Star Wars** (1977), *The Black Hole* is best remembered for the technical ingenuity (it was shot in Technovision and 70 mm) which went into its making, than for the ludicrous dialogue the characters exchange as they teeter on the edge of the Black Hole of the title. Schell is the meglomaniac mad scientist (a cross between Jules Verne's Captain Nemo and Morbius from **Forbidden Planet**, 1956) who, having transformed his rebellious crew into mechanical slaves, is intending to enter the Black Hole he's been observing for some time. Against him are ranged the crew of the deep space research vessel, the *Palamino*, which includes Mimieux, Forster, Perkins and the mandatory would-be chirpy robot. The film's most interesting element, the melding of man and machine, a recurrent theme of modern Science Fiction, is hardly touched on in Rosebrook and Day's screenplay which simply alternates action with the most heavy-handed dialogue imaginable, made even more so by the constant stream of references to the likes of Goethe and Cicero. Accordingly, the film's climax, the descent into the Black Hole, though spectacular, has no dramatic power at all.

Maximilian, Schell's robot henchman, was based on the drawings of the Devil in Disney's *Fantasia* (1940).

d Gary Nelson *p* Ron Miller *s* Jeb Rosebrook, Gerry Day *c* Frank Phillips *se* Art Cruickshank, Joe Hale, Danny Lee, Terence Saunders, Peter Ellenshaw *lp* Maximilian Schell, Anthony Perkins, Robert Forster, Joseph Bottoms, Yvette Mimieux, Ernest Borgnine

The Brood

(MUTUAL PRODS/ELGIN INTERNATIONAL; CAN) 91 min

Another of Cronenberg's 'institutional' horrors – the obsessive trail can be traced clearly back through **Rabid** (1976) and **The Parasite Murders** (1974) to such works as **Stereo** (1969)

Right: Gil Gerard and Twiki on the planet of Anarchia in the juvenile Buck Rogers in the 25th Century.

and **Crimes of the Future** (1970) – but, despite much of its action being centred on psychoplasmic therapist Reed's experimental Somafree clinic, this apparently more deeply personal film truly focusses on the institution of the family. The human body remains the manifest site of terror insofar as its potentials for perverse growth and replication are realized on the screen, but the source of the traumas that cause both cancerous mutations and the birth of a brood of murderous 'children of rage' is identified explicitly as the nuclear social unit. Eggar is the mentally disturbed wife and mother, left uneasily by husband Hindle in the 'progressive' therapeutic care of Reed, whose family variously fall prey to the attentions of hideously homicidal midgets (finally revealed as the tangible products of Eggar's neuroses, made flesh). Hinds is her 'real' daughter, herself undergoing a traumatic introduction to the tensions and terrors of family life, experiencing a grotesquely extreme version of the familial hostilities that seem destined to continue and develop through the generations. One might quibble with the hints of misogyny (the sins of the mothers?) in Cronenberg's psycho-sexual scheme of things, but the power he generates in visualizing another psycho-genetic experiment gone gorily awry is almost overwhelming. To put it another way – there's a second filmographical line converging towards Cronenberg's own that runs from the sober documentary-drama of the Ken Loach/R.D. Laing, *Family Life* (1971) through generic variants as diverse as Nicolas Roeg's *Don't Look Now* (1973) and Alfred Sole's *Communion* (1976). In *The Brood* both lines collide with a disturbing impact.

d/s David Cronenberg *p* Claude Heroux *c* Mark Irwin *se* Jack Young, Dennis Pike *lp* Oliver Reed, Samantha Eggar, Art Hindle, Cindy Hinds, Nuala Fitzgerald, Robert Silverman

Buck Rogers in the 25th Century (U) 89 min

Co-scripted and developed by Larson, who also masterminded the **Battlestar Galactica** film (1978) and teleseries, this remake of the **Buck Rogers** (1939) serial is yet another telefilm masquerading as a feature film in Europe. Gerard is the cheerful Buck Rogers, Gray the colourless heroine, all pearly teeth and lipgloss but little else, and Hensley the untiringly evil Princess Ardela whose plans to conquer Earth Buck foils with a mixture of old-fashioned heroics and modern technology (provided by the insufferably charming robot, Twiki). Juvenile oriented, like its *Battlestar Galactica*

The robot Maximilian and his becloaked humanoid henchmen in the aweful The Black Hole.

stablemate, the film skirts the sexual liaison between Gerard and Hensley, a character clearly based on **Barbarella** (1967), which the script perpetually teases. Similarly, in place of the irony of someone from this century saving the 25th, writers Larson and Stevens, with capable assistance from Haller, seem content to merely pile incident upon incident in clear imitation of **Star Wars** (1977), the film's true progenitor.

d Daniel Haller *p* Richard Caffey *s* Glen A. Larson, Leslie Stevens *c* Frank Beascoechea *se* Peter Gibbons-Fly, Alex Funke, Keith White, Ray Monahan, John Moulds, David Robman, Charles Shuman, David Stypes, David M. Garber, Wayne Smith, Cubic Corporation, Bud Ewing, Jack Faggard *lp* Gil Gerard, Pamela Hensley, Erin Gray, Henry Silva, Tim O'Connor, Joseph Wiseman

Cerne Slunce *aka* The Black Sun

(STUDIO BARRANDOV; CZECH) 135 min

This is a remake, by the same director, of the dreamily fascinating **Krakatit** (1948), a classic story by Karel Capek about the misuse of atomic power. Overlong and glossily produced, it has none of the strangely lyrical aspects of the old version and frequently strays into James Bond territory. The story is that of a scientist who discovers a new source of energy, krakatit, but whose invention is stolen by a younger and more personally ambitious man (which echoes **Giperboloid Ingenera Garina**, 1965). An American-based multinational company is also trying to obtain the substance, which is about as large as a golf ball. The ambitious scientist brings about a neutron-bomb type of explosion, killing people but leaving property virtually untouched, and the old inventor has to make a new life for himself in a small village where people still know how life should be lived.

d/co-s Otakar Varvra *co-s* Jiri Sotala *c* Miroslav Ondricek *lp* Radoslav Hrzobohaty, Jiri Thomas, Rudolph Hrusinsky, Magda Vasaryova, Gunther Naumann, Vladimir Sneral

The China Syndrome (IPC FILMS) 122 min

Conceived of as Science Fiction, *The China Syndrome* quickly became science fact when, within a couple of weeks of its opening, the story of the failure of a faulty nuclear reactor it told was echoed in the breakdown of the power station at Three Mile Island, Pennsylvania. Fonda, the moving force behind the film, is careful to base her anti-nuclear polemic on the developing realizations of the characters rather than simply preaching at her audience in the manner of, say, Arch Oboler. She plays the initially opportunistic television news-reporter trying to advance from human interest to hard news stories and Lemmon (whose disintegration from loyal corporation man to distraught incoherent and near terrorist anticipates his performance in *Missing*, 1982) is the engineer whose growing suspicions about 'his' power plant fuse with Fonda's. The film's message, the corruption of big business, is commonplace, but one which remains timely in the wake of the renewed debate about nuclear power that the near-disaster at Three Mile Island rekindled.

d/co-s James Bridges *p* Michael Douglas *co-s* Mike Gray, T.S. Cook *c* James Crabe *se* James F. Liles, Henry Millar Jnr *lp* Jane Fonda, Jack Lemmon, Michael Douglas, Scott Brady, James Hampton, Peter Donat

The Dark (FILM VENTURES INTERNATIONAL) 92 min
In marked contrast to **The Day Time Ended** (1979), Cardos' other version of **Close Encounters of the Third Kind** (1977) which collapsed in a heap of ineptly mounted special effects, this outing sees Cardos approaching his material in the restrained manner of his best film, the intriguing **Kingdom of the Spiders** (1977). In this he is greatly aided by a strong cast (which includes Devane and Crosby as the author and TV newscaster respectively who set out to track down the blue-jeaned alien) and Whitmore's literate screenplay which fills in the spaces between the alien's murderous attacks on the inhabitants of Santa Monica to good effect.

The film was to have been directed by Tobe Hopper of *The Texas Chainsaw Massacre* (1974) fame, who was replaced just before shooting commenced.

d John 'Bud' Cardos *p* Edward L. Montoro, Dick Clark *s* Stanford Whitmore *c* John Morrill *lp* William Devane, Cathy Lee Crosby, Richard Jaeckel, Keenan Wynn, Jacquelyn Hyde, Warren Kemmerling, Biff Elliott

The Day Time Ended
(COMPASS INTERNATIONAL/MANSON INTERNATIONAL)
scope 80 min
In the wake of **Star Wars** (1977) *et al* the role of special effects has become central, rather than merely supportive, to the success of numerous films. Projects have been created to show off special effects and in turn special effects have been expected to salvage the silliest of ideas that otherwise would have been left alone. *The Day Time Ended* is a case in point. Unlike Cardos' earlier film, **Kingdom of the Spiders** (1977) which wore its small budget with a jaunty air, this outing is simply too ambitious for the special effects available. Without them, it's just a silly film. Davis, Malone, Mitchum, Lafferty and Ryan are the family who move into an isolated house only to discover that what they mistook for vandalism was caused by aliens attempting to warn Earth of its imminent destruction. The references to Steven Spielberg, back to **Close Encounters of the Third Kind** (1977) and forward to **E.T.** and *Poltergeist* (both 1982) abound, but the special effects, which include cardboard cutouts of prehistoric monsters fighting, a humanoid playmate for Ryan's six-year-old and a supposedly perfect 'city of light and crystal' are so crudely animated as to destroy any belief in the plot. The result is a film with no sense of wonder at all.

d John 'Bud' Cardos *p/co-s* Wayne Schmidt *co-s* J. Larry Carroll, David Schmoeller *c* John Morrill *se* Paul W. Gentry, Pete Kuran, Rich Bennette *lp* Jim Davis, Chris Mitchum, Dorothy Malone, Marcey Lafferty, Natasha Ryan, Scott Kolden

Az Erod *aka* **The Fortress**
(HUNGAROFILM; HUN) 92 min
Apparently written by Hernadi for Miklös Jancso well before the release of **Westworld** (1973), this misanthropic fantasy about a holiday camp touches on the same ground. The establishment, located on a private estate, is called Victory Line and offers a special form of participatory entertainment. Bored tourists may come and organize wargames, but they soon discover that the corpses produced are real ones, which causes a temporary panic before the survivors really get into the spirit of things. The proceedings often turn to black comedy and in the end the State steps in, closes the camp but recruits its female director to train commando units for a larger scale war. The ensemble acting of the holidaymakers is finely tuned and appropriately callous.

Michael Douglas and Jane Fonda as the intrepid reporters in The China Syndrome.

Left: *Susan Anton as the* Goldengirl.

d/co-s Miklos Szinetar   co-s Gyula Hernadi   c Miklos Biro
lp Bella Tanai, Sandor Oszter, Jozsef Madaras, Istvan
Kovacs, Adam Rajhona, Ferenc Bacs, Gyoergy Tarjan

Goldengirl (BACKSTAGE PRODUCTIONS) 104 min

This silly film owes its genesis less to the Frankenstein myth
or tales of the Nazis' genetic experiments (both of which are
put to use in Kohn's vapid script) than in the producer's
desire to milk the ill-fated 1980 Moscow Olympics for all the
free publicity possible. Thus it is fitting that the political
pressures that ended America's participation in the event
should have all but drowned this weak outing which sends its
heroine to Moscow alone.

Anton is unconvincing as the goldengirl of the title whose
image is sold to a cartel of businessmen, in a faint echo of
George Cuker's classic comedy, *Pat and Mike* (1952), by her
geneticist father (Jurgens) in order to raise the necessary
money to make a 'superwoman' out of her through a mixture
of drugs and psychological treatments. Coburn is the manager
they hire who falls for her after she has won her third gold
medal 'her way'.

d Joseph Sargent   p Danny O'Donovan   s John Kohn
c Steven Larner   lp James Coburn, Susan Anton, Robert
Culp, Curt Jurgens, Leslie Caron, Harry Guardino

Golem aka The Golem

(ZESPOLY FILMOWE/PERSPEKTY UNIT; POL)
sepia and col   92 min

The most recent variation on the Golem theme can be located
somewhere between **Invasion of the Body Snatchers** (1956)
and Tarkovsky's paranoid epic **Stalker** (1979). Szulkin's film
is a Golem in reverse. After an atomic war, 'doctors'
programme a new human race totally controlled by technology in their every movement. One creature, Pernat (Walczewski) is the odd one out in that his transformation failed. He
lives as an outsider in an alien environment, irritating the
doctors as well as his neighbours. One administrator,
Holtrum (Dmochowski) pursues experiments with the creation of an artificial human being by means of his alchemist's
oven. Pernat becomes identified, gradually, with such a
creature as his identification number is seen to bring alive a
golem-type figure looking just like him. Shot mostly in sepia,
the film's main target appears to be the notion that forms of
mass communication mould reality and programme people
into a life of ordinary madness. Echoes of Kafka reverberate,
strengthened by elements of the extremely vital though
disturbing tradition of Polish surrealism.

For the sake of completeness, it is worth noting a Japanese
equivalent of the Golem legend, where the demon creature is
called Majin. It appears in Kimiyoshi Yasuda's *Daimajin*
(1966) and Kenji Misumi's *Daimajin Ikaru* (1966). A similar
creature, Bas-Celik, appeared in the Yugoslav film by Voja
Nanovic, *Cudotvorni Mac* (1950). The last time a golem had
appeared in an East European film was Brdecka's contribution, **Prazske Noci** (1968) and the feature **Cisaruv Pekar**
(1951).

Janda received a Silver Asteroid for her performance as the
mad friend of the 'hero' at the Trieste festival of 1981.

d/co-s Piotr Szulkin   co-s Tadeusz Sobo   c Zygmunt
Samosiuk   lp Marek Walczewski, Krystyna Janda, Joanna
Zolkowska, Krzystof Majchrzak, Mariusz Dmochowski,
Wieslaw Drzewica, Henryk Bak, Jan Nowicki, Wojciech
Pszoniak

Die Hamburger Krankheit

(HALLELUJAH FILM/SND; WG, FR)   113 min

The motif of the sudden disease epidemic as a metaphor for
systems of political control and dissent has been used expertly
by Romero in **The Crazies** (1973) and goes back to **Invasion
of the Body Snatchers** (1956). Fleischmann's version is an
awkwardly naïve exploitation of the plot device. The basic
idea is that Hamburg has to be quarantined to contain a
mysterious disease that has broken out in Germany's leading
sin bin. A group of 'social misfits' breaks out and, pursued by
the authorities, spreads the epidemic. That longhaired youth
could somehow be seen as a dangerous challenge to the State
was a myth about ten years out-of-date by the time the film
was made, relegating the basic premise of the movie to the
realm of media clichés. In addition, the only redeemable
character is killed off halfway through the story, reducing the
rest to woolly meandering. A sporadic insertion of outlandish
imagery, possibly due to Topor's peculiarly black humour,
simply highlights how unimaginative the rest of the film is.
The only interest remaining is the game of identifying famous
figures (Haag, Arabal and others) as they pass through the
frame.

d/co-s Peter Fleischmann   co-s Otto Jaegersberg, Roland
Topor   c Colin Mounier   lp Carline Seisser, Helmut Griem,
Ulrich Wildgruber, Fernando Arabal, Rainer Langhans, Tilo
Prueckner, Rosl Zech, Romy Haag, Leopold Hainisch

H.G. Wells' The Shape of Things to Come

(SOTTC FILM PRODUCTIONS/CFI INVESTMENTS; CAN)
98 (95) min

Conceived of as a sequel to **Things to Come** (1936) this
juvenile space opera has little in common with either William
Cameron Menzies' film or H.G. Wells' novel. It is set just
after a nuclear war on Earth, which leaves the recently
established Moon base as the last bastion of humanity.
Palance is the renegade who seizes control of Delat Three, the
source of Radio Q2, the drug the Moon colonists need to
combat the radiation sickness that is spreading from the
Earth, and Lynley, Morse and Campbell, in company with a
would-be cheerful robot 'Sparks', are amongst those who do
'what a spaceperson must do'.

d George McCowan   p William Davison   s Martin Lager
c Reginald Morris   se Wally Gentleman, Bill Wood
lp Jack Palance, Carol Lynley, Barry Morse, Nicholas
Campbell, John Ireland, Eddie Benton

Hi No Tori-2772 aka Space Firebird 2772 aka Phoenix
2772 (TEZUKA/TOHO; JAP)   122 min

Like the similar Japanese animated feature, **Uchusenkan
Yamato** (1977), this cosmic cartoon has an excess of divergent
plotting and irritatingly episodic character development. The
main thrust has a space shark ship scouring the stars to try to
capture the phoenix-like firebird monster that's creating
universal havoc, and return it to a dying Earth where its
life-blood may be used to scientifically rejuvenate the planet.

*Jack Palance in George
McCowan's juvenile
space opera that owes
little beyond its title,
H.G. Wells' The
Shape of Things to
Come, to Wells.*

Too much time is spent, however, logging the would-be 'cute' antics of the hero's alien 'pets', and setting up a conflict between heroic adventurer Godoh and his ludicrously named scientist brother, Rock Schlock, while the mythological monster itself jars among the surrounding futurism. The animation is, typically, economy-minded and skimpily achieved, though the aim of international exploitation is clearly signalled in the fact that all the human figures have decidedly non-Oriental features.

d/s Osamu Tezuku, Suguru Sugiyama *p* Kiichi Akitagawa *c* Iwao Yamaki

Incontri Molto Ravvicinati *aka* **Very Close Encounters of the Fourth Kind** (MIDIA CINEMATOGRAFICA; IT) 86 min
Baxa is Emanuelle Charier, the most unlikely Professor of Astronomical Physics, who in company with a friend, Zanchi, meets three humanoid 'aliens' in the woods near her cottage and indulges in the most predictable of encounter group sessions in this lacklustre sexploitation offering. The film's weak excuse for the lengthy scenes of couplings with the aliens is that they are in fact three students (in drag as it were) previously dismissed from Baxa's class for continually interrupting her lectures with questions about the sexual proclivities of space creatures. In short, routine Italian soft porn cashing in on **Close Encounters of the Third Kind** (1977).

d/co-s Mario Garriazzo *p/co-s* Augusto Finocchi *c* Aldo Greci *lp* Maria Baxa, Monica Zanchi, Marina Duania, Mario Maranza

Mad Max

(MAD MAD PTY; AUST) Todd-AO 35 100 (91) min
An Australian exploitation movie in the manner of Roger Corman's New World productions, such as Paul Bartel's **Death Race 2000** (1975), *Mad Max* has a plot that is pared down even by New World standards. Gibson, in the title role, is a cop in a near future where violence is the norm, who turns vigilante to trace the marauding motorcycle gang who killed his wife. Using only a minimum of blood and gore, its reputation notwithstanding, Miller fragments his story into a series of shock sequences in which his ever-mobile camera involves the audience directly in the action in the manner of John Carpenter. It is this that makes the car and motorbike crashes, mounted with real élan by Grant Page, so powerful.

Wisely, Miller never explains what kind of society his characters inhabit, beyond glimpses of the ramshackle police headquarters; like the machines he celebrates and mourns, the film is an example of pure style. An even better sequel followed in 1981, **Mad Max 2.**

d/co-s George Miller *p* Byron Kennedy *co-s* James McCausland *c* David Eggby *se* Chris Murray *lp* Mel Gibson, Joanne Samuel, Hugh Keays-Byrne, Steve Bisley, Tim Burns, Roger Ward

Meteor (PALADIUM PICTURES) pv 107 min
An asteroid on collision course with Earth and theatening the end of the world is one of the oldest themes of Science Fiction cinema. **The Comet** (1910) is the first recorded example of the sub-genre which includes such interesting works as **Verdens Undergang** (1916), which highlighted the social unrest that accompanied the projected end of the world, and the superb special effects of **Deluge** (1933) and **When Worlds Collide** (1951). In comparison to these, Neame's film is a decidedly minor affair, substituting melodrama (can East and West work together to shoot the meteor to bits and save the world?) and romance (between Connery's American scientist and Woods' Soviet interpreter) for any sense of cosmic catastrophe. Even the special effects by Robinson, who'd been responsible for the destruction of Los Angeles in *Earthquake* (1974), are routine compared to those of *Deluge* or *When Worlds Collide.*

Mad Max, *the beginnings of Australian exploitation movies.*

d Ronald Neame *p* Arnold Orgolini, Theodore Parvin *s* Stanley Mann, Edmund H. North *c* Paul Lohmann *se* William Cruse, Margo Anderson, Robert Staples, Glen Robinson *lp* Sean Connery, Natalie Wood, Karl Malden, Brian Keith, Trevor Howard, Henry Fonda

Misson Galactica: The Cylon Attack

(GLEN A. LARSON PRODUCTIONS/U) 107 min
A clumsy film that betrays its television origins in every frame, this sequel to **Battlestar Galactica** (1978) lacks even the verve of the earlier (tele)film. Greene is the commander of the Battlestar Galactica, still leading his wagontrain of battered spaceships in search of Earth. Bridges is the commander of the *Pegasus* whose over-ambitious plans to destroy the Cylons, a robot force akin to the Daleks of the *Doctor Who* teleseries, bent on destroying humanity, nearly lead to disaster until Luke Skywalker lookalikes Benedict and Hatch come to the rescue at the last minute.

d Vince Edwards, Christian I. Nyby II *p* David J. O'Connell *s* Glen A. Larson, Jim Carlson, Terrence McDonnell *c* Frank Thackery, H. John Penner *se* David H. Garber, Wayne Smith *lp* Richard Hatch, Dirk Benedict, Lorne Greene, Lloyd Bridges, Herbert Jefferson Jnr

Moonraker

(EON PRODUCTIONS/LES PRODUCTIONS ARTISTES ASSOCIES; GB, FR) pv 126 min
The eleventh Bond film, one of the longest running series devoted to the exploits of a single character outside the world of B movies, this entry sees Moore's Bond finally make it into outer space. As ever, the plot is as fantastical as any thirties serial and the special effects as baroque as possible. Indeed the film's one novel idea is in having Kiel's Jaws (returning from **The Spy Who Loved Me,** 1977) transformed by love and joining the side of the goodies to help Moore put an end to Lonsdale's plans of world domination with a peculiar mix of Amazonian troops and a race of pure beings bred on his private space station. Nonetheless, the film's most interesting feature is Bond's clear invulnerability. In contrast to Christopher Reeve's **Superman** (1978) who, although invincible as the man of steel is made dramatic through his possession of a second, bumbling persona, newspaperman Clark Kent, Bond is clearly conceived as a cartoon character pure and simple.

d Lewis Gilbert p Albert R. Broccoli s Christopher Wood c Jean Tournier se Derek Meddings, Paul Wilson, Robin Browne, Michel François Films, Jean Berard, Louis Lapeyre, John Evans, John Richardson, René Albouze, Serge Ponvianne lp Roger Moore, Lois Chiles, Michael Lonsdale, Richard Kiel, Corinne Clery, Emily Bolton

La Mort en Direct aka Death Watch

(SELTA FILM/LITTLE BEAR/SARA FILM/GAUMONT/ANTENNE 2/ TV 15; FR, WG) pv 130 min

An oddly disappointing film, *La Mort en Direct* yokes together, but doesn't develop any further, ideas from such disparate sources as **La Decima Vittima** (1965) and **Terminal Man** (1974) for its story of a man (Keitel) with a television camera implanted in his head observing – and transmitting as a soap opera of the future – the approach to death of the incurably ill Schneider. Clearly intended as an assault on the media, whose intrusion into private life Tavernier sees as debasing, the film fails (especially in contrast to his earlier, and remarkably similar *L'Horloger de St Paul*, 1973, which allows its central character more space to breathe and thus to achieve his own destiny) because the characters are straitjacketed by a plot whose formula-ridden twists and turns are not of their making. Thus the dénouement, in which it is revealed that Schneider and Keitel have been used by Stanton and Schneider's illness is curable, falls flat. Similarly the near future Tavernier imagines, in which death has been banished by medical science, is hardly substantiated by the film's images of urban blight.

The best moments are Keitel's sufferings when he is deprived of the necessary light he requires to keep his TV-camera eyes functioning, which give his later decision to temporarily blind himself (rather than transmit Schneider's pain) a heroic aspect the film's plot then sadly undercuts.

A former film critic, Tavernier is the co-author of the influential *Trente Ans du Cinéma Américain*.

d/p/co-s Bertrand Tavernier co-s David Rayfiel c Pierre-William Glenn lp Romy Schneider, Harvey Keitel, Harry Dean Stanton, Max Von Sydow, Thérèse Liotard, Bernard Wicki, Caroline Langrishe, William Russell

Otel 'U Pogibshchego Alpinista aka The Dead Mountaineer Hotel (TALLINNFILM; USSR) scope 90 min

An intriguing thriller set in an isolated hotel high in the snowy Ala-Tau mountains of Kazakhstan. A police inspector is summoned to the hotel but he finds no crime, only an odd collection of guests. Gradually, he begins to discover that he is being confronted by bizarre events and that he is surrounded by people from another planet. The rest of the movie is like a chess game in which the detective tries to find out what the rules of the game might be as he attempts to adapt his mode of thinking and detecting to an environment in which normal human logic does not apply. Based on a story by the

Strugatskys, who were also responsible for the narrative of Tarkovsky's **Stalker** (1979), the film skilfully uses the conventions of the detective story, designed to establish or restore the rules of normality, to underline the notion, all too rarely acknowledged in Science Fiction, that a different social existence also must entail a radically different notion of consciousness, of thought, of psychology and 'character'. Since it is the task of the detective to reconstruct the coherence of a story, the film shows that 'stories' involving people from radically different social orders simply cannot be told in story-forms developed by and for our own societies. Although the film, as a 20th-century story-form, necessarily must betray the radicality of its own premise, the ingenuous script, ably directed by the leading Estonian film-maker, fully deserved the prize awarded to it by the jury of the Trieste festival of 1980.

d Grigori Kromarov s Boris Strugatsky, Arkady Strugatsky c Yuri Sillart lp Uldis Putsitis, Yuri Yarvet, Lembit Peterson, Mikk Mikiver, K. Sebris, I. Kriauzaite, S. Puik, T. Khyarm

Phantasm (NEW BREED PRODUCTIONS INC.) 90 (89) min

An engaging low-budget shocker in the mould of John Carpenter's *Halloween* (1979) with the twist that the indestructible mysterious 'Tall Man' (Scrimm) is using a nearby cemetery as a source of raw material with which to create a legion of *homunculi* as part of his plan for world domination, *Phantasm* is directed with verve by Coscarelli. Baldwin is the orphaned teenager who observes the strange goings-on and investigates the dark mausoleum which Scrimm uses as his base. The film's highlight is Scrimm's finger, hacked off by Baldwin when Scrimm tries to capture him with the aid of his futuristic 'silver sphere', returning to life with its homicidal inclinations intact. Coscarelli directs with an eye to humour as well as horror to good effect.

d/p/s/c Don Coscarelli se Paul Pepperman lp Michael Baldwin, Bill Thornbury, Reggie Bannister, Angus Scrimm, Kathy Lester, Terrie Kalbus, Ken Jones

Prophecy (PAR) pv 102 (100) min

From one perspective the culmination of the revenge-of-nature cycle of films of the seventies, if only because it evinces genuine concern about the effects of mercury poisoning on nature, *Prophecy*, nonetheless, is probably best remembered as yet another of director Frankenheimer's disastrous attempts to rehabilitate himself in Hollywood in the seventies by playing the genre game.

Foxworth is the committed doctor sent by the US Environmental Protection Agency to investigate reports of industrial pollution in the backwoods of Maine from a lumber mill that is causing friction between the mill's employees and the local indians. He finds the forest wildlife mutating ferociously, including a bear grown to Godzilla proportions. A tedious sub-plot centres on Foxworth's wife (Shire, the younger sister of Francis Ford Coppola and wife of noted Hollywood composer, David Shire) and her worries that the child she is carrying will be contaminated. The predictable climax sees Foxworth kill the mutant bear only for another to rear into view behind the film's end titles.

d John Frankenheimer *p* Robert L. Rosen *s* David Seltzer *c* Harry Stradling Jnr *se* Robert Dawson *lp* Talia Shire, Robert Foxworth, Armand Assante, Richard Dysart, Victoria Racimo, George Clutesi

Quintet (LION'S GATE GILMS/FOX) 118 min

Altman's film starts promisingly enough with Newman appearing out of nowhere with his pregnant wife only to have her promptly killed as the result of a wrong move in the game of Quintet that the survivors of the nuclear holocaust – that has brought upon a new Ice Age – play, only to collapse into metaphysical small talk. The Quintet players (Gassman, Andersson and Van Pallandt), fiddling while Rome freezes and dogs feast on corpses outside are contrasted neatly enough with Newman's loner, but the over-complex and talkative script leaves the international cast (many of which seem to have difficulty speaking in English) with little to do but parrot their lines and hope. Only Rey as the referee and Andersson as the player who falls for Newman, are able to make anything of their parts. The best thing about the movie is Boffety's startling cinematography.

d/p/co-s Robert Altman *co-s* Frank Barhydt, Patricia Resnick *c* Jean Boffety *se* Tom Fisher, John Thomas *lp* Paul Newman, Vittorio Gassman, Fernando Rey, Bibi Andersson, Nina Van Pallandt, Brigitte Fossey

Ratataplan (VIDES CINEMATOGRAFICA; IT) 100 min

In this crazy comedy director Nichetti plays a young Milanese engineer, Colombo, who suffers from a far too creative imagination to remain in gainful employment for any length of time. Even a stint in a radical theatre group ends in chaos as the rural audience destroys the scenery in an orgiastic riot. Colombo then builds a robot-duplicate of himself, dressed up

The game's the thing – Bibi Andersson in Quintet.

as the perfect specimen of the disco generation, which proceeds to achieve all the success that eluded its creator, especially in the area of amorous relations. However, at the crucial moment of Angelillo's seduction, the robot blows a fuse and turns into a mess of smouldering cables. The happy end is provided by Nichetti and Finocchiaro finding they are happy sharing a magical world bearing little relation to the real one.

Nichetti worked as a mime artist at the famous Piccolo Theatre before joining Bruno Bozzetto, Italy's main producer of comic animation – an experience which left its imprint on the design of the gags in this crazy comedy. He also founded a theatre collective, Quellidigrock, the members of which provided the cast for this, his first feature film. The movie was enthusiastically received for its inventiveness and anarchic humour, receiving a prize at the 1980 Venice film festival. Topor contributed a cameo part as the company director who falls victim to a heart attack, a role in keeping with the sick, and often cruel, black humour cartoons he contributed to many magazines and books, including *Hara Kiri*, the successful French journal that set out to offend as many people as possible.

d/s Maurizio Nichetti *p* Franco Cristaldi, Nicola Carraro *c* Mario Battistoni *lp* Maurizio Nichetti, Angela Finocchiaro, Edy Angelillo, Lidia Biondi, Roland Topor, Giorgio White, Umberto Gallone, Enrico Grazioli

The Ravagers (COL) 91 min

A commercial disaster, this is a vapid blending of *Death Wish* (1974) and **Mad Max** (1979). Set in the post-nuclear-holocaust world of 1991, it stars Harris as the loner whose wife is raped and murdered by a gang of motorcyclists. To secure his revenge he joins forces with Carney's dedicated band of hopefuls who are trying to lay the foundations of a new civilization on a deserted aircraft carrier. Directed in the vulgar style of Compton's Southern-vigilante films (*Macon County Line*, 1974 and *Return to Macon County*, 1975) and limply scripted by Sanford, the film updates the vigilante theme to no purpose and wastes its strong cast.

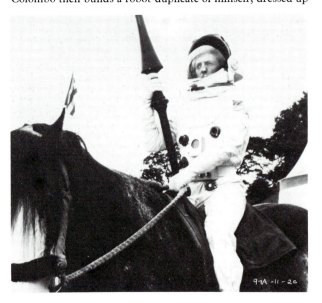

Left: *Dennis Dugan prepares for battle in* The Spaceman and King Arthur.

d Richard Compton *p* John W. Hyde *s* Donald Sanford
c Vincent Saizis *lp* Richard Harris, Art Carney, Alana
Hamilton, Ernest Borgnine, Ann Turkel, Woody Strode

The Spaceman and King Arthur *aka* UFO *aka*
Unidentified Flying Oddball (WALT DISNEY) 93 min

Confidently directed by Mayberry, this is a pleasant re-
working of Mark Twain's oft-filmed novel, *A Connecticut
Yankee in King Arthur's Court*. Dugan is the reluctant
astronaut who, with his humanoid robot Hermes, is whisked
back to the 16th century where the duo do battle with Dale's
evil Mordred on behalf of More's King Arthur. Tait's
efficient screenplay and the ensemble playing of the cast of
British comics are nicely pitched, the occasional excess of
sentimentality aside.

Twain's novel, first filmed as a straight fantasy in 1921, was
filmed in 1931 as **A Connecticut Yankee** and in 1949, with
Bing Crosby in the title role, as **A Connecticut Yankee in
King Arthur's Court.**

d Russ Mayberry *p* Ron Miller *s* Don Tait *c* Paul
Beeson *se* Cliff Culley, Ron Ballanger, Michael
Collins *lp* Dennis Dugan, Jim Dale, Ron Moody, Kenneth
More, John Le Mesurier, Sheila White

Stalker (MOSFILM; USSR) b/w and col 161 min

A more pessimistic version of themes familiar from the same
director's **Solaris** (1971): the subjectivity of men's relation to
their environment and the fearful temptation of wanting to see
one's dreams embodied in reality. The two obsessions can
make for good cinema (as in Fritz Lang's work) but also can
lead easily towards a narcissistic hall of mirrors entrapping the
film-maker into sterile navel-gazing and philosophical plati-
tudes. Adapting a Boris and Arkady Strugatsky story,
Roadside Picnic, Tarkovsky tells of a mysterious Zone that has
appeared in the middle of a country that has become an
industrial wasteland. It is forbidden to enter the Zone, but a
stalker (Kaidanovsky), drawn to the place, acts as a guide to a
writer (Solonitsyn) and a scientist (Grinko) who want to find
the Room that can make dreams come true and which is said
to be in the heart of the Zone. However, the Zone is also
presented as full of traps and as a terrain that constantly
moves and changes in the presence of humans. When, after an
anxiety ridden journey, they arrive at the threshold of the
Room, the professor wants to destroy it in case it is misused
and the writer fears to go in because his fantasies may be
unworthy. The three confusedly scuffle with each other
before returning to prosaic reality. Back with his family, the
stalker bemoans his isolation and complains that soon no-one
will share his faith in the Room. The Room functions as the
planet Solaris did, except that now, knowing what the special
place offers, the intrepid voyagers turn back, preferring to
keep the fantasy of there being such a place rather than enter
it. The philosophical platitude underpinning the story was
enounced over a century ago by R.L. Stevenson: 'To travel
hopefully is a better thing than to arrive.' However, the
visualization of that maxim is striking, with desolate landscapes causing unspecified anxieties expertly conveyed with
eerie lighting and slow, menacing camera movements alternating with uncomfortably long fixed shots, constantly
suggesting a sense of an observing presence which may or may
not be malignant.

*Aleksandr Kaidanovsky
in the title role of
Tarkovsky's bleak*
Stalker.

d Andrei Tarkovsky   *s* Boris Strugatsky, Arkady Strugatsky
c Aleksandr Knyazhinsky   *lp* Aleksandr Kaidanovsky,
Anatoly Solonitsyn, Nikolai Grinko, Alisa Freindlikh,
Natasha Abramova, F. Yurma, E. Kostin, R. Rendi

Star Trek – The Motion Picture (PAR) pv 132 min
In Britain, the Campaign for Real Ale managed the near
impossible when in the late seventies it staunched the spread
of gassy beer and brought about the wholesale return to
popularity of traditional ales. It was a massive victory against
the entrenched interests of the big brewers for such a small
consumer group, but was as nothing compared to the fervour
of the 'Trekkies', as the fans of the *Star Trek* teleseries dubbed
themselves, who throughout the seventies kept the teleseries
on American and British television through endless repeats
(despite the fact that after only three seasons on NBC it had
been cancelled) and had their constant pressures finally
rewarded by the translation of the show from the small to
large screen.

Sadly, for non-trekkies at least, the translation, though a
huge box-office winner, was not entirely a success. Livingstone's screenplay sees the crew of the *Enterprise* (Shatner,
Nimoy, Kelley and most of the minor characters) defending
Earth in the 23rd century from an alien which takes on the
form of new crewmember Khambatta. It transpires that the
alien has in the past consumed an old voyager space probe that
was collecting information about the solar system and,
frustrated in its desire for companionship – Earth hasn't
responded to its signals – is threatening Earth with destruction. Wise, wisely sidestepping the weighty issues that so
bogged down **The Black Hole** (1979), concentrates on the
impressive-looking hardware and on transforming his alien,
called V'ger, into an emotional human being. Certainly it is a
more interesting film than the director's earlier **The
Andromeda Strain** (1970). The climax sees the union of
Khambatta and her old flame Collins which satisfies the
alien's need for companionship.

Ironically, even though the film's plot mirrors the reflective
feel of the teleseries which was always at its best when thought
rather than action was central, in the simple process of
transforming the world of the small screen to that of the large
screen, the domestic cosiness of the original is lost.

A sequel followed in 1982, **Star Trek II: The Wrath of
Khan.**

d Robert Wise   *p* Gene Roddenberry   *s* Harold Livingstone
co-c Richard H. Kline, (matte paintings) Mathew Yuricich
co-c/co-se Richard Yuricich   *co-se* Douglas Trumbull, John
Dykstra, Dave Stewart, Don Baker, Robert Swarthe, Harry
Moreau   *lp* William Shatner, Leonard Nimoy, DeForest
Kelley, Persis Khambatta, Stephen Collins, James Doohan

Starcrash (COL/AIP/FILM ENTERPRISE) 91 min
A blatant melding of **Star Wars** (1977) and **Barbarella** (1967),
this lunatic piece of Science Fiction features the scantily
clothed Munro as Stella Star (!) who, aided by Gortner and
the obligatory robot, does battle with Spinell in defence of the
Universe. The acting is rudimentary and the special effects
hardly special but Cozzi's breakneck direction and the
serial-like action are surprisingly appealing.

d/co-s Lewis Coates (Luigi Cozzi)   *co-p/co-s* Nat
Wachsberger   *co-p* Patrick Wachsberger   *c* Paul Beeson,
Robert D'Ettorre   *se* Studio Quattro, Armando Valcauda,
Matteo Verzini, Germano Natali   *lp* Marjoe Gortner,
Caroline Munro, Christopher Plummer, Joe Spinell, David
Hasselhoff, Robert Tessier

Supersonic Man (ALMENA FILMS; SP) 88 min
Beneath the veneer of obvious influences such as **Star Wars**
(1977) and **Superman – The Movie** (1978), this is essentially
a muscleman movie in the long tradition of the Hercules/
wrestler movies that exists in the Latin cinema. Crudely
plotted, it stars Coby in the title role as a Superman lookalike
from a distant galaxy who comes complete with a second
identity as a private eye. Mitchell is the mad scientist who
wouldn't be out of place in a thirties serial and Polakow the
Lois Lane lookalike. Piquer's direction is routine but the
special effects of Prosper and Ruiz surprisingly good.

d/co-s Piquer Simon (Juan Piquer)   *co-p/co-s* Tonino Moi
co-p Dick Randall, Faruk Alatan   *c* John (Juan) Marine
se Jack Elkubi, Miguel Villa, Frank (Francisco) Prosper,
Emil (Emilio) Ruiz   *lp* Michael Coby, Cameron Mitchell,
Diana Polakow, Richard Yesteran, Frank Brana, Javier de
Campos

*Persis Khambatta leads
(left to right) Leonard
Nimoy, Stephen
Collins, William
Shatner and DeForest
Kelley to a rendezvous
with the mysterious alien
force in Star Trek –
The Motion Picture.*

*Left: Caroline Munro
as Stella Star, a
latterday Barbarella,
with her pet robot Elle in
danger in the enjoyable
Starcrash.*

Time After Time (WB/ORION) pv 112 min

Meyer, a novelist whose pleasant pastiche of the world of
Sherlock Holmes, *The Seven Per Cent Solution* (1976) was
badly let down by director Herbert Ross, here picks up the
megaphone himself for this similarly joky conflation of the
careers of H.G. Wells (McDowell) and Jack the Ripper
(Warner). The intricate plot features Warner escaping from
the police and 1893 in McDowell's time machine and
McDowell pursuing him to San Francisco and 1979 where
Warner immediately finds himself at home amidst the sleazy
neon lights of the town's red-light district and the sexual
liberation of the new age in which he finds himself. Meyer
directs labouredly for the most part, making cheap jokes out
of the contrast between the utopian future McDowell clearly
expects and the reality of San Francisco in 1979. Only in the
affair between Steenburgen (who gives a splendid performance) and McDowell does Meyer show the delicate touch
needed to make the film work.

In 1983, Meyer directed the powerful telefilm *The Day
After*, a film in the tradition of **The War Game** (1965), which
caused an uproar in America for its depiction of the aftermath
of a nuclear war.

d/s Nicholas Meyer   *p* Herb Jaffe   *c* Paul Lohmann
se Larry Fuentes, Jim Blount   *lp* Malcolm McDowell, David
Warner, Mary Steenburgen, Charles Cioffi, Kent Williams,
Andonia Katsaros

L'Umanoide *aka* The Humanoid

(MEROPE; IT) 100 (99) min

Yet another would-be **Star Wars** (1977), this Italian offering
features Kennedy as the mad scientist bent on domination of
the known Universe who is foiled by Golob (played by Kiel as
an extention of his Jaws persona in the James Bond films),
Yeh's tiny Tibetan mystic and Clery, who in company with
Kennedy's girlfriend, Bach, is yet another refugee from
Bondage. The plot is ridiculously convoluted so as to allow
Kennedy to take control of Kiel and transform him into the
humanoid of the title, and the direction crude. Nonetheless
the film has its moments of enjoyable delirium.

d George B. Lewis   *p* Giorgio Venturini   *s* Adriano
Bolzoni, Aldo Lado   *c* Silvano Ippoliti   *se* Studio 4, Studio
Verzini, Ermanno Biamonte, Anthony M. Dawson (Antonio
Margheriti), Armando Valcauda   *lp* Richard Kiel, Corinne
Clery, Leonard Mann, Barbara Bach, Arthur Kennedy,
Marco Yeh

Zombie 2 *aka* Zombie Flesh Eaters

(VARIETY FILMS; IT) 91 (89) min

This incompetent Italian borrowing of the central idea of
George Romero's **Night of the Living Dead** (1968) wastes too
much time on (implausibly) explaining the whys and where-
fores of its zombies to be ever truly scaring. The opening, a
boat adrift in New York with its echoes of *Nosferatu* (1922), is
fine, but once Farrow and McCulloch voyage to the island,
where her father has been assisting Johnson's doctor, the
horrors become too predictable, as is the tired direction of
Fulci.

d Lucio Fulci   *p* Ugo Tucci, Fabrizio De Angelis   *s* Elisa
Briganti   *c* Sergio Salvati   *se* Giannetto De Rossi
lp Tisa Farrow, Ian McCulloch, Richard Johnson, Al Cliver,
Auretta Gay, Stefania D'Amario

The 1980s

Science Fiction Triumphant

The Science Fiction boom of the seventies continued un-abated into the eighties but, in America at least, several significant changes in attitude to the genre occurred. In mainstream Hollywood a new conservatism was visible as producers and studios attempted, in the main with great commercial success, simply to replay successful hits. **Superman** (1978), **Star Trek** (1979), **Alien** (1979) and **Star Wars** (1977) all spawned (several) sequels, while *Star Wars* itself was parodied by Mel Brooks in **Spaceballs** (1987), and *Alien* was undoubtedly the most imitated film of the decade. Similarly, most of the decade's big successes were repeated: hence the sequels to **Cocoon** and **Back to the Future** (both 1985). Few of these sequels, with the notable exception of **Return of the Jedi** (1983), which infused a genuine element of pulp poetry into the simple heroics of *Star Wars*, matched the originals. The same was true of most of the other examples of the new conservatism, the remakes of fifties' classics that included **The Thing** (1982), **Invaders From Mars** (1986) and **Not of This Earth** (1988).

More interesting and influential was **E.T.** (1982), which both spawned numerous imitations (e.g. **MAC and Me**, 1988) and introduced the one new cross-genre theme of the decade, the family in peril. Generally given a comic inflection (in contrast to Horror films dealing with the subject), films like **Honey, I Shrunk the Kids** (1989) confirmed that Science Fiction had not lost the social function it developed in the fifties, the decade in which, to all intents and purposes, it became a genre.

At the exploitation end of the market the most significant film was **Mad Max** (1979), the success of which led to a pair of big-budget sequels and, in the same manner, the genre's other great independent success, **Night of the Living Dead** (1968), laid the ground rules for numerous imitative low-budget outings in similar post-holocaust settings. While most of the exploitation films of the period aimed simply at reproducing the formulae of mainstream success, with further emphasis on sex and violence, it was notable that a few were more pessimistic than their mainstream models (John Carpenter's **They Live**, 1988). Even more were self-reflective, often celebrating their fifties-like tattiness, and witty (though sadly too often only in part) in a manner infrequently found in big-budget films. While rarely truly dangerous, in the style of David Cronenberg's **Videodrome** (1982), films like **The Wizard of Speed and Time** (1988), **Liquid Sky** (1982) and **Earth Girls Are Easy** (1988) suggested that the tyranny of the special effects department, a feature of so many films of the late seventies and early eighties, was over and that a more probing attitude to the fears of the day was at hand.

Agency   (RSL FILMS; CAN)   94 min
A plodding thriller adapted from Paul Gottlieb's novel of the same title, this probably made its way to the screen less on merit than as a convenient tax-shelter project. Mitchum is the malign manipulator behind a plot to use subliminal messages encoded in TV ads for a kids' breakfast drink to back political candidates of his choice. Rubinek and Majors are his ad agency underlings who smell a rat and risk all to expose him. Every plot twist is predictable, and all the cast, bar the perky Rubinek, merely go through the motions at what seems like a snail's pace.

d George Kaczender   *p* Robert Lantos, Stephen J. Roth
s Noel Hynd   *c* Miklos Lente   *lp* Robert Mitchum, Lee Majors, Valerie Perrine, Saul Rubinek, Alexandra Stewart, Hayward Morse

Altered States   (WB)   102 min
Once an (unlikely sounding) Arthur Penn project, *Altered States* gained Russell, lost Chayevsky behind a pseudonym after the contours of his novel began to get swamped in psychedelia, and emerged as an awesomely idiotic fusion of Science Fiction, naked-ape horror and hippie trip: exactly the sort of tenuously justified light-show extravaganza to be expected from the director of *Tommy* (1975) and sundry other flashy stabs at anchoring the evocative in crushingly literalistic imagery. The justification here is Hurt's research scientist Eddie Jessup, a dedicated seeker after heightened forms of consciousness who'll try anything from sacred Mexican hallucinogens to laboratory-based sensory deprivation tests to earn himself glimpses of heaven, hell and all the altered images between; and who ends up overdosing on psychic regression while immersed in the lab tank to the extent that he physically mutates to monkeydom and beyond. Sorely tried wife Brown eventually pulls him back from the brink of disappearing into the evolutionary black hole, while Balaban and Haid stand thanklessly around in white coats proffering unheeded warnings and looking suitably distraught at Hurt's metamorphoses.

d Ken Russell   *p* Howard Gottfried   *s* Sidney Aaron (Paddy Chayevsky)   *c* Jordan Cronenweth   *se* Bran Ferren, Robbie Blalack, Jamie Shourt, Chuck Gaspar   *lp* William Hurt, Blair Brown, Bob Balaban, Charles Haid, Miguel Godreau

The Apple *aka* Star-Rock   (CANNON)   pv   94 (92) min
An inane Science Fiction musical from the dedicated team who've inflicted umpteen versions of *Lemon Popsicle* (1977) on the world, this begins at the 1994 Worldvision Song Contest and thereafter essays a decidedly un-magical mystery tour through the clichés of youth-culture dissent before expiring in interplanetary escapism. Sheybal is the promoter

Previous pages: E.T. The Extra-Terrestrial (1982), Science Fiction triumphant in the eighties.

Darlanne Fleugel and android in Battle Beyond the Stars, *Roger Corman's biggest budgeted film to date. Although scripted by the inventive John Sayles, it is only intermittently interesting, a testament to Corman's growing conservatism as a producer as his budgets grew larger.*

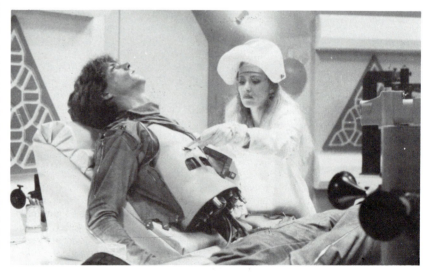

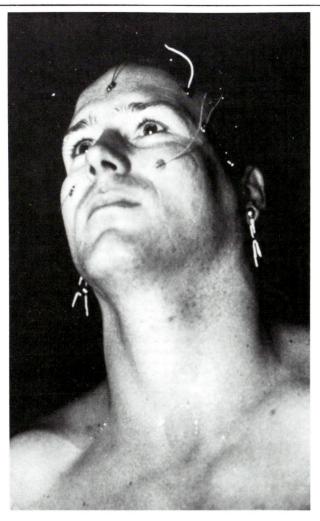

brainwashing the masses through muzak and Gilmour the wet balladeer whose love songs promise liberation. The flashily mounted farrago of nonsense is not even enlivened by such patent absurdities as the casting of Ackland as an aged, outlawed hippie; and the film's production values would be disdained by almost any disco.

d/co-p/s Menahem Golan   *co-p* Yoram Globus   *c* David Gurfinkel   *lp* Catherine Mary Stuart, George Gilmour, Grace Kennedy, Allan Love, Joss Ackland, Vladek Sheybal

Battle Beyond the Stars   (NEW WORLD)   103 min
Costing $5 million, *Battle Beyond the Stars* is the biggest budgeted production of Roger Corman's New World studios to date. Cost-conscious as ever, when John Dykstra (of **Star Wars,** 1977, fame) asked $2 million to do the special effects, Corman built his own studio and special effects' department for half of Dysktra's fee and subsequently rented it out at great profit to other film-makers (notably John Carpenter who shot **Escape from New York,** 1981, there).

The film was scripted by Sayles, who'd earlier written **Piranha** (1978) for New World and subsequently directed the pleasing *The Return of the Secaucus Seven* (1979) to a warm critical reception. On Corman's instructions, the basic plotline was *The Magnificent Seven* (1960) in space. The film was a commercial success despite the over-concentration on hardware and special effects at the expense of character. Thomas is the Akirian youth who journeys in search of mercenaries to help defend his planet from Saxon's gloriously excessive warlord who threatens to destroy it within a week unless the Akirians turn over their wealth to him. Amongst the mercenaries are Vaughn (reprising his doomed gunfighter from *The Magnificent Seven*), Peppard's scotch-gulping space

cowboy and Danning's **Barbarella** (1967) lookalike Valkyrie maiden. Murakami's direction lacks the deft touch needed to bring either the stereotyped characters or Sayles' occasional witticisms to life. The result is a film whose script presumably was inventive but which, in the course of its relatively expensive production, fell prey to the innate conservatism of Corman the producer. In 1983, Corman produced **Space Raiders** whose sole reason for existing was to re-use the special effects of *Battle Beyond the Stars*.

d Jimmy T. Murakami   *p* Ed Carlin   *s* John Sayles   *c* Daniel Lacambre, (miniatures) George D. Dodge, Dennis Skotak   *se* New World Studio   *lp* Richard Thomas, Robert Vaughn, John Saxon, George Peppard, Sybil Danning, Darlanne Fluegel

The Chain Reaction
(PALM BEACH PICTURES; AUST)   92 min
A frenzied action thriller tracking the violent conflict over desperate attempts to expose and cover up a serious release of irradiated nuclear waste, *The Chain Reaction* apes the visual attack of **Mad Max** (1979) but, in so doing, glosses topical fears with a patina of glib sensationalism. The extent of authoritarian investment in secrecy and misinformation over any nuclear issue is made more than adequately clear by the shock-cut cinematography that peppers the narrative and the echoes of films like George Romero's **The Crazies** (1973). But the heroics of those trying to spread the truth seem absurd, and the faith in the media's power (or willingness) to wrap up the narrative – they witness the closing stages of a deadly chase – and conclusively blow the cover-up is decidedly naïve.

d/s Ian Barry   *p* David Elfick   *c* Russell Boyd   *lp* Steve Bisley, Arna-Maria Winchester, Ross Thompson, Ralph Cotterill, Hugh Keays-Byrne

Conquest of the Earth
(GLEN A. LARSON PRODUCTIONS/U)   99 min
The third film derived from the *Battlestar Galactica* teleseries, *Conquest of the Earth*, like its predecessors **Battlestar Galactica** (1978) and **Mission Galactica: The Cylon Attack** (1979), was cobbled together from episodes of the teleseries for theatrical release in Europe. The resulting anonymous film sees Greene, having at last located Earth, trying to make contact with Reed's scientist and so prepare Earth for the imminent Cylon attack while at the same time keep Earth's location a secret from the Cylons by destroying their probe before it can communicate with its base. The idea of Galactica crewmembers McCord and Van Dyke being mistaken for anti-nuclear demonstators when they try to reach Reed gives a fair indication of the level of wit at work. Wolfman Jack guests as himself.

d Sidney Hayers, Sigmund Neufeld Jnr, Barry Crane   *p* Jeff Freilich, Frank Lupo, Gary B. Winters   *s* Glen A. Larson   *c* Frank P. Beascoechea, Mario DiLeo, Ben Colman   *se* David M. Garber, Wayne Smith   *lp* Kent McCord, Barry Van Dyke, Robyn Douglass, Lorne Greene, Patrick Stuart, Robbie Rist, Robert Reed, John Colicos

Dr Heckyl and Mr Hype   (CANNON)   99 min
Scripted 'with apologies to Robert Louis Stevenson' and with at least some of the lunatic verve that characterized Griffith's vintage work for Roger Corman – *A Bucket of Blood* (1959) and **The Little Shop of Horrors** (1960) included – this perversion of the 'Jekyll and Hyde' formula has Reed metamorphozing from ugly-but-nice chiropodist Heckyl to dashing-but-nasty ladykiller Hype after OD-ing on a wonder slimming potion in a failed suicide attempt. Amid the subsequent patchily hilarious convolutions of sex, violence and scrambled identities, Reed for once hams enjoyably and Griffith clearly relishes the opportunity to 'return' to his touchingly zany Z-grade roots, still showing all the camp

cultists who've appeared in the intervening years that they've a lot to learn about sustaining a tone of engaging weirdness.

d/s Charles B. Griffith   *p* Menahem Golan, Yoram Globus   *c* Robert Carras   *lp* Oliver Reed, Sunny Johnson, Mel Welles, Maia Danziger, Jackie Coogan, Virgil Frye

The Empire Strikes Back

(LUCASFILM/FOX)   pv   124 min

The second of the trilogy that began with **Star Wars** (1977) and concludes with **Return of the Jedi** (1983), *The Empire Strikes Back* is the least interesting of the films. Its $32 million budget and Oscar-winning special effects testify to its technical polish but the characters are never developed beyond the cardboard cut-outs of *Star Wars*. In the manner of the James Bond films, it falls into the trap of committing itself to the spectacular at the expense of the personal. Even though Kasdan's and Brackett's screenplay spends more of its time on the individual adventures of Hamill, Ford and Fisher, they remain stereotypes.

The film's one success, and pointer to the future, is Prowse's Darth Vader whose dark presence dominates the picture, giving it the weighty centre it so desperately needs. Moreover, with the revelation that Vader is Luke's father, the film edges closer to the mythic, giving the *Star Wars* legend the beginnings of a sense of complexity beyond the simple-minded serial verities of Good versus Evil, that Richard Marquand would further develop in the masterful *Return of the Jedi*. It is this aspect, reflected in the narrative's classic cliff-hanging ending (Ford preserved alive awaiting rescue in the next instalment) that gives what is otherwise merely an efficient sequel a certain resonance.

d Irvin Kershner   *p* Gary Kurtz   *s* Leigh Brackett, Lawrence Kasdan   *c* Peter Suschitzky   *se* Brian Johnson, Richard Edlund   *lp* Mark Hamill, Harrison Ford, Carrie Fisher, Billy Dee Williams, David Prowse, Anthony Daniels, Frank Oz, Kenny Baker, Alec Guinness, James Earl Jones (voice of Vader), Peter Mayhew

The Falls   (BFI; GB)   185 min

Doubts as to whether ornithology, structuralism or statistics constitute the sort of sciences on which generic fiction might be based keep several early Greenaway films out of this volume. Such disciplines are as much a part of the world of *The Falls* as they are of, say, *A Walk Through H* or *Vertical Features Remake* (both 1978), but this epic catalogue of improbable personae can at least be appropriated for Science Fiction scrutiny on the wholly speculative assumption that the Violent Unknown Event to which the 92 subjects bear witness might stand equally for Genesis or Apocalypse (even if, as is more likely the case, this is the ultimate inexplicable VUE). Ninety-two capsule biographies of people whose surnames are

prefixed by the letters F-A-L-L, numerous jokes, several excursions into the lore of birds and much counterfeit erudition all add up to eccentricity raised to the level of a science. This whimsicality contrasts with Greenaway's best film to date, *The Draughtsman's Contract* (1982), in which the odd world its characters inhabit is drawn with a bravura formalism.

d/s Peter Greenaway   *c* Mike Coles, John Rosenberg

The Fiendish Plot of Fu Manchu

(ORION/PLAYBOY PRODUCTIONS)   108 min

A sad last film for Sellers whose comic talents are all but buried by the shambling script and direction, *The Fiendish Plot of Fu Manchu* also marked the last entry (so far) in the long-running saga of Fu Manchu. Sellers plays both Sax Rohmer's arch criminal, this time trying to steal the crown jewels, a vital ingredient in the 'elixir vitae' by which he keeps eternally young, and Nayland Smith his old enemy. Even the climax, Seller's Fu Manchu rejuvenated as an outrageous parody of Elvis Presley compares unfavourably with Sellers' impersonation of the singer on record in the sixties.

d Piers Haggard   *p* Zev Braun, Leland Nolan   *s* Jim Moloney, Rudy Dochtermann   *c* Jean Tournier   *se* Richard Parker   *lp* Peter Sellers, Helen Mirren, David Tomlinson, Sid Caesar, Simon Williams, John Le Mesurier

The Final Countdown   (BRYNA COMPANY)   pv   105 min

An opportunity for Douglas to furrow his brow over the ethics of tampering with a subject as weighty as history itself, this film for his own production company bears all the hallmarks of an overgrown tele-feature. The aircraft carrier USS *Nimitz* is manoeuvring in Pacific waters under Douglas' command, with observer Sheen aboard, when it is enveloped in a bizarre storm and emerges intact in 1941, with all reconnaissance evidence pointing to the imminent cataclysm of Pearl Harbor. To intervene – or not to intervene – in the course of events becomes the question on everyone's mind, with doomed politician Durning determined to cheat his ordained fate, but everyone else mulling the dilemma as if it were Hamlet's own. The script's let-out clauses are legion, however, and, in a very belated bit of opportunist mystification, Farentino's character is suggested as some sort of *deus ex machina* after a second

Left: *Peter Sellers with Helen Mirren in the* terrible The Fiendish Plot of Fu Manchu, *a sad last film for Sellers.*

Mark Hamill riding a Tauntaun on Hoth the ice planet in The Empire Strikes Back, *the second part of the* Star Wars (1977) *trilogy.*

Sam J. Jones, American footballer extraordinaire and the saviour of Earth in Flash Gordon.

time-warp has returned the *Nimitz* to the present day and obviated the need for decision-making. Countdowns have their own tension, but in this one director Taylor merely goes through the motions.

d Don Taylor *p* Peter Vincent Douglas *s* David Ambrose, Gerry Davis, Thomas Hunter, Peter Powell *c* Victor J. Kemper *se* Maurice Binder *lp* Kirk Douglas, Martin Sheen, Katharine Ross, James Farentino, Ron O'Neal, Charles Durning

Flash Gordon
(STARLING PRODUCTIONS/FAMOUS FILMS; GB)
Todd-AO 115 (113) min

In the manner of **Flesh Gordon** (1974), this camp remake of the classic 1936 serial over-relies on sex appeal. Thus, though it faithfully follows the serial's plot for the most part, it has none of the mythological appeal of Frederick Stephani's chapterplay which drew out the perversity of Alex Raymond's original comic strip both in the interactions of the various paired characters and in the elaborate décor of Mongo and its environs. In its place Hodges puts a knowingness and literalness that works completely against the sense of pulp poetry so essential if we are to believe in Flash (Jones), Dale Arden (Anderson) and Zharkov (Topol). Semple's script, like that for De Laurentiis' other remake, *King Kong* (1976), is similarly bland, its occasional witticisms notwithstanding.

The score was composed and performed by the rock group Queen who also had a British top ten hit with the film's theme song, 'Flash', in 1981.

d Michael Hodges *p* Dino De Laurentiis *s* Lorenzo Semple Jnr *c* Gil Taylor *se* Frank Van Der Veer, Barry Nolan, George Gibbs *lp* Sam J. Jones, Melody Anderson, Topol, Max Von Sydow, Brian Blessed, Ornella Muti

Fukkatsu No Hi *aka* Virus
(HARUKI KADOKAWA FILMS; JAP) 155 min

Directed by Fukasaku who was responsible for the first Japanese-American co-production, **Gamma Sango Uchu Daisakusen** (1968) and the inventive **Uchu Kara No Messeji** (1978), Japan's most expensive production until *Fukkatsu No Hi*, this disturbing film marks a further development beyond the ecological concerns that dominated Japanese Science Fiction of the seventies. Here it is not the world's ecology that is threatened but humanity itself from the combination of an East German invented virus intended for bacteriological

warfare that is accidentally let loose and the American military who ready their nuclear forces as the virus spreads worldwide. The chilling climax sees the world's population reduced to some 800 people, including Hussey, Svenson and Kusakari, living perilously in the Arctic wastes, protected from the still malignant virus by the freezing cold.

d/co-s Kinji Fukasaku *p* Haruki Kadakawa *co-s* Koji Takada, Gregory Knapp *c* Daisaku Kimura *lp* Masao Kusakari, Olivia Hussey, Bo Svenson

Galaxina (MARIMAR/CROWN INTERNATIONAL) 95 min
A lethargic intergalactic spoof movie that attracted more attention than it deserved when its American opening coincided with the murder of former Playmate and starlet Stratten (subsequently the centre of an all-too-predictable Hollywood death-cult focus, via the telefilm *Death of a Centrefold* (1981) and Bob Fosse's *Star '80* (1983)), who here plays a robot navigator aboard the police cruiser *Infinity*, patrolling the busy space-lanes of 3008. A mission to planet Altar 1 to retrieve the powerful 'Blue Star' provides the basis for the script's hit-and-miss parodic digressions – taking in encounters with bikers and westerners as well as the usual cheap shots at recent mega-hits – while Stratten's android charms begin to stir Macht's interest in a romance which has to overcome the handicap of the robot not being totally equipped as a female. Solid professional jobs on camera and effects' work are insufficient to rescue the bitty script and haphazard direction, and it's not hard to see here the same wavering hand that guided the inane *Van Nuys Boulevard* (1979).

d/s William Sachs *p* Marilyn J. Tenser *c* Dean Cundy *lp* Stephen Macht, Dorothy Stratten, James David Hinton, Avery Schreiber

Hangar 18 (SUNN CLASSIC) 97 min
Underpinning its UFO-logy with a rather more literal set of post-Watergate assumptions than those that informed the ostensibly similar **Capricorn One** (1977), and trying to come across as a cynical version of **Close Encounters of the Third Kind** (1977), this slapdash fiction from the team more used to turning out Sunn Classic's speculative 'documentaries' is the most sluggish of straight-faced satires. Collins and Hampton are the astronauts, targeted by the White House as scapegoats for the loss of a space shuttle which has actually collided with a UFO, who try to blow the politically expedient, conspiratorial cover-up of the alien craft's crash-landing in Texas and subsequent secretion in a remote air-base's Hangar 18. Vaughn is the typically steely and sinister politician trying to stem any news leak by fair means or foul, and McGavin the NASA investigator who decides to side with Collins after discovering and decoding alien plans to invade the USA. The abrupt defeatism of the final plot twist – all evidence is simply bombed to destruction on White House orders – is both predictable and wholly symptomatic of the complacency Conway exhibits throughout in his inept juggling of genre styles and spectacle.

d James L. Conway *p* Charles E. Sellier Jnr *s* Steven Thornley *c* Paul Hipp *se* Harry Woolman *lp* Darren McGavin, Robert Vaughn, Gary Collins, James Hampton, Joseph Campanella, Steven Keats

Herbie Goes Bananas (WALT DISNEY) 93 min
In the company of an equally cute teenage pickpocket (Garay), Herbie, the Volkswagen with a mind of its own, foils Vernon's plans to loot a lost Inca city of its gold in this tired offering in the once charming series that began life with the phenomenally successful **The Love Bug** (1969). Set amidst a succession of picturesque locations the film sees its human cast reduced to standing on the sidelines as Herbie goes through his well-groomed paces.

d Vincent McEveety *p* Ron Miller *s* Don Tait *c* Frank Phillips *se* Art Cruickshank, Danny Lee *lp* Cloris Leachman, Charles Martin Smith, John Vernon, Stephan W. Burns, Elyssa Davalos, Richard Jaeckel, Joaquin Garay

Inseminoid (JUPITER FILM PRODUCTIONS; GB) 92 min
This low-budget version of **Alien** (1979) features Geeson in the thankless role of an archaeologist who is raped and gives birth to a mutant offspring on a distant planet. Conceived by director Warren and his writers as a headlong catalogue of murder and violence in outer space in which narrative clarity is wholly dispensable, the film fails, not least because the (interchangeable) characters are too vapid and one-dimensional to be taken seriously.

d Norman J. Warren *p* Richard Gordon, David Speechley *s* Nick Maley, Gloria Maley *c* John Metcalfe *se* Oxford Scientific Films, Camera Effects *lp* Robin Clarke, Jennifer Ashley, Stephanie Beacham, Judy Geeson, Steven Grives, Barry Houghton

Nightmare City *aka* **City of the Walking Dead**
(LOTUS INTERNATIONAL/DIALCHI FILM PRODUCCIONES; SP, IT) 92 min
Better known under its re-release title, *City of the Walking Dead* (which, to make matters even more confusing, carries the copyright date of 1984) this exploitation film is derived in equal parts from George Romero's **Night of the Living Dead** (1968) and **The China Syndrome** (1979). A radiation leak at a nuclear power plant causes people to become bloodsucking vampire monsters – they need to replenish their rapidly decaying red blood cells – that attack the local airport. Mexican star Stiglitz is the television newscaster who witnesses the attack and whose report is censored by Ferrer's authoritarian general. Lenzi's direction is workmanlike but the script is far too predictable and the acting routine at best.

d Umberto Lenzi *p* Diego Alchimede *s* Piero Regnoli, Toni Corti *c* Hans Burman *lp* Hugo Stiglitz, Laura Trotter, Francisco Rabal, Mel Ferrer, Maria Rosario Omaggio

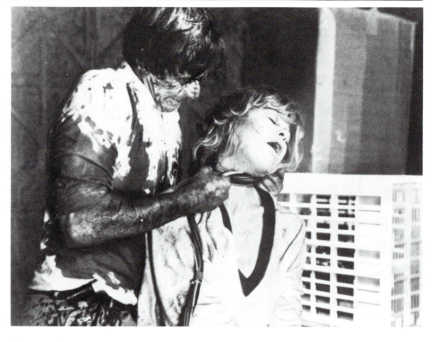

The Nude Bomb (U/TIME-LIFE FILMS) 94 min
The most surprising thing about this spin-off from the *Get Smart* teleseries is its date, 1980. Created by Mel Brooks and Buck Henry, the series, a highly inventive parody of the legion of superspies who trailed in the wake of James Bond, ran from 1965 to 1969. In 1980, the bumbling, forever apologetic Adams – one catchphrase was 'I'm sorry about that Chief' – is decidedly out of time, a point made even more evident by both the film's title and the presence of Kristel (the original *Emmanuelle*, 1974) as his co-star. With Brooks in charge the film might have made sense, but as it is *The Nude Bomb* is simply redundant. The clumsy screenplay sees Adams, Kristel, Howard and a bizarre array of gadgetry combating Gassman, who has devised a bomb that will destroy all known clothes' fabrics and thus leave the world naked, and his army of clones.

d Clive Donner *p* Jennings Lang *s* Arne Sultan, Bill Dana, Leonard B. Stern *c* Harry L. Wolf *se* Whitey Krumm, Richard Lea *lp* Don Adams, Sylvia Kristel, Vittorio Gassman, Andrea Howard, Rhonda Fleming, Dana Elcar

Saturn 3
(TRANSCONTINENTAL FILM PRODUCTIONS; GB) 87 (86) min
Begun by set designer John Barry, who'd designed several of the Bond films, but completed by Donen when Barry died in mid-production, *Saturn 3* features an 8-foot robot (built by Chilvers from a drawing by Leonardo Da Vinci no less) lusting after ex-Charlie's Angel Fawcett. The film's best performance comes from Keitel as the deranged scientist who brings a brutish credibility to his dreams of creating a super-race of robots that completely over-balances the film and leaves Douglas as the ageing but virile defender of Fawcett with little to do but grin and grimace. The film's one interesting ploy is the idea, little followed up, of a robot assuming the personality of its creator.

d/p Stanley Donen *s* Martin Amis *c* Billy Williams *se* Colin Chilvers, Roy Spencer, Terry Schubert, Jeff Luff *lp* Farrah Fawcett, Kirk Douglas, Harvey Keitel, Douglas Lambert, Ed Bishop, Christopher Muncke

Scanners (FILMPLAN INTERNATIONAL; CAN) 103 min
The exploding head movie. For all its deadly telepathic duels and fleshy pyrotechnics, Cronenberg's characteristic Science Fiction horror/thriller touches base most tellingly in the

Above: Judy Geeson finally murdered by Robin Clarke in Norman J. Warren's Inseminoid, *a low-budget version of* Alien *(1979).*

Left: The Nude Bomb, a failed attempt to revive sixties-type humour in the eighties.

Right: Scanners: the *exploding head movie.*

realms of pharmaceutical politics and sibling psycho-drama. The human scanners are people blessed (or damned) with the deadly power to lock into another's central nervous system at will, who have polarized in response to their common capabilities into units of quasi-fascist nasties and peaceable opposition underground. Hero scanner Lack passes bewildered through the hands of the first group before joining the second and leading their last-ditch resistance, piecing together the strands of conspiracy that link McGoohan's ComSec research agency with the Biochemical Amalgamated drug plant, and discovering that a thalidomide-like tranquillizer called ephemerol is responsible for the spread of the scanning facility among pregnant women and their offspring. In the process, he also discovers that he and his megalomaniac brother, Ironside, were the original foetal guinea-pigs in the irresponsible medical experiment that gave rise to scanning. Battle, of course, has to be joined.

Alan Arkin as Simon *in Marshall Brickman's engaging, if decidedly flawed, comedy.*

A cruelly black humour runs throughout – in the off-centre dialogue and brilliant physical casting as much as in such set-pieces as Lack *telephonically* scanning a computer's 'nervous system' to explosive effect – while the orchestration of tension and ability to toy with audience expectations is little short of masterly. Outstripping such second cousins as *Carrie* (1976), *Patrick* (1978) and *The Fury* (1978) with its effects and effectiveness, *Scanners* also signalled the virtual end of the telekinetic thriller cycle by pushing it to its limit, as if Science Fiction *per se* were turning violently on its upstart mutant offspring, and seeing it off.

Below: *Farrah Fawcett in the grip of Hector the robot who lusts after her in* Saturn 3.

d/s David Cronenberg   *p* Claude Heroux   *c* Mark Irwin *se* Dick Smith, Gary Zeller, Henry Pierrig   *lp* Stephen Lack, Jennifer O'Neill, Patrick McGoohan, Michael Ironside, Lawrence Dane, Robert Silverman

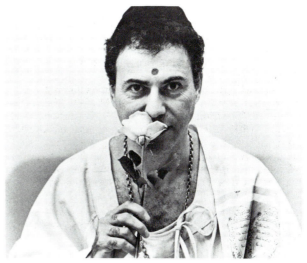

Scared to Death
(LONE STAR/MALONE PRODUCTIONS)   95 (87) min
This half-homage/half-heisted monster movie, which trades on a high corpse count, inevitably takes to the sewers for its final chase. Standing in here as an Earthbound version of Giger's 'alien' is actor Kermit Eller in a rubber suit, playing the synthesized genetic organism (Syngenor) which has gone on the rampage after the death of its scientific progenitor and is feeding its own pod-borne offspring with human life fluids. Stinson is the ex-cop-cum-novelist and Janotta the genetics student who give chase.

d/s/co-se William Malone   *p* Rand Marlis, Gil Shelton *c* Patrick Prince   *co-se* Robert Short   *lp* John Stinson, Diana Davidson, Jonathan David Moses, Toni Janotta

Simon   (ORION)   97 min
The directorial début of former Woody Allen script collaborator Brickman, this failed, flailing satire on scientific irresponsibility and the cult of the television guru contrives to have Arkin's bumbling psychology professor subjected to sensory deprivation and regression techniques by the bored scientists at the think-tank Institute of Advanced Concepts and brainwashed into believing that he is really an extra-terrestrial from Nebula Orion with a message for the world. As a gag framework this is promising, but Brickman's pretensions to having 'ideas' about 'issues' are about all that glue together the disconnectedly joky scenes illustrating the human awe of hardware and apparent blindness to dehumanization, and it's left to Arkin's natural skill with grimace and gesture to salvage some laughs from the débris. Graubert is the girl who stands by him.

d/s Marshall Brickman p Martin Bregman c Adam Holender lp Alan Arkin, Madeline Kahn, Austin Pendleton, Judy Graubert, William Finley, Wallace Shawn

Superman II
(DOVEMEAD/INTERNATIONAL FILM PRODUCTIONS; GB)
pv 127 min

Superman II takes the humanizing of the man of steel, commenced in **Superman – The Movie** (1978) a stage further by having Reeve at one point forego his invulnerability for love of Kidder's Lois Lane. Set against this human drama, Lester (who took over from Richard Donner, the director of *Superman-The Movie*), gleefully elaborates, in the style of his sixties pop art films (notably *The Knack* and *Help!*, both 1965), a cardboard cut-out world comprising such cultural icons as the Eiffel Tower, Mount Rushmore, Coca-Cola signs and a truck emblazoned with the Marlboro trademark. It is this consumerist paradise that is threatened with extermination by the three supergoons from Krypton led by Stamp's malevolent General Zod. Lester pushes the parallels between Superman minus his powers and an emasculated America – and this at the time of the Iranian hostage affair – into the realms of comic-strip absurdity. At one point the president of America (Marshall) is seen cringing before Stamp's all-in-black thirties-style supervillain and the climax sees a revived and victorious Superman carefully replacing the dome on the White House before seeking out the trucker who sent him flying when he'd lost his powers.

More importantly, the elevation of the dilemma of love (ie sex) or superpowers that Clark Kent/Superman faces as the central dramatic issue of the film gives it more space to breathe and allows Lester to mount the most theatrical of set-pieces (as in the final confrontation between Superman and Zod and company, which is watched by the terrified population of Metropolis). Along with this Hackman's Lex Luthor, in terms of plot a minor villain in league with the Krypton rebels, is allowed free play, in the manner of court jester to Superman's indecisive hero.

d Richard Lester p Pierre Spengler s Mario Puzo, David Newman, Leslie Newman c Geoffrey Unsworth, Bob Paynter se Roy Field, Colin Chilvers, Zoran Perisic lp Christopher Reeve, Gene Hackman, Ned Beatty, Margot Kidder, Terence Stamp, E. G. Marshall

Above: Richard Pascoe (left), Ian Bannen, Lynn-Holly Johnson (blindfolded) and Frances Cuka in the bland The Watcher in the Woods.

Taiyo o Nusunda Otoko *aka* The Man Who Stole the Sun (KITTY FILMS; JAP) 130 min

A wonderfully audacious black comedy idea underpins this Japanese 'New Wave' movie, but Hasegawa and Schrader (brother of Paul, with whom he has written) can't quite spin it out coherently or develop it to a convincing conclusion within the excessive running time. Pop singer Sawada plays a school science teacher who graduates from blackboard demonstrations to manufacturing his own atom bomb at home, and threatens the government with its detonation if his absurd demands – that the TV networks be allowed to transmit baseball games to their end, rather than having to cut them off at a rigid closedown time and that the Rolling Stones be allowed to play live in Japan, despite their drug-busts record – aren't met. Sawada's also engaged in a cat-and-mouse battle of wits and wills with detective Sugawara (a veteran of numerous yakuza movies), and an offbeat romance with a kooky disc jockey. His inevitable downfall, however, is followed by some ridiculous plot leaps – he manages to steal back his bomb from the police – and the film ends more like an action quickie. The culture-clash casting works well, and the initial tone of perverse capering is fine; it's merely a shame that imagination runs out too early.

d/co-s Kazuhiko Hasegawa co-s Leonard Schrader c Tatsuo Suzuki lp Kenji Sawada, Bunta Sugawara, Kimiko Ikegami, Yonosuke Ito

The Watcher in the Woods
(WALT DISNEY) 83 (100) min

Briefly released in 1980, but almost immediately withdrawn for some re-shooting (under the uncredited direction of Disney stalwart Vincent McEveety) and extensive re-editing, this hybrid fairy-tale horror involving a benign alien as the observer of the title suffers much the same creative (but unproductive) schizophrenia in its conception as the later, more substantial Disney-backed terror fantasy *Something Wicked This Way Comes* (1982). Basically, the Disney studio has always been in the business of reassurance – so for all the mysterious disturbances befalling the family (dad McCallum, mom Baker, kids Johnson and Richards) that rents Davis' old English home, one is constantly aware that no real threat to that unit is being posed. Indeed, the narrative's Science

Christopher Reeve in search of a telephone booth in Superman II.

Fiction aspect actually allows for the restitution of another family unit – with the sketchily characterized alien accomplishing the reunion of Davis with her own daughter, missing for 30 years while trapped in another dimension. The presence of production personnel from the reaches of tele-fantasy (such as co-scripter Clemens, trailing an admirable reputation from the likes of *The Avengers*) seems to have no effect on the blandness of the fantasy, which never comes close to the realms touched by Disney's classic cartoon features.

d John Hough *p* Ron Miller *s* Brian Clemens, Harry Spalding, Rosemary Anne Sisson *c* Alan Hume *lp* Bette Davis, David McCallum, Carroll Baker, Lynn-Holly Johnson, Kyle Richards, Ian Bannen, Frances Cuka

Without Warning (FILMWAYS) 89 min

A resolutely down-market don't-go-in-the-woods terror movie that replaces the usual blade-wielding maniac or overgrown freak-of-nature with an aggressive alien flinging blood-sucking organisms at its catalogue of hapless victims. Nutter and Nelson are the teenage campers in peril, ignoring dire warnings from the grizzled backwoods' veterans (Ralph Meeker sharing cameo duties with Mitchell and Brand) and eventually setting off in confused pursuit of the other-worldly visitor with crazed gas-station owner Palance and equally unbalanced saloon-keeper Landau. Much effects' work later (concentrated on the colourfully oozing interaction of flying parasites and flesh), Clark concludes on the secondhand warning that 'there's more critters up there a 'waiting'.

d/p Greydon Clark *s* Lyn Freeman, Daniel Grodnik, Ben Nett, Steve Mathis *c* Dean Cundy *lp* Jack Palance, Martin Landau, Tarah Nutter, Christopher S. Nelson, Cameron Mitchell, Neville Brand

Zvyozdnyi Inspector *aka* The Star Inspector
(MOSFILM; USSR) scope 81 min

An oddly archaic space thriller reminiscent of silent Hollywood serials with less frenetic physical action. As in Kluge's masterful **Der Grosse Verhau** (1970), the setting is a distant future in which private companies conduct their shady operations involving space hijacks and interplanetary terrorism. But the intergalactic police force is Russian instead of a gigantic multiplanet company, and the villains bear Anglo-Saxon names. Inspector Lazarev (Ivashov) investigates a crime that resulted in the destruction of a space station. Suspicions rest on scientists associated with the Mainhaus Company. It is the job of the Russian team, including a token non-Russian presence, to re-establish order in the galaxy and to curb private enterprise.

A movie obviously predicated on Cold War fantasies, it relies on a strangely outdated iconography familiar from similar Hollywood films but also draws on the old European and American *Boy's Own* comic-strip imagery for its villains, dressing up the main antagonist in vaguely Egyptian clothing and using images of white robed women that would have been appropriate in a Mary Pickford movie of a Wilkie Collins novel. Whereas Kluge's film projects present trends into the future, thus pinpointing dangers in the current situation, this Russian movie locates pulp fiction stereotypes of a colonial past in the future, producing an adventure story that illustrates the thesis that most anticipatory stories are in fact merely dislocated fragments of images and narratives encountered in childhood or adolescence, a motif most strongly treated in **Solaris** (1971).

co-d/co-s Mark Kovalyov *co-d* Vladimir Polin *co-s* Vladislav Smirnov *c* Vladimir Fastenko *lp* Vladimir Ivashov, Yuri Gusev, Timofei Spivak, Valentina Titova, Emmanuil Vitorgan

Alien Contamination (CANNON; IT) 85 min

Featuring a cyclops from Mars that somehow inveigles an ex-astronaut (Rauch) into helping spread its eggs all over the Earth – crating them as cargoes of coffee – this is little more than a witless rewrite of the Dracula story, that owes several of its most 'imaginative' scenes to Murnau's classic *Nosferatu* (1922). The alien threat is discovered when a ship laden with the eggs docks in New York with every member of its crew dead. The unlikely team of Rauch's former Mars-mission buddy McCulloch, a Brooklyn cop (Mase) and a government security agent (Monroe) is assembled to track the contamination back to the South American equivalent of Transylvania. With badly dubbed dialogue and regular recourse to abattoir effects, this is about par for the Cinecitta course, though it is enlivened by an effective score from Dario Argento's regular accompanists, Goblin.

d/s Lewis Coates (Luigi Cozzi) *p* Claudio Mancini *c* Giuseppe Pinori *lp* Ian McCulloch, Louise Monroe, Siegfried Rauch, Martin Mase, Lisa Hahn

Alligator (ALLIGATOR ASSOCIATES/GROUP I) 91 min

This film infuses one of the hoariest of creature-feature plot structures with genuine wit and nicely insolent political wisdom. Sayles again proves that as much craftsmanlike care goes into the writing of his genre vehicles – such as **Piranha** (1978) or **Battle Beyond the Stars** (1980) – as into his prize-winning fiction or personally generated film projects like *The Return of the Secaucus Seven* (1979), *Lianna* and *Baby, It's You* (both 1983). Here reunited with director Teague after the Dillinger-inspired gangster flick *The Lady In Red* (1979), he builds on the old urban myth about baby alligators thriving in the sewers after being discarded as pets via the toilet, and gives us a memorable monster-'gator in Ramon – grown both massive and voracious by being fed, unwittingly, dead pets from a scientific lab's hormone experiments, and then graduating to human victims. (Indeed, Ramon entered this particular eco-system in 1968, and now in his teenage years emerges from the underground to spectacularly gnaw his way through and up the social heirarchy, having thrived on the latter's tainted detritus.)

Forster, a cop with a nightmare past, leads the hunt and Riker tags along not only as an academic specializing in reptilia or as romantic interest, but as the adult self of the child whose pet Ramon originally was. Jagger is the corrupt research head who uses the old-boy network to shift the blame and obstruct the chase, and who provides Ramon with one of his tastiest meals in a gloriously ironic scene of celebratory carnage. With fifties paranoia filtered through post-'68

The 30-foot hero of Alligator, a film which benefits greatly from John Sayles' witty script.

prisms, every sub-generic convention of the old mutant-movie is revived only to be subtly radicalized and re-packaged with a contagious relish.

d Lewis Teague *p* Brandon Chase *s* John Sayles
c Joseph Mangine *se* Richard O. Helmer *lp* Robert Forster, Robin Riker, Michael Gazzo, Dean Jagger, Henry Silva, Bart Braverman

Bells *aka* Murder by Phone *aka* The Calling
(CO-CO FILM PRODUCTIONS; CAN) 79 min
Its promising premise – a killer is despatching his apparently arbitrary victims via a device that transmits through the telephone system – notwithstanding, this Canadian production wastes its cast in a failed, belated attempt to milk the post-Watergate vogue for paranoid thrillers. Science teacher Chamberlain and his former mentor Houseman lead the trail to the higher echelons of Morse's Inter-World Telephone Company, while cops and Botsford tag breathlessly along. Essaying little more than a catalogue of hand-set designs, veteran director Anderson confirms the decline in his fortunes signalled by **Logan's Run** (1976), while scripters Shryack and Butler return to the one-gag formula with which they underpinned *The Car* (1977), as if they'd never been involved in the nicely judged playfulness of Clint Eastwood's *The Gauntlet* (1977).

d Michael Anderson *p* Robert Cooper *s* Dennis Shryack, Michael Butler, John Kent Harrison *c* Reginald Morris *lp* Richard Chamberlain, John Houseman, Sara Botsford, Robin Gammell, Barry Morse, Gary Reineke

Cherez Ternii k Zvezdam *aka* Per Aspera ad Astra
(GORKI; USSR) scope 2 parts 146 min
A long ecological Science Fiction film in two parts, *Niya-Iskusstvennyi Chelovek* and *Angely Kosmosa*, directed by Viktorov, who made the children's space opera **Moskva – Kassiopeia** (1974) and its sequel **Otroki vo Vselennoi** (1975). The story falls relatively easily into two sections. First, cosmonauts bring to Earth the sole survivor of an alien spacecraft, Niya (Metelkina), where she stays as the guest of the chief cosmonaut's family. The charmingly beautiful and somewhat ethereal Niya learns about life on Earth in a series of sequences told with tenderness and humour, until a message comes from her planet asking the Earth for assistance. The second part chronicles the adventures of the mission sent to help the planet Dessa conquer its virulent pollution problems. Plot complications involve the tyrannical ruler of Dessa and the possibility that the aid mission has fallen into a trap. Full of references to conditions and preoccupations in the USSR (including the echo of Soviet involvement in Afghanistan) the film is lighter and more humorous than would appear from the subtitled version. The stories unfold at a slow, rhythmical pace which acquires a fascination all of its own, avoiding both mawkishness (the hero and the heroine do not fall into a clinch at the end) and an excessive reliance on special effects to paper over the cracks of a creaky narrative. A refreshing, relaxing and entertaining movie which uses imagination and an interesting approach to the characters, as well as well-constructed adventure scenes, to captivate the viewers.

Metelkina was awarded a Silver Asteroid in Trieste 1982 for her performance.

d/co-s Richard Viktorov *co-s* Kir Bulychev *c* Alexander Rybin *lp* Elena Metelkina, Nadezhda Sementsova, Vadim Ledogorov, Alexander Lazarev, Alexander Mikhailov, Uldis Lieldidzh, Elena Fadeyeva, Vaclav Dvorzetski, Gleb Strinzhenov, Nikolai Timofeev

The Creature Wasn't Nice *aka* Starship
(CREATURE FEATURE PRODUCTIONS) 88 min
A misbegotten attempt to do for space horrors, especially *Alien* (1979), what *Airplane!* (1980) had done for the *Airport* series, this low-budget parody misses rather more often than it hits with its scattershot humour. The crew of madcaps (Williams, Kimmel, Graham) and tongue-in-cheek veterans (Nielsen, MacNee) is as likeable a bunch of outer-space adventurers as you could wish, but their experiences with an alien life-form that transmutes into a monster (Kurowski) just don't prompt any truly sustained humour. When a scene in which the creature is hooked up to a computer and begins performing a song and dance act entitled 'I Want to Eat Your Face' is regarded as a highlight, you know the movie's in trouble.

d/s Bruce Kimmel *p* Mark Haggard *c* Denny Lavil *lp* Cindy Williams, Bruce Kimmel, Leslie Nielsen, Gerrit Graham, Patrick MacNee, Ron Kurowski

Dead and Buried (AVCO EMBASSY) 95 min
Seemingly content to give one original twist to zombie legend and the 'living dead' sub-genre (by having its ambulatory corpses the beneficiaries of scientific reincarnation, as practised by coroner/undertaker and former pathologist Albertson), this slice of graphic terror from the screenwriters of **Alien** (1979) and the director of the inventive British horror **Death Line** (1972) settles early into a routine shocker, with sheriff Farentino counting the corpses and wondering what his wife (Anderson) has to do with turning the township of Potters Bluff into a genuinely deadly tourist trap. Winston's makeup effects carry the movie but amid the scare tactics is at least one solid piece of resonant characterization, with Albertson's mad-scientist figure not only cast physically against type, but also embodying a double-barrelled taste for both nostalgia and necrophilia, operating on the undead to the strains of thirties swing tunes.

d Gary A. Sherman *p/co-s* Ronald Shusett *co-s* Dan O'Bannon *c* Steve Poster *se* Knott Limited *lp* James Farentino, Melody Anderson, Jack Albertson, Dennis Redfield, Nancy Locke Hauser

Kurt Russell as Snake Plissken in John Carpenter's disappointing Escape from New York.

Above: *Androids Andy Kaufman and Bernadette Peters with their 'uncle' Catskill (left) and 'son' in* Heartbeeps, *Alan Arkush's inventive comedy.*

d/co-s John Carpenter   *p* Larry Franco, Debra Hill
co-s Nick Castle   *c* Dean Cundey   *se* New World/Venice,
Roy Arbogast, Pat Patterson, Eddie Surkin, Gary Zink
lp Kurt Russell, Lee Van Cleef, Ernest Borgnine, Donald
Pleasance, Isaac Hayes, Harry Dean Stanton, Season Hubley

Gosti iz Galaksije *aka* Visitors from the Galaxy

(ZAGREB FILM/JADRAN FILM; YUG)   90 min
A juvenile special effects' fable from former animator
Vukotic, whose animated short *Ersatz* was an Oscar-winner in
1958. The simple but eventful plot has a youthful author
conjuring his fictional alien characters to life, and this trio
playing havoc with the boy and his fellow townsfolk as they
exercise their special extra-terrestrial powers, before restoring
normality by turning back time. The effects' work, done in
Czechoslovakia, is integrated well into the action, which has
the air of a fairy-tale despite its Science Fiction aspects.

d/co-s Dusan Vukotic   *co-s* Milos Macourek   *c* Jiri Macak
lp Zarko Potocnjak, Ljubisa Samardzic, Lucie Zulova

Heartbeeps   (U)   79 min

Arkush's unique robotic romance is an under-rated gem of
corny charm: silly, sentimental and sluggish but wholly
likeable. Kaufman and Peters – bravely encased from head to
toe in vacu-formed plastic – are state-of-the-art domestic
robots, designed respectively for valet and poolside service
duties, who escape the service-bay shelf and the likelihood of
reprogramming to test their inklings of emotion and trek off
into the woods in search of a sunset. While a pursuit chase
proceeds in virtual slow motion, they build themselves a
spare-part junior robot and complete their alternative family
with an accompanying 'uncle' – an ageing android comedian
with a steady supply of Borscht Belt jokes (credited to the
repertoire of Henny Youngman). Much metallic mooning
later, after excursions into junkyard consumerism and recog-
nizably 'human' anxiety, they make the supreme touching
sacrifice for their kid's future. Hill's script packs in all the
yearning of an out-of-time *Wizard of Oz* (1939), John
Williams' score is almost tear-jerkingly manipulative in
helping anthropomorphize the tin man and his mate, and the
leading couple perform wonders with stylized gestures and
movement.

d Allan Arkush   *p* Michael Phillips   *s* John Hill   *c* Charles
Rosher Jnr   *se* Jaimie Shourt, Robert Baladack, Albert
Whitlock   *lp* Andy Kaufman, Bernadette Peters, Randy
Quaid, Kenneth McMillan, Melanie Mayron, Christopher
Guest

Heavy Metal   (COL)   90 min

Despite his indubitably herculean efforts at co-ordinating
numerous international animation crews for this opportunistic
thrash at welding adolescent sub-cultural enthusiasms for
comic-book art and headbanging rock, Potterton seems
destined to remain better remembered for his simpler
combination of Buster Keaton and a railway handcart in the
Canadian short *The Railroader* (1965). Between liberal sprink-
lings of Science Fiction, mysticism, dystopianism, gothic
horror, soft-core sex and sword and sorcery – drawn in a
bewilderingly violent clash of styles – lies a tangle of
connections not made; while over them is cast a fog of risibly
portentous juvenile gibberish. Through an octet of ill-
matched episodes, a tenuous narrative about the influence of
the evil jewel, the Loch-Nar, wanders in and out of focus,
while a Manhattan cabbie, a musclemen, a mass murderer, a
bomber crew, a Pentagon secretary, an amorous robot and
barbarian hordes flit across the animation cells (and any
notion of continuity) to little coherent purpose beyond that of
exciting momentary titillation or terror.

   Some of the imaginative draughtsmanship of individual
sequences is noteworthy (that of Angus McKie, especially),

Escape from New York

(AVCO EMBASSY/INTERNATIONAL FILM INVESTORS/GOLDCREST
FILMS INTERNATIONAL/CITY FILMS)   PV   99 min
Despite its marvellous night-time opening with Carpenter's
camera stalking the perimeter wall of Manhattan Island
(transformed as the opening titles tell us into a maximum
security prison whose 3 million inhabitants prowl the streets
in packs) before introducing us to Russell's Snake Plissken,
Escape from New York, a few sequences apart, is a disappointing movie. If the opening demonstrates Carpenter's ability to
make exposition literally thrilling, the film's subsequent
developments see him satisfied with the most routine of
solutions to the over-complicated plotlines he's set himself;
and this from the maker of **Dark Star** (1974) and *Assault on
Precinct 13* (1976).

   Russell (a one-time teenage star at the Disney studios) is
suitably sullen as the war hero turned felon offered a chance of
freedom if he can rescue Pleasance's President who has
crashed in Manhattan Island within 24 hours (and has an
explosive device implanted in his neck that will only be
de-activated on his return). But the other roles are mere
cyphers. Thus Borgnine's Cabbie is 'the old ham', Hubley,
'the beauty', Hayes, the gang leader who holds Pleasance
captive, in a piece of racial stereotyping if ever there was one,
'the beast' while Stanton is even called 'the Brain'. Once he's
got Russell inside Manhattan, Carpenter seems unsure of
what to do. Accordingly, the film veers first this way then that
before settling down to a series of set-pieces (the escape of the
'crazies', the fight Hayes stages between Russell and one of
his stooges) before Russell makes his escape with a bewildered
Pleasance.

but the heavy hands of screenwriters Goldberg and Blum – previously responsible for such Reitman-produced comedies as *Meatballs* (1979) and *Stripes* (1981) – effectively quash any sense of expectation raised by seeing the likes of Dan O'Bannon named among the source writers. It's symptomatic of the film's failure that Murakami's live-action début with **Battle Beyond the Stars** (1980) easily exhibited more genuine comic-strip energy than anything he cranked into motion here with his top-and-tail framing sequences.

d Gerald Potterton (*sequences d* Jimmy T. Murakami, Harold Whitaker, Pino Van Lamsweerde, Jack Stokes, Paul Sabella, Julian Szuchopa, Barrie Nelson, John Halas, John Bruno) *p* Ivan Reitman *s* Dan Goldberg, Len Blum *design* Thomas Warkentin, Angus McKie, Bernie Wrightson, Richard Corben, Juan Gimenez, Lee Mishkin

The Incredible Shrinking Woman
(LIJA PRODUCTIONS/U) 88 min
A listless film, this twist on the classic **The Incredible Shrinking Man** (1957) transforms the terror of that film into a would-be satire on the world of big business and the media. Thus, unlike either Richard Matheson's original novel or Jack Arnold's film, both of which proceed by cataloguing the growing horrors of the familiar, as Grant Williams shrinks and shrinks, writer Wagner and director Schumacher spend far too much time explaining why Tomlin starts shrinking (a new perfume is spilt on her) and then making public her private dilemma. The Arnold film was made from the point of view of Grant Williams, this from the point of view of a detached observer. In the course of this radical shift of emphasis any paranoia implicit in the central situation is lost. In its place Wagner attempts to inject humour (camp references to **The Creature from the Black Lagoon**, 1954, and the like), a 'feminist' statement (the perfume responsible for Tomlin's condition is called 'Sexpot') and a convoluted plot, but to little effect.

d Joel Schumacher *p* Hank Moonjean *s* Jane Wagner *c* Bruce Logan *se* Roy Arbogast, Guy Faria, David Kelsey *lp* Lily Tomlin, Charles Grodin, Ned Beatty, Henry Gibson, Elizabeth Wilson, Mark Blankfield

Io e Caterina
(ITALIAN INTERNATIONAL FILM/CARTHAGO FILM/RAI; IT, FR) 117 min
A formulaic Italian farce of the sort Sordi has been making for years, this warrants mention for the fact that it introduces a robot – the Caterina of the title – into the predictable permutations of chauvinist sex comedy. Programmed for maximum pliancy as a domestic helpmate that's less likely to demur than wife, mistress or maid, Caterina oversteps her functions by blowing an amorous fuse for Sordi, and becoming jealous over his new girlfriend Fenech. Infused with a token (wholly specious) cybernetic 'feminism', Caterina takes her revenge on her 'master' in a way that's not so much sinister as indicative of the double standard machismo/fear-of-the-female that underpins the whole genre.

d/co-s Alberto Sordi *p* Fulvio Lucisano, Tarak Ben Ammar *co-s* Rodolfo Sonego *c* Sergio D'Offizi *lp* Alberto Sordi, Edwige Fenech, Catherine Spaak, Valeria Valeri, Rossano Brazzi

Inferno dei Morti-Viventi *aka* Zombie Creeping Flesh
(BEATRICE FILM/FILMS DARA; IT, SP) 99 min
This cheerless and gratuitously gory film sinks its intriguing premise of the Third World biting back (literally) in a morass of incoherence and incompetence. The HOPE research centre in Papua, New Guinea ostensibly exists for the scientific benefit of underdeveloped nations, but in fact the synthetic food made there is intended to have the effect of cutting back the world's overpopulation by reviving cannibalistic urges in the Third World. When the toxic gases start to leak, its work-force are turned into flesh-eating zombies. The contagious artificial plague claims as its next victims both the military personnel (led by Garfield) intent on a cover-up and

Taarna the avenging warrior queen of Heavy Metal.

Left: *Lily Tomlin is* The Incredible Shrinking Woman.

the media persons, including Newton's spunky reporter, bent on an exposé, before threatening global apocalypse.

Mattei's *grand guignol* direction betrays his supposed concern for the Third World, revealing in its place the cynicism of the pure exploitation film.

d Vincent Dawn (Bruno Mattei) *p* Sergio Cortona
s Claudio Fragasso, J. M. Cunilles *c* John Cabrera
se Giuseppe Ferrranti *lp* Margit Evelyn Newton, Frank Garfield, Selan Karay, Robert O'Neil, Gaby Renom

Light Years Away
(LPA-PHENIX/SLOTINT-SSR; FR, SWITZ) 107 min
A surprisingly bland film, *Light Years Away*, though it features a character called Jonas (played by Ford) and is set in the year 2000, bears little relation to *Jonas Qui Aura 25 Ans en l'An 2000* (1976), Tanner's best film to date. Where the images and narrative of that film, scripted by John Berger (as have been the best of Tanner's films), were tightly organized, *Light Years Away*, Tanner's first literary adaptation, rambles far too much. The result is a film that fails to create a real sense of the mythic that it strives so desperately for.

Howard is the crotchety old man who transforms his deserted garage into a dream factory in which he attempts to become a latterday Icarus and Ford the youngster who makes a home for himself in the surrounding wreckage and eventually becomes Howard's puzzled acolyte. Tanner cleverly makes Howard's dream an eccentric rather than heroic matter, treating his first successful attempt at flight in a marvellously matter-of-fact way, but the beauty of the film's images are not sufficient recompense for its slim content.

d/s Alain Tanner *p* Pierre Heros *c* Jean-François Robin
lp Trevor Howard, Mick Ford, Odile Schmitt, Louis Samier, Joe Pilkington, John Murphy, Jerry O'Brien, Vincent Smith

Looker (LADD CO.) pv 94 min
A wildly overplotted Science Fiction thriller that self-consciously stirs motifs from Crichton's earlier **Westworld** (1973) and **Coma** (1978) into its maddeningly complex mix, *Looker* takes on such topics as subliminal TV advertising and three-dimensional computer simulation and pushes them one stage past the state-of-the-art into a mystery of murder and corporate corruption where, almost inevitably, they're strangled in the maze of narrative loose ends. Finney is the plastic surgeon under suspicion for the murder of several models who've taken his treatment, who decides to crack the case for himself, and finds himself drawn into the orbit of the researches carried out by Coburn's Reston Industries conglomerate. It transpires that the models have been replicated by computer, and utilized in a series of mind-bending, hypnotic tele-ads with which Coburn claims he can sell

anything. Light-pulse stun-gun in hand, Finney eventually closes the case with a slapstick shoot-out. Crichton's tone fluctuates wildly between satire and shock, while he deliberately emphasizes the bewildering tanglement of plot development by incorporating a great deal of cartoonish chasing and stuntwork, and muddling up humans and their computer-generated counterparts. A supporting cast of former *Playboy* Playmates provides a flimsy commercial safety net. The title is an acronym for *Light Ocular Oriented Kinetic Energetic Responsers*.

d/s Michael Crichton *p* Howard Jeffrey *c* Paul Lohmann
lp Albert Finney, James Coburn, Susan Dey, Leigh Taylor-Young, Dorian Harewood, Darryl Hickman

Mad Max 2 *aka* The Road Warrior
(KENNEDY MILLER ENTERTAINMENT; AUST) pv 96 min
The most influential genre movie of recent years – at least in terms of the number of cheap rip-offs that over-invest in replicating its spare narrative form while (in)conveniently ignoring the consummate skill with which Miller animates its cockeyed mythological resonances – *Mad Max 2* defines itself modestly enough as an exploitation feature by sheer dint of admitting to its sequel status. This is one sequel (to **Mad Max**, 1979) that outstrips its fine model in every sense, though. Embittered one-time cop Gibson, having survived his past ordeals, now finds himself at the centre of a post-holocaust western, being gradually persuaded to ride to the aid of a beleaguered circle of civilization under siege and attack by savage hordes. Since World War III, petrol has become the golden commodity in a skeletal society still slavishly attached to its automobile culture – a culture which has been subject to exotic fetishism, by the barbarian bikers at any rate. Gibson's the man to run the last tanker convoy past their blockade, if only he'll commit himself to the cause and avail himself of the unconventional assistance proffered by Spence's eccentric autogyro pilot and Minty's triumphantly un-moppet-like Feral Kid.

The inventive characterizations and vivid caricatures meet in superb cross-genre, comic-strip combat, with Miller cutting brilliantly throughout on grotesquely incisive action and near-parodic ultra-violence, his stunt team performing wonders with scenes of high-speed homicide, Brian May's score pacing the mayhem to a heightened pulse-rate, and the Australian desert providing the most convincing post-apocalyptic landscape imaginable. A neatly ironic coda draws nothing so mundane as a moral, only applause for a movie scaled perfectly to its means, and for one that most definitely, breathtakingly, *moves*.

d/co-s George Miller *p* Byron Kennedy *co-s* Terry Hayes, Brian Hannant *c* Dean Semler *se* Jeffrey Clifford, Roger Cowland, Melinda Brown *lp* Mel Gibson, Bruce Spence, Kjell Nilsson, Emil Minty, Virginia Hey, Vernon Wells

Malevil (NEF DIFFUSION/STELLA FILMS/A2/FILMS GIBE/
TELECIP; FR, WG) pv 119 min
Robert Merle's post-nuclear parable comes across as a slightly broken-backed affair in de Chalonge's film adaptation, with a genuinely disturbing first half having its cumulative effect dissipated by recourse to conventional melodramatics once the group of survivors that emerges from the wine-cellars of an old chateau comes into conflict with the fascist 'tunnel people'. The contrast between the idyllic-looking French countryside and the gaunt, charred wasteland that replaces it after the horrific blast is well captured in Penzer's cinematography, but the social struggles that are played out against this frightening backdrop are simplistic in the extreme.

d/co-s Christian de Chalonge *p* Claude Nedjar *co-s* Pierre Dumayet *c* Jean Penzer *lp* Michel Serrault, Jacques Dutronc, Robert Dhery, Hanns Zischler, Jean-Louis Trintignant, Jacques Villeret

Below: Mad Max 2, one of the few sequels to be better than the original and one of the most influential exploitation films of the eighties.

Memoirs of a Survivor

(MEMORIAL FILMS/NATIONAL FILM FINANCE CORP./EMI; GB)
115 min

For all its good intentions, this adaptation of Doris Lessing's novel (not one of her major sequence of Science Fiction novels, *Canopus in Argos: Archives*) is a decided failure. In its central contrast between an idyllic past and a frightening present, it mirrors the substance of former editor Gladwell's earlier film, *Requiem for a Village* (1975). But where, in that film, Gladwell animated his past in a series of extraordinary images (the dead rising from their graves in their Sunday best, for example), *Memoirs of a Survivor* gives him no such leeway. Indeed, Lessing's essentially personal novel is concerned less with a contrast between past (represented by the cold emotional world of a Victorian family) and the present (represented by the breakdown of the social order) than in escaping both. In simplifying this into an escape into the past (Christie's 'D' walks through the wall of her shabby flat into the past at the climax), Gladwell deforms the novel by centering on the decaying urban world of the near future which Christie observes. The novel is further undercut by the resolutely realist stance of Gladwell and cinematographer Lassally which denies us any access to the literary/metaphysical speculation going on in Christie's head.

d/co-s David Gladwell   *p* Michael Medwin, Penny Clark   *co-s* Kerry Crabbe   *c* Walter Lassally   *se* Effects Associates   *lp* Julie Christie, Christopher Guard, Leonie Mellinger, Debbie Hutchings, Nigel Hawthorne, Pat Keen

Mindwarp: An Infinity of Terror *aka* Planet of Horrors *aka* Galaxy of Terror   (NEW WORLD)   80 min

An effects-heavy space horror exploitation piece that conflates borrowings from **Alien** (1979), **Forbidden Planet** (1956) and even George Orwell's novel *1984*, by pitting its neurotic crew of astronauts against a whole array of monsters from the id as they tramp the inhospitable terrain of a distant planet in search of a missing ship. Production values considerably outstrip the screenplay in quality as the film degenerates rapidly into a catalogue of gruesome killings that culminates in a grotesque scene of rape (by giant worm). All the mock-Freudian psycho-babble amounts to is an excuse for the gore.

d/co-s B. D. Clark   *co-p/co-s* Marc Siegler   *co-p* Roger Corman   *c* Jacques Haitkin   *lp* Edward Albert, Erin Moran, Ray Walston, Zalman King, Robert Englund, Taaffe O'Connell

Modern Problems   (FOX)   91 min

Though it was a surprising hit (grossing over $15 million on its initial release) – a testament to Chase's drawing power at the box office – this is a disappointing film. It's a heartless and largely laughless comedy about an all-round loser (Chase)

The miners at work in Con-Am 27 in Outland, *a re-working of* High Noon *(1952) as a space opera.*

revenging himself mercilessly on 'friends' after he develops telekinetic powers as a consequence of being smothered in spilt nuclear waste. The 'problems' are the film's own, and they have less to do with bad taste than with sheer bad film-making.

d/co-s Ken Shapiro   *p* Alan Greisman, Michael Shamberg   *co-s* Tom Sherohman, Arthur Sellers   *c* Edmond Koons   *lp* Chevy Chase, Patti D'Arbanville, Mary Kay Place, Dabney Coleman, Nell Carter, Brian Doyle-Murray

Outland   (LADD CO.; GB)   pv   109 min

A straightforward transposition of *High Noon* (1952) into outer space, complete with digital clocks counting down the arrival time of the hired killers, *Outland* suffers from writer/director Hyams' one-dimensional approach to both plot and character. In contrast to **Capricorn One** (1977) which saw Hyams failing to meld together his disparate plotlines, in *Outland* he excludes anything not immediately germane to either plot or character (with the sole exception of décor which is overlongingly examined as if to prove that the film really is set on Io, the third moon of Jupiter). The result is a film whose characters verge on being the stereotyped clichés that populate the B western.

Connery is the honest marshall determined 'to do what a man's gotta do', Markham, his wife who wants to quit, Sternhagen the doctor who saves the day and Boyle the manager feeding his miners a dangerous drug which induces suicidal tendencies in order to raise the production rate.

d/s Peter Hyams   *p* Richard A. Roth   *c* Stephen Goldblatt   *se* Roy Field, John Stears, Bob Harman   *lp* Sean Connery, Peter Boyle, Frances Sternhagen, Kika Markham, Clarke Peters, Steven Berkoff

Piranha II: Flying Killers

(BROUWERSGRACHT INVESTMENTS/CHAKO FILM CO.; NETH)
95 min

An unofficial sequel to **Piranha** (1978), John Sayles and Joe Dante's witty small-fry riposte to *Jaws* (1975), this Dutch-financed, Italian-crewed film once more accounts for its killer-fish threat by invoking military scientific research. It looks like it could have done with a little more science itself in the special effects department, with the winged marine life giving the awesome impression of haddock with dentures as they decimate sundry revellers on a jolly Caribbean isle. Director Cameron went on to make **The Terminator** (1984), **Aliens** (1986) and **The Abyss** (1989).

Left: The well-intentioned but disappointing Memoirs of a Survivor.

d James Cameron *p* Chako Van Leuwen, Jeff Schechtman
s H. A. Milton *c* Roberto D'Ettorre Piazzoli *se* Giannetto
De Rossi *lp* Tricia O'Neil, Steve Marachuk, Lance
Henricksen, Ricky G. Paull

The Protectors, Book 1 *aka* Angel of H.E.A.T.
(STUDIOS PAN IMAGO) 93 min
A ragged soft-core spy spoof, designed as a showcase for porn
star Chambers as a low-budget Modesty Blaise, this even
failed to create interest among America's down-market
distributors. Megalomaniac villain Jesse employs libidinous
androids and high-tech communications in his plot for global
takeover, while the good guys (led by parallel teams headed
by Chambers and genuine B-queen Woronov) crack arch
jokes and offer unconvincing martial arts' skills in opposition.
More time, inevitably, is extended on the skin-flick tease than
on anything that might make the plot remotely interesting.

d/p Myrl A. Schreibman *s* Helen Sanford *c* Jacques
Haitkin *lp* Marilyn Chambers, Stephen Johnson, Mary
Woronov, Milt Kogan, Dan Jesse, Remy O'Neill

Sengoku Jietai *aka* Time Slip (TOEI; JAP) 139 min
Not quite the surreal joy that its imaginatively handled
time-warp plot suggests it could have been – there's an excess
of extraneous cross-cutting and a dire western soft-rock score
– this is nonetheless a neat action adventure along comic-strip
lines. The basic Science Fiction wrinkle has a training squad
of contemporary Japanese soldiers suddenly transported back
in time to the 16th century and forced to engage with massed
ranks of samurai warriors. Commander Chiba decides the
only way back to the present for him and his men is to
deliberately alter the course of history, so that nature will
reject the threat to its status quo, and to achieve this he tries
making a military play for control of the country. The ensuing
battles are well choreographed (by Chiba), bloodily swashbuckling affairs of technological weaponry against sheer
weight of blade-wielding numbers; and they're played out to a
definite (and perhaps surprising) conclusion, thus sparing the
audience the anti-climax, common to the likes of **The Final
Countdown** (1980), of a second time-slip solving the
dilemma.

Below: *The violent
world of Terry Gilliam:*
Time Bandits.

d Kosei Saito *p* Haruki Kadokawa *s* Toshio Kaneda, Ryo
Hanmura *c* Iwao Isayama *lp* Sonny Chiba, Isao Natsuki,
Miyuki Ono, Jana Okada

Supersnooper *aka* Super Fuzz
(TRANS-CINEMA TV; IT) 106 (94) min
Presumably budgeted with no allowance to purchase the
rights to a genuine comic-book superhero, this Italian-
backed, American-shot comedy throws the ever-watchable
Hill into the slipstream of **Superman – The Movie** (1978) as a
cop accidentally blessed with super-powers after being
exposed to mega-radiation tests. Carrying on the tradition of
the Trinity westerns by being paired with a rotund co-lead
(Borgnine here replacing Bud Spencer), Hill blasts into action
against mobster Lawrence and survives several attempts to
execute him in a frame-up. Most heroically of all, he wrestles
with some abysmally slapdash special effects and a host of
less-than-inspired gag sequences.

d/co-s Sergio Corbucci *p* Maximilian Wolkoff
co-s Sabatino Giuffini *c* Silvano Ippoliti *lp* Terence Hill
(Mario Girotti), Ernest Borgnine, Joanne Dru, Marc
Lawrence, Julie Gordon

Threshold (PARAGON; CAN) 106 min
A serious, mutedly dramatic problem picture about the
dilemmas surrounding experimentation on the boundaries of
new medical technology, this classy Canadian production
refuses to tread into the horror-hospital territory of **Coma**
(1978) or mere medical melodrama, and, perhaps accordingly,
found that its solid focus on character studies failed to connect
commercially. Sutherland is the heart surgeon defying his
hospital board to give patient Winningham one last shot at life
with a transplanted mechanical heart invented by Goldblum,
and it is these three who become the objects of the film's
scrutiny as they each face the implications of the operation
and its success. Sutherland is a rock of heel-digging dedication under fire for his disobedience, Willingham tortuously
comes to terms with her feelings of not being completely
human, and Goldblum welcomes his sudden celebrity status
with open arms, providing some much-needed light relief for
the film. Director Pearce and writer Salter both bring
impressive documentary-drama backgrounds to bear on the
film's conception and execution – the former made the
pioneer western *Heartland* (1979), and the latter includes
among his many credits the script for Michael Ritchie's
Downhill Racer (1969) – while cameraman Brault is also better
known as a director of both fact-based dramas and straight
documentaries. So, appropriately enough, this film proved
prescient in the short term rather than embodying a
long-range speculation – Dr Robert Jarvis, who designed the
heart used in the film, was also responsible for the first
artificial transplant ever performed on a human.

d Richard Pearce *p* John Slan, Michael Burns *s* James
Salter *c* Michel Brault *lp* Donald Sutherland, Mare
Winningham, Jeff Goldblum, John Marley, Sharon
Ackerman, Michael Lerner

Time Bandits (HANDMADE FILMS; GB) 113 min
Utilizing the trusty Science Fiction element of ruptures in the
space/time continuum, this partly Pythonesque romp features
a sextet of renegade dwarfs adventuring through the cosmic
fabric in the wide-eyed company of English schoolboy Craig
Warnock, scraping their way through absurd encounters with
history and legend, and generally upsetting the equanimity of
Richardson's gentlemanly Supreme Being. It has some of the
genuine comic cruelty of classic fable in the half-sophisti-
cated, half-slapstick episodics, and there's an acute tension
between the conventions of children's film-making and those
of the family horror film. A true curio of small people, big
themes and red herrings – a close live-action approximation of
Gilliam's more customary Freudian cartoonery.

d/p/co-s Terry Gilliam   *co-s* Michael Palin   *c* Peter Biziou
se John Bunker   *lp* David Rappaport, Kenny Baker, Ian
Holm, John Cleese, Ralph Richardson, David Warner

Wojna Swiatow – Nastepne Stulecie *aka* The War of the Worlds – Next Century

(ZESPOLY FILMOWE/PERPEKTY UNIT; POL)   98 min

Like Szulkin's first feature film (**Golem**, 1979), this is in part
a satire on the media. But where Szulkin's interest in the
earlier film was in the ability of the media to mould opinion,
his interest here is explicitly with censorship and the invasion
of Poland. Accordingly, though the film is dedicated to H.G.
Wells and Orson Welles (whose 1938 radio adaptation of
Wells' *War of the Worlds* caused a mass panic on the east coast
of America) and set in the year 1999, its concerns are far more
immediate and all the more powerful for being so.

Szulkin's script focuses on a local TV reporter (Wilhelmi)
who witnesses the arrival of the Martians on Earth and is used
by the authorities to legitimize the invasion. Similar in part to
The Monitors (1968), but far more controlled, the film
follows Wilhelmi's desperate attempts to tell an unconcerned
and uncomprehending public the truth. The bitter conclusion
has Wilhelmi's show trial being televised on the 'Now Better
News Show' that replaced his own news programme.

The film was (pointedly) premiered at the 1981 Gdansk
Film festival.

d/s Piotr Szulkin   *c* Zygmunt Samosiak   *lp* Roman
Wilhelmi, Krystyna Janda, Mariusz Dmochowski, Jerzy
Stuhr, Bozena Dykiel, Morek Walcewski

Airplane II: The Sequel   (PAR)   84 min

Abandoned by the three co-pilots who made the original
lunatic parody of airborne disaster flicks such a rare delight,
this sequel strays into Science Fiction territory by being set
aboard a Moon-bound space shuttle but essentially it's little
more than an action replay of its predecessor, with the laughs
concomitantly muted in reaction to hearing and seeing the
same jokes and sight gags so reverently reproduced. As Hays
wrestles with recalcitrant technology to shift his ship from
collision course with the sun and attempt an (of course)
impossible lunar landing, and Hagerty similarly exercises
herself with the usual collection of hysterical passengers, brief
snatches of the music from **Battlestar Galactica** (1978) add to
the cosy sense of all-round knowing familiarity.

d/s Ken Finkleman   *p* Howard W. Koch   *c* Joe Biroc
se Phil Kellison, Robert N. Dawson   *lp* Robert Hays, Julie
Hagerty, Lloyd Bridges, William Shatner, Rip Torn, Peter
Graves

Android   (NEW WORLD/ANDROID PRODUCTIONS)   80 min

One of the wittiest, most pleasurable movies of its year
regardless of genre, *Android* infuses exploitation-movie material with grace and, almost equally paradoxically, presents in
Opper's remarkable performance as the eponymous Max 404
one of the most delightfully memorable, roundedly human
characters in recent Science Fiction film.

Max is the creation of, and assistant to, an apparently
typical mad scientist (Kinski), whose orbiting research station
becomes a temporary refuge for a trio of escaped criminals,
one of whom (Howard) Max falls in love with. At least, that
is, he relates to her in a style approximating that of James
Stewart – whose courtship scenes in the old Frank Capra
movie *It's a Wonderful Life* (1946) Max has repeatedly studied
during his copious video research into life on Earth. Much
mayhem and many revelations later (and the film *is* conventionally action-packed, even if it truly takes off on its nuances
and subtler ironies), Max is grieving over his murdered lover
until finding a new partner in Cassandra (Kirchner), the
female android Kinski had groomed to replace him and who
now points out to him that Earth is but a star-flight away.

The humanization of Max 404 is a slyly funny and acutely
resonant process, and the tyro film-makers (graduates of both
academic film studies *and* the Roger Corman school of
shoestring production) skilfully fit his superlative star turn
into a telling network of relationships that speak volumes
about knowledge and power (and even class). Though the
genre hardware isn't shoddy, pure talent is the principal
special effect on view.

Airplane II: the
Sequel, *little more than
a replay of* Airplane!

d Aaron Lipstadt   *p* Mary Ann Fisher   *s* James Reigle, Don
Opper   *c* Tim Suhrstedt   *se* New World Effects, Steven B.
Caldwell   *lp* Don Opper, Klaus Kinski, Brie Howard,
Norbert Weisser, Crofton Hardester, Kendra Kirchner

Battletruck *aka* Warlords of the 21st Century

(NEW WORLD)   91 min

A fast-paced actioneer along the lines of **Mad Max 2** (1981),
with an ecological undercurrent and more subtlety than might
be expected in its characterizations, this under-rated entry in
the future-wars cycle represents an intriguing mesh of
production elements. An American production, shot in New
Zealand, it employs some fine talent from Britain, with
Cockliss following up his Children's Film Foundation feature
The Glitterball (1977) and second-unit work on **The Empire
Strikes Back** (1980), and cameraman Menges stepping out of
the comparative shadows of radical/liberal British tele-drama.
With neither exhibiting any culture-shock inhibition, the
schematic plot of fuel-foraging baddies battling peaceable new
pioneers after the 'oil wars' rips along nicely, with lone biker
Beck and runaway villain's daughter McEnroe rallying to the
cause of alternative energies against the gang led by the
latter's dad (Wainwright) and his gas-guzzling supertruck.
The messages never get in the way of the mayhem, but the
reverse is also true – and even the ironies of so much clear
momentum are aired with a sharp wit.

d/co-s Harley Cockliss   *p* Lloyd Phillips, Rob Whitehouse
co-s Irving Austin, John Beech   *c* Chris Menges
lp Michael Beck, Annie McEnroe, James Wainwright, John
Ratzenberger, Bruno Lawrence

Big Meat Eater

(BCD ENTERTAINMENT CORP.; CAN)   82 min

A throwback to fifties invasion films, but with the post-
Watergate twist that the aliens' success is dependent on
Taylor's zombified mayor's adeptness at bribery and corruption, *Big Meat Eater* is an engaging oddity. Surprisingly
unviolent, Windsor's film is at its best at its most absurd, as in
the mountainous Miller's rendition of 'Baghdad Boogie'

(complete with three belly dancers who appear from nowhere and disappear immediately after the conclusion of the number) in front of the furnace in which he intends to dispose of Taylor's body. Equally charming is the unlikely plot: the waste from butcher's Dawson's septic tank forms radioactive baloneum which the hovering aliens want so they raise Taylor from the dead to build them, through his connivery, a plant to extract the baloneum only to be beaten by Gillies (the son of the crooked building contractor Taylor employs), who uses the baloneum to convert his car into a rocketship from which he guns down the aliens in their cupcake of a flying saucer. As this synopsis suggests, the film's narrative flourishes are extravagantly orchestrated with little regard for cohesion. In place of this, Windsor offers his characters enough space to have fun in.

The result, if perhaps too unstructured to be successful, is thoroughly enjoyable, a tribute in equal parts to Windsor's benign anarchic direction and the enthusiastic cast, especially Dawson's cheery butcher whose 'Pleased to meet you . . . meat to please you' refrain sums up the sense of humour of the whole venture.

d/co-s Chris Windsor   *p/co-s* Laurence Keane   *co-s* Phil Savath   *c* Doug McKay   *se* Michael Dorsey, Iain Best, Jim Bridge   *lp* George Dawson, Big Miller, Andrew Gillies, Stephen Dimopoulous, Georgina Hegedos, Ida Carnevali, Sharon Wahl, Howard Taylor

Blade Runner   (LADD CO.)   pv   117 min

Less concerned with fidelity to his credited inspiration, Philip K. Dick's novel *Do Androids Dream of Electric Sheep?*, than with creating a futuristic *film noir* (replete with replicant *femmes fatales* and laconic violence on the rain-slicked mean streets of Chinatown, 2019-style), Scott blows a sizeable budget on perversely trying to match the scales of B-pic plotting and state-of-the-art production design. Overwhelmed by the magnificent sets and attention-grabbing visuals, the slim narrative of troubleshooter Rick Deckard (Ford) hunting down a group of semi-humanized robot replicants often threatens to disappear completely, especially when enigmatic fragments of Dick's original conception are re-introduced without explanation; and the recourse to voice-over musings from the hero smacks of a pre-release loss of confidence as much as of a generic homage. Though Ford makes an adequate stab at reviving the trench-coated cop role, the *noir* fatalism that does manage to cut through the smoky neon haze is largely supplied by his robot antagonists, programmed for only a four-year life span precisely lest they engage in introspection and revolt. The sleekly enigmatic Young, the lithely doll-like Hannah (and even the sinuous charmer Cassidy) represent nice, deadly puzzles for our hero, while Hauer virtually steals the film with his curiously moving presence as a renegade Aryan replicant who's fighting blindly for more time to appeal against his DOA destiny.

d Ridley Scott   *p* Michael Deeley   *s* Hampton Fancher, David Peoples   *c* Jordan Cronenweth   *se* Douglas Trumbull, Richard Yuricich, David Dryer   *lp* Harrison Ford, Rutger Hauer, Sean Young, Edward James Olmos, Daryl Hannah, M. Emmet Walsh, Joanna Cassidy

Chronopolis

(PRODUCTIONS DU CIRQUE/INA/AAA; FR)   70 min

The result of five years' intricate labour by Polish-born animator Kamler, this brilliant triumph of stop-motion technique shames many live-action pictures with both the

Joanna Cassidy in flight through Chinatown circa 2019 in Ridley Scott's ambitious Blade Runner, *a film that sadly spends far too much time on its sets and not enough on its characters.*

evocative power of its design and the relative sophistication of its Science Fiction narrative, genuinely creating its very own universe of possibilities and playful speculation. The title refers to a phantasmagoric city lost in space, inhabited by *ennui*-laden immortals who distract themselves from the unchanging routines of eternity by synthesizing time itself into a visible, tangible state, and using it in their abstract cosmic sports. Michel Lonsdale's brief voice-over introduction sets the broad parameters of the action, but the subsequent choreography of metamorphozing clay and fabric, operating entirely within its own future-tense rules, requires no grounding in human explication. Ironically enough, Kamler's most essential piece of movie technology was his 1920-vintage camera.

d/p/s/c/animation/design Piotr Kamler *graphics* Diane Chretien, Maria Tatarczuk, Babette Vimenet

Crosstalk (WALL TO WALL PTY.; AUST) 82 min

This pedestrian thriller features a domestic computer as not only the plot's McGuffin – its valuable patent is fought over by its temporarily housebound inventor (Day) and his villainous one-time business partners – but also as the hero(ine?). A bland cast mouthing dull dialogue come across as poor foils to the advanced technology, an automation/surveillance system which exercises Day's time and energies to the point where his wife (Downie) becomes jealous of it, but which eventually proves equal to the task of deciding for itself who should profit from its considerable capacities. 'Witnessing' a murder, the computer takes its time reacting (playing a star-smart game of camera-hogging as it cogitates cybernetically), but makes its decisive intervention at the crucial moment for the besieged family, to have both its former master and his doubting spouse expressing undying gratitude to the marvels of 'moral' machinery. The script isn't particularly logical, but some apt scoring (by Chris Neal) and interesting camerawork make Egerton's début feature as interesting as it is intriguing.

d/co-s Mark Egerton *p* Errol Sullivan *co-s* Linda Lane, Denis Whitburn *c* Vincent Monton *lp* Gary Day, Penny Downie, Brian McDermott, Peter Collingwood, Kim Deacon

E.T. The Extra-Terrestrial (U) 115 min

Neatly described by *Variety* as 'the best Disney film Disney never made' – and indeed from its opening nocturnal chase through the woods the film is shot through with allusions to the world of Disney – *E.T.* is an even more triumphant piece of film-making than Spielberg's **Close Encounters of the Third Kind** (1977). For all its many splendours, however, it is the lesser of the two films. Whereas in *Close Encounters* Richard Dreyfuss is the ordinary man who escapes his mundane life by dint of his commitment to his dreams and is liberated by dreaming, Thomas' Elliott (E . . . T) is a child who loses himself in his dreams. Dreyfuss is a man in an adult world who has kept his childlike sense of wonder alive at great cost (to those around him, notably his family, indeed he could be Thomas' father at one remove, as well as himself) and is rewarded for his faith by a miracle as great as the parting of the Red Sea. Thomas is merely a lonely child whose world is dominated, not by commitment to dreaming but by the lack of a father. As such the character may accurately reflect Spielberg's own childhood – he has called *E.T.* his most personal and autobiographical film – but in comparison to Dreyfuss, Thomas is not called upon to defend his dreams, merely to protect and assist the extra-terrestrial that takes up residence in his toy cupboard and becomes his new plaything.

The evocation of childhood is masterful (the film is virtually completely shot from hip height, a literalization of a child's perspective) as is the way Spielberg effortlessly moves from terror through comedy and death to climax on the 'magic' BMX bike ride. But, whereas in *Close Encounters*

E.T. The Extra-Terrestrial *and its resonant, simple imagery: fatherless children, a dying plant, the cosmos and Earth.*

Spielberg was careful to stress the different responses (and needs) of the various characters (scientist, mother, dreamer, etc) involved with the meeting with the aliens, *E.T.* is far more one-dimensional, far more emotional, as in the over-stressing of the empathy between E.T. and Thomas, for example (as children deserted by fathers?). Similarly, the film's religious overtones (the death, resurrection and ascension of E.T.) which led it to be joyously quoted (as if the Bible?) by born-again Americans, like its strangely unmotivated narrative, suggest that Spielberg was working very close to his unconscious. In a sense, the film is similar to John Ford's *The Sun Shines Bright* (1953), a movie whose narrative collapses under the strain of Ford's attempts to articulate his idealized society. Of course, *E.T.* does not collapse, but then its aspirations are far more modest. Like Judy Garland's Dorothy in *The Wizard of Oz* (1939), Thomas learns that, even without a father, there's no place like home, but whereas she has to be courageous, ingenious and caring, has to go on a quest to find home (like Dreyfuss in *Close Encounters*), Thomas is only really called upon to be caring. Similarly, for all its celebration of wonder and innocence, in *E.T.* too much is explained – Elliott needs a father, gets E.T. – and too much is too close to the surface for the sense of mystery of the power of the imagination and man's dreams (Dreyfuss' vision in mashed potato) to remain.

The film's major achievements are in the simplicity and directness of its vision and Spielberg's ability to both articulate that vision and transfer to the audience/screen relationship the E.T./Elliott empathy (the film is very affecting). Its major weakness, however, is the comfortableness of that vision, which Spielberg has interrogated himself in *Poltergeist* (1982) which he wrote and produced but strangely did not direct.

d/co-p Steven Spielberg *co-p* Kathleen Kennedy *s* Melissa Mathison *c* Allen Daviou *se* Industrial Light and Magic, Dennis Muren *lp* Henry Thomas, Dee Wallace, Peter Coyote, Robert MacNaughton, Drew Barrymore, K.C. Martel, Sean Frye, Tom Howell, Erika Eleniak

Firefox (WB) 136 min

This gloriously tongue-in-cheek thriller of Cold War simplicities and absurdist complexities about acting and identity, features Eastwood trying on numerous images for size and the reproduction of the **Star Wars** (1977) dogfight sequence. Eastwood's special effects' crew engineer the film's climax brilliantly as he and the plane he's stolen – a supersonic Russian MiG fighter plane whose weaponry is activated by its pilot's thought processes – ward off all attackers. The script is routine and Eastwood's direction hardly inspiring but the sheer pace of the film and Eastwood's gaunt image overcome almost everything in the manner of an unabashed star-vehicle.

d/p Clint Eastwood   *s* Alex Lasker, Wendell Wellman
c Bruce Surtees   *se* John Dykstra, Chuck Gaspar, Karl Baumgartaer   *lp* Clint Eastwood, Freddie Jones, Warren Clarke, Nigel Hawthorne, Kai Wulff, Kenneth Colley

Forbidden World *aka* Mutant   (NEW WORLD)   86 min

Though critics expended much energy on pointing out the generic antecedents of, and visible influences on, Ridley Scott's **Alien** (1979), they could have had more fun predicting the mass of celluloid that would subsequently exploit that monster-movie mega-hit. If a couple of Italian cheapies were inevitable, Corman's New World was always a likely candidate to be early on the scene, and sure enough Holzman's movie works as a virtual low-budget replay of Scott's for much of its length, with its growing mutant dining on space research scientists and performing some pretty disgusting tricks with its alien organs. The nausea factor is heightened by Holzman's skill in creating and sustaining tension and by some convincing special effects' and makeup work, but it reaches its highpoint with a script climax of blacker-than-black absurdity. One of the terrorized scientists is about to expire from cancer anyway, so he makes the supreme sacrifice his own way: he orders investigating troubleshooter Vint to cut out his tumour-ridden liver and feed it to the creature, which promptly overdoses spectacularly on the potent carcinogen. No more need really be said: this is the sort of *tour de force* that becomes an instant legend purely on the strength of being 'the one where. . .'.

d Allan Holzman   *p* Roger Corman   *s* Tim Curnen
c Tim Suhrstedt   *lp* Jesse Vint, June Chadwick, Dawn Dunlap, Linden Chiles, Fox Harris, Raymond Oliver

Jekyll and Hyde . . . Together Again   (PAR)   87 min

The directorial début of veteran television comedy writer Belson (who scripted the hilarious telefilm of a comedy western, *Evil Roy Slade*, 1971, amongst others), this is undoubtedly one of the jauntiest re-workings of Robert Louis Stevenson's classic story. Updated to the present, Belson's movie features Blankfield as the intense surgeon who, when

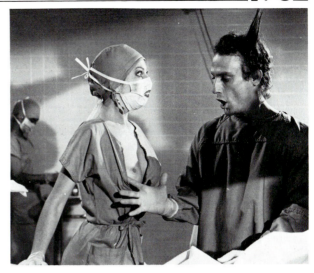

transformed into his alter ego Hyde, rejects his square girlfriend Armstrong in favour of the punk charms of Errickson. The strong supporting cast includes McGuire as Armstrong's miserly father and Thomerson as the narcissistic plastic surgeon who is his own best patient.

Belson's scattergun approach to his material produces a few duds but the sheer jollity of the production is appealing.

d/co-s Jerry Belson   *p* Lawrence Gordon   *co-s* Monica Johnson, Harvey Miller, Michael Leeson   *c* Philip Lathrop
lp Mark Blankfield, Bess Armstrong, Krista Errickson, Tim Thomerson, Michael McGuire

Kamikaze *aka* Kamikaze '89

(REGINA ZEIGLER/TRIO FILM/OASE FILM; WG)   106 min
The final acting appearance from Fassbinder – very much at home among numerous members of his own repertory company and former behind-the-camera colleagues – inevitably adds intrigue to Gremm's deliberately enigmatic hybrid, a futuristic (1989) thriller developed from the novel *Death on the 31st Floor* by much-lauded Swedish detective specialist Per Wahloo. In a half-recognizable urban world of bizarre high-tech and post-punk, Fassbinder is the surly police lieutenant, under murderous fire from all angles as he approaches the riddle of a bomb-threatened high-rise block with a hidden extra floor. Rather too obtuse and playfully sleazy for its own good, the film works as an exercise in scrambled styles and cross-genre characterization, but it hardly comes close to matching the *frissons* of intellectual excitement occasioned by Fassbinder's own directorial sortie into Science Fiction, the two-part tele-feature *Welt am Draht* (1973). That said, the Edgar Froese/Tangerine Dream score is very apt in its electronic iciness.

d/co-s Wolf Gremm   *p* Regina Ziegler   *co-s* Robert Katz
c Xaver Schwarzenberger   *lp* Rainer Werner Fassbinder, Gunther Kaufmann, Boy Gobert, Arnold Marquis, Brigitte Mira, Frank Ripploh

Liquid Sky   (Z FILMS INC)   118 min

An awesomely perverse low-budget attempt by classically trained Soviet émigré film-maker Tsukerman to chart the outer limits of New York's New Wave never-never land, this chic soft-core Science Fiction black comedy is a genuine aliens'-eye-view of the latest mutation of the evergreen cultural combination sex'n'drugs'n'rock'n'roll. Tracked from a voyeuristic distance by a single-minded German UFO-logist, a miniature flying saucer descends on the patio roof of an apartment shared by a lesbian performance artist (Sheppard) and her bisexual fashion-model lover (Carlisle). The unseen intergalactic visitors, it transpires, take sustenance from heroin, in which Sheppard occasionally deals, but will also make do with feeding on a similar chemical compound formed in the human brain at the very moment of orgasm. As Carlisle is besieged with disturbing regularity by would-be seducers or rapists of both sexes – who thus tend to come and go (dematerializing in a blaze of solarized light-show imagery) simultaneously – she soon becomes aware of her avenging sexual power, and even contrives to make deadly love to her own alter ego, in the guise of the sullenly obnoxious male model Jimmy (also played by Carlisle), before surrendering to the saucer and hovering heavenwards.

Tsukerman and his cohorts cut through the narcissist sub-culture with a fairly sharp satirical edge, and develop several strands of suitably off-the-wall wit, though in carefully laying their own artfully posed provocations they come very close to creating the classic exploitation condition of having their cake and eating it. That said, however, the saucer's dinky, the sex is kinky, and you could never imagine Tarkovsky having this much fun in the forbidden zone.

d/p/co-s Slava Tsukerman   *co-s* Nina Kerova, Anne Carlisle
c/se Yuri Neyman   *lp* Anne Carlisle, Paula Sheppard, Susan Doukas, Otto von Wernherr

Les Maîtres du Temps

(TELECIP/TF1/SSR/SWF/WDR; FR, SWITZ, WG)   78 min
Far superior to **Wizards** (1977) or **Heavy Metal** (1981), Laloux's return to the animated Science Fiction feature format (and the novels of Stefan Wul – this time *L'Orphelin de Perdide*) unfortunately also marks a step back from his own hit of nearly a decade earlier, **La Planète Sauvage** (1973). With renowned genre artist Moebius stepping into the shoes of Roland Topor as chief graphic designer, the portents during production (mainly accomplished in Hungarian studios) were good, but in visualizing the motley heroic crew of a space cruiser on a rescue mission the film-makers opted for a bland consistency that's at curious odds with the obvious care taken over bringing to life the various episodic encounters that interrupt their journey. The script too, on which crime novelist Manchette tries to prove his versatility, is an affair of *déjà vu* and murky metaphysics, with a studiedly enigmatic anti-climax that's almost a parody of **2001 – A Space Odyssey** (1968). A long-drawn-out trip in more ways than one.

d/co-s René Laloux   *p* Roland Gritti, Jacques Dercourt
co-s Moebius (Jean Giraud), Jean-Patrick Manchette
se Sandor Reisenbuchler

1990: I Guerrieri del Bronx *aka* Bronx Warriors *aka* 1990: Bronx Warriors   (DEAF FILM INTERNATIONAL; IT)

pv   84 min
A clear rip-off of **Escape from New York** (1981) and *The Warriors* (1979), which also awkwardly accommodates a misplaced homage to Mickey Spillane in the figure of Morrow's fascist cop Hammer, this Italian piece of urban futurism is as riddled with narrative non-sequiturs as it is devoid of cinematic imagination or élan. The Bronx of 1990 has supposedly been surrendered to the street gangs, while Manhattan remains a 'civilized' corporate fiefdom, but for her own (no doubt) good reasons, uptown heiress (Girolami) crosses the bridge and seems to be enjoying a spot of slumming with an improbably balletic biker. Hammer's sent in after her, but would be happier simply blowing away every bit of scum in his former home turf – which he gets his chance to do after the heiress becomes kidnap currency between rival gangs, her biker goes walkabout through scavenger territory to secure allies his own gang aren't too keen on, a club-footed truckdriver turns informer, and everyone conveniently congregates at the palace of top-dog Ogre (Williamson) to get themselves incinerated. From costuming to camerawork and score to secondhand style, this is one Cinecitta carbon copy that's flat, baroque *and* berserk.

d/co-s Enzo G. Castellari   *p* Fabrizio De Angelis
co-s Dardana Sacchetti, Elisa Livia Briganti   *c* Sergio Salvati
lp Vic Morrow, Mark Gregory, Stefania Girolami, Fred Williamson, Christopher Connelly

Paradis pour Tous   (AJ FILMS/FILMS A2; FR)   110 min

Having fringed Science Fiction with several of his earlier, under-rated intrigues based on the eruption of the *fantastique* into everyday reality – *La Vie à l'Envers* (1964), *Jeu de Massacre* (1967), *Traitement de Choc* (1973) and *Armaguedon* (1977) – Jessua makes a valid appearance here with a work that both loosely fits the mad-scientist category and operates as an imaginative development of the classic premise of

Anne Carlisle as the bisexual fashion-model in the startling Liquid Sky.

The SS Enterprise *in flight in* Star Trek II: The Wrath of Khan.

Invasion of the Body Snatchers (1956). By tragic irony the final film of the talented Dewaere, who committed suicide before its release, *Paradis pour Tous* actually begins with Dewaere's insurance salesman making an unsuccessful attempt on his own life. As a result, he's exposed by experimenting doctor Dutronc to the new anti-depressant process of 'flashing', and finds himself permanently relieved of all feelings of anxiety and stress, returned to the world in a state of constant, unquestioning equanimity that drives wife Cottençon and most people he encounters into a frenzy. By the time Dutronc realizes just what he's unleashed – his 'patients' have been stripped of their consciences – the men with the deadly fixed smile are in a position to give him a dose of his own medicine, and to plot a more widespread application of the treatment. Strangely enough, given this film's close relation to his previous work, Jessua's direction proves a little too flat to tease truly disturbing resonances from his conceit; but as a film trying to walk the line between suspense and satire, it's a bravely eccentric try.

d/p/co-s Alain Jessua   *co-s* André Ruellan   *c* Jacques Robin *lp* Patrick Dewaere, Jacques Dutronc, Fanny Cottençon, Stephane Audran, Philippe Leotard, Jeanne Goupil

Parasite   (CHARLES BAND)   85 min

Alien (1979) meets **Mad Max** (1979) meets Cronenberg's **The Parasite Murders** (1974) in this catch-all post-holocaust scenario slapped together to get in quick on the predicted 3-D renaissance. Glaudini (best remembered as the star of Jon Jost's Los Angeles features) scientifically develops a parasite strain at precisely the moment he finds himself caught between para-military forces and mutant punks, and his slithery creation proves itself adept at nibbling away at its victims from the inside. Narrative logic has little purchase on this cheaply assembled universe, where eye-strain effects are all, and even the opportunity to showcase the talents of ex-Runaway Currie is thrown away among silliness.

d/p Charles Band   *s* Alan J. Adler, Michael Shoob, Frank Levering   *c* Mac Ahlberg   *se* Doug White   *lp* Robert Glaudini, Demi Moore, Luca Bercovici, Cherie Currie

Star Trek II: The Wrath of Khan

(PAR)   pv   114 (113) min

Right: Starflight One, *a disaster pic in outer space from Jerry Jameson who specialized in the sub-genre.*

A lacklustre sequel to **Star Trek – The Motion Picture** (1979). Going rather less boldly than they used to on TV – and considerably less so than cherishably megalomaniac villain Khan (Montalban) – the veteran crew of the starship *Enterprise* creak out of contemplative retirement to find several of their stray space seeds bearing thorny fruit.

Literally, because Meyer's film plays essentially as a sequel to the 'Space Seed' TV episode of 1967, with Khan's cosmic renegade blasting back into understandably wrathful action from his prison-planet exile, and metaphorically, with Admiral Kirk discovering the corny upshot of his youthful wild oats living with lost love Besch on a threatened planet. If Freud finds his way between the comic-strip frame lines here, courtesy of the familial traumas that ensue, he turns out to be in good company – Khan's instrument of revenge turns out to be a destructively wielded Genesis device, while his chosen transport, the commandeered USS *Reliant*, provides a blatant acronymic link with Cold War polarities. Meyer directs flatly, aping a primitivism that the teleseries didn't possess, and even fails to invest Spock's climactic self-sacrifice with any sense other than that of a teasing hook for yet another sequel. Montalban, hyping up some half-forgotten characterization of an Indian Chief into a slyly convincing space savage, is the only possible reason for seeing the movie. 'It might just be a particle of pre-animate matter caught up in the matrix' reads one damage report aboard the *Enterprise*, but the problems run much deeper than that.

In the wake of the film's commercial success a further sequel, *Star Trek III*, was announced.

d Nicholas Meyer   *p* Robert Sallin   *s* Jack B. Sowards *c* Gayne Rescher   *se* Edward A. Ayer, Martin Becker, Gary F. Bentley, Fred Brauer, Peter G. Evangelatos, William Purcell, Harry Stewart   *lp* William Shatner, Leonard Nimoy, Ricardo Montalban, Bibi Besch, Paul Winfield, DeForest Kelley

Starflight One

(ORGOLINI-NELSON PRODUCTIONS/ORION)   115 min

All too accurately described on its brief theatrical release as **Airplane II** (1982) without laughs, this really is a crippled straggler in the small-screen disaster movie genre, masquerading as an awed tribute to NASA's latest technological marvel, the space shuttle *Columbia*. Starflight One is a new rocket-powered plane, pressed prematurely into trans-Pacific service by its backers against the advice of its designer, which is disabled and spun into space orbit after an uncomfortably close encounter with a pirate communications satellite. Many hiccups and much tension later, both the plane and the bulk of its passengers are duly rescued by *Columbia*. The script is pure formula corn – with the hardware being granted heroic status almost by default – and for all one can tell, Jameson might well have directed in his sleep; an impression strengthened by knowledge of his reputation as *the* disaster-movie specialist in the world of tele-features with movies like *Hurricane, Terror on the 40th Floor, Superdome* and *A Fire in the Sky*, amongst others.

d Jerry Jameson   *p* Peter Nelson, Arnold Orgolini *s* Robert Malcolm Young   *c* Hector Figueroa   *se* John Dykstra, Terry Frazee   *lp* Lee Majors, Hal Linden, Lauren Hutton, Ray Milland, Robert Webber, Michael Sacks

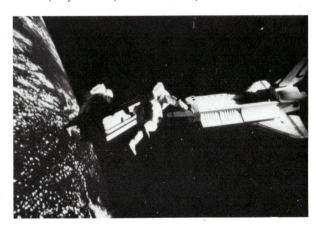

Jeff Bridges (right) dragged into the electronic innards of Tron.

Swamp Thing (EMBASSY) 90 Min

Stepping aside from such effective horrors as *The Last House on the Left* (1972), *The Hills Have Eyes* (1977) and *Deadly Blessing* (1981), Craven here detours into an enthusiastic homage to fifties monster-movies and comic-book aesthetics, but shows himself less comfortable with juvenile gee-whizzery than with adult nightmares. The plot has scientist Wise working in the Louisiana bayous on a suitably manic government project to develop vegetable cells with animal nuclei, and his formula being accidentally spilt all over him when Jourdan's baddies try to steal it. Mutating into the semi-vegetable 'swamp thing' (played by Durock) with healing powers in its green fingers, he becomes the intended prize in a knockabout chase between Jourdan and his henchmen and government agent Barbeau. The latter's panache and a wavering strand of very camp humour keep the film above the quicksands, but Craven shows real uncertainty about his audience's tastes and tolerances.

d/s Wes Craven *p* Benjamin Melniker, Michael E. Uslan *c* Robin Goodwin *se* William Munns *lp* Louis Jourdan, Adrienne Barbeau, Ray Wise, Dick Durock, David Hess, Nicholas Worth

The Thing

(U/TURMAN-FOCTER PRODUCTIONS) pv 109 min

A surprising failure, this is a revision (a revision rather than a remake because it goes directly back to John W. Campbell's original story, which features a shape-changing alien, for its inspiration) of Howard Hawks' classic **The Thing** (1951). Where Hawks in his elegant simplification of Campbell's story had created a confrontation between an isolated group and the carnivorous alien they discover in the Arctic and mistakenly revive and then played out that confrontation in terms of the different notions of humanity it represents for different members of the group, Carpenter's film is clearly in the mould, if not the style, of **Alien** (1979). Thus the dramatic tension of the film, once it is ascertained that the alien can take over humans at will, quickly becomes a question of 'who next?'. Even more surprising, in contrast to the wit and invention of **Dark Star** (1974), The Thing has no discernible style. Instead, in the manner of **Escape from New York** (1981), the narrative seems little more than an excuse for the various set-pieces of special effects and Russell's hero is no more than a cypher compared to Kenneth Tobey's rounded character in Howard Hawks' The Thing, let alone to the marvellous array of characters in *Dark Star*. The result is Carpenter's most unsatisfying film to date.

d John Carpenter *p* Davis Foster, Lawrence Turman *s* Bill Lancaster *c* Dean Cundey *se* Albert Whitlock, Roy Arbogast, Leroy Routly, Michael A. Clifford, Rob Bottin *lp* Kurt Russell, A. Wilford Brimley, T.K. Carter, David Clennon, Keith David, Richard Dysart, Charles Hallahan

Time Walker

(DIMITRI VILLARD PRODUCTIONS/WESCOM PRODUCTIONS) 83 min

A hackneyed variant on the old horror-movie standbys, the mummy picture and the monster-on-campus flick, this cheapie was partly distributed in the US by New World, but completely lacks the insolent verve that characterizes many of that studio's home-bred hybrids. The Science Fiction angle is introduced in the conceit that Tutankhamen's tomb also contains the body of the extra-terrestrial that killed the pharaoh – so it's an alien that rises, conventionally bandaged, from its sarcophagus when it's over-exposed to an American college lab's X-rays. Setting off in deadly pursuit of the gem-like transmitter crystals stolen from its side, with astounded academic Murphy in hot pursuit, the alien displays an un-mummy-like turn of speed on the ground, but spends most of the film simply zapping assorted students with its fatal fungoid touch. Kennedy gauchely embraces all the clichés of the embalmed formula, right down to representing the alien's point-of-view through a green camera filter.

d Tom Kennedy *p* Dimitri Villard, Jason Williams *s* Karen Levitt, Tom Friedman *c* Robbie Greenberg *lp* Ben Murphy, Nina Axelrod, Kevin Brophy, Austin Stoker, James Karen

Tron

(WALT DISNEY/LISBERGER-KUSHNER PRODUCTIONS) Super pv 96 min

In effect a video version of **Fantastic Voyage** (1966) with Bridges boldly going down the mean streets of a computer's circuits to do battle with its power-mad Master Control Programme (MCP) and with the merciless angularities of computer graphics replacing the more voluptuous and romantic hills and dales of the interior of the human body, *Tron*, despite its occasionally winning humour, fails because it substitutes the verities of the video game for the more sinister complexities of the computer Bridges actually enters. Accordingly the beguiling speed with which Lisberger gets his hero inside ENCOM and the deftness of the explanations of what happens to him inside, notwithstanding, the film quickly loses its metaphorical force – for indeed we clearly are being 'taken over' by computers – and descends into becoming yet another exotic adventure story. In great part this is due to the clichéd characters, such as Warner's Sark and the MCP who is yet another snarling, malevolent would-be world dictator.

Lisberger's aims are clearly higher, as seen in the last thrilling shot, a city panorama with its streets forming yet another grid pattern in which we humans are imprisoned, but the film's execution only too rarely matches these aspirations. Indeed, the project seems to mirror the crisis of confidence of the Disney studio which, since the disaster of **The Black Hole** (1979), has tried to diversify away from the solid family fare of **Herbie Goes to Monte Carlo** (1977) and **Return from Witch Mountain** (1978) into the dangerous territory of big budgets and rather more adventurous scripts with too much caution ever to be really successful.

d/s Steven Lisberger *p* Donald Kushner *c* Bruce Logan *se* Richard Taylor, Harrison Ellenshaw *lp* Jeff Bridges, David Warner, Bruce Boxleitner, Cindy Morgan, Barnard Hughes, Dan Shor, Peter Jurasik, Tony Stephano

Turkey Shoot (HEMDALE/FGH; AUST) scope 93 (87) min
An out-and-out gore-drenched exploiter, this gruesome Australian horror borrows its plot framework from a combination of *The Hounds of Zaroff* (1932) and Peter Watkins' **Punishment Park** (1971) and weakly tries to justify itself as a vision of the future, where social 'deviants' – Hussey's shopgirl, Stoner's prostitute and Railsback's 'freedom fighter' – are sent to Camp 97 for re-education, but end up as the human prey in warden Thatcher's (Craig) sadistic bloodsports (no coherent allegory apparent). Styleless and most notable only for following the lead of **Mad Max** (1979) in eschewing the spuriously arty gloss with which most new Australian movies of the period were coated, *Turkey Shoot* was much cut on its British release, and became a bone of contention in the US between the censors and the distributors, with the former claiming that sequences they had deleted had merely been reinserted into release prints by the latter.

Videodrome, David Cronenberg's disturbing evocation of the video age.

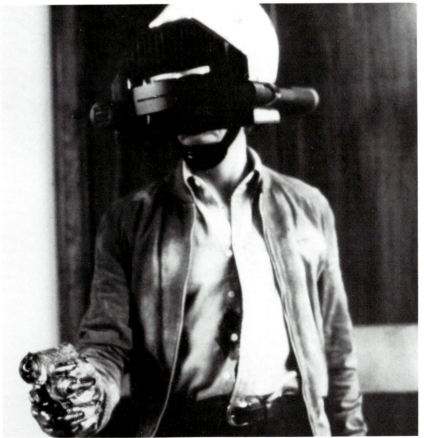

d Brian Trenchard-Smith *p* Anthony I. Ginnane, William Fayman *s* Jon George, Neill Hicks *c* John McLean *lp* Steve Railsback, Olivia Hussey, Michael Craig, Carmen Duncan, Linda Stoner

Videodrome (FILMPLAN INTERNATIONAL; CAN) 89 min
As audacious in its formal refusal to disentangle medium and message as it is provocative in scrambling politics and pornography, Cronenberg's ragged speculation on the video-age future acts both as the first McLuhanite horror movie and as a cheekily joky reprise of motifs from his own substantial generic *oeuvre* to date. Adopting the highly unstable first-person perspective of voyeuristically inclined video-freak and cable station controller Woods, Cronenberg takes us on a truly discomfiting trip through the outer limits of TV programming and the viewing psyche – sado-erotic fantasies populate both – and first investigates, then penetrates, the charged space between subject and screen. Woods, hooked on the apparent pirate broadcasts of the shadowy Videodrome channel, finds himself immersed not only in ideological conspiracy (hypnotized by TV signals) but also in evolutionary turmoil (hallucinating his own genetic adaptation to video's primacy, and developing a brand new orifice in which to receive 'living' software). And with Cronenberg giving no indication where 'reality' might be situated in this complex scheme, we can't help but share Woods' dread, and possibly deadly, fascination. The film's disgust factor is high, but it's also compulsive, and therein lies the intricacy of Cronenberg's boldly conceptualized sortie into the very debates about representations of sex and violence that have so often sprung up around his own previous films (each here 'quoted' in some bit of nightmarish comedy). A black punning humour hardly lightens the tone – though it occasionally carries the film into the distinguished company of works like Michael Powell's *Peeping Tom* (1959) and Kubrick's **A Clockwork Orange** (1971) – but the film's eventual incoherence as an 'argument' or as articulating a 'position' is in many ways its saving grace. Now Cronenberg's definitively opened up this particular can of worms, it's up to the audience (for film, TV, or video) to do their own fishing.

d/s David Cronenberg *p* Claude Héroux *c* Mark Irwin *se* Rick Baker, Michael Lennick, Frank Carere *lp* James Woods, Deborah Harry, Sonja Smits, Peter Dvorsky, Les Carlson, Jack Creley

Xtro (ASHLEY PRODUCTIONS/ AMALGAMATED FILM ENTERPRISES; GB) 86(80) min
A meandering plotline that seems set on raising, and then abruptly dropping, all the issues of the currently fashionable horror-in-the-family cycle, and a budgetary stringency that makes for extremely variable special effects are but two of the drawbacks to this British monster movie. Working some irony out of a situation of literal 'alienation', the theme of Davenport's first feature, *Whispers of Fear* (1974), the film follows the return home of a man (Sayer) – (re)born full-grown from a hapless woman raped by an alien – after he has been abducted by a UFO. Infecting his son with alien spores, and setting in motion a chain of killings and transformations, Sayers discovers that home is no longer where his heart is, and eventually begins to revert to his alien shape; but not before leaving his wife (Stegers) with a brood of lookalike offspring. So much of the movie is a matter of outright mimicry of motifs from recent genre hits (including a lot of undigested Cronenberg), and so little of it is blessed with either imagination or coherence, that it's hard to credit it as the responsibility of producer Forstater, whose **The Glitterball** (1977) remains so memorable.

d Harry Bromley Davenport *p* Mark Forstater *s* Iain Cassie, Robert Smith *c* John Metcalfe *se* Tom Harris, Francis Coates *lp* Bernice Stegers, Philip Sayer, Danny Brainin, Simon Nash

Blue Thunder

(RASTAR/GORDON CARROLL PRODUCTIONS)   pv   110 min

One of Badham's pair of technological thrillers (the other being **War Games,** 1983) that cover their politically dubious premises – deadly hardware possessing a strictly neutral value that's only rendered sinister through 'abuse' – in a camouflaging plethora of derivatively choreographed (and ostensibly reassuring) action. Here the hardware is a super-sophisticated police surveillance-and-attack helicopter – an urban **Firefox** (1982), set to all intents and purposes, in a film which borrows more than its share of motifs from the Eastwood film and sadly none from the O'Bannon co-scripted **Dark Star** (1974). McDowell's right-wing colonel is conspiring to use it to incite and then bloodily quell Los Angeles ghetto unrest; Scheider's troubled Vietnam veteran is out to stop him, proving to be the 'responsible' finger on the trigger after he steals the plane, blows the conspiracy, and dogfights his way to heroism between the skyscrapers. A running joke about high-level voyeurism, and a final (albeit brief) screen appearance by Oates are among the few moments of relief from celebratory aerobatics and the rudimentary ideology.

d John Badham   *p* Gordon Carroll   *s* Dan O'Bannon, Don Jakoby   *c* John A. Alonzo   *lp* Roy Scheider, Warren Oates, Daniel Stern, Malcolm McDowell, Candy Clark, Joe Santos

Born in Flames

(LIZZIE BORDEN/JEROME FOUNDATION/CAPS/YOUNG
FILM-MAKERS)   80 min

Set in the near future in an America ruled by 'The Party' after a democratic revolution which has changed little, *Born in Flames* is one of the most unusual feminist films of recent years, particularly for its espousal of 'pleasure' as a necessary element in radical film-making. Shot on 16mm and made with a ridiculously small budget, Borden eschews the detailed images of the future of a film like **Blade Runner** (1982) in favour, *à la* **Alphaville** (1965), of imaginatively using contemporary New York to suggest a sense of the future. Similarly, she uses her

Blue Thunder, *John Badham's hymn to technology and companion piece to* War Games *(1983).*

budgetary constraints to create out of the fast mix of rapid editing, harsh close-ups and a strident music track, an effective allegory for our times.

The thrust of the narrative follows the disenchantment of various groups – party officials, the Women's Army and guerrillas – with the new status quo, their eventual coming together around the issue of Satterfield's death in detention and the laying of the groundwork for a new revolution, seen in the closing images of the explosion set off at the World's Trade Center. This structure is further reflected in the film's plot in which the various groups, first seen in isolation, slowly interact.

The film is also of interest for the way it evolved during its lengthy production – it took some five years to complete – as it changed from a film devoted to white women to include black women and general women's issues. The result is a testament, in radical film-making at least, of the primacy of experience and reflection over the (possible) deadweight of a finished script.

d/p/s Lizzie Borden   *c* Ed Bowes, Al Santana
se Hisa Tayo   *lp* Honey, Adele Bertei, Jeanne Satterfield, Flo Kennedy, Hillary Hurst, Pat Murphy, Katheryn Biglow, Becky Johnston

Brainstorm   (JF/MGM/UA)   pv   106 min

Almost abandoned by its studio backers after Wood died tragically during production, Trumbull's special effects' showcase unavoidably prompts the thought that it might better have been aborted at the drawing-board stage. The Super Panavision process it was designed to introduce does indeed add a clarity and definition to the 70mm screen image, but the film's fatal flaw is that its narrative does little more than replicate the sense of a technical demonstration, hinging as it does on the invention of a hi-tech system for the recording of physical, emotional and intellectual sensations from the brain that can then be re-experienced by anyone else when replayed.

Developed experimentally by pioneers Fletcher and Walken, the 'brainstorm' device soon attracts the attention of the military, and the death from natural causes of Fletcher gives them their chance to move in and take the project over for nefarious refinement. Fletcher, however, dies while still linked to the recorder, and the initially complacent Walken's growing obsession with replaying her last tape – and thereby experiencing vicariously the sensations of death – brings him into a conflict with his new paymasters that's critically exacerbated when he's locked out of his own lab. Eventually, reducing the labs to chaos with his mastery of their computer systems, Walken taps in to the tape to earn his glimpse of heaven.

Left: *Douglas Trumbull's* Brainstorm, *which covers much of the same territory as David Cronenberg's far more disturbing* Videodrome *(1982).*

There's really very little to enthuse over. Wood's final role is fairly marginal, the central 'brainstorm' visions (for which the projected image widens) veer between Cinerama-style travelogue material and sub-**2001 – A Space Odyssey** (1968) psychedelics, and the film's few attempts at humour are either ploddingly protracted – as when a lab technician overdoses on orgasm after pirating a tape made by someone else while making love – or predicated on slapdash slapstick.

d/p Douglas Trumbull *s* Robert Stitzel, Philip Frank Messina *c* Richard Yuricich *se* Robert Spurlock, Eric Allard, Margin Bresin *lp* Christopher Walken, Natalie Wood, Louise Fletcher, Cliff Robertson

The Dead Zone (DEG) 103 min

After the commercial failure of the intensely personal **Videodrome** (1982), Cronenberg began to seek ways of accommodating his own vision into the movie mainstream, ultimately reaping the dividend of **The Fly** (1986) and *Dead Ringers* (1988). Here, as a gun-for-hire, he was handed Stephen King's novel and displayed his ability to make an ordinary film by turning in a professional, perfectly acceptable little movie that, like his drag race picture *Fast Company* (1976), stands out among his distinctive, original movies.

Johnny Smith (Walken), a teacher who awakens from his 5-year crash-induced coma with the unnerving power to visualize potential disasters, is recognizable as one of Cronenberg's tortured psychic heroes, with each use of his gift debilitating him further, but the Everyman stamp of his name – as opposed to Cronenberg's Adrian Tripod, Max Renn, Cameron Vale, Seth Brundle or Doctor Mantle – marks him as one of King's 'ordinary' protagonists in extraordinary situations.

Boam's screenplay condenses the novel's tapestry into a rather clumsily strung procession of episodes, as Johnny discovers his powers, helps the police track down the Castle Rock killer and confronts the power-hungry, folksy politician (Sheen) he knows will start World War Three if elected to the presidency. The Cronenbergian elements are diluted: snowy Canadian locations double for King's New England, but the bleak landscape is given a homey horror movie character by old wooden houses; the visions punctuate the story, but never subvert the film's reality as completely as do those of

De Lift, Dick Maas' engaging addition to the revenge-of-the-machine cycle of films.

Videodrome so that, even before the plot reveals that the horrors can be averted, it is obvious that they are 'safe'; and Johnny's ESP-driven *angst* is reduced to banality by an introductory sequence showing him as a happy-go-lucky, ordinary guy before the accident ruins his life.

d David Cronenberg *p* Debra Hill *s* Jeffrey Boam *c* Mark Irwin *se* Jon Belyeu *lp* Christopher Walken, Martin Sheen, Brooke Addams, Herbert Lom, Tom Skerritt, Colleen Dewhurst, Anthony Zerbe

Le Dernier Combat aka The Last Battle

(LES FILMS DU LOUP; FR) scope b/w 92 min

The directorial début of Besson (who subsequently went on to make the superior *Subway*, 1985), *Le Dernier Combat* reworks the disaster images of high-tech buildings prodding through huge sand dunes so familiar from the works of J. G. Ballard to create one of the most unusual entry-into-manhood movies of recent times. Set in the near future after an unspecified catastrophe that has left small groups of mute humans barely surviving off the few remaining stocks of food, the film and its characters are unconcerned with the hows and whys of their predicament. They simply act. Thus what might have been a story about the rebirth of civilization, as Jolivet escapes from one set of ruins in search of companionship and after a string of adventures finds a mate, becomes in Bessons' hands no more (and no less) than a rite of passage in which Jolivet proves himself a worthy inhabitant of the surreal world he has fallen heir to. The result is a fine film, all the better for its refusal to look back and instead, like its characters, make playthings of the obsolete objects that populate it.

d/p/co-s Luc Besson *co-s* Pierre Jolivet *c* Carlo Varini *lp* Pierre Jolivet, Jean Bousie, Fritz Wepper, Jean Reno, Maurice Lamy

Halloween III: Season of the Witch

(DINO DE LAURENTIIS) pv 98 min

The first film in the series initiated by Carpenter's masterly shocker, *Halloween* (1979) to utilize a Science Fiction premise, *Halloween* III had its serious internal contradictions (commerce versus coherence) exposed from the moment the writer of the Quatermass films, veteran Nigel Kneale, decided to remove his name from the screenplay credits, with its reception thereafter always tempered by speculation about the film that might have been.

The marriage of mysticism and the microchip at the film's heart – a demonic Irish-American toy manufacturer incorporates a killer device in the popular children's Halloween masks he's marketing, to be triggered by a TV commercial code – is swamped by the emphasis on maintaining a quota of gory shock effects. Yet the break from the psycho-killer formula is welcome, and there's much pleasing ingenuity on display in the yoking of such disparate models as **Invasion of the Body Snatchers** (1956) and even Don Siegel's *Telefon* (1977) to the unstoppable paranoia bandwagon. A nice sense of absurdity, too, in the throwaway notion of malevolent robotic leprechauns.

d/s Tommy Lee Wallace *p* Debra Hill, John Carpenter *c* Dean Cundey *se* Jon G. Belyeu *lp* Tom Atkins, Stacey Nelkin, Dan O'Herlihy

Krull

(COL/TED MANN-RON SILVERMAN PROD./BARCLAYS INDUSTRIAL MERCANTILE FINANCE LTD; GB) 121 min

A likeable, if lightweight, blend of sword and sorcery and Science Fiction, *Krull* follows the travails of Marshall and his unlikely band of helpers in search of the enormous Black Beast who has kidnapped Marshall's fiancée, Anthony. The result, clearly intended as a fairy tale (the Black Beast, in particular, is hardly characterized at all), is an oddly innocent, almost

chivalrous film. It's as though director Yates and writer Sherman, in their efforts to avoid the pyrotechnics of **Star Wars** (1977) and its sequels, left out the mythic confrontation between Good and Evil that gave those films' special effects a degree of meaning beyond the merely spectacular. All that is left is a few engaging characters (notably Bresslaw's melancholy giant and Jones' tetchy prophet) who surround the pallid hero and heroine and some nicely judged sequences.

d Peter Yates *p* Ron Silverman *s* Stanford Sherman
c Peter Suschitzky *se* Derek Meddings, John Evans, Mark Meddings *lp* Ken Marshall, Lysette Anthony, Freddie Jones, Francesca Annis, Alun Armstrong, David Battley, Bernard Bresslaw, Liam Neeson

De Lift *aka* The Lift (SIGMA FILMS; NETH) 99 min

An engaging addition to the growing number of revenge-of-the-machine films, *De Lift* features a murderous electronic elevator, programmed by an 'organic computer' with dim views of the humans who use, and deface, the elevator without thinking. Stapel is the maintenance engineer who becomes suspicious after a couple of questionable deaths in the lift and Van Ammelrooy the graduate of the Lois Lane school of journalism who helps his investigations.

The situation is an all too familiar one and the green slime that is the organic computer is not sufficiently characterized to be really terrifying, but Maas twists his material first this way then that to pleasantly confound our expectations. Thus Stapel and Van Ammelrooy don't have the affair that seems on the cards (though Stapel's wife leaves him thinking they do) and, even after the truth about the elevator has been established, the various representatives of authority remain as ineffectual as before, so preparing the way for Stapel's climactic foray into the lift shaft which Maas orchestrates in a delightfully old-fashioned manner.

d/s Dick Maas *p* Mathijs Van Heijningen *c* Marc Felperlaan *se* Leo Cahn, Rene Stouthamer *lp* Huub Stapel, Willeke Van Ammelrooy, Josine Van Dalsum, Piet Romer, Hans Veerman, Siem Vroom, Serge-Henri Valcke

The Man With Two Brains
(ASPEN FILM SOCIETY) 93 (86) min

A spoof on Curt Siodmak's novel *Donovan's Brain* (previously filmed 'straight' as **The Lady and the Monster**, 1944; **Donovan's Brain**, 1953; and **Vengeance**, 1962), this is a minor but nonetheless enjoyable outing. Martin is the brain surgeon who falls for the body of Turner's dumb blonde and the mind of Anne Uumellmahaye and solves his problem by putting Anne's mind in Turner's body. Running through the narrative are parodies of various genres, the best of which is the take off of the psycho killer with the various victims of the elevator killer turning to the subjective camera and recognizing not an important character in the film but a television personality.

Both Martin and Turner (who appears throughout the film in an extraordinary range of undergarments) make the best of their characters while cinematographer Chapman bathes the images in pastel colours that succeed in papering over the many implausibilities of the script.

d/co-s Carl Reiner *p* David V. Picker *co-s* Steve Martin, George Gipe *c* Michael Chapman *se* Allen Hall
lp Steve Martin, Kathleen Turner, David Warner, Paul Benedict, Richard Brestoff, George Furth

Metalstorm: The Destruction of Jared-Syn
(ALBERT BAND INTERNATIONAL) 84 min

The third dimension is about all that's added here to the apparently infinitely exploitable mechanics of **Mad Max 2** (1981) and **Star Wars** (1977). The team responsible for the earlier 3-D effort **Parasite** (1982) here offer Byron as a peace-keeping ranger of the future, despatched on an obscure interplanetary mission to wrest a powerful crystal from the evil desert dwellers led by Preston, and engaging in all the usual western-on-wheels manoeuvres between grotesque encounters. One or two unexpected ocular assaults apart, there's no panache, no poetry and, worst of all, no point.

d/co-p Charles Band *co-p/s* Alan J. Adler *c* Mac Ahlberg
lp Jeffrey Byron, Tim Thomerson, Kelly Preston, Mike Preston, Richard Moll

Never Say Never Again

(WOODCOTE/TALIAFILM PROD.; GB)   pv   134 min

Unlike **Casino Royale** (1967) which attempted to satirize the James Bond saga to death and failed miserably, *Never Say Never Again* is a far more modest and enjoyable film. Its aims, best expressed in its title which is a joke at the expense of Connery who, when he quit the role of James Bond, said he'd never return to it, are simply to gently guy the Bond series to the profit of all concerned, including the audience. Accordingly, from the opening remarks of McCowen's Q to Connery ('Let's get back to the gratuitous sex and violence') on, with great suppleness, the film-makers manage to both further lionize Connery and, with his connivance, gently poke fun at Bond (who at the film's beginning is sent to a health farm because, in the view of Fox's charmingly dotty M, he's past it).

In fact, a remake of **Thunderball** (1965), the twin successes of the movie are Connery's effortless demonstration that, toupée or not, he *is* James Bond, and its re-structuring of the Bond myth, downgrading the lavish special effects of the Roger Moore Bonds (such as **Moonraker**, 1979, and the non Science Fiction *Octopussy*, 1983) in favour of Q's decidedly cut-price gadgets and, more interestingly, far more rounded characters, such as Brandauer's gloriously demented Largo, and human action. Accordingly, the plot, Brandauer's dreams of world conquest through the two nuclear missiles he's hijacked, is broken down into a series of set scenes, all mounted with the knowingness that Kershner demonstrated in *Loving* (1970) and the efficiency of **The Empire Strikes Back** (1980). Not surprisingly, the result is a celebration of old-fashioned Hollywood film-making at its most enjoyable and professional, good acting, efficient direction and, above all, good humour.

d Irvin Kershner   p Jack Schwartzman   s Lorenzo Semple Jnr   c Douglas Slocombe   se Don Dryer, Ian Wingrove   lp Sean Connery, Klaus Maria Brandauer, Max Von Sydow, Barbara Carrera, Kim Basinger, Bernie Casey, Alec McCowen, Edward Fox, Pamela Salem, Rowan Atkinson

I Nuovi Barbari *aka* The New Barbarians

(DEAF FILM INTERNATIONAL; IT)   91 min

A blatant Cinecitta rip-off of **Mad Max 2** (1981) from indefatigable (and inept) cover-artist Castellari, who has had more pseudonyms than original cinematic ideas in a lengthy career stretching back to his days in the spaghetti sagebrush as E.G. Rowland. Even here, he directs as Castellari, co-scripts as Enzo Girolami and acts under the name of Thomas Moore. The sort of work to inspire cult enthusiasts to rapture, this dire post-holocaust western pits lone desert warriors Skorpion (Brent) and Nadir (Williamson) against marauding nihilist gay bikers, and arbitrarily drags in stray wisps of religious allegory and homophobic venom amid the incompetently stunted ultra-violence and half-cock perversions of the George Miller model.

Techno-Rollbikes in action in the jaunty Spacehunter: Adventures in the Forbidden Zone.

d/co-s Enzo G. Castellari   p Fabrizio De Angelis   co-s Tito Carpi   c Fausto Zuccoli   lp Timothy Brent, George Eastman, Fred Williamson, Anna Kanakis

Prisoners of the Lost Universe

(MARCEL-ROBERTSON PRODUCTIONS/UNITED MEDIA FINANCE; GB)   91 (90) min

A cutprice alternative world adventure. Lenz and Hatch are the TV journalist and martial arts champion/electrician respectively who save the world of Vonya from its evil ruler Saxon and Hendel's renegade mad scientist. Sadly, Marcel offers the most predictable of alternative worlds – this one's mostly Middle Ages – while the script is even duller: 'Please Miss Madison, the matter transmitter is a finely calibrated instrument'.

d/co-s Terry Marcel   p/co-s Harry Robertson   c Derek Browne   se Ray Hanson   lp Richard Hatch, Kay Lenz, John Saxon, Peter O'Farrell, Ray Charleson, Kenneth Hendel

Return of the Jedi   (LUCASFILM)   132 min

The final chapter in the trilogy that also comprises **Star Wars** (1977) and **The Empire Strikes Back** (1980), *Return of the Jedi* is the best of the series. According to Lucas, the originator and owner of the *Star Wars* property, the series is projected to run nine episodes in three disconnected series, of which the trilogy is chapters four, five and six. Thus it would seem, and the text of the film confirms, that *Return of the Jedi* represents the conclusion of the stories of Luke Skywalker, Princess Leia, Han Solo, C-3PO, R2-D2, Darth Vader and the rest of the characters introduced in *Star Wars*.

The film has its lapses. The Ewoks, for example, are clearly manufactured as lovable little teddy bears and in particular the sequence where Wicket (Warwick Davis) knocks himself over in the middle of a fight against the stormtroopers, though it always brings forth a roar of appreciation in the cinema, is too calculated a piece of film-making. Similarly, some of the special effects of the second half are only competent, especially in comparison to the perfectly judged sequence at the Sarlac Pit which begins with R2-D2 magicking Hamill's light sabre out of nowhere and must be one of the classic action set-pieces in the history of the cinema. But set against this is Lucas' marvellous recreating of the original story of *Star Wars*, the destruction of the Death Star by the democratic rebels with the added twist that this time the characters, especially Luke Skywalker and Darth Vader, are given the mythic dimension they so sorely lacked in the earlier film. At the centre of this transformation lies the double revelation that Vader is Luke's father and Princess Leia is Luke's sister. Thus, at one stroke, and with an economy that is breath-taking, the impersonal battle of Good versus Evil is given a mythical dimension which makes Hamill's Luke Skywalker no longer the simple, earnest hero he began life as but a man who must outfight his father in battle and yet save him – in *Return of the Jedi* even 'the Force', previously one of the more embarrassingly juvenile elements of the series, is given an added dimension too. This voyage into the mythic makes Luke a true hero, one whose acts bring salvation to those around him but can find no peace himself. For as well as losing/saving his father and finally losing Leia to Solo (as if that was ever in doubt) *Return of the Jedi* ends with Luke completely adrift, minus even the support of the various father figures who have supported him throughout the trilogy, his uncle, Guinness' Ben Kenobi and even Oz's Yoda. Fittingly, the film ends with Luke alone gazing at his father's burning funeral pyre before joining the victory celebrations at the Ewok village. Of course, this fairy tale is only pulp poetry but its success is all the more remarkable for the unlikely beginnings it had in the simple gee-whizz heroics of *Star Wars*.

Furthermore, Marquand's restrained direction marvellously unites this deeply resonant personal story with the traditional verities of space opera that supports it. Thus once the characters have been triumphantly re-assembled after the setting free of Ford's Han Solo from Jabba the Hut, Marquand and writers Kasdan and Lucas first send them on their separate ways and then cross-cut between the three climaxes they set up, Luke's battle with Vader inside the Death Star, the rebel fleet attacking the Death Star and the battle of Endor to knock out the defensive screen erected around the Death Star. Each intercutting between these battles accelerates the narrative pace and intensifies the other battles, melding everything together and creating a sense of emotional urgency that is finally satisfied by the victorious conclusion of all three battles. It is this interrogation of the adventure story until it finally slips into legend in the mythic confrontation of son and father that makes *Return of the Jedi* such a triumphant conclusion and envoi to the world of *Star Wars*.

d Richard Marquand   *p* Howard Kazanjian   *s* Lawrence Kasdan, George Lucas   *c* Alan Hume   *se* Richard Edlund, Dennis Muren, Ken Ralston, Roy Arbogast   *lp* Mark Hamill, Harrison Ford, Carrie Fisher, Billy Dee Williams, Anthony Daniels, Peter Mayhew, Ian McDiarmid, Frank Oz, David Prowse, James Earl Jones (voice of Vader), Alec Guinness

Space Raiders

(NEW WORLD/MILLENIUM PRODUCTIONS)   82 min
As if making an attempt on his own house record for cheap, quickie B-picture production, Corman here hands Cohen (who was also responsible for the scrappy screenplay of Cirio Santiago's **Stryker**, 1983) the thankless assignment of creating a new feature out of and around the special effects' footage first used in his comparatively big-budget space western **Battle Beyond the Stars** (1980). The technique had worked a few years before for Joe Dante and Allan Arkush on the delightful *Hollywood Boulevard* (1980), which made a satiric virtue out of its near-incoherence, but this time around Cohen is clearly unequal to the task.

The space-battle shots are poorly integrated with the new (well, secondhand) narrative, which pits the freelance raiders of the title against the evil 'Company' (read as 'Empire') and their lethal robot command ship (Death Star?), and takes depressing detours down the byways of space sentimentality by lumbering the heroes with a cute stowaway kid to return to his home planet. Plentiful **Star Wars** (1977) quotes apart, the incestuous nature of the whole enterprise is finally sealed by such details as having Edwards' Colonel Hawkins much given to swigging beer from anachronistic ring-pull cans, in witless homage to George Peppard's scotch-gulping space cowboy in *Battle Beyond the Stars*.

d/s Howard R. Cohen   *p* Roger Corman   *c* Alec Hirschfeld   *lp* Vince Edwards, David Mendenhall, Patsy Pease, Thom Christopher, Drew Snyder, Dick Miller

Spacehunter: Adventures in the Forbidden Zone

(COL/DELPHI PRODUCTIONS)   90 min
Appearing just as the second great 3-D boom seems to be losing its novelty value at the international box-office, *Spacehunter* is the sort of fun movie that could well have done without additional optical gimmickry. Still, having survived against all odds the collective travails of six writers (two for the original story), two directors (dependable veteran Johnson replaced Jean Lafleur a fortnight into shooting) and several title changes (*Road Gangs* and *Adventures in the Creep Zone* were earlier working handles), it wears its clear borrowings from umpteen recent screen hits with a jaunty air of embattled resilience.

Strauss plays a kind of cosmic, 22nd-century Indiana Jones embroiled in a plot of rollicking space-western resonance on forbidding planet Terra Eleven, battling mutant tribes and sundry savage nasties, initially for bounty, then for almost the

sheer hell of it. Gathering stock sidekicks along the way (though losing his female android mate), Strauss ends up despatching planetary dictator Overdog to his just desserts and blowing Graveyard City to stardust, before blasting off in optimistic search of a sequel.

d Lamont Johnson   *p* Don Carmody, André Link, John Dunning   *s* David Preston, Edith Rey, Dan Goldbert, Len Blum   *c* Frank Tidy   *se* Darrell Martin, Gene Warren, Gary Gentley   *lp* Peter Strauss, Molly Ringwald, Ernie Hudson, Andrea Marcovicci, Michael Ironside

Strange Invaders   (ORION/EMI)   94 min

The supposed centrepiece of a touted trilogy from Laughlin and Condon – but an only tangentially related follow-up to the same duo's nightmarish psycho-thriller *Strange Behaviour* (1981) – this Science Fiction oddity combines affectionate genre satire and outright horror in its linking of alien visitations in 1958 and the present, but maintains a classily un-ruffled air of imaginative fantasy throughout all its shifts in tone. Basically the story has aliens, on their initial exploration of the planet, assuming the bodies of mid-western farmers and returning in that form in up-to-date New York on a search for a couple of stay-behinds, also sought by bemused professor Le Mat (who married one and fathered another) and inquisitive scandal-sheet hackette Allen. Culture clash naturally takes many forms, and the deceptiveness of surface appearances is remarkably illustrated in one of the numerous shock scenes when an incognito alien decides to 'unmask' itself, but the real surprise is that such prime 'body-snatchers' exploitation fodder is here galvanized with gorgeously fluent detailing in performance, design and direction.

d/co-s Michael Laughlin   *p* Walter Coblenz   *co-s* William Condon   *c* Louis Horvath   *se* John Muto, Robert Skotak   *lp* Paul Le Mat, Nancy Allen, Diana Scarwid, Michael Lerner, Louise Fletcher, Wallace Shawn, Fiona Lewis

Stryker   (HCI INTERNATIONAL PICTURES; PHIL)   84 min

Yet another cut-rate futuristic actioneer modelled on **Mad Max 2** (1981) this Filipino offering is, if anything, even more ridiculous than its Italian competitor, **I Nuovi Barbari** (1983). Establishing itself as post-holocaust by using stock documentary footage of an American test mushroom for its opening scene, this soon resolves itself into a dimly plotted conflict over water, and the subtle political dilemma of whether it should be shared or hoarded. The film's principal features are much macho posturing from both Sandor and the brutish villains, much female flesh on the sidelines, including former Playmate Monique St Pierre, and a totally withering sense of *déjà vu* throughout.

Richard Pryor (left) watches in disbelief as Christopher Reeve is entranced by a piece of synthetic kryptonite in Superman III.

The veteran Santiago used to turn out at least halfway decent movies for Roger Corman's New World from his Filipino base including *Fly Me, Savage!* (both 1973), *TNT Jackson* (1975) and the like.

d/p Cirio H. Santiago   *s* Howard R. Cohen   *c* Ricardo Remias   *lp* Steve Sandor, Andria Savio, William Ostrander, Michael Lane, Julie Gray

Superman III (DOVEMEAD/CANTHARUS; GB) pv 125 min
No longer are we simply begged to believe that a man can fly. Rather, Lester turns his first truly autonomous entry in the Salkinds' money-spinning series into a fully credible demonstration that comic strips can move, giving Reeve's split personality a real hard day's night by fragmenting his physique and psyche one stage further and staging an ironic slug-out between Superman's baser instincts and Clark Kent's super-ego. No longer, either, are we expected to be naïvely awestruck by the mythological resonances and epic intimations so stressfully interwoven in parts **I** (1978) and **II** (1980). This second sequel is a comparative model of economical narrative coherence, with the only distractions from an essential shaggy-dog joke on the disparate scales of ambition being some pleasurable detours through the Lester back-catalogue of slapstick sight-gags, offbeat romance, and the lengthways scrutiny of popular legend.

The supervillain this time around is a pointedly Earthbound man of corporate capital (Vaughn), exploiting the formerly unemployable Pryor's new-found computer wizardry as he tries to play multinational monopoly with such handy commodities as coffee and oil, and launching a pre-emptive strike against Superman with a dose of synthetic kryptonite whose impurities reveal the Man of Steel to be not entirely stainless. For a while refusing to 'do that nice stuff anymore', and neglecting new love Lana Lang (O'Toole) for the upfront charms of Stephenson's Lorelei, the tarnished hero eventually pulls himself together to take on Vaughn's cybernetic alter-ego in the sort of man-against-machine combat that Lester nicely guys within the film as little more than advanced video-arcade material.

The film's hardly an unalloyed delight, but its air of playfulness and distinct lack of pomp or pretension are appealing.

d Richard Lester   *p* Pierre Spengler   *s* David Newman, Leslie Newman   *c* Robert Paynter   *se* Roy Field, Colin Chilvers, Martin Gutteridge, Brian Warner   *lp* Christopher Reeve, Richard Pryor, Annette O'Toole, Robert Vaughn, Pamela Stephenson, Annie Ross

Testament
(ENTERTAINMENT EVENTS/AMERICAN PLAYHOUSE) 89 min
Beneficiary of a rare exhibition tie-in between a major distributor (Paramount) and America's public TV system, this soberly restrained, brilliantly acted adaptation of Carol Amen's magazine story *The Last Testament* charts the effects of a nuclear World War III on the small Californian town of Hamlin, whose inhabitants all survive the distant blasts, but gradually begin succumbing to radiation sickness and reacting in variously resigned ways to their morbid fate. Littman's feature début begins by establishing strongly a profile of the sheer normality of Hamlin, and after the community finds itself isolated and apparently doomed, it is the complete lack of sensationalism in both script and direction which sets the film apart from most post-holocaust speculative fiction, with a strong focus on the older generations trying to somehow explain to the children the experience of life that they'll now never have. The senses of loss, waste and futility are registered through faces, looks and gestures rather than shock footage, and Alexander in particular contributes a tremendously moving performance.

d/co-p Lynee Littman   *co-p* Jonathan Bernstein   *s* John Sacret Young   *c* Steven Poster   *lp* Jane Alexander, William Devane, Ross Harris, Roxana Zal, Lukas Haas, Lilia Skala

Timerider: The Adventures of Lyle Swann
(ZOOMO PRODUCTIONS/JENSEN-FARLEY PICTURES) 92 min
With an endearing lack of subtlety, this cheerful little programmer from ex-Monkee-cum-country star Nesmith

The computer display screens of NORAD show evidence of a surprise nuclear attack in War Games.

turns current fascinations with the space western on their head, employing the Science Fiction standby of the time-warp as an excuse to let loose a biker in the Wild West. The result is every bit as daft as that achieved by George Romero's *Knightriders* (1982) (jousting bikers accommodating their outlaw sensibilities to Arthurian codes), but Dear seems unable to decide whether to go for all-out incongruity in developing his culture-clash premise, and rather fudges the point of the meeting between a fairly dumb 20th-century technocrat and a merely functionally evil band of primitive desperadoes. Ward is the timerider, Coyote the outlaw who takes a fancy to Ward's bike and Bauer the unusually passive heroine.

d/co-s William Dear *p* Harry Gites *co-s* Michael Nesmith *c* Larry Pizer *se* Computer Camera Service *lp* Fred Ward, Belinda Bauer, Peter Coyote, Ed Lauter, L. Q. Jones

War Games

(MGM/UA/SHERWOOD PRODUCTIONS) 113 min
Doing little to develop the grisly gallows humour implicit in its central conceit of nuclear war being waged as a kids'-play video game, *War Games* rather conventionally exploits current arcane fascinations and apocalyptic fears to produce a melodramatic mix of adventure and suspense. Broderick is the teenage home-computer wiz, showing off to girlfriend Sheedy when he accidentally taps in to America's nuclear defence computer (WOPR, or 'whopper', if you like) and innocently convinces it of an imminent Soviet attack. Many fraught misunderstandings later, Broderick forestalls American retaliation by appealing to the independently functioning WOPR's sense of logic, cueing the literal spelling out of the movie's message – 'A strange game. The only winning move is not to play' – but failing to dispel or question the Cold War clichés that underpin almost all the script's, admittedly spectacular, convolutions.

d John Badham *p* Harold Schneider *s* Lawrence Lasker, Walter F. Parkes *c* William A. Fraker *lp* Matthew Broderick, Dabney Coleman, Ally Sheedy, John Wood, Barry Corbin, Dennis Lipscomb

Yor: The Hunter from the Future

(DIAMANT FILM; IT) 88 min
An Italian production largely shot in Turkey, this juvenile outing appears to be suffering from schizophrenia about whether it's a prehistoric epic or a futuristic fantasy, but decides to play it both ways by having its loin-clothed muscleman hero develop murderous prowess with both a rudimentary axe and laser technology, and having both a dinosaur and a spaceship make guest appearances. If this and Hercules are anything to go by, *Conan the Barbarian* (1981) will have as much to answer for in the near future as does **Mad Max 2** (1981) currently. Sadly the film has little of the visual delirium of Margheriti's earlier essays in Science Fiction, notably **Il Pianeta degli Uomoni Spenti** (1961) and **I Criminali della Galassia** (1965).

d/co-s Anthony M. Dawson (Antonio Margheriti) *p* Michele Marsala *co-s* Robert Bailey *c* Marcello Masciochi *lp* Reb Brown, Corrine Clery, John Steiner

The Adventures of Buckaroo Banzai Across the 8th Dimension (SHERWOOD) pv 102 min

A bewildering but rather likeable *non sequitur* of a movie that drops the audience into a self-contained and elaborate world, as if it were the last episode of an incredibly complicated

serial. Buckaroo Banzai (Weller) is a Japanese-American genius who divides his time between neuro-surgery, particle physics, rock 'n' roll and saving the Earth from extra-dimensional invaders. When Rastafarians from another world inform him that the crazy Dr Emilio Lizardo (Lithgow) has been taken over by a megalomaniac alien with plans for galactic conquest, Buckaroo and The Hong Kong Cavaliers, his team of trusty cowboy scientist sidekicks, swing into action. While the good guys play it dead straight, Lithgow chews up the scenery, as an alien whose invasion force hypnotized Orson Welles into putting out the **War of the Worlds** radio broadcast to cover up their initial landing on Earth in 1939; meanwhile Barkin contributes another one of her fractured waif performances as a heroine who has to be talked out of a public suicide by the supercool hero during a rock gig.

'Now wait a minute here': The Adventures of Buckaroo Banzai Across the 8th Dimension.

With an excellent and varied cast, uniformly clever costumes by Aggie Guerrard Rogers, impressively spiny seashell spaceships and a host of dialogue felicities, this is endearing enough to justify its instant mythologizing of itself by incorporating into its plot a huge merchandizing campaign featuring a fan club (The Blue Blaze Irregulars), comic books, video games and rock records. But this is tempered by enough blankly impenetrable weirdness and frustrating inanity to suggest that waiting for the sequel promised in the end credits – *Buckaroo Banzai Versus the World Crime League* – will prove as fruitful as waiting for the one similarly promised at the end of **Doc Savage – The Man of Bronze** (1975).

d/co-p W.D. Richter *co-p* Neil Canton *s* Earl Mac Rauch *c* Fred J. Koenkamp *se* Peter Kuran/VCE, Dream Quest Images *lp* Peter Weller, John Lithgow, Ellen Barkin, Christopher Lloyd, Jeff Goldblum, Clancy Brown, Lewis Smith, Robert Ito, Matt Clark, Pepe Serna, Dan Hedaya, Mariclare Costello

The Brother from Another Planet

(A-TRAIN FILMS)   108 min

For all its failings, Sayles' film succeeds by the force of the sheer fun and humour that runs through it. Morton is the mute alien who materializes in New York in black human form, discovers alienation, puts paid to a drugs racket and after disposing of the pair of bounty hunters after him (one of which is played by Sayles himself) decides to stay. If the strand of social comment – Morton on Ellis Island hearing the voices of previous generations of aliens arriving in America or looking at an image of a runaway slave and comparing his plight to the slave's – seems strained in the manner of *Lianna* (1982), Sayles plays the genre games to the hilt. Shot on a budget of less than $200,000 but looking far plusher, *The Brother from Another Planet* freewheels its way through Harlem, turning this way then that with the same ease that Morton fixes the video games.

d/s John Sayles   *p* Peggy Rajski, Maggie Renzi   *c* Ernest R. Dickerson   *lp* Joe Morton, Tom Wright, Caroline Aaron, Herbert Newsome, Dee Dee Bridgewater, Darryl Edwards, Leonard Jackson

C.H.U.D.

(BONIME ASSOCIATES/NEW WORLD)   110(87) min

The title is an acronym for either Cannibalistic Humanoid Underground Dwellers or Contamination Hazard Urban Disposal, signalling that the premise of this ambitious, but broken-backed, monster movie is that the regulation Unscrupulous Chemical Company has been dumping its toxic waste in the New York sewers and mutating winos into flesh-eating goblins.

Although the central characters – a vengeful cop (Curry), an anti-establishment photojournalist (Heard), a skid-row preacher (Stern) – are more interesting than is usual in formula monster movies, and Caglione's bug-eyed monsters are welcome creations, the film suffers from its attenuated storyline and an accumulation of blatantly unlikely plot twists. The shortened version is an extensive recutting, which goes so far as to take an attack sequence from the middle of the film and place it at the end to provide the regulation 'the-horror-is-not-over' finish. The lesser follow-up, *C.H.U.D. II: Bud the Chud* (1989) was more straightforwardly comic.

d Douglas Cheek   *p* Larry Abrams   *s* Parnell Hall   *c* Peter Stein   *se* John Caglione Jr   *lp* John Heard, Daniel Stern, Christopher Curry, Kim Griest, J.C. Quinn, George Martin, Laure Mattos, Brenda Currin

City Limits

(SHO FILMS/VIDEOFORM PICTURES/ISLAND ALIVE)   85 min

This disappointing follow-up to **Android** (1982) has pace, humour and some visual invention, but nothing much new to add to the post-holocaust genre.

In the future, as in **Gas-s-s-s** (1970) and **Logan's Run** (1976), all adults – with the exception of James Earl Jones – have died and cowboy kid Stockwell goes to the Big City to join a street gang, led by Larson, and to fight an unscrupulous faction, led by junior fascist Benson, who are taking over. Similar in its setting, plot and style to such spaghetti **Mad Max** clones as **1990: I Guerrieri del Bronx** (1982) and **I Nuovi Barbari** (1983), the film has a good cast, but its script is a lazy assemblage of societal breakdown clichés, and it winds up with a pretty ordinary battle, featuring plentiful bike action and whizzing model aeroplanes.

Right: Danger threatens from a Cannibalistic Humanoid Underground Dweller in C.H.U.D.

d Aaron Lipstadt   *p* Rupert Harvey, Barry Opper   *s* Don Opper   *c* Tim Suhrstedt   *se* Special Effects Unlimited   *lp* Darrell Larson, John Stockwell, Kim Cattrall, Robby Benson, James Earl Jones, Rae Dawn Chong, John Diehl, Danny de la Paz, Tony Plana

Dark Enemy   (CHILDREN'S FILM UNIT; GB)   97 min

The Children's Film Unit, a well-established British institution that has produced a series of admirable low-budget features, here turns its attention to the Dark Times, when a small agrarian community, living a self-sufficient existence in an isolated valley, is dying out. The adults fall prey to mysterious plagues, while in the surrounding woods sub-human Moon Children prowl. As in **Teenage Cavemen** (1958), the film depicts an apparently historical primitive society in which the youngsters of the tribe are baffled by a set of taboos handed down by their elders, and then finally reveals that the world we are seeing is actually the near future, after a nuclear holocaust. The inevitable roughness of the production, with children employed as key technicians, actually adds to the mock medieval feel of the film, and the performances of the young cast are natural and unforced. Director Finbow's handling of the action scenes is uncertain, but *Dark Enemy* is an admirable, thoughtful, quietly haunting little movie.

d/p Colin Finbow   *s* Children's Film Unit   *c* Andrew Fleury   *lp* David Haig, Douglas Storm, Martin Laing, Chris Chescoe, Jennifer Harrisson, Helen Mason, Rory MacFarquhar, Cerian Van Doorninck

DefCon 4   (NEW WORLD; CAN)   89 min

Another post-nuke movie, following the plot premise of *The Aftermath* (1980), *DefCon 4* has a spacecraft returning to Earth after World War Three and pitching the astronauts into a brutal new society. The competent captain is hauled out and eaten by savages, leaving the confused lady doctor (Zann) and a wimpish button-pusher (Chaykin) to forage in a world overrun by preppy militarists, cannibalistic scum and mad Scotsmen. More realistic and hard-bitten than most fun-in-the-wasteland movies, this opens with the space station – an orbital missile platform – living through the five-minute war in a state of panic, and then shows an Earth convincingly covered in mud with a despairing, despondent bunch of survivors.

d/co-p/s Paul Donovan   *co-p* B.A. Gillian, Maura O'Connell   *c* Doug Connell, Les Kriszan   *se* Keith Currie   *lp* Leone Zann, Maury Chaykin, Kate Lynch, Tim Choate, Kevin King, Jeff Pustil, Alan MacGillivray

2019: Dopo la Caduta di New York aka Due Mille Dicianuove aka After the Fall of New York

(NUOVA DANIA CINEMATOGRAFICA/LES FILMS DU GRIFFON/MEDUSA/IMPEX FILMS; IT,FR) 99 (95) min

An episodic post holocaust comic-strip adventure, this features Sopkiw as Parsifal sent by the failing President of the Pan American Confederation (Purdom) to find the last fertile woman left on Earth. Slackly directed with little sense of the devasted Earth the script suggests, the film all too often retreats to such tried and tested clichés as rats when the suspense flags. Geer, Ecclesia, Eastman and Monnier are Sopkiw's sidekicks.

d/co-s Martin Dolman (Sergio Martino) p Luciano Martino co-s Julian Berry, Gabriel Rossini c Giancarlo Ferrando se Paolo Ricci lp Michael Sopkiw, Valentine Monnier, Roman Geer, George Eastman, Louis Ecclesia, Anna Kanakis, Edmund Purdom

Dune

(DINO DE LAURENTIIS PRODUCTIONS/U) Todd AO 140 (136) min

A brave attempt to bring Frank Herbert's novel, a landmark of modern Science Fiction, to the screen, *Dune* finally fails, ironically because Lynch is too faithful to the sprawling work to do it justice. At various times a project for Roger Corman, Ridley Scott and Alexandro Jodorowsky (who got the closest of the three to making it), the film was finally offered to Lynch who in *Eraserhead* (1978) demonstrated a similar cosmic imagination to Herbert's, albeit on a far more intimate scale. Thus, it is all the more surprising that as well such bizarre creations as the maggot-like Supreme Being, the giant sandworms and (most successful of all) McMillan's bloated villain, Lynch opts for a relatively straightforward narrative in which much of the complex political underpinning of Herbert's world is presented in an expository rather than dramatic fashion. As a result much of the film, its breathtaking visuals notwithstanding, is dramatically flat.

MacLachlan is Paul Atreides, whose family is given the governorship of the desert planet of Dune on which is mined the spice *melange* – the key commodity of life. However, on their arrival on Dune, the Atreides family is virtually wiped out by McMillan's Evil Baron Harkonnen and MacLachlan flees to the desert where he unites the Fremen tribesmen and sets out to wrest control of Dune from the Harkonnen family. However, too much screen time is given to the religious underpinnings – the idea of MacLachlan as a Messiah and the feudal pageantry of Herbert's world – of this simple adventure story on a grand scale. Similarly, Lynch wastes his strong supporting cast (which includes the likes of Ferrer, Sting, Annis and Phillips) in a barrage of cameo roles that only serve to clutter and further confuse the narrative.

d/s David Lynch p Raffaella De Laurentiis c Freddie Francis se Carlo Rambaldi, Barry Nolan lp Francesca Annis, Leonardo Cimino, Jose Ferrer, Kyle MacLachlan, Sting, Sian Phillips, Kenneth McMillan, Max Von Sydow, Dean Stockwell

The Ewok Adventure aka Caravan of Courage

(LUCASFILMS/KORTY FILMS) 120 (97) min

Little but an excuse to put the cuddly Ewoks on display for what might be called the nursery audience, this unsophisticated adventure story – two children, Walker and Miller, rescue their parents from the giant Gorak with the help of a tribe of Ewoks – is utterly charmless. Much shortened after its initial previews,

Kyle MacLachan (left) and Sting do battle in Dune.

and hence in need of Ives' narration to explain what is happening, the film is a betrayal of the innocence and cinematic imagination of the **Star Wars** (1977) trilogy at its best. In their place, writer Carrou opts for sub-Disney heroics which director Korty fleshes out in the sketchiest of fashions.

d/c John Korty   *p* Thomas G. Smith   *s* Bob Carrou
se Michael Pangrazio   *lp* Burl Ives (narrator), Eric Walker, Warwick Davis, Aubree Miller, Fionnula Flanagan, Guy Boyd

Firestarter (U) 114 min

Because her parents took part in an unethical drug experiment conducted by a covert US government agency, little Barrymore has the power to set fire to anything and anyone when she gets angry, and might conceivably be able to 'crack the world in half, like a plate'. With her slightly psychic father (Keith), she is hunted down by the nattily dressed Establishment bad guys and imprisoned in a research station. After much child abuse, All Hell (predictably) Breaks Loose as she unlooses fireballs and destroys spy chief Sheen's headquarters in a traditional mini-inferno.

An obvious adaptation of one of Stephen King's effective but unexceptional shockers – like many of his psi-based stories, it takes a Science Fiction concept and plays it as a cross between horror and blockbusting thriller – this film proves unable to bring to the screen the many things in the novel which do work. John Rainbird, the hideously scarred American Indian psychopathic secret agent, is unforgettably disturbing in print (and would seem to have been written for B-movie villain Richard Lynch) but, as hammed by Scott, he comes across as an almost comic figure. Similarly the lesser characters, King's touching representatives of fragile ordinariness in the book, come over as jus' plain folks refugees from *The Waltons*, played with an 'aw shucks' twang by Keith, Carney and Fletcher. Director Lester has more control over the endless inferno stunts than over his temperamental cast, but his sure hand with action and a few effective moments in the first half-hour cannot do much for this stodgy, repetitive, slow burn of a movie.

d Mark L. Lester   *p* Frank Capra Jr   *s* Stanley Mann
c Giuseppe Ruzzolini   *se* Mike Wood, Jeff Jarvis   *lp* Drew Barrymore, George C. Scott, David Keith, Heather Locklear, Martin Sheen, Art Carney, Louise Fletcher, Freddie Jones, Moses Gunn, Antonio Fargas

Forbrydelsens Element *aka* The Element of Crime
(PER HOLST FILMPRODUKTION; DEN) 104 min

'Do you believe I'm in the middle of Europe screwing a Volkswagon 9200?' asks a voice-over, as cop hero Elphick makes love with strumpet Lai on the bonnet of a car in an amber-tinted rainstorm. The semi-retired investigator is summoned from a Cairo of whirling ceiling fans to a Europe of floods, dereliction and rampant skinheads to solve a series of child murders. Employing Professor Knight's theories of empathetic detection, Elphick gets on the trail of the murderer and ultimately becomes him. Like **Alphaville** (1965), this finds a fantastical future in contemporary locations, using areas of Copenhagen shot entirely in shades of yellow to represent a continent struck by the same type of ambiguous, possibly mystical disaster that had blighted the France of *Le Dernier Combat* (1983). While the film has something of the feel of J. G. Ballard's more abstract Science Fictions – the uneasy feel coming perhaps from the use of a British cast who speak peculiar English among accented continentals – it suffers from a somnolent pace.

Explaining the colour scheme, von Trier remarked that Denmark was known only for blue films, 'so I think I make a yellow one'. *Epidemic* (1987), von Trier's follow-up, tackles similar themes, and embeds its Science Fiction vision of a plague-devastated Europe in a film-within-a-film section.

d/co-s Lars von Trier   *p* Per Holst   *co-s* Niels Vørsel   *c* Tom Elling   *se* Peter Høimark   *lp* Michael Elphick, Me Me Lai, Esmond Knight, Jerrold Wells, Ahmed El Shenawi, Astrid Henning-Jensen, Janos Hersko

Iceman (U) pv 99 min

An arctic oil-drilling team discovers the perfectly preserved body of a Neanderthal man (Lone). He is revived at a nearby cryogenics facility, where a conflict arises between deep-freeze surgeon Crouse, who sees the find as a way of furthering her science, and anthropologist Hutton, who wants to study Lone's prehistoric way of life. Like its scientists, the film has a lot of trouble thinking of something to do with its Neanderthal once it has got through the elaborate and interesting process of reviving him. The opening sequences are stunning, with crystal-clear photography of awesome Arctic locations, tense and authentic scientific small-talk, an underplayed and convincing set of conflicts within the scientific team, and a script that takes care of all the scientific footnotes through the well-staged, not-too-incredible defrosting scene. However, once the iceman is up and about – placed in a convenient vivarium for study – the film has a melodramatic torment-and-escape plot that serves to cut off any more interesting avenues of drama.

Thanks to Lone's perky and inventive performance, the film manages to present an anthropologically realistic, non-clichéd view of the caveman. The prehistoric survivor proves as curious and sociable as ex-hippie scientist Hutton, introducing himself with a grunted name before the anthropologist has even tried to establish contact, and enthusiastically banging a rock during a campfire singalong of late sixties songs. In contrast to the lumbering primitivism of *Quest for Fire* (1982), the film allows its Neanderthal to define his proto-humanity through quite sophisticated behaviour, displaying resigned understanding when Hutton refuses to let him buy Crouse with a shiny piece of plumbing, or scratching a picture of his wife and children in the earth. But the finale, with Lone running amok and dying in the snow, is a throwback to the monster-on-the-loose silliness of *Trog* (1971).

d Fred Schepisi   *p* Patrick Palmer, Norman Jewison   *s* Chip Proser, John Drimmer   *c* Ian Baker   *se* Michael Westmore   *lp* Timothy Hutton, John Lone, Lindsay Crouse, Josef Sommer, David Strathairn, Philip Akin, Danny Glover, James Tolkan

The Ice Pirates (MGM/UA) 94 min

Given that the space opera genre inaugurated by **Star Wars** (1977) has largely been concerned with locating the elements of familiar, action-oriented genres in pulp Science Fiction settings, it is hardly surprising to find here that streamlined space cruisers are manned by a rowdy crew of cutlass-waving swashbucklers in knee-boots. Pirate Urich and his lusty crew specialize in raiding the convoys of Carradine's Templars, which carry vast chunks of the ice upon which the sect has a monopoly, but are only too keen on setting out in search of a near-legendary, water-rich planet. Although the conceit is stretched a mite thin by the slightly-too-broad comic hijinx, this does quite cleverly use the leftovers of the pirate movie in an outer space context, mixing high- and low-tech to allow for charming corollaries, both major (Huston's performance as a lean pirate queen is worthy of *The Black Swan*, 1942, or *Anne of the Indies*, 1951) and minor (the livestock given free range of the spaceship).

The production has a definite hand-me-down feel, from the re-use of the miniature city that wasn't very convincing in **Logan's Run** (1976) to the clips from **Rollerball** (1975) that provide entertainment for the space travellers. But while those earlier MGM movies failed to grasp the potential for the eccentric within pot-boiling Science Fiction, *The Ice Pirates* jauntily throws around ideas with an insane light-heartedness that is perfectly in the pulp tradition. The finale is especially pleasing with its mix of hokum heroism, cheap laughs and scientific playfulness, as the characters enter a time-warp which ages the hero to the point where Urich is replaced by Hank Worden, but which allows the good guys to be saved by a son who has been conceived, born and grown to dashing manhood in two minutes' screen time.

d/co-s Stewart Raffill   *p* John Foreman   *co-s* Stanford Sherman   *c* Matthew F. Leonetti   *se* Russ Hessey, Gene Grigg, Michael McCracken, Shawn McCracken   *lp* Robert Urich, Mary Crosby, Michael D. Roberts, Anjelica Huston, John Matuszak, Ron Perlman, John Carradine, Natalie Core

Impulse (ABC) 99(91) min

Sutcliffe, USA, is just another ordinary, agrarian Mid-West community where people chug beer in a dingy little saloon and get their ailments treated by the folksy old doctor (Cronyn) who brought them into the world. Nothing ever happens, until an earthquake ruptures some subterranean toxic waste storage tanks and everyone starts acting strangely. When her mother attempts an over-the-phone suicide, guilt-ridden dancer Tilly returns home with her doctor boyfriend (Matheson) in tow, and gets involved again in her family's economic and emotional depressions. A respectable citizen takes a leak on Matheson's car on Main Street at noon; a frustrated queue-stander suddenly decides to rob the bank; Tilly's old flame (Paxton) proves his love for her by breaking his fingers; a harassed mother watches while her children try to burn their best friend to death ('You think it's easy having kids?' she whines); the Sheriff shoots dead a kid who has broken into a parking meter; and Cronyn treats an incontinent patient, who is getting on his nerves, by suffocation.

A quieter version of **The Crazies** (1973), this never does pay off with the expected apocalypse, although the gradual accumulation of odd detail is affecting. In the film's best twist, it's the normal Matheson – not the brooding Paxton – who becomes the last-reel threat to the heroine, a change signalled by a creepy little moment as the ostensible hero poses in front of the mirror with one of Paxton's macho leather jackets.

d Graham Baker   *p* Tim Zinnemann   *s* Bart Davis, Don Carlos Dunaway   *c* Thomas Del Ruth   *se* Tom Fisher, Greg Curtis   *lp* Meg Tilly, Tim Matheson, John Karlen, Hume Cronyn, Bill Paxton, Amy Stryker, Claude Earl Jones, Robert Wightman

Mary Crosby (centre) and Robert Urich (right) flee from The Ice Pirates.

The Last Starfighter (LORIMAR/U) pv 101 min

A cheap and cheerful **Star Wars** (1977) clone of an actioner blessed with a strong cast and a simple idea, *The Last Starfighter* is far better a film than it should be. Guest is the video ace, Preston (a superb performance) the humanoid alien who invites him to help defend the Empire from Snow and his renegades once he's seen Guest's prowess on the 'Starfighter' video game and O'Herlihy is Guest's reptile-like navigator. The replacement of model animation with computer animation for the outer-space dogfights lessens their drama, but then there is never any doubt that the Empire will be saved once the over-elaborate plot, which includes a robot replacing Guest on Earth while he's in deep space, has been unwound to the full.

Writer Betuel subsequently graduated to directing with the equally engaging **My Science Project** (1985).

d Nick Castle   *p* Gary Adelson, Edward O. Denault   *s* Jonathan Betuel   *se* Kevin Pike, Michael Lantieri, Darrell D. Pritchett, James Dale Camomille, Joseph C. Sasgen   *lp* Lance Guest, Dan O'Herlihy, Robert Preston, Catherine Mary Stewart, Barbara Bossom, Norman Snow

The Lost Empire (HARWOOD) 78 min

A serial-style programmer made with a lot of dash and humour, this pits three hard-boiled adventuresses against Dr Sin Do (Scrimm), an immortal mad doctor who has an island enclave full of superscientific death equipment. Vincz is a tough female cop, de la Croix an Indian priestess with mystical inclinations, and Aames a fluffy-haired, gutsy ex-convict. Mixing jokey feminism with Russ Meyer-style busty exploitation, the film tries to have it both ways, but is at its most enjoyable when playing around with the leftovers of the Fu Manchu or *kung fu* genre. Wynorski, a Corman protégé, later specialized in sequels and remakes.

d/p/s Jim Wynorski   *c* Jacques Haitkin   *se* Steve Neill, Ernest D. Farino   *lp* Melanie Vincz, Raven de la Croix, Angela Aames, Paul Coufos, Bob Tessier, Angus Scrimm, Angelique Pettyjohn

Dan O'Herlihy as the gung-ho alien in the cheap and cheerful The Last Starfighter.

Night of the Comet (ATLANTIC 9000)   95 min

A witty pastiche of fifties Science Fiction films, from the minatory introductory narration to its judicious use of genre clichés such as the heroine being saved because she's with her boyfriend pirating a print of **It Came from Outer Space** (1953) when those exposed to the light of a passing comet are either turned to piles of dust or homicidal zombies, *Night of the Comet* is a wonderful example of what can be done with a low budget and high expectations. The storyline is simplicity itself – teenagers battle zombies in a deserted Los Angeles and then set about laying down the foundations of civilization. Similarly the special effects are limited to red filters and a few hand-me-down zombies. But writer/director Eberhardt brings his characters to life with such verve that the film is compelling. In particular, the slow transformation of the hedonistic teenagers into middle-class conservatives conscious of their responsibility to mankind is finely handled, as is the repeated inversion of stereotypes, such as Beltran's Chicano and Woronov's tragic *femme fatale*, while Lewis, eyes twitching like mad even under his dark glasses makes the perfect mad scientist.

d/s Thom Eberhardt   *p* Andrew Lane, Wayne Crawford
c Arthur Albert   *se* Court Wizard, John Eggett
lp Robert Beltran, Catherine Mary Stewart, Kelli Maroney, Sharon Farrell, Mary Woronov, Geoffrey Lewis

Nineteen Eighty-Four

(UMBRELLA-ROSENBLOOM/VIRGIN FILMS; GB)   110 min
Launched, in the words of its executive producer, Marvin J. Rosenblum, with 'the greatest marketing hook that there ever was for a movie: a film of *Nineteen Eighty-Four* made *in* 1984', in retrospect most of the film's successes (and some of its failures) belong to the marketing department. Thus, the film was actually finished and (just) shown in 1984, featured the last performance of Burton and, on the debit side, the debate about its score – after Dominic Muldowney's music was used in the previews it was largely replaced by music from the rock duo the Eurythmics at the behest of Virgin – kept the film in the news

John Hurt looks at the future in 1984.

during the first half of 1985. Turning to the film itself, apart from the bold device of imagining the future in terms of what life might look like 40 years on seen from 1948 (the year George Orwell completed the book) director Radford has, like Michael Anderson before him, trivialized Orwell's novel. His film is far superior to Anderson's 1956 version, but, like that, reduces what was intended as a savage satire on the growth of authoritarianism, what was clearly a political work, into a melodrama pure and simple.

Hurt is Winston Smith, the doubter who turns to self-expression (his diary) and then love out of boredom with the ways of Big Brother before being re-educated by Burton and left to live out his life as a wreck, and Hamilton the obscure object of his desire.

d/s Michael Radford   *p* Simon Perry   *c* Roger Deakins
se Ian Scoones   *lp* John Hurt, Richard Burton, Suzanna Hamilton, Cyril Cusak, George Fisher, James Walker

The Philadelphia Experiment

(NEW WORLD PICTURES/CINEMA GROUP VENTURE/
NEW PICTURES GROUP)   101 min
Based on a work of 'speculative non-fiction' by the authors of *The Bermuda Triangle*, William I. Moore and Charles Berlitz, this is a silly piece of hokum. That said, Raffill (replacing John Carpenter, who became executive producer) undercuts the complex time-warp structure behind his material to produce a straight-ahead adventure yarn, a sort of **The Final Countdown** (1980) in reverse. In this he is aided by the central performances of Parée as one of the seamen from 1943 yanked into 1984 when an experiment to make ships invisible to radar goes wrong and Allen (whose character name, Allison Hayes, is a homage to the star of **Attack of the 50 Foot Woman**, 1958) as the spunky girl who helps Parée and shipmate Di Cicco. Treating the plotline – having been sent to the future by Christmas' failed experiment Parée discovers an elderly Christmas about to conclude a potentially more disastrous experiment – as little but an excuse for a series of adventures and culture clashes – confronted with television of the eighties Parée decides he's happier with reruns of Abbott and Costello movies! – Raffill manages to produce a better movie than the material deserves.

d Stewart Raffill   p Joel B. Michaels, Douglas Curtis
s William Gray, Michael Janover   c Dick Bush   se Special
Effects Unlimited Inc   lp Michael Pareé, Nancy Allen,
Bobby Di Cicco, Michael Currie, Louise Latham, Kene
Holliday, Joe Dorsey

Red Dawn (VALKYRIE/MGM/UA) 114 min

In the near future, Russian paratroops land in the Rockies,
and the United States, its missile bases taken out with surgical
nuclear strikes, is occupied by Soviet and Cuban troops. The
youth of a small town – played by 'Brat Pack' regulars
Swayze, Sheen, Howell, Thompson and Grey – takes to the
hills and forms a resistance movement in the spirit of Milius'
beloved Mountain Men and Teddy Roosevelt's Rough Riders.

A controversial film for its supposed rabid anti-
communism, this is actually a rightist libertarian's wish-
fulfilment fantasy of a situation. In it Americans can be the
underdog movie heroes again, rather than the oppressor, as is
pointed out by the character of the Cuban commander
(O'Neal), who is unable to make the switch from insurgence
to occupation that this latest posting has entailed. Merely
competent as an action movie, the film has unfortunately
camp cameos from dignified archetypal Americans like
Johnson, Stanton (who howls 'avenge me' from behind the
fence of his internment camp) and Boothe, but actually builds
up a fairly convincing picture of a Soviet America, where
Alexander Nevski (1938) is playing at the town's cinema and
the rebel faction is named after a high school football team. A
similar scenario was used in the teleseries *Amerika*.

d/co-s John Milius   p Buzz Feitshans, Barry Beckerman
co-s Kevin Reynolds   c Ric Waite   se Tom Fisher, Dale
L. Martin   lp Patrick Swayze, C. Thomas Howell, Lea
Thompson, Charlie Sheen, Darren Dalton, Jennifer Grey,
Brad Savage, Doug Toby, Ben Johnson, Harry Dean Stanton,
William Smith, Ron O'Neal, Vladek Sheybal, Powers Boothe

Repo Man (EDGE CITY PRODUCTIONS) 92 min

A bizarre and wholly engaging mix of Science Fiction and *film
noir* tied together with an acerbic strand of social comment,
Repo Man is a striking directorial début for Cox. Dean Stanton is
the repossession man who inhabits the murky underworld of
Los Angeles and Estevez his apprentice. They hear of a battered
'64 Chevy Malibu, owned by crazed nuclear scientist Harris,
the boot of which emits a blinding white light when opened that
is sought after by various government agents, led by the metal-
handed Barnes, the Rodriguez brothers and assorted LA punks,
and set out to repossess it. Superbly shot by Muller and
organized by Cox, who handles the complex narrative with
ease, *Repo Man*, for all its cinematic borrowings, has a style that
is wholly its own. This is especially evident in the damning view
of the superannuated hippies, such as Estevez's parents
perpetually stoned as they watch the broadcasts of TV evan-
gelist Reverend Larry (Bruce White), who exist on the fringes
of, but know nothing of, the murky world around them.

d/s Alex Cox   p Jonathan Wacks, Peter McCarthy
c Robby Muller   se Robby Knott, Roger George   lp Emilio
Estevez, Harry Dean Stanton, Tracey Walter, Susan Barnes,
Fox Harris, Del Zamora, Eddie Velez, Olivia Barash

Runaway (TRI-STAR/DELPHI PRODUCTIONS) 100 (97) min

An engaging effort from Crichton, *Runaway* makes up for its
over-reliance on clichés (a villain who wouldn't be out of place
in a thirties serial, the black sidekick and Selleck's vertigo, for
example) by sheer visual exuberance. Set in the near future, the
film has Selleck as a world-weary cop responsible for dealing
with defective robots and Simmons (neatly parodying his former persona in the rock group Kiss) as the evil genius set on
transforming domestic robots into killing machines. Superficially similar to **Blade Runner** (1982), in fact the film's
theme, summed up by Selleck's comment, 'Let me tell you the
way the world is. Nothing works right', is akin to that of

*'Brat Pack' regulars
Patrick Swayze
(left), C. Thomas
Howell (centre) and
Charlie Sheen as
American guerrillas
fighting the Commies
in the pre-glasnost
Red Dawn.*

Emilio Estevez at the wheel in Repo Man, *a delicious meld of Science Fiction,* film noir *and punk music.*

Crichton's first feature **Westworld** (1973). Sadly, apart from the lengthy climax in which Selleck is trapped in a freight elevator and menaced by clackety robot spiders, Crichton does little to illustrate his theme. The result is a minor film.

d/s Michael Crichton *p* Michael Rachmill *c* John A. Alonzo *se* John Thomas, Special Effects Unlimited, Broggie Elliott Animation *lp* Tom Selleck, Cynthia Rhodes, Gene Simmons, Kirstie Alley, Stan Shaw, Joey Cramer, G.W. Bailey

Seksmisja *aka* The Sex Mission
(ZESPOLY FILMOWE, KADR; POL) 128(121,90) min
A decidedly odd film, *Seksmisja* raises the question of what function Science Fiction films have in Eastern Europe and Poland in particular. On the one hand it seems to be a corrosive comedy about a future Poland based on deceit with the populace as mindless zombies, and as such is presumably highly topical. Another view might see the film as a feminist comedy in which the film's world, a future in which men have been banished and history rewritten so that Einstein was a woman, Adam tempted Eve in the Garden of Eden and so forth, and the male heroes' position when they wake up from an hibernation experiment to this women only world, is intended as a parody of the present. And lastly it can be seen as a *Carry On* type farce with Lukaszewicz and Stuhr as the males who finally ogle and bed their way back to the natural order (in which males are superior). Certainly the film offers evidence for all three readings. Thus, for instance there is so much female flesh on display it is hard to imagine the film-makers did not see the project as simply titillating its male audiences, and yet the drift of the film is clearly critical of the world it imagines. Accordingly, one is left thinking that either the confusions in the film are simply that, confusions, or that, from a Western perspective, an essential interpretative key is missing.

Although Machulski's future does not compare to the high-tech of recent Hollywood Science Fiction, the script is erratic (especially in the last section) and the acting (in particular that of Stuhr) is weak, the film is far better than one might expect given the dottiness of its central premise.

d/co-s Juliusz Machulski *co-s* Jolanta Hartwig, Pavel Hajny *c* Jerzy Lukaszewicz *lp* Olgierd Lukaszewicz, Jerzy Stuhr, Bozena Strjkowna, Bogulslaw Pawelec, Hanna Stankowna

Star Trek III - The Search for Spock
(PAR/CINEMA GROUP VENTURE) pv70mm 105 min
The third and silliest of the *Star Trek* movies, *Star Trek III* is also in many ways the most interesting. A direct sequel to the previous outing, **Star Trek II - The Wrath of Kahn** (1982) which saw the death of Spcck (Nimoy), this film is structured around the absence of Nimoy's Spock, seen throughout the film in teasing glimpses, and culminates with his re-creation. What makes all this the more interesting is that the film is directed by Nimoy (not unsurprisingly with real conviction) and that the film's victim is the series nominal hero, Shatner's Kirk, who in the course of the film loses his ship, son and career that Spock might mysteriously be reborn. Circling around this pathological storyline is a subplot in which the series regulars take on the Klingons lead by Lloyd's Kruge, and numerous special effects.

d Leonard Nimoy *p* Harve Bennett *s* John Hickridge *c* Charles Correll *se* Bob Dawson, Rocky Gehr *lp* Leonard Nimoy, William Shatner, DeForest Kelly, James Doohan, Walter Koenig, James B. Sikking, Christopher Lloyd, Dame Judith Anderson

Starman (COL/DELPHI PRODUCTIONS II) 115 min
The opening sequence, Voyager II rolling through the galaxy with its messages of goodwill and friendship to the strains of the Rolling Stones singing 'I Can't Get No Satisfaction', momentarily suggests that this might be another **Dark Star** (1974) from director Carpenter. Such hopes are soon defused, but if *Starman* is a minor film, unlike **The Thing** (1982), it is at least modest rather than pretentious and in Bridges' alien in human form it has a genuinely sympathetic character. A more intimate film than its inspiration, **Close Encounters of the Third Kind** (1977), it follows the attempts of Bridges, who's taken the form of Allen's recently deceased husband, to get back to his rendezvous point while being chased by the authorities, represented by the bellicose Jaeckel and liberal Smith. The developing love between Bridges and Allen (both of whom turn in fine performances) is imaginatively handled, however the chase itself, like the finale which apes that of *Close Encounters*, is all too predictable.

d John Carpenter *p* Larry J. Franco *s* Bruce A. Evans, Raynold Gideon *se* Industrial Light & Magic, Rick Baker *lp* Jeff Bridges, Karen Allen, Charles Martin Smith, Richard Jaeckel, Robert Phalen, Tony Edwards

Supergirl (ARTISTRY LTD/CANTHARUS PRODUCTIONS; GB)
pv70mm 124 min
This is an insipid addition to the Salkind Brothers' series of films devoted to the exploits of The Man of Steel that commenced with **Superman** (1978). Significantly, whereas in the Superman films the fate of the Universe was seen from the perspective of Earth, and Margot Kidder's Lois Lane was a spikey go-getter of a reporter, Slater's Supergirl is little but an innocent ingénue and the fate of the Universe is seen from the perspective of Krypton (in actual fact one of its 'satellites', Argo). Thus, as one critic has put it, what 'by all the conventions of the genre ought at least to be a Manichean struggle between Good and Evil ... becomes a banal case of romantic rivalry, the clash of the Titans reduced to a cat fight over a landscape gardener'.

Jeff Bridges and Karen Allen as the star-crossed lovers of Starman.

Slater is Supergirl/Linda Clark who comes to Earth in search of the Omegahedron, a Kryptonite power source which has fallen into the hands of Dunaway's amateur witch, and Ward the gardener Slater 'steals' from Dunaway (whose camp performance is the best in the film) so unleashing the Omegahedron's powers. Sundry visits to the Phantom Zone and cameos from the likes of O'Toole and Farrow fail to lift the film while the special effects, the flying sequences apart, testify to the Salkinds' desire, like Sam Katzman before them, to milk the Superman legend at minimal cost.

d Jeannot Szwarc *p* Timothy Burrill *s* David Odell
c Alan Hume *se* John Evans *lp* Helen Slater, Faye Dunaway, Peter O'Toole, Mia Farrow, Brenda Vaccaro, Peter Cook, Simon Ward

SwordKill *aka* **Ghost Warrior** (EMPIRE) 81(80) min
A swift cash-in on **Iceman** (1984) that is actually rather more entertaining than the model. Fujioka is the samurai, preserved in ice since 1552, who is revived in Los Angeles and gets involved with mad scientists, street gangs and police dragnets. The opening, in the snowbound wastes of medieval Japan, is decidedly cod-Kurosawa, but once the film gets to the present day its modern situations cleverly echo those that the hero faced in the past. With amiable two-dimensional performances, crisply directed fight scenes, and Ahlberg's unfussy visual style, this has an enjoyable comic book feel as it rips through its unlikely script. A bonus is provided by an elaborate, mock-Japanese score turned in by Richard Band, the most prolific and talented composer in mid-eighties exploitation movies.

d Larry Carroll *p* Charles Band *s* Tim Curnen *c* Mac Ahlberg *se* Roger George, Bob Short *lp* Hiroshi Fujioka, John Calvin, Janet Julian, Charles Lampkin, Frank Schuller, Bill Morey, Andy Wood

The Terminator
(CINEMA 84/PACIFIC WESTERN PRODUCTIONS) 107 min
Unlike Italian exploitation films of the eighties which for the most part are simply low-budget versions of their models, *The Terminator*, though it borrows freely (mostly from **Mad Max II**, 1981 and **Blade Runner**, 1982), does so with a wit and elegance completely missing from a film like **1990: I Guerrieri del Bronx** (1982). Both producer Hurd and director Cameron who wrote the film together are veterans of Roger Corman's New World productions: Cameron worked on the special effects of **Escape from New York** (1981) and **Battle Beyond the Stars** (1980) and Hurd was Corman's assistant before getting involved in production.

Schwarzenegger is the part-man, part-machine sent back to 1984 from a nuclear-devastated 2029 ruled by Machines to eliminate the mother of a yet-to-be-born saviour of mankind, Biehn the guerilla fighter from 2029 who tries to stop him and Hamilton the damsel in distress. All are excellent as are the special effects (especially Schwarzenegger's phoenix-like rebirth from a blazing wreck at the film's climax). But it is the relentless narrative drive of the movie, in which incident is piled on incident, that is so thrilling.

d/co-s James Cameron *p/co-s* Gale Ann Hurd *c* Adam Greenberg *se* Fantasy II Film Effects *lp* Arnold Schwarzenegger, Michael Biehn, Linda Hamilton, Paul Winfield, Lance Henrikson, Dick Miller, Bess Mota

Trancers *aka* Future Cop
(LEXYN PRODUCTIONS) 85(76) min
An imaginative exploitation pic, this is far superior to Band's previous outings (which include **Laserblast**, 1978, **Parasite**, 1982 and **Metalstorm: The Destruction of Jared-Syn**, 1983). Thomerson is the embittered cop from the future who returns to the Los Angeles of 1985 to put paid to Stefani's time

Arnold Schwarzenegger is The Terminator.

travelling mystic who plans to eliminate the ancestors of the benign rulers of Los Angeles of 2247 with the aid of his army of zombie-like 'trancers'. The plot is over-complex and highly unlikely but the narrative line is pleasingly taut and the characters, especially Hunt as the bemused Girl Friday who discovers Thomerson has 'borrowed' her boyfriend's body, are given space to breathe. Similarly, the quotes from films as diverse as **Rabid** (1976) and *Chinatown* (1974) are well done.

d/p Charles Band *s* Danny Bilson, Paul De Meo *c* David Boyd *lp* Tim Thomerson, Helen Hunt, Michael Stefani, Art Le Fleur, Thelma Hopkins, Richard Herd, Anne Seymour

2010 (MGM/UA) pv70mm 116 min
The long-awaited sequel to **2001** (1968), *2010* begins as though it intends to answer the questions posed by the earlier film only to quickly descend to a glossy adventure outing in which the mysteries of what is happening amongst the rings of Jupiter are paralleled by the threat of the destruction of the Earth as tension grows between the USA and USSR.

Scheider and Mirren are the leaders of a joint American-Russian expedition sent to examine the spaceship 'Discovery' still in orbit around Jupiter. They are vouchsafed visions of Dullea and warnings to leave quickly, before their persistence leads to Jupiter's destruction (rather than the Earth's). Although Hyams' functional direction (which is in complete contrast to Stanley Kubrick's stately approach) defuses the more mystical elements of Arthur C. Clarke's original novel, his script fails to find anything but the highly unoriginal unite-or-die theme to replace it with. As a result the film is forever in the shadow of Kubrick's earlier work, to which it appears to be little but an unconsidered appendage.

d/p/s/c Peter Hyams   *lp* Roy Scheider, Helen Mirren, Keir Dullea, John Lithgow, Bob Balaban, Madolyn Smith

1985

The Adventures of Mark Twain

(HARBOUR TOWN)   90 min

In 1910, determined that his death shall coincide, as did his birth, with the passing of Halley's Comet, Sam Clemens/Mark Twain (voiced by Whitmore) constructs a Jules Verne-style flying machine that is half-dirigible and half-riverboat. Tom Sawyer, Becky Thatcher and Huck Finn, Twain's most famous characters, get wind of this marvel and, along with Huck's faithful frog Homer, stow away on board. They are treated to the great man's reminiscences and to dramatizations of some of his stories ('The Celebrated Jumping Frog of Calaveras County', 'The Private Lives of Adam and Eve'), but begin to suspect that the Mysterious Stranger, a representative of Clemens' darker side, is also aboard.

The first full-length feature in Claymation – the dimensional animation process that Vinton has perfected in his short *Closed Mondays* and in the Nome King sequences of *Return to Oz* (1985) – this is technically a triumph, with rich characterizations, fabulous backgrounds, and fascinating Plasticine movements. Furthermore, the film has the courage to tackle 'difficult' material, mixing whimsy with philosophy, rather than take the easy Spielberg-Lucas razzle-dazzle route. Despite a peppering of Twain's crusty wit, the film is a bit gloomy for the children at which it seems to be aimed, dealing as it does more with the complicated misanthropies of Twain's later books than the nostalgic childishness of his most famous works. It's also rather lopsided in its story construction, and probably requires of the viewer too much knowledge of the great man's works.

d/p/se Will Vinton   *s* Susan Shadburne   *c* (uncredited) *lp* James Whitmore, Michele Mariana, Gary Krug, Chris Ritchie

Baby – The Secret of the Lost Legend

(TOUCHSTONE)   95 min

Unscrupulous palaentologist McGoohan discovers that there are dinosaurs still living in a remote stretch of African jungle, and sets out to track one down. However, leggy zoologist Young and her cute husband Katt get there first, and make friends with Mama, Papa and Baby Brontosaurus. In the millions of years since their supposed extinction, the brontosauri have apparently evolved the kind of monogamous sit-com family unknown among reptiles, but familiar from all those Disney True-Life adventures.

This is another attempt to adapt the successful formula of **E.T.: The Extra-Terrestrial** (1982), in which an orphaned special effects creation is adopted by the liberal human heroes and protected from a caricatured villain. It falls down because the lumbering robot monsters are never convincingly alive, and because the soggy screenplay reinforces any number of groundless stereotypes – from the belief that it's all right to take off your bra or be machine-gunned in a children's movie if you're black, to the common fallacy that all Englishmen called 'Nigel' are effete wimps. Notable only for McGoohan's ham villainy and Young's fetching jungle wear.

d B.W.L. Norton   *p* Jonathan T. Taplin   *s* Clifford and Ellen Green   *c* John Alcott   *se* Isidoro Raponi, Roland Tantin   *lp* William Katt, Sean Young, Patrick McGoohan, Julian Fellowes, Kyalo Mativo, Hugh Quarshie

Back to the Future

(U/AMBLIN ENTERTAINMENT)   116 min

Deservedly a huge box-office success. At the centre of this pointed piece of nostalgia is the charming notion that the repressed fifties were a paradise compared to the liberal eighties. This is best seen in the lovingly created backdrops to the action. Thus the small town cinema that in 1955 is showing Ronald Reagan in *Cattle Queen of Montana* (1954) has become a porno-house in 1985, the car showroom selling Studebakers in 1955 sells Toyotas in 1985 and the comfortable drugstore becomes an aerobics gym.

The storyline is simplicity itself: teenager Fox travels back to the fifties in a Heath-Robinson/De Lorean time machine, courtesy of joyfully crazed scientist Lloyd, to make a man of his high-school slob of a father (Glover) and so make him a fit partner for his mother (Thompson) who, to complicate matters, falls for Fox, a very 'knowing' young man by fifties standards. Masterfully orchestrated by Zemkis, who makes of his hero a knight in shining armour rather than the Merlin Jones lookalike he might have been in other hands, the film neatly alternates between knockabout humour and nostalgia before sending Fox, his mission accomplished, 'back to the future'.

d/co-s Robert Zemkis   *co-p/co-s* Bob Gale   *co-p* Neil Canton   *c* Dean Cunedy   *se* Kevin Pike   *lp* Michael J. Fox, Christopher Lloyd, Crispin Glover, Lea Thompson, Claudia Wells, Thomas F. Wilson

Black Moon Rising   (NEW WORLD)   100(99) min

An old John Carpenter script from the seventies – witness some liftshaft-dangling *à la* **Dark Star** (1974) and Hawksian cameraderie as in *Assault on Precinct 13* (1976) – is here dressed up as an enjoyable high-tech *film noir*, with superthief Jones forced to go after the Black Moon, a streamlined car in which a macguffin has been concealed. Cokliss does well by the black and white visual scheme, poaching from *The Big Combo* (1955) a stunt in which a deaf character is killed in subjective silence, and the fine cast enjoy themselves in their hard-boiled roles, especially Hamilton as a Bacall-style heroine and Vaughn as the Establishment villain. Essentially a heist movie with Science Fiction gimmickry, it has a sustained and effective climax, which builds up to the spectacular aerial punchline of the Black Moon crashing through the air.

d Harley Cokliss   *p* Joel B. Michaels, Douglas Curtis *s* John Carpenter, Desmond Nakano, William Gray *c* Mischa Suslov   *se* Special Effects Unlimited   *lp* Tommy Lee Jones, Linda Hamilton, Robert Vaughn, Richard Jaeckel, Lee Ving, Bubba Smith, Dan Shor, William Sanderson, Keenan Wynn, Nick Cassavetes

Right: *The high-tech car of* Black Moon Rising.

Brazil

(BRAZIL PRODUCTIONS; GB)   142 min

Sharing a similar vision of the near future as **Nineteen Eighty-Four** (1984), a future full of forties trappings, but shot through with a wicked surrealism that is missing from Michael Radford's film, *Brazil* is undoubtedly Gilliam's best movie to date. Pryce is the mother-dominated hapless clerk who takes refuge in adolescent fantasies in which he is part-Icarus, part-Siegfried and wholly the hero *par excellence* only to be dragged slowly but surely into the oppressive machinations of a shaky bureaucracy threatened by anarchists. Like **The Time Bandits** (1981), full of nastiness and excremental humour, but far more organized, *Brazil* also benefits from a superb cast – Richardson's sleek bureaucrat, De Niro, the film's real super-hero, Holm as the paranoid department chief, Palin's torturer and, best of all, Helmond as Pryce's beauty-conscious mother bent on holding back the ravages of time – and a restrained script from Gilliam, Stoppard and McKeown. More surprising is the wistful edge to the film, highlighted in the evocative title song, and the longing for a return to more innocent times that lies behind the, often vicious, surface of the film.

d/co-s Terry Gilliam   *p* Arnon Michan   *co-s* Tom Stoppard, Charles McKeown   *c* Roger Pratt   *se* George Gibbs   *lp* Jonathan Pyrce, Robert De Niro, Michael Palin, Kim Greist, Katherine Helmond, Ian Holm, Ian Richardson

The Bride

(COL/DELPHI III PRODUCTIONS)   119 (118) min

An unsuccessful revision rather than a remake of the classic **The Bride of Frankenstein** (1935), Fonveille's script recasts Mary Shelley's classic novel as a modern fairy story with Beals as a decidedly modern woman. Sting (who shot to acting fame in director Roddam's *Quadrophenia*, 1979) is the arrogant Baron who lusts after his creation and Brown (a fine performance) the monster, but the acting honours go to Rappaport's vagabond dwarf who befriends Brown and the likes of Veruschka, Alexei Sayle and Quentin Crisp who all produce neat cameos. More jarring than the reinterpretation of the material is the look of the film which forgoes the gothic atmosphere more usually associated with the Frankenstein legend for a more intimate romantic feel only to then climax in the genre cliché of Brown and Beals collapsing in each other's arms on top of the castle Frankenstein.

d Franc Roddam   *p* Victor Drai   *s* Lloyd Fonveille
c Stephen H. Burum   *lp* Sting, Jennifer Beals, Clancy Brown, David Rappaport, Geraldine Page, Anthony Higgins

Chopping Mall *aka* Killbots

(CONCORDE/NEW HORIZON)   76 min

Patterned a bit too obviously on TV movie *Trapped* (1973), this enjoyable little suspense movie features a group of teenagers partying in a mall, who find themselves locked in with a trio of robot security guards that look like the mechanical creation from **Short Circuit** (1986), but which have gone haywire.

Despite its derivative nature and basic teens-getting-killed plot, the film is quite fun. Babyfat princess Maroney is, as in **Night of the Comet** (1984), a cute crackshot heroine ('My Dad's a Marine'), Bartel and Woronov do a clever cameo in their roles from *Eating Raoul* (1982), and Miller rides again in his 'Walter Paisley' persona from *A Bucket of Blood* (1959). The villainous robots move like Daleks, but display a sense of humour as they blurt out meaningless supermarket courtesies while they slaughter teenagers. The effects are exemplary for a low-budget production, with a finely crafted exploding head, although one notes the money-saving re-use of stock footage from **Attack of the Crab Monsters** (1956) and the theme song from *Streetwalkin'* (1984).

d/s Jim Wynorski   *p* Julie Corman   *c* Tom Richmond
se Robert Short   *lp* Kelli Maroney, Tony O'Dell, John Terlesky, Russell Todd, Barbara Crampton, Paul Bartel, Mary Woronov, Dick Miller, Gerrit Graham, Mel Welles

Escaping the future in swashbuckling fashion in Brazil.

Below: *Quentin Crisp (left) and Sting bring the perfect woman to life in* The Bride.

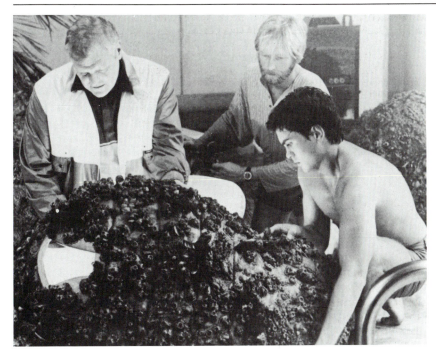

Brian Dennehey and Tyrone Power Jnr gaze in wonder at the dessicated body of a fellow Antarean in Cocoon

Cocoon

(FOX/ZANUCK BROWN PRODUCTIONS) 117 min

Clearly intended as another *Splash*, director Howard's summer hit of 1984, *Cocoon* for all its enjoyable whimsy, strains too hard (and borrows too lazily from other films) to be successful. Dennehey leads a quartet of aliens in human guise (that includes Raquel Welch's daughter Tahnee and Tyrone Power Jnr) whose mission is to revive and rescue a group of aliens lying underwater in boulder-like cocoons off the Florida coast. To do this, they specially treat the water of the indoor swimming pool of the house they've rented and which unbeknownst to them is the private playground of three members of a nearby retirement home, Ameche, Brimley (who gives the film's best performance) and Cronyn. As a result the three senior citizens are rejuvenated. It's at this point that Howard's handling of the plot turns coarse as the senior citizens turn to break dancing and the like. As a result, the essential innocence of the story is lost and the finale, with some thirty odd members of the retirement home travelling back with the aliens, is forced.

d Ron Howard *p* Richard D. Zanuck, David Brown, Lili Fini Zanuck *s* Tom Benedek, *c* Don Peterman *se* Industrial Light & Magic *lp* Don Ameche, Wilfred Brimley, Hume Cronyn, Brian Dennehey, Jack Gilford, Steve Guttenberg, Jessica Tandy

A Colpi di Luce *aka* Lightblast

(OVERSEAS FILMGROUP; IT) 85 min

Yet another inept outing from Italian action king Castellari, this stars Estrada (of the teleseries *Chips* fame) as the man given the task of saving San Francisco from evil scientist Pritchard and his deadly laser gun. The action sequences are well enough mounted and the actors are called on to do little but grin (Estrada) or leer (Pritchard) by way of characterization but all too quickly the silliness of the project becomes apparent.

d/co-s Enzo G. Castellari *p* Galliano Juso, Achille Manzotti *co-s* Tito Carpi *c* Sergi D'Offizi *lp* Erik Estrada, Michael Pritchard, Thomas Moore, Peggy Rowe, Bob Taylor

Creature (U/KINGS ROAD PRODUCTIONS) 107 min

A confused film, *Creature* seems unsure whether it's about scientist O'Toole's attempt to re-create his dead wife from cells which he's preserved for some 30 years, or his attempts to resus-

D.A.R.Y.L., child of the future

citate Madsen, the girlfriend of his assistant Spano, when she goes into a coma. Another strand is Hemingway who offers to help O'Toole out of love for him. O'Toole is suitably nutty as the scientist who loves American football almost as much as his dead wife, but the film's tone, which oscillates from light comedy to near-tragedy, makes the character too slight to take seriously at any level.

d Ivan Passer *p* Stephen Freidman *s* Jeremy Leven *c* Robbie Greenberg *lp* Peter O'Toole, Mariel Hemingway, Vincent Spano, Virginia Madsen, David Ogden Stiers, John Dehner, Karen Kopins

D.A.R.Y.L. (PAR) pv 99 min

Oliver is Daryl (Data Analyzing Robot Youth Lifeform) who finds refuge in the foster home run by Hurt and McKean only to have his 'natural' parents – research scientists Sommer and Walker – come to take him home in this lightweight Disney-esque offering. Efficiently made, though low on suspense, the film is at its best in the second half when Oliver shows off his robotic powers.

d Simon Wincer *p* John Heyman *s* David Ambrose, Allan Scott, Jeffrey Ellis *c* Frank Watts *se* Adrian Carr *lp* Mary Beth Hurt, Michael McKean, Barett Oliver, Kathryn Walker, Josef Sommer, Colleen Camp, Ron Frazier

Desert Warrior

(RODEO PRODUCTIONS) 85 min

Shot in the Philippines, this is an unimaginative exploitation version of the **Mad Max** (1979) and its sequels. Watkins is a poor replacement for Mel Gibson in the role of the hero who, with female bounty-hunter Banks and psychic Grovenor brings law to a lawless future and finally rescues his sister who spends most of the film being raped by all and sundry baddies. In place of the action pieces and verve of the original, director Santiago offers little but nudity and more nudity.

d/p Ciro H. Santiago *s* Frederick Bailey *c* uncredited *lp* Gary Watkins, Laura Banks, Lynda Weismeier, Linda Grovenor

Enemy Mine (KINGS ROAD/FOX) 108(93) min

During a minor skirmish in a war between Earth and the planet Dracon, fighter pilots Quaid, an Earthman, and Gossett, a Drac, shoot each other down and crashland on the

inhospitable, desolate, dangerous planet of Fyrine IV. After trying to kill each other, the human and the alien learn that they must co-operate in order to survive the meteor showers, the sand-dwelling omnivores and the bleak loneliness that threaten them. At first distrustful of the lizard creature, Quaid becomes its friend when Gossett reads pearls of alien wisdom from a Holy Drac Filofax and explains the proud heritage of his people. However, the war soon intervenes.

Rather that conceive of something genuinely otherworldly, this adaptation of Barry B. Longyear's Science Fiction magazine story merely shifts the plot of John Boorman's *Hell in the Pacific* (1968) to an alien world, which strangely makes the film feel a lot like *Robinson Crusoe on Mars* (1964). Despite some stolid attempts at giving the Drac a culture of its own, the film fails to resonate, because the invented squabble between humanity and a race of hermaphrodite reptiles has none of the overtones of any of the genuine conflicts – between American and Japanese, cowboy and Indian, white and black – that are timidly evoked. That said, director Petersen and his trusty special effects team create a convincing alien world populated by tentacled turtles, and the script is no worse than many an episode of *Star Trek*. The two leads, alone on screen for most of the film, do well under the circumstances, and the make-up, and the moments of embarrassing sentiment and philosophy (heavily pruned in the non-American release prints), are mercifully outweighed by exciting scenes with rocketships, monsters and evil galactic slave-drivers.

d Wolfgang Petersen *p* Stephen Friedman *s* Edward Khmara *c* Tony Imi *se* ILM, Chris Walas *lp* Dennis Quaid, Lou Gossett Jr, Brion James, Richard Marcus, Carolyn McCormick

Escape from the Bronx
(FULVIA FILMS; IT) 89 min
A belated sequel to **1990: I Guerrieri del Bronx** (1982) and like that film full of borrowings from John Carpenter's **Escape from New York** (1981), this is an inept Cinecittà actioneer. Gregory is the hi-tech gunman who saves the residents of the decaying Bronx from extermination by Silva and exposes the rapacious plans of Moore's financier who wants to build luxury housing there, and D'Obici the crusading reporter and heroine. After kidnapping Moore with assistance from Brent, the narrative all but collapses into a series of extended shootouts. In short, a spaghetti Western in Science Fiction clothing.

d/co-s Enzo G. Castellari *p* Fabrizio De Angelis *co-s* Titi Carpi *c* Blasco Giurato *se* Corridori *lp* Mark Gregory, Henry Silva, Valeria D'Obici, Timothy Brent, Paolo Malco, Thomas Moore

Explorers
(EDWARD S.FELDMAN PRODUCTIONS/INDUSTRIAL LIGHT & MAGIC) 109 min
In his directorial début, *Hollywood Boulevard* (1976), Dante paid homage to the cut-price charms of Roger Corman and his New World productions; in *Explorers* he celebrates the whole spectrum of American popular culture and fifties Science Fiction in particular. His device for this is Wak, the most offbeat alien since the beachball alien of John Carpenter's **Dark Star** (1974), whose total knowledge of mankind is derived from intercepting American television signals and who is accordingly reluctant to visit Earth because in all the Science Fiction films he's seen aliens are attacked once they make their presence on Earth known. The result is a gleeful pot pourri of popular culture, from Bugs Bunny to Little Richard, whose 'All Around the World' is performed by Picardo's Wak as his party piece. If the first half of the film, in which adolescents Hawke, Phoenix and Presson jerrybuild themselves a spaceship, is slow, the movie comes into its own once the teenage heroes meet Wak and Neek (Rickert).

d Joe Dante *p* Edward S. Feldman *s* Eric Luke *c* John Hora *se* Industrial Light & Magic *lp* Ethan Hawke, River Phoenix, Jason Presson, Amanda Peterson, Dick Miller, Robert Picardo, Leslie Rickert

Joey Cramer mounts the steps of the alien spaceship in Flight of the Navigator.

Fists of Steel *aka* Atomic Cyborg
(NATIONAL CINEMATOGRAFICA/DANIA FILM/MEDUSA) 95 min
'You made one mistake, Tanner,' claims the killer cyborg hero (Greene) just before he rips out corporate villain Saxon's heart. 'You thought you could own me by controlling my brain; what you didn't realize is that you don't own a man until you control his heart.' Oddly, given that this is a blatant imitation of **The Terminator** (1984) – it even features a Schwarzenegger-lookalike in the lead role – the film doesn't reveal until very late in the plot that its on-the-run, conscience-stricken hit man hero *is* a cyborg. While cheap, it's fairly well thought-out as Science Fiction, with a near future setting where acid rain eats into cars in the eastern USA and blue-suited conservationists have a chance for victory in the next election, and there are several clever throwaways, like the mention that the hero was a victim of the war in Guatemala in 1987.

After the opening, in which Greene refuses to carry out an unethical assassination, the movie relocates from the city to the familiar splendours of Arizona – often visited by low-budget Italian movies – and turns into a prototype for Sylvester Stallone's *Over the Top* (1987), as Greene becomes an arm-wrestling champion by besting perennial Italian supporting thug Montefiore. Saxon sends Dutch killer Cassinelli, a cadre of dark-helmeted bikers and a cyborg killer bimbo after Greene, and the invincible hero vanquishes all the villains in a mildly bloody manner. The end title reads, 'It was a day in the future, the era of the cyborg had begun.' Directed capably by Martino, one of the more reliable spaghetti Science Fiction specialists, this also has a decent score by Claudio Simonetti of Goblin.

d/p/co-s Martin Dolman (Sergio Martino) *co-s* Elisabeth Parker Jr, Paul Saska *c* John McFerrand *se* Sergio Stivaletti *lp* Daniel Greene, Janet Agren, Claudio Cassinelli, George Eastman (Luigi Montefiore), John Saxon, Robert Ben, Pat Monti, Donald O'Brien, Amy Werba

Flight of the Navigator (WALT DISNEY) 89 min

In 1978, a child (Cramer) is sent to meet his younger brother on the way home through the woods, and disappears. Eight years later he shows up again – four hours older – and the US Government's scientific spies link his mysterious absence to the recent discovery of a boiled-sweet-shaped flying saucer. Brought together in a hush-hush base, the child renews an acquaintance with the talking spaceship (voiced by an uncredited Reubens) that has been wiped from his memory, and finds himself impressed to serve aboard the craft as 'navigator', cueing an efficient but hardly magical special effects extravaganza as the saucer is pursued across country.

One of a wave of high school Science Fiction films that came out of Hollywood in the mid-eighties, which side steps the interesting misfits of **Explorers** (1985) and **Weird Science** (1985) and tries to cater to a vast pre-yuppie audience of squeaky-clean dullards, whose idea of high-tech is a dog-catching-frisbee contest. Being the Disney entry in the cycle, it features a happy family where all problems can be resolved with a few hugs and declarations of love, and turns the government agency – traditionally a force for evil in this sub-genre, from **E.T.: The Extra Terrestrial** (1982) to **D.A.R.Y.L** (1985) – into a mildly over-authoritarian but well-intentioned group of concerned adults. The strangest aspect of this mainly faceless movie is that it manages to get nostalgic about – of all years – 1978, with Cramer wistfully yearning for Jimmy Carter and the Bee-Gees in a manner that might have something to do with the fact that 1978 was the year Kleiser last had a hit movie, *Grease*. Painless but unmemorable.

d Randal Kleiser *p* Robby Wald, Dimitri Villard *s* Michael Burton, Matt McManus *c* James Glennon *se* Cinema Research Corporation, Fantasy II *lp* Joey Cramer, Veronica Cartwright, Cliff De Young, Sarah Jessica Parsons, Matt Adler, Howard Hesseman, Paul Reubens

Frankenstein's Great-Aunt Tillie

(TILLIE/FILMIER PRODUCTIONS; MEX) 93 min

A farce rather than a parody, Gold's film succeeds, despite the occasional slip, by its sheer exuberance. Pleasence is Franken-stein and Furneaux his great-aunt (who has kept her looks through a judicious use of rejuvenating cream) who return to the family mansion to find the town council plotting to repossess it for non-payment of taxes. Add to this, a house for wayward girls, the first stirrings of woman's emancipation, Furneaux's attempt to win the first Trans-Balkan Road Race and a marvellous performance from Pleasence and the result is a charming film that mixes slapstick with throwaway asides and puns with real gusto. Zsa Zsa Gabor makes a guest appearance.

d/p/s Myron J. Gold *c* Miguel Garzon *lp* Donald Pleasence, Yvonne Furneaux, June Wilkinson, Rod Colbin, Garnett Smith

Gojira *aka* Godzilla 1985 (TOHO) 87 min

'Godzilla,' mutters the Japanese Prime Minister, 'I was hoping I would never hear that name again.' This is at once a remake of the original **Gojira** (1954) and an alternative sequel that ignores the follow-ups produced between **Gojira No Gyakushu** (1955) and **Mekagojira No Gyakushu** (1975). As with the original film, the American release print has been shorn of some of the sermonizing, and spiced up with scenes of an American newsman (Burr returning to his old role) and some Generals sipping Dr Pepper – who heavily sponsored the re-edit – and contributing helpful advice. Thirty years after his original ravaging of Tokyo, Godzilla returns to trample again, and the Japanese resist pressure from the USA and Russia, who want to use unthinkable nuclear weapons against the beast. There are moments of effective tension-building in the first half-hour – a doomed Russian submarine attacked by a large object, Burr in his home having a

premonition of disaster – but once Godzilla gets ashore and in full view, 'that strangely innocent and tragic monster' becomes the whole show, smashing everything until a scientist, who has noted how similar the monster's brain is to that of a seagull, lures him into an active volcano with an electronic birdcall.

The special effects are elaborate and pleasantly busy after the manner of Gerry Anderson's *Thunderbirds* teleseries, with plentiful explosions, smashed buildings and trampled toy vehicles. The dubbed and American-added dialogue offers some humour: 'I hear you lost your parents to Godzilla thirty years ago, I imagine that has made you bitter,' says a journalist to a scientist; 'He sunk a Russian sub single-handed,' muses an American soldier, 'I say put a uniform on him and sign him up'; and, in a twisted bit of straining for significance, the intrepid birdcall expert concludes of the monster, 'He's a product of civilization. Men are the only monsters. Godzilla is like a living nuclear weapon, destined to walk the Earth forever ... a victim of the modern nuclear age.' Some prints have Marv Newland's hilarious 30-second short *Bambi Meets Godzilla* (1969) spliced on before the credits.

d Kohji Hashimoto, R.J. Kizer *p* Tomoyuki Tanaka, Anthony Randel *s* Shuichi Nagahara, Lisa Tomei *c* Kazutami Hara, Takashi Yamamoto, Toshimitsu Ohneda *se* Nobuyuki Yasumaru *lp* Raymond Burr, Keiju Kobayashi, Ken Tanaka, Yasuko Sawagachi, Shin Takumaa, Eitaro Ozawa

Lifeforce

(LONDON CANNON FILMS; GB) 101 min

A truly bad movie. In place of the neo-existential philosophizing of Colin Wilson's cult novel, *The Space Vampires*, on which it is based, director Hooper and his writers, O'Bannon and Jakoby,

The kiss of life/death in Tobe Hooper's silly Lifeforce.

piles cliché upon cliché about Ye Olde England while indulging in the most reactionary representations of sexuality.

May is the Space Girl, discovered by a joint Anglo-American space team, led by Railsback, investigating Halley's Comet, who on being brought to Earth comes back to life and sets about vampirizing the inhabitants of London for their lifeforce. Completely naked for most of the film to no purpose beyond our voyeuristic delight, May simply wanders through the film and London pursued by Railsback, with whom she's in telepathic communication, and Firth's police inspector who seems more like a refugee from Agatha Christie country than a modern policeman. Add to this the ludicrous over-acting by all concerned (the actors' collective revenge on a script that would have been old-fashioned in 1950?) and the result is a real contender in the worst big-budget movie ever stakes.

Hooper, whose best film remains the landmark *Texas Chainsaw Massacre* (1974) directs with an irritating penchant for tilted camera angles. The special effects by Dykstra (of **Star Wars**, 1977, fame) are chilling.

d Tobe Hooper   *p* Menahem Golan, Yoram Globus
s Dan O'Bannon, Don Jakoby   *c* Alan Hume   *se* John Dykstra   *lp* Steve Railsback, Peter Firth, Frank Finlay, Mathilda May, Michael Gothard, Nicholas Ball, Patrick Stewart

Lorca and the Outlaws

(LORCA FILM PRODUCTIONS: GB)   100 min
A lacklustre **Star Wars** (1977) inspired quickie – director Christian worked on *Star Wars* and **Alien** (1979) as a set designer – *Lorca* pits a band of rebels led by Tarrant against Cotterill and his military police droids on the desert planet Ordessa. Shot in Australia, the film looks good but the script, which even includes an imitation C-3PO, and its cardboard characters give the actors little to work with. The best thing is the music from Genesis member Tony Banks.

d/co-s Roger Christian   *p* Michael Guest   *co-s* Matthew Jacobs   *c* John Metcalfe   *lp* John Tarrant, Donogh Rees, Deep Roy, Cassandra Webb, Ralph Cotterill, Hugh Keays-Byrne

Mad Max Beyond Thunderdome

(KENNEDY-MILLER PRODUCTIONS; AUST)   pv   107 min
The third and most sumptuous of the series that began with **Mad Max** (1979) and **Mad Max II** (1981). Unlike the earlier films which had spare, stripped-down narratives and merely suggested the social organization of the post apocalptic world Gibson's hero stalked, *Beyond Thunderdome* has a classic Hollywood storyline and a particularized vision of the ramshackle future that beckons after the bombs have been dropped. Accordingly, although Miller still borrows and refurbishes material from a variety of genres, especially the Western, with impish delight, the film lacks the demented charm of the earlier outings. In place of that, Miller and his co-director Ogilvie have opted for a plot that moves from set-piece to set-piece and the same 'gee whizz' special effects and heroics of **Star Wars** (1977).

Gibson, robbed in a thrilling opening squence by Spence's flying scavenger, arrives in Bartertown in search of his stolen possessions and immediately falls foul of its ruler, Aunt Entity, played with verve by veteran soul songstress Turner. Exiled to the desert, he falls in with a tribe of children waiting for a saviour to fly them to salvation and with the aid of Spence and Rossitto's dwarf scientist he does just that. Bartertown is wonderfully imagined and the set-pieces exciting enough but the whole is decidedly less than the sum of its parts.

co-d/p/co-s George Miller   *co-d* George Ogilvie   *co-s* Terry Hayes   *c* Dean Semler   *se* Steve Courtly, Alan Maxwell
lp Mel Gibson, Tina Turner, Angelo Rossitto, Helen Buday, Bruce Spence, Adam Cockbourn, Paul Larsson

Tina Turner (left of centre) as Aunt Entity in Mad Max Beyond Thunderdome.

Christopher Collet with the world's first home-made nuclear bomb in The Manhattan Project.

The Manhattan Project *aka* Deadly Game
(FOX) 118 min

Miffed because his real-estate-agent mother is dating nuclear physicist Lithgow, high school genius Collet decides to turn in a science project that will really impress his teachers, by building his own nuclear device. He steals a bottle of weapons-grade plutonium from Lithgow's top-secret research station, in a neatly constructed heist sequence, and assembles a working atomic bomb, which he takes to a New York science fair. The government soon catches on, and sets out to track him down, leading to a race-against-time climax in which he has to defuse his own bomb before half America blows up. Clearly inspired by the success of **War Games** (1983), this is wittily co-scripted by Woody Allen's sometime collaborator Brickman ('They could lock you in a room,' Lithgow warns Collet, 'and throw the room away') and directed by him with old-style Hollywood efficiency. It is mercifully free of the teenage nerd antics that blight such contemporaries as **Real Genius** (1985) and **My Science Project** (1985), and features one of Lithgow's credibly eccentric performances. He is one of the few screen actors who can really make an impact with a punchline, delivered after the world has narrowly been saved, like 'Well, that was interesting.' However, it is finally a cop-out because of its refusal to consider the bomb as anything more than a gadget. Like **War Games**, it could do with a healthy dose of political anger in place of its wish-fulfilment liberalism.

d/co-s Marshall Brickman *p* Jennifer Ogden *co-s* Thomas Baum *c* Billy Williams *se* Bran Ferren *lp* John Lithgow, Christopher Collet, Cynthia Nixon, Jill Eikenberry, John Mahoney

Morons from Outer Space
(THORN EMI; GB) 97(91) min

A silly film, this betrays all the faults of a television idea stretched to feature film length. Written by Smith and Jones (of the *Not the Nine O'Clock News* British comedy series), its central idea is that far from being geniuses by Earth's standards, visitors from space might well be morons. So far so good, but in detailing the adventures of Bown, Pearce, Smith and Nail (who gives the film's best performance as the ultra-ultra idiot) director Hodges and his writers rely too much on parodic references to the likes of **Close Encounters of the Third Kind** (1977) and try too hard for a transatlantic feel – the first half of the film is set in the UK, the second in the USA. The result, a few enjoyable gags aside, is a sad waste of the undeniable talents on display.

d Mike Hodges *p* Barry Hanson *s* Griff Rhys Jones, Mel Smith *c* Phil Meheaux *se* David Speed *lp* Mel Smith, Griff Rhys Jones, Paul Bown, Joanne Pearce, Jimmy Nail, Dinsdale Landen, James B. Sikking

My Science Project
(TOUCHSTONE FILMS) 94 min

An engaging comedy, if only for Hopper's wonderful hippie science teacher, complete with VW van and Country Joe and the Fish cassettes, who on his return from 'the headwaters of creation' announces 'the future is a groove', *My Science Project*, like **Weird Science** (1985) takes for its subject the adolescent goings on of a group of high-school students. Stockwell is the hero who builds a time travel machine from a military junkyard, Stevens his wisecracking buddy with whom he gets lost in the web of time and Zerneck the romantic interest. The plot is thin – Stockwell and his cronies rescuing Zerneck from the likes of Neanderthal men, Nazis and a Godzilla lookalike – but Betuel directs energetically enough and Stevens' one liners come fast enough to paper over the cracks.

d/s Jonathan Betuel *p* Jonathan Taplin *c* David M. Walsh *se* John B. Mansbridge *lp* John Stockwell, Danielle von Zerneck, Fisher Stevens, Dennis Hopper, Rapheal Sbarge, Barry Corbin

O-Bi, O-Ba – Koniec Cywilizacji
aka **The End of Civilization**
(POLISH FILM CORPORATION, PERSPECTYWA UNIT; POL) 88 min

Set in a post-nuclear-holocaust world in which the ragged remnants of mankind wait for a Noah's Ark to take them to salvation, this is an austere film. Stuhr is the hero who tries to establish if there is any truth behind the myth, Janda the pragmatic woman who prefers life as a whore to a doubtful future and Dmochowski the engineer who knows the Ark will bring no salvation – and indeed when it finally comes it explodes bringing an end to the Earth. Highly theatrically constructed, the bleak future it envisages is all the better for being suggested (often with comic inflections) rather presented in great detail. Certainly in contrast to most Science Fiction films of the eighties, it retains the questioning element that made the genre so fruitful in the fifties.

d/s Piotr Szulkin *c* Witbold Sobocinski *lp* Jerzy Stuhr, Krystyna Janda, Kalina Jedrusik, Mariusz Dmochowski, Jan Nowicki, Henryk Bista

Operation Dead End (OKO/CINEVOX) 92 min

Similar in its premise to *Chosen Survivors* (1974), this glossy German production has three volunteers put in a fall-out shelter on an island contaminated by nerve gas for a supposed sixty days to study the psychological stress effects of nuclear war and close confinement. As usual the scientists, led inevitably by the chilly Diffring, don't tell the test subjects all the facts, and the experiment soon falls apart. A live weasel turns up in the shelter, one subject turns out to have suicidal tendencies, and, in between attempts to beat up and rape each

other, the characters try to force the scientists, who are watching them all the time via closed-circuit television, to airlift them out. The setting and set-up are interesting and atmospheric, but as the melodramatic plot is worked out, one gets the feeling that the film would have been more interesting if the experiment *hadn't* been disrupted and had proceeded as planned.

d/co-s Nikolai Mullerschoen   *p* Dieter Geissler
co-s Stanislav Barabas   *c* Jacques Steyn   *lp* Isabelle Willer, Uwe Oxchsenknecht, Hannes Jaenicke, Gunter Maria Halmer, Felix von Manteuffel, Anton Diffring

The Quiet Earth
(CINEPRO/PILLSBURY FILMS; NZ)   100 min
An imaginative twist on the man alone theme, *The Quiet Earth* stars Lawrence as the scientist who wakes up to discover he's apparently the only man alive in an unchanged world as the result of a malfunctioning science project. Superbly directed by Murphy, who made the chilling *Utu* (1983), which also starred Lawrence, the film develops a strong sense of mystery when Lawrence finds two other survivors, Routledge and Smith. In place of the sermonizing tone of most similar films, Murphy uses the situation to explore the characters.

d Geoff Murphy   *co-p/co-s* Sam Pillsbury   *co-p* Don Reynolds   *co-s* Bruno Lawrence, Bill Baer   *c* James Bartle   *se* Ken Durey   *lp* Bruno Lawrence, Alison Routledge, Peter Smith

Rage War *aka* The Dungeonmaster *aka* Digital Dreams
(EMPIRE)   77 min
Less a film than a strung-together series of effects test reels and audition pieces, this multi-directed portmanteau is about a computer genius (Byron) who is mind-linked to his computer X-CALBR-8 and who is forced to travel through time and space as a heroic warrior in a quest to rescue his girlfriend (Wing) from a sorcerer (Moll), who decrees that the hero must face seven challenges. In rapid succession, Byron bests a giant

stone idol, an imp with a horde of tame zombies, a Satanic Heavy Metal group, some defrosted horror luminaries (Jack the Ripper, the Wolf Man, the Mummy), a skid-row slasher in downtown LA, a demon-angel, and a band of post-holocaust desert marauders. Too fast and varied to be as boring as Band's **Metalstorm: The Destruction of Jared-Syn** (1983), but not as spirited as the best of Empire's Science Fiction quickies, **Trancers** (1984) and **Zone Troopers** (1985).

co-d Steve Ford   *co-d/p/co-s* Charles Band   *co-d/co-s* Rose-Marie Turko, Peter Manoogian, Ted Nicolaou   *co-s* Allen Actor, Jeffrey Byron   *co-d/co-s/co-se* David Allen, John Buechler *c* Mac Ahlberg   *lp* Jeffrey Byron, Richard Moll, Leslie Wing, Gina Calabrese, Daniel Dion, WASP, Phil Fondacaro

Real Genius   (TRI-STAR/DELPHI III)   scope   106 min
Fifteen-year-old superbrain Jarret is admitted to Pacific Tech, an élite school for budding Oppenheimers and Frankensteins, and finds it inhabited by the same array of nerds, studs and jocks found in most low-IQ teen movie halls of learning. In addition to palling around with crazy cut-up Kilmer, getting off with hyperactive Louise Brooks lookalike Meyrink and wondering what the silent hippie is doing in his wardrobe, Jarret is co-opted by his reptilian professor (Atherton) into helping devise a fiendish laser weapon for the government. An acceptable teenage slob comedy with some scientific frills, and a comically creepy performance from Atherton as the glamourboy mad scientist with his own TV show and an ambition to take over the SDI programme. In the era of *Top Gun* (1986), it is refreshing to see a film aimed at young people which assumes that the US Government is rotten through and through and shouldn't be allowed to play with war toys.

d Martha Coolidge   *p* Brian Grazer   *s* Neal Israel, Pat Proft, Peter Torokvei   *c* Vilmos Zsigmond   *se* Syd Dutton, Bill Taylor   *lp* Val Kilmer, Gabe Jarret, Michelle Meyrink, William Atherton, Patti d'Arbanville, Robert Prescott, Louis Giambalvo

Val Kilmer (left) and Gabe Jarret in the enjoyable teenage slob comedy movie Real Genius.

The Return of Captain Invincible

(WILLARRA/SEVEN KEYS PRODUCTIONS; AUST) pv 91 min
Made in 1982, but not released until 1985, this is a witty *homage* to the verities of serialdom. Arkin is the super-hero who fell foul of Joe McCarthy in the fifties (his red cape is cited as evidence of Communist leanings). Discovered as a tramp in Sydney, in response to a plea from his president, he once more puts on his cape and shorts to stop Lee's Mr Midnight and his plans to restore New York to a state of racial purity. Directed by Mora with an affectionate use of B movie clichés and marvellously inventive in its use of stock footage, unlike **Airplane II: The Sequel** (1981), the movie is more than a string of jokes simply laid end to end.

d Philippe Mora *p/co-s* Andrew Gaty *co-s* Steven E. De Souza *c* Mike Malloy *se* Monty Feiguth *lp* Alan Arkin, Christopher Lee, Kate Fitzpatrick, Bill Hunter, Michael Pate, John Bluthal, David Argue

Il Risveglio di Paul *aka* Paul's Awakening

(SIGLA EMME; IT) 85 min
This is virtually a one man film. Saponaro, a former director of television commercials, as well as handling the writing, producing and directing chores, takes the leading role as the French Decathlon champion of 1945 who's projected into the future. The world of 2262 is ruled by machines which keep their human slaves in order through drugs and Olympic-like circuses in which athletes from the past compete. In common with Italian Science Fiction of the sixties, but not the exploitation pics of the seventies and eighties, this future is stylishly imagined (by set designer Nini Migliotta) which gives added substance to the comic book action of the storyline in which Saponaro fights for his freedom and O'Feeney against sundry villains (including a drugged O'Feeney) in the film's climax. A minor but enjoyable movie.

d/p/s Michele Saponaro *c* Riccardo Pizzocchere
lp Michele Saponaro, Bianca O'Feeney, Thomas Wu Tao Ling

Shadey

(LARKSPUR/FILM FOUR INTERNATIONAL; GB) 106 min
Oliver Shadey (Sher), a bankrupt small businessman, has the psychic power of recording precognitive and long-range visions on camera film. He approaches tycoon Macnee, in the hope of profiting from his abilities so that he can afford a sex-change operation, but finds himself handed over to military intelligence, and embroiled in a plot that involves hypocritical members of the aristocracy, a kidnap, incest, castration, rampant insanity and fantasy touches. From its mildly interesting psi premise, this attempt at 'surrealist black comedy' spins off an extraordinarily annoying and ill-constructed storyline, mixing tiresomely obvious comedy with outmoded whinges about obvious targets (big business, the military, spies, rock video, South Africa). A collection of impressive performers associated with various television genres are ill-used in dotty cameo appearances, and Sher, in his first major film role, turns in an embarrassing exercise in Chaplinesque self-indulgence, complete with drag scene and would-be comic castration.

d Philip Saville *p* Otto Plaschkes *s* Snoo Wilson *c* Roger Deakins *se* George Gibbs, Terry Cox *lp* Anthony Sher, Billie Whitelaw, Patrick Macnee, Katharine Helmond, Larry Lamb, Leslie Ash, Bernard Hepton, Jesse Birdsall

Starchaser: The Legend of Orin

(COLEMAN-ROSENBLATT) 100 min
A 3-D cartoon feature following the exploits of Orin, a young slave, who rebels against a race of robot masters when he finds a magical swordhilt and is told by a spectral old man that his destiny is to free his people. Falling in with a Han Solo-esque cynical spacefaring adventurer, Orin sets out to overthrow the outer space tyrant. A stereotypical mix of magic and superscience in the **Star Wars** (1977) tradition, with the Arthurian hero defeating robotic villains. While Orin's little blind brother is as fey a Tiny Tim type as ever there was, the film thankfully cuts down on the glutinous aspects of the plot and sticks to the business of saving the galaxy. It is even grown-up enough to kill off the hero's girlfriend in an early scene – he finds another in the course of his adventures – and to feature some mild bad language and sexual innuendo. The space battles are mostly predictable and repetitive, but there is one genuinely scary/funny sequence in Orin's encounter with organ-hunting cyborgs, and the vocal characterizations are excellent throughout, if let down by the cheapskate US/Korean TV-style animation.

d/p Steven Han *s* Jeffrey Scott *c* Charles Flekal *lp* Joe Colligan, Carmen Argenziano, Noelle North, Anthony Delongis, Les Tremayne

Star Crystal (SKOURAS/WOSTER) 93 min

An ultra-low-budget imitation of **Alien** (1979). In 2032, a routine expedition to Mars unearths a rock that seems to be packed with circuitry and splits open to reveal a crystal which, when taken aboard a spaceship, turns into a slimy creature that kills most of the crew. The hand puppet attacks with tentacles on strings, and bottom-drawer actors rush around a New World surplus spaceship mouthing idiotic dialogue. The movie is memorable only for its benevolent final twist, in which the monster accesses the ship's computer and reads the gospels, whereupon it converts to Christianity and turns into an E.T.-type lovable alien, who humbly begs the forgiveness of the survivors for its previous murderous behaviour.

d/co-s Lance Lindsay *p/co-s* Eric Woster *c* uncredited
se Lance Abernathy *lp* C. Justin Campbell, Faye Bolt, John Smith

The Stuff (LARCO) 93 min

As nifty a satire on fast food as you'll ever see, *The Stuff* features Moriarty, Marcovicci and 11-year-old Bloom as industrial saboteurs on the track of a parasitic yogurt-like dessert that eats people from inside out once ingested. Directed with panache by Cohen (maker of **It's Alive**, 1973 and **It Lives Again**, 1978 – both classics of the genre), the movie eschews hardware and hi-tech special effects in favour of wit and elegance, if one can talk

Anthony Sher is Shadey.

of elegance in the context of a film in which hideous gaping mouths full of white goo are a regular occurrence. In short, a minor masterpiece.

d/s Larry Cohen   *p* Paul Kurta   *c* Paul Glickman
se Steve Neill, Rick Stratton, Ed French   *lp* Michael Moriarty, Andrea Marcovicci, Paul Sorvino, Scott Bloom, Garrett Morris, Danny Aiello

The Titan Find *aka* Creature
(TIFIN PRODUCTIONS)   97 (93) min
Briefly enlivened by a cameo from Kinski, this is a dull and plodding version of **Alien** (1979). Ivar is the space captain who finds a creature on Titan that decimates his crew before he can kill it and jet back home with Schaal and Salinger. Sadly, apart from Kinski who clearly understands that parody is the only way to deal with such a wooden script and cardboard characters, everybody else treats the story seriously.

d/co-p/co-s William Malone   *co-p* William Dunn   *co-s* Alan Reed   *c* Harry Mathias   *se* L.A. Effects Group   *lp* Stan Ivar, Wendy Schaal, Lyman Ward, Robert Jaffe, Annette McCarthy, Klaus Kinski, Diane Salinger

Trouble in Mind   (RAINCITY/ISLAND ALIVE)   112 min
Like John Frankenheimer's *99 & 44/100% Dead* (1974), this has a deliberately ordinary ganster movie plot – about an ex-cop (Kristofferson) trying to look out for a woman (Singer) whose husband (Carradine) is getting mixed up with the crime empire of Divine – and sets it against the possibly futuristic background of a changed America. Like the earlier film, it uses Seattle as its mythical background, here called Rain City.

Soldiers in Russian-style uniforms prowl the streets searching for recruits, and the fashions are a strange mix of the forties, the fifties and eighties. A comedy of muddled relationships after the manner of Rudolph's *Choose Me* (1984), this is a rich collage of bizarre character details and obscure semi-jokes: Kristofferson toils over a cardboard model of a slum as he tries to put the world to rights, while Carradine literally transforms from Tom Joad to Frank N. Furter with each scene. The screenplay crackles with smart lines ('When your ship comes in, I'll see there's a dock strike'), and Rudolph's blues-scored, lovingly-coloured direction makes its self-contained world appealing and charming, if still tinged with threat and menace.

d/s Alan Rudolph   *p* Carolyn Pfeiffer, David Blocker
c Toyomuchi Kurita   *se* Bob Burns   *lp* Kris Kristofferson, Keith Carradine, Lori Singer, Genevieve Bujold, Joe Morton, Divine, George Kirby, John Consdine, Dirk Blocker

Underworld *aka* Transformations
(GREEN MAN; GB)   100 min
An admirable attempt to make a stylish British exploitation movie, *Underworld* doesn't quite come off. It follows **Blade Runner** (1982) and *Diva* (1982) by cribbing from the right sources – Hollywood thrillers of the forties, Italian horrors of the sixties – but rock promo graduate Pavlou is all too obviously still working in a medium that demands that everything be essentially pointless.

Hardboiled ex-hoodlum Lamb is hired by gangland king-pin Berkoff to track down Cowper, everybody's favourite heroin-addicted teenage prostitute. It turns out that the girl

Keith Carradine (left) and Joe Morton in Alan Rudolph's futuristic crime movie Trouble in Mind.

Kelly LeBrock as the Barbie doll come devastatingly to life with Anthony Michael Hall in Weird Science.

has been abducted from Pitt's brothel by underground-dwelling mutants with rubbery faces, and that the macguffin everyone is really after is a wonder drug invented by seedy scientist Elliott, which makes people transform into the image of their wildest dreams.

There's a lot of action, but only one scary fight with a werewolf-type thing is actually exciting; the rest of the chasing and battling being designed simply to show off the performers' rock star-like ability to jump about gymnastically to keep some movement in the frame. The story comes from Barker, who would later make a notable directorial début with *Hellraiser* (1987), but only Elliott's mad doctor and a few minor thugs suggest the kind of perverse quirkiness which is his speciality. The rest of the actors are just posing, as in Lamb's wimpy tough-guy act, or Berkoff's ludicrous attempt to be Sydney Greenstreet and Alf Garnett rolled into one. The electro-droning score by the group Freur is quite horrible, and the sub-**Scanners** (1980) climax, in which Elliott is supposed spectacularly to mutate to death, is botched by Litton's special effects and the leaving-around of too many loose plot ends.

d George Pavlou   *p* Kevin Attew, Don Hawkins, Al Burgess
s Clive Barker   *c* Sid McCartney   *se* Peter Litton
lp Denholm Elliott, Larry Lamb, Nicola Cowper, Stephen Berkoff, Miranda Richardson, Art Malik, Ingrid Pitt

Warning Sign

(FOX/BARWOOD-ROBBINS PRODUCTIONS)   100 min
Barwood's directorial debut pits Waterson as the lone cop up against the results of a deadly plague when a culture from which it was intended to manufacture biological weapons is accidentally spilt at an American top secret research laboratory. The germ makes homicidal monsters out of those contaminated. Quinlan is Waterson's wife trapped in the research establishment when it's quarantined and Kotto the military bigwig trying to hush matters up.

Directed at breakneck speed by Barwood, at the cost of any tension, the film is too one-dimensional to engage one's attention for long, though Cunedy's cinematography manages to find new angles for the seemingly endless sequences of people desperately trying to get out of the laboratory.

d/co-s Hal Barwood   *p* Jim Bloom   *co-s* Matthew Robbins   *c* Dean Cunedy   *lp* Sam Waterson, Kathleen Quinlan, Yaphet Katto, Jeffrey de Munn, Richard Dysart, G.W. Bailey

Weird Science   (U)   94 min

A Science Fiction variant on the teenagers-in-search-of-sex films, this lacklustre outing from *National Lampoon* alumnus Hughes features Hall and Mitchell-Smith as the adolescent nerds who create LeBrock (by animating a Barbie Doll with a computer!) to fulfil their fantasies only to have her turn into an elder sister, so scared of her do they become, and guide them to maturity and more suitable partners.

Sadly, LeBrock (reprising her role in Gene Wilder's *The Woman in Red*, 1984) has too little to do in the only too predictable script beyond offering the traditionally threatening image of active female sexuality.

d/s John Hughes   *p* Joel Silver   *c* Matthew F. Leonetti
lp Anthony Michael Hall, Kelly LeBrock, Ilan Mitchell-Smith, Bill Paxton, Suzanne Synder, Judie Aronson

Zone Troopers   (EMPIRE/ALTAR)   86 min

'He's a million miles from home, he doesn't speak the language, and people are trying to kill him,' says hard-bitten US army Sgt Stone (Thomerson) of the crash-landed insectoid alien that his buddies have stumbled across while caught behind the enemy lines in Italy during World War Two – 'sound familiar?' With co-writers Bilson and De Meo promoted to director and producer, and most of the cast returning from the excellent **Trancers** (1984), this is obviously Empire's attempt to repeat the success of the earlier movie. Crossbreeding genres again, this emerges as a perfect pastiche of the forties war movie – with correspondent Manard doing an imitation of Ernie Pyle, while doughboys Van Patten and La Fleur play the roles that would once have gone to Robert Walker or William Bendix, and Thomerson giving another wittily hard-boiled performance as the Iron Sarge, who is built into a mythic figure of Duke Wayne proportions. The monster – a *Dr Who*-style man in a suit – is something of a disappointment, but its *Astounding Science Fiction*-style forties spaceship is wonderful, and other effective period touches include a brief fantasy sequence with a genuine forties-style vamp in elbow-length gloves, and clever use of the 'Kilroy was here' joke. Richard Band provides a score that imitates the ominous style of forties war films but also throws in some big band swing for one spirited battle, after La Fleur has socked the passing Adolf Hitler on the nose. A charmingly lunatic enterprise.

d/co-s Danny Bilson   *p/co-s* Paul De Meo   *c* Mac Ahlberg
se John Carl Buechler   *lp* Tim Thomerson, Timothy Van Patten, Art La Fleur, Biff Manard, William Paulson

Aliens   (FOX)   137 min

A rarity among sequels, *Aliens* elaborates upon the haunted-house-in-space success of **Alien** (1979) by replaying all the monstrous highlights of the earlier film in the context of a different transplanted-to-space genre. Borrowing heavily from the Sam Fuller-style combat movie, Cameron, working from an outline by Walter Hill and David Giler, has Ripley (Weaver) revived after fifty-seven years in suspended animation, and packed off to the planet of the eggs to help a group of battle-hardened space marines deal with a further outbreak of alien activity. As in the traditional World War Two movie, the marines include representatives from every possible minority group, updated to include women and androids. The plot essentially concerns a patrol, with the group wandering into danger and being picked off in a series of engagements with the enemy, until a representative survivor faces up to the main menace and triumphs, signifying the superiority of the Allied way of life. Although Cameron is plainly in love with the mix of cinematic and military hardware – one of the most pleasing devices is a perfect fusion of the two, an M–16 mounted on a steadicam harness – the film presents its marines not as the indestructible superheroes of the contemporary earthbound action movie (Cameron had co-written *Rambo: First Blood, Part 2*, 1985) but as cannon fodder thrown away by conscienceless corporation men back on Earth. When told that she needn't worry because she is being protected by well-trained troops, a blank-faced child (Henn) chillingly says, 'That won't make any difference.'

The finish has Weaver in a robotic forklift-truck suit clashing head-on with the egg-laying Queen Alien in order to rescue the little girl, demonstrating the superiority of one brand of maternalism over the other. The extra length is used to advantage to fill in the characterizations – Weaver's Ripley being softened since the first film, and made a real person rather than an emblematic survivor – and to build up the suspense before the all-out battle scenes, which demonstrate the significant advances in special effects since the astonishing first film. Cameron, fresh from **The Terminator** (1984), stirs his own concerns – with hard-boiled heroines, biomechanics, political paranoia and relentless suspense – into the set-up of the first movie, not quite matching Ridley Scott's detailing of the deadbeat futuristic background, but certainly one-upping him insofar as suspense, character, gritty dialogue, action and explosions are concerned.

d/s James Cameron   *p* Gale Anne Hurd   *c* Adrian Biddle *se* Stan Winston, Bob & Dennis Skotak, John Richardson, Doug Beswick   *lp* Sigourney Weaver, Michael Biehn, Bill Paxton, Lance Henriksen, Jenette Goldstein, Paul Reiser, Carrie Henn, William Hope, Al Matthews

Biggles (COMPACT/YELLOWBILL; GB) 92 min
Evidently Captain W.E. Johns' sterling British aviator hero wasn't considered commercial enough on his own merits to be worth a movie, and so this intermittently likeable but unredeemably daft movie throws in a lot of gimmicky Science Fiction material. Doddery old Cushing, a British Government man who lives inside Tower Bridge, approaches a frozen food entrepreneur (Hyde-White) and tells him that he is somehow the 'time twin' of James Bigglesworth (Dickson), the World War One air ace and saviour of democracy. Hyde-White keeps being struck by blue lightning and whisked back to the mud of France, whenever Biggles is in mortal danger. Since, back in 1917, Biggles is trying to stop the beastly Hun from using a dastardly secret weapon to win the war, and is getting into mortal danger every other moment, there is plenty of time-tripping. In an obvious bit of budget-cutting silliness, Biggles is brought to the 1980s for a stretch of the film, where his leather flying gear blends in with the London street punks and he is able to hijack a police helicopter on the grounds that 'If you can fly a Sopwith Camel, you can fly *anything*!'

An astonishing film, with Dickson exactly right as the square-jawed Biggles – not too camp, but not too starched either – and his well-remembered heroic pals equally well cast. But, as a Biggles movie, it is a disappointment. It boasts only one measly biplane dogfight, has almost no death-defying aerial stunts, is stuck with a fingernails-down-a-blackboard disco score, and is far more interested in the time-travel sit-com side of the story than in the vintage derring-do. However, this keeps offering surprising and effective little moments: Cushing lurking in a *film noir* alley as a black cat crosses his path; the modern heroine (Hutchison) squirting Mace into the face of an *Achtung*–shouting sausage-eater; Gilbert doing some fine sneering as the iron-masked German air ace; a black-tie launch for Hyde-White's horrible line of 'Celebrity TV Dinners'; a character being brought back from

Mother to the rescue: Sigourney Weaver saves Carrie Henn in Aliens.

the dead by God; and one classic dialogue exchange – heroine: 'Tell me this is some crazy dream like *Fantasy Island*?'; hero: 'Come on now, it's not that bad, it's only World War One!'

d John Hough   *co-p/co-s* Kent Walwin   *co-p* Pom Oliver *co-s* John Groves   *c* Ernest Vincze   *se* David Harris *lp* Neil Dickson, Alex Hyde-White, Peter Cushing, Fiona Hutchison, Marcus Gilbert, William Hootkins, Alan Polonsky, Michael Siberry, James Saxon, Daniel Flynn

Breeders (TYCIN) 77 min
Shot in New York City by a bargain basement offshoot of Charles Band's Empire pictures, this is a throwback to the **Alien** (1979) rip-offs of the early eighties, with production values and technical attributes on a par with the Ted V. Mikels or Andy Milligan zero-budget disasters of the sixties and seventies. A series of virgins in the big city is being raped by an acid-dripping inhuman that lives in the tunnels under

the Empire State Building. A cop on the case (Lewman) and a black woman doctor (Farley) try to puzzle it out in endless dialogue sequences, which fill in between the exploitational scenes of nudity or violence. All the virgins have to be undressed before being abused – cueing a series of aerobics scenes, showers and nude phone-calls – and afterwards feel compelled to go into the tunnels to wallow in an alien slime paddling pool, while a possessed doctor (Kincaid) explains the plot. With amateurish performances and shaky production values, this is among the worst Science Fiction movies of the eighties. Incredibly, Kincaid and his associates were able to crank out several similar items: *Mutant Hunt* (1986), *Robot Holocaust* (1986) and *Necropolis* (1987).

d/s Tim Kincaid   *p* Cynthia DePaula   *c* Arthur D. Marks   *se* Ed French   *lp* Teresa Farley, Lance Lewman, Frances Raines, Natalie O'Connell, Tim Kincaid, LeeAnne Baker

Critters   (NEW LINE/SMART EGG/SHO FILMS)   86(85) min
Critters is a typical eighties attempt to recapture the feel of fifties Science Fiction monster movies like *It Came from Outer Space* (1953) and *Invaders From Mars* (1953), with slightly higher-tech effects than the originals, and a slightly tongue-in-cheek script distancing it from the deliberately stereotypical characterizations and ominous mumblings about the threat from 'out there'. A group of Krites – furry tumbleweeds with lots of teeth – escape from an intergalactic prison and head for the universal backwater planet, Earth. On a Kansas farm, a very normal family finds its homestead under siege as the

Jeff Goldblum and the matter transmitter that will transform him into The Fly.

hungry, dangerous nuisances close in. Mom (Stone), Dad (Bush) and Sis (Van Der Velde) get variously disabled in the struggle, and it's down to a bratty kid (Grimes) to fend off the monsters with his home-made fireworks. Meanwhile, a pair of shapeshifting alien bounty hunters have come to town in order to round up the Krites, and the village idiot (Opper) is trying to convince the Sheriff (Walsh) that spacemen really *are* communicating with him through the fillings in his teeth.

Like **The Terminator** (1984) before it, *Critters* takes its direct inspiration from the TV series *The Outer Limits*, in this case the 'Zanti Misfits' episode, which is recalled by a character name and which featured human-faced insects that were a lot more unnerving than the sort-of cuddly monsters featured here. The film has fine special effects, a nicely caricatured small town setting and a few neat gags about its shape-changing aliens, but it is a little too derivative to pass muster with the best of retro-chic Science Fiction (**Alligator**, 1981, **Strange Invaders**, 1982) simply because it concentrates on serving up the recipe as before with more obvious humour, rather than straining for the mix of paranoia, black and white anxiety and pulp poetry that distinguishes the best of the originals. It was successful enough to have a sequel, Mick Garris's *Critters 2: The Main Course* (1988).

d/co-s Stephen Herek   *p* Rupert Harvey   *co-s* Dominic Muir, Don Opper   *c* Tim Suhrstedt   *se* Charlie & Steve Chiodo   *lp* Dee Wallace Stone, M. Emmet Walsh, Billy Green Bush, Scott Grimes, Nadine Van Der Velde, Don Opper, Billy Zane, Ethan Phillips, Terrence Mann

Eliminators   (EMPIRE/ALTAR)   96 min
'We have been dissecting the very building blocks of the universe. Since when have we been concerned with compassion?' A cyborg (Reynolds), a ninja (Lee), a hard-boiled adventurer (Prine), a tough lady scientist (Crosby) and a cute robot called SPOT travel up a Mexican river to the jungle enclave of mad scientist Dotrice in order to thwart his fiendish plan to go back in time and take over as Emperor of Rome, thus changing the course of history for the worst. Although Prine and Dotrice seem to have been let in on the jokes of a typically witty pulp script by Bilson and De Meo, screenwriters of **Trancers** (1984) and **Zone Troopers** (1985), this is one of Empire's lesser pot-boilers, with a deal too much repetitive slogging-through-the-undergrowth and a storyline that doesn't really get anywhere.

d Peter Manoogian   *p* Charles Band   *s* Danny Bilson, Paul De Meo   *c* Mac Ahlberg   *se* Quick Silver FX Studio   *lp* Andrew Prine, Denise Crosby, Roy Dotrice, Patrick Reynolds, Conan Lee

The Fly   (FOX/BROOKSFILMS)   96 min
Compared to the facelessness of Cronenberg's previous 'mainstream' project, **The Dead Zone** (1983), *The Fly*, although a remake, is a very personal film, returning to the obsessional examinations of bodily metamorphosis and scientific experimentation that run throughout the director's *oeuvre*. Seth Brundle (Goldblum), the gawky scientist who invents teleportation as a way of getting round his chronic motion sickness, emerges from the telepod in which he has been fused with the molecules of an interfering fly, not as an insect-headed monstrosity, like David Hedison in the original film (1958), but as a super-improved version of himself. However, after he has demonstrated his prowess as a sexual athlete and a bar-room arm-wrestler, he finds himself gradually transforming, decomposing and otherwise losing his humanity as he develops into Brundlefly, a literal fusion of Brundle and the fly. Typical of Cronenberg is the combination of graphic sickness and good humour that accompanies Brundle's metamorphosis, which he is at pains always to treat in a philosophical, questioning manner ('Do you know that insects have no politics,' he remarks. 'I'd like to be the first

insect politician.'). Goldblum, in an Oscar-nominated performance, tosses off nervous remarks about his collection of dropped-off body parts, gives an amusingly disgusting, TV chef-like demonstration of the fly-like manner in which he consumes a doughnut, hums 'I Know an Old Lady Who Swallowed a Fly' and treats his mutation as a voyage of discovery.

Although it is a showcase for the make-up effects of Walas and his crew, and was Cronenberg's biggest production, the film is a surprisingly compressed, intimate work. It has only three main characters and one main set, and makes do with the metamorphosis and a restrained eternal triangle relationship, without feeling the need to invent melodramatic contrivances to extend the action (this monster doesn't go on a rampage to up the film's body count, unlike Eric Stoltz in the sequel, **The Fly II**, 1988). One unnecessary dream sequence, involving a maggot baby, apart – a similar flaw recurs in Cronenberg's otherwise excellent *Dead Ringers* (1988) – this is a perfectly structured, tightly inner-directed film, at once funny, poignant and horrific. Like many of Cronenberg's rigorously intelligent horrors, it can be read as a metaphor for the processes of disease and ageing, and finally comes to an acceptance of the perishability of human tissue as the transformed-beyond-possibility Brundle accepts death, like Lon Chaney's Wolf Man, at the hands of one who loves him, the neurotic heroine Veronia Quaife (Davis).

d/co-s David Cronenberg *p* Stuart Cornfeld *co-s* Charles Edward Pogue *c* Mark Irwin *se* Chris Walas *lp* Jeff Goldblum, Geena Davis, John Getz, Joy Boushel

Hellfire (MANLEY) 89 min
'Half a century of this atomic age has left us with forty-nine and a half states and no Middle East in this world.' An ambitious generic mix along the lines of **Trancers** (1984), *Hellfire* doesn't quite come together, although it has several incidental felicities. In 1997, Hellfire, a revolutionary new power source, is a controversial issue, with a gang of terrorists destroying a space station in an attempt to stop the project, which could produce pollution-free energy but also tends to induce spontaneous human combustion. Private eye McGregor is hired by a cool blonde (Miller) to investigate her murderous tycoon brother, who is in control of Hellfire, and finds himself caught between various double-crossing factions. 'How am I supposed to operate when my client is a bigger mystery than the case?' laments the hero, who comes complete with such hard-boiled accoutrements as a voice-over narration, a sleazy apartment, a best friend in the force, an assortment of underworld contacts and a tendency to get beaten up. There's an understated and quite effective future vision in the background – in a police station, complainants have to take a number and wait – but the up-front storyline suffers from Murray's clumsiness with actors and action scenes, and, although the sparkly combustion trick is fairly impressive, the futuristic vehicles aren't at all convincing.

d/s William Murray *p* Howard Foulkrod *c* Dennis Peters *se* David DiPietro, Geoff Langloh, Eric Princz *lp* Kenneth McGregor, Sharon Mason, Julie Miller, Jon Maurice, Joseph White, Stephen Caldwell, Edward Fallon, Mickey Shaughnessy

Howard the Duck *aka* Howard . . . A New Breed of Hero
(LUCASFILM/U) 110 min
Based on the cultish/hip/weird Marvel Comics series of the mid-seventies, this $50 million movie was such a disaster in the US that the title was changed and an advertising campaign designed overseas in an attempt to de-emphasize (indeed, to totally conceal) the lead character's duckness. Something went terribly wrong with this adaptation, which replaces the original's snappy verve with childishness but doesn't quite make the film into a Lucasfilmstyle kiddie epic.

Howard (played by a succession of midgets in a suit, and voiced by Zien) is a disillusioned ad exec/would-be songwriter living the life of a swinging bachelor in a world where ducks have evolved into the dominant species. One evening, he is plucked from his home by a laser beam and transported across the stars to a filthy back alley in downtown Cleveland, Ohio. After getting extremely friendly with rock 'n' roller Thompson, who favours *very* short skirts, Howard tries to make his way on the new planet and discover how the hell he got there. However, no sooner has friendly scientific genius Jones admitted that the laser was one of his experiments than he starts turning into one of the Dark Overlords of the Universe, a scorpion-tailed monster whose ambition is to destroy everything and rule the ruins. Only Howard stands between the monster and the end of the world.

The duck himself – who would have been far more effective if done as a Roger Rabbit cartoon character – is by far the weakest aspect of the film, despite a few neat wisecracks, and his near-bestial relationship with Thompson is never resolved in the rush to play it safe. Jones, however, is wonderful as the scientist-turned monster, and the Dark Overlords are impressive monstrosities, which makes Howard's eventual defeat of them even more unbelievable.

d/co-s Willard Huyck *p/co-s* Gloria Katz *c* Bobby Byrne *se* ILM *lp* Lea Thompson, Jeffrey Jones, Tim Robbins, Chip Zien, Paul Guilfoyle, Liz Sagal

Invaders From Mars (CANNON) scope 99 min
This is an expensive, needless remake of William Cameron Menzies' 1953 classic, clogged with excellent special effects and dragged down by its insistence on staying faithful even to the flaws of the original film. Menzies was forced to tack on an 'it's-all-a-dream' ending and to use endless military stock footage to pad out the running time. Hooper not only reuses the hokey cop-out finish, but also expensively restages extensive and pointless soldiers-rushing-around scenes that make the movie seem interminable.

A kid (Carson) suspects his parents have been taken over by aliens, who are hiding under the sandpit, and appeals for help from his sympathetic teacher (Black) and a gruff general (Karen). Hooper imposes his own personality on the film only through the character of the alien-dominated science teacher (Fletcher), whose van is a miniature version of the stuffed animal-decorated house of *The Texas Chainsaw Massacre* (1973), and who is glimpsed echoing the aliens of the *V* series by swallowing a live frog.

Howard the Duck *in flight.*

Great sets, pity about the movie: Invaders From Mars.

The film reproduces Menzies' striking set designs, but Hooper's cluttered, unsubtle approach is at odds with the original's sparse eeriness. The only major attempt at updating the material is in the effects, which are plentiful and spectacular. However, the head-in-a-fishbowl Supreme Martian Intelligence of the 1953 film, a throwaway prop in a school basement here, is somehow more unsettling than Hooper's faced-brain-on-a-stalk. Only Newman and Bottoms, as the possessed parents, have any idea of the genre's requirements, with the rest of the one-note performances comparing badly even with the makeshift acting of Helena Carter, Arthur Franz and Morris Ankrum in the original. Unlike **Invasion of the Body Snatchers** (1978), **The Thing** (1982) and **The Fly** (1986) and like **Gojira** (1985), **The Blob** (1988) and **Not of This Earth** (1988), this is a remake which really has nothing to add to the original movie and is thus forced to flounder in the wake of a cheaper, less self-conscious, but fundamentally more powerful film.

d Tobe Hooper *p* Menahem Golan, Yoram Globus *s* Dan O'Bannon, Don Jakoby *c* Daniel Pearl *se* Apogee, John Dykstra, Stan Winston *lp* Karen Black, Hunter Carson, Timothy Bottoms, Laraine Newman, James Karen, Bud Cort, Louise Fletcher

Kamikaze

(LES FILMS DU LOUP/ARP/GAUMONT; FR) scope 89 min
Less a style-heavy thriller after the manner of such French eighties hits as *Diva* (1982) and **Mauvais Sang** (1986) than a throwback to the seventies international cycle of Science Fiction-tinged paranoia movies. Like such American movies as *The Parallax View* (1974) and *Winter Kills* (1979) or the home-grown *Écoute Voir* (1979), *Kamikaze* mixes bizarre assassination hardware and computerized complications with the traditional, down-at-heel strengths of the *policier*, as it follows its two central characters through their own labyrinths.

Galabru, an unemployed mad scientist obsessed with television, invents a Flash Gordon-style ray gun cannon which, when pointed at the screen, can kill anyone appearing live. When the smarmy link-men and -women on French afternoon TV start getting blasted in the middle of their announcements, rumpled *flic* Bohringer gets on the case with the aid of a roomful of boffins and sets out to track down the unknown killer. Meanwhile, Galabru is getting more and more paranoid, prompting his loving niece – with whom he shares a dark old house – to become suspicious. And Bohringer notices that the government is paying unhealthy attention to this particular murder investigation.

Galabru is outstanding as the mad murderer, starting out as a sympathetic loser getting back at the smug mannequins who simper all over his TV set ('I was right, wasn't I?' he asks, when finally confronted by his nemesis), before turning into a major psychopath who whites his face and dresses up as a Mishima-style samurai, demonstrating an extraordinary callousness to achieve his ends by murdering his own niece when she catches him with his superweapon. Bohringer is a typically anti-bureaucratic French cop hero, bewildered by the high-tech frills of the case, as explained by a Quatermass-style conclave of experts, but able to crack it by methodical footwork, although he is finally frustrated by the intervention of a state apparatus even more oppressive and casually brutal than the madman he's after. It's a fun film, tinged with seriousness, but, like Claude Chabrol's murderous TV quiz show host movie *Masques* (1986), the blackness of its central idea might have been funnier set against the horrors of British or American television rather than the notoriously tasteful and inoffensive French networks.

d/co-s Didier Grousset *p/co-s* Luc Besson *c* Jean François Robin *se* Georges Demetrou, Pierre Foury, Jacky Dufour *lp* Richard Bohringer, Michel Galabru, Dominique Lavanant, Riton Liebman, Kim Massee, Harry Cleven, Romane Bohringer

Mauvais Sang *aka* **The Night Is Young** (LES FILMS PLAIN CHANT/SPOROFILMS/FR3 FILMS/UNITÉ 3; FR) 119 min
In 2058, climatic conditions are being affected by the return of Halley's Comet, and France is being swept by an AIDS-style disease, which is spread by couples who have sex without being in love. Despite the minimally evoked futuristic setting – perhaps an echo of **Alphaville** (1965) – the film is essentially an Art Movie that dawdles its way through a plot similar to that of *Rififi* (1954), as punk Lavant is recruited by a gang of crooks to plan and execute a daring heist, the object of the robbery being a serum which can cure the disease. With a pair of achingly beautiful actresses (Binoche, Delpy) thrown away in undercharacterized girlfriend roles, and some understated playing from old pros Piccoli and Meyer, this is an uninvolving, posy adolescent's movie that takes forever to get around to its climax. In a bizarre and unsuccessful attempt at humour, the finish finds Lavant borrowing a trick from *Blazing Saddles* (1974), as he holds himself hostage while the police surround the building. Pretty, but infuriating.

d/s Léos Carax *p* Philippe Diaz *c* Jean-Yves Escoffier *se* Guy Trielli *lp* Michel Piccoli, Juliette Binoche, Denis Lavant, Hans Meyer, Julie Delpy

Maximum Overdrive (DEG) 97 min
'If you don't take your hand off me, you're gonna be wipin' your ass with a hook next time you take a dump!' While King's script, from his own short story 'Trucks', has much of the profane grittiness of hiš prose, his début as a director is hardly notable.

The Earth passes through the tail of a comet, and all the machinery in the world rebels against mankind, penning up a small group of characters in a southern roadside diner. The situation is modelled on that of **Night of the Living Dead** (1968), with ominous-looking lorries replacing zombies as the menace, but King never approaches Romero's grip on his subject. The occasional scenes of machines uprising – an automated cashpoint calls a cameoing King an asshole, a coke machine beans a football coach with a deadly can, a pitch-roller squashes a kid – are fairly impressive 'gags', but don't integrate into the not very suspenseful siege situation, and, despite the professional work of Estevez and Hingle, the characters don't become more than swearing stick figures before they meet their mainly bloody demises.

d/s Stephen King *p* Martha Schumacher *c* Armando Nanuzzi *se* Steve Galick, Dean Gates *lp* Emilio Estevez, Pat Hingle, Laura Harrington, Yeardley Smith, John Short, Ellen McElduff, J.C. Quinn, Christopher Murney, Holter Graham

Midnight Movie Massacre (WILLIAMS) 85 min
A patchwork movie pieced together by Kansas City nostalgia entrepreneur Williams, this reuses various key props and images from fifties Science Fiction movies to little effect. Originally intended as a satire of the old *Space Patrol* TV series, in the manner of the title segment of *Amazon Women on the Moon* (1987), with authentic fifties stars Robert Clarke and Ann Robinson and a horde of Republic-style tincan robots, the film was begun by Larry Jacobs and left unfinished. As it stands, the footage from the spoof, in which Commander Cory (Staffer), cadet Happy (Hutsler) and a future glamour girl (Robbins) return to the 1950s to foil a mad scientist's plan to change the past, is seen on the screen in a 1956 movie theatre while various broad, unfunny comic skits, directed by Stock, are taking place in the audience.

A real-live Martian, who looks something like the creature from **It Came from Outer Space** (1953) with added tentacles, shows up in a flying saucer and wanders around the theatre gorily murdering people in graphic, but completely unconvincing, splatter sequences. Padded out with trailer footage from **Cat Women of the Moon** (1953) and **Devil Girl from**

Yeardley Smith in Maximum Overdrive.

Mars (1954), this amateurish production becomes something of an ordeal thanks to several of the worst running jokes in motion picture history – one involving snot, the other featuring a gluttonous patron (Case) who ultimately disposes of the real Martian by eating it – although the pastiche rock 'n' roll songs are in fact surprisingly good.

d Mark Stock, Larry Jacobs *p* Wade Williams *s* Roger Branit, John Chadwell, David Houston, Mark Stock *c* David Dart, Nicholas Von Sternberg *se* Ken Wheatly *lp* Robert Clarke, Ann Robinson, David Staffer, Tom Hutsler, Margie Robbins, Brad Bittiker, Charity Case

Monster in the Closet (TROMA) 87 min
This mediocre Science Fiction/horror comedy humiliates and misuses the old-timers it wheels on as 'guest stars'. Carradine does a demeaning turn as a blind idiot and is killed before the credits, and Stevens is required to go topless in a *Psycho* (1960) parody shower scene.

A monster is travelling from closet to closet, killing people, and a heroic Clark Kent-lookalike reporter (Grant) gets put on the case, and discovers that, in addition to being a murderous reptile from another dimension, the monster is gay. The most amusing of several attempts to thwart the beast comes in a televised appeal by the heroine (DuBarry), who entreats the viewers to destroy every closet in America in order to shut the monster out.

The creature itself is a surprisingly detailed man-in-a-suit thing in direct line of descent from **The Creature from the Black Lagoon** (1954) and **Alien** (1979), but the *Airplane!* (1980) style parade of cameo performers fails to get much humour out of the done-to-death fifties pastiche.

d/s Bob Dahlin *p* David Levy, Peter Bergquist *c* Ronald W. McLeish *se* William Stout, Doug Beswick *lp* Donald Grant, Denise DuBarry, Henry Gibson, Claude Akins, Howard Duff, Donald Moffat, Paul Dooley, John Carradine, Frank Ashmore, Paul White, Jesse White, Stella Stevens

Right: The restless calm of Offret.

Night of the Creeps *aka* Homecoming Night
(TRI-STAR) 88 min

'The good news is that your dates are here,' snarls cop Atkins to some huddled co-eds, 'the bad news is that they're dead.' This is a jokey retread of the fifties Science Fiction film, wittily scripted – if with an over-reliance on in-jokes, like naming all the characters after horror movie directors – but only adequately directed by Dekker, who would pull the elements together much better for his subsequent *The Monster Squad* (1987). In a fifties opening sequence, a cop has to deal at the same time with a faithless girlfriend who has ditched him for a football-playing hunk, a mad axeman who has just escaped from the asylum and is running loose, and a test tube from outer space which has crash-landed in the vicinity, disgorging a horde of wriggly, brain-eating parasites. In the present day, some frat pledges at Corman University steal an alien-infested corpse that has been deep-frozen for twenty-five years, and the horror starts up again. Although it has a superfluity of 'B' picture ideas, it all boils down to some pretty standard zombie riffs with the odd exploding brainpan, humorous suicide attempt or alien-dominated axe murderer to liven it up. Dekker's characterizations, especially of the hero's crippled best friend (Marshal), are rather sturdier than the rest of the flippant screenplay, and the performers are more animated than usual. More distinctive a pastiche than *Return of the Living Dead* (1985) or **Critters** (1986), both of which it resembles, this is still too derivative to make much of an impression.

d/s Fred Dekker   *p* Charles Gordon   *c* Robert C. New
se Ted Rae   *lp* Jason Lively, Steve Marshal, Jill Whitlow, Tom Atkins, Wally Taylor, Bruce Solomon, Dick Miller

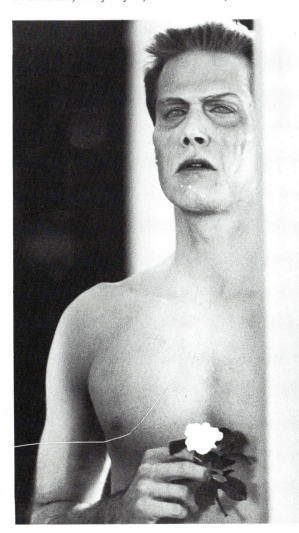

A zombie stalks in Night of the Creeps.

Offret *aka* The Sacrifice
(SWEDISH FILM INSTITUTE/ARGOS; SWED/FR)   149 min

When World War Three destroys the world, a Swedish intellectual (Josephson) living in a remote rural area promises God that he will destroy his life if the deity takes back the nuclear holocaust. He wakes up to find that the devastation was either all a nightmare or has indeed been revoked by divine intervention, whereupon he burns down his house as a sacrifice to save everyone else. Tarkovsky's last film features his distinctive traits of inordinate length and long-held static shots, but otherwise blends in – through the use of familiar actors, settings, themes and technicians – with the works of Ingmar Bergman. *Skammen* (1968) is especially evoked by the confrontation of the withdrawn ascetic with a violent war, and the conclusion that even a tortured genius can retreat only so far from the world, while the endless dinner table conversations and icy relationships recall all Bergman's island-set psychodramas. Reduced to the bare bones of its plot and content, *Offret* contrives to 'say' less about its subject than *The Day the World Ended* (1955), although several of its stretches are undeniably fascinating and resonant. This is especially true of the war itself, conveyed by characters moving from window to window as unseen missiles whizz past the house, the monochrome flashes of the ravaged world that encroaches upon the hero's bleak but settled existence, and the extraordinary one-take sequence at the end, when Josephson carries out his part of the bargain.

d/s Andrei Tarkovsky   *p* Katinka Farago   *c* Sven Nykvist
se Svenska Stungruppen   *lp* Erland Josephson, Susan Fleetwood, Valérie Mairesse, Alan Edwall

Pisma Myortvoi Chelovyeka *aka* Letters From a Dead Man   (LENFILM; USSR)   87 min

'You're the last of the humanists, in other words, of the prehistoric mammoths.' Russia's contribution to the serious post-nuclear drama cycle, epitomized by TV productions like *The Day After* (1983), **Testament** (1983) and *Threads* (1984), perhaps inevitably opts for the doom and gloom approach contained in Stalin's famous remark that 'the survivors would envy the dead'. Shaken survivors with battered street clothes, pasty faces and ragged hair huddle in an orange-lit cavern and mumble about their misery, while water drips on the soundtrack. In contrast to most Western World War Three

'I think we take a left here': Number Five and Ally Sheedy in Short Circuit.

stories, the nuclear holocaust here hasn't demolished the apparatus of the state – a bald official issues passes to those who have a stronger chance of survival; there are still military checkpoints; and, while everyone grumbles about it, these survivors are dutifully working for the preservation of an old order rather than the establishment of a new.

Outside the bunker, the film goes into a grainy, blue-tinged monochrome, and decontamination-suited troops summarily execute offenders who are found supporting a black market in tinned food or painkillers. Despite the deliberately non-specific setting – the character names suggest Scandinavia rather than Russia – the impression is that this is less a prophetic vision of nuclear war, as are Western movies, than a bitter caricature of contemporary Soviet life before *glasnost*. The punchline, in which the scientist narrator passes on the spirit of Christmas (?) to the children of the apocalypse, and his voice is replaced by that of one of the children recounting his legend, is oddly reminiscent of that of **Mad Max 2** (1981). It's sometimes moving, but its despair is almost bland and the post-holocaust alienation effects prevent it from working up the angry charge that Western movies have.

d/co-s Konstantin Lpoushansky *p* Raisa Proskuryakova, Yuri Golinchik *co-s* Vyacheslav Ribakov, Boris Strugatsky *c* Nikolai Pokoptsev *se* A. Filaretov, I. Krinsky *lp* Rolan Bikov, I. Riklin, V. Mikhailov, A. Sabinin, N. Gryakalova

Prison Ship *aka* **Starslammer: The Escape** *aka* **Prison Ship: Starslammer** (VIKING FILMS) 88 min
As Ray's would-be camp quickies go, this is fairly enjoyable. Like the legendary and barely-seen *Space Sluts in the Slammer* (1987), this locates the clichés of the women-behind-bars exploitation genre of *Caged Heat* (1974) or *The Concrete Jungle* (1982) in a threadbare outer space. With leftover space footage from Harris' **Dark Star** (1974) and one monster borrowed from **The Deadly Spawn** (1983), this is obviously a cheapskate production, but it gets quite a bit of humour out of

its stunt of placing the familiar elements of the women's prison story – a one-eyed sadistic trusty, a corrupt warden, a revolutionary doctor, the fresh fish who toughens up after a hazing, the final escape-riot scene – in a new surrounding. Ray has a brief cameo as a torturer who won a prize as a child for squashing a record number of tribbles, while Carradine is the President of the Universe in another walk-on, which leaves hard-boiled villain Hagen to carry the acting weight of the movie. One scene takes place on Planet Arous, home of **Brain from Planet Arous** (1958). The sex and violence are amusingly gratuitous, the in-jokes are better placed than usual and the idea is fun, leaving only the familiar cast and production inadequacies to let the movie down.

d Fred Olen Ray *p* Jack H. Harris *s* Michael D. Sonye *c* uncredited *se* Brett Nixon *lp* Ross Hagen, Sandy Brooke, Susan Stokey, Dawn Wildsmith, John Carradine, Aldo Ray, Bobbie Bresee, Johnny Legend, Eric Caidin

Short Circuit (TRI-STAR) pv 98 min
Badham's fuzzy-minded technophilia, previously seen in **Blue Thunder** (1983) and **War Games** (1983), resurfaces in this film, in which the director yet again justifies his fascination with the cinematic delights of death-dealing gadgetry through a plot in which a machine designed as an instrument of mass devastation is bent to the slightly anachronistic cause of peace and love. Here, the mechanical star is Number Five, a military robot who is struck by magical lightning and develops self-awareness, deserting from his martinet masters to pal around with boy genius Guttenberg and scatty modern miss Sheedy, while the Evil Establishment sets out to track it down and smash it to pieces. There is some sort of progression, in that the moral judgement is neither imposed by a conventional screen hero (as in *Blue Thunder*) nor coaxed out of the machine through simplistic rational argument (as in *War Games*), but is generated spontaneously within the sentient circuits of Number Five just as arbitrarily as the

'No, we turn right': the teenage astronauts of Space Camp.

Frankensteinian lightning bolt brings it to life. This gradual shift towards a species of mechanist mysticism is matched by Badham's loss of the suspense movie verve that made his earlier variations on the theme work as streamlined entertainments (if not as assessments of the role of the machine in modern society).

Following the lead of the awkward middle section of **E.T.: The Extra-Terrestrial** (1982), which is virtually reprised in the initial sheltering of Number Five by Sheedy, and the rather more accomplished teen movie asides of *War Games*, Badham here makes the general tone of the film sit-com bland. The corporate villains are buffoons who pose no threat to the resourceful robot or his friends, and Guttenberg and Sheedy demonstrate their proven amiability in vacuum-filling roles. Given that Number Five is capable of a wide range of expression, it is unfortunate that the script's demands on him – impersonations of John Travolta, John Wayne, Elmer Fudd and George Raft – are so minimal. Furthermore, it is unfortunate and distasteful that Stevens, in the role of Guttenberg's East Indian sidekick, should be allowed to resuscitate the Peter Sellers caricature, complete with 'goodness gracious me' malapropisms, which has been unacceptable on the grounds of racism even on British television since the early seventies.

d John Badham   *p* David Foster, Lawrence Turman
s S.S. Wilson, Brent Maddock   *c* Nick McClean   *se* Eric Allard   *lp* Ally Sheedy, Steve Guttenberg, Fisher Stevens, Austin Pendleton, G.W. Baily, Brian MacNamara, Tim Blaney

Space Camp (ABC) 108 min

Unfortunately released in the wake of the *Challenger* space shuttle disaster, this pro-NASA teen movie deservedly splashed down and sank without trace. A group of misfit kids at a summer training camp for wanna-be astronauts – a studious girl, a bimbo who isn't as stupid as she pretends, a cocky nerd who discovers responsibility, a stock black kid, and a truly annoying brat (Phoenix) who thinks he is Luke Skywalker – are semi-accidentally blasted into outer space, thanks to the intervention of a cute robot, and have to get back on their own. With annoying junior characters driving Skerritt and Capshaw to exasperation, this juggles predictable dumb comedy with embarrassing self-help homilies. In addition to its other demerits, it is saddled with surprisingly bad special effects, with many a matt fringe on view.

Right: The Voyage Continues: Star Trek IV.

d Harry Winer   *p* Patrick Baily, Walter Coblenz
s W.W. Wicket (pseud?), Casey T. Mitchell   *c* William A. Fraker   *se* Barry Nolan   *lp* Kate Capshaw, Lea Thompson, Kelly Preston, Larry B. Scott, Leaf Phoenix, Tate Donovan, Tom Skerritt, Barry Primus, Terry O'Quinn

Star Trek IV: The Voyage Home *aka* The Voyage Home: Star Trek IV (PAR) pv 119 min

After spending an inordinate amount of time tying up plot threads left over from the last two movies, this takes the regular crew of the destroyed *Enterprise* back to the twentieth century to kidnap a pair of extinct whales, which need to be transported to the twenty-third century in order to talk a mysterious space probe out of destroying the Earth. Although the time trip allows for some discreet humour – Kirk adopting a profane eighties vocabulary that he has learned from 'the literature of the period, the collected works of Jacqueline Susann, the novels of Harold Robbins' ('the giants,' observes Spock) – that is an improvement over the sombre tone of the first three films, *The Voyage Home* is still stuck with the cast's advancing years, the astounding fact that Doohan and Koenig still haven't perfected their Scots or Russian accents, a storyline awash with major plot-holes, dead spots and eco-blather, and clichés carried over from the original TV series. Shatner, given twenty-four hours to save the world, still finds time to take the heroine (Hicks) out for a romantic dinner, whereupon he goes back on his earlier buffoonery by lapsing into his usual pompous pose and trotting out chat-up lines from D.H. Lawrence.

The trendy green overtones of the plot have echoes of those TV episodes that embarrassingly tried to address the Vietnam question or the counterculture without offending anyone, and lead to some impassioned and overly earnest save-the-whale pleading, plus a throwaway snide remark about the twentieth century's 'brief but disastrous flirtation with nuclear fission'. This is all very well if your civilization is powered by non-existent dilithium crystals, but otherwise not terribly helpful. There is also some attempt to patronize the eighties for the Cold War, which hardly sits well with a script that includes not only evil Russian whalers but also a Klingon-Federation confrontation that excuses Kirk's *Top Gun* (1986) style adventuring and makes the Federation of United Planets seem more than ever like a United States of Outer Space.

d Leonard Nimoy   *p/co-s* Harve Bennett   *co-s* Steve Meerson, Peter Krikes, Nicholas Meyer   *c* Don Peterman   *se* ILM   *lp* William Shatner, Leonard Nimoy, DeForrest Kelly, Catherine Hicks, James Doohan, George Takei, Walter Koenig, Nichelle Nichols

Terminus (CAT PRODUCTIONS/LES FILMS DU CHEVAL DE FER/
INITIAL GROUPE/FILMS A2/CBL FILMPRODUKTION; FR/WG)
110(83) min
This is a muddled collection of over-familiar elements, with
steel-handed Hallyday taking over from martyred Allen as the
driver of a 'ferroglider' (an armoured mobile home) in a
futuristic road sport like the ones seen in **Death Race 2000**
(1975) or *Bronx lotta finale* (1984). Prochnow has several roles
as villains who are clones of each other, and the film features a
child genius who is attempting to use the heroes to rescue his
sister. It also features the usual Nazi-type villains, and
plentiful unimpressive stuntwork as customized and
armoured vehicles chase each other. It is more expensive
and better cast than the average Italian post-holocaust
quickie, but still repetitive (even in its truncated British
release print). Allen, who brings a touch of life to the film, is
killed off fairly early in the action, leaving Prochnow's
overacting and Hallyday's impassivity to bounce off each
other to little effect.

d/co-s Pierre William Glenn   *co-s* Patrice Duvic   *c* Jean-
Claude Vicquery   *se* Christian Talenton   *lp* Johnny
Hallyday, Karen Allen, Jurgen Prochnow, Gabriel Damon,
Julie Glenn

TerrorVision (EMPIRE/ALTAR)   83(72) min
A mutant monster from outer space is beamed to earth and
emerges from the many television sets in the house of
satellite-dish-obsessed Graham and Woronov, hungrily menacing the entire family. A jokey, cartoony horror comic with a
cardboard vision of Outer Space – the monster comes from
Planet Pluton – and lots of in-gags about cheap Science Fiction
movies piped in by Elvira-style horror movie host Edwards,
TerrorVision is in the spirit of the incredibly-detailed *MAD*
magazine strips of the fifties. Graham and Woronov seethe with a
frenzy of consumerist sexuality as they add more and more
gadgets to their garishly tasteless house, and are appropriately
punished with incorporation into the writhing, many-headed
monster; Remsen's Granpa is a survivalist crusading to solve the
world hunger problem by encouraging everyone to eat lizards'
tails, because (of course) they grow back after they've been eaten;
and even the kids, traditionally better at dealing with aliens, from
The Blob (1958) to **E.T.: The Extra-Terrestrial** (1982), are
cartoon creations who fully deserve to get eaten in the finale. The
grinning creature is well in tune with the cartooned human
characters, and Nicolaou even finds room for a few moments of
genuine eeriness, when a character swims through a jacuzzi
towards the beckoning, no-longer-human head of his girlfriend.

d/s Ted Nicolaou   *p* Albert Band   *c* Romano Albani
se John Buechler   *lp* Mary Woronov, Gerrit Graham, Diane
Franklin, Chad Allen, Jonathan Gries, Jennifer Richards,
Alejandro Rey, Bert Remsen, Randi Brooks

Transformers: The Movie (SUNBOW/MARVEL)   85 min
This is a feature-length cartoon designed to show off the
entire range of Transformer toys – ingenious robots that can
be disjointed and reassembled either as superheroically
endowed humanoid giant robots, or as a variety of items
including trucks, ghetto-blasters, sportscars, ack-ack guns
and motorcycles – put out by the Hasbro toy company. Given
that it is torn between the need to tell a story and the need to
demonstrate its characters' transforming capabilities, as in a
toy advert, this has an incredibly complicated storyline which
somewhat resembles a thumbnail sketch of the twentieth
century history of the Balkans. A war between the Autobots
(good transformers) and Decepticons (bad transformers) is
complicated by the arrival of Unicron, a planet-sized mechanical omnivore voiced by Orson Welles, who enlists a certain
faction of Decepticons to help him get hold of the Autobots'
Matrix of Power. Also involved are such minor races as the
Dinobots (robot dinosaurs), the Sharkticons (robot sea
monsters), the Quintessons (evil tentacled things) and the
Junkions (scrap metal robots) plus two token human beings.
Dialogue is mainly on the speech bubble level of 'I've got
better things to do tonight than die' or 'Let this mark the end
of the cybertronic wars', and it's all scored with pulsing,
neverending, undistinguished rock courtesy of Vince DiCola.

d Nelson Shin   *p* Joe Bacal, Tom Griffin   *s* Ron Friedman
c Masatoshi Fukui   *se* Masayuki Kawachi, Shoji Sato
lp Eric Idle, Judd Nelson, Leonard Nimoy, Robert Stack,
Lionel Stander, Orson Welles, Scatman Crothers

The Vindicator *aka* **Frankenstein 1990**
(LEVY; CAN)   90 min
A well-produced but fundamentally silly and uninteresting
version of **The Terminator** (1984), with a mad scientist
murdering a colleague and then reviving him inside a space
suit that makes him indestructible. Naturally, the monster
goes on a Frankensteinian rampage, killing Hells' Angels,
befriending a little boy, visiting his own grieving widow, and
killing off the scientists who have done him wrong. The
special effects are impressive, but the humourless script and
performances are directly off the rack, with only Grier as a
hard-nosed bounty hunter adding any life to a generally
robotic cast.

d Jean-Claude Lord   *p* Don Carmody, John Dunning
s Edith Rey, David Preston   *c* Debra Karen
se Stan Winston   *lp* Terri Austin, Richard Cox, Maury
Chaykin, Pam Grier, David McIlwraith

When the Wind Blows
(MELTDOWN/FILM FOUR INTERNATIONAL)   84 min
Before turning his best-selling graphic novel into a screenplay, Raymond Briggs made an interim radio adaptation, with
the unfortunate effect that this cartoon is shackled to the
non-stop chatter of its two characters. Jim (Mills) and Hilda
(Ashcroft) live in Sussex, and are concerned with the build-up
to World War Three. They follow the advice given in official
pamphlets, but the aftermath of the Bomb proves considerably worse than they have been told, and they are left on
their own. Moaning about international crises they haven't
bothered to be interested in, misled by memories of the
blitzed cameraderie of the last war and somewhat unfairly
patronized by the film, the working class couple is shattered
to learn that nuclear holocaust means that the milk stops
being delivered, they can't use the flush toilet and the curtains
are all destroyed. While Murakami, director of the live-action

*Left: Product-
placement reaches
Science Fiction:*
Transformers: The
Movie.

When the Wind
Blows.

Battle Beyond the Stars (1980), makes use of state-of-the-art cartoon technology to make the best use of three-dimensional sets in the medium since *Hoppity Goes to Town* (1941), the film still has a certain middle-class CND smugness about it, with *Sir* John Mills and *Dame* Peggy Ashcroft trying to sound thick as typical 'ordinary' people, and a dirge-like David Bowie theme song.

d Jimmy T. Murakami   *p* John Coates   *s* Raymond Briggs   *c* Pete Turner, Maureen Simons, Roger Chandler, Roy Watford   *se* Camera Effects, Peerless Films   *lp* John Mills, Peggy Ashcroft

Whoops Apocalypse (ITC; GB)   91 min
Adapted from the considerably more amusing television serial, this is an attempt to make a sort of *Carry On Dr Strangelove*, with a bunch of British comedians involved in the build-up to World War Three. It manages to be as witless and annoying as any British gutter comedy can be, with an endless parade of fag jokes, fart jokes, bared bottoms and alternative comedians saying 'fuck' a lot. The flashpoint here is a caricature of the Falklands crisis, with Prime Minister Cook, a lunatic obsessed with pixies, sending a fleet to a Central American dependency that has been overrun by Lom, which leads to a marine confrontation similar to the punchline of *The Bedford Incident* (1965) as the camp submariner (Richardson) accidentally gives the order to end the world. The crucial cop-out is that, while **Dr Strangelove** (1964) achieved its chilling comedy by presenting a selection of high-ranking madmen who were frighteningly good at their jobs, this presents simply an assortment of clowns and cartoon psychopaths who take the world to war. Given the real-life political

Right: Alexei Sayle in the disappointing Whoops Apocalypse.

situation at the time of production and the perceived need to make inroads into the US box office, there is something decidedly compromised in its following of *Dr Strangelove* by

depicting a US president (Swit) who is a well-meaning liberal who tries to avert the catastrophe.

d Tom Bussmann   *p* Brian Eastman   *s* Andrew Marshall, David Renwick   *c* Ron Robson   *se* Peter Hutchinson, J.B. Jones   *lp* Loretta Swit, Peter Cook, Michael Richards, Rik Mayall, Alexei Sayle, Ian Richardson, Herbert Lom, Joanne Pearce

Batteries Not Included (AMBLIN/U) 106 min

A single dilapidated brownstone stands in a wasteland that used to be 8th Street, New York, its tenants under pressure from capitalists and thugs to sell out and make way for a tower block. Then a pair of frisbee-sized flying saucers arrive, perhaps in answer to the prayers of diner chef Frank Riley (Cronyn), and start fixing things. The lady flying saucer (!) is pregnant (!?) and gives births to triplets (£?*&$%!!), one of which is still-born and has to be revived by an ex-prizefighter janitor. In addition to seeing off the property developers, the saucers cheer up a pregnant Hispanic, an unfashionable artist and Frank's daffy wife Faye (Tandy). Like **Harry and the Hendersons** (1987), this Steven Spielberg-produced slice of whimsy (originally intended as an episode of his half-hour *Amazing Stories* TV show) is a by-the-numbers re-assembly of the ingredients of **E.T.: The Extra-Terrestrial** (1982).

Again, we have superb special effects in the service of a sugary comedy/soap opera (*The Love Bug*, 1969, *Blackbeard's Ghost*, 1968) of the kind Walt Disney pioneered in the sixties, and a vision of the world that brooks no problems so deep that they can't be solved with a smile and some childish sense of wonder. In this case, one particularly objects to the trivialization of Faye's senility, and the credibility gap is exacerbated by the fact that the script makes absolutely no connection between the *deus ex machina* spaceships and the troubles of their earthly friends. As with **Cocoon** (1985), it's a shame that such terrific senior citizen players as Cronyn and Tandy are stuck with such unrewarding material, but they do manage to put it over with a conviction unmatched by the rest of the cast. There's a nice big band score by James Horner, though.

d/co-s Matthew Robbins *p* Ronald L. Schwary *co-s* Brad Bird, Brent Maddock, S.S. Wilson *c* John McPherson *se* ILM *lp* Hume Cronyn, Jessica Tandy, Elizabeth Pena, Frank McRae, Michael Carmine, Dennis Boutsikaris, Tom Aldredge

Le Big Bang *aka* The Big Bang

(ZWANZ/COMEDA; FR/BELG) 90(76) min

When it looks as if World War Four – fought between the male population of the USSSR, a combination of Russia and America, and the women of Vaginia, a matriarchy ruled by a multi-breasted hag – will destroy the fabric of the Universe, dustbinman superhero Fred, who is powered by a lightbulb in his navel, is sent to Earth to stop the trouble, and encounters a race of human beings who have literally had their asses blown off in a nuclear war. A witless cartoon with pornographic and scatological jokes, a relentless stupidity, and dialogue gems like 'I didn't come 300 light years to get fucked by a homo!' In the end, Earth has an orgy and the universe is destroyed.

d Picha *p* Boris Zsulzinger *s* Tony Hendra *c* Philippe Benoit, Michel Bertiaux, Jean-Claude Callet, Daved Ferre, Bernard Forestier, Krikel Hamel, Pascal Jardin, Richard Kuziemsky, Pierre Mialaret *se* Pascal Roulin *lp* David Lander, Carole Androfsky, Marshall Efron, Alice Pleyten, Marvin Silbersher

Blue Monkey *aka* Insect *aka* Invasion of the Body Suckers

(SPECTRAFILM; CAN) 98 min

A contagious disease leads to the quarantining of an urban hospital, which coops up cop hero Railsback, some doctors and a soap operatic bunch of patients with a giant insect from Micronesia, which has hatched out of a casualty and accidentally been fed a growth hormone by an irksome brat with leukaemia. The hospital is as equipped with corridors and boiler rooms as the spaceship from **Alien** (1979), and also happens to have handy a super-laser unit that comes in useful when the monster has to be defeated. The result is a silly big bug movie with a few comedy scenes to make it seem more

Jessica Tandy and the tiny flying saucer that enlivens her life in Batteries Not Included.

tongue-in-cheek than it actually is. The insect prowls in subjective camera, the clichés come thick and fast, and Fruet again demonstrates that his directorial flair might be better applied to a real screenplay rather than a warmed-over collection of fifties cast-offs.

d William Fruet *p* Martin Walters *s* George Goldsmith *s* Brenton Spencer *se* Steve Neill *lp* Steve Railsback, Gwynyth Walsh, Susan Anspach, John Vernon, Joe Flaherty, Robin Duke, Don Lake, Sandy Webster

Creepozoids (URBAN CLASSICS) 71 min

'It's an incredible protein chemical, it's probably impossible.' Like the Italian *Rats: Notte di terrore* (1984), this features a group of post-holocaust wanderers who find themselves in a subterranean bunker where scientific experiments have created a monstrous mutation.

Yet another low-budget spin-off from **Alien** (1979), *Creepozoids* features a unit of deserting soldiers picked off by giant rats, a slimy monster and the monster's fanged baby. Quigley gets in the obligatory nude shower scene, and the monsters are trotted out at regular intervals, but it's a drearily directed, cramped and uninteresting quickie, spotlighting the usual extended vomiting sequences and plentiful footage-wasting wandering around in the dark. The title achieved some sort of immortality when Stephen King used it (albeit misspelled) as a recurrent expression in his novel *The Dark Half*.

d/co-p/co-s David DeCoteau *co-p* John Schouweiler *co-s* Burford Hauser *c* Thomas Callaway *se* Thom Floutz, Peter Carsillo *lp* Linnea Quigley, Ken Abraham, Michael Aranda, Richard Hawkins, Kim McKamy, Joi Wilson

Evil Spawn *aka* Metamorphosis *aka* Deadly Sting *aka* Alive By Night (CAMP) 73 min

Like the somewhat superior **Rejuvenator** (1988), this attempts to crossbreed *Sunset Boulevard* (1950) and **The Wasp Woman** (1960), as ageing movie star Bobbie Bresee ('My tits are as good as they ever were, and I can act') is given a rejuvenation serum by a psychopathic fan that turns her into a ridiculous monster. It opens with two prologues, one (featuring Carradine as a mad scientist) which may be from an unconnected unfinished movie, and then confines itself to the area around Bresee's swimming pool, alternating exploitative nudity and gore with low-budget in-jokes, but without enough verve to carry it off. Bresee is frankly not up to Susan Cabot standards, let alone Gloria Swanson's level, and the effects are blatantly ludicrous.

d/s Kenneth J. Hall   *p* Anthony Brewster   *c* Christopher Condon   *se* Cleve Hall   *lp* Bobbie Bresee, Drew Godderis, John Terrence, Donna Shock (Dawn Wildsmith), Jerry Fox, Pamela Gilbert, John Carradine, Forrest J. Ackerman

Friendship's Death   (MODELMARK/BFI)   78 min

In Black September – 1970 – in Amman, Jordan, a British reporter (Paterson) meets an elegantly adrift young woman, Friendship (Swinton), who turns out to be an extra-terrestrial envoy. Somehow misdirected, like Klaatu in **The Day the Earth Stood Still** (1951), she was supposed to make contact with the forces of internationalism and deliver a message dissuading the human race from self-destruction, but she has landed in the Middle East rather than the Massachusetts Institute of Technology and her sense of mission is changed by what she sees there. At first agonized when she feels a kinship for the typewriter that Paterson mistreats, she soon comes to identify with the stateless Palestinians and joins the PLO.

An expansion by film theorist Wollen of his own short story, this is an almost entirely interior film, relieved only by library news footage of the great events taking place outside the hotel room where Paterson and Swinton are closeted discussing humanity. While it is a difficult film to respond to warmly, the issues it raises remain with one thanks to the resourceful, cool performances of Paterson and Swinton, who remain alone on camera for almost the entire length of the movie.

d/s Peter Wollen   *p* Colin McCabe   *c* Witold Stok   *lp* Bill Paterson, Tilda Swinton, Patrick Bauchau, Ruby Baker, Joumania Gill

Harry and the Hendersons *aka* Bigfoot and the Hendersons   (AMBLIN/U)   111 min

Despite another superb monster costume from Baker, and the usual fine Lithgow performance, *Harry and the Hendersons* is just another gooey xerox of **E.T.: The Extra-Terrestrial** (1982) and *Splash!* (1984).

The Hendersons, a typical WASP family in the Steven Spielberg vein, run over a Bigfoot (Hall) while vacationing in the woods, and take it home to Seattle, where they call the creature Harry and help it escape from a nasty French scientist (Suchet) who wants to vivisect the amiable creature. When Harry gets lost in the big city, Dad (Lithgow) feels responsible for his slow-witted, hairy pal and sets out to find him before Suchet and some rifle-nut hunters catch up with him.

The script comes on like an extended sit-com pilot, and never really outgrows its lame sight gags and cloying sentiment. In his early screen career, Bigfoot was usually found either in appalling low-budget wandering-in-the woods bores (*Big Foot*, 1971, *Curse of Bigfoot*, 1972, *Creature from Black Lake*, 1976), pseudo-documentaries (*Legend of Boggy Creek*, 1973, *Bigfoot – Man or Beast?*, 1975, *In Search of Bigfoot*, 1976) or in video nasties (*Shriek of the Mutilated*, 1974, *Night of the Demon*, 1980); *Harry and the Hendersons*, his big-budget breakthrough movie, suggests that it's back to the Z-feature woods in future.

d/co-p/co-s William Dear   *co-p* Richard Vane   *co-s* William E. Martin, Ezra D. Rappaport   *c* Allen Daviau   *se* ILM, Rick Baker   *lp* John Lithgow, Melinda Dillon, Margaret Langrick, Joshua Rudoy, Kevin Peter Hall, David Suchet, Lainie Kazan, Don Ameche, M. Emmet Walsh

Hell Comes to Frogtown   (NEW WORLD)   86 min

A lightly likeable post-holocaust parody, with wrestler Piper, who boasts a terrible seventies haircut that no one else could get away with, as one of the last potent men in a world where a female-dominated America is in a population war. Captured by bespectacled warrior Bergman, Piper is taken into the wasteland to rescue and impregnate some fertile maidens being held captive by a band of frog-headed mutants. Most of the humour focuses below the belt on Piper's 'loaded weapon', which is encased in an electrified jockstrap that Bergman can activate to keep him under control, and there are plenty of traditional escapes, shoot-outs, fights and chases. While Piper is simply thuggish as the hero, Bergman brings a few almost subtle touches to her unusually restrained role.

co-d/co-p/co-c Donald G. Jackson   *co-d* R.J. Kizer   *co-p/s* Randall Frakes   *co-c* Enrico Picard   *se* Steve Wang   *lp* Roddy Piper, Sandahl Bergman, Cec Verrell, William Smith, Rory Calhoun, Nicholas Worth, Kristi Somers

InnerSpace   (AMBLIN/WB)   120 min

Quaid, a drunken test pilot with all the Wrong Stuff, volunteers in a fit of pique for a top-secret project whereby he is scientifically miniaturized so that he can be injected into the bloodstream of a rabbit. However, Silicon Valley spies raid the laboratory just after miniaturization and a fleeing scientist, trying to keep the secret out of the villains' hands, injects Quaid into the ass (cheap laugh) of hypochrondriac super-market clerk Short.

A play-it-safe movie for Dante, coming between the ambitious commercial failures of **Explorers** (1985) and *The 'burbs* (1988), *InnerSpace* spoofs **Fantastic Voyage** (1966) without matching the earlier film's colourful charm, and rather oddly combines fairly grim violence (a villain is digested in Short's acidic stomach) with knockabout humour. For a while, it seems to be trying to remedy all the holes and inaccuracies of Richard Fleischer's movie – the interior body sequences make use of drabber, more abstract, more convincing effects, which skilfully combine models with actual microphotography – but eventually the script drops this and comes up with lapses of logic every bit as obvious of those in the first movie. The film is mainly concerned with the comedy thriller aspect, as Short is pursued by the villains, while Quaid tries to tutor him from within about how to be a man, but too often the initially credible characterizations evaporate when the time comes for a cheap joke or an action scene.

d Joe Dante   *p* Michael Finnell   *s* Jeffrey Boam, Chip Proser   *c* Andrew Laszlo   *se* ILM   *lp* Martin Short, Dennis Quaid, Meg Ryan, Kevin McCarthy, Fiona Lewis, Vernon Wells, Robert Picardo, Wendy Schaal, William Schallert, Henry Gibson, Dick Miller, Ken Tobey

Right: The mysteries of InnerSpace.

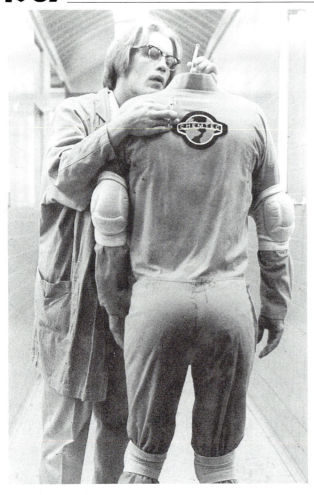

Making Mr Right (ORION) 98 min

A public relations consultant (Magnusson) is hired by an electronics corporation to design a personality for Ulysses (Malkovich), a human-seeming robot created in his own image by a scientist (also Malkovich) for a rigorous deep-space voyage. With a similar premise to **Tobor the Great** (1954), this actually plays more like an update of such robotic comedies as **The Perfect Woman** (1949) as Magnusson and the android fall in love, with the innocently Frankensteinian creation – Magnusson's character name is Frankie Stone – becoming involved in the romantically complex inter-relationships of the heroine's family, lovers and friends. A stylish screwball romance, this is lightly enjoyable but suffers from the usual American comedy problem of feeling the need for 'serious relief', as the film stops dead from time to time to make elementary comments about the fraughtness of human relationships.

d Susan Seidelman   *p* Mike Wise, Joel Tuber   *s* Floyd Byars, Laurie Frank   *c* Edward Lachman   *se* Bran Ferren   *lp* John Malkovich, Ann Magnusson, Glenne Headly, Ben Masters, Laurie Metcalf, Polly Bergen

Masters of the Universe (CANNON) 106 min

'It's about the importance of trust and friendship, of cameraderie and ideals,' claimed director Goddard of this, the first live-action movie to be based on a line of toys (as previously seen in the cartoon *The Secret of the Sword*, 1985). On the planet Eternia, Skeletor (Langella) has breached Castle Grayskull, subjugated to his will the Sorceress who supports the Good Guys, and sworn to make He-Man (Lundgren) – a beefcake-in-bondage hero who looks like a surfing Nazi bodybuilder – kneel before his throne. He-Man and a few loyal pals, including a dwarf (Barty), a crusty old warrior (Cypher), and a warrior girl (Field), zap themselves to the vicinity of a chili take-away place in California, where they get mixed up with a wistful waitress (Cox) and her dumbo musician boyfriend, who mistakes the key to ultimate power everyone is after for 'one of those new Japanese synthesizers'. Skeletor sends his green-eyed girlfriend Evil-Lyn (Foster) and a bunch of killer Darth Vader clones to Earth to get hold of the macguffin. A highly derivative space opera, with hand-

Left: *John Malkovich makes final adjustments in* Making Mr Right.

Dolph Lundgren and his many muscles, with Bill Barty, in Masters of the Universe.

It's Alive III: Island of the Alive (WB/LARCO) 92 min

This is probably the messiest of Cohen's messy movies, held together only by the premise of the earlier films in the series – **It's Alive** (1973), **It Lives Again** (1978) – and by another of Moriarty's wigged-out performances. The amazing hash of a plot brings on a new set of characters every quarter of an hour and keeps changing its tack, with bewildering effect. It opens with a pastiche of the abortion debate, as the Supreme Court decides that the mutants have the right to life and has them banished to an offshore island, while Moriarty, who has fathered a monster with Black, becomes a celebrity by writing a book about his experience. Later, several expeditions are sent to the island, a group of corporate villains who want to get rid of the evidence of their genetically damaging products, and a scientific group who take Moriarty along. After some stalking around the undergrowth, in which the grown-up mutants are seen as rubber-suited monsters, the film detours to Cuba with Moriarty, while transporting mutants to Miami where, suffering from measles, they hunt out Black for love and understanding.

This mixes the ludicrous with the telling, alternating frankly stupid monster-on-the-loose sequences with genuinely daring scenes, like the painful moment in which bimbo Landon freaks out when she realizes just what her casual singles bar pick-up Moriarty is famous for. With an interesting cast, Cohen's usual off-centre wit and enough varied action to keep it moving, this is at least strange enough to be compulsive. Nobody but Cohen could make a film like this; but, then again, nobody but Cohen would want to.

d/s Larry Cohen   *p* Paul Stader   *c* Daniel Pearl   *se* William Hedge   *lp* Michael Moriarty, Karen Black, Laurene Landon, James Dixon, Gerritt Graham, MacDonald Carey, Neal Israel, Art Lund, Anne Dane

The headless torso of Michael Des Barres attacks Catherine Mary Stewart in Nightflyers.

me-down costumes, plot devices, music and dialogue, this is hampered by its bathetic attempt at epic seriousness – somewhat undone when the major action scene turns out to be a scrappy laser fight in a Los Angeles guitar shop that hardly counts as qualification for any of the participants to claim mastery of the universe – and by the embarrassingly camp characterizations.

d Gary Goddard   *p* Menahem Golan, Yoram Globus *s* David Odell   *c* Hanania Baer, William Neil   *se* Richard Edlund, Boss Film Corporation   *lp* Dolph Lundgren, Frank Langella, Meg Foster, Billy Barty, Courteney Cox, James Tolkan, Christina Pickles, Jon Cypher, Chelsea Field

Nightflyers (VISTA FILMS) 89 min

'This ship is alive,' warns hologram Praed, 'it's a seething, malignant presence and it hates all of you.' A disappointing adaptation of George R.R. Martin's very cinematic novella, this is a sloppy **Aliens** (1986) imitation, with Praed's dead clone mother reincarnated as a spaceship's controlling compu-ter – sometimes projected in the image of poseur psychic Des Barres – and murdering one by one a crew recruited by scientist Standing to seek out a mysterious and vast lifeform passing through the galaxy. It has a competent cast – Praed and Des Barres aside – and the ship is an impressively gothic backdrop, but it's essentially a series of mechanized splatter scenes, distantly reminiscent of **Gog** (1954), as the characters are colourfully killed by gadgetry in pop video-style sequ-ences. A passable time-waster, but a good deal less startling than it should have been.

d T.C. Blake (Robert Collector)   *p/s* Robert Jaffe   *c* Shelly Johnson   *se* Robert Short, Fantasy II   *lp* Catherine Mary Stewart, Michael Praed, John Standing, Lisa Blount, Glenn Whitrow, James Avery, Helene Udy, Annabel Brooks, Michael Des Barres

Pathos *aka* **A Taste for Fear** *aka* **Obsession: A Taste for Fear** (TITANUS/REITALIA; IT) 89 min

A glossy, cosmopolitan whodunit along the lines of *The Eyes of Laura Mars* (1978) or *Sotto i vestite niente* (1987). Hey is the bisexual fashion/art photographer on the track of a transves-tite psychopath who has been murdering her model lovers. Whereas the other entries in this cycle leaven their Helmut Newton-style obsession with stylish but mild s/m with psychic frills, this opts for a near-future setting, with much use of video-clip imagery and technology to create a decadent world of luxury perched atop a steamy sub-city of poverty and crime. The science fictional elements include streamlined cars, a computerized wardrobe that coordinates outfits for its mistress, a police-issue zap gun and some high-tech video disc equipment used to crack a clue left on videoed messages of the murders, but they are mainly an excuse for the kind of foggy backlighting and graphics effects familiar from rock video and TV commercials. As usual in this genre, Raffanini seems to align himself visually with the attitude towards violent/erotic art/pornography that is explicitly condemned in the script through the character of the moralistic, designer-stubbled cop (Mucari) on the case, for whom Hey falls. With its retro-chic look, and a trendy music score that ranges from Gershwin to Grace Jones, the film is obviously an exercise in Euro-style, but it also seems like an excuse to truss up a series of gorgeous fashion models in expensively torn clothes for the delectation of the audience.

d Piccio Raffanini   *p* Jacques Lipkau Boyard   *s* Lidia Ravera   *c* Romano Albani   *se* Michele Radice   *lp* Virginia Hey, Gerard Darmon, Kid Creole, Goia Scola, Carlo Mucari, Dario Parisini, Carin McDonald, Tegan Clive, Eva Grimaldi

Predator (FOX) pv 106 min

A faceless, machine-assembled bicep movie, cross-breeding *Rambo: First Blood, Part 2* (1985) with **Alien** (1979), as a group of covert action commandos in the Central American jungles, led by Schwarzenegger, are picked off one by one by an alien big-game hunter who tracks down human beings for sport. The *Most Dangerous Game* (1932) premise is remark-ably similar to that of **Without Warning** (1980), but the plot is worked out in an elementary, predictable fashion, winding up with an effective battle between Schwarzenegger and Win-ston's impressive alien monster (Hall). As in most of his vehicles, Schwarzenegger takes a few time-outs to romance a non-Aryan heroine (Carrillo) and to demonstrate that he is not as right-wing as Chuck Norris, in this case by affirming that he would only destroy an entire guerilla village on a rescue mission and that he would never have bombed Libya. This has plenty of big-budget razzle-dazzle – especially some heat-vision optical effects to show the alien's point of view, and a very interesting masking device that helps the creature

Right: *Arnold Schwarzenegger (left) is the* Predator.

blend into the jungle – and the action man explosions and suffering are well-staged by McTiernan, but it refuses to be anything more than a violent, noisy comic book and so fails to be as thrilling as more ambitious Science Fiction muscle epics like **The Terminator** (1984) and **RoboCop** (1987).

d John McTiernan *p* Lawrence Gordon, Joel Silver, John Davis *s* Jim Thomas, John Thomas *c* Donald McAlpine, Leon Sanchez *se* R. Greenberg, Stan Winston *lp* Arnold Schwarzenegger, Carl Weathers, Elpidia Carrillo, Bill Duke, Jesse Ventura, Sonny Landham, Richard Chaves, R.G. Armstrong, Shane Black, Kevin Peter Hall

Project X (FOX) 103(91) min

Mixing several *Tomorrow's World* items – chimps being taught sign language, the use of primates in flight simulation tests, the dangers of looking after nuclear reactors – this tries to come up with a green-tinged knockabout comedy, as misfit pilot Broderick gets outraged enough by the mistreatment of the intelligent chimpanzees being used in unethical experiments to help them escape. Directed without too much enthusiasm by Kaplan, this is further demonstration that chimpanzees are not as endearing as film-makers would have us believe they are. Ironically, given the subject matter, the film was controversial because of the alleged on-set mistreatment of its simian stars.

d Jonathan Kaplan *p* Walter F. Parkes, Lawrence Lasker *s* Stanley Weiser *c* Dean Cundey *se* Michael Fink *lp* Matthew Broderick, Helen Hunt, Bill Sadler, Johnny Ray McGhee, Jonathan Stark, Robin Gammell, Stephen Lang, Jean Smart

RoboCop (ORION) 102 min

One of the best Science Fiction/action movies of the decade, *RoboCop* marvellously combines the gung-ho vigilante vengeance plot necessary to capture a mass audience with a rigorously well worked-out futuristic environment, an engagingly cynical view of a big business-dominated America and a handful of genuinely science fictional ideas about the

Peter Weller is RoboCop.

interface between technology and humanity. Murphy (Weller), an idealistic cop in the near future, is shot to pieces in downtown Detroit, but the corporation which has just privatized the city's law enforcement agencies has a use for the leftovers. His limbs are replaced, his body is armoured and his brain is wiped and partially replaced with a computer, and soon he is back on the streets as RoboCop, an automated warrior on the beat, who politely solves any and all crimes that he comes across. Typical of his mechanical but humane approach is an incident in which he calmly disposes of a mugger who has been terrorizing a woman, and picks up the damsel in distress, informing her, 'You have been emotionally traumatized, I'll alert the nearest rape crisis centre.' Gradually, however, RoboCop comes to distrust the cynical coporation men (Cox, Ferrer) who have control of him – and who have programmed him not to intervene whenever an official of the corporation is breaking the law – and to regain part of his lost humanness.

Amid the brilliantly choreographed action and violence, Verhoeven even finds time for a little understated sentiment, as the armoured colossus lumbers around the home he used to own or eats babyfood while talking to his ex-partner (Allen). In addition to the conspiracy-revenge storyline, in which RoboCop tracks down corruption, from the criminals who killed him right up to the corporate executive who runs them, the film includes plenty of detail about its invented future. Television commercials, overheard newscasts, infantile sitcoms ('I'll buy that for a dollar') and legal details all hint at the kind of cyberpunk world that has given birth to RoboCop Following **Blade Runner** (1982) and **The Terminator** (1985), this adapts some of the ideas of written Science Fiction – from

Left: Matthew Broderick, Helen Hunt and chimpanzee in Project X.

Isaac Asimov to Philip K. Dick – with regards to robotics and their effect on society. In addition to the RoboCop, the film features an extremely menacing non-anthropomorphic law enforcement droid which has to be disabled, in one of many superb action sequences, by the cyborg who has made it obsolete. As its melodramatically evil villains suggest, this is essentially a comic strip movie; but it's a *great* comic strip movie.

d Paul Verhoeven p Arne Schmidt s Edward Neumeier, Michael Miner c Jost Vocano se Rob Bottin lp Peter Weller, Nancy Allen, Ronny Cox, Dan O'Herlihy, Kurtwood Smith, Miguel Ferrer, Robert DoQui, Ray Wise

The Running Man (TAFT/BARISH) 101 min

Adapted from a novel that Stephen King wrote under his 'Richard Bachman' pseudonym, this is in direct line of descent from **La Decima Vittima** (1965) and *Le Prix du Danger* (1984) – both of which were adapted from Robert Sheckley stories that influenced King – in its depiction of a future gladiatorial sport made popular as a television game show. Schwarzenegger plays an honest cop who bucks the system in a tyrannical future and is framed for mass murder, whereupon he is given the choice of execution or participation in a TV show ('I am your court-appointed theatrical agent,' announces one functionary), in which he is chased through the wastelands of a city on the skids by a group of colourfully costumed celebrity warriors. By overcoming his opponents in spectacular duels, Schwarzenegger wins the support of the viewing public and becomes the focus of a revolutionary movement, which wants to expose the game as the fraud it is in order to bring down the government. With its rather obvious satire of game shows – real-life host Deacon plays a character much like himself – and facile message about pandering to violence-loving audiences, it is a very minor piece of work, which fails even to work up the suspense that King handles quite well, and does especially badly by an interesting supporting cast.

d Paul Michael Glaser p Tim Zinnemann, George Linder s Steven E. deSouza c Thomas Del Ruth se Gary Gutierrez lp Arnold Schwarzenegger, Maria Conchita Alonso, Yaphet Kotto, Jim Brown, Jesse Ventura, Erland Van Lidth, Richard Dawson, Mick Fleetwood, Dweezil Zappa, Professor Toru Tanaka

Spaceballs (BROOKSFILMS/MGM) 96 min

Brooks' largely redundant spoof of the *Star Wars* series fails to be either a clever pastiche of a well-loved genre (like his **Young Frankenstein**, 1974) or a genuinely inventive, tasteless comic skit (like his *Blazing Saddles*, 1974). Limiting itself to one particular movie, the film fails even to parody George Lucas as well as Ernie Fosselius had done in his hilarious short *Hardware Wars* (1978).

President Skroob (Brooks) of the planet Spaceball is trying, with the help of the evil Lord Dark Helmet (Moranis), to kidnap Princess Vespa (Zuniga) of Drudia. To her rescue comes space trucker Lone Starr (Pullman) and his man-dog sidekick Barf (Candy), who need the money to pay off gangster Pizza the Hut. Along the way, Starr meets with small green Jewish sage Yogurt (Brooks again) and is taught to use the power of the Schwartz. Zuniga's bratty performance ('I'm rich, I don't have to put up with this') and one or two mildly amusing jokes about Lucas' merchandising fever ('We'll meet again in the sequel, *Spaceballs II: The Search for More Money*') aside, this is a real failure, wasting its talented cast on a script that could be classified a laugh-free zone, and even Brooks, greedily playing his usual two roles, seems tired of his own jokes. The special effects – which include skits on **Planet of the Apes** (1968) and **Alien** (1979) – are elaborate and impressive, but a lot less funny than Fosselius' flying toasters and electric irons.

Right: Mel Brooks (right), Rick Moranis (centre) as the dastardly Dark Helmet, and George Wyner in the only mildly funny parody of Star Wars, Spaceballs.

d/p/co-s Mel Brooks co-s Thomas Meehan, Ronny Graham c Nick McLean se Apogee Inc, ILM lp Bill Pulman, John Candy, Daphne Zuniga, Rick Moranis, Mel Brooks, Dick Van Patten, George Wyner, John Hurt

Superman IV: The Quest for Peace
(CANNON) 93 min

An unfortunate retread for the *Superman* series, passed from the Salkinds to Cannon, ambitiously and ill-advisedly asking the hero to tackle a serious subject. A Metropolis schoolboy writes to Superman (Reeve) asking him to stop the arms race, whereupon the superhero decides to enforce disarmament on all the nations of the world. Meanwhile, newly escaped archvillain Lex Luthor (Hackman) has created a nuclear-powered and evil Superman clone (Pillow) in order to take over the world. In a sub-plot that is unfortunately rather more interesting than the weighty issues, Clark Kent and Lois Lane (Kidder) have to deal with a sleazy media millionaire (Wanamaker) who has taken over the *Daily Planet* and turned it into a supermarket tabloid edited by his airhead daughter (Hemingway).

Cannon persuaded Reeve to return to the role by allowing him to co-author the story, which then proved a problem because it was both embarrassingly bad and embroiled him in a plagiarism suit that dragged on for years. The attempt to deal in kiddie terms with nuclear weapons makes for lots of annoying, maudlin speeches and a truly banal cop-out ending, and the promising business about the *Planet* take-over fizzles out amid such unlikely plot twists as a Rupert Murdoch-style tabloid tycoon running an anti-nuclear editorial and Hemingway's crush on the bespectacled Clark. The special effects are astonishingly variable, with some very ugly process work, and the titanic clash between Superman and the ridiculously named Nuclear Man falls particularly flat.

d Sidney J. Furie p Menahem Golan, Yoram Globus s Lawrence Kohner, Mark Rosenthal c Ernest Day se Olsen, Lane & White lp Christopher Reeve, Gene Hackman, Margot Kidder, Jackie Cooper, Mariel Hemingway, Mark Pillow, Sam Wanamaker, Marc McClure, Jon Cryer

World Gone Wild (APOLLO) 95 min

This is another remake of *The Magnificent Seven* (1961) in a Science Fiction setting, although this exchanges the space opera universe of **Battle Beyond the Stars** (1980) for a **Mad Max 2** (1981) post-holocaust wasteland. In 2087, fifty years after World War Three, the world is a rain-starved desert, and all-in-white guru Derek (Ant), who reads to his followers from *The Wit and Wisdom of Charles Manson*, is terrorizing the community of Lost Wells. After taking some abuse, leftover hippie headman Dern and schoolteacher Stewart visit the big city to recruit mercenaries to defend the village, and return with a hero (Paré) and some sidekicks. Although it is an American production, shot in Arizona, it looks very much like such Italian action films as **I Nuovi Barbari** (1983) and the similarly water-themed *Barbari 3000* (1983).

With a rare sympathetic role, albeit as a patriotic cannibal, for pockmarked perennial exploitation villain James, and a few eccentric moments – like a final struggle that leaves Paré on the sidelines while a minor character kills Ant, and Jimi Hendrix's 'Star-Spangled Banner' plays on the soundtrack – this is a tolerable quickie, but its painless violence and plentiful explosions give it the feel of an episode of *The A-Team* with a few castrations, throat-cuttings and bullet squibs thrown in. In a predictable fade-out, echoing those of *The Rainmaker* (1956) and *3:10 to Yuma* (1957), all the problems are solved as the clouds break to end the drought.

d Lee H. Katzin *p* Robert L. Rosen *s* Jorge Zamorra
c Don Burgess *se* Cliff Wenger *lp* Bruce Dern, Michael
Paré, Catherine Mary Stewart, Adam Ant, Anthony James,
Rick Podell, Julius Carry III, Alan Autry

1988

Akira (AKIRA; JAP) scope 124 min

This videogame-style feature cartoon is adapted from Otomo's best-selling run of comic books, following the adventures of Akira, a young psychic biker, in a post-holocaust Tokyo of the twenty-first century. There has been a nuclear war, and a new city has been constructed on the old, creating an environment of social decay, similar to that in **Blade Runner** (1982), complete with colourful street gangs, whizzing vehicles, terrorist outrages and plentiful action. With kinetic, computer-assisted animation, this has some remarkable visions of the future, even if the human characters are as stiff and two-dimensional as is traditional in transpacific cartoons. A booming Dolby soundtrack, with multi-layered effects, is an especial asset.

d/co-s Katsuhiro Otomo *co-s* Izo Hashimoto *c* Katsuji
Misawa *se* Takashi Nakamura *lp* Mitsuo Iwara, Nozomu
Sasaki, Mami Koymara, Taro Ishida

Alien From L.A. *aka* Odeon (CANNON) 87 min

This is a runaway production intended to salvage some of the sets and performers from Cannon's **Journey to the Center of the Earth** (1989) remake. When the fairly high-budget film was stalled on its South African/Zimbabwean locations, Cannon despatched Pyun, the post-holocaust specialist of *Radioactive Dreams* (1986) and **Cyborg** (1989), to make this ineffectually jokey variation on the Jules Verne premise.

The mousy heroine (Ireland), a Californian bimbo with an irritating voice (which, in a tiresome running gag, gives everyone a headache), travels to Africa when her explorer father (Haines) disappears and falls down a hole, which leads directly to the lost city of Atlantis. At the mid-point, cover girl Ireland sheds her glasses and hairdo and is made over into her glamorous self without becoming any more endearing. The Atlanteans are, as in **Warlords of Atlantis** (1978), emigrants from Outer Space who sport impeccable British accents, and their society is a repressive state dressed up in punk *noir* oddments. In an insulting final twist to the story, it all turns out to be a dream. Ireland cameoed in the same role in *Journey to the Center of the Earth* when it was eventually resumed and finished, making the remake also a sequel to a dream.

d Albert Pyun *p* Menahem Golan, Yoram Globus *s* Debra
Ricci, Regina Davis *c* Tom Fraser *se* Fantasy II *lp* Kathy
Ireland, Thom Mathews, Don Michael Paul, Linda Kerridge,
Richard Haines, William R. Moses, Janie du Plessis, Deep
Roy

Alien Nation *aka* Outer Heat (FOX) 90 min

In the near-future, a flying saucer lands in California, disgorging a horde of potato-headed alien refugees from an outer space slave state. The Newcomers, impolitely called 'slags', are half-assimilated into American society, some trying to become all-American family types, others getting mixed up in big-time crime or street-gang delinquency.

While the plot premise is fascinating, the film unfortunately chooses to be just another entry in the 1988 cycle of cop buddy movies (*Red Heat*, *The Presidio*, *Off Limits*, **The Hidden**, *Dead Heat*), with a bigoted human detective (Caan) partnered by enthusiastic alien policeman Patinkin. The plot is the same as that of *Red Heat* or *The Presidio*, with alien entrepreneur Stamp mixed up in a drug deal that can turn Newcomers into raging psychopaths. Much of the background detail of the alien-Americans' lifestyle – complete with Coca-Cola advertisements targeted at them, bars which serve rancid milk as an intoxicant, a selection of silly names slapped on the Newcomers by unsympathetic Ellis Island officials – is pointed and interesting, but the formulaic cop action story, although helped by the fine performances of the leads, gets in the way and the ending, with Stamp dissolving in seawater, is especially formulaic. The film led the following year to a television series.

d Graham Baker *p* Gale Anne Hurd, Richard Kobritz
s Rockne S. O'Bannon *c* Adam Greenberg *se* Stan Winston
Studios *lp* James Caan, Mandy Patinkin, Terence Stamp,
Kevyn Major Howard, Leslie Bevis, Peter Jason

Left: *Mandy Patinkin (left) and James Caan as the odd couple in the buddy movie* Alien Nation.

The Blob (TRI-STAR) 92 min

Middle America is under attack again, in this remake of the 1958 cult movie, as an archetypal small town is invaded by a hungry smudge of ooze that absorbs anything it comes across, and expands into a globbering mass of protoplasmic nastiness that shoots out killer tendrils, snacks on necking teens and generally rips up the countryside. The hero is Brian (played by Matt Dillon's less talented brother), a leather-jacketed hoodlum whose sensitive underside is heavily telegraphed and who teams up, after the death of a secondary hero (played by Ione Skye's also less talented brother Leitch), with cheerleader Smith to kick some slime, when it looks as if the feckless authorities won't do anything to deal with the crisis. This high-tech, special effects-clogged remake puts its jelly monster through far more rigorous paces than the original, and allows it to do more spectacular eviscerating and absorbing in a series of star-turn effects sequences that suck victims down plugholes or reduce them to slime-covered skeletons in moments.

Other remakes of fifties Science Fiction hits – **Invasion of the Body Snatchers** (1978), **The Thing** (1982), **The Fly** (1986) – embroider their originals and create genuine updates of their premises, but this *Blob* follows **Godzilla 1985** (1985) and **Invaders From Mars** (1986) by being simply a more expensive elaboration without an original idea to its credit, with special effects far in advance of the earlier film but a dramatic structure wedded to the crudeness of the fifties quickie, but without its charm. To compound its hackneyed characterizations – evil government scientist, cool rebel, football hero, drunken preacher – and gloopy effects, modelled on those of John Carpenter's *The Thing*, this throws in images and sequences ripped off at random from **Them!** (1954), **E.T.: The Extra-Terrestrial** (1982), and **Aliens** (1986). *The Blob* is a pleasant diversion when its monster is in action, and mildly irritating the rest of the time, but, in the end, the new multi-purpose monster is somehow less fearsome and less interesting than the almost childishly simple slime from the original film.

d/co-s Chuck Russell   *p* Jack H. Harris   *co-s* Frank Darabont   *c* Mark Irwin   *se* Dream Quest Images, Lyle Conway   *lp* Shawnee Smith, Kevin Dillon, Donovan Leitch, Jeffrey DeMunn, Candy Clark, Art La Fleur, Sharon Spelman, Del Close

The Caller (EMPIRE) 98 min

A nondescript man (McDowell) with a British accent calls upon isolated housewife Smith in her woodland house and they exchange politely barbed dialogue, menacing each other. Absurdly minor issues are debated at length, and various gruesome and/or horrific possibilities are ominously raised, only to be left dangling. Of a hatbox, McDowell wonders 'Whoever heard of a hat leaking? I think you've got something else in here – something that goes *under* a hat . . .' For an hour and twenty minutes, this plays like a Pinteresque variant on *Sleuth* (1972), as the two characters circle verbally around each other, and the audience tries to figure out what is going on, and then the finale takes it straight into the *Twilight Zone* for some Science Fiction licks that have previously been unguessable.

An extremely well-written little drama, perfectly played by Smith and McDowell, which is rich in unnervingly wrong details that finally add up – a reference to 'the war', which doesn't seem to sit with the Smith character's age, turns out not to refer to Vietnam but to an alien invasion, for instance. The finale features some reasonably well-handled horror effects that sit somewhat uneasily with the more subtle flavour of the rest of the film.

d Arthur Seidelmann   *p* Frank Yablans   *s* Michael Sloan   *c* Armando Nannuzzi   *se* John Carl Buechler   *lp* Malcolm McDowell, Madolyn Smith

Cherry 2000 (ORION/ERP) 93 min

Shelved uncompleted for several years, this **Mad Max 2** (1981) imitation begins promisingly, with an interestingly detailed future, but degenerates into the standard driving-

A victim of The Blob *comes to a sticky end.*

around-and-shooting hijinx, when it gets out into the desert. In 2017, singles bar patrons have to bring demo tapes to show their sexual prowess, and exchange complicated contracts with one-night pick-ups, and so the bland hero (Andrews) is in love with his Cherry 2000, a robot. When Cherry malfunctions, Andrews hires tough tracker Griffith to take him through the wasteland to a derelict factory where he can get a replacement. Finally, after a good deal of uninteresting action, Andrews decides he prefers real women to robots and falls for the fetchingly red-headed heroine.

Although exploitation favourites Thomerson and James make showy villains and there are pleasing cameos from old-timers Johnson and Carey to make the Western connection, this is still an ordinary, ultimately pointless exercise along the lines of countless Italian and Filipino future desert warrior movies, or even of such home-grown American programmers as **World Gone Wild** (1987) and **Cyborg** (1989). De Jarnatt followed up with the far superior nuclear crisis drama **Miracle Mile** (1989).

d Steve de Jarnatt   *p* Edward R. Pressmann   *s* Michael Almereyda   *c* Jacques Haitkin   *lp* Melanie Griffith, David Andrews, Ben Johnson, Tim Thomerson, Brion James, Pamela Gidley, Harry Carey Jr

Cocoon: The Return (FOX) 116 min

Even as sequels go, *Cocoon: The Return* is extraordinarily scrappy. With the return from outer space of the entire cast from **Cocoon** (1985), the script does a ridiculous series of gyrations in order to find things for them all to do. Again, the thin Science Fiction premise is used to justify all manner of violations of logic and sense. The cocoons arbitrarily left at the bottom of the sea at the end of the last film are equally arbitrarily raised without fuss at the beginning of this, and the characters dawdle on their own emotional hang-ups without getting caught up in the race-against-time to rescue the one alien who has been unleashed, and who is being examined by scientist Cox.

Stritch, unfetchingly crammed into a leotard, is added to the roster of old-timers, and fails to strike any sparks with the gloomily rubber-faced Gilford, while the talented likes of Cronyn, Ameche and Brimley shuffle through TV movie-style mawkishness as they confront their various problems and, of the women, only Tandy is given a sub-plot worthy of the

name. Brimley and his grandson, Guttenberg and Welch – whose performance is irresistibly reminiscent in its dullness of her mother's in **Fantastic Voyage** (1966) – and Cox and her pet alien exist in self-contained sections of the film that really don't have anything to do with the fuzzy central plot, which winds up with a replay of the rescue-the-alien finale of *Splash!* (1983). The faceless Petrie, replacing Ron Howard as director, is uncomfortable with the mixture of heart-warming sentiment and glowing aliens, but at least the finish reverses the depressingly whimsical finale of the original, by suggesting that there could be a fruitful life for old people on Earth, although the film otherwise does little to suggest this is so.

d Daniel Petrie   *p* Richard D. Zanuck, David Brown   *s* Stephen McPherson   *c* Tak Fujimoto   *se* ILM   *lp* Don Ameche, Wilford Brimley, Hume Cronyn, Jack Gilford, Steve Guttenberg, Maureen Stapleton, Jessica Tandy, Gwen Verdon, Elaine Stritch, Courtney Cox, Tahnee Welch, Brian Dennehy

Back on Earth, Don Ameche (left), Hume Cronyn (centre) and Wilford Brimley head for the beach in Cocoon: The Return.

DeepStar Six (CAROLCO) 100 min

The first to be released of several competing underwater Science Fiction movies, this, like the more expensive **Leviathan** (1989), slavishly apes the plot of **Alien** (1979). The crew of the undersea missile base spends its time quoting Emerson, exchanging hilarious dialogue ('Have you ever heard of photomigration?'; 'What do you say, if it's a boy we name it after the captain?'; 'Please God, let my baby live!'), having sex in the shower, bickering, making stupid mistakes, panicking and getting gorily killed. The monster, which looks like a giant, scaly, three-lipped prawn, causes surprisingly few of the deaths, which tend to involve defective hatches chopping people in half, the sweaty claustrophobic (Ferrer) accidentally jamming a raft-inflating cartridge into a scientist, who blows up like a balloon, and – that old submarine movie favourite – bloody decompression.

Cunningham, who kicked off the *Friday the 13th* series, virtually reruns the 1980 initial outing, down to the hokey, but still effective, last-minute shock sequence. The film also follows the conventions of the *Voyage to the Bottom of the Sea* TV series, including the blatantly silly monster suit, the consoles that shoot out sparks whenever anything goes wrong, the female characters who are supposed to be high-powered

Left: Marius Weyers *and* Miguel Ferrer *in* DeepStar Six, *the first to be released of several underwater Science Fiction outings of the eighties.*

geniuses but act like nervous teenagers, and the sprays of water that come through the walls whenever the sub is ruptured.

d/co-p Sean S. Cunningham   *co-p* Patrick Markey   *s* Lewis Abernathy, Geoff Miller   *c* Mac Ahlberg   *se* Mark Shostrom   *lp* Taurean Blacque, Nancy Everhard, Greg Evigan, Miguel Ferrer, Nia Peeples, Matt McCoy, Cindy Pickett, Marius Weyers

Dr Alien *aka* I Was a Teenage Sex Mutant
(PHANTOM)   87 min
'Maybe it was stupid to challenge a mentally superior being holding a ray gun,' whines the geeky hero (Jacoby), 'but I was pissed!' College student Jacoby is injected with a green liquid by his science teacher (Landers), who happens to be an alien on Earth studying human sexuality so that she can help repopulate her world, and grows a tentacle from his forehead which makes him irresistible to women, thus getting him into trouble with his steady girlfriend. He also unbends enough to quit his bespectacled nerdiness and join a rock band, The Sex Mutants, who come on like crazy, but then turn out to be mild MOR wimps. The film comes complete with cameos by starlets Bauer, Quigley and Stevens as an all-girl band called The Tang-Poons, clips from DeCoteau's earlier **Creepozoids** (1987), topless co-eds jiggling in the girls' locker-room, very brief roles for down-on-their-luck luminaries Williams and Donahue, and endless bad rock music. A typically unbearable college nerd comedy with Science Fiction overtones.

d/co-p Dave DeCoteau   *co-p* John Schouweiler   *s* Kenneth J. Hall   *c* Nicholas Von Sternberg   *se* John Vulich   *lp* Billy Jacoby, Judy Landers, Olivia Narash, Stuart Franklin, Raymond O'Connor, Arlene Golonka, Julie Gray, Jim Hackett, Troy Donahue, Ginger Lynn Allen, Michelle Bauer, Linnea Quigley, Edy Williams, Elizabeth Kaitan

Doin' Time on Planet Earth   (CANNON)   85 min
Although its general witlessness and preoccupation with high school kids trying to get laid is on a par with such monster nerd comedies as **Dr Alien** (1988), this misfire comedy aspires to be an off-the-wall drama of literal alienation along the more intriguing lines of unclassifiable pictures like *UFOria* (1980), *Static* (1986) and *Society* (1989). Strouse is the misfit younger brother of a clean-cut hunk due to marry into a socially prominent family, and whose computer informs him that the reason he feels so out of place with his family is that he is an extra-terrestrial. West and Azzara turn up claiming to be fellow aliens, explaining that all the world's space cadets, misfits and losers are the descendants of ancient astronauts, and that Strouse is destined to pilot their spaceship – disguised as his father's revolving restaurant – back to the stars. In the busy finale, Strouse concludes that Planet Earth needs weirdoes like him, and the whole plot fizzles out. While there is an intriguing basic idea in Star's screenplay, the film falls down for its lack of decent jokes and because of its below-par performances. Matthau is the son of Walter, and recruits various distinguished friends of the family for walk-on roles.

d Charles Matthau   *p* Menahem Golan, Yoram Globus   *s* Darren Star   *c* Timothy Suhrstedt   *se* Bill Millar   *lp* Nicholas Strouse, Hugh Gillin, Gloria Henry, Hugh O'Brian, Martha Scott, Timothy Patrick Murphy, Adam West, Candy Azzara, Roddy McDowell, Maureen Stapleton

Earth Girls Are Easy   (KESTREL/ODYSSEY)   100 min
Adapted from Brown's comic song, this is a confection of bright colours, fifties kitsch Science Fiction trappings, poolside parties and *Carry On* humour. Hollywood manicurist Davis is having trouble with her unresponsive, fickle fiancé (Rocket) when a spaceship crash-lands in her swimming pool and disgorges three colourful, hairy, fun-loving aliens who move in for the weekend while the pool is being drained. After a trip to the beauty shop – where sidekick-screenwriter-singer Brown holds court and shaves the creatures into reasonable approximations of humanity – everyone goes out on the town. Mac (Goldblum), the least hyperactive of the aliens, falls for Davis and cars get crashed between the more original comic sequences.

A zippy cross between **My Stepmother is an Alien** (1988) and *Beach Blanket Bingo* (1965), this proves that Temple *can* still do the job, although his arm-waving staging of Brown's material proves that he still can't really handle the musical numbers which sunk his earlier *Absolute Beginners* (1986). With a basic plot reminiscent of **Pajama Party** (1964), in which Martian Tommy Kirk romanced Annette Funicello, this film is less interested in the Science Fiction comedy side of it all than in the extravagantly painted nails, gaudy clothes and stoned slang of the Valley setting. Davis and Goldblum are a fetching couple again, and add some notes of sanity to the whole thing, which is otherwise eternally in danger of collapsing under the weight of its own jokiness. Nonetheless, a colourful, distinctive movie and fast enough to get round its dud jokes, badly mixed songs and general predictability.

d Julien Temple   *p* Tony Garnett   *s* Julie Brown, Charlie Coffey   *c* Oliver Stapleton   *se* Bob Clark   *lp* Geena Davis, Jeff Goldblum, Julie Brown, Jim Carrey, Damon Wayans, Charles Rocket, Michael McKean

The Fly II   (BROOKSFILMS/FOX)   pv   104 min
Essentially a remake of **Return of the Fly** (1959), in which the son of the scientist-turned-monster of the first film takes over his father's researches into teleportation. He also turns into a human-fly composite and indulges in a conventional monster-on-the-loose rampage, slaughtering a group of melodramatic secondary characters who deserve what they get, and partici-pates in an especially hokey, unlikely and annoying cop-out ending. Cast holdover Getz, who had his hand and foot dissolved in fly vomit in the first film (hence his bitter remark that his compassion had 'cost me an arm and a leg'), performs the same function of plot-explainer as Vincent Price did in the fifties. Stoltz is perfectly acceptable as the newborn son of the Jeff Goldblum character from **The Fly** (1986) who attains adulthood in five years, never sleeps, has a genius-capacity

It's party time in Earth Girls Are Easy.

So this is matter transformation: The Fly II.

intelligence and is doomed by a plot contrivance and some caricatured corporate baddies to turn into an insectoid monstrosity.

All the highlights of the first film – the impressive telepods, the increasingly monstrous make-up, the inside-out animals, the offbeat romance – are recaptured, but on top of them we get an overly involved plot and a set of gross villains who don't really do anything to make the hero's plight more upsetting, but are useful for providing cannon fodder to the make-up boys, who get their kicks dissolving faces off skulls, crushing heads under liftshafts and the like. As directed by former make-up effects man Walas – who does a surprisingly solid job – this is a wastefully good movie. Given that the whole business of making a sequel to *The Fly* is unrewarding and pointless, the picture comes up with a reasonable script (if a silly storyline), mainly well-turned dialogue, generally good performances (heroine Zuniga is particularly good), some gloopy horror sequences, a fair approximation of the Cronenberg visual style and a seriousness of intent that *almost* makes the ending work.

d/se Chris Walas   *p* Steven-Charles Jaffe   *s* Mick Garris, Jim Wheat, Ken Wheat, Frank Darabont   *c* Robin Vidgeon
lp Eric Stoltz, Daphne Zuniga, Lee Richardson, John Getz, Frank Turner, Ann Marie Lee, Gary Chalk, Harley Cross

The Hidden   (NEW LINE/HERON)   97 min
Beginning forcefully with a security camera's view of a bank, as a normal-seeming stockbroker violently robs it, this then cuts to a dynamic, if familiar, car chase as the hold-up man, who is host to a body-swapping alien parasite, wrecks half the police cars in Los Angeles; he then laughs as he is multiply shot by a horde of marksmen, his entire torso erupting (as do

many of the film's characters) with special effects squibs. Then it segues into a token bit of *Alien*-style sliminess, as the convincing slug-like creature oozes out of a patently plastic head and squirms into its next victim's equally plastic mouth. Only then does it slot a touch uncomfortably into the 1988–9 run of mismatched buddy-cop movies – *Red Heat, Alien Nation, The Presidio, K-9, Lethal Weapon 2* – as the literally spaced-out Gallagher (MacLachlen), an alien policeman on the trail of the parasite, teams up with the fast-talking but aggressively normal Beck (Nouri). Their relationship provides whatever spine the movie has to hang its action on, but never really takes fire, mainly because Nouri's entirely conventional tough cop fails to provide any character details to match MacLachlen's fairly clever performance, as the alien lawman nauseated by beer and bewildered by Alka-Seltzer. The crucial 'relationship' sequence, in which Nouri has MacLachlen over to his suburban home to meet his adoring wife and adorable daughter over an awkward dinner, during which MacLachlen reveals his personal reason for tracking the alien, is, in any case, a simple steal from the far spikier one in *Lethal Weapon* (1987).

The film seems to suggest that the universe is entirely peopled with strange creatures, who nevertheless conform to American stereotypes – honest cops with buddies, solid family men, psychopathic serial killers, grudge-bearing snitches, and redneck bigots ('Altairians are a *filthy* people!' snaps the villain). Where the film does work, however, is in its depiction of its alien fiend, whose *modus operandi* bears some resemblance to that of Steve Gallagher's similarly police-themed novel *The Valley of Lights*, and whose precedents also include the Martian invaders of the serial **The Purple Monster Strikes** (1945) and the body-swapping assassins of the Red Galaxy Collective's short *The Idiot* (1983). With the

Right: *Michael Nouri (top) and Kyle MacLachlen as the odd couple in the buddy movie* The Hidden.

minimum of actual monster footage, and a clever combination of six actors and a dog, the film still manages to give its invader a convincingly psychotic personality, marked by a fondness for heavy metal music (particularly jarring when a middle-aged, blue-collar host is toting a ghettoblaster), fast red Ferraris and random violence, finally calming down only when it decides that being President of the USA could offer it more chance to wreak havoc than a simple joyride of carnage.

d Jack Sholder   *p* Robert Shaye, Gerald T. Olson, Michael Meltzer   *s* Bob Hunt   *c* Jacques Haitkin   *se* Dream Quest Images, Kevin Yagher   *lp* Kyle MacLachlen, Michael Nouri, Claudia Christian, Clarence Felder, Clu Gulager, Ed O'Ross, William Boyett, Richard Brooks, Larry Cedar

Incident at Raven's Gate *aka* Encounter at Raven's Gate (FGH INTERNATIONAL; AUS)   scope   93 min

In the Australian Outback things are out of joint. Cassette players disgorge the wrong music. Dead birds fall out of the sky. Water evaporates mysteriously. Sheep die. Huge circular burns appear in isolated pastures. And there are lights in the sky. On an isolated farm, petty offender Vidler is sweating out his probation on his tyrannical brother's payroll and trying half-heartedly to resist the temptation of his dissatisfied sister-in-law (Griffin). Vidler's problems are compounded by the local football thugs, who think he's stolen their trophy; and the local psycho opera-loving cop, who is obsessed with the barmaid with whom Vidler's having an affair, has an assortment of good reasons to make his life hell. And what's going on down at Raven's Gate? At first, a hush-hush evil government project like the one in *Endangered Species* (1982) seems likely, but the ambiguous finale suggests that intangible alien visitors are to blame. Following such under-appreciated genre items as *Long Weekend* (1977), *The Last Wave* (1978), *Razorback* (1984) and *Ground Zero* (1988), this conspiracy-cum-UFO movie locates its bizarre storyline in a dried-up, mean-spirited rural Australia.

The film starts a trifle awkwardly with an unnecessary flashback structure, and risks alienating Spielberg spoon-fed audiences with its refusal to provide complete explanations for all its manifestations, but is otherwise an outstanding, atmospheric nail-biter. As in the best fifties Science Fiction cheapies – **It Came from Outer Space** (1953) is the particular touchstone being evoked – the fantastical elements are used to bring out the tensions of the human characters. This works

here because the characters are credible before being forced into exaggerated behaviour by the strange phenomena, and because director De Heer has a strong feeling for the loneliness, frustration and boredom of dead-end life on a dried-up farmstead. In particular, the pressures on the already uptight policeman that turn him into a dangerous menace compete with the influence of the offscreen aliens as the source of the horror, so that the film wavers between the psycho movie and the alien encounter genre. It makes good use of widescreen landscape, and even if it doesn't trot out tentacled monstrosities, it does have a few impressively unsettling moments in the invaded-transformed Raven's Gate farmhouse.

d/co-p/co-s Rolf De Heer   *co-p/co-s* Marc Rosenberg
c Richard Michalak   *se* Jon Armstrong   *lp* Steven Vidler, Celine Griffin, Ritchie Singer, Vincent Gil, Saturday Rosenberg, Terry Camilleri, Max Cullen

Killer Klowns from Outer Space

(TRANSWORLD/SARLUI-DIAMANT)   88 min

'Maybe they aren't clowns,' someone theorizes about the alien invaders, 'maybe they were here a long time ago, and that's where our idea of clowns comes from.' The hero pithily, and all too aptly, replies, 'Then how come they aren't *funny*?' Like **Critters** (1986), whose special effects team took over the writing, producing and direction here, this is a spoof of fifties Science Fiction which has a marvellous idea for its monstrous menace, but wastes it on yet another unnecessary remake of **The Blob** (1958). Aside from Dano, as the old man who is first to get killed, and Vernon, as the teen-hating cop who refuses to believe the monsters are loose, the cast is comprised of small-talent youngsters who run around between the 'gag'

A Killer Klown from Outer Space.

special effects pretending there is a storyline to follow. The aliens are grotesque clowns who arrive in a circus-tent-shaped flying saucer and wrap their victims' corpses in candyfloss, using such carnival accessories as tied-balloon tracker dogs and shadow-puppet dinosaurs to track and trick their human prey. Although one or two of the jokes work, the film lacks the sick visual humour that its imaginatively designed monsters deserve. Although the movie looks interesting, its meandering storyline and uninvolving characterizations prove yet again that special effects and movie buff in-jokes can't by themselves sustain a film.

d/co-p/co-s Stephen Chiodo *co-p* Edward Chiodo
co-s/se Charles Chiodo   *c* Alfred Taylor   *lp* Grant Cramer,
Suzanne Snyder, John Allen Nelson, Royal Dano, John Vernon,
Michael Siegel, Peter Licassi

MAC and Me (ORION) 93 min

A cute alien with big glass eyes and a squeaky whistle is stranded on Earth and takes refuge with a lonely little boy and his family, who protect him when he is hunted down by the evil authorities. This time out, the alien has a missing set of parents and a sister (the aliens have the nuclear family too), the little boy (Calegory) is crippled, and in the finale it's the human who dies and is resurrected by the alien rather than the other way around. That's about all that distinguishes this – in terms of plot, at least – from its obvious inspiration, Steven Spielberg's **E.T.: The Extra-Terrestrial** (1982), although, in terms of script, acting, action, special effects, music and everything else, it is overwhelmingly inferior to its model.

MAC – an acronym for Mysterious Alien Creature – has a large repertoire of facial movements and rod-puppet gimmicks, but it's still resolutely a high-tech piece of hardware rather than a living creature. The kids are well down the standard of a Disney TV show, and the adults barely get a look-in. A credit that reads 'and Ronald McDonald as Himself' suggests that product placement might account for a large proportion of the budget: in one major scene, the kids all boogie on down to McDonald's for a big hip-hop party with Ronald himself in attendance, and the patrons and staff of the place help MAC to escape from the bad guys; and there's also a major plot strand that deals with MAC's sole means of sustenance – Coca-Cola – with plenty of lingering shots of alien fingers grasping cans as the carbonated drink keeps them alive. Like **Short Circuit 2** (1988), this ends with the complete assimilation of its non-human characters as they take the oath of allegiance and become US citizens.

d/s Stewart Raffill   *p* R.J. Louis   *c* Nick McLean   *se* Martin J. Becker   *lp* Christine Ebersole, Jonathan Ward, Katrina Caspary, Luren Stanley, Jade Calegory

Moontrap (SHAPIRO-GLICKENHAUS) 86 min

Another **Alien** (1979) variant, distinguished from the pack only by its slightly unusual near-future setting. Astronauts Koenig and Campbell, depressed because NASA is winding down, are recalled to duty to check out an ancient moonbase staffed by mechanical pods which sprout into equipment-cannibalizing robot monsters. Koenig defrosts and falls for a humanoid alien (Lombardi), who is cryogenetically preserved in the robots' lair, while Campbell, the only engaging actor on view, is killed off too early. Although busy, this is a dull movie, with sluggish action scenes that move like an astronaut in reduced gravity, and plenty of pointless zapping and shooting. The robots are nicely designed, but overfamiliar, and they aren't called upon to do anything of special interest.

d/p Robert Dyke   *s* Tex Ragsdale   *c* Peter Klein   *se* Gary Jones   *lp* Walter Koenig, Bruce Campbell, Leigh Lombardi, Robert Kurcz, John J. Saunders, Reavis Graham, Tom Case, Judy Levitt

My Stepmother is an Alien (COL) 108 min

Aykroyd, an astronomer intent on proving there's life on other planets, accidentally beams a blast of energy into an adjacent galaxy. He gets fired and, thanks to a screenwriter's implausible device, an entire civilization is doomed to be destroyed unless he sends another beam. The aliens dress up one of their number, Celeste (Basinger), as the most desirable woman in the world and send her down to Earth in a flying saucer, accompanied by a tentacled eyeball in a handbag. She

Left: Dan Aykroyd (centre) protects his alien wife, Kim Basinger, and daughter, Alyson Hannigan, from another set of aliens in My Stepmother is an Alien.

The ultimate in product placement: MAC, *the hero of* MAC and Me, *lives on Coca-Cola.*

Moontrap, *another* Alien *variant.*

who tries to cover up, and he gets to take part in an impressive roach-man transformation, which pays off with him treading on his own just-popped eyeball. It has just enough humour – a character stamping on insects to the tune of 'La Cucuracha' – to undercut its solemnly silly science, and Winkless stages the whole thing with brisk efficiency.

d Terence H. Winkless   *p* Julie Corman   *s* Robert King
c Ricardo Jacques Gale   *se* uncredited   *lp* Robert Lansing, Lisa Langlois, Franc Luz, Terri Treas, Stephen Davies, Diana Bellamy, Jack Collins

Nightfall   (CONCORDE/NEW HORIZONS)   82 min
Based on Isaac Asimov's famous 1941 short story 'Nightfall', this film adaptation is an unmitigated disaster. It blends the low-budget cost-cutting typical of Roger Corman's Concorde outfit with the humourless high art pretension of director Mayersberg's début feature, *Captive* (1986). Set on a planet with three suns, the film follows a society on the brink of collapse as a 3,000-year period of light is coming to a brief end with an eclipse, which a blind prophet (Kanner) believes will mean the end of civilization. Birney, the planet's scientific leader, is embroiled in a footage-wasting eternal triangle that winds up with murder. Filmed in 'experimental architectural environments' in Arizona, the movie tries to reuse some of the techniques mastered by Nicolas Roeg on the Mayersberg-scripted **The Man Who Fell to Earth** (1976), but consistently trips over into unintentional humour.

d/s Paul Mayersberg   *p* Julie Corman   *c* Dariusz Wolsky
se Chuck Comisky   *lp* David Birney, Sarah Douglas, Alexis Kanner, Andra Millian, Starr Andreeff, Charles Hayward, Jonathan Emerson, Susie Lindemann, Russell Wiggins

Not of This Earth   (CONCORDE)   80 min
An exact remake of the outstanding 1956 Corman 'B' picture, this is less distinctive than Wynorski's notionally original **The Lost Empire** (1984) and **Chopping Mall** (1985), with porno star Lords, and bland Roberts, failing to match Beverly Garland and Paul Birch as a nurse and her alien patient. 'No man on Earth should be able to live with as low an amount of red corpuscles as you have.' Not only does this open with a collage of clips from Roger Corman-produced Science Fiction monster movies (**Piranha**, 1978, *Humanoids From the Deep*, 1980, **Forbidden World**, 1982), but one of the action sequences is lifted wholsale from *Hollywood Boulevard* (1976), itself one of Corman's patchwork jobs. The dialogue yanks in a reference to AIDS for 'contemporary relevance', although the blood disease theme was present in the original.

d/co-p/co-s Jim Wynorski   *co-p* Murray Miller   *co-s* R.J. Robertson   *c* Zoran Hockstatter   *se* uncredited   *lp* Traci Lords, Arthur Roberts, Lenny Juliano, Ace Mask, Roger Lodge, Michael Delano

The Phantom Empire
(AMERICAN INDEPENDENT)   83 min
Nominally a remake of the 1935 serial, this follows a motley expedition into Bronson Caverns to discover the lost city of R'lyeh, encountering Danning as a leather-suited alien queen accompanied by Robby the Robot, a group of ragged mutants, some barbarian bimbos in fur bikinis, a selection of stop-motion dinosaurs borrowed from *Planet of Dinosaurs* (1978) and lots of familiar cave corridors. Despite all the in-jokes, and a mainly amiable cast, this is a repetitive and dreary exploitation film, typical of Ray (*Cyclone*, 1987, *Hollywood Chainsaw Hookers*, 1988, *Beverly Hills Vamp*, 1989) – tame and pointless. The end credits boast 'Filmed on Location at the Center of the Earth', and threateningly add 'Coming Soon – *Phantom Empire II: The Land Where Time Said "Fuck"* '.

crashes a party thrown by Aykroyd's obnoxious brother, and hurls herself at the scientist, bewildering everyone with her obvious unfamiliarity with terrestrial ways, as she ignores the canapés to snack on the butts smouldering in an ashtray. After a whirlwind courtship, during which Basinger catches up on Earthling sexual habits by copying porno movies, and goes through all the leftover alien-on-Earth shtick from *My Favourite Martian* and *Mork and Mindy*, the alien and human are married. But her civilization is still doomed unless Aykroyd gets his job back, and his daughter (Hannigan) suspects something is amiss with her new stepmother when she finds her eating batteries.

Aykroyd flounders in a role with a one to nine ratio of smart one-liners against fudged routines, sentimental tripe and simple balderdash, and Basinger is so spaced out that one gets the impression that rather than playing an alien she is doing a distasteful impersonation of a mentally retarded person. Typical of the film is a finale in which these characters' idea of trying to save the Earth from destruction turns out to involve miming to an old Jimmy Durante routine. Despite some excellent special effects spaceships and hardware, this is Science Fiction at its worst – it's one of those films where characters can do anything the plot requires because they're aliens – and, despite four credited screenwriters, it barely raises a titter as comedy. On the plus side, there's one witty remark about Switzerland.

d Richard Benjamin   *p* Ronald Parker, Franklin R. Levy
s Jerico Weingrod, Herschel Weingrod, Timothy Harris, Jonathan Reynolds   *c* Richard H. Kline   *se* John Dykstra   *lp* Dan Aykroyd, Kim Basinger, Jon Lovitz, Alyson Hannigan, Joseph Maher, Amy Prentiss

The Nest   (CONCORDE)   88 min
'It's kind of hard to exterminate a species that's been around for sixty million years when the only natural predators it's got is me, your foot and a strip of sticky paper.' This is a capable terror-by-bug movie, encompassing the fifties retro feel of such seventies outings as **Squirm** (1976), and the high-tech splatter-effects of **The Fly** (1986). On an offshore island, an unscrupulous corporation has been breeding a strain of cannibal cockroaches as an alternative to insecticides, and the experiment has gone disastrously wrong, unleashing a horde of killer bugs on the community. The characterizations are more interesting than usual, and the film takes its time before it lets the bug effects get out of hand. Lansing is the Mayor

d/p/co-s Fred Olen Ray *co-s* T.L. Lankford *c* Gary
Graver *se* Mark D. Wolf, Paul M. Rinehard *lp* Ross
Hagen, Jeffrey Combs, Dawn Wildsmith, Robert Quarry,
Susan Chambers, Michelle Bauer, Russ Tamblyn, Sybil
Danning

Purple People Eater

(MOTION PICTURE CORPORATION OF AMERICA) 92 min
Joining the ranks of *Alice's Restaurant* (1969), *Ode to Billy Joe*
(1976) and *Convoy* (1978), this anodyne children's film is
based on a hit record, Sheb Woolley's 1958 American
chart-topper about a 'one-eyed, one-horned flying purple
people eater' who comes to earth to join a rock 'n' roll band.
In addition to playing rock music through the horn in his
head, Purple – a succession of midgets in a furry muppet suit
– befriends a socially retarded kid (Harris) and helps him gain
self-confidence by starting up a minipop group. He pitches in
to organize a benefit concert for old folks, like Beatty and
Winters, who are about to be thrown out of their homes by a
nasty property developer. After minimal complications, the
Save Our Seniors concert is a success and the Mayor (Richard)
passes a law making it illegal to evict senior citizens from
their homes for any reason whatsoever. The final singalong
rendition of the title song is notable in that it must be the only
time Little Richard has ever been upstaged on film, as he gets
out one measly scat-sung line and has the microphone
snatched from his hand by a nearby tot who takes over the
lyrics. The burbly score features bland rearrangements of an
assortment of fifties tunes – 'Rockin' Robin', 'Twist It Up',
'The Birds and the Bees', 'Good Golly Miss Molly' – and
Chubby Checker does a guest appearance with the clean kids'
combo. Woolley's song is used, to rather more sinister effect,
in *Parents* (1988). Other great Science Fiction pop hits, as yet
unfilmed, include Billy Lee Riley's 'Flying Saucers Rock 'n'
Roll', Creedence Clearwater Revival's 'It Came Out of the
Sky' and David Bowie's 'Space Oddity'.

d/s Linda Shayne *p* Brad Revoy, Steve Sabler *c* Peter
Deming *se* The Chiodo Brothers *lp* Ned Beatty, Neil
Patrick Harris, Shelley Winters, Peggy Lipton, James
Houghton, Thora Birch, Little Richard, Chubby Checker

The Rejuvenator *aka* Rejuvenatrix

(JEWEL) 86 min
Like the inferior **Evil Spawn** (1987), this combines the plots
of *Sunset Boulevard* (1950) and **The Wasp Woman** (1960), as
an obsessive scientist distils an elixir of life from cranial
matter at the behest of an ageing movie star (Lanko), who
turns into a seductive young beauty but also, from time to
time, into a spectacularly repulsive monster. The characters
are all clichés, and the script trots out lots of silly plot twists
and lines – 'Your theories of regenerative pathology border on
the insane!' – but the film is played surprisingly and
effectively straight. From *Sunset Boulevard* the film even lifts
the character of the Germanic butler (Hogue) obsessively
devoted to his mistress, while the monster-on-the-loose
business is efficiently done.

d/co-s Brian Thomas Jones *p* Steven Mackler *co-s* Simon
Nuchtern *c* James McCalmont *se* Edward French
lp Vivian Lanko, John MacKay, James Hogue, Katell
Pleven, Marcus Powell, Jessica Dublin

Return of the Killer Tomatoes

(FOUR SQUARE PRODUCTIONS/NEW WORLD) 90 min
This sequel to **Attack of the Killer Tomatoes** (1978)
continually undercuts itself with references to its supposedly
humorous badness. These include a framing story about a
screening of the sequel on afternoon television, a false start
when *Big-Breasted Girls Go to the Beach and Take Their Tops
Off* is accidentally laced into the projector, and a finale in
which gun-toting carrots invade the studio as a vanguard of

*Ned Beatty takes
Purple and the gang
for a ride in* Purple
People Eater.

their own invasion. The actual story takes place ten years after
the first film, when tomatoes have been made illegal in
America, and deals with a couple of young pizza chefs who
realize that Dr Gangreen (Astin) has been conducting
unorthodox tomato experiments, involving subjecting vegetables to music, which can turn tomatoes into human beings.
The appealingly daft Mistal is a human-shaped tomato girl
who falls for the hero (Stark), and convinces him that
vegetables aren't all bad, and there's also a furry tomato called
F.T. which heroically throws itself on a hand-grenade in the
finale. The film is constantly interrupted by jokes in the style
of *Blazing Saddles* (1974), whereby the film-makers run out of
money and have to resort to extreme product placement to
make up the budget, or are persecuted by an official from the
Screen Actors' Guild. The end credits promise a Part III:
Killer Tomatoes Go to Paris. It's enthusiastic, but not terribly
amusing.

d/co-s John De Bello *p/co-s* Stephen Peace *co-s* Constantine
Dillon *c* Stephen Kent Welch *se* Dean Andolsek, Ron
Coons, Gary Schnuckle, Michael Bishop *lp* Anthony Stark,
George Clooney, Karen Mistal, Steve Lundquist, John Astin,
Charlie Jones, 'Rock' Peace

Short Circuit 2 (TRI-STAR) 110 min
With its original director John Badham replaced by TV
Science Fiction stalwart Kenneth Johnson (*The Bionic
Woman*, *The Incredible Hulk*, *V*), and the original co-stars
Steve Guttenberg and Ally Sheedy dispatched to an off-screen
limbo, this by-the-numbers sequel to an already formulaic hit

has been reduced to a virtual double act between Johnny Five, the tiresomely whacky sentient robot, and Stevens' embarrassing reincarnation of a Peter Sellers-style Indian buffoon. Although the demeaning nature of Stevens' role – complete with lines like 'It is being slower than mole's asses in January' – is emphasized, especially in the excruciating comic courtship sequences with the WASP heroine (Gibb), the robot comes off slightly better in the sequel than he did in **Short Circuit** (1986), thanks to a variety of useful gadgets (like a hang-glider that sprouts when the robot falls out of a building) and some nice comic by-play, with the characters played by experienced hands McKean and Weston. However, the script is still lacking actual jokes, the robot still mainly manages to be irritating and, like *Beverly Hills Cop 2* (1987) and *'Crocodile' Dundee 2* (1988), **Short Circuit 2** assumes that the way to go about following up a successful comedy is to downplay the humour and shoe-horn its unlikely hero into a plot heavy with caper mechanisms and straightforward, unparodied action movie business.

d Kenneth Johnson   *p* David Foster, Lawrence Turman
s S.S. Wilson, Brent Maddock   *c* John McPherson   *se* Eric Allard   *lp* Fisher Stevens, Michael McKean, Cynthia Gibb, Jack Weston, Dee McCafferty, Dave Hemblem

Slugs – The Movie   (DISTER FILMS; SP)   92 min

Shaun Hutson's paperback original horror novel is here turned into an equally rotten, although marginally more entertaining, splatter movie, set in America but made by, and starring, swarthy Spaniards. Meat-eating slugs are mutated by contact with toxic waste and menace a town until a he-man health inspector, a geeky scientist and an intrepid sewer patrolman set out to burn the creatures to death. There are the usual cartoonish and inept gore scenes – a restaurant patron's head explodes when he's infected with slug flukes from the salad, a courting couple are eaten alive – but it's difficult to make slugs swarming on raw meat (or, in one

Johnny Five does his homework in Short Circuit 2.

scene, attacking a hamster) seem very horrible. The film's only entertaining quality is its Hispanic tackiness, which almost suggests the kind of deliberately ugly art direction favoured by John Waters, as a big business deal is discussed around a tiny table in a pizza joint, the interior furnishings are Dayglo seventies hideous, and the performers all seem like refugees from 'only a minute from this cinema' Indian restaurant commercials. Magnano, the mother of producer De Laurentiis, has her last screen role in an unbilled cameo.

d/co-p Juan Piquer Simón   *co-p* José A. Escrivá, Francesca De Laurentiis   *s* Ron Gantman   *c* Julio Bragado   *se* Carlo de Marchis   *lp* Michael Garfield, Santiago Alvarez, Philip Machale, Alicia Moro, Kim Terry, Concha Cuetos, Emilio Linder, Silvana Magnano

A Switch in Time *aka* Norman's Awesome Experience   (NORSTAR/SALTER STREET; CAN)   90 min

A pleasant time travel comedy in which a scientist (McCann), an obnoxious model (Paton) and a trendy fashion photographer (Lussier) are zapped in a Swiss research station and find themselves in Helvetia, a province of the Roman Empire, where McCann introduces steel, rocketry, balloons and rock 'n' roll to a depressed tribe whom he encourages to rebel against the Romans. In contrast to such outright fantasies as *Roman Scandals* (1933) and *Fiddlers Three* (1944), this presents a grimy, archaeologically correct vision of a bleak past – where the Romans are Fellini-esque decadents who speak in subtitled Latin – but it still emerges as a wish-fulfilment fantasy as the hero defeats the might of the Empire. Argentina effectively stands in for Switzerland, and Donovan reveals more of the grit and ambition that make *Siege* (1983) and **DefCon 4** (1984) unusually effective exploitation movies.

d/s/co-p Paul Donovan   *co-p* Peter Simpson   *c* Vic Sarin   *lp* Tom McCann, Laurie Paton, Jacques Lussier, Lee Broker, David Hemblen, Armando Capo, Brian Downey

They Live   (ALIVE)   pv   93 min

A bizarre Science Fiction social satire-cum-thick-ear action movie. Nada (Piper) is one of the new American hobos, a loser in the eighties boom, who comes to a big city with only a backpack, looking for work. He stumbles over a revolutionary movement hiding out in a skid-row church, and gets hold of a pair of sunglasses that enable him to see the real world. It's in black and white ('They colorized us,' someone protests) and every billboard and magazine carries a message encouraging the human race to lust for money, stay passive and knuckle under to authority. It all turns out to be the work of alien exploiters, who have melted-to-the-skull faces and are masquerading as the rich and powerful. They have bought the Earth by offering a select few humans immense material wealth to sell the rest of us out, and are thus behind the Reaganite-yuppie me-first generation. Nada reacts badly to this news, and takes a pump shotgun to a bank, declaring, 'I have come here to chew bubblegum and kick ass, and I'm all out of bubblegum', before blowing away a couple of the monsters. Hunted as a psycho killer, he tries to find the remnants of the revolution, and convince tele-exec Foster to join the struggle against the Gucci overlords whose fancy watches are actually teleportation devices and who plan to asset-strip the planet before moving on to their next victims.

It begins almost like a modern *The Grapes of Wrath* (1940), with Carpenter and regular collaborator Alan Howarth providing an evocative harmonica-based down-at-heel blues score, as Nada wanders around the flipside of the Reagan revolution, where migrant workers watch numbing TV shows around trashcan fires on a travellers' site. When it gets science fictional, the film is a jokey rewrite of **Invasion of the Body Snatchers** (1954) or *The Invaders* teleseries, with its cynical idea that the aliens would be able to buy converts to their cause. Among its clever conceits are a monochrome reality

just like a fifties film, complete with flying saucers out of **The Day the Earth Stood Still** (1951), low-tech mind-control devices on top of traffic lights and an interdimensional transport system that's just as dull as any earthly airport. *They Live* is stronger on ideas than plot, but Carpenter has convinced his largely unfamiliar cast to have fun with their roles, and he hasn't lost his affinity for good old-fashioned action. A particular highlight is the prolonged back-alley fight scene, in which Nada tries to persuade his best friend Frank (David) to try on the glasses, and which progresses from a simple movie slugfest into a hilarious parody of professional wrestling and knuckle-headed stubbornness, but also manages to make an effective political point about the underclass being too busy beating each other up to start a revolution. The pay-off, which depends on that old serial standby, the machine-which-can-be-blown-up-to-foil-the-plot, is a bit disappointing, but otherwise *They Live* signals a refreshing return by Carpenter to his inventive low-budget roots.

d John Carpenter   *p* Larry Franco   *s* Frank Armitage (John Carpenter)   *c* Gary B. Kibbe   *se* Jim Danforth   *lp* Roddy Piper, Keith David, Meg Foster, George (Buck) Flower, Peter Jason, Raymond St Jacques, Sy Richardson

Watchers   (CONCORDE/CENTAUR; CAN)   92 min
The premise of Dean R. Koontz's competent novel is that the scheming government has created a new breed of genetically engineered *Gestalts*, consisting of a telepathic dog, an eyeball-gouging ape and a human psychopath. This film adaptation is a kind of combination of *Lassie Come Home* (1943) and **Predator** (1987) that picks up Koontz's basic idea and then throws it away amid a parade of monster movie clichés. It opens with an unexplained explosion, which lets the dog and the beast out of maximum security and is

forgotten by the screenplay thereafter. The dog, nicknamed Furface, finds refuge with a tousle-haired teen (Haim). The monster wanders around, ripping up anyone who gets in the way and poking their eyes out for no apparent reason. Enter psycho Ironside, who works for a shadowy Washington agency that definitely isn't supposed to be the CIA, and who has been genetically altered to be even nastier than the monster.

There's an annoying attempt to make us care about the boy and the dog element of the plot, which is scuppered by Haim's unsympathetic performance and the silliness of the dog's Scrabble-playing, computer-programming and one-bark-for-yes communications. The monster on the loose sequences are typical low-budget cheats: lots of boring shots of the subjective camera crashing through the undergrowth intercut with glimpses of someone in a shaggy Bigfoot outfit. There are contrived gore scenes every reel or so, in which various disposable characters wander on screen with T-shirts marked 'Next Victim' and mutter a bit before the hairy arms reach into frame and yank bodily parts off them. Schlock-meister producer Roger Corman's usual saving graces – sick humour, a lively cast and spirited direction – are absent here, and the whole thing is so slackly assembled that it resembles a made-for-TV movie with clips from some forgotten video nasty spliced in at random.

d Jon Hess   *co-/co-sp* Damian Lee   *co-p* David Mitchell   *co-s* Bill Freed   *c* Richard Leiterman   *se* Dean Lockwood   *lp* Corey Haim, Barbara Williams, Michael Ironside, Lala, Duncan Fraser, Blu Mankuma, Colleen Winto, Norman Browning

The Wizard of Speed and Time
(SHAPIRO-GLICKENHAUS)   95 min
This has about half an hour of marvellous footage and half an hour of utter crap, the balance being a weird cocktail of the two. Mike Jittlov, a Los Angeles independent film-maker who specializes in pixilation/animation effects and tends to write, direct, edit and star in his films, here takes the best bits of his dazzling shorts, throws in a few more startling moments, and wraps them up in a semi-autobiographical story about a fictional film-maker called Mike Jittlov (Jittlov), who is trying to crank out some effects footage for a TV special, despite the efforts of a villainous producer. Shot over a period of a

Left: Reality revealed in They Live.

Boy (Corey Haim) and dog together in Watchers.

The Wizard of Speed and Time.

marvellously in a more realistic, sweaty, high-tech mode, as a nuclear submarine is bumped by something unidentified and lodged on an undersea ledge. The Navy hires deep-sea oil engineer Bud Brigman (Ed Harris) and his estranged wife Lindsey (Mary Elizabeth Mastrantonio), who designed the submarine rig Bud captains, to go down into the abyss and check out the sub for survivors. To complicate things, they get landed with Lieutenant Coffey (Biehn), a paranoid who reacts badly to the extreme depth and has to calm his shaking hands by carving chunks out of his arm. Mysterious creatures float around the submarine, and Mastrantonio thinks they represent a Non-Terrestrial Intelligence. Biehn, however, who has picked up a nuclear warhead from the downed ship, thinks they're a Russian secret weapon and plots to give the NTIs a big hot hello.

For its first two hours or so, *The Abyss* is first-rate: shot under impossibly gruelling conditions, it is a damp, claustrophobic widescreen movie, full of frail people straining with thick iron bulkheads or being crushed by tons of rushing water as their tincans rupture. There is one absolutely magical alien special effect involving a seawater pseudopod that explores the rig, but the main business of the film is unbearable suspense. It keeps tossing new problems at its heroes, and Cameron really punishes his cast as the dramatic

decade, the bulk of the work being done in 1983 and 1987, this has an obvious piecemeal feel – an overdubbed joke makes fun of Thomas, who became a big star in *Miami Vice* subsequent to filming his scenes – and never remotely coheres, descending to embarrassment in a finale which turns maudlin, as the film-maker makes a special plea for men of vision like himself trapped in the heartless movie business.

Jittlov himself is a toothy, charming figure, who comes across like a more personable Pee-Wee Herman, with his caseful of gadgets and tricks, and his best early works combine Science Fiction in-jokes and imagery with simple but astonishing camera techniques. The Hollywood satire – which includes information on the difficulties an independent film-maker faces when he comes up against the monolithic Hollywood unions, the police force and unscrupulous big bucks merchants – sometimes clicks, although it seems rather indulgent to include it in a film apparently aimed primarily at children, over whose heads this strand of the picture certainly goes. There are some extremely clumsy comedy routines and one or two of the supporting players – probably friends and relations of those involved in the production – are simply appalling. On the whole, it's a doggily likeable movie, but there's an edge of desperation about it that is offputting. For instance, Jittlov uses subliminal cuts to deliver propagandist messages like 'Advance the creative spirit'. The green-gowned Wizard character that Jittlov plays in the film-within-a-film was better served by the original, Academy Award-nominated short.

d/s/se Mike Jittlov   *p* Richard Kaye, Deven Chierighino *c* Russ Carpenter   *lp* Mike Jittlov, Richard Kaye, Lucky Straecker, Paige Moore, Brian Lucas, Philip Michael Thomas, Steve Brodie, Michael Thomas, Frank LaLoggia

1989

The Abyss (FOX) 140 min
Weighing in at upwards of $50 million, *The Abyss*, writer-director Cameron's follow-up to **The Terminator** (1984) and **Aliens** (1986), is by far the most substantial of the late eighties school of underwater Science Fiction/action/monster movies (**Deepstar Six** (1988), **La Grieta**, **Leviathan**, *Lords of the Deep*, *The Hunt for Red October*, all 1989). It gets things right at the outset with a pre-credits ping of a sonar that evokes the campy sub-aqua Science Fiction of TV series like *Stingray* and *Voyage to the Bottom of the Sea*, and then sets up its plot

Right: *Perils of the deep:* The Abyss.

contrivances pile up – at one point, the hero has to deal with his marital crisis, a raving psychotic waving an atom bomb, a topside hurricane, possibly threatening space creatures, a leaky submarine, extreme cold, a diminishing oxygen supply and failing electricity, all at the same time. Weirdly, the film's problem is that it revs up the tension so much that, like one character's submersible sinking into the high pressure of the titular Abyss, it finally bursts. The climax, as Harris – who, in a truly squirm-inducing twist, has to drown himself in an oxygenated fluid in order to breathe in the deeps – descends to defuse the bomb and meet the aliens, just doesn't work. The inevitable reconciliation with Mastrantonio and the choked-through-tears communications – when it seems one or both of the lovers is going to die – simply provoke laughter, and the awe-inspiring special effects finish rings hollow because, as nowhere else in this or any previous Cameron film, things turn out to be better than they seem. Cameron's strongest suit as a film-maker is his hitherto unshakeable belief in the essential malevolence of the universe and the consequent resilience of his heroes and heroines, but here he turns unconvincingly at the last moment into a Spielbergian sentimentalist.

d/s James Cameron   *p* Gale Anne Hurd   *c* Mikael Salomon   *se* Dream Quest Images, Industrial Light & Magic, Fantasy II Film Effects   *lp* Ed Harris, Mary Elizabeth Mastrantonio, Michael Biehn, Leo Burmeister, Todd Graf, John Bedford Lloyd, J.C. Quinn, Kimberly Scott, Captain Kidd Brewer Jr

Back to the Future, Part II

(AMBLIN ENTERTAINMENT/U)   108 min

Unlike most sequels, this really does play like the next episode of a serial, to the extent of winding up on a cliffhanger and a trailer for the forthcoming *Back to the Future, Part III* (1990). It opens with the last five minutes of the first film, as Marty McFly (Fox), who is just back from 1955, is whisked off to 2015 by mad scientist Lloyd in his time-travelling De Lorean, in order to sort out some trouble with his as yet unborn children. After a spell in a chipper future of flying skateboards and eighties nostalgia, which could almost come from an optimistic fifties Science Fiction novel, the film whips back to an alternate 1985, caused by some tampering with the past, to discover that the small town setting has been converted into a violent hellhole resembling a cross between the fantasy sequence from *It's a Wonderful Life* (1947) and an urban nightmare like *The Warriors* (1979), where all the streets are covered with white body outlines. The heroes are then forced to go back again to 1955 to the events of **Back to the Future** (1985) to fill in some interesting narrative gaps, as Fox tries to prevent the villain (Wilson) from taking advantage of an almanac of future sports results, handed to him by his time-tripping future self while trying to avoid himself. The finish sets up another bout of time-twisting in the next instalment, where Fox has to go back to the Old West to rescue Lloyd and be around at the founding of the town.

The film lacks the blend of nostalgic detail and bizarre (bordering on the incestuous) family feeling that gave the first film heart as well as flash, but it replaces that with a plotline that never lets up, a wealth of interesting detail in all its time zones, and some mind-bending concepts. It is a subtle development from the fifties feel of the original, in that it uses many of the devices and jokes from fifties *written* Science Fiction – fifties Science Fiction movies were very different from what was going on in the magazines – and is very much in the spirit of writers like Fritz Leiber, Philip K. Dick, Alfred Bester and Fredric Brown, who were reshaping literary Science Fiction in the Eisenhower years. Thus, the film provides a weird and appealing blend of nostalgia and anticipation. Some of the characters get lost in the narrative reshuffle, with Marty's love interest (Shue) mainly being left

Christopher Lloyd explains time in the hilarious Back to the Future, Part II.

asleep on the porch during the action, but Fox and his nemesis (Wilson) get to appear as several versions of themselves in elaborate make-up. Breathlessly paced, this almost matches the feel of such Eastern European paradox-mongers as **Zabil Jsem Einsteina, Panove** (1970) and *Tomorrow, I'll Wake Up and Scald Myself With Tea* (1979).

d Robert Zemkis   *co-p* Neil Canton   *co-p/s* Bob Gale   *c* Dean Cunedy   *se* Michael Lantieri   *lp* Michael J. Fox, Christopher Lloyd, Lea Thompson, Thomas F. Wilson, Elizabeth Shue

Batman

(WB/GUBER-PETERS COMPANY/POLYGRAM PICTURES)   126 min

Burton signals his approach to the world of *Batman* with his first vision of Gotham City, a tainted Metropolis of **Blade Runner** (1982) styled neon and steam, which resembles a forties vision of a hellish future and is populated by unwary victims and criminals. A family from out of town – bumbling parents and a wide-eyed son – falls prey to a pair of psychotic muggers, and a black bat shape detaches itself from the shadows to descend upon the petty villains, wreaking a rough justice and telling the criminals to spread the word about the Batman. The film sees Batman (Keaton) and the Joker (Nicholson) as dramatic antitheses; not only is the Joker created partially due to Batman's frightening him into falling into a vat of chemicals, but the young Jack Napier, who will become the disfigured criminal, is the mugger who kills Bruce Wayne's family, presented as an echo of the innocents of the first sequence, and triggers off the neuroses that lead young Bruce to become the fearsome Batman. For most of the film, the authorities of Gotham City are as keen to track down the vigilante as the Joker, and the Laurel and Hardy-style one-upmanship that characterizes the relationship of hero and villain is nicely crystallized in the moment, at once funny and genuinely chilling, in which the Joker, annoyed by the headline WINGED FREAK TERRORIZES CITY chortles, 'Terrorizes? Wait until they get a load of me?'

During the production of the film there was a great deal of hostility generated in the fan press by the selection of a director and star known best for their comedy work, on the

Vorsprung durch Technik. This machine kills very efficiently, as William Hootkins is about to find out in Hardware.

The Handmaid's Tale

(CINECOM-BIOSCOP; US-WG) 108 min

Pinter's script distils Margaret Atwood's dystopian vision of a future America run on fundamental-sexist principles to yet another colour-coded warning, laced annoyingly with pseudo-revolutionary guff that wouldn't seem out of place in the more honestly pulpy context of **Planet of the Apes** (1968) or **Logan's Run** (1976).

Fertile Richardson, a would-be escapee from an American Christian-fascist state called Gilead, is trained in a prison-come-school to serve as the handmaid of regime official Duvall and wife Dunaway. A surrogate mother whose function in the sterile family is rigidly defined, she is required to bear Duvall a child or face capital punishment. Duvall's impotence forces her to take house functionary Quinn as a lover, and to plot with him the assassination of Duvall, after which, in conventional against-the-system melodrama fashion, she joins the rebels in the hills and is reunited with her own lost child.

Although the rituals and jargon of Atwood's award-winning novel – evangelical public hangings, undiscussed disappearances, biblically sanctioned and joyless troilism – are retained, and there are strong secondary performances from McGovern as a lesbian convicted of 'gender treachery' and Tennant as a nannyish state inquisitor, Schlondorff and Pinter frame everything in the tritest imaginable terms, including a ridiculously unconvincing feel-good ending that undercuts the rigid pessimism of the rest of the picture. Richardson, trapped in a submissive role that unconvincingly turns into a forceful heroine by the finale, is unimpressive, while Duvall and Dunaway – arch-hypocrites who preach iron discipline and Christian family values while Duvall sneaks off to a decadent élite nightspot and Dunaway encourages Richardson's affair with Quinn – act no more convincingly than the ruling classes of **Metropolis** (1926) did. Like many 'mainstream' dystopias, including *Nineteen Eighty-Four* and *Brave New World*, this suffers from the author's lack of interest in the Science Fiction angle, so that we have to take on trust the ecological disasters that have rendered most women in the world barren but don't seem to have affected their well-scrubbed health in any other way or to have taken any toll at all on the environment.

d Volker Schlondorff   *p* Daniel Wilson   *s* Harold Pinter
c Igor Luther   *lp* Natasha Richardson, Robert Duvall, Faye Dunaway, Aidan Quinn, Elizabeth McGovern, Victoria Tennant, Blanche Baker, Traci Lind

Hardware   (WICKED FILMS; UK) 95 min

Although made with all the high-concept intensity one expects from a pop promo graduate like tyro writer-director Stanley, *Hardware* is essentially as patchwork a movie as its villain. Besides the obvious bits from **The Terminator** (1984) and **Mad Max 2** (1981), it has a regeneration sequence similar to *Hellraiser* (1986) – even employing the same effects house – a few oddments of *Le Dernier Combat* (1983), plenty of *Halloween* (1978), scraps of **RoboCop** (1987), 'guilty pleasure' flashes of **Saturn 3** (1980) and frills from innumerable heavy-metal videos. Art fans even get a glimpse of the incredible Survival Research videos, not to mention dollops of heavy metal and cameos by Lemmy from Motorhead, and the voice of Iggy Pop. The film's derivative nature even prompted the last-minute inclusion of a credit to an obscure British comic story, from which the script was allegedly plagiarized.

Sometime in the blighted future, a desert scavenger finds a few leftover robot bits and sells them to a soldier (McDermott), who gives them to his sculptress girlfriend (Travis), who incorporates them in her latest despairing industrial construction. The spares turn out to be part of the Mark 13, a people-destroying machine that can repair itself and has been overloaded with apocalyptic impulses, and the sculpture turns into a killer robot that stalks the girl around her messy apartment. A blubbery voyeur from next door (Hootkins)

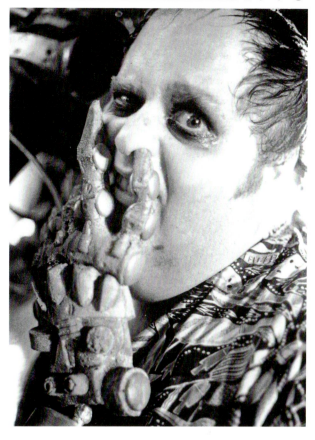

turns up at precisely the wrong moment, as do some downstairs neighbours annoyed by the racket, but this eventually becomes another lady-and-the-monster game of stalk-and-slash as Travis fights back, ultimately besting and demolishing the robot in Science Fiction splatter style. On its limited means and after a slowish start, this delivers the goods a lot more efficiently than the multi-million **RoboCop 2** (1990) and once the robot is up and killing, it turns into a very effective piece of knee-jerk shock-suspense, as the monster keeps coming back for one more assault and the heroine has to prove herself even more resourceful. Maybe just a touch too arty in its compositions and thin in its characterizations for its own good, but a very nice try.

d/s Richard Stanley   *p* Paul Trybits, Joanne Sellar
c Steven Chivers   *se* Image Animation   *lp* Dylan McDermott, Stacey Travis, John Lynch, William Hootkins, Lemmy, Carl McCoy, Oscar James

Highlander II: The Quickening

(DAVIS/PANZER) 104 (87) min

While Mulcahy's *Highlander* (1985) was a sword and sorcery fantasy about a group of immortals with mystic powers, this sequel – whose screenplay contradicts the premise and many details of the original – is a Science Fiction film. It rationalizes immortals Connor MacLeod (Lambert) and Ramirez (Connery) as aliens exiled from the Planet Zeist 500 years ago (even though the first film clearly established that they were Earth-born and that Connery was 2,000 years old) and at the same time bestows on Lambert the power to pray the expensive, but dead, Connery back to life for a singularly pointless cameo walk-through appearance.

Set in 2024, the film's slapdash storyline has to do with a radiation shield that the now-aged Lambert has helped to construct around the world to compensate for the destruction of the ozone layer, which has turned the planet into a tropical hell with rainy, **Blade Runner** (1982)-inspired retro-fitted cities. The shield is being maintained by an evil corporation,

Christopher Lambert and sword in Highlander II: The Quickening.

despite the fact that the ozone layer has magically replenished itself (one of the film's throwaway notions), prompting Lambert, who is rejuvenated after a tussle with a pair of geekish alien hit-men, to join eco-terrorist Madsen in the struggle to overthrow the shield.

Meanwhile, General Katana (Ironside), the dictator of Zeist, has arrived on Earth to dispose of Lambert, his old enemy, whom he has left alone for 500 years before deciding on a whim to finish him off. Many pointless action scenes later, the villain is decapitated and the shield easily destroyed in a remarkably abrupt climax. Although Mulcahy stages screen-filling sword-fights and spectacular fireworks on huge and imaginative Argentinian sets, this film is doomed by a screenplay more pathetic than that of the lowliest Lary Buchanan or Ed Wood poverty-row programmer. Perhaps the most disastrous sequel in Science Fiction cinema.

d Russell Mulcahy *p* Peter Davis, William Panzer *s* Peter Bellwood *c* Phil Meheux *se* John Richardson *lp* Christopher Lambert, Sean Connery, Virginia Madsen, Michael Ironside, John C. McGinley, Allan Rich

Jetsons – the Movie (HANNA-BARBERA/U) 83 min
Originally conceived in 1962 as a simple mirror-image of their television stablemates *The Flintstones* – the typical American sit-com family unit shifted into the far future rather than the remote past – *The Jetsons* ran as a half-hour cartoon show for only one season before cancellation, although producers Hanna-Barbera revived the show, with most of the original voice artists, in the mid-eighties. This feature version is a strange meld of the technologically up-to-the-moment – computer-animated space cities, an irritating pop and rap score, an MTV-cum-*Yellow Submarine* fantasy song sequence, a post-**Star Wars** (1977) race of cloyingly cute teddy bear aliens, and an ecology-minded plot – and the socially out-moded, as the Jetsons themselves remain locked in a fifties ideal of Dad going to work, Mom spending the day shopping and a maid (albeit a robot) to do the housework. With a

storyline that finds little room for real conflict, and characters who have never really registered in the way that the Flintstones managed to, this is ultimately a high-tech exercise in tedium, which its pre-teen audience might find bewildering rather than charming.

d/p William Hanna, Joseph Barbera *s* Dennis Marks *c* Daniel Bunn *se* Perpetual Motion Pictures *lp* George O'Hanlon, Mel Blanc, Penny Singleton, Tiffany, Patric Zimmerman

Lord of the Flies (CASTLE ROCK) 90 min
While Peter Brook's 1963 version of William Golding's near-future allegory was clod-hopping in the extreme, it still managed to be more flavoursome in its arty way than this Americanized remake. Golding's English choir, marooned on a rocky island and reverting to savagery, is replaced by a cadre of American military school brats, whose screen image from *End as a Man* (1959) to *The Lords of Discipline* (1982) has always been so brutal and violent that they hardly seem to need to revert to the Stone Age.

Getty is the conscience-stricken junior hero, a pouting pretty-boy in this reading, while the rest of the cadets come on like refugees from Stephen King's *Children of the Corn* (1983). Peck shows up for a hilarious one-line cameo as the airman whose arrival shocks the children out of their feeding frenzy. Typical of the clumsy up-dating and transatlanticizing of the novel is the change of victim Pipoly's nickname from 'Piggy' to 'Miss Piggy', while dialogue references to Rambo and *ALF* stick out uncomfortably from the unaltered but now over-familiar plotline. British director Hook, making his second feature, compromises all down the line, turning out a film that satisfies neither the GCSE syllabus requirements of the novel's readers nor the commercial dictates of a Hollywood produc-tion. An abandoned treatment of the Golding novel – to be written by Nigel Kneale, directed by Seth Holt, and produced by Kenneth Tynan – remains a tantalizing might-have-been movie.

d Harry Hook *p* Ross Milloy *s* Sara Schiff *c* Martin Fuhrer *lp* Balthazar Getty, Chris Furrh, Daniel Pipoly, Andrew Taft, Edward Taft, Gary Rule, Bob Peck

Lovers Beyond Time
(GREEK FILM CENTRE; GREECE) 85 min

Luridly advertised as 'where sex meets Science Fiction', this is a softcore porno time-travel romance executed with Greek solemnity, its stuffy posiness defusing a potentially intriguing plotline. Heroine Skaza, a music business functionary searching for a reclusive composer, suffers from spontaneous orgasms at embarrassing moments, and seems to be haunted by a lover (Roussel) who vanished three years ago. It turns out, of course, that the composer and the ex-lover are one and the same, but in an unravelling knot of complications it emerges that Roussel is using a time machine to go back to the period of the love affair and make love to Skaza, causing the orgasms in the present day, then extending the trick to murdering the girl's best friend and her husband in the past, thus subtracting them from her current life. Things get even more out of hand and the storyline collapses into multiple paradoxes when it turns out that the original Roussel died three years ago, but managed to bring his younger self from the past to the present to take over his scheme to win the girl back. And it winds up with the single Roussel and two Skazas posing nude as they are zapped by the machine, which resembles a glowing gazebo, into the void.

Like most time-twisting tales, this is severely in need of an ending, and while Skaza's solo sex scenes are spectacularly silly, Roussel's stubbled Myles O'Keeffe lookalike time traveller is a gloomy, uninvolving protagonist.

d/p Dimitris Panayotatos *s* Petros Markaris *c* Tassos Alexakis *lp* Benoit Roussel, Christine Skaza, Takis Moschos, Nadia Deliyanni, Dimitris Poulikakos

Meet the Applegates *aka* The Applegates
(NEW WORLD) 89 min

A family of Brazilian cockroaches that can assume human form invades small-town USA, intent on stopping the destruction of the rain forest by blowing up a nuclear power plant, but gradually the Applegates – who have taken their ideas of Americana from a fifties Dick and Jane primer – are seduced and led astray by the corruption of the nineties, father (Begley Jr) having an affair with the secretary, mother (Channing) becoming a credit-spending alcoholic, daughter Sally getting pregnant and then turning gay, son Johnny getting into drugs.

Lehmann's first feature, *Heathers* (1989), was so precise in its comic cruelty that the film naturally became more serious than its appearance would suggest; however, this skit on the fifties sit-com and big bug movies is so knockabout in its humour that the supposed serious content – several too many eco-blather speeches about how insects treat the world better than humans – is impossible to take. Nevertheless this wayward movie has a great deal of charm, thanks to four perfect performances from the Applegates themselves – with the under-used Begley Jr and Channing showing what they can do if given real material to work with, as opposed to the time-waste roles both of them tend to be cast in, and Jacoby and (especially) Cooper both managing to be marvellously bright and perky in their first incarnations, then gradually, amusingly, going bad as the influence of America sinks in.

The film manages to make interestingly light of the were-cockroaches, with perfect home-maker Jane proudly serving 'rancid trash' to her adoring family, and snarled dialogue putting the situation in perspective, as when Johnny talks about Sally's lesbian girlfriend with the remark, 'But how's she going to react when a kid with a black exoskeleton starts calling her "Daddy"?'

Pardon my antennae are showing. Ed Begley Jr in Meet the Applegates.

A few of the supporting players, notably Coleman in a one-joke transvestite skit that flops, let the side down, but the film has a perfect echt-fifties look, and a genuinely warm feel for its naive characters, so that the final effect really is not that far removed from the life- and lifestyle-affirming Doris Day-Rock Hudson-James Garner movies it lampoons.

d/co-s Michael Lehmann *p* Denise Di Novi *co-s* Redbeard Simmons *c* Mitchell Dubin *se* Kevin Yagher *lp* Ed Begley Jr, Stockard Channing, Cami Cooper, Dabney Coleman, Bobby Jacoby, Glenn Shadix, Susan Barnes

Megaville (WHITE NOISE) 95 min

This is an impressive little picture updating some of the feel of Jean-Luc Godard's **Alphaville** (1965) in its vision of a transformed future America, played oddly but effectively by current-day Switzerland, divided into independent zones. The hero (Zane) is sent by a dying Big Brother (Travanti) into the wide open city of Megaville, where forms of electronic entertainment illegal in a puritan country are still widely available, on a mission that requires him to impersonate a media-manipulating criminal as he searches for a device that enables the user to experience other people's experiences, memories and fantasies. As in the contemporary **Total Recall** (1990), the hero is gradually led to question his own identity, in this case coming to wonder, in Philip K. Dick style, whether he is indeed the criminal he is supposed to be replacing. A cold and cynical film, with a supporting cast of well-played sinister characters, it winds up with a bleak absurdist moment worthy of an EC comic, as Zane is murdered in the desert by his mentor (Quinn), but manages to handcuff his corpse to the killer's foot, anchoring him so that he will die too.

d/s Peter Lehner *p* Christina Schmidlin *c* Zoltan David *lp* Billy Zane, J. C. Quinn, Grace Zabriskie, Kristen Cloke, Daniel J. Travanti, Stefan Gierasch

Miracle Mile (HEMDALE) 88 min

Shifting unfashionably from wistful comedy to outright panic, this dares to take an unconventional, and hardly reassuring, approach to familiar subject matter. On Miracle Mile, a stretch of Los Angeles freeway near the prehistoric LaBrea tar pits, trombonist Edwards has just overslept and missed a late-night date with Winningham, the girl he has been looking for all his

life. Turning up at 4.30 in the morning at the diner where he was due to meet her at midnight, he answers a ringing call-phone and receives a panic-stricken message from a soldier in a missile silo somewhere, who claims that World War Three is going to start within the hour. Unsure but half-convinced, Edwards shares the news with the rest of the late-nighters in the diner, and gradually the ripples of panic spread throughout the city as zero hour approaches. While others are organizing a futile and insane dash for Antarctica, Edwards decides to make a bid at finding and rescuing Winningham, making up in one hour for the life he thinks he has wasted.

A worst-case scenario rethinking of *1941* (1980), *Miracle Mile* has some of the eccentric drive and taut plotting of *After Hours* (1986), but is mainly a movie original, confronting the End of the World with a mix of black humour, deeply felt anger and honest sentiment. Wonderfully acted by a large cast of star bit-players, who were obviously just keen on being in this particular movie, this may not exactly be cheerful, but it tackles an important issue in an approachable, individual way and its overall impact is quietly devastating.

d/s Steve DeJarnatt *p* Eileen Stringer *c* Theo Van De Sande *se* Jena Holman *lp* Anthony Edwards, Mare Winningham, Denise Crosby, John Agar, Lou Hancock, Mykel T. Williamson, Kelly Minter, Robert DoQui, Danny de la Paz, Brian Thompson, Jenette Goldstein

Moon 44 (CEBTROPOLIS FILMPRODUKTION; WG) 99 min
This is an outer space version of two mutually exclusive earthbound genres, the prison picture and the fighter pilot movie, even stirring in some teen nerd geniuses for 'youth appeal'. In the future, mining companies run the universe and there are wars going on between them. Paré is the Shakespeare-reading unshaven hunk cop sent to Moon 44 – we never find out what it is the 44th moon of – to discover who is stealing expensive mining equipment. The colony, run by a haggard McDowell, is defended by a cadre of rough, tough fighter jocks. The problem is that all the pilots have been killed and so they are being replaced by 'volunteers' from the prisons of Earth, muscle-bound scumbags who enjoy terrorizing the irritating teenage brains who navigate their fighter-plane-cum-helicopter ships.

Half of the film comprises prison clichés – the brutalized sensitive lad gets back at the thug who raped him in the showers and then hangs himself in his cell – and the rest comprises air force clichés, with pilots crashing 'copters into each other and blasting robot invaders from rival corporations. Paré broods, and the plot unravels in unwieldy dollops, but it's a thudding bore despite adequate special effects and effectively cramped production design.

d/co-p Roland Emmerich *co-p/co-s* Dean Heyde *co-s* Oliver Eberle *c* Karl Walter Undenlaub *se* Robert G. Brown *lp* Michael Paré, Lisa Eichhorn, Malcolm McDowell, Brian Thompson, Dean Devlin, Stephen Geoffreys, Leon Rippy

Night of the Living Dead (21ST CENTURY) 89 min
George A. Romero's 1968 classic, which had already been expanded upon by two official sequels and sundry imitations and parodies, was hardly in need of a colour remake (it has, after all, already suffered colourization). Indeed this was undertaken partly because a rights quirk meant that if the original production team did *not* undertake a remake, then anyone else could have stepped in and done so. However, given that cavil, this is as good a job as one might have the right to expect, compressing the major plot points of the original movie into its first four-fifths and then coming up with a potent and disturbing new set of last-minute twists, vaguely indebted to *Straw Dogs* (1972), which cap the heroine's declaration of the zombies that 'we are them and they are us' with a startling, ambiguous and callous offhand murder.

Top Gun *goes into orbit:* Moon 44.

Revising his original screenplay, Romero shears away much of the 'scientific' explanation, sixties social satire and commentary on the media reaction to the crisis, concentrating instead on the acute divisions among the small group of survivors cooped up in a farmhouse caused by the rising of the dead. While the black hero (Todd) and his bigoted adversary (Towles) remain essentially as they were, even to the point of seeming to be men out of their time, the heroine (Tallman) is given a post-Sigourney Weaver attitude. Her shock-trauma reaction to the death of her brother and the attack of the flesh-eating ghouls is not to become an instant catatonic but to turn into a supercompetent guerilla fighter, whose effective anti-zombie violence is finally and devastatingly seen to be as insane a reaction as her predecessor's simple crawling into a psychological shell.

Make-up supremo Savini, in his directorial debut, surprisingly but intelligently refrains from going as overboard into zombie gore gags as **Dawn of the Dead** (1978) and *Day of the Dead* (1985), and even plays the siege situation more for suspense than for the blend of social comedy and splatter that has come to characterize the series. With resources unavailable to the original movie – an effective original score rather than stock music cuts, convincing make-up for the monster extras, consistent lighting, professional actors – he even manages to bring up to standard the sometimes ropy qualities of the first film. Cannily, Romero and Savini don't reproduce exactly the shocks of the original, the shambling wino in the graveyard in the first scene turning out to be exactly that and merely a precursor to the unexpected appearance from another part of the screen of the first attacking zombie. However, the film does have too many hand-through-the-window shock tricks. Moreover – like any potential remake of **Invasion of the Body Snatchers** (1956), *A Bout de Souffle* (1959) or *La Maschera del Demoniuo* (1960) – the original was both so much a creation of its time and an important, influential and excellent work that has withstood the test of time, that any remake, no matter how fine, is doomed to be just a footnote.

d Tom Savini *p* John A. Russo, Russ Streiner *s* George A. Romero *c* Frank Prinzi *se* John Vulich, Everett Burrell *lp* Tony Todd, Pat Tallman, Tom Towles, William Butler, Katie Finneran, McKee Anderson, Bill Moseley

Peacemaker

(GIBRALTAR RELEASING/MENTONE PICTURES) 90 min
Similar to **Dark Angel** (1990), itself similar to **The Hidden** (1988), itself similar to **Brain from Planet Arous** (1958), itself indebted to Hal Clement's novel *Needle*, this is a competent actioner, with yet another extra-terrestrial cop and killer team loose on Earth. The only notable twist is that both the aliens – recently crash-landed and unshaven macho man Edwards, and gun-toting twenty-years assimilated brooder Forster – claim to be the cop and that the other is an extra-terrestrial serial killer. However, there is never any doubt, thanks to medical examiner heroine Shepard's attraction to Edwards, that Forster – who has slipped through a timewarp just prior to arrival and is scheming to get hold of Edwards' functional spaceship to replace his own crashed vehicle – is the villain. A pleasant timewaster, this perhaps relies too much on repetitive and familiar chases and explosions, rather than let its fine cast do much with their roles.

d/s Kevin S. Tenney   *p* Andrew Lane, Wayne Crawford
c Thomas Jewett   *se* John Blake   *lp* Robert Forster, Lance Edwards, Hilary Shepard, Robert Davi, Bert Remsen

Predator 2   (FOX)   108 min

The premise that was hackneyed in the original **Predator** (1987) – a big-game hunter from outer space goes after a well-trained and armed team of he-men for sport – is here combined with the currently fashionable rogue cop and anti-drugs themes (instead of the jungle, this is set in a 1997 Los Angeles ghetto overrun by warring drugs cartels). The result is a machine-tooled piece of undeniable entertainment which resembles a patchwork quilt of eighties Science Fiction and action successes but still, like Gordon and Silver's *Die Hard 2* (1990), leaves a faintly hollow feeling at its fade-out. Its self-referential aspects range from the extremely neat in-joke of having the skull of one of the creatures from the *Alien* films on display with the predator's other trophies in his flying saucer, to the employment of Morton Downey Jr as an 'in-your-face' television newsman who allows for some **RoboCop**-style satire on a degraded future media. Meanwhile production designer Lawrence G. Paull provides a variation on the steamy, multi-ethnic, on-the-skids future city he devised for **Blade Runner** (1982). However, with the intervention of the semi-invisible creature, whose shimmering outline is an impressively weird but somewhat over-used effect, the movie gradually transforms into a straightforward body count picture, as a succession of eccentric characters – the strangest of whom is Lockhart's dreadlocked voodoo priest drug king – wander into the grips of the monster and are colourfully but repetitively disposed of.

Given that it's a sequel, the film perhaps wastes too much time on its 'mystery' angle, as tough cop Glover laboriously comes to the conclusion that an alien is behind the murders and Hopkins works up to the shock revelation of what the creature's face looks like, which will hardly be a shock to anyone who saw the first film. Hopkins takes advantage of his monster's rampages to stage some striking Grand Guignol tableaux, like the smashed penthouse full of dangling skinned corpses. But the last reels degenerate further into a conflation of the battles from **Aliens** (1986), as Busey's space-suited team gets picked off, and the original *Predator*, as Glover sweatily but unconvincingly tries to follow in Man Mountain Arnie's footsteps by triumphing over the fanged giant.

d Stephen Hopkins   *p* Lawrence Gordon, Joel Silver
s Jim & John Thomas   *c* Peter Leavy   *se* Stan Winston
lp Danny Glover, Maria Conchita Alonso, Gary Busey, Bill Paxton, Ruben Blades, Calvin Lockhart, Kevin Peter Hall, Robert Davi, Adam Baldwin

RoboCop 2   (ORION)   116 min

This sequel was manufactured by exactly the same process as its hero back in Part One. The premise of **RoboCop** (1987) has been taken out, tortured for a while, shot full of holes and mechanically revived as a soulless, ungainly, clanking, expensive walking disaster. In a summer of disappointing sequels, *RoboCop 2* was right down there with *Re-Animator 2* (1990) and *Another 48 Hrs* (1990) as a trashing of an efficient-to-beloved original.

Culprit Number One must be comics author Frank Miller Jr (*The Dark Knight Returns*), whose ideas were extensively plundered for the first film, but who here shows himself totally incapable of handling his own second-hand material in any

Danny Glover (left) and Gary Busey as the buddy-buddy cops in Predator 2.

cinematic way. This straggles on for thirteen minutes longer than the original, robocopping out at every opportunity, as it inverts the intriguing political cynicism of the first film to come up with yet another conservative anti-drugs picture heavily laden with overkill.

The villain this time is Cain (Noonan), a hippie who is distributing the powerful new dope Nuke to the citizens of Detroit. He gets killed three-quarters of the way through, and his brain is unbelievably selected for insertion into RoboCop 2, a super-destructive cyborg intended to outclass the outmoded first edition. RoboCop (Weller) has meanwhile been pottering about in the background, absent for large stretches of the action, trying hard to get some personal trauma in the film so that Culprit Number Two, director Kershner, can claim to have made a 'relationship movie' rather than yet another excuse to blow things up and mutilate people. The film thuds across the screen, occasionally raising a flicker of interest with a spoof TV commercial, with too many supporting characters intriguing against each other, and repetitively involving its hero in machine-gun shoot-outs that lead nowhere, while RoboCop himself alternates between Nazi superthug and annoying wimp. Charbonneau has a major role as RoboCop's police physician, but is uncredited, suggesting that she was brought in to fill in for Allen's heroine in some scenes after Allen's rumoured walk-out.

d Irvin Kershner *p* Jon Davison *s* Frank Miller, Walon Green *c* Mark Irwin *se* Peter Kuran, Phil Tippett, Rob Bottin *lp* Peter Weller, Nancy Allen, Dan O'Herlihy, Tom Noonan, Patricia Charbonneau, Belinda Bauer, Gabriel Damon, John Glover

The Salute of the Jugger *aka* The Blood of Heroes
(US-AUST) 92 min
This is yet another post-apocalypse Science Fiction movie without any special effects, but with plenty of plot licks borrowed from the **A Boy and His Dog** (1975), the *Mad Max* series, and the run of pictures – **Rollerball** (1975), **Death Race 2000** (1975), **The Running Man** (1987) – about how popular gladiatorial sports will be in the twenty-first century. In an Australian desert littered with tribal communities and rusting scrap metal, a roving team of battered juggers – the term is never really explained – challenges a succession of local boys to take part in 'The Game', which is a combination of rugby, basketball, gratuitous violence, s-m gear and dog-skull tossing. Veteran Hauer, who was once a big star jugger in a fascist underground city, is egged on by newcomer Chen to go back to the big leagues and challenge the grudge-holding bad guys to a new match.

Unfocused and trite, this film manages to be dull even in the action scenes, because jugging is even more boring than most real-life sports and fails to serve any particular credible function in the banal and familiar future society that the film creates. *Rollerball*, *Death Race 2000* and *The Running Man* – none of which qualify as masterpieces – all spent some time on the reasons why people would be interested in playing or watching their invented gladiatorial sports, but *Salute of the Jugger* just needs an excuse for fights. The characters are thin – so much so that the rubber scars everyone wears are constantly threatening to peel off – the ending at once predictable and pointless, the horrors have no resonance, and first-time director Peoples (screenwriter of **Blade Runner** (1982), *Ladyhawke* (1985), **Predator** (1987) and **Leviathan** (1989)) manages to turn out a movie with no sense of humour whatsoever, much less any Science Fiction imagination or muscle-flexing excitement.

d/s David Peoples *p* Charles Roven *c* David Eggby *se* Neville Maxwell *lp* Rutger Hauer, Joan Chen, Vincent Phillip D'Onofrio, Delroy Lindo, Hugh Keays-Byrne, Gandhi McIntire, Max Fairchild

Shadowzone (EMPIRE) 88 min
Although this competent, low-budget Science Fiction horror item from the Charles Band stable is essentially yet another rip-off of **Alien** (1979), with more than a few similarities to the already imitative **Forbidden World** (1982), it has a pleasantly cramped feel and an offbeat scientific background reminiscent of the *Outer Limits* television series.

An army investigator (Beecroft) probes into a mysterious death in a sealed-off underground base where a group of vaguely mad scientists, led by the always-welcome Hong and Fletcher, are conducting research into long-term sleep. After some fairly suspenseful licks in the opening, as everyone tries to conceal the truth from the blockhead hero, it develops that the sleepers, as in *From Beyond* (1985), have become gateways to another dimension and have summoned a shape-changing pasta creature with red goulash eyeballs, who slaughters its way through the supporting cast. Cardone, who made the effective slasher *The Slayer* (1980), handles the conventional story with some claustrophobic flair, after the manner of either version of **The Thing**, and the setting is more detailed and interesting than the familiar space stations and sewers favoured by this species of monster. The title, as with most Band coinages (**Laserblast**, 1978, **Metalstorm**, 1983, **Swordkill**, 1984) is meaningless.

d/s J. S. Cardone *p* Carol Kottenbrook *c* Karen Grossman *lp* Louise Fletcher, David Beecroft, James Hong, Shawn Wetherly, Miguel Nunez, Maureen Flaherty

Rutger Hauer in
Salute of the Jugger.

Wanna light?
Spontaneous
Combustion.

Spaced Invaders (SMART EGG) 100 min

On the fiftieth anniversary of Orson Welles' *War of the Worlds* broadcast, an Illinois radio station puts the play out again, and the signal happens to be picked up by a passing spaceship crewed by a lost unit of the Martian Space Navy. They are fooled into thinking that their comrades are mounting a mass invasion of the Earth and zapp down to Big Bean, Ill., in order to join in the fun. With their cheery catchphrase, 'prepare to die, Earth scum', they romp around on Hallowe'en night, getting mixed up with trick-or-treaters, farm closures, a gas-pump attendant dressed as Zorro, a deadly discipline robot and some cutesy kids. This being a PG film, the aliens don't actually hurt anyone – not even the dog or the town's grasping bank manager – even though the Earth seems frequently threatened with total devastation. Among the earthling characters are a creaky old farmer (Dano), a square-jawed sheriff (Barr), a cute blonde girl dressed as an alien (Harris) and a lisping black kid in a duck costume (Anderson), and since it's Hallowe'en night the locals predictably assume that the aliens are just trick-or-treaters.

Although it's way too long for its slight premise, and the aliens aren't as well characterized as they might be – the one who does a Jack Nicholson impersonation, complete with a Lakers T-shirt and cool shades, comes off best – *Spaced Invaders* finishes by being quite an enjoyable and amusing movie. Suffused with a shaggy dog amiability that sees everything turn out all right in the end, despite the attempts of a metal jellyfish to get serious with its deathray, the film sneaks by quite pleasantly.

d/co-s Patrick Read Johnson *p* Luigi Cingolani *co-s* Scott Alexander *c* James L. Carter *se* John Criswell, Greg Johnson, Frank Ceglia *lp* Royal Dano, Douglas Barr, Ariana Richards, J. J. Anderson, Judith Harris

Spontaneous Combustion (TAURUS/MGM) 92 min

This is further evidence, in this case literal, of Hooper's creative burn-out, with promising subject matter botched by an incoherent script, uncertain performances and a general feeling that major scenes have been left out of the final cut. It opens in 1955, with a young couple deliberately being exposed to radiation during a desert A-bomb test, in order to gauge the effectiveness of a serum against irradiation. The couple produce a child, but then mysteriously burn up, allowing the boy to grow up into a confused young man (Dourif) whose life is completely manipulated by Hughes-style billionaire Prince. For no apparent reason, Dourif starts to exhibit many of the symptoms of pyrokinesis familiar from *Firestarter* (1984), and his rages result in the (mainly off-screen) torching of supporting characters who irritate him. Finally, he confronts Prince and is informed that he has been bred especially to be 'America's Atomic Man', the cleanest imaginable killing machine, and turns into a monster who has a brief rampage to tie up a few of the loose plot ends by killing minor villains, before he melts down entirely, saving the life of his similarly afflicted girlfriend (Bain).

A mix of paranoia and the paranormal, this trots out yet another purposeless conspiracy theory to no good end, and spends so much of its time being ominous that a lot of the minor details – a young student who presents Dourif with his long-dead father's watch, for instance – never do get explained. Even the human melt-down sequences are rather ineffectually staged, with padded and flinching stuntmen substituting for the performers and little in the way of fiery flourishes.

d/co-s Tobe Hooper *p* Jim Rogers *co-s* Howard Goldberg *c* Levie Isaacks *se* Stephen Brooks, Apogee Productions Inc *lp* Brad Dourif, Cynthia Bain, William Prince, Dey Young, Melinda Dillon, Jon Cypher

Teenage Mutant Ninja Turtles

(LIMELIGHT) 93 min

Teenage Mutant Ninja Turtles takes its slender joke too far. Originally conceived by comics creators Kevin Eastman and Peter Laird as a hip, ridiculous parody of the superhero genre, the turtles somehow took off with the pre-teen market, replacing the wishy-washy Care Bears in the affections of millions, and spun off into an animated TV series and sundry other manifestations. This movie version rushes through the characters' origins after the fashion of such recent comic-to-film transfers as **Swamp Thing** (1982), *The Punisher* (1990) and **Batman** (1989), from all of which it borrows. It then gets down to the business of pitting its four pizza-loving Bill-and-Ted-talking amphibian heroes against the Shredder (Sato), a ninja master with a Darth Vader hat and voice, for perhaps the mildest martial arts action ever seen on the screen. In between, it manages to express a typically conservative early nineties Bush-era set of values, with feckless kids going along with a criminal patriarch because of the weakness of their family values, and a few sneeringly racist jokes – 'What's the matter, did I fall behind on my Sony payments?' snaps heroine Hoag when confronted by ordinary ninjas – that express resentment at Japan's economic strength even while the film is plundering Japan's popular culture.

Directed rather fuzzily by Barron, as a belated follow-up to his similarly flabby-whimsical début *Electric Dreams* (1984), this betrays its low budget with makeshift non-star performances, generally lame wisecracks and grainy look, although the Henson Creature Shop's work on the titular turtles remains impressive. The film is doggily endearing while it is introducing its characters, but increasingly tiresome thereafter, as it can't make up its mind whether it is parodying the crowd-pleasing heroics of its characters or presenting them straight. Unlike *Batman* or **Superman – the Movie** (1978), this never does find a proper balance between self-parody and the right stuff, and hence flounders somewhat through its elementary and contrived plot until its unimpressive climax, in which the supposedly awesome villain happily falls off a building into a garbage grinder *before* the big fight we might legitimately have been expecting. Compounding the lack of flair in the martial arts sequences are the film's problems with its characters, who strut and drop the occasional teenage buzzword, but are never remotely convincing as teenagers, mutants, ninjas or turtles, leaving them stranded on the screen as big green muppets with different coloured headbands. In the end, the artistically named creatures are highly reminiscent of the early seventies Godzilla movies, in which lovable monsters in baggy foam rubber suits befriended lost children and smashed things up in orgies of destruction that somehow never hurt anyone.

d Steve Barron *p* Kim Dawson, Simon Fields, David Chan *s* Todd W. Langen, Bobby Herbeck *c* John Fenner *se* Henson Creature Shop *lp* Judith Hoag, Eleas Koteas, Josh Pais, Michelan Sisti, Lief Tilden, David Forman, Michael Tunrey, James Sato

Tetsuo *aka* Tin Man (KAIJU THEATRE; JAP) 67 min

Tetsuo, a common Japanese given name, can be written with the characters for 'metal' and 'man', and this astonishing 16mm black and white movie is the body-horror cyber-punk tale of monster mutants who fuse flesh and steel in an increasingly creaky and agonized ecstasy of transformation.

In an industrial Japanese Hell, a scrapheap casualty who enjoys ramming bits of iron pipe into open wounds is trashed in a hit-and-run accident, and causes the responsible couple to turn into hideous half-man, half-machine, all-monster creations and alternately to indulge in frenzied and painful sexual congress or try to drill, slash, hack and splatter each other to bits. Finding a metal spike in his cheek while shaving, the salary man driver gradually mutates in competition with the underground geek, and an uptight female commuter and his girlfriend are also dragged along the evolutionary path.

With monster costumes that come across as the X-rated equivalent of the tatty grotesque outfits that used to crop up on *Dr Who* ('The Claws of Axos') or *Lost in Space* ('The Great Vegetable Rebellion'), this film features some of the strongest stuff seen on the screen in recent years, especially when the nominal hero sprouts an uncontrollable pneumatic-drill penis and his girlfriend rides him to a messy death, redecorating the wall behind her. It winds up with a pixilated battle through the streets of town, as the two main mutants chase and hack each other with Marvel Comics verve, finally resolving to spread their biomechanical perversion across the city. Painful, funny, pretentious and pointed, *Tetsuo* goes beyond almost anything else currently being made in the mainstream, harking back to the Kurosawa of *Do'des-ka Den* (1970), the Cronenberg of **Videodrome** (1982) or the Lynch of *Eraserhead* (1976). In its stylized, shrieking kabuki horror, *Tetsuo* establishes Shinya, a fringe theatre director and rock promoter, as a potential dingbat genius.

d/p/s/co-c/se Tsukamoto Shinya   *co-c* Fujiwara Kei
lp 'Tomorrow' Taguchi, Fujiwara Kei, Kanaoko Nobu, Tsukamoto Shinya, Musaka Naomesa

Total Recall   (CAROLCO)   113 min

Perhaps the most expensive movie ever made, this clearly attempted to be also one of the most successful, combining an above-the-title star who has the highest profile among modern action men, a director fresh from a major cult success, a fully detailed Science Fiction background lavishly straddling two imagined worlds, a complicated and much-retailored screenplay that has been through nearly 10 years of development, and, perhaps most importantly, an almost non-stop parade of action, destruction, stuntwork and violence.

In the future, Douglas Quaid (Schwarzenegger) has been having bad dreams about Mars, where he has never been. He visits Rekall Inc, a holiday service that provides its customers with artificial memories of visits to exotic places, and signs up for a fantasy vacation as a secret agent on Mars, but becomes psychotic before the memories can be injected. Suddenly, his best friend from work and his wife Stone try to kill him, and he is pursued by a ruthless assassin in the pay of Cox, the dictator of Mars. Quaid escapes and is given a video message from himself, which tells him that his real name is Hauser and that he is a former associate of Cox's who has joined the rebellion on Mars and has vital information locked in his head, but that Cox has had his mind re-programmed with fake memories of an ordinary life on Earth to get rid of him. Following a trail left by himself in his Hauser incarnation, Quaid makes his way to Mars and meets the girl of his dreams (Ticotin), continually finding that all his beliefs about the world are being pulled out from under him.

Taking off from the comic book goriness of **RoboCop** (1987), this finds Verhoeven straying back almost to the sheer nastiness of *Flesh & Blood* (1986), with almost every sequence constructed around or containing some fresh atrocity. While the film favours such old favourite over-the-top tropes as the graphic special-effects death and the gunning-down of faceless hordes of extras – with Schwarzenegger even using the bullet-riddled corpse of one bystander as a shield during a shoot-out in a subway station – it also takes care to elevate even the most standard act of violence to the level of ultra-brutality by turning up the sound effects in the martial arts movie style. This emphasis on violence is indicative of the coarse tone of the film, but does have a cumulative effect that, in a roundabout way, manages to get fairly close to the paranoid spirit of Philip K. Dick.

The protagonist of 'We Can Remember It For You Wholesale', the original story, is a typical Dick-style everyman, a Walter Mitty-ish character whose literal dream holiday makes him doubt his whole identity and history. Casting the obviously invulnerable Schwarzenegger in the role has necessitated a strange re-thinking, whereby the first act, when we are supposed to take Douglas Quaid for an ordinary building labourer, is a transparent fiction, granting the more obvious fantasy of the secret agent storyline a level of reality that is surprisingly apt, given the film's neat attempts to make it seem like the kind of exotic movie-style plot that a no one like Quaid might select for his Rekall dream. When Schwarzenegger

Make My Day: Arnie
in Total Recall.

explodes into action one has the sense of a role being stripped away and the real man – or, at least, Schwarzenegger's pre-manufactured hero image – coming to the fore. Likewise, the stiffly played and pathetic domestic scene at the very beginning of the film, which most audiences take as evidence that the star's acting ability cannot stretch to playing a happily married man, is indeed as false and hollow as we perceive it to be. It is marvellously contradicted in the sequence where the bewildered Quaid comes home to tell Stone about his terrible experience, only to have her turn from concerned and clichéd perfect wife into a murderous assassin who convinces him that all his memories are a lie.

One of the major surprises of the film is that, unlike **Blade Runner** (1982), it approximates to Dick's demented plotting, even new-minting twists and turns entirely in the spirit of the late author. In particular, the sequence in which a mild-mannered boffin and Stone turn up in Quaid's Martian hotel room and try to convince him that he is still dreaming – 'Do you really believe that you're an invincible secret agent who's the victim of a giant conspiracy to convince him that he's an ordinary construction worker?' – has a Dick-like feel. It forces one to reassess the unlikely but crowd-pleasing action heroics that have gone before and, later, to question whether, despite Quaid's decision to accept his adventure as reality, what we see on screen, especially the vast *deus ex machina* ending featuring **2001** (1968)-style alien artefacts, is the hero's subjective or objective reality. Even more clever, however, is the revelation that Hauser, Quaid's previous incarnation, is, in fact, the villain of the movie, partly because it brilliantly clears up a niggling plot doubt – if Hauser has turned traitor, why hasn't Cox simply killed him rather than gone through the whole false identity business? – and partly because it makes genuinely unexpected and ingenious use of Schwarzenegger's by-no-means entirely sympathetic image.

Subverting itself at all levels, the film has an excuse for most of its flaws – after all, if the whole Martian section is possibly Quaid's fantasy, then the tacky mutant make-up, the underdeveloped secondary characterizations, the hokey joke lines that Schwarzenegger uses when he kills people ('screw you,' he sneers as he drills a minor baddy with a boring instrument), the non-stop incredible plot twists, and the regulation unbelievable escapes are entirely in keeping with his limited imagination. The huge budget allows for a profusion of genuinely Science Fictional touches, like the secretary's colour-changing nail polish; the automated fat lady disguise that Quaid adopts on his attempt to bluff his way through Mars immigration; the thumb-press safe deposit boxes; the skull-implant tracer – which has to be painfully withdrawn through the hero's nose – that the villains use to keep tabs on Quaid; the X-ray corridor that reveals concealed weapons; and the hologram tennis player that Stone uses as an exercise aid. While it is ingenious and entertaining, rather than likeable and inspiring, **Total Recall** nevertheless stands as state-of-the-art film Science Fiction for 1990.

d Paul Verhoeven *co-p* Buzz Feitshans *co-p/co-s* Ronald Shusett *co-s* Dan O'Bannon, Gary Goldman *c* Jost Vacano *se* Rob Bottin *lp* Arnold Schwarzenegger, Rachel Ticotin, Sharon Stone, Ronny Cox, Michael Ironside, Marshall Bell

1991

Alligator 2: The Mutation
(GROUP 1) 92 min

'I understand that you're professionals,' the hero tells experts as the mutant-on-a-rampage crisis escalates, 'but this is not a professional alligator.' This made-for-video picture from the director of **Watchers** (1988) is less a sequel to the well-regarded **Alligator** (1981) than a lacklustre remake. Though adequately cast, with Bologna an acceptable substitute for Robert Forster as the befuddled cop on the case and Stone fine as his helpful scientist wife, this outing suffers from a script which exactly follows the clichéd plot of *Alligator* but fails to match John Sayles's witty dialogue and offbeat characterization. Railsback is the property-developing toxic waste dumper

responsible for the mutation in the first place, while Lynch takes the man-of-the-match award in the old Henry Silva role as a Cajun gator hunter who confronts the immobile rubber monster in the sewers.

d Jon Hess *p* Brandon Chase *s* Curt Allen *c* Joseph Mangine *se* Bob McKee *lp* Joseph Bologna, Dee Wallace Stone, Richard Lynch, Woody Brown, Holly Gagnier, Bill Daily, Steve Railsback, Brock Peters

Appleseed
(GAINAX/AIC/CENTRE STUDIO/TOHOKUSHINSHA/BANDAI/MOVIC; JAP) 71 min

Based on a *manga* by Masumune Shirow, creator of the popular *Dominion: Tank Police* series, this is the usual *anime* mix: little girls with big guns, hulking robo-warrior suits, a future city, chases and fights, cyborg computer jocks, shrill characters and a plot that sets up numberless future episodes. In a premise which prefigures **Demolition Man** (1993), the utopian city of Olympus has been established in the ruins of a ravaged future earth. The inhabitants have to recruit hardened survivors from the wastelands to form a special police unit to fight ambiguous terrorists out to destroy the status quo. The heroes are an elfin but spunky young girl and her lumbering cyborg best friend-partner, stock characters whose sexless relationship gives the film a curiously childlike feel despite its cynicism and violence.

That said, the selling point is the spectacular high-tech urban warfare which explodes between the sociological speculation and buddy-bonding.

d/s Kazuyoshi Katayama *p* Taro Maki, Sugita Asushi, Masaki Sawanobori, Miura Tohru *se* Shizuo Kurahashi

Bill & Ted's Bogus Journey
(ORION) 93 min

In the far future, megalomaniac Ackland has decided to reverse the ending of **Bill & Ted's Excellent Adventure** (1989) by sending back in time evil robot doubles of the braindead valley dudes, played again by Reeves and Winter, with orders to wreck their chance of winning the Battle of the Bands contest, and thus forestall the utopian pastel future Bill and Ted will create with their horrible rock music. The evil robots kidnap the originals and throw them off a *Star Trek* location mountain to their deaths, whereupon Bill and Ted have to face the Grim Reaper

Hey you want tidy or should we trash some more? - Alex Winter (left) and Keanu Reeves as robots in Bill & Ted's Bogus Journey.

Solveig Dommartin and William Hurt in the bewildering Bis ans Ende der Welt.

(Sadler) and visit both Heaven and Hell before returning to Earth as ghosts to set things to rights. The result is less funny than the original, but surprisingly a rather smoother movie, with something approaching a plot and characters and far more visual imagination than the scrappy but hilarious original. The stupidity quotient is as high as before: a Bergman spoof has Bill and Ted challenge Death to games of Battleship, Cluedo and Twister, while Ben Franklin, Confucius and Einstein pass the time in Heaven playing charades (Einstein wins by guessing *Smokey and the Bandit 3: Smokey is the Bandit*) and Hell features a nice turn by a gleefully malign Easter Bunny.

d Peter Hewitt *p* Scott Kroopf *s* Ed Solomon, Chris Matheson *c* Oliver Wood *se* Kevin Yagher, Stan Parks, Richard Yuricich *lp* Keanu Reeves, Alex Winter, William Sadler, Joss Ackland, Pam Grier

Bis ans Ende der Welt *aka* Until the End of the World
(ROAD MOVIES/ARGOS/VILLAGE ROADSHOW; G-FR-AUST) 158 min
This overlong Science Fiction art film sets out to be the ultimate road movie. In 1999, with the Earth endangered by an out-of-control Star Wars satellite, various characters – enigmatic wanderer Dommartin (the actress co-wrote the original story with Wenders), mystery criminal Hurt, Dommartin's ex-lover (Neill), a private eye (Vogler), some bank robbers, Hurt's parents (Moreau, von Sydow) – traipse from Venice to France to Berlin to Lisbon to Tokyo to San Francisco to the Australian outback, revolving around each other and such macguffins as stolen money, various prices on Hurt's head, sundered relationships, computerized person-trackers and, finally, a camera device invented by von Sydow which can help the blind see and also transmit images from one brain to another. This invention has driven von Sydow into retreat, since he has a paranoia movie fear of US government intervention: 'It can take visual information straight from the brain. Once they can do that, they can suck out your dreams and look at them like television.' Hurt, gradually going blind, comes to depend on von Sydow's device which, when the explosion of the satellite convinces him the world has ended, opens the way into Aboriginal dreamworlds.

Wenders builds the film on references to his earlier works ('Weren't you the angel in Lisbon?') which sometimes come close to self-plagiarism. The result is a half-hearted attempt to mimic the generic forms of the international conspiracy thriller and the apocalyptic Science Fiction film.

d/co-s Wim Wenders *p* Jonathan Taplin, Anatole Dauman, Paulo Branco *co-s* Peter Carey *c* Robby Muller *se* FuturEffects *lp* Solveig Dommartin, William Hurt, Sam Neill, Jeanne Moreau, Max von Sydow, Chick Ortega, Rüdiger Vogler, Allen Garfield, Lois Chiles, David Gulpilil, Ryu Chishu

Critters 3
(NEW LINE/OH FILMS) 86 min
Though this third series entry relocates from the small town of the earlier films to the big city, it is a scaled-down effort, turning away from the large-scale effects and sprawling plots of **Critters** (1986) and *Critters 2: The Main Course* (1988). Novelist Schow works in a few smart lines and re-uses riffs from his much nastier monster-in-a-tenement book *The Shaft*. However, lack of resources, a cast of nonentities (including future star DiCaprio) and feeble monster stuff (anyone for a farting monster joke?) doom this to the video tape bargain bin. It was shot back-to-back with *Critters 4* (1992), a marginally superior effort written by Schow and Joseph Lyle and directed by producer Harvey, with a slightly superior cast (Angela Bassett, Brad Dourif, Eric Da Re) and a *Dr Who*-style off-Earth space station setting.

d Kristine Peterson *p* Rupert Harvey, Barry Opper *s* David J. Schow *c* Tom Callaway *se* Charles Chiodo, Stephen Chiodo, Edward Chiodo *lp* Aimee Brooks, John Calvin, Dan Opper, Katherine Cortez, Leonardo DiCaprio, Geoffrey Blake

Dollman
(FULL MOON ENTERTAINMENT) 86 min
'Thirteen inches tall, with an attitude,' runs the tag-line for this odd attempt at gritty fantasy.

On a far-away planet Brick Bardo (Thomerson) is the toughest cop in the neighbourhood, then he and his floating head arch-enemy are zapped down to the South Bronx where they are caught up in a struggle between a crack-dealing gang and a pretty widow's neighbourhood watch scheme. Thomerson reprises his hardboiled but sly hero from **Trancers** (1984) as a pissed-off Brick, who does his level best not to be cute as he blasts villains' knee-caps and saves the day. While the downsizing of the story from galactic import to just another gang war 'n' the hood is surprisingly workable, there is a major drawback in Pyun's lack of the effects resources available to **Honey, I Shrunk the Kids** (1989), which means the hero is

A womb with a fuse:
Renée Soutendijk in
Eve Of Destruction.

almost never seen in the same frame as the big people. After a cameo in Full Moon's **Bad Channels** (1992), Thomerson's Brick encounters the monsters from *Demonic Toys* (1991) in Charles Band's economical, stock footage-filled multi-sequel *Dollman vs the Demonic Toys* (1993).

d Albert Pyun *p* Cathy Gesualdo *s* Chris Roghair *c* George Mooradian *lp* Tim Thomerson, Jackie Earle Haley, Kamala Lopez, Humberto Ortiz, Nicholas Guest, Judd Omen

Eve of Destruction

(INTERSCOPE) 98 min

At once a rip-off of **The Terminator** (1984) and a get-in-there-first cash-in on the famously expensive but development-hellbound spec script *The Ticking Man*, this casts Soutendijk in a dual role as a repressed scientist and as her creation, a robot hoyden with a thermo-nuclear womb. The military gyndroid goes out of control during a test and starts chomping down on rednecks, causing road accidents and machine-gunning innocent bystanders. Counter-terrorist Hines, in an uncommitted performance, has twenty-four hours to track down the robot before she detonates. Despite Soutendijk's impressive presence and a workable premise, *Eve of Destruction* fails to come up with interesting material for its robo-babe and sadly has a climax which bears more resemblance to a damp squib than a doomsday device.

d/co-s Duncan Gibbins *p* David Madden *co-s* Yale Udoff *c* Alan Hume *se* Steve Galich *lp* Renée Soutendijk, Gregory Hines, Michael Greene, Kurt Fuller, John M. Jackson, Loren Haynes, Ross Malinger

Fantasy

(COMBRIDGE; AUST) 80 min

This is a rare sexploitation film with a decent story, a proper plot, a bizarre sense of humour and almost acceptable acting. If the sweaty sexual scenes intended as the money shots were not so ordinary, this Australian peculiarity might have had genuine cult potential. Frustrated wife Chilton meets her dream lover, suave experimental psychologist Borgonon, and persuades him to live out her familiar sexual fantasies, apparently derived from *Emmanuelle* and Mickey Rourke, for a month. In return, she agrees to fulfil his considerably stranger desires, which involve her in a psycho-drama experiment that requires her to take the part of a short-skirted maid in a fetishist re-creation of turn-of-the-century erotica, with clinical psychologists enlisted as the supporting stable-lads, decadent aristocrats and hypersexed servants. Several American features (*Indecent Behaviour*, 1993, *Sins of Desire*, 1993) also use sexology to borderline Science Fiction ends.

co-d/p/c Geoffrey Brown *co-d/s* Derek Strahan *lp* Colin Borgonon, Clare Chilton, Jane Darley-Jones, Julia Binns, Brendan Strahan, Elizabeth Stewart

Gojira Tai Kingu Gidora *aka* Godzilla Versus King Ghidorah

(TOHO; JAP) scope 105 min

Following his reappearance in the revisionary sequel-cum-remake **Gojira** (1985), the titan of Kaiju Eiga has starred in a fresh series of adventures which introduce or reintroduce monster foes and edge Godzilla back into his role as protector of his nation and young children. Omori's *Gojira Tai Biollante* (1989) pits Godzilla against a surreal mutant which cross-breeds Hedora of **Gojira Tai Hedora** (1971) with a giant rose and the heart of a little girl. This sequel revives the three-headed evil dragon of **Ghidrah** (1965). A US relaunch for the series, produced by Columbia, has been repeatedly announced, but was put on hold in 1995 following the departure of director Jan DeBont from the project.

In 1992, Japan is visited by a flying saucer from the future, and time travellers announce that the country will shortly be destroyed by Godzilla but can be saved if two contemporary characters, a writer (Toyohara) and a psychic (Odaka), travel back with them to WWII to help remove from a Pacific island the regular dinosaur mutated in 1954 into Godzilla by atom bomb tests. The mission is accomplished, teleporting the dinosaur just after he has patriotically helped a lost Japanese unit see off an overwhelmingly superior American force, but the future people leave behind three gremlin creatures which combine and mutate into Ghidorah, who replaces Godzilla in history and devastates Japan with even greater ferocity. It turns out that the time travellers have in fact been trying to prevent Japan from growing into a superpower which dominates the 23rd century. The shifted dinosaur has spontaneously mutated into an even more powerful Godzilla and clashes with Ghidorah. A Japanese girl (Nakagawa) from the future has a change of heart and, in another confusing reversal, turns the battered Ghidorah into a cyborg which she pilots in battle against Godzilla to save the country.

Also mixed up in the amazingly complex if simple-minded plot is an American cyborg along the lines of **The Terminator** (1984) and a throwaway joke involving Steven Spielberg's supposed father which explains the director's obsession with UFOs and dinosaurs. After the relative solemnity of the first two new series entries, this is a throwback to the colourful, childish Godzilla pictures of the late sixties and early seventies, with composer Akira Ifukube lifting themes from his old scores and human characters who are either heroic and cheerful or evil and scowling. Retained from *Biollante* is an interesting streak of anti-Americanism, with WWII GIs and meddlers from the future depicted as cowardly, vicious and inept. The film's strong suits are some of the most spectacular city-destroying yet, a steroided-out and bigger-jawed look for the remutated Godzilla and pleasantly expansive sumo battles between its impressive monsters.

d/s Kazuki Omori *p* Tomoyuki Tanaka *c* Yoshinori Sekiguchi *se* Koichi Kawakita *lp* Anna Nakagawa, Kosuke Toyohara, Megumi Odaka, Kiwako Harada, Shoji Kabayashi, Koichi Ueda, Masahiko Sasaki, Chuck Wilson

Now get on down and feel the burn - The Guyver.

The Guyver *aka* Mutronics
(IMPERIAL ENTERTAINMENT/YUZNA; US-JAP) 92 min
Originally a Japanese comic book by Yoshiki Takaya, *The Guyver* was first transposed by Koichi Ishiguro into a series of Japanese animated episodes which were released directly to video. This live-action movie is a simplified distillation of the video series, morphing the property from a bizarre Japanese Science Fiction superhero saga into an American monster movie featuring incredible rubber mutation special effects but little else of note. Uncharismatic judo expert Armstrong stumbles on a mysterious, never-explained device which attaches to his body and periodically coats him with monster-proof armour which augments his fighting skills so he can cope when everyone else metamorphoses into Zoanoids – scaly, slimy, clawed, fanged, bad-tempered creatures from another dimension. Between ten-minute tag-wrestling monster scenes, there is barely room for any story or characterization, let alone the complex multi-generational epic of the *manga* original.

In a lame extension of his Herbert West role from *Re-Animator* (1985), Combs appears as 'Dr East', while fellow Yuzna veteran Gale is the evil corporate head who turns into a two-storey scorpion for the finale. The equally colourless David Hayter replaces Armstrong in Wang's makeshift, but more solemn follow-up *Guyver: Dark Hero* (1994).

d/se Screaming Mad George, Steve Wang *p* Brian Yuzna *s* Jon Purdy *c* Levie Isaacks *lp* Jack Armstrong, Mark Hamill, Vivian Wu, Jimmy Walker, David Gale, Jeffrey Combs, Linnea Quigley, Michael Berryman, Spice Williams

Harley Davidson and the Marlboro Man
(MGM) 98 min
Two drifters, a philosophical biker known as Harley Davidson (Rourke) and an ex-rodeo cowboy who chooses to be called the Marlboro Man (Johnson), pull off an armoured car robbery to pay off the mortgage on their favourite bar. Their haul turns out not to be money but a cache of Crystal Dream, a fantastically addictive and lethal new drug, which drags them into a war with a corrupt banker and his team of super-assassins. A would-be comic strip action movie – whose 1996 owes less to the Science Fiction of **Mad Max** (1979) or **Blade Runner** (1982) than the 'imaginary America' seen in *99 and 44/100 % Dead* (1974), *Streets of Fire* (1984) and **Trouble in Mind** (1985) – this needed the demented directorial enthusiasm and skill at arms of a Walter Hill.

In a promisingly camp introductory reel, a succession of macho characters are brought on with grand barfight entrances and there are constant gratuities like a stripper on a motorcycle, a muscle-straining arm-wrestling match, Rourke politely foiling a hold-up, cowboy Johnson beating off a crowd of enraged Indians with a pool cue, and the coolly robotic hit team in monk-like kevlar slickers formation-jumping over a burning motorcycle. But the film gets seriously bogged down with its mix of Science Fiction, Western, heist and good ole boy themes. It's as if someone had decided to crossbreed *Butch Cassidy and the Sundance Kid* (1967), *Angels Hard As They Come* (1971), *Charley Varrick* (1972) and **Prayer of the Rollerboys** (1991). Understandably, an opening caption declares 'No company has approved, sponsored or endorsed the title or content of this film.'

d Simon Wincer *p* Jere Henshaw *s* Don Michael Paul *c* David Eggby *se* Terry Frazee *lp* Mickey Rourke, Don Johnson, Chelsea Field, Daniel Baldwin, Giancarlo Esposito, Vanessa Williams, Robert Ginty, Tia Carrere, Julis Harris, Big John Studd, Tom Sizemore

Late for Dinner
(CASTLE ROCK/NEW LINE/GRANITE) 93 min
In 1962, fleeing from a misunderstanding with the law, unemployed milkman Wimmer and his slightly retarded brother-in-law Berg run into a scientist who tries out his cryogenic process on them until they can be defrosted in a future where Wimmer won't be in trouble with the law and Berg can get the

kidney transplant which will restore his mind. Revived in 1991, the simple-minded heroes try to go home, only to find Wimmer's daughter is now older than him, and that his wife (Harden) is a successful businesswoman on the point of retirement and mildly involved with a senior citizen.

Surprisingly, *Late for Dinner* – aside from an inevitable Ronald Reagan joke – doesn't play its Rip Van Winkle theme for fish-out-of-water comedy, but instead opts to tread in the eternal love footsteps of *Ghost* (1990) with an emotional climax as Wimmer and Harden work out their drastically-interrupted relationship. Once the plot reaches the future, the Science Fiction angle is left on ice, along with the *deus ex machina* cryogenics characters who take a discreet fade never to turn up again. The lack of smarts of the well-played central characters is sometimes touching but often requires dollops of explanation that slow the already stately pace to a dead halt. Only marginally successful and deeply unoriginal – everything that doesn't come from the *When the Sleeper Wakes* chestnut seems cribbed from *Of Mice and Men* – this soft-centered film nonetheless remains likeable.

d/co-p W.D. Richter *co-p* Dan Lupovitz *s* Mark Andrus *c* Peter Sova *se* Stan Parks *lp* Brian Wimmer, Peter Berg, Marcia Gay Harden, Colleen Flynn, Kyle Secor, Michael Beach, Peter Gallagher, Colin Friel

Lensman

(STREAMLINE PICTURES; JAP) 107 min
The space operas of E.E. 'Doc' Smith have had a great influence on the development of Science Fiction writing. Sadly this tardy *anime* adaptation, loosely taken from the 1937 novel *Galactic Patrol*, owes more to Smith's imitators, with an especial debt to **Star Wars** (1977) and DC's *Green Lantern* comics, rather than Smith himself.

In 2500, the peaceful Galactic Alliance is threatened by the Boskonian Empire, a group of militarist bad guys led by the evil Helmuth. Kimball Kinnison, farmboy son of a former galactic patrolman, is given a powerful and mystic device by a fallen hero, a lens inset in Kinnison's hand which somehow gives him great powers. The *Star Wars* parallels continue as Kinnison hooks up with a spunky heroine who has Carrie Fisher hairy earmuffs, a loveable dustbin-shaped robot and a hairy thug with a good heart to engage in impressive if empty computer-generated deep space battle scenes. A monotonous procession of amazing incidents give the feel of a plot running around between sequels, especially when the characters wind up in a discotheque Smith would not have recognized so an irritating comic relief disc jockey can cue a batch of embarrassing songs. The strident but bland post-*Star Wars* feel prevents *Lensman* from working up any nostalgic buzz about Smith's by-passed thirties futurism while the one-note characters prevent any involvement with the sophisticated animation technology used to power the occasionally awesome visuals.

d Yoshiaki Kawajiri, Kazuyuki Hirokawa *p* Akihiko Ito, Mitsuru Kaneko, Michihiro Tomii, Tadami Watanabe *s* Soji Yoshikawa *c* Ben Yamaki

Liquid Dreams

(NORTHERN ARTS ENTERTAINMENT) 92 (111) min
A style-heavy futurist thriller set in a self-contained urban pleasure palace where taxi dancer Daly rises through the ranks to become a star of Neuro-Vid, a new hypnotic art-form which cross-breeds rock video, brainwashing and sadomasochist strip-tease. While investigating the death of her sister, the heroine mixes with a brutal cop ('If I'd wanted your opinion, I would have scraped it off the sidewalk'), a superpimp with no genitals, various glamorously-doomed women and a clutch of

You may not believe it but boxer shorts were considered real neat in 1962 - *Brian Wimmer and Peter Berg in* Late for Dinner.

Yet another ordinary roller-skating vigilante teen Science Fiction anti-drugs picture - Prayer of the Rollerboys.

sneering secondary slime, including Bartel's familiar pervert, John Waters regular Stole and punk rocker Doe. Manos creates an impressively nightmarish world, but the plot has a certain obviousness and too many atmospheric sequences are so slowly paced as to prompt the audience to actual dreams.

d/co-s Mark Manos *p* Zane W. Levitt, Diane Firestone *co-s* Zack David *c* Sven Kirsten *lp* Candice Daly, Richard Steinmetz, Barry Dennen, Juan Fernandez, Tracey Walter, Frankie Thorn, Mink Stole, Paul Bartel, John Doe

Poison

(BRONZE EYE) 85 min
Underground film-maker Haynes, best known for making *Superstar: The Karen Carpenter Story* (1987) with a cast of Barbie Dolls, interweaves three storylines: a Jean Genet-derived gay prison tale ('Homo'), a black-and-white mad science pastiche ('Horror') and a fake documentary about a little boy's Fortean disappearance ('Hero'). The strands are arbitrarily shuffled together so any connections between them remain obscure. The monster sequence, presumably intended as a comment on AIDS, is a distant parody of **The Hideous Sun Demon** (1959) though its venereal concerns are more Cronenbergian: an infected scientist (Maxwell) spreads a leprous mutating disease while he broods melodramatically. A commendably strange but slight effort, most notable for the extreme buggery and thuggery of its prison segment.

d/s Todd Haynes *p* Christine Vachon *c* Maryse Alberti *se* Scott Sliger *lp* Larry Maxwell, Susan Norman, Al Quagliata, Edith Meeks, Millie White, Scott Renderer, James Lyons

Prayer of the Rollerboys

(GAGA/FOX LORBER/JVC) 94 min
An ordinary roller-skating vigilante teen Science Fiction anti-drugs picture, with Haim infiltrating cool-coated skate psychos to get even with their neo-Nazi leader (Collet). The characterizations are cliché to the max and the futuristic background resembles *Blade Runner: the Home Movie*, but this is really doomed to the remainder racks because it doesn't even have the spectacular stuntwork that might have distinguished it. As skating Science Fiction goes, it is almost as bad as *Solarbabies* (1986) and *Roller Blade* (1986).

d Rick King *p* Robert Mickelson *s* Peter Iliff *c* Phedon Papamichael *se* Special Effects Unlimited *lp* Corey Haim, Patricia Arquette, Christopher Collet, J.C. Quinn, Julius Harris, Devin Clark, Mark Pelegrino

The Rocketeer

(WALT DISNEY/SILVER SCREEN PARTNERS IV) scope 116 (108) min
In 1938, daredevil stunt pilot Campbell, an All-American boy with a rebellious cowlick and a chiselled chin, accidentally comes into possession of an experimental and dangerous rocket backpack, designed by Howard Hughes (O'Quinn), which can make a man fly. Adding a helmet created out of an art deco radio set by his crusty mentor (Arkin), Campbell becomes the leather-jacketed rocketeer. Neville Sinclair (Dalton), an Errol Flynn-style swashbuckling movie star who is also a Nazi saboteur, wants to get his hands on the rocket suit, and has a gang of hoodlums, a Zeppelin full of stormtroopers and a lumbering monster in the exact image of forties B-picture fiend Rondo Hatton to help him, not to mention a line in smarmy chat-up that he applies to the hero's bosomy but naive girl (Connelly).

Based on Dave Stevens's retro-chic 1981 comic book, itself inspired by **King of the Rocket Men** (1949), *The Rocketeer* lacks the knowing, self-consciously hip tone that mars such attempts to revive serial thrills as *Dick Tracy* (1989) and *The Shadow* (1994). It lovingly deploys the furniture of the thirties (diners shaped like bulldogs, flying circuses) and offers in Campbell a stalwart hero whose slight dullness is highly reminiscent of Buster Crabbe. Dalton's villain is funny, but never overbalances the film to the hero's detriment in the manner of Jack Nicholson's Joker or Alan Rickman's Sheriff of Nottingham. With plentiful action, climaxing with derring-do on a doomed dirigible, and lots of snappy dialogue, this perfectly captures the innocence and pep of thirties adventure movies.

d Joe Johnston *p* Lawrence Gordon, Charles Gordon, Lloyd Levin *s* Danny Bilson, Paul De Meo *c* Hiro Narita *se* ILM *lp* Bill Campbell, Jennifer Connelly, Timothy Dalton, Alan Arkin, Terry O'Quinn, Paul Sorvino, Ed Lauter

Rojin Z *aka* Roujin Z

(TOKYO THEATRES CO/THE TELEVISION INC/MOVIC CO/TV ASAHI/SONY MUSIC ENTERTAINMENT; JAP) 78 min
Directed by Kitakubo, this big-screen Japanese cartoon was written and designed by Otomo, the comic book visionary behind the breakthrough *anime*, **Akira** (1988). The result is a unique reworking of Japan's traditional city-stomping giant monsters and super-transforming battle robots, informed and complicated by another singularly Japanese obsession, the dignified care of the elderly.

In a sunlit near-future ostensibly more pleasant than the cyberpunk hell of *Akira*, a government research project develops a fully-automated hospital bed to take care of the elderly with maximum efficiency and minimum compassion. The scientists have unethically used a human brain in the controlling computer and given the bed the capability of defending itself by adding on extra bits of machinery. Medical drama swiftly turns to **Tetsuo** (1990)-like spectacle as the robot bed runs around (there's a nifty monorail chase) and comes up against its military-minded opposite number. Half-way through, the script's suggestion that the all-machine bed (which feeds, washes, entertains and ignores its hapless charge) is an abomination is contradicted by the strangely touching, if actually equally disturbing, idea of dead wives' brains looking after their decrepit husbands. Not quite *Ozu Meets Ultraman*, *Rojin Z* nevertheless takes an unusual (if simplistic) social tack into the familiar and likeable business of having huge robots smash property.

d Hiroyuki Kitakubo *p* Yasuhito Nomura, Yasuku Kazama, Yoshiaki Motoya *s* Katsuhiro Otomo *c* Hideo Okazaki *se* Kenichi Abe

*It's good to talk –
(from right) William
Shatner, DeForest
Kelley, Christopher
Plummer and Michael
Dorn in* Star Trek VI.

Star Trek VI: The Undiscovered Country

(PAR) 110 min

To simultaneously rescue the series from the disaster of **Star Trek V: The Final Frontier** (1989) and provide 'something special' in honour of the 25th Anniversary of the original series, Meyer opts for the bluntest imaginable attempt at linking the universe of the Federation with that of the America on which it is so blatantly patterned, even making its President sound like George Bush. With its own Gorbachov, Siberia, hard-liners, show trials, Chernobyl and *glasnost*, the Klingon Empire (once vaguely Mongolian) is reconfigured as an exact, not to say uninteresting, equivalent of the disintegrating Soviet Union.

After years of cold war, Klingon Chancellor Warner offers to forge a peace with the Federation, and the *Enterprise* is sent to escort him to the negotiating table. Warner is assassinated and Klingon-hating Kirk (Shatner) is framed, prompting his shipmates to rescue him from a prison planet. Spock (Nimoy) realizes his Vulcan protégé (Cattrall) is a traitor in league with Klingon reactionary Plummer, and the heroes break up a conspiracy to destroy the talks. Even given the heavy-handed paralleling, this is a thudding, lumbering and self-indulgent picture, dragged down at every turn by the weight of years of illogical mediocrity, as if the series' notional Science Fiction aspects pre-empted the need for characters, stories or universe to make dramatic sense.

Much is made of the conflicting demands of friendship and politics, but there is no possibility that the supposedly unemotional Spock (after all these years, clearly a mush-hearted softie) would rate the future of the universe as more important than rescuing his friends. Despite the noble attempt to wind down with a finale that hands over the baton to the crew of *Star Trek: The Next Generation*, the universe of the *Star Trek* series has so firmly established its rules that it is inconceivable that anyone, no matter how important in plot terms, could be valued more highly than the seven leads of the original show, who remain middling TV actors stranded amid the big-budget, big-screen glitz of the movies. This is especially notable when an uncredited Christian Slater pops in for a cameo bit-part in a scene with Takei's Sulu: in any other movie Slater would be the star and Takei barely rate notice as a spear-carrier, but here their positions are reversed.

Otherwise, camp is about all the series has to offer, with Meyer playing inside jokes by having Spock quote Sherlock Holmes ('an ancestor of mine'), and Shatner turning in a tubbily mercurial performance which is the perfect synthesis of ham and self-parody, especially in his love-tussle with alien Iman, who turns into a replica of him. Typical of Roddenberry is the autodidact's reverence for superficial erudition, as demonstrated by the cast's fondness for throwing out-of-context Shakespeare quotes at each other during verbal or actual battles. The most significant turn of the endless verbiage is a confusion about the sub-title, with all the characters confidently asserting that Shakespeare was talking about the future when actually Hamlet's 'undiscovered country' is *death*.

d/co-s Nicholas Meyer *p* Ralph Winter, Steven Charles Jaffe *co-s* Danny Martin Flinn *c* Hiro Narita *se* Industrial Light and Magic *lp* William Shatner, Leonard Nimoy, DeForest Kelley, Kim Cattrall, Christopher Plummer, David Warner, James Dooha, George Takei, Nichelle Nichols, Michael Dorn, Iman

Steel and Lace

(CINEMA HOME VIDEO) 92 min

A predictable, adequate entry in the mini-cycle of girlie Terminator movies that includes *The Annihilator* (1986), *Programmed to Kill* (1987) and **Eve of Destruction** (1991). Also a revenge-for-rape drama, it follows concert pianist Wren, who commits suicide when Ceveris, the rich swine who abused her, is acquitted on the testimony of his associates. Resurrected as a glamorous killer cyborg by her Frankensteinian scientist brother (Davison), Wren seduces and slaughters Ceveris's accomplices while a courtroom sketch artist (Haiduk) and her cop boyfriend (Naughton) puzzle over the gruesome murders. The plot is obvious but the characterizations and performances are above average for the budget level, as are the elaborately horrid disembowelling or decapitating devices.

d Ernest Farino *p* John Schouweiler, David DeCoteau *s* Joseph Dougherty, Dave Edison *c* Thomas L. Callaway *se* S.O.T.A. F/X *lp* Bruce Davison, Clare Wren, Stacy Haiduk, David Naughton, Michael Ceveris, David L. Lander

Street Asylum (MEDUSA) 94 (89) min

'If we could send messages to the animal part of the brain, recharge them and then send them back, then man could become this unstoppable fighting machine' is the central premise of this engaging if sleazy action-exploitation movie, with a sense of politics and a streak of black humour. The script by critic Powers is well-handled by Brown, who also directs erotic thrillers as 'A. Gregory Hippolyte' and hardcore as 'Gregory Dark'.

Cop Hauser – star also of Brown's *Dead Man Walking* (1987), a post-apocalypse remake of *The Searchers* (1956) – is wounded and recruited into Strike Squad, an LAPD unit with devices implanted into their spines which turn them periodically into psychotics with ESP. A side-effect of the process is suicidal mania, leading to an effective scene as Hauser's partner (Richardson) self-destructs. Hauser has his girlfriend (Vasquez) carve the bug out of his back so he can track down the politicos who have masterminded the plan. Liddy is the main villain, a mayoral candidate who enjoys beating up would-be dominatrixes, while Cord is the police chief who has sanctioned the scheme. Also involved in a relishable cameo is James as a mad street preacher. There are striking pre-Rodney King sequences of LA cops summarily executing minor offenders and Brown, a surprisingly intelligent director, makes good use of flash images.

d Gregory Brown *p* Walter Gernert *s* John Powers *c* Paul Desatoff *lp* Wings Hauser, Alex Cord, G. Gordon Liddy, Roberta Vasquez, Sy Richardson, Brion James, Jesse Doran

Suburban Commando

(NEW LINE) 91 min

This is quite a bright little picture. Professional wrestler Hogan, in his first film after gaining acting experience in the ring, is Shep Ramsey, an intergalactic good guy marooned on Earth during a lull in a **Star Wars** (1977)-style space crusade. He rents an apartment in the home of Lloyd, a put-upon middle-class suburban Dad, and sets about cleaning up the neighbourhood, Lloyd's life, the planet and the universe in roughly that order. While Hogan learns about the joys of Earth and Lloyd finds out whether he has the right stuff by joining the hero on do-gooding endeavours, a pair of alien bounty hunters are on their way.

With a deliberately stupid plot line and a low budget, this should by rights be as ho-hum a kiddie comedy as **Spaced Invaders** (1990) or **Jetsons – the Movie** (1990), but something somewhere goes right with script and direction, and the laughs miraculously keep coming. Hogan, bursting with muscle and cartoonish facial contortions, is an amiably ridiculous hero, amusingly perplexed by the complications of a 1990s suburbia where little girls with cats stuck in trees and leering local bullies refuse to act predictably. Lloyd, as ever, is one of the most professional laugh-milkers in the business, bumbling through the story and coming out on top.

d Burt Kennedy *p* Howard Gottfried *s* Frank Cappello *c* Patrick J. Swovelin, Ken Lambkin, Richard Clabaugh, Charlie Liberman *se* Perpetual Motion Pictures *lp* Hulk Hogan, Christopher Lloyd, Shelley Duvall, William Ball, Laura Mooney, Larry Miller, Roy Dotrice, Christopher Neame

Teenage Mutant Ninja Turtles II: The Secret of the Ooze (NEW LINE) 87 min

Hurriedly-produced to get into theatres before the titular amphibian superheroes went the way of the Cabbage Patch Dolls and pet rocks, this sequel starts off as if it might possibly be an improvement on the muddy, unengaging original. However, even though Warner pops in as a waste-dumping mad scientist to provide some acting, the film dispenses with anything more than a basic capture-escape-and-confrontation plot as the four interchangeable heroes and their self-righteous rat sensei, aided by a drippy TV newslady (Turco) and an irritating pizza-delivering pint-sized martial artist (Reyes), clash with Darth Vader croak-alike villain Shredder and a horde of singularly useless ninjas who specialize in suddenly turning up in large numbers and getting beaten senseless. With Vanilla Ice dropping in for a drippy rap club finale, and a pair of goofy monsters going on a tame rampage, this hits all the bases, cuing cereal packet tie-ins, but forgets that there has to be a film inside the phenomenon to keep the merchandising juggernaut going.

d Michael Pressman *p* Thomas K. Gray, Kim Dawson, David Chan *s* Todd W. Langen *c* Shelly Johnson *se* Jim Henson's Creature Shop *lp* Paige Turco, Michelan Sisti, Lief Tilden, Kenn Troum, Mark Caso, Ernie Reyes Jr, David Warner, François Chau, Kevin Clash

David Warner discovers how a turtle becomes a teenage mutant ninja turtle in Teenage Mutant Ninja Turtles II.

Terminator 2: Judgment Day

(CAROLCO/PACIFIC WESTERN/LIGHTSTORM) 136 min

Tipping the scales at a reputed $100m, this was allegedly the most expensive movie ever made to its date. More to the point, the money is all visible on screen in exploding vehicles, wrecked buildings, monster effects and sheer sweaty action.

It opens with an intriguing re-run of the first movie's premise as a gigantic cyborg (Schwarzenegger) and a slimline ordinary joe (Patrick) are zapped back from the future, to seek out ten-year-old John Connor (Edward Furlong), son of the heroine (Hamilton) of **The Terminator** (1984), and struggle over his life, with the balance of a future that may or may not be ruined by a cataclysmic war between man and machines up for grabs. The twist is that the fresh-faced Patrick is the mechanical villain. Schwarzenegger, in biker leathers and mean shades, is reprogrammed to protect Furlong and gets to reveal, between extensive carnage, that biomechanical killing machines from the future have their sensitive sides.

The rewriting of the star's persona smacks of a commercial sop to the *Kindergarten Cop* (1990) audience, but the reversal pays off when it comes to the cop-uniformed villain, constructed from a liquid metal that can shape itself into anything it wants and also pull itself back together if blasted apart. A high-tech version of the Blob, utilizing astonishing and surreal CGI effects, Patrick's T-1000 stands as one of the great monsters of the cinema. Like all Cameron movies, this shuffles its character stuff out of the way in the first two-thirds, then delivers a succession of untoppable climaxes routinely out-awesomed by the next set-piece. It may be less satisfying than the more idea-driven original, but it still sends firepower fans into Action Flick Heaven as Arnie does his shotgun twirl.

d/p/co-s James Cameron *co-s* William Wisher *c* Adam Greenberg *se* ILM, Fantasy II Film Effects, Stan Winston, Joseph Viskocil *lp* Arnold Schwarzenegger, Linda Hamilton, Edward Furlong, Robert Patrick, Earl Boen, Joe Morton, Xander Berkeley

Tetsuo II: Bodyhammer

(KAIJU THEATRE/TOSHIBA EMI; JAP) 83 min

In this sequel-cum-remake, Tsukamoto ups the budgetary stakes on **Tetsuo** (1990) by adding colour, length and a script that supports its primal imagery and spectacular mutations with a proliferation of incident and something approaching a backstory in the 'origin' sequence that explains, if not rationally, where the first film's mutants came from. However, the alterations are cosmetic, serving, like the iron shell Taguchi grows, to make the project sturdier rather than alter or even extend the subject matter. Tsukamoto films in colour but deliberately limits the palette to oily blacks, battleship greys and the occasional blotches of blue, green and dark red, giving the effect if not of monochrome then of a minimally tinted comic-strip.

Given the film's fondness for taking left-overs and twisting them into new organisms, it is entirely apt that Tsukamoto should choose to borrow heavily, taking from David Cronenberg's **Scanners** (1980) the skeleton plot of a flesh-twisting sibling conflict between the mutating rival sons of a mad visionary scientist. A suit-and-glasses Japanese urban man (Taguchi) is targeted by an undergound movement of mutating skinheads who kidnap and horribly murder his young son. Assaulted with a rivet-gun, Taguchi begins to mutate, sprouting pipe-like guns from his chest and gradually turning into a human tank. An internal coup in the mutant faction brings to power a sleek young monster (Tsukamoto) who enters into a personal conflict with Taguchi, his long-lost brother.

This time, Tsukamoto blunts the brutal sexuality that was a part of the original protagonist's mutations – displacing that aspect of the film onto the mutant brothers' flashback father, who is seen murdering his wife while making love – and plumps instead to present Taguchi, star of the earlier movie, in a reincarnated but altered version of his old role. Taguchi more completely comes to control his new body than the

Schwarzenegger prepares for the end while Linda Hamilton and Edward Furlong look to the future in Terminator 2.

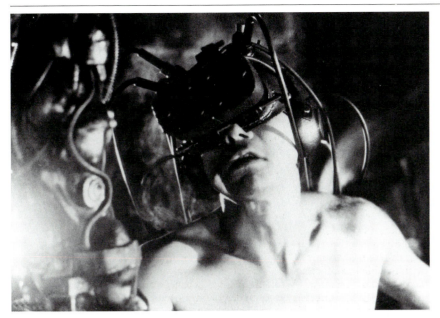

Tetsuo II –
*The melding of man
and machine.*

'salary man' of *Tetsuo*, deftly using the cluster of guns that burst from his chest and, in a masterly stroke, exploding tentacles from his head that neatly drill into the shaven heads of the villain's disciples, rather than be carried away, as his predecessor was, by the uncontrollable urges of his drill-bit penis. The emotional palette is extended slightly to include Taguchi's grief at the callous slaughter of his son and Kanaoka's steadfast love for her cyborg husband, but these turn out to be minor tweaks on the machine, which chiefly consists of loving examinations of mutants who seem the illegitimate offspring of surrealist sculpture and Kaiju Eiga monster movies. With its humorous and repulsive special effects, accompanied by an appropriately grinding soundtrack, the film piles more and more debris on Taguchi, finally signalling his continued individuality by leaving his eyes alive in the dead mass of metal meat, as in **The Quatermass Xperiment** (1955), but also, in a wittily grotesque touch, by allowing him to retain his blinding white and bizarrely expressive human teeth.

d/s/co-c Shinya Tsukamoto *p* Fuminori Shishido, Fumio Kurokawa *co-c* Fumikazu Oda, Katsunori Yokayoma *se* Takashi Oda, Ken Takahama, Akira Fukaya *lp* Tomoroh Taguchi, Nobu Kanaoka, Shinya Tsukamoto, Keinosuke Tomioka, Sujin Kim, Min Tanaka

Timebomb
(MGM/UA) 96 min
A reworking of *The Manchurian Candidate* (1962) and *The Parallax View* (1974) for the **Total Recall** (1990) era, which effectively means draining out the satire and piping in bland ideas about standardized militarist conspiracies while dotting the mystery with sporadic shoot-outs, punch-ups and Patsy-on-top sex scenes.

Mild watchmaker Biehn suffers flashes which suggest his character is a construct, and eventually his personality peels away to reveal the CIA-trained zombie hit man underneath. Accompanied by Kensit as a Hungarian psychoanalyst given to sensitive insights like shouting 'you're mad', Biehn fights off hordes of equally mind-wiped killers and tries to prevent Jordan and Culp assassinating an anti-corruption, honest politician who is unbelievably about to be appointed Attorney General by a President we assume to be George Bush. Director Nesher does better by the explosions and massacres than in his post-holocaust Sandahl Bergman version of *She* (1985) and the set decoration features a nifty brainwashing tank in the tradition of **A Clockwork Orange** (1971) and **Altered States** (1980), but this is still a throwaway B picture. In the end, we are reassured 'never again will common criminals be licensed to act in the name of this country'.

d/s Avi Nesher *p* Raffaella DeLaurentiis *c* Anthony B. Richmond *se* Richard Malzahn *lp* Michael Biehn, Patsy Kensit, Tracy Scoggins, Robert Culp, Richard Jordan, Raymond St Jacques, Billy Blanks

Timescape *aka* Disaster in Time *aka* The Grand Tour
(WILD STREET) 99 min
A rare intelligent Science Fiction movie without excess comedy or monsters, adapted from 'Vintage Season', a classic 1946 novella by Lawrence O'Donnell and C.L. Moore. Daniels, the widowed owner of a small hotel overlooking a nondescript town, is pestered by a strangely remote tour group who insist on booking the place out of season. Gradually, he realizes his guests are actually tourists from the future on a field trip to the sites of famous disasters. When a meteor ploughs into town and a subsequent gas explosion kills his daughter, Daniels steals a time-machine-cum-passport and loops back a day to talk himself into making things come out right, despite the future people's attempts to preserve history.

This has its soapy side as widowed drunk Daniels reassembles his personal life while rescuing people, but the well-thought-out script is full of clever reversals – the time travellers dress in bizarre clownish outfits we take to be their native costume as they leave the present, but these turn out to be disguises for the next stop on their tour, a Mardi Gras fire in New Orleans – and is well-served by an unobtrusively excellent everyman performance from Daniels.

d/s David N. Twohy *p* John A. O'Connor *c* Harry Mathias *se* SPFX Inc. *lp* Jeff Daniels, Ariana Richards, Emilia Crow, Nicholas Guest, Jim Haynie, Marilyn Lightstone, George Murdock

Trancers 2
(FULL MOON ENTERTAINMENT) 86 min
This sequel to the best B picture of the eighties brings back the creative team behind the first picture, with the vital exception of screenwriters Paul De Meo and Danny Bilson, who graduated from cheapies to writing **The Rocketeer** (1991) and the TV series *The Flash*. Band had already attempted a sequel in one episode of the never-completed compilation movie *Pulse Pounders* (1988), but this picks up the threads dropped by **Trancers** (1984) with Thomerson back as Jack Deth, a grumpy cop from the future stuck in modern Los Angeles, battling a horde of zombie cultists disguised as eco-activists led by Lynch, the brother of the villain of the first film. His life is complicated by the arrival of his dead wife (Ward) from the future, which gives him problems with his living wife in the present (Hunt). Villains Lynch, Beswick and Combs are underused, but there are plenty of good jokes and character bits, plus an unexpectedly emotional conclusion as Deth resolves his romantic complications. Though it lacks the first film's concise brilliance and conceptual flair, this is nevertheless a fun Science Fiction actioner.

Trancers 3 (1993), directed by C. Courtney Joyner, continues the storyline with Deth shifted up the line to the next decade, where he tracks down a mad militarist (Andy Robinson) whose process for turning soldiers into killer zombies will eventually lead to the creation of the trancers. The series took a new, disappointing direction with *Trancers 4: Jack of Swords* (1994) and *Trancers 5: Sudden Deth* (1995), shot back-to-back in Romania by David Nutter. In a mild imitation of *Army of Darkness* (1993), Deth is zapped into a medieval parallel universe where he sides with Robin Hood-ish rebels against vampire trancers who have Shakespearean names. Thomerson's cynical hero remains a delight throughout, but the feeble swashbuckling fantasy is no replacement for the snappy Science Fiction time-twisting.

d/p Charles Band *s* Jackson Barr *c* Adolfo Bartoli *lp* Tim Thomerson, Helen Hunt, Megan Ward, Richard Lynch, Biff Manard, Martine Beswick, Jeffrey Combs, Alyson Croft, Art La Fleur, Barbara Crampton

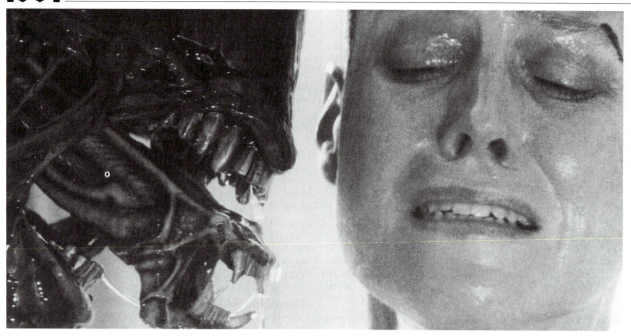

Alien3.

Xtro II: The Second Encounter

(NEW LINE; CAN) 92 min

'I think we have better things to do with tax-payers' money than to attempt to transport personnel to parallel dimensions,' complains a bureaucrat in the early stages of this acceptable, unexceptional programmer. Intended as a follow-up to Bromley-Davenport's 1982 British **Alien** (1979) imitation, this *Second Encounter* has no ostensible connection with its supposed prequel, instead mimicking almost exactly the minor **Shadowzone** (1990). The sole survivor of an expedition into another dimension returns, incubating a monster that escapes from her body and terrorizes an underground complex, which – in a steal from **The Andromeda Strain** (1970) – has sealed itself off and is run by an impersonal computer. The director of the project turns megalomaniacal and Vincent tries to cope with another dull hero role, while Buckman and a group of firepower-toting soldiers who recall the cast of **Aliens** (1986) climb lift-shafts or ventilation shafts in doomed escape attempts and play touch tag in the corridors with the regulation oily, stringy, toothy monster. Competent but entirely derivative.

d Harry Bromley-Davenport *co-p* Lloyd A. Simandl *co-p/s* John A. Curtis *c* Nathaniel Massey *se* Charlie Grant, Wane Dang *lp* Jan-Michael Vincent, Paul Koslo, Tara Buckman, Jano Frandsen, Nicholas Lea, W.F. Wadden

Alien3 (FOX) scope 115 min

A piece of awkward exposition eliminates the other left-over characters from **Aliens** (1986) in computer read-out asides and brings Ripley (Weaver) and a handy alien egg to a prison planet populated by religious fanatics. Conceived by Vincent Ward (one of many writers and directors to come and go on the project) as a medieval space epic, the script was scaled down so it could be shot in the familiar disused ironworks of the future. Rock video graduate Fincher employs a grainy brown sludginess that tries for atmosphere but comes off as simply murky. The shaven-head theme allows Weaver to look striking in Joan of Arc poses, but also serves to render the rest of the cast, in contrast with the well-fleshed monster munchies of the earlier films, totally anonymous.

The few attempts at character (Dance gets an emotional speech as Weaver's brief love interest but is swiftly killed by the monster) come off as unfortunately gigglesome. Weaver, who took the two-dimensional character from **Alien** (1979) and gave her real depth in the first sequel, goes over old ground

with a new haircut, being required by an idiotic script not to tell anyone she thinks there's a monster on the loose until well after heads have been crunched to pulp and acid-blood dripped all over the show. The film hurries towards an absurd 'transcendent' finale – which owes much to **Terminator 2** (1991) – in which Weaver falls into a furnace to save the universe from the alien bursting through her chest, but consists mainly of interchangeable characters running around dark corridors while a fish-eye lens monster chases them.

With the raising of stakes between the first two films and coming after James Cameron's all-out war with dozens of monsters, *Alien3* finds it hard to make much of its lone dog-shaped alien, especially since the beast seems to have come not from the finale of the last film but from a script conference in Development Hell that began when Renny Harlin was going to direct from a script by William Gibson.

d David Fincher *p* Gordon Carroll *p/co-s* David Giler, Walter Hill *co-s* Larry Ferguson *c* Alex Thomson *se* Richard Edlund, George Gibbs, Alec Gillis, Tony Woodruff Jr *lp* Sigourney Weaver, Charles S. Dutton, Charles Dance, Paul McGann, Brian Glover, Lance Henriksen, Ralph Brown, Danny Webb, Pete Postlethwaite

Arcade

(FULL MOON ENTERTAINMENT) 85 min

This is a Charles Band-backed stab at the demonic video game genre due to become cliché of the 1990s. Cells from the brain of an abused kid are incorporated into a new game that trendily uses Virtual Reality trickery to suck in a group of teens – not badly played by growing-up kid stars – who have to be rescued by neurotic games novice Ward. The heroine, traumatized by the death of her Mom (Farrell), alternately duels with and tries to understand the guiding spirit of the gameworld. The VR sequences make ingenious but obviously cheap use of limited computer animation and a lot of chroma-key video trickery which gives it the look of a British kids' TV show like *Knightmare* or *Terror Towers*, complete with winged skeleton computer cartoons. Despite a couple of false endings, this has trouble stretching itself even to the minimal running time typical of Full Moon. Fully aware that it can't decide how its plot works, the script has someone ask 'Is it supernatural evil that you're fighting or is it space aliens or something?'

d Albert Pyun *p* Cathy Gesualdo *s* David S. Goyer *c* George Mooradian *se* Digital Fantasy *lp* Megan Ward, Peter Billingsley, Seth Green, Humberto Ortiz, Norbert Weisser, Sharon Farrell, John DeLancie

Bad Channels

(FULL MOON ENTERTAINMENT) 88 min

Talk Radio (1988) meets *Dr Who* in this lively, scrappy Science Fiction quickie from the Charles Band stable. Wildman disc jockey Hipp, broadcasting on the 666 frequency finds his studio invaded by an encrusted space creature with a head the size of a Volkswagen and a robot sidekick along the lines of the aliens who advertised instant mashed potatoes on British TV. Everyone listening assumes Hipp's alien invasion monologue is another wild and crazy promotional stunt, but the monster uses radio waves to zero in on the channel's more babelicious listeners, hypnotize them with sub-standard glam rock video clips featuring the Blue Oyster Cult and suck them into the studio where they are shrunk down to a fifth of their normal size and put in test tubes as a preparation for something ghastly the script never explains. Everything falls apart in the end and green fungus, Punch and Judy snake-heads, mucho explosions, a very loud soundtrack and rotten jokes splurge all over the screen. It is vaguely watchable if purposeless, with a post-credits cameo by tiny Tim Thomerson, walking in from **Dollman** (1991) to pick up shrunken waitress Jane Behr so they can co-star in Band's audacious *Dollman vs the Demonic Toys* (1993).

d Ted Nicolau *p* Keith Payson *s* Jackson Barr *c* Adolfo Bartoli *se* Criswell Productions *lp* Paul Hipp, Martha Quinn, Aaron Lustig, Ian Patrick Williams, Charlie Spradling, Sonny Davis

Batman Returns

(WARNERS) 126 min

This grotesque and weird picture represents a darkening of tone of Burton's grim **Batman** (1989). It opens with a deformed baby being flushed down the sewers and proceeds to deal with three characters so twisted and malformed by family circumstances, urban life and unendurable emotional stress that they adopt animal totems and dress up in fetishist outfits to torture each other. Replacing Jack Nicholson's Joker is DeVito's Penguin, a flipper-handed misfit in a spherical tuxedo who proudly shrieks 'I'm not a human being, I'm an animal' and earns a moving Viking funeral with an honour guard of real penguins.

While the Penguin conspires with white-quiffed Walken to get elected Mayor and ruin the city, Bruce Wayne (Keaton, leaner and sharper) is intrigued by the presence of Pfeiffer's Catwoman. A put-upon secretary who has survived being pushed off a skyscraper by Walken and woken up with an aggressive new personality, she converts an old mac into a slinky cat-suit and takes a whip to anyone who gets in her way. Shorn of Kim Basinger's deadweight heroine, Prince's unnecessary songs (Danny Elfman's almost continual score is a grim delight) and several supporting characters, this is tighter, and more imaginative and affecting, than *Batman*. After the animated **Batman: Mask of the Phantasm** (1993), the franchise passed to the mercies of Joel Schumacher, considered by many to be the worst A-list director in Hollywood, for *Batman Forever* (1995).

d/co-p Tim Burton *co-p* Denise DiNovi *s* Daniel Waters *c* Stefan Czapsky *se* Michael Fink, 4-Ward productions, Stan Winston, Mike Reedy *lp* Michael Keaton, Danny DeVito, Michelle Pfeiffer, Christopher Walken, Michael Gough, Michael Murphy, Pat Hingle

Dongfang San Xia *aka* The Heroic Trio

(CHINA ENTERTAINMENT/PAKA HILL; HONG KONG) 82 min

This is a patchwork of Eastern and Western influences, taking aboard Japanese *anime* and traditional Hong Kong fantasy martial arts along with the American superhero genre. A quasi-supernatural subterranean entity (Shiguan) kidnaps male children of diluted royal blood, intending to make one puppet emperor of China while raising the rest as cannibalistic killer serfs. In the city above, the baby-napping – which is carried out by Invisible Woman (Yeoh), who has been pressed into the villain's service – gets the attention of contrasting super-heroines: Wonder Woman (Mui), the altruistic and agile alter ego of a policeman's meek wife, and Thief Taker (Cheung), a shotgun-wielding mercenary bounty huntress. It turns out that the three super-women have a complex, interlocked backstory whereby each is a possible sister figure for both of the others, and finally Invisible Woman (red leotard, cloak of invisibility) joins with Wonder Woman (domino mask, thigh-boots) and

Unnaturals unite: Danny DeVito as the Penguin, surely Tim Burton's most appealing creation to date, and Michelle Pfeiffer as Catwoman in Batman Returns.

Thief Taker (knee-pads, cycle shorts, cool shades) to take on the Evil Master, who is incinerated but emerges as a **Terminator** (1984)-like skeleton to fight to the last.

A good-humoured superhero saga with occasional touches of cruelty – during the mercy-killing of the Master's flesh-eating slaves, the victims urinate in terror – and a great deal of basic incoherence, introducing all three of its heroines as if their origins and powers were already well-established in decades' worth of earlier films and comics. Producer Ching, mastermind of the *Mr Vampire* series, takes over from director To for the knockabout action scenes, which find the three *gamine kung fu* divas tumbling through the air in exhilarating three-way battles, taking time to add a little camp humour as they touch up their clothes and make-up before presenting themselves to an adoring public. To, Ching and the three stars returned in *Heroic Trio II* (1993), aka *The Executioners*, which has a darker, future city setting and a downbeat finale in which one of the winsome trio is apparently permanently killed.

d Johnny To [Du Qifeng] *p* Ching Siu-Tung [Cheng Xiodong] *s* Sandy Shaw [Shao Liqiong] *c* Poon Hang-Sang, Tom Lau *se* Bai Le, 3000cc Productions *lp* Anita Mui [Mei Yanfang], Magie Cheung [Zhang Manyu], Michelle Yeoh [Yang Ziqiong], Damian Lau [Liu Songren], Paul Chin [Qin Pei], James Pak [Bai Shiqian], Ren Shiguan

Encino Man *aka* California Man

(HOLLYWOOD PICTURES/TOUCHWOOD PACIFIC PARTNERS) 88 min
An early entry in a wave of Bill & Ted/Wayne & Garth cash-ins that proliferated in the early 1990s, climaxing perhaps with the axiomatic *Dumb and Dumber* (1994). Taking the premise of **Iceman** (1984) or *Trog* (1971) and transforming it into a nerd comedy, which had already been done in **Schlock** (1973), the film has a desperate high school loser (Astin) unearth a frozen Cro-Magnon man (Fraser) while digging a swimming pool in his backyard. The archaeological find thaws out and returns to life, whereupon Astin and his equally ditzy best friend (Shore) shave him, wash him, dress him and take him to school. He is passed off as 'Linkovich Chombofsky', an Estonian exchange student, on the mistaken assumption that a confusion of 'Estonia' and 'Stone Age' is amusing.

Between homilies about how it is more important to be yourself than cool, Link becomes the most popular guy in school, thus earning the enmity of the local jocks and even upsetting Astin when he moves in on the girl (Ward) our hero wants to take to the prom. The plot advances by mechanical lurches based on the emotional temperature of a self-centred

Brendan Fraser (centre) as Encino Man.

dweeb who deserves all the humiliation showered on him. The wildman comedy mainly consists of characters opening their mouths wide and going 'aaaaahhhhh' in perilous situations. Drenched in snippets from chart hits and stuck with a trio of charmless central performances, this mainly serves to demonstrate that a smattering of excellent dude slang and a dopey fantasy premise don't make a sure-fire hit.

d Les Mayfield *p* George Zaloom *s* Shawn Schepps *c* Robert Brinkmann *se* Dennis Dion *lp* Sean Astin, Brendan Fraser, Pauly Shore, Megan Ward, Robin Tunney, Mariette Hartley, Richard Masur

Forever Young

(WARNERS) 101 min
In 1939, test pilot Gibson fails to propose marriage to his life-long love (Glasser) just before a road accident puts her in a supposedly irreversible coma, which prompts him to volunteer for pal Wendt's cryogenesis experiment. Fifty years later, he wakes up forgotten in a military storehouse when an interfering kid (Wood) messes with his deep-sleep capsule. Bewildered, he winds up lodging with Wood's single mother, overworked nurse Curtis, and tries to find out what has happened since he went under. Skipping most of the obvious man-out-of-time jokes, this gentle fantasy romance (pre-empted by the cheaper **Late for Dinner**, 1991) concentrates on the impact on a typical nineties dysfunctional family of the perfect Gibson, a thirties movie hero in a cool flying jacket who unexpectedly refrains from becoming Curtis's love interest but nevertheless helps her get her life together.

There is a sticky bit of male bonding as Gibson teaches Wood to fly an airplane in his treehouse and the contrivances pile up along with the make-up latex that comes into play as the years start to catch up with Gibson, but for the most part this is an irresistible star vehicle. Gibson, his handsomeness for once suited to a role, is more relaxed and likeable than usual as the modest hero and, thanks to Glasser's supernaturally wonderful cameo, his lifelong romantic yearning is entirely understandable even down to the doddery, love-conquers-all reunion finale. It has nicely hokey period flying stunts with throttle-back action and against-the-deadline daredeviltry but for the most part this works through its honest and affecting emotional sequences, with the bruised and cynical Curtis on hand to take the edge off the whimsy.

d Steve Miner *p* Bruce Davey *s* Jeffrey Abrams *c* Russell Boyd *se* Greg Cannom, Image Special Effects *lp* Mel Gibson, Jamie Lee Curtis, Elijah Wood, Isabel Glasser, George Wendt, Joe Morton, Nicholas Surovy, David Marshall Grant

Left: Mel Gibson as the test pilot who is Forever Young.

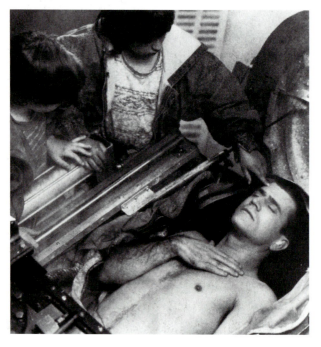

Fortress

(FORTRESS FILMS/VILLAGE ROADSHOW/DAVIS ENTERTAINMENT; US-AUST) 95 min

A futuristic prison movie, with bits and pieces of **Zero Population Growth** (1971), *Terminal Island* (1973), **Turkey Shoot** (1982), *Ghosts ... of the Civil Dead* (1988), *Wedlock* (1991) and **Alien3** (1992) floating around in the multi-authored script stew.

In a fascist future, America has strict population control laws: hero Lambert and wife Locklin are sentenced to 31 years apiece in an underground prison when they try to have a second baby after the death of their first. The social speculation is got out of the way quickly in the first minutes and then Gordon gets down to the business of replaying prison movie clichés. In the escape-proof fortress, inmates are injected with a gadget which causes extreme pain or can be exploded. Logic takes a back seat to gruesome effects: the intestinators are implanted in the stomach rather than the head or the heart simply so there can be an ucky sequence in which the good guys get rid of the devices by magnetically working them up through gullets.

Despite laser bars and robot guards, things are much as in most penitentiary pictures: weaselly informants, a sadistic warden (Smith), thuggish would-be rapists, an imprisoned genius (Combs), lots of fistfights and a big break-out at the end. The villain, the cyborg warden who realizes he too is imprisoned in the fortress, is not only more interesting than the hero but more sympathetic, with Smith turning in a performance that easily eclipses Lambert's *franglais* machismo. It is also strange that after stressing the escape-proof claustrophobia of the setting the movie should opt for a finale out in the wide open spaces where Lambert tackles a monster truck. An honest B picture that functions well on its own comic book terms.

I Can't Get No Satisfaction – Mick Jagger in Freejack.

d Stuart Gordon p John Davis, John Flock s Steve Feinberg, Troy Neighbors c David Eggby se Tad Pride, Paul Gentry lp Christopher Lambert, Loryn Locklin, Kurtwood Smith, Tom Towles, Jeffrey Combs, Lincoln Kilpatrick, Clifton Gonzales Gonzalez, Vernon Wells

Freddie as F.R.O.7

(HOLLYWOOD ROAD FILMS; GB) 91 min

This animated feature offers a bizarre, unsuccessful fusion of outdated fairytale cutes with even more anachronistic sixties Bond parody. A French prince, turned into a frog by his evil auntie, becomes a dashing superspy – voiced with a terrible French accent by Kingsley in perhaps the most humiliating role awarded to an Oscar winner – and is borrowed by the Brits to tackle the mysterious disappearance of major tourist attractions. Accompanied by a debby karate expert with the voice of Agutter and an all-purpose Scots sidekick with one of Sessions' many accents, Freddie stows away on Big Ben as it is stolen by El Supremo, a cartoon Blessed, and discovers that the auntie (Whitelaw), now turned into a big snake, is behind it all. An overlong hack at overfamiliar material that manages its secret agent parody without the flair of the UK TV cartoon *Dangermouse*. Despite a starry voice cast, it suffers from the usual faults of modern animated movies: unmemorable characters, third-hand jokes, excruciating songs, and that music which tells you what to feel when the film fails to be funny or moving enough.

d/co-p/co-s Jon Acevski co-p Norman Priggen co-s David Ashton c Rex Neville se Les Newstead, Colin Hughes lp Ben Kingsley, Jenny Agutter, Billie Whitelaw, John Sessions, Brian Blessed

Freejack

(MORGAN CREEK) 109 min

Robert Sheckley, whose major strengths as a Science Fiction writer are a satiric streak and a fondness for fully developed crazy ideas, seems doomed in the cinema to find his ironic tales of future media jungles turned into dim-witted action movies. *Freejack*, from his 1959 novel of a comic afterlife *Immortality, Inc.*, follows **La Decima Vittima** (1965) and *Le Prix du Danger*

(1983) in erasing almost all of the spark and strangeness of Sheckley's original in favour of a thick-ear game of touch-tag between a bewildered Estevez and a corpse-like Jagger, presided over by the discarnate spectre of Hopkins. Racing car driver Estevez disappears in a car crash, but finds himself whisked to the year 2009 by Jagger, a mercenary hired by a corporation to provide a healthy body (a 'freejack') from the past for possession by recently-deceased plutocrat Hopkins. Estevez escapes and finds the world much changed, with cities divided into combat zones and heavily-policed corporate enclaves. Pursued by several factions of baddies, he tracks down his surprised girlfriend (Russo) and penetrates the corporation to confront his nemesis.

While influenced by **Total Recall** (1989), this is rooted in the pre-Spielberg/Lucas film Science Fiction of the seventies, when similarly cinema-suited original novels were hammered into a dispiriting succession of action pictures like **The Omega Man** (1971), **Soylent Green** (1973), **Logan's Run** (1976) and **Damnation Alley** (1977). At one point the plot literally comes to a halt so Jagger can capture Estevez but let him go on a whim just to keep the story moving. But worse is the fact that the film's hellish future is less detailed and effective than the quickest Charles Band movie. Plummer is amusing as a hard-boiled nun who quotes the 'turn the other cheek' dictum before kneeing a corporate goon in the groin with 'But, of course, our Saviour never really had to deal with assholes like you.'

d Geoff Murphy co-p/co-s Ronald Shusett co-p Stuart Oken co-s Steven Pressfield, Dan Gilroy c Amir Mokri se Dream Quest Images lp Emilio Estevez, Mick Jagger, Rene Russo, Amanda Plummer, Anthony Hopkins, Jonathan Banks, David Johansen

Gauyat Sandiu Haplui *aka* Saviour of the Soul

(TEAM WORK PRODUCTION HOUSE; HONG KONG) scope 89 min
In this Eastern action extravaganza, a Japanese Science Fiction kung fu comic is turned into a Hong Kong martial arts fantasy that owes something in its basics (superguys kinetically slugging it out in eerily-lit warehouses to pounding music) to *Highlander* (1986) but moves so fast that it's hard to follow the plot closely enough to pick out the gaping holes. In the future, the evil but stylish Silver Fox (Kwok) and his zombie-like followers ('the Horrible Angels') tangle with high-kicking (and sometimes flying) heroine Mui, her twin sister, a perky brat girl, a pantomime dame and bounty-hunting good guy Lau. Wildly fantastical, with astonishing set-pieces like Silver Fox's genocidal attack on a jail to rescue a confederate and neat little touches like the bullet that sucks all the air out of a room. Typical of the slyly humorous tough talk is one dying villain's vow, 'I'll pay you in my next life.'

d Corey Yuen (Yuen Kwai) *p* David Lai *s* Kar-wai Wong
c Peter Pau *lp* Andy Lau, Anita Mui, Aaron Kwok, Kenny Bee

Gojira Tai Mosura *aka* Godzilla Versus Mothra

(TOHO; JAP) scope 104 mins
'If the world lives to see another century, please remember what Mothra did for you and the planet you live on.' With each new entry, the revived *Gojira* series comes more closely to resemble the colourful, childish, incoherent monster rallies of the sixties. Notionally a remake of **Mosura Tai Gojira** (1964), this is more like the original **Mosura** (1961) with Godzilla roped in as a guest star. A meteor crashes in the sea off Japan, threatening the ecological balance of the planet and awakening not only Godzilla, dormant since **Gojira Tai Kingu Gidora** (1991), but also the twin monsters Battra and Mothra. An Indiana Jones-style artefact thief (Bessho) is blackmailed by his government agent ex-wife (Kobayashi) into leading an expedition to the island where Mothra's egg lies. The expedition, backed by an unscrupulous corporation, discovers the Cosmos, ten-inch-high twin singing princesses (Imamura, Osawa) who explain that they are survivors of a space-borne pre-human race who fell from grace when they tampered with the balance of nature, prompting the Earth to unleash the protective spirit of Battra.

The plot confusingly changes Godzilla from the semi-benign nationalist monster of the last entry into a simple city-stomping menace, as characterless as the unseen meteor which turns out to be the real danger. In compensation, Mothra and Battra are rather complex, light and dark incarnations of apparently antagonistic spirits who finally make truce among the ruins and jointly overcome Godzilla. Battra, a sinister presence, even turns out to be destined to save the Earth from the meteor and his death forces Mothra to take on that role in an unusually poetic finale, accompanied by the singing mannikins, as the great moth departs for space in a golden haze to defend the world. The large-scale city-smashing, monster-battling and tag-wrestling scenes are among the best in the genre, with nostalgic use of decades-old monster themes by Akira Ifukube and an iconic recasting of sixties Kaiju Eiga regular Takarada.

d Takao Okawara *p* Tomoyuki Tanaka *s* Kazuki Omori
c Masahiro Kishimoto *se* Koichi Kawakita *lp* Tetsuya Bessho, Satomi Kobayashi, Akira Takarada, Keiko Imamura, Sayaka Osawa, Megumi Odaka

Honey, I Blew Up the Kid

(DISNEY) 89 min
This is a by-the-numbers sequel to **Honey, I Shrunk the Kids** (1989), hard to hate but impossible to love. Kleiser reassembles the ingredients of the first film with all the personality of a McDonald's employee putting together a Big Mac, using references to **The Amazing Colossal Man** (1958) rather than **The Incredible Shrinking Man** (1957) as a giant toddler (the Shalikar twins) invades Las Vegas for the finale. The pre-digested cuteness is heavy on family values as irresponsible scientist Moranis accidentally zaps his two-year-old with an enlarging ray, prompting him to go on a tame rampage, but everything is sorted out – perhaps in a reference to **Gorgo** (1961) – by the arrival of a giant Mom. The players, who include Bridges as a paternalist tycoon, barely get a joke apiece as the film clumps from one effects set-piece to another, but the seamless gigantism

Honey, I blew up the kid – Rick Moranis in Honey, I Blew Up the Kid.

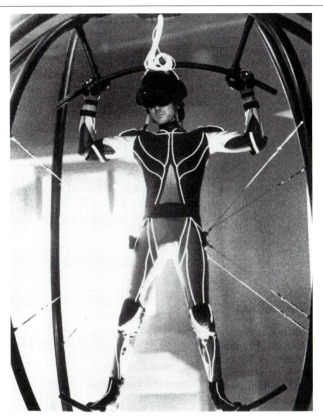

Pierce Brosnan in The Lawnmower Man.

Memoirs of an Invisible Man

(WARNER/CORNELIUS/CANAL+/REGENCY/ALCOR) 99 min
Before video-taping his life story, an empty presence with Chase's voice one-ups previous screen invisible men by unwrapping a stick of bubble gum, chewing it thoroughly and blowing a bubble. After this, the film slips into a standard romantic comedy thriller vein, with Carpenter doing the facelessly efficient hired gun act last seen on **Starman** (1984). Chase, a feckless businessman, is caught napping by an industrial accident that turns him see-through, whereupon CIA psycho Neill tries to capture him for nefarious purposes. Fortunately, Chase hooks up with a glamorously unbelievable anthropologist (Hannah), and they fall in love in between escapes, disguises, stunts and tricks.

With several of its best images – the slow unwrapping of a bandaged head to reveal nothing, villains pursuing a fleeing pair of trousers – lifted directly from **The Invisible Man** (1933), this hardly makes much use of H.F. Saint's ambitious source novel, content to let Chase trot out his usual smarmy schtick. There are effective effects: the partially-invisible building where the accident takes place, a disembodied make-up mask floating eyeless in the air, Chase accidentally wiping the make-up off his lips in a restaurant, Chase as a bubble-shape in the rain, Chase smoking a cigarette that outlines his lungs, Chase digesting and vomiting Chinese food. In a device that works surprisingly well, the audience often sees Chase though everyone in the film, including Chase himself, can't.

While it is a blandly entertaining picture, the possibly interesting character point that Chase's Nick Halloway was such an average loser that he was invisible even before he became invisible is simply raised in the dialogue and forgotten.

d John Carpenter *p* Bruce Bodner, Dan Kolsrud *s* Robert Collector, Dana Olson, William Goldman *c* William A. Fraker *se* ILM *lp* Chevy Chase, Daryl Hannah, Sam Neill, Michael McKean, Stephen Tobolowsky, Jim Norton

Mindwarp

(FANGORIA) 91 min
Though it does feature wet gore sequences involving vomited leeches and a giant grinding machine, the first feature backed by *Fangoria* magazine turns out not to be a horror picture but a mildly inventive exercise in low-rent Science Fiction with a frame story likely to be imitated frequently in the nineties. In a white-on-white underground futureworld that harks back to **THX 1138** (1970), all citizens are plugged into Infinisynth, a VR-style escapist medium, and only heroine Alicia, who has developed a unique and side-issued ability to hop from dream to dream, is unhappy about the situation. After a confrontation with the master of the machine, Alicia is ejected into a wilderness of **Mad Max 2** (1981) deserts, a wandering hard-bitten hero (Campbell), skeletons on poles, cannibal mutants and B-picture clichés.

sequences are curiously flat, antiseptic and uninvolving, with all the sense of wonder of a chroma-key weather forecast map. So good-natured and wholesome that it can't bear seriously to endanger any of its characters and therefore never works up any suspense. There are in-jokes about Godzilla, *Citizen Kane* (1941) and *Raiders of the Lost Ark* (1981).

d Randal Kleiser *p* Dawn Steel, Edward S. Feldman *s* Thom Eberhardt, Peter Elbling, Garry Goodrow *c* John Hora *se* Thomas G. Smith *lp* Rick Moranis, Marcia Strassman, Robert Oliveri, Daniel Shalikar, Joshua Shalikar, Lloyd Bridges, John Shea, Amy O'Neill, Kenneth Tobey

The Lawnmower Man

(ALLIED VISION/LANE PRINGLE; US-GB) 108 min
Mad scientist Brosnan, upset because the Evil Government has used his Virtual Reality experiments to turn chimps into homicidal maniacs, quits his job and hangs around the house in a VR wetsuit, playing the high-tech equivalent of video games. After his wife walks out, he turns his work to noble ends inspired by **Charly** (1968), raising the intelligence of a mentally handicapped gardener (Fahey) to genius level. The process also turns Fahey into a telekinetic homicidal maniac who justifies the film's Stephen King associations by exterminating various horrible secondary characters who have tormented him.

The fashionable VR stuff allows flashy visual effects, but actually has nothing to do with the plot, though the movie keeps coming up with interesting technical bits and bobs, especially when villains are turned into electronic bubbles and dispersed. Fahey and Brosnan try hard to be serious, peering intently as they suffer for science, but no amount of effects glitz, name-dropping or emotional angst disguises the fact that this is essentially a George Zucco picture for the nineties, tarting up the premise of *The Monster and the Girl* (1941) or *The Mad Ghoul* (1943). King successfully sued to have the title changed from *Stephen King's The Lawnmower Man*, Leonard supervised a two-and-a-quarter-hour director's cut for video, and a sequel arrived in *Lawnmower Man II: CyberGod* (1995).

Bet You Can't Do This One – Chevy Chase in Memoirs of an Invisible Man.

d/co-s/co-se Brett Leonard *p/co-s/co-se* Gimel Everett *c* Russell Carpenter *lp* Jeff Fahey, Pierce Brosnan, Jenny Wright, Mark Bringleson, Geoffrey Lewis, Jeremy Slate

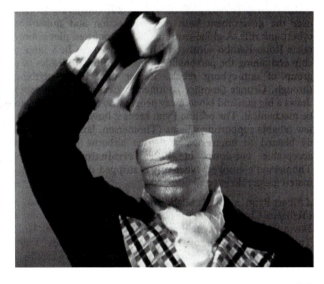

Of course, the whole action plot turns out to be just a more realistic level of illusion, a twist which would be more satisfying if the film did not include scenes within the heroine's fantasy where she is not present and which therefore could have no existence within her tailor-made dream. The perhaps-intentionally hokey central section has Alicia discovering that her long-lost father (Scrimm) is now the cowled tyrant of the mutant gang and duelling with him – 'I never imagined I could devour my own child, but I can. Here, I can do anything and it's wonderful' – for apparent mastery of the monsters but actually auditioning for her new role as ruler of the Infinisynth system. *Fangoria*'s other features are the vampire movie *Children of the Night* (1991) and the mad scientist quickie *Severed Ties* (1991).

d Steve Barnett *p* Christopher Webster *s* Henry Dominic *c* Peter Fernberger *lp* Bruce Campbell, Angus Scrimm, Marta Alicia, Elizabeth Kent, Mary Becker

Mom and Dad Save the World

(WARNER) 88 min
Despite a likeable cast, this comedy from the authors of the *Bill & Ted* films remains somewhat flat. Replacing the teenage dudes are a middle-class sit-com couple plucked from their suburban home into a Science Fiction universe patterned on the *Flash Gordon* serials because Emperor Tod Spengo (Lovitz) of the the Planet Spengo, which is populated entirely by idiots, has decided that Mom (Garr) is the most desirable woman in the universe and must become his bride, which forces placid Dad (Jones) to become a heroic warrior and overthrow the tyrant so the rightful heir (Idle) can be restored. Jones and Garr, perfect incarnations of the bemused Americans Dave Berg drew for *MAD* magazine in the 1970s, underplay to the strength of the script while Lovitz, who resembles Rick Moranis cubed, overdoes everything as the infantile ruler of an imbecilic galactic empire.

The old-fashioned universe is nicely evoked by rebels in silly bird-masks, races of midget dog- and fish-people, killer mushrooms, medieval uniforms, death-rays and ungainly spaceships, but after **Flesh Gordon** (1974), **Star Wars** (1976) and **Flash Gordon** (1980), there really is not enough left to be parodied. Mom and Dad, who narrate while showing the stultifying slides of their outer space adventure, are actually a far richer source of satire and insight than the more fantastical elements of the picture.

d Greg Beeman *p* Michael Phillips *s* Chris Matheson, Ed Solomon *c* Jacques Haitkin *se* Tony Gardner *lp* Jeffrey Jones, Terri Garr, Jon Lovitz, Thalmus Rasulala, Wallace Shawn, Eric Idle, Dwier Brown, Kathy Ireland

Nemesis

(SHAH-JENSEN/IMPERIAL) 95 min
Action-packed but incomprehensible, this dresses up the old **Futureworld** (1976) premise of androids conspiring to take over the government with non-stop action and numerous cyberpunk riffs. A globe-trotting, deeply confused plot mainly takes Robo-Rambo Gruner to Indonesia where he's after a chip containing the personality of his ex-girlfriend, leader of a group of anti-cyborg rebels. Rather than think anything through, Gruner (another continental kick-boxing wannabe) draws a big gun and blows away people who mostly turn out to be mechanical. The prolific Pyun keeps it busy and loud and a few reliable supporting villains (Thomerson, James) get messily blasted to fragments, while the airborne ending is an acceptable cut-down of **The Terminator** (1984) as Thomerson's crooked cyber-cop is stripped down to an animated gadget skeleton.

d Albert Pyun *p* Ash R. Shah, Eric Karson, Tom Karnowski *s* Rebecca Charles *c* George Mooradian *se* Terry Frazee, David Barton, Fantasy II Film Effects *lp* Oliver Gruner, Tim Thomerson, Cary-Hirooyuki Tagawa, Merele Kennedy, Yuji Okumoto, Brion James, Vince Klyn

Oliver Gruner as the cyborg killer in Nemesis.

Neon City

(KODIAK) 103 min
Taking the Western associations of the post-Holocaust action movie to extremes, this is a remake of *Stagecoach* (1939). In 2053, a 'transport' carries an assortment of outcasts through poisoned wastelands, where they are attacked by 'skins', Indian-style mutant marauders, and have to survive sunburst storms of deadly weather. The plot and characters of John Ford's film are jumbled in the rewrite: the doctor is the absconding criminal, the whisky drummer is carrying futuristic drugs. Hero Ireland, roughly taking the George Bancroft part, is a bounty hunter taking a recaptured fugitive to Neon City to face the law, which bizarrely casts Vanity in the John Wayne role. Competently directed by Markham, who also cameos, this is an adequate video item, surprisingly respectful of its source, down to the extent of naming a character 'Dicky Devine' (Sanders) and shooting action scenes in Fordian Utah locations.

d/co-s Monte Markham *p* Wolf Schmidt *co-s* Buck Finch, Jeff Begun *c* Keith Holland *lp* Michael Ironside, Vanity, Lyle Alzado, Valerie Wildman, Nick Klar, Julie Landau, Arsenio 'Sonny' Trinidad, Richard Sanders

Project: Shadowchaser

(NAR/EGM; US-GB) 97 min
This is another exploitation cross-breed, with the elements of *Die Hard* (1988) and **The Terminator** (1984) shuffled together to provide 97 minutes of bang-bang cheap thrills. In a premise that prefigures **Demolition Man** (1993), future criminal Kove, best known as the baddie in *The Karate Kid* (1984), is defrosted from a cryogenic prison and sent into a high-rise hospital where android terrorist Zagarino, a Dolph Lundgren clone, is holding to ransom the president's daughter (Foster). A complication arises in that Kove is not the super-competent commando he is supposed to be, but the foul-up who was stashed in the adjacent cryo-tube. Ackland, the mad scientist responsible for manufacturing the killer hunk, grins evilly in the background, setting up a predictable but effective last-minute twist. Unexceptional B-grade fodder, but watchable; filmed in the UK with a convincing American setting, and with some nice sparks between Kove and the always-welcome Foster. The same team's *Project Shadowchaser II* (1994) is even closer to *Die Hard*, as Zagarino, the only returning cast member, takes over a nuclear weapons decommissioning plant over Christmas and is foiled by a drunken janitor, a babe scientist and a spotty kid.

d/co-p John Eyres *co-p* Geoff Griffiths *s* Stephen Lister *c* Alan M. Trow *se* Brian Smithies *lp* Martin Kove, Meg Foster, Frank Zagarino, Paul Koslo, Joss Ackland, Ricco Ross

Prototype aka Prototype X29A

(FILM TOWN ENTERTAINMENT) 98 min

Trudging glumly in the bootsteps of **The Terminator** (1984) this plays like a throwback to the Italian **Mad Max** (1979) imitations of the early eighties. In the usual yob-overrun California wasteland of 2057, crippled and emasculated ex-soldier Tossberg volunteers for a process which will turn him into an armoured cyborg because he thinks it will help him reunite with Lenhart, an enhanced woman he shares VR erotic dreams with, but it turns out that he is programmed to track her down and kill her. Dingy visuals, murky scripting, vague characters and a lack of actual action renders the whole thing remarkably unexciting. The same team proceeded to the marginally better **APEX** (1993).

d/co-p/s Phillip Roth *co-p* Gian-Carlo Scandiuzzi, Ron Schmidt, Gary Jude Burkart *c* Mark W. Gray *se* George Temple, Robert J. Marino *lp* Lane Lenhart, Robert Tossberg, Brenda Swanson, Paul Coulj, Mitchell Cox

Seedpeople

(FULL MOON ENTERTAINMENT) 86 min

'Let's see if you bleed chlorophyll,' vows one crackpot defender of the Earth in this ill-thought-out film that is clearly inspired by **Invasion of the Body Snatchers** (1956) but which has the presumption to include the credit 'based on an idea by Charles Band'. Intrepid but dull-witted meteor specialist Hennings investigates a small town where giant peach stones have fallen from the sky and hatched out three **Critters** (1986)-style troublemaking tumbleweeds which assume the forms of the American Gothic townsfolk to reduce the special effects budget but occasionally resume their alien plant monster shape and are susceptible to ultra-violet light. With many plot points (the hero's breathless narration as he explains it all to the FBI, a truckful of deadly seed-pods exporting terror to all America) lifted from *Body Snatchers*, uninspiring performers, cardboard characters, sub-*Muppet* effects and an overall air of pointlessness, this is among the least interesting of the prolific Band's output. Immediately upstaged by Abel Ferrara's **Body Snatchers** (1993).

d Peter Manoogian *p* Anne Kelly *s* Jackson Barr *c* Adolfo Bartoli *se* Magical Media Industries, Inc *lp* Sam Hennings, Andrea Roth, Dane Witherspoon, Dave Dunard, Anne Betancourt, Holly Fields, Bernard Kates, Sonny Carl Davis

Solar Crisis aka Kuraishisu Niju-Goju Nen

(TRIMARK/GAKKEN NHK; US-JAP) 118 min

Like **Fukkatsu No Hi** (1980), this is basically a Japanese movie, based on a popular novel (by Kawata), restructured and dotted with 'international' guest stars to play down the heroic role of a Japanese character (Bessho) and spotlight American performers who are compelled to play characters enmeshed in a subtly wrong set of codes of honour and emotion. On top of the usual problems of such international hybrids, compounded by the built-in ridiculousness of the disaster-from-space genre, this was beset by production troubles that prompted Sarafian to sign the film with the Directors Guild of America all-purpose pseudonym.

In the future, scientists predict that a solar flare will soon destroy the Earth. Heston ('I can do anything I want to, I'm the Admiral') masterminds a scheme to save the world by firing an anti-matter bomb into the Sun to trigger the flare early so it will shoot harmlessly into space, but zillionaire villain Boyle, who doesn't believe the pessimist prognosis and sees an opportunity for profit, tries to sabotage the mission. The disaster movie plot, which has some echoes of **The Day the Earth Caught Fire** (1961) and **Meteor** (1979), cuts between several sets of characters in crisis situations. Space commander Matheson, Heston's son, leads the potential *kamikaze* mission and has to deal with bio-engineered Schofield, who has been brainwashed to serve Boyle, along the way. Heston, meanwhile, hooks up with desert rat Palance on Earth as he searches for his grandson (Nemec), who has gone missing.

Aside from a loony Palance performance, the cast are uniformly earnest as they cope with dialogue that sounds as if it has been translated ('The cremation of the planet is at hand', 'I don't give a Martian's ass about anything except the performance of my ship', 'Goddamnit, tell me you love me before you leave the room'). Paul Williams adds a strange touch as the voice of an insecure bomb who harks back to **Dark Star** (1974) but oddly plays for pathos rather than humour. The effects-heavy finale depicts a descent into the fires of the Sun that is not quite the **2001** (1968) trip it would like to be and strangely omits depiction of the flare. Though it has quality optics and an expansive Maurice Jarre score, this still feels like an outdated quickie, down to preposterous character names like Admiral 'Skeet' Kelso and Freddy the Bomb.

d Alan Smithee (Richard C. Sarafian) *p* Richard Edlund, James Nelson, Tsuneyuki Morishima *s* Joe Gannon, Crispan Bolt, Takeshi Kawata *c* Russ Carpenter *se* Neil Krepela *lp* Tim Matheson, Charlton Heston, Peter Boyle, Annabel Schofield, Jack Palance, Corin Nemec, Dorian Harweood, Tetsuya Bessho

Split Second

(CHALLENGE/MUSE; GB) 91 min

London, 2008. The Thames has risen, society is crumbling and the Metropolitan Police employ psychopaths, including Hauer, to track serial killers. Global warming has clearly also had an effect on the atoms that bind together plots, because this slasher movie has an almost random approach to its traditional story. Inexplicable events, disappearing characters, logical lapses and downright silliness tumble together. Coffee-drinking hard-man Hauer and comics-reading Scots intellectual Duncan

are brawling buddy cops on the trail of a heart-eating villain who carves astrological symbols on what's left of the chests of his victims. Various solutions are raised, involving mutant DNA and the Devil, but the killer turns out to be a regulation **Alien** (1979)-imitation Big Monster With Teeth who gets righteously splattered in a tube train-set finale (directed by Ian Sharp).

Mostly directed at a rapid plod by Tony Maylam, the film consists mainly of characters colliding in the middle of the screen to snarl would-be hard-bitten dialogue at each other. As a video trash action picture, this at least offers up all the requisite chewed hearts, naked people, big guns and monsters. Hauer tries to look cool in sunglasses that can hardly be much help in the murksome world of the future, while Duncan's enthusiastic performance accounts for the sole touch of character and humour.

d Tony Maylam *p* Laura Gregory *s* Gary Scott Thompson *c* Clive Tickner *se* Stephen Norrington *lp* Rutger Hauer, Kim Cattrall, Neil Duncan, Michael J. Pollard, Alun Armstrong, Pete Postlethwaite, Ian Dury

Three Tornadoes *aka* Blue Tornado

(CLEMI CINEMATOGRAFICA; IT) 96 min

When his best buddy disappears in a cloud of flying light blobs, NATO flier Benedict becomes obsessed with UFOs and initiates further close encounters, irking his cover-up-minded superiors and finally climbing a European mountain on foot for the feeblest imaginable alien epiphany. With a proliferation of barking Euro-accents, one of Kensit's trademarked embarrassing heroine performances and acres of *Top Gun*-style stock footage, this hardware-heavy aviation movie is more reminiscent of the very uninteresting *Project UFO* TV series, with its simple (and cheap) bright lights in place of even cheesy alien effects, than the 1990s reincarnation of the UFO investigation-government conspiracy drama of *The X-Files*. Benedict has at least had a decent haircut since **Battlestar Galactica** (1978) but still acts like a square-jawed sequoia. He subsequently starred in the similar but slightly better cable TV movie *Official Denial* (1993).

d/co-s Tony B. Dobb (Antonio Bido) *p* Giovanni di Clemente *co-s* Gino Capone *c* Maurizio Dell'Orco *lp* Dirk Benedict, Patsy Kensit, Ted McGinley, David Warner

Universal Soldier

(CAROLCO) scope 103 min

A no-brain Saturday night action flick gung-ho enough to have the most lily-livered peacenik howling for blood, **Universal Soldier** backs up its second-string hulks with a Stallone-sized budget, then sets them loose on a script which mixes Science Fiction, martial arts, exploding gas stations, sadistic wisecracks and post-'Nam angst.

In Vietnam, a bleeding heart private (Van Damme) scrags a psycho sergeant (Lundgren) who has been collecting ears from innocent bystanders. Then, in the film's present, the deep-frozen dead are revived for use in an experimental military programme whereby well-trained zombies are let loose with enormous weapons and deployed every time a terrorist incident threatens the integrity of the USA. Wires get crossed and muscleheads revert to their old personalities: Van Damme hares across country with a journalist (Walker) in search of the truth, while Lundgren slaughters all and sundry in an extended 'Nam flashback while giving out with terrible one-liners ('I'm all ears').

Emmerich, half-way between the Euro-dreariness of **Moon 44** (1990) and the epic tosh of **Stargate** (1994), turns in a well put-together if standardized nineties genre film. Both he-men are given a chance to get away from their direct-to-video roots: Van Damme, so proud of his bottom that he makes sure it appears in each of his films, does sub-**RoboCop** (1987) bewilderment but cuts loose whenever he gets to show off high kicks, while Lundgren, an unhappy good guy in **Masters of the Universe** (1987) or **Dark Angel** (1990), demonstrates that nature and his hairdresser have suited him perfectly to Nazi genegineered baddie roles. The action is interrupted only be pre-digested plot chunks and Linda Hamilton-lookalike Walker's irritating hyperactivity. The 1992 theme of time-interrupted relationships (**Late for Dinner**, **Freejack**) is exercised as Van Damme, who sounds more like a soldier killed in Indochina in 1954 than Vietnam in 1969, gets sensitive en route to a reunion with his parents. Lundgren, a foot and a hairstyle taller than the hero, gnashes his teeth until a last-reel punch-up involving do-it-yourself steroids and a multi-pronged farm implement.

d Roland Emmerich *p* Allen Shapiro, Craig Bamgarten, Joel B. Michaels *s* Richard Rothstein, Christopher Leitch, Dean Devlin *c* Karl Walter Lindenlaub *se* Kit West *lp* Jean-Claude Van Damme, Dolph Lundgren, Ally Walker, Ed O'Ross, Jerry Orbac, Leon Rippy, Tico Wells, Tiny Lister Jr

1993

Accion Mutante

(EL DESEO/CIBY 3000; SP) scope 94 min

In 2012, beautiful people are under attack (sperm banks are blown up, aerobic classes mown down by gunfire, body-builders executed) by a terrorist cell known as Accion Mutante. Led by disfigured genius Resines, AM consist of cripples, retards, Siamese twins and hunchbacks. Angry at a world dominated by mineral water and diets, they kidnap Feder, daughter of a wholemeal bread tycoon, from her high society wedding (which, with its absurd clothes and bubblegum music is the single sequence that suggests an Almodóvar influence) and head off to Planet Abraxas to collect a ransom. En voyage Resines double-crosses his bungling comrades and feeds them all to the monster cat. Crash-landing on the desert planet, Resines and the increasingly dependent Feder encounter sundry maniacs while Feder's father closes in and a surviving Siamese twin, seeking revenge for his brother's murder, hobbles after them.

Eyes Right – (left to right) Jean-Claude Van Damme, Dolph Lundgren and Tiny Lister Jr in Universal Soldier.

Terrorist Antonio Resines kidnaps beautiful person Frédérique Feder in the quirky Accion Mutante.

The opening reel swiftly delineates its appealing premise of a handicapped vigilante group (their logo is a wheelchair-bound stick figure brandishing a rifle), providing its grungy heroes with a coolly anarchic TV-style credits sequence complete with an obnoxious 'Accion Mutante' rap and an evocative snippet of Lalo Schifrin's *Mission: Impossible* theme. However, when the terrorists get into a spaceship, the film abandons its ostensible idea and sticks rather too closely to the plot of *No Orchids for Miss Blandish* (especially Robert Aldrich's adaptation of James Hadley Chase, *The Grissom Gang*, 1971). As it straggles across a familiar desert planetscape, *Accion Mutante* even resembles one of the dozens of **Mad Max** (1979) imitations churned out in the early eighties by Italy, the Philippines or Charles Band. Isolated images (a smiling dead Siamese twin strung up by a lynch mob while his living brother kicks) recapture the grim humour of the opening, but rather more sequences go beyond black comedy into actual nastiness (a retarded child slicing away at Resines with a razor-blade then pouring salt and vinegar into the wounds). Also highly unfunny is the abuse Feder (who has her lips stapled together for a long stretch of the film) is required to take, ostensibly because of her class but which seems actually to express a streak of unattractive misogyny (there are notably no female mutants) that co-exists uncomfortably with the editorializing on behalf of the hideous. Officially a promising first film, this feels more like a disappointing second one.

d/co-s Alex de la Iglesia *p* Augustin Almodóvar, Pedro Almodóvar *co-s* Jorge Guerriaechevarria *c* Carles Gusi *se* Oliver Gleyze, Yves Domenjoud, Jean-Baptiste Bonetto, Bernard-André le Boetti *lp* Antonio Resines, Frédérique Feder, Alex Angulo, Juan Viadas, Kara Elejalde, Saturnina Garcia, Fernando Guellén

APEX

(GREEN COMMUNICATIONS/REPUBLIC) 103 min

'Time is a strange thing. No matter what happens, no matter what you do, things change and nothing can quite be the same again.' A **Terminator** (1984) rip-off from the makers of **Prototype** (1992) this expends a goodly portion of its low budget on neat morphing effects. However the action mainly consists of uncharismatic no-name players yomping around an orange-filter desert shooting at clunky robots. Time-travelling Keats visits 1973 from 2073 and returns to find he has accidentally created an alternate future where things are terrible, an AIDS-like plague ravages the land, killer robots wage war on humanity, his meek wife (Russell) is an Amazon rebel, and everyone speaks in tough-talk clichés ('I'll slap your ass so hard, your first child'll be born dizzy'). Despite its time-twisting premise (echoed in **Philadelphia Experiment II**, 1993), this is a rather simplistic, humourless and cramped Science Fiction actioner.

d/co-s Philip J. Roth *p* Talaat Captan *co-s* Ronald Schmidt *c* Mark W. Gray *se* Altered Anatomy FX *lp* Richard Keats, Mitchell Cox, Lisa Ann Russell, Marcus Aurelius, Adam Lawson

Batman: Mask of the Phantasm

(WAR) 77 min

Though this spin-off from the excellent animated *Batman* TV series is too dark to catch audiences who flocked to *The Lion King*, it certainly stands as the best cartoon feature of 1993. Better-plotted than Tim Burton's live action movies, it shares their semi-tragic characterization of the schizoid superhero and a love of the art deco gothic of Gotham City.

A brooding Bruce Wayne (Conroy) is haunted by an old flame (Delaney) who returns to his life just as the Phantasm, an even scarier vigilante, starts a murderous crusade against Gotham's gangsters. In *Casablanca* (1943) style, the film flashes back to the early days of Batman's career as he almost calls off his war against crime when the temptation of normal life is nearly too great to resist. In a moment more emotionally powerful than anything in Burton's films, Bruce talks to his parents' grave, trying to back out of his vow to fight crime, pleading 'I'm sorry, but it just doesn't hurt so much any more ... I never expected to be happy.' Later the film closes bleakly with Batman and the Phantasm marooned in their isolation, lives ruined by the need to avenge dead parents.

Though it focuses on the character elements, *Mask of the Phantasm* does not skimp on action and black humour, with a bravura finale as Batman battles the Joker (a wildly ranting Hamill) in the ruins of an outmoded City of the Future exhibit.

d Eric Radomski, Bruce W. Timm *p* Benjamin Melniker, Michael Uslan *s* Michael Reeves, Alan Burnett, Paul Dini, Martin Pako *lp* Kevin Conroy, Dana Delaney, Mark Hamill, Hart Bochner, Stacy Keach, Abe Vigoda, Efrem Zimbalist Jr

Body Snatchers (WAR) scope 87 min

Addressing the universal personal and political fear that individuals or society can easily lose the essentials of humanity and become soulless 'pods', the body snatchers concept is one of the great pop myths of the post-war world. Jack Finney's 1955 novel *The Body Snatchers*, filmed by Don Siegel and Philip Kaufman as **Invasion of the Body Snatchers** (1956, 1978), is a property that can usefully be remade every fifteen years. This third version, developed at various times by Larry Cohen and Stuart Gordon, is less faithful to Finney's plot than the earlier films but still elaborates on his basic theme.

Body Snatchers is set on an army base which already imposes an uncomfortable degree of conformity on characters, as regimentation finally becomes a nightmarish melange of chanting platoons and sweeping searchlights. This bold stroke increases political resonance and allows for gung ho action with helicopters and missiles, including a marvellously ambiguous and hollow triumph at the finale. Rather than a medical-scientific investigator hero, the protagonist is Anwar, teenage daughter of an Environment Protection Agency boffin (Kinney) who is investigating the storage of toxic materials in an army installation.

At the outset, the heroine's family is screamingly dysfunctional, emphasizing the calming, soothing influence of the pod people, who replace alcoholics with teetotallers and threaten to turn Anwar from a sulky, intolerant teen into an ideal daughter. In an amazingly creepy scene, Anwar's little brother is revealed as the only real human in his infants' class when all the other children produce identical finger-paintings. On the fair assumption that the audience already knows the premise, *Body Snatchers* does not explain the alien invasion but simply shows it with gloopily effective effects as the pods sprout tendrils which swarm disgustingly around sleeping victims' faces as the replacement person is formed. Post-production studio tampering is suggested by the sudden segue at the mid-way point from oblique hints to non-stop action but Ferrara, in a rare medium budget excursion, shows he can make a smooth-looking, perfectly-paced film as well as he can handle spiky, zero-expense items like *Bad Lieutenant* (1992). His acute ear for character tensions deftly captures the untidy human emotions that the pods live without, as Anwar loses her messy family and friends, paying off with a helicopter defenestration (a dodgy process shot, sadly) that violates the deepest taboos of the American cinema as she is forced to jettison her brother.

The writing and acting are remarkable for mid-budget Science Fiction: a 'truth' game between Anwar and soldier Wirth, apparently an irrelevant aisde, sets up resonances that pay off throughout the film, as Wirth's tendency to hide his feelings enables him to pass among the pods and Anwar is forced to learn how to shoot 'people'. Tilly, remarkable as an alternately calm and screeching pod queen, delivers a keynote speech for the unease of the 1990s: 'Where are you going to go, where are you going to run, where are you going to hide? Nowhere, because there's no one like *you* left.'

d Abel Ferrara *p* Robert H. Solo *s* Nicholas St John, Stuart Gordon, Dennis Paoli *c* Bojan Bazeli *se* Tom Burman & Bari Dreiband-Burman Spfx *lp* Gabrielle Anwar, Terry Kinney, Meg Tilly, Billy Wirth, Forrest Whitaker, R. Lee Ermey, Christine Elise

Carnosaur
(CONCORDE) 82 min
In a characteristically ingenious exploitation move, Roger Corman set out to cash in on **Jurassic Park** (1993) by buying the rights to a paperback by Harry Adam Knight (John Brosnan) which dealt with genetically engineered dinosaurs well before Michael Crichton tackled the subject, then casting Diane Ladd, the mother of Steven Spielberg's leading lady Laura Dern, as a mad scientist responsible for bringing some lumbering dino-puppets into the world. However, in an era when major studios stage lavishly-mounted throwaway exploitation pictures in the Corman style (cf: **Tremors**, 1989), this cutprice effort fails to make much of its promising material, lumbered as it is with dinosaurs that look like 1960s *Dr Who* effects and move like Sooty or Kermit. Simon, who made the promising *Brain Dead* (1990), drops in a few cynical touches and some sick comedy scenes: a group of environmentalist protesters padlock themselves to bulldozers and can't escape when a dinosaur trundles up to chomp down on them. Ladd, as the mad scientist who hopes dinosaurs will replace mankind, hams outrageously, but the rest of the cast, headed by Sbarge as a drunken Sheriff, fail to make an impression

Given the ineptitude of the effects and the slapdash plot, Simon is forced to crib irrelevant bits of business from *Humanoids From the Deep* (1980) as dino embryos hatch in human women and explode through chests and **The Crazies** (1973) as decontamination-suited government hit men turn up and wipe out all the characters to cover up the disaster. Naturally, it was a big enough video hit to prompt *Carnosaur 2* (1994), an even sillier rip-off of **Aliens** (1986).

d/s Adam Simon *p* Mike Eliott *c* Keith Holland *se* John Carl Buechler *lp* Diane Ladd, Raphael Sbarge, Jennifer Runyon, Harrison Page, Clint Howard

Class of 1999 II: The Substitute
(VIDMARK) 90 min
'Sadistic behaviour should not be condoned. Especially when you're not trained to do it properly.' A cheap sequel to **Class of 1999** (1990), beefed up with effects footage from the original, with one clever plot twist that could conceivably just be an excuse not to spend money on more expensive robo-carnage. Smart-suited kickboxer Mitchell goes from school to school, intimidating and murdering rebellious pupils, tracked by a government agent who thinks the substitute teacher is the last of the military robot/teachers who rebelled in the first movie. In the finale, it turns out that Mitchell is just a mad scientist's brainwashed son who wears super-efficient body armour and *believes* he's a robot. Mitchell, who totes a book of his father's sensitively militarist poetry, gets friendly with Dulaney, a teacher on the point of testifying in a murder case involving a student. He is brought down during a paintball battle he has used as an excuse to wipe out the delinquents, but Dulaney takes up his murderous crusade. Flatly directed, drearily cast and too full of overfamiliar explosions.

d/p Spiro Razatos *s* Mark Sevi *lp* Sasha Mitchell, Nick Cassavetes, Caitlin Dulaney, Jack Knight, Gregory West

Coneheads (PAR) 86 min
'If I were not concerned about incarceration by human authority figures, I would apply such pressure to your blunt skull to terminate your life functions.' A comedy loser spun off from the *Saturday Night Live* sketches, with Aykroyd and Curtin recreating their roles as the barking, bald, pointy-headed aliens from the planet Remulak who pass in New Jersey by posing as French. The usual TV spin-off failings are evidenced by an utter failure to come up with a plot that does more than string together all the old characters and schtick. Among the strands experimented with and thrown away are immigration official McKean's attempts to catch the illegal aliens, the rebellion of

Pretentious, moi? – Dan Aykroyd and Jane Curtin with child in Coneheads.

teenage Conehead daughter Burke against old world values, and a trip back to outer space for a trial by combat in which Aykroyd uses his Earth-learned golf skills to defeat an impressive animated monster. Many *SNL* cast members pop up in pointless cameos. The aliens-in-suburbia premise was done better in **Meet the Applegates** (1990).

d Steve Barron *p* Lorne Michaels *s* Tom Davis, Dan Aykroyd, Bonnie Turner, Terry Turner *c* Francis Kenny *se* Phil Tippett *lp* Dan Aykroyd, Jane Curtin, Michelle Burke, Laraine Newman, Michael McKean, Chris Farley

Cyborg 2: Glass Shadow

(VIDMARK/ANGLO-AMERICAN) 99 min

Though Jean-Claude Van Damme is glimpsed in almost subliminal flashbacks from **Cyborg** (1989), this follow-up abjures the original's desert survivalism for a cheapo **Blade Runner** (1982) urban look and strangles its plot with a complex backstory that makes it seem like a sequel to another movie.

Sylvester Stallone is the Demolition Man.

Koteas, the dullest leading man of the 1990s, fails to fill Van Damme's kickboxing boots as a macho mercenary who falls for runaway robotrix Jolie and is pursued by bounty hunting psycho Drago, overacting enthusiastically in the service of corporate villain Garfield, as they all search for legendery cyborg Palance, who is mostly seen as a pair of disembodied lips on TV sets. The corporate *noir* scenario and the macguffin of 'glass shadow' – a liquid explosive that can be injected into cyborgs to make them walking bombs who explode on orgasm – are quickly forgotten in favour of a standard escape scenario as Koteas and Jolie survive gladiatorial combat to head for freedom in Africa, where Koteas grows old tended by the eternally youthful robot girl. Schroeder at least tries for some visual sophistication to dress up the idiot plot; he also directed *Cyborg 3* (1994), with Zach Galligan, Richard Lynch and Malcolm McDowell.

d/co-s Michael Schroeder *p* Raju Patel, Alain Silver *co-s* Ron Yanover, Mark Geldman *c* Jamie Thompson *se* KNB *lp* Angeline Jolie, Elias Koteas, Jack Palance, Allen Garfield, Karen Shepherd, Billy Drago

Cyborg Cop (NU IMAGE) 97 min

Acceptable video nonsense from Firstenberg, director of *Ninja III: The Domination* (1984) and *Breakin' II: Electric Boogaloo* (1984). Less the expected **RoboCop** (1987) rip-off than an old-fashioned B movie, with impassive martial artist Bradley investigating the disappearance of his secret agent brother (Swart) on a scenic Caribbean island. Yorkshire-accented mastermind Rhys-Davies, in a performance that makes Brian Blessed look like Scott Tracy, has turned the missing man into a steel-skulled killer cyborg for use as an international assassin. Despite a few nice touches, like the sparks that fly whenever Bradley shoves a circular saw into a robot's head, this is strictly fodder. *Cyborg Cop 2* duly arrived in 1994.

d Sam Firstenberg *p* Danny Lerner *s* Greg Latter *c* Joseph Wein *se* Image Animation *lp* David Bradley, John Rhys-Davies, Alonna Shaw, Rufus Swart, Todd Jensen

Death Machine

(FUGITIVE FEATURES/ENTERTAINMENT/VICTOR; GB) 98 min

Though it aspires to seem influenced by Ridley Scott and James Cameron, with a monster which combines design elements of **Alien** (1979) and **The Terminator** (1984), *Death Machine* is more in the tradition of earlier second generation cyber-thrillers like **Hardware** (1990) and **Split Second** (1992).

In the future, the new CEO (Pouget) of the Chaank Corporation discovers that renegade mad scientist Dourif has unethically created a multi-purpose battlefield robot called the Warbeast, which he is not above using in personal power plays. The plot is simplicity itself as the Warbeast shreds its way through the cast at the Chaank Corporation.

The film lacks the brisk economy of its predecessors, spinning out its *Die Hard*-with-a-robot plot well beyond the 85

minutes it merits and failing to sustain suspense beyond a few odd spurts of action. By trying for expansive action rather than being content with the claustrophobia of *Hardware*, this stretches admirable effects and stunts a little too thinly. The occasional budgetary skimp undermines the impact: a potentially strong confrontation, out of **Blade Runner** (1982) and *Die Hard* (1988), atop the skyscraper during a heavy storm, loses its nerve-shredding factor through a lack of overhead shots to emphasize how high up the characters are and how precarious their dangling is. Also handicapping the film is a sappy fanboy attitude, epitomized by in-joke character names (Raimi, Dante, Scott, etc), which prevents involvement with characters who are merely compounded of gag references and traits that tend to be either bathetic (Pouget is especially afraid of the Warbeast because it reminds her of the kitchen disposal unit that killed her daughter) or running jokes.

d/s Stephen Norrington *p* Dominic Anciano *c* John de Borman *se* Lost in Space *lp* Ely Pouget, Brad Dourif, William Hootkins, John Sharian

Demolition Man (WARNER/SILVER) 115 min

Silver's commitment to explosions and wisecracking action heroes suggests he may well remain King of the No Brain Movie until the 21st century. That said, although his films never threaten to pack heavy intellectual firepower, a thread of wry, sly, self-parodic cleverness runs through his work. Accordingly while *Demolition Man* blows up enough things to keep the video generation off the fast-forward button, it also elaborates on the knowingness of *Die Hard* (1988) and *Road House* (1989). Moreover it manages to get away with the jokiness that doomed Silver's *Hudson Hawk* (1991) and the non-Silver *Last Action Hero* (1993) to megaturkey status. For the first time in a decade, a Stallone film edged past Arnie in the hipness stakes, pulling off a joke about President Schwarzenegger which pays back *Last Action Hero*'s alternate-world gag casting of Stallone in **Terminator 2** (1991). Stallone does a better job of being funny than in his conventional comedies (*Oscar*, 1991, *Stop! or My Mom Will Shoot*, 1992) but still gets to bungee-jump with a machine-gun into a blazing riot.

The plot is a variation on a theme that dates back to **Buck Rogers** (1939), but is merely an excuse to pit Sly against a lightly-caricatured pastel future. Cryo-imprisoned nineties steroid supercop John Spartan (Stallone) is revived in an idyllic but oppressive future to track down his old enemy, psychopath Simon Phoenix (Snipes). Stallone must save the city of San Angeles from old-style terrorism by applying equally old-fashioned heroic ultra-violence. Hardly a serious attempt at social prophecy, this is a rare effort to get away from the now-cliché urban hells of **Blade Runner** (1982) or **The Terminator** (1984) and come up with an open air mall, PC-dominated alternative vision of the future. The fight scenes are interspersed with genuinely clever jokes about action movies and California triviality: a Golden Oldies station replays 1990s ad jingles, irritatingly omnipresent swear boxes chide 20th-century barbarians for their non-PC/non-PG language, the brainwashing rehabilitation process unlooses Stallone from cryo-sleep as an expert knitter and Leary's rebel leader advocates meat-eating and chain-smoking.

If the action is not quite as well handled by debuting pop video man Brambilla as it might be if James Cameron or John McTiernan were holding the megaphone, it still delivers enough carnage and property damage to pass as a multiplex picture. But it's the skewed, imaginative, sick comedy worldview – courtesy of *Hudson Hawk* scripter Waters – that gives it distinction.

d Mario Brambilla *p* Joel Silver, Michael Levy, Howad Kazanjian *s* Daniel Waters, Robert Reneau, Peter M. Lenkov *c* Alex Thomson *se* Michael J. McAlister, Kimberley K. Nelson, Christopher S. Watts, Mary E. Walter, Courtney M. Campbell *lp* Sylvester Stallone, Wesley Snipes, Sandra Bullock, Nigel Hawthorne, Benjamin Bratt, Bob Gunton, Glenn Shadix, Denis Leary, Grand L. Bush

Diki Vostok *aka* The Wild East

(STUDIO KINO; KAZAKHSTAN) 100 (97) min
Like the American outings **World Gone Wild** (1987) and **New Eden** (1994), this Russian action film is a minimally Science Fictional retread of *The Magnificent Seven* (1961) with outlaw bikers persecuting a settlement of 'solar children' at a time 'long, long ago in the late 20th century' and macho mercenaries headed up by a slicker-clad hero named 'the Wanderer' defending them.

Aside from remotely Dovzhenko-ish hymns to hard-working agricultural collectives (a dying heroine tells her survivors to 'buy some grain and a tractor'), this is exactly like the rash of desert-set wasteland warrior movies that flooded the world in the wake of **Mad Max** (1979). In the final confrontation, the Wanderer's nemesis dresses as a scythe-wielding Death and Nugmanov indulges in rock video mannerisms like dipping water and slo-mo slashes. Most of the build-up consists of stunt men being knocked off bikes or vehicles being blown up. Slavish in its aping of Western models, the film is full of characters who dress up as cowboys or Nazis and almost gets round to saying that this is not a mature or useful thing to do.

d/co-p/s Rashid Nugmanov *co-p/c* Mourat Nougmanov *lp* Zhanna Isina, Konstantin Fyodorov, Gennadi Shatunov, Alexander Aksyonov, Konstantin Shamshurin

Equinox

(SC ENTERTAINMENT INTERNATIONAL) scope 110 min
An urban fantasy in the vein of Rudolph's similarly-bewildering **Trouble in Mind** (1985), this is set in Empire City, an American community (played by Minneapolis) that exists either in the near future or an alternative present, where magic and romance co-exist with seediness and *noir* despair. A nurse (Ferrell) pieces together the story of twins (both Modine) separated at birth, a sleek hoodlum and a meek garage man. Born of an impossibly romantic liaison between a European aristocrat and a ballet dancer, the twins revolve around each other in a bizarre tangle that is resolved in a strange restaurant shoot-out and a trip to the Grand Canyon for an astonishing final image.

As usual with Rudolph, the precise meaning is obscure, but the supporting cast and the incidental detail are amazing: Ward as a crime czar who watches a non-stop porno channel with a stock market crawl, Walsh as an ex-vaudevillian garage owner, Tomei as a brassy doomed hooker, Singer as an obsessive lottery contestant and Boyle as the nice Modine's shrinking girlfriend. Thought for the Day: 'Duck is my favourite chicken except for turkey.'

d/s Alan Rudolph *p* David Blocker *c* Elliot Davis *se* Randall Balsmeyer *lp* Matthew Modine, Lara Flynn Boyle, Fred Ward, Tyra Ferrell, Marisa Tomei, Kevin J. O'Connor, Tate Donovan, Lori Singer, M. Emmett Walsh, Gailard Sartain

Fire in the Sky

(PAR) scope 109 min
Though it carries the heart-sinking 'based on a true story' preface, this is a surprisingly strong UFO drama, at once the story of a close encounter of the ghastly kind and a portrait of a rural community turning upon its outcasts. In 1975, a bunch of check-shirted working-men drive back from a hard day's logging in depressed middle America. When a spaceship-type apparition looms overhead, one man (Sweeney) gets out of the pick-up to investigate and the others chicken-heartedly leave him behind as a light grapple descends to abduct him. With Sweeney missing, Sheriff Garner wants to pin a murder rap on his workmates, forcing the men to go back on their decision to keep the experience quiet.

The film could quite interestingly play out this story with no further aliens necessary as Sweeney's best friend (Patrick) falls apart from his own guilt and the town's suspicion. Sweeney reappears in a dazed and battered condition and remembers his painful experiences. As with all the 'alien' scenes, his version of events is bracketed by a flashback to leave the question of belief open to the audience, but the suffering he undergoes in the belly of the saucer one-ups anything in **Close Encounters of the Third Kind** (1977) or **Communion** (1990). In a nightmare sequence with the intensity of *The Texas Chain Saw Massacre* (1973), ambiguously malevolent aliens torture or examine the helpless human in a grimy, oozing zero-gee laboratory, employing an especially unpleasant optical probe. No answers are given, with Garner remaining a sceptic at the fade-out, allowing the film's real strength to emerge in its depiction of the uneasy, unidealized woodsmen as they stick together or fall apart. With clever casting of Science Fiction icons Patrick (**Terminator 2**, 1991) and Thomas (**E.T.**, 1982), this has eyes on the stars but boasts an authentically tangled human story as Sweeney, who suffers the worst, gets his life together while Patrick, living with the guilt of leaving his friend, winds up as a hermit in a shack.

d Robert Lieberman *p* Joe Wizan, Todd Black *s* Tracy Tormé *c* Bill Pope *se* ILM *lp* D.B. Sweeney, Robert Patrick, Craig Sheffer, James Garner, Henry Thomas, Peter Berg, Kathleen Wilhoite, Bradley Gregg, Noble Willingham

Freaked

(FOX) 79 min
Pitched somewhere between a John Waters film and *Wayne's World* (1992), this has a certain *Film Threat* attitude, undermining its supposed subtext and character arcs just as much as everything else, cramming in joke after joke in a largely successful attempt at being impolite. An obnoxious TV star (Winter), employed as a corporate spokesman by the Everything But Shoes Company, is turned into a half-gargoyle monster by redneck carny showman-cum-Dr Moreau Quaid, who uses toxic gloop provided by EBS CEO Sadler to create a menagerie of bizarre creatures. Some of the make-up monsters are deliberately cheesy (Mr T as a bearded lady), but others are quite elaborate (evoking the cartoon grotesques of Basil Wolverton).

The eclectic casting suggests that Winter and Stern have called in a lot of favours to get this personal picture made. An unbilled Reeves, Winter's partner in the *Bill & Ted* films, plays a Dog Boy who seems to be a skit on the Bela Lugosi role from **Island of Lost Souls** (1932), while a glamorous pinhead clearly evokes *Freaks* (1933). Among the clever ideas are a live mouse used as a computer accessory, the heroic death of Mr Sockhead (a human hand puppet voiced by Bobcat Goldthwait), a pair of gun-toting rastafarian eyeballs ('I and I') and a parody of *Friday the 13th* (1979) as Quaid-cum-Shields revives several times from apparent death to attack again. On the downside, there are too many fart gags. Mostly forgivable.

d/co-s Alex Winter, Tom Stern *p* Harry J. Ulfland, Mary Jane Ulfland *co-s* Tim Burns *c* Jamie Thompson *se* Tony Gardner, Steve Johnson, Screaming Mad George *lp* Alex Winter, Randy Quaid, Megan Ward, William Sadler, Brooke Shields, Mr T, Keanu Reeves

I forecast happiness: Bill Murray in the superb Groundhog Day.

Groundhog Day

(COL) scope 101 min

This encouragingly successful comedy, which oscillates between the moods of *It's a Wonderful Life* (1946) and *The Twilight Zone*, is an interesting test case for definitions of Science Fiction. Cynical weatherman Murray, assigned against his will to cover a groundhog ceremony in Punxatawney, Pennsylvania, finds himself trapped in a cycle of repetition, endlessly reliving one single day in a town he hates.

'What if there is no tomorrow,' Murray laments, 'there wasn't one today.' With an irritating burst of Sonny and Cher's 'I Got You, Babe' that comes to take on a cosmic malevolence as the clock radio ticks over to 6.00 AM, Murray is constantly hauled back to start over again, progressing through puzzlement, delight, despair, rapture and melancholy as he reshuffles trivial incidents, lives as if there were no consequences, commits perfect crimes, survives suicides, learns skills, saves lives, seduces women, comes to feel like a God, and experiences repeated failure as his cunning attempts to charm his producer (MacDowell) into bed always pay off with a slap in the face.

Aside from a single dud scene with Murray in fancy dress as a spaghetti Western cowboy, this is miraculously flawless, intellectually and emotionally daring as it deals with an idea of Resnais-like complexity within the invisible conventions of Hollywood romantic comedy. Murray, apparently building on the interesting failure of *Scrooged* (1988), is remarkably subtle as the unhappy wiseacre who progresses through irresponsibility and frustration to become a better person. As Murray comes to a perfect knowledge of the limited slice of time given him, he is allowed to explore his own personality, making this a rare mainstream analysis of the need to outgrow solipsism. It is also notable that the film never falls into the syrupiness that flaws *Sleepless in Seattle* (1993), with Ramis and Murray always leavening the heart interest with tart, deflating jokes that are at once funny and grow out of the characters rather than seeming imposed on them.

No scientific or magical explanation is offered and the resolution, in which Murray escapes from his time bubble only when he finally lives the day perfectly, can be interpreted as a divine reward for his Scrooge-like conversion or a random passing of an arbitrary time-space continuum anomaly. Given the refusal to get involved with the mechanics of its fantastical premise, the film's concentration on character and redemption are squarely within the fable-like conventions of classic fantasy, but it works out the implications of its set-up with an admirable rigour that sets it beside the most logical idea-based Science Fiction. A precedent within genre is the 1990 short *12:01*, based on a Richard Lupoff short story, which was expanded into a 1993 television movie that was perhaps unfairly labelled a rip-off of **Groundhog Day**, while the theme was unworkably mauled over into a non-fantastic Dana Carvey vehicle *Clean Slate* (1994).

d/co-p/co-s Harold Ramis *co-p* Trevor Albert *co-s* Danny Rubin *c* John Bailey *se* Tom Ryba *lp* Bill Murray, Andie MacDowell, Chris Elliott, Stephen Toblowsky, Brian Doyle-Murray, Rick Ducommun

The Hidden II

(NEW LINE) 91 min

Less a sequel than a mop-up operation, this opens with a full quarter-of-an-hour of footage from the climax of **The Hidden** (1988), which notably contains more action than the entire new footage. Fifteen years later, the body-hopping alien villain of the first film is rampaging through low-rent locations, causing trouble at underlit raves in Los Angeles, and a fresh alien cop (Sbarge) teams up with Hodge, the daughter of the combined heroes of the first film, to track and destroy the nasty. Hodge introduces Sbarge to human pleasures like brushing teeth and having sex, and he explains that the chief difference between his world and Earth is that they don't have Chinese food. This is yet another video-driven attempt to turn a modest hit into a franchise.

d/s Seth Pinsker *p* Michael Meltzer, David Helpern *c* Bryan England *se* Todd Masters *lp* Raphael Sbarge, Kate Hodge, Jovin Montanaro, Christopher Murphy, Michael Weldon, Michael A. Nickles

Invisible: The Chronicles of Benjamin Knight

(FULL MOON ENTERTAINMENT) 80 min

Though not identified as such by the title or packaging, this is a sequel to **Mandroid** (1993), shot back-to-back with the earlier quickie and picking up characters and plot threads where they were dropped with a serial-like rigour rare in the era of remakes disguised as sequels. Shot in Romania like the *Subspecies* series or the later *Trancers* sequels, this Charles Band movie can't afford much in the way of spectacular effects for its invisible hero (Dellafemina), who went see-through in a *Mandroid* sub-plot, and has surprisingly little to do in his own movie. The skimping is compensated for by including a giant robot, a scarred master fiend, an asylum-full of depraved loonies and a finale in which belly-dancing genius heroine Nash sword-fights to the death with mad scientist villain Lowens.

d Jack Ersgard *p* Vlad Paunescu, Oana Paunescu *s* Earl Kenton *c* Christiano Pogany *se* Alchemy FX *lp* Brian Cousins, Jennifer Nash, Michael Dellafemina, Curt Lowens, David Kaufman, Alan Oppenheimer

Jurassic Park

(AMBLIN/U) 127 min

The narrative motor of *Jurassic Park* is the overlap of irreconcilable agendas: the creation and collapse of its eponymous theme park requires input from caring paleontologists, Frankensteinian genetic engineers, chaos doomsayers, 'blood-sucking lawyers', wide-eyed children, ferocious predators and a fatherly multi-millionaire. Similar conflicts and contrasting motives power the conversion of Crichton's best-selling novel into a Spielberg 'event' movie and make this blockbuster at once an all-but-infallible entertainment and a demonstration of the theory, espoused by Goldblum's character, that things go wrong exponentially.

After a decade of literary adaptations, *Indiana Jones* sequels and oddments like *Always* (1990), Spielberg needed to re-establish himself as a commercial and creative giant, setting up the one-two move that climaxed with the Oscar knock-out of *Schindler's List* (1994). Given this circumstance, *Jurassic Park* is almost identikit 'Spielberg': the paring-down of a monster bestseller into a suspense machine (*Jaws*, 1975); the mix of a popular science-childhood sense of wonder perennial with state-of-the-art effects to reimagine the familiars of 1950s B Science Fiction (**Close Encounters of the Third Kind**, 1977); the jungle adventure littered with incredible perils, gruesome deaths and indomitable heroes (*Raiders of the Lost Ark*, 1981); and big-eyed creatures who range from toothily murderous to beatifically benevolent (**E.T.**, 1983, *Gremlins*, 1984). Add to this a John Williams score, glowing epiphanies (Dern as much as the children is called upon to gape in tearful amazement), textbook suspense (a character clinging to a dead electric fence as someone unknowingly switches on the power), one all-too-true key speech ('you can't think this through, there are some things you have to feel'), and slapstick sadism involving caricatures nobody cares about (the gross spy is blinded and gutted, the pockmarked lawyer is plucked from the toilet) and you have the Spielberg blockbuster.

However, the input of Crichton (a novelist who is himself a director and who laid down the basics of this plot with his first feature, **Westworld**, 1973), is also vital. As in all of Crichton's works, in print or on film, technological achievements are ultimately dangerous because human motives and skills are incapable of keeping pace with pure scientific advances. Ian Malcolm, played with a scene-stealing glee by Goldblum so the expository lumps go down painlessly, is Crichton's signature character: a scientist who actually has a theory about why nothing ever goes right. Like James Cameron (who was also influenced by *Westworld*), Crichton has a technophobic vision that can only be brought to the screen by triumphs of technology no

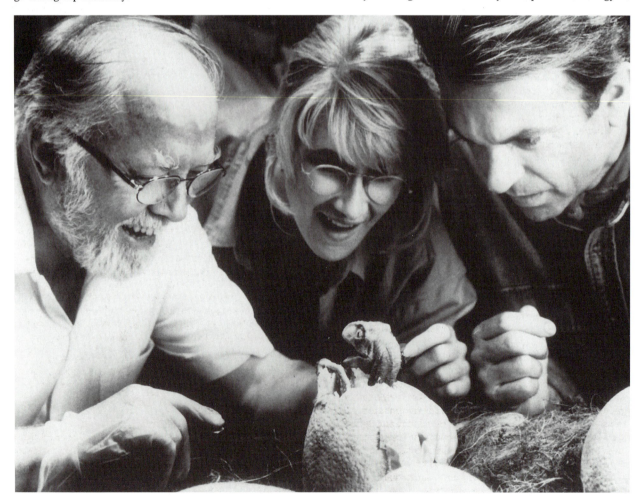

It's a velociraptor – (left to right) Richard Attenborough, Laura Dern and Sam Neill look forward to the past in Jurassic Park.

less astonishing than genetically recreating dinosaurs or constructing androids in the image of Yul Brynner. *Jurassic Park* was seen by millions for its effects alone, and the combination of CGI, puppetwork and animation goes beyond the previous high water marks of Willis H. O'Brien's *King Kong* (1932) or Ray Harryhausen's *Valley of Gwangi* (1969). However, just as a group of diverse experts under the direction of a showman are responsible for the genengineering (rather than the Frankenstein figures of fifties Science Fiction or Roger Corman's cash-in, **Carnosaur**, 1993), lone visionaries like O'Brien and Harryhausen have been replaced by teams of multi-skilled employees whose collective achievement lacks the individual heart of Kong. A further irony is that *Jurassic Park* makes extensive use of the robotics and image-engineering processes Crichton himself predicted (and saw disastrous consequences for) in *Westworld*, **Looker** (1981) and *Rising Sun* (1993).

The most significant change between Crichton's novel and Spielberg's film is the transformation of John Hammond from an unsympathetic capitalist into a cuddly cod Scots visionary played by Attenborough (irresistibly recalling Dr Dolittle). The novel is an Awful Warning with a *gosh-wow-dinosaurs!* undercurrent, but the film is quite properly in love with its beasties as a narrative necessity and as a prelude to the inclusion of a *Jurassic Park* ride on the Universal Studio Tour. In tune with Spielberg's mind-numbingly ignorant proclamation 'this is not Science Fiction, it's Science Eventuality', the film presents its prehistoric animals seriously, employing advisors to ensure that the dinosaurs act more like real dinosaurs than the *Jaws* shark did a real Great White. Neill's explanatory lectures about the way saurians probably had more in common with birds than reptiles smugly underline the film's authenticity. Even the saur-hating hunter Peck, as he is about to be devoured, breathes 'clever girl' (all the monsters are female) in appreciation of the hunter's trick the velociraptors have used to trap him. Just as *Close Encounters* crossbred 'true life' UFO stories with fifties Jack Arnold, this is informed by dino-buff Spielberg's genre heritage: images and lines deliberately recall *King Kong*, Ray Bradbury's 'The Foghorn' (filmed as **The Beast From 20,000 Fathoms**, 1953), *Dinosaurus!* (1960) and **When Dinosaurs Ruled the Earth** (1969). No matter how smarmy and syrupy kid-hating Neill's transformation into a fantasy father might be, it's hard to resist such primal moments as his calling to a herd of brachiosaurs with a Bradbury-ish honk only to be answered by a charming animal who takes the sugar off the scene by sneezing quantities of slime over a little girl.

Many annoying things about the film constitute survival traits in an international marketplace that would like a new monster to depose *E.T.* in the quarter-of-a-billion dollars club. The softening of the novel so only secondary characters are killed, the switch from nightmare horror to clean chase, the down-playing of any critique of entertainment capitalism and pointless science (Crichton's Hammond has a lengthy speech about why it makes more economic sense to recreate dinosaurs than cure cancer), the welcome inclusion of Dern in shorts and the abandonment of internal script logic in favour of a storyline which demonstrates its own chaos theory compromise the film as drama but widen its appeal. The surprise, as usual, is that painstaking effects co-exist with extraordinary clumsiness: in adapting the novel, many sub-plots are pruned but extremely awkward factors (the ability of dinosaurs spontaneously to change sex and thus breed beyond their controlled populations) are confusingly retained though they serve no narrative function. Like Jurassic Park, *Jurassic Park* is ultimately unable safely to contain its attractions, but the dinosaurs are still magnificent: the tyrannosaurus attack during a night storm, a fleeing herd of gallimimuses, the gremlin-like collared dilophosaurus cautiously killing its prey and the game of velociraptor hide-and-seek must stand as definitive. However, the most deeply-felt and emotionally complex shot of the film – a pan from a rack of now-unsaleable cutesy dinosaur merchandise to the dejected Hammond – raises issues the media monolith that is a nineties big studio blockbuster could never address.

Ally Sheedy in Man's Best Friend.

d Steven Spielberg *p* Kathleen Kennedy, Gerald R. Molen *s* Michael Crichton, David Koepp *c* Dean Cundey *se* ILM *lp* Sam Neill, Laura Dern, Richard Attenborough, Jeff Goldblum, Bob Peck, Martin Ferrero, B.D. Wong, Samuel L. Jackson, Wayne Knight

Knights

(MOONSTONE ENTERTAINMENT) 89 min

This is another Science Fiction action quickie from the inexhaustible Pyun (**Cyborg**, 1989, **Captain America**, 1990, **Arcade**, 1991, **Nemesis**, 1992, **Hong Kong '97**, 1994) set in a red-filtered Monument Valley passing itself off as a quasi-medieval future where vampire cyborg Henriksen, one of the best value-for-money villains in low budget features, ravages the land with his cadre of evil henchmen.

Long, a surfer chick in tight red shorts, apprentices with grizzled and frequently disassembled good guy robot Kristofferson, to learn how to jump up in the air and kick in the heads of evil cyborgs. Because financing ran out before a suitably apocalyptic climax could be filmed, *Knights* avoids the big battle it seems to be building towards and concludes with Long continuing on her quest as a narration promises further adventures. Dialogue is all on the level of 'You are destined for great things. Within your heart, all dreams are possible.'

d/s Albert Pyun *p* Tom Karnovski *c* George Mooradian *se* David Barton *lp* Kris Kristofferson, Kathy Long, Lance Henriksen, Scott Paulin, Gary Daniels, Tim Thomerson

Man's Best Friend

(NEW LINE/ROVEN-CAVELLO) 87 min

TV reporter Sheedy breaks into a vivisection lab to investigate the scientific torturing of animals and liberates Max, a super-intelligent guard dog who has been gene-spliced by mad scientist Henriksen. Grateful when the dog sees off a mugger (by ripping out his throat), Sheedy takes him home to her understandably dog-hating boyfriend. While Henriksen shouts at the cops that the dog has to be found before he has 'a psychotic episode', Sheedy tries to make the mutt inconspicuous in suburbia. Things go awry as Max starts swallowing cats whole, date-raping next door's collie (with 'Puppy Love' on the soundtrack) and sabotaging cars. Emerging from an encounter with an oxyacetylene torch as a scarred freak, Max is compelled by feelings of rejection to go for Sheedy.

Thanks to ludicrous plotting, Max is given super-powers as the mechanical script pits him against a dog's traditional enemies: cats, mailmen, dog-catchers, a junkyard owner. The film veers between *Beethoven* (1992) sentiment and dumb-ass comedy ('What about my dog?' Henriksen asks the cops, 'have you got any leads?'), then throws in insane Science Fiction (because he has chameleon DNA, Max can become invisible!) and unpleasant gore (Max pisses acid in people's faces). In a final confrontation back at the lab, Sheedy's new dog saves the day through its habit of fiddling with plugs, but a last moment twist (lifted from *Turner and Hooch*, 1990) brings a litter of potential sequels into the world.

d/s John Lafia *p* Bob Engelman *c* Mak Irwin *se* Frank Ceglia *lp* Ally Sheedy, Lance Henriksen, Robert Costanzo, John Cassini, Fredric Lehne

Mandroid

(FULL MOON ENTERTAINMENT) 81 min
'Gentlemen, meet the Mandroid unit. Powerful, indestructible. With only one purpose: to help us in the laboratory.' Charles Band's indebtedness to Marvel Comics is well to the fore in this shot-in-Romania quickie, which introduces characters whose powers and plights are pretty obviously based on Iron Man, Dr Doom and Invisible Girl. A cluttered plot introduces a batch of characters who recur in **Invisible: The Chronicles of Benjamin Knight** (1993), as a succession of lab accidents turn clean-cut scientist Cousins into a cripple who links with a remote-control robot warrior who can fight his battles for him, mad scientist Lowens into a scarred fiend who wears a metal mask ('My nerve endings are destroyed, I feel nothing') and sidekick Dellafemina into a periodic invisible man. The busy but underpopulated plot offers competent no-name actors reading word balloons and endless gun battles while the Mandroid, which looks like a prop left over from **The Black Hole** (1979), lumbers around ruins seeing off Lowens's stuntmen legions.

d Jack Ersgard *co-p/c* Vlad Paunescu *co-p* Oana Paunescu *s* Earl Kenton, Jackson Barr *se* Alchemy FX, Michael B. Deak *lp* Brian Cousins, Jane Caldwell, Michael Dellafemina, Curt Lowens, Patrick Ersgard, Costel Constantin

The Meteor Man

(MGM/TINSEL TOWNSEND) 100 min
An overly gentle black-themed superhero parody. Director-star Townsend plays a meek inner-city teacher exposed to a glowing meteor which gives him Superman-like powers, though his fear of heights means he never flies more than a few feet above ground level.

Persuaded by the neighbourhood watch committee to use his super powers in the service of an anti-crime campaign that pits him against the local gangs, he is confronted by various toughs who are not as hard or realistic as they would be in a grown-up film, enabling him to pull a happy ending out of his cape. With black stars in cameos (Jones, Guillaume, Cosby) and a genial air, this is likeable and watchable but never really takes flight, coming across like a *Cosby Show* version of the sort of comedies Fred MacMurray used to make for Disney which were aptly characterized in *Matinee* (1992) as 'flying rubber professor movies'.

d/s Robert Townsend *p* Loretha C. Jones *c* John A. Alonzo *se* ILM *lp* Robert Townsend, Marla Gibbs, Eddie Griffin, Robert Guillaume, James Earl Jones, Bill Cosby, Frank Gorshin, Sinbad, Luther Vandross

Robert Townsend is The Meteor Man.

Monolith

(EGM) 96 min
Another imitation of **The Hidden** (1987), made by the team responsible for **Project: Shadowchaser** (1992). Buddy cops Frost and Paxton track a body-hopping alien parasite on the cheap streets of LA, drawn into the case when a distrait female Russian scientist tries to murder a child who is the current host of the creature. Hurt provides ham as a whispery government agent whose cadre of besuited hit men cause the heroes more trouble than the pyrokinetic monster, evoking the now-traditional cover-up conspiracy angle associated with stranded aliens. The film has an explosion every few minutes but never comes up with a fresh plot twist, and the leads' wisecracking relationship is more like bickering than banter.

d John Eyres *p* Geoff Griffiths *s* Stephen Lister *c* Alan M. Trou *se* Nick Davis *lp* Bill Paxton, Lindsay Frost, Louis Gossett Jr, John Hurt

Philadelphia Experiment II

(TRIMARK) 98 min
A belated sequel to the 1984 movie, with Johnson taking over from Michael Parée as the WWII sailor time-warped to the future by a US Navy experiment. Chilly scientist Graham resumes the Philadelphia experiment in the hope of rendering US aircraft radar-invisible, but succeeds only in sending a

stealth bomber, complete with nuclear weapons, back to Nazi Germany, where his own father (also Graham) uses it to win the War, creating a parallel timeline. Johnson is sucked into the alternate America and falls in with the rebels, battling an alternate Graham's fascist minions and travelling back in time to help cancel out this continuum. It is blessed with a quite complex bit of time-twisting, though the personal story is over-reliant on golden-suffused visions of little league baseball that are supposed to represent the best of the America wiped out by a Nazi victory. Graham is showy in three roles, notably as the cowboy-hatted and sneering *gauleiter* of fascist America, and the art directors do an effective job of imagining the architecture and lifestyle of a Nazified USA, complete with shuffling slave workers out of **Metropolis** (1926) and insistent propaganda slogans.

The Hitler Victorious theme is very common in literature (Sarban's *The Sound of His Horn*, Philip Dick's *The Man in the High Castle*, Len Deighton's *SS/GB*) but has been underused in film, yielding only *It Happened Here* (1966) and the TV productions *An Englishman's Castle* (1978) and *Fatherland* (1994).

d Stephen Cornwell *p* Mark Levinson, Doug Curtis *s* Kevin Rock, Nick Paine *c* Ronn Schmidt *se* Frank Ceglia *lp* Brad Johnson, Gerritt Graham, Marjean Holden, James Greene, Geoffrey Blake, Cyril O'Reilly

Prehysteria

(MOONBEAM ENTERTAINMENT) 86 min

The first production of a new unit set up by Charles Band to produce 'family' fantasy films. In a plot premise intended to capitalize on **Jurassic Park** (1993) but actually closer in feel to Roger Corman's *Munchies* (1987), sleazy Lee discovers sacred dinosaur eggs in a South American temple and they accidentally come into the possession of widowed niceguy paleontologist Cullen. The eggs hatch into adequate if cute effects creatures which are adopted by Cullen's kids: O'Brien names the tyrannosaur Elvis because 'rex means "king"' while a Woody Woodpecker-ish pterodactyl baby is named Madonna. Lee and some Disney-ish thugs try to kidnap the creatures so they can be commercially exploited by sending them to Hollywood or putting them in the zoo but the blandly suburban heroes (who co-opt a replacement Mom) turn them into the wild. Successful enough on video to merit a sequel, *Prehysteria 2* (1995). Moonbeam's most notable follow-up, which is thematically similar, is the fantasy *Dragonworld* (1994).

co-d/p Charles Band *co-p* Albert Band *s* Greg Suddeth, Mark Goldstein *c* Adolfo Bartoli *se* David Allen Productions *lp* Brett Cullen, Colleen Morris, Samantha Mills, Austin O'Brien, Tony Longo, Stephen Lee, Stuart Fratkin

Scanner Cop

(IMAGE) 94 min

'Try not to dream too loud.' Producer David exploited David Cronenberg's **Scanners** (1980) by producing a couple of back-to-back Canadian sequels *Scanners II: The New Order* (1991) and *Scanners III: The Takeover* (1992), which conform to the template of the original and seem structured around exploding heads. Relocating to Los Angeles, this is an attempt to change the direction of the franchise, with David taking over as director and expunging the last tinges of Cronenberg's visionary conspiracy in favour of a straightforward plot. Weak-chinned Quinn stars as a rookie cop with telepathic powers who takes on Lynch, a scarred mad brain surgeon who is using a *Manchurian Candidate* (1961) process to turn decent citizens into cop killers. It zips along pleasantly to its head-bursting climax, with some interesting dream sequences as the brainwashed killers see cops as monsters, but suffers from a feeble supporting cast and a perfunctory script. Only Lynch has any fun at all, but a lone madman assisted only by an evilly glam tarot reader is hardly a fearsome enough opponent for the super-powered hero.

d/p Pierre David *s* John Bryant, George Saunders *c* Jacques Haitkin *se* John Carl Buechler, MMI *lp* Daniel Quinn, Darlanne Fluegel, Richard Lynch, Mark Rolston, Hilary Shepard, Brion James

Shopping

(IMPACT/CHANNEL 4/POLYGRAM KUZUI) 107 min

After a sentence for joy-riding, teenage outlaw Billy (Law) is picked up from jail by his Irish girlfriend (Frost), who has stolen the car she comes to meet him in. On the way back to their urban wasteland home, the couple, looking more like slumming models than homeless desperadoes, rip off a BMW and play high-speed touch-tag with police cars. Law, whose need for speed has replaced his sex drive, is almost an artist, crashing a car into a superstore just to steal a kettle, which makes him a threat to mini-tycoon Pertwee, who is organizing the local youth into an army of systematic looters.

Though the subject is torn, as they say, from the headlines and the tie-in album is a canny assembly of 1993 sounds (Law's darkest secret is ownership of a Spandau Ballet tape), this resorts to Science Fiction as a mythologizing cop-out. The story is rooted not in the real-life depressed inner cities that have produced the nihilist joy-riding culture but in the familiar nebulous near future backdrop of *The Warriors* (1979) or **Streets of Fire** (1984) where urchins stand around dustbin bonfires and a decayed music hall has turned into a video game warren. *Shopping* is flawed by budgetary stinginess: the burning of a Porsche has to be conveyed by a shot of a steering wheel on fire and the climax is truncated *before* Law can ram a fortified mall, cheating the audience out of the destruction Jackie Chan or Arnold Schwarzenegger would guarantee. Anderson scored enough with this debut to land the job of filming a video game in *Mortal Kombat* (1995).

d/s Paul Anderson *p* Jeremy Bolt *c* Tony Imi *se* Vendetta FX *lp* Jude Law, Sadie Frost, Sean Pertwee, Fraser James, Sean Bean, Marianne Faithfull, Jonathan Pryce

Skeeter

(NEW LINE/AUGUST/TEAM PLAYERS/KAR) 95 min

'I've grown real tired of your save-the-world philosophy, you burned-out old pinhead.' Buzzing in shortly after **Ticks** (1993), this is another nineties rip-off of the seventies movies that tried to recapture the feel of fifties big bug films but with pollution replacing radiation as the reason for the rampage of killer insects.

Because property developer Robinson has been unethical with his toxic waste, ridiculous toy mosquitoes, which are rubbery but go squish when swatted, attack redneck locals. Napier is the crooked Sheriff and Pollard overacts as usual as a loon who enjoys being bitten, but the acting weight falls on the inadequate shoulders of Melanie Griffith's redheaded sister Tracy, who does a lot of running around. Very cheap and not very exciting.

d/co-s Clark Brandon *co-p* James Glenn Dudelson, Kelly Andrea Rubin *co-p/c* John Lambert *co-s* Lanny Horn *se* Frank H. Isaacs *lp* Tracy Griffith, Charles Napier, Michael J. Pollard, Jay Robinson, William Sanderson, Eloy Casados, John Putch

Super Mario Bros.

(LIGHTMOTIVE/ALLIED FILMMAKERS/CINERGI) scope 104 min

The first film adapted from rather than into a Nintendo cartridge, *Super Mario Bros.* is shrill, hectic and tiresome, with little story, less excitement and, as it turned out, no audience.

Millions of years ago, a meteor caused time to fissure around Manhattan, resulting in a cramped parallel universe where, as in Brian Aldiss's novel *The Malacia Tapestry*, humanity has evolved from dinosaurs rather than apes. Lizard King Koopa (Hopper) kidnaps fugitive Princess Daisy (Mathis), who has been raised from an egg by nuns in our world. She has just caught the attention of Luigi Mario (Leguiziamo), younger

With nary a pause to identify the heroes (distinguishable only by colour-coded bandanas and personalized weaponry), this whisks heroine Turco off to medieval Japan via a sacred carriage lamp and then despatches the reptile quartet to rescue her from the plot of a sub-Kurosawa *Shogun* replay as feudal Lord Shimono conspires with English pirate Wilson to make life miserable for the peasantry. The plot consists of one damn thing after another as modern characters mix it with samurai sword-swingers and razor-edged martial arts weapons are whipped around without ever cutting anyone open. The throwaway wit of the premise has been scraped off and replaced by embarrassing moral homilies and the standard of writing and direction declined to a level that suggests despairing realization that no matter how bad a *Turtles* film might be, it still has a fanatically eager captive audience.

d/s Stuart Gillard *p* Thomas K. Gray, Kim Dawson, David Chan *c* David Gurfinkel *se* Perpetual Motion Pictures, All Effects Company *lp* Elias Koteas, Paige Turco, Stuart Wilson, Shab Shimono, Vivian Wu, Mark Caso, Matt Hill, Jim Raposa, David Fraser

Ticks

(FIRST LOOK PICTURES) 85 min
An old-fashioned Big Bug horror conceived in the seventies by effects man Beswick, this borrows elements from the eighties slasher cycle, specifically *The Campsite Massacre* (1981), as a group of troubled inner-city teens go on a wilderness weekend to be attacked by oversized blood-sucking insects.

What is more interesting is the starting point of the film, marijuana farmers spraying 'plant steroid' on the undergrowth. This lends the acceptably exciting movie a reactionary undercurrent. In the seventies marijuana producers would have been the good guys and the insects would have been blamed on big business. The insect effects are reasonably convincing, and there's a lively forest fire finale with the survivors besieged in a shack by the horrors and menaced by extreme hippie villains, while an added frill (borrowed, admittedly, from **The Nest**, 1988) has a character metamorphose into a scaly part-insect creature. Screamy Dolenz exercises her lungs as the preppy heroine.

d Tony Randel *p* Brian Yuzna *s* Brent V. Friedman *c* Steve Grass *se* Doug Beswick *lp* Rosalind Allen, Ami Dolenz, Seth Green, Virginia Keehne, Ray Oriel, Peter Scolari, Clint Howard

Timerunner

(CINEMAX; CAN) 88 min
A convoluted action movie, this aims for **The Terminator** (1984) but falls nearer British teleseries *Blake's 7*. Future space jockey Hamill, still trading on his Luke Skywalker image, is zapped to the present during an alien invasion only to find advance scouts of the extra-terrestrial nasties have already infiltrated the US government. With turncoat spacelady Chong, Hamill flees from a bleached blond assassin and tries to protect his pregnant mother from killers so he can be safely born and save the world. Given that presidential candidate James is named John Neila (spell it backwards), it takes a surprisingly long time for supposed genius Hamill to spot him as the villain. With six credited writers and plot holes you could teleport a space shuttle through, this is lively but dull.

d/co-s Michael Mazo *co-p* Lloyd A. Simandl *co-p/co-s* John Curtis *co-s* Chris Hyde, Greg Derochie, Ron Tarrant, Ian Bray *c* Danny Nowak *se* John Gajdecki *lp* Mark Hamill, Brion James, Rae Dawn Chong, Marc Bauer, Gordon Tipple, Allen Forget

U.F.O.

(POLYGRAM/GEORGE FORSTER; GB) 79 min
Northern comedian Roy 'Chubby' Brown is kidnapped by a flying saucer and convicted of crimes against womankind by

A video game is a video game not a film:
Super Mario Bros.

brother and business partner of mustachioed Mario Mario (Hoskins), and the dedicated plumbers set out to rescue her. Hauled into the parallel world along with a shard of meteor that powers the plot, the Brothers blunder around theme park rides trying to save the girl. The few good lines are snatched by Hopper, who (partnered by the supposedly lizardy but notably mammalian Shaw) handles the villainy as if there were a real film to back him up rather than a melange of fungus-strewn, leftover **Batman** (1989) sets populated by ridiculous special effects and shouting humans. Occasionally, an effect (a pet-size dinosaur, transformations, disintegrations) raises interest, but there is never any sense that this is more than a technical showreel interspersed with Three Stooges cast-off routines. Produced by Eberts and Joffé, usually so smug about their commitment to Serious Quality Subjects, this is a grotesque imitation of a nineties blockbuster. It was followed into the malls by more game-derived films, *Street Fighter* (1995), *Double Dragon* (1995) and *Mortal Kombat*(1995).

d Rocky Morton, Annabel Jankel *p* Jake Eberts, Roland Joffé *s* Parker Bennett, Terry Runté, Ed Solomon *c* Dean Semler *se* Christopher Francis Woods, Patrick Tatopoulos *lp* Bob Hoskins, John Leguiziamo, Dennis Hopper, Samantha Mathis, Fiona Shaw, Fisher Stevens, Richard Edson, Lance Henriksen

Teenage Mutant Ninja Turtles III

(GOLDEN HARVEST/CLEARWATER/GARY PROPPER) 96 min
From underground comix to prepube omnipresence, the Turtles have outlasted the boom-and-bust of their original craze to such an extent that the thirty-ish nostalges of 2010 will probably be as misty-eyed over tattered tie-ins as the nineties generation is over *Thunderbirds*. That said the merchandising juggernaut needs sturdier engines than this sequel to perpetuate its thrall over pre-teen playgrounds.

feminist aliens, then sentenced in a pre-emption of **Junior** (1994) to live through multiple pregnancies. The result is a DIY vehicle for the video-only foulmouth comic who gets to sing songs like 'I'm a Cunt' and 'I'm As Sick As Fuck' between the expected jokes about planets called Clitoris ('it's right next to Uranus') and some occasional almost amusing callousness ('Chub, can you record a personal message for my baby brother ... he's in a coma.' 'Wake up you dozy cunt!').

The sort of comedy that elicits more groans than laughs, *U.F.O.* is not quite as stupid as it seems: the plot turns the tables on Chubby so every crass sexist joke ('I hope your tampon turns into an 'edgehog') is answered by an equally crass anti-sexist joke turning on male stupidity ('Who needs a wife, anyway? Anyone can boil the fuckin' toast.'), and the finale even finds the hero redeemed by motherhood. Not a great movie by any standards, this low-budget exercise in fish 'n' chip-stained end-of-the-pier slobbery still has more chuckles than any five Eddie Murphy vehicles put together.

d Tony Dow *p* Simon Wright *s* Richard Hall, Simon Wright, Roy 'Chubby' Brown *c* Paul Wheeler *se* Alan Whibley *lp* Roy 'Chubby' Brown, Sara Stockbridge, Amanda Symons, Shirley Anne Field, Elizabeth Hickling, Roger Lloyd Pack, Sue Lloyd

We're Back!: A Dinosaur's Story

(AMBLIN/U) 72 min

Based on the novel by Hudson Talbott, this is a pleasant-enough cartoon feature, and a far less sticky exercise in animated dinophilia than the Spielberg-Lucas-Don Bluth *The Land Before Time* (1988) and quite probably a notch or two funnier than the prehistoricana of *The Flintstones* (1994).

A scientist from the future arrives in pre-history, having picked up on his 'wish radio' a universal desire among modern children to see real live dinosaurs, and feeds a group of creatures with 'brain grain', a cereal that makes them intelligent and apparently robs them of their desire or need to prey on lesser species. In the present, these altered dinosaurs pal around with a pair of lost children, a street kid and a neglected debutante, and have a brush with an evil professor who runs a circus. Given that Spielberg has made as many monster movies and heart-warming family films, there's a touch of hypocrisy in the film's condemnation of the evil scientist because he trades in fear and only wants to use the dinosaurs to frighten people. Competent rather than gripping.

d Dick Zondag, Ralph Zondag, Phil Nibbelink, Simon Wells *p* Stephen Hickner *s* John Patrick Shanley *se* American Film Technologies Inc *lp* John Goodman, Walter Cronkite, Julia Child, Kenneth Mars, Martin Short, Rhea Perlman, Felicity Kendal

Wilder Napalm

(TRI-STAR) 109 min

Given that there were already *two* pyrokinetic screwball comedies on the video racks (*Nice Girls Don't Explode*, 1987, *Pyrates*, 1991), it's hard to see why anyone would feel the need to add another effort to the tiny sub-sub-genre. Howard and Quaid star as firestarting brothers in love with the same woman, convicted arsonist Winger. Howard overdos the cringing meekness, Winger is all affected mannerisms and Quaid, as the villainous 'Dr Napalm' who lusts after his brother's wife, does Jack Nicholson. At one point, Quaid explains the plot in terms of an analysis of the sit-com *Bewitched*, which is flattering to the thinness of the premise and the stridency of the performances. In the end, after a lot of chat and some barbershop numbers from a quartet of singing firemen, the brothers square off for a 'Flame On' battle that destroys a carnival but isn't spectacular enough to redeem the dullness of what has gone before.

d Glenn Gordon Caron *p* Mark Johnson, Stuart Cornfield *s* Vince Gilligan *c* Jerry Hartleben *lp* Debra Winger, Dennis Quaid, Arliss Howard, M. Emmett Walsh, Jim Varney, Mimi Lieber

Now remember, all for one and one for all – Teenage Mutant Ninja Turtles III.

1993

The Wind of Amnesia *aka* A Wind Named Amnesia
(HIDEYUCHI KIKUCHI/ASAHI SONORAMA/RIGHT STUFF
OFFICE/JHV; JAP) 83 min

This is superior *anime* adapted from a *manga* by Hideyuki Kikuchi, with a highly unusual apocalypse scenario and far more imaginative post-collapse situations than usual.

In the late 1990s, a wind passes around the world robbing almost all of humanity of its memories, leaving mankind wordless brutes stranded among the buildings and robot devices of a literally forgotten civilization. Wataru, a Japanese San Franciscan, is taught a little of what has gone by a dying cyborg, the survivor of bio-weaponry experiments, and sets out alone on a quest to revisit the cities of America, imparting the knowledge he has.

Joined by the ethereal, white-haired Sophia, Wataru encounters a primitive New York where tribes are prepared to sacrifice virgins to an automated demolition machine and an enclosed dome city where two inhabitants are forced to live out many scenarios to satisfy a computer programmed to protect an entire population. In both locales, the settings for episode-like stops in the road movie plot, Wataru encounters couples who seem to have a romantic relationship but who turn out to be father and daughter, and Sophia, who confesses that she is one of the aliens who have mind-wiped humanity, finally reminds Wataru about love-making, presumably giving him the power to ensure the survival of humanity. Though it has the usual elfin sexuality and rampaging robot menaces, this is an oddly poetic and sentimental film, refusing to indulge in excesses of sex and violence as it struggles to find a humanist message in its end-of-the-world scenario.

d/co-s Kazuo Yamazaki *p* Hisaro Kuriyama, Makato Shioya, Koreyasu Norimizu *co-s* Yoshiako Kawajiri, Kenji Kurata *c* Kinichi Ishikawa *se* Hideo Kurahashi

1994

Attack of the 50 Ft. Woman
(HBO) 89 min

Like most 'cult' movies, **Attack of the 50 Foot Woman** (1958) is an unrepeatable mix of the dreadful and the wonderful. This effort, made for Home Box Office but given a theatrical release outside the US, tries to recapture the cheesy magic of the original, retailoring the shoddy old script as a vehicle for Hannah, replacing unintentional comedy and accidental feminism with deliberate spoofing and a blatant foregrounding of subtext.

Hannah is the neglected wife of a philandering swine who gets her own back on hubby (Baldwin) when an alien alters her metabolism so she grows to giant size. The original movie paid off mercilessly with deaths all round, but this comes up with a contrived happy finish for everyone: condemning Baldwin not to a good squashing but an eternity of wearing a *Star Trek* uniform in a male consciousness-raising encounter group.

The original film boasted an impressive poster depicting a scene not in the film, with Allison Hayes bestriding a freeway, tossing cars around. This puts that moment on screen, but after such a long wait, it is a disappointingly tame rampage. The long-limbed, beautiful but awkward Hannah is well cast, but is not much of a comedian. The original version runs 65 minutes, while this hammers its idea into the ground with an extra 24 minutes of padding. Without being very good, the original *50 Foot Woman* is a classic; without being very bad, this film is a waste of space.

d Christopher Guest *p* Debra Hill *s* Joseph Daugherty *c* Russell Carpenter *se* Fantasy II Film Effects *lp* Daryl Hannah, Daniel Baldwin, William Windom, Frances Fisher, Christi Conaway, Paul Benedict

Digital Man
(GREEN COMMUNICATIONS/SCI-FI PRODUCTIONS/REPUBLIC)
92 min

Following the same team's **Prototype** (1992) and **APEX** (1993), this is a cyberpunk spaghetti Western with macho characters yomping around the desert firing very heavy hand-held weaponry at clunking robo-terminator villains.

Digital Man (Hues), an experimental android, is deployed against a group of terrorists and then seems to go rogue, prompting a devious general (Lauter) to send a team of armour-plated hi-tech soldiers into the wilderness to reclaim the macguffin codes. A slight advance on Roth's literally characterless previous films in that the budget has been stretched to a few familiar players who add a welcome touch of professional eccentricity to the usual parade of high-kicking surfer/martial artist/whatever types who handle the dreary action scenes.

d/co-s Phillip Roth *p* Talaat Captan *co-s* Ronald Schmidt *c* Harris Done *se* Todd Masters Effects, Mach Universe, David Wainstain, David Hopkins *lp* Ken Olandt, Kristen Dalten, Matthias Hues, Adam Baldwin, Ed Lauter, Paul Gleason, Susan Tyrell

The Fantastic Four
(CORMAN/CONSTANTIN) 93 min

'Hi Mrs Storm, can Johnny and Susan go to outer space with us?' Made cheaply and then shelved so Constantin could retain the rights to do a big-budget version, this adaptation of the Stan Lee-Jack Kirby Marvel comic has every right to be even worse than the TV pilot **Spider-Man** (1977) and Cannon's take on **Captain America** (1990). Actually it isn't such a bad comic book movie. Characters like Mr Fantastic, who can elongate his body, and the Human Torch, who seems made of living flame, cry out for CGI wizardry but get by on lo-tech short-cuts (gloves on the end of broom-handles), while the look of the rock-like Thing (Smith) and the fiendish Dr Doom (Culp) is dead right.

The script retells the characters' origins, establishing the Fantastic Four and Dr Doom and their complex relationships. Reed Richards (Hyde-Whyte) and Doom collaborate on a science project which malfunctions, turning Doom into a scarred and embittered mad genius who wears a metal mask. Then Richards crews an experimental spacecraft, taking along his fiancée Sue Storm (Staab), her brother Johnny (Underwood) and test pilot Ben Grimm (Trigger), exposing them to cosmic radiation that turns them into Mr Fantastic, Invisible Girl, the Human Torch and the Thing. The plot is complicated by a minor super-villain called the Jeweller, who replaces Marvel's Mole Man but looks more like a low-rent Penguin, then has time for some of the character interaction that distinguished the original as the Thing leaves the group while feeling sorry for himself because his super-powers have also turned him into a monster. Given the brief running time, there is then only time for the heroes to solidify their group status in a battle with Doom and his dress-alike minions before the finale.

Cheapness aside, this is a rare comic book movie that respects its source enough to cast performers who approximate the look and tone of the original characters.

d Oley Sassone *p* Steven Rabinier *s* Craig J. Neuus, Kevin Rock *c* Mark Parry *se* Mr Film, Billips Communications, Optic Nerve *lp* Alex Hyde-White, Rebecca Staab, Joseph Culp, Jay Underwood, Michael Bailey Smith, George Gaynes, Ian Trigger

The High Crusade
(OVERSEAS FILM GROUP/CENTROPOLIS/CLAUSSEN+WÖBKE; G)
87 min

Adapted from Poul Anderson's likeable 1960 novel, *The High Crusade* was unfortunately shot on the cheap by a crew little skilled in the fine arts of comedy or special effects.

A maverick, an icon and an actress combine to create a great poster: Junior.

control of Hong Kong, this sadly makes very little of its fascinating backdrop and concentrates instead on the sub-John Woo tribulations of Patrick, a British-trained ethical assassin, as he learns to make a commitment during a convoluted but predictable set of double crosses and reversals. Pyun regulars James and Thomerson offer some strange support, with James adopting a misjudged Bertie Wooster accent and Thomerson scratching his head as an American who has to have everything explained to him.

d Albert Pyun *p* Gary Schmoeller *s* Randall Fontana *c* George Mooradian *se* Paul Staples, John Chan, Rolando Salem *lp* Robert Patrick, Brion James, Ming-Na Wen, Tim Thomerson, Andrew Divoff

Junior

(NORTHERN LIGHTS) 110 min

Clearly delighted with its originality, this high concept drama about a pregnant man actually has Arnold Schwarzenegger following an example set by Marcello Mastroianni in *L'Événement le plus important depuis que l'Homme a marché sur la Lune* (*A Slightly Pregnant Man*, 1972), Nigel Planer in *Frankenstein's Baby* (1990) and even Roy 'Chubby' Brown in **U.F.O.** (1993).

Reuniting the director and star of the more engaging *Twins* (1988), which was also about a bizarre medical experiment, the film has fertility researchers Schwarzenegger and DeVito losing their funding and lab space to rival Thompson and carrying on independently. Fertilizing one of Thompson's eggs with Schwarzenegger's sperm, DeVito creates an embryo which Schwarzenegger agrees to incubate in his own body for a trial period. During pregnancy, Schwarzenegger's body chemistry and psychology alter and he winds up carrying the child to term, giving birth through a Caesarean. Mildly amusing throughout, with expert performances, this suffers from its essential pointlessness beyond the actual concept. In short, a better poster than a film.

d/p Ivan Reitman *s* Kevin Wade, Chris Conrad *c* Adam Greenberg *se* Matthew W. Mungle, Russell Seifert, John E. Jackson *lp* Arnold Schwarzenegger, Danny DeVito, Emma Thompson, Frank Langella, Pamela Reed, Judy Collins

Mary Shelley's Frankenstein

(AMERICAN ZOETROPE/TRI-STAR/JAPAN SATELLITE BROADCASTING/INDIEPROD) 123 min

As the film's very title indicates, this is an attempt to recapture the buzz of Coppola's *Bram Stoker's Dracula* (1992) by imposing Mills & Boon romantic content and elementary psychobabble on a reasonably if smugly faithful adaptation of a classic novel.

The extraordinarily attenuated narrative laboriously prefaces the Monster's *bildungsroman* sufferings with a lengthy account of Victor's upbringing and family tragedy. Frankenstein (Branagh) is driven to create life in the laboratory because his mother (Lunghi) has died in childbirth, an imposition as feeble though less ironic than the supposition of **The Fly** (1986) that Seth Brundle invents teleportation because he suffers from severe motion sickness.

Victor and Elizabeth (Bonham-Carter) swoon over each other in period costumes in time-outs from the choreographed laboratory scenes, but the real relationship – quite properly – is between Victor and the Creature (DeNiro), given a homoerotic angle (Branagh is the first screen Frankenstein to perform his experiments with his shirt off) in a spectacular if silly creation scene which involves shocking the new-made being to life with electric eels and man and monster grappling nude in quantities of slime. DeNiro's surprisingly subdued and sadly staid monster fails to evoke the physical or emotional stature of the character: he has one memorable leaping entrance on an icy mountainside but comes off as bathetic in the melodramatic language-learning sequence which features an inaptly cuddly Briers as the blind recluse.

In an attempt to ape the style of *Monty Python* or *Les Visiteurs* (1992), the dim and loony inhabitants of a medieval English castle encounter a *Dr Who*-reject midget alien (Carrington). Thick knight Overton, encouraged by a monk (Rhys-Davies) and a supposed French ambassador (des Barres), commandeers Carrington's spaceship and sets out for the Crusades, intending to retake Jerusalem for Christendom with the marvellous extra-terrestrial weapons. The spaceship whizzes out into the cosmos, where the knockabout crusaders become embroiled in a galactic empire that consists of two Scots-dubbed dwarves in rubber masks who keep coming out with witty lines on a level of 'their brains are even smaller than our willies'. Oddly, executive producer Roland Emmerich devoted an enormous budget to the inordinately thin **Stargate** premise, doling out comparatively meagre resources to Anderson's novel, which had the potential to be a far more spectacular and rewarding space opera.

d Holger Neuhäuser, Klaus Knoesel *p* Roland Emmerich, Jakob Claussen, Thomas Wöbke *s* Jürgen Egger, Robert G. Brown *c* Wolfgang Aicholzer *se* Karl-Heinz Christmann, Magicmove, Birger Lauber *lp* John Rhys-Davies, Rick Overton, Michael des Barres, Catherine Punch, Patrick Brymer, Debbie Lee Carrington

Hong Kong '97

(TRIMARK) 90 min

For obvious reasons, there are few film entries in the Very Near Future sub-genre of political Science Fiction, which allows for intricate speculation and editorializing but is handicapped by limited shelf life. Set specifically between June 30th and July 30th, 1997, during the period when China resumes

In a divergence from the text that evokes James Whale in content, Terence Fisher in style and Roger Corman to the point of imitation, Victor sews the murdered Elizabeth's head onto the body of the hanged Justine (McDowell) and is caught in a tug-of-love with the monster over this patchwork reanimate, who drenches her wedding dress in lamp oil and immolates herself to burn down yet another Frankenstein house. Framed by Quinn's arctic voyage and cluttered with extraneous relatives and hangers-on (who mainly get killed), this is a drab, big-budget melodrama enlivened only by occasional passages of camp. Few Frankenstein films are as deeply reactionary, with the punch-line coming when Quinn learns his lesson from Branagh's awful example, deciding that all this science is a bad thing and turning his ship away from the ice floes to return to a civilization where surgery is performed without anaesthetic and the natural process of birth is as bloody and doomed a business as the unnatural activities of mad scientists.

d Kenneth Branagh *p* Francis Ford Coppola, James V. Hart, John Veitch *s* Steph Lady, Frank Darabont *c* Roger Pratt *se* Daniel Parker, Richard Conway *lp* Robert DeNiro, Kenneth Branagh, Helena Bonham-Carter, Tom Hulce, Aidan Quinn, Richard Briers, John Cleese, Ian Holm, Robert Hardy, Cherie Lunghi, Celia Imrie, Trevyn McDowell

New Eden

(MTE/U) 88 min
2237. This starts as yet another futuristic prison movie as idealist Baldwin and survivalist Bowen are dumped on a penal planet to fend for themselves, but then turns into an even more overfamiliar battle-in-the-ruins action movie, born of **Mad Max 2** (1981) and *Seven Samurai* (1954) but copied almost exactly from **World Gone Wild** (1987). Baldwin inspires a farming community to irrigate their crops and revives the family unit by settling down with Bonet. After several raids, he has to ditch his pacifism and take lessons from a nomadic warrior (Bell) to learn to defend civilization from Bowen's marauding Sand Pirates. Rather low-key, with a villain who doesn't even have the heart to be really nasty to the hero until the blah finale and the usual primitive wilderness that is somehow complete with petrol-driven armoured dune buggies and laser guns.

d Alan Metzger *p* Harvey Frand *s* Dan Gordon *c* Geoffrey Erb *se* Mark Byers *lp* Stephen Baldwin, Lisa Bonet, Tobin Bell, Michael Bowen, Janet Hubert-Whitten

No Escape

(PLATINUM) 115 min
Filmed in Australia as *Penal Colony*, this continues a mini-genre of shot-down-under futuristic prison movies: **Turkey Shoot** (1982), *Ghosts ... of the Civil Dead* (1988), **Fortress** (1992). With *Lord of the Flies* tribal culture and *Mad Max* post-apocalypse gear, it owes an great debt to early visions of alternatives to prison, Peter Watkins' **Punishment Park** (1971) and (especially) Stephanie Rothman's *Terminal Island* (1973). To *No Escape*'s discredit, it ignores Rothman's ideas about redemptive communal society and the inefficiency of savage violence as an agent of control and opts instead for the easy way out of non-stop action.

In 2022, soldier Liotta is unjustly convicted of war crimes and sentenced to Absalom, an island where dangerous prisoners are left to their own devices. He survives an encounter with Wilson, insane leader of a barbarian faction, and enters an *Iron John* self-help group-cum-*Swiss Family Robinson* stockade ruled by the visionary Henriksen. Aspiring to an action-hero laurel, Liotta is lumbered with a clumsy backstory signalled by

In the midnight hour: Kenneth Branagh as Doctor Frankenstein in Mary Shelley's Frankenstein.

flaming visions and acts throughout as a dispenser of cool carnage without ever deciding if his primary duty is to escape and clear his name or to succeed Henriksen as saviour of the redeemable cons.

The first reel offers glimpses of huge sets and futuristic helicopters, but when it gets to Absalom, the film becomes a conventional jungle adventure. There is a hint of depth in Henriksen's character, a saint everyone believes to be innocent but who sadly admits he is indeed a wife-murderer, and in his insistence on the redemptive powers of self-sufficiency, but all the other characters are thick-ear stereotypes played by hammy British character actors and sentimentally macho Americans.

A homily about the possibility of establishing a genuine society within the framework of a prison (the crux of *Terminal Island*) is quickly ditched in favour of a *Boys' Own* display of POW escape attempts and a ready abandonment of progress when there is the chance of a war-whooping bit of a scrap.

d Martin Campbell *p* Gale Anne Hurd *s* Michael Gaylin, Joel Gross *c* Phil Meheux *se* David Hardie *lp* Ray Liotta, Stuart Wilson, Kevin Dillon, Lance Henriksen, Michael Lerner, Kevin J. O'Connor, Don Henderson, Jack Shepherd, Ian McNeice, Ernie Hudson

Oneamisu No Tsubasa *aka* The Wings of Honneamise

(MANGA/HEOLO LTD/ANIMAZE; JAP) 121 min

Set on another Earth where unrecognizable but archetypal nations go through familiar power politics and space remains unconquered, *Oneamisu* is a successful entry in one of the trickiest Science Fiction sub-genres, convincingly creating a world neither of the past nor the future yet divorced from the real present. Without fantasy elements (or even much scientific invention), it manages remarkably to envision a consistent, varied world in which every object (aircraft, trains, uniforms, windows, cup, TV broadcasts, newspapers, books, money, spoons) is recognizable but somehow different from designs that actually exist. The Kingdom of Honneamano has elements of Imperial Japan and the United States but can truly stand in for neither, serving as an amalgam of any society with a tendency towards the dystopian.

Shiro, an idealistic young Honneamise citizen, joins the Royal Space Force, a demoralized service suffering ridicule after twenty years of failing to put an astronaut in orbit. When the RSF commander announces that a man will finally be launched into space, only Shiro volunteers. Like much downbeat futuristic Science Fiction, from *Brave New World* through *Fahrenheit 451* to *1984* and much of the work of Philip K. Dick, this follows a fairly privileged member of an unjust society as he comes to realize how extensive are the problems of the masses he has barely seen. However, Shiro does not react by joining the oft-mentioned but barely-seen 'radicals' but by throwing himself into the dream of space flight, embracing the enthusiasm of the eccentric and naive boffins who have stuck by the programme through years of neglect, rallying his comrades to defy the cynical purpose of their masters and turning the space flight into a plea for international peace, telling the world there are no borders visible from orbit.

It is disappointing that the visual and political sophistication of the film should be diluted by the most banal religious message imaginable (hardly vitiated by the film's invention of a non-specific religion, complete with creation myth, to go with its non-specific politics) as Shiro and his almost-interestingly-characterized girlfriend exhort passersby and the entire planet to have faith in God.

d/s Hiroyuki Yamaga *p* Hirohiko Sueyoshi, Hiroaki Inoue *c* Hiroshi Isagawa

Ray Liotta (left) fights for his life in No Escape.

Pet Shop

(MOONBEAM ENTERTAINMENT) 85 min

This is a U certificate invasion from schlockmeister Charles Band's kids movie division. Aliens in ten-gallon hats that conceal their third eyes take over a mid-Western pet shop and give cutesy muppet creatures which transform into regular pets to a batch of annoying children, plotting evilly to beam the kids into outer space where they will be pets for alien brats. Pathetic el cheapo monster effects, a no-name cast, Witness Protection Scheme jokes lifted from *My Blue Heaven* (1990) and kid kulture yocks that feel like the *Double Deckers* on Prozac. Innocuous but offensively bad.

d Hope Ferello *p* Albert Band, Debra Dion, Peter von Sholly *s* Mark Goldstein, Greg Suddeth, Brent Friedman *c* Karen Grossman *se* Mark Rappaport, Alchemy FX *lp* Leigh Ann Orsi, Terry Kiser, Spencer Vrooman, Joanne Baron, David Wagner

The Puppet Masters

(DISNEY) scope 109 min

This is a belated authorized adaptation of Robert A. Heinlein's 1951 novel of the same title. The novel was the progenitor of the 'Body Snatchers' sub-genre and inspired a low budget rip-off **The Brain Eaters** (1958).

Slug-like aliens land in Iowa and embed themselves in the brains of locals, establishing a mind-controlled beachhead. A government agency tries to resist the invasion, with intelligence chief Sutherland forced to rely on his estranged son (Thal) in the crisis and NASA extraterrestrial expert Warner providing scientific advice. An almost superior shocker the film loses its way during the second half as the darkly serious atmosphere gets replaced by an awkward romance between Thal and Warner. At the same time stupid plot contrivances are glossed over for the sake of maintaining a driving narrative momentum towards the high-flying climax and the weak twist ending. There are subtleties – a CGI flying saucer seen only as a reflection in a hub-cap – but some major set-pieces are fudges, with the alien hive depicted as a tacky mass of net curtains, plastic tendrils and styrofoam sheeting.

d Stuart Orme *p* Ralp Winter *s* Ted Elliott, Terry Rossio, David S. Goyer *se* Greg Cannom *lp* Donald Sutherland, Eric Thal, Julie Warner, Keith David, Will Patton, Yaphet Kotto, Andrew Robinson

RoboCop 3 (ORION) 104 min

This is an advance on the expensive, disappointing mess of **RoboCop 2** (1990) only insofar as it is a cheap, disappointing mess. Residual goodwill from the original **RoboCop** (1987) has been stripped by sequels, comic books, an animated series and a TV spin-off.

In a devolution of the surprisingly sophisticated comic book politics of the first film, the Evil American Corporation has been taken over by an Evil Japanese Corporation and mercenaries led by another well-spoken Brit (Castle) are massacring the homeless in downtown Detroit. The script, co-written by comics guru Miller, busily introduces a host of new characters, from feisty homeless terrorists to creepy corporate types, then, as an afterthought, squeezes in RoboCop himself (Burke) for a silly and not-very-well-done finale in which he sprouts a flying pack and zooms through the air. The hero's partner (Allen) is killed off early to make room for younger, less talented, less interesting femme interest, bimbo scientist Hennessy and cute computer whizz Ryan.

Dekker holds back the violence to get a 15 rating, though this means major plot points like the murders of Ryan's parents are almost completely lost, and misinterprets Paul Verhoeven's satire by having all the supporting cast overact like sit-com geeks. Though Burke is as skilled as Peter Weller in acting with only his grim mouth, he's less comfortable with hardware. Weller's RoboCop was a living monolith but Burke's is a lumbering action figure; it's obvious from the tricky way Dekker films Robo getting into cars or climbing through manholes that it is actually impossible for anyone in that suit to perform simple human tasks like sitting down much less take on dozens of heavily-armed bad guys.

d/co-s Fred Dekker *p* Patrick Crowley *co-s* Frank Miller *c* Gary B. Kibbe *se* VCE, Phil Tippett, Rob Bottin *lp* Robert Burke, Nancy Allen, Rip Torn, John Castle, Jill Hennessy, C.C.H. Pounder, Mako, Robert Do'Qui, Remy Ryan

Pleased to meet you – Robert Burke, as RoboCop, and Robert Do'Qui in RoboCop 3.

Patrick Stewart (left) and Brent Spiner at the helm in Star Trek: Generations.

Star Trek: Generations

(PAR) 118 min

Having exhausted the big-screen potential of the saggy original *Star Trek* cast, this tries to extend the franchise by roping in the merely craggy cast of the sequel television series *Star Trek: The Next Generation*.

In an extended prologue, James T. Kirk (Shatner) is apparently killed while performing an act of familiar heroism. 70 years later, Captain Jean-Luc Picard (Stewart) of the new *Enterprise* leads his crew into an investigation of outer space dirty-dealing that involves mad scientist McDowell, whose scheme to get into a pseudo-scientific version of Heaven called the Nexus involves wiping out an entire inhabited planet and everyone on the starship. Picard is sucked into a time-space anomaly that feels like the *Reader's Digest* version of the last reel of **2001** (1968) but is also entirely in tune with the pompous religious impulses often exercised by the late Gene Roddenberry and meets Kirk, whereupon the two captains get together and go back in time to thwart McDowell.

As in all known *Star Trek* films, the patchwork plot and overreliance on unearned sentimentality about the continuing characters means this plays badly to anyone but the core fan audience. There are dollops of trite character stuff about the shallow sufferings Kirk and Picard have brought upon themselves by lifetimes of being inflexibly heroic and dedicated, which serve to prod the usually-excellent Stewart into displaying bad acting muscles almost the size of Shatner's well-developed hambone. Seven years after being cast for their freshness and vigour, the *Next Generation* crew look ship-worn and fed-up. Aside from Spiner's Data, an android given human emotions in a more than usually tired sub-plot, the supporting cast are mainly relegated to bit-parts. On the plus side, McDowell clearly enjoys being a galactic bastard and there are spectacular special effects, including yet another destruction of the *Enterprise*.

d David Carson *p* Rick Berman *s* Ronald D. Moore, Brannon Braga *c* John A. Alonzo *se* ILM *lp* Patrick Stewart, William Shatner, Jonathan Frakes, Brent Spiner, Malcolm McDowell, LeVar Burton, Whoopee Goldberg, Marina Sirtis, Gates McFadden, Michael Dorn, James Doohan, Walter Koenig

Stargate

(LE STUDIO CANAL+/CENTROPOLIS/CAROLCO) 121 min

Enormous production values, in seamless special effects and an old-fashioned deployment of vast sets and armies of extras, are here harnessed in the service of an amazingly ramshackle script that recycles pulpy chunks of the lesser Science Fiction stories of the thirties and the lost world romances of Rider Haggard. Surprisingly it almost works.

A large alien artefact is discovered in Egypt in 1928. Years later, archaeologist Spader works out that if the giant circle is aligned properly, the thing serves as a gateway to another part of the universe. A military team led by traumatized Marine Russell is despatched to an alien desert world settled by apparent ancient Egyptians and ruled tyrannically by Ra (Davidson), a possessed pharaonic version of Ming the Merciless.

The 'heart-warming' business of Russell making friends with a desert urchin who replaces his dead son is extremely tiresome, but the equally cliché relationship of the eager Spader and a local girl is a more acceptable evocation of the native romances of Hollywood sarong epics. Davidson, a limited performer who has miraculously found another part only he could play, swans about in Egyptian frocks and a computer-generated shapeshifting head-dress, emerging from a *Dr Phibes*-style

hi-tech resuscitating sarcophagus to add a welcome note of Edgar Rice Burroughs-ish camp to the surprisingly stolid desert rebellion plot. There is a smug element of unattractive patronizing as slaves whipped up against their masters act like every American administration's fantasy of a grateful Third World populace begging for military aid and presumably capable of abandoning the system which is all they've ever known for a simulation of parliamentary democracy. The triteness of it all is such that Spader's decision to stay behind with his native girl prompts less romantic admiration than wonderment that anyone would volunteer to spend the rest of his life on a planet without dentists.

d/co-s Roland Emmerich *p* Joel B. Michaels, Oliver Eberle *co-p/co-s* Dean Devlin *c* Karl Walter Lingenlaub *se* Kit West, Cinema Research Corporation *lp* Kurt Russell, James Spader, Jaye Davidson, Viveca Lindfors, Alexis Cruz

T-Force

(PM ENTERTAINMENT) 90 min
In the future, a cadre of anti-terrorist androids play *Die Hard* (1986) at an embassy siege and accidentally kill a few too many hostages along with the bad guys, prompting the Mayor of Los Angeles (Gray) to order their decommission, whereupon they exceed the bounds of their programming by revolting and escaping, vowing to bring down a law they have decided is corrupt. Robot-hating human cop Scalia and his cyborg partner Lurie set out to track down the renegade robo-cyberterminator types, and plenty of cheap explosions ensue as the bigoted human learns to respect his manufactured sidekick between battles on vacant lots. Competent, unexceptional stuff, typical of the martial arts/killer robot quickies that

swarmed on video in the mid-nineties. Against the odds, McDonald manages some pathos as the female robot but Johnston's preening fascist rebel is laughable.

d/co-p Richard Pepin *co-p* Joseph Merhi *s* Jacobsen Hart *c* Ken Blakey *se* Makeup and Effects Labs, Inc *lp* Jack Scalia, Evan Lurie, Erin Gray, Bobby Johnston, Deron McBee, Jennifer McDonald

Timecop

(LARGO/JVC/SIGNATURE/RENAISSANCE/DARK HORSE) 98 min
Hyams handles *Timecop* with exactly the expected ordinary skill, never treating Van Damme to the kind of semi-mythic treatment given him by John Woo on *Hard Target* (1993) though allowing for more specifically Jean-Claude bits of business, like a leap to do a mid-air splits in the kitchen to avoid being electrocuted. With a blithely paradox-heavy time travel scenario, nipping at the heels of the *Terminators* and the *Back to the Futures*, this is exactly the sort of film a comic book company eager to expand into features would come up with.

In 1994, following the invention of a time travel process, America establishes the Time Enforcement Commission, a police which will prevent miscreants tampering with the past. As the ambitious Senator Silver volunteers to head the TEC committee, Washington policeman Van Damme is attacked by mysterious hit men from the future who murder his wife (Sara). In 2004, the embittered Van Damme is a timecop and Silver has been subverting the past to finance a presidential campaign. Learning of a major anomaly in 1994, Van Damme is sent back to discover Silver conspiring with his younger self to fix the future so he will win the election and sees a chance to thwart the villain *and* set his life straight. In a typical bit of have-it-all plotting, the finale finds the hero returned to his

Right: Welcome II
The Terrordome.

present to find all the likeable characters who have been killed
returned to life without even a memory of the threat posed by
the vanished Silver.

While its time-twisting is on a superficial TV movie level,
Timecop is a worthy post-modern action movie. It is so confident of its conventions that it can spring surprises: Reuben, a
young black woman with an attitude, is so clearly in the spirit
of the feisty ethnic partners Arnie is often given that it is a genuine shock that she turns out (albeit shakily) to be a wrong 'un.
And there is a 'Scenes We'd Like to See' moment when Van
Damme thinks of the appropriate witticism ('freeze') a scene
after he has despatched a vile baddie by icing his arm and
breaking him apart with a far less satisfying one-liner. Effects-
wise, the movie has little new to offer, though the paradox-dri-
ven disposal of the villain as his two incarnations wind together
in a time implosion is suitably gruesome in a fairly fresh manner.

d/c Peter Hyams *p* Moshe Dimant, Sam Raimi, Robert
Tapert *s* Mark Verheiden *se* VIFX *lp* Jean-Claude Van
Damme, Mia Sara, Ron Silver, Bruce McGill, Gloria Reuben,
Scott Bellis

Welcome II The Terrordome
(NON ALIGNED COMMUNICATIONS/CHANNEL 4/METRO TARTAN)
94 min
This no-budget near-future political drama suffers from shrill-
ness as it tries to graft elements of black history and race conflict onto a sub-standard action scenario.

A group of Ibo slaves, newly transplanted to North Carolina in
1652, walk into the sea, still shackled, and are reincarnated in the
Terrordome, a futuristic ghetto of drug-dealing, violence and

Below: *A kickboxer is
a kickboxer is a
kickboxer – Jean-
Claude Van Damme
in* Timecop.

suffering. The plot revolves around a young mother (Llewellyn)
trying to keep her children out of the drugs business run by
their father (Joseph) while disapproving of the liaison between
Joseph's sidekick (Nonyela) and a white woman (Burrows) he
has impregnated. It all ends with a race riot, the miscarrying of
Burrows's mixed race baby and the peaceful reincarnation of
all the characters back in Africa. A review in *Interzone* noted
'the script is a breathtakingly incompetent farrago of incoherent clichés, offensively vacuous rhetoric and elementary
filmwriting blunders . . . the hate-filled images, uncritical
incitement to mob violence and crude substitution of gangsta
confrontation but undermine the case by presenting black rad-
icalism as a movement of unreasoning emotion, anarchy and
destruction.'

d/s Ngozi Onwurah *p* Simon Onwurah *c* Alwin H. Kuchler
lp Suzette Llewellyn, Saffron Burrows, Felix Joseph, Valentine
Nonyela, Ben Wynter, Sian Martin

Appendix 1

All-Time Science Fiction Rental Champs

This list below is compiled from *Variety*'s 1994 ranking of *All-Time Rental Champs* and *Daily Variety*'s *Film Rentals From A To Z, 1915-1994*, published in January 1995. Where the *Daily Variety* ranking adds new titles and updates figures in the *Variety* list these figures have been used. However, where a film included in the *Variety* list was omitted from the *Daily Variety* list it has still been included in the list below. It is unclear why these titles were omitted from the *Daily Variety* list.

The list includes films which have secured rentals (i.e. distributors' receipts, not ticket sales) in America and Canada of over $5 million. *Variety* suggests as a rough guide that foreign rentals 'sometimes equal or slightly surpass American and Canadian rentals'. Thus, doubling the figures listed here would give an indication of world-wide rentals. The figures relate, in the main, to the first release of a title. In the case of some older titles a successful re-release could well have significantly increased rental revenue. It is also worth pointing out that these figures do not include non-theatrical revenue, for example from television or video sales, which are substantial. Needless to say the list is biased in favour of recent titles and their higher seat prices.

		in thousands of dollars
1	E.T. The Extra-Terrestrial 1982	228,619
2	Jurassic Park 1993	208,000
3	Star Wars 1977	193,777
4	Return of the Jedi 1983	169,193
5	Batman 1989	150,500
6	The Empire Strikes Back 1980	141,672
7	Terminator 2: Judgment Day 1991	112,500
8	Back to the Future 1985	105,496
9	Batman Returns 1992	100,100
10	Superman - The Movie 1978	82,800
11	Close Encounters of the Third Kind 1977	82,750
12	Back to the Future, Part II 1989	72,320
13	Honey, I Shrunk the Kids 1989	72,007
14	Teenage Mutant Ninja Turtles 1990	67,650
15	Superman II 1980	65,100
16	Total Recall 1990	63,511
17	Star Trek IV: The Voyage Home 1986	56,820
18	Star Trek - The Motion Picture 1979	56,000
19	Back to the Future, Part III 1990	49,072
20	Aliens 1986	43,753
21	Teenage Mutant Ninja Turtles II 1991	41,900
22	The Rocky Horror Picture Show 1975	40,420
23	Alien 1979	40,300
24	Star Trek II: The Wrath of Khan 1982	40,000
	Cocoon 1985	40,000
26	Star Trek III - The Search for Spock 1984	39,000
27	Young Frankenstein 1974	38,823
28	War Games 1983	38,520
29	Superman III 1983	37,200
30	Star Trek VI: The Undiscovered Country 1991	36,000
31	Moonraker 1979	33,924
32	Groundhog Day 1993	32,500
33	Alien3 1992	31,762
34	Predator 1987	31,000
35	Stargate 1994	29,293
36	The Abyss 1989	28,800
37	Thunderball 1965	28,621
38	Star Trek: Generations 1994	28,487
39	Never Say Never Again 1983	28,200
40	Honey, I Blew Up the Kid 1992	27,417
41	Star Trek V: The Final Frontier 1989	27,035
42	2001 - A Space Odyssey 1968	25,522
43	Demolition Man 1993	25,500
44	The Black Hole 1979	25,437
45	The China Syndrome 1979	25,342
46	Firefox 1982	25,000
47	Forever Young 1992	24,400
48	The Spy Who Loved Me 1977	24,365
49	RoboCop 1987	24,037
50	The Rocketeer 1991	23,179
51	The Love Bug 1969	23,150
52	Goldfinger 1964	22,998
53	RoboCop 2 1990	22,505
54	Blue Thunder 1983	21,890
55	Time Bandits 1981	20,534
56	Timecop 1994	20,211
57	2010 1984	20,187
58	Teenage Mutant Ninja Turtles III 1993	19,869
59	Diamonds Are Forever 1971	19,727
60	You Only Live Twice 1967	19,389
61	Spaceballs 1987	19,027
62	Red Dawn 1984	17,938
63	Mad Max Beyond Thunderdome 1985	17,900
64	Short Circuit 1986	17,878
65	Harry and the Hendersons 1987	17,430
66	Bill & Ted's Bogus Journey 1991	17,249
67	A Clockwork Orange 1971	17,000
	Herbie Rides Again 1974	17,000
69	The Terminator 1984	16,822
70	Bill & Ted's Excellent Adventure 1989	16,802
71	Tron 1982	16,704
72	Blade Runner 1982	16,650
73	Dune 1984	16,560
74	The Running Man 1987	16,335
75	Universal Soldier 1992	16,000
76	Predator 2 1990	15,700
77	Batteries Not Included 1987	15,416
78	Planet of the Apes 1968	15,000
79	Flash Gordon 1980	14,879
80	Modern Problems 1981	14,800
81	Coma 1978	14,539
82	Herbie Goes to Monte Carlo 1977	14,000
83	Starman 1984	13,730
84	InnerSpace 1987	13,700
85	The Lawnmower Man 1992	13,600
86	The Last Starfighter 1984	13,148
87	Altered States 1980	12,500
88	Capricorn One 1977	12,000
89	Escape from New York 1981	11,715
90	The Absent-Minded Professor 1961	11,426
91	Airplane II: The Sequel 1982	11,341

92	*Mad Max 2* 1981	11,300
93	*20,000 Leagues Under the Sea* 1954	11,267
94	*Invasion of the Body Snatchers* 1978	11,133
95	*Heavy Metal* 1981	10,754
96	*Buck Rogers in the 25th Century* 1979	10,746
97	*Son of Flubber* 1963	10,450
98	*Casino Royale* 1967	10,200
99	*Howard the Duck* 1986	10,154
100	*Super Mario Bros.* 1993	10,020
101	*Weird Science* 1985	10,009
102	*Outland* 1981	10,000
103	*The Thing* 1982	9,814
104	*Escape to Witch Mountain* 1974	9,500
105	*The Man with the Golden Gun* 1974	9,441
106	*Logan's Run* 1976	9,426
107	*The Incredible Shrinking Woman* 1981	9,201
108	*On Her Majesty's Secret Service* 1969	9,117
109	*Rollerball* 1975	9,055
110	*The Fly II* 1988	8,750
111	*Krull* 1983	8,744
112	*Beneath the Planet of the Apes* 1969	8,600
113	*Short Circuit 2* 1988	8,500
114	*The Cat from Outer Space* 1978	8,488
115	*Sleeper* 1973	8,254
116	*Spacehunter: Adventures in the Forbidden Zone* 1983	8,131
117	*The Nude Bomb* 1980	8,112
118	*Superman IV: The Quest for Peace* 1987	8,100
119	*The Boys from Brazil* 1978	8,000
	Herbie Goes Bananas 1980	8,000
121	*The Andromeda Strain* 1970	7,913
122	*The Swarm* 1978	7,700
	Project X 1987	7,700
124	*Masters of the Universe* 1987	7,683
125	*Cocoon: The Return* 1988	7,400
126	*Return from Witch Mountain* 1978	7,398
127	*The Silencers* 1965	7,350
128	*Westworld* 1973	7,283
129	*Charly* 1968	7,260
130	*Halloween III: Season of the Witch* 1983	7,239
131	*Our Man Flint* 1965	7,200
132	*It's Alive* 1973	7,100
133	*Baby – The Secret of the Lost Legend* 1985	6,832
134	*The Final Countdown* 1980	6,702
135	*Leviathan* 1989	6,581
136	*Scanners* 1980	6,569
137	*Time After Time* 1979	6,500
138	*Doctor No* 1962	6,435
139	*Battlestar Galactica* 1978	6,396
140	*Murderer's Row* 1966	6,350
141	*The Computer Wore Tennis Shoes* 1969	6,000
	Meteor 1979	6,000
143	*Phantasm* 1979	5,812
144	*Night of the Comet* 1984	5,800
145	*Hangar 18* 1980	5,760
146	*Escape from the Planet of the Apes* 1971	5,560
147	*Barbarella* 1967	5,500
	Fantastic Voyage 1966	5,500
	Wild in the Streets 1968	5,500
150	*Flesh Gordon* 1974	5,300
	My Stepmother is an Alien 1988	5,300
152	*Million Dollar Duck* 1971	5,250
	Death Race 2000 1975	5,250
154	*They Live* 1988	5,246
155	*The Birds* 1963	5,090
156	*Dr Strangelove, or How I Learned to Stop Worrying and Love the Bomb* 1964	5,000
	In Like Flint 1967	5,000
	The Fiendish Plot of Fu Manchu 1980	5,000
	Lifeforce 1985	5,000
	Space Camp 1986	5,000

Note: The figure for *Close Encounters of the Third Kind* is a conflation of the rentals for the original 1977 movie and the 1980 re-released *Special Edition*. The figure for *Blade Runner* (1982) and the 'director's cut' released in 1992 is similarly conflated.

Appendix 2

Critics' Top Tens

The definitional problems of Science Fiction as a genre are once again well illustrated in these Top Tens. For convenience sake I have marked with an asterisk (*) those films which are not included in this volume of the *Encyclopedia*.

Brian W Aldiss

Brian Aldiss is a Science Fiction writer and critic. His novels include *Hothouse*, *Report on Probability A* and *Greybeard* and he is also the author of the adventurous and stimulating history of Science Fiction, *Billion Year Spree*.

The films are listed in order of preference.

Solaris 1971
Doctor Strangelove 1964
L'Annee Dernière a Marienbad 1961*
Capricorn One 1977
Westworld 1973
Metropolis 1926
Gladiatorerna 1969
Things to Come 1936
A Clockwork Orange 1971
Alien 1979

'Making a list like this immediately invites a second list, featuring neglected pets which might or might not be SF, but who cares. Like Spielberg's *Duel* (1971), and of course the original *King Kong* (1933), whose theme of the beast from the subconscious erupting in the midst of a civilization – well, New York – is so grand it ought to be SF. None of the fifties wave of SF films reaches my list; there was not quite room for *The Incredible Shrinking Man* (1957). The ten I have chosen offer fresh viewpoints on life, are often startling, even on successive showings, and rate rather well merely as Cinema. But they are minority tastes; if the SF Cinema is to retain vitality and subversive intent, it must remain a minority taste and not try to hit the warm hearts of Middle America.'

Ramsey Campbell

Ramsey Campbell is a novelist and critic whose recent works include *Incarnate*, *Obsession*, *The Hungry Moon*, *The Influence* and *Ancient Images*. He has written widely about film, and is Britain's leading author of short ghost-horror stories.

The films are listed chronologically.

Things to Come 1936
The Thing 1951
Forbidden Planet 1956
Invasion of the Body Snatchers 1956
The Incredible Shrinking Man 1957
2001 – A Space Odyssey 1968
Dark Star 1974
Close Encounters of the Third Kind (original version) 1977
Stalker 1979
The Fly 1986

'Of course I thought of *Metropolis*, but omitted it partly on the basis that I'm fonder of maybe as many as ten of Lang's other films. I do regret having no room for the James Whale *Frankenstein* films, not to mention *God Told Me To*, but as with horror I'll allow myself just one television film, the BBC serial of *Quatermass and the Pit*, which gives Kneale's ideas more room to breathe than the Hammer version did.'

Arthur C. Clarke

Arthur C. Clarke is a prolific Science Fiction novelist and science writer. Amongst his many publications are *The City and the Stars*, *The Sentinel* (which formed the basis of *2001 – A Space Odyssey*) and *Rendevous With Rama*.

The films are listed in no particular order.

Metropolis 1926
Things to Come 1936
Frankenstein 1931
King Kong 1933*
Forbidden Planet 1956
The Thing 1951
The Day the Earth Stood Still 1951
2001 – A Space Odyssey 1968
Close Encounters of the Third Kind, The Special Edition 1980
Alien 1979
Blade Runner 1982

'The above is a rough-cut of my best: I may change my mind on some, but not many . . . There's no way I can keep it to ten films – and I'm still brooding about *Return of the Jedi* (1983), *Star Trek II – The Wrath of Khan* (1982), *E.T. The Extra-Terrestrial* (1982) etc. Actually it would make more sense to make two lists: Most Important and Best.'

Nigel Floyd

Nigel Floyd is a critic and broadcaster.
The films are listed in alphabetical order.

Aliens 1986
Blade Runner 1982
Brazil 1985
The Day the Earth Stood Still 1951
The Incredible Shrinking Man 1957
Invasion of the Body Snatchers 1956
The Man Who Fell to Earth 1976
Metropolis 1926
Quatermass II 1957
2001 – A Space Odyssey 1968

'Obvious choices, for the most part, with the possible exception of James Cameron's *Aliens*, which I prefer to Ridley Scott's predictable killing-by-numbers original. Scott's atmospheric but incoherent *Blade Runner*, on the other hand, virtually reinvented the look of the modern Science Fiction movie, despite being a travesty of Philip K. Dick's novel *Do Androids Dream of Electric Sheep?* Similarly incoherent, but visually and intellectually dazzling, Nicholas Roeg's *The Man Who Fell to Earth* is one of the few "serious" Science Fiction pictures of recent years to have stood the test of time.'

Denis Gifford

Denis Gifford is a contributor to this book. *Frankenstein* is omitted as being considered a horror picture.

The films are listed in alphabetical order.

Close Encounters of the Third Kind 1977
Flash Gordon 1936
Invasion of the Body Snatchers 1956
The Invisible Man 1933
Metropolis 1926
Star Wars 1977
Superman – The Movie 1978
Things to Come 1936
2001 – A Space Odyssey 1968
War of the Worlds 1953

Phil Hardy

The films are listed in no particular order.

The Man Who Fell to Earth 1976
The Thing 1951
Not of This Earth 1957
Flash Gordon 1936
The Parasite Murders 1974
Alphaville 1965
Quatermass II 1957
Metropolis 1926
Silent Running 1971
Dark Star 1974
Der Grosse Verhau 1970

'My concern has been to pinpoint resonant moments in the history of the Science Fiction film. Accordingly I have bypassed many of the accepted highpoints of the genre: any history that only covers the peaks is no more than an introduction to its subject and the time is long gone when Science Fiction, both literature and film, needed a mere introduction. Nonetheless, with a couple of exceptions, the films I've chosen are hardly undiscovered gems. It is the context they form, the tradition they represent, that I hope is informative. It is a tradition in which special effects are of secondary importance to ideas and in which ideas are filmically realized rather than merely stated. Hence the absence of recent blockbusters like *Star Wars* (1977), which for all their self-conscious charm lack the innocence that gives wing to the pulp poetry of *Flash Gordon*; and the absence of *2001 – A Space Odyssey* (1968) which for all its incidental splendours lacks the controlled imagination of the likes of *Metropolis* or *Alphaville*. Hence the presence of films like *Dark Star*, *Silent Running* and *Der Grosse Verhau* which simply have the feel of Science Fiction literature (a rare occurence on the Science Fiction screen) and *The Parasite Murders* and *The Man Who Fell to Earth* which are both ruthless and relentless in their "what if" speculations and vibrantly achieved as films. And lastly, hence *The Thing*, *Not of This Earth* and *Quatermass II*, beacons still shining bright from the fifties, *the* decade in the history of the Science Fiction film.'

Harry Harrison

Harry Harrison is a Science Fiction writer and anthologist. Amongst his many books are The *Stainless Steel Rat, Bill the Galactic Hero, Make Room! Make Room!* (which formed the basis of the film *Soylent Green*) and *The Transatlantic Tunnel, Hurrah!*.

'I find it difficult to list a top ten, but I will name the best SF film ever done. H.G. Wells' *Things to Come* (1936). In California I showed it to a class I was doing for teachers of SF in high schools. It was a beautifully clean print. The film itself still holds up; the acting, writing, direction – even the sets and the model work. I think it belongs in the top ten best films of all time – and is certainly *the* SF classic.'

Stefan Jaworzyn

Stefan Jaworzyn is editor of *Shock Xpress*. He is the lead guitarist of Skullflower, and manager of Shock Records, a company which specializes in 'Horrible Grinding Noises'. He is co-organizer of Shock Around the Clock, Britain's most prestigious horror film event.

The films are listed alphabetically.

Blade Runner 1982
A Clockwork Orange 1971
Frankenstein 1931
Frankenstein Meets the Space Monster 1965
Kiss Me Deadly 1955
Mad Max 2 1981
Plan 9 from Outer Space 1956
Quatermass and the Pit 1967
The Thing 1982
Things to Come 1936
Videodrome 1982

Alan Jones

Alan Jones writes extensively about Science Fiction and horror movies.

The films are listed in order of preference.

Blade Runner 1982
2001 – A Space Odyssey 1968
RoboCop 1987
Videodrome 1982
Danger: Diabolik 1967
Mad Max 2 1981
A Clockwork Orange 1971
Demon Seed 1977
Star Wars 1977
Alien 1979

Stephen Jones

Stephen Jones is a freelance writer, editor, and film publicist for such movies as *Hellbound: Hellraiser II* and *Night Life*.

The films are listed in order of preference.

Quatermass and the Pit 1967
Invaders from Mars 1953
Things to Come 1936
Blade Runner 1982
The Thing 1982
Dune 1984
Aliens 1986
A Clockwork Orange 1971
Star Wars 1977
Back to the Future 1985

'The Science Fiction movie is a genre that has really only come into its own during the past decade or so, thanks to the incredible advances made in cinematic special effects. The above list reflects these changes, with only one film representing the fifties Science Fiction boom (although I do have a great fondness for *War of the Worlds* (1953) and *It Came from Outer Space* (1953)). *Things to Come* is on there because it has a truly epic scope, although a longer list would have included Lang's equally visionary *Metropolis* (1926). In retrospect, Science Fiction movies from the sixties are not particularly inspiring, although *Doctor Strangelove, or How I Learned to Stop Worrying and Love the Bomb* (1964), *Terrore nello Spazio* (1965) and *Planet of the Apes* (1968) would always win out, if only for their inherent weirdness, over such techno-tedium as Kubrick's *2001 – A Space Odyssey* (1968).

I would also have liked to include (just for their entertainment value) such recent titles, combining fast-paced narrative with state-of-the-art effects, as *The Final Programme* (1973), *Invasion of the Body Snatchers* (1978) – like Carpenter's *The Thing*, much better than the original – *Time After Time* (1979), *Mad Max 2* (1981), *The Terminator* (1984), *Explorers* (1985) and *RoboCop* (1987).'

Tony Masters

Tony Masters is a contributor to this book.
The films are listed in order of preference.

Alien 1979
Planet of the Apes 1968
The Birds 1963
Close Encounters of the Third Kind 1977
Fahrenheit 451 1966
The Illustrated Man 1968
On The Beach 1959
Quatermass and the Pit 1967
2001 – A Space Odyssey 1968
A Clockwork Orange 1971

'As a novelist, mood and atmosphere appeal to me even more than a well-conceived plot, interesting structure or good characterization. My top ten films, therefore, tend to be those that are very atmospheric, or those that happen to set a certain original mood. Some of the films are flawed, but it is the fragments, the little sparks of originality, that makes me love them so much.'

Tom Milne

Tom Milne is the author of *Mamoulian* and editor of *Godard on Godard* and several other books.
The films are listed in order of preference.

The Man Who Fell to Earth 1976
Alphaville 1965
Invasion of the Body Snatchers 1956
La Jetée 1963
The Incredible Shrinking Man 1957
Je T'Aime, Je T'Aime 1967
Quintet 1979
Forbidden Planet 1956
Fahrenheit 451 1966
Dark Star 1974

'I have excluded films which, for all their SF connections, I consider belong more properly to horror. Thus, there is no place for *King Kong* (1933), *The Island of Lost Souls* (1932), *The Bride of Frankenstein* (1935), *Mad Love* (1935), *Les Yeux Sans Visage* (1959) or *The Birds* (1963). Basically, Science Fiction in the cinema seems to me to be suffering from a case of arrested development. Too narrow a focus on alien invaders, BEMs, technological marvels; too little inclination to explore in the (often amused) wake of writers like Philip K. Dick, Sturgeon, Leiber, Bester, Simak, Farmer, Kuttner, Fred Brown. God preserve us from any more pieces of stupid butchery like Ridley Scott's *Blade Runner* (1982) which, in the interests of commercial viability, reduce the simplicity, originality and charm of their source novels to pure formula.

Kim Newman

Kim Newman is a contributor to this book.
The films are listed in no particular order.

Trancers 1984
Invasion of the Body Snatchers 1956
The Thing 1951
The Invisible Man 1933
Doctor Strangelove 1964
The Damned 1961
The Man Who Fell to Earth 1976
Kiss Me Deadly 1955
The Terminator 1984
The Manchurian Candidate 1962★

Peter Nicholls

Peter Nicholls is the editor of *The Encyclopedia of Science Fiction*, the essential reference book to the literary genre, and the author of *Fantastic Cinema*.
The lists are in chronological order.

THE TOP TEN
King Kong 1933★
Forbidden Planet 1956
2001 – A Space Odyssey 1968
Solaris 1971
The Parasite Murders 1974/*The Brood* 1979/*Videodrome* 1982
The Man Who Fell to Earth 1976
Close Encounters of the Third Kind 1977
Blade Runner 1982
The Thing 1982
Strange Invaders 1983

THE SECOND TEN
Metropolis 1926
Invasion of the Body Snatchers 1956
The Birds 1963
It's Alive 1973
Westworld 1973
God Told Me To! 1976
Star Wars 1977
Alien 1979
The Empire Strikes Back 1980
E.T. The Extra-Terrestrial 1982

THE THIRD TEN
Bride of Frankenstein 1935
This Island Earth 1955
The Incredible Shrinking Man 1957
Dr Strangelove 1964
Barbarella 1967
Je T'Aime, Je T'Aime 1967
Planet of the Apes 1968
Quintet 1979
Mad Max 2 1981

'As you can see, my "short" list comes to 32 films, so just for the hell of it, I've given you a second ten, and a third ten as well. *King Kong* is the *classic* monster movie, and holds up amazingly well. It can still move the watcher to tears. The SF boom of the 1950s was great at the time, but a lot of them have not weathered well, so I include only *Forbidden Planet* from this period. *2001* revolutionized the genre. *Solaris* is intelligent, mysterious, very beautiful. I cannot separate my three favourite Cronenberg shockers; all are amusing, black, disgusting and say something important about the world in SF imagery. *The Man Who Fell to Earth* is a more interesting alien visitor than *E.T.*, and almost as cuddly. *Close Encounters* is a classic fairy tale/obsession myth. *Blade Runner* (whose hero is surely an android too, in the most interesting subtext for years) makes the future come to life like no other movie. *The Thing* is not only bizarre; it is a faithful adaptation of an SF classic, and is the last word on the horror of loss of identity, and technically brilliant as well.'

David Pirie

David Pirie is a screenwriter, novelist and critic. He is the author of *Mystery Story*, *A Heritage of Horror* and the editor of *Anatomy of the Movies*.
The films are listed in order of preference.

Invasion of the Body Snatchers 1956
Quatermass II 1957
The Incredible Shrinking Man 1957
Close Encounters of the Third Kind 1977

2001 – A Space Odyssey 1968
Superman – The Movie 1978
Alphaville 1965
Them! 1954
Westworld 1973
The Thing 1951
Alien 1979

'Master-craftsmen like Kubrick and Spielberg have made great SF movies but for all their virtuosity, they still for me just lack the edge of those film-makers and writers of the fifties whose gut instinct occasionally channeled the anxieties of an age. It is doubtful if there can ever again be films of such pure paranoia as my top three. Technically of course they look very rough today, but they still convey a tension that is almost impossible to recreate. And two of them have the additional advantage of the theme of alien possession, which is among the richest of all cinematic metaphors.'

Paul Taylor

Paul Taylor is a contributor to this book.
The films are listed in alphabetical order.

Android 1982
Bride of Frankenstein 1935
Dark Star 1974
The Incredible Shrinking Man 1957
Invaders from Mars 1953
Invasion of the Body Snatchers 1956
Mad Max 2 1981
The Man Who Fell to Earth 1976
Not of This Earth 1957
The Parasite Murders 1974

'Ten not-quite-arbitrary evocations of pleasure from a genre I still can't define or even always recognize. That they're (almost) all sound films from North America – *Mad Max 2* travels on a forged passport anyway – is intensely irritating, slightly embarrassing, yet probably only a few decimal points off representational accuracy. A British entry would have to be chosen from among *The Quatermass Xperiment* (1955), *Scream and Scream Again* (1969) or *The War Game* (1965); a vintage Fritz Lang or something like Fassbinder's long-form telemovie *Welt am Draht* (1973) might lead the generally more playful European contingent. It's a matter of regret that there's no room for a true creature-feature – either *Them!* (1954) or a John Sayles-scripted variant would fit the bill – a marginal sci-horror from either Larry Cohen or George Romero, or a plainly daft personal indulgence like *Heartbeeps* (1981). And it's a matter of total confusion on my part whether or not *Eraserhead* (1976) could be co-opted for Science Fiction – if so, regard that list as eleven strong. There's little to add about the ten actually listed: a contemporary bias is obvious; the Cronenberg title stands for most of his fascinating, troubling work; only one film sneaks in for primarily extra-cinematic resonances '

Bill Warren

Bill Warren is the author of *Keep Watching the Skies!*

top eleven
in order by length of title

Blade Runner
Forbidden Planet
War of the Worlds
The Invisible Man
The Star Wars Trilogy
2001 – A Space Odyssey
The Quatermass Quartet
The Man Who Fell to Earth
Close Encounters of the Third Kind
Invasion of the Body Snatchers (both)
Dr Strangelove, or How I Learned to Stop Worrying and Love the Bomb

Runners-up

E.T.
Alien
Them!
Solaris
Metropolis
*Innerspace**
The Road Warrior
Planet of the Apes
A Clockwork Orange
Village of the Damned
The Day the Earth Stood Still
The Incredible Shrinking Man
The Thing from Another World
The Day the Earth Caught Fire

'My criteria for inclusion? Simply films I like. I made no efforts to be fair, to include titles from each continent, from each era. I didn't even try to think of titles that I would want if I were stranded on a desert island with a videotape player. If I had bent in that direction, the list would be even longer.

I realize that my top 'ten' list really consists of sixteen movies, and includes one (*Quatermass/The Quatermass Conclusion*) that doesn't belong in there. But I see no reason to limit myself to an arbitrary number – and no good way of getting the fourth *Quatermass* film out of there. And because the two *Body Snatchers* films work their effects so differently, but each so well, I didn't want to have to choose between them. (I think the Kauffman version is probably a better movie, but the Siegel version is much more in tune with its time.)

Naturally there are some films that are, by rigid definition, Science Fiction that are not in this list (*King Kong*, *Alien*, *Bride of Frankenstein*, Cronenberg's *The Fly*), which I consider to be outstanding. But that's what the horror list is for, of course.

Science Fiction itself is a very slippery term to define, not to mention 'best'. If you had asked me in 1956 what the best Science Fiction films were, I would unhesitatingly have named *It Came from Beneath the Sea* and *Creature with the Atom Brain*; at thirteen, those were not just the best Science Fiction movies I had ever seen, but (I thought) the best movies of *any* sort. Five years from now, the above list will shift around too. Perhaps *Zontar, the Thing from Venus* or *Battle Beneath the Earth* are due for re-examination.'

French Critics

A compilation of the movies mentioned in the six Top Tens first published in *Demain La Science Fiction*. It is reprinted here as a comparison to the contemporary Top Ten lists and as reminder of the way in which the Science Fiction film was seen before *Star Wars* (1977).

1 *2001 – A Space Odyssey* 1968

2 *The Bride of Frankenstein* 1935

3 *Invasion of the Body Snatchers* 1956
Metropolis 1926
Silent Running 1971
This Island Earth 1955
War of the Worlds 1953

4 *Chikyu Boeigun* 1957
The Day the Earth Stood Still 1951
Forbidden Planet 1956
King Kong 1933★
Phase IV 1973
Planet of the Apes 1968
The Time Machine 1960
Village of the Damned 1960

5 *Alphaville* 1965
The Birds 1963

Day of the Triffids 1963
Frankenstein 1931
Futureworld 1976
The Incredible Shrinking Man 1957
Je T'Aime, Je T'Aime 1967
La Jetée 1963
The Lost World 1925★
Quatermass and the Pit 1967
Quatermass II 1957
The Quatermass Xperiment 1955

Der Schweigende Stern 1960
Soylent Green 1973
The Thing 1951
20,000 Leagues Under the Sea 1954
Voyage dans la Lune 1909
Westworld 1973
X – The Man with X-Ray Eyes 1963
Zardoz 1973

Appendix 3

Science Fiction Oscars

The following is a list of all Oscars awarded to Science Fiction films, and of all performances nominated for Oscars, in the sound period.

1932

Oscar: Best actor Frederic March, *Doctor Jekyll and Mr Hyde*
Nominations: Writing (adaptation) Percy Heath, Samuel Hoffenstein, *Doctor Jekyll and Mr Hyde*; Cinematography Karl Struss, *Doctor Jekyll and Mr Hyde*

1935

Nomination: Sound recording Gilbert Kurland, *The Bride of Frankenstein*

1940

Nominations: Special effects John P. Fulton, Bernard B. Brown, William Hedgecoch, *The Invisible Man Returns*; Farciot Edouard, Wallace Kelly, *Dr Cyclops*

1941

Nomination: Cinematography (black and white) Joseph Ruttenberg, *Dr Jekyll and Mr Hyde*

1942

Nomination: Special effects John P. Fulton, Bernard B. Brown, *The Invisible Agent*

1950

Oscar: Special effects Lee Zavitz, *Destination Moon*

1951

Oscar: Special effects Gordon Jennings, *When Worlds Collide*
Nomination: Cinematography (colour) John F. Seitz, W. Howard Greene, *When Worlds Collide*

1952

Nomination: Writing (screenplay) Roger MacDougall, John Dighton, Alexander Mackendrick, *The Man in the White Suit*

1953

Oscar: Special effects Gordon Jennings, *War of the Worlds*
Nominations: Sound recording Paramount Sound Department, *War of the Worlds*; Film editing Everett Douglas, *War of the Worlds*

1954

Oscars: Art direction/Set direction John Meehan, Emile Kuri, *20,000 Leagues Under the Sea*; Special effects Ub Iwerks, *20,000 Leagues Under the Sea*
Nominations: Film editing Elmo Williams, *20,000 Leagues Under the Sea*; Special effects Ralph Ayers, *Them!*

1955

Nomination: Special effects A. Arnold Gillespie, Irving Ries, Wesley C. Miller, *Forbidden Planet*

1959

Nominations: Art direction/Set direction (colour) Lyle R. Wheeler, Franz Bachelin, Herman Blumenthal, Walter M. Scott, Joseph Kish, *Journey to the Centre of the Earth*; Sound 20th Century Fox Sound Department, *Journey to the Centre of the Earth*; Special effects L.B. Abbott, James B. Gorden, Carl Faulkner, *Journey to the Centre of the Earth*; Film editing Frederic Knudtson, *On the Beach*; Best scoring (of a dramatic or comedy picture) Ernest Gold, *On the Beach*

1960

Oscar: Special effects Gene Warren, Tim Baar, *The Time Machine*
Nomination: Art direction/Set decoration Hal Pereira, Walter Tyler, Sam Comer, Arthur Krams, *Visit to a Small Planet*

1963

Nomination: Special visual effects Ub Iwerks, *The Birds*

1964

Oscar: Sound effects Norman Wanstall, *Goldfinger*
Nominations: Best picture *Dr Strangelove*; Best actor Peter Sellers, *Dr Strangelove*; Best director Stanley Kubrick, *Dr Strangelove*; Writing (screenplay based on material from another medium) Stanley Kubrick, Peter George, Terry Southern, *Dr Strangelove*

1965

Oscar: Special visual effects John Stears, *Thunderball*

1966

Oscars: Special visual effects Art Cruickshank, *Fantastic Voyage*; Art direction/Set direction Jack Martin Smith, Dale Hennesy, Walter M. Scott, Stuart A. Reiss, *Fantastic Voyage*; Best documentary *The War Game*
Nominations: Cinematography (colour) Ernest Laszlo, *Fantastic Voyage*; Cinematography (black and white) James Wong Howe, *Seconds*; Film editing William B. Murphy, *Fantastic Voyage*; Sound effects Walter Ross, *Fantastic Voyage*

1968

Oscars: Best actor Cliff Robertson, *Charly*; Special visual effects Stanley Kubrick, *2001 – A Space Odyssey*; Honorary Award for makeup created by John Chambers, *Planet of the Apes*
Nominations: Best director Stanley Kubrick, *2001 – A Space Odyssey*; Writing (story and screenplay) Stanley Kubrick, Arthur C. Clarke, *2001 – A Space Odyssey*; Art direction/Set decoration Tony Masters, Harry Lange, Ernie Archer, *2001 – A Space Odyssey*; Costume design Morton Haack, *Planet of the Apes*; Best original score Jerry Goldsmith, *Planet of the Apes*; Film editing Fred Feitshans, Eve Newman, *Wild in the Streets*

1969

Oscar: Special visual effects Robbie Robertson, *Marooned*
Nominations: Cinematography Daniel Fapp, *Marooned*; Sound Les Fresholtz, Arthur Piantadosi, *Marooned*

1970

Nominations: Best documentary *Erinnerungen an die Zukunft*

1971

Nominations: Best picture *A Clockwork Orange*; Best director Stanley Kubrick, *A Clockwork Orange*; Film editing Bill Butler, *A Clockwork Orange*; Sound Gordon K. McCallum, John Mitchell, Alfred J. Overton, *Diamonds Are Forever*;

Film editing Stuart Gilmore, John W. Holmes, *The Andromeda Strain*; Art direction/Set decoration Boris Leven, William Tuntke, Ruby Levitt, *The Andromeda Strain*; Special visual effects Jim Danforth, Roger Dicken, *When Dinosaurs Ruled the Earth*

1973

Nominations: Sound Richard Portman, Lawrence O. Jost, *The Day of the Dolphin*; Best original dramatic score Georges Delerue, *The Day of the Dolphin*

1974

Nomination: Writing (screenplay adapted from other material) Gene Wilder, Mel Brooks, *Young Frankenstein*; Sound Richard Portman, Gene Cantamessa, *Young Frankenstein*

1976

Oscar: Special award for visual effects Lyle B. Abbott, Glen Robinson, Mathew Yuricich, *Logan's Run*
Nomination: Art direction/Set decoration Dale Hennesy, Robert de Vestel, *Logan's Run*

1977

Oscars: Art Direction/Set decoration John Barry, Norman Reynolds, Leslie Dilley, Roger Christian, *Star Wars*; Film editing Paul Hirsch, Marcia Lucas, Richard Chew, *Star Wars*; Visual effects John Stears, John Dykstra, Richard Edlund, Grant McCune, Robert Blalack, *Star Wars*; Costume design John Mollo, *Star Wars*; Sound Don MacDougall, Ray West, Bob Minkler, Derek Ball, *Star Wars*; Best original score John Williams, *Star Wars*; Special achievement award for sound effect creations Benjamin Burtt Jnr, *Star Wars*; Cinematography Vilmos Zsigmond, *Close Encounters of the Third Kind*; Special achievement award for sound effects editing Frank Warner, *Close Encounters of the Third Kind*
Nominations: Best picture *Star Wars*; Best director George Lucas, *Star Wars*; Steven Spielberg, *Close Encounters of the Third Kind*; Best supporting actor Alec Guinness, *Star Wars*; Best supporting actress Melinda Dillon, *Close Encounters of the Third Kind*; Best screenplay (written directly for the screen) George Lucas, *Star Wars*; Film editing Michael Kahn, *Close Encounters of the Third Kind*; Art direction/Set decoration Joe Alves, Don Lomino, Phil Abramson, *Close Encounters of the Third Kind*; Sound Robert Knudson, Robert J. Glass, Don MacDougall, Gene S. Cantamessa, *Close Encounters of the Third Kind*; Visual effects Roy Arbogast, Douglas Trumbull, Mathew Yuricich, Gregory Jein, Richard Yuricich, *Close Encounters of the Third Kind*; Best original score John Williams, *Close Encounters of the Third Kind*

1978

Oscar: Special achievement award for visual effects Les Bowie, Colin Chilvers, Denys Coops, Roy Field, Derek Meddings, Zoran Perisic, *Superman – The Movie*
Nominations: Best actor Laurence Olivier, *The Boys from Brazil*; Film editing Robert E. Swink, *The Boys from Brazil*; Stuart Baird, *Superman – The Movie*; Best original score John Williams, *Superman – The Movie*; Jerry Goldsmith, *The Boys from Brazil*; Sound Gordon K. McCallum, Graham Hartstone, Nicholas Le Messurier, Roy Chairman, *Superman – The Movie*; Costume design Paul Zastupnevich, *The Swarm*

1979

Oscar: Visual effects H.R. Giger, Carlo Rambaldi, Brian Johnson, Nick Allder, Denys Ayling, *Alien*
Nominations: Best actor Jack Lemmon, *The China Syndrome*; Best actress Jane Fonda, *The China Syndrome*; Best original screenplay Mike Gray, T.S. Cook, James Bridges, *The China Syndrome*; Cinematography Frank Phillips, *The Black Hole*;

Visual effects Peter Ellenshaw, Art Cruickshank, Eustace Lycett, Danny Lee, Harrison Ellenshaw, Joe Hale, *The Black Hole*; Douglas Trumbull, John Dykstra, Richard Yuricich, Robert Swarthe, Dave Stewart, Grant McCune, *Star Trek – The Motion Picture*; Derek Meddings, Paul Wilson, John Evans, *Moonraker*; Art direction George Jenkins, Arthur Jeph Parker, *The China Syndrome*; Michael Seymour, Les Diller, Roger Christian, Ian Whittaker, *Alien*; Harold Michelson, Joe Jennings, Leon Harris, John Vallone, Linda Descenna, *Star Trek – The Motion Picture*; Sound William McCaughey, Aaron Rochin, Michael J. Kohut, Jack Solomon, *Meteor*; Best original score Jerry Goldsmith, *Star Trek – The Motion Picture*

1980

Oscars: Sound Bill Varney, Steve Maslow, Greg Landaker, Peter Sutton, *The Empire Strikes Back*; Special achievement award for visual effects Brian Johnson, Richard Edlund, Dennis Muren, Bruce Nicholson, *The Empire Strikes Back*
Nominations: Art direction/Set decoration Norman Reynolds, Leslie Dilley, Harry Lange, Alan Tomkins, Michael Ford, *The Empire Strikes Back*; Sound Arthur Piantadosi, Les Fresholtz, Michael Minkler, Willie D. Burton, *Altered States*; Best original score John Williams, *The Empire Strikes Back*; John Corigliano, *Altered States*

1981

Nomination: Sound John K. Wilkinson, Robert W. Glass Jnr, Robert M. Thirlwell, Robin Gregory, *Outland*

1982

Oscars: Best visual effects Carlo Rambaldi, Dennis Muren, Kenneth F. Smith, *E.T. The Extra-Terrestrial*; Sound Buzz Knudson, Robert Glass, Don Digirolamo, Gene Cantamessa, *E.T. The Extra-Terrestrial*; Sound effects editing Ben Burtt, Charles L. Campbell, *E.T. The Extra-Terrestrial*; Best original score John Williams, *E.T. The Extra-Terrestrial*
Nominations: Best picture *E.T. The Extra-Terrestrial*; Best director Steven Spielberg, *E.T. The Extra-Terrestrial*; Best screenplay (written for the screen) Melissa Mathison, *E.T. The Extra-Terrestrial*; Cinematography Allen Daviau, *E.T. The Extra-Terrestrial*; Film editing Carol Littleton, *E.T. The Extra-Terrestrial*; Art direction/Set decoration Lawrence G. Paull, David Snyder, Linda Descenna, *Blade Runner*; Visual effects Douglas Trumbull, Richard Yuricich, David Dryer, *Blade Runner*; Costume design Elois Jenssen, *Tron*; Sound Michael Minkler, Bob Minkler, Lee Minkler, Jim La Rue, *Tron*

1983

Nominations: Best actress Jane Alexander, *Testament*; Best original screenplay Lawrence Lasker, Walter F. Parkes, *War Games*; Best cinematography William A. Fraker, *War Games*; Best film editing Frank Morriss, Edward Abroms, *Blue Thunder*; Best original score John Williams, *Return of the Jedi*; Art direction/Set direction Norman Reynolds, Fred Hole, James Schoppe, Michael Ford, *Return of the Jedi*; Best sound Ben Burtt, Gary Summers, Randy Thom, Tony Dawe, *Return of the Jedi*; Michael J. Koht, Carlos de Larios, Aaron Rochin, Willie D. Burton, *War Games*; Best sound editing Ben Burtt, *Return of the Jedi*

1984

Nominations: Best actor Jeff Bridges, *Starman*; Best art direction Albert Brenner, Rick Simpson, *2010*; Best costume design Patricia Norris, *2010*; Best makeup Michael Westmore, *2010*; Best sound Bill Varney, Steve Masslow, Kevin O'Connell, Nelson Stoll, *Dune*; Michael J. Kohut, Aaron Rochin, Carlos de Larios, Gene S. Cantamessa, *2010*; Best visual effects Richard Edlund, Neil Krepela, George Jensen, Mark Stetson, *2010*

1985

Oscars: Best supporting actor Don Ameche, *Cocoon*; Best visual effects Ken Ralston, Ralph McQuarrie, Scott Farrar, David Barry, *Cocoon*

Nominations: Best original screenplay Robert Zemeckis, Bob Gale, *Back to the Future*; Terry Gilliam, Tom Stoppard, Charles McKeown, *Brazil*; Best original song Chris Hayes, Johnny Colla, Huey Lewis, 'Power of Love', *Back to the Future*; Best art direction Norman Garwood (art direction), Maggie Gray (set decoration), *Brazil*; Best sound Bill Varney, B. Tennyson Sebastian II, Robert Thirlwell, William B. Kaplan, *Back to the Future*; Best sound effects editing Charles L. Campbell, Robert Rutledge, *Back to the Future*

1986

Oscars: Best visual effects Robert Skotak, Stan Winston, John Richardson, Suzanne Benson, *Aliens*; Best makeup Chris Walas, Stephen Dupuis, *The Fly*; Best sound effects editing Don Sharpe, *Aliens*

Nominations: Best actress Sigourney Weaver, *Aliens*; Best cinematography Don Peterman, *Star Trek IV: The Voyage Home*; Best film editing Ray Lovejoy, *Aliens*; Best original score James Horner, *Aliens*; Leonard Rosenman, *Star Trek IV: The Voyage Home*; Best art direction Peter Lamont (art direction), Crispian Sallis (set decoration), *Aliens*; Best sound Graham V. Hartstone, Nicolas Le Messurier, Michael A. Carter, Roy Charman, *Aliens*; Terry Porter, Dave Hudson, Mel Metcalfe, Gene S. Cantamessa, *Star Trek IV: The Voyage Home*; Best sound effects editing Mark Mangini, *Star Trek IV: The Voyage Home*

1987

Oscars: Best visual effects Denis Muren, William George, Harley Jessup, Kenneth Smith, *InnerSpace*; Best makeup Rick Baker, *Harry and the Hendersons*

Nominations: Best visual effects Joel Hynek, Robert M. Greenberg, Richard Greenberg, Stan Winston, *Predator*; Best film editing Frank J. Urioste, *RoboCop*; Best sound Michael J. Kohut, Carlos DeLarios, Aaron Rochin, Robert Wald, *RoboCop*

1989

Oscars: Best art direction Anton Furst (art direction), Peter Young (set decoration), *Batman*; Best sound Don Bassman, Kevin F. Cleary, Richard Overton, Lee Orloff, *The Abyss*

Nominations: Best cinematography Mikael Salomon, *The Abyss*; Best visual effects John Bruno, Dennis Muren, Hoyt Yeatman, Dennis Skotak, *The Abyss*; Ken Ralston, Michael Lantieri, John Bell, Steve Gawley, *Back to the Future, Part II*; Best art direction Leslie Dilley (art direction), Anne Kuljian (set decoration), *The Abyss*

1990

Oscar: Best visual effects Eric Brevig, Rob Bottin, Tim McGovern, Alex Funke, *Total Recall*

Nominations: Best sound Nelson Stoll, Michael J. Kohut, Carlos deLarios, Aaron Rochin, *Total Recall*; Best sound effects editing Stephen H Flick, *Total Recall*

1991

Oscars: Best visual effects Dennis Muren, Stan Winston, Gene Warren Jr, Robert Skotak, *Terminator 2: Judgment Day*; Best makeup Stan Winston, Jeff Dawn, *Terminator 2: Judgment Day*; Best sound Tom Johnson, Gary Rydstrom, Gary Summers, Lee Orloff, *Terminator 2: Judgment Day*; Best sound effects editing Gary Rydstrom, Gloria S. Borders, *Terminator 2: Judgment Day*

Nominations: Best cinematography Adam Greenburg, *Terminator 2: Judgment Day*; Best film editing Conrad Buff, Mark Goldblatt, Richard A. Harris, *Terminator 2: Judgment Day*; Best makeup Michael Mills, Edward French, Richard Snell, *Star Trek VI: The Undiscovered Country*; Best sound effects editing George Watters II, F. Hudson Miller, *Star Trek VI: The Undiscovered Country*

1992

Nominations: Best visual effects Richard Edlund, Alec Gillis, Tom Woodruff Jr, George Gibbs, *Alien3*; Michael Fink, Craig Barron, John Bruno, Dennis Skotak, *Batman Returns*; Best makeup Ve Neill, Ronnie Specter, Stan Winston, *Batman Returns*

1993

Oscars: Best visual effects Dennis Muren, Stan Winston, Phil Tippett, Michael Lantieri, *Jurassic Park*; Best sound Gary Summers, Gary Rydstrom, Shawn Murphy, Ron Judkins, *Jurassic Park*; Best sound effects editing Gary Rydstrom, Richard Hymns, *Jurassic Park*

1994

Nominations: Best original song Carole Bayer Sager, James Newton Howard, James Ingram, Patty Smyth, 'Look What Love Has Done', *Junior*; Best makeup Daniel Parker, Paul Engelen, Carol Hemming, *Mary Shelley's Frankenstein*

Appendix 4

Select Bibliography

Amelio, Ralph J, *Hal in the Classroom: Science Fiction Films*, Pflaum Publishing, Ohio, 1974

Ash, Brian (ed), *The Visual Encyclopaedia of Science Fiction*, Pan, London, 1977

Atkins, Thomas R, *Science Fiction Films*, Monarch Press, New York, 1976

Baxter, John, *Science Fiction in the Cinema*, The Tantivy Press, London; A. S. Barnes & Co, New York, 1970

Bouyxou, J P, *La Science-Fiction au Cinéma*, Union Générale d'Editions, Paris, 1971

Brosman, John, *Future Tense*, Macdonald & Janes, London, 1978

Edelson, Edward, *Visions of Tomorrow*, Doubleday, New York, 1975

Frank, Alan, *Sci-Fi Now*, Octopus, London, 1978

Gasca, Luis, *Cine y Ciencia-Ficción*, Libres de Sinera SA, Barcelona, 1969, reprinted and revised Editorial Planeta, Barcelona, 1975

Gasca, Luis, *Fantascienza e Cinema*, Gabrièle Mazzotta Editore, Milan, 1972

Geduld, Harry M and Gottesman, Ronald (eds), *Robots, Robots, Robots*, New York Graphic Society, Boston, 1978

Gifford, Denis, *Science Fiction Film*, Studio Vista/Dutton Pictureback, London, 1971

Glut, Donald F, *The Frankenstein Legend*, The Scarecrow Press, Metuchen, New Jersey, 1973

Harry, Bill, *Heroes of the Spaceways*, Omnibus Press, London, 1981

Hickman, Morgan Gail, *The Films of George Pal*, A.S. Barnes & Co, New York; Yoseloff, London, 1977

Johnson, William (ed), *Focus on the Science Fiction Film*, Prentice Hall, New York, 1972

Kolodynski, Andrzej, *Filmy Fantastyczno-naukowe*, Wydawnictwa Artystyczne i Filmowe, Warsaw, 1972

Lee, Walt, *Reference Guide to Fantastic Films, Science Fiction, Fantasy and Horror, Vols 1, 2 & 3*, Chelsea-Lee Books, London, 1972, 1973, 1974

Manchel, Frank, *Great Science Fiction Films*, Franklin Watts, New York/London, 1976

Mank, William Gregory, *It's Alive, The Classic Cinema Saga of Frankenstein*, Tantivy Press, London, 1981

Menningen, Juergen, *Filmbuch Science Fiction*, Verlag M. DuMont Schauberg, Germany, 1975

Menville, Douglas, *A Historical and Critical Survey of the Science Fiction Film*, Arno Press, New York, 1975

Menville, Douglas and Reginald, R, *Things to Come, An Illustrated History of the Science Fiction Film*, Times Books, New York, 1977

Mongini, G, *Storia del Cinema di Fantascienza, Vols I and II*, Fanucci, Rome, 1976, 1977

Nicholls, Peter (ed), *The Encyclopaedia of Science Fiction*, Granada, London, 1979

Nicholls, Peter, *Fantastic Cinema*, Ebury Press, London, 1984

Parish, James Robert and Pitts, Michael R, *The Great Science Fiction Pictures*, The Scarecrow Press, Metuchen, New Jersey, 1977

Pickard, Roy, *Science Fiction in the Movies, an A-Z*, Frederick Muller, London, 1978

Pohl, Frederik and Pohl, Frederik IV, *Science Fiction Studies in Film*, Ace, New York, 1981

Rovin, Jeff, *A Pictorial History of Science Fiction Films*, Citadel Press, US, 1975

Rovin, Jeff, *From Jules Verne to Star Trek*, Drake, New York, 1977

Rovin, Jeff, *The Science Fiction Collectors Catalog*, Barnes, San Diego; Tantivy Press, London, 1982

Schlockoff, Alain (ed), *Demain la Science Fiction*, a special issue of *Cinéma d'Aujourd'hui*, Paris, 1976

Seymour, Simon, *Mad Scientists, Weird Doctors and Time Travellers in Movies, TV and Books*, Lippincott, New York, 1981

Siegel, Richard and Saurès, J C, *Alien Creatures*, Reed Books, Los Angeles, 1978

Sobchack, Vivien Carol, *The Limits of Infinity: The American Science Fiction Film*, A.S. Barnes & Co, New York; Yosselof, London, 1980

Sternberg, Jacques, *Une Succursale du Fantastique Nommée Science Fiction*, Le Terrain Vague, Paris

Stoker, John, *The Illustrated Frankenstein*, Westbridge Books, Newton Abbot, 1980

Strick, Philip, *Science Fiction Movies*, Octopus, London, 1976

Strickland, A W and Ackerman, Forrest J, *A Reference Guide to American Science-Fiction Films, Vol. I*, US, 1981

Warren, Bill, *Keep Watching the Skies, Vol I 1950-1957*, McFarland, North Carolina, 1982

Willis, Donald C, *Horror and Science Fiction Films: A Checklist*, The Scarecrow Press, New York, 1972

Wright, Gene, *The Science Fiction Image*, Columbus Books, New York, 1983

Zanotto, Piero, *La Fantascienza*, R.A.D.A.R., Venice, 1967

Index

Titles in italic are attributed English-language titles for films for which the original title is unknown.

509

510